ISBN 978-0-484-42373-1
PIBN 10193839

FB &c Ltd, Dalton House, 60 Windsor Avenue, London, SW19 2RR.
Company number 08720141. Registered in England and Wales.

For support please visit www.forgottenbooks.com

Blackwood's Universal Library of Standard Authors.

THE

COMPLETE POETICAL WORKS

OF

GRAY, BEATTIE, BLAIR, COLLINS, THOMSON, AND KIRKE WHITE.

With Fine Steel Portrait of Gray

AND A FAC-SIMILE OF THE MS. OF HIS POEMS, AND OTHER ILLUSTRATIONS.

LONDON:
JAMES BLACKWOOD & CO., PATERNOSTER ROW.

GLASGOW:
C. L. WRIGHT,
PRINTER.

THE

POETICAL WORKS

OF

THOMAS GRAY.

CONTENTS.

One Morn I m
, Along the Heath, &
, Another came; nor
, Nor up the Lawn,
The next with
, Slow thro' the Chur
, Approach & read, fo
, Graved on the Ston
*
Epitap

Here rests his Head
A Youth, to Fortune
Fair Science frown'd
And Melancholy m
Large was his Bo
Heav'n did a Recomp
He gave to Mis'ry a
He gain'd from Hea
No farther seek t
Or draw his Frailties
(There they alike in
The Bosom of his Fat

Insert.

There scatter'd oft,
By Hands unseen, ar
The Red-breast loves
And little Footsteps l

Some
Even
And it
For
Dost
If cha
Some k
Hap
, Oft ha
, Brushi
, To meet
, There
, That w
, His list
, And por

The Boast of Heraldry, the Pomp of Pow'r,
And all that Beauty, all that Wealth, e'er gave
Awaits alike th' inevitable Hour.
The Paths of Glory lead but to the Grave.
Forgive, ye Proud, th' involuntary Fault, Nor You : impute to These the
If Memory to these no Trophies raise, Mem'ry o'er their Tomb
Where thro' the long-drawn Isle, & fretted Vault
The pealing Anthem swells the Note of Praise.
Can storied Urn, or animated Bust
Back to its Mansion call the fleeting Breath?
Can Honour's Voice provoke the silent Dust,
Or Flattery sooth the dull cold Ear of Death?
Perhaps in this neglected Spot is laid
Some Heart once pregnant with celestial Fire,
Hands, that the Reins of Empire might have sway'd, Rod
Or waked to Ecstasy the living Lyre.
But Knowledge to their Eyes her ample Page
Rich with the Spoils of Time did ne'er unroll;
Chill Penury repress'd their noble Rage,
And froze the genial Current of the Soul.
Full many a Gem of purest Ray serene
The dark unfathom'd Caves of Ocean bear:
Full many a Flower is born to blush unseen,
And wast its Sweetness on the desert Air.
Some Village-Hampden, that with dauntless Breast
The little Tyrant of his Fields withstood;
Some mute inglorious Milton here may rest,
Some Cromwell guiltless of his Country's Blood.
Th' Applause of list'ning Senates to command,
The Threats of Pain & Ruin to despise,
To scatter Plenty o'er a smiling Land,
And read their Hist'ry in a Nation's Eyes
Their Lot forbad: nor circumscribed alone
Their growing Virtues, but their Crimes confined;
Forbad to wade thro' Slaughter to a Throne,
Or shut the Gates of Mercy on Mankind,

The struggling Pangs of conscious Truth to hide,
To quench the Blushes of ingenuous Shame,
Or heap the Shrine of Luxury & Pride
With Incense, kindled at the Muse's Flame.
Far from the madding Crowd's ignoble Strife,
Their sober Wishes never learn'd to stray;
Along the cool sequester'd Vale of Life
They kept the noiseless Tenour of their Way.
Yet ev'n these Bones from Insult to protect
Some frail Memorial still erected nigh,
With uncouth Rhimes & shapeless Sculpture deck'd,
Implores the passing Tribute of a Sigh.
Their Name, their Years, spelt by th' unletter'd Muse,
The Place of Fame & Elegy supply:
And many a holy Text around she strews,
That teach the rustic Moralist to die.
For who to dumb Forgetfulness a Prey,
This pleasing anxious Being e'er resign'd,
Left the warm Precincts of the chearful Day,
Nor cast one longing ling'ring Look behind?
On some fond Breast the parting Soul relies,
Some pious Drops the closing Eye requires;
Even from the Tomb the Voice of Nature cries, no
And in our Ashes glow their wonted Fires. Ev'n live
For Thee, who mindful of th' unhonour'd Dead
Dost in these Lines their artless Tale relate;
If chance, by lonely Contemplation led,
Some kindred Spirit shall inquire thy Fate,
Haply some hoary-headed Swain may say,
'Oft have we seen him at the Peep of Dawn
'Brushing with hasty Steps the Dews away
'To meet the Sun upon the upland Lawn.
'There at the Foot of yonder nodding Beech
'That wreathes its old fantastic Roots so high,
'His listless Length at Noontide would he stretch,
'And pore upon the Brook that babbles by.

, Hard by yon Wood, now smiling as in Scorn,
, Mutt'ring his wayward Fancies, would he rove;
, Now drooping, woeful-wan, like one forlorn,
, Or crazed with Care, or cross'd in hopeless Love.

, One Morn I miss'd him from the custom'd Hill,
, Along the Heath, & near his fav'rite Tree;
, Another came; nor yet beside the Rill,
, Nor up the Lawn, nor at the Wood was he.

, The next with Dirges due in sad Array
, Slow thro' the Churchway Path we saw him born
, Approach & read (for thou can'st read) the Lay
, Graved on the Stone beneath yon aged Thorn.

* *

Epitaph

Here rests his Head upon the Lap of Earth
A Youth, to Fortune & to Fame unknown
Fair Science frown'd not on his humble Birth,
And Melancholy mark'd him for her own.

Large was his Bounty, & his Soul sincere;
Heav'n did a Recompense as largely send:
He gave to Mis'ry all he had, a Tear
He gain'd from Heav'n ('twas all he wish'd) a Friend

No farther seek his Merits to disclose,
Or draw his Frailties from their dread Abode,
(There they alike in trembling Hope repose)
The Bosom of his Father, & his God.

Insert & *

There scatter'd oft, the earliest of the Year,
By Hands unseen, are Show'rs of Violets found:
The Red-breast loves to build, & warble there,
And little Footsteps lightly print the Ground.

Omitted in 1751

From the Original in the hand writing of Thomas Gray.

Elegy, written in a Country-Church Yard - 1750

The Curfeu tolls the Knell of parting Day,
The lowing Herd wind slowly o'er the Lea,
The Plowman homeward plods his weary Way,
And leaves the World to Darkness & to me.

Now fades the glimm'ring Landscape on the Sight,
And all the Air a solemn Stillness holds;
Save where the Beetle wheels his droneing Flight,
Or drowsy Tinklings lull the distant Folds.

Save that from yonder ivy mantled Tower
The mopeing Owl does to the Moon complain
Of such, as wand'ring near her secret Bower
Molest her ancient solitary Reign.

Beneath those rugged Elms, that Yewtree's shade,
Where heaves the Turf in many a mould'ring Heap,
Each in his narrow Cell for ever laid
The rude Forefathers of the Hamlet sleep.

The breezy Call of incense-breathing Morn,
The Swallow twitt'ring from the straw-built Shed,
The Cock's shrill Clarion, & the eechoing Horn,
No more shall rouse them from their lowly Bed.

For them no more the blazing Hearth shall burn,
Or busy Huswife ply her evening Care,
No Children run to lisp their Sire's Return,
Nor climb his Knees the envied Kiss to share.

Oft did the Harvest to their Sickle yield
Their Furrow oft the stubborn Glebe has broke:
How jocund did they drive their Team a-field!
How bow'd the Woods beneath their sturdy Stroke!

Let not Ambition mock their useful Toil,
Their homely Joys & Destiny obscure;
Nor Grandeur hear with a disdainful Smile
The short & simple Annals of the Poor.

* publish'd in Feb: 7. 1751 by Dodsley & went thro' four Editions in two months, & afterwards a fifth, 6th, 7th & 8th, 9th & 10th & 11th, printed also in 1753 with Mr Bentley's Designs, of wch there is a 2d Edition & again by Dodsley in his Miscellany, Vol. 4th & in a Scotch Collection call'd the Union. translated into Latin by Chr. Anstey Esq, & the Revd Mr Roberts, & publish'd in 1762; & again in the same year by Rob: Lloyd M.A.

slowly o'er the Lea,
nd plods his weary Way,
to Darkness & to me
n'ring Landscape on the Sight.
lemn Stillness holds,
wheels his droning Flight,
lull the distant Folds;
er ivy mantled Tower
to the Moon complain
near her secret Bower
itary Reign.
Elms, that Yewtree's shade,
in many a mould'ring Heap,
l for ever laid
l the Hamlet sleep.
ncense-breathing Morn,
from the straw-built Shed,
, & the ecchoing Horn,
m from their lowly Bed,
blazing Hearth shall burn,
r evening Care,
their Sire's Return,
envied Kiss to share.
their Sickle yield
ubborn Glebe has broke;
ve their Team a-field,
eneath their sturdy Stroke!
their useful Toil,
stiny obscure;
a disdainful Smile,
als of the Poor.

went thro' some Editions: in two Months; & afterwards a fifth, 6th 7th & 8th, 9th & 10th & 11th printed also in 1753 with Mr Bentley's Designs, of which there is a 2d Edition & again by Dodsley in his Miscellany, Vol: 4th & in a Scotch Collection call'd the Union. translated into Latin by Chr: Anstey Esq, & the Revd Mr Roberts, & publish'd in 1762; & again in the same year by Rob: Lloyd M: A:

MEMOIR.

THE life of this poet, whose classic taste has imprinted a stamp of purity and elegance on the few, too few poems he has left us, does not present much incident. It was chiefly passed in the literary seclusion of a college, interrupted only by short excursions to the residences of his friends. We meet with no adventures or fluctuations of fortune; he lived a life of learned leisure, congenial to his natural disposition, and the effects of which are only to be regretted, inasmuch as, by the constant contemplations of the masterpieces of antiquity, his taste became so exquisitely sensitive, as to render him too captious on the merits of his own productions and too distrustful of his own genius.

Thomas Gray was born in Cornhill, in the city of London, on the 26th of December, 1716. His father, who was a money scrivener, was in good circumstances, although by imprudence and ignorance he impaired rather than improved his paternal fortune, and at his death left his family somewhat straitened in their means. Thomas was the sole survivor of many children, the rest having all died in their infancy. He was educated at Eton school, under the care of Mr. Antrobus, his maternal uncle, who was at that time one of the assistant masters. From Eton he proceeded to St. Peter's College, Cambridge, in the year 1734, where he continued till April 1738, when he took a set of chambers in the Temple, with the intention of studying the law, but this design was soon laid aside. Mr. Horace Walpole, who had been his schoolfellow at Eton, invited Mr. Gray to accompany him on a foreign tour; he accepted the proposal, but on his return did not resume his juridical studies.

Mr. Gray set out on his travels with Mr. Walpole early in 1739, and continued abroad till the summer of 1741. In this space of time he and Mr. Walpole visited almost all the places in France and Italy which usually attract the notice of travellers, and the letters of Mr. Gray, which have been preserved, give many lively sketches of the scenes which passed before him. They are, however, the letters of a young man, and are tinctured with the *affected* ease which was then fashionable in polite society; the ground he went over has been so repeatedly described, that we have forborne from republishing them. In the course of his correspondence he communicated several Latin poems and fragments of poems to his friend Mr. West, a young man of great talent, and an old fellow-collegian, who died early; but as they were never made public by Mr. Gray, or received the last polish from his hand, it would not be right to publish them unconnected with the letters that accompanied them.

An unfortunate dispute which occurred between the travellers, led to their separation at Reggio. Gray's own character is not ill depicted by himself in a letter to Mr. West, and we give it, since it affords a pretty fair idea of his epistolary style at that time:—

"As I am recommending myself to your love, methinks I ought to send you my picture (for I am no more what I was, some circumstances excepted, which I hope I need not particularize to you); you must add, then, to your former idea, two years of age, a reasonable quantity of dulness, a great deal of silence, and something that rather resembles, than is, thinking; a confused notion of many strange and fine things that have swum before my eyes for some time, *a want of love for general society*, indeed an inability to it. On the good side you may add a sensibility for what others feel, and indulgence for their faults or weaknesses, a love of truth, and detestation of everything else. Then you are to deduct a little impertinence, a little laughter, a great deal of pride, and some spirits. These are all the alterations I know of, you perhaps may find more. Think not that I have been obliged for this reformation of manners to reason or reflection, but to a severer schoolmistress, Experience. One has little merit in learning her lessons, for one cannot well help it; but they are more useful than others, and imprint themselves in the very heart."

Walpole, on the other hand, was a man made for society. The aim of his studies was, to shine; whilst, the more Gray knew, the more shrinking he became. The difference was afterwards (in 1744) accommodated through the intervention of a lady, who wished well to both parties; and it is to Walpole's honour that, after the death of Gray, he enjoined Mr. Mason, who took on himself the task of editing the works and writing the memoirs of the poet, "to charge him (Mr. Walpole) with the chief blame in the quarrel;" confessing, "that more attention and complaisance, more deference to a warm friendship, superior judgment, and prudence might have prevented a rupture that gave much uneasiness to them both, and a lasting concern to the survivor."

After quitting Mr. Walpole, Gray proceeded homewards, visiting in his way Venice, Padua, Milan, Turin, and Lyons. Shortly after his return his father died, leaving his family, though not in embarrassed circumstances, yet not so easy as to enable his son to prosecute his studies in the law without becoming burdensome to his mother and aunt; and he determined to retire to Cambridge and reside at his college, a mode of life congenial to his retired disposition and studious habits, and to which he ever afterwards adhered. He now began to turn his attention to English poetry, and in June, 1742, wrote his "Ode on the Spring," the first English poem he ever completed. This is a singular fact in the life of a man who was afterwards so distinguished for the singular excellence of his English poetry; it is probably to be attributed to his unceasing study of the classic writers, and early habits of Latin composition, at Eton, which led him to prefer that language as the medium of his poetic thoughts; after he had awakened his English Muse, he abandoned his classic lyre, and wrote no more Latin poetry. His Ode to Spring, which was written at Stoke Pogis, near Windsor, the residence of his mother and aunts, was sent to his friend Mr. West, who had just sunk under the attacks of consumption, from which he had long suffered. Three weeks before, he had written to Mr. Gray, upbraiding him in a lively vein for his melancholy, and ending, "Vale, et vive paulisper cum vivis." He was now lying dead, but Mr. Gray was not aware of his decease, when, as had been usual with the friends, he sent his ode to one whose ear was now cold in death. The circumstance is recorded in his common-place book. Mr. West's death occasioned the elegant sonnet which is inserted in the collection of poems. The "Ode on a distant Prospect of Eton College," and the "Ode to Adversity," were both composed in the following August; and there is reason for believing that the "Elegy in a Country Churchyard," was begun, if not ended, about the same time. As it now stands the conclusion was of a later date, but before it was published Mr. Gray made several alterations in the original poem. He did not put the finishing hand to it till 1750. In the interval he wrote but little poetry; the "Ode on the Death of a favourite Cat," written for Mr. Walpole, and a fragment of an intended essay on the Connexion of Government and Education, seem to be the sole fruits of this period. He gave himself up to his favourite studies, and in connexion with this pursuit he projected and made some progress with a chronology, which he brought from the 30th Olympiad, where it begins, to the 113th, that is, 332 years. This laborious work was formed much in the manner of the President Henault's "Histoire de France." Every page consisted of nine columns: one for the Olympiad, the next for the Archons, the third for the public affairs of Greece, the three next for the Philosophers, and the three last for Poets, Historians, and Orators. It does not appear to have been ever carried further.

The "Elegy in a Country Churchyard," being handed about in manuscript, excited great admiration, and was the occasion of introducing the poet to the acquaintance of Lady Cobham, who lived at the mansion-house at Stoke Pogis, and who commissioned Lady Schaub and Miss Speed to make the visit commemorated in the "Long Story." The elegy found its way to a magazine, and, to prevent imperfect versions from getting abroad, Mr. Gray immediately caused an authentic copy to be published by Mr. Dodsley, who had three years before performed the same office for the "Ode on a distant Prospect of Eton College." The other pieces appeared at various periods, and being afterwards collected, were published during Mr. Gray's life-time in London, and also at Glasgow. It was, however, no object of Mr. Gray's ambition to appear as an author; his pleasure consisted in a life of learned leisure, in which he could indulge his various studies without the cares and vexations, the flattery and vituperation, the almost constant attendants of literary fame. His natural disposition was retiring, and he was not fond of notoriety. The world has been a loser by this sensitiveness, for the stores of knowledge he acquired in most branches of learning, except mathematical science, for which he never had any inclination, were such as to enable him to have done much for the improvement and instruction of mankind, especially in the field of history, ancient and modern, in which he was deeply learned. He is an instance in which we may, without being uncharitable, wish that he had been either a little richer or a little poorer. Poverty would have compelled him to open up his stores, and riches would have prevented the fancied necessity of proving that he only wrote for amusement, (an assertion he was very desirous of having believed,) by writing very little.

The publication of his poems, especially the Elegy, which ran through eleven editions, at once established his fame, and in 1757, a mark of royal approbation was exhibited in the offer of the post of Poet Laureate, vacant by the death of Colley Cibber; but this Mr. Gray declined to accept, considering the office degraded by the unworthy hands through which it had passed. In 1762 he applied for the more congenial post of Professor of Modern Languages and History at Cambridge, but without success, the office having been already disposed of. It was, however, bestowed upon him, without solicitation, on the next vacancy, in 1768; but although he held it nearly three years, he never entered upon its duties. He indeed prepared an admirable sketch of an inaugural speech, and proposed a plan of private instruction to the students, since successfully followed up, but ill health prevented him from realising his wishes. He had long been subject to distressing attacks of hereditary gout, which would in all probability have put an end to his life much sooner, had not his habits been extremely temperate; he combated the disease by exercise, and found great benefit from the excursions he was in the habit of taking every summer, and of which many pleasing records are to be found in his letters, but the enemy was too strong, and on the 24th July, 1771, he was attacked, whilst at dinner in the college hall, with the gout in his stomach; he lingered till the evening of the 31st, when he expired, in the 55th year of his age.

Of his writings little need here be said. They have become part of the standard literature of the nation; their merits and demerits have been canvassed again and again; and the true poetic fire and taste displayed in them, their classic correctness of diction, and the fine imagination which is so conspicuous, have been the just themes of praise. His almost fastidious nicety in the choice of language has been regretted as too strong a curb on his Pegasus, as a restraint on that fancy, which when indulged soars to the heavens, but when checked falls lame and lifeless to the ground. He was never satisfied with his work, and touched and retouched, till the life of the original conception was sometimes almost destroyed. But his poems are, notwithstanding, all very noble compositions, and have, in assuming their eminent station in the literature of Great Britain, received but their just meed of praise.

His studies were very varied, and pursued with great diligence; many subjects he not only mastered but improved by his researches. He had acquired a taste for botany from his uncle while young, and it was throughout his life a favourite amusement; in his later years he pursued his researches in natural history, and turned much of his attention to zoology, and acquired a fund of knowledge in that science, which he successfully applied to the illustration of Aristotle and others of the ancients. He was a perfect adept in heraldry, and he found a not uncongenial pursuit in the study of the ancient architecture of the kingdom; on this subject he communicated some remarks to Mr. Belham, who inserted them in his History of Ely. He was also a proficient in music, of which he had an excellent theoretic knowledge; he was not a finished, although a pleasing performer on the harpsichord, which he was wont to accompany with his voice very agreeably. He was a connoisseur in painting and sculpture. In a word, there was no branch of polite literature or of the elegant arts of which he did not possess a competent if not a profound knowledge; and knowing what he could do, we must ever regret that indolence or diffidence prevented him from doing more.

Mr. Mason, the friend and biographer of the poet, has adopted a character of him, drawn by the Rev. Mr. Temple, rector of St. Glauvais, in Cornwall. We follow his example, and thus conclude our memoir:—

"Perhaps he was the most learned man in Europe. He was equally acquainted with the elegant and profound parts of science, and that not superficially, but thoroughly. He knew every branch of history, both natural and civil; had read all the original historians of England, France, and Italy; and was a great antiquarian. Criticism, metaphysics, morals, politics, made a principal part of his plan of study; voyages and travels of all sorts were his favourite amusement; and he had a fine taste in painting, prints, architecture, and gardening. With such a fund of knowledge his conversation must have been equally instructing and entertaining; but he was also a good man, a well-bred man, a man of virtue and humanity. There is no character without some speck, some imperfection; and I think the greatest defect in his was an affectation in delicacy, or rather effeminacy, and a visible fastidiousness, or contempt and disdain of his inferiors in science. He also had in some degree that weakness which disgusted Voltaire so much in Mr. Congreve: though his mind was enlarged, his heart softened, his virtue strengthened; the world and mankind were shown to him without a mask; and he was taught to consider everything as trifling, and unworthy of the attention of a wise man, except the pursuit of knowledge, and the practice of virtue, in that state wherein God hath placed us."

THE

Poetical Works

OF

THOMAS GRAY.

ODE I.

ON THE SPRING.

Lo! where the rosy-bosom'd Hours,
  Fair Venus' train, appear,
Disclose the long-expecting flowers,
  And wake the purple year!
The Attic warbler pours her throat,
Responsive to the cuckoo's note,
The untaught harmony of spring;
  While, whisp'ring pleasure as they fly,
  Cool Zephyrs through the clear blue sky
Their gather'd fragrance fling.

Where'er the oak's thick branches stretch
  A broader browner shade;
Where'er the rude and moss-grown beech
  O'er-canopies the glade,
Beside some water's rushy brink
With me the Muse shall sit, and think
(At ease reclined in rustic state)
  How vain the ardour of the Crowd,
  How low, how little are the Proud,
How indigent the Great!

Still is the toiling hand of Care:
  The panting herds repose:
Yet hark, how through the peopled air
  The busy murmur glows!
The insect youth are on the wing,
Eager to taste the honied spring,
And float amid the liquid noon:
  Some lightly o'er the current skim,
  Some show their gaily-gilded trim
Quick-glancing to the sun.

To Contemplation's sober eye
  Such is the race of Man;
And they that creep, and they that fly,
  Shall end where they began.
Alike the Busy and the Gay
But flutter through life's little day,
In Fortune's varying colours drest:
  Brush'd by the hand of rough Mischance,
  Or chill'd by Age, their airy dance
They leave, in dust to rest.

Methinks I hear in accents low
  The sportive kind reply:
Poor moralist! and what art thou?
  A solitary fly!
Thy joys no glittering female meets,
No hive hast thou of hoarded sweets,
No painted plumage to display:
  On hasty wings thy youth is flown;
  Thy sun is set, thy spring is gone—
We frolic, while 'tis May.

ODE II.

ON THE DEATH OF A FAVOURITE CAT,

Drowned in a Tub of Gold Fishes.

'Twas on a lofty vase's side,
Where China's gayest art had dyed
The azure flowers, that blow;
  Demurest of the tabby kind,
  The pensive Selima reclined,
Gazed on the lake below.

Her conscious tail her joy declared;
The fair round face, the snowy beard,
The velvet of her paws,
  Her coat, that with the tortoise vies,
  Her ears of jet, and emerald eyes,
She saw; and purr'd applause.

Still had she gazed; but 'midst the tide
Two angel forms were seen to glide,
The Genii of the stream:
  Their scaly armour's Tyrian hue
  Through richest purple to the view
Betray'd a golden gleam.

The hapless Nymph with wonder saw:
A whisker first and then a claw,
With many an ardent wish,
  She stretch'd in vain to reach the prize.
  What female heart can gold despise!
What Cat's averse to fish!

Presumptuous Maid! with looks intent
Again she stretch'd, again she bent,
Nor knew the gulf between.
  (Malignant Fate sat by, and smiled)
  The slipp'ry verge her feet beguiled,
She tumbled headlong in.

Eight times emerging from the flood,
She mew'd to every wat'ry God,
Some speedy aid to send.
  No Dolphin came, no Nereid stirr'd:
  Nor cruel Tom, nor Susan heard.
A Fav'rite has no friend!

From hence, ye Beauties, undeceived,
Know, one false step is ne'er retrieved,
And be with caution bold.
  Not all that tempts your wand'ring eyes
  And heedless hearts, is lawful prize;
Nor all, that glisters, gold.

ODE III.

ON A DISTANT PROSPECT OF ETON COLLEGE

Ἄνθρωπος ἱκανὴ πρόφασις εἰς τὸ δυστυχεῖν.

MENANDER.

Ye distant spires, ye antique towers,
  That crown the wat'ry glade,
Where grateful Science still adores
  Her Henry's [1] holy shade;
And ye, that from the stately brow
Of Windsor's heights th' expanse below
Of grove, of lawn, of mead survey,
  Whose turf, whose shade, whose flowers among
  Wanders the hoary Thames along
His silver-winding way!

Ah happy hills! ah pleasing shade!
  Ah fields beloved in vain,
Where once my careless childhood stray'd
  A stranger yet to pain!
I feel the gales that from ye blow
A momentary bliss bestow,
As waving fresh their gladsome wing,
  My weary soul they seem to soothe,
  And, redolent of joy and youth,
To breathe a second spring.

Say, Father Thames, for thou hast seen
  Full many a sprightly race
Disporting on thy margent green
  The paths of pleasure trace,
Who foremost now delight to cleave
With pliant arm thy glassy wave?
The captive linnet which enthrall?
  What idle progeny succeed
  To chase the rolling circle's speed,
Or urge the flying ball?

While some on earnest business bent
  Their murm'ring labours ply
'Gainst graver hours, that bring constraint
  To sweeten liberty:
Some bold adventurers disdain
The limits of their little reign,
And unknown regions dare descry:
  Still as they run they look behind,
  They hear a voice in every wind,
And snatch a fearful joy.

Gay hope is theirs, by fancy fed,
  Less pleasing when possest;
The tear forgot as soon as shed,
  The sunshine of the breast:
Theirs buxom health of rosy hue,
Wild wit, invention ever-new,
And lively cheer of vigour born;
  The thoughtless day, the easy night,
  The spirits pure, the slumbers light
That fly th' approach of morn.

Alas! regardless of their doom,
  The little victims play!
No sense have they of ills to come,
  Nor care beyond to-day:
Yet see how all around 'em wait
The Ministers of human fate,
And black Misfortune's baleful train!
  Ah, show them where in ambush stand
To seize their prey the murd'rous band!
  Ah, tell them they are men!

These shall the fury Passions tear,
  The vultures of the mind,
Disdainful Anger, pallid Fear,
  And Shame that skulks behind;
Or pining Love shall waste their youth,
Or Jealousy with rankling tooth,
That inly gnaws the secret heart,
  And Envy wan, and faded Care,
  Grim-visaged comfortless Despair,
And Sorrow's piercing dart.

Ambition this shall tempt to rise,
  Then whirl the wretch from high,
To bitter Scorn a sacrifice,
  And grinning Infamy.
The stings of Falsehood those shall try,
And hard Unkindness' alter'd eye,
That mocks the tear it forced to flow;
  And keen Remorse with blood defiled,
  And moody Madness laughing wild
Amid severest woe.

Lo, in the vale of years beneath
  A grisly troop are seen,
The painful family of Death,
  More hideous than their Queen:
This racks the joints, this fires the veins,
That every labouring sinew strains,
Those in the deeper vitals rage:
  Lo, Poverty, to fill the band,
  That numbs the soul with icy hand,
And slow-consuming Age.

To each his suff'rings: all are men,
  Condemn'd alike to groan;
The tender for another's pain,
  Th' unfeeling for his own.
Yet ah! why should they know their fate!
Since sorrow never comes too late,
And happiness too swiftly flies.
  Thought would destroy their paradise.
  No more; where ignorance is bliss,
'Tis folly to be wise.

[1] King Henry the Sixth, founder of the College.

ODE IV.

TO ADVERSITY.

———————Ζῆνα
Τὸν φρονεῖν βροτοὺς ὁδώ-
σαντα, τῷ πάθει μαθεῖν
Θέντα κυρίως ἔχειν.
ÆSCHYLUS, *in Agamemnone.*

DAUGHTER of Jove, relentless Power,
Thou Tamer of the human breast,
Whose iron scourge and tort'ring hour
The Bad affright, afflict the Best!
Bound in thy adamantine chain
The Proud are taught to taste of pain,
And purple Tyrants vainly groan
With pangs unfelt before, unpitied and alone.

When first thy Sire to send on earth
Virtue, his darling Child, design'd,
To thee he gave the heav'nly Birth,
And bade to form her infant mind
Stern rugged Nurse! thy rigid lore
With patience many a year she bore:
What sorrow was, thou bad'st her know,
And from her own she learn'd to melt at others' woe.

Scared at thy frown terrific, fly
Self-pleasing Folly's idle brood,
Wild Laughter, Noise, and thoughtless Joy,
And leave us leisure to be good.
Light they disperse, and with them go
The summer Friend, the flatt'ring Foe;
By vain Prosperity received,
To her they vow their truth, and are again believed.

Wisdom in sable garb array'd,
Immersed in rapt'rous thought profound,
And Melancholy, silent maid,
With leaden eye, that loves the ground,
Still on thy solemn steps attend:
Warm Charity, the general Friend,
With Justice, to herself severe,
And Pity, dropping soft the sadly-pleasing tear.

Oh, gently on thy Suppliant's head,
Dread Goddess, lay thy chast'ning hand!
Not in thy Gorgon terrors clad,
Nor circled with the vengeful Band
(As by the Impious thou art seen)
With thund'ring voice, and threat'ning mien,
With screaming Horror's funeral cry,
Despair, and fell Disease, and ghastly Poverty.

Thy form benign, oh Goddess, wear,
Thy milder influence impart,
Thy philosophic Train be there
To soften, not to wound my heart.
The generous spark extinct revive,
Teach me to love and to forgive,
Exact my own defects to scan,
What others are to feel, and know myself a Man.

ODE V.

THE PROGRESS OF POESY.

Pindaric.[1]

Φωνᾶντα συνετοῖσιν ἐς
Δὲ τὸ πᾶν ἑρμηνέων χατίζει.
PINDAR, *Olymp II.*

I. 1.

AWAKE, Æolian lyre, awake,
And give to rapture all thy trembling strings.
[2] From Helicon's harmonious springs
A thousand rills their mazy progress take:
The laughing flowers, that round them blow,
Drink life and fragrance as they flow.
Now the rich stream of music winds along
Deep, majestic, smooth, and strong,
Through verdant vales, and Ceres' golden reign:
Now rolling down the steep amain,
Headlong, impetuous, see it pour:
The rocks, and nodding groves, rebellow to the roar

I. 2.

[3] Oh! Sovereign of the willing soul,
Parent of sweet and solemn-breathing airs,
Enchanting shell! the sullen Cares,
And frantic Passions, hear thy soft control.
On Thracia's Hills the Lord of War
Has curb'd the fury of his car,
And dropp'd his thirsty lance at thy command.
Perching on the sceptred hand
Of Jove, thy magic lulls the feather'd king
With ruffled plumes, and flagging wing·
Quench'd in dark clouds of slumber lie
The terror of his beak, and lightnings of his eye.

I. 3.

[4] Thee the voice, the dance, obey,
Temper'd to thy warbled lay.
O'er Idalia's velvet-green
The rosy-crowned Loves are seen
On Cytherea's day
With antic Sport, and blue-eyed Pleasures,
Frisking light in frolic measures;
Now pursuing, now retreating,
Now in circling troops they meet
To brisk notes in cadence beating
Glance their many-twinkling feet. [clare
Slow melting strains their Queen's approach de
Where'er she turns the Graces homage pay.
With arms sublime, that float upon the air,
In gliding state she wins her easy way:
O'er her warm cheek, and rising bosom, move
The bloom of young Desire and purple light of Love.

[1] When the author first published this and the following Ode, he was advised, even by his friends, to subjoin some few explanatory notes; but had too much respect for the understanding of his readers to take that liberty.

[2] The subject and simile, as usual with Pindar, are united. The various sources of poetry, which gives life and lustre to all its touches, are here described; its quiet majestic progress enriching every subject (otherwise dry and barren) with a pomp of diction and luxuriant harmony of numbers; and its more rapid and irresistible course, when swoln and hurried away by the conflict of tumultuous passions.

[3] Power of harmony to calm the turbulent sallies of the soul. The thoughts are borrowed from the first Pythian of Pindar.

[4] Power of harmony to produce all the graces of motion in the body.

II. 1.

Man's feeble race what ills await!
Labour, and Penury, the racks of Pain,
Disease, and Sorrow's weeping train,
And Death, sad refuge from the storms of Fate!
The fond complaint, my Song, disprove,
And justify the laws of Jove.
Say, has he giv'n in vain the heav'nly Muse?
Night, and all her sickly dews,
Her Spectres wan, and Birds of boding cry,
He gives to range the dreary sky:
Till down the eastern cliffs afar
Hyperion's march they spy, and glittering shafts of war.

II. 2.

[2] In climes beyond the solar road,
Where shaggy forms o'er ice-built mountains roam,
The Muse has broke the twilight-gloom
To cheer the shivering Native's dull abode.
And oft, beneath the od'rous shade
Of Chili's boundless forests laid,
She deigns to hear the savage Youth repeat
In loose numbers wildly sweet
Their feather-cinctured Chiefs, and dusky Loves.
Her track, where'er the Goddess roves,
Glory pursue, and generous Shame,
Th' unconquerable Mind, and Freedom's holy flame.

II. 3.

[3] Woods, that wave o'er Delphi's steep,
Isles, that crown th' Ægean deep,
Fields, that cool Ilissus laves,
Or where Mæander's amber waves
In lingering Lab'rinths creep,
How do your tuneful Echoes languish,
Mute, but to the voice of Anguish!
Where each old poetic Mountain
Inspiration breathed around;
Ev'ry shade and hallow'd Fountain
Murmur'd deep a solemn sound:
Till the sad Nine in Greece's evil hour
Left their Parnassus for the Latian plains.
Alike they scorn the pomp of tyrant Power,
And coward Vice, that revels in her chains.
When Latium had her lofty spirit lost,
They sought, oh Albion! next thy sea-encircled coast.

III. 1.

Far from the sun and summer-gale,
In thy green lap was Nature's[4] Darling laid,
What time, where lucid Avon stray'd,
To him the mighty Mother did unveil
Her awful face: the dauntless Child
Stretch'd forth his little arms, and smiled.
"This pencil take," she said, "whose colours clear
Richly paint the vernal year:
Thine too these golden keys, immortal Boy!
This can unlock the gates of Joy;
Of Horror that, and thrilling Fears,
Or ope the sacred source of sympathetic Tears."

III. 2.

Nor second He[5], that rode sublime
Upon the seraph-wings of Ecstacy,
The secrets of th' Abyss to spy.
He pass'd the flaming bounds of Place and Time:
The living Throne, the sapphire-blaze,
Where Angels tremble, while they gaze,
He saw; but blasted with excess of light,
Closed his eyes in endless night.
Behold where Dryden's less presumptuous car
Wide o'er the fields of Glory bear
Two Coursers of ethereal race,
With necks in thunder clothed, and long-resounding pace.

III. 3.

Hark, his hands the lyre explore!
Bright-eyed Fancy hovering o'er
Scatters from her pictured urn
Thoughts, that breathe, and words, that burn.
[6] But ah! 'tis heard no more——
Oh! Lyre divine, what daring Spirit
Wakes thee now? though he inherit
Nor the pride, nor ample pinion,
[7] That the Theban eagle bear,
Sailing with supreme dominion
Through the azure deep of air:
Yet oft before his infant eyes would run
Such forms, as glitter in the Muse's ray
With orient hues, unborrow'd of the Sun:
Yet shall he mount, and keep his distant way
Beyond the limits of a vulgar fate,
Beneath the Good how far—but far above the Great.

ODE VI.

THE BARD

Pindaric.[8]

I. 1.

"RUIN seize thee, ruthless King!
Confusion on thy banners wait!
Though fann'd by Conquest's crimson wing,
They mock the air with idle state.
Helm, nor Hauberk's[9] twisted mail,
Nor e'en thy virtues, Tyrant, shall avail

[1] To compensate the real and imaginary ills of life, the Muse was given to mankind by the same Providence that sends the day by its cheerful presence to dispel the gloom and terrors of the night.

[2] Extensive influence of poetic genius over the remotest and most uncivilised nations: its connexion with liberty, and the virtues that naturally attend on it.—(See the Erse, Norwegian, and Welch Fragments; the Lapland and American Songs.)

[3] Progress of poetry from Greece to Italy, and from Italy to England. Chaucer was not unacquainted with the writings of Dante or of Petrarch. The Earl of Surrey and Sir Thomas Wyatt had travelled in Italy, and formed their taste there; Spenser imitated the Italian writers; Milton improved on them: but this school expired soon after the Restoration, and a new one arose on the French model, which has subsisted ever since.

[4] Shakspeare.

[5] Milton.

[6] We have had in our language no other odes of the sublime kind, than that of Dryden on St. Cecilia's day: for Cowley (who had his merit) yet wanted judgment, style, and harmony for such a task. That of Pope is not worthy of so great a man. Mr. Mason, indeed, of late days, has touched the true chords, and with a masterly hand in some of his Choruses,—above all in the last of Caractacus:

"Hark! heard ye not yon footstep dread?" &c.

[7] Pindar.

[8] This Ode is founded on a tradition current in Wales, that Edward the First, when he completed the conquest of that country, ordered all the Bards that fell into his hands to be put to death.

[9] The Hauberk was a texture of steel ringlets, or rings interwoven, forming a coat of mail, that sat close to the body, and adapted itself to every motion.

To save thy secret soul from nightly fears,
From Cambria's curse, from Cambria's tears!"
Such were the sounds, that o'er the crested pride
Of the first Edward scatter'd wild dismay,
As down the steep of Snowdon's[1] shaggy side
He wound with toilsome march his long array.
Stout Glo'ster[2] stood aghast in speechless trance:
"To arms!" cried Mortimer[3], and couch'd his quiv'ring lance.

I. 2

On a rock, whose haughty brow
Frowns o'er old Conway's foaming flood,
Robed in the sable garb of woe,
With haggard eyes the Poet stood;
(Loose his beard, and hoary hair
Stream'd, like a meteor, to the troubled air)
And with a Master's hand, and Prophet's fire,
Struck the deep sorrows of his lyre.
"Hark, how each giant-oak, and desert cave,
Sighs to the torrent's awful voice beneath!
O'er thee, oh King! their hundred arms they wave,
Revenge on thee in hoarser murmurs breathe;
Vocal no more, since Cambria's fatal day,
To high-born Hoel's harp, or soft Llewellyn's lay.

I. 3.

"Cold is Cadwallo's tongue,
That hush'd the stormy main:
Brave Urien sleeps upon his craggy bed:
Mountains, ye mourn in vain
Modred, whose magic song
Made huge Plinlimmon bow his cloud-topp'd head.
On dreary Arvon's shore[4] they lie,
Smear'd with gore, and ghastly pale:
Far, far aloof th' affrighted ravens sail;
The famish'd Eagle[5] screams, and passes by.
Dear lost companions of my tuneful art,
Dear, as the light that visits these sad eyes,
Dear, as the ruddy drops that warm my heart,
Ye died amidst your dying country's cries—
No more I weep. They do not sleep.
On yonder cliffs, a grisly band,
I see them sit; they linger yet,
Avengers of their native land:
With me in dreadful harmony they join,
And[6] weave with bloody hands the tissue of thy line."

[1] *Snowdon* was a name given by the Saxons to that mountainous tract which the Welch themselves call *Craigian-eryri*: it included all the highlands of Caernarvonshire and Merionethshire, as far east as the river Conway. R. Hygden, speaking of the castle of Conway, built by King Edward the First, says, "Ad ortum amnis Conway ad clivum montis Erery;" and Matthew of Westminster, (ad ann. 1283,) "Apud Aberconway ad pedes montis Snowdoniæ fecit erigi castrum forte."

[2] Gilbert de Clare, surnamed the Red, Earl of Gloucester and Hertford, son-in-law to King Edward.

[3] Edmond de Mortimer, Lord of Wigmore.

They both were *Lords-Marchers*, whose lands lay on the borders of Wales, and probably accompanied the King in this expedition.

[4] The shores of Caernarvonshire opposite to the Isle of Anglesea.

[5] Camden and others observe, that eagles used annually to build their aerie among the rocks of Snowdon, which from thence (as some think) were named by the Welch *Craigian-eryri*, or the crags of the eagles. At this day (I am told) the highest point of Snowdon is called *the eagle's nest*. That bird is certainly no stranger to this island, as the Scots, and the people of Cumberland, Westmoreland, &c., can testify: it even has built its nest in the Peak of Derbyshire. See Willoughby's Ornithol. published by Ray.

[6] See the Norwegian Ode, that follows.

II. 1.

'Weave the warp, and weave the woof,
The winding-sheet of Edward's race.
Give ample room, and verge enough
The characters of hell to trace.
Mark the year, and mark the night,
When Severn shall re-echo with affright
The shrieks of death, through Berkley's roof that ring,
Shrieks of an agonizing King!
She-wolf[8] of France, with unrelenting fangs,
That tear'st the bowels of thy mangled Mate,
From thee be born,[9] who o'er thy country hangs
The scourge of Heav'n! What Terrors round him wait!
Amazement in his van, with Flight combined,
And Sorrow's faded form, and Solitude behind.

II. 2.

'Mighty Victor, mighty Lord,
Low on his funeral couch he lies![10]
No pitying heart, no eye, afford
A tear to grace his obsequies.
Is the sable Warrior fled?[11]
Thy son is gone. He rests among the Dead.
The Swarm, that in thy noon-tide beam were born?
Gone to salute the rising Morn.
Fair[12] laughs the Morn, and soft the Zephyr blows,
While proudly riding o'er the Azure realm
In gallant trim the gilded Vessel goes;
Youth on the prow, and Pleasure at the helm;
Regardless of the sweeping Whirlwind's sway,
That, hush'd in grim repose, expects his evening prey.

II. 3.

'Fill high the sparkling bowl,[13]
The rich repast prepare;
Reft of a crown, he yet may share the feast:
Close by the regal chair
Fell Thirst and Famine scowl
A baleful smile upon their baffled Guest.
Heard ye the din of battle bray,[14]
Lance to lance, and horse to horse?
Long years of havoc urge their destined course,
And through the kindred squadrons mow their way.
Ye Towers of Julius,[15] London's lasting shame,
With many a foul and midnight murder fed,
Revere his Consort's faith,[16] his Father's fame,[17]
And spare the meek Usurper's holy head![18]

[7] Edward the Second, cruelly butchered in Berkley Castle.

[8] Isabel of France, Edward the Second's adulterous queen.

[9] Triumphs of Edward the Third in France.

[10] Death of that King, abandoned by his children, and even robbed in his last moments by his courtiers and his mistress.

[11] Edward, the Black Prince, dead some time before his father.

[12] Magnificence of Richard the Second's reign. See Froissart, and other contemporary writers.

[13] Richard the Second (as we are told by Archbishop Scroop and the confederate lords in their manifesto, by Thomas of Walsingham, and all the older writers) was starved to death. The story of his assassination by Sir Piers, of Exon, is of much later date.

[14] Ruinous civil wars of York and Lancaster.

[15] Henry the Sixth, George Duke of Clarence, Edward the Fifth, Richard Duke of York, &c., believed to be murdered secretly in the Tower of London. The oldest part of that structure is vulgarly attributed to Julius Cæsar.

[16] Margaret of Anjou, a woman of heroic spirit, who struggled hard to save her husband and her crown.

[17] Henry the Fifth.

[18] Henry the Sixth, very near being canonized. The line of Lancaster had no right of inheritance to the crown.

Above, below, the rose of snow,[1]
  Twined with her blushing foe, we spread:
The bristled Boar[2] in infant-gore
  Wallows beneath the thorny shade.
Now, Brothers, bending o'er th' accursed loom,
Stamp we our vengeance deep, and ratify his doom.

III. 1.

'Edward, lo! to sudden fate
  (Weave we the woof. The thread is spun.)
Half of thy heart[3] we consecrate.
  (The web is wove. The work is done.)'
"Stay, oh stay! nor thus forlorn
Leave me unbless'd, unpitied, here to mourn:
In yon bright track, that fires the western skies,
They melt, they vanish from my eyes.
But oh! what solemn scenes, on Snowdon's height
  Descending slow, their glittering skirts unroll?
Visions of glory, spare my aching sight,
  Ye unborn Ages, crowd not on my soul!
No more our long-lost Arthur[4] we bewail.
All-hail, ye genuine Kings![5] Britannia's Issue, hail!

III. 2.

"Girt with many a Baron bold,
  Sublime their starry fronts they rear;
And gorgeous Dames, and Statesmen old
  In bearded majesty, appear.
In the midst a Form divine!
Her eye proclaims her of the Briton-Line;
Her lion-port,[6] her awe-commanding face,
Attemper'd sweet to virgin-grace.
What strings symphonious tremble in the air,
  What strains of vocal transport round her play!
Hear from the grave, great Taliessin[7], hear!
  They breathe a soul to animate thy clay.
Bright Rapture calls, and soaring, as she sings,
Waves in the eye of Heav'n her many-colour'd wings.

III. 3.

"The verse adorn again
  Fierce War, and faithful Love,
And Truth severe, by fairy Fiction drest.
  In buskin'd[8] measures move
Pale Grief, and pleasing Pain,
With Horror, Tyrant of the throbbing breast.
A voice[9] as of the Cherub-Choir,
  Gales from blooming Eden bear;
  And distant warblings[10] lessen on my ear,
That lost in long futurity expire.
Fond impious Man, think'st thou yon sanguine cloud,
  Raised by thy breath, has quench'd the Orb of day?
To morrow he repairs the golden flood,
  And warms the nations with redoubled ray.
Enough for me: With joy I see
  The different doom our Fates assign.
Be thine Despair, and sceptred Care;
  To triumph, and to die, are mine."
He spoke, and headlong from the mountain's height
Deep in the roaring tide he plunged to endless night.

ODE VII.

FOR MUSIC[11]

Irregular.

I.

"Hence, avaunt, ('tis holy ground)
  Comus, and his midnight-crew,
And Ignorance with looks profound,
  And dreaming Sloth of pallid hue,
Mad Sedition's cry profane,
Servitude that hugs her chain,
Nor in these consecrated bowers
Let painted Flatt'ry hide her serpent-train in Flowers.
Nor Envy base, nor creeping Gain
Dare the Muse's walk to stain,
While bright-eyed Science watches round:
Hence, away, 'tis holy ground!

II.

From yonder realms of empyrean day
Bursts on my ear th' indignant lay:
There sit the sainted Sage, the Bard divine,
The Few, whom Genius gave to shine
Through every unborn age, and undiscovered clime.
Rapt in celestial transport they,
Yet hither oft a glance from high
They send of tender sympathy
To bless the place, where on their opening soul
First the genuine ardour stole.
'Twas Milton struck the deep-toned shell,
And, as the choral warblings round him swell,
Meek Newton's self bends from his state sublime,
And nods his hoary head, and listens to the rhyme.

III.

"Ye brown o'er-arching Groves,
That Contemplation loves,
Where willowy Camus lingers with delight!
  Oft at the blush of dawn
  I trod your level lawn,
Oft woo'd the gleam of Cynthia silver-bright
In cloisters dim, far from the haunts of Folly,
With Freedom by my side, and soft-eyed Melancholy."

[1] The white and red roses, devices of York and Lancaster.

[2] The silver Boar was the badge of Richard the Third; whence he was usually known, in his own time, by the name of *the Boar*.

[3] Eleanor of Castile died a few years after the conquest of Wales. The heroic proof she gave of her affection for her lord is well known. The monuments of his regret, and sorrow for the loss of her, are still to be seen at Northampton, Geddington, Waltham, and other places.

[4] It was the common belief of the Welch nation, that King Arthur was still alive in Fairy-Land, and should return again to reign over Britain.

[5] Both Merlin and Taliessin had prophesied, that the Welch should regain their sovereignty over this island; which seemed to be accomplished in the House of Tudor.

[6] Speed, relating an audience given by Queen Elizabeth to Paul Dzialinski, Ambassador of Poland, says, "And thus she, lion-like rising, daunted the malapert orator no less with her stately port and majestical deporture, than with the tartnesse of her princelie checkes."

[7] Taliessin, chief of the bards, flourished in the sixth century. His works are still preserved, and his memory held in high veneration among his countrymen.

[8] Shakspeare.

[9] Milton.

[10] The succession of poets after Milton's time.

[11] This Ode was performed in the Senate-House at Cambridge, July 1, 1769, at the Installation of his Grace Augustus Henry Fitzroy, Duke of Grafton, Chancellor of the University.

IV.

But hark! the portals sound, and pacing forth
With solemn steps and slow,
High Potentates, and Dames of royal birth,
And mitred Fathers in long order go:
Great [1] Edward, with the lilies on his brow
From haughty Gallia torn,
And [2] sad Chatillon, on her bridal morn
That wept her bleeding Love, and princely [3] Clare,
And [4] Anjou's Heroine, and [5] the paler Rose,
The rival of her crown and of her woes,
And [6] either Henry there,
The murder'd Saint, and the majestic Lord,
That broke the bonds of Rome.
(Their tears, their little triumphs o'er,
Their human passions now no more,
Save Charity, that glows beyond the tomb)
All that on Granta's fruitful plain
Rich streams of regal bounty pour'd,
And bade these awful fanes and turrets rise,
To hail their Fitzroy's festal morning come;
And thus they speak in soft accord
The liquid language of the skies:—

V.

"What is Grandeur, what is Power?
Heavier toil, superior pain.
What the bright reward we gain?
The grateful memory of the Good.
Sweet is the breath of vernal shower,
The bee's collected treasures sweet,
Sweet music's melting fall, but sweeter yet
The still small voice of Gratitude."

I.

Foremost and leaning from her golden cloud
The [7] venerable Marg'ret see!
"Welcome, my noble Son, (she cries aloud)
To this, thy kindred train, and me:
Pleased in thy lineaments we trace
[8] A Tudor's fire, a Beaufort's grace.
Thy liberal heart, thy judging eye,
The flower unheeded shall descry,

[1] Edward the Third; who added the *fleur de lys* of France to the arms of England. He founded Trinity College.

[2] Mary de Valentia, Countess of Pembroke, daughter of Guy de Chatillon Comte de St. Paul in France: of whom tradition says, that her husband, Audemar de Valentia, Earl of Pembroke, was slain at a tournament on the day of his nuptials. She was the foundress of Pembroke College, or Hall, under the name of Aula Mariæ de Valentia.

[3] Elizabeth be Burg, Countess of Clare, was wife of John de Burg, son and heir of the Earl of Ulster, and daughter of Gilbert de Clare, Earl of Gloucester, by Joan of Acres, daughter of Edward the First. Hence the poet gives her the epithet of "princely." She founded Clare Hall.

[4] Margaret of Anjou, wife of Henry the Sixth, foundress of Queen's College. The poet has celebrated her conjugal fidelity in the former Ode: V. Epode 2nd, line 13th.

[5] Elizabeth Widville, wife of Edward the Fourth, (hence called the paler Rose, as being of the House of York.) She added to the foundation of Margaret of Anjou.

[6] Henry the Sixth and Eighth. The former the founder of King's, the latter the greatest benefactor to Trinity College.

[7] Countess of Richmond and Derby; the mother of Henry the Seventh, foundress of St. John's and Christ's Colleges.

[8] The countess was a Beaufort, and married to a Tudor: hence the application of this line to the Duke of Grafton, who claims descent from both these families.

And bid it round heav'n's altars shed
The fragrance of its blushing head:
Shall raise from earth the latent gem
To glitter on the diadem.

VII.

"Lo, Granta waits to lead her blooming band,
Not obvious, not obtrusive, She
No vulgar praise, no venal incense flings;
Nor dares with courtly tongue refined
Profane thy inborn royalty of mind:
She reveres herself and thee.
With modest pride to grace thy youthful brow
The laureate wreath, [9] that Cecil wore, she brings,
And to thy just, thy gentle hand
Submits the Fasces of her sway,
While Spirits blest above and Men below
Join with glad voice the loud symphonious lay.

VIII.

"Through the wild waves as they roar
With watchful eye and dauntless mien
Thy steady course of honour keep,
Nor fear the rocks, nor seek the shore:
The Star of Brunswick smiles serene,
And gilds the horrors of the deep.'

ODE VIII.

THE FATAL SISTERS.

From the Norse-Tongue [10].

Now the Storm begins to lower,
(Haste, the loom of Hell prepare,)
Iron-sleet of arrowy shower
Hurtles in the darken'd air.

[9] Lord Treasurer Burleigh was Chancellor of the University, in the reign of Queen Elizabeth.

[10] To be found in the Orcades of Thormodus Torfæus; Hafniæ, 1697, folio: and also in Bartholinus.

Vitt er orpit fyrir valfalli, &c.

For the better understanding the first of these Odes, the reader is to be informed, that in the eleventh century Sigurd, Earl of the Orkney Islands, went with a fleet of ships, and a considerable body of troops, into Ireland, to the assistance of *Sictryg with the silken beard,* who was then making war on his father-in-law Brian, King of Dublin: the Earl and all his forces were cut to pieces, and Sictryg was in danger of a total defeat; but the enemy had a greater loss by the death of Brian, their king, who fell in the action. On Christmas-day, (the day of the battle,) a native of Caithness, in Scotland, saw at a distance a number of persons on horseback riding full speed towards a hill, and seeming to enter into it. Curiosity led him to follow them, till looking through an opening in the rocks he saw twelve gigantic figures resembling women: they were all employed about a loom; and as they wove, they sung the following dreadful song; which, when they had finished, they tore the web into twelve pieces, and (each taking her portion) galloped six to the north and as many to the south. These were the Valkyriur, female divinities, servants of Odin (or Woden) in the Gothic mythology. Their name signifies *choosers of the slain.* They were mounted on swift horses, with drawn swords in their hands; and in the throng of battle selected such as were destined to slaughter, and conducted them to Valkalla, the hall of Odin, or paradise of the brave; where they attended the banquet, and served the departed heroes with horns of mead and ale.

Glitt'ring lances are the loom,
Where the dusky warp we strain,
Weaving many a Soldier's doom,
Orkney's woe, and Randver's bane.

See the grisly texture grow,
('Tis of human entrails made,)
And the weights, that play below,
Each a gasping Warrior's head.

Shafts for shuttles, dipt in gore,
Shoot the trembling cords along.
Sword, that once a Monarch bore,
Keep the tissue close and strong.

Mista black, terrific Maid,
Sangrida, and Hilda see,
Join the wayward work to aid:
'Tis the woof of victory.

Ere the ruddy sun be set,
Pikes must shiver, javelins sing,
Blade with clattering buckler meet,
Hauberk crash, and helmet ring.

(Weave the crimson web of war)
Let us go, and let us fly,
Where our Friends the conflict share,
Where they triumph, where they die.

As the paths of fate we tread,
Wading through th' ensanguined field:
Gondula, and Geira, spread
O'er the youthful King your shield.

We the reins to slaughter give,
Ours to kill, and ours to spare:
Spite of danger he shall live.
(Weave the crimson web of war.)

They, whom once the desert-beach
Pent within its bleak domain,
Soon their ample sway shall stretch
O'er the plenty of the plain.

Low the dauntless Earl is laid,
Gored with many a gaping wound:
Fate demands a nobler head;
Soon a King shall bite the ground.

Long his loss shall Eirin weep,
Ne'er again his likeness see;
Long her strains in sorrow steep,
Strains of Immortality!

Horror covers all the heath,
Clouds of carnage blot the sun.
Sisters, weave the web of death;
Sisters, cease; the work is done.

Hail the task, and hail the hands!
Songs of joy and triumph sing!
Joy to the victorious bands;
Triumph to the younger King.

Mortal, thou that hear'st the tale,
Learn the tenor of our song.
Scotland, through each winding vale
Far and wide the notes prolong.

Sisters, hence with spurs of speed:
Each her thundering falchion wield;
Each bestride her sable steed.
Hurry, hurry to the field.

ODE IX.

THE DESCENT OF ODIN[1].

From the Norse Tongue.

Uprose the King of Men with speed,
And saddled straight his coal-black steed;
Down the yawning steep he rode,
That leads to [2]Hela's drear abode.
Him the Dog of Darkness spied,
His shaggy throat he open'd wide,
While from his jaws, with carnage fill'd,
Foam and human gore distill'd:
Hoarse he bays with hideous din,
Eyes that glow, and fangs that grin:
And long pursues, with fruitless yell,
The Father of the powerful spell.
Onward still his way he takes,
(The groaning earth beneath him shakes,)
Till full before his fearless eyes
The portals nine of hell arise.
Right against the eastern gate,
By the moss-grown pile he sate;
Where long of yore to sleep was laid
The dust of the prophetic Maid.
Facing to the Northern clime,
Thrice he traced the Runic rhyme;
Thrice pronounced, in accents dread,
The thrilling verse that wakes the Dead;
Till from out the hollow ground
Slowly breathed a sullen sound.

Pr. What call unknown, what charms presume
To break the quiet of the tomb?
Who thus afflicts my troubled sprite,
And drags me from the realms of night?
Long on these mould'ring bones have beat
The winter's snow, the summer's heat,
The drenching dews and driving rain.
Let me, let me sleep again.
Who is he, with voice unblest,
That calls me from the bed of rest?

O. A Traveller, to thee unknown;
Is he that calls, a Warrior's Son.
Thou the deeds of light shalt know;
Tell me what is done below,
For whom yon glitt'ring board is spread,
Drest for whom yon golden bed.

Pr. Mantling in the goblet see
The pure bev'rage of the bee;
O'er it hangs the shield of gold;
'Tis the drink of Balder bold:
Balder's head to death is giv'n.
Pain can reach the Sons of Heav'n!
Unwilling I my lips unclose:
Leave me, leave me to repose.

O. Once again my call obey.
Prophetess, arise, and say,
What dangers Odin's Child await,
Who the Author of his fate.

[1] The original is to be found in Bartholinus, De Causis Contemnendæ Mortis; Hafniæ, 1689, quarto.

Upreis Odinn allda gautr, &c.

[2] *Niflheimr*, the hell of the Gothic nations, consisted of nine worlds, to which were devoted all such as died of sickness, old age, or by any other means than in battle: over it presided Hela, the goddess of death.

Pr. In Hoder's hand the Hero's doom:
His brother sends him to the tomb.
Now my weary lips I close:
Leave me, leave me to repose.

O. Prophetess, my spell obey,
Once again arise, and say,
Who th' Avenger of his guilt,
By whom shall Hoder's blood be spilt.

Pr. In the caverns of the west,
By Odin's fierce embrace comprest,
A wond'rous Boy shall Rinda bear,
Who ne'er shall comb his raven-hair,
Nor wash his visage in the stream,
Nor see the sun's departing beam;
Till he on Hoder's corse shall smile
Flaming on the fun'ral pile.
Now my weary lips I close:
Leave me, leave me to repose.

O. Yet awhile my call obey.
Prophetess, awake, and say,
What Virgins these, in speechless woe,
That bend to earth their solemn brow,
That their flaxen tresses tear,
And snowy veils, that float in air.
Tell me whence their sorrows rose:
Then I leave thee to repose.

Pr. Ha! no Traveller art thou,
King of Men, I know thee now,
Mightiest of a mighty line——

O. No boding Maid of skill divine
Art thou, nor Prophetess of good;
But mother of the giant-brood!

Pr. Hie thee hence, and boast at home,
That never shall Inquirer come
To break my iron-sleep again;
Till [1] Lok has burst his tenfold chain.
Never, till substantial Night
Has reassumed her ancient right;
Till wrapp'd in flames, in ruin hurl'd,
Sinks the fabric of the world.

ODE X.

THE TRIUMPHS OF OWEN [2].

From the Welch.

Owen's praise demands my song,
Owen swift, and Owen strong;
Fairest flower of Roderic's stem,
[3] Gwyneth's shield, and Britain's gem.
He nor heaps his brooded stores,
Nor on all profusely pours;
Lord of every regal art,
Liberal hand, and open heart.

Big with hosts of mighty name,
Squadrons three against him came;
This the force of Eirin hiding,
Side by side as proudly riding,
On her shadow long and gay
[4] Lochlin ploughs the wat'ry way;
There the Norman sails afar
Catch the winds, and join the war:
Black and huge along they sweep,
Burthens of the angry deep.

Dauntless on his native sands
[5] The Dragon-Son of Mona stands;
In glitt'ring arms and glory drest,
High he rears his ruby crest.
There the thund'ring strokes begin,
There the press, and there the din;
Talymalfra's rocky shore
Echoing to the battle's roar.
[6] Check'd by the torrent-tide of blood
Backward Meinai rolls his flood;
While, heap'd his master's feet around,
Prostrate Warriors gnaw the ground.
Where his glowing eye-balls turn,
Thousand Banners round him burn.
Where he points his purple spear,
Hasty, hasty Rout is there,
Marking with indignant eye
Fear to stop, and Shame to fly.
There Confusion, Terror's Child,
Conflict fierce, and Ruin wild,
Agony, that pants for breath,
Despair and honourable Death.

ODE XI.

THE DEATH OF HOEL.

From the Welch [7].

Had I but the torrent's might,
With headlong rage and wild affright
Upon Deïra's squadrons hurl'd,
To rush, and sweep them from the world!

Too, too secure in youthful pride,
By them my friend, my Hoel, died,
Great Cian's Son: of Madoc old
He ask'd no heaps of hoarded gold;
Alone in Nature's wealth array'd,
He ask'd, and had the lovely Maid.

To Cattraeth's vale in glitt'ring row
Twice two hundred Warriors go;
Every Warrior's manly neck
Chains of regal honour deck,

[1] *Lok* is the evil being, who continues in chains till the *Twilight of the Gods* approaches, when he shall break his bonds; the human race, the stars, and sun, shall disappear; the earth sink in the seas, and fire consume the skies: even Odin himself and his kindred deities shall perish. For a farther explanation of this mythology, see "Introduction à l'Histoire de Dannemarc, par Mons. Mallet," 1755, quarto; or rather a translation of it, published in 1770, and entitled, "Northern Antiquities," in which some mistakes in the original are judiciously corrected.

[2] From Mr. Evans's Specimens of the Welch poetry; London, 1764, quarto. Owen succeeded his father Griffith in the principality of North Wales, A.D. 1120. This battle was fought near forty years afterwards.

[3] North Wales.

[4] Denmark.

[5] The red dragon is the device of Cadwallader, which all his descendants bore on their banners.

[6] This and the three following lines are not in the former editions, but are now added from the author's MS.

[7] Of Aneurim, styled the monarch of the Bards. He flourished about the time of Taliessin, A.D. 570. This ode is extracted from the Gododin, (see Mr. Evans' Specimens, p. 71 and 73) and now first published.

Wreath'd in many a golden link:
From the golden cup they drink
Nectar, that the bees produce,
Or the grape's ecstatic juice.

Flush'd with mirth and hope they burn:
But none from Cattraeth's vale return,
Save Aëron brave, and Conan strong,
(Bursting through the bloody throng)
And I, the meanest of them all,
That live to weep, and sing their fall.

SONNET

ON THE DEATH OF MR. RICHARD WEST.

In vain to me the smiling Mornings shine,
And redd'ning Phœbus lifts his golden fire:
The birds in vain their amorous descant join;
Or cheerful fields resume their green attire
These ears, alas! for other notes repine,
A different object do these eyes require:
My lonely anguish melts no heart but mine;
And in my breast the imperfect joys expire.
Yet Morning smiles the busy race to cheer,
And new-born pleasure brings to happier men:
The fields to all their wonted tribute bear:
To warm their little loves the birds complain:
I fruitless mourn to him, that cannot hear,
And weep the more, because I weep in vain.

EPITAPH I.

ON MRS. CLARKE.[1]

Lo! where this silent Marble weeps,
A Friend, a Wife, a Mother sleeps;
A Heart, within whose sacred cell
The peaceful Virtues loved to dwell.
Affection warm, and faith sincere,
And soft humanity were there.
In agony, in death resign'd,
She felt the Wound she left behind.
Her infant Image, here below,
Sits smiling on a Father's woe:
Whom what awaits, while yet he strays
Along the lonely vale of days?
A Pang, to secret sorrow dear;
A Sigh; an unavailing Tear;
Till Time shall ev'ry grief remove,
With Life, with Memory, and with Love.

EPITAPH II.[2]

ON SIR WILLIAM WILLIAMS.

Here, foremost in the dangerous paths of fame,
Young Williams fought for England's fair renown;
His mind each muse, each grace adorn'd his frame,
Nor Envy dared to view him with a frown.
At Aix his voluntary sword he drew,
There first in blood his infant honour seal'd;
From fortune, pleasure, science, love he flew,
And scorn'd repose when Britain took the field.

With eyes of flame, and cool undaunted breast,
Victor he stood on Bellisle's rocky steeps——
Ah! gallant youth! this marble tells the rest,
Where melancholy Friendship bends, and weeps.

[1] This lady, the wife of Dr. Clarke, physician at Epsom, died April 27, 1757; and is buried in the church of Beckenham, Kent.

[2] This epitaph (hitherto unpublished) was written at the request of Mr. Frederick Montagu, who intended to have inscribed it on a monument at Bellisle, at the siege of which this accomplished youth was killed, 1761; but from some difficulty attending the erection of it, this design was not executed.

ELEGY

WRITTEN IN A COUNTRY CHURCH-YARD.

The Curfew tolls the knell of parting day,
The lowing herds wind slowly o'er the lea,
The ploughman homeward plods his weary way,
And leaves the world to darkness and to me.

Now fades the glimmering landscape on the sight,
And all the air a solemn stillness holds,
Save where the beetle wheels his droning flight,
And drowsy tinklings lull the distant folds;

Save that, from yonder ivy-mantled tower,
The moping owl does to the moon complain
Of such, as wand'ring near her secret bower,
Molest her ancient solitary reign.

Beneath those rugged elms, that yew-tree's shade,
Where heaves the turf in many a mould'ring heap,
Each in his narrow cell for ever laid,
The rude Forefathers of the hamlet sleep.

The breezy call of incense-breathing Morn,
The swallow twitt'ring from the straw-built shed,
The cock's shrill clarion, or the echoing horn,
No more shall rouse them from their lowly bed

For them no more the blazing hearth shall burn,
Or busy housewife ply her evening care:
No children run to lisp their sire's return,
Or climb his knees the envied kiss to share.

Oft did the harvest to their sickle yield,
Their furrow oft the stubborn glebe has broke;
How jocund did they drive their team afield!
How bow'd the woods beneath their sturdy stroke!

Let not Ambition mock their useful toil,
Their homely joys, and destiny obscure;
Nor Grandeur hear with a disdainful smile
The short and simple annals of the poor.

The boast of heraldry, the pomp of power,
And all that beauty, all that wealth e'er gave,
Await alike th' inevitable hour:
The paths of glory lead but to the grave.

Nor you, ye Proud, impute to these the fault,
If Memory o'er their tomb no trophies raise,
Where through the long-drawn aisle and fretted vault
The pealing anthem swells the note of praise.

Can storied urn or animated bust
Back to its mansion call the fleeting breath
Can Honour's voice provoke the silent dust.
Or Flatt'ry soothe the dull cold ear of Death?

Perhaps in this neglected spot is laid
  Some heart once pregnant with celestial fire;
Hands, that the rod of empire might have sway'd,
  Or waked to ecstacy the living lyre.

But knowledge to their eyes her ample page
  Rich with the spoils of time did ne'er unroll;
Chill Penury repress'd their noble rage,
  And froze the genial current of the soul.

Full many a gem, of purest ray serene,
  The dark unfathom'd caves of ocean bear:
Full many a flower is born to blush unseen,
  And waste its sweetness on the desert air.

Some village-Hampden, that with dauntless breast
  The little Tyrant of his fields withstood;
Some mute inglorious Milton here may rest,
  Some Cromwell guiltless of his country's blood.

Th' applause of list'ning senates to command,
  The threats of pain and ruin to despise,
To scatter plenty o'er a smiling land,
  And read their hist'ry in a nation's eyes,

Their lot forbade: nor circumscribed alone
  Their growing virtues, but their crimes confined;
Forbade to wade through slaughter to a throne,
  And shut the gates of mercy on mankind;

The struggling pangs of conscious truth to hide,
  To quench the blushes of ingenuous shame.
Or heap the shrine of Luxury and Pride
  With incense kindled at the Muse's flame.

Far from the madding crowd's ignoble strife,
  Their sober wishes never learn'd to stray;
Along the cool sequester'd vale of life
  They kept the noiseless tenour of their way.

Yet ev'n these bones from insult to protect
  Some frail memorial still erected nigh,
With uncouth rhymes and shapeless sculpture deck'd,
  Implores the passing tribute of a sigh.

Their name, their years, spelt by the unletter'd muse,
  The place of fame and elegy supply:
And many a holy text around she strews,
  That teach the rustic moralist to die.

For who, to dumb Forgetfulness a prey,
  This pleasing anxious being e'er resign'd,
Left the warm precincts of the cheerful day,
  Nor cast one longing ling'ring look behind?

On some fond breast the parting soul relies,
  Some pious drops the closing eye requires;
Ev'n from the tomb the voice of Nature cries,
  Ev'n in our Ashes live their wonted Fires.

For thee who, mindful of th' unhonour'd Dead,
  Dost in these lines their artless tale relate;
If chance, by lonely Contemplation led,
  Some kindred Spirit shall inquire thy fate,

Haply some hoary-headed Swain may say—
  "Oft have we seen him at the peep of dawn
Brushing with hasty steps the dews away
  To meet the sun upon the upland lawn.

"There at the foot of yonder nodding beech
  That wreathes its old fantastic roots so high,
His listless length at noontide would he stretch,
  And pore upon the brook that babbles by.

"Hard by yon wood, now smiling as in scorn,
  Mutt'ring his wayward fancies he would rove;
Now drooping, woful wan, like one forlorn,
  Or crazed with care, or cross'd in hopeless love.

"One morn I miss'd him on the 'custom'd hill,
  Along the heath and near his fav'rite tree;
Another came; nor yet beside the rill,
  Nor up the lawn, nor at the wood was he:

"The next, with dirges due in sad array
  Slow through the church-yard path we saw him borne.
Approach and read (for thou canst read) the lay,
  Graved on the stone beneath yon aged thorn."

THE EPITAPH.

HERE rests his head upon the lap of Earth
  A Youth, to Fortune and to Fame unknown:
Fair Science frown'd not on his humble birth,
  And Melancholy mark'd him for her own.

Large was his bounty, and his soul sincere,
  Heav'n did a recompense as largely send:
He gave to Mis'ry all he had, a tear,
  He gain'd from Heav'n ('twas all he wish'd) a friend.

No farther seek his merits to disclose,
  Or draw his frailties from their dread abode,
(There they alike in trembling hope repose,)
  The bosom of his Father and his God.

TRANSLATION FROM STATIUS.

THIRD in the labours of the Disc came on,
With sturdy step and slow Hippomedon;
Artful and strong he poised the well-known weight,
By Phlegyas warn'd, and fired by Mnestheus' fate,
That to avoid, and this to emulate.
His vigorous arm he tried before he flung,
Braced all his nerves, and every sinew strung:
Then with a tempest's whirl and wary eye,
Pursued his cast, and hurl'd the orb on high;
The orb on high tenacious of its course,
True to the mighty arm that gave it force,
Far overleaps all bound, and joys to see
Its ancient lord secure of victory.
The theatre's green height and woody wall
Tremble ere it precipitates its fall,
The ponderous mass sinks in the cleaving ground,
While vales and woods and echoing hills rebound.
As when from Ætna's smoking summit broke,
The eyeless Cyclops heaved the craggy rock;
Where Ocean frets beneath the dashing oar,
And parting surges round the vessel roar;
'Twas there he aim'd the meditated harm,
And scarce Ulysses scaped his giant arm.
A tiger's pride the victor bore away,
With native spots and artful labour gay,
A shining border round the margin roll'd
And calm'd the terrors of his claws in gold.

Cambridge, May 8, 1736.

SONG.[1]

Thyrsis, when he left me, swore
  Ere the Spring he would return—
Ah! what means the op'ning flower?
  And the bud that decks the thorn?
'Twas the nightingale that sung!
'Twas the lark that upward sprung!

Idle notes! untimely green!
  Why such unavailing haste?
Gentle gales and skies serene
  Prove not always Winter past.
Cease, my doubts, my fears to move—
Spare the honour of my love.

A LONG STORY.

In Britain's isle, no matter where,
  An ancient pile of building stands[2]:
The Huntingdons and Hattons there
  Employ'd the pow'r of fairy hands

To raise the ceiling's fretted height,
  Each pannel in achievements clothing,
Rich windows that exclude the light,
  And passages, that lead to nothing.

Full oft within the spacious walls,
  When he had fifty winters o'er him,
My grave lord-keeper[3] led the brawls;
  The seal and maces danced before him.

His bushy beard, and shoe-strings green,
  His high-crown'd hat, and satin doublet,
Moved the stout heart of England's queen,
  Though Pope and Spaniard could not trouble it.

What, in the very first beginning!
  Shame of the versifying tribe!
Your hist'ry whither are you spinning!
  Can you do nothing but describe?

A house there is (and that's enough)
  From whence one fatal morning issues
A brace of warriors, not in buff,
  But rustling in their silks and tissues.

The first came cap-à-pie from France,
  Her conquering destiny fulfilling,
Whom meaner beauties eye askance,
  And vainly ape her art of killing.

The other amazon kind Heaven
  Had arm'd with spirit, wit, and satire:
But Cobham had the polish giv'n,
  And tipp'd her arrows with good-nature.

To celebrate her eyes, her air——
  Coarse panegyrics would but tease her;
Melissa is her *nom de guerre;*
  Alas, who would not wish to please her!

With bonnet blue and capuchine,
  And aprons long they hid their armour,
And veil'd their weapons bright and keen
  In pity to the country farmer.

Fame in the shape of Mr. P—t
  (By this time all the parish know it)
Had told, that thereabouts there lurk'd
  A wicked imp they call a poet:

Who prowl'd the country far and near,
  Bewitch'd the children of the peasants,
Dried up the cows, and lamed the deer,
  And suck'd the eggs, and kill'd the pheasants.

My lady heard their joint petition,
  Swore by her coronet and ermine,
She'd issue out her high commission
  To rid the manor of such vermin.

The heroines undertook the task,
  Through lanes unknown, o'er stiles they ventured,
Rapp'd at the door, nor stay'd to ask,
  But bounce into the parlour enter'd.

The trembling family they daunt,
  They flirt, they sing, they laugh, they tattle,
Rummage his mother, pinch his aunt,
  And up stairs in a whirlwind rattle.

Each hole and cupboard they explore,
  Each creek and cranny of his chamber,
Run hurry-skurry round the floor,
  And o'er the bed and tester clamber;

Into the drawers and china pry,
  Papers and books, a huge imbroglio!
Under a tea-cup he might lie,
  Or creased, like dog's-ears, in a folio.

On the first marching of the troops,
  The Muses, hopeless of his pardon,
Convey'd him underneath their hoops,
  To a small closet in the garden.

So rumour says: (who will, believe.)
  But that they left the door a-jar,
Where, safe and laughing in his sleeve,
  He heard the distant din of war.

Short was his joy. He little knew
  The pow'r of magic was no fable;
Out of the window, whisk! they flew,
  But left a spell upon the table.

The words too eager to unriddle,
  The poet felt a strange disorder:
Transparent bird-lime form'd the middle,
  And chains invisible the border.

[1] This was written, at the request of Miss Speed, to an old air of Geminiani: the thought from the French.

[2] The mansion-house at Stoke Pogis, then in the possession of Viscountess Cobham. The style of building, which we now call Queen Elizabeth's, is here admirably described, both with regard to its beauties and defects; and the third and fourth stanzas delineate the fantastic manners of her time with equal truth and humour. The house formerly belonged to the Earls of Huntingdon and the family of Hatton.

[3] Sir Christopher Hatton, promoted by Queen Elizabeth for his graceful person and fine dancing. G.—Brawls were a sort of figure-dance, then in vogue, and probably deemed as elegant as our modern cotillions, or still more modern quadrilles.

So cunning was the apparatus,
  The powerful pot-hooks did so move him,
That, will he, nill he, to the great house
  He went, as if the devil drove him.

Yet on his way (no sign of grace,
  For folks in fear are apt to pray)
To Phœbus he preferr'd his case,
  And begg'd his aid that dreadful day.

The godhead would have back'd his quarrel;
  But with a blush, on recollection,
Own'd that his quiver and his laurel
  'Gainst four such eyes were no protection.

The court was sate, the culprit there;
  Forth from their gloomy mansions creeping
The Lady Janes and Jones repair,
  And from the gallery stand peeping:

Such as in silence of the night
  Come (sweep) along some winding entry,
(Styack[1] has often seen the sight)
  Or at the chapel-door stand sentry:

In peaked hoods[2] and mantles tarnish'd,
  Sour visages, enough to scare ye,
High dames of honour once, that garnish'd
  The drawing-room of fierce Queen Mary.

The peeress comes. The audience stare,
  And doff their hats with due submission:
She curtsies, as she takes her chair,
  To all the people of condition.

The bard, with many an artful fib,
  Had in imagination fenced him,
Disproved the arguments of Squib,[3]
  And all that Groom[4] could urge against him.

But soon his rhetoric forsook him,
  When he the solemn hall had seen;
A sudden fit of ague shook him,
  He stood as mute as poor Macleane.[5]

Yet something he was heard to mutter,
  "How in the park beneath an old tree
(Without design to hurt the butter,
  Or any malice to the poultry),

"He once or twice had penn'd a sonnet;
  Yet hoped, that he might save his bacon:
Numbers would give their oaths upon it,
  He ne'er was for a conjuror taken."

The ghostly prudes with haggard face
  Already had condemn'd the sinner.
My lady rose, and with a grace——
  She smiled, and bade him come to dinner.

"Jesu-Maria! Madam Bridget,
  Why, what can the Viscountess mean?
(Cried the square-hoods in woeful fidget)
  The times are alter'd quite and clean!

"Decorum's turn'd to mere civility;
  Her air and all her manners show it.
Commend me to her affability!
  Speak to a commoner and poet!"

[*Here 500 stanzas are lost.*]

And so God save our noble king,
  And guard us from long-winded lubbers.
That to eternity would sing,
  And keep my lady from her rubbers.

---

1 The housekeeper. G.

2 The description is here excellent, and I should think would please universally.

3 Groom of the chamber. G.

4 The steward. G.

5 A famous highwayman, hanged the week before.

HYMN TO IGNORANCE.

A FRAGMENT.

Hail, Horrors, hail! ye ever gloomy bowers,
Ye gothic fanes, and antiquated towers,
Where rushy Camus' slowly-winding flood
Perpetual draws his humid train of mud:
Glad I revisit thy neglected reign,
Oh take me to thy peaceful shade again.

  But chiefly thee, whose influence breathed from high
Augments the native darkness of the sky;
Ah Ignorance! soft salutary power!
Prostrate with filial reverence I adore.
Thrice hath Hyperion roll'd his annual race,
Since weeping I forsook thy fond embrace.
Oh say, successful dost thou still oppose
Thy leaden Ægis 'gainst our ancient foes?
Still stretch, tenacious of thy right divine,
The massy sceptre o'er thy slumb'ring line?
And dews Lethean through the land dispense
To steep in slumbers each benighted sense?
If any spark of wit's delusive ray
Break out, and flash a momentary day,
With damp, cold touch forbid it to aspire,
And huddle up in fogs the dangerous fire.

  Oh say—she hears me not, but careless grown,
Lethargic nods upon her ebon throne.
Goddess! awake, arise, alas my fears!
Can powers immortal feel the force of years?
Not thus of old, with ensigns wide unfurl'd,
She rode triumphant o'er the vanquish'd world;
Fierce nations own'd her unresisted might,
And all was ignorance, and all was night.

  Oh sacred age! Oh times for ever lost!
(The schoolman's glory, and the churchman boast.)
For ever gone—yet still to Fancy new,
Her rapid wings the transient scene pursue,
And bring the buried ages back to view.

  High on her car, behold the grandam ride
Like old Sesostris with barbaric pride;
* * * * a team of harness'd monarchs bend——

AGRIPPINA:

AN UNFINISHED TRAGEDY.

DRAMATIS PERSONÆ.

AGRIPPINA, *the Empress-mother.*
NERO, *the Emperor.*
POPPÆA, *believed to be in love with Otho.*
OTHO, *a young man of quality, in love with Poppæa.*
SENECA, *the Emperor's Preceptor.*
ANICETUS, *Captain of the Guards.*
DEMETRIUS, *the Cynic, friend to Seneca.*
ACERONIA, *Confidante to Agrippina.*

SCENE.—*The Emperor's Villa at Baiæ.*

The drama opens with the indignation of Agrippina, at receiving her son's orders from Anicetus to remove from Baiæ, and to have her guard taken from her. At this time Otho, having conveyed Poppæa from the house of her husband Rufus Crispinus, brings her to Baiæ, where he means to conceal her among the crowd; or, if his fraud is discovered, to have recourse to the Emperor's authority; but, knowing the lawless temper of Nero, he determines not to have recourse to that expedient, but on the utmost necessity. In the mean time he commits her to the care of Anicetus, whom he takes to be his friend, and in whose age he thinks he may safely confide. Nero is not yet come to Baiæ; but Seneca, whom he sends before him, informs Agrippina of the accusation concerning Rubellius Plancus, and desires her to clear herself, which she does briefly; but demands to see her son, who, on his arrival, acquits her of all suspicion, and restores her to her honours. In the mean while Anicetus, to whose care Poppæa had been entrusted by Otho, contrives the following plot to ruin Agrippina: he betrays his trust to Otho, and brings Nero, as it were by chance, to the sight of the beautiful Poppæa; the Emperor is immediately struck with her charms, and she, by a feigned resistance, increases his passion; though, in reality, she is from the first dazzled with the prospect of empire, and forgets Otho: she therefore joins with Anicetus in his design of ruining Agrippina, soon perceiving that it will be for her interest. Otho, hearing that the Emperor had seen Poppæa, is much enraged; but not knowing that this interview was obtained through the treachery of Anicetus, is readily persuaded by him to see Agrippina in secret, and acquaint her with his fears that her son Nero would marry Poppæa. Agrippina, to support her own power, and to wean the Emperor from the love of Poppæa, gives Otho encouragement, and promises to support him. Anicetus secretly introduces Nero to hear their discourse; who resolves immediately on his mother's death, and by Anicetus's means, to destroy her by drowning. A solemn feast, in honour of their reconciliation, is to be made: after which she being to go by sea to Bauli, the ship is so contrived as to sink or crush her; she escapes by accident, and returns to Baiæ. In this interval, Otho has an interview with Poppæa; and being duped a second time by Anicetus and her, determines to fly with her into Greece, by means of a vessel which is to be furnished by Anicetus; but he, pretending to remove Poppæa on board in the night, conveys her to Nero's apartment: she there encourages and determines Nero to banish Otho, and finish the horrid deed he had attempted on his mother. Anicetus undertakes to execute his resolves; and, under pretence of a plot upon the Emperor's life, is sent with a guard to murder Agrippina, who is still at Baiæ in imminent fear, and irresolute how to conduct herself. The account of her death, and the Emperor's horror and fruitless remorse, finishes the drama.

I refer the reader to the 13th and 14th books of the Annals of Tacitus for the facts on which this story is founded: by turning to that author, he will easily see how far the poet thought it necessary to deviate from the truth of history. I shall only further observe, that as such a fable could not possibly admit of any good character, it is terror only, and not pity, that could be excited by this tragedy, had it been completed. Yet it was surely capable of exciting this passion in a supreme degree, if what the critics tell us be true that crimes, which illustrious persons commit, affect us from the very circumstance of their rank, because we unite with that our fears for the public weal.

ACT I.—SCENE 1.

AGRIPPINA, ACERONIA.

AGRIPPINA.

'TIS well, begone! your errand is performed:
[*Speaks as to Anicetus entering.*
The message needs no comment. Tell your master,
His mother shall obey him. Say you saw her
Yielding due reverence to his high command:
Alone, unguarded, and without a lictor,
As fits the daughter of Germanicus.
Say, she retired to Antium; there to tend
Her household cares, a woman's best employment
What if you add, how she turn'd pale, and trembled
You think, you spied a tear stand in her eye,
And would have dropp'd, but that her pride restrain'd it?
(Go! you can paint it well) 'twill profit you,
And please the stripling. Yet 't would dash his joy
To hear the spirit of Britannicus
Yet walks on earth; at least there are who know
Without a spell to raise, and bid it fire
A thousand haughty hearts, unused to shake
When a boy frowns, nor to be lured with smiles
To taste of hollow kindness, or partake
His hospitable board: they are aware
Of th' unpledged bowl, they love not aconite.

ACERONIA.

He's gone; and much I hope these walls alone,
And the mute air, are privy to your passion.
Forgive your servant's fears, who sees the danger
Which fierce resentment cannot fail to raise
In haughty youth, and irritated power.

AGRIPPINA.

And dost thou talk to me—to me! of danger,
Of haughty youth, and irritated power;
To her that gave it being, her that arm'd
This painted Jove, and taught his novice hand
To aim the forked bolt; while he stood trembling,
Scared at the sound, and dazzled with its brightness!
'Tis like, thou hast forgot, when yet a stranger
To adoration, to the grateful steam
Of flattery's incense, and obsequious vows
From voluntary realms, a puny boy,
Deck'd with no other lustre than the blood

Of Agrippina's race, he lived unknown
To fame, or fortune; haply eyed at distance
Some edileship, ambitious of the power
To judge of weights and measures; scarcely dared
On expectation's strongest wing to soar
High as the consulate, that empty shade
Of long-forgotten liberty! when I
Oped his young eye to bear the blaze of greatness;
Show'd him where empire tower'd, and bade him
strike
The noble quarry. Gods! then was the time
To shrink from danger; fear might then have worn
The mask of prudence: but a heart like mine,
A heart that glows with the pure Julian fire—
If bright Ambition from her craggy seat
Display the radiant prize, will mount undaunted,
Gain the rough heights, and grasp the dangerous
honour.

ACERONIA.

Through various life I have pursued your steps,
Have seen your soul, and wonder'd at its daring:
Hence rise my fears. Nor am I yet to learn
How vast the debt of gratitude, which Nero
To such a mother owes; the world, you gave him,
Suffices not to pay the obligation.
I well remember too (for I was present)
When in a secret and dead hour of night,
Due sacrifice perform'd with barb'rous rites
Of mutter'd charms, and solemn invocation,
You bade the Magi call the dreadful powers,
That read futurity, to know the fate
Impending o'er your son: their answer was,
If the son reign, the mother perishes.
Perish (you cried) the mother! reign the son!
He reigns, the rest is heaven's; who oft has bade
Ev'n when its will seem'd wrote in lines of blood,
Th' unthought event disclose a whiter meaning.
Think too how oft in weak and sickly minds
The sweets of kindness lavishly indulged
Rankle to gall; and benefits too great
To be repaid, sit heavy on the soul,
As unrequited wrongs. The willing homage
Of prostrate Rome, the senate's joint applause,
The riches of the earth, the train of pleasures,
That wait on youth, and arbitrary sway;
These were your gift, and with them you bestow'd
The very power he has to be ungrateful.

AGRIPPINA.

Thus ever grave, and undisturb'd reflection
Pours its cool dictates in the madding ear
Of rage, and thinks to quench the fire it feels not.
Say'st thou I must be cautious, must be silent,—
And tremble at the phantom I have raised?
Carry to him thy timid counsels: he
Perchance may heed 'em. Tell him too, that one,
Who had such liberal power to give, may still
With equal power resume that gift, and raise
A tempest, that shall shake her own creation
To its original atoms—tell me! say
This mighty emperor, this dreaded hero,
Has he beheld the glittering front of war?
Knows his soft ear the trumpet's thrilling voice,
And outcry of the battle? Have his limbs
Sweat under iron harness? Is he not
The silken son of dalliance, nursed in ease
And pleasure's flowery lap?—Rubellius lives,
And Sylla has his friends, though school'd by fear
To bow the supple knee, and court the times
With shows of fair obeisance: and a call,
Like mine, might serve belike to wake pretensions
Drowsier than theirs, who boast the genuine blood
Of our imperial house.

ACERONIA.

Did I not wish to check this dangerous passion,
I might remind my mistress that her nod
Can rouse eight hardy legions, wont to stem
With stubborn nerves the tide, and face the rigour
Of bleak Germania's snows. Four, not less brave,
That in Armenia quell the Parthian force
Under the warlike Corbulo, by you
Mark'd for their leader: these, by ties confirm'd,
Of old respect and gratitude, are yours.
Surely the Masians too, and those of Egypt,
Have not forgot your sire: the eye of Rome
And the Prætorian camp have long revered,
With 'custom'd awe, the daughter, sister, wife,
And mother of their Cæsars.

AGRIPPINA.

Ha! by Juno,
It bears a noble semblance. On this base
My great revenge shall rise: or say we sound
The trump of liberty? there will not want,
Even in the servile senate, ears to own
Her spirit-stirring voice; Soranus there,
And Cassius; Vetus too, and Thrasea,
Minds of the antique cast, rough, stubborn souls,
That struggle with the yoke. How shall the spark
Uuquenchable, that glows within their breasts,
Blaze into freedom, when the idle herd
(Slaves from the womb, created but to stare,
And bellow in the Circus) yet will start,
And shake 'em at the name of liberty,
Stung by a senseless word, a vain tradition,
As there were magic in it? wrinkled beldams
Teach it their grandchildren, as somewhat rare
That anciently appear'd, but when, extends
Beyond their chronicle—oh! 'tis a cause
To arm the hand of childhood, and rebrace
The slacken'd sinews of time-wearied age.
Yes, we may meet, ingrateful boy, we may!
Again the buried genius of old Rome
Shall from the dust uprear his reverend head,
Roused by the shout of millions: there before
His high tribunal thou and I appear.
Let majesty sit on thy awful brow,
And lighten from thy eye: around thee call
The gilded swarm that wantons in the sunshine
Of thy dull favour; Seneca be there
In gorgeous phrase of labour'd eloquence
To dress thy plea, and Burrhus strengthen it
With his plain soldier's oath, and honest seeming.
Against thee, liberty and Agrippina:
The world, the prize; and fair befall the victors.
But soft! why do I waste the fruitless hours
In threats unexecuted? Haste thee, fly
These hated walls, that seem to mock my shame,
And cast me forth in duty to their lord.

ACERONIA.

'Tis time we go, the sun is high advanced,
And, ere mid-day, Nero will come to Baiæ.

AGRIPPINA.

My thought aches at him; not the basilisk
More deadly to the sight, than is to me
The cool injurious eye of frozen kindness.
I will not meet its poison. Let him feel
Before he sees me.

ACERONIA.

Why then stays my sovereign,
Where he so soon may——

AGRIPPINA.

Yes, I will be gone,
But not to Antium—all shall be confess'd,
Whate'er the frivolous tongue of giddy fame
Has spread among the crowd; things that, but whisper'd,
Have arch'd the hearer's brow, and riveted
His eyes in fearful ecstacy: no matter
What; so 't be strange, and dreadful.—Sorceries,
Assassinations, poisonings—the deeper
My guilt, the blacker his ingratitude.
  And you, ye manes of ambition's victims,
Enshrined Claudius, with the pitied ghosts
Of the Syllani, doom'd to early death,
(Ye unavailing horrors, fruitless crimes!)
If from the realms of night my voice ye hear,
In lieu of penitence, and vain remorse,
Accept my vengeance. Though by me ye bled,
He was the cause. My love, my fears for him
Dried the soft springs of pity in my heart,
And froze them up with deadly cruelty.
Yet if your injured shades demand my fate,
If murder cries for murder, blood for blood,
Let me not fall alone: but crush his pride,
And sink the traitor in his mother's ruin!

[*Exeunt.*

SCENE II.

OTHO, POPPÆA.

OTHO.

Thus far we're safe. Thanks to the rosy queen
Of amorous thefts: and had her wanton son
Lent us his wings, we could not have beguiled
With more elusive speed the dazzled sight
Of wakeful jealousy. Be gay securely!
Dispel, my fair, with smiles, the tim'rous cloud
That hangs on thy clear brow. So Helen look'd,
So her white neck reclined, so was she borne
By the young Trojan to his gilded bark
With fond reluctance, yielding modesty,
And oft reverted eye, as if she knew not
Whether she fear'd, or wished to be pursued.

* * * * * *

FRAGMENT OF AN ETHICAL ESSAY.

——Πόταγ' ὦ γαθέ; τὰν γὰρ ἀοιδὰν
Οὔτι πω εἰς Αἴδαν γε τὸν ἐκλελαθόντα φυλάξεις.

THEOCRITUS.

As sickly plants betray a niggard earth,
Whose barren bosom starves her gen'rous birth,
Nor genial warmth, nor genial juice retains
Their roots to feed, and fill their verdant veins:
And as in climes, where Winter holds his reign,
The soil, though fertile, will not teem in vain,
Forbids her gems to swell, her shades to rise,
Nor trusts her blossoms to the churlish skies:
So draw mankind in vain the vital airs,
Unform'd, unfriended, by those kindly cares,
That health and vigour to the soul impart,
Spread the young thought, and warm the opening heart:
So fond Instruction on the growing powers
Of nature idly lavishes her stores,
If equal Justice with unclouded face
Smile not indulgent on the rising race,
And scatter with a free, though frugal hand
Light golden showers of plenty o'er the land:
But Tyranny has fix'd her empire there,
To check their tender hopes with chilling fear,
And blast the blooming promise of the year.
  This spacious animated scene survey,
From where the rolling orb, that gives the day,
His sable sons with nearer course surrounds
To either pole, and life's remotest bounds.
How rude soe'er th' exterior form we find,
Howe'er opinion tinge the varied mind,
Alike, to all the kind, impartial Heav'n
The sparks of truth and happiness has giv'n:
With sense to feel, with memory to retain,
They follow pleasure, and they fly from pain;
Their judgment mends the plan their fancy draws,
Th' event presages, and explores the cause;
The soft returns of gratitude they know,
By fraud elude, by force repel the foe;
While mutual wishes, mutual woes endear
The social smile and sympathetic tear.
  Say, then, through ages by what fate confined
To different climes seem different souls assign'd?
Here measured laws and philosophic ease
Fix, and improve the polish'd arts of peace.
There industry and gain their vigils keep,
Command the winds, and tame th' unwilling deep.
Here force and hardy deeds of blood prevail;
There languid pleasure sighs in every gale.
Oft o'er the trembling nations from afar
Has Scythia breathed the living cloud of war;
And, where the deluge burst, with sweepy sway
Their arms, their kings, their gods were roll'd away.
As oft have issued, host impelling host,
The blue-eyed myriads from the Baltic coast.
The prostrate South to the destroyer yields
Her boasted titles and her golden fields:
With grim delight the Brood of winter view
A brighter day, and heavens of azure hue,
Scent the new fragrance of the breathing rose,
And quaff the pendent vintage as it grows.
Proud of the yoke, and pliant to the rod,
Why yet does Asia dread a monarch's nod,
While European freedom still withstands
Th' encroaching tide, that drowns her lessening
And sees far off with an indignant groan [lands
Her native plains, and empires once her own.
Can opener skies and suns of fiercer flame
O'erpower the fire, that animates our frame;
As lamps, that shed at eve a cheerful ray,
Fade and expire beneath the eye of day?
Need we the influence of the northern star
To string our nerves and steel our hearts to war?
And, where the face of nature laughs around,
Must sick'ning virtue fly the tainted ground?

Unmanly thought! what seasons can control,
What fancied zone can circumscribe the soul,
Who, conscious of the source from whence she
springs,
By reason's light, on resolution's wings,
Spite of her frail companion, dauntless goes
O'er Lybia's deserts and through Zembla's snows?
She bids each slumb'ring energy awake,
Another touch, another temper take,
Suspends th' inferior laws, that rule our clay:
The stubborn elements confess her sway;
Their little wants, their low desires, refine,
And raise the mortal to a height divine.
Not but the human fabric from the birth
imbibes a flavour of its parent earth.
As various tracts enforce a various toil,
The manners speak the idiom of their soil.
An iron race the mountain-cliffs maintain,
Foes to the gentler genius of the plain:
For where unwearied sinews must be found
With side-long plough to quell the flinty ground
To turn the torrent's swift-descending flood,
To brave the savage rushing from the wood,
What wonder, if to patient valour train'd
They guard with spirit. what by strength they
gain'd?
And while their rocky ramparts round they see,
The rough abode of want and liberty,
(As lawless force from confidence will grow)
Insult the plenty of the vales below?
What wonder, in the sultry climes, that spread,
Where Nile redundant o'er his summer-bed
From his broad bosom life and verdure flings,
And broods o'er Egypt with his wat'ry wings,
If with advent'rous oar and ready sail
The dusky people drive before the gale;
Or on frail floats to neighb'ring cities ride,
That rise and glitter o'er the ambient tide.

* * * *

COMMENTARY.[1]

The author's subject being *The necessary Alliance between a good Form of Government and a good Mode of Education, in order to produce the Happiness of Mankind*, the poem opens with two similes; an uncommon kind of exordium: but which, I suppose, the poet intentionally chose, to intimate the analogical method he meant to pursue in his subsequent reasonings. 1st, He asserts that men without education are like sickly plants in a cold or barren soil, (line 1 to 5, and 8 to 12); and, 2dly, he compares them, when unblest with a just and well-regulated government, to plants that will not blossom or bear fruit in an unkindly and inclement air (l. 5 to 9, and l. 13 to 22). Having thus laid down the two propositions he means to prove, he begins by examining into the characteristics which (taking a general view of mankind) all men have in common one with another (l. 22 to 39); they covet pleasure and avoid pain (l. 31); they feel gratitude for benefits (l. 34); they desire to avenge wrongs, which they effect either by force or cunning (l. 35); they are linked to each other by their common feelings, and participate in sorrow and in joy (l. 36, 37). If, then, all the human species agree in so many moral particulars, whence arises the diversity of national characters? This question the poet puts at line 38, and dilates upon it to l. 64. Why, says he, have some nations shown a propensity to commerce and industry; others to war and rapine; others to ease and pleasure? (l. 42 to 46.) Why have the Northern people overspread, in all ages, and prevailed over the Southern? (l. 46 to 58.) Why has Asia been, time out of mind, the seat of despotism, and Europe that of freedom? (l. 54 to 64.) Are we from these instances to imagine men necessarily enslaved to the inconveniences of the climate where they were born? (l. 64 to 72.) Or are we not rather to suppose there is a natural strength in the human mind, that is able to vanquish and break through them? (l. 72 to 84.) It is confessed, however, that men receive an early tincture from the situation they are placed in, and the climate which produces them (l. 84 to 88). Thus the inhabitants of the mountains, inured to labour and patience, are naturally trained to war (l. 88 to 96); while those of the plain are more open to any attack, and softened by ease and plenty (l. 96 to 99). Again, the Egyptians, from the nature of their situation, might be the inventors of home-navigation, from a necessity of keeping up an intercourse between their towns during the inundation of the Nile (l. 99 to ****). Those persons would naturally have the first turn to commerce, who inhabited a barren coast like the Tyrians, and were persecuted by some neighbouring tyrant; or were driven to take refuge on some shoals, like the Venetian and Hollander; their discovery of some rich island, in the infancy of the world, described. The Tartar, hardened to war by his rigorous climate and pastoral life, and by his disputes for water and herbage in a country without land-marks, as also by skirmishes between his rival clans, was consequently fitted to conquer his rich Southern neighbours, whom ease and luxury had enervated: yet this is no proof that liberty and valour may not exist in southern climes, since the Syrians and Carthaginians gave noble instances of both; and the Arabians carried their conquests as far as the Tartars. Rome also (for many centuries) repulsed those very nations, which, when she grew weak, at length demolished[2] her extensive empire.****

[1] Compiled from Mr. Gray's notes and papers.

[2] The reader will perceive that the commentary goes further than the text. The reason for which is, that the editor (Mr. Mason,) found it so on the paper from which he formed that comment; and, as the thoughts seemed to be those which Mr. Gray would have next graced with the harmony of his numbers, he held it best to give them in continuation. There are other maxims on different papers. all apparently relating to the same subject, which are too excellent to be lost; these, therefore, (as the place in which he meant to employ them cannot be ascertained) I shall subjoin to this note, under the title of detached sentiments.

"Man is a creature not capable of cultivating his mind but in society, and in that only where he is not a slave to the necessities of life.

"Want is the mother of the inferior arts, but Ease that of the finer; as eloquence, policy, morality, poetry, sculpture, painting, architecture, which are the improvements of the former.

"The climate inclines some nations to contemplation and pleasure; others to hardship, action, and war; but not so as to incapacitate the former for courage and discipline, or the latter for civility, politeness, and works of genius.

SKETCH OF HIS OWN CHARACTER.[1]

Too poor for a bribe, and too proud to importune,
He had not the method of making a fortune:
Could love and could hate, so was thought somewhat odd;
No very great Wit, he believed in a God.
A Post or a Pension he did not desire,
But left Church and State to Charles Townshend and Squire[2].

"It is the proper work of education and government united to redress the faults that arise from the soil and air.

"The principal drift of education should be to make men *think* in the northern climates, and *act* in the southern.

"The different steps and degrees of education may be compared to the artificer's operations upon marble; it is one thing to dig it out of the quarry, and another to square it; to give it gloss and lustre, call forth every beautiful spot and vein, shape it into a column, or animate it into a statue.

"To a native of free and happy governments his country is always dear:

'He loves his old hereditary trees.'—COWLEY.

While the subject of a tyrant has no country; he is therefore selfish and base-minded; he has no family, no posterity, no desire of fame; or, if he has, of one that turns not on its proper object.

"Any nation that wants public spirit, neglects education, ridicules the desire of fame, and even of virtue and reason, must be ill governed.

"Commerce changes entirely the fate and genius of nations, by communicating arts and opinions, circulating money, and introducing the materials of luxury; she first opens and polishes the mind, then corrupts and enervates both that and the body.

"Those invasions of effeminate southern nations by the warlike northern people seem (in spite of all the terror, mischief, and ignorance, which they brought with them) to be necessary evils; in order to revive the spirit of mankind, softened and broken by the arts of commerce, to restore them to their native liberty and equality, and to give them again the power of supporting danger and hardship; so a comet, with all the horrors that attend it as it passes through our system, brings a supply of warmth and light to the sun, and of moisture to the air.

"The doctrine of Epicurus is ever ruinous to society; it had its rise when Greece was declining, and perhaps hastened its dissolution, as also that of Rome; it is now propagated in France and in England, and seems likely to produce the same effect in both.

"One principal characteristic of vice in the present age is the contempt of fame.

"Many are the uses of good fame to a generous mind: it extends our existence and example into future ages; continues and propagates virtue, which otherwise would be as short-lived as our frame; and prevents the prevalence of vice in a generation more corrupt even than our own. It is impossible to conquer that natural desire we have, of being remembered; even criminal ambition and avarice, the most selfish of all passions, would wish to leave a name behind them."

I find also among these papers a single couplet much too beautiful to be lost, though the place where he meant to introduce it cannot be ascertained; it must, however, have made a part of some description of the effect which the Reformation had on our national manners:

When love could teach a monarch to be wise,
And gospel-light first dawn'd from BULLEN'S eyes.

Thus, with all the attention that a connoisseur in painting employs in collecting every slight outline, as well as finished drawing, which led to the completion of some capital picture, I have endeavoured to preserve every fragment of this great poetical design. It surely deserved this care, as it was one of the noblest which Mr. Gray ever attempted; and also, as far as he carried it into execution, the most exquisitely finished. That he carried it no further is, and must ever be, a most sensible loss to the republic of letters.

[1] This was written in 1761, and was found in one of his pocket-books.

[2] At that time Fellow of St. John's College, Cambridge, and afterwards Bishop of St. David's

THE

POETICAL WORKS

OF

DR. JAMES BEATTIE.

LIFE OF JAMES BEATTIE.

JAMES BEATTIE was born at Laurencekirk, in the county of Kincardine, Scotland, on the 25th day of October, 1735. His father, who was a farmer of no considerable substance, is said to have had a turn for reading and versifying; but, as he died in 1742, when his son was only seven years of age, his example could have had little influence on his child.

Young Beattie was sent early to the only school his birth-place afforded, where he passed his time under the instructions of a tutor named Milne, whom he used to represent as a "good grammarian, and tolerably skilled in the Latin language, but destitute of taste, as well as of some other qualifications essential to a good teacher." He is said to have preferred Ovid as a school author, whom Mr. Beattie gladly exchanged for Virgil. That author he had been accustomed to read with great delight in Ogilvy's and Dryden's translations, as he did Homer in that of Pope; and these, with Thomson's Seasons and Milton's Paradise Lost, of all which he was very early fond, probably gave him that taste for poetry which he afterwards cultivated with so much success. Even in his school days he was inclined to making verses, and, among his play-fellows, went by the name of "the Poet."

He obtained great proficiency in his studies at school, and on his removal in 1749 to the Marischal College, Aberdeen, he appeared with great credit, and obtained the first of those bursaries or exhibitions which are left for the use of students whose parents are unable to support the entire expenses of academical education. Here he pursued his studies with unremitting diligence, and he accumulated a much more various stock of general knowledge than is usual. The only science in which he made no extraordinary proficiency was mathematics; although he performed the requisite exercises in it, he gladly forsook them to return to subjects of taste or general literature. In every other branch of academical study, he never was satisfied with what he learned within the walls of the college. His private reading was extensive and various, and his taste inclined him to the cultivation of those branches on which his future celebrity was to depend.

In 1753, he took his degree of M.A.; and being anxious to relieve his elder brother, who had hitherto provided for his support, from a longer continuance of that burden, he in August in the same year accepted the humble office of school-master and parish-clerk to the parish of Fordoun, adjoining to Laurencekirk. This he regarded as only a temporary arrangement, his intention being to obtain admission into the church, the only path by which he conceived he could obtain an independence; and with this view he attended the divinity lectures at Marischal College during the winter. His leisure hours he employed on some poetical attempts, which, as they were published in the "Scots Magazine," with his initials, and sometimes with his place of abode, must have contributed to make him yet better known and respected.

While the church seemed his only prospect, and one which he never contemplated with satisfaction, there occurred in 1757, a vacancy for one of the masters of the grammar-school of Aberdeen, a situation of considerable importance in all respects. On this occasion Mr. Beattie was advised to become a candidate; but he was diffident of his qualifications, and did not think himself so retentive of the grammatical niceties of the Latin language as to be able to answer readily any question that might be put to him by older and more experienced judges. In every part of life, it may be here observed, Mr. Beattie appears to have formed an exact estimate of his own talents; and in the present instance he failed just where he expected to fail, rather in the circumstantial than the essential requisites for the situation to which he aspired. The other candidate was accordingly preferred. But Mr. Beattie's attempt was attended with so little loss of reputation, that a second vacancy occurring a few months after, and two candidates appearing both unqualified for the office, it was presented to him by the magistrates in the most handsome manner, without the form of a trial, and he immediately entered upon it in June 1758.

In 1760 he published proposals for his first volume of poems, which appeared early in 1771. It consisted partly of originals, and partly of the pieces formerly printed in the Scots Magazine, but altered and corrected: a practice which Dr. Beattie carried almost to excess in all his poetical works. This volume met with a very favourable reception, and procured for its author at once a high poetical reputation, but he was himself so little satisfied with it as to destroy every copy he could procure; and some years after, when his taste and judgment became fully matured, he refused to acknowledge above four of the poems, namely: Retirement, the Ode to Hope, the Elegy on a Lady, and the Hares, and these he almost re-wrote before he would permit them to be printed with the Minstrel.

In September 1760 he was appointed professor of philosophy in Marischal College, an office which he held until his death. In 1765 he published his "Judgment of Paris," which was unfavourably received; and in the next year he printed his poem "On the Talk of erecting a Monument to Churchill in Westminster Abbey:" but it was not until 1770 that he produced his Essay on Truth, a work which added greatly to his reputation. This work led to an extended acquaintance with the literati of England, for hitherto his fame had been chiefly confined to his own country; but when he first visited London in 1771, he formed an acquaintance with many men of the first eminence. Among other marks of respect, the university of Oxford conferred the degree of LL.D. on the author; and on his second arrival in London, he was most graciously received by his Majesty, who not only bestowed a pension on him. but admitted him to the honour of a private conference. Many years after, when Dr. Beattie went to pay his respects to his Majesty, he was still received with every mark of condescension and kindness.

A few months after the appearance of the Essay on Truth, he published the first book of the Minstrel, but without his name. It immediately received the stamp of public favour, which has never been withdrawn, and quickly ran through four editions. The second appeared in 1774.

Dr. Beattie published several other works in prose; but after the publication of the Minstrel, he suffered his muse to be idle. His Essays, his work on the Evidences of the Christian Religion, and "Elements of Moral Science," the latter being an abstract of the lectures he had delivered in his capacity of professor of philosophy, all added to the high reputation he had already obtained.

The latter years of Dr. Beattie's life were clouded by misfortune. His wife, who was the daughter of the rector or head master of the grammar-school of Aberdeen, was seized by insanity, and was obliged to be placed in confinement. His eldest son, James Hay Beattie, was a youth of very extraordinary endowments, and uncommon moral excellence. He was so successfully trained by his father, as to be made his assistant in the professorial chair at the age of nineteen; and he was become the most intimate friend and beloved companion of his revered parent, when he fell into a decline, which carried him off in 1790, at the age of 22. This grievous loss was followed, in 1796, by that of his younger son, Montague Beattie, in his eighteenth year. The unhappy father was unable to bear up under his accumulated sorrow. The latter years of his life were a blank of existence, which terminated at Aberdeen on the 18th August, 1803, in the 68th year of his age. Dr. Beattie was amiable and exemplary in every department of private life, and fulfilled the duties of his public station in such a manner as to confer honour and credit upon the University in which he was a professor.

THE
Poetical Works
OF
JAMES BEATTIE, LL.D.

THE MINSTREL;
OR, THE PROGRESS OF GENIUS.

PREFACE.

The design was, to trace the progress of a poetical genius, born in a rude age, from the first dawning of fancy and reason, till that period at which he may be supposed capable of appearing in the world as a minstrel—that is, as an itinerant poet and musician;—a character which, according to the notions of our forefathers, was not only respectable, but sacred.

I have endeavoured to imitate Spenser in the measure of his verse, and in the harmony, simplicity, and variety of his composition. Antique expressions I have avoided; admitting, however, some old words where they seemed to suit the subject: but I hope none will be found that are now obsolete, or in any degree not intelligible to a reader of English poetry.

To those who may be disposed to ask what could induce me to write in so difficult a measure, I can only answer, that it pleases my ear, and seems, from its gothic structure and original, to bear some relation to the subject and spirit of the poem. It admits both simplicity and magnificence of sound and of language, beyond any other stanza that I am acquainted with. It allows the sententiousness of the couplet, as well as the more complex modulation of blank verse. What some critics have remarked, of its uniformity growing at last tiresome to the ear, will be found to hold true only when the poetry is faulty in other respects.

BOOK I.

Ah! who can tell how hard it is to climb
The steep where Fame's proud temple shines afar;
Ah! who can tell how many a soul sublime
Has felt the influence of malignant star,
And waged with Fortune an eternal war;
Check'd by the scoff of Pride, by Envy's frown,
And Poverty's unconquerable bar,
In life's low vale remote has pined alone,
Then dropt into the grave, unpitied and unknown!

And yet the languor of inglorious days
Not equally oppressive is to all;
Him, who ne'er listen'd to the voice of praise,
The silence of neglect can ne'er appal.
There are, who, deaf to mad Ambition's call,
Would shrink to hear th' obstreperous trump of Fame;
Supremely blest, if to their portion fall
Health, competence, and peace. Nor higher aim
Had he, whose simple tale these artless lines proclaim.

The rolls of fame I will not now explore;
Nor need I here describe, in learned lay,
How forth the Minstrel fared in days of yore,
Right glad of heart, though homely in array;
His waving locks and beard all hoary grey:
While from his bending shoulder, decent hung
His harp, the sole companion of his way,
Which to the whistling wind responsive rung:
And ever as he went some merry lay he sung.

Fret not thyself, thou glittering child of pride,
That a poor villager inspires my strain;
With thee let Pageantry and Power abide;
The gentle Muses haunt the sylvan reign,
Where through wild groves at eve the lonely swain
Enraptured roams, to gaze on Nature's charms.
They hate the sensual, and scorn the vain,
The parasite their influence never warms,
Nor him whose sordid soul the love of gold alarms.

Though richest hues the peacock's plumes adorn,
Yet horror screams from his discordant throat;
Rise, sons of harmony, and hail the morn,
While warbling larks on russet pinions float:
Or seek at noon the woodland scene remote,
Where the grey linnets carol from the hill.
O let them ne'er, with artificial note,
To please a tyrant, strain the little bill,
But sing what Heaven inspires, and wander where they will.

Liberal, not lavish, is kind Nature's hand;
Nor was perfection made for man below;
Yet all her schemes with nicest art are plann'd,
Good counteracting ill, and gladness woe:
With gold and gems if Chilian mountains glow,
If bleak and barren Scotia's hills arise;
There plague and poison, lust and rapine grow;
Here peaceful are the vales, and pure the skies,
And freedom fires the soul and sparkles in the eyes.

Then grieve not thou, to whom th' indulgent Muse
Vouchsafes a portion of celestial fire:
Nor blame the partial Fates, if they refuse
Th' imperial banquet, and the rich attire.
Know thine own worth, and reverence the lyre.
Wilt thou debase the heart which God refined?
O! let thy heaven-taught soul to heaven aspire,
To fancy, freedom, harmony, resign'd;
Ambition's groveling crew for ever left behind.

Canst thou forego the pure ethereal soul,
In each fine sense so exquisitely keen,
On the dull couch of Luxury to loll,
Stung with disease, and stupified with spleen;
Fain to implore the aid of Flattery's screen,
Even from thyself thy loathsome heart to hide,
(The mansion then no more of joy serene,)
Where fear, distrust, malevolence, abide,
And impotent desire, and disappointed pride?

O how canst thou renounce the boundless store
Of charms which Nature to her votary yields!
The warbling woodland, the resounding shore,
The pomp of groves, and garniture of fields;
All that the genial ray of morning gilds,
And all that echoes to the song of even,
All that the mountain's sheltering bosom shields,
And all the dread magnificence of Heaven,
O how canst thou renounce, and hope to be forgiven?

These charms shall work thy soul's eternal health,
And love, and gentleness, and joy, impart.
But these thou must renounce, if lust of wealth
E'er win its way to thy corrupted heart:
For ah! it poisons like a scorpion's dart;
Prompting th' ungenerous wish, the selfish scheme,
The stern resolve unmoved by pity's smart,
The troublous day, and long distressful dream.—
Return! my roving muse, resume thy purposed theme.

There lived in Gothic days, as legends tell,
A shepherd-swain, a man of low degree;
Whose sires, perchance, in Fairyland might dwell,
Sicilian groves, or vales of Arcady;
But he, I ween, was of the north countrie[1]:
A nation famed for song, and beauty's charms;
Zealous, yet modest; innocent, though free;
Patient of toil; serene amidst alarms;
Inflexible in faith; invincible in arms.

The shepherd-swain of whom I mention made,
On Scotia's mountains fed his little flock;
The sickle, scythe, or plough, he never sway'd;
An honest heart was almost all his stock;
His drink the living water from the rock:
The milky dams supplied his board, and lent
Their kindly fleece to baffle winter's shock;
And he, though oft with dust and sweat besprent,
Did guide and guard their wanderings, wheresoe'er they went.

From labour health, from health contentment springs:
Contentment opes the source of every joy.
He envied not, he never thought of, kings;
Nor from those appetites sustain'd annoy,
That chance may frustrate, or indulgence cloy:
Nor Fate his calm and humble hopes beguiled;
He mourn'd no recreant friend, nor mistress coy,
For on his vows the blameless Phœbe smiled,
And her alone he loved, and loved her from a child.

No jealousy their dawn of love o'ercast,
Nor blasted were their wedded days with strife;
Each season look'd delightful as it pass'd,
To the fond husband, and the faithful wife.
Beyond the lowly vale of shepherd life
They never roam'd; secure beneath the storm
Which in Ambition's lofty land is rife,
Where peace and love are canker'd by the worm
Of pride, each bud of joy industrious to deform.

The wight, whose tale these artless lines unfold,
Was all the offspring of this humble pair:
His birth no oracle or seer foretold;
No prodigy appear'd in earth or air,
Nor aught that might a strange event declare.
You guess each circumstance of EDWIN's birth:
The parents' transport, and the parent's care;
The gossip's prayer for wealth, and wit, and worth;
And one long summer-day of indolence and mirth.

And yet poor Edwin was no vulgar boy,
Deep thought oft seem'd to fix his infant eye.
Dainties he heeded not, nor gaude, nor toy,
Save one short pipe of rudest minstrelsy:
Silent when glad; affectionate, though shy:
And now his look was most demurely sad;
And now he laugh'd aloud, yet none knew why.
The neighbours stared and sigh'd, yet bless'd the lad:
Some deem'd him wondrous wise, and some believed him mad.

But why should I his childish feats display?
Concourse, and noise, and toil, he ever fled;
Nor cared to mingle in the clamorous fray
Of squabbling imps; but to the forest sped,
Or roam'd at large the lonely mountain's head,
Or, where the maze of some bewilder'd stream
To deep untrodden groves his footsteps led,
There would he wander wild, till Phœbus' beam,
Shot from the western cliff, released the weary team.

Th' exploit of strength, dexterity, or speed,
To him nor vanity nor joy could bring.
His heart, from cruel sport estranged, would bleed
To work the woe of any living thing,
By trap or net; by arrow, or by sling.
These he detested; those he scorn'd to wield:
He wish'd to be the guardian, not the king,
Tyrant far less, or traitor of the field;
And sure the sylvan reign unbloody joy might yield!

[1] There is hardly an ancient ballad or romance wherein a minstrel or a harper appears, but he is characterised, by way of eminence, to have been "of the north countrie." It is probable that under this appellation were formerly comprehended all the provinces to the north of the Trent. See Percy's Essay on the English Minstrels.

Lo! where the stripling, rapt in wonder, roves
Beneath the precipice o'erhung with pine;
And sees, on high, amidst th' encircling groves,
From cliff to cliff the foaming torrents shine:
While waters, woods, and winds, in concert join,
And Echo swells the chorus to the skies.
Would Edwin this majestic scene resign
For aught the huntsman's puny craft supplies?
Ah! no: he better knows great Nature's charms
to prize.

And oft he traced the uplands, to survey,
When o'er the sky advanced the kindling dawn,
The crimson cloud, blue main, and mountain grey,
And lake, dim gleaming on the smoky lawn:
Far to the west the long long vale withdrawn,
Where twilight loves to linger for a while;
And now he faintly kens the bounding fawn,
And villager abroad at early toil.
But lo! the sun appears! and heaven, earth,
ocean, smile.

And oft the craggy cliff he loved to climb,
When all in mist the world below was lost.
What dreadful pleasure! there to stand sublime,
Like shipwreck'd mariner on desert coast,
And view th' enormous waste of vapour, toss'd
In billows, lengthening to th' horizon round,
Now scoop'd in gulfs, with mountains now emboss'd!
And hear the voice of mirth and song rebound,
Flocks, herds, and water-falls, along the hoar pro-
found!

In truth he was a strange and wayward wight,
Fond of each gentle, and each dreadful scene.
In darkness, and in storm, he found delight;
Nor less, than when on ocean-wave serene
The southern Sun diffused his dazzling shene[1].
Even sad vicissitude amused his soul:
And if a sigh would sometimes intervene,
And down his cheek a tear of pity roll,
A sigh, a tear, so sweet, he wish'd not to control.

"O ye wild groves, O where is now your bloom!"
(The Muse interprets thus his tender thought)
"Your flowers, your verdure, and your balmy gloom,
Of late so grateful in the hour of drought!
Why do the birds, that song and rapture brought
To all your bowers, their mansions now forsake?
Ah! why has fickle chance this ruin wrought?
For now the storm howls mournful thro' the brake,
And the dead foliage flies in many a shapeless flake.

"Where now the rill, melodious, pure, and cool,
And meads, with life, and mirth, and beauty crown'd!
Ah! see, th' unsightly slime, and sluggish pool,
Have all the solitary vale embrown'd;
Fled each fair form, and mute each melting sound,
The raven croaks forlorn on naked spray:
And hark! the river, bursting every mound,
Down the vale thunders, and with wasteful sway
Uproots the grove, and rolls the shatter'd rocks
[away.

"Yet such the destiny of all on Earth:
So flourishes and fades majestic Man.
Fair is the bud his vernal morn brings forth,
And fostering gales awhile the nursling fan.

[1] Brightness, splendour. The word is used by some late writers as well as by Milton.

O smile, ye heavens serene! ye mildews wan,
Ye blighting whirlwinds, spare his balmy prime,
Nor lessen of his life the little span:
Borne on the swift, though silent, wings of Time
Old age comes on apace to ravage all the clime.

"And be it so. Let those deplore their doom
Whose hope still grovels in this dark sojourn;
But lofty souls, who look beyond the tomb,
Can smile at Fate, and wonder how they mourn.
Shall Spring to these sad scenes no more return?
Is yonder wave the Sun's eternal bed?
Soon shall the orient with new lustre burn,
And Spring shall soon her vital influence shed,
Again attune the grove, again adorn the mead.

"Shall I be left forgotten in the dust,
When Fate, relenting, lets the flower revive?
Shall Nature's voice, to man alone unjust,
Bid him, though doom'd to perish, hope to live?
Is it for this fair Virtue oft must strive
With disappointment, penury and pain?
No: Heaven's immortal spring shall yet arrive,
And Man's majestic beauty bloom again,
Bright thro' th' eternal year of Love's triumphant
reign."

This truth sublime his simple sire had taught--
In sooth, 'twas almost all the shepherd knew—
No subtile nor superfluous lore he sought,
Nor ever wish'd his Edwin to pursue.
"Let man's own sphere," said he, "confine his view
Be man's peculiar work his sole delight."
And much, and oft, he warn'd him to eschew
Falsehood and guile, and aye maintain the right;
By pleasure unseduced, unawed by lawless might.

"And, from the prayer of Want and plaint of Woe,
O never, never turn away thine ear!
Forlorn, in this bleak wilderness below,
Ah! what were man, should Heaven refuse to hear!
To others do (the law is not severe)
What to thyself thou wishest to be done.
Forgive thy foes; and love thy parents dear,
And friends, and native land: nor those alone—
All human weal and woe learn thou to make thine
own."

See, in the rear of the warm sunny shower,
The visionary boy from shelter fly;
For now the storm of summer-rain is o'er,
And cool, and fresh, and fragrant is the sky:
And, lo! in the dark east, expanded high,
The rainbow brightens to the setting Sun!
Fond fool, that deem'st the streaming glory nigh,
How vain the chase thine ardour has begun!
'Tis fled afar, ere half thy purposed race be run.

Yet couldst thou learn that thus it fares with age,
When pleasure, wealth, or power, the bosom warm,
This baffled hope might tame thy manhood's rage,
And disappointment of her sting disarm.
But why should foresight thy fond heart alarm!
Perish the lore that deadens young desire;
Pursue, poor imp! th' imaginary charm,
Indulge gay hope, and fancy's pleasing fire:
Fancy and hope too soon shall of themselves
expire.

When the long-sounding curfew from afar
Loaded with loud lament the lonely gale,
Young Edwin, lighted by the evening star,
Lingering and listening, wander'd down the vale.
There would he dream of graves, and corses pale;
And ghosts that to the charnel-dungeon throng,
And drag a length of clanking chain, and wail,
Till silenced by the owl's terrific song,
Or blast that shrieks by fits the shuddering aisles along.

Or when the setting Moon, in crimson dyed,
Hung o'er the dark and melancholy deep,
To haunted stream, remote from man, he hied,
Where Fays of yore their revels wont to keep;
And there let Fancy rove at large, till sleep
A vision brought to his entranced sight.
And first, a wildly murmuring wind 'gan creep
Shrill to his ringing ear; then tapers bright,
With instantaneous gleam, illumed the vault of night.

Anon, in view a portal's blazon'd arch
Arose: the trumpet bids the valves unfold;
And forth a host of little warriors march,
Grasping the diamond lance, and targe of gold.
Their look was gentle, their demeanour bold,
And green their helms, and green their silk attire;
And here and there, right venerably old,
The long-robed minstrels wake the warbling wire,
And some with mellow breath the martial pipe inspire.

With merriment and song, and timbrels clear,
A troop of dames from myrtle bowers advance;
The little warriors doff the targe and spear,
And loud enlivening strains provoke the dance.
They meet, they dart away, they wheel askance:
To right, to left, they thrid the flying maze;
Now bound aloft with vigorous spring, then glance
Rapid along: with many-colour'd rays
Of tapers, gems, and gold, the echoing forests blaze.

The dream is fled. Proud harbinger of day,
Who scaredst the vision with thy clarion shrill,
Fell chanticleer! who oft hath reft away
My fancied good, and brought substantial ill!
O to thy cursed scream, discordant still,
Let harmony aye shut her gentle ear:
Thy boastful mirth let jealous rivals spill,
Insult thy crest, and glossy pinions tear,
And ever in thy dreams the ruthless fox appear.

Forbear, my Muse. Let love attune thy line.
Revoke the spell. Thine Edwin frets not so:
For how should he at wicked chance repine,
Who feels from every change amusement flow!
Ev'n now his eyes with smiles of rapture glow
As on he wanders through the scenes of morn,
Where the fresh flowers in living lustre blow,
Where thousand pearls the dewy lawns adorn,
A thousand notes of joy in every breeze are borne.

But who the melodies of morn can tell?
The wild brook babbling down the mountain side;
The lowing herd; the sheepfold's simple bell;
The pipe of early shepherd dim descried
In the lone valley; echoing far and wide
The clamorous horn along the cliffs above!
The hollow murmur of the ocean-tide;
The hum of bees, the linnet's lay of love,
And the full choir that wakes the universal grove.

The cottage-curs at early pilgrim bark;
Crown'd with her pail the tripping milkmaid sings;
The whistling ploughman stalks afield; and, hark!
Down the rough slope the ponderous waggon rings;
Through rustling corn the hare astonish'd springs;
Slow tolls the village-clock the drowsy hour,
The partridge bursts away on whirring wings;
Deep mourns the turtle in sequester'd bower,
And shrill lark carols clear from her aërial tour.

O Nature, how in every charm supreme!
Whose votaries feast on raptures ever new!
O for the voice and fire of seraphim,
To sing thy glories with devotion due!
Blest be the day I 'scaped the wrangling crew
From Pyrrho's maze, and Epicurus' sty;
And held high converse with the godlike few,
Who to th' enraptured heart, and ear, and eye,
Teach beauty, virtue, truth, and love, and melody

Hence! ye, who snare and stupify the mind,
Sophists, of beauty, virtue, joy, the bane!
Greedy and fell, though impotent and blind,
Who spread your filthy nets in Truth's fair fane,
And ever ply your venom'd fangs amain!
Hence to dark Error's den, whose rankling slime
First gave you form! Hence! lest the Muse should deign
(Though loth on theme so mean to waste a rhyme)
With vengeance to pursue your sacrilegious crime.

But hail, ye mighty masters of the lay,
Nature's true sons, the friends of man and truth!
Whose songs sublimely sweet, serenely gay,
Amused my childhood, and inform'd my youth:
O let your spirit still my bosom soothe,
Inspire my dreams, and my wild wanderings guide;
Your voice each rugged path of life can smooth,
For well I know, where-ever ye reside
There harmony, and peace, and innocence abide.

Ah me! neglected on the lonesome plain,
As yet poor Edwin never knew your lore,
Save when, against the winter's drenching rain
And driving snow, the cottage shut the door.
Then, as instructed by tradition hoar,
Her legend when the beldame 'gan impart,
Or chant the old heroic ditty o'er,
Wonder and joy ran thrilling to his heart!
Much he the tale admired, but more the tuneful art.

Various and strange was the long-winded tale;
And halls, and knights, and feats of arms display'd;
Or merry swains, who quaff the nut-brown ale,
And sing enamour'd of the nut-brown maid;
The moonlight revel of the fairy glade;
Or hags, that suckle an infernal brood,
And ply in caves th' unutterable trade[1],
'Midst fiends and spectres, quench the Moon in blood,
Yell in the midnight storm, or ride th' infuriate flood.

---

[1] Allusion to Shakspeare:—

Macbeth. How now, ye secret, black, and midnight hags,
What is't ye do?

Witches. A deed without a name.

MACBETH, Act iv. Scene I.

But when to horror his amazement rose,
A gentler strain the beldame would rehearse,
A tale of rural life, a tale of woes,
The orphan-babes, and guardian uncle fierce.
O cruel! will no pang of pity pierce
That heart, by lust of lucre sear'd to stone?
For sure, if aught of virtue last, or verse,
To latest times shall tender souls bemoan
Those hopeless orphan-babes by thy fell arts undone.

Behold, with berries smear'd, with brambles torn[1],
The babes now famish'd lay them down to die:
Amidst the howl of darksome woods forlorn,
Folded in one another's arms they lie;
Nor friend nor stranger hears their dying cry:
"For from the town the man returns no more."
But thou, who Heaven's just vengeance darest defy,
This deed with fruitless tears shalt soon deplore,
When Death lays waste thy house, and flames consume thy store.

A stifled smile of stern vindictive joy
Brighten'd one moment Edwin's starting tear,
"But why should gold man's feeble mind decoy,
And innocence thus die by doom severe?"
O Edwin! while thy heart is yet sincere,
Th' assaults of discontent and doubt repel:
Dark even at noontide is our mortal sphere;
But let us hope; to doubt is to rebel;
Let us exult in hope, that all shall yet be well.

Nor be thy generous indignation check'd,
Nor check'd the tender tear to Misery given;
From Guilt's contagious power shall that protect,
This soften and refine the soul for heaven.
But dreadful is their doom, when doubt has driven
To censure Fate, and pious Hope forego:
Like yonder blasted boughs by lightning riven,
Perfection, beauty, life, they never know,
But frown on all that pass, a monument of woe.

Shall he, whose birth, maturity, and age,
Scarce fill the circle of one summer day,
Shall the poor gnat, with discontent and rage
Exclaim that Nature hastens to decay,
If but a cloud obstruct the solar ray,
If but a momentary shower descend!
Or shall frail man Heaven's dread decree gainsay,
Which bade the series of events extend
Wide through unnumber'd worlds, and ages without end!

One part, one little part, we dimly scan
Through the dark medium of life's feverish dream;
Yet dare arraign the whole stupendous plan,
If but that little part incongruous seem:
Nor is that part perhaps what mortals deem;
Oft from apparent ill our blessings rise.
O then renounce that impious self-esteem,
That aims to trace the secrets of the skies;
For thou art but of dust; be humble, and be wise.

Thus Heaven enlarged his soul in riper years,
For Nature gave him strength, and fire, to soar,
On Fancy's wing above this vale of tears;
Where dark cold-hearted sceptics, creeping, pore
Through microscope of metaphysic lore:
And much they grope for Truth, but never hit.
For why? Their powers, inadequate before,
This idle art makes more and more unfit;
Yet deem they darkness light, and their vain blunders wit.

[1] See the fine old ballad, called "The Children in the Wood."

Nor was this ancient dame a foe to mirth:
Her ballad, jest, and riddle's quaint device
Oft cheer'd the shepherds round their social hearth;
Whom levity or spleen could ne'er entice
To purchase chat, or laughter, at the price
Of decency. Nor let it faith exceed,
That Nature forms a rustic taste so nice.
Ah! had they been of court or city breed,
Such delicacy were right marvellous indeed.

Oft, when the winter storm had ceased to rave,
He roam'd the snowy waste at even, to view
The cloud stupendous, from th' Atlantic wave
High-towering, sail along th' horizon blue:
Where, 'midst the changeful scenery, ever new,
Fancy a thousand wondrous forms descries,
More wildly great than ever pencil drew,
Rocks, torrents, gulfs, and shapes of giant size,
And glitt'ring cliffs on cliffs, and fiery ramparts rise.

Thence musing onward to the sounding shore,
The lone enthusiast oft would take his way,
Listening, with pleasing dread, to the deep roar
Of the wide-weltering waves. In black array
When sulphurous clouds roll'd on th' autumnal day,
Even then he hasten'd from the haunt of man,
Along the trembling wilderness to stray,
What time the lightning's fierce career began,
And o'er heaven's rending arch the rattling thunder ran.

Responsive to the sprightly pipe, when all
In sprightly dance the village youth were join'd,
Edwin, of melody aye held in thrall,
From the rude gambol far remote reclined,
Soothed with the soft notes warbling in the wind:
Ah then, all jollity seem'd noise and folly.
To the pure soul by Fancy's fire refined,
Ah, what is mirth but turbulence unholy,
When with the charm compared of heavenly melancholy.

Is there a heart that music cannot melt?
Alas! how is that rugged heart forlorn;
Is there, who ne'er those mystic transports felt
Of solitude and melancholy born?
He needs not woo the muse; he is her scorn.
The sophist's rope of cobweb he shall twine;
Mope o'er the schoolman's peevish rage; or mourn,
And delve for life in Mammon's dirty mine;
Sneak with the scoundrel fox, or grunt with glutton swine.

For Edwin, Fate a nobler doom had plann'd;
Song was his favourite and first pursuit.
The wild harp rang to his advent'rous hand,
And languish'd to his breath the plaintive flute.
His infant muse, though artless, was not mute:
Of elegance as yet he took no care;
For this of time and culture is the fruit;
And Edwin gain'd at last this fruit so rare:
As in some future verse I purpose to declare.

Meanwhile, whate'er of beautiful, or new,
Sublime, or dreadful, in earth, sea, or sky,
By chance, or search, was offer'd to his view,
He scann'd with curious and romantic eye.
Whate'er of lore tradition could supply
From gothic tale, or song, or fable old,
Roused him, still keen to listen and to pry.
At last, though long by penury controll'd,
And solitude, his soul her graces 'gan unfold.

Thus on the chill Lapponian's dreary land,
For many a long month lost in snow profound,
When Sol from Cancer sends the season bland,
And in their northern cave the storms are bound:
From silent mountains, straight, with startling sound,
Torrents are hurl'd; green hills emerge: and lo!
The trees with foliage, cliffs with flowers are crown'd;
Pure rills through vales of verdure warbling go;
And wonder, love, and joy, the peasant's heart o'erflow.[1]

Here pause, my gothic lyre, a little while.
The leisure hour is all that thou canst claim.
But on this verse if MONTAGUE should smile,
New strains ere long shall animate thy frame,
And her applause to me is more than fame;
For still with truth accords her taste refined.
At lucre or renown let others aim,
I only wish to please the gentle mind
Whom Nature's charms inspire, and love of human kind.

BOOK II.

OF chance or change O let not man complain,
Else shall he never never cease to wail;
For, from the imperial dome, to where the swain
Rears the lone cottage in the silent dale,
All feel th' assault of Fortune's fickle gale;
Art, empire, Earth itself, to change are doom'd;
Earthquakes have raised to heaven the humble vale,
And gulfs the mountain's mighty mass entomb'd;
And where th' Atlantic rolls wide continents have bloom'd.[2]

But sure to foreign climes we need not range,
Nor search the ancient records of our race,
To learn the dire effects of time and change,
Which in ourselves, alas! we daily trace.
Yet at the darken'd eye, the withered face,
Or hoary hair, I never will repine:
But spare, O Time, whate'er of mental grace,
Of candour, love, or sympathy divine,
Whate'er of fancy's ray or friendship's flame is mine.

So I, obsequious to Truth's dread command,
Shall here without reluctance change my lay,
And smite the gothic lyre with harsher hand;
Now when I leave that flowery path for aye,
Of childhood, where I sported many a day,
Warbling and sauntering carelessly along;
Where every face was innocent and gay,
Each vale romantic, tuneful every tongue,
Sweet, wild, and artless all, as Edwin's infant song.

"Perish the lore that deadens young desire,"
Is the soft tenor of my song no more.
Edwin, though loved of Heaven, must not aspire
To bliss, which mortals never knew before.
On trembling wings let youthful fancy soar,
Nor always hunt the sunny realms of joy:
But now and then the shades of life explore;
Though many a sound and sight of woe annoy,
And many a qualm of care his rising hopes destroy.

Vigour from toil, from trouble patience grows.
The weakly blossom, warm in summer bower,
Some tints of transient beauty may disclose;
But soon it withers in the chilling hour.
Mark yonder oaks! Superior to the power
Of all the warring winds of Heaven they rise,
And from the stormy promontory tower,
And toss their giant arms amid the skies,
While each assailing blast increase of strength supplies.

And now the downy cheek and deepen'd voice
Gave dignity to Edwin's blooming prime;
And walks of wider circuit were his choice,
And vales more mild, and mountains more sublime
One evening, as he framed the careless rhyme,
It was his chance to wander far abroad,
And o'er a lonely eminence to climb,
Which heretofore his foot had never trode;
A vale appear'd below, a deep retired abode.

Thither he hied, enamour'd of the scene;
For rocks on rocks piled, as by magic spell:
Here scorch'd with lightning, there with ivy green.
Fenced from the north and east this savage dell:
Southward a mountain rose with easy swell,
Whose long long groves eternal murmur made;
And toward the western sun a streamlet fell,
Where, through the cliffs, the eye, remote, survey'd
Blue hills, and glittering waves, and skies in gold array'd.

Along this narrow valley you might see
The wild deer sporting on the meadow ground,
And, here and there, a solitary tree,
Or mossy stone, or rock with woodbine crown'd.
Oft did the cliffs reverberate the sound
Of parted fragments tumbling from on high;
And from the summit of that craggy mound
The perching eagle oft was heard to cry,
Or on resounding wings to shoot athwart the sky.

One cultivated spot there was, that spread
Its flowery bosom to the noonday beam,
Where many a rose-bud rears its blushing head,
And herbs for food with future plenty teem.
Sooth'd by the lulling sound of grove and stream,
Romantic visions swarm on Edwin's soul:
He minded not the Sun's last trembling gleam,
Nor heard from far the twilight curfew toll;
When slowly on his car these moving accents stole.

"Hail, awful scenes, that calm the troubled breast,
And woo the weary to profound repose!
Can passion's wildest uproar lay to rest,
And whisper comfort to the man of woes?
Here Innocence may wander, safe from foes,
And Contemplation soar on seraph wings.
O solitude! the man who thee foregoes,
When lucre lures him, or ambition stings,
Shall never know the source whence real grandeur springs.

"Vain man! is grandeur given to gay attire?
Then let the butterfly thy pride upbraid:
To friends, attendants, armies, bought with hire?
It is thy weakness that requires their aid
To palaces, with gold and gems inlaid?
They fear the thief, and tremble in the storm:
To hosts, through carnage who to conquest wade?
Behold the victor vanquish'd by the worm!
Behold, what deeds of woe the locust can perform.

[1] "Spring and autumn are hardly known to the Laplanders. About the time the sun enters Cancer, their fields, which a week before were covered with snow, appear on a sudden full of grass and flowers."—SCHEFFER'S *History of Lapland*, p. 16.

[2] See Plato's Timæus.

"True dignity is his, whose tranquil mind
Virtue has raised above the things below;
Who, every hope and fear to Heaven resign'd,
Shrinks not though Fortune aim her deadliest blow."
This strain from 'midst the rocks was heard to flow,
In solemn sounds. Now beam'd the evening star:
And from embattled clouds emerging slow
Cynthia came riding on her silver car;
And hoary mountain-cliffs shone faintly from afar.

Soon did the solemn voice its theme renew,
(While Edwin rapt in wonder listening stood:)
"Ye tools and toys of tyranny, adieu,
Scorn'd by the wise and hated by the good!
Ye only can engage the servile brood
Of Levity and Lust, who all their days,
Ashamed of truth and liberty, have woo'd,
And hugg'd the chain, that, glittering on their gaze,
Seems to outshine the pomp of Heaven's empyreal [blaze.

"Like them, abandon'd to Ambition's sway,
I sought for glory in the paths of guile;
And fawn'd and smiled, to plunder and betray,
Myself betray'd and plunder'd all the while;
So gnaw'd the viper the corroding file;
But now, with pangs of keen remorse, I rue
Those years of trouble and debasement vile.
Yet why should I this cruel theme pursue!
Fly, fly, detested thoughts, for ever from my view!

"The gusts of appetite, the clouds of care,
And storms of disappointment, all o'erpast,
Henceforth no earthly hope with Heaven shall share
This heart, where peace serenely shines at last.
And if for me no treasure be amass'd,
And if no future age shall hear my name,
I lurk the more secure from fortune's blast,
And with more leisure feed this pious flame,
Whose rapture far transcends the fairest hopes of [fame.

"The end and the reward of toil is rest,
Be all my prayer for virtue and for peace.
Of wealth and fame, of pomp and power possess'd,
Who ever felt his weight of woe decrease?
Ah! what avails the lore of Rome and Greece,
The lay heaven-prompted, and harmonious string,
The dust of Ophir, or the Tyrian fleece,
All that art, fortune, enterprise, can bring,
If envy, scorn, remorse, or pride the bosom wring!

"Let Vanity adorn the marble tomb
With trophies, rhymes, and scutcheons of renown,
In the deep dungeon of some gothic dome,
Where night and desolation ever frown.
Mine be the breezy hill that skirts the down;
Where a green grassy turf is all I crave,
With here and there a violet bestrown,
Fast by a brook, or fountain's murmuring wave;
And many an evening sun shine sweetly on my [grave.

"And thither let the village swain repair;
And, light of heart, the village maiden gay,
To deck with flowers her half-dishevell'd hair,
And celebrate the merry morn of May.
There let the shepherd's pipe the live-long day
Fill all the grove with love's bewitching woe;
And when mild Evening comes in mantle grey,
Let not the blooming band make haste to go;
No ghost, nor spell, my long and last abode shall know.

"For though I fly to 'scape from Fortune's rage,
And bear the scars of envy, spite, and scorn,
Yet with mankind no horrid war I wage,
Yet with no impious spleen my breast is torn:
For virtue lost, and ruin'd man, I mourn.
O man! creation's pride, Heaven's darling child,
Whom Nature's best, divinest gifts adorn,
Why from thy home are truth and joy exiled,
And all thy favourite haunts with blood and tears [defiled!

"Along yon glittering sky what glory streams!
What majesty attends Night's lovely queen!
Fair laugh our valleys in the vernal beams;
And mountains rise, and oceans roll between,
And all conspire to beautify the scene.
But, in the mental world, what chaos drear;
What forms of mournful, loathsome, furious mien!
O when shall that eternal morn appear,
These dreadful forms to chase, this chaos dark to [clear!

"O thou, at whose creative smile, yon heaven,
In all the pomp of beauty, life, and light,
Rose from th' abyss; when dark Confusion driven
Down, down the bottomless profound of night,
Fled, where he ever flies thy piercing sight!
O glance on these sad shades one pitying ray,
To blast the fury of oppressive might,
Melt the hard heart to love and mercy's sway,
And cheer the wandering soul, and light him on the [way!"

Silence ensued: and Edwin raised his eyes
In tears, for grief lay heavy at his heart.
"And is it thus in courtly life," he cries,
"That man to man acts a betrayer's part?
And dares he thus the gifts of Heaven pervert,
Each social instinct, and sublime desire?
Hail Poverty! if honour, wealth, and art,
If what the great pursue, and learn'd admire,
Thus dissipate and quench the soul's ethereal fire!"

He said, and turn'd away; nor did the sage
O'erhear, in silent orisons employ'd.
The youth, his rising sorrow to assuage,
Home as he hied, the evening scene enjoy'd:
For now no cloud obscures the starry void;
The yellow moonlight sleeps on all the hills[1];
Nor is the mind with startling sounds annoy'd;
A soothing murmur the lone region fills,
Of groves, and dying gales, and melancholy rills.

But he from day to day more anxious grew,
The voice still seem'd to vibrate on his ear.
Nor durst he hope the hermit's tale untrue;
For man he seem'd to love, and Heaven to fear;
And none speaks false, where there is none to hear.
"Yet, can man's gentle heart become so fell!
No more in vain conjecture let me wear
My hours away, but seek the hermit's cell;
'Tis he my doubt can clear, perhaps my care dispel."

At early dawn the youth his journey took,
And many a mountain pass'd and valley wide,
Then reach'd the wild; where, in a flowery nook,
And seated on a mossy stone, he spied
An ancient man: his harp lay him beside.
A stag sprang from the pasture at his call,
And, kneeling, lick'd the wither'd hand that tied
A wreath of woodbine round his antlers tall,
And hung his lofty neck with many a floweret small.

[1] How sweet the moonlight sleeps upon this bank.—SHAKS.

And now the hoary sage arose, and saw
The wanderer approaching: innocence
Smiled on his glowing cheek, but modest awe
Depress'd his eye, that fear'd to give offence.
"Who art thou, courteous stranger, and from whence?
Why roam thy steps to this sequester'd dale?"
"A shepherd-boy," the youth replied; "far hence
My habitation; hear my artless tale;
Nor levity nor falsehood shall thine ear assail.

"Late as I roam'd, intent on Nature's charms,
I reach'd at eve this wilderness profound;
And, leaning where yon oak expands her arms,
Heard these rude cliffs thine awful voice rebound,
(For in thy speech I recognise the sound.)
You mourn'd for ruin'd man, and virtue lost,
And seem'd to feel of keen remorse the wound,
Pondering on former days by guilt engross'd,
Or in the giddy storm of dissipation toss'd.

"But say, in courtly life can craft be learn'd,
Where knowledge opens, and exalts the soul?
Where Fortune lavishes her gifts unearn'd,
Can selfishness the liberal heart control?
Is glory there achieved by arts, as foul
As those that felons, fiends, and furies plan?
Spiders ensnare, snakes poison, tigers prowl:
Love is the godlike attribute of man.
O teach a simple youth this mystery to scan,—

"Or else the lamentable strain disclaim,
And give me back the calm, contented mind;
Which, late, exulting, view'd in Nature's frame
Goodness untainted, wisdom unconfined,
Grace, grandeur, and utility combined.
Restore those tranquil days, that saw me still
Well pleased with all, but most with humankind:
When Fancy roam'd through Nature's works at will,
Uncheck'd by cold distrust, and uninform'd of ill."

"Wouldst thou," the sage replied, "in peace return
To the gay dreams of fond romantic youth,
Leave me to hide, in this remote sojourn,
From every gentle ear the dreadful truth:
For if my desultory strain with ruth
And indignation make thine eyes o'erflow,
Alas! what comfort could thy anguish soothe,
Shouldst thou the extent of human folly know.
Be ignorance thy choice, where knowledge leads to [woe.

"But let untender thoughts afar be driven;
Nor venture to arraign the dread decree.
For know, to man, as candidate for heaven,
The voice of the Eternal said, Be free:
And this divine prerogative to thee
Does virtue, happiness, and Heaven convey;
For virtue is the child of liberty,
And happiness of virtue; nor can they
Be free to keep the path, who are not free to stray.

"Yet leave me not. I would allay that grief,
Which else might thy young virtue overpower,
And in thy converse I shall find relief,
When the dark shades of melancholy lower;
For solitude has many a dreary hour,
Even when exempt from grief, remorse, and pain:
Come often then; for, haply, in my bower,
Amusement, knowledge, wisdom thou may'st gain:
If I one soul improve, I have not lived in vain."

And now, at length, to Edwin's ardent gaze
The Muse of history unrols her page.
But few, alas! the scenes her art displays,
To charm his fancy, or his heart engage.
Here chiefs their thirst of power in blood assuage,
And straight their flames with tenfold fierceness burn:
Here smiling Virtue prompts the patriot's rage,
But lo, ere long, is left alone to mourn,
And languish in the dust, and clasp the abandon'd [urn!

"Ambition's slippery verge shall mortals tread,
Where ruin's gulf unfathom'd yawns beneath!
Shall life, shall liberty be lost," he said,
"For the vain toys that pomp and power bequeath:
The car of victory, the plume, the wreath,
Defend not from the bolt of fate the brave:
No note the clarion of renown can breathe,
To alarm the long night of the lonelygrave,
Or check the headlong haste of time's o'erwhelming [wave.

"Ah, what avails it to have traced the springs,
That whirl of empire the stupendous wheel!
Ah, what have I to do with conquering kings,
Hands drench'd in blood, and breasts begirt with [steel!
To those, whom Nature taught to think and feel,
Heroes, alas! are things of small concern;
Could History man's secret heart reveal,
And what imports a heaven-born mind to learn,
Her transcripts to explore what bosom would not [yearn!

"This praise, O Cheronean sage [1], is thine!
(Why should this praise to thee alone belong?)
All else from Nature's moral path decline,
Lured by the toys that captivate the throng;
To herd in cabinets and camps, among
Spoil, carnage, and the cruel pomp of pride;
Or chant of heraldry the drowsy song,
How tyrant blood, o'er many a region wide,
Rolls to a thousand thrones its execrable tide.

"O who of man the story will unfold,
Ere victory and empire wrought annoy,
In that elysian age (misnamed of gold)
The age of love, and innocence, and joy,
When all were great and free! man's sole employ
To deck the bosom of his parent earth;
Or toward his bower the murmuring stream decoy,
To aid the flow'ret's long-expected birth,
And lull the bed of peace, and crown the board of [mirth.

"Sweet were your shades, O ye primeval groves!
Whose boughs to man his food and shelter lent,
Pure in his pleasures, happy in his loves,
His eye still smiling, and his heart content.
Then, hand in hand, health, sport, and labour went.
Nature supplied the wish she taught to crave.
None prowl'd for prey, none watch'd to circumvent.
To all an equal lot Heaven's bounty gave:
No vassal fear'd his lord, no tyrant fear'd his slave.

"But ah! the historic Muse has never dared
To pierce those hallow'd bowers: 'tis Fancy's beam
Pour'd on the vision of the enraptured bard,
That paints the charms of that delicious theme.
Then hail sweet Fancy's ray! and hail the dream
That weans the weary soul from guilt and woe!
Careless what others of my choice may deem,
I long, where Love and Fancy lead, to go
And meditate on Heaven, enough of Earth I know."

[1] Plutarch

"I cannot blame thy choice," the sage replied,
"For soft and smooth are Fancy's flowery ways.
And yet, even there, if left without a guide,
The young adventurer unsafely plays.
Eyes dazzled long by fiction's gaudy rays
In modest truth no light nor beauty find.
And who, my child, would trust the meteor-blaze,
That soon must fail, and leave the wanderer blind,
More dark and helpless far, than if it ne'er had [shined?

"Fancy enervates, while it soothes, the heart,
And, while it dazzles, wounds the mental sight:
To joy each heightening charm it can impart,
But wraps the hour of woe in tenfold night.
And often, where no real ills affright,
Its visionary fiends, an endless train,
Assail with equal or superior might,
And through the throbbing heart, and dizzy brain,
And shivering nerves, shoot stings of more than [mortal pain.

"And yet, alas! the real ills of life
Claim the full vigour of a mind prepared,
Prepared for patient, long, laborious strife,
Its guide experience, and truth its guard.
We fare on Earth as other men have fared.
Were they successful? Let not us despair.
Was disappointment oft their sole reward?
Yet shall their tale instruct, if it declare [to bear.
How they have borne the load ourselves are doom'd

"What charms the historic Muse adorn, from spoils,
And blood, and tyrants, when she wings her flight,
To hail the patriot prince, whose pious toils
Sacred to science, liberty, and right,
And peace, through every age divinely bright,
Shall shine the boast and wonder of mankind!
Sees yonder Sun, from his meridian height,
A lovelier scene, than virtue thus enshrined
In power, and man with man for mutual aid com- [bined?

"Hail sacred Polity, by Freedom rear'd!
Hail sacred Freedom, when by law restrain'd!
Without you what were man? A groveling herd,
In darkness, wretchedness, and want enchain'd.
Sublimed by you, the Greek and Roman reign'd
In arts unrivall'd: O, to latest days,
In Albion may your influence unprofaned
To godlike worth the generous bosom raise,
And prompt the sage's lore, and fire the poet's lays!

"But now let other themes our care engage.
For lo, with modest yet majestic grace,
To curb Imagination's lawless rage,
And from within the cherish'd heart to brace,
Philosophy appears! The gloomy race
By Indolence and moping Fancy bred,
Fear, Discontent, Solicitude, give place,
And Hope and Courage brighten in their stead,
While on the kindling soul her vital beams are shed.

"Then waken from long lethargy to life[1]
The seeds of happiness, and powers of thought;
Then jarring appetites forego their strife,
A strife by ignorance to madness wrought.
Pleasure by savage man is dearly bought
With fell revenge, lust that defies control,
With gluttony and death. The mind untaught
Is a dark waste, where fiends and tempests howl:
As Phœbus to the world, is science to the soul.

"And reason now through number, time, and space,
Darts the keen lustre of her serious eye,
And learns, from facts compared, the laws to trace,
Whose long progression leads to Deity.
Can mortal strength presume to soar so high!
Can mortal sight, so oft bedimm'd with tears,
Such glory bear!—for lo, the shadows fly
From Nature's face; confusion disappears,
And order charms the eye, and harmony the ears!

"In the deep windings of the grove, no more
The hag obscene and grisly phantom dwell;
Nor in the fall of mountain-stream, or roar
Of winds, is heard the angry spirit's yell;
No wizard mutters the tremendous spell,
Nor sinks convulsive in prophetic swoon;
Nor bids the noise of drums and trumpets swell,
To ease of fancied pangs the labouring Moon,
Or chase the shade that blots the blazing orb of noon.

"Many a long-lingering year, in lonely isle,
Stunn'd with the eternal turbulence of waves,
Lo, with dim eyes, that never learn'd to smile,
And trembling hands, the famish'd native craves
Of Heaven his wretched fare; shivering in caves,
Or scorch'd on rocks, he pines from day to day;
But Science gives the word; and lo, he braves
The surge and tempest, lighted by her ray,
And to a happier land wafts merrily away!

"And even where Nature loads the teeming plain
With the full pomp of vegetable store,
Her bounty, unimproved, is deadly bane:
Dark woods and rankling wilds, from shore to shore,
Stretch their enormous gloom; which to explore
Ev'n Fancy trembles, in her sprightliest mood;
For there, each eye-ball gleams with lust of gore,
Nestles each murderous and each monstrous brood,
Plague lurks in every shade, and steams from every flood.

"'Twas from Philosophy man learn'd to tame
The soil, by plenty to intemperance fed.
Lo, from the echoing axe, and thundering flame,
Poison and plague and yelling rage are fled!
The waters, bursting from their slimy bed,
Bring health and melody to every vale:
And from the breezy main, and mountain's head,
Ceres and Flora, to the sunny dale,
To fan their glowing charms, invite the fluttering gale.

"What dire necessities on every hand
Our art, our strength, our fortitude require!
Of foes intestine what a numerous band
Against this little throb of life conspire!
Yet Science can elude their fatal ire
Awhile, and turn aside Death's levell'd dart,
Soothe the sharp pang, allay the fever's fire,
And brace the nerves once more, and cheer the heart,
And yet a few soft nights and balmy days impart.

[1] The influence of the philosophic spirit in humanising the mind, and preparing it for intellectual exertion and delicate pleasure;—in exploring, by the help of geometry, the system of the universe;—in banishing superstition;—in promoting navigation, agriculture, medicine, and moral and political science.

"Nor less to regulate man's moral frame
Science exerts her all-composing sway.
Flutters thy breast with fear, or pants for fame,
Or pines, to indolence and spleen a prey,
Or avarice, a fiend more fierce than they?
Flee to the shade of Academus' grove;
Where cares molest not, discord melts away
In harmony, and the pure passions prove
How sweet the words of Truth, breathed from the
lips of Love.

"What cannot Art and Industry perform,
When Science plans the progress of their toil!
They smile at penury, disease, and storm;
And oceans from their mighty mounds recoil.
When tyrants scourge, or demagogues embroil
A land, or when the rabble's headlong rage
Order transforms to anarchy and spoil,
Deep versed in man the philosophic sage
Prepares with lenient hand their frenzy to assuage.

"'Tis he alone, whose comprehensive mind,
From situation, temper, soil, and clime
Explored, a nation's various powers can bind,
And various orders, in one form sublime
Of policy, that 'midst the wrecks of time,
Secure shall lift its head on high, nor fear
The assault of foreign or domestic crime,
While public faith, and public love sincere,
And industry and law maintain their sway severe."

Enraptured by the hermit's strain, the youth
Proceeds the path of Science to explore.
And now, expanded to the beams of truth,
New energies and charms unknown before
His mind discloses: Fancy now no more
Wantons on fickle pinion through the skies;
But, fix'd in aim, and conscious of her power,
Aloft from cause to cause exults to rise,
Creation's blended stores arranging as she flies.

Nor love of novelty alone inspires,
Their laws and nice dependences to scan;
For, mindful of the aids that life requires,
And of the services man owes to man,
He meditates new arts on Nature's plan;
The cold desponding breast of sloth to warm,
The flame of industry and genius fan,
And emulation's noble rage alarm,
And the long hours of toil and solitude to charm.

But she, who set on fire his infant heart,
And all his dreams, and all his wanderings shared
And bless'd, the Muse, and her celestial art,
Still claim the enthusiast's fond and first regard.
From Nature's beauties variously compared
And variously combined, he learns to frame
Those forms of bright perfection[1], which the bard,
While boundless hopes and boundless views inflame,
Enamour'd consecrates to never-dying fame.

Of late, with cumbersome, though pompous show,
Edwin would oft his flowery rhyme deface,
Through ardour to adorn: but Nature now
To his experienced eye a modest grace
Presents, where ornament the second place
Holds, to intrinsic worth and just design
Subservient still. Simplicity apace
Tempers his rage: he owns her charm divine,
And clears the ambiguous phrase, and lops the
unwieldy line.

Fain would I sing (much yet unsung remains)
What sweet delirium o'er his bosom stole,
When the great shepherd of the Mantuan plains[2]
His deep majestic melody 'gan roll:
Fain would I sing what transport stormed his soul,
How the red current throbb'd his veins along,
When, like Pelides, bold beyond control,
Without art graceful, without effort strong,
Homer raised high to heaven the loud, the im-
petuous song.

And how his lyre, though rude her first essays,
Now skill'd to soothe, to triumph, to complain,
Warbling at will through each harmonious maze,
Was taught to modulate the artful strain,
I fain would sing: but ah! I strive in vain.
Sighs from a breaking heart my voice confound,
With trembling step, to join yon weeping train
I haste, where gleams funereal glare around,
And, mix'd with shrieks of woe, the knells of death
resound.

Adieu, ye lays, that Fancy's flowers adorn,
The soft amusement of the vacant mind!
He sleeps in dust, and all the Muses mourn,
He, whom each virtue fired, each grace refined,
Friend, teacher, pattern, darling of mankind!
He sleeps in dust[3]. Ah, how shall I pursue
My theme! To heart-consuming grief resign'd,
Here on his recent grave I fix my view,
And pour my bitter tears. Ye flowery lays, adieu!

Art thou, my *Gregory*, for ever fled!
And am I left to unavailing woe!
When fortune's storms assail this weary head,
Where cares long since have shed untimely snow!
Ah, now for comfort whither shall I go?
No more thy soothing voice my anguish cheers:
Thy placid eyes with smiles no longer glow,
My hopes to cherish, and allay my fears.
'Tis meet that I should mourn: flow forth afresh,
my tears!

[1] General ideas of excellence, the immediate archetypes of sublime imitation, both in painting and in poetry. See Aristotle's Poetics, and the Discourses of Sir Joshua Reynolds.

[2] Virgil.

[3] This excellent person died suddenly on the 10th of February, 1773. The conclusion of the poem was written a few days after.

POEMS.

TO

MRS. MONTAGU,

THESE

LITTLE POEMS,

NOW REVISED AND CORRECTED FOR THE LAST TIME,

ARE,

WITH EVERY SENTIMENT OF ESTEEM AND GRATITUDE,

MOST RESPECTFULLY INSCRIBED

BY THE AUTHOR.

ADVERTISEMENT.

January, 1777.

Having lately seen in print some poems ascribed to me which I never wrote, and some of my own inaccurately copied, I thought it would not be improper to publish, in this little volume, all the verses of which I am willing to be considered as the author. Many others I did indeed write in the early part of my life; but they were in general so incorrect, that I would not rescue them from oblivion, even if a wish could do it.

Some of the few now offered to the public would perhaps have been suppressed, if in making this collection I had implicitly followed my own judgment. But in so small a matter, who would refuse to submit his opinion to that of a friend?

It is of no consequence to the reader to know the date of any of these little poems. But some private reasons determined the author to add, that most of them were written many years ago, and that the greater part of the *Minstrel*, which is his latest attempt in this way, was composed in the year 1768.

ODE TO PEACE.

I. 1.

Peace, heaven-descended maid! whose powerful voice
From ancient darkness call'd the morn,
Of jarring elements composed the noise,
When Chaos from his old dominion torn,
With all his bellowing throng,
Far, far was hurl'd the void abyss along;
And all the bright angelic choir
To loftiest raptures tuned the heavenly lyre,
Pour'd in loud symphony the impetuous strain;
And every fiery orb and planet sung,
And wide through night's dark desolate domain
Rebounding long and deep the lays triumphant rung.

I. 2.

Oh, whither art thou fled, Saturnian reign?
Roll round again, majestic years!
To break fell Tyranny's corroding chain,
From Woe's wan cheek to wipe the bitter tears,
Ye years, again roll round!
Hark from afar what loud tumultuous sound,
While echoes sweep the winding vales,
Swells full along the plains, and loads the gales!
Murder deep roused, with the wild whirlwind's haste
And roar of tempest, from her cavern springs,
Her tangled serpents girds around her waist,
Smiles ghastly-stern, and shakes her gore-distilling wings.

I. 3.

Fierce up the yielding skies
The shouts redoubling rise:
Earth shudders at the dreadful sound,
And all is listening trembling round.
Torrents, that from yon promontory's head
Dash'd furious down in desperate cascade,
Heard from afar amid the lonely night
That oft have led the wanderer right,
Are silent at the noise.
The mighty ocean's more majestic voice,
Drown'd in superior din, is heard no more;
The surge in silence sweeps along the foamy shore.

II. 1.

The bloody banner streaming in the air,
Seen on yon sky-mix'd mountain's brow,
The mingling multitudes, the madding car
Pouring impetuous on the plain below,
War's dreadful lord proclaim.
Bursts out by frequent fits the expansive flame;
Whirl'd in tempestuous eddies flies
The surging smoke o'er all the darken'd skies.
The cheerful face of heaven no more is seen,
Fades the morn's vivid blush to deadly pale,
The bat flits transient o'er the dusky green,
Night's shrieking birds along the sullen twilight sail.

II. 2.

Involved in fire-streak'd gloom the car comes on,
The mangled steeds grim Terror guides;
His forehead writhed to a relentless frown,
Aloft the angry power of battles rides:
Grasp'd in his mighty hand
A mace tremendous desolates the land;
Thunders the turret down the steep,
The mountain shrinks before its wasteful sweep:
Chill Horror the dissolving limbs invades;
Smit by the blasting lightning of his eyes,
A bloated paleness beauty's bloom o'erspreads,
Fades every flowery field, and every verdure dies.

II. 3.

How startled Frenzy stares,
Bristling her ragged hairs!
Revenge the gory fragment gnaws;
See, with her griping vulture-claws
Imprinted deep, she rends the opening wound!
Hatred her torch blue-streaming tosses round;
The shrieks of agony and clang of arms
Re-echo to the fierce alarms
Her trump terrific blows.
Disparting from behind, the clouds disclose
Of kingly gesture a gigantic form,
That with his scourge sublime directs the whirling storm.

III. 1.

Ambition, outside fair! within more foul
Than fellest fiend from Tartarus sprung,
In caverns hatch'd, where the fierce torrents roll
Of Phlegethon, the burning banks along,
Yon naked waste survey:
Where late was heard the flute's mellifluous lay:
Where late the rosy-bosom'd Hours
In loose array danced lightly o'er the flowers;
Where late the shepherd told his tender tale;
And waked by the soft-murmuring breeze of morn
The voice of cheerful labour fill'd the dale;
And dove-eyed Plenty smiled, and waved her liberal horn.

III. 2.

Yon ruins, sable from the wasting flame,
But mark the once replendent dome;
The frequent corse obstructs the sullen stream,
And ghosts glare horrid from the sylvan gloom.
How sadly-silent all!
Save where outstretch'd beneath yon hanging wall
Pale Famine moans with feeble breath,
And Torture yells, and grinds her bloody teeth—
Though vain the muse, and every melting lay,
To touch thy heart, unconscious of remorse!
Know, monster, know, thy hour is on the way,
I see, I see the years begin their mighty course.

III. 3.

What scenes of glory rise
Before my dazzled eyes!
Young Zephyrs wave their wanton wings,
And melody celestial rings:
Along the lilied lawn the nymphs advance,
Flush'd with love's bloom, and range the sprightly dance.
The gladsome shepherds on the mountain-side,
Array'd in all their rural pride,
Exalt the festive note,
Inviting Echo from her inmost grot—
But ah! the landscape glows with fainter light,
It darkens, swims, and flies for ever from my sight.

IV. 1.

Illusions vain! Can sacred Peace reside
Where sordid gold the breast alarms,
Where cruelty inflames the eye of Pride,
And Grandeur wantons in soft Pleasure's arms!
Ambition! these are thine:
These from the soul erase the form divine;
These quench the animating fire,
That warms the bosom with sublime desire.
Thence the relentless heart forgets to feel,
Hate rides tremendous on the o'erwhelming brow,
And midnight Rancour grasps the cruel steel,
Blaze the funereal flames, and sound the shrieks of Woe.

IV. 2.

From Albion fled, thy once-beloved retreat,
What region brightens in thy smile,
Creative Peace, and underneath thy feet
Sees sudden flowers adorn the rugged soil?
In bleak Siberia blows,
Waked by thy genial breath, the balmy rose?
Waved over by thy magic wand,
Does life inform fell Lybia's burning sand?
Or does some isle thy parting flight detain,
Where roves the Indian through primeval shades:
Haunts the pure pleasures of the woodland reign,
And led by reason's ray the path of Nature treads?

IV. 3.

On Cuba's utmost steep,[1]
Far leaning o'er the deep,
The goddess' pensive form was seen.
Her robe of Nature's varied green
Waved on the gale; grief dimm'd her radiant eyes,
Her swelling bosom heaved with boding sighs:
She eyed the main; where, gaining on the view,
Emerging from the ethereal blue,
Midst the dread pomp of war,
Gleam'd the Iberian streamer from afar.
She saw; and on refulgent pinions borne
Slow wing'd her way sublime, and mingled with the morn.

THE

TRIUMPH OF MELANCHOLY.

Memory, be still! why throng upon the thought
These scenes deep-stain'd with Sorrow's sable dye?
Hast thou in store no joy-illumined draught,
To cheer bewilder'd Fancy's tearful eye?

Yes—from afar a landscape seems to rise,
Deck'd gorgeous by the lavish hand of Spring;
Thin gilded clouds float light along the skies,
And laughing Loves disport on fluttering wing.

How blest the youth in yonder valley laid!
Soft smiles in every conscious feature play,
While to the gale low-murmuring through the glade
He tempers sweet his sprightly-warbling lay.

Hail Innocence! whose bosom, all serene,
Feels not fierce passion's raving tempest roll!
Oh ne'er may Care distract that placid mien!
Oh ne'er may Doubt's dark shades o'erwhelm thy soul!

Vain wish! for lo, in gay attire conceal'd,
Yonder she comes! the heart-inflaming fiend!
(Will no kind power the helpless stripling shield!)
Swift to her destined prey see Passion bend!

O smile accurst, to hide the worst designs!
Now with blithe eye she woos him to be blest,
While round her arm unseen a serpent twines—
And lo, she hurls it hissing at his breast!

And, instant, lo, his dizzy eye-ball swims
Ghastly, and reddening darts a threatful glare:
Pain with strong grasp distorts his writhing limbs,
And Fear's cold hand erects his bristling hair!

Is this, O life, is this thy boasted prime!
And does thy spring no happier prospect yield!
Why gilds the vernal sun thy gaudy clime,
When nipping mildews waste the flowery field!

How memory pains! Let some gay theme beguile
The musing mind, and soothe to soft delight.
Ye images of woe, no more recoil;
Be life's past scenes wrapt in oblivious night.

[1] This alludes to the discovery of America by the Spaniards under Columbus. These ravagers are said to have made their first descent on the islands in the Gulf of Florida, of which Cuba is one.

Now when fierce Winter, arm'd with wasteful power,
Heaves the wild deep that thunders from afar,
How sweet to sit in this sequester'd bower,
To hear, and but to hear, the mingling war!

Ambition here displays no gilded toy
That tempts on desperate wing the soul to rise,
Nor Pleasure's flower-embroider'd paths decoy,
Nor Anguish lurks in Grandeur's gay disguise.

Oft has Contentment cheer'd this lone abode
With the mild languish of her smiling eye;
Here Health has oft in blushing beauty glow'd,
While loose-robed Quiet stood enamour'd by.

E'en the storm lulls to more profound repose:
The storm these humble walls assails in vain;
Screen'd is the lily when the whirlwind blows,
While the oak's stately ruin strows the plain.

Blow on, ye winds! Thine, Winter, be the skies,
Roll the old ocean, and the vales lay waste:
Nature thy momentary rage defies;
To her relief the gentler seasons haste.

Throned in her emerald car see Spring appear!
(As Fancy wills, the landscape starts to view)
Her emerald car the youthful Zephyrs bear,
Fanning her bosom with their pinions blue.

Around the jocund Hours are fluttering seen;
And lo, her rod the rose-lipp'd power extends!
And lo, the lawns are deck'd in living green,
And Beauty's bright-eyed train from heaven descends!

Haste, happy days, and make all nature glad—
But will all nature joy at your return?
Say, can ye cheer pale Sickness' gloomy bed,
Or dry the tears that bathe the untimely urn?

Will ye one transient ray of gladness dart
'Cross the dark cell where hopeless slavery lies?
To ease tired Disappointment's bleeding heart,
Will all your stores of softening balm suffice?

When fell Oppression in his harpy fangs
From Want's weak grasp the last sad morsel bears,
Can ye allay the heart-wrung parent's pangs,
Whose famish'd child craves help with fruitless tears?

For ah! thy reign, Oppression, is not past.
Who from the shivering limbs the vestment rends?
Who lays the once-rejoicing village waste,
Bursting the ties of lovers and of friends?

O ye, to Pleasure who resign the day,
As loose in Luxury's clasping arms you lie,
O yet let pity in your breast bear sway,
And learn to melt at Misery's moving cry.

But hop'st thou, Muse, vain-glorious as thou art,
With the weak impulse of thy humble strain,
Hop'st thou to soften Pride's obdurate heart,
When Errol's bright example shines in vain?

Then cease the theme. Turn, Fancy, turn thine eye,
Thy weeping eye, nor further urge thy flight;
Thy haunts, alas! no gleams of joy supply,
Or transient gleams, that flash, and sink in night.

Yet fain the mind its anguish would forego—
Spread then, historic Muse, thy pictured scroll;
Bid thy great scenes in all their splendour glow,
And swell to thought sublime th' exalted soul.

What mingling pomps rush boundless on the gaze!
What gallant navies ride the heaving deep!
What glittering towns their cloud-wrapt turrets raise!
What bulwarks frown horrific o'er the steep!

Bristling with spears, and bright with burnish'd shields,
Th' embattled legions stretch their long array;
Discord's red torch, as fierce she scours the fields,
With bloody tincture stains the face of day.

And now the hosts in silence wait the sign.
How keen their looks whom Liberty inspires!
Quick as the goddess darts along the line,
Each breast impatient burns with noble fires.

Her form how graceful! In her lofty mien
The smiles of Love stern Wisdom's frown control;
Her fearless eye, determined though serene,
Speaks the great purpose, and th' unconquer'd soul.

Mark, where Ambition leads the adverse band,
Each feature fierce and haggard, as with pain!
With menace loud he cries, while from his hand
He vainly strives to wipe the crimson stain.

Lo, at his call, impetuous as the storms,
Headlong to deeds of death the hosts are driven;
Hatred, to madness wrought, each face deforms,
Mounts the black whirlwind, and involves the heaven.

Now, Virtue, now thy powerful succour lend,
Shield them for Liberty, who dare to die—
Ah Liberty! will none thy cause befriend?
Are these thy sons, thy generous sons, that fly?

Not Virtue's self, when Heaven its aid denies,
Can brace the loosen'd nerves, or warm the heart;
Not Virtue's self can still the burst of sighs,
When festers in the soul Misfortune's dart.

See where, by heaven-bred terror all dismay'd,
The scattering legions pour along the plain!
Ambition's car with bloody spoils array'd
Hews its broad way, as Vengeance guides the rein.

But who is he, that, by yon lonely brook
With woods o'erhung and precipices rude[1],
Abandon'd lies, and with undaunted look
Sees streaming from his breast the purple flood?

Ah Brutus! ever thine be Virtue's tear!
Lo, his dim eyes to Liberty he turns
As, scarce supported on her broken spear,
O'er her expiring son the goddess mourns.

Loose to the wind her azure mantle flies,
From her dishevel'd locks she rends the plume;
No lustre lightens in her weeping eyes,
And on her tear-stain'd cheek no roses bloom.

Meanwhile the world, Ambition, owns thy sway,
Fame's loudest trumpet labours in thy praise;
For thee the Muse awakes her sweetest lay,
And Flattery bids for thee her altars blaze.

[1] Such, according to the description given by Plutarch, was the scene of Brutus's death.

Nor in life's lofty bustling sphere alone,
The sphere where monarchs and where heroes toil,
Sink Virtue's sons beneath Misfortune's frown,
While Guilt's thrill'd bosom leaps at Pleasure's
smile;

Full oft, where Solitude and Silence dwell
Far, far remote amid the lowly plain,
Resounds the voice of Woe from Virtue's cell.
Such is man's doom, and Pity weeps in vain.

Still grief recoils—How vainly have I strove
Thy power, O Melancholy, to withstand!
Tired I submit; but yet, O yet remove,
Or ease the pressure of thy heavy hand.

Yet for a while let the bewilder'd soul
Find in society relief from woe;
O yield a while to Friendship's soft control;
Some respite, Friendship, wilt thou not bestow!

Come, then, Philander! for thy lofty mind
Looks down from far on all that charms the great;
For thou canst bear, unshaken and resign'd,
The brightest smiles, the blackest frowns of Fate:

Come thou, whose love unlimited, sincere,
Nor faction cools, nor injury destroys;
Who lend'st to Misery's moans a pitying ear,
And feel'st with ecstacy another's joys:

Who know'st man's frailty; with a favouring eye,
And melting heart, behold'st a brother's fall;
Who, unenslaved by custom's narrow tie,
With manly freedom follow'st reason's call.

And bring thy Delia, softly-smiling fair,
Whose spotless soul no sordid thoughts deform;
Her accents mild would still each throbbing care,
And harmonize the thunder of the storm:

Though blest with wisdom and with wit refined,
She courts not homage, nor desires to shine;
In her each sentiment sublime is join'd
To female sweetness, and a form divine.

Come, and dispel the deep-surrounding shade:
Let chasten'd mirth the social hours employ;
O catch the swift-wing'd hour before 'tis fled,
On swiftest pinion flies the hour of joy.

Even while the careless disencumber'd soul
Dissolving sinks to joy's oblivious dream,
Even then to time's tremendous verge we roll
With haste impetuous down life's surgy stream.

Can Gaiety the vanish'd years restore,
Or on the withering limbs fresh beauty shed,
Or soothe the sad inevitable hour,
Or cheer the dark dark mansions of the dead?

Still sounds the solemn knell in fancy's ear
That call'd Cleora to the silent tomb;
To her how jocund roll'd the sprightly year!
How shone the nymph in beauty's brightest bloom!

Ah! Beauty's bloom avails not in the grave,
Youth's lofty mien, nor age's awful grace;
Moulder unknown the monarch and the slave,
Whelm'd in th' enormous wreck of human race.

The thought-fix'd portraiture, the breathing bust,
The arch with proud memorials array'd,
The long-lived pyramid shall sink in dust
To dumb oblivion's ever-desert shade.

Fancy from comfort wanders still astray.
Ah, Melancholy! how I feel thy power!
Long have I labour'd to elude thy sway!
But 'tis enough, for I resist no more.

The traveller thus, that o'er the midnight waste
Through many a lonesome path is doom'd to roam,
Wilder'd and weary sits him down at last;
For long the night, and distant far his home.

ELEGY.

Tired with the busy crowds, that all the day
Impatient throng where Folly's altars flame,
My languid powers dissolve with quick decay,
Till genial Sleep repair the sinking frame.

Hail, kind reviver! that canst lull the cares,
And every weary sense compose to rest,
Lighten th' oppressive load which anguish bears,
And warm with hope the cold desponding breast.

Touch'd by thy rod, from Power's majestic brow
Drops the gay plume; he pines a lowly clown;
And on the cold earth stretch'd, the son of Woe
Quaffs Pleasure's draught and wears a fancied crown.

When roused by thee, on boundless pinions borne,
Fancy to fairy scenes exults to rove,
Now scales the cliff gay-gleaming on the morn,
Now sad and silent treads the deepening grove;

Or skims the main, and listens to the storms,
Marks the long waves roll far remote away;
Or mingling with ten thousand glittering forms,
Floats on the gale, and basks in purest day.

Haply, ere long, pierced by the howling blast,
Through dark and pathless deserts I shall roam,
Plunge down th' unfathom'd deep, or shrink aghast
Where bursts the shrieking spectre from the tomb

Perhaps loose Luxury's enchanting smile
Shall lure my steps to some romantic dale,
Where Mirth's light freaks th' unheeded hours be-
And airs of rapture warble in the gale. [guile

Instructive emblem of this mortal state!
Where scenes as various every hour arise
In swift succession, which the hand of Fate
Presents, then snatches from our wondering eyes.

Be taught, vain man, how fleeting all thy joys,
Thy boasted grandeur, and thy glittering store;
Death comes, and all thy fancied bliss destroys,
Quick as a dream it fades, and is no more.

And, sons of Sorrow! though the threatening storm
Of angry Fortune overhang a while,
Let not her frowns your inward peace deform;
Soon happier days in happier climes shall smile.

Through Earth's throng'd visions while we toss for-
'Tis tumult all, and rage, and restless strife; [lorn,
But these shall vanish like the dreams of morn,
When Death awakes us to immortal life.

EPITAPH

ON ***** *******.[1]

Escaped the gloom of mortal life, a soul
Here leaves its mouldering tenement of clay,
Safe, where no cares their whelming billows roll,
No doubts bewilder, and no hopes betray.

Like thee, I once have stemm'd the sea of life;
Like thee, have languish'd after empty joys;
Like thee, have labour'd in the stormy strife;
Been grieved for trifles, and amused with toys.

Yet for a while 'gainst Passion's threatful blast
Let steady Reason urge the struggling oar;
Shot through the dreary gloom the morn at last
Gives to thy longing eye the blissful shore.

Forget my frailties, thou art also frail;
Forgive my lapses, for thyself may'st fall;
Nor read unmoved my artless tender tale,
I was a friend, O man, to thee, to all.

EPITAPH[2].

Nov. 1, 1757.

TO THIS GRAVE IS COMMITTED
ALL THAT THE GRAVE CAN CLAIM
OF TWO BROTHERS, ***** AND ********[3],
WHO, ON THE VII OF OCTOBER, MDCCLVII,
BOTH UNFORTUNATELY PERISHED IN THE *** WATER:
THE ONE IN HIS XXII, THE OTHER IN HIS XVIII, YEAR.
THEIR DISCONSOLATE FATHER, ***** ******,
ERECTS THIS MONUMENT TO THE MEMORY OF
THESE AMIABLE YOUTHS;
WHOSE EARLY VIRTUES PROMISED
UNCOMMON COMFORT TO HIS DECLINING YEARS,
AND SINGULAR EMOLUMENT TO SOCIETY.

O thou! whose steps in sacred rev'rence tread
These lone dominions of the silent dead;
On this sad stone a pious look bestow,
Nor uninstructed read this tale of woe;
And while the sigh of sorrow heaves thy breast,
Let each rebellious murmur be suppress'd;
Heaven's hidden ways to trace, for us, how vain!
Heaven's wise decrees how impious to arraign!
Pure from the stains of a polluted age,
In early bloom of life, they left the stage:
Not doom'd in lingering woe to waste their breath,
One moment snatch'd them from the power of Death:
They lived united, and united died;
Happy the friends, whom Death cannot divide!

[1] James Beattie. This epitaph was intended for himself.—C.

[2] This epitaph is engraven on a tomb-stone in the churchyard of Lethnet, in the shire of Angus.

[3] Two young men of the name of Leitch, who were drowned in crossing the river Southesk. It is not very obvious why their names should be concealed in the first edition of these poems.—C.

SONG,

IN IMITATION OF SHAKSPEARE'S

"Blow, blow, thou winter wind," &c.

Blow, blow, thou vernal gale!
Thy balm will not avail
To ease my aching breast;
Though thou the billows smooth,
Thy murmurs cannot soothe
My weary soul to rest.

Flow, flow, thou tuneful stream!
Infuse the easy dream
Into the peaceful soul;
But thou canst not compose
The tumult of my woes,
Though soft thy waters roll.

Blush, blush, ye fairest flowers!
Beauties surpassing yours
My Rosalind adorn;
Nor is the Winter's blast,
That lays your glories waste,
So killing as her scorn.

Breathe, breathe, ye tender lays,
That linger down the maze
Of yonder winding grove;
O let your soft control
Bend her relenting soul
To pity and to love.

Fade, fade, ye flowerets fair!
Gales, fan no more the air!
Ye streams forget to glide!
Be hush'd, each vernal strain;
Since nought can soothe my pain,
Nor mitigate her pride.

RETIREMENT.

1758.

When in the crimson cloud of even
The lingering light decays,
And Hesper on the front of Heaven
His glittering gem displays;
Deep in the silent vale, unseen,
Beside a lulling stream,
A pensive youth, of placid mien,
Indulged this tender theme:—

"Ye cliffs, in hoary grandeur piled
High o'er the glimmering dale;
Ye woods, along whose windings wild
Murmurs the solemn gale;
Where Melancholy strays forlorn,
And Woe retires to weep,
What time the wan Moon's yellow horn
Gleams on the western deep.

"To you, ye wastes, whose artless charms
Ne'er drew ambition's eye,
'Scaped a tumultuous world's alarms,
To your retreats I fly.
Deep in your most sequester'd bower
Let me at last recline,
Where Solitude, mild, modest power,
Leans on her ivied shrine.

"How shall I woo thee, matchless fair!
Thy heavenly smile how win?
Thy smile that smooths the brow of care,
And stills the storm within.

O wilt thou to thy favourite grove
Thine ardent votary bring,
And bless his hours and bid them move
Serene, on silent wing?

"Oft let Remembrance soothe his mind
With dreams of former days,
When in the lap of Peace reclined
He framed his infant lays:
When Fancy roamed at large, nor Care
Nor cold Distrust alarm'd,
Nor Envy with malignant glare
His simple youth had harm'd.

"Twas then, O Solitude! to thee
His early vows were paid,
From heart sincere, and warm and free,
Devoted to the shade.
Ah why did Fate his steps decoy
In stormy paths to roam,
Remote from all congenial joy!—
O take the wanderer home.

"Thy shades, thy silence now be mine,
Thy charms my only theme;
My haunt the hollow cliff, whose pine
Waves o'er the gloomy stream.
Whence the scared owl on pinions gray
Breaks from the rustling boughs,
And down the lone vale sails away
To more profound repose.

"O, while to thee the woodland pours
Its wildly-warbling song,
And balmy from the bank of flowers
The Zephyr breathes along;
Let no rude sound invade from far,
No vagrant foot be nigh,
No ray from Grandeur's gilded car
Flash on the startled eye.

"But if some pilgrim through the glade
Thy hallow'd bowers explore,
O guard from harm his hoary head,
And listen to his lore;
For he of joys divine shall tell,
That wean from earthly woe,
And triumph o'er the mighty spell
That chains his heart below.

"For me, no more the path invites
Ambition loves to tread;
No more I climb those toilsome heights,
By guileful Hope misled;
Leaps my fond fluttering heart no more
To Mirth's enlivening strain;
For present pleasure soon is o'er,
And all the past is vain."

ELEGY,

WRITTEN IN THE YEAR 1758.

Still shall unthinking man substantial deem
The forms that fleet through life's deceitful dream?
Till at some stroke of Fate the vision flies,
And sad realities in prospect rise;
And, from elysian slumbers rudely torn,
The startled soul awakes, to think and mourn.

O ye, whose hours in jocund train advance,
Whose spirits to the song of gladness dance,
Who flowery plains in endless pomp survey,
Glittering in beams of visionary day;
O, yet while Fate delays th' impending woe,
Be roused to thought, anticipate the blow;
Lest, like the lightning's glance the sudden ill
Flash to confound, and penetrate to kill;
Lest, thus encompass'd with funereal gloom,
Like me, ye bend o'er some untimely tomb,
Pour your wild ravings in Night's frighted ear,
And half pronounce Heaven's sacred doom severe.

Wise, beauteous, good! O every grace combined,
That charms the eye, or captivates the mind!
Fresh as the floweret opening on the morn,
Whose leaves bright drops of liquid pearl adorn!
Sweet as the downy-pinion'd gale, that roves
To gather fragrance in Arabian groves!
Mild as the melodies at close of day,
That heard remote along the vale decay!
Yet, why with these compared? What tints so fine,
What sweetness, mildness, can be match'd with [thine?
Why roam abroad, since recollection true
Restores the lovely form to fancy's view?
Still let me gaze, and every care beguile,
Gaze on that cheek, where all the Graces smile;
That soul-expressing eye, benignly bright,
Where Meekness beams ineffable delight;
That brow, where Wisdom sits enthroned serene,
Each feature forms, and dignifies the mien:
Still let me listen, while her words impart
The sweet effusions of the blameless heart,
Till all my soul, each tumult charm'd away,
Yields, gently led, to Virtue's easy sway,

By thee inspired, O Virtue, age is young,
And music warbles from the faltering tongue:
Thy ray creative cheers the clouded brow,
And decks the faded cheek with rosy glow,
Brightens the joyless aspect, and supplies
Pure heavenly lustre to the languid eyes:
But when youth's living bloom reflects thy beams,
Resistless on the view the glory streams,
Love, wonder, joy, alternately alarm,
And beauty dazzles with angelic charm.

Ah, whither fled? ye dear illusions, stay!
Lo, pale and silent lies the lovely clay.
How are the roses on that cheek decay'd,
Which late the purple light of youth display'd!
Health on her form each sprightly grace bestow'd!
With life and thought each speaking feature glow'd.
Fair was the blossom, soft the vernal sky;
Elate with hope, we deem'd no tempest nigh:
When lo, a whirlwind's instantaneous gust
Left all its beauties withering in the dust.

Cold the soft hand that sooth'd Woe's weary head!
And quench'd the eye, the pitying tear that shed!
And mute the voice, whose pleasing accents stole,
Infusing balm, into the rankled soul!
O Death, why arm with cruelty thy power,
And spare the idle weed, yet lop the flower?
Why fly thy shafts in lawless error driven?
Is Virtue then no more the care of Heaven?
But peace, bold thought! be still, my bursting [heart!
We, not Eliza, felt the fatal dart.

Escaped the dungeon, does the slave complain,
Nor bless the friendly hand that broke the chain?
Say, pines not Virtue for the lingering morn,
On this dark wild condemn'd to roam forlorn!
Where Reason's meteor-rays, with sickly glow,
O'er the dun gloom a dreadful glimmering throw;
Disclosing dubious to th' affrighted eye
O'erwhelming mountains tottering from on high,
Black billowy deeps in storms perpetual toss'd,
And weary ways in wildering labyrinths lost.

O happy stroke that burst the bonds of clay,
Darts through the rending gloom the blaze of day,
And wings the soul with boundless flight to soar,
Where dangers threat and fears alarm no more.

Transporting thought! here let me wipe away
The tear of Grief, and wake a bolder lay.
But ah! the swimming eye o'erflows anew;
Nor check the sacred drops to Pity due;
Lo, where in speechless, hopeless anguish, bend
O'er her loved dust, the parent, brother, friend!
How vain the hope of man: but cease thy strain,
Nor sorrow's dread solemnity profane;
Mix'd with yon drooping mourners, on her bier
In silence shed the sympathetic tear.

ODE TO HOPE.

I. 1.

O THOU, who glad'st the pensive soul,
More than Aurora's smile the swain forlorn,
Left all night long to mourn
Where desolation frowns, and tempests howl;
And shrieks of woe, as intermits the storm,
Far o'er the monstrous wilderness resound,
And 'cross the gloom darts many a shapeless form,
And many a fire-eyed visage glares around:—
O come, and be once more my guest:
Come, for thou oft thy suppliant's vow hast heard,
And oft with smiles indulgent cheer'd
And soothed him into rest.

I. 2.

Smit by thy rapture-beaming eye
Deep flashing through the midnight of their mind,
The sable bands combined,
Where Fear's black banner blots the troubled sky,
Appall'd retire. Suspicion hides her head,
Nor dares th' obliquely gleaming eyeball raise:
Despair, with gorgon-figured veil o'erspread,
Speeds to dark Phlegethon's detested maze.
Lo, startled at the heavenly ray,
With speed unwonted Indolence upsprings,
And, heaving, lifts her leaden wings,
And sullen glides away:

I. 3.

Ten thousand forms, by pining Fancy view'd,
Dissolve.—Above the sparkling flood
When Phœbus rears his awful brow,
From lengthening lawn and valley low
The troops of fen-born mists retire.
Along the plain
The joyous swain
Eyes the gay villages again,
And gold-illumined spire;
While on the billowy ether borne
Floats the loose lay's jovial measure;
And light along the fairy Pleasure,
Her green robes glittering to the morn,
Wantons on silken wing. And goblins all
To the damp dungeon shrink, or hoary hall,
Or westward, with impetuous flight,
Shoot to the desert realms of their congenial night.

II. 1.

When first on childhood's eager gaze
Life's varied landscape, stretch'd immense around,
Starts out of night profound,
Thy voice incites to tempt th' untrodden maze.
Fond he surveys thy mild maternal face,
His bashful eye still kindling as he views,
And, while thy lenient arm supports his pace,
With beating heart the upland path pursues;
The path that leads, where, hung sublime,
And seen afar, youth's gallant trophies, bright
In Fancy's rainbow ray, invite
His wingy nerves to climb.

II. 2.

Pursue thy pleasurable way,
Safe in the guidance of thy heavenly guard,
While melting airs are heard,
And soft-eyed cherub-forms around thee play:
Simplicity, in careless flowers array'd,
Prattling amusive in his accent meek;
And Modesty, half turning as afraid,
The smile just dimpling on his glowing cheek!
Content and Leisure, hand in hand
With Innocence and Peace, advance, and sing;
And Mirth, in many a mazy ring,
Frisks o'er the flowery land.

II. 3.

Frail man, how various is thy lot below!
To-day though gales propitious blow,
And Peace, soft-gliding down the sky,
Lead Love along, and Harmony,
To-morrow the gay scene deforms;
Then all around
The thunder's sound
Rolls rattling on through heaven's profound,
And down rush all the storms.
Ye days, that balmy influence shed,
When sweet childhood, ever sprightly,
In paths of pleasure sported lightly,
Whither, ah whither are ye fled?
Ye cherub train, that brought him on his way,
O leave him not 'midst tumult and dismay;
For now youth's eminence he gains;
But what a weary length of lingering toil remains!

III. 1.

They shrink, they vanish into air.
Now Slander taints with pestilence the gale;
And mingling cries assail,
The wail of Woe, and groan of grim Despair.
Lo! wizard Envy from his serpent eye
Darts quick destruction in each baleful glance;
Pride smiling stern, and yellow Jealousy,
Frowning Disdain, and haggard Hate advance;
Behold, amidst the dire array,
Pale wither'd Care his giant stature rears,
And lo! his iron hand prepares
To grasp its feeble prey.

III. 2.

Who now will guard bewilder'd youth
Safe from the fierce assault of hostile rage?
Such war can Virtue wage,
Virtue, that bears the sacred shield of Truth?
Alas! full oft on Guilt's victorious car
The spoils of Virtue are in triumph borne;
While the fair captive, mark'd with many a scar,
In long obscurity, oppress'd, forlorn,
Resigns to tears her angel form.
Ill-fated youth, then whither wilt thou fly?
No friend, no shelter now is nigh,
And onward rolls the storm.

III. 3.

But whence the sudden beam that shoots along?
Why shrink aghast the hostile throng?
Lo, from amidst affliction's night,
Hope bursts all radiant on the sight:
Her words the troubled bosom soothe.
"Why thus dismay'd?
Though foes invade,
Hope ne'er is wanting to their aid
Who tread the path of truth.
'Tis I, who smooth the rugged way,
I, who close the eyes of Sorrow,
And with glad visions of to-morrow
Repair the weary soul's decay. [heart,
When Death's cold touch thrills to the freezing
Dreams of Heaven's opening glories I impart,
Till the freed spirit springs on high
In rapture too severe for weak mortality."

PYGMÆO-GERANO-MACHIA:

THE BATTLE OF THE PYGMIES AND CRANES.

FROM THE LATIN OF ADDISON.

1762.

The pigmy-people, and the feather'd train,
Mingling in mortal combat on the plain,
I sing. Ye Muses! favour my designs,
Lead on my squadrons, and arrange the lines;
The flashing swords and fluttering wings display,
And long bills nibbling in the bloody fray;
Cranes darting with disdain on tiny foes, [woes.
Conflicting birds and men, and war's unnumber'd

The wars and woes of heroes six feet long
Have oft resounded in Pierian song.
Who has not heard of Colchos' golden fleece,
And Argo mann'd with all the flower of Greece?
Of Thebes' fell brethren, Theseus stern of face,
And Peleus' son unrivall'd in the race,
Æneas, founder of the Roman line,
And William, glorious on the banks of Boyne?
Who has not learn'd to weep at Pompey's woes,
And over Blackmore's epic page to doze?
'Tis I, who dare attempt unusual strains,
Of hosts unsung, and unfrequented plains;
The small shrill trump, and chiefs of little size,
And armies rushing down the darken'd skies.

Where India reddens to the early dawn,
Winds a deep vale from vulgar eye withdrawn:
Bosom'd in groves the lowly region lies,
And rocky mountains round the border rise.
Here, till the doom of fate its fall decreed,
The empire flourish'd of the pygmy breed;
Here Industry perform'd, and Genius plann'd,
And busy multitudes o'erspread the land.
But now to these lone bounds if pilgrim stray,
Tempting through craggy cliffs the desperate way,
He finds the puny mansion fallen to earth,
Its godlings mouldering on the abandon'd hearth;
And starts, where small white bones are spread
'Or little footsteps lightly print the ground;' [around,
While the proud crane her nest securely builds,
Chattering amid the desolated fields.

But different fates befel her hostile rage,
While reign'd, invincible through many an age,
The dreaded pygmy: roused by war's alarms,
Forth rush'd the madding mannikin to arms.
Fierce to the field of death the hero flies;
The faint crane fluttering flaps the ground, and dies;
And by the victor borne (o'erwhelming load!)
With bloody bill loose-dangling marks the road.
And oft the wily dwarf in ambush lay,
And often made the callow young his prey; [smiled,
With slaughter'd victims heap'd his board, and
T' avenge the parent's trespass on the child.
Oft, where his feather'd foe had rear'd her nest,
And laid her eggs and household gods to rest,
Burning for blood, in terrible array,
The eighteen-inch militia burst their way;
All went to wreck; the infant foeman fell,
When scarce his chirping bill had broke the shell.

Loud uproar hence, and rage of arms arose,
And the fell rancour of encountering foes;
Hence dwarfs and cranes one general havoc whelms,
And Death's grim visage scares the pigmy realms.
Not half so furious blazed the warlike fire
Of mice, high theme of the Mæonian lyre;
When bold to battle march'd th' accoutred frogs,
And the deep tumult thunder'd through the bogs:
Pierced by the javelin bulrush on the shore,
Here agonizing roll'd the mouse in gore;
And there the frog (a scene full sad to see!)
Shorn of one leg, slow sprawl'd along on three;
He vaults no more with vigorous hops on high,
But mourns in hoarsest croaks his destiny.

And now the day of woe drew on apace,
A day of woe to all the pygmy race,
When dwarfs were doom'd (but penitence was vain)
To rue each broken egg, and chicken slain.
For, roused to vengeance by repeated wrong,
From distant climes the long-bill'd legions throng
From Strymon's lake, Cayster's plashy meads,
And fens of Scythia, green with rustling reeds,
From where the Danube winds through many a land,
And Mareotis laves th' Egyptian strand,
To rendezvous they waft on eager wing,
And wait assembled the returning spring.
Meanwhile they trim their plumes for length of flight,
Whet their keen beaks, and twisting claws, for fight;
Each crane the pygmy power in thought o'erturns,
And every bosom for the battle burns.

When genial gales the frozen air unbind,
The screaming legions wheel, and mount the wind;
Far in the sky they form their long array,
And land and ocean stretch'd immense survey
Deep deep beneath; and, triumphing in pride,
With clouds and winds commix'd, innumerous ride:
'Tis wild obstreperous clangour all, and heaven
Whirls, in tempestuous undulation driven.

Nor less th' alarm that shook the world below,
Where march'd in pomp of war th' embattled foe:
Where mannikins with haughty step advance,
And grasp the shield, and couch the quivering lance:
To right and left the lengthening lines they form,
And rank'd in deep array await the storm.

High in the midst the chieftain-dwarf was seen,
Of giant stature, and imperial mien:
Full twenty inches tall, he strode along,
And view'd with lofty eye the wondering throng:
And while with many a scar his visage frown'd,
Bared his broad bosom, rough with many a wound
Of beaks and claws, disclosing to their sight
The glorious meed of high heroic might.
For with insatiate vengeance he pursued,
And never-ending hate, the feathery brood.

Unhappy they, confiding in the length
Of horny beak, or talon's crooked strength,
Who durst abide his rage; the blade descends,
And from the panting trunk the pinion rends:
Laid low in dust the pinion waves no more,
The trunk disfigured stiffens in its gore.
What hosts of heroes fell beneath his force!
What heaps of chicken carnage mark'd his course!
How oft, O Strymon, thy lone banks along,
Did wailing Echo waft the funeral song!

And now from far the mingling clamours rise,
Loud and more loud rebounding through the skies.
From skirt to skirt of heaven, with stormy sway,
A cloud rolls on, and darkens all the day.
Near and more near descends the dreadful shade,
And now in battailous array display'd,
On sounding wings, and screaming in their ire,
The cranes rush onward, and the fight require.

The pygmy warriors eye with fearless glare
The host thick swarming o'er the burthen'd air;
Thick swarming now, but to their native land
Doom'd to return a scanty straggling band.—
When sudden, darting down the depth of heaven,
Fierce on th' expecting foe the cranes are driven,
The kindling frenzy every bosom warms,
The region echoes to the crash of arms:
Loose feathers from th' encountering armies fly,
And in careering whirlwinds mount the sky.
To breathe from toil upsprings the panting crane,
Then with fresh vigour downward darts again.
Success in equal balance hovering hangs.
Here, on the sharp spear, mad with mortal pangs,
The bird transfix'd in bloody vortex whirls,
Yet fierce in death the threatening talon curls;
There, while the life-blood bubbles from his wound,
With little feet the pygmy beats the ground;
Deep from his breast the short short sob he draws,
And dying curses the keen-pointed claws.
Trembles the thundering field, thick cover'd o'er
With falchions, mangled wings, and streaming gore,
And pygmy arms, and beaks of ample size,
And here a claw, and there a finger lies.

Encompass'd round with heaps of slaughter'd foes,
All grim in blood the pygmy champion glows,
And on th' assailing host impetuous springs,
Careless of nibbling bills, and flapping wings;
And 'midst the tumult, wheresoe'er he turns,
The battle with redoubled fury burns;
From ev'ry side th' avenging cranes amain
Throng, to o'erwhelm this terror of the plain.
When suddenly (for such the will of Jove)
A fowl enormous, sousing from above,
The gallant chieftain clutch'd, and, soaring high,
(Sad chance of battle!) bore him up the sky.
The cranes pursue, and clustering in a ring,
Chatter triumphant round the captive king.
But ah! what pangs each pygmy bosom wrung,
When, now to cranes a prey, on talons hung,
High in the clouds they saw their helpless lord,
His wriggling form still lessening as he soar'd.

Lo! yet again, with unabated rage,
In mortal strife the mingling hosts engage.
The crane with darted bill assaults the foe,
Hovering; then wheels aloft to 'scape the blow:
The dwarf in anguish aims the vengeful wound,
But whirls in empty air the falchion round.

Such was the scene, when 'midst the loud alarms
Sublime th' eternal Thunderer rose in arms.
When Briareus, by mad ambition driven,
Heaved Pelion huge, and hurl'd it high at Heaven,
Jove roll'd redoubling thunders from on high,
Mountains and bolts encounter'd in the sky;
Till one stupendous ruin whelm'd the crew,
Their vast limbs weltering wide in brimstone blue.

But now at length the pygmy legions yield,
And wing'd with terror fly the fatal field.
They raise a weak and melancholy wail,
All in distraction scattering o'er the vale.
Prone on their routed rear the cranes descend;
Their bills bite furious, and their talons rend:
With unrelenting ire they urge the chase,
Sworn to exterminate the hated race.
'Twas thus the pygmy name, once great in war,
For spoils of conquer'd cranes renown'd afar,
Perish'd. For, by the dread decree of Heaven,
Short is the date to earthly grandeur given,
And vain are all attempts to roam beyond
Where fate has fix'd the everlasting bound.
Fallen are the trophies of Assyrian power,
And Persia's proud dominion is no more;
Yea, though to both superior far in fame,
Thine empire, Latium, is an empty name.

And now with lofty chiefs of ancient time,
The pygmy heroes roam th' elysian clime.
Or, if belief to matron-tales be due,
Full oft, in the belated shepherd's view,
Their frisking forms, in gentle green array'd,
Gambol secure amid the moonlight glade.
Secure, for no alarming cranes molest,
And all their woes in long oblivion rest:
Down the deep vale, and narrow winding way,
They foot it featly, ranged in ringlets gay:
'Tis joy and frolic all, where'er they rove,
And Fairy-people is the name they love.

THE HARES.

A FABLE.

Yes, yes, I grant the sons of Earth
Are doom'd to trouble from their birth.
We all of sorrow have our share:
But say, is yours without compare?
Look round the world; perhaps you'll find
Each individual of our kind
Press'd with an equal load of ill,
Equal at least. Look further still,
And own your lamentable case
Is little short of happiness.
In yonder hut that stands alone
Attend to Famine's feeble moan;
Or view the couch where Sickness lies,
Mark his pale cheek, and languid eyes,
His frame by strong convulsion torn,
His struggling sighs, and looks forlorn.
Or see, transfix'd with keener pangs,
Where o'er his hoard the miser hangs;
Whistles the wind; he starts, he stares!
Nor Slumber's balmy blessing shares;
Despair, Remorse, and Terror roll
Their tempests on his harass'd soul.

But here perhaps it may avail
T' enforce our reasoning with a tale.

Mild was the morn, the sky serene,
The jolly hunting band convene,

The beagle's breast with ardour burns,
The bounding steed the champaign spurns,
And Fancy oft the game descries
Through the hound's nose, and huntsman's eyes.

Just then, a council of the hares
Had met, on national affairs.
The chiefs were set; while o'er their head
The furze its frizzled covering spread.
Long lists of grievances were heard,
And general discontent appear'd.
" Our harmless race shall every savage
Both quadruped and biped ravage?
Shall horses, hounds, and hunters still
Unite their wits to work us ill?
The youth, his parents' sole delight,
Whose tooth the dewy lawns invite,
Whose pulse in every vein beats strong,
Whose limbs leap light the vales along,
May yet ere noontide meet his death,
And lie dismember'd on the heath.
For youth, alas! nor cautious age,
Nor strength, nor speed, eludes their rage.
In every field we meet the foe,
Each gale comes fraught with sounds of woe;
The morning but awakes our fears,
The evening sees us bathed in tears.
But must we ever idly grieve,
Nor strive our fortunes to relieve?
Small is each individual's force:
To stratagem be our recourse;
And then, from all our tribes combined,
The murderer to his cost may find
No foes are weak, whom Justice arms,
Whom Concord leads, and Hatred warms.
Be roused; or liberty acquire,
Or in the great attempt expire."—
He said no more, for in his breast
Conflicting thoughts the voice suppress'd:
The fire of vengeance seem'd to stream
From his swoln eyeballs' yellow gleam.

And now the tumults of the war,
Mingling confusedly from afar,
Swell in the wind. Now louder cries
Distinct of hounds and men arise.
Forth from the brake, with beating heart,
Th' assembled hares tumultuous start,
And, every straining nerve on wing,
Away precipitately spring.
The hunting band, a signal given,
Thick thundering o'er the plain are driven,
O'er cliff abrupt, and shrusby mound,
And river broad, impetuous bound:
Now plunge amid the forest shades,
Gluce through the opening of the glades
Now o'er the level valley sweep,
Now with short step strain up the steep;
While backward from the hunter's eyes
The landscape like a torrent flies.
At last an ancient wood they gain'd,
By pruner's axe yet unprofaned.
High o'er the rest, by Nature rear'd,
The oak's majestic boughs appear'd;
Beneath, a copse of various hue
In barbarous luxuriance grew.
No knife had curb'd the rambling sprays,
No hand had wove th' implicit maze.
The flowering thorn, self-taught to wind,
The hazel's stubborn stem intwined,
And bramble twigs were wreath'd around,
And rough furze crept along the ground.
Here sheltering from the sons of murther,
The hares drag their tired limbs no further.

But lo! the western wind ere long
Was loud, and roar'd the woods among;
From rustling leaves and crashing boughs
The sound of woe and war arose.
The hares distracted scour the grove,
As terror and amazement drove;
But danger, wheresoe'er they fled,
Still seem'd impending o'er their head.
Now crowded in a grotto's gloom,
All hope extinct, they wait their doom.
Dire was the silence, till, at length,
Even from despair deriving strength,
With bloody eye and furious look,
A daring youth arose and spoke.

" O wretched race, the scorn of Fate,
Whom ills of every sort await!
O, cursed with keenest sense to feel
The sharpest sting of every ill!
Say ye, who, fraught with mighty scheme,
Of liberty and vengeance dream,
What now remains? To what recess
Shall we our weary steps address,
Since Fate is evermore pursuing
All ways, and means to work our ruin?
Are we alone, of all beneath,
Condemn'd to misery worse than death?
Must we, with fruitless labour, strive
In misery worse than death to live?
No. Be the smaller ill our choice:
So dictates Nature's powerful voice.
Death's pang will in a moment cease;
And then, All hail, eternal peace!"
Thus while he spoke, his words impart
The dire resolve to every heart.

A distant lake in prospect lay,
That, glittering in the solar ray,
Gleam'd through the dusky trees, and shot
A trembling light along the grot.
Thither with one consent they bend,
Their sorrows with their lives to end,
While each, in thought, already hears
The water hissing in his ears.
Fast by the margin of the lake,
Conceal'd within a thorny brake,
A linnet sate, whose careless lay
Amused the solitary day.
Careless he sung, for on his breast
Sorrow no lasting trace impress'd;
When suddenly he heard a sound
Of swift feet traversing the ground.
Quick to the neighbouring tree he flies,
Thence trembling casts around his eyes;
No foe appear'd, his fears were vain;
Pleased he renews the sprightly strain.

The hares, whose noise had caused his fright,
Saw with surprise the linnet's flight.
" Is there on earth a wretch," they said,
" Whom our approach can strike with dread?"
An instantaneous change of thought
To tumult every bosom wrought.
So fares the system-building sage,
Who, plodding on from youth to age,
At last on some foundation-dream
Has rear'd aloft his goodly scheme,

And proved his predecessors fools,
And bound all nature by his rules;
So fares he in that dreadful hour,
When injured Truth exerts her power,
Some new phenomenon to raise,
Which, bursting on his frighted gaze,
From its proud summit to the ground
Preves the whole edifice unsound.

"Children," thus spoke a hare sedate,
Who oft had known th' extremes of fate,
"In slight events the docile mind
May hints of good instruction find.
That our condition is the worst,
And we with such misfortunes curst
As all comparison defy,
Was late the universal cry;
When lo! an accident so slight
As yonder little linnet's flight
Has made your stubborn heart confess
(So your amazement bids me guess)
That all our load of woes and fears
Is but a part of what he bears.
Where can he rest secure from harms,
Whom even a helpless hare alarms?
Yet he repines not at his lot,
When past, the danger is forgot:
On yonder bough he trims his wings,
And with unusual rapture sings:
While we, less wretched, sink beneath
Our lighter ills, and rush to death.
No more of this unmeaning rage,
But hear, my friends, the words of age.

"When by the winds of autumn driven
The scatter'd clouds fly 'cross the Heaven,
Oft have we, from some mountain's head,
Beheld th' alternate light and shade
Sweep the long vale. Here hovering lowers
The shadowy cloud; there downwards pours,
Streaming direct, a flood of day,
Which from the view flies swift away;
It flies, while other shades advance,
And other streaks of sunshine glance.
Thus chequer'd is the life below
With gleams of joy and clouds of woe.
Then hope not, while we journey on,
Still to be basking in the sun:
Nor fear, though now in shades ye mourn
That sunshine will no more return
If, by your terrors overcome,
Ye fly before th' approaching gloom,
The rapid clouds your flight pursue,
And darkness still o'ercasts your view.
Who longs to reach the radiant plain
Must onward urge his course amain;
For doubly swift the shadow flies,
When 'gainst the gale the pilgrim plies.
At least be firm, and undismay'd
Maintain your ground! the fleeting shade
Ere long spontaneous glides away,
And gives you back th' enlivening ray.
Lo, while I speak, our danger past!
No more the shrill horn's angry blast
Howls in our ear; the savage roar
Of war and murder is no more.
Then snatch the moment fate allows,
Nor think of past or future woes."
He spoke; and hope revives; the lake
That instant one and all forsake,
In sweet amusement to employ
The present sprightly hour of joy.

Now from the western mountain's brow,
Compass'd with clouds of various glow,
The Sun a broader orb displays,
And shoots aslope his ruddy rays.
The lawn assumes a fresher green,
And dew-drops spangle all the scene.
The balmy zephyr breathes along,
The shepherd sings his tender song.
With all their lays the groves resound,
And falling waters murmur round,
Discord and care were put to flight,
And all was peace, and calm delight.

EPITAPH:

BEING PART OF AN INSCRIPTION FOR A MONUMENT TO BE ERECTED BY A GENTLEMAN TO THE MEMORY OF HIS LADY.

Farewell, my best-beloved! whose heavenly mind
Genius with virtue, strength with softness join'd;
Devotion, undebased by pride or art,
With meek simplicity, and joy of heart;
Though sprightly, gentle; though polite, sincere;
And only of thyself a judge severe;
Unblamed, unequall'd in each sphere of life,
The tenderest daughter, sister, parent, wife.
In thee their patroness th' afflicted lost;
Thy friends, their pattern, ornament, and boast!
And I—but ah, can words my loss declare,
Or paint th' extremes of transport and despair!
O thou, beyond what verse or speech can tell,
My guide, my friend, my best-beloved, farewell!

ODE

ON LORD H**'S BIRTH-DAY.

A Muse, unskill'd in venal praise,
Unstain'd with flattery's art;
Who loves simplicity of lays
Breathed ardent from the heart;
While gratitude and joy inspire,
Resumes the long-unpractised lyre,
To hail, O, H * *, thy natal morn:
No gaudy wreath of flowers she weaves,
But twines with oak the laurel leaves,
Thy cradle to adorn.

For not on beds of gaudy flowers
Thine ancestors reclined,
Where sloth dissolves, and spleen devours
All energy of mind.
To hurl the dart, to ride the car,
To stem the deluges of war,
And snatch from fate a sinking land:
Trample th' invader's lofty crest,
And from his grasp the dagger wrest,
And desolating brand:

'Twas this that raised th' illustrious line
To match the first in fame!
A thousand years have seen it shine
With unabated flame:

Have seen thy mighty sires appear
Foremost in glory's high career,
The pride and pattern of the brave.
Yet, pure from lust of blood their fire,
And from ambition's wild desire,
They triumph'd but to save.

The Muse with joy attends their way
The vale of peace along;
There to its lord the village gay
Renews the grateful song.
Yon castle's glittering towers contain
No pit of woe, nor clanking chain,
Nor to the suppliant's wail resound;
The open doors the needy bless,
Th' unfriended hail their calm recess,
And gladness smiles around.

There to the sympathetic heart
Life's best delights belong,
To mitigate the mourner's smart,
To guard the weak from wrong.
Ye sons of luxury, be wise:
Know, happiness for ever flies
The cold and solitary breast;
Then let the social instinct glow,
And learn to feel another's woe,
And in his joy be blest.

O yet, ere Pleasure plant her snare
For unsuspecting youth;
Ere Flattery her song prepare
To check the voice of Truth;
O may his country's guardian power
Attend the slumbering infant's bower,
And bright, inspiring dreams impart;
To rouse th' hereditary fire,
To kindle each sublime desire,
Exalt, and warm the heart.

Swift to reward a parent's fears,
A parent's hopes to crown,
Roll on in peace, ye blooming years,
That rear him to renown;
When in his finish'd form and face
Admiring multitudes shall trace
Each patrimonial charm combined,
The courteous yet majestic mien,
The liberal smile, the look serene,
The great and gentle mind.

Yet, though thou draw a nation's eyes,
And win a nation's love,
Let not thy towering mind despise
The village and the grove.
No slander there shall wound thy fame,
No ruffian take his deadly aim,
No rival weave the secret snare:
For Innocence with angel smile,
Simplicity that knows no guile,
And Love and Peace are there.

When winds the mountain oak assail,
And lay its glories waste,
Content may slumber in the vale,
Unconscious of the blast.
Through scenes of tumult while we roam,
The heart, alas! is ne'er at home,
It hopes in time to roam no more;
The mariner, not vainly brave,
Combats the storm, and rides the wave,
To rest at last on shore.

Ye proud, ye selfish, ye severe,
How vain your mask of state!
The good alone have joy sincere,
The good alone are great:
Great, when, amid the vale of peace,
They bid the plaint of sorrow cease,
And hear the voice of artless praise;
As when along the trophied plain
Sublime they lead the victor train,
While shouting nations gaze.

THE HERMIT.

At the close of the day, when the hamlet is still,
And mortals the sweets of forgetfulness prove,
When nought but the torrent is heard on the hill,
And nought but the nightingale's song in the grove:
'Twas thus, by the cave of the mountain afar,
While his harp rung symphonious, a hermit began:
No more with himself or with nature at war,
He thought as a sage, though he felt as a man.

"Ah! why, all abandon'd to darkness and woe,
Why, lone Philomela, that languishing fall?
For spring shall return, and a lover bestow,
And sorrow no longer thy bosom inthral:
But, if pity inspire thee, renew the sad lay,
Mourn, sweetest complainer! man calls thee to mourn;
O soothe him, whose pleasures like thine pass away:
Full quickly they pass—but they never return.

"Now gliding remote, on the verge of the sky,
The Moon half extinguish'd her crescent displays:
But lately I mark'd, when majestic on high
She shone, and the planets were lost in her blaze.
Roll on, thou fair orb, and with gladness pursue
The path that conducts thee to splendour again;
But man's faded glory what change shall renew?
Ah fool! to exult in a glory so vain!

"'Tis night, and the landscape is lovely no more;
I mourn, but, ye woodlands, I mourn not for you;
For morn is approaching, your charms to restore,
Perfumed with fresh fragrance, and glittering with dew:
Nor yet for the ravage of winter I mourn;
Kind Nature the embryo blossom will save;
But when shall spring visit the mouldering urn!
O when shall it dawn on the night of the grave!

"'Twas thus, by the glare of false science betray'd,
That leads, to bewilder; and dazzles, to blind;
My thoughts wont to roam, from shade onward to shade,
Destruction before me, and sorrow behind.
'O pity, great Father of Light,' then I cried,
'Thy creature who fain would not wander from thee;
Lo, humbled in dust, I relinquish my pride:
From doubt and from darkness thou only canst free!'

"And darkness and doubt are now flying away,
No longer I roam in conjecture forlorn.
So breaks on the traveller, faint, and astray,
The bright and the balmy effulgence of morn.
See Truth, Love, and Mercy, in triumph descending,
And nature all glowing in Eden's first bloom!
On the cold cheek of Death smiles and roses are blending,
And Beauty immortal awakes from the tomb."

TO THE

RIGHT HON. LADY CHARLOTTE GORDON,

DRESSED IN A TARTAN SCOTCH BONNET, WITH PLUMES, &C.

Why, lady, wilt thou bind thy lovely brow
With the dread semblance of that warlike helm,
That nodding plume, and wreath of various glow,
That graced the chiefs of Scotia's ancient realm?

Thou knowest that Virtue is of power the source,
And all her magic to thy eyes is given;
We own their empire, while we feel their force,
Beaming with the benignity of heaven.

The plumy helmet, and the martial mien,
Might dignify Minerva's awful charms;
But more resistless far th' Idalian queen—
Smiles, graces, gentleness, her only arms.

ON THE REPORT OF A MONUMENT TO BE ERECTED IN WESTMINSTER ABBEY, TO THE MEMORY OF A LATE AUTHOR. (CHURCHILL.)

Written in 1765.

[PART OF A LETTER TO A PERSON OF QUALITY.]

—Lest your lordship, who are so well acquainted with everything that relates to true honour, should think hardly of me for attacking the memory of the dead, I beg leave to offer a few words in my own vindication.

If I had composed the following verses with a view to gratify private resentment, to promote the interest of any faction, or to recommend myself to the patronage of any person whatsoever, I should have been altogether inexcusable. To attack the memory of the dead from selfish considerations, or from mere wantonness of malice, is an enormity which none can hold in greater detestation than I. But I composed them from very different motives; as every intelligent reader, who peruses them with attention, and who is willing to believe me upon my own testimony, will undoubtedly perceive. My motives proceeded from a sincere desire to do some small service to my country, and to the cause of truth and virtue. The promoters of faction I ever did, and ever will consider as the enemies of mankind: to the memory of such I owe no veneration: to the writings of such I owe no indulgence.

Your lordship knows that (Churchill) owed the greatest share of his renown to the most incompetent of all judges, the mob: actuated by the most unworthy of all principles, a spirit of insolence, and inflamed by the vilest of all human passions, hatred to their fellow-citizens. Those who joined the cry in his favour, seemed to me to be swayed rather by fashion than by real sentiment: he therefore might have lived and died unmolested by me, confident as I am that posterity, when the present unhappy dissentions are forgotten, will do ample justice to his real character. But when I saw the extravagant honours that were paid to his memory, and heard that a monument in Westminster Abbey was intended for one whom even his admirers acknowledge to have been an incendiary and a debauchee, I could not help wishing that my countrymen would reflect a little on what they were doing, before they consecrated, by what posterity would think the public voice, a character, which no friend to virtue or true taste can approve. It was this sentiment, enforced by the earnest request of a friend, which produced the following little poem; in which I have said nothing of (Churchill's) manners that is not warranted by the best authority; nor of his writings, that is not perfectly agreeable to the opinion of many of the most competent judges in Britain.

(Aberdeen), January 1765.

Bufo, begone! with thee may faction's fire,
That hatch'd thy salamander-fame expire.
Fame, dirty idol of the brainless crowd,
What half-made moon-calf can mistake for good!
Since shared by knaves of high and low degree;
Cromwell and Catiline; Guido Faux, and thee.

By nature uninspired, untaught by art;
With not one thought that breathes the feeling heart,
With not one offering vow'd to Virtue's shrine,
With not one pure unprostituted line;
Alike debauch'd in body, soul, and lays;—
For pension'd censure, and for pension'd praise,
For ribaldry, for libels, lewdness, lies,
For blasphemy of all the good and wise:
Coarse violence in coarser doggrel writ,
Which bawling blackguards spell'd, and took for wit:
For conscience, honour, slighted, spurn'd, o'erthrown:
Lo, Bufo shines the minion of renown.

Is this the land that boasts a Milton's fire,
And magic Spenser's wildly warbling lyre!
The land that owns th' omnipotence of song,
When Shakspeare whirls the throbbing heart along?
The land, where Pope, with energy divine,
In one strong blaze bade wit and fancy shine:
Whose verse, by Truth in Virtue's triumph borne
Gave knaves to infamy, and fools to scorn;
Yet pure in manners, and in thought refined,
Whose life and lays adorn'd and bless'd mankind!
Is this the land, where Gray's unlabour'd art
Soothes, melts, alarms, and ravishes the heart:
While the lone wanderer's sweet complainings flow
In simple majesty of manly woe:
Or while, sublime, on eagle-pinion driven,
He soars Pindaric heights, and sails the waste of heaven!
Is this the land, o'er Shenstone's recent urn
Where all the Loves and gentler Graces mourn!
And where, to crown the hoary bard of Night[1]
The Muses and the Virtues all unite?
Is this the land, where Akenside displays
The bold yet temperate flame of ancient days;
Like the rapt sage[2], in genius as in theme,
Whose hallow'd strain renown'd Ilyssus' stream:
Or him, the indignant bard[3], whose patriot ire,
Sublime in vengeance, smote the dreadful lyre:
For truth, for liberty, for virtue warm,
Whose mighty song unnerved a tyrant's arm,
Hush'd the rude roar of discord, rage, and lust,
And spurn'd licentious demagogues to dust.

Is this the queen of realms! the glorious isle,
Britannia, blest in Heaven's indulgent smile:
Guardian of truth, and patroness of art,
Nurse of th' undaunted soul, and generous heart!

[1] Dr. Young. [2] Plato.
[3] Alcæus. See Akenside's Ode on Lyric Poetry.

Where, from a base unthankful world exiled,
Freedom exults to roam the careless wild:
Where taste to science every charm supplies,
And genius soars unbounded to the skies!

And shall a Bufo's most polluted name
Stain her bright tablet of untainted fame?
Shall his disgraceful name with theirs be join'd,
Who wish'd and wrought the welfare of their kind?
His name accurst, who leagued with Wilkes and hell,
Labour'd to rouse, with rude and murderous yell,
Discord the fiend, to toss rebellion's brand,
To whelm in rage and woe a guiltless land:
To frustrate wisdom's, virtue's noblest plan,
And triumph in the miseries of man.

Driveling and dull, when crawls the reptile Muse
Swoln from the sty, and rankling from the stews,
With envy, spleen, and pestilence replete,
And gorged with dust she lick'd from Treason's feet:
Who once, like Satan, raised to heaven her sight,
But turn'd abhorrent from the hated light:—
O'er such a Muse shall wreaths of glory bloom?
No—shame and execration be her doom.

Hard-fated Bufo! could not dulness save
Thy soul from sin, from infamy thy grave?
Blackmore and Quarles, those blockheads of renown,
Lavish'd their ink, but never harm'd the town.
Though this, thy brother in discordant song,
Harass'd the ear, and cramp'd the labouring tongue:
And that, like thee, taught staggering prose to stand,
And limp on stilts of rhyme around the land.
Harmless they dozed a scribbling life away,
And yawning nations own'd th' innoxious lay;
But from thy graceless, rude, and beastly brain
What fury breathed th' incendiary strain?

Did hate to vice exasperate thy style?
No—Bufo match'd the vilest of the vile.
Yet blazon'd was his verse with Virtue's name—
Thus prudes look down to hide their want of shame:
Thus hypocrites to truth, and fools to sense,
And fops to taste, have sometimes made pretence:
Thus thieves and gamesters swear by honour's laws:
Thus pension-hunters bawl "their country's cause:"
Thus furious *Teague* [Burke] for moderation raved,
And own'd his soul to liberty enslaved.

Nor yet, though thousand cits admire thy rage,
Though less of fool than felon marks thy page:
Nor yet, though here and there one lonely spark
Of wit half brightens through th' involving dark,
To show the gloom more hideous for the foil,
But not repay the drudging reader's toil;
(For who for one poor pearl of clouded ray
Through Alpine dunghills delves his desperate way?)
Did genius to thy verse such bane impart?
No. 'Twas the demon of thy venom'd heart
(Thy heart with rancour's quintessence endued),
And the blind zeal of a misjudging crowd.

Thus from rank soil a poison'd mushroom sprung,
Nursling obscene of mildew and of dung:
By Heaven design'd on its own native spot
Harmless to enlarge its bloated bulk, and rot.
But Gluttony th' abortive nuisance saw;
It roused his ravenous undiscerning maw:
Gulp'd down the tasteless throat, the mess abhorr'd
Shot fiery influence round the maddening board.

O had thy verse been impotent as dull,
Nor spoke the rancorous heart, but lumpish scull;
Had mobs distinguish'd, they who howl'd thy fame,
The icicle from the pure diamond's flame,
From fancy's soul thy gross imbruted sense,
From dauntless truth thy shameless insolence,
From elegance confusion's monstrous mass,
And from the lion's spoils the sculking ass,
From rapture's strain the drawling doggrel line,
From warbling seraphim the grunting swine;—
With gluttons, dunces, rakes, thy name had slept,
Nor o'er her sullied fame Britannia wept:
Nor had the Muse, with honest zeal possess'd,
T' avenge her country, by thy name disgraced,
Raised this bold strain for virtue, truth, mankind,
And thy fell shade to infamy resign'd.

When frailty leads astray the soul sincere,
Let mercy shed the soft and manly tear.
When to the grave descends the sensual sot,
Unnamed, unnoticed, let his carrion rot.
When paltry rogues, by stealth, deceit, or force,
Hazard their necks, ambitious of your purse:
For such the hangman wreaths his trusty gin,
And let the gallows expiate their sin.
But when a ruffian, whose portentous crimes
Like plagues and earthquakes terrify the times,
Triumphs through life, from legal judgment free,
For hell may hatch what law could ne'er foresee
Sacred from vengeance shall his memory rest?—
Judas though dead, though damn'd, we still detest.

THE JUDGMENT OF PARIS.

(*Published in* 1765.)

Far in the depth of Ida's inmost grove,
 A scene for love and solitude design'd;
Where flowery woodbines wild by Nature wove
 Form'd the lone bower, the royal swain reclined.

All up the craggy cliffs, that tower'd to Heaven,
 Green waved the murmuring pines on every side
Save where, fair opening to the beam of even,
 A dale sloped gradual to the valley wide.

Echo'd the vale with many a cheerful note;
 The lowing of the herds resounding long,
The shrilling pipe, and mellow horn remote,
 And social clamours of the festive throng.

For now, low hovering o'er the western main,
 Where amber clouds begirt his dazzling throne,
The Sun with ruddier verdure deck'd the plain;
 And lakes, and streams, and spires triumphant shone.

And many a band of ardent youths were seen,
 Some into rapture fired by glory's charms,
Or hurl'd the thundering car along the green,
 Or march'd embattled on in glittering arms.

Others more mild, in happy leisure gay,
 The darkening forest's lonely gloom explore,
Or by Scamander's flowery margin stray,
 Or the blue Hellespont's resounding shore.

But chief the eye to Ilion's glories turn'd,
 That gleam'd along th' extended champaign far,
And bulwarks, in terrific pomp adorn'd,
 Where Peace sat smiling at the frowns of War.

Rich in the spoils of many a subject-clime,
In pride luxurious blazed th' imperial dome;
Tower'd mid th' encircling grove the fane sublime;
And dread memorials mark'd the hero's tomb,

Who from the black and bloody cavern led
The savage stern, and sooth'd his boisterous breast;
Who spoke, and Science rear'd her radiant head,
And brighten'd o'er the long benighted waste;

Or, greatly daring in his country's cause,
Whose heaven-taught soul the awful plan design'd,
Whence Power stood trembling at the voice of laws;
Whence soar'd on Freedom's wing th' ethereal mind.

But not the pomp that royalty displays,
Nor all th' imperial pride of lofty Troy,
Nor Virtue's triumph of immortal praise
Could rouse the languor of the lingering boy.

Abandon'd all to soft Œnone's charms,
He to oblivion doom'd the listless day;
Inglorious lull'd in Love's dissolving arms,
While flutes lascivious breathed th' enfeebling lay.

To trim the ringlets of his scented hair;
To aim, insidious, Love's bewitching glance;
Or cull fresh garlands for the gaudy fair,
Or wanton loose in the voluptuous dance:

These were his arts; these won Œnone's love,
Nor sought his fettered soul a nobler aim.
Ah why should beauty's smile those arts approve,
Which taint with infamy the lover's flame!

Now laid at large beside a murmuring spring,
Melting he listen'd to the vernal song,
And Echo listening waved her airy wing,
While the deep winding dales the lays prolong:

When, slowly floating down the azure skies,
A crimson cloud flash'd on his startled sight;
Whose skirts gay-sparkling with unnumber'd dyes
Launch'd the long billowy trails of flickery light.

That instant hush'd was all the vocal grove,
Hush'd was the gale, and every ruder sound,
And strains aërial, warbling far above,
Rung in the ear a magic peal profound.

Near, and more near, the swimming radiance roll'd;
Along the mountains stream the lingering fires,
Sublime the groves of Ida blaze with gold,
And all the Heaven resounds with louder lyres.

The trumpet breathed a note: and all in air,
The glories vanish'd from the dazzled eye;
And three ethereal forms, divinely fair,
Down the steep glade were seen advancing nigh.

The flowering glade fell level where they moved;
O'erarching high the clustering roses hung,
And gales from heaven on balmy pinion roved,
And hill and dale with gratulation rung.

The *first* with slow and stately step drew near,
Fix'd was her lofty eye, erect her mien:
Sublime in grace, in majesty severe,
She look'd and moved a goddess and a queen.

Her robe along the gale profusely stream'd,
Light lean'd the sceptre on her bending arm;
And round her brow a starry circlet gleam'd,
Heightening the pride of each commanding charm.

Milder the *next* came on with artless grace,
And on a javelin's quivering length reclined:
T' exalt her mien she bade no splendour blaze,
Nor pomp of vesture fluctuate on the wind

Serene, though awful, on her brow the light
Of heavenly wisdom shone: nor roved her eyes,
Save to the shadowy cliff's majestic height,
Or the blue concave of th' involving skies.

Keen were her eyes to search the inmost soul:
Yet Virtue triumph'd in their beams benign,
And impious Pride oft felt their dread control,
When in fierce lightning flash'd the wrath divine.[1]

With awe and wonder gazed th' adoring swain;
His kindling cheeks great Virtue's power confess'd;
But soon 'twas o'er, for Virtue prompts in vain,
When Pleasure's influence numbs the nerveless breast.

And now advanced the *queen of melting joy*,
Smiling supreme in unresisted charms:
Ah then, what transports fired the trembling boy!
How throbb'd his sickening frame with fierce alarms!

Her eyes in liquid light luxurious swim,
And languish with unutterable love.
Heaven's warm bloom glows along each bright'ning limb,
Where fluttering bland the veil's thin mantlings rove.

Quick, blushing as abash'd, she half withdrew:
One hand a bough of flowering myrtle waved,
One graceful spread, where, scarce conceal'd from view,
Soft through the parting robe her bosom heaved.

"Offspring of Jove supreme! beloved of heav'n!
Attend." Thus spoke the empress of the skies.
"For know, to thee, high fated prince, 'tis given
Through the bright realms of Fame sublime to rise,

"Beyond man's boldest hope; if nor the wiles
Of Pallas triumph o'er the ennobling thought;
Nor Pleasure lure with artificial smiles
To quaff the poison of her luscious draught,—

"When Juno's charms the prize of beauty claim,
Shall aught on earth, shall aught in heav'n contend?
Whom Juno calls to high triumphant fame,
Shall he to meaner sway inglorious bend?

"Yet lingering comfortless in lonesome wild,
Where Echo sleeps mid cavern'd vales profound,
The pride of Troy, Dominion's darling child,
Pines while the slow hour stalks its sullen round.

"Hear thou, of Heaven unconscious! From the blaze
Of glory, stream'd from Jove's eternal throne,
Thy soul, O mortal, caught the inspiring rays
That to a god exalt Earth's raptured son.

[1] This is agreeable to the theology of Homer, who often represents Pallas as the executioner of divine vengeance.

"Hence the bold wish, on boundless pinion borne,
That fires, alarms, impels the maddening soul;
The hero's eye, hence, kindling into scorn,
Blasts the proud menace, and defies control.

"But, unimproved, Heaven's noblest boons are vain,
No sun with plenty crowns the uncultured vale:
Where green lakes languish on the silent plain,
Death rides the billows of the western gale.

"Deep in yon mountain's womb, where the dark cave
Howls to the torrent's everlasting roar,
Does the rich gem its flashy radiance wave?
Or flames with steady ray the imperial ore?

"Toil deck'd with glittering domes yon champaign wide,
And wakes yon grove-embosom'd lawns to joy,
And rends the rough ore from the mountain's side,
Spangling with starry pomp the thrones of Troy.

"Fly these soft scenes. Even now, with playful art,
Love wreathes the flowery ways with fatal snare.
And nurse the ethereal fire that warms thy heart,
That fire ethereal lives but by thy care.

"Lo, hovering near on dark and dampy wing,
Sloth with stern patience waits the hour assign'd,
From her chill plume the deadly dews to fling,
That quench Heaven's beam, and freeze the cheerless mind.

"Vain, then, the enlivening sound of Fame's alarms,
For Hope's exulting impulse prompts no more:
Vain even the joys that lure to Pleasure's arms,
The throb of transport is for ever o'er.

"O who shall then to Fancy's darkening eyes
Recall the Elysian dreams of joy and light?
Dim through the gloom the formless visions rise,
Snatch'd instantaneous down the gulf of night.

"Thou, who securely lull'd in youth's warm ray
Mark'st not the desolations wrought by Time,
Be roused or perish. Ardent for its prey
Speeds the fell hour that ravages thy prime.

"And, midst the horrors shrined of midnight storm,
The fiend Oblivion eyes thee from afar,
Black with intolerable frowns her form,
Beckoning the embattled whirlwinds into war.

"Fanes, bulwarks, mountains, worlds, their tempest whelms:
Yet glory braves unmoved the impetuous sweep.
Fly then, ere hurl'd from life's delightful realms,
Thou sink to Oblivion's dark and boundless deep.

"Fly then, where Glory points the path sublime,
See her crown dazzling with eternal light!
'Tis Juno prompts thy daring steps to climb,
And girds thy bounding heart with matchless might.

"Warm in the raptures of divine desire,
Burst the soft chain that curbs the aspiring mind:
And fly, where Victory, borne on wings of fire,
Waves her red banner to the rattling wind.

"Ascend the car. Indulge the pride of arms,
Where clarions roll their kindling strains on high,
Where the eye maddens to the dread alarms,
And the long shout tumultuous rends the sky.

"Plunged in the uproar of the thundering field,
I see thy lofty arm the tempest guide:
Fate scatters lightning from thy meteor shield,
And Ruin spreads around the sanguine tide.

"Go, urge the terrors of thy headlong car
On prostrate Pride, and Grandeur's spoils o'erthrown,
While all amazed even heroes shrink afar,
And hosts embattled vanish at thy frown.

"When glory crowns thy godlike toils, and all
The triumph's lengthening pomp exalts thy soul,
When lowly at thy feet the mighty fall,
And tyrants tremble at thy stern control:

"When conquering millions hail thy sovereign might,
And tribes unknown dread acclamation join:
How wilt thou spurn the forms of low delight!
For all the ecstacies of Heaven are thine:

"For thine the joys that fear no length of days,
Whose wide effulgence scorns all mortal bound:
Fame's trump in thunder shall announce thy praise,
Nor bursting worlds her clarion's blast confound."

The goddess ceased, not dubious of the prize:
Elate she mark'd his wild and rolling eye,
Mark'd his lip quiver, and his bosom rise,
And his warm cheek suffused with crimson dye.

But Pallas now drew near. Sublime, serene
In conscious dignity, she view'd the swain:
Then, love and pity softening all her mien,
Thus breathed with accents mild the solemn strain.

"Let those, whose arts to fatal paths betray,
The soul with passion's gloom tempestuous blind,
And snatch from Reason's ken the auspicious ray
Truth darts from Heaven to guide the exploring mind.

"But Wisdom loves the calm and serious hour,
When Heaven's pure emanation beams confess'd:
Rage, ecstacy, alike disclaim her power,
She woos each gentler impulse of the breast.

"Sincere the unalter'd bliss her charms impart,
Sedate the enlivening ardours they inspire:
She bids no transient rapture thrill the heart,
She wakes no feverish gust of fierce desire.

"Unwise, who, tossing on the watery way,
All to the storm the unfetter'd sail devolve:
Man more unwise resigns the mental sway,
Borne headlong on by passion's keen resolve.

"While storms remote but murmur on thine ear,
Nor waves in ruinous uproar round thee roll,
Yet, yet a moment check thy prone career,
And curb the keen resolve that prompts thy soul.

"Explore thy heart, that, roused by Glory's name,
Pants all enraptured with the mighty charm—
And, does Ambition quench each milder flame?
And is it conquest that alone can warm?

"To indulge fell Rapine's desolating lust,
To drench the balmy lawn in streaming gore,
To spurn the hero's cold and silent dust—
Are these thy joys? Nor throbs thy heart for more?

"Pleased canst thou listen to the patriot's groan,
And the wild wail of Innocence forlorn?
And hear the abandon'd maid's last frantic moan,
Her love for ever from her bosom torn?

"Nor wilt thou shrink, when Virtue's fainting breath
Pours the dread curse of vengeance on thy head?
Nor when the pale ghost bursts the cave of death,
To glare distraction on thy midnight bed?

"Was it for this, though born to regal power,
Kind Heaven to thee did nobler gifts consign,
Bade Fancy's influence gild thy natal hour,
And bade Philanthropy's applause be thine?

"Theirs be the dreadful glory to destroy,
And theirs the pride of pomp, and praise suborn'd,
Whose eye ne'er lighten'd at the smile of Joy,
Whose cheek the tear of Pity ne'er adorn'd:

"Whose soul, each finer sense instinctive quell'd,
The lyre's mellifluous ravishment defies:
Nor marks where Beauty roves the flowery field,
Or Grandeur's pinion sweeps the unbounded skies.

"Hail to sweet Fancy's unexpressive charm!
Hail to the pure delights of social love!
Hail, pleasures mild, that fire not while ye warm,
Nor rack the exulting frame, but gently move.

"But Fancy soothes no more, if stern Remorse
With iron grasp the tortured bosom wring.
Ah then, even Fancy speeds the venom's course,
Even Fancy points with rage the maddening sting.

"Her wrath a thousand gnashing fiends attend,
And roll the snakes, and toss the brands of Hell:
The beam of Beauty blasts: dark Heavens impend
Tottering: and Music thrills with startling yell.

"What then avails, that with exhaustless store
Obsequious Luxury loads thy glittering shrine?
What then avails, that prostrate slaves adore,
And Fame proclaims thee matchless and divine?

"What though bland Flattery all her arts apply?
Will these avail to calm the infuriate brain?
Or will the roaring surge, when heaved on high,
Headlong hang, hush'd, to hear the piping swain?

"In health how fair, how ghastly in decay
Man's lofty form! how heavenly fair the mind
Sublimed by Virtue's sweet enlivening sway!
But ah! to guilt's outrageous rule resign'd,

"How hideous and forlorn! when ruthless Care
With cankering tooth corrodes the seeds of life,
And deaf with passion's storms when pines Despair,
And howling furies rouse the eternal strife.

"O, by thy hopes of joy that restless glow,
Pledges of Heaven! be taught by Wisdom's lore:
With anxious haste each doubtful path forego,
And life's wild ways with cautious fear explore.

"Straight be thy course: nor tempt the maze that leads
Where fell Remorse his shapeless strength conceals,
And oft Ambition's dizzy cliff he treads,
And slumbers oft in Pleasure's flowery vales.

"Nor linger unresolved: Heaven prompts the choice;
Save when Presumption shuts the ear of Pride:
With grateful awe attend to Nature's voice,
The voice of Nature Heaven ordain'd thy guide.

"Warn'd by her voice, the arduous path pursue,
That leads to Virtue's fane a hardy band:
What, though no gaudy scenes decoy their view,
Nor clouds of fragrance roll along the land?

"What, though rude mountains heave the flinty way?
Yet there the soul drinks light and life divine,
And pure aërial gales of gladness play,
Brace every nerve, and every sense refine.

"Go, prince, be virtuous, and be blest. The throne
Rears not its state to swell the couch of Lust:
Nor dignify Corruption's daring son,
To o'erwhelm his humbler brethren of the dust.

"But yield an ampler scene to Bounty's eye,
An ampler range to Mercy's ear expand:
And, midst admiring nations, set on high
Virtue's fair model, framed by Wisdom's hand.

"Go then: the moan of Woe demands thine aid:
Pride's licensed outrage claims thy slumbering ire:
Pale Genius roams the bleak neglected shade,
And battening Avarice mocks his tuneless lyre.

"Even Nature pines by vilest chains oppress'd:
The astonish'd kingdoms crouch to Fashion's nod.
O ye pure inmates of the gentle breast,
Truth, Freedom, Love, O where is your abode?

"O yet once more shall Peace from Heaven return,
And young Simplicity with mortals dwell!
Nor Innocence the august pavilion scorn,
Nor meek Contentment fly the humble cell!

"Wilt thou, my prince, the beauteous train implore,
Midst Earth's forsaken scenes once more to bide?
Then shall the shepherd sing in every bower,
And Love with garlands wreathe the domes of Pride.

"The bright tear starting in the impassion'd eyes
Of silent gratitude: the smiling gaze
Of gratulation, faltering while he tries
With voice of transport to proclaim thy praise;

"The ethereal glow that stimulates thy frame,
When all the according powers harmonious move,
And wake to energy each social aim,
Attuned spontaneous to the will of Jove;

"Be these, O man, the triumphs of thy soul;
And all the conqueror's dazzling glories slight,
That meteor-like o'er trembling nations roll,
To sink at once in deep and dreadful night.

"Like thine, yon orb's stupendous glories burn
With genial beam; nor, at the approach of even,
In shades of horror leave the world to mourn,
But gild with lingering light the impurpled Heaven."

Thus while she spoke, her eye, sedately meek,
Look'd the pure fervour of maternal love.
No rival zeal intemperate flush'd her cheek—
Can Beauty's boast the soul of wisdom move?

Worth's noble pride can Envy's leer appal,
Or staring Folly's vain applauses soothe?
Can jealous Fear Truth's dauntless heart enthral?
Suspicion lurks not in the heart of Truth.

And now the shepherd raised his pensive head:
Yet unresolved and fearful roved his eyes,
Scared at the glances of the awful maid;
For young unpractised Guilt distrusts the guise

Of shameless Arrogance—His wavering breast,
Though warm'd by Wisdom, own'd no constant fire;
While lawless Fancy roam'd afar, unblest
Save in the oblivious lap of soft Desire.

When thus the queen of soul-dissolving smiles:
"Let gentler fate my darling prince attend;
Joyless and cruel are the warrior's spoils,
Dreary the path stern Virtue's sons ascend.

"Of human joy full short is the career,
And the dread verge still gains upon your sight:
While idly gazing, far beyond your sphere,
Ye scan the dream of unapproach'd delight:

"Till every sprightly hour, and blooming scene,
Of life's gay morn unheeded glides away,
And clouds of tempests mount the blue serene,
And storms and ruin close the troublous day.

"Then still exult to hail the present joy,
Thine be the boon that comes unearn'd by toil:
No froward vain desire thy bliss annoy,
No flattering hope thy longing hours beguile.

"Ah! why should man pursue the charms of Fame,
For ever luring, yet for ever coy?
Light as the gaudy rainbow's pillar'd gleam,
That melts illusive from the wondering boy!

"What though her throne irradiate many a clime,
If hung loose-tottering o'er th' unfathom'd tomb?
What though her mighty clarion, rear'd sublime,
Display the imperial wreath, and glittering plume?

"Can glittering plume, or can th' imperial wreath
Redeem from unrelenting fate the brave?
What note of triumph can her clarion breathe,
T' alarm th' eternal midnight of the grave?

"That night draws on: nor will the vacant hour
Of expectation linger as it flies:
Nor Fate one moment unenjoy'd restore:
Each moment's flight how precious to the wise!

"O shun th' annoyance of the bustling throng,
That haunt with zealous turbulence the great;
There coward Office boasts th' unpunished wrong,
And sneaks secure in insolence of state.

"O'er fancied injury Suspicion pines,
And in grim silence gnaws the festering wound;
Deceit the rage-embitter'd smile refines,
And Censure spreads the viperous hiss around.

"Hope not, fond prince, though Wisdom guard thy throne,
Tho' Truth and Bounty prompt each generous aim,
Though thine the palm of peace, the victor's crown,
The Muse's rapture, and the patriot's flame:

"Hope not, though all that captivates the wise,
All that endears the good exalt thy praise:
Hope not to taste repose; for Envy's eyes
At fairest worth still point their deadly rays.

"Envy, stern tyrant of the flinty heart,
Can aught of Virtue, Truth, or Beauty charm?
Can soft Compassion thrill with pleasing smart,
Repentance melt, or Gratitude disarm?

"Ah no. Where Winter Scythia's waste enchains,
And monstrous shapes roar to the ruthless storm,
Not Phœbus' smile can cheer the dreadful plains,
Or soil accursed with balmy life inform.

"Then, Envy, then is thy triumphant hour,
When mourns Benevolence his baffled scheme:
When Insult mocks the clemency of Power,
And loud Dissention's livid firebrands gleam:

"When squint-eyed Slander plies th' unhallow'd tongue,
From poison'd maw when Treason weaves his line,
And Muse apostate (infamy to song!)
Grovels, low-muttering at Sedition's shrine.

"Let not my prince forego the peaceful shade,
The whispering grove, the fountain and the plain:
Power, with th' oppressive weight of pomp array'd,
Pants for simplicity and ease in vain.

"The yell of frantic Mirth may stun his ear,
But frantic Mirth soon leaves the heart forlorn:
And Pleasure flies that high tempestuous sphere,
Far different scenes her lucid paths adorn.

"She loves to wander on th' untrodden lawn,
Or the green bosom of reclining hill,
Soothed by the careless warbler of the dawn,
Or the lone plaint of ever-murmuring rill.

"Or from the mountain-glade's aërial brow,
While to her song a thousand echoes call,
Marks the wild woodland-wave remote below,
Where shepherds pipe unseen, and waters fall.

"Her influence oft the festive hamlet proves,
Where the high carol cheers the exulting ring;
And oft she roams the maze of wildering groves,
Listening th' unnumber'd melodies of Spring.

"Or to the long and lonely shore retires;
What time, loose-glimmering to the lunar beam,
Faint heaves the slumberous wave, and starry fires
Gild the blue deep with many a lengthening gleam.

"Then to the balmy bower of Rapture borne,
While strings self-warbling breathe elysian rest,
Melts in delicious vision, till the morn
Spangle with twinkling dew the flowery waste.

"The frolic Moments, purple-pinion'd, dance
Around, and scatter roses as they play:
And the blithe Graces, hand in hand, advance,
Where, with her loved compeers she deigns to stray.

"Mild Solitude, in veil of rustic dye,
Her sylvan spear with moss-grown ivy bound:
And Indolence, with sweetly-languid eye,
And zoneless robe that trails along the ground.

But chiefly Love—O thou, whose gentle mind,
Each soft indulgence Nature framed to share,
Pomp, wealth, renown, dominion, all resign'd,
O haste to Pleasure's bower, for Love is there.

"Love, the desire of gods! the feast of Heaven!
Yet to Earth's favour'd offspring not denied!
Ah, let not thankless man the blessing given
Enslave to Fame, or sacrifice to Pride.

"Nor I from Virtue's call decoy thine ear;
Friendly to Pleasure are her sacred laws:
Let Temperance' smile the cup of gladness cheer;
That cup is death, if he withhold applause.

"Far from thy haunt be Envy's baneful sway,
And Hate, that works the harass'd soul to storm;
But woo Content to breathe her soothing lay,
And charm from Fancy's view each angry form.

"No savage joy th' harmonious hours profane!
Whom Love refines, can barbarous tumults please?
Shall rage of blood pollute the sylvan reign?
Shall Leisure wanton in the spoils of Peace?

"Free let the feathery race indulge the song,
Inhale the liberal beam, and melt in love;
Free let the fleet hind bound her hills along,
And in pure streams the watery nations rove.

"To joy in Nature's universal smile
Well suits, O man, thy pleasurable sphere;
But why should Virtue doom thy years to toil?
Ah, why should Virtue's law be deem'd severe?

"What meed, Beneficence, thy care repays?
What, Sympathy, thy still returning pang?
And why his generous arm should Justice raise,
To dare the vengeance of a tyrant's fang?

"From thankless spite no bounty can secure;
Or froward wish of discontent fulfil,
That knows not to regret thy bounded power,
But blames with keen reproach thy partial will.

"To check th' impetuous all-involving tide
Of human woes, how impotent thy strife!
High o'er thy mounds devouring surges ride,
Nor reck thy baffled toils, or lavish'd life.

"The bower of bliss, the smile of love be thine,
Unlabour'd ease, and leisure's careless dream.
Such be their joys, who bend at *Venus'* shrine,
And own her charms beyond compare supreme."

Warm'd as she spoke, all panting with delight,
Her kindling beauties breathed triumphant bloom;
And Cupids flutter'd round in circlets bright,
And Flora pour'd from all her stores perfume.

"Thine be the prize," exclaim'd th' enraptured youth,
"Queen of unrivall'd charms, and matchless joy."—
O blind to fate, felicity and truth!—
But such are they, whom Pleasure's snares decoy.

The Sun was sunk; the vision was no more;
Night downward rush'd tempestuous at the frown
Of Jove's awaken'd wrath: deep thunders roar,
And forests howl afar and mountains groan;

And sanguine meteors glare athwart the plain;
With horror's scream the Ilian towers resound,
Raves the hoarse storm along the bellowing main,
And the strong earthquake rends the shuddering ground.

THE WOLF AND SHEPHERDS,

A FABLE.

(Written in 1757, and first published in 1766.)

Laws, as we read in ancient sages,
Have been like cobwebs in all ages.
Cobwebs for little flies are spread,
And laws for little folks are made;
But if an insect of renown,
Hornet or beetle, wasp or drone,
Be caught in quest of sport or plunder,
The flimsy fetter flies in sunder.

Your simile perhaps may please one
With whom wit holds the place of reason:
But can you prove that this in fact is
Agreeable to life and practice?

Then hear what in his simple way
Old Æsop told me t' other day.
In days of yore, but (which is very odd)
Our author mentions not the period,
We mortal men, less given to speeches,
Allow'd the beasts sometimes to teach us.
But now we all are prattlers grown,
And suffer no voice but our own;
With us no beast has leave to speak,
Although his honest heart should break.
'Tis true your asses and your apes,
And other brutes in human shapes,
And that thing made of sound and show
Which mortals have misnamed a beau,
(But in the language of the sky
Is call'd a two-legg'd butterfly)
Will make your very heartstrings ache
With loud and everlasting clack,
And beat your auditory drum,
Till you grow deaf, or they grow dumb.

But to our story we return:
'Twas early on a summer morn,
A wolf forsook the mountain-den,
And issued hungry on the plain.
Full many a stream and lawn he pass'd,
And reach'd a winding vale at last;
Where from a hollow rock he spied
The shepherds drest in flowery pride.
Garlands were strow'd, and all was gay,
To celebrate a holiday.
The merry tabor's gamesome sound
Provoked the sprightly dance around.
Hard by a rural board was rear'd,
On which in fair array appear'd
The peach, the apple, and the raisin,
And all the fruitage of the season.
But, more distinguish'd than the rest,
Was seen a wether ready drest,
That smoking, recent from the flame,
Diffused a stomach-rousing steam.
Our wolf could not endure the sight,
Courageous grew his appetite:
His entrails groan'd with tenfold pain,
He lick'd his lips and lick'd again;
At last, with lightning in his eyes,
He bounces forth, and fiercely cries,
"Shepherds! I am not given to scolding,
But now my spleen I cannot hold in:
By Jove, such scandalous oppression
Would put an elephant in passion.

You, who your flocks (as you pretend)
By wholesome laws from harm defend,
Which make it death for any beast,
How much soe'er by hunger press'd,
To seize a sheep by force or stealth,
For sheep have right to life and health;
Can you commit, uncheck'd by shame,
What in a beast so much you blame?
What is a law if those who make it
Become the forwardest to break it?
The case is plain: you would reserve
All to yourselves, while others starve.
Such laws from base self-interest spring,
Not from the reason of the thing—"

He was proceeding, when a swain
Burst out:—"And dares a wolf arraign
His betters, and condemn their measures,
And contradict their wills and pleasures?
We have establish'd laws, 'tis true,
But laws are made for such as you.
Know, sirrah, in its very nature
A law can't reach the legislature,
For laws, without a sanction join'd,
As all men know, can never bind:
But sanctions reach not us the makers,
For who dares punish us though breakers?
'Tis therefore plain beyond denial,
That laws were ne'er design'd to tie all,
But those, whom sanctions reach alone;
We stand accountable to none.
Besides, 'tis evident, that, seeing
Laws from the great derive their being,
They as in duty bound should love
The great, in whom they live and move,
And humbly yield to their desires:
'Tis just, what gratitude requires.
What suckling dandled on the lap
Would tear away its mother's pap?
But hold—Why deign I to dispute
With such a scoundrel of a brute?
Logic is lost upon a knave,
Let action prove the law our slave."

An angry nod his will declared
To his gruff yeomen of the guard;
The full-fed mongrels, train'd to ravage,
Fly to devour the shaggy savage.

The beast had now no time to lose
In chopping logic with his foes;
"This argument," quoth he, "has force,
And swiftness is my sole resource."

He said, and left the swains their prey
And to the mountains scour'd away.

TRANSLATIONS.

ANACREON. ODE XXII.

Παρὰ τὴν σκιὴν, Βάθυλλε,
Κάθισον·—κ. τ. λ.

Bathyllus, in yonder lone grove
All carelessly let us recline:
To shade us the branches above
Their leaf-waving tendrils combine;
While a streamlet inviting repose
Soft-murmuring wanders away,
And gales warble wild through the boughs:
Who there would not pass the sweet day?

THE BEGINNING OF

THE FIRST BOOK OF LUCRETIUS.

Æneadum Genetrix —— v. 1—45.

Mother of mighty Rome's imperial line,
Delight of man, and of the powers divine,
Venus, all bounteous queen! whose genial power
Diffuses beauty in unbounded store
Through seas, and fertile plains, and all that lies
Beneath the starr'd expansion of the skies.
Prepared by thee, the embryo springs to day,
And opes its eyelids on the golden ray.
At thy approach, the clouds tumultuous fly,
And the hush'd storms in gentle breezes die;
Flowers instantaneous spring; the billows sleep;
A wavy radiance smiles along the deep;
At thy approach, th' untroubled sky refines,
And all serene Heaven's lofty concave shines.
Soon as her blooming form the Spring reveals,
And Zephyr breathes his warm prolific gales,
The feather'd tribes first catch the genial flame,
And to the groves thy glad return proclaim.
Thence to the beasts the soft infection spreads;
The raging cattle spurn the grassy meads,
Burst o'er the plains, and frantic in their course
Cleave the wild torrents with resistless force.
Won by thy charms, thy dictates all obey,
And eager follow where thou lead'st the way.
Whatever haunts the mountains, or the main,
The rapid river, or the verdant plain,
Or forms its leafy mansion in the shades,
All, all thy universal power pervades,
Each panting bosom melts to soft desires,
And with the love of propagation fires.
And since thy sovereign influence guides the reins
Of nature, and the universe sustains;
Since nought without thee bursts the bonds of night,
To hail the happy realms of heavenly light;
Since love, and joy, and harmony are thine,
Guide me, O goddess, by thy power divine,
And to my rising lays thy succour bring,
While I the universe attempt to sing.
O may my verse deserved applause obtain
Of him, for whom I try the daring strain,
My Memmius, him, whom thou profusely kind
Adorn'st with every excellence refined.
And that immortal charms my song may grace,
Let war, with all its cruel labours, cease;
O hush the dismal din of arms once more,
And calm the jarring world from shore to shore.
By thee alone the race of man foregoes
The rage of blood, and sinks in soft repose:
For mighty Mars, the dreadful god of arms,
Who wakes or stills the battle's dire alarms,
In love's strong fetters by thy charms is bound,
And languishes with an eternal wound.

Oft from his bloody toil the god retires
To quench in thy embrace his fierce desires.
Soft on thy heaving bosom he reclines,
And round thy yielding neck transported twines;
There fix'd in ecstacy intense surveys
Thy kindling beauties with insatiate gaze,
Grows to thy balmy mouth, and ardent sips
Celestial sweets from thy ambrosial lips.
O, while the god with fiercest raptures blest
Lies all dissolving on thy sacred breast,
O breathe thy melting whispers to his ear,
And bid him still the loud alarms of war.
In these tumultuous days, the Muse, in vain,
Her steady tenour lost, pursues the strain,
And Memmius' generous soul disdains to taste
The calm delights of philosophic rest;
Paternal fires his beating breast inflame,
To rescue Rome, and vindicate her name.

HORACE, BOOK II. ODE X.

Rectius vives, Licini——.

Wouldst thou through life securely glide,
Nor boundless o'er the ocean ride;
Nor ply too near th' insidious shore,
Scared at the tempest's threat'ning roar.
The man who follows Wisdom's voice,
And makes the golden mean his choice,
Nor plunged in antique gloomy cells
'Midst hoary desolation dwells;
Nor to allure the envious eye
Rears his proud palace to the sky.
The pine, that all the grove transcends,
With every blast the tempest rends;
Totters the tower with thund'rous sound,
And spreads a mighty ruin round;
Jove's bolt with desolating blow
Strikes the ethereal mountain's brow.
The man, whose stedfast soul can bear
Fortune indulgent or severe,
Hopes when she frowns, and when she smiles
With cautious fear eludes her wiles.
Jove with rude winter wastes the plain,
Jove decks the rosy spring again.
Life's former ills are overpast,
Nor will the present always last.
Now Phœbus wings his shafts, and now
He lays aside th' unbended bow,
Strikes into life the trembling string,
And wakes the silent Muse to sing.
With unabating courage, brave
Adversity's tumultuous wave;
When too propitious breezes rise,
And the light vessel swiftly flies,
With timid caution catch the gale,
And shorten the distended sail.

HORACE, BOOK III. ODE XIII.

O Fons Blandusiæ——.

Blandusia! more than crystal clear!
Whose soothing murmurs charm the ear!
Whose margin soft with flowrets crown'd
Invites the festive band around,
Their careless limbs diffused supine,
To quaff the soul-enlivening wine.
To thee a tender kid I vow,
That aims for fight his budding brow;
In thought, the wrathful combat proves,
Or wantons with his little loves:
But vain are all his purposed schemes,
Delusive all his flattering dreams;
To-morrow shall his fervent blood
Stain the pure silver of thy flood.
When fiery Sirius blasts the plain,
Untouch'd thy gelid streams remain.
To thee, the fainting flocks repair,
To taste thy cool reviving air;
To thee, the ox with toil opprest,
And lays his languid limbs to rest.
As springs of old renown'd, thy name,
Blest fountain! I devote to fame;
Thus while I sing in deathless lays
The verdant holm, whose waving sprays,
Thy sweet retirement to defend,
High o'er the moss-grown rock impend,
Whence prattling in loquacious play
Thy sprightly waters leap away.

THE PASTORALS OF VIRGIL.
PASTORAL I.[1]

Non ita certandi cupidus, quam propter amorem
Quod te imitari aveo——.
Lucret. lib. iii.

MELIBŒUS, TITYRUS.

MELIBŒUS.

Where the broad beech an ample shade displays,
Your slender reed resounds the sylvan lays,

[1] It has been observed by some critics who have treated of pastoral poetry, that, in every poem of this kind, it is proper that the scene or landscape connected with the little plot or fable on which the poem is founded, be delineated with at least as much accuracy as is sufficient to render the description particular and picturesque. How far Virgil has thought fit to attend to such a rule, may appear from the remarks which the translator has subjoined to every pastoral.

The scene of the first pastoral is pictured out with great accuracy. The shepherds Melibœus and Tityrus are represented as conversing together beneath a spreading beech-tree. Flocks and herds are feeding hard by. At a little distance we behold on the one hand a great rock, and on the other a fence of flowering willows. The prospect, as it widens, is diversified with groves, and streams, and some tall trees, particularly elms. Beyond all these appear marshy grounds and rocky hills. The ragged and drooping flock of the unfortunate shepherd, particularly the she-goat which he leads along, are no inconsiderable figures in this picture.—The time is the evening of a summer day, a little before sunset. See, of the original, v. 1, 5, 9, 52, 54, 57, 59, 81, &c.

This pastoral is said to have been written on the following occasion:—Augustus, in order to reward the services of his veterans, by means of whom he had established himself in the Roman empire, distributed among them the lands that lay contiguous to Mantua and Cremona. To make way for these intruders, the rightful owners, of whom Virgil was one, were turned out; but our poet, by the intercession of Mecænas, was reinstated in his possessions. Melibœus here personates one of the unhappy exiles, and Virgil is represented under the character of Tityrus.

O happy Tityrus! while we, forlorn,
Driven from our lands, to distant climes are borne,
Stretch'd careless in the peaceful shade you sing,
And all the groves with Amaryllis ring.

TITYRUS.

This peace to a propitious god I owe;
None else, my friend, such blessings could bestow.
Him will I celebrate with rites divine,
And frequent lambs shall stain his sacred shrine.
By him, these feeding herds in safety stray;
By him, in peace I pipe the rural lay.

MELIBŒUS.

I envy not, but wonder at your fate,
That no alarms invade this blest retreat;
While neighbouring fields the voice of woe resound,
And desolation rages all around.
Worn with fatigue I slowly onward bend,
And scarce my feeble fainting goats attend.
My hand this sickly dam can hardly bear,
Whose young new-yean'd (ah once a hopeful pair!)
Amid the tangling hazels as they lay,
On the sharp flint were left to pine away.
These ills I had foreseen, but that my mind
To all portents and prodigies was blind.
Oft have the blasted oaks foretold my woe;
And often has the inauspicious crow,
Perch'd on the wither'd holm, with fateful cries
Scream'd in my ear her dismal prophecies.
But say, O Tityrus, what god bestows
This blissful life of undisturb'd repose?

TITYRUS.

Imperial Rome, while yet to me unknown,
I vainly liken'd to our country-town,
Our little Mantua, at which is sold
The yearly offspring of our fruitful fold;
As in the whelp the father's shape appears,
And as the kid its mother's semblance bears:
Thus greater things my inexperienced mind
Rated by others of inferior kind.
But she, 'midst other cities, rears her head
High, as the cypress overtops the reed.

MELIBŒUS.

And why to visit Rome was you inclined?

TITYRUS.

'Twas there I hoped my liberty to find.
And there my liberty I found at last,
Though long with listless indolence opprest;
Yet not till Time had silver'd o'er my hairs,
And I had told a tedious length of years;
Nor till the gentle Amaryllis charm'd[1],
And Galatea's love no longer warm'd.
For (to my friend I will confess the whole)
While Galatea captive held my soul,
Languid and lifeless all I dragg'd the chain,
Neglected liberty, neglected gain.
Though from my fold the frequent victim bled,
Though my fat cheese th' ungrateful city fed,
For this I ne'er perceived my wealth increase;
I lavish'd all, her haughty heart to please.

MELIBŒUS.

Why Amaryllis pined, and pass'd away
In lonely shades the melancholy day;
Why to the gods she breathed incessant vows;
For whom her mellow apples press'd the boughs,
So late, I wonder'd—Tityrus was gone,
And she (ah luckless maid!) was left alone.
Your absence every warbling fountain mourn'd,
And woods and wilds the wailing strains return'd.

TITYRUS.

What could I do? to break th' enslaving chain
All other efforts had (alas!) been vain;
Nor durst my hopes presume, but there, to find
The gods so condescending and so kind.
'Twas there these eyes the Heaven-born youth[1] beheld,
To whom our altars monthly incense yield:
My suit he even prevented, while he spoke,
"Manure your ancient farm, and feed your former flock."

MELIBŒUS.

Happy old man! then shall your lands remain,
Extent sufficient for th' industrious swain!
Though bleak and bare yon ridgy rocks arise,
And lost in lakes the neighbouring pasture lies,
Your herds on wonted grounds shall safely range,
And never feel the dire effects of change.
No foreign flock shall spread infecting bane
To hurt your pregnant dams, thrice happy swain!
You by known streams and sacred fountains laid
Shall taste the coolness of the fragrant shade.
Beneath yon fence, where willow-boughs unite,
And to their flowers the swarming bees invite,
Oft shall the lulling hum persuade to rest,
And balmy slumbers steal into your breast;
While warbled from this rock the pruner's lay
In deep repose dissolves your soul away;
High on yon elm the turtle wails alone,
And your loved ring-doves breathe a hoarser moan.

TITYRUS.

The nimble harts shall graze in empty air,
And seas retreating leave their fishes bare,
The German dwell where rapid Tigris flows,
The Parthian banish'd by invading foes
Shall drink the Gallic Arar, from my breast
Ere his majestic image be effaced.

MELIBŒUS.

But we must travel o'er a length of lands,
O'er Scythian snows, or Afric's burning sands;
Some wander where remote Oäxes laves
The Cretan meadows with his rapid waves;
In Britain some, from every comfort torn,
From all the world removed, are doom'd to mourn.
When long long years have tedious roll'd away,
Ah! shall I yet at last, at last survey
My dear paternal lands, and dear abode,
Where once I reign'd in walls of humble sod!
These lands, these harvests must the soldier share!
For rude barbarians lavish we our care!
How are our fields become the spoil of wars!
How are we ruin'd by intestine jars!
Now, Melibœus, now ingraff the pear,
Now teach the vine its tender sprays to rear!—
Go then, my goats!—go, once a happy store
Once happy!—happy now (alas!) no more!
No more shall I, beneath the bowery shade
In rural quiet indolently laid,
Behold you from afar the cliffs ascend,
And from the shrubby precipice depend;
No more to music wake my melting flute,
While on the thyme you feed, and willow's wholesome shoot.

[1] The refinements of Taubmannus, De la Cerda, and others, who will have Amaryllis to signify Rome, and Galatea to signify Mantua, have perplexed this passage not a little: if the literal meaning be admitted, the whole becomes obvious and natural.

[1] Augustus Cæsar.

TITYRUS.

This night at least with me you may repose
On the green foliage, and forget your woes.
Apples and nuts mature our boughs afford,
And curdled milk in plenty crowns my board.
Now from yon hamlets clouds of smoke arise,
And slowly roll along the evening skies;
And see projected from the mountain's brow
A lengthen'd shade obscures the plains below.

PASTORAL II[1].

ALEXIS.

YOUNG Corydon for fair Alexis pined,
But hope ne'er gladden'd his desponding mind;
Nor vows nor tears the scornful boy could move,
Distinguish'd by his wealthier master's love.
Oft to the beech's deep embowering shade
Pensive and sad this hapless shepherd stray'd;
There told in artless verse his tender pain
To echoing hills and groves, but all in vain.
In vain the flute's complaining lays I try;
And am I doom'd, unpitying boy, to die?
Now to faint flocks the grove a shade supplies,
And in the thorny brake the lizard lies;
Now Thestylis with herbs of savoury taste
Prepares the weary harvest-man's repast;
And all is still, save where the buzzing sound
Of chirping grasshoppers is heard around;
While I, exposed to all the rage of heat,
Wander the wilds in search of thy retreat.
Was it not easier to support the pain
I felt from Amaryllis' fierce disdain?
Easier Menalcas' cold neglect to bear,
Black though he was, though thou art blooming fair?
Yet be relenting, nor too much presume,
O beauteous boy, on thy celestial bloom;
The sable violet[2] yields a precious dye,
While useless on the field the withering lilies lie.
Ah cruel boy! my love is all in vain,
No thoughts of thine regard thy wretched swain.
How rich my flock thou carest not to know,
Nor how my pails with generous milk o'erflow.
With bleat of thousand lambs my hills resound,
And all the year my milky stores abound.
Not Amphion's lays were sweeter than my song,
Those lays that led the listening herds along;
And if the face be true I lately view'd,
Where calm and clear the uncurling ocean stood,
I lack not beauty, nor could'st thou deny,
That even with Daphnis I may dare to vie.
O deign at last, amid these lonely fields,
To taste the pleasures which the country yields;
With me to dwell in cottages resign'd,
To roam the woods, to shoot the bounding hind;
With me the weanling kids from home to guide
To the green mallows on the mountain side;
With me in echoing groves the song to raise,
And emulate even Pan's celestial lays.
Pan taught the jointed reed its tuneful strain,
Pan guards the tender flock, and shepherd swain.
Nor grudge, Alexis, that the rural pipe
So oft hath stain'd the roses of thy lip:
How did Amyntas strive thy skill to gain!
How grieve at last to find his labour vain!
Of seven unequal reeds a pipe I have,
The precious gift which good Damœtas gave:
'Take this,' the dying shepherd said, 'for none
Inherits all my skill save thou alone.'
He said; Amyntas murmurs at my praise,
And with an envious eye the gift surveys.
Besides, as presents for my soul's delight
Two beauteous kids I keep bestreak'd with white,
Nourish'd with care, nor purchased without pain;
A ewe's full udder twice a day they drain.
These to obtain oft Thestylis hath tried
Each winning art, while I her suit denied;
But I at last shall yield what she requests,
Since thy relentless pride my gifts detests.
'Come, beauteous boy, and bless my rural bowers,
For thee the nymphs collect the choicest flowers:
Fair Nais culls amid the bloomy dale
The drooping poppy, and the violet pale,
To marigolds the hyacinth applies,
Shading the glossy with the tawny dyes:
Narcissus' flower with daffodil entwined,
And cassia's breathing sweets to these are join'd,
With every bloom that paints the vernal grove,
And all to form a garland for my love.
Myself with sweetest fruits will crown thy feast;
The luscious peach shall gratify thy taste,
And chestnut brown (once high in my regard,
For Amaryllis this to all preferr'd;
But if the blushing plum thy choice thou make,
The plum shall more be valued for thy sake.)
The myrtle wreathed with laurel shall exhale
A blended fragrance to delight thy smell.
Ah Corydon! thou rustic, simple swain!
Thyself, thy prayers, thy offers, all are vain.
How few, compared with rich Iolas' store,
Thy boasted gifts, and all thy wealth how poor!
Wretch that I am! while thus I pine forlorn,
And all the livelong day, inactive mourn,
The boars have laid my silver fountains waste,
My flowers are fading in the southern blast.—
Fly'st thou, ah foolish boy, the lonesome grove?
Yet gods for this have left the realms above.
Paris with scorn the pomp of Troy survey'd,
And sought the Idæan bowers and peaceful shade.
In her proud palaces let Pallas shine;
The lowly woods and rural life be mine.
The lioness all dreadful in her course
Pursues the wolf, and he with headlong force

---

[1] The chief excellency of this poem consists in its delicacy and simplicity. Corydon addresses his favourite in such a purity of sentiment as one would think might effectually discountenance the prepossessions which generally prevail against the subject of this eclogue. The nature of his affection may easily be ascertained from his ideas of the happiness which he hopes to enjoy in the company of his beloved Alexis.

O tantum libeat ———

&c. O deign at last, amid these lonely fields, &c.

It appears to have been no other than that friendship which was encouraged by the wisest legislators of ancient Greece as a noble incentive to virtue, and recommended by the example even of Agesilaus, Pericles, and Socrates; an affection wholly distinct from the infamous attachments that prevailed among the licentious. The reader will find a full and satisfying account of this generous passion in Dr. Potter's Antiquities of Greece, book iv. ch. 9. Mons. Bayle, in his Dictionary, at the article Virgile, has at great length vindicated our poet from the charge of immorality which the critics have grounded upon this pastoral.—The scene of the pastoral is a grove interspersed with beech-trees; the season, harvest.

[2] vaccinium (here translated violet) yielded a purple colour, used in dying the garments of slaves, according to Plin. l. xvi. c. 28.

Flies at the wanton goat, that loves to climb
The cliff's steep side, and crop the flowering thyme;
Thee Corydon pursues, O beauteous boy:
Thus each is drawn along by some peculiar joy.
Now evening soft comes on; and homeward now
From field the weary oxen bear the plough.
The setting sun now beams more mildly bright,
The shadows lengthening with the level light.
While with love's flame my restless bosom glows,
For love no interval of ease allows.
Ah Corydon! to weak complaints a prey!
What madness thus to waste the fleeting day!
Be roused at length; thy half-pruned vines demand
The needful culture of thy curbing hand.
Haste, lingering swain, the flexile willows weave,
And with thy wonted care thy wants relieve.
Forget Alexis' unrelenting scorn,
Another love thy passion will return.

PASTORAL III.

MENALCAS, DAMŒTAS, PALÆMON[1].

MENALCAS.

To whom belongs this flock, Damœtas, pray:
To Meliboeus?

DAMŒTAS.

No: the other day
The shepherd Ægon gave it me to keep.

MENALCAS.

Ah still neglected, still unhappy sheep[2]!
He plies Neæra with assiduous love,
And fears lest she my happier flame approve;
Meanwhile this hireling wretch (disgrace to swains!)
Defrauds his master, and purloins his gains,
Milks twice an hour, and drains the famish'd dams,
Whose empty dugs in vain attract the lambs.

DAMŒTAS.

Forbear on men such language to bestow.
Thee, stain of manhood! thee, full well I know.
I know, with whom—and where—[3] (their grove defiled
The nymphs revenged not, but indulgent smiled)
And how the goats beheld, then browsing near,
The shameful sight with a lascivious leer.

MENALCAS.

No doubt, when Mycon's tender trees I broke,
And gash'd his young vines with a blunted hook.

DAMŒTAS.

Or when conceal'd behind this ancient row
Of beech, you broke young Daphnis' shafts and bow,
With sharpest pangs of rancorous anguish stung
To see the gift conferr'd on one so young;
And had you not thus wreaked your sordid spite,
Of very envy you had died outright.

MENALCAS.

Gods! what may masters dare, when such a pitch
Of impudence their thievish hirelings reach:
Did I not, wretch, (deny it if you dare,)
Did I not see you Damon's goat ensnare?
Lycisca bark'd; then I the felon spied,
And 'Whither slinks yon sneaking thief?' I cried.
The thief discover'd, straight his prey forsook,
And skulk'd amid the sedges of the brook.

DAMŒTAS.

That goat my pipe from Damon fairly gained.
A match was set, and I the prize obtain'd.
He own'd it due to my superior skill,
And yet refused his bargain to fulfil.

MENALCAS.

By your superior skill—the goat was won!
Have you a jointed pipe, indecent clown!
Whose whizzing straws with harshest discord jarr'd,
As in the streets your wretched rhymes you marr'd.

DAMŒTAS.

Boasts are but vain. I'm ready, when you will,
To make a solemn trial of our skill.
I stake this heifer, no ignoble prize;
Two calves from her full udder she supplies,
And twice a day her milk the pail o'erflows;
What pledge of equal worth will you expose?

MENALCAS.

Aught from the flock I dare not risk; I fear
A cruel step-dame, and a sire severe,
Who of their store so strict a reckoning keep,
That twice a day they count the kids and sheep.
But, since you purpose to be mad to-day,
Two beechen cups I scruple not to lay
(Whose far superior worth yourself will own),
The labour'd work of famed Alcimedon.
Raised round the brims by the engraver's care
The flaunting vine unfolds its foliage fair;
Entwined the ivy's tendrils seem to grow,
Half-hid in leaves its mimic berries glow;
Two figures rise below, of curious frame,
Conon, and—what's that other sage's name,
Who with his rod described the world's vast round,
Taught when to reap, and when to till the ground?
At home I have reserved them unprofaned,
No lip has e'er the glossy polish stain'd.

DAMŒTAS.

Two cups for me that skilful artist made;
Their handles with acanthus are array'd;
Orpheus is in the midst, whose magic song
Leads in tumultuous dance the lofty groves along.
At home I have reserved them unprofaned,
No lip has e'er their glossy polish stain'd.
But my pledged heifer if aright you prize,
The cups so much extoll'd you will despise.

MENALCAS.

These arts, proud boaster, all are lost on me;
To any terms I readily agree.
You shall not boast your victory to-day,
Let him be judge who passes first this way:
And see the good Palæmon! trust me, swain,
You'll be more cautious how you brag again.

DAMŒTAS.

Delays I brook not; if you dare, proceed;
At singing no antagonist I dread.
Palæmon, listen to the important songs,
To such debates attention strict belongs.

---

[1] The contending shepherds, Menalcas and Damœtas, together with their umpire Palæmon, are seated on the grass, not far from a row of beech-trees. Flocks are seen feeding hard by. The time of the day seems to be noon; the season, between spring and summer.

[2] Throughout the whole of this altercation, notwithstanding the untoward subject, the reader will find in the original such a happy union of simplicity and force of expression and harmony of verse, as it is vain to look for in an English translation.

[3] The abruptness and obscurity of the original is here imitated.

PALÆMON.

Sing then. A couch the flowery herbage yields:
Now blossom all the trees, and all the fields;
And all the woods their pomp of foliage wear,
And Nature's fairest robe adorns the blooming year,
Damœtas first the alternate lay shall raise:
The inspiring Muses love alternate lays.

DAMŒTAS.

Jove first I sing; ye Muses, aid my lay;
All Nature owns his energy and sway;
The Earth and Heavens his sovereign bounty share,
And to my verses he vouchsafes his care.

MENALCAS.

With great Apollo I begin the strain,
For I am great Apollo's favourite swain;
For him the purple hyacinth I wear,
And sacred bay to Phœbus ever dear.

DAMŒTAS.

The sprightly Galatea at my head
An apple flung, and to the willows fled;
But as along the level lawn she flew,
The wanton wish'd not to escape my view.

MENALCAS.

I languish'd long for fair Amyntas' charms,
But now he comes unbidden to my arms,
And with my dogs is so familiar grown,
That my own Delia is no better known.

DAMŒTAS.

I lately mark'd where midst the verdant shade
Two parent-doves had built their leafy bed;
I from the nest the young will shortly take,
And to my love a handsome present make.

MENALCAS.

Ten ruddy wildings, from a lofty bough,
That through the green leaves beam'd with yellow [glow,
I brought away, and to Amyntas bore:
To-morrow I shall send as many more.

DAMŒTAS.

Ah the keen raptures! when my yielding fair
Breathed her kind whispers to my ravish'd ear!
Waft, gentle gales, her accents to the skies,
That gods themselves may hear with sweet surprise.

MENALCAS.

What, though I am not wretched by your scorn!
Say, beauteous boy, say can I cease to mourn,
If, while I hold the nets, the boar you face,
And rashly brave the dangers of the chase?

DAMŒTAS.

Send Phyllis home, Iolas, for to-day
I celebrate my birth, and all is gay;
When for my crop the victim I prepare,
Iolas in our festival may share.

MENALCAS.

Phyllis I love; she more than all can charm,
And mutual fires her gentle bosom warm:
Tears, when I leave her, bathe her beauteous eyes;
A long, a long adieu, my love!' she cries.

DAMŒTAS.

The wolf is dreadful to the woolly train,
Fatal to harvests is the crushing rain,
To the green woods the winds destructive prove,
To me the rage of mine offended love.

MENALCAS.

The willow's grateful to the pregnant ewes,
Showers to the corns, to kids the mountain-brows;
More grateful far to me my lovely boy,
In sweet Amyntas centres all my joy.

DAMŒTAS.

Even Pollio deigns to hear my rural lays;
And cheers the bashful Muse with generous praise:
Ye sacred Nine, for your great patron feed
A beauteous heifer of the noblest breed.

MENALCAS.

Pollio the art of heavenly song adorns;
Then let a bull be bred with butting horns,
And ample front, that bellowing spurns the ground,
Tears up the turf, and throws the sands around.

DAMŒTAS.

Him whom my Pollio loves may nought annoy,
May he like Pollio every wish enjoy;
O may his happy lands with honey flow,
And on his thorns Assyrian roses blow!

MENALCAS.

Who hates not foolish Bavius, let him love
Thee, Mævius, and thy tasteless rhymes approve'
Nor needs it thy admirer's reason shock
To milk the he-goats, and the foxes yoke.

DAMŒTAS.

Ye boys, on garlands who employ your care,
And pull the creeping strawberries, beware,
Fly for your lives, and leave that fatal place,
A deadly snake lies lurking in the grass.

MENALCAS.

Forbear, my flocks, and warily proceed,
Nor on that faithless bank securely tread;
The heedless ram late plunged amid the pool,
And in the sun now dries his reeking wool.

DAMŒTAS.

Ho, Tityrus! lead back the browsing flock,
And let them feed at distance from the brook;
At bathing-time I to the shade will bring
My goats, and wash them in the cooling spring.

MENALCAS.

Haste, from the sultry lawn the flocks remove
To the cool shelter of the shady grove:
When burning noon the curdling udder dries,
The ungrateful teats in vain the shepherd plies.

DAMŒTAS.

How lean my bull in yonder mead appears,
Though the fat soil the richest pasture bears!
Ah Love! thou reign'st supreme in every heart,
Both flocks and shepherds languish with thy dart.

MENALCAS.

Love has not injured my consumptive flocks,
Yet bare their bones, and faded are their looks:
What envious eye hath squinted on my dams,
And sent its poison to the tender lambs?

DAMŒTAS.

Say in what distant land the eye descries
But three short ells of all the expanded skies:
Tell this, and great Apollo be your name;
Your skill is equal, equal be your fame.

MENALCAS.

Say in what soil a wondrous flower is born,
Whose leaves the sacred names of kings adorn;
Tell this, and take my Phyllis to your arms,
And reign the unrivall'd sovereign of her charms.

PALÆMON.

'Tis not for me these high disputes to end;
Each to the heifer justly may pretend.
Such be their fortune, who so well can sing [spring.
From love what painful joys, what pleasing torments
Now, boys, obstruct the course of yonder rill;
The meadows have already drunk their fill.

PASTORAL IV[1].

POLLIO.

Sicilian Muse, sublimer strains inspire,
And warm my bosom with diviner fire!
All take not pleasure in the rural scene,
In lowly tamarisks, and forests green.
If sylvan themes we sing, then let our lays
Deserve a consul's ear, a consul's praise.

The age comes on, that future age of gold
In Cuma's mystic prophecies foretold.
The years begin their mighty course again,
The Virgin now returns, and the Saturnian reign.
Now from the lofty mansions of the sky
To Earth descends a heaven-born progeny.
Thy Phœbus reigns, Lucina, lend thine aid,
Nor be his birth, his glorious birth, delay'd!
An iron race shall then no longer rage,
But all the world regain the golden age.
This child, the joy of nations, shall be born
Thy consulship, O Pollio, to adorn:
Thy consulship these happy times shall prove,
And see the mighty months begin to move:
Then all our former guilt shall be forgiven,
And man shall dread no more the avenging doom of Heaven.

The son with heroes and with gods shall shine,
And lead, enroll'd with them, the life divine.
He o'er the peaceful nations shall preside,
And his sire's virtues shall his sceptre guide.
To thee, auspicious babe, the unbidden earth
Shall bring the earliest of her flowery birth;
Acanthus soft in smiling beauty gay,
The blossom'd bean, and ivy's flaunting spray.
The untended goats shall to their homes repair,
And to the milker's hand the loaded udder bear.
The mighty lion shall no more be fear'd,
But graze innoxious with the friendly herd.
Sprung from thy cradle fragrant flowers shall spread,
And, fanning bland, shall wave around thy head.
Then shall the serpent die, with all his race:
No deadly herb the happy soil disgrace:
Assyrian balm on every bush shall bloom,
And breathe in every gale its rich perfume.

But when thy father's deed thy youth shall fire,
And to great actions all thy soul inspire,
When thou shalt read of heroes and of kings,
And mark the glory that from virtue springs;
Then boundless o'er the far-extended plain
Shall wave luxuriant crops of golden grain,
With purple grapes the loaded thorn shall bend,
And streaming honey from the oak descend.
Nor yet old fraud shall wholly be effaced;
Navies for wealth shall roam the watery waste;
Proud cities fenced with towery walls appear,
And cruel shares shall earth's soft bosom tear:
Another Tiphys o'er the swelling tide
With steady skill the bounding ship shall guide;
Another Argo with the flower of Greece
From Colchos' shore shall waft the golden fleece;
Again the world shall hear war's loud alarms,
And great Achilles shine again in arms.

When riper years thy strengthen'd nerves shall brace,
And o'er thy limbs diffuse a manly grace,
The mariner no more shall plough the deep,
Nor load with foreign wares the trading ship;
Each country shall abound in every store,
Nor need the products of another shore.
Henceforth no plough shall cleave the fertile ground,
No pruning-hook the tender vine shall wound;
The husbandman, with toil no longer broke,
Shall loose his ox for ever from the yoke.
No more the wool a foreign dye shall feign,
But purple flocks shall graze the flowery plain,
Glittering in native gold the ram shall tread,
And scarlet lambs shall wanton on the mead.

In concord join'd with fate's unalter'd law
The Destinies these happy times foresaw,
They bade the sacred spindle swiftly run,
And hasten the auspicious ages on.

O dear to all thy kindred gods above!
O thou, the offspring of eternal Jove!
Receive thy dignities, begin thy reign,
And o'er the world extend thy wide domain.
See nature's mighty frame exulting round,
Ocean, and earth, and heaven's immense profound!
See nations yet unborn with joy behold
Thy glad approach, and hail the age of gold!

O would the immortals lend a length of days,
And give a soul sublime to sound thy praise;
Would Heaven this breast, this labouring breast inflame
With ardour equal to the mighty theme;
Not Orpheus with diviner transports glow'd,
When all her fire his mother-muse bestow'd;
Nor loftier numbers flow'd from Linus' tongue,
Although his sire Apollo gave the song;
Even Pan, in presence of Arcadian swains,
Would vainly strive to emulate my strains.

Repay a parent's care, O beauteous boy,
And greet thy mother with a smile of joy;
For thee, to loathing languors all resign'd,
Ten slow-revolving months thy mother pined.
If cruel fate thy parents' bliss denies[1],
If no fond joy sits smiling in thine eyes,
No nymph of heavenly birth shall crown thy love
Nor shalt thou share the immortal feast above.

---

[1] In this fourth pastoral no particular landscape is delineated. The whole is a prophetic song of triumph. But as almost all the images and allusions are of the rural kind, it is no less a true bucolic than the others; if we admit the definition of a pastoral, given us by an author of the first rank*, who calls it "A poem in which any action or passion is represented by its effects upon country life."

It is of little importance to inquire on what occasion this poem was written. The spirit of prophetic enthusiasm that breathes through it, and the resemblance it bears in many places to the Oriental manner, makes it not improbable that our poet composed it partly from some pieces of ancient prophecy that might have fallen into his hands, and that he afterwards inscribed it to his friend and patron Pollio, on occasion of the birth of his son Saloninus.

* The author of the Rambler.

[1] This passage has perplexed all the critics. Out of a number of significations that have been offered, the translator has pitched upon one, which he thinks the most agreeable to the scope of the poem and most consistent with the language of the original. The reader who wants more particulars on this head may consult Servius, De La Cerda, or Ruæus.

PASTORAL V [1].

MENALCAS, MOPSUS.

MENALCAS.

SINCE you with skill can touch the tuneful reed,
Since few my verses or my voice exceed;
In this refreshing shade shall we recline,
Where hazels with the lofty elms combine?

MOPSUS.

Your riper age a due respect requires,
'Tis mine to yield to what my friend desires;
Whether you choose the zephyr's fanning breeze,
That shakes the wavering shadows of the trees;
Or the deep-shaded grotto's cool retreat:—
And see yon cave screen'd from the scorching heat,
Where the wild vine its curling tendrils weaves,
Whose grapes glow ruddy through the quivering
leaves.

MENALCAS.

Of all the swains that to our hills belong,
Amyntas only vies with you in song.

MOPSUS.

What, though with me that haughty shepherd
Who proudly dares Apollo's self defy? [vie,

MENALCAS.

Begin; let Alcon's praise inspire your strains [2],
Or Codrus' death, or Phyllis' amorous pains,
Begin, whatever theme your Muse prefer.
To feed the kids be, Tityrus, thy care.

MOPSUS.

I rather will repeat that mournful song,
Which late I carved the verdant beech along;
(I carved and trill'd by turns the labour'd lay)
And let Amyntas match me if he may.

MENALCAS.

As slender willows where the olive grows,
Or sordid shrubs when near the scarlet rose,
Such (if the judgment I have form'd be true)
Such is Amyntas when compared with you.

MOPSUS.

No more, Menalcas; we delay too long,
The grot's dim shade invites my promised song.
When Daphnis fell by fate's remorseless blow [3],
The weeping nymphs poured wild the plaint of wo;
Witness, O hazel-grove, and winding stream,
For all your echoes caught the mournful theme.
In agony of grief his mother prest
The clay-cold carcass to her throbbing breast,
Frantic with anguish wail'd his hapless fate,
Raved at the stars, and Heaven's relentless hate.
'Twas then the swains in deep despair forsook
Their pining flocks, nor led them to the brook;
The pining flocks for him their pastures slight,
Nor grassy plains nor cooling streams invite.
The doleful tidings reach'd the Libyan shores,
And lions mourn'd in deep repeated roars.
His cruel doom the woodlands wild bewail,
And plaintive hills repeat the melancholy tale.
'Twas he, who first Armenia's tigers broke,
And tamed their stubborn natures to the yoke;
He first with ivy wrapt the thyrsus round,
And made the hills with Bacchus' rites resound [4].
As vines adorn the trees which they entwine,
As purple clusters beautify the vine,
As bulls the herd, as corn the fertile plains,
The godlike Daphnis dignified the swains.
When Daphnis from our eager hopes was torn
Phœbus and Pales left the plains to mourn.
Now weeds and wretched tares the crop subdue,
Where store of generous wheat but lately grew.
Narcissus' lovely flower no more is seen,
No more the velvet violet decks the green;
Thistles for these the blasted meadow yields,
And thorns and frizzled burs deform the fields.
Swains, shade the springs, and let the ground be
drest
With verdant leaves; 'twas Daphnis' last request.
Erect a tomb in honour to his name,
Mark'd with this verse to celebrate his fame:
'The swains with Daphnis' name this tomb adorn,
Whose high renown above the skies is borne;
Fair was his flock, the fairest on the plain,
The pride, the glory of the sylvan reign.'

MENALCAS.

Sweeter, O bard divine, thy numbers seem
Than to the scorched swain the cooling stream,
Or soft on fragrant flow'rets to recline,
And the tired limbs to balmy sleep resign. [praise
Blest youth! whose voice and pipe demand the
Due but to thine, and to thy master's lays.
I in return the darling theme will choose,
And Daphnis' praises shall inspire my Muse;
He in my song shall high as Heaven ascend,
High as the Heavens, for Daphnis was my friend.

MOPSUS.

His virtues sure our noblest numbers claim;
Nought can delight me more than such a theme,
Which in your song new dignity obtains;
Oft has our Stimichon extoll'd the strains.

MENALCAS.

Now Daphnis shines, among the gods a god,
Struck with the splendours of his new abode.
Beneath his footstool far remote appear
The clouds slow-sailing, and the starry sphere. [ring,
Hence lawns and groves with gladsome raptures
The swains, the nymphs, and Pan in concert sing.
The wolves to murder are no more inclined,
No guileful nets ensnare the wandering hind,
Deceit and violence and rapine cease,
For Daphnis loves the gentle arts of peace.
From savage mountains shouts of transport rise
Borne in triumphant echoes to the skies;
The rocks and shrubs emit melodious sounds,
Through nature's vast extent the god, the god re-
bounds.
Be gracious still, still present to our prayer;
Four altars, lo! we build with pious care,
Two for the inspiring god of song divine,
And two, propitious Daphnis, shall be thine.

[1] Here we discover Menalcas and Mopsus seated in an arbour formed by the interwoven twigs of a wild vine. A grove of hazels and elms surrounds this arbour. The season seems to be summer. The time of the day is not specified.

[2] From this passage it is evident that Virgil thought pastoral poetry capable of a much greater variety in its subjects than some modern critics will allow.

[3] It is the most general and most probable conjecture, that Julius Cæsar is the Daphnis, whose death and deification are here celebrated. Some, however, are of opinion, that by Daphnis is meant a real shepherd of Sicily of that name, who is said to have invented bucolic poetry, and in honour of whom the Sicilians performed yearly sacrifices.

[1] This can be applied only to Julius Cæsar; for it was he who introduced at Rome the celebration of the Bacchanalian revels.—Servius.

Two bowls white-foaming with their milky store,
Of generous oil two brimming goblets more,
Each year we shall present before thy shrine,
And cheer the feast with liberal draughts of wine;
Before the fire when winter-storms invade,
In summer's heat beneath the breezy shade:
The hallow'd bowls with wines of Chios crown'd,
Shall pour their sparkling nectar to the ground.
Damœtas shall with Lyctian[1] Ægon play,
And celebrate with festive strains the day.
Alphesibœus to the sprightly song
Shall like the dancing Satyrs trip along.
These rites shall still be paid, so justly due,
Both when the nymphs receive our annual vow,
And when with solemn songs and victims crown'd,
Our lands in long procession we surround.
While fishes love the streams and briny deep,
And savage boars the mountain's rocky steep,
While grasshoppers their dewy food delights,
While balmy thyme the busy bee invites;
So long shall last thine honours and thy fame,
So long the shepherds shall resound thy name.
Such rites to thee shall husbandmen ordain,
As Ceres and the god of wine obtain.
Thou to our prayers propitiously inclined
Thy grateful suppliants to their vows shalt bind.

MOPSUS.

What boon, dear shepherd, can your song requite?
For nought in nature yields so sweet delight.
Not the soft sighing of the southern gale,
That faintly breathes along the flowery vale;
Nor, when light breezes curl the liquid plain,
To tread the margin of the murmuring main;
Nor melody of streams, that roll away
Through rocky dales, delights me as your lay.

MENALCAS.

No mean reward, my friend, your verses claim:
Take then this flute that breathed the plaintive theme
Of Corydon[2]; when proud Damœtas[3] tried
To match my skill, it dash'd his hasty pride.

MOPSUS.

And let this sheep-crook by my friend be worn,
Which brazen studs in beamy rows adorn;
This fair Antigenes oft begg'd to gain,
But all his beauty, all his prayers were vain.

PASTORAL VI[4].

SILENUS.

My sportive Muse first sung Sicilian strains,
Nor blush'd to dwell in woods and lowly plains.
To sing of kings and wars when I aspire,
Apollo checks my vainly-rising fire.
'To swains the flock and sylvan pipe belong,
Then choose some humbler theme, nor dare heroic song.'
The voice divine, O Varus, I obey,
And to my reed shall chant a rural lay;
Since others long thy praises to rehearse,
And sing thy battles in immortal verse.

Yet if these songs which Phœbus bids me write,
Hereafter to the swains shall yield delight,
Of thee the trees and humble shrubs shall sing,
And all the vocal grove with Varus ring
The song inscribed to Varus' sacred name
To Phœbus' favour has the justest claim.

Come then, my Muse, a sylvan song repeat.
'Twas in his shady arbour's cool retreat
Two youthful swains the god Silenus found,
In drunkenness and sleep his senses bound,
His turgid veins the late debauch betray;
His garland on the ground neglected lay,
Fallen from his head; and by the well-worn ear
His cup of ample size depended near.
Sudden the swains the sleeping god surprise,
And with his garland bind him as he lies,
(No better chain at hand,) incensed so long
To be defrauded of their promised song.
To aid their project, and remove their fears,
Ægle, a beauteous fountain-nymph appears;
Who while he hardly opes his heavy eyes,
His stupid brow with bloody berries dyes.
Then smiling at the fraud, Silenus said,
'And dare you thus a sleeping god invade?
To see me was enough; but haste, unloose
My bonds; the song no longer I refuse;
Unloose me, youths; my song shall pay your pains;
For this fair nymph another boon remains.'

He sung; responsive to the heavenly sound
The stubborn oaks and forests dance around,
Tripping the Satyrs and the Fauns advance,
Wild beasts forget their rage, and join the general dance.
Not so Parnassus' listening rocks rejoice,
When Phœbus raises his celestial voice;
Nor Thracia's echoing mountains so admire,
When Orpheus strikes the loud-lamenting lyre.

For first he sung of Nature's wond'rous birth;
How seeds of water, air, and flame, and earth,
Down the vast void with casual impulse hurl'd,
Clung into shapes, and form'd this fabric of the world.
Then hardens by degrees the tender soil,
And from the mighty mound the seas recoil.
O'er the wide world new various forms arise;
The infant Sun along the brighten'd skies
Begins his course, while Earth with glad amaze
The blazing wonder from below surveys.
The clouds sublime their genial moisture shed,
And the green grove lifts high its leafy head.
The savage beasts o'er desert mountains roam,
Yet few their numbers, and unknown their home.
He next the blessed Saturnian ages sung;
How a new race of men from Pyrrha sprung[1];
Prometheus' daring theft, and dreadful doom,
Whose growing heart devouring birds consume.
Then names the spring, renown'd for Hylas' fate,
By the sad mariners bewail'd too late;
They call on Hylas with repeated cries,
And Hylas, Hylas, all the lonesome shore replies.
Next he bewails Pasiphaë (hapless dame!)
Who for a bullock felt a brutal flame.
What fury fires thy bosom, frantic queen!
How happy thou, if herds had never been!
The maids, whom Juno, to avenge her wrong[2],
Like heifers doom'd to low the vales along,

[1] Lyctium was a city of Crete.

[2] See Pastoral second. [3] See Pastoral third.

[4] The cave of Silenus, which is the scene of this eclogue, is delineated with sufficient accuracy. The time seems to be the evening; at least the song does not cease till the flocks are folded, and the evening star appears.

[1] See Ovid. Met. lib. i.

[2] Their names were Lysippe, Ipponoë, and Cyrianassa. Juno, to be avenged of them for preferring their own beauty to hers, struck them with madness, to such a degree, that they imagined themselves to be heifers.

Ne'er felt the rage of thy detested fire,
Ne'er were polluted with thy foul desire;
Though oft for horns they felt their polish'd brow,
And their soft necks oft fear'd the galling plough.
Ah wretched queen! thou roam'st the mountain-waste,
While, his white limbs on lilies laid to rest,
The half-digested herb again he chews,
Or some fair female of the herd pursues.
'Beset, ye Cretan nymphs, beset the grove,
And trace the wandering footsteps of my love.
Yet let my longing eyes my love behold,
Before some favourite beauty of the fold
Entice him with Gortynian [1] herds to stray,
Where smile the vales in richer pasture gay.'
He sung how golden fruit's resistless grace
Decoy'd the wary virgin from the race [2].
Then wraps in bark the mourning sisters round [3],
And rears the lofty alders from the ground.
He sung, while Gallus by Permessus [4] stray'd,
A sister of the Nine the hero led
To the Aonian hill; the choir in haste
Left their bright thrones, and hail'd the welcome guest.
Linus arose, for sacred song renown'd,
Whose brow a wreath of flowers and parsley bound;
And 'Take' he said, 'this pipe, which heretofore
The far-famed shepherd of Ascræa [5] bore;
Then heard the mountain-oaks its magic sound,
Leap'd from their hills, and thronging danced around.
On this thou shalt renew the tuneful lay,
And grateful songs to thy Apollo pay,
Whose famed Grynæan [6] temple from thy strain
Shall more exalted dignity obtain.'
Why should I sing unhappy Scylla's fate [7]?
Sad monument of jealous Circe's hate!
Round her white breast what furious monsters roll,
And to the dashing waves incessant howl:
How from the ships that bore Ulysses' crew [8]
Her dogs the trembling sailors dragg'd and slew.
Of Philomela's feast why should I sing [9],
And what dire chance befel the Thracian king?
Changed to a lapwing by th' avenging god,
He made the barren waste his lone abode,
And oft on soaring pinions hover'd o'er
The lofty palace then his own no more.

The tuneful god renews each pleasing theme
Which Phœbus sung by blest Eurotas' stream;
When blest Eurotas gently flow'd along,
And bade his laurels learn the lofty song.
Silenus sung; the vocal vales reply,
And heavenly music charms the listening sky.
But now their folds the number'd flocks invite,
The star of evening sheds its trembling light,
And the unwilling heavens are wrapt in night.

[1] Gortyna was a city of Crete. See Ovid. Ars. Am. lib. i.

[2] Atalanta. See Ovid. Met. lib. x.

[3] See Ovid. Met. lib. ii.

[4] A river in Bœotia arising from Mount Helicon, sacred to the Muses.

[5] Hesiod.

[6] Grynium was a maritime town of the Lesser Asia, where were an ancient temple and oracle of Apollo.

[7] See Virgil. Æn. iii.

[8] See Hom. Odyss. lib. xii.

[9] See Ovid. Met. lib. vi.

PASTORAL VII [1].

MELIBŒUS, CORYDON, THYRSIS.

MELIBŒUS.

Beneath a holm that murmur'd to the breeze,
The youthful Daphnis lean'd in rural ease;
With him two gay Arcadian swains reclined,
Who in the neighbouring vale their flocks had join'd,
Thyrsis, whose care it was the goats to keep,
And Corydon, who fed the fleecy sheep;
Both in the flowery prime of youthful days,
Both skill'd in single or responsive lays.
While I with busy hand a shelter form
To guard my myrtles from the future storm,
The husband of my goats had chanced to stray;
To find the vagrant out I take my way.
Which Daphnis seeing cries, 'Dismiss your fear,
Your kids and goats are all in safety here;
And if no other care require your stay,
Come, and with us unbend the toils of day
In this cool shade; at hand your heifers feed,
And of themselves will to the watering speed;
Here fringed with reeds slow Mincius winds along,
And round yon oak the bees soft murmuring throng.'
What could I do? for I was left alone,
My Phyllis and Alcippe both were gone,
And none remain'd to feed my weanling lambs,
And to restrain them from their bleating dams:
Betwixt the swains a solemn match was set,
To prove their skill, and end a long debate.
Though serious matters claim'd my due regard,
Their pastime to my business I preferr'd.
To sing by turns the Muse inspired the swains,
And Corydon began the alternate strains.

CORYDON.

Ye nymphs of Helicon, my sole desire!
O warm my breast with all my Codrus' fire.
If none can equal Codrus' heavenly lays,
For next to Phœbus he deserves the praise,
No more I ply the tuneful art divine,
My silent pipe shall hang on yonder pine.

THYRSIS.

Arcadian swains, an ivy wreath bestow,
With early honours crown your poet's brow;
Codrus shall chafe, if you my songs commend,
Till burning spite his tortured entrails rend;
Or amulets, to bind my temples, frame,
Lest his invidious praises blast my fame.

CORYDON.

A stag's tall horns, and stain'd with savage gore
This bristled visage of a tusky boar,
To thee, O virgin-goddess of the chase,
Young Mycon offers for thy former grace.
If like success his future labours crown,
Thine, goddess, then shall be a nobler boon;
In polish'd marble thou shalt shine complete,
And purple sandals shall adorn thy feet.

[1] The scene of this pastoral is as follows. Four shepherds, Daphnis in the most distinguished place, Corydon, Thyrsis, and Melibœus, are seen reclining beneath a holm. Sheep and goats intermixed are feeding hard by. At a little distance Mincius fringed with reeds appears winding along. Fields and trees compose the surrounding scene. A venerable oak, with bees swarming around it, is particularly distinguished. The time seems to be the forenoon of a summer-day.

THYRSIS.

To thee, Priapus[1], each returning year,
This bowl of milk, these hallow'd cakes, we bear;
Thy care, our garden, is but meanly stored,
And mean oblations all we can afford.
But if our flocks a numerous offspring yield,
And our decaying fold again be fill'd,
Though now in marble thou obscurely shine,
For thee a golden statue we design.

CORYDON.

O Galatea, whiter than the swan,
Loveliest of all thy sisters of the main,
Sweeter than Hybla, more than lilies fair!
If ought of Corydon employ thy care,
When shades of night involve the silent sky,
And slumbering in their stalls the oxen lie,
Come to my longing arms, and let me prove
The immortal sweets of Galatea's love.

THYRSIS.

As the vile sea-weed scatter'd by the storm,
As he whose face Sardinian herbs deform[2],
As burs and brambles that disgrace the plain,
So nauseous, so detested, be thy swain,
If when thine absence I am doom'd to bear
The day appears not longer than a year.
Go home, my flocks, ye lengthen out the day;
For shame, ye tardy flocks, for shame, away!

CORYDON.

Ye mossy fountains, warbling as ye flow:
And softer than the slumbers ye bestow,
Ye grassy banks! ye trees with verdure crown'd,
Whose leaves a glimmering shade diffuse around!
Grant to my weary flocks a cool retreat,
And screen them from the summer's raging heat;
For now the year in brightest glory shines,
Now reddening clusters deck the bending vines.

THYRSIS.

Here's wood for fuel; here the fire displays
To all around its animating blaze;
Black with continual smoke our posts appear;
Nor dread we more the rigour of the year,
Than the fell wolf the fearful lambkins dreads,
When he the helpless fold by night invades;
Or swelling torrents, headlong as they roll,
The weak resistance of the shatter'd mole.

CORYDON.

Now yellow harvests wave on every field,
Now bending boughs the hoary chestnut yield,
Now loaded trees resign their annual store,
And on the ground the mellow fruitage pour;
Jocund, the face of Nature smiles, and gay;
But if the fair Alexis were away,
Inclement drought the hardening soil would drain,
And streams no longer murmur o'er the plain.

THYRSIS.

A languid hue the thirsty fields assume,
Parch'd to the root the flowers resign their bloom,
The faded vines refuse their hills to shade,
Their leafy verdure wither'd and decay'd:
But if my Phyllis on these plains appear,
Again the groves their gayest green shall wear,
Again the clouds their copious moisture lend,
And in the genial rain shall Jove descend.

[1] This deity presided over gardens.

[2] It was the property of this poisonous herb to distort the features of those who had eaten of it in such a manner, that they seemed to expire in an agony of laughter.

CORYDON.

Alcides' brows the poplar-leaves surround,
Apollo's beamy locks with bays are crown'd,
The myrtle, lovely queen of smiles, is thine,
And jolly Bacchus loves the curling vine;
But while my Phyllis loves the hazel-spray,
To hazel yield the myrtle and the bay.

THYRSIS.

The fir, the hills; the ash adorns the woods;
The pine, the gardens; and the poplar, floods.
If thou, my Lycidas, wilt deign to come,
And cheer thy shepherd's solitary home,
The ash so fair in woods, and garden-pine,
Will own their beauty far excell'd by thine.

MELIBŒUS.

So sung the swains, but Thyrsis strove in vain;
Thus far I bear in mind th' alternate strain.
Young Corydon acquired unrivall'd fame,
And still we pay a deference to his name.

PASTORAL VIII[1].

DAMON, ALPHESIBŒUS.

Rehearse we, Pollio, the enchanting strains
Alternate sung by two contending swains.
Charm'd by their songs, the hungry heifers stood
In deep amaze, unmindful of their food;
The listening lynxes laid their rage aside,
The streams were silent, and forgot to glide.
O thou, where'er thou lead'st thy conquering host,
Or by Timavus[2], or th' Illyrian coast!
When shall my Muse, transported with the theme,
In strains sublime my Pollio's deeds proclaim;
And celebrate thy lays by all admired,
Such as of old Sophocles' Muse inspired!
To thee, the patron of my rural songs,
To thee my first, my latest lay belongs.
Then let this humble ivy-wreath enclose,
Twined with triumphal bays, thy godlike brows.
What time the chill sky brightens with the dawn,
When cattle love to crop the dewy lawn,
Thus Damon to the woodlands wild complain'd,
As 'gainst an olive's lofty trunk he lean'd.

DAMON.

Lead on the genial day, O star of morn!
While wretched I, all hopeless and forlorn,
With my last breath my fatal woes deplore,
And call the gods by whom false Nisa swore;
Though they, regardless of a lover's pain,
Heard her repeated vows, and heard in vain.
Begin, my pipe, the sweet Mænalian strain[3].

Blest Mænalus! that hears the pastoral song
Still languishing its tuneful groves along!

[1] In this eighth pastoral no particular scene is described. The poet rehearses the songs of two contending swains, Damon and Alphesibœus. The former adopts the soliloquy of a despairing lover: the latter chooses for his subject the magic rites of an enchantress forsaken by her lover, and recalling him by the power of her spells.

[2] A river in Italy.

[3] This intercalary line (as it is called by the commentators) which seems to be intended as a chorus or burden to the song, is here made the last of a triplet, that it may be as independent of the context and the verse in the translation as it is in the original.—Mænalus was a mountain in Arcadia.

That hears th' Arcadian god's celestial lay,
Who taught the idly-rustling reeds to play!
That hears the singing pines! that hears the swain
Of love's soft chains melodiously complain!
Begin, my pipe, the sweet Mænalian strain.

Mopsus the willing Nisa now enjoys—
What may not lovers hope from such a choice!
Now mares and griffins shall their hate resign,
And the succeeding age shall see them join
In friendship's tie; now mutual love shall bring
The dog and doe to share the friendly spring.
Scatter thy nuts, O Mopsus, and prepare
The nuptial torch to light the wedded fair.
Lo, Hesper hastens to the western main!
And thine the night of bliss—thine, happy swain!
Begin, my pipe, the sweet Mænalian strain.

Exult, O Nisa, in thy happy state!
Supremely blest in such a worthy mate;
While you my beard detest, and bushy brow,
And think the gods forget the world below:
While you my flock and rural pipe disdain,
And treat with bitter scorn a faithful swain.
Begin, my pipe, the sweet Mænalian strain.

When first I saw you by your mother's side,
To where our apples grew I was your guide:
Twelve summers since my birth had roll'd around,
And I could reach the branches from the ground.
How did I gaze!—how perish!—ah how vain
The fond bewitching hopes that soothed my pain!
Begin, my pipe, the sweet Mænalian strain.

Too well I know thee, Love. From Scythian snows,
Or Lybia's burning sands the mischief rose.
Rocks adamantine nursed this foreign bane,
This fell invader of the peaceful plain.
Begin, my pipe, the sweet Mænalian strain.

Love taught the mother's[1] murdering hand to kill,
Her children's blood love bade the mother spill.
Was love the cruel cause[2]? Or did the deed
From fierce unfeeling cruelty proceed?
Both fill'd her brutal bosom with their bane;
Both urged the deed, while Nature shrunk in vain.
Begin, my pipe, the sweet Mænalian strain.

Now let the fearful lamb the wolf devour;
Let alders blossom with Narcissus' flower;
From barren shrubs let radiant amber flow;
Let rugged oaks with golden fruitage glow;
Let shrieking owls with swans melodious vie;
Let Tityrus the Thracian numbers try,
Outrival Orpheus in the sylvan reign,
And emulate Arion on the main.
Begin, my pipe, the sweet Mænalian strain.

Let land no more the swelling waves divide;
Earth, be thou whelm'd beneath the boundless tide;
Headlong from yonder promontory's brow
I plunge into the rolling deep below.
Farewell, ye woods! farewell, thou flowery plain!
Hear the last lay of a despairing swain:
And cease, my pipe, the sweet Mænalian strain.

Here Damon ceased. And now, ye tuneful Nine,
Alphesibœus' magic verse subjoin,
To his responsive song your aid we call;
Our power extends not equally to all.

[1] Medea.

[2] This seems to be Virgil's meaning. The translator did not choose to preserve the conceit on the words *puer* and *mater* in his version; as this (in his opinion) would have rendered the passage obscure and unpleasing to an English reader.

ALPHESIBŒUS.

Bring living waters from the silver stream,
With vervain and fat incense feed the flame;
With this soft wreath the sacred altars bind,
To move my cruel Daphnis to be kind,
And with my phrensy to inflame his soul;
Charms are but wanting to complete the whole.
Bring Daphnis home, bring Daphnis to my arms,
O bring my long-lost love, my powerful charms.

By powerful charms what prodigies are done!
Charms draw pale Cynthia from her silver throne;
Charms burst the bloated snake, and Circe's[1] guests
By mighty magic charms were changed to beasts.
Bring Daphnis home, bring Daphnis to my arms,
O bring my long-lost love, my powerful charms.

Three woollen wreaths, and each of triple dye,
Three times about thy image I apply,
Then thrice I bear it round the sacred shrine;
Uneven numbers please the powers divine.
Bring Daphnis home, bring Daphnis to my arms,
O bring my long-lost love, my powerful charms.

Haste, let three colours with three knots be join'd,
And say, 'Thy fetters, Venus, thus I bind.'
Bring Daphnis home, bring Daphnis to my arms,
O bring my long-lost love, my powerful charms.

As this soft clay is harden'd by the flame,
And as this wax is soften'd by the same,
My love, that harden'd Daphnis to disdain,
Shall soften his relenting heart again.
Scatter the salted corn, and place the bays,
And with fat brimstone light the sacred blaze.
Daphnis my burning passion slights with scorn,
And Daphnis in this blazing bay I burn.
Bring Daphnis home, bring Daphnis to my arms,
O bring my long-lost love, my powerful charms.

As when, to find her love, a heifer roams
Through trackless groves, and solitary glooms;
Sick with desire, abandon'd to her woes,
By some lone stream her languid limbs she throws;
There in deep anguish wastes the tedious night,
Nor thoughts of home her late return invite:
Thus may he love, and thus indulge his pain,
While I enhance his torments with disdain.
Bring Daphnis home, bring Daphnis to my arms,
O bring my long-lost love, my powerful charms.

These robes beneath the threshold here I leave,
These pledges of his love, O Earth, receive.
Ye dear memorials of our mutual fire,
Of you my faithless Daphnis I require.
Bring Daphnis home, bring Daphnis to my arms,
O bring my long-lost love, my powerful charms.

These deadly poisons, and these magic weeds,
Selected from the store which Pontus breeds,
Sage Mœris gave me; oft I saw him prove
Their sovereign power; by these, along the grove
A prowling wolf the dread magician roams;
Now gliding ghosts from the profoundest tombs
Inspired he calls; the rooted corn he wings,
And to strange fields the flying harvest brings.
Bring Daphnis home, bring Daphnis to my arms,
O bring my long-lost love, my powerful charms.

These ashes from the altar take with speed,
And treading backwards cast them o'er your head
Into the running stream, nor turn your eye.
Yet this last spell, though hopeless, let me try.

[1] See Hom. Odyss. lib. x

But nought can move the unrelenting swain,
And spells, and magic verse, and gods are vain.
Bring Daphnis home, bring Daphnis to my arms,
O bring my long-lost love, my powerful charms.

Lo, while I linger, with spontaneous fire
The ashes redden, and the flames aspire!
May this new prodigy auspicious prove!
What fearful hopes my beating bosom move!
Hark! does not Hylax bark?—ye powers supreme,
Can it be real, or do lovers dream?—
He comes, my Daphnis comes! forbear my charms;
My love, my Daphnis flies to bless my longing arms.

PASTORAL IX[1].

LYCIDAS, MŒRIS.

LYCIDAS.

Go you to town, my friend? this beaten way
Conducts us thither.

MŒRIS.

Ah! the fatal day,
The unexpected day at last is come,
When a rude alien drives us from our home.
Hence, hence, ye clowns, th' usurper thus commands,
To me you must resign your ancient lands.
Thus helpless and forlorn we yield to fate;
And our rapacious lord to mitigate
This brace of kids a present I design,
Which load with curses, O ye powers divine!

LYCIDAS.

'Twas said, Menalcas with his tuneful strains
Had saved the grounds of all the neighbouring swains,
From where the hill, that terminates the vale,
In easy risings first begins to swell,
Far as the blasted beech that mates the sky,
And the clear stream that gently murmurs by.

MŒRIS.

Such was the voice of fame; but music's charms,
Amid the dreadful clang of warlike arms,
Avail no more than the Chaonian dove,
When down the sky descends the bird of Jove.
And had not the prophetic raven spoke
His dire presages from the hollow oak,
And often warn'd me to avoid debate,
And with a patient mind submit to fate,
Ne'er had thy Mœris seen this fatal hour,
And that melodious swain had been no more.

LYCIDAS.

What horrid breast such impious thoughts could breed!
What barbarous hand could make Menalcas bleed!
Could every tender Muse in him destroy,
And from the shepherds ravish all their joy!
For who but he the lovely nymphs could sing,
Or paint the valleys with the purple spring?
Who shade the fountains from the glare of day?
Who but Menalcas could compose the lay,
Which, as we journey'd to my love's abode,
I softly sung to cheer the lonely road?
'Tityrus, while I am absent, feed the flock[1],
And, having fed, conduct them to the brook,
(The way is short, and I shall soon return)
But shun the he-goat with the butting horn.'

MŒRIS.

Or who could finish the imperfect lays
Sung by Menalcas to his Varus' praise?
'If fortune yet shall spare the Mantuan swains,
And save from plundering hands our peaceful plains,
Nor doom us sad Cremona's fate to share,
(For ah! a neighbour's wo excites our fear)
Then high as Heaven our Varus' fame shall rise,
The warbling swans shall bear it to the skies.'

LYCIDAS.

Go on, dear swain, these pleasing songs pursue;
So may thy bees avoid the bitter yew,
So may rich herds thy fruitful fields adorn,
So may thy cows with strutting dugs return.
Even I with poets have obtain'd a name,
The Muse inspires me with poetic flame;
The applauding shepherds to my songs attend,
But I suspect my skill, though they commend.
I dare not hope to please a Cinna's ear,
Or sing what Varus might vouchsafe to hear.
Harsh are the sweetest lays that I can bring,
So screams a goose where swans melodious sing.

MŒRIS.

This I am pondering, if I can rehearse
The lofty numbers of that labour'd verse.
'Come, Galatea, leave the rolling seas;
Can rugged rocks and heaving surges please?
Come, taste the pleasures of our sylvan bowers,
Our balmy-breathing gales and fragrant flowers.
See, how our plains rejoice on every side,
How crystal streams through blooming valleys glide:
O'er the cool grot the whitening poplars bend,
And clasping vines their grateful umbrage lend.
Come, beauteous nymph, forsake the briny wave;
Loud on the beach let the wild billows rave.'

LYCIDAS.

Or what you sung one evening on the plain—
The air, but not the words, I yet retain.

MŒRIS.

'Why, Daphnis, dost thou calculate the skies,
To know when ancient constellations rise?
Lo, Cæsar's star its radiant light displays,
And on the nations sheds propitious rays.

[1] This and the first eclogue seem to have been written on the same occasion. The time is a still evening. The landscape is described at the 97th line of this translation. On one side of the highway is an artificial arbour, where Lycidas invites Mœris to rest a little from the fatigue of his journey: and at a considerable distance appears a sepulchre by the way-side, where the ancient sepulchres were commonly erected.

The critics with one voice seem to condemn this eclogue as unworthy of its author; I know not for what good reason. The many beautiful lines scattered through it would, one might think, be no weak recommendation. But it is by no means to be reckoned a loose collection of incoherent fragments; its principal parts are all strictly connected, and refer to a certain end, and its allusions and images are wholly suited to pastoral life. Its subject, though uncommon, is not improper; for what is more natural, than that two shepherds, when occasionally mentioning the good qualities of their absent friend, particularly his poetical talents, should repeat such fragments of his songs as they recollected?

[1] These lines, which Virgil has translated literally from Theocritus, may be supposed to be a fragment of the poem mentioned in the preceding verses; or, what is more likely, to be spoken by Lycidas to his servant; something similar to which may be seen Past. 5, v. 20, of this translation.—The original is here remarkably explicit, even to a degree of affectation. This the translator has endeavour to imitate.

On the glad hills the reddening clusters glow,
And smiling plenty decks the plains below.
Now graff thy pears; the star of Cæsar reigns,
To thy remotest race the fruit remains.'
The rest I have forgot, for length of years
Deadens the sense, and memory impairs.
All things in time submit to sad decay;
Oft have we sung whole summer suns away.
These vanish'd joys must Mœris now deplore,
His voice delights, his numbers charm, no more;
Him have the wolves beheld, bewitch'd his song [1],
Bewitch'd to silence his melodious tongue.
But your desire Menalcas can fulfil,
All these, and more, he sings with matchless skill.

LYCIDAS.

These faint excuses which my Mœris frames
But heighten my desire.—And now the streams
In slumber-soothing murmurs softly flow;
And now the sighing breeze hath ceased to blow.
Half of our way is past, for I descry
Bianor's tomb just rising to the eye [2].
Here in this leafy arbour ease your toil,
Lay down your kids, and let us sing the while:
We soon shall reach the town; or, lest a storm
Of sudden rain the evening sky deform,
Be yours to cheer the journey with a song,
Eased of your load, which I shall bear along.

MŒRIS.

No more, my friend; your kind entreaties spare,
And let our journey be our present care;
Let fate restore our absent friend again,
Then gladly I resume the tuneful strain.

PASTORAL X [3].

GALLUS.

To my last labour lend thy sacred aid,
O Arethusa: that the cruel maid
With deep remorse may read the mournful song,
For mournful lays to Gallus' love belong.
(What Muse in sympathy will not bestow
Some tender strains to soothe my Gallus' wo?)
So may thy waters pure of briny stain
Traverse the waves of the Sicilian main.
Sing, mournful Muse, of Gallus' luckless love,
While the goats browse along the cliffs above.
Nor silent is the waste while we complain,
The woods return the long-resounding strain.
Whither, ye fountain-nymphs, were ye withdrawn,
To what lone woodland, or what devious lawn,
When Gallus' bosom languish'd with the fire
Of hopeless love, and unallay'd desire?
For neither by the Aonian spring you stray'd,
Nor roam'd Parnassus' heights, nor Pindus' hallow'd shade.
The pines of Mænalus were heard to mourn,
And sounds of wo along the groves were borne;
And sympathetic tears the laurel shed,
And humbler shrubs declined their drooping head.
All wept his fate, when to despair resign'd
Beneath a desert cliff he lay reclined.
Lyceus' rocks were hung with many a tear,
And round the swain the flocks forlorn appear.
Nor scorn, celestial bard, a poet's name;
Renown'd Adonis by the lonely stream
Tended his flock.—As thus he lay along,
The swains and awkward neatherds round him throng.
Wet from the winter-mast Menalcas came.
All ask, what beauty raised the fatal flame.
The god of verse vouchsafed to join the rest;
He said, 'What phrensy thus torments thy breast?
While she, thy darling, thy Lycoris, scorns
Thy proffer'd love, and for another burns,
With whom o'er winter-wastes she wanders far,
'Midst camps, and clashing arms, and boisterous war.'
Sylvanus came, with rural garlands crown'd,
And waved the lilies long, and flowering fennel round.
Next we beheld the gay Arcadian god;
His smiling cheeks with bright vermilion glow'd.
'For ever wilt thou heave the bursting sigh?
Is love regardful of the weeping eye?
Love is not cloy'd with tears; alas, no more
Than bees luxurious with the balmy flower,
Than goats with foliage, than the grassy plain
With silver rills and soft refreshing rain.'
Pan spoke; and thus the youth with grief opprest;
'Arcadians, hear, O hear my last request;
O ye, to whom the sweetest lays belong,
O let my sorrows on your hills be sung:
If your soft flutes shall celebrate my woes,
How will my bones in deepest peace repose!
Ah, had I been with you a country-swain,
And pruned the vine, and fed the bleating train;
Had Phyllis, or some other rural fair,
Or black Amyntas been my darling care;
(Beauteous though black; what lovelier flower is seen
Than the dark violet on the painted green?)
These in the bower had yielded all their charms,
And sunk with mutual raptures in my arms:
Phyllis had crown'd my head with garlands gay,
Amyntas sung the pleasing hours away.
Here, O Lycoris, purls the limpid spring,
Bloom all the meads, and all the woodlands sing;
Here let me press thee to my panting breast,
Till youth, and joy, and life itself be past.
Banish'd by love, o'er hostile lands I stray,
And mingle in the battle's dread array;
Whilst thou, relentless to my constant flame,
(Ah could I disbelieve the voice of fame!)
Far from thy home, unaided and forlorn,
Far from thy love, thy faithful love, art borne,
On the bleak Alps with chilling blasts to pine,
Or wander waste along the frozen Rhine.
Ye icy paths, O spare her tender form!
O spare those heavenly charms, thou wintry storm

[1] In Italia creditur luporum visus esse noxios; vocemque homini quem priores contemplentur adimere ad præsens.—Plin. *H. N.* viii. 22.

[2] Bianor is said to have founded Mantua.—Servius.

[3] The scene of this pastoral is very accurately delineated. We behold the forlorn Gallus stretched along beneath a solitary cliff, his flocks standing round him at some distance. A group of deities and swains encircle him, each of whom is particularly described. On one side we see the shepherds with their crooks; next to them the neatherds, known by the clumsiness of their appearance; and next to these Menalcas with his clothes wet, as just come from beating or gathering wintermast. On the other side we observe Apollo with his usual insignia; Sylvanus crowned with flowers, and brandishing in his hand the long lilies and flowering fennel; and last of all Pan, the god of shepherds, known by his ruddy smiling countenance, and the other peculiarities of his form.

Gallus was a Roman of very considerable rank, a poet of no small estimation, and an intimate friend of Virgil. He loved to distraction one Cytheris, (here called Lycoris,) who slighted him, and followed Antony into Gaul.

'Hence let me hasten to some desert-grove,
And soothe with songs my long-unanswer'd love.
I go, in some lone wilderness to suit
Eubœan lays to my Sicilian flute.
Better with beasts of prey to make abode
In the deep cavern, or the darksome wood;
And carve on trees the story of my wo,
Which with the growing bark shall ever grow.
Meanwhile with woodland-nymphs, a lovely throng,
The winding groves of Mænalus along
I roam at large; or chase the foaming boar;
Or with sagacious hounds the wilds explore,
Careless of cold. And now methinks I bound
O'er rocks and cliffs, and hear the woods resound;
And now with beating heart I seem to wing
The Cretan arrow from the Parthian string—
As if I thus my phrensy could forego,
As if love's god could melt at human wo.
Alas! nor nymphs nor heavenly songs delight—
Farewell, ye groves! the groves no more invite.
No pains, no miseries of man can move
The unrelenting deity of love.
To quench your thirst in Hebrus' frozen flood,
To make the Scythian snows your drear abode;
Or feed your flock on Ethiopian plains,
When Sirius' fiery constellation reigns,
(When deep-imbrown'd the languid herbage lies,
And in the elm the vivid verdure dies)
Were all in vain. Love's unresisted sway
Extends to all, and we must Love obey.'

'Tis done; ye Nine, here ends your poet's strain,
In pity sung to soothe his Gallus' pain.
While leaning on a flowery bank I twine
The flexile osiers, and the basket join.
Celestial Nine, your sacred influence bring,
And soothe my Gallus' sorrows while I sing:
Gallus, my much beloved! for whom I feel
The flame of purest friendship rising still:
So by a brook the verdant alders rise,
When fostering zephyrs fan the vernal skies.

Let us be gone; at eve, the shade annoys
With noxious damps, and hurts the singer's voice;
The juniper breathes bitter vapours round,
That kill the springing corn, and blast the ground.
Homeward, my sated goats, now let us hie;
Lo beamy Hesper gilds the western sky.

END OF DR. BEATTIE'S POEMS.

THE GRAVE

BY ROBERT BLAIR.

WITH BIOGRAPHICAL MEMOIR.

LIFE OF ROBERT BLAIR.

THE life of a poet, one of the "genus irritabile," most frequently presents to us a varied picture; too often the excitable spirit, whose inspired outpourings are destined to delight present and future ages, is itself a prey to distresses frequently real, in the every day sense of the word, but as frequently caused, or at least exaggerated, by the same high imagination from whence so much of the beautiful and excellent has been drawn. To this rule, which we fear must be regarded as the general one, governing the fate of the gifted sons of genius, there are many exceptions, but the fact of there being exceptions, must rank such examples very high in the scale of humanity. The body too often cripples the workings of the intellect; and oftener still does the ardent soul wear out the earthly frame that bars it from its native heaven. In both cases the world loses, for the spirit is in both overborne.

The poet whose life we are now about to sketch, was one who listened more to the calls of duty, than to the voice of fame. Had he pursued the path of Parnassus, he would have ascended very high, if he failed to touch the summit; as it was, he, at a bound, attained a point which has been seldom gained by a single effort. But more sacred duties recalled his attention from the Muses, and while we regret the sacrifice of the poet, we reverence the memory of the man.

Robert Blair was the eldest son of the Rev. David Blair, one of the ministers of Edinburgh, and chaplain to the king. His mother was Euphemia Nisbet, daughter of Archibald Nisbet of Carfin. His grandfather was the Rev. Robert Blair, one of the most distinguished Scottish clergymen in the time of the civil wars. He was born at Edinburgh, in 1699, received a liberal education in its university, and afterwards travelled on the Continent. In 1731 he was ordained minister at Athelstaneford, in the county of East Lothian, where he resided the remainder of his days.

He lived in the style of a gentleman, and was much respected by all the men of rank, talent, and property in his neighbourhood. He enjoyed his independent fortune as a man of learning, elegant manners, and polished taste would choose to do. He distinguished himself in the study of botany, particularly in the culture of flowers; and was well versed in optical and microscopical knowledge, on which subjects he corresponded regularly with several eminent men of science. In the exercise of his pastoral functions his assiduity was unremitting; pious and fervent in devotion, warm and earnest in preaching, he performed the duties of his sacred office with the seriousness of a divine, and the zeal of a poet.

In 1738 he married Isabella Law, daughter of Mr. Law of Elvingston, a lady of uncommon beauty, and amiable manners. It appears that this marriage was the result of a family connexion and a long acquaintance. Her father, who had been professor of moral philosophy in the University of Edinburgh, was his relation, and had been nominated one of Mr Blair's tutors in his father's will. The fruits of this marriage were one daughter and five sons, of whom the fourth, named Robert, was the most celebrated. He was bred to the profession of the law in Scotland, and for many years held the highly honourable situation of Dean of the Faculty of Advocates. In 1810, on the resignation of Lord President Campbell, he was appointed by the king to the high station of Chief Justice of the Court of Session: which post he filled with consummate ability until his death, which took place in 1812.

Although Mr. Blair never neglected his important duties for the sake of literature, which he would so much have adorned, he kept up a correspondence with many of the most celebrated characters of his age. His taste was particularly directed to subjects of natural history, on which he maintained a long correspondence with that celebrated naturalist, Henry Barker, Esq F.R.S., an intelligent, upright, and benevolent man, who was particularly attentive to the improvement of natural science, and very solicitous for the prosecution of useful discoveries. Another of Blair's friends and correspondents was Mr. Callender of Craigforth, as appears by a copy of verses addressed to him in Callender's "Lugubres Cantus." He lived likewise on terms of the strictest intimacy with Colonel Gardiner, who died on the field of Prestonpans, on the 21st of September, 1745, an extraordinary man, who is perhaps better known to the general reader by the perusal of "Waverley," than by Dr. Doddridge's curious memoir.

Besides the friends already mentioned, Blair numbered Watts and Doddridge, two men whom it is unnecesary further to particularize, among his intimates. A letter to Doddridge, opening the correspondence, has been preserved, and we transcribe it, since it relates to the poem which occupies the subsequent pages. It is dated, Athelstaneford, February 25, 1741-2.

"You will be justly surprised with a letter from one whose name is not so much as known to you: nor shall I offer to make an apology. Though I am entirely unacquainted with your person, I am no stranger to your merit as an author; neither am I altogether unacquainted with your personal character, having often heard honourable mention made of you by my much respected and worthy friends, Colonel Gardiner and Lady Frances. About ten months ago, Lady Frances did me the favour to transmit to me some manuscript hymns of yours, with which I was wonderfully delighted. I wish I could, on my part, contribute in any measure to your entertainment, as you have sometimes done to mine in a very high degree. And that I may show how willing I am to do so, I have desired Dr. Watts to transmit you a manuscript poem of mine, intituled *The Grave*, written, I hope, in a way not unbecoming my profession as a minister of the gospel, though the greatest part of it was composed several years before I was clothed with so sacred a character. I was urged by some friends here, to whom I showed it, to make it public; nor did I decline it, provided I had the approbation of Dr. Watts, from whom I have received many civilities, and for whom I had ever entertained the highest regard. Yesterday I had a letter from the doctor, signifying his approbation of the piece in a manner most obliging. A great deal less from him would have done me no small honour. But, at the same time, he mentions to me, that he had offered it to two booksellers of his acquaintance, who, he tells me, did not care to run the risk of publishing it. They can scarcely think (considering how critical an age we live in, with respect to such kind of writings), that a person living three hundred miles from London could write so as to be acceptable to the fashionable and polite. Perhaps it may be so; though, at the same time, I must say, in order to make it more generally liked, I was obliged sometimes to go cross to my own inclination, well knowing, that whatever poem is written on a serious argument, must, on that very account, be under peculiar disadvantages; and therefore proper arts must be used to make such a piece go down with a licentious age, which cares for none of those things. I beg pardon for breaking in on moments precious as yours, and hope you will be so kind as to give me your opinion of the poem."

Two other poems, written by Mr. Blair, besides "The Grave," were printed during his lifetime; the first being an elegiac poem on the death of his father-in-law, the other a version of a pious ode of Florentus Holusenus; but neither of these possesses sufficient merit to justify republication. "The Grave" was first printed in London in 1743, and was reprinted at Edinburgh in 1747, and since that time it has deservedly been ranked among our "Standard" works.

There is a nervous energy throughout the poem, of a very singular character. The diction has been, not unreasonably, compared to that of the finest passages of Shakspeare, but it is deficient in the grace which that great master imparted to the didactic portions of his works: nevertheless it is a production of considerable elegance, and so excellent in its matter, that few who have once read it attentively will be satisfied with a single perusal.

The author died in the forty-seventh year of his age, having lived a useful life; and neglecting not in scorn, or proud humility, but for conscience' sake, the excellent poetical gifts he possessed, and devoting the powers of a fine and beneficent mind to the unpretending, but arduous duties of a parish priest. Whatever the world may have lost by this self-denial, may be recompensed by the lessons to be derived from the very paucity of incidents in his life.

He sought not, he desired not, the fame which embalms his memory; and his poem, beautiful in itself, becomes doubly interesting when the pure character of the writer, his virtues, and his modesty, are brought home to our minds

THE GRAVE.

A Poem.

BY ROBERT BLAIR.

WHILST some affect the sun, and some the shade,
Some flee the city, some the hermitage ;
Their aims as various as the roads they take
In journeying through life ; the task be mine
To paint the gloomy horrors of the Tomb ;
The appointed place of rendezvous, where all
These travellers meet. Thy succours I implore,
Eternal King ! whose potent arm sustains
The keys of hell and death. The Grave, dread thing !
Men shiver when thou'rt nam'd : nature appalled
Shakes off her wonted firmness. Ah ! how dark
Thy long-extended realms, and rueful wastes,
Where nought but silence reigns, and night, dark night,
Dark as was chaos ere the infant sun
Was roll'd together, or had tried his beams
Athwart the gloom profound ! the sickly taper,
By glimm'ring through thy low-brow'd misty vaults,
Furr'd round with mouldy damps, and ropy slime,
Lets fall a supernumerary horror,
And only serves to make thy night more irksome !
Well do I know thee by thy trusty yew,
Cheerless, unsocial plant ! that loves to dwell
'Midst sculls and coffins, epitaphs, and worms ;
Where light-heel'd ghosts, and visionary shades,
Beneath the wan cold moon (as fame reports)
Embodied thick, perform their mystic rounds.
No other merriment, dull tree ! is thine.

See yonder hallow'd fane ! the pious work
Of names once famed, now dubious or forgot,
And buried 'midst the wreck of things which were;
There lie interr'd the more illustrious dead.
The wind is up : hark ! how it howls ! methinks,
Till now I never heard a sound so dreary.
Doors creak, and windows clap, and night's foul bird,
Rook'd in the spire, screams loud, the gloomy aisles,
Black plaster'd, and hung round with shreds of scutcheons
And tatter'd coats of arms, send back the sound,
Laden with heavier airs, from the low vaults,
The mansions of the dead ! Roused from their slumbers,
In grim array the grisly spectres rise,
Grin horrible, and obstinately sullen
Pass and repass, hush'd as the foot of night !
Again the screech owl shrieks; ungracious sound !
I'll hear no more ; it makes one's blood run chill.

Quite round the pile, a row of reverend elms,
Coeval near with that, all ragged show,
Long lash'd by the rude winds ; some rift half down
Their branchless trunks, others so thin a-top
That scarce two crows could lodge in the same tree.
Strange things, the neighbours say, have happen'd here.
Wild shrieks have issued from the hollow tombs ;
Dead men have come again, and walked about ;
And the great bell has toll'd, unrung, untouch'd !
Such tales their cheer, at wake or gossiping,
When it draws near the witching time of night.

Oft in the lone church-yard at night I've seen,
By glimpse of moon-shine, checquering through the trees,
The school-boy, with his satchel in his hand,
Whistling aloud to bear his courage up,
And lightly tripping o'er the long flat stones
(With nettles skirted and with moss o'ergrown)
That tell in homely phrase who lies below.
Sudden he starts ! and hears, or thinks he hears,
The sound of something purring at his heels.
Full fast he flies, and dares not look behind him,
Till out of breath he overtakes his fellows ;
Who gather round, and wonder at the tale
Of horrid apparition, tall and ghastly,
That walks at dead of night, or takes his stand
O'er some new-open'd grave ; and, strange to tell,
Evanishes at crowing of the cock !

The new-made widow too, I've sometimes spied,
Sad sight! slow moving o'er the prostrate dead:
Listless she crawls along in doleful black,
While bursts of sorrow gush from either eye,
Fast falling down her now untasted cheek.
Prone on the lowly grave of the dear man
She drops; while busy meddling memory,
In barbarous succession, musters up
The past endearments of their softer hours,
Tenacious of its theme. Still, still she thinks
She sees him, and indulging the fond thought,
Clings yet more closely to the senseless turf,
Nor heeds the passenger who looks that way.

Invidious Grave! how dost thou rend in sunder
Whom love has knit, and sympathy made one!
A tie more stubborn far than nature's band.
Friendship! mysterious cement of the soul!
Sweetener of life and solder of society!
I owe thee much. Thou hast deserved from me
Far, far beyond what I can ever pay.
Oft have I proved the labours of thy love,
And the warm efforts of the gentle heart
Anxious to please. O! when my friend and I
In some thick wood have wander'd heedless on,
Hid from the vulgar eye; and sat us down
Upon the sloping cowslip-cover'd bank,
Where the pure limpid stream has slid along
In grateful errors through the under-wood,
Sweet murmuring; methought, the shrill-tongued thrush
Mended his song of love; the sooty blackbird
Mellow'd his pipe, and soften'd every note;
The eglantine smelt sweeter, and the rose
Assumed a dye more deep; whilst every flower
Vied with its fellow-plant in luxury
Of dress. O! then the longest summer's day
Seem'd too, too much in haste; still the full heart
Had not imparted half: 'twas happiness
Too exquisite to last. Of joys departed,
Not to return, how painful the remembrance

Dull Grave! thou spoil'st the dance of youthful blood,
Strik'st out the dimple from the cheek of mirth,
And every smirking feature from the face;
Branding our laughter with the name of madness.
Where are the jesters now? the men of health
Complexionally pleasant? where the droll,
Whose very look and gesture was a joke
To clapping theatres and shouting crowds,
And made e'en thick-lipp'd musing Melancholy
To gather up her face into a smile
Before she was aware? Ah! sullen now,
And dumb as the green turf that covers them!

Where are the mighty thunderbolts of war,
The Roman Cæsars and the Grecian chiefs,
The boast of story? Where the hot-brain'd youth,
Who the tiara at his pleasure tore
From kings of all the then-discover'd globe;
And cried, forsooth, because his arm was hamper'd,
And had not room enough to do its work?
Alas! how slim—dishonourably slim!
And cramm'd into a space we blush to name—
Proud royalty! how alter'd in thy looks!
How blank thy features, and how wan thy hue!
Son of the morning! whither art thou gone?
Where hast thou hid thy many-spangled head,
And the majestic menace of thine eyes,
Felt from afar? Pliant and powerless now:
Like new-born infant bound up in his swathes,
Or victim tumbled flat upon his back,
That throbs beneath the sacrificer's knife;
Mute must thou bear the strife of little tongues,
And coward insults of the base-born crowd,
That grudge a privilege thou never hadst,
But only hoped for in the peaceful Grave—
Of being unmolested and alone!
Arabia's gums and odoriferous drugs,
And honours by the heralds duly paid
In mode and form, e'en to a very scruple;
O cruel irony! these come too late;
And only mock whom they were meant to honour!
Surely, there's not a dungeon slave that's buried
In the highway, unshrouded and uncoffin'd,
But lies as soft, and sleeps as sound, as he.
Sorry pre-eminence of high descent
Above the baser born, to rot in state!

But see! the well-plumed hearse comes nodding on,
Stately and slow; and properly attended
By the whole sable tribe, that painful watch
The sick man's door, and live upon the dead,
By letting out their persons by the hour
To mimic sorrow, when the heart's not sad!
How rich the trappings, now they're all unfurl'd
And glittering in the sun! Triumphant entries
Of conquerors, and coronation pomps,
In glory scarce exceed. Great gluts of people
Retard the unwieldy show; whilst from the casements,
And houses' tops, ranks behind ranks close wedged
Hang bellying o'er. But tell us, why this waste?
Why this ado in earthing up a carcass
That's fallen into disgrace, and in the nostril
Smells horrible? Ye undertakers! tell us,
'Midst all the gorgeous figures you exhibit,
Why is the principal conceal'd, for which
You make this mighty stir? 'Tis wisely done,
What would offend the eye in a good picture,
The painter casts discreetly into shades.

Proud lineage! now how little thou appear'st!
Below the envy of the private man!
Honour, that meddlesome officious ill,
Pursues thee e'en to death! nor there stops short
Strange persecution! when the Grave itself
Is no protection from rude sufferance.

Absurd! to think to over-reach the Grave,
And from the wreck of names to rescue ours!
The best concerted schemes men lay for fame
Die fast away; only themselves die faster.
The far-famed sculptor and the laurell'd bard,
These bold insurancers of deathless fame,
Supply their little feeble aids in vain.
The tapering pyramid, the Egyptian's pride,
And wonder of the world! whose spiky top
Has wounded the thick cloud, and long outlived
The angry shaking of the winter's storm;
Yet, spent at last by the injuries of Heaven,
Shatter'd with age and furrow'd o'er with years,
The mystic cone, with hieroglyphics crusted
At once gives way. O lamentable sight!
The labour of whole ages lumbers down,
A hideous and mis-shapen length of ruins!
Sepulchral columns wrestle but in vain
With all-subduing Time: his cankering hand
With calm deliberate malice wasteth them.

Worn on the edge of days, the brass consumes,
The busto moulders, and the deep cut marble,
Unsteady to the steel, gives up its charge!
Ambition, half convicted of her folly,
Hangs down the head, and reddens at the tale!

Here all the mighty troublers of the earth,
Who swam to sovereign rule through seas of blood;
The oppressive, sturdy, man-destroying villains,
Who ravaged kingdoms, and laid empires waste,
And in a cruel wantonness of power
Thinn'd states of half their people, and gave up
To want the rest; now, like a storm that's spent,
Lie hush'd, and meanly sneak behind the covert.
Vain thought! to hide them from the general scorn,
That haunts and dogs them like an injured ghost
Implacable. Here too the petty tyrant,
Whose scant domains geographer ne'er noticed,
And, well for neighbouring grounds, of arm as short;
Who fix'd his iron talons on the poor,
And griped them like some lordly beast of prey,
Deaf to the forceful cries of gnawing hunger,
And piteous plaintive voice of misery;
(As if a slave were not a shred of nature,
Of the same common substance with his lord;)
Now tame and humble, like a child that's whipp'd,
Shakes hands with dust, and calls the worm his kinsman;
Nor pleads his rank and birthright. Under ground
Precedency's a jest; vassal and lord,
Grossly familiar, side by side consume.

When self-esteem, or others' adulation,
Would cunningly persuade us we were something
Above the common level of our kind,
The Grave gainsays the smooth-complexion'd flattery,
And with blunt truth acquaints us what we are.

Beauty! thou pretty plaything! dear deceit!
That steals so softly o'er the stripling's heart,
And gives it a new pulse unknown before!
The Grave discredits thee. Thy charms expunged,
Thy roses faded, and thy lilies soil'd,
What hast thou more to boast of. Will thy lovers
Flock round thee now, to gaze and do thee homage?
Methinks I see thee with thy head low laid,
Whilst surfeited upon thy damask cheek,
The high-fed worm, in lazy volumes roll'd,
Riots unscared. For this was all thy cantion?
For this thy painful labours at thy glass,
T' improve those charms, and keep them in repair,
For which the spoiler thanks thee not? Foul feeder!
Coarse fare and carrion please thee full as well,
And leave as keen a relish on the sense.
Look, how the fair one weeps! the conscious tears
Stand thick as dew-drops on the bells of flowers:
Honest effusion! the swoln heart in vain
Works hard to put a gloss on its distress.

Strength too! thou surly, and less gentle boast
Of those that loud laugh at the village ring!
A fit of common sickness pulls thee down
With greater ease than e'er thou didst the stripling
That rashly dared thee to the unequal fight.
What groan was that I heard? deep groan indeed,
With anguish heavy laden! let me trace it:
From yonder bed it comes, where the strong man,
By stronger arm belabour'd, gasps for breath
Like a hard hunted beast. How his great heart
Beats thick! his roomy chest by far too scant
To give the lungs full play! What now avail
The strong-built sinewy limbs, and well-spread shoulders?
See, how he tugs for life, and lays about him,
Mad with his pain! eager he catches hold
Of what comes next to hand, and grasps it hard,
Just like a creature drowning! hideous sight!
O how his eyes stand out, and stare full ghastly!
Whilst the distemper's rank and deadly venom
Shoots like a burning arrow 'cross his bowels,
And drinks his marrow up. Heard you that groan?
It was his last. See how the great Goliath,
Just like a child that brawl'd itself to rest,
Lies still. What mean'st thou then, O mighty boaster,
To vaunt of nerves of thine? What means the bull,
Unconscious of his strength, to play the coward,
And flee before a feeble thing like man;
That, knowing well the slackness of his arm,
Trusts only in the well-invented knife!

With study pale, and midnight vigils spent,
The star-surveying sage close to his eye
Applies the sight-invigorating tube;
And, travelling through the boundless length of space,
Marks well the courses of the far-seen orbs,
That roll with regular confusion there,
In ecstacy of thought. But ah! proud man!
Great heights are hazardous to the weak head:
Soon, very soon, thy firmest footing fails,
And down thou dropp'st into that darksome place,
Where nor device nor knowledge ever came.
Here the tongue-warrior lies! disabled now,
Disarm'd, dishonour'd, like a wretch that's gagg'd,
And cannot tell his ails to passers-by.
Great man of language! whence this mighty change,
This dumb despair, and drooping of the head?
Though strong Persuasion hung upon thy lip,
And sly Insinuation's softer arts
In ambush lay about thy flowing tongue,
Alas how chop-fallen now! thick mists and silence
Rest, like a weary cloud, upon thy breast
Unceasing. Ah! where is the lifted arm,
The strength of action, and the force of words,
The well-turu'd period, and the well-tuned voice,
With all the lesser ornaments of phrase?
Ah! fled for ever, as they ne'er had been!
Razed from the book of fame; or, more provoking,
Perhaps some hackney hunger-bitten scribbler
Insults thy memory, and blots thy tomb
With long flat narrative, or duller rhymes,
With heavy halting pace that drawl along—
Enough to rouse a dead man into rage,
And warm, with red resentment, the wan cheek.

Here the great masters of the healing art,
Those mighty mock defrauders of the tomb,
Spite of their juleps and catholicons,
Resign to fate! Proud Æsculapius' son,
Where are thy boasted implements of art,
And all thy well-cramm'd magazines of health?
Nor hill, nor vale, as far as ship could go,
Nor margin of the gravel-bottom'd brook,
Escaped thy rifling hand! from stubborn shrubs
Thou wrung'st their shy retiring virtues out,
And vex'd them in the fire; nor fly, nor insect,

Nor writhy snake, escaped thy deep research.
But why this apparatus? why this cost?
Tell us, thou doughty keeper of the grave,
Where are thy recipes and cordials now,
With the long list of vouchers for thy cures!
Alas! thou speak'st not. The bold impostor
Looks not more silly, when the cheat's found out.

Here the lank-sided miser, worst of felons!
Who meanly stole (discreditable shift!)
From back and belly too their proper cheer;
Eased of a tax it irk'd the wretch to pay
To his own carcass, now lies cheaply lodged,
By clamorous appetites no longer teased,
Nor tedious bills of charges and repairs.
But ah! where are his rents, his comings in?
Aye! now you've made the rich man poor indeed!
Robb'd of his gods, what has he left behind?
O cursed lust of gold! when for thy sake
The fool throws up his interest in both worlds,
First starv'd in this, then damn'd in that to come!

How shocking must thy summons be, O Death!
To him that is at ease in his possessions!
Who, counting on long years of pleasure here,
Is quite unfurnish'd for that world to come!
In that dread moment, how the frantic soul
Raves round the walls of her clay tenement,
Runs to each avenue, and shrieks for help,
But shrieks in vain! how wishfully she looks
On all she's leaving, now no longer her's!
A little longer, yet a little longer,
O might she stay to wash away her stains,
And fit her for her passage! mournful sight!
Her very eyes weep blood, and every groan
She heaves is big with horror! but the foe,
Like a staunch murderer steady to his purpose,
Pursues her close through every lane of life,
Nor misses once the track, but presses on;
Till, forced at last to the tremendous verge,
At once she sinks to everlasting ruin.

Sure 'tis a serious thing to die! my soul,
What a strange moment must it be, when near
Thy journey's end, thou hast the gulf in view!
That awful gulf no mortal e'er repass'd
To tell what's doing on the other side!
Nature runs back and shudders at the sight,
And every life-string bleeds at thoughts of parting!
For part they must—body and soul must part!
Fond couple! link'd more close than wedded pair.
This wings its way to its Almighty Source,
The witness of its actions, now its judge;
That drops into the dark and noisome grave,
Like a disabled pitcher of no use.

If death were nothing, and nought after death;
If when men died, at once they ceased to be,
Returning to the barren womb of nothing,
Whence first they sprung; then might the debauchee,
Untrembling, mouth the Heavens; then might the drunkard
Reel over his full bowl, and when 'tis drain'd
Fill up another to the brim, and laugh
At the poor bug-bear Death; then might the wretch
That's weary of the world, and tired of life,
At once give each inquietude the slip,
By stealing out of being when he pleased,
And by what way, whether by hemp or steel:—
Death's thousand doors stand open. Who could force
The ill-pleased guest to sit out his full time,
Or blame him if he goes? Sure he does well
That helps himself as timely as he can,
When able. But, if there's an hereafter—
And that there is, conscience, uninfluenced
And suffer'd to speak out, tells every man—
Then must it be an awful thing to die;
More horrid yet to die by one's own hand.
Self-murder! name it not; our island's shame;
That makes her the reproach of neighb'ring states.
Shall nature, swerving from her earliest dictate,
Self-preservation, fall by her own act?
Forbid it, Heaven! let not, upon disgust,
The shameless hand be foully crimson'd o'er
With blood of its own lord! Dreadful attempt!
Just reeking from self-slaughter, in a rage
To rush into the presence of our Judge!
As if we challenged him to do his worst,
And matter'd not his wrath. Unheard-of tortures
Must be reserved for such: these herd together;
The common damn'd shun their society,
And look upon themselves as fiends less foul.
Our time is fix'd, and all our days are number'd!
How long, how short, we know not: this we know,
Duty requires we calmly wait the summons,
Nor dare to stir till Heaven shall give permission:
Like sentries that must keep their destined stand.
And wait th' appointed hour till they're relieved.
Those only are the brave that keep their ground,
And keep it to the last. To run away
Is but a coward's trick: to run away
From this world's ills, that at the very worst
Will soon blow o'er, thinking to mend ourselves,
By boldly venturing on a world unknown,
And plunging headlong in the dark—'tis mad!
No frenzy half so desperate as this.

Tell us, ye dead! will none of you, in pity
To those you left behind disclose the secret?
O! that some courteous ghost would blab it out,
What 'tis you are, and we must shortly be.
I've heard that souls departed have sometimes
Forewarn'd men of their death. 'Twas kindly done
To knock and give th' alarum. But what means
This stinted charity? 'tis but lame kindness
That does its work by halves. Why might you not
Tell us what 'tis to die? Do the strict laws
Of your society forbid your speaking
Upon a point so nice? I'll ask no more.
Sullen, like lamps in sepulchres, your shine
Enlightens but yourselves. Well—'tis no matter:
A very little time will clear up all,
And make us learn'd as you are, and as close.

Death's shafts fly thick! Here falls the village swain,
And there his pamper'd lord! The cup goes round,
And who so artful as to put it by?
'Tis long since death had the majority;
Yet, strange, the living lay it not to heart!
See yonder maker of the dead man's bed,
The sexton, hoary-headed chronicle!
Of hard unmeaning face, down which ne'er stole
A gentle tear; with mattock in his hand
Digs thro' whole rows of kindred and acquaintance
By far his juniors! scarce a scull's cast up,
But well he knew its owner, and can tell
Some passage of his life. Thus hand in hand

The sot has walk'd with Death twice twenty years ;
And yet ne'er younker on the green laughs louder,
Or clubs a smuttier tale ; when drunkards meet,
None sings a merrier catch, or lends a hand
More willing to his cup. Poor wretch ! he minds not
That soon some trusty brother of the trade
Shall do for him what he has done for thousands.

On this side, and on that, men see their friends
Drop off, like leaves in autumn ; yet launch out
Into fantastic schemes, which the long livers
In the world's hale and undegenerate days
Could scarce have leisure for ; fools that we are !
Never to think of Death and of ourselves
At the same time !—as if to learn to die
Were no concern of ours. O more than sottish !
For creatures of a day, in gamesome mood
To frolic on eternity's dread brink,
Unapprehensive ; when, for aught we know,
The very first swoln surge shall sweep us in !
Think we, or think we not, time hurries on
With a resistless unremitting stream,
Yet treads more soft than e'er did midnight thief,
That slides his hand under the miser's pillow,
And carries off his prize. What is this world ?
What, but a spacious burial-field unwall'd,
Strew'd with Death's spoils, the spoils of animals
Savage and tame, and full of dead men's bones ?
The very turf on which we tread once lived ;
And we that live must lend our carcasses
To cover our own offspring : in their turns,
They too must cover theirs. 'Tis here all meet!
The shiv'ring Icelander, and sun-burnt Moor;
Men of all climes, that never met before,
And of all creeds, the Jew, the Turk, the Christian.
Here the proud prince, and favourite yet prouder,
His sov'reign's keeper, and the people's scourge,
Are huddled out of sight ! Here lie abash'd
The great negotiators of the earth,
And celebrated masters of the balance,
Deep read in stratagems and wiles of courts ,
Now vain their treaty-skill ! Death scorns to treat.
Here the o'erloaded slave flings down his burden
From his gall'd shoulders; and, when the stern tyrant,
With all his guards and tools of power about him,
Is meditating new unheard-of hardships,
Mocks his short arm, and quick as thought escapes,
Where tyrants vex not, and the weary rest.
Here the warm lover, leaving the cool shade,
The tell-tale echo, and the babbling stream,
Time out of mind the fav'rite seats of love,
Fast by his gentle mistress lays him down,
Unblasted by foul tongue. Here friends and foes
Lie close, unmindful of their former feuds.
The lawn-robed prelate, and plain presbyter,
Erewhile that stood aloof, as shy to meet,
Familiar mingle here, like sister streams
That some rude interposing rock has split.
Here is the large-limb'd peasant ; here the child
Of a span long, that never saw the sun,
Nor press'd the nipple, strangled in life's porch.
Here is the mother with her sons and daughters ;
The barren wife ; and long-demurring maid,
Whose lonely unappropriated sweets
Smil'd like yon knot of cowslips on the cliff,
Not to be come at by the willing hand.
Here are the prude severe, and gay coquette,
The sober widow, and young green virgin,
Cropp'd like a rose before 'tis fully blown,
Or half its worth disclosed. Strange medley here!
Here garrulous old age winds up his tale ;
And jovial youth, of lightsome vacant heart,
Whose every day was made of melody,
Hears not the voice of mirth; the shrill-tongued shrew,
Meek as the turtle-dove, forgets her chiding.
Here are the wise, the generous, and the brave ;
The just, the good, the worthless, and profane ;
The downright clown, and perfectly well-bred ;
The fool, the churl, the scoundrel, and the mean ;
The supple statesman, and the patriot stern ;
The wrecks of nations and the spoils of time,
With all the lumber of six thousand years !

Poor man ! how happy once in thy first state,
When yet but warm from thy great Maker's hand,
He stamp'd thee with his image, and, well pleased,
Smiled on his last fair work ! Then all was well :
Sound was the body, and the soul serene ;
Like two sweet instruments, ne'er out of tune,
That play their several parts. Nor head nor heart
Offer'd to ache ; nor was there cause they should,
For all was pure within. No fell remorse,
Nor anxious castings up of what might be,
Alarm'd his peaceful bosom. Summer seas
Show not more smooth, when kiss'd by southern winds,
Just ready to expire. Scarce importuned,
The generous soil, with a luxuriant hand,
Offer'd the various produce of the year,
And every thing most perfect in its kind.
Blessed, thrice blessed days ! but, ah, how short!
Bless'd as the pleasing dreams of holy men,
But fugitive, like those, and quickly gone.
O slippery state of things ! What sudden turns,
What strange vicissitudes, in the first leaf
Of man's sad history ! to-day most happy,
And ere to-morrow's sun has set, most abject !
How scant the space between these vast extremes!
Thus fared it with our sire ; not long he enjoy'd
His paradise ! scarce had the happy tenant
Of the fair spot due time to prove its sweets,
Or sum them up, when straight he must be gone,
Ne'er to return again ! And must he go ?
Can nought compound for the first dire offence
Of erring man ? Like one who is condemn'd,
Fain would he trifle time with idle talk,
And parley with his fate. But 'tis in vain.
Not all the lavish odours of the place,
Offer'd in incense, can procure his pardon,
Or mitigate his doom. A mighty angel,
With flaming sword, forbids his longer stay,
And drives the loit'rer forth ; nor must he take
One last and farewell round. At once he lost
His glory and his God ! If mortal now,
And sorely maim'd, no wonder—Man has sinn'd !
Sick of his bliss, and bent on new adventures,
Evil he would needs try ; nor tried in vain.
Dreadful experiment !—destructive measure !—
Where the worst thing could happen, is success !
Alas ! too well he sped ; the good he scorn'd
Stalked off reluctant, like an ill-used ghost,
Not to return ; or, if it did, its visits,
Like those of angels, short, and far between :
Whilst the black dæmon, with his hell-'scaped train,
Admitted once into its better room,
Grew loud and mutinous, nor would be gone;
Lording it o'er the man, who now too late
Saw the rash error which he could not mend ;

An error fatal not to him alone,
But to his future sons, his fortune's heirs.
Inglorious bondage! human nature groans
Beneath a vassalage so vile and cruel,
And its vast body bleeds through every vein.

What havoc hast thou made, foul monster, Sin!
Greatest and first of ills! the fruitful parent
Of woes of all dimensions! but for thee
Sorrow had never been. All noxious things
Of vilest nature, other sorts of evils,
Are kindly circumscribed, and have their bounds.
The fierce volcano, from its burning entrails
That belches molten stone and globes of fire,
Involved in pitchy clouds of smoke and stench,
Mars the adjacent fields for some leagues round,
And there it stops. The big swoln inundation,
Of mischief more diffusive, raving loud,
Buries whole tracts of country, threat'ning more;
But that too has its shore it cannot pass.
More dreadful far than these; sin has laid waste,
Not here and there a country, but a world;
Despatching at a wide-extended blow
Entire mankind, and for their sakes defacing
A whole creation's beauty with rude hands;
Blasting the foodful grain, and loaded branches,
And marking all along its way with ruin!
Accursed thing! O where shall fancy find
A proper name to call thee by, expressive
Of all thy horrors? Pregnant womb of ills!
Of temper so transcendantly malign,
That toads and serpents of most deadly kind
Compared to thee are harmless! Sicknesses
Of every size and symptom, racking pains,
And bluest plagues are thine! See how the fiend
Profusely scatters the contagion round!
While deep-mouth'd Slaughter, bellowing at her heels,
Wades deep in blood new spilt; yet for to-morrow
Shapes out new work of great uncommon daring,
And inly pines till the dread blow be struck.

But hold! I've gone too far; too much discover'd
My father's nakedness and nature's shame.
Here let me pause; and drop an honest tear,
One burst of filial duty, and condolence,
O'er all those ample deserts Death hath spread,
This chaos of mankind! O great man-eater!
Whose every day is carnival, not sated yet!
Unheard-of epicure, without a fellow!
The veriest gluttons do not always cram;
Some intervals of abstinence are sought
To edge the appetite; thou seekest none.
Methinks the countless swarms thou hast devour'd,
And thousands that each hour thou gobblest up,
This, less than this, might gorge thee to the full,
But ah! rapacious still, thou gap'st for more;
Like one, whole days defrauded of his meals,
On whom lank Hunger lays his skinny hand,
And whets to keenest eagerness his cravings;
As if Diseases, Massacres, and Poison,
Famine, and War, were not thy caterers.

But know, that thou must render up thy dead,
And with high interest too! they are not thine;
But only in thy keeping for a season,
Till the great promised day of restitution;
When loud diffusive sound from brazen trump
Of strong-lung'd cherub shall alarm thy captives,
And rouse the long, long sleepers into life,
Day-light, and liberty.——
Then must thy gates fly open, and reveal the minds
That lay long forming under ground,
In their dark cells immured; but now full ripe,
And pure as silver from the crucible,
That twice has stood the torture of the fire,
And inquisition of the forge. We know
Th' illustrious Deliverer of mankind,
The Son of God, thee foil'd. Him in thy power
Thou couldst not hold; self-vigorous he rose,
And, shaking off thy fetters, soon retook
Those spoils his voluntary yielding lent:
(Sure pledge of our releasement from thy thrall!)
Twice twenty days he sojourn'd here on earth,
And show'd himself alive to chosen witnesses,
By proofs so strong, that the most slow assenting
Had not a scruple left. This having done,
He mounted up to Heaven. Methinks I see him
Climb the aerial heights, and glide along
Athwart the severing clouds; but the faint eye,
Flung backwards in the chase, soon drops its hold,
Disabled quite, and jaded with pursuing.
Heaven's portals wide expand to let him in;
Nor are his friends shut out; as some great prince
Not for himself alone procures admission,
But for his train; it was his royal will
That where he is, there should his followers be.
Death only lies between: a gloomy path!
Made yet more gloomy by our coward fears;
But nor untrod, nor tedious; the fatigue
Will soon go off. Besides, there's no bye-road
To bliss. Then why, like ill-condition'd children,
Start we at transient hardships in the way
Which leads to purer air and softer skies,
And a ne'er-setting sun? Fools that we are!
We wish to be where sweets unwith'ring bloom;
But straight our wish revoke, and will not go.
So have I seen upon a summer's even,
Fast by the rivulet's brink a youngster play;
How wishfully he looks to stem the tide!
This moment resolute, next unresolved,
At last, he dips his foot; but, as he dips,
His fears redouble, and he runs away
From th' inoffensive stream, unmindful now
Of all the flowers that paint the further bank,
And smiled so sweet of late. Thrice welcome Death!
That, after many a painful bleeding step,
Conducts us to our home, and lands us safe
On the long-wish'd for shore. Prodigious change!
Our bane turn'd to a blessing! Death disarm'd,
Loses its fellness quite; all thanks to him
Who scourged the venom out! Sure the last end
Of the good man is peace! How calm his exit!
Night-dews fall not more gently to the ground,
Nor weary worn-out winds expire so soft.
Behold him in the ev'ning-tide of life,
A life well spent, whose early care it was
His riper years should not upbraid his green:
By unperceived degrees he wears away;
Yet, like the sun, seems larger at his setting.
High in his faith and hopes, look how he reaches
After the prize in view! and, like a bird
That's hamper'd, struggles hard to get away:
While the glad gates of sight are wide expanded
To let new glories in, the first fair fruits
Of the fast-coming harvest! Then—O then!
Each earth-born joy grows vile, or disappears,
Shrunk to a thing of nought. O how he longs
To have his passport sign'd, and be dismiss'd!

'Tis done—and now he's happy! The glad soul
Has not a wish uncrown'd. E'en the lag flesh
Rests too in hope of meeting once again
Its better half, never to sunder more.
Nor shall it hope in vain: the time draws on
When not a single spot of burial-earth,
Whether on land or in the spacious sea,
But must give back its long committed dust
Inviolate; and faithfully shall these
Make up the full account; not the least atom
Embezzled, or mislaid, of the whole tale.
Each soul shall have a body ready furnish'd;
And each shall have his own. Hence, ye profane!
Ask not, how this can be. Sure the same power
That rear'd the piece at first, and took it down,
Can re-assemble the loose scatter'd parts,
And put them as they were. Almighty God
Has done much more; nor is his arm impair'd
Through length of days; and what he can he will:
His faithfulness stands bound to see it done.
When the dread trumpet sounds, the slumb'ring dust,
Not unattentive to the call, shall wake;
And ev'ry joint possess its proper place,
With a new elegance of form, unknown
To its first state. Nor shall the conscious soul
Mistake its partner; but, amidst the crowd,
Singling its other half, into its arms
Shall rush, with all the impatience of a man
That's new come home, who having long been absent,
With haste runs over ev'ry different room,
In pain to see the whole. Thrice happy meeting!
Nor time, nor death, shall ever part them more.
'Tis but a night, a long and moonless night;
We make the grave our bed, and then are gone!

Thus at the shut of even, the weary bird
Leaves the wide air, and in some lonely brake
Cowers down, and dozes till the dawn of day;
Then claps his well-fledged wings and bears away.

END OF THE GRAVE.

THE

POETICAL WORKS

OF

WILLIAM COLLINS.

CONTENTS.

MEMOIR.

WILLIAM COLLINS, who, to use the vivid language of Hazlitt, "is, of all the minor poets, probably the one who has shown the most of the highest qualities of poetry, and who excites the most intense interest in the bosom of the reader; who soars into the regions of imagination, and occupies the highest peaks of Parnassus," was born at Chichester on the 25th Dec., 1720. He was the son of a respectable hatter in that city. In 1733 he was admitted scholar of Winchester College, and at nineteen was elected, upon the foundation, to New College in Oxford. There was, however, no vacancy, and in the mean time he was admitted a commoner of Queen's College, and subsequently, in July, 1741, his tutor, being very sensible of his merits, procured his admission to Magdalen College, as a demy. Whilst yet at college, he directed his attention chiefly to poetry, and published an epistle to Sir Thomas Hanmer on his edition of Shakspeare; and the Persian, or as they have since been entitled, the Oriental Eclogues.

It is a melancholy task to trace the brief career of this highly-gifted man. In 1744 he quitted the university, and proceeded to London a mere literary adventurer, and with feelings so delicate, nerves so finely strung, as to render him very unfit to fight his way to fame. His head was full of projects, and amongst others he published proposals for a "History of the Revival of Learning," a subject which he was well able to have treated in a masterly manner, but which was not pursued further than the "proposals," probably from want of encouragement. His life in London was very irregular and unsettled. He in fact lived the life which is now understood as that of "a young man about town;" he ruined his health and expended the little money he possessed. But still he was not idle, and besides the fine odes he has left us, which were published by Mr. Millar, and met with even less success than his Eclogues, he wrote numerous other poems, which were condemned by his fastidious taste, and after being read to a friend or two were irrevocably destroyed, for he would never permit a copy to be taken.

The odes were published in 1746, but falling still-born from the press, he was discouraged and quite disheartened, and being at the same time in great pecuniary difficulties, he sought a refuge abroad. He first called in all the unsold copies of his odes and burnt them, and then, raising a few guineas on a projected translation of Aristotle's Poetics, he retreated from the assaults of bailiffs, into the country, and afterwards went abroad to his uncle, Lieutenant-colonel Martin, then with the army in Germany. This gentleman dying soon afterwards, left his nephew a legacy of £2000, a sum which was to him riches, but which he did not live to spend. The first use he made of it was to repay Millar all the loss upon the publication of the odes, and to other booksellers the sums advanced upon the speculated translation of Aristotle. But he lived not to give the world further proofs of his fine genius. His mind and body had been too deeply wounded for recovery. He fell into a melancholy condition, and although he did not become absolutely insane, yet it was found necessary for some time to put him under the restraint of a lunatic asylum. Death came to his relief in 1756, but he died in his sister's arms, and felt the consolation of a sister's love.

When the poet was dead, his value began to be appreciated, and the demand for his poems became general, and they quickly rose to that station which they have ever since retained. The noble Ode to the Passions, in particular, was extolled by the critics, and recited in the theatres; and his Oriental Eclogues, which he himself was wont to condemn, and, in allusion to some supposed errors * in the representation of Eastern imagery and manners, often called his Irish Eclogues, were recognised as possessing all the qualities proper to that style of poetry, and, although that be not much in unison with more modern taste, yet we still find delight in the fine touches of natural feeling there displayed, and we admire the chaste and nervous diction which adorns them. We cannot read of the solitary Hassan, toiling in the desert and lamenting the hour "When first from Schiraz walls he bent his way," without participating in his fears, and dreading that each step will reveal the awful foot-print of the lion.

Dr. Johnson, who knew and loved Collins, thus depicted his character:—"The appearance of Collins was decent and manly; his knowledge considerable, his views extensive, his conversation elegant, and his disposition cheerful. He was a man of extensive literature, and of vigorous faculties. He was acquainted not only with the learned tongues, but with the Italian, French, and Spanish languages. He had employed his mind chiefly upon works of fiction, and subjects of fancy; and, by indulging some peculiar habits of thought, was eminently delighted with those flights of imagination which pass the bounds of nature, and to which the mind is reconciled only by a passive acquiescence in popular traditions. He loved fairies, genii, giants, and monsters; he delighted to rove through the meanders of enchantment, to gaze on the magnificence of golden palaces, to repose by the waterfalls of Elysian gardens. This was, however, the character rather of his inclination than his genius; the grandeur of wildness, and the novelty of extravagance, were always desired by him, but were not always attained. Yet, as diligence is never wholly lost, if his efforts sometimes caused harshness and obscurity, they likewise produced in happier moments sublimity and splendour.

"This idea which he had formed of excellence, led him to oriental figures and allegorical imagery; and perhaps while he was intent upon description, he did not sufficiently cultivate sentiment. His poems are the production of a mind not deficient in fire, nor unfurnished with knowledge either of books or life, but somewhat obstructed in its progress by deviation in quest of mistaken beauties. His morals were pure, and his opinions pious: in a long continuance of poverty and long habits of dissipation, it cannot be expected that any character should be exactly

* He had been led to imagine that he had committed some gross blunders in his description of Eastern manners &c., whereas they are really singularly correct.

uniform. There is a degree of want by which the freedom of agency is almost destroyed; and long association with fortuitous companions will at last relax the strictness of truth, and abate the fervour of sincerity. That this man, wise and virtuous as he was, passed always unentangled through the snares of life, it would be prejudice and temerity to affirm; but it may be said that at least he preserved the source of action unpolluted, that his principles were never shaken, that his distinctions of right and wrong were never confounded, and that his faults had nothing of malignity or design, but proceeded from some unexpected pressure or casual temptation.

"After his return from France, the writer of this character paid him a visit at Islington, where he was waiting for his sister, whom he had directed to meet him: there was then nothing of disorder discernible in his mind by any but himself; but he had withdrawn from study, and travelled with no other book than an English Testament, such as children carry to the school: when his friend took it into his hand, out of curiosity to see what companion a man of letters had chosen: 'I have but one book,' says Collins, 'but it is the best.' Such was the fate of Collins, with whom I once delighted to converse, and whom I yet remember with tenderness."

A monument, executed by Flaxman, who was then lately returned from Rome, was erected by public subscription to the memory of Collins. The poet is represented as just recovered from one of those fits of frenzy, to which he was unhappily subject, and in a calm and reclining posture, seeking refuge from his misfortunes in the consolations of the Gospel, while his lyre and one of the first of his poems lie neglected on the ground. The following epitaph by Hayley is inscribed below:—

"Ye who the merits of the dead revere,
Who hold misfortune's sacred genius dear,
Regard this tomb, where Collins, hapless name
Solicits kindness with a double claim.
Though Nature gave him, and though Science taught
The fire of Fancy, and the reach of thought,
Severely doom'd to Penury's extreme,
He pass'd in madd'ning pain life's fev'rish dream,
While rays of genius only served to show
The thick'ning horror, and exalt his woe.
Ye walls that echo'd to his frantic moan,
Guard the due records of this grateful stone;
Strangers to him, enamour'd of his lays,
This fond memorial to his talents raise.
For this the ashes of a bard require,
Who touch'd the tend'rest notes of Pity's lyre;
Who join'd pure faith to strong poetic powers,
Who, in reviving Reason's lucid hours,
Sought on one book his troubled mind to rest,
And rightly deem'd the book of God the best."

THE
Poetical Works
OF
WILLIAM COLLINS.

ORIENTAL ECLOGUES.

ECLOGUE I.

SELIM; OR, THE SHEPHERD'S MORAL.

SCENE—*A Valley near Bagdat.* TIME—*The Morning.*

YE Persian maids! attend your poet's lays,
And hear how shepherds pass their golden days.
Not all are blest, whom Fortune's hand sustains
With wealth in courts: nor all that haunt the plains:
Well may your hearts believe the truths I tell;
'Tis virtue makes the bliss where'er we dwell.

Thus Selim sung, by sacred Truth inspired;
Nor praise, but such as Truth bestow'd, desired:
Wise in himself, his meaning songs convey'd
Informing morals to the shepherd maid;
Or taught the swains that surest bliss to find,
What groves nor streams bestow, a virtuous mind.

When sweet and blushing, like a virgin bride,
The radiant morn resumed her orient pride;
When wanton gales along the valleys play,
Breathe on each flower, and bear their sweets away;
By Tigris' wand'ring waves he sat, and sung
This useful lesson for the fair and young.

"Ye Persian dames," he said, "to you belong,
Well may they please, the morals of my song:
No fairer maids, I trust, than you are found,
Graced with soft arts, the peopled world around!
The morn that lights you, to your love supplies
Each gentler ray delicious to your eyes:
For you those flowers her fragrant hands bestow,
And yours the love that kings delight to know.
Yet think not these, all beauteous as they are,
The best kind blessings Heaven can grant the fair!
Who trust alone in beauty's feeble ray,
Boast but the worth Bassora's pearls display;
Drawn from the deep, we own their surface bright,
But, dark within, they drink no lustrous light:
Such are the maids, and such the charms they boast,
By sense unaided, or to virtue lost.
Self-flattering sex! your hearts believe in vain,
That love shall blind, when once he fires the swain;
Or hope a lover by your faults to win,
As spots on ermine beautify the skin:
Who seeks secure to rule, be first her care
Each softer virtue that adorns the fair;
Each tender passion man delights to find,
The loved perfections of a female mind!

"Blest were the days when wisdom held her reign,
And shepherds sought her on the silent plain;
With Truth she wedded in the secret grove,
Immortal Truth! and daughters bless'd their love.

"O haste, fair maids! ye Virtues, come away,
Sweet Peace and Plenty lead you on your way!
The balmy shrub for you shall love our shore,
By Ind excell'd or Araby no more.

"Lost to our fields, for so the Fates ordain,
The dear deserters shall return again.
Come thou, whose thoughts as limpid springs are clear,
To lead the train, sweet Modesty! appear:
Here make thy court amidst our rural scene,
And shepherd-girls shall own thee for their queen.
With thee be Chastity, of all afraid,
Distrusting all, a wise, suspicious maid;
But man the most—not more the mountain doe
Holds the swift falcon for her deadly foe.
Cold is her breast like flowers that drink the dew;
A silken veil conceals her from the view.
No wild desires amidst thy train be known,
But Faith, whose heart is fix'd on one alone:
Desponding Meekness, with her downcast eyes,
And friendly Pity, full of tender sighs:
And Love, the last: by these your hearts approve,
These are the virtues that must lead to love."

Thus sung the swain; and ancient legends say,
The maids of Bagdat verified the lay:
Dear to the plains, the Virtues came along,
The shepherds loved, and Selim bless'd his song.

ECLOGUE II.

HASSAN; OR, THE CAMEL-DRIVER.

SCENE—*The Desert*. TIME—*Mid-day*.

In silent horror o'er the boundless waste
The driver Hassan with his camels pass'd:
One cruise of water on his back he bore,
And his light scrip contain'd a scanty store;
A fan of painted feathers in his hand,
To guard his shaded face from scorching sand.
The sultry sun had gain'd the middle sky,
And not a tree and not a herb was nigh;
The beasts, with pain, their dusty way pursue,
Shrill roar'd the winds, and dreary was the view!
With desperate sorrow wild, th' affrighted man
Thrice sigh'd, thrice struck his breast, and thus began:
Sad was the hour and luckless was the day,
When first from Schiraz' walls I bent my way!

"Ah! little thought I of the blasting wind,
The thirst or pinching hunger that I find!
Bethink thee, Hassan, where shall thirst assuage,
When fails this cruise, his unrelenting rage?
Soon shall this scrip its precious load resign!
Then what but tears and hunger shall be thine?

"Ye mute companions of my toils, that bear
In all my griefs a more than equal share!
Here, where no springs in murmurs break away,
Or moss-crown'd fountains mitigate the day,
In vain ye hope the dear delights to know,
Which plains more blest, or verdant vales bestow:
Here rocks alone and tasteless sands are found,
And faint and sickly winds for ever howl around.
Sad was the hour, and luckless was the day,
When first from Schiraz' walls I bent my way!

"Curst be the gold and silver which persuade
Weak men to follow far fatiguing trade!
The lily peace outshines the silver store,
And life is dearer than the golden ore:
Yet money tempts us o'er the desert brown,
To every distant mart and wealthy town.
Full oft we tempt the land, and oft the sea;
And are we only yet repaid by thee?
Ah! why was ruin so attractive made,
Or why fond man so easily betray'd?
Why heed we not, while mad we haste along,
The gentle voice of Peace, or Pleasure's song?
Or wherefore think the flowery mountain's side,
The fountain's murmurs, and the valley's pride,
Why think we these less pleasing to behold
Than dreary deserts, if they lead to gold?
Sad was the hour, and luckless was the day,
When first from Schiraz' walls I bent my way!

"Oh cease, my fears!—all frantic as I go,
When thought creates unnumber'd scenes of woe;
What if the lion in his rage I meet!—
Oft in the dust I view his printed feet;
And, fearful! oft, when day's declining light
Yields her pale empire to the mourner night,
By hunger roused he scours the groaning plain,
Gaunt wolves and sullen tigers in his train:
Before them Death with shrieks directs their way,
Fills the wild yell, and leads them to their prey.
Sad was the hour, and luckless was the day,
When first from Schiraz' walls I bent my way!

"At that dread hour the silent asp shall creep,
If aught of rest I find, upon my sleep:
Or some swoln serpent twist his scales around,
And wake to anguish with a burning wound.
Thrice happy they, the wise contented poor,
From lust of wealth, and dread of death secure!
They tempt no deserts, and no griefs they find;
Peace rules the day where reason rules the mind.
Sad was the hour, and luckless was the day,
When first from Schiraz' walls I bent my way!

"O hapless youth! for she thy love hath won,
The tender Zara will be most undone!
Big swell'd my heart, and own'd the powerful maid,
When fast she dropt her tears, as thus she said:
'Farewell the youth whom sighs could not detain,
Whom Zara's breaking heart implored in vain!
Yet as thou goest may every blast arise
Weak, and unfelt as these rejected sighs!
Safe o'er the wild, no perils may'st thou see,
No griefs endure, nor weep, false youth, like me!'
Oh let me safely to the fair return,
Say, with a kiss, she must not, shall not mourn;
Oh! let me teach my heart to lose its fears,
Recall'd by Wisdom's voice, and Zara's tears!"

He said, and call'd on Heaven to bless the day
When back to Schiraz' walls he bent his way.

ECLOGUE III.

ABRA; OR, THE GEORGIAN SULTANA.

SCENE—*A Forest*. TIME—*The Evening*.

In Georgia's land, where Tefflis' towers are seen,
In distant view along the level green,
While evening dews enrich the glittering glade,
And the tall forests cast a longer shade,
What time 'tis sweet o'er fields of rice to stray,
Or scent the breathing maize at setting day;
Amidst the maids of Zagen's peaceful grove,
Emyra sung the pleasing cares of love.
Of Abra first began the tender strain,
Who led her youth with flocks upon the plain:
At morn she came her willing flocks to lead,
Where lilies rear them in the watery mead:
From early dawn the live-long hours she told,
Till late at silent eve she penn'd the fold.
Deep in the grove, beneath the secret shade,
A various wreath of odorous flowers she made:
Gay-motley'd pinks and sweet jonquils[1] she chose,
The violet blue that on the moss-bank grows;
All sweet to sense, the flaunting rose was there:
The finish'd chaplet well adorn'd her hair.

Great Abbas chanced that fated morn to stray,
By love conducted from the chase away;
Among the vocal vales he heard her song,
And sought the vales and echoing groves among:
At length he found, and woo'd the rural maid;
She knew the monarch, and with fear obey'd.
Be every youth like royal Abbas moved,
And every Georgian maid like Abra loved!

1 These flowers are found in very great abundance in some of the provinces of Persia.

The royal lover bore her from the plain;
Yet still her crook and bleating flock remain:
Oft, as she went, she backward turn'd her view,
And bade that crook and bleating flock adieu,
Fair, happy maid! to other scenes remove,
To richer scenes of golden power and love!
Go, leave the simple pipe, and shepherd's strain;
With love delight thee, and with Abbas reign.
Be every youth like royal Abbas moved,
And every Georgian maid like Abra loved!

Yet, 'midst the blaze of courts she fix'd her love
On the cool fountain, or the shady grove;
Still with the shepherd's innocence her mind
To the sweet vale and flowery mead inclined;
And oft as Spring renew'd the plains with flowers,
Breathed his soft gales, and led the fragrant hours,
With sure return she sought the sylvan scene,
The breezy mountains, and the forests green.
Her maids around her moved, a duteous band!
Each bore a crook all rural in her hand:
Some simple lay, of flocks and herds they sung;
With joy the mountain and the forest rung.
Be every youth like royal Abbas moved,
And every Georgian maid like Abra loved!

And oft the royal lover left the care
And thorns of state, attendant on the fair;
Oft to the shades and low-roof'd cots retired,
Or sought the vale where first his heart was fired:
A russet mantle, like a swain, he wore,
And thought of crowns and busy courts no more.
Be every youth like royal Abbas moved,
And every Georgian maid like Abra loved!

Blest was the life that royal Abbas led:
Sweet was his love, and innocent his bed.
What if in wealth the noble maid excel?
The simple shepherd girl can love as well.
Let those who rule on Persia's jewel'd throne
Be famed for love, and gentlest love alone:
Or wreathe, like Abbas, full of fair renown,
The lover's myrtle with the warrior's crown.
O happy days! the maids around her say:
O haste, profuse of blessings, haste away!
Be every youth like royal Abbas moved,
And every Georgian maid like Abra loved!

ECLOGUE IV.

AGIB AND SECANDER; OR THE FUGITIVES.

SCENE—*A Mountain in Circassia.* TIME—*Midnight.*

In fair Circassia, where, to love inclined,
Each swain was blest, for every maid was kind;
At that still hour, when awful midnight reigns,
And none but wretches haunt the twilight plains;
What time the Moon had hung her lamp on high,
And pass'd in radiance through the cloudless sky;
Sad o'er the dews two brother shepherds fled,
Where wildering fear and desperate sorrow led:
Fast as they press'd their flight, behind them lay
Wild ravaged plains, and valleys stole away.
Along the mountain's bending sides they ran,
Till faint and weak Secander thus began:

SECANDER.

Oh, stay thee, Agib, for my feet deny,
No longer friendly to my life, to fly.
Friend of my heart! Oh turn thee and survey,
Trace our long flight through all its length of way!
And first review that long-extended plain,
And yon wide groves, already pass'd with pain!
Yon ragged cliff, whose dangerous path we tried!
And last this lofty mountain's weary side!

AGIB.

Weak as thou art, yet hapless must thou know
The toils of flight or some severer woe!
Still as I haste, the Tartar shouts behind,
And shrieks and sorrows load the saddening wind:
In rage of heart, with ruin in his hand,
He blasts our harvests, and deforms our land.
Yon citron grove, whence first in fear we came,
Droops its fair honours to the conquering flame:
Far fly the swains, like us, in deep despair,
And leave to ruffian bands their fleecy care.

SECANDER.

Unhappy land! whose blessings tempt the sword,
In vain, unheard, thou call'st thy Persian lord!
In vain thou court'st him, helpless, to thine aid,
To shield the shepherd, and protect the maid!
Far off, in thoughtless indolence resign'd,
Soft dreams of love and pleasure soothe his mind,
'Midst fair sultanas lost in idle joy,
No wars alarm him, and no fears annoy.

AGIB.

Yet these green hills, in summer's sultry heat,
Have lent the monarch oft a cool retreat.
Sweet to the sight is Zabran's flowery plain,
And once by maids and shepherds loved in vain!
No more the virgins shall delight to rove
By Sargis' banks, or Irwan's shady grove;
On Tarkie's mountains catch the cooling gale,
Or breathe the sweets of Aly's flowery vale:
Fair scenes! but, ah! no more with peace possest,
With ease alluring, and with plenty blest!
No more the shepherds' whitening tents appear,
Nor the kind products of a bounteous year;
No more the date, with snowy blossoms crown'd!
But Ruin spreads her baleful fires around.

SECANDER.

In vain Circassia boasts her spicy groves,
For ever famed for pure and happy loves:
In vain she boasts her fairest of the fair,
Their eyes' blue languish, and their golden hair.
Those eyes in tears their fruitless grief must send;
Those hairs the Tartar's cruel hand shall rend.

AGIB.

Ye Georgian swains, that piteous learn from far
Circassia's ruin, and the waste of war;
Some weightier arms than crooks and staffs prepare,
To shield your harvests, and defend your fair:
The Turk and Tartar like designs pursue,
Fix'd to destroy, and steadfast to undo.
Wild as his land, in native deserts bred,
By lust incited, or by malice led,
The villain Arab, as he prowls for prey,
Oft marks with blood and wasting flames the way
Yet none so cruel as the Tartar foe,
To death inured, and nursed in scenes of woe.

He said: when loud along the vale was heard
A shriller shriek, and nearer fires appear'd.
Th' affrighted shepherds through the dews of night,
Wide o'er the moonlight hills renew'd their flight.

ODES,

DESCRIPTIVE AND ALLEGORICAL.

ODE TO PITY.

O THOU! the friend of man assign'd,
With balmy hands his wounds to bind,
And charm his frantic woe:
When first Distress, with dagger keen,
Broke forth to waste his destined scene,
His wild unsated foe!

By Pella's bard, a magic name,
By all the griefs his thought could frame,
Receive my humble rite:
Long, Pity, let the nations view
Thy sky-worn robes of tenderest blue,
And eyes of dewy light!

But wherefore need I wander wide
To old Ilissus' distant side,
Deserted stream and mute?
Wild Arun[1] too has heard thy strains,
And Echo, midst my native plains,
Been soothed by Pity's lute.

There first the wren thy myrtles shed
On gentlest Otway's infant head,
To him thy cell was shown;
And while he sung the female heart,
With youth's soft notes unspoil'd by art,
Thy turtles mix'd their own.

Come, Pity! come; by Fancy's aid,
Ev'n now my thoughts, relenting maid,
Thy temple's pride design:
Its southern site, its truth complete,
Shall raise a wild enthusiast heat
In all who view the shrine.

There Picture's toil shall well relate,
How chance, or hard involving fate,
O'er mortal bliss prevail:
The buskin'd Muse shall near her stand,
And sighing prompt her tender hand,
With each disastrous tale.

There let me oft, retired by day,
In dreams of passion melt away,
Allow'd with thee to dwell:
There waste the mournful lamp of night,
Till, Virgin, thou again delight
To hear a British shell!

ODE TO FEAR.

THOU, to whom the world unknown
With all its shadowy shapes is shown;
Who seest appall'd th' unreal scene,
While Fancy lifts the veil between:
Ah Fear! ah, frantic Fear!
I see, I see thee near.
I know thy hurried step, thy haggard eye!
Like thee I start, like thee disorder'd fly!
For, lo! what monsters in thy train appear!
Danger, whose limbs of giant mould
What mortal eye can fix'd behold?
Who stalks his round, and hideous form,
Howling amidst the midnight storm;
Or throws him on the ridgy steep
Of some loose hanging rock to sleep:
And with him thousand phantoms join'd,
Who prompt to deeds accursed the mind:
And those, the fiends, who near allied,
O'er Nature's wounds, and wrecks preside;
While Vengeance, in the lurid air,
Lifts her red arm, exposed and bare:
On whom that ravening brood of Fate,
Who lap the blood of Sorrow, wait;
Who, Fear, this ghastly train can see,
And look not madly wild, like thee?

EPODE.

In earliest Greece, to thee, with partial choice,
The grief-full Muse address'd her infant tongue;
The maids and matrons, on her awful voice,
Silent and pale, in wild amazement hung.

Yet he, the bard[2] who first invoked thy name,
Disdain'd in Marathon its power to feel:
For not alone he nursed the poet's flame,
But reach'd from Virtue's hand the patriot's steel.

But who is he, whom later garlands grace,
Who left awhile o'er Hybla's dews to rove,
With trembling eyes thy dreary steps to trace.
Where thou and furies shared the baleful grove?

Wrapt in thy cloudy veil th' incestuous queen[3]
Sigh'd the sad call her son and husband heard,
When once alone it broke the silent scene,
And he the wretch of Thebes no more appear'd.

O Fear! I know thee by my throbbing heart,
Thy withering power inspired each mournful line,
Though gentle Pity claim her mingled part,
Yet all the thunders of the scenes are thine!

ANTISTROPHE.

Thou who such weary lengths hast past,
Where wilt thou rest, mad Nymph! at last?
Say, wilt thou shroud in haunted cell,
Where gloomy Rape and Murder dwell?
Or in some hallow'd seat,
'Gainst which the big waves beat,
Hear drowning seamen's cries in tempests brought!
Dark Power! with shuddering, meek, submitted thought,
Be mine to read the visions old,
Which thy awakening bards have told.

And, lest thou meet my blasted view,
Hold each strange tale devoutly true;
Ne'er be I found, by thee o'er-awed,
In that thrice-hallow'd eve abroad,

[1] A river in Sussex.

[2] Æschylus.

[3] Jocasta.

When ghosts, as cottage-maids believe,
Their pebbled beds permitted leave,
And goblins haunt from fire, or fen,
Or mine, or flood, the walks of men!

O thou, whose spirit most possest
The sacred seat of Shakspeare's breast!
By all that from thy prophet broke,
In thy divine emotions spoke!
Hither again thy fury deal,
Teach me but once like him to feel:
His cypress wreath my meed decree,
And I, O Fear, will dwell with thee!

ODE TO SIMPLICITY.

O THOU by Nature taught
To breathe her genuine thought,
In numbers warmly pure, and sweetly strong:
Who first on mountains wild,
In Fancy, loveliest child,
Thy babe, and Pleasure's, nursed the powers of [song!

Thou, who with hermit heart
Disdain'st the wealth of art,
And gauds, and pageant weeds, and trailing pall:
But com'st a decent maid,
In Attic robe array'd,
O chaste, unboastful nymph! to thee I call!

By all the honey'd store
On Hybla's thymy shore,
By all her blooms, and mingled murmurs dear,
By her, whose love-lorn woe,
In evening musings slow,
Soothed sweetly sad Electra's poet's ear:

By old Cephisus' deep,
Who spread his wavy sweep
In warbled wanderings round thy green retreat,
On whose enamell'd side,
When holy Freedom died,
No equal haunt allured thy future feet.

O sister meek of Truth,
To my admiring youth
Thy sober aid and native charms infuse!
The flowers that sweetest breathe.
Though beauty cull'd the wreath,
Still ask thy hand to range their order'd hues.

While Rome could none esteem
But Virtue's patriot theme,
You loved her hills, and led her laureate band;
But staid to sing alone
To one distinguish'd throne,
And turu'd thy face, and fled her alter'd land.

No more, in hall or bower,
The Passions own thy power,
Love, only Love, her forceless numbers mean:
For thou hast left her shrine,
Nor olive more, nor vine,
Shall gain thy feet to bless the servile scene.

Though taste, though genius, bless
To some divine excess,
Faint's the cold work till thou inspire the whole:
What each, what all supply,
May court, may charm our eye,
Thou! only thou canst raise the meeting soul!

Of these let others ask,
To aid some mighty task,
I only seek to find thy temperate vale:
Where oft my reed might sound
To maids and shepherds round,
And all thy sons, O Nature! learn my tale.

ODE ON THE POETICAL CHARACTER.

As once, if not with light regard,
I read aright that gifted bard,
(Him whose school above the rest
His loveliest Elfin queen has blest)
One, only one, unrivall'd fair [1],
Might hope the magic girdle wear,
At solemn tourney hung on high,
The wish of each love-darting eye.

Lo! to each other nymph in turn applied,
As if, in air unseen, some hovering hand,
Some chaste and angel-friend to virgin-fame,
With whisper'd spell had burst the starting band,
It left unblest her loathed dishonour'd side;
Happier, hopeless fair, if never
Her baffled hand with vain endeavour
Had touch'd that fatal zone, to her denied!

Young Fancy thus, to me divinest name,
To whom, prepared and bathed in heaven,
The cest of amplest power is given,
To few the god-like gift assigns,
To gird their blest prophetic loins,
And gaze her visions wild, and feel unmix'd her flame.

The band, as fairy legends say,
Was wove on that creating day,
When He, who call'd with thought to birth
Yon tented sky, this laughing earth,
And drest with springs, and forests tall,
And pour'd the main engirting all,
Long by the loved enthusiast woo'd
Himself in some diviner mood,
Retiring, sat with her alone,
And placed her on his sapphire throne,
The whiles, the vaulted shrine around,
Seraphic wires were heard to sound,
Now sublimest triumph swelling,
Now on love and mercy dwelling;
And she, from out the veiling cloud,
Breathed her magic notes aloud:
And thou, thou rich-hair'd youth of morn,
And all thy subject life was born!
The dangerous Passions kept aloof,
Far from the sainted growing woof;
But near it sat ecstatic Wonder,
Listening the deep applauding thunder:
And Truth, in sunny vest array'd,
By whose the Tarsel's eyes were made;
And the shadowy tribes of Mind,
In braided dance their murmurs join'd,
And all the bright uncounted Powers,
Who feed on heaven's ambrosial flowers.
Where is the bard, whose soul can now
Its high presuming hopes avow?
Where he who thinks, with rapture blind,
This hallow'd work for him design'd?

[1] Florimel. See Spenser, Leg.

High on some cliff, to heaven up-piled,
Of rude access, of prospect wild,
Where, tangled round the jealous steep,
Strange shades o'erbrow the valleys deep,
And holy Genii guard the rock,
Its glooms embrown, its springs unlock,
While on its rich ambitious head
An Eden like his own, lies spread,
I view that oak, the fancied glades among,
By which, as Milton lay, his evening ear,
From many a cloud that dropp'd ethereal dew
Night sphered in heaven its native strains could hear;
On which that ancient trump he reach'd was hung:
Thither oft his glory greeting,
From Waller's myrtle shades retreating,
With many a vow from Hope's aspiring tongue,
My trembling feet his guiding steps pursue;
In vain—Such bliss to one alone,
Of all the sons of soul was known,
And Heaven, and Fancy, kindred powers,
Have now o'erturn'd th' inspiring bowers,
Or curtain'd close such scene from every future view.

ODE, WRITTEN IN THE YEAR MDCCXLVI.

How sleep the brave, who sink to rest,
By all their country's wishes blest!
When Spring, with dewy fingers cold,
Returns to deck their hallow'd mould,
She there shall dress a sweeter sod
Than Fancy's feet have ever trod.

By Fairy hands their knell is rung,
By forms unseen their dirge is sung:
There Honour comes, a pilgrim gray
To bless the turf that wraps their clay,
And Freedom shall awhile repair,
To dwell a weeping hermit there!

ODE TO MERCY.

STROPHE.

O Thou! who sit'st a smiling bride
By Valour's arm'd and awful side,
Gentlest of sky-born forms, and best adored:
Who oft, with songs, divine to hear,
Win'st from his fatal grasp the spear,
And hidest in wreaths of flowers his bloodless sword!
Thou who, amidst the deathful field,
By godlike chiefs alone beheld,
Oft with thy bosom bare art found,
Pleading for him, the youth who sinks to ground:
See, Mercy, see! with pure and loaded hands,
Before thy shrine my country's Genius stands,
And decks thy altar still, though pierced with many a wound!

ANTISTROPHE.

When he whom even our joys provoke,
The Fiend of Nature join'd his yoke,
And rush'd in wrath to make our isle his prey;
Thy form, from out thy sweet abode,
O'ertook him on his blasted road,
And stopp'd his wheels, and look'd his rage away.
I see recoil his sable steeds,
That bore him swift to savage deeds,
Thy tender melting eyes they own;
O maid! for all thy love to Britain shown,
Where Justice bars her iron tower,
To thee we build a roseate bower,
Thou, thou, shalt rule our queen, and share our monarch's throne!

ODE TO LIBERTY.

STROPHE.

Who shall awake the Spartan fife,
And call in solemn sounds to life
The youths, whose locks divinely spreading,
Like vernal hyacinths in sullen hue,
At once the breath of fear and virtue shedding,
Applauding Freedom loved of old to view?
What new Alcæus, fancy-blest,
Shall sing the sword, in myrtles drest,
At Wisdom's shrine awhile its flame concealing,
(What place so fit to seal a deed renown'd?)
Till she her brightest lightnings round revealing,
It leap'd in glory forth, and dealt her prompted wound!
O Goddess! in that feeling hour,
When most its sounds would court thy ears,
Let not my shell's misguided power
E'er draw thy sad, thy mindful tears.
No, Freedom! no, I will not tell
How Rome, before thy weeping face,
With heaviest sound, a giant statue, fell,
Push'd by a wild and artless race
From off its wide ambitious base,
When Time his Northern sons of spoil awoke,
And all the blended work of strength and grace,
With many a rude repeated stroke,
And many a barbarous yell, to thousand fragments broke!

EPODE I.

Yet even, where'er the least appear'd,
Th' admiring world thy hand revered:
Still, 'midst the scatter'd states around,
Some remnants of her strength were found;
They saw, by what escaped the storm,
How wondrous rose her perfect form,
How in the great, the labour'd whole,
Each mighty master pour'd his soul;
For sunny Florence, seat of art,
Beneath her vines preserved a part.
Till they, whom Science loved to name,
(Oh! who could fear it?) quench'd her flame.
And lo, an humbler relic laid
In jealous Pisa's olive shade!
See small Marino joins the theme,
Though least, not last in thy esteem;
Strike, louder strike th' ennobling strings
To those, whose merchant-sons were kings;
To him, who, deck'd with pearly pride,
In Adria weds his green-hair'd bride:
Hail, port of glory, wealth, and pleasure!
Ne'er let me change this Lydian measure:
Nor e'er her former pride relate,
To sad Liguria's bleeding state.
Ah, no! more pleased thy haunts I seek,
On wild Helvetia's mountains bleak
(Where, when the favour'd of thy choice,
The daring archer heard thy voice,

Forth from his eyrie roused in dread,
The ravening eagle northward fled.)
Or dwell in willow'd meads more near,
With those [1] to whom thy stork is dear:
Those whom the rod of Alva bruised,
Whose crown a British queen refused,
The magic works, thou feel'st the strains,
One holier name alone remains;
The perfect spell shall then avail,
Hail, nymph! adored by Britain, hail!

ANTISTROPHE.

Beyond the measure vast of thought,
The works, the wizard Time has wrought!
The Gaul, 'tis held of antique story,
Saw Britain link'd to his now adverse strand[2],
No sea between, nor cliff sublime and hoary,
He pass'd with unwet feet through all our land,
To the blown Baltic then, they say,
The wild waves found another way,
Where Orcas howls, his wolfish mountains rounding,
Till all the banded west at once 'gan rise,
A wide wild storm even Nature s self confounding,
Withering her giant sons with strange uncouth surprise.
This pillar'd earth, so firm ana wide,
By winds and inward labours torn,
In thunders dread was push'd aside,
And down the shouldering billows borne.
And see like gems her laughing train,
The little isles on every side;
Mona [3], once hid from those who search the main,
Where thousand elfin shapes abide,
And Wight who checks the westering tide,
For thee consenting Heaven has each bestow'd,
A fair attendant on her sovereign pride:
To thee this blest divorce she owed,
For thou hast made her vales thy loved, thy last abode.

SECOND EPODE.

Then too, 'tis said, a hoary pile,
'Midst the green navel of our isle,
Thy shrine in some religious wood,
O soul-enforcing Goddess! stood;
There oft the painted native's feet,
Were wont thy form celestial meet:
Though now with hopeless toil we trace
Time's backward rolls, to find its place;

[1] The Dutch, amongst whom there are very severe penalties for those who are convicted of killing this bird. They are kept tame in almost all their towns, and particularly at the Hague; of the arms of which they make a part. The common people of Holland are said to entertain a superstitious sentiment, that if the whole species of them should become extinct, they should lose their liberties.

[2] This tradition is mentioned by several of our old historians. Some naturalists too have endeavoured to support the probability of the fact by arguments drawn from the correspondent disposition of the two opposite coasts.

[3] There is a tradition in the Isle of Man, that a mermaid becoming enamoured of a young man of extraordinary beauty, took an opportunity of meeting him one day as he walked on the shore, and opened her passion to him, but was received with a coldness, occasioned by his horror and surprise at her appearance. This, however, was so misconstrued by the sea-lady, that in revenge for his treatment of her she punished the whole island with a mist, so that all who attempted to carry on any commerce with it either never arrived at it, but wandered up and down the sea, or were upon a sudden wrecked upon its cliffs.

Whether the fiery-tressed Dane,
Or Roman's self, o'erturn'd the fane;
Or in what heaven-left age it fell;
'Twere hard for modern song to tell.
Yet still, if Truth those beams infuse,
Which guide at once, and charm the Muse,
Beyond yon braided clouds that lie,
Paving the light-embroider'd sky,
Amidst the bright pavilion'd plains,
The beauteous model still remains.
There happier than in islands blest,
Or bowers by Spring or Hebe drest,
The chiefs who fill our Albion's story,
In warlike weeds, retired in glory,
Hear their consorted Druids sing
Their triumphs to th' immortal string.

How may the poet now unfold,
What never tongue or numbers told?
How learn, delighted and amazed,
What hands unknown that fabric raised
Ev'n now, before his favour'd eyes,
In gothic pride it seems to rise!
Yet Græcia's graceful orders join,
Majestic through the mix'd design:
The secret builder knew to choose
Each sphere-found gem of richest hues:
Whate'er heaven's purer mould contains,
When nearer suns emblaze its veins;
There on the walls the Patriot's sight
May ever hang with fresh delight,
And, graved with some prophetic rage,
Read Albion's fame through every age.

Ye forms divine! ye laureate band
That near her inmost altar stand,
Now soothe her to her blissful train,
Blithe Concord's social form to gain:
Concord, whose myrtle wand can steep
Even Anger's blood-shot eyes in sleep!
Before whose breathing bosom's balm,
Rage drops his steel, and storms grow calm;
Here let our sires and matrons hoar
Welcome to Britain's ravaged shore,
Our youths, enamour'd of the fair,
Play with the tangles of her hair,
Till, in one loud applauding sound,
The nations shout to her around,
Oh how supremely art thou blest!
Thou, lady, thou shalt rule the West!

ODE TO A LADY,

ON THE DEATH OF COLONEL CHARLES ROSS, IN THE ACTION AT FONTENOY

Written May 1745.

While, lost to all his former mirth,
Britannia's Genius bends to earth,
And mourns the fatal day;
While stain'd with blood he strives to tear,
Unseemly, from his sea-green hair,
The wreaths of cheerful May:

The thoughts which musing Pity pays,
And fond Remembrance loves to raise,
Your faithful hours attend:
Still Fancy, to herself unkind,
Awakes to grief the soften'd mind,
And points the bleeding friend.

By rapid Scheldt's descending wave,
His country's vows shall bless the grave,
Where'er the youth is laid;
That sacred spot the village hind
With every sweetest turf shall bind,
And Peace protect the shade.

O'er him, whose doom thy virtues grieve,
Aërial forms shall sit at eve,
And bend the pensive head!
And, fallen to save his injured land,
Imperial Honour's awful hand
Shall point his lonely bed!

The warlike dead of every age,
Who fill the fair recording page,
Shall leave their sainted rest:
And, half-reclining on his spear,
Each wondering chief by turns appear,
To hail the blooming guest.

Old Edward's sons, unknown to yield,
Shall crowd from Cressy's laurell'd field,
And gaze with fix'd delight:
Again for Britain's wrongs they feel,
Again they snatch the gleamy steel,
And wish th' avenging fight.

But lo, where, sunk in deep despair,
Her garments torn, her bosom bare
Impatient Freedom lies!
Her matted tresses madly spread,
To every sod which wraps the dead,
She turns her joyless eyes.

Ne'er shall she leave that lowly ground,
Till notes of triumph bursting round,
Proclaim her reign restored:
Till William seek the sad retreat,
And bleeding at her sacred feet,
Present the sated sword.

If, weak to soothe so soft a heart,
These pictured glories nought impart,
To dry thy constant tear;
If yet, in Sorrow's distant eye,
Exposed and pale thou see'st him lie,
Wild war insulting near:

Where'er from time thou court'st relief,
The Muse shall still, with social grief,
Her gentlest promise keep;
Even humble Harting's cottaged vale
Shall learn the sad repeated tale,
And bid her shepherds weep.

ODE TO EVENING.

If aught of oaten stop, or pastoral song,
May hope, chaste Eve, to soothe thy modest ear,
Like thy own solemn springs,
Thy springs, and dying gales,

O nymph reserved! while now the bright-hair'd sun
Sits in yon western tent, whose cloudy skirts,
With brede ethereal wove,
O'erhang his wavy bed:

Now air is hush'd, save where the weak-eyed bat
With short shrill shriek flits by on leathern wing,
Or where the beetle winds
His small but sullen horn,

As oft he rises 'midst the twilight path,
Against the pilgrim borne in heedless hum:
Now teach me, maid composed,
To breathe some soften'd strain,

Whose numbers stealing through thy dark'ning vale,
May not unseemly with its stillness suit,
As, musing slow, I hail
Thy genial loved return!

For when thy folding-star arising shows
His paly circlet, at his warning lamp
The fragrant Hours, and Elves
Who slept in buds the day,

And many a Nymph who wreathes her brows with sedge,
And sheds the freshening dew, and, lovelier still,
The pensive Pleasures sweet
Prepare thy shadowy car.

Then let me rove some wild and heathy scene,
Or find some ruin 'midst its dreary dells,
Whose walls more awful nod
By thy religious gleams.

Or if chill blust'ring winds, or driving rain,
Prevent my willing feet, be mine the hut,
That, from the mountain's side,
Views wilds and swelling floods,

And hamlets brown, and dim-discover'd spires,
And hears their simple bell, and marks o'er all
Thy dewy fingers draw
The gradual dusky veil.

While Spring shall pour his showers, as oft he wont,
And bathe thy breathing tresses, meekest Eve!
While Summer loves to sport
Beneath thy lingering light:

While sallow Autumn fills thy lap with leaves,
Or Winter, yellow through the troublous air,
Affrights thy shrinking train,
And rudely rends thy robes:

So long, regardful of thy quiet rule,
Shall Fancy, Friendship, Science, smiling Peace,
Thy gentlest influence own,
And love thy favourite name!

ODE TO PEACE.

O THOU! who badest thy turtles bear
Swift from his grasp thy golden hair,
And sought'st thy native skies;
When War, by vultures drawn from far,
To Britain bent his iron car,
And bade his storms arise!

Tired of his rude tyrannic sway,
Our youth shall fix some festive day,
His sullen shrines to burn:
But thou, who hear'st the turning spheres,
What sounds may charm thy partial ears,
And gain thy blest return!

O Peace! thy injured robes upbind!
O rise, and leave not one behind
Of all thy beamy train:
The British lion, goddess sweet;
Lies stretch'd on earth to kiss thy feet,
And own thy holier reign.

Let others court thy transient smile,
But come to grace thy western isle,
By warlike Honour led!
And, while around her ports rejoice,
While all her sons adore thy choice,
With him for ever wed!

THE MANNERS.

AN ODE.

Farewell, for clearer ken design'd,
The dim-discover'd tracts of mind;
Truths which, from action's paths retired,
My silent search in vain required!
No more my sail that deep explores,
No more I search those magic shores,
What regions part the world of soul,
Or whence thy streams, Opinion, roll:
If e'er I round such fairy field,
Some power impart the spear and shield,
At which the wizard Passions fly,
By which the giant Follies die!

Farewell the porch, whose roof is seen,
Arch'd with th' enlivening olive's green:
Where Science, prank'd in tissued vest,
By Reason, Pride, and Fancy drest,
Comes like a bride, so trim array'd,
To wed with Doubt in Plato's shade!

Youth of the quick uncheated sight,
Thy walks, Observance, more invite!
O thou, who lovest that ampler range,
Where life's wide prospects round thee change,
And, with her mingled sons allied,
Throw'st the prattling page aside;
To me in converse sweet impart,
To read in man the native heart,
To learn, where Science sure is found,
From Nature as she lives around:
And gazing oft her mirror true,
By turns each shifting image view!
Till medding Art's officious lore
Reverse the lessons taught before,
Alluring from a safer rule,
To dream in her enchanted school;
Thou, Heaven, whate'er of great we boast,
Hast blest this social science most.

Retiring hence to thoughtful cell,
As Fancy breathes her potent spell,
Not vain she finds the charmful task,
In pageant quaint, in motley mask;
Behold, before her musing eyes,
The countless Manners round her rise;
While ever varying as they pass,
To some Contempt applies her glass:
With these the white-robed Maids combine,
And those the laughing Satyrs join!
But who is he whom now she views,
In robe of wild contending hues?
Thou by the Passions nursed; I greet
The comic sock that binds thy feet!

O Humour, thou whose name is known
To Britain's favour'd isle alone:
Me too amidst thy band admit,
There where the young-eyed healthful Wit,
(Whose jewels in his crisped hair
Are placed each other's beams to share,
Whom no delights from thee divide)
In laughter loosed attends thy side!

By old Miletus[1], who so long
Has ceased his love-inwoven song:
By all you taught the Tuscan maids,
In changed Italia's modern shades:
By him[2], whose knight's distinguish'd name,
Refined a nation's lust of fame;
Whose tales even now, with echoes sweet,
Castilia's Moorish hills repeat:
Or him[3], whom Seine's blue nymphs deplore,
In watchet weeds on Gallia's shore;
Who drew the sad Sicilian maid,
By virtues in her sire betray'd:
O Nature boon, from whom proceed
Each forceful thought, each prompted deed;
If but from thee I hope to feel,
On all my heart imprint thy seal!
Let some retreating Cynic find
Those oft-turn'd scrolls I leave behind,
The Sports and I this hour agree,
To rove thy sceneful world with thee!

THE PASSIONS

AN ODE FOR MUSIC.

When Music, heavenly maid, was young,
While yet in early Greece she sung,
The Passions oft, to hear her shell,
Throng'd around her magic cell,
Exulting, trembling, raging, fainting,
Possess'd beyond the Muse's painting;
By turns they felt the glowing mind
Disturb'd, delighted, raised, refined.
Till once, 'tis said, when all were fired,
Fill'd with fury, rapt, inspired,
From the supporting myrtles round
They snatch'd her instruments of sound,
And, as they oft had heard apart
Sweet lessons of her forceful art,
Each, for Madness ruled the hour,
Would prove his own expressive power.

First Fear, his hand its skill to try,
Amid the chords bewilder'd laid,
And back recoil'd, he knew not why,
Even at the sound himself had made.

Next Anger rush'd, his eyes on fire,
In lightnings own'd his secret stings,
In one rude clash he struck the lyre,
And swept with hurried hand the strings.

With woful measures wan Despair—
Low sullen sounds his grief beguiled,
A sullen, strange, and mingled air,
'Twas sad by fits, by starts 'twas wild.

[1] Alluding to the Milesian Tales, some of the earliest romances. [2] Cervantes.

[3] Monsieur Le Sage, author of the incomparable Adventures of Gil Blas de Santillane, who died in Paris in the year 1745.

But thou, O Hope! with eyes so fair,
What was thy delighted measure?
Still it whisper'd promised pleasure,
And bade the lovely scenes at distance hail!
Still would her touch the strain prolong,
And from the rocks, the woods, the vale,
She call'd on Echo still through all the song;
And where her sweetest theme she chose,
A soft responsive voice was heard at every close,
And Hope enchanted smiled, and waved her golden hair.

And longer had she sung,—but, with a frown,
Revenge impatient rose,
He threw his blood-stain'd sword in thunder down,
And, with a withering look,
The war-denouncing trumpet took,
And blew a blast so loud and dread,
Were ne'er prophetic sounds so full of woe.
And ever and anon he beat
The doubling drum with furious heat;
And though sometimes, each dreary pause between,
Dejected Pity at his side,
Her soul-subduing voice applied,
Yet still he kept his wild unalter'd mien,
While each strain'd ball of sight seem'd bursting from his head.

Thy numbers, Jealousy, to nought were fix'd,
Sad proof of thy distressful state!
Of differing themes the veering song was mix'd,
And now it courted Love, now raving call'd on Hate.
With eyes upraised, as one inspired,
Pale Melancholy sat retired,
And from her wild sequester'd seat,
In notes by distance made more sweet,
Pour'd through the mellow horn her pensive soul:
And dashing soft from rocks around,
Bubbling runnels join'd the sound;
Through glades and glooms the mingled measure stole,
Or o'er some haunted streams with fond delay,
Round a holy calm diffusing,
Love of peace and lonely musing,
In hollow murmurs died away.

But O! how alter'd was its sprightlier tone!
When Cheerfulness, a nymph of healthiest hue,
Her bow across her shoulders flung,
Her buskins gemm'd with morning dew,
Blew an inspiring air that dale and thicket rung,
The hunter's call to Faun and Dryad known;
The oak-crown'd Sisters, and their chaste-eyed Queen,
Satyrs and Sylvan boys were seen,
Peeping from forth their alleys green;
Brown Exercise rejoiced to hear,
And Sport leapt up, and seized his beechen spear.

Last came Joy's ecstatic trial;
He with viny crown advancing,
First to the lively pipe his hand address'd;
But soon he saw the brisk awakening viol,
Whose sweet entrancing voice he loved the best.
They would have thought who heard the strain,
They saw in Tempe's vale her native maids,
Amidst the festal sounding shades,
To some unwearied minstrel dancing,
While, as his flying fingers kiss'd the strings,
Love framed with Mirth, a gay fantastic round,
Loose were her tresses seen, her zone unbound:
And he, amidst his frolic play,
As if he would the charming air repay,
Shook thousand odours from his dewy wings.

O Music, sphere-descended maid,
Friend of Pleasure, Wisdom's aid,
Why, goddess, why to us denied,
Lay'st thou thy ancient lyre aside?
As in that loved Athenian bower,
You learn'd an all-commanding power,
Thy mimic soul, O nymph endear'd!
Can well recall what then it heard.
Where is thy native simple heart,
Devote to virtue, fancy, art?
Arise, as in that elder time,
Warm, energetic, chaste, sublime!
Thy wonders, in that god-like age,
Fill thy recording Sister's page—
'Tis said, and I believe the tale,
Thy humblest reed could more prevail,
Had more of strength, diviner rage,
Than all which charms this laggard age,
E'en all at once together found
Cecilia's mingled world of sound—
O bid our vain endeavours cease,
Revive the just designs of Greece;
Return in all thy simple state!
Confirm the tales her sons relate!

AN EPISTLE,

ADDRESSED TO SIR THOMAS HANMER,

On his Edition of Shakspeare's Works.

While born to bring the Muse's happier days,
A patriot's hand protects a poet's lays,
While nursed by you she sees her myrtles bloom
Green and unwither'd o'er his honour'd tomb;
Excuse her doubts, if yet she fears to tell
What secret transports in her bosom swell:
With conscious awe she hears the critic's fame,
And blushing hides her wreath at Shakspeare's name.
Hard was the lot those injured strains endured,
Unown'd by science, and by years obscured:
Fair Fancy wept; and echoing sighs confess'd
A fixed despair in every tuneful breast.
Not with more grief th' afflicted swains appear,
When wintry winds deform the plenteous year:
When lingering frosts the ruin'd seats invade,
Where Peace resorted, and the Graces play'd.

Each rising art by just gradation moves,
Toil builds on toil, and age on age improves:
The Muse alone unequal dealt her rage,
And graced with noblest pomp her earliest stage.
Preserved through time, the speaking scenes impart
Each changeful wish of Phædra's tortured heart:
Or paint the curse that mark'd the [1] Theban's reign,
A bed incestuous, and a father slain.
With kind concern our pitying eyes o'erflow,
Trace the sad tale, and own another's woe.

[1] The Œdipus of Sophocles.

To Rome removed, with wit secure to please,
The comic sisters kept their native ease.
With jealous fear declining Greece beheld
Her own Menander's art almost excell'd!
But every Muse essay'd to raise in vain
Some labour'd rival of her tragic strain;
Ilissus' laurels, though transferr'd with toil,
Droop'd their fair leaves, nor knew th' unfriendly
soil.

As arts expired, resistless Dulness rose;
Goths, priests, or Vandals,—all were learning's
Till [1] Julius first recall'd each exiled maid, [foes,
And Cosmo own'd them in th' Etrurian shade:
Then deeply skill'd in love's engaging theme,
The soft Provençal pass'd to Arno's stream:
With graceful ease the wanton lyre he strung,
Sweet flow'd the lays—but love was all he sung.
The gay description could not fail to move:
For, led by nature, all are friends to love.

But Heaven, still various in its works, decreed
The perfect boast of time should last succeed.
The beauteous union must appear at length,
Of Tuscan fancy, and Athenian strength:
One greater Muse Eliza's reign adorn,
And even a Shakspeare to her fame be born!

Yet, ah! so bright her morning's opening ray,
In vain our Britain hoped an equal day!
No second growth the western isle could bear,
At once exhausted with too rich a year.
Too nicely Jonson knew the critic's part;
Nature in him was almost lost in art.
Of softer mould the gentle Fletcher came,
The next in order, as the next in name,
With pleased attention 'midst his scenes we find
Each glowing thought that warms the female mind;
Each melting sigh, and every tender tear,
The lover's wishes, and the virgin's fear.
His [2] every strain the Smiles and Graces own;
But stronger Shakspeare felt for man alone:
Drawn by his pen, our ruder passions stand
Th' unrivall'd picture of his early hand.

[3] With gradual steps, and slow, exacter France
Saw art's fair empire o'er her shores advance:
By length of toil a bright perfection knew,
Correctly bold, and just in all she drew.
Till late Corneille, with [4] Lucan's spirit fired,
Breathed the free strain, as Rome and he inspired:
And classic Judgment gain'd to sweet Racine
The temper'd strength of Maro's chaster line.

But wilder far the British laurel spread,
And wreaths less artful crown our poet's head.
Yet he alone to every scene could give
Th' historian's truth, and bid the manners live.
Waked at his call, I view with glad surprise
Majestic forms of mighty monarchs rise.
There Henry's trumpets spread their loud alarms,
And laurell'd Conquest waits her hero's arms.

Here gentler Edward claims a pitying sigh,
Scarce born to honours, and so soon to die!
Yet shall thy throne, unhappy infant! bring
No beam of comfort to the guilty king:
The [5] time shall come, when Glo'ster's heart shall
bleed,
In life's last hours, with horror of the deed:
When dreary visions shall at last present
Thy vengeful image in the midnight tent:
Thy hand unseen the secret death shall bear,
Blunt the weak sword, and break th' oppressive
spear.

Where'er we turn, by Fancy charm'd, we find
Some sweet illusion of the cheated mind.
Oft, wild of wing, she calls the soul to rove
With humbler nature in the rural grove;
Where swains contented own the quiet scene,
And twilight fairies tread the circled green:
Dress'd by her hand the woods and valleys smile,
And spring diffusive decks th' Enchanted Isle.

O more than all in powerful genius blest,
Come, take thine empire o'er the willing breast!
Whate'er the wounds this youthful heart shall feel,
Thy songs support me, and thy morals heal!
There every thought the poet's warmth may raise,
There native music dwells in all the lays.
Oh, might some verse with happiest skill persuade
Expressive Picture to adopt thine aid!
What wondrous draughts might rise from every
page!
What other Raphaels charm a distant age!

Methinks even now I view some free design,
Where breathing Nature lives in every line:
Chaste and subdued the modest lights decay,
Steal into shades, and mildly melt away.
—And see, where [6] Antony, in tears approved,
Guards the pale relics of the chief he loved:
O'er the cold corse the warrior seems to bend,
Deep sunk in grief, and mourns his murder'd
friend!
Still as they press he calls on all around;
Lifts the torn robe, and points the bleeding wound.

But [7] who is he, whose brows exalted bear
A wrath impatient, and a fiercer air?
Awake to all that injured worth can feel,
On his own Rome he turns th' avenging steel.
Yet shall not war's insatiate fury fall
(So Heaven ordains it) on the destined wall.
See the fond mother, 'midst the plaintive train,
Hung on his knees, and prostrate on the plain!
Touch'd to the soul, in vain he strives to hide
The son's affection in the Roman's pride:
O'er all the man conflicting passions rise,
Rage grasps the sword, while Pity melts the eyes

Thus, generous Critic, as thy bard inspires,
The sister Arts shall nurse their drooping fires;
Each from his scenes her stores alternate bring,
Blend the fair tints, or wake the vocal string:
Those Sibyl-leaves, the sport of every wind,
(For poets ever were a careless kind)
By thee disposed, no farther toil demand,
But, just to Nature, own thy forming hand.

---

[1] Julius II. the immediate predecessor of Leo X.

[2] Their characters are thus distinguished by Mr. Dryden.

[3] About the time of Shakspeare, the poet Hardy was in great repute in France. He wrote, according to Fontenelle, six hundred plays. The French poets after him applied themselves in general to the correct improvement of the stage, which was almost totally disregarded by those of our own country, Jonson excepted.

[4] The favourite author of the elder Corneille.

[5] "Tempus erit Turno, magno cùm optaverit emptum Intactum Pallanta," &c.

[6] See the tragedy of Julius Cæsar.

[7] Coriolanus. See Mr. Spence's dialogue on the Odyssey.

So spread o'er Greece, th' harmonious whole unknown,
Even Homer's numbers charm'd by parts alone.
Their own Ulysses scarce had wander'd more,
By winds and waters cast on every shore:
When raised by fate, some former Hanmer join'd
Each beauteous image of the boundless mind;
And bade, like thee, his Athens ever claim
A fond alliance with the Poet's name.

DIRGE IN CYMBELINE.

SUNG BY GUIDERUS AND ARVIRAGUS OVER FIDELLE, SUPPOSED TO BE DEAD.

To fair Fidelle's grassy tomb
Soft maids and village hinds shall bring
Each opening sweet, of earliest bloom,
And rifle all the breathing Spring.

No wailing ghost shall dare appear
To vex with shrieks this quiet grove,
But shepherd lads assemble here,
And melting virgins own their love.

No wither'd witch shall here be seen,
No goblins lead their nightly crew;
The female fays shall haunt the green,
And dress thy grave with pearly dew!

The red-breast oft at evening hours
Shall kindly lend his little aid,
With hoary moss, and gather'd flowers,
To deck the ground where thou art laid.

When howling winds, and beating rain,
In tempests shake the sylvan cell;
Or 'midst the chase on every plain,
The tender thought on thee shall dwell.

Each lonely scene shall thee restore,
For thee the tear be duly shed;
Beloved, till life can charm no more;
And mourn, till Pity's self be dead.

ODE ON THE DEATH OF MR. THOMSON.

THE SCENE OF THE FOLLOWING STANZAS IS SUPPOSED TO LIE ON THE THAMES, NEAR RICHMOND.

I.

In yonder grave a Druid lies,
Where slowly winds the stealing wave!
The year's best sweets shall duteous rise
To deck its poet's sylvan grave!

II.

In yon deep bed of whisp'ring reeds
His airy harp [1] shall now be laid,
That he, whose heart in sorrow bleeds,
May love through life the soothing shade.

III.

Then maids and youths shall linger here,
And, while its sounds at distance swell,
Shall sadly seem in Pity's ear
To hear the woodland pilgrim's knell.

IV.

Remembrance oft shall haunt the shore
When Thames in summer wreaths is drest,
And oft suspend the dashing oar
To bid his gentle spirit rest!

V.

And oft as Ease and Health retire
To breezy lawn, or forest deep,
The friend shall view yon whitening [2] spire,
And 'mid the varied landscape weep.

VI.

But thou, who own'st that earthy bed,
Ah! what will every dirge avail?
Or tears which Love and pity shed,
That mourn beneath the gliding sail!

VII.

Yet lives there one, whose heedless eye
Shall scorn thy pale shrine glimm'ring near;
With him, sweet bard, may Fancy die,
And joy desert the blooming year.

VIII.

But thou, lorn stream, whose sullen tide
No sedge-crown'd sisters now attend,
Now waft me from the green hill's side
Whose cold turf hides the buried friend!

IX.

And see, the fairy valleys fade,
Dun Night has veil'd the solemn view!
Yet once again, dear parted shade,
Meek Nature's child, again adieu!

X.

[3] The genial meads, assign'd to bless
Thy life, shall mourn thy earl doom!
There hinds and shepherd girls shall dress
With simple hands thy rural tomb.

XI.

Long, long, thy stone and pointed clay
Shall melt the musing Briton's eyes:
O vales, and wild woods! shall he say,
In yonder grave your Druid lies!

VERSES

WRITTEN ON A PAPER WHICH CONTAINED A PIECE OF BRIDE-CAKE.

Ye curious hands, that hid from vulgar eyes,
By search profane shall find this hallow'd cake,
With virtue's awe forbear the sacred prize,
Nor dare a theft, for love and pity's sake!

This precious relic, form'd by magic power,
Beneath the shepherd's haunted pillow laid,
Was meant by love to charm the silent hour,
The secret present of a matchless maid.

The Cyprian queen, at Hymen's fond request,
Each nice ingredient chose with happiest art;
Fears, sighs, and wishes of th' enamour'd breast,
And pains that please, are mix'd in every part.

[1] The harp of Æolus, of which see a description in the Castle of Indolence.

[2] Richmond church.

[3] Mr. Thomson resided in the neighbourhood of Richmond some time before his death.

With rosy hand the spicy fruit she brought,
  From Paphian hills, and fair Cytherea's isle ;
And temper'd sweet with these the melting thought,
  The kiss ambrosial, and the yielding smile.

Ambiguous looks, that scorn and yet relent,
  Denials mild, and firm unalter'd truth ;
Reluctant pride, and amorous faint consent,
  And meeting ardours, and exulting youth.

Sleep, wayward god ! hath sworn, while these remain,
  With flattering dreams to dry his nightly tear,
And cheerful Hope, so oft invoked in vain,
  With fairy songs shall soothe his pensive ear.

If, bound by vows to Friendship's gentle side,
  And fond of soul, thou hopest an equal grace,
If youth or maid thy joys and griefs divide,
  O, much entreated, leave this fatal place !

Sweet Peace, who long hath shunn'd my plaintive day
  Consents at length to bring me short delight ;
Thy careless steps may scare her doves away,
  And Grief with raven note usurp the night.

AN ODE.

ON THE POPULAR SUPERSTITIONS OF THE HIGHLANDS OF SCOTLAND.

I.

Home! thou return'st from Thames, whose Naiads long
  Have seen thee ling'ring with a fond delay,
  'Mid those soft friends, whose hearts some future
Shall melt, perhaps, to hear thy tragic song. [day
Go, not unmindful of that cordial youth,[2]
  Whom, long endear'd, thou leavest by Lavant's
Together let us wish him lasting truth, [side ;
  And joy untainted with his destined bride.
Go ! nor regardless, while these numbers boast
  My short-lived bliss, forget my social name ;
But think, far off, how, on the southern coast,
  I met thy friendship with an equal flame !
Fresh to that soil thou turn'st, where ev'ry vale
  Shall prompt the poet, and his song demand:
To thee thy copious subjects ne'er shall fail ;
  Thou need'st but take thy pencil to thy hand,
  And paint what all believe, who own thy genial land.

II.

There must thou wake perforce thy Doric quill ;
  'Tis Fancy's land to which thou sett'st thy feet ;
  Where still, 'tis said, the fairy people meet,
Beneath each birken shade, on mead or hill.
There each trim lass, that skims the milky store,
  To the swart tribes their creamy bowls allots ;
By night they sip it round the cottage-door,
  While airy minstrels warble jocund notes.
There, every herd, by sad experience, knows
  How, wing'd with fate, their elf-shot arrows fly,
When the sick ewe her summer food foregoes,
  Or, stretch'd on earth, the heart-smit heifers lie.
Such airy beings awe the untutor'd swain :
  Nor thou, though learn'd, his homelier thoughts neglect ;
Let thy sweet Muse the rural faith sustain ;
  These are the themes of simple, sure effect,
That add new conquests to her boundless reign,
And fill, with double force, her heart-commanding strain.

III.

Even yet preserved, how often may'st thou hear,
  Where to the pole the Boreal mountains run,
  Taught by the father to his list'ning son,
Strange lays, whose power had charm'd a Spenser's ear.
At ev'ry pause, before thy mind possest,
  Old Runic bards shall seem to rise around,
With uncouth lyres, in many-colour'd vest,
  Their matted hair with boughs fantastic crown'd:
Whether thou bid'st the well-taught hind repeat
  The choral dirge that mourns some chieftain brave,
When ev'ry shrieking maid her bosom beat,
  And strew'd with choicest herbs his scented grave ;
Or whether, sitting in the shepherd's shiel,[3]
  Thou hear'st some sounding tale of war's alarms;
When at the bugle's call, with fire and steel,
  The sturdy clans pour'd forth their brawny swarms,
  And hostile brothers met to prove each other's arms.

IV

'Tis thine to sing, how, framing hideous spells,
  In Skye's lone isle, the gifted wizard-seer,
  Lodged in the wintry cave, with Fate's fell spear,
Or in the depth of Uist's dark forest dwells :
  How they, whose sight such dreary dreams engross,
With their own vision oft astonish'd droop,
  When, o'er the wat'ry strath or quaggy moss,
They see the gliding ghosts unbodied troop.
  Or, if in sports, or on the festive green,
Their destined glance some fated youth descry,
  Who now, perhaps, in lusty vigour seen,
And rosy health, shall soon lamented die.
  For them the viewless forms of air obey,
Their bidding heed, and at their beck repair.
  They know what spirit brews the stormful day,
And heartless, oft like moody madness, stare
To see the phantom train their secret work prepare.

V.

Or on some bellying rock that shades the deep,
  They view the lurid signs that cross the sky,
  Where, in the west, the brooding tempests lie .
And hear their first, faint, rustling pennons sweep.
Or in the arched cave, where deep and dark
  The broad, unbroken billows heave and swell,

[1] Addressed to the Rev. John Home, author of the tragedy of "Douglas," &c.—Ed.

[2] A gentleman of the name of Barrow, who introduced Home to Collins.

[3] A summer hut, built in the high part of the mountains, to tend their flocks in the warm season, when the pasture is fine.

In horrid musings rapt, they sit to mark
The lab'ring moon; or list the nightly yell
Of that dread spirit, whose gigantic form
The seer's entranced eye can well survey,
Through the dim air who guides the driving storm,
And points the wretched bark, its destined prey.
Or him who hovers on his flagging wing
O'er the dire whirlpool, that, in ocean's waste,
Draws instant down whate'er devoted thing
The failing breeze within its reach hath placed—
The distant seaman hears. and flies with trembling haste.

VI.

Or, if on land the fiend exerts his sway,
Silent he broods o'er quicksand, bog or fen,
Far from the shelt'ring roof and haunts of men,
When witched darkness shuts the eye of day,
And shrouds each star that wont to cheer the night;
Or if the drifted snow perplex the way,
With treach'rous gleam he lures the fated wight,
And leads him flound'ring on and quite astray.

VII.

To monarchs dear, some hundred miles astray,
Oft have they seen Fate give the fatal blow!
The seer, in Skye, shriek'd as the blood did flow,
When headless Charles warm on the scaffold lay!
As Boreas threw his young Aurora forth,
In the first year of the first George's reign,
And battles raged in welkin of the North,
They mourn'd in air, fell, fell rebellion slain!
And as, of late, they joy'd in Preston's fight,
Saw, at sad Falkirk, all their hopes near crown'd!
They raved! divining, through their second sight,
Pale, red Culloden, where these hopes were drown'd!
Illustrious William! Britain's guardian name!
One William saved us from a tyrant's stroke;
He, for a sceptre, gain'd heroic fame,
But thou, more glorious, Slavery's chain hast broke,
To reign a private man, and bow to Freedom's yoke!

VIII.

These, too, thou'lt sing! for well thy magic muse
Can to the topmost heaven of grandeur soar;
Or stoop to wail the swain that is no more!
Ah homely swains! your homeward steps ne'er lose;
Let not dank "Will" mislead you to the heath;
Dancing in mirky night, o'er fen and lake,
He glows, to draw you downward to your death,
In his bewitch'd, low, marshy, willow brake;
What though far off, from some dark dell espied,
His glimmering mazes cheer th' excursive sight,
Yet turn, ye wanderers, turn your steps aside,
Nor trust the guidance of that faithless light;
For watchful, lurking, mid th' unrustling reed,
At those mirk hours the wily monster lies,
And listens oft to hear the passing steed,
And frequent round him rolls his sullen eyes,
If chance his savage wrath may some weak wretch surprise.

IX.

Ah, luckless swain! o'er all unblest, indeed!
Whom late bewilder'd in the dank, dark fen,
Far from his flocks, and smoking hamlet, then!
To that sad spot where hums the sedgy weed:
On him, enraged, the fiend, in angry mood,
Shall never look with pity's kind concern,
But instant, furious, raise the whelming flood
O'er its drown'd banks, forbidding all return!
Or if he meditate his wish'd escape,
To some dim hill that seems uprising near,
To his faint eye, the grim and grisly shape,
In all its terrors clad, shall wild appear.
Mean time the wat'ry surge shall round him rise,
Pour'd sudden forth from ev'ry swelling source!
What now remains but tears and hopeless sighs?
His fear-shook limbs have lost their youthly force,
And down the waves he floats, a pale and breathless corse!

X.

For him in vain his anxious wife shall wait,
Or wander forth to meet him on his way;
For him in vain at to-fall of the day,
His babes shall linger at th' unclosing gate!
Ah, ne'er shall he return! Alone if night,
Her travell'd limbs in broken slumbers steep!
With drooping willows drest, his mournful sprite
Shall visit sad, perchance, her silent sleep:
Then he, perhaps, with moist and wat'ry hand
Shall fondly seem to press her shudd'ring cheek,
And with his blue swoln face before her stand,
And shiv'ring cold, these piteous accents speak:
"Pursue, dear wife! thy daily toils pursue,
At dawn or dusk, industrious as before;
Nor e'er of me one helpless thought renew,
While I lie welt'ring on the osier'd shore,
Drown'd by the Kelpie's [1] wrath, nor e'er shall aid thee more!"

XI.

Unbounded is thy range; with varied skill
Thy Muse may, like those feath'ry tribes which spring
From their rude rocks, extend her skirting wing
Round the moist marge of each cold Hebrid isle,
To that hoar pile [2] which still its ruin shows:
In whose small vaults a pigmy-folk is found,
Whose bones the delver with his spade upthrows
And culls them, wond'ring, from the hallow'd ground!
Or thither [3], where beneath the show'ry west,
The mighty kings of three fair realms are laid:
Once foes, perhaps, together now they rest;
No slaves revere them, and no wars invade:
Yet frequent now, at midnight solemn hour,
The rifted mounds their yawning cells unfold,
And forth the monarchs stalk with sov'reign pow'r,
In pageant robes, and wreath'd with sheeny gold,
And on their twilight tombs aërial council hold.

---

[1] The water-fiend.

[2] One of the Hebrides is called "The Isle of Pigmies," where it is reported that several miniature bones of the human species have been dug up in the ruins of the chapel there.

[3] Icolmkill, one of the Hebrides, where near sixty of the ancient Scottish, Irish, and Norwegian kings are interred.

XII.

But, oh! o'er all, forget not Kilda's race,
On whose bleak rocks, which brave the wasting tides,
Fair Nature's daughter, Virtue, yet abides.
Go! just as they, their blameless manners trace!
Then to my ear transmit some gentle song,
Of those whose lives are yet sincere and plain,
Their bounded walks the rugged cliffs along,
And all their prospect but the wintry main.
With sparing temp'rance at the needful time,
They drain the scented spring; or, hunger-prest,
Along th' Atlantic rock, undreading, climb,
And of its eggs despoil the Solan's[1] nest.
Thus, blest in primal innocence they live,
Sufficed, and happy with that frugal fare
Which tasteful toil and hourly danger give.
Hard is their shallow soil, and bleak and bare;
Nor ever vernal bee was heard to murmur there!

XIII.

Nor need'st thou blush that such false themes engage
Thy gentle mind, of fairer stores possest;
For not alone they touch the village breast,
But fill'd in elder time th' historic page.
There Shakspeare's self, with every garland crown'd,
Flew to those fairy climes his fancy sheen,
In musing hour; his wayward sisters found,
And with their terrors drest the magic scene.
From them he sung, when, 'mid his bold design,
Before the Scot, afflicted and aghast!
The shadowy kings of Banquo's fated line,
Through the dark cave in gleamy pageant pass'd.
Proceed! nor quit the tales which, simply told,
Could once so well my answ'ring bosom pierce;
Proceed, in forceful sounds, and colour bold,
The native legends of thy land rehearse:
To such adapt thy lyre, and suit thy powerful verse.

[1] An aquatic bird, on the eggs of which the inhabitants of St. Kilda, another of the Hebrides, chiefly subsist.

XIV.

In scenes like these, which, daring to depart
From sober truth, are still to Nature true,
And call forth fresh delight to Fancy's view,
Th' heroic Muse employ'd her Tasso's art!
How have I trembled, when, at Tancred's stroke,
Its gushing blood the gaping cypress pour'd!
When each live plant with mortal accents spoke,
And the wild blast upheaved the vanish'd sword!
How have I sat, when piped the pensive wind,
To hear his harp by British Fairfax strung!
Prevailing poet! whose undoubting mind
Believed the magic wonders which he sung!
Hence, at each sound, imagination glows!
Hence, at each picture, vivid life starts here!
Hence his warm lay with softest sweetness flows;
Melting, it flows, pure, murm'ring, strong and clear,
And fills th' impassion'd heart, and wins th' harmonious ear!

XV.

All hail! ye scenes, that o'er my soul prevail!
Ye splendid friths and lakes, which, far away,
Are by smooth Annan[2] fill'd, or past'ral Tay[3]
Or Don's[4] romantic springs, at distance, hail!
The time shall come, when I, perhaps, may tread
Your lowly glens, o'erhung with spreading broom,
Or o'er your stretching heaths, by Fancy led;
Or o'er your mountains creep in awful gloom!
Then will I dress once more the faded bower,
Where Jonson[5] sate in Drummond's classic shade:
Or crop, from Tiviotdale, each lyric flower,
And mourn, on Yarrow's banks, where Willy's laid!
Meantime, ye pow'rs that on the plains which bore
The cordial youth, on Lothian's plains, attend!—
Where'er Home dwells, on hill, or lowly moor,
To him I lose your kind protection lend,
And, touch'd with love like mine, preserve my absent friend!

[2] [3] [4] Three rivers in Scotland.

[5] Ben Jonson paid a visit on foot, in 1619, to the Scot poet Drummond, at his seat of Hawthornden, within fo miles of Edinburgh.

THE

POETICAL WORKS

OF

JAMES THOMSON.

CONTENTS.

BIOGRAPHICAL NOTICE

OF

JAMES THOMSON.

BY SAMUEL JOHNSON, LL.D.

James Thomson, the son of a minister well esteemed for his piety and diligence, was born September 7, 1700, at Ednam, in the shire of Roxburgh, of which his father was pastor. His mother, whose name was Hume,* inherited, as co-heiress, a portion of a small estate. The revenue of a parish in Scotland is seldom large; and it was probably in commiseration of the difficulty with which Mr Thomson supported his family, having nine children, that Mr Riccarton, a neighbouring minister, discovering in James uncommon promises of future excellence, undertook to superintend his education and provide him books.

He was taught the common rudiments of learning at the school of Jedburg, a place which he delights to recollect in his poem of *Autumn;* but was not considered by his master as superior to common boys, though in those early days he amused his patron and his friends with poetical compositions; with which, however, he so little pleased himself, that on every new-year's day he threw into the fire all the productions of the foregoing year.

From the school he was removed to Edinburgh, where he had not resided two years when his father died, and left all his children to the care of their mother, who raised upon her little estate what money a mortgage could afford, and removing with her family to Edinburgh, lived to see her son rising into eminence.

The design of Thomson's friends was to breed him a minister. He lived at Edinburgh, as at school, without distinction or expectation, till at the usual time he performed a probationary exercise by explaining a psalm. His diction was so poetically splendid, that Mr Hamilton, the professor of divinity, reproved him for

* His mother's name was Beatrix Trotter. His grandmother's name was Hume.

speaking language unintelligible to a popular audience; and he censured one of his expressions as indecent, if not profane.

This rebuke is reported to have repressed his thoughts of an ecclesiastical character, and he probably cultivated with new diligence his blossoms of poetry, which, however, were in some danger of a blast; for, submitting his productions to some who thought themselves qualified to criticise, he heard of nothing but faults; but finding other 'udges more favourable, he did not suffer himself to sink into despondence.

He easily discovered that the only stage on which a poet could appear with any hope of advantage was London; a place too wide for the operation of petty competition and private malignity, where merit might soon become conspicuous, and would find friends as soon as it became reputable to befriend it. A lady who was acquainted with his mother advised him to the journey, and promised some countenance or assistance, which at last he never received; however, he justified his adventure by her encouragement, and came to seek in London patronage and fame.

At his arrival he found his way to Mr Mallet, then tutor to the sons of the Duke of Montrose. He had recommendations to several persons of consequence, which he had tied up carefully in his handkerchief; but as he passed along the street, with the gaping curiosity of a new-comer, his attention was upon every thing rather than his pocket, and his magazine of credentials was stolen from him.

His first want was a pair of shoes. For the supply of all his necessities, his whole fund was his *Winter*, which for a time could find no purchaser, till at last Mr Millar was persuaded to buy it at a low price, and this low price he had for some time reason to regret; but by accident Mr Whatley, a man not wholly unknown among authors, happening to turn his eye upon it, was so delighted that he ran from place to place celebrating its excellence. Thomson obtained likewise the notice of Aaron Hill, whom, being friendless and indigent, and glad of kindness, he courted with every expression of servile adulation.

Winter was dedicated to Sir Spencer Compton, but attracted no regard from him to the author, till Aaron Hill awakened his attention by some verses addressed to Thomson, and published in one of the newspapers, which censured the great for their neglect of ingenious men. Thomson then received a present of twenty guineas, of which he gives this account to Mr Hill:

'I hinted to you in my last, that on Saturday morning I was with Sir Spencer Compton. A certain gentleman, without my desire, spoke to him concerning me; his answer was, that I had never come near him. Then the gentleman put the question, if he desired that I should wait on him? He returned, he did. On this, the gentleman gave me an introductory letter to him. He received me in what they commonly call a civil manner, asked me some commonplace questions, and made me a present of twenty guineas. I am very ready to own that the present was larger than my performance deserved, and shall ascribe it to his generosity, or any other cause, rather than the merit of the address.'

The poem, which being of a new kind, few would venture at first to like, by degrees gained upon the public; and one edition was very speedily succeeded by another.

Thomson's credit was now high, and every day brought him new friends; among others, Dr Rundle, a man afterwards unfortunately famous, sought his acquaintance, and found his qualities such, that he recommended him to the Lord Chancellor Talbot.

Winter was accompanied in many editions not only with a preface and dedication, but with poetical praises by Mr Hill, Mr Mallet (then Malloch), and Mira, the fictitious name of a lady once too well known. Why the dedications are, to *Winter* and the other seasons, contrarily to custom, left out in the collected works, the reader may inquire.

The next year (1727) he distinguished himself by three publications: of *Summer*, in pursuance of his plan; of *A Poem on the Death of Sir Isaac Newton*, which he was enabled to perform as an exact philosopher by the instruction of Mr Gray; and of *Britannia*, a kind of poetical invective against the ministry, whom the nation then thought not forward enough in resenting the depredations of the Spaniards. By this piece he declared himself an adherent to the opposition, and had therefore no favour to expect from the court.

Thomson, having been some time entertained in the family of the Lord Binning, was desirous of testifying his gratitude by making him the patron of his *Summer*; but the same kindness which had first disposed Lord Binning to encourage him, determined him to refuse the dedication, which was by his advice addressed to Mr Dodington, a man who had more power to advance the reputation and fortune of a poet.

Spring was published next year, with a dedication to the Countess of Hertford; whose practice it was to invite every summer some poet into the country, to hear her verses and assist her studies. This honour was one summer conferred on Thomson, who took more delight in carousing with Lord Hertford and his friends than assisting her ladyship's poetical operations, and therefore never received another summons.

Autumn, the season to which the *Spring* and *Summer* are preparatory, still remained unsung, and was delayed till he published (1730) his works collected.

He produced in 1727 the tragedy of *Sophonisba*, which raised such expectation, that every rehearsal was dignified with a splendid audience, collected to anticipate the delight that was preparing for the public. It was observed, however, that nobody was much affected, and that the company rose as from a moral lecture.

It had upon the stage no unusual degree of success. Slight accidents will operate upon the taste of pleasure. There is a feeble line in the play:

'O Sophonisba, Sophonisba, O!'

This gave occasion to a waggish parody:

'O Jemmy Thomson, Jemmy Thomson, O!'

which for a while was echoed through the town.

I have been told by Savage, that of the prologue to *Sophonisba* the first part was written by Pope, who could not be persuaded to finish it; and that the concluding lines were added by Mallet.

Thomson was, not long afterwards, by the influence of Dr Rundle, sent to travel with Mr Charles Talbot, the eldest son of the chancellor. He was yet young enough to receive new impressions, to have his opinions rectified, and his views enlarged; nor can he be supposed to have wanted that curiosity which is inseparable from an active and comprehensive mind. He may therefore now be supposed to have revelled in all the joys of intellectual luxury; he was every day feasted with instructive novelties; he lived splendidly without expense; and might expect when he returned home a certain establishment.

At this time a long course of opposition to Sir Robert Walpole had filled the nation with clamours for liberty, of which no man felt the want, and with care for liberty, which was not in danger. Thomson, in his travels on the continent, found or fancied so many evils arising from the tyranny of other governments, that he resolved to write a very long poem, in five parts, upon liberty.

While he was busy on the first book, Mr Talbot died; and Thomson, who had been rewarded for his attendance by the place of secretary of the briefs, pays in the initial lines a decent tribute to his memory.

Upon this great poem two years were spent, and the author congratulated himself upon it, as his noblest work; but an author and his reader are not always of a mind. Liberty called in vain upon her votaries to read her praises and reward her encomiast: her praises were condemned to harbour spiders and to gather dust: none of Thomson's performances were so little regarded.

The judgment of the public was not erroneous: the recurrence of the same images must tire in time; an enumeration of examples to prove a position which nobody denied, as it was from the beginning superfluous, must quickly grow disgusting.

The poem of *Liberty* does not now appear in its original state; but, when the author's works were collected after his death, was shortened by Sir George Lyttelton, with a liberty which, as it has a manifest tendency to lessen the confidence of society, and to confound the characters of authors, by making one man write by the judgment of another, cannot be justified by any supposed propriety of the alteration, or kindness of the friend—I wish to see it exhibited as its author left it.*

* 'A poem to the memory of Mr Congreve, inscribed to her Grace Henrietta Duchess of Marlborough, London, printed for J. Millar, and sold at his shop near the Horse Guards: 1729, price six-

Thomson now lived in ease and plenty, and seems for a while to have suspended his poetry; but he was soon called back to labour by the death of the chancellor, for his place then became vacant; and though the Lord Hardwick delayed for some time to give it away, Thomson's bashfulness or pride, or some other motive perhaps not more laudable, withheld him from soliciting; and the new chancellor would not give him what he would not ask.

He now relapsed to his former indigence; but the Prince of Wales was at that time struggling for popularity, and by the influence of Mr Lyttelton, professed himself the patron of wit: to him Thomson was introduced, and being gaily interrogated about the state of his affairs, said, 'that they were in a more poetical posture than formerly;' and had a pension allowed him of one hundred pounds a-year.

Being now obliged to write, he produced (1738)* the tragedy of *Agamemnon*, which was much shortened in the representation. It had the fate which most commonly attends mythological stories, and was only endured, but not favoured. It struggled with such difficulty through the first night, that Thomson, coming late to his friends with whom he was to sup, excused his delay by telling them how the sweat of his distress had so disordered his wig that he could not come till he had been refitted by a barber.

He so interested himself in his own drama, that, if I remember right, as he sat in the upper gallery, he accompanied the players by audible recitation, till a friendly hint frighted him to silence. Pope countenanced *Agamemnon* by coming to it the first night, and was welcomed to the theatre by a general clap: he had much regard for Thomson, and once expressed it in a poetical epistle sent to Italy; of which, however, he abated the value by translating some of the lines into his epistle to Arbuthnot.†

About this time the act was passed for licensing plays, of which the first operation was the prohibition of *Gustavus Vasa*, a tragedy of Mr Brooke, whom the public recompensed by a very liberal subscription; the next was the refusal of *Edward and Eleonora*, offered by Thomson. It is hard to discover why either play should have

pence;' and a poetical address 'To Love,' both by Thomson, and neither included in any existing edition of his works, have been printed by the Percy Society, under the zealous care of Mr Peter Cunningham.

* It is not generally known that in this year an edition of Milton's *Areopagitica* was published by Millar, to which Thomson wrote a preface.

† A part of the prologue to this play, the lines marked in the printed copies by inverted commas, was prohibited to be spoken by the licenser. The 'words of fear' were these:

'As such our fair attempt, we hope to see
Our judges, here at least, from influence free;
One place unbiass'd yet by party rage,
Where only honour votes—the British stage.
We ask for justice, for indulgence sue:
Our best, last license must proceed from you.'

been obstructed. Thomson likewise endeavoured to repair his loss by a subscription, of which I cannot now tell the success.

When the public murmured at the unkind treatment of Thomson, one of the ministerial writers remarked, that 'he had taken a *liberty* which was not agreeable to *Britannia* in any *season.*'

He was soon after employed, in conjunction with Mr Mallet, to write the mask of *Alfred*, which was acted before the prince at Cliefden House.

His next work (1745) was *Tancred and Sigismunda*, the most successful of all his tragedies, for it still keeps its turn upon the stage. It may be doubted whether he was, either by the bent of nature or habits of study, much qualified for tragedy. It does not appear that he had much sense of the pathetic; and his diffusive and descriptive style produced declamation rather than dialogue.

His friend Mr Lyttelton was now in power, and conferred upon him the office of surveyor-general of the Leeward Islands; from which, when his deputy was paid, he received about three hundred pounds a year.

The last piece that he lived to publish was the *Castle of Indolence*, which was many years under his hand, but was at last finished with great accuracy. The first canto opens a scene of lazy luxury that fills the imagination.

He was now at ease, but was not long to enjoy it; for, by taking cold on the water between London and Kew, he caught a disorder which, with some careless exasperation, ended in a fever that put an end to his life, August 27, 1748. He was buried in the church of Richmond, without an inscription; but a monument has been erected to his memory in Westminster Abbey.

Thomson was of a stature above the middle size, and 'more fat than bard beseems,' of a dull countenance, and a gross, unanimated, uninviting appearance; silent in mingled company, but cheerful among select friends, and by his friends very tenderly and warmly beloved.

He left behind him the tragedy of *Coriolanus*, which was, by the zeal of his patron, Sir George Lyttelton, brought upon the stage for the benefit of his family, and recommended by a prologue, which Quin, who had long lived with Thomson in fond intimacy, spoke in such a manner as showed him 'to be,' on that occasion, 'no actor.' The commencement of this benevolence is very honourable to Quin, who is reported to have delivered Thomson, then known to him only for his genius, from an arrest by a very considerable present; and its continuance is honourable to both; for friendship is not always the sequel of obligation.* By this tragedy a considerable sum was

* Quin, learning that Thomson was in great distress, visited him, and told him he was in his debt. Thomson, who did not suppose that any man could owe him a single farthing, answered, with the jealousy of misfortune, somewhat peevishly; and he thought the assertion was meant to deride him. Quin answered, 'Sir, I am one of the many who are in your debt for the pleasure

raised, of which part discharged his debts, and the rest was remitted to his sisters, whom, however removed from them by place or condition, he regarded with great tenderness.

The benevolence of Thomson was fervid,* but not active: he would give on all occasions what assistance his purse would supply; but the offices of intervention or solicitation he could not conquer his sluggishness sufficiently to perform. The affairs of others, however, were not more neglected than his own. He had often felt the inconveniences of idleness, but he never cured it; and was so conscious of his own character, that he talked of writing an Eastern tale 'of the man who loved to be in distress.'

Among his peculiarities was a very unskilful and inarticulate manner of pronouncing any lofty or solemn composition. He was once reading to Dodington, who, being himself a reader eminently elegant, was so much provoked by his odd utterance, that he snatched the paper from his hands, and told him that he did not understand his own verses.

The biographer of Thomson has remarked, that an author's life is best read in his works: his observation was not well-timed. Savage, who lived much with Thomson,† once told me, he heard a lady remarking that she could gather from his works three parts of his character; that he was 'a great lover, a great swimmer, and rigorously abstinent:' but, said Savage, he knows not any love but that of the sex; he was, perhaps, never in cold water in his life; and he indulges himself in all the luxury that comes within his reach. Yet Savage always spoke with the most eager praise of his social qualities, his warmth and constancy of friendship, and his adherence to his first acquaintance when the advancement of his reputation had left them behind him.

As a writer, he is entitled to one praise of the highest kind: his mode of thinking and of expressing his thoughts is original. His blank verse is no more the blank verse of Milton, or of any other poet, than the rhymes of Prior are the rhymes of Cowley. His numbers, his pauses, his diction, are of his own growth, without transcription, without imitation. He thinks in a peculiar train, and he thinks always as a man of genius; he looks round on nature and on life with the eye which Nature bestows only on a poet: the eye that distinguishes, in every thing presented to its view, whatever there is on which imagination can delight to be detained, and with a mind that at once comprehends the vast and attends to the minute.

which your poem of the *Seasons* has afforded us, and you will give me leave to discharge my portion of it now that there is fit opportunity;' and so saying, presented him with a note for £100.

* 'He had the most benevolent heart that ever warmed the human breast.'—SMOLLETT, *History of England*, xiii. 433.

† 'Several references to the two poets,' writes Mr Peter Cunningham, 'occur in a curious little volume of letters, quite overlooked by Sir Harris Nicolas, and equally so by Mr Corney, entitled "A Collection of Letters never before printed, written by Alexander Pope, Esq., and other ingenious gentlemen, to the late Aaron Hill, Esq. 1751." 12mo, pp. 88. Among these letters are fourteen from Thomson to Hill.'

The reader of *The Seasons* wonders that he never saw before what Thomson shows him, and that he never yet has felt what Thomson impresses.

His is one of the works in which blank verse seems properly used. Thomson's wide expansion of general views, and his enumeration of circumstantial varieties, would have been obstructed and embarrassed by the frequent intersections of the sense, which are the necessary effects of rhyme.

His descriptions of extended scenes and general effects bring before us the whole magnificence of nature, whether pleasing or dreadful. The gaiety of spring, the splendour of summer, the tranquillity of autumn, and the horror of winter, take in their turns possession of the mind. The poet leads us through the appearances of things as they are successively varied by the vicissitudes of the year, and imparts to us so much of his own enthusiasm, that our thoughts expand with his imagery, and kindle with his sentiments. Nor is the naturalist without his part in the entertainment; for he is assisted to recollect and to combine, to range his discoveries, and to amplify the sphere of his contemplation.

The great defect of *The Seasons* is want of method; but for this I know not that there was any remedy. Of many appearances subsisting all at once, no rule can be given why one should be mentioned before another; yet the memory wants the help of order, and the curiosity is not excited by suspense or expectation.

His diction is in the highest degree florid and luxuriant, such as may be said to be to his images and thoughts 'both their lustre and their shade;' such as invest them with splendour, through which, perhaps, they are not always easily discerned. It is too exuberant, and sometimes may be charged with filling the ear more than the mind.

These poems, with which I was acquainted at their first appearance, I have since found altered and enlarged by subsequent revisals, as the author supposed his judgment to grow more exact, and as books or conversation extended his knowledge and opened his prospects. They are, I think, improved in general; yet I know not whether they have not lost part of what Temple calls their 'race;' a word which, applied to wines in its primitive sense, means the flavour of the soil.

Liberty, when it first appeared, I tried to read, and soon desisted. I have never tried again, and therefore will not hazard either praise or censure.

The highest praise which he has received ought not to be suppressed. It is said by Lord Lyttelton, in the prologue to his posthumous play, that his works contained

'No line which, dying, he could wish to blot.'

SPRING.

Et nunc omnis ager, nunc omnis parturit arbos,
Nunc frondent silvæ, nunc formosissimus annus.—VIRG.

TO

THE RIGHT HONOURABLE THE COUNTESS OF HERTFORD.

MADAM,

I have always observed that, in addresses of this nature, the general taste of the world demands ingenious turns of wit, and disguised artful periods, instead of an open sincerity of sentiment flowing in a plain expression. From what secret impatience of the justest praise, when bestowed on others, this often proceeds, rather than a pretended delicacy, is beyond my purpose here to inquire; but, as nothing is more foreign to the disposition of a soul sincerely pleased with the contemplation of what is beautiful and excellent, than wit and turn, I have too much respect for your Ladyship's character, either to touch it in that gay trifling manner, or venture on a particular detail of those truly amiable qualities of which it is composed. A mind exalted, pure, and elegant—a heart overflowing with humanity, and the whole train of virtues thence derived, that give a pleasing spirit to conversation—an engaging simplicity to the manners, and form the life to harmony—are rather to be felt and silently admired than expressed. I have attempted, in the following poem, to paint some of the most tender beauties and delicate appearances of Nature, how much in vain your Ladyship's taste will, I am afraid, but too soon discover; yet would it still be a much easier task to find expression for all that variety of colour, form, and fragrance which enrich the Season I describe, than to speak the many nameless graces and native riches of a mind capable so much at once to relish solitude and adorn society. To whom then could these sheets be more properly inscribed than to you, MADAM, whose influence in the world can give them the protection they want, while your fine imagination and intimate acquaintance with *Rural Nature* will recommend them with the greatest advantage to your favourable notice? Happy, if I have hit any of those images and correspondent sentiments, your calm evening walks in the most delightful retirement have oft inspired. I could add too, that as this poem grew up under your encouragement, it has therefore a natural claim to your patronage. Should you read it with approbation, its music shall not droop; and should it have the good fortune to deserve your smiles, its roses shall not wither. But, where the subject is so tempting, lest I begin my poem before the dedication is ended, I here break short and beg leave to subscribe myself with the highest respect, MADAM,

Your most obedient, humble servant,
JAMES THOMSON.

ARGUMENT.

The subject proposed. Inscribed to the Countess of Hertford. The season is described as it affects the various parts of nature, ascending from the lower to the higher; with digressions arising from the subject. Its influence on inanimate matter, on vegetables, on brute animals, and lastly on man; concluding with a dissuasive from the wild and irregular passion of love, opposed to that of a pure and happy kind.

COME gentle Spring, etherial mildness, come,
And from the bosom of yon dropping cloud,
While music wakes around, veil'd in a shower
Of shadowing roses, on our plains descend.
O Hertford! fitted or to shine in courts
With unaffected grace, or walk the plain
With innocence and meditation join'd
In soft assemblage, listen to my song,
Which thy own season paints, when Nature all
Is blooming and benevolent, like thee.
And see where surly Winter passes off,
Far to the north, and calls his ruffian blasts:
His blasts obey, and quit the howling hill,
The shatter'd forest and the ravaged vale,
While softer gales succeed, at whose kind touch,
Dissolving snows in livid torrents lost,
The mountains lift their green heads to the sky.
As yet the trembling year is unconfirm'd,

And Winter oft at eve resumes the breeze,
Chills the pale morn, and bids his driving sleets
Deform the day delightless : so that scarce
The bittern knows his time, with bill ingulf'd
To shake the sounding marsh ; or from the shore
The plover, when to scatter o'er the heath,
And sing their wild notes to the listening waste.
At last from Aries rolls the bounteous sun,
And the bright Bull receives him. Then no more
The expansive atmosphere is cramp'd with cold ;
But, full of life and vivifying soul, [thin,
Lifts the light clouds sublime, and spreads them
Fleecy, and white, o'er all-surrounding heaven.
Forth fly the tepid airs ; and unconfined,
Unbinding earth, the moving softness strays.
Joyous, the impatient husbandman perceives
Relenting Nature, and his lusty steers [plough
Drives from their stalls, to where the well-used
Lies in the furrow, loosen'd from the frost.
There, unrefusing, to the harness'd yoke
They lend their shoulder, and begin their toil,
Cheer'd by the simple song and soaring lark,
Meanwhile incumbent o'er the shining share
The master leans, removes the obstructing clay,
Winds the whole work, and sidelong lays the glebe.
While through the neighbouring fields the sower stalks
With measured step, and, liberal, throws the grain
Into the faithful bosom of the ground,
The harrow follows harsh, and shuts the scene.
Be gracious, Heaven ! for now laborious man
Has done his part. Ye fostering breezes, blow !
Ye softening dews, ye tender showers, descend !
And temper all, thou world-reviving sun,
Into the perfect year ! Nor ye who live
In luxury and ease, in pomp and pride,
Think these lost themes unworthy of your ear :
Such themes as these the rural Maro sung
To wide-imperial Rome, in the full height
Of elegance and taste, by Greece refined.
In ancient times the sacred plough employ'd
The kings and awful fathers of mankind :
And some, with whom compared your insect tribes
Are but the beings of a summer's day,
Have held the scale of empire, ruled the storm
Of mighty war ; then, with unwearied hand,
Disdaining little delicacies, seized
The plough, and greatly independent lived.
Ye generous Britons, venerate the plough !
And o'er your hills, and long withdrawing vales,
Let Autumn spread his treasures to the sun,
Luxuriant and unbounded. As the sea,
Far through his azure turbulent domain,
Your empire owns, and from a thousand shores
Wafts all the pomp of life into your ports,
So with superior boon may your rich soil,
Exuberant, Nature's better blessings pour
O'er every land, the naked nations clothe,
And be the exhaustless granary of a world !
Nor only through the lenient air this change,
Delicious, breathes ; the penetrative sun,
His force deep-darting to the dark retreat
Of vegetation, sets the steaming power
At large, to wander o'er the verdant earth,
In various hues ; but chiefly thee, gay green !
Thou smiling Nature's universal robe !
United light and shade ; where the sight dwells
With growing strength, and ever-new delight.
From the moist meadow to the wither'd hill,
Led by the breeze, the vivid verdure runs,
And swells, and deepens to the cherish'd eye.
The hawthorn whitens ; and the juicy groves
Put forth their buds, unfolding by degrees,
Till the whole leafy forest stands display'd
In full luxuriance to the sighing gales ;
Where the deer rustle through the twining brake,
And the birds sing conceal'd. At once array'd
In all the colours of the flushing year,
By Nature's swift and secret-working hand,
The garden glows, and fills the liberal air
With lavish fragrance ; while the promised fruit
Lies yet a little embryo unperceived
Within its crimson folds. Now from the town
Buried in smoke, and sleep, and noisome damps,
Oft let me wander o'er the dewy fields, [drops
Where freshness breathes, and dash the trembling
From the bent bush, as through the verdant maze
Of sweet-briar hedges I pursue my walk ;
Or taste the smell of dairy ; or ascend
Some eminence, Augusta, in thy plains,
And see the country, far diffused around,
One boundless blush, one white-empurpled shower
Of mingled blossoms ; where the raptured eye
Hurries from joy to joy, and, hid beneath
The fair profusion, yellow Autumn spies.
If, brush'd from Russian wilds, a cutting gale
Rise not, and scatter from his humid wings
The clammy mildew ; or, dry-blowing, breathe
Untimely frost ; before whose baleful blast
The full-blown Spring through all her foliage
Joyless and dead, a wide-dejected waste. [shrinks,
For oft, engender'd by the hazy north,
Myriads on myriads, insect armies warp
Keen in the poisoned breeze ; and wasteful eat,
Through buds and bark, into the blacken'd core,
Their eager way. A feeble race ! yet oft
The sacred sons of vengeance, on whose course
Corrosive famine waits, and kills the year.
To check this plague, the skilful farmer chaff
And blazing straw before his orchard burns ;
Till, all involved in smoke, the latent foe
From every cranny suffocated falls :
Or scatters o'er the blooms the pungent dust
Of pepper, fatal to the frosty tribe :
Or, when the envenom'd leaf begins to curl,
With sprinkled water drowns them in their nest ;
Nor, while they pick them up with busy bill,
The little trooping birds unwisely scares.
Be patient, swains ; these cruel-seeming winds
Blow not in vain. Far hence they keep repress'd
Those deepening clouds on clouds, surcharged with
That o'er the vast Atlantic hither borne, [rain,
In endless train, would quench the summer-blaze.
And, cheerless, drown the crude unripen'd year.
The north-east spends his rage ; he now shut up
Within his iron cave, the effusive south
Warms the wide air, and o'er the void of heaven
Breathes the big clouds with vernal showers distent.
At first a dusky wreath they seem to rise,
Scarce staining ether ; but by swift degrees,
In heaps on heaps, the doubling vapour sails
Along the loaded sky, and mingling deep
Sits on the horizon round a settled gloom :
Not such as wintry storms on mortals shed,
Oppressing life ; but lovely, gentle, kind,
And full of every hope and every joy,
The wish of Nature. Gradual sinks the breeze
Into a perfect calm, that not a breath
Is heard to quiver through the closing woods
Or rustling turn the many-twinkling leaves

Of aspen tall. The uncurling floods, diffused,
In glassy breadth, seem through delusive lapse
Forgetful of their course. 'Tis silence all
And pleasing expectation. Herds and flocks
Drop the dry sprig, and, mute-imploring, eye
The falling verdure. Hush'd in short suspense,
The plumy people streak their wings with oil,
To throw the lucid moisture trickling off,
And wait the approaching sign to strike at once
Into the general choir. Even mountains, vales,
And forests seem, impatient, to demand
The promised sweetness. Man superior walks
Amid the glad creation, musing praise,
And looking lively gratitude. At last
The clouds consign their treasures to the fields;
And, softly shaking on the dimpled pool
Prelusive drops, let all their moisture flow,
In large effusion, o'er the freshen'd world.
The stealing shower is scarce to patter heard
By such as wander through the forest walks,
Beneath the umbrageous multitude of leaves.
But who can hold the shade, while Heaven descends
In universal bounty, shedding herbs,
And fruits, and flowers, on Nature's ample lap?
Swift Fancy fired anticipates their growth;
And, while the milky nutriment distils,
Beholds the kindling country colour round.
Thus all day long the full-distended clouds
Indulge their genial stores, and well shower'd earth
Is deep enrich'd with vegetable life;
Till, in the western sky, the downward sun
Looks out, effulgent, from amid the flush
Of broken clouds, gay-shifting to his beam.
The rapid radiance, instantaneous, strikes
The illumined mountain, through the forest streams,
Shakes on the floods, and in a yellow mist,
Far smoking, o'er the interminable plain,
In twinkling myriads lights the dewy gems.
Moist, bright, and green, the landscape laughs around.
Full swell the woods; their every music wakes,
Mix'd in wild concert with the warbling brooks
Increased, the distant bleatings of the hills,
And hollow lows responsive from the vales,
Whence blending all the sweeten'd zephyr springs.
Meantime, refracted from yon eastern cloud,
Bestriding earth, the grand ethereal bow
Shoots up immense; and every hue unfolds
In fair proportion, running from the red
To where the violet fades into the sky.
Here, awful Newton, the dissolving clouds
Form, fronting on the sun, thy showery prism:
And to the sage-instructed eye unfold
The various twine of light, by thee disclosed
From the white mingling maze. Not so the boy;
He wondering views the bright enchantment bend,
Delightful, o'er the radiant fields, and runs
To catch the falling glory; but amazed
Beholds the amusive arch before him fly,
Then vanish quite away Still night succeeds,
A soften'd shade, and saturated earth
Awaits the morning beam, to give to light,
Raised through ten thousand different plastic tubes,
The balmy treasures of the former day.
Then spring the living herbs, profusely wild,
O'er all the deep-green earth, beyond the power
Of botanist to number up their tribes;
Whether he steals along the lonely dale,
In silent search; or through the forest, rank
With what the dull incurious weeds account,
Bursts his blind way; or climbs the mountain rock,
Fired by the nodding verdure of its brow.
With such a liberal hand has Nature flung
Their seeds abroad, blown them about in winds,
Innumerous mix'd them with the nursing mould,
The moistening current, and prolific rain.
But who their virtues can declare? who pierce,
With vision pure, into these secret stores
Of health, and life, and joy? the food of man,
While yet he lived in innocence, and told
A length of golden years; unflesh'd in blood
A stranger to the savage arts of life,
Death, rapine, carnage, surfeit and disease;
The lord, and not the tyrant, of the world.
The first fresh dawn then waked the gladden'd [race
Of uncorrupted man, nor blush'd to see
The sluggard sleep beneath its sacred beam;
For their light slumbers gently fumed away,
And up they rose as vigorous as the sun,
Or to the culture of the willing glebe,
Or to the cheerful tendance of the flock. [sport,
Meantime the song went round; and dance and
Wisdom and friendly talk, successive stole,
Their hours away; while in the rosy vale
Love breathed his infant sighs, from anguish free,
And full replete with bliss; save the sweet pain
That, inly thrilling, but exalts it more.
Nor yet injurious act, nor surly deed,
Was known among those happy sons of Heaven;
For reason and benevolence were law.
Harmonious Nature too look'd smiling on:
Clear shone the skies, cool'd with eternal gales,
And balmy spirit all. The youthful sun
Shot his best rays, and still the gracious clouds
Dropp'd fatness down; as o'er the swelling mead
The herds and flocks, commixing, play'd secure.
This when, emergent from the gloomy wood,
The glaring lion saw, his horrid heart
Was meeken'd, and he join'd his sullen joy;
For music held the whole in perfect peace;
Soft sigh'd the flute; the tender voice was heard,
Warbling the varied heart; the woodlands round
Applied their choir; and winds and waters flow'd
In consonance. Such were those prime of days.
But now those white unblemish'd manners
The fabling poets took their golden age, [whence
Are found no more amid these iron times,
These dregs of life! now the distemper'd mind
Has lost that concord of harmonious powers
Which forms the soul of happiness; and all
Is off the poise within: the passions all
Have burst their bounds; and Reason half extinct
Or impotent, or else approving, sees
The foul disorder. Senseless, and deform'd,
Convulsive Anger storms at large; or pale,
And silent, settles into fell Revenge.
Base Envy withers at another's joy,
And hates that excellence it cannot reach.
Desponding Fear of feeble fancies full,
Weak and unmanly, loosens every power.
Even Love itself is bitterness of soul,
A pensive anguish pining at the heart;
Or, sunk to sordid interest, feels no more
That noble wish, that never-cloy'd desire,
Which, selfish joy disdaining, seeks alone
To bless the dearer object of its flame.
Hope sickens with extravagance; and Grief,
Of life impatient, into madness swells,
Or in dead silence wastes the weeping hours.
These, and a thousand mix'd emotions more,
From ever-changing views of good and ill,

Form'd infinitely various, vex the mind
With endless storm: whence, deeply rankling, grows
The partial thought, a listless unconcern,
Cold, and averting from our neighbour's good;
Then dark Disgust, and Hatred, winding wiles,
Coward Deceit, and ruffian Violence;
At last, extinct each social feeling, fell
And joyless Inhumanity pervades
And petrifies the heart. Nature disturb'd
Is deem'd, vindictive, to have changed her course.
  Hence, in old dusky time, a deluge came:
When the deep-cleft disparting orb, that arch'd
The central waters round, impetuous rush'd,
With universal burst, into the gulf,
And o'er the high-piled hills of fractured earth
Wide dash'd the waves, in undulation vast:
Till, from the centre to the streaming clouds,
A shoreless ocean tumbled round the globe.
  The seasons since have, with severer sway,
Oppress'd a broken world; the Winter keen
Shook forth his waste of snows: and summer shot
His pestilential heats. Great Spring, before,
Green'd all the year; and fruits and blossoms blush'd,
In social sweetness, on the self-same bough.
Pure was the temperate air; an even calm,
Perpetual, reign'd, save what the zephyrs bland
Breathed o'er the blue expanse: for then nor storms
Were taught to blow, nor hurricanes to rage;
Sound slept the waters; no sulphureous glooms
Swell'd in the sky and sent the lightning forth;
While sickly damps and cold autumnal fogs
Hung not, relaxing on the springs of life.
But now, of turbid elements the sport,
From clear to cloudy toss'd, from hot to cold,
And dry to moist, with inward-eating change,
Our drooping days are dwindled down to nought,
Their period finish'd ere 'tis well begun.
  And yet the wholesome herb neglected dies;
Though with the pure exhilarating soul
Of nutriment and health, and vital powers,
Beyond the search of art, 'tis copious blest.
For, with hot ravine fired, ensanguined man
Is now become the lion of the plain,
And worse. The wolf, who from the nightly fold
Fierce drags the bleating prey, ne'er drunk her milk,
Nor wore her warming fleece; nor has the steer,
At whose strong chest the deadly tiger hangs,
E'er plough'd for him. They too are temper'd high,
With hunger stung and wild necessity,
Nor lodges pity in their shaggy breast.
But man, whom Nature form'd of milder clay,
With every kind emotion in his heart,
And taught alone to weep; while from her lap
She pours ten thousand delicacies, herbs,
And fruits, as numerous as the drops of rain,
Or beams that gave them birth: shall he, fair form'
Who wears sweet smiles, and looks erect on heaven,
E'er stoop to mingle with the prowling herd,
And dip his tongue in gore? The beast of prey,
Blood-stain'd, deserves to bleed: but you, ye flocks,
What have you done? ye peaceful people, what,
To merit death? you, who have given us milk
In luscious streams, and lent us your own coat
Against the Winter's cold? and the plain ox,
That harmless, honest, guileless animal,
In what has he offended? he, whose toil,
Patient and ever ready, clothes the land
With all the pomp of harvest; shall he bleed,
And struggling groan beneath the cruel hands
Even of the clown he feeds? and that, perhaps,
To swell the riot of the autumnal feast,
Won by his labour? Thus the feeling heart
Would tenderly suggest: but 'tis enough,
In this late age, adventurous, to have touch'd
Light on the numbers of the Samian sage.
High Heaven forbids the bold presumptuous strain
Whose wisest will has fix'd us in a state
That must not yet to pure perfection rise.
  Now when the first foul torrent of the brooks,
Swell'd with the vernal rains, is ebb'd away;
And whitening, down their mossy-tinctured stream
Descends the billowy foam: now is the time,
While yet the dark-brown water aids the guile,
To tempt the trout. The well-dissembled fly,
The rod fine-tapering with elastic spring,
Snatch'd from the hoary steed the floating line,
And all thy slender watery stores prepare.
But let not on thy hook the tortured worm,
Convulsive, twist in agonising folds;
Which, by rapacious hunger swallow'd deep,
Gives, as you tear it from the bleeding breast
Of the weak, helpless, uncomplaining wretch,
Harsh pain and horror to the tender hand.
  When with his lively ray the potent sun
Has pierced the streams, and roused the finny race,
Then, issuing cheerful, to thy sport repair;
Chief should the western breezes curling play,
And light o'er ether bear the shadowy clouds,
High to their fount, this day, amid the hills,
And woodlands, warbling round, trace up the brooks;
The next, pursue their rocky-channel'd maze,
Down to the river, in whose ample wave
Their little naiads love to sport at large.
Just in the dubious point, where with the pool
Is mixed the trembling stream, or where it boils
Around the stone, or from the hollow'd bank
Reverted plays in undulating flow,
There throw, nice-judging, the delusive fly:
And, as you lead it round in artful curve,
With eye attentive mark the springing game.
Straight as above the surface of the flood
They wanton rise, or urged by hunger leap,
Then fix, with gentle twitch, the barbed hook:
Some lightly tossing to the grassy bank,
And to the shelving shore slow-dragging some,
With various hand proportion'd to their force.
If yet too young, and easily deceived,
A worthless prey scarce bends your pliant rod,
Him, piteous of his youth and the short space
He has enjoy'd the vital light of heaven
Soft disengage, and back into the stream
The speckled captive throw. But should you lure
From his dark haunt, beneath the tangled roots
Of pendent trees, the monarch of the brook,
Behoves you then to ply your finest art.
Long time he, following cautious, scans the fly;
And oft attempts to seize it, but as oft
The dimpled water speaks his jealous fear.
At last, while haply o'er the shaded sun
Passes a cloud, he, desperate, takes the death,
With sullen plunge. At once he darts along,
Deep-struck, and runs out all the lengthen'd line;
Then seeks the farthest ooze, the sheltering weed,
The cavern'd bank, his old secure abode;
And flies aloft, and flounces round the pool,
Indignant of the guile. With yielding hand,

That feels him still, yet to his furious course
Gives way, you, now retiring, following now,
Across the stream, exhaust his idle rage;
Till floating broad upon his breathless side,
And to his fate abandon'd, to the shore
You gaily drag your unresisting prize.
Thus pass the temperate hours; but when the sun
Shakes from his noon-day throne the scattering clouds,
Even shooting listless languor through the deeps,
Then seek the bank where flowering elders crowd,
Where scatter'd wild the lily of the vale
Its balmy essence breathes, where cowslips hang
The dewy head, where purple violets lurk,
With all the lowly children of the shade:
Or lie reclined beneath yon spreading ash,
Hung o'er the steep: whence, borne on liquid wing,
The sounding culver shoots: or where the hawk,
High, in the beetling cliff, his eyry builds.
There let the classic page thy fancy lead
Through rural scenes, such as the Mantuan swain
Paints in the matchless harmony of song;
Or catch thyself the landscape, gliding swift
Athwart imagination's vivid eye;
Or by the vocal woods and waters lull'd,
And lost in lonely musing, in the dream,
Confused, of careless solitude, where mix
Ten thousand wandering images of things,
Soothe every gust of passion into peace;
All but the swellings of the soften'd heart,
That waken, not disturb, the tranquil mind.
Behold yon breathing prospect bids the Muse
Throw all her beauty forth. But who can paint
Like Nature? Can imagination boast,
Amidst its gay creation, hues like hers;
Or can it mix them with that matchless skill,
And lose them in each other, as appears
In every bud that blows? If fancy then
Unequal fails beneath the pleasing task,
Ah, what shall language do? ah, where find words
Tinged with so many colours, and whose power,
To life approaching, may perfume my lays
With that fine oil, those aromatic gales,
That inexhaustive flow continual round?
Yet, though successless, will the toil delight.
Come then, ye virgins and ye youths, whose hearts
Have felt the raptures of refining love;
And thou, Amanda, come, pride of my song!
Form'd by the Graces, loveliness itself!
Come with those downcast eyes sedate and sweet,
Those looks demure, that deeply pierce the soul,
Where, with the light of thoughtful reason mix'd,
Shines lively fancy and the feeling heart;
Oh come! and while the rosy-footed May
Steals blushing on, together let us tread
The morning dews, and gather in their prime
Fresh blooming flowers, to grace thy braided hair,
And thy loved bosom that improves their sweets.
See, where the winding vale its lavish stores,
Irriguous spreads. See, how the lily drinks
The latent rill, scarce oozing through the grass,
Of growth luxuriant; or the humid bank,
In fair profusion, decks. Long let us walk,
Where the breeze blows from yon extended field
Of blossom'd beans. Arabia cannot boast
A fuller gale of joy, than, liberal, thence
Breathes through the sense, and takes the ravish'd [soul.
Nor is the mead unworthy of thy foot,
Full of fresh verdure, and unnumber'd flowers,
The negligence of Nature, wide, and wild;
Where undisguised by mimic Art, she spreads
Unbounded beauty to the roving eye.
Here their delicious task the fervent bees,
In swarming millions, tend: around, athwart,
Through the soft air, the busy nations fly,
Cling to the bud, and, with inserted tube,
Suck its pure essence, its ethereal soul;
And oft, with bolder wing, they soaring dare
The purple heath, or where the wild thyme grows,
And, yellow, load them with the luscious spoil.
At length the finish'd garden to the view
Its vistas opens, and its alleys green.
Snatch'd through the verdant maze the hurried eye
Distracted wanders; now the bowery walk
Of covert close, where scarce a speck of day
Falls on the lengthen'd gloom, protracted sweeps;
Now meets the bending sky; the river now
Dimpling along, the breezy-ruffled lake,
The forest darkening round, the glittering spire,
The ethereal mountain and the distant main.
But why so far excursive? when at hand,
Along these blushing borders, bright with dew,
And in yon mingled wilderness of flowers,
Fair-handed Spring unbosoms every grace,
Throws out the snow-drop and the crocus first;
The daisy, primrose, violet darkly blue,
And polyanthus of unnumber'd dyes:
The yellow wall-flower, stain'd with iron brown;
And lavish stock that scents the garden round:
From the soft wing of vernal breezes shed,
Anemones: auriculas, enrich'd
With shining meal o'er all their velvet leaves;
And full ranunculus, of glowing red.
Then comes the tulip-race, where beauty plays
Her idle freaks; from family diffused
To family, as flies the father-dust,
The varied colours run, and, while they break
On the charm'd eye, the exulting florist marks,
With secret pride, the wonders of his hand.
No gradual bloom is wanting; from the bud,
First-born of Spring, to Summer's musky tribes:
Nor hyacinths, of purest virgin white,
Low-bent, and blushing inward; nor jonquils,
Of potent fragrance; nor Narcissus fair,
As o'er the fabled fountain hanging still;
Nor broad carnations, nor gay-spotted pinks;
Nor, shower'd from every bush, the damask rose.
Infinite numbers, delicacies, smells,
With hues on hues expression cannot paint,
The breath of Nature, and her endless bloom.
Hail, Source of Being! Universal Soul
Of heaven and earth! Essential Presence, hail!
To Thee I bend the knee: to Thee my thoughts,
Continual, climb; who, with a master-hand,
Hast the great whole into perfection touch'd.
By Thee the various vegetative tribes,
Wrapt in a filmy net, and clad with leaves,
Draw the live ether, and imbibe the dew:
By Thee disposed into congenial soils
Stands each attractive plant, and sucks and swells
The juicy tide; a twining mass of tubes.
At Thy command the vernal sun awakes
The torpid sap, detruded to the root
By wintry winds, that now in fluent dance,
And lively fermentation, mounting, spreads
All this innumerous-colour'd scene of things.
As rising from the vegetable world
My theme ascends, with equal wing ascend,
My panting Muse! and hark, how loud the woods
Invite you forth in all your gayest trim.

Lend me your song, ye nightingales! oh, pour
The mazy-running soul of melody
Into my varied verse! while I deduce,
From the first note the hollow cuckoo sings,
The symphony of Spring, and touch a theme
Unknown to fame, —the passion of the groves.

When first the soul of love is sent abroad,
Warm through the vital air, and on the heart
Harmonious seizes, the gay troops begin,
In gallant thought, to plume the painted wing,
And try again the long-forgotten strain
At first faint-warbled; but no sooner grows
The soft infusion prevalent and wide,
Than, all alive, at once their joy o'erflows
In music unconfined. Up-springs the lark,
Shrill-voiced, and loud, the messenger of morn:
Ere yet the shadows fly, he mounted sings
Amid the dawning clouds, and from their haunts
Calls up the tuneful nations. Every copse
Deep-tangled, tree irregular, and bush
Bending with dewy moisture o'er the heads
Of the gay choristers that lodge within,
Are prodigal of harmony. The thrush
And wood-lark, o'er the kind contending throng
Superior heard, run through the sweetest length
Of notes; when listening Philomela deigns
To let them joy, and purposes, in thought
Elate, to make her night excel their day.
The black-bird whistles from the thorny brake;
The mellow bullfinch answers from the grove:
Nor are the linnets o'er the flowering furze
Pour'd out profusely, silent. Join'd to these
Innumerous songsters, in the freshening shade
Of new-sprung leaves their modulations mix
Mellifluous. The jay, the rook, the daw,
And each harsh pipe, discordant heard alone,
Aid the full concert: while the stock-dove breathes
A melancholy murmur through the whole.

'Tis love creates their melody, and all
This waste of music is the voice of love,
That even to birds, and beasts, the tender arts
Of pleasing teaches. Hence the glossy kind
Try every winning way inventive love
Can dictate, and in courtship to their mates
Pour forth their little souls. First, wide around,
With distant awe, in airy rings they rove,
Endeavouring by a thousand tricks to catch
The cunning, conscious, half averted glance
Of the regardless charmer. Should she seem,
Softening, the least approvance to bestow,
Their colours burnish, and, by hope inspired,
They brisk advance; then, on a sudden struck,
Retire disorder'd; then again approach;
In fond rotation spread the spotted wing,
And shiver every feather with desire.

Connubial leagues agreed, to the deep woods
They haste away, all as their fancy leads,
Pleasure, or food, or secret safety prompts;
That Nature's great command may be obey'd:
Nor all the sweet sensations they perceive
Indulged in vain. Some to the holly-hedge
Nestling repair, and to the thicket some:
Some to the rude protection of the thorn
Commit their feeble offspring. The cleft tree
Offers its kind concealment to a few,
Their food its insects, and its moss their nests.
Others apart, far in the grassy dale
Or roughening waste, their humble texture weave.
But most in woodland solitudes delight,
In unfrequented glooms or shaggy banks,
Steep, and divided by a babbling brook,
Whose murmurs soothe them all the live-long day,
When by kind duty fix'd. Among the roots
Of hazel, pendent o'er the plaintive stream,
They frame the first foundation of their domes:
Dry sprigs of trees, in artful fabric laid,
And bound with clay together. Now 'tis nought
But restless hurry through the busy air,
Beat by unnumber'd wings. The swallow sweeps
The slimy pool, to build his hanging house
Intent. And often, from the careless back
Of herds and flocks, a thousand tugging bills
Pluck hair and wool; and oft when unobserved,
Steal from the barn a straw: till soft and warm,
Clean and complete, the habitation grows.

As thus the patient dam assiduous sits,
Not to be tempted from her tender task
Or by sharp hunger or by smooth delight,
Though the whole loosen'd Spring around her blows,
Her sympathising lover takes his stand
High on the opponent bank, and ceaseless sings
The tedious time away; or else supplies
Her place a moment, while she sudden flits
To pick the scanty meal. The appointed time
With pious toil fulfill'd, the callow young,
Warm'd and expanded into perfect life,
Their brittle bondage break, and come to light,
A helpless family, demanding food
With constant clamour. O what passions then.
What melting sentiments of kindly care,
On the new parents seize! away they fly
Affectionate and undesiring bear
The most delicious morsel to their young;
Which equally distributed, again
The search begins. Even so a gentle pair
By fortune sunk, but form'd of generous mould,
And charm'd with cares beyond the vulgar breast,
In some lone cot, amid the distant woods,
Sustain'd alone by providential Heaven,
Oft, as they weeping eye their infant train,
Check their own appetites, and give them all.

Nor toil alone they scorn: exalting love,
By the great Father of the Spring inspired,
Gives instant courage to the fearful race,
And to the simple, art. With stealthy wing,
Should some rude foot their woody haunts molest,
Amid a neighbouring bush they silent drop,
And whirring thence, as if alarm'd, deceive
The unfeeling schoolboy. Hence, around the head
Of wandering swain, the white-wing'd plover wheels
Her sounding flight, and then directly on
In long excursion skims the level lawn,
To tempt him from her nest. The wild-duck, hence,
O'er the rough moss, and o'er the trackless waste
The heath-hen flutters, pious fraud! to lead
The hot-pursuing spaniel far astray.

Be not the Muse ashamed here to bemoan
Her brothers of the grove, by tyrant man
Inhuman caught, and in a narrow cage
From liberty confined, and boundless air.
Dull are the pretty slaves, their plumage dull,
Ragged, and all its brightening lustre lost;
Nor is that sprightly wildness in their notes,
Which, clear and vigorous, warbles from the beech.
Oh then, ye friends of love and love-taught song,
Spare the soft tribes, this barbarous art forbear,
If on your bosom innocence can win,
Music engage, or piety persuade.

But let not chief the nightingale lament
Her ruin'd care, too delicately framed

To brook the harsh confinement of the cage.
Oft, when returning with her loaded bill,
The astonish'd mother finds a vacant nest,
By the hard hand of unrelenting clowns
Robb'd, to the ground the vain provision falls;
Her pinions ruffle, and, low-drooping, scarce
Can bear the mourner to the poplar shade;
Where, all abandon'd to despair, she sings
Her sorrows through the night; and, on the bough,
Sole-sitting, still at every dying fall
Takes up again her lamentable strain
Of winding woe; till, wide around, the woods
Sigh to her song, and with her wail resound.
But now the feather'd youth their former bounds,
Ardent, disdain; and, weighing oft their wings,
Demand the free possession of the sky:
This one glad office more, and then dissolves
Parental love at once, now needless grown:
Unlavish Wisdom never works in vain.
'Tis on some evening, sunny, grateful, mild,
When nought but balm is breathing through the woods,
With yellow lustre bright, that the new tribes
Visit the spacious heavens, and look abroad
On Nature's common far as they can see,
Or wing, their range and pasture. O'er the boughs
Dancing about, still at the giddy verge
Their resolution fails; their pinions still,
In loose libration stretch'd, to trust the void
Trembling refuse; till down before them fly
The parent guides, and chide, exhort, command,
Or push them off. The surging air receives
Its plumy burden; and their self-taught wings
Winnow the waving element. On ground
Alighted, bolder up again they lead,
Farther and farther on, the lengthening flight;
Till vanish'd every fear, and every power
Roused into life and action, light in air
The acquitted parents see their soaring race
And once rejoicing never know them more.
High from the summit of a craggy cliff,
Hung o'er the deep, such as amazing frowns
On utmost Kilda's* shore, whose lonely race
Resign the setting sun to Indian worlds,
The royal eagle draws his vigorous young,
Strong-pounced, and ardent with paternal fire.
Now fit to raise a kingdom of their own,
He drives them from his fort, the towering seat,
For ages, of his empire; which in peace,
Unstain'd, he holds, while many a league to sea
He wings his course and preys in distant isles.
Should I my steps turn to the rural seat,
Whose lofty elms, and venerable oaks,
Invite the rook, who high amid the boughs,
In early Spring, his airy city builds,
And ceaseless caws amusive; there, well-pleased,
I might the various polity survey
Of the mix'd household kind. The careful hen
Calls all her chirping family around,
Fed and defended by the fearless cock,
Whose breast with ardour flames, as on he walks,
Graceful, and crows defiance. In the pond
The finely-checker'd duck before her train
Rows garrulous. The stately-sailing swan
Gives out his snowy plumage to the gale;
And, arching proud his neck, with oary feet
Bears forward fierce, and guards his osier-isle,
Protective of his young. The turkey nigh, [spreads
Loud threatening, reddens; while the peacock

* The farthest of the Western Islands of Scotland.

His every-colour'd glory to the sun,
And swims in radiant majesty along.
O'er the whole homely scene, the cooing dove
Flies thick in amorous chase, and wanton rolls
The glancing eye, and turns the changeful neck.
While thus the gentle tenants of the shade
Indulge their purer loves, the rougher world
Of brutes, below, rush furious into flame,
And fierce desire. Through all his lusty veins
The bull, deep-scorch'd, the raging passion feels.
Of pasture sick, and negligent of food,
Scarce seen, he wades among the yellow broom,
While o'er his ample sides the rambling sprays
Luxuriant shoot; or through the mazy wood
Dejected wanders, nor the enticing bud
Crops, though it presses on his careless sense.
And oft, in jealous maddening fancy rapt,
He seeks the fight and, idly butting, feigns
His rival gored in every knotty trunk.
Him should he meet, the bellowing war begins:
Their eyes flash fury; to the hollow'd earth,
Whence the sand flies, they mutter bloody deeds,
And, groaning deep, the impetuous battle mix:
While the fair heifer, balmy-breathing, near,
Stands kindling up their rage. The trembling steed,
With his hot impulse seized in every nerve,
Nor heeds the rein, nor hears the sounding thong:
Blows are not felt; but tossing high his head,
And by the well known joy to distant plains
Attracted strong, all wild he bursts away;
O'er rocks, and woods, and craggy mountains flies,
And, neighing, on the aërial summit takes
The exciting gale; then, steep-descending, cleaves
The headlong torrents foaming down the hills,
Even where the madness of the straiten'd stream
Turns in black eddies round: such is the force
With which his frantic heart and sinews swell.
Nor undelighted by the boundless Spring
Are the broad monsters of the foaming deep:
From the deep ooze and gelid cavern roused,
They flounce and tumble in unwieldy joy.
Dire were the strain, and dissonant, to sing
The cruel raptures of the savage kind;
How, by this flame their native wrath sublimed,
They roam, amid the fury of their heart,
The far-resounding waste in fiercer bands,
And growl their horrid loves. But this the theme
I sing, enraptured, to the British Fair,
Forbids, and leads me to the mountain brow,
Where sits the shepherd on the grassy turf,
Inhaling, healthful, the descending sun.
Around him feeds his many-bleating flock,
Of various cadence; and his sportive lambs,
This way and that convolved, in friskful glee,
Their frolics play. And now the sprightly race
Invites them forth; when swift, the signal given,
They start away, and sweep the massy mound
That runs around the hill; the rampart once
Of iron war, in ancient barbarous times,
When disunited Britain ever bled,
Lost in eternal broil: ere yet she grew
To this deep-laid indissoluble state,
Where Wealth and Commerce lift their golden
And o'er our labours Liberty and Law, [heads;
Impartial, watch; the wonder of a world!
What is this mighty breath, ye sages, say,
That, in a powerful language, felt, not heard,
Instructs the fowls of heaven, and through their breast
These arts of love diffuses? What, but God!

Inspiring God ! who boundless Spirit all,
And unremitting Energy, pervades,
Adjusts, sustains, and agitates the whole.
He ceaseless works alone ; and yet alone
Seems not to work : with such perfection framed
Is this complex stupendous scheme of things.
But, though conceal'd to every purer eye
Th' informing Author in his works appears :
Chief, lovely Spring, in thee, and thy soft scenes,
The smiling God is seen ; while water, earth,
And air, attest his bounty ; which exalts
The brute creation to this finer thought,
And, annual, melts their undesigning hearts
Profusely thus in tenderness and joy.
Still let my song a nobler note assume,
And sing the infusive force of Spring on man.
When heaven and earth, as if contending, vie
To raise his being, and serene his soul,
Can he forbear to join the general smile
Of nature ? Can fierce passions vex his breast,
While every gale is peace, and every grove
Is melody ? Hence ! from the bounteous walks
Of flowing Spring, ye sordid sons of earth,
Hard, and unfeeling of another's woe,
Or only lavish to yourselves, away !
But come, ye generous minds, in whose wide thought,
Of all his works, creative Bounty burns
With warmest beam ; and on your open front
And liberal eye sits, from his dark retreat
Inviting modest Want. Nor, till invoked,
Can restless Goodness wait ; your active search
Leaves no cold wintry corner unexplored ;
Like silent-working Heaven, surprising oft
The lonely heart with unexpected good.
For you the roving spirit of the wind
Blows Spring abroad ; for you the teeming clouds
Descend in gladsome plenty o'er the world ;
And the sun sheds his kindest rays for you,
Ye flower of human race ! In these green days,
Reviving Sickness lifts her languid head ;
Life flows afresh ; and young-eyed Health exalts
The whole creation round. Contentment walks
The sunny glade, and feels an inward bliss
Spring o'er his mind, beyond the power of kings
To purchase. Pure serenity apace
Induces thought, and contemplation still.
By swift degrees the love of Nature works,
And warms the bosom ; till at last sublimed
To rapture, and enthusiastic heat,
We feel the present Deity and taste
The joy of God to see a happy world !
These are the sacred feelings of thy heart,
Thy heart inform'd by reason's purer ray,
O Lyttelton, the friend ! thy passions thus
And meditations vary, as at large, [stray'st ;
Courting the Muse, through Hagley Park thou
The British Tempe ! There along the dale,
With woods o'erhung, and shagg'd with mossy rocks,
Whence on each hand the gushing waters play,
And down the rough cascade white-dashing fall,
Or gleam in lengthen'd vista through the trees,
You silent steal ; or sit beneath the shade
Of solemn oaks, that tuft the swelling mounts
Thrown graceful round by Nature's careless hand,
And, pensive, listen to the various voice
Of rural peace ; the herds, the flocks, the birds,
The hollow-whispering breeze, the plaint of rills,
That, purling down amid the twisted roots
Which creep around, their dewy murmurs shake
On the soothed ear. From these abstracted oft,
You wander through the philosophic world,
Where in bright train continual wonders rise
Or to the curious or the pious eye.
And oft, conducted by historic truth,
You tread the long extent of backward time ,
Planning, with warm benevolence of mind,
And honest zeal unwarp'd by party rage,
Britannia's weal ; how from the venal gulf
To raise her virtue, and her arts revive.
Or, turning thence thy view, these graver thoughts
The Muses charm : while, with sure taste refined,
You draw th' inspiring breath of ancient song,
Till nobly rises, emulous, thy own.
Perhaps thy loved Lucinda shares thy walk,
With soul to thine attuned. Then Nature all
Wears to the lover's eye a look of love ;
And all the tumult of a guilty world,
Toss'd by ungenerous passions, sinks away.
The tender heart is animated peace,
And as it pours its copious treasures forth
In varied converse, softening every theme,
You, frequent-pausing, turn, and from her eyes,
Where meeken'd sense, and amiable grace,
And lively sweetness dwell, enraptured, drink
That nameless spirit of ethereal joy,
Unutterable happiness ! which love
Alone bestows, and on a favour'd few.
Meantime you gain the height, from whose fair brow
The bursting prospect spreads, immense, around :
And snatch'd o'er hill and dale, and wood and lawn,
And verdant field, and darkening heath between,
And villages embosomed soft in trees,
And spiry towns by surging columns mark'd
Of household smoke, your eye excursive roams :
Wide-stretching from the hall, in whose kind haunt
The Hospitable Genius lingers still,
To where the broken landscape, by degrees,
Ascending, roughens into rigid hills ;
O'er which the Cambrian mountains, like far clouds
That skirt the blue horizon, dusky rise.
Flush'd by the spirit of the genial year,
Now from the virgin's cheek a fresher bloom
Shoots, less and less, the live carnation round ;
Her lips blush deeper sweets : she breathes of
youth ;
The shining moisture swells into her eyes,
In brighter flow ; her wishing bosom heaves
With palpitations wild ; kind tumults seize
Her veins, and all her yielding soul is love.
From the keen gaze her lover turns away,
Full of the dear ecstatic power, and sick
With sighing languishment. Ah then, ye fair !
Be greatly cautious of your sliding hearts :
Dare not the infectious sigh : the pleading look,
Downcast and low, in meek submission dress'd,
But full of guile. Let not the fervent tongue,
Prompt to deceive, with adulation smooth,
Gain on your purposed will. Nor in the bower,
Where woodbines flaunt, and roses shed a couch,
While Evening draws her crimson curtains round,
Trust your soft minutes with betraying man.
And let the aspiring youth beware of love,
Of the smooth glance beware ; for 'tis too late
When on his heart the torrent-softness pours.
Then wisdom prostrate lies, and fading fame
Dissolves in air away ; while the fond soul,
Wrapp'd in gay visions of unreal bliss,
Still paints the illusive form ; the kindling grace ;
The enticing smile ; the modest-seeming eye,
Beneath whose beauteous beams, belying heaven,

Lurk searchless cunning, cruelty, and death ;
And still, false-warbling in his cheated ear,
Her siren voice, enchanting, draws him on
To guileful shores, and meads of fatal joy.
Even present, in the very lap of love
Inglorious laid ; while music flows around,
Perfumes, and oils, and wine, and wanton hours ;
Amid the roses fierce Repentance rears
Her snaky crest : a quick-returning pang [still,
Shoots through the conscious heart; where honour
And great design, against the oppressive load
Of luxury, by fits, impatient heave.
But absent, what fantastic woes, aroused,
Rage in each thought, by restless musing fed,
Chill the warm cheek, and blast the bloom of life !
Neglected fortune flies ; and, sliding swift,
Prone into ruin fall his scorn'd affairs.
'Tis nought but gloom around : the darken'd sun
Loses his light : the rosy-bosomed Spring
To weeping fancy pines ; and yon bright arch,
Contracted, bends into a dusky vault.
All Nature fades extinct; and she alone,
Heard, felt, and seen, possesses every thought,
Fills every sense, and pants in every vein.
Books are but formal dulness, tedious friends ;
And sad amid the social band he sits,
Lonely, and unattentive. From his tongue
The unfinish'd period falls : while, borne away
On swelling thought, his wafted spirit flies
To the vain bosom of his distant fair ;
And leaves the semblance of a lover, fix'd
In melancholy site, with head declined,
And love-dejected eyes. Sudden he starts,
Shook from his tender trance, and restless runs
To glimmering shades, and sympathetic glooms ;
Where the dun umbrage o'er the falling stream,
Romantic, hangs ; there through the pensive dusk
Strays, in heart-thrilling meditation lost,
Indulging all to love : or on the bank
Thrown, amid drooping lilies, swells the breeze
With sighs unceasing, and the brook with tears.
Thus in soft anguish he consumes the day,
Nor quits his deep retirement, till the moon
Peeps through the chambers of the fleecy east
Enlighten'd by degrees, and in her train
Leads on the gentle Hours ; then forth he walks,
Beneath the trembling languish of her beam,
With soften'd soul, and woos the bird of eve
To mingle woes with his ; or, while the world
And all the sons of care lie hush'd in sleep,
Associates with the midnight shadows drear ;
And, sighing to the lonely taper, pours
His idly-tortured heart into the page
Meant for the moving messenger of love ;
Where rapture burns on rapture, every line
With rising frenzy fired. But, if on bed
Delirious flung, sleep from his pillow flies.
All night he tosses, nor the balmy power
In any posture finds ; till the grey morn
Lifts her pale lustre on the paler wretch,
Exanimate by love : and then perhaps
Exhausted nature sinks awhile to rest,
Still interrupted by distracted dreams,
That o'er the sick imagination rise,
And in black colours paint the mimic scene.
Oft with the enchantress of his soul he talks ;
Sometimes in crowds distress'd ; or if retired
To secret winding flower-enwoven bowers,
Far from the dull impertinence of man,
Just as he, credulous, his endless cares
Begins to lose in blind oblivious love,
Snatch'd from her yielded hand, he knows not how,
Through forest huge, and long unravel'd heaths
With desolation brown, he wanders waste,
In night and tempest wrapp'd ; or shrinks aghast,
Back, from the bending precipice ; or wades
The turbid stream below, and strives to reach
The farther shore ; where, succourless and sad,
She with extended arms his aid implores ;
But strives in vain : borne by the outrageous flood
To distance down, he rides the ridgy wave,
Or whelm'd beneath the boiling eddy sinks.
These are the charming agonies of love,
Whose misery delights. But through the heart
Should jealousy its venom once diffuse,
'Tis then delightful misery no more,
But agony unmix'd, incessant gall,
Corroding every thought, and blasting all
Love's paradise. Ye fairy prospects, then,
Ye beds of roses, and ye bowers of joy,
Farewell ! Ye gleamings of departed peace,
Shine out your last ! the yellow-tinging plague
Internal vision taints, and in a night
Of livid gloom imagination wraps.
Ah then ! instead of love-enliven'd cheeks,
Of sunny features, and of ardent eyes
With flowing rapture bright, dark looks succeed,
Suffused and glaring with untender fire ;
A clouded aspect, and a burning cheek,
Where the whole poison'd soul, malignant, sits,
And frightens love away. Ten thousand fears
Invented wild, ten thousand frantic views
Of horrid rivals, hanging on the charms
For which he melts in fondness, eat him up
With fervent anguish and consuming rage.
In vain reproaches lend their idle aid,
Deceitful pride, and resolution frail,
Giving false peace a moment. Fancy pours,
Afresh, her beauties on his busy thought,
Her first endearments twining round the soul,
With all the witchcraft of ensnaring love.
Straight the fierce storm involves his mind anew,
Flames through the nerves, and boils along the veins ;
While anxious doubt distracts the tortured heart :
For even the sad assurance of his fears
Were ease to what he feels. Thus the warm youth,
Whom love deludes into his thorny wilds,
Through flowery-tempting paths, or leads a life
Of fever'd rapture, or of cruel care ;
His brightest aims extinguish'd all, and all
His lively moments running down to waste.
But happy they ! the happiest of their kind !
Whom gentler stars unite, and in one fate
Their hearts, their fortunes, and their beings blend.
'Tis not the coarser tie of human laws,
Unnatural oft, and foreign to the mind,
That binds their peace, but harmony itself,
Attuning all their passions into love ;
Where friendship full exerts her softest power,
Perfect esteem enliven'd by desire
Ineffable, and sympathy of soul ;
Thought meeting thought, and will preventing will,
With boundless confidence : for nought but love
Can answer love, and render bliss secure.
Let him, ungenerous, who, alone intent
To bless himself, from sordid parents buys
The loathing virgin, in eternal care,
Well-merited, consume his nights and days :
Let barbarous nations, whose inhuman love

Is wild desire, fierce as the suns they feel;
Let eastern tyrants from the light of heaven
Seclude their bosom-slaves, meanly possess'd
Of a mere lifeless violated form:
While those whom love cements in holy faith,
And equal transport, free as nature live,
Disdaining fear. What is the world to them,
Its pomp, its pleasure, and its nonsense all,
Who in each other clasp whatever fair
High fancy forms, and lavish hearts can wish;
Something than beauty dearer, should they look
Or on the mind, or mind-illumined face:
Truth, goodness, honour, harmony, and love,
The richest bounty of indulgent heaven?
Meantime a smiling offspring rises round,
And mingles both their graces. By degrees,
The human blossom blows: and every day,
Soft as it rolls along, shows some new charm,
The father's lustre, and the mother's bloom.
Then infant reason grows apace, and calls
For the kind hand of an assiduous care.
Delightful task! to rear the tender thought,
To teach the young idea how to shoot,
To pour the fresh instruction o'er the mind,
To breathe the enlivening spirit, and to fix
The generous purpose in the glowing breast.
Oh, speak the joy! ye, whom the sudden tear
Surprises often, while you look around,
And nothing strikes your eye but sights of bliss,
All various Nature pressing on the heart:
An elegant sufficiency, content,
Retirement, rural quiet, friendship, books,
Ease and alternate labour, useful life,
Progressive virtue, and approving Heaven.
These are the matchless joys of virtuous love;
And thus their moments fly. The Seasons thus,
As ceaseless round a jarring world they roll,
Still find them happy; and consenting Spring
Sheds her own rosy garland on their heads:
Till evening comes at last, serene and mild;
When after the long vernal day of life,
Enamour'd more, as more remembrance swells
With many a proof of recollected love,
Together down they sink in social sleep;
Together freed, their gentle spirits fly
To scenes where love and bliss immortal reign.

SUMMER

Jam clarus occultum Andromedæ pater
Ostendit ignem: jam Procyon furit
Et stella vesani Leonis,
Sole dies referente siccos.
Jam pastor umbras cum grege languido,
Rivumque fessus quærit, et horridi
Dumeta Sylvani: caretque
Ripa vagis taciturna ventis.—HOR.

TO

THE RIGHT HONOURABLE MR. DODINGTON,

ONE OF THE LORDS OF HIS MAJESTY'S TREASURY, ETC.

SIR,

It is not my purpose, in this address, to run into the common track of dedicators, and attempt a panegyric which would prove *ungrateful* to you, too *arduous* for me, and *superfluous* with regard to the world. To you it would prove *ungrateful*, since there is a certain generous delicacy in men of the most distinguished merit, disposing them to avoid those praises they so powerfully attract: and when I consider that a *character*, in which the VIRTUES, the GRACES, and the MUSES join their influence, as much exceeds the expression of the most elegant and judicious pen as the finished *beauty* does the representation of the pencil, I have the best reasons for declining such an *arduous* undertaking, as, indeed, it would be *superfluous* in itself; for what reader need to be told of those great abilities in the management of public affairs, and those amiable accomplishments in private life, which you so eminently possess? The general voice is loud in the praise of so many virtues, though posterity alone will do them justice; but may you, SIR, live long to illustrate your own fame by your own actions, and by them be transmitted to future times as the BRITISH MÆCENAS.

Your example has recommended POETRY, with the greatest grace, to the admiration of those who are engaged in the highest and most active scenes of life; and this, though confessedly the least considerable of those exalted qualities that dignify your character, must be particularly pleasing to *one* whose only hope of being introduced to your regard is through the recommendation of an ART in which you are a master.—But I forget what I have been declaring above, and must therefore turn my eyes to the following sheets. I am not ignorant that, when offered to your perusal, they are put into the hands of one of the finest, and consequently the most indulgent, judges of the age; but as there is no mediocrity in POETRY, so there should be no limits to its ambition.—I venture directly on the trial of my fame. If what I here present you has any merit to gain your approbation, I am not afraid of its success; and if it fails of your notice, I give it up to its just fate.—This advantage at least I secure to myself, an occasion of thus publicly declaring that I am, with the profoundest veneration, SIR,

Your most devoted, humble servant,

JAMES THOMSON

ARGUMENT.

The subject proposed. Invocation. Address to Mr. Dodington. An introductory reflection on the motion of the heavenly bodies; whence the succession of the seasons. As the face of nature in this season is almost uniform, the progress of the poem is a description of a summer's day. The dawn. Sun-rising. Hymn to the sun. Forenoon. Summer insects described. Haymaking. Sheep-shearing. Noon-day. A woodland retreat. Group of herds and flocks. A solemn grove; how it affects a contemplative mind. A cataract, and rude scene. View of summer in the torrid zone. Storm of thunder and lightning. A tale. The storm over, a serene afternoon. Bathing. Hour of walking. Transition to the prospect of a rich well-cultivated country; which introduces a panegyric on Great Britain. Sunset. Evening. Night. Summer meteors. A comet. The whole concluding with the praise of philosophy.

FROM brightening fields of ether fair disclosed,
Child of the Sun, refulgent Summer comes,
In pride of youth, and felt through Nature's depth:

He comes attended by the sultry Hours,
And ever-fanning breezes, on his way ;
While, from his ardent look, the turning Spring
Averts her blushful face ; and earth, and skies,
All-smiling, to his hot dominion leaves.
Hence, let me haste into the mid-wood shade,
Where scarce a sunbeam wanders through the gloom ;
And on the dark-green grass, beside the brink
Of haunted stream, that by the roots of oak
Rolls o'er the rocky channel, lie at large,
And sing the glories of the circling year.
Come, Inspiration ! from thy hermit seat,
By mortal seldom found ; may Fancy dare,
From thy fix'd serious eye, and raptured glance
Shot on surrounding heaven, to steal one look
Creative of the Poet, every power
Exalting to an ecstacy of soul.
And thou, my youthful Muse's early friend,
In whom the human graces all unite :
Pure light of mind, and tenderness of heart ;
Genius, and wisdom : the gay social sense,
By decency chastised ; goodness and wit,
In seldom-meeting harmony combined ;
Unblemish'd honour, and an active zeal
For Britain's glory, liberty, and man :
O Dodington ! attend my rural song,
Stoop to my theme, inspirit every line,
And teach me to deserve thy just applause.
With what an awful world-revolving power
Were first the unwieldy planets launch'd along
The illimitable void ! thus to remain,
Amid the flux of many thousand years,
That oft has swept the toiling race of men
And all their labour'd monuments away,
Firm, unremitting, matchless, in their course ;
To the kind-temper'd change of night and day,
And of the seasons ever stealing round,
Minutely faithful : such the All-perfect hand
That poised, impels, and rules the steady whole !
When now no more the alternate Twins are fired,
And Cancer reddens with the solar blaze,
Short is the doubtful empire of the night ;
And soon, observant of approaching day,
The meek-eyed Morn appears, mother of dews,
At first faint-gleaming in the dappled east :
Till far o'er ether spreads the widening glow ;
And, from before the lustre of her face, [step,
White break the clouds away. With quicken'd
Brown Night retires : young Day pours in apace,
And opens all the lawny prospect wide.
The dripping-rock, the mountain's misty top,
Swell on the sight, and brighten with the dawn.
Blue, through the dusk, the smoking currents shine ;
And from the bladed field the fearful hare
Limps, awkward ; while along the forest glade
The wild deer trip, and often turning gaze
At early passenger Music awakes
The native voice of undissembled joy ;
And thick around the woodland hymns arise
Roused by the cock, the soon-clad shepherd leaves
His mossy cottage, where with peace he dwells ;
And from the crowded fold, in order, drives
His flock, to taste the verdure of the morn.
Falsely luxurious ! will not man awake ;
And, springing from the bed of sloth, enjoy
The cool, the fragrant and the silent hour,
To meditation due and sacred song ?
For is there aught in sleep can charm the wise ?
To lie in dead oblivion, losing half
The fleeting moments of too short a life ;
Total extinction of the enlighten'd soul !
Or else to feverish vanity alive,
Wilder'd, and tossing through distemper'd dreams ?
Who would in such a gloomy state remain
Longer than nature craves, when every Muse
And every blooming pleasure waits without,
To bless the wildly-devious morning-walk ?
But yonder comes the powerful King of Day,
Rejoicing in the east. The lessening cloud,
The kindling azure, and the mountain's brow
Illumed with fluid gold, his near approach
Betoken glad. Lo ! now, apparent all,
Aslant the dew-bright earth, and colour'd air,
He looks in boundless majesty abroad ;
And sheds the shining day, that burnish'd plays
On rocks, and hills, and towers, and wandering streams,
High-gleaming from afar. Prime cheerer, Light !
Of all material beings first, and best !
Efflux divine ! Nature's resplendent robe !
Without whose vesting beauty all were wrapt
In unessential gloom ; and thou, O Sun !
Soul of surrounding worlds ! in whom best seen
Shines out thy Maker ! may I sing of thee ?
'Tis by thy secret, strong, attractive force,
As with a chain indissoluble bound,
Thy system rolls entire : from the far bourne
Of utmost Saturn, wheeling wide his round
Of thirty years, to Mercury, whose disk
Can scarce be caught by philosophic eye,
Lost in the near effulgence of thy blaze.
Informer of the planetary train !
Without whose quickening glance their cumbrous
Were brute unlovely mass, inert and dead, [orbs
And not, as now, the green abodes of life !
How many forms of being wait on thee,
Inhaling spirit ; from the unfetter'd mind,
By thee sublimed, down to the daily race,
The mixing myriads of thy setting beam !
The vegetable world is also thine,
Parent of Seasons ! who the pomp precede
That waits thy throne, as through thy vast domain,
Annual, along the bright ecliptic road,
In world-rejoicing state, it moves sublime.
Meantime the expecting nations, circled gay
With all the various tribes of foodful earth,
Implore thy bounty, or send grateful up
A common hymn : while, round thy beaming car,
High seen, the Seasons lead, in sprightly dance
Harmonious knit, the rosy-finger'd Hours,
The Zephyrs floating loose, the timely Rains,
Of bloom ethereal the light-footed Dews,
And soften'd into joy the surly Storms.
These, in successive turn, with lavish hand,
Shower every beauty, every fragrance shower,
Herbs, flowers, and fruits ; till kindling at thy touch,
From land to land is flush'd the vernal year.
Nor to the surface of enliven'd earth,
Graceful with hills and dales, and leafy woods,
Her liberal tresses, is thy force confined :
But, to the bowel'd cavern darting deep,
The mineral kinds confess thy mighty power.
Effulgent, hence the veiny marble shines ; [War
Hence Labour draws his tools ; hence burnish'd
Gleams on the day ; the nobler works of Peace
Hence bless mankind, and generous Commerce
The round of nations in a golden chain. [binds
The unfruitful rock itself, impregn'd by thee,
In dark retirement forms the lucid stone.

The lively diamond drinks thy purest rays,
Collected light, compact; that, polish'd bright,
And all its native lustre let abroad,
Dares, as it sparkles on the fair-one's breast,
With vain ambition emulate her eyes.
At thee, the ruby lights its deepening glow,
And with a waving radiance inward flames.
From thee the sapphire, solid ether, takes
Its hue cerulean; and, of evening tinct,
The purple-streaming amethyst is thine.
With thy own smile the yellow topaz burns.
Nor deeper verdure dyes the robe of Spring,
When first she gives it to the southern gale,
Than the green emerald shows. But, all combined,
Thick through the whitening opal play thy beams;
Or, flying several from its surface, form
A trembling variance of revolving hues,
As the site varies in the gazer's hand.
The very dead creation, from thy touch,
Assumes a mimic life. By thee refined,
In brighter mazes the relucent stream
Plays o'er the mead. The precipice abrupt,
Projecting horror on the blacken'd flood,
Softens at thy return. The desert joys,
Wildly, through all his melancholy bounds.
Rude ruins glitter; and the briny deep,
Seen from some pointed promontory's top
Far to the blue horizon's utmost verge,
Restless, reflects a floating gleam. But this,
And all the much-transported Muse can sing,
Are to thy beauty, dignity, and use,
Unequal far; great delegated Source
Of light, and life, and grace, and joy below!
How shall I then attempt to sing of Him!
Who, Light himself, in uncreated light
Invested deep, dwells awfully retired
From mortal eye or angel's purer ken,
Whose single smile has, from the first of time,
Fill'd, overflowing, all those lamps of Heaven,
That beam for ever through the boundless sky:
But, should he hide his face, the astonish'd sun,
And all the extinguish'd stars, would loosening reel
Wide from their spheres, and Chaos come again.
And yet was every faltering tongue of man,
Almighty Father! silent in thy praise,
Thy works themselves would raise a general voice,
Even in the depth of solitary woods
By human foot untrod; proclaim thy power,
And to the choir celestial Thee resound,
The eternal cause, support, and end of all!
To me be Nature's volume broad-display'd;
And to peruse its all-instructing page,
Or, haply catching inspiration thence,
Some easy passage, raptured, to translate,
My sole delight; as through the falling glooms
Pensive I stray, or with the rising dawn
On Fancy's eagle wing, excursive, soar.
Now, flaming up the heavens, the potent sun
Melts into limpid air the high-raised clouds,
And morning fogs, that hover'd round the hills
In party-colour'd bands; till wide unveil'd
The face of Nature shines, from where earth seems,
Far-stretch'd around, to meet the bending sphere.
Half in a blush of clustering roses lost,
Dew-dropping Coolness to the shade retires;
There, on the verdant turf, or flowery bed,
By gelid founts and careless rills to muse;
While tyrant Heat, dispreading through the sky,
With rapid sway, his burning influence darts
On man, and beast, and herb, and tepid stream.
Who can unpitying see the flowery race,
Shed by the morn, their new-flush'd bloom resign,
Before the parching beam? so fade the fair,
When fevers revel through their azure veins.
But one, the lofty follower of the sun,
Sad when he sets, shuts up her yellow leaves,
Drooping all night; and, when he warm returns,
Points her enamour'd bosom to his ray.
Home, from his morning task, the swain retreats;
His flock before him stepping to the fold;
While the full udder'd mother lows around
The cheerful cottage, then expecting food,
The food of innocence and health! The daw,
The rook, and magpie, to the grey-grown oaks
That the calm village in their verdant arms,
Sheltering, embrace, direct their lazy flight;
Where on the mingling boughs they sit embower'd,
All the hot noon, till cooler hours arise.
Faint, underneath, the household fowls, convene;
And, in a corner of the buzzing shade,
The house-dog, with the vacant grey-hound lies,
Outstretch'd, and sleepy. In his slumbers one
Attacks the nightly thief, and one exults
O'er hill and dale; till, waken'd by the wasp,
They starting snap. Nor shall the Muse disdain
To let the little noisy summer race
Live in her lay, and flutter through her song:
Not mean though simple; to the sun allied,
From him they draw their animating fire.
Waked by his warmer ray, the reptile young
Come wing'd abroad; by the light air upborne,
Lighter, and full of soul. From every chink
And secret corner, where they slept away
The wintry storms; or rising from their tombs,
To higher life; by myriads, forth at once,
Swarming they pour; of all the varied hues
Their beauty-beaming parent can disclose.
Ten thousand forms, ten thousand different tribes,
People the blaze. To sunny waters some
By fatal instinct fly; where on the pool
They, sportive, wheel; or, sailing down the stream
Are snatch'd immediate by the quick-eyed trout,
Or darting salmon. Through the greenwood glade
Some love to stray; there lodged, amused, and fed,
In the fresh leaf. Luxurious, others make
The meads their choice, and visit every flower,
And every latent herb: for the sweet task,
To propagate their kinds, and where to wrap,
In what soft beds, their young yet undisclosed,
Employs their tender care. Some to the house,
The fold, and dairy, hungry, bend their flight;
Sip round the pail, or taste the curdling cheese;
Oft, inadvertent, from the milky stream
They meet their fate; or, weltering in the bowl,
With powerless wings around them wrapt, expire.
But chief to heedless flies the window proves
A constant death; where, gloomily retired,
The villain spider lives, cunning, and fierce,
Mixture abhorr'd! Amid a mangled heap
Of carcases, in eager watch he sits
O'erlooking all his waving snares around.
Near the dire cell the dreadless wanderer oft
Passes, as oft the ruffian shows his front;
The prey at last ensnared, he dreadful darts,
With rapid glide, along the leaning line;
And, fixing in the wretch his cruel fangs,
Strikes backward, grimly pleased: the fluttering [wing
And shriller sound declare extreme distress,
And ask the helping hospitable hand.
Resounds the living surface of the ground:

Nor undelightful is the ceaseless hum,
To him who muses through the woods at noon ;
Or drowsy shepherd, as he lies reclined,
With half-shut eyes, beneath the floating shade
Of willows grey, close-crowding o'er the brook.
Gradual, from these what numerous kinds
Evading even the microscopic eye ! [descend,
Full Nature swarms with life ; one wondrous mass
Of animals, or atoms organized,
Waiting the vital breath, when Parent-Heaven
Shall bid his spirit blow. The hoary fen,
In putrid steams, emits the living cloud
Of pestilence. Through subterranean cells,
Where searching sunbeams scarce can find a way,
Earth animated heaves. The flowery leaf
Wants not its soft inhabitants. Secure,
Within its winding citadel, the stone
Holds multitudes. But chief the forest-boughs,
That dance unnumber'd to the playful breeze,
The downy orchard, and the melting pulp
Of mellow fruit, the nameless nations feed
Of evanescent insects. Where the pool
Stands mantled o'er with green, invisible
Amid the floating verdure millions stray.
Each liquid too, whether it pierces, soothes,
Inflames, refreshes, or exalts the taste,
With various forms abounds. Nor is the stream
Of purest crystal, nor the lucid air,
Though one transparent vacancy it seems,
Void of their unseen people. These, conceal'd
By the kind art of forming Heaven, escape
The grosser eye of man ; for, if the worlds
In worlds enclosed should on his senses burst,
From cates ambrosial, and the nectar'd bowl,
He would abhorrent turn, and in dead night,
When silence sleeps o'er all, be stunn'd with noise.
Let no presuming impious railer tax
Creative Wisdom, as if aught was form'd
In vain, or not for admirable ends.
Shall little haughty Ignorance pronounce
His works unwise, of which the smallest part
Exceeds the narrow vision of her mind ?
As if upon a full proportion'd dome,
On swelling columns heaved the pride of art,
A critic-fly, whose feeble ray scarce spreads
An inch around, with blind presumption bold,
Should dare to tax the structure of the whole.
And lives the man, whose universal eye
Has swept at once the unbounded scheme of things,
Mark'd their dependence so, and firm accord,
As with unfaltering accent to conclude
That this availeth nought ? Has any seen
The mighty chain of beings, lessening down
From Infinite Perfection to the brink
Of dreary nothing, desolate abyss !
From which astonish'd thought recoiling turns ?
Till then alone let zealous praise ascend,
And hymns of holy wonder, to that Power
Whose wisdom shines as lovely on our minds,
As on our smiling eyes his servant sun.
Thick in yon stream of light, a thousand ways,
Upward, and downward, thwarting, and convolved,
The quivering nations sport ; till tempest-wing'd,
Fierce Winter sweeps them from the face of day.
Even so luxurious men, unheeding, pass
An idle summer life in fortune's shine,
A season's glitter ! Thus they flutter on
From toy to toy, from vanity to vice ;
Till, blown away by death, oblivion comes
Behind, and strikes them from the book of life.

Now swarms the village o'er the jovial mead ;
The rustic youth, brown with meridian toil,
Healthful and strong ; full as the summer rose
Blown by prevailing suns, the ruddy maid,
Half-naked, swelling on the sight, and all
Her kindled graces burning o'er her cheek.
Even stooping age is here ; and infant hands
Trail the long rake, or, with the fragrant load
O'ercharged, amid the kind oppression roll.
Wide flies the tedded grain ; all in a row
Advancing broad, or wheeling round the field,
They spread the breathing harvest to the sun,
That throws refreshful round a rural smell :
Or, as they rake the green-appearing ground,
And drive the dusky wave along the mead,
The russet hay-cock rises thick behind,
In order gay. While heard from dale to dale,
Waking the breeze, resounds the blended voice
Of happy labour, love, and social glee.
Or rushing thence, in one diffusive band,
They drive the troubled flocks, by many a dog
Compell'd, to where the mazy-running brook
Forms a deep pool ; this bank abrupt and high,
And that fair-spreading in a pebbled shore.
Urged to the giddy brink, much is the toil,
The clamour much, of men, and boys, and dogs,
Ere the soft fearful people to the flood
Commit their woolly sides. And oft the swain,
On some impatient seizing, hurls them in :
Embolden'd then, nor hesitating more,
Fast, fast, they plunge amid the flashing wave,
And, panting, labour to the farthest shore.
Repeated this, till deep the well-wash'd fleece
Has drunk the flood, and from his lively haunt
The trout is banish'd by the sordid stream ;
Heavy, and dripping, to the breezy brow
Slow move the harmless race : where, as they spread
Their swelling treasures to the sunny ray,
Inly disturb'd, and wondering what this wild
Outrageous tumult means, their loud complaints
The country fill ; and, toss'd from rock to rock
Incessant bleatings run around the hills.
At last, of snowy white, the gather'd flocks
Are in the wattled pen, innumerous, press'd,
Head above head : and ranged in lusty rows
The shepherds sit, and whet the sounding shears.
The housewife waits to roll her fleecy stores,
With all her gay-dress'd maids attending round.
One, chief, in gracious dignity enthroned,
Shines o'er the rest, the pastoral queen, and rays
Her smiles, sweet-beaming, on her shepherd king ;
While the glad circle round them yield their souls
To festive mirth, and wit that knows no gall.
Meantime, their joyous task goes on apace :
Some mingling stir the melted tar, and some,
Deep on the new-shorn vagrant's heaving side,
To stamp the master's cypher ready stand ;
Others the unwilling wether drag along ;
And, glorying in his might, the sturdy boy
Holds by the twisted horns the indignant ram.
Behold where bound, and of its robe bereft,
By needy man, that all-depending lord,
How meek, how patient, the mild creature lies !
What softness in its melancholy face,
What dumb complaining innocence appears !
Fear not, ye gentle tribes, 'tis not the knife
Of horrid slaughter that is o'er you waved ;
No, 'tis the tender swain's well guided shears,
Who having now, to pay his annual care,

Borrow'd your fleece, to you a cumbrous load,
Will send you bounding to your hills again.
A simple scene! yet hence Britannia sees
Her solid grandeur rise: hence she commands
The exalted stores of every brighter clime,
The treasures of the Sun without his rage:
Hence, fervent all, with culture, toil, and arts,
Wide glows her land: her dreadful thunder hence
Rides o'er the waves sublime, and now, even now,
Impending hangs o'er Gallia's humbled coast;
Hence rules the circling deep, and awes the world.
'Tis raging noon; and, vertical, the sun
Darts on the head direct his forceful rays.
O'er heaven and earth, far as the ranging eye
Can sweep, a dazzling deluge reigns; and all
From pole to pole is undistinguish'd blaze.
In vain the sight, dejected, to the ground
Stoops for relief; thence hot ascending steams
And keen reflection pain. Deep to the root
Of vegetation parch'd, the cleaving fields
And slippery lawn an arid hue disclose,
Blast Fancy's bloom, and wither e'en the soul.
Echo no more returns the cheerful sound
Of sharpening scythe: the mower, sinking, heaps
O'er him the humid hay, with flowers perfumed;
And scarce a chirping grasshopper is heard
Through the dumb mead. Distressful Nature pants.
The very streams look languid from afar;
Or, through the unshelter'd glade, impatient, seem
To hurl into the covert of the grove.
All-conquering Heat, oh, intermit thy wrath!
And on my throbbing temples potent thus
Beam not so fierce! incessant still you flow,
And still another fervent flood succeeds,
Pour'd on the head profuse. In vain I sigh,
And restless turn, and look around for night;
Night is far off; and hotter hours approach.
Thrice happy he! who on the sunless side
Of a romantic mountain, forest-crown'd,
Beneath the whole collected shade reclines:
Or in the gelid caverns, woodbine-wrought,
And fresh-bedew'd with ever-spouting streams,
Sits coolly calm; while all the world without,
Unsatisfied, and sick, tosses in noon.
Emblem instructive of the virtuous man,
Who keeps his temper'd mind serene and pure,
And every passion aptly harmonized,
Amid a jarring world with vice inflamed.
Welcome, ye shades! ye bowery thickets hail!
Ye lofty pines! ye venerable oaks!
Ye ashes wild, resounding o'er the steep!
Delicious is your shelter to the soul,
As to the hunted hart the sallying spring,
Or stream full-flowing, that his swelling sides
Laves, as he floats along the herbaged brink.
Cool, through the nerves, your pleasing comfort glides;
The heart beats glad; the fresh-expanded eye
And ear resume their watch; the sinews knit;
And life shoots swift through all the lighten'd limbs.
Around the adjoining brook, that purls along
The vocal grove, now fretting o'er a rock,
Now scarcely moving through a reedy pool,
Now starting to a sudden stream, and now
Gently diffused into a limpid plain;
A various group the herds and flocks compose,
Rural confusion! On the grassy bank
Some ruminating lie; while others stand
Half in the flood, and often bending sip
The circling surface. In the middle droops
The strong laborious ox, of honest front,
Which incomposed he shakes; and from his sides
The troublous insects lashes with his tail,
Returning still. Amid his subjects safe,
Slumbers the monarch-swain; his careless arm
Thrown round his head, on downy moss sustain'd;
Here laid his scrip, with wholesome viands fill'd;
There, listening every noise, his watchful dog.
Light fly his slumbers, if perchance a flight
Of angry gad-flies fasten on the herd,
That startling scatters from the shallow brook,
In search of lavish stream. Tossing the foam,
They scorn the keeper's voice, and scour the plain,
Through all the bright severity of noon;
While from their labouring breasts a hollow moan
Proceeding, runs low-bellowing round the hills.
Oft in this season too the horse, provoked,
While his big sinews full of spirits swell,
Trembling with vigour, in the heat of blood,
Springs the high fence; and, o'er the field effused,
Darts on the gloomy flood, with steadfast eye,
And heart estranged to fear: his nervous chest,
Luxuriant, and erect, the seat of strength,
Bears down the opposing stream; quenchless his thirst:
He takes the river at redoubled draughts,
And with wide nostrils, snorting, skims the wave.
Still let me pierce into the midnight depth
Of yonder grove, of wildest largest growth;
That, forming high in air a woodland choir,
Nods o'er the mount beneath. At every step,
Solemn and slow, the shadows blacker fall,
And all is awful listening gloom around.
These are the haunts of Meditation, these
The scenes where ancient bards the inspiring breath
Ecstatic, felt; and, from this world retired
Conversed with angels, and immortal forms,
On gracious errands bent; to save the fall
Of virtue struggling on the brink of vice;
In waking whispers, and repeated dreams,
To hint pure thought, and warn the favour'd soul
For future trials fated to prepare;
To prompt the poet, who devoted gives
His muse to better themes; to soothe the pangs
Of dying worth, and from the patriot's breast
(Backward to mingle in detested war,
But foremost when engaged) to turn the death;
And numberless such offices of love,
Daily, and nightly, zealous to perform.
Shook sudden from the bosom of the sky,
A thousand shapes or glide athwart the dusk,
Or stalk majestic on. Deep-roused, I feel
A sacred terror, a severe delight,
Creep through my mortal frame; and thus, methinks,
A voice, than human more, the abstracted ear
Of Fancy strikes. "Be not of us afraid,
Poor kindred man! thy fellow-creatures, we
From the same Parent-Power our beings drew,
The same our Lord, and laws, and great pursuit.
Once some of us, like thee, through stormy life,
Toil'd, tempest-beaten, ere we could attain
This holy calm, this harmony of mind,
Where purity and peace immingle charms.
Then fear not us; but with responsive song,
Amid these dim recesses, undisturb'd
By noisy folly and discordant vice,
Of Nature sing with us, and Nature's God.
Here frequent, at the visionary hour,
When musing midnight reigns or silent noon,
Angelic harps are in full concert heard,

And voices chanting from the wood-crown'd hill,
The deepening dale, or inmost sylvan glade:
A privilege bestow'd by us, alone,
On Contemplation, or the hallow'd ear
Of poet, swelling to seraphic strain."
And art thou, Stanley *, of that sacred band?
Alas, for us too soon! though raised above
The reach of human pain, above the flight
Of human joy; yet, with a mingled ray
Of sadly pleased remembrance, must thou feel
A mother's love, a mother's tender woe,
Who seeks thee still, in many a former scene;
Seeks thy fair form, thy lovely beaming eyes,
Thy pleasing converse, by gay lively sense
Inspired, where moral wisdom mildly shone
Without the toil of art; and virtue glow'd,
In all her smiles, without forbidding pride.
But, O thou best of parents! wipe thy tears;
Or rather to Parental Nature pay
The tears of grateful joy, who for a while
Lent thee this younger self, this opening bloom
Of thy enlighten'd mind and gentle worth.
Believe the Muse: the wintry blast of death
Kills not the buds of virtue; no, they spread
Beneath the heavenly beam of brighter suns,
Through endless ages, into higher powers.
Thus up the mount, in airy vision rapt,
I stray, regardless whither, till the sound
Of a near fall of water every sense
Wakes from the charm of thought: swift-shrinking back,
I check my steps, and view the broken scene.
Smooth to the shelving brink a copious flood
Rolls fair and placid, where collected all,
In one impetuous torrent, down the steep
It thundering shoots, and shakes the country round.
At first, an azure sheet, it rushes broad;
Then whitening by degrees, as prone it falls,
And, from the loud-resounding rocks below,
Dash'd in a cloud of foam, it sends aloft
A hoary mist, and forms a ceaseless shower.
Nor can the tortured wave here find repose;
But, raging still amid the shaggy rocks,
Now flashes o'er the scatter'd fragments, now
Aslant the hollow'd channel rapid darts;
And falling fast from gradual slope to slope,
With wild infracted course and lessen'd roar,
It gains a safer bed, and steals, at last,
Along the mazes of the quiet vale.
Invited from the cliff, to whose dark brow
He clings, the steep-ascending eagle soars,
With upward pinions through the flood of day,
And, giving full his bosom to the blaze,
Gains on the sun; while all the tuneful race
Smit by afflictive noon, disorder'd droop,
Deep in the thicket; or from bower to bower,
Responsive, force an interrupted strain.
The stock-dove only through the forest coos,
Mournfully hoarse; oft ceasing from his plaint,
Short interval of weary woe! again
The sad idea of his murder'd mate,
Struck from his side by savage fowler's guile,
Across his fancy comes; and then resounds
A louder song of sorrow through the grove.
Beside the dewy border let me sit,
All in the freshness of the humid air;
There in that hollow'd rock, grotesque and wild,
An ample chair moss-lined, and over head
By flowering umbrage shaded; where the bee
Strays diligent, and with the extracted balm
Of fragrant woodbine loads his little thigh.
Now, while I taste the sweetness of the shade,
While Nature lies around deep-lull'd in noon,
Now come, bold Fancy, spread a daring flight,
And view the wonders of the torrid zone:
Climes unrelenting! with whose rage compared
Yon blaze is feeble, and yon skies are cool.
See, how at once the bright-effulgent sun,
Rising direct, swift chases from the sky
The short-lived twilight, and with ardent blaze
Looks gaily fierce through all the dazzling air:
He mounts his throne; but kind before him sends,
Issuing from out the portals of the morn,
The general breeze †, to mitigate his fire
And breathe refreshment on a fainting world.
Great are the scenes, with dreadful beauty crown'd
And barbarous wealth, that see, each circling year,
Returning suns and double seasons pass ‡;
Rocks rich in gems, and mountains big with mines,
That on the high equator ridgy rise,
Whence many a bursting stream auriferous plays:
Majestic woods, of every vigorous green,
Stage above stage, high-waving o'er the hills;
Or to the far horizon wide diffused,
A boundless deep immensity of shade.
Here lofty trees, to ancient song unknown,
The noble sons of potent heat and floods
Prone-rushing from the clouds, rear high to heaven
Their thorny stems, and broad around them throw
Meridian gloom. Here, in eternal prime,
Unnumber'd fruits, of keen delicious taste
And vital spirit, drink amid the cliffs,
And burning sands that bank the shrubby vales,
Redoubled day, yet in their rugged coats
A friendly juice to cool its rage contain.
Bear me, Pomona, to thy citron groves,
To where the lemon and the piercing lime,
With the deep orange, glowing through the green
Their lighter glories blend. Lay me reclined
Beneath thy spreading tamarind, that shakes,
Fann'd by the breeze, its fever-cooling fruit.
Deep in the night the massy locust sheds,
Quench my hot limbs; or lead me through the maze,
Embowering endless, of the Indian fig;
Or, thrown at gayer ease on some fair brow,
Let me behold, by breezy murmurs cool'd,
Broad o'er my head the verdant cedar wave,
And high palmetos lift their graceful shade.
Or, stretch'd amid these orchards of the sun,
Give me to drain the cocoa's milky bowl,
And from the palm to draw its freshening wine,
More bounteous far than all the frantic juice
Which Bacchus pours! Nor, on its slender twigs
Low-bending, be the full pomegranate scorn'd:
Nor, creeping through the woods, the gelid race
Of berries. Oft in humble station dwells
Unboastful worth, above fastidious pomp.
Witness, thou best anana, thou the pride
Of vegetable life, beyond whate'er
The poets imaged in the golden age:

* A young lady, well known to the author, who died at the age of eighteen, in the year 1738.

† Which blows constantly between the tropics from the east, or the collateral points, the north-east and south-east; caused by the pressure of the rarefied air on that before it, according to the diurnal motion of the sun from east to west.

‡ In all climates between the tropics, the sun, as he passes and repasses in his annual motion, is twice a year vertical, which produces this effect.

Quick let me strip thee of thy tufty coat,
Spread thy ambrosial stores, and feast with Jove!
From these the prospect varies. Plains immense
Lie stretch'd below, interminable meads,
And vast savannahs, where the wandering eye,
Unfix'd, is in a verdant ocean lost.
Another Flora there, of bolder hues,
And richer sweets, beyond our garden's pride,
Plays o'er the fields, and showers with sudden hand
Exuberant Spring ; for oft these valleys shift
Their green-embroider'd robe to fiery brown,
And swift to green again, as scorching suns,
Or streaming dews and torrent rains, prevail.
Along these lonely regions, where, retired
From little scenes of art, great Nature dwells
In awful solitude, and nought is seen
But the wild herds that own no master's stall,
Prodigious rivers roll their fattening seas,
On whose luxuriant herbage, half-conceal'd,
Like a fallen cedar, far-diffused his train,
Cased in green scales, the crocodile extends.
The flood disparts : behold ! in plaited mail,
Behemoth rears his head. Glanced from his side,
The darted steel in idle shivers flies ;
He fearless walks the plain, or seeks the hills,
Where, as he crops his varied fare, the herds,
In widening circle round, forget their food,
And at the harmless stranger wondering gaze.
Peaceful, beneath primeval trees, that cast
Their ample shade o'er Niger's yellow stream,
And where the Ganges rolls his sacred wave ;
Or 'mid the central depth of blackening woods,
High-raised in solemn theatre around,
Leans the huge elephant : wisest of brutes !
O truly wise, with gentle might endow'd,
Though powerful, not destructive . Here he sees
Revolving ages sweep the changeful earth,
And empires rise and fall ; regardless he
Of what the never-resting race of men
Project: thrice-happy! could he 'scape their guile,
Who mine, from cruel avarice, his steps ;
Or with his towery grandeur swell their state,
The pride of kings ! or else his strength pervert,
And bid him rage amid the mortal fray,
Astonish'd at the madness of mankind.
Wide o'er the winding umbrage of the floods,
Like vivid blossoms glowing from afar,
Thick swarm the brighter birds; for Nature's hand,
That with a sportive vanity has deck'd
The plumy nations, there her gayest hues
Profusely pours But, if she bids them shine,
Array'd in all the beauteous beams of day,
Yet, frugal still, she humbles them in song.*
Nor envy we the gaudy robes they lent
Proud Montezuma's realm, whose legions cast
A boundless radiance waving on the sun,
While Philomel is ours ; while in our shades,
Through the soft silence of the listening night,
The sober-suited songstress trills her lay.
But come, my Muse, the desert-barrier burst,
A wild expanse of lifeless sand and sky,
And, swifter than the toiling caravan,
Shoot o'er the vale of Sennar, ardent climb
The Nubian mountains, and the secret bounds
Of jealous Abyssinia boldly pierce.
Thou art no ruffian, who beneath the mask
Of social commerce comest to rob their wealth ;
No holy fury thou, blaspheming Heaven,
With consecrated steel to stab their peace,
And through the land, yet red from civil wounds,
To spread the purple tyranny of Rome.
Thou, like the harmless bee, mayst freely range
From mead to mead bright with exalted flowers,
From jasmine grove to grove mayst wander gay,
Through palmy shades and aromatic woods,
That grace the plains, invest the peopled hills,
And up the more than Alpine mountains wave.
There on the breezy summit, spreading fair
For many a league ; or on stupendous rocks,
That from the sun-redoubling valley lift,
Cool to the middle air, their lawny tops ;
Where palaces, and fanes, and villas rise ;
And gardens smile around, and cultured fields ;
And fountains gush ; and careless herds and flocks
Securely stray; a world within itself,
Disdaining all assault : there let me draw
Ethereal soul, there drink reviving gales,
Profusely breathing from the spicy groves,
And vales of fragrance ; there at distance hear
The roaring floods and cataracts, that sweep
From disembowel'd earth the virgin gold ;
And o'er the varied landscape, restless, rove,
Fervent with life of every fairer kind :
A land of wonders ! which the sun still eyes
With ray direct, as of the lovely realm
Enamour'd, and delighting there to dwell. [noon,
How changed the scene ! In blazing height of
The sun, oppress'd, is plunged in thickest gloom.
Still horror reigns, a dreary twilight round
Of struggling night and day malignant mix'd.
For to the hot equator crowding fast,
Where, highly rarefied, the yielding air
Admits their stream, incessant vapours roll,
Amazing clouds on clouds continual heap'd ;
Or whirl'd tempestuous by the gusty wind,
Or silent borne along, heavy, and slow,
With the big stores of steaming oceans charged.
Meantime, amid these upper seas, condensed
Around the cold aërial mountain's brow,
And by conflicting winds together dash'd,
The thunder holds his black tremendous throne:
From cloud to cloud the rending lightnings rage ;
Till, in the furious elemental war
Dissolved, the whole precipitated mass
Unbroken floods and solid torrents pours.
The treasures these, hid from the bounded search
Of ancient knowledge, whence, with annual pomp,
Rich king of floods ! o'erflows the swelling Nile.
From his two springs, in Gojam's sunny realm,
Pure-welling out, he through the lucid lake
Of fair Dambea rolls his infant stream.
There, by the Naiads nursed, he sports away
His playful youth, amid the fragrant isles,
That with unfading verdure smile around.
Ambitious, thence the manly river breaks ;
And gathering many a flood, and copious fed
With all the mellow'd treasures of the sky,
Winds in progressive majesty along:
Through splendid kingdoms now devolves his maze,
Now wanders wild o'er solitary tracts
Of life-deserted sand; till, glad to quit
The joyless desert, down the Nubian rocks,
From thundering steep to steep, he pours his urn,
And Egypt joys beneath the spreading wave
His brother Niger too, and all the floods
In which the full-form'd maids of Afric lave
Their jetty limbs ; and all that from the tract

*In all the regions of the torrid zone, the birds, though more beautiful in their plumage, are observed to be less melodious than ours.

Of woody mountains stretch'd thro' gorgeous Ind
Fall on Cor'mandel's coast, or Malabar;
From Menam's* orient stream, that nightly shines
With insect lamps, to where Aurora sheds
On Indus' smiling banks the rosy shower:
All, at this bounteous season, ope their urns,
And pour untoiling harvest o'er the land.
Nor less thy world, Columbus, drinks, refresh'd,
The lavish moisture of the melting year.
Wide o'er his isles the branching Oronoque
Rolls a brown deluge, and the native drives
To dwell aloft on life-sufficing trees,
At once his dome, his robe, his food, and arms.
Swell'd by a thousand streams, impetuous hurl'd
From all the roaring Andes, huge descends
The mighty Orellana. Scarce the Muse
Dares stretch her wing o'er this enormous mass
Of rushing water; scarce she dares attempt
The sea-like Plata, to whose dread expanse,
Continuous depth, and wondrous length of course,
Our floods are rills. With unabated force,
In silent dignity they sweep along,
And traverse realms unknown, and blooming wilds,
And fruitful deserts, worlds of solitude,
Where the sun smiles, and seasons teem in vain,
Unseen, and unenjoy'd. Forsaking these,
O'er peopled plains they fair-diffusive flow,
And many a nation feed, and circle safe,
In their soft bosom, many a happy isle;
The seat of blameless Pan, yet undisturb'd
By Christian crimes and Europe's cruel sons.
Thus pouring on they proudly seek the deep,
Whose vanquish'd tide, recoiling from the shock,
Yields to this liquid weight of half the globe,
And Ocean trembles for his green domain.
But what avails this wondrous waste of wealth?
This gay profusion of luxurious bliss?
This pomp of Nature? what their balmy meads,
Their powerful herbs, and Ceres void of pain?
By vagrant birds dispersed, and wafting winds,
What their unplanted fruits? what the cool draughts,
The ambrosial food, rich gums, and spicy health,
Their forests yield? Their toiling insects what?
Their silky pride, and vegetable robes?
Ah! what avail their fatal treasures, hid
Deep in the bowels of the pitying earth,
Golconda's gems, and sad Potosi's mines,
Where dwelt the gentlest children of the sun?
What all that Afric's golden rivers roll,
Her odorous woods, and shining ivory stores?
Ill-fated race! the softening arts of peace,
Whate'er the humanising Muses teach;
The godlike wisdom of the temper'd breast;
Progressive truth, the patient force of thought;
Investigation calm, whose silent powers
Command the world; the light that leads to Heaven;
Kind equal rule, the government of laws,
And all-protecting freedom, which alone
Sustains the name and dignity of man:
These are not theirs. The parent sun himself
Seems o'er this world of slaves to tyrannise;
And, with oppressive ray the roseate bloom
Of beauty blasting, gives the gloomy hue,
And feature gross: or worse, to ruthless deeds,
Mad jealousy, blind rage, and fell revenge,
Their fervid spirit fires. Love dwells not there,
The soft regards, the tenderness of life,
The heart-shed tear, the ineffable delight
Of sweet humanity: these court the beam
Of milder climes; in selfish fierce desire,
And the wild fury of voluptuous sense,
There lost. The very brute-creation there
This rage partakes, and burns with horrid fire.
Lo! the green serpent, from his dark abode,
Which e'en imagination fears to tread,
At noon forth-issuing, gathers up his train
In orbs immense, then, darting out anew,
Seeks the refreshing fount, by which, diffused,
He throws his folds: and while, with threatening tongue
And deathful jaws erect, the monster curls
His flaming crest, all other thirst appall'd,
Or shivering flies, or check'd at distance stands,
Nor dares approach. But still more direful he,
The small close-lurking minister of fate,
Whose high-concocted venom through the veins
A rapid lightning darts, arresting swift
The vital current. Form'd to humble man,
This child of vengeful Nature! there, sublimed
To fearless lust of blood, the savage race
Roam, licensed by the shading hour of guilt,
And foul misdeed, when the pure day has shut
His sacred eye. The tiger darting fierce
Impetuous on the prey his glance has doom'd;
The lively-shining leopard, speckled o'er
With many a spot, the beauty of the waste;
And, scorning all the taming arts of man,
The keen hyena, fellest of the fell;
These rushing from the inhospitable woods
Of Mauritania, or the tufted isles
That verdant rise amid the Lybian wild,
Innumerous glare around their shaggy king,
Majestic, stalking o'er the printed sand;
And with imperious and repeated roars,
Demand their fated food. The fearful flocks
Crowd near the guardian swain; the nobler herds,
Where round their lordly bull, in rural ease,
They ruminating lie, with horror hear
The coming rage. The awaken'd village starts;
And to her fluttering breast the mother strains
Her thoughtless infant. From the pirate's den,
Or stern Morocco's tyrant fang, escaped,
The wretch half wishes for his bonds again;
While, uproar all, the wilderness resounds,
From Atlas eastward to the frighted Nile.
Unhappy he, who from the first of joys,
Society, cut off, is left alone
Amid this world of death. Day after day,
Sad on the jutting eminence he sits,
And views the main that ever toils below;
Still fondly forming in the farthest verge,
Where the round ether mixes with the wave,
Ships, dim-discover'd, dropping from the clouds;
At evening to the setting sun he turns
A mournful eye, and down his dying heart
Sinks helpless; while the wonted roar is up,
And hiss continual through the tedious night.
Yet here, even here, into these black abodes
Of monsters, unappall'd, from stooping Rome,
And guilty Cæsar, Liberty retired,
Her Cato following through Numidian wilds:
Disdainful of Campania's gentle plains,
And all the green delights Ausonia pours,
When for them she must bend the servile knee,
And fawning take the splendid robber's boon.
Nor stop the terrors of these regions here.
Commission'd demons oft, angels of wrath,

* The river that runs through Siam, on whose banks a vast multitude of those insects called fire-flies make a beautiful appearance at night.

Let loose the raging elements. Breathed hot
From all the boundless furnace of the sky,
And the wide glittering waste of burning sand,
A suffocating wind the pilgrim smites
With instant death. Patient of thirst and toil,
Son of the desert! even the camel feels,
Shot through his wither'd heart, the fiery blast.
Or from the black-red ether, bursting broad,
Sallies the sudden whirlwind. Straight the sands,
Commoved around, in gathering eddies play;
Nearer and nearer still they darkening come:
Till, with the general all-involving storm
Swept up, the whole continuous wilds arise;
And by their noon-day fount dejected thrown,
Or sunk at night in sad disastrous sleep,
Beneath descending hills the caravan
Is buried deep. In Cairo's crowded streets
The impatient merchant, wondering, waits in vain,
And Mecca saddens at the long delay.
  But chief at sea, whose every flexile wave
Obeys the blast, the aërial tumult swells.
In the dread ocean, undulating wide,
Beneath the radiant line that girts the globe,
The circling Typhon, whirl'd from point to point,
Exhausting all the rage of all the sky,
And dire Ecnephia*, reign. Amid the heavens,
Falsely serene, deep in a cloudy speck†
Compress'd, the mighty tempest brooding dwells;
Of no regard save to the skilful eye,
Fiery and foul, the small prognostic hangs
Aloft, or on the promontory's brow
Musters its force. A faint deceitful calm,
A fluttering gale, the demon sends before,
To tempt the spreading sail. Then down at once,
Precipitant, descends a mingled mass
Of roaring winds, and flame, and rushing floods.
In wild amazement fix'd the sailor stands.
Art is too slow: by rapid fate oppress'd,
His broad-wing'd vessel drinks the whelming tide,
Hid in the bosom of the black abyss.
With such mad seas the daring Gama‡ fought,
For many a day, and many a dreadful night,
Incessant, labouring round the stormy Cape;
By bold ambition led, and bolder thirst
Of gold. For then from ancient gloom emerged
The rising world of trade: the Genius, then,
Of navigation, that, in hopeless sloth,
Had slumber'd on the vast Atlantic deep,
For idle ages, starting, heard at last
The Lusitanian prince§; who, Heaven-inspired,
To love of useful glory roused mankind,
And in unbounded commerce mix'd the world.
  Increasing still the terrors of these storms,
His jaws horrific arm'd with threefold fate,
Here dwells the direful shark. Lured by the scent
Of steaming crowds, of rank disease, and death,
Behold! he rushing cuts the briny flood,
Swift as the gale can bear the ship along;
And, from the partners of that cruel trade
Which spoils unhappy Guinea of her sons,

* Typhon and Ecnephia, names of particular storms or hurricanes, known only between the tropics.

† Called by sailors the Ox-eye, being in appearance at first no bigger.

‡ Vasco de Gama, the first who sailed round Africa, by the Cape of Good Hope, to the East Indies.

§ Don Henry, third son to John the First, King of Portugal. His strong genius to the discovery of new countries was the chief source of all the modern improvements in navigation.

Demands his share of prey, demands themselves.
The stormy fates descend: one death involves
Tyrants and slaves; when straight, their mangled limbs
Crashing at once, he dyes the purple seas
With gore, and riots in the vengeful meal.
  When o'er this world, by equinoctial rains
Flooded immense, looks out the joyless sun,
And draws the copious steam, from swampy fens,
Where putrefaction into life ferments,
And breathes destructive myriads! or from woods,
Impenetrable shades, recesses foul,
In vapours rank and blue corruption wrapt,
Whose gloomy horrors yet no desperate foot
Has ever dared to pierce; then, wasteful, forth
Walks the dire power of pestilent disease.
A thousand hideous fiends her course attend,
Sick Nature blasting, and to heartless woe,
And feeble desolation, casting down
The towering hopes and all the pride of man.
Such as, of late, at Carthagena quench'd
The British fire. You, gallant Vernon, saw,
The miserable scene; you, pitying, saw
To infant weakness sunk the warrior's arm;
Saw the deep-racking pang, the ghastly form,
The lip pale-quivering, and the beamless eye
No more with ardour bright: you heard the groans
Of agonising ships, from shore to shore;
Heard nightly plunged amid the sullen waves
The frequent corse; while on each other fix'd,
In sad presage, the blank assistants seem'd,
Silent, to ask, whom Fate would next demand.
  What need I mention those inclement skies,
Where, frequent o'er the sickening city, Plague,
The fiercest child of Nemesis divine,
Descends? From Ethiopia's poison'd woods,
From stifled Cairo's filth, and fetid fields
With locust-armies putrifying heap'd||,
This great destroyer sprung. Her awful rage
The brutes escape; man is her destined prey,
Intemperate man! and o'er his guilty domes
She draws a close incumbent cloud of death;
Uninterrupted by the living winds,
Forbid to blow a wholesome breeze; and stain'd
With many a mixture by the sun, suffused,
Of angry aspect. Princely wisdom, then,
Dejects his watchful eye; and from the hand
Of feeble justice, ineffectual, drop
The sword and balance: mute the voice of joy,
And hush'd the clamour of the busy world.
Empty the streets, with uncouth verdure clad;
Into the worst of deserts sudden turn'd
The cheerful haunt of men: unless escaped
From the doom'd house, where matchless horror reigns,
Shut up by barbarous fear, the smitten wretch,
With frenzy wild, breaks loose; and loud to Heaven
Screaming, the dreadful policy arraigns,
Inhuman, and unwise. The sullen door
Yet uninfected, on its cautious hinge
Fearing to turn, abhors society:
Dependants, friends, relations, Love himself,
Savage by woe, forget the tender tie,
The sweet engagement of the feeling heart.
But vain their selfish care: the circling sky,
The wide enlivening air, is full of fate;
And, struck by turns, in solitary pangs
They fall, unblest, untended, and unmourn'd.

|| These are the causes supposed to be the first origin of the plague, in Dr. Mead's elegant book on that subject

Thus o'er the prostrate city black Despair
Extends her raven wing; while to complete
The scene of desolation, stretch'd around,
The grim guards stand, denying all retreat,
And give the flying wretch a better death.
Much yet remains unsung: the rage intense
Of brazen-vaulted skies, of iron fields,
Where drought and famine starve the blasted year:
Fired by the torch of noon to tenfold rage,
The infuriate hill that shoots the pillar'd flame,
And, roused within the subterranean world,
The expanding earthquake, that resistless shakes
Aspiring cities from their solid base,
And buries mountains in the flaming gulf.
But 'tis enough; return, my vagrant Muse:
A nearer scene of horror calls thee home.
Behold, slow-settling o'er the lurid grove,
Unusual darkness broods, and, growing, gains
The full possession of the sky, surcharged.
With wrathful vapour, from the secret beds,
Where sleep the mineral generations, drawn.
Thence nitre, sulphur, and the fiery spume
Of fat bitumen, steaming on the day,
With various-tinctured trains of latent flame,
Pollute the sky, and in yon baneful cloud
A reddening gloom, a magazine of fate,
Ferment; till, by the touch ethereal roused,
The dash of clouds, or irritating war
Of fighting winds, while all is calm below,
They furious spring. A boding silence reigns,
Dread through the dun expanse; save the dull sound
That from the mountain, previous to the storm,
Rolls o'er the muttering earth, disturbs the flood,
And shakes the forest-leaf without a breath.
Prone, to the lowest vale, the aërial tribes
Descend: the tempest-loving raven scarce
Dares wing the dubious dusk. In rueful gaze
The cattle stand, and on the scowling heavens
Cast a deploring eye; by man forsook,
Who to the crowded cottage hies him fast,
Or seeks the shelter of the downward cave.
'Tis listening fear, and dumb amazement all:
When to the startled eye the sudden glance
Appears far south, eruptive through the cloud;
And following slower, in explosion vast,
The Thunder raises his tremendous voice.
At first, heard solemn o'er the verge of heaven,
The tempest growls; but as it nearer comes,
And rolls its awful burden on the wind,
The lightnings flash a larger curve, and more
The noise astounds: till over head a sheet
Of livid flame discloses wide; then shuts,
And opens wider; shuts and opens still
Expansive, wrapping ether in a blaze.
Follows the loosen'd aggravated roar,
Enlarging, deepening, mingling; peal on peal
Crush'd horrible, convulsing heaven and earth.
Down comes a deluge of sonorous hail,
Or prone-descending rain. Wide-rent, the clouds
Pour a whole flood; and yet, its flame unquench'd,
The unconquerable lightning struggles through
Ragged and fierce, or in red whirling balls,
And fires the mountains with redoubled rage.
Black from the stroke, above, the smouldering pine
Stands a sad shatter'd trunk; and, stretch'd below,
A lifeless group the blasted cattle lie:
Here the soft flocks, with that same harmless look
They wore alive, and ruminating still
In fancy's eye; and there the frowning bull,
And ox half-raised. Struck on the castled cliff,
The venerable tower and spiry fane
Resign their aged pride. The gloomy woods
Start at the flash, and from their deep recess,
Wide-flaming out, their trembling inmates shake.
Amid Carnarvon's mountains rages loud
The repercussive roar: with mighty crash,
Into the flashing deep, from the rude rocks
Of Penmanmaur heap'd hideous to the sky,
Tumble the smitten cliffs: and Snowden's peak,
Dissolving, instant yields his wintry load.
Far seen, the heights of heathy Cheviot blaze,
And Thule bellows through her utmost isles.
Guilt hears appall'd, with deeply-troubled thought;
And yet not always on the guilty head
Descends the fated flash. Young Celadon
And his Amelia were a matchless pair;
With equal virtue form'd, and equal grace,
The same, distinguish'd by their sex alone:
Hers, the mild lustre of the blooming morn,
And his, the radiance of the risen day.
They loved: but such their guileless passion was
As in the dawn of time inform'd the heart
Of innocence and undissembling truth.
'Twas friendship, heighten'd by the mutual wish;
The enchanting hope, and sympathetic glow,
Beam'd from the mutual eye. Devoting all
To love, each was to each a dearer self;
Supremely happy in the awaken'd power
Of giving joy. Alone, amid the shades,
Still in harmonious intercourse they lived
The rural day, and talk'd the flowing heart,
Or sigh'd and look'd unutterable things.
So pass'd their life, a clear united stream,
By care unruffled; till, in evil hour,
The tempest caught them on the tender walk,
Heedless how far and where its mazes stray'd,
While, with each other blest, creative love
Still bade eternal Eden smile around.
Presaging instant fate, her bosom heaved
Unwonted sighs, and, stealing oft a look
Of the big gloom, on Celadon her eye
Fell tearful, wetting her disorder'd cheek.
In vain assuring love, and confidence
In Heaven, repress'd her fear; it grew, and shook
Her frame near dissolution. He perceived
The unequal conflict, and, as angels look
On dying saints, his eyes compassion shed,
With love illumined high. "Fear not," he said,
"Sweet innocence! thou stranger to offence,
And inward storm! He, who yon skies involves
In frowns of darkness, ever smiles on thee
With kind regard. O'er thee the secret shaft
That wastes at midnight, or the undreaded hour
Of noon, flies harmless; and that very voice,
Which thunders terror through the guilty heart,
With tongues of seraphs whispers peace to thine.
'Tis safety to be near thee sure, and thus
To clasp perfection!" From his void embrace,
(Mysterious Heaven!) that moment, to the ground,
A blacken'd corse, was struck the beauteous maid
But who can paint the lover, as he stood,
Pierced by severe amazement, hating life,
Speechless, and fix'd in all the death of woe!
So (faint resemblance!) on the marble tomb,
The well-dissembled mourner stooping stands,
For ever silent, and for ever sad.
As from the face of heaven the shatter'd clouds
Tumultuous rove, the interminable sky
Sublimer swells, and o'er the world expands
A purer azure. Through the lighten'd air

A higher lustre and a clearer calm,
Diffusive, tremble ; while, as if in sign
Of danger past, a glittering robe of joy,
Set off abundant by the yellow ray,
Invests the fields, and Nature smiles revived.
'Tis beauty all, and grateful song around,
Join'd to the low of kine, and numerous bleat
Of flocks thick-nibbling through the clover'd vale.
And shall the hymn be marr'd by thankless man,
Most favour'd ! who with voice articulate
Should lead the chorus of this lower world ;
Shall he, so soon forgetful of the Hand
That hush'd the thunder, and serenes the sky,
Extinguish'd feel that spark the tempest waked,
That sense of powers exceeding far his own,
Ere yet his feeble heart has lost its fears ?
Cheer'd by the milder beam, the sprightly youth
Speeds to the well-known pool, whose crystal depth
A sandy bottom shows. Awhile he stands
Gazing the inverted landscape, half afraid
To meditate the blue profound below ;
Then plunges headlong down the circling flood.
His ebon tresses and his rosy cheek
Instant emerge ; and through the obedient wave,
At each short breathing by his lip repell'd,
With arms and legs according well, he makes,
As humour leads, an easy-winding path ;
While, from his polish'd sides, a dewy light
Effuses on the pleased spectators round.
This is the purest exercise of health,
The kind refresher of the summer heats ;
Nor, when cold Winter keens the brightening flood,
Would I, weak-shivering, linger on the brink.
Thus life redoubles, and is oft preserved,
By the bold swimmer, in the swift illapse
Of accident disastrous. Hence the limbs
Knit into force ; and the same Roman arm,
That rose victorious o'er the conquer'd earth,
First learn'd, while tender, to subdue the wave.
Even from the body's purity the mind
Receives a secret sympathetic aid.
Close in the covert of a hazel copse,
Where, winded into pleasing solitudes,
Runs out the rambling dale, young Damon sat,
Pensive, and pierced with love's delightful pangs.
There to the stream that down the distant rocks
Hoarse murmuring fell, and plaintive breeze that play'd
Among the bending willows, falsely he
Of Musidora's cruelty complain'd.
She felt his flame ; but deep within her breast,
In bashful coyness, or in maiden pride,
The soft return conceal'd, save when it stole
In side-long glances from her downcast eye,
Or from her swelling soul in stifled sighs.
Touch'd by the scene, no stranger to his vows,
He framed a melting lay to try her heart ;
And, if an infant passion struggled there,
To call that passion forth. Thrice happy swain !
A lucky chance, that oft decides the fate
Of mighty monarchs, then decided thine.
For lo ! conducted by the laughing Loves,
This cool retreat his Musidora sought :
Warm in her cheek the sultry season glow'd ;
And, robed in loose array she came to bathe
Her fervent limbs in the refreshing stream.
What shall he do ? In sweet confusion lost,
And dubious flutterings, he awhile remain'd ;
A pure ingenuous elegance of soul,
A delicate refinement, known to few.
Perplex'd his breast, and urged him to retire :
But love forbade. Ye prudes in virtue, say,
Say, ye severest, what would you have done ?
Meantime, this fairer nymph than ever blest
Arcadian stream, with timid eye around
The banks surveying, stripp'd her beauteous limbs,
To taste the lucid coolness of the flood.
Ah then ! not Paris on the piny top
Of Ida panted stronger, when aside
The rival goddesses the veil divine
Cast unconfined, and gave him all their charms,
Than, Damon, thou ; as from the snowy leg,
And slender foot, the inverted silk she drew ;
As the soft touch dissolved the virgin zone ;
And through the parting robe, the alternate breast,
With youth wild-throbbing, on thy lawless gaze
In full luxuriance rose. But, desperate youth,
How durst thou risk the soul-distracting view,
As from her naked limbs, of glowing white,
Harmonious swell'd by Nature's finest hand,
In folds loose-floating fell the fainter lawn ;
And fair-exposed she stood, shrunk from herself,
With fancy blushing, at the doubtful breeze
Alarm'd, and starting like the fearful fawn ?
Then to the flood she rush'd ; the parted flood
Its lovely guest with closing waves received ;
And every beauty softening, every grace
Flushing anew, a mellow lustre shed :
As shines the lily through the crystal mild ;
Or as the rose amid the morning dew,
Fresh from Aurora's hand, more sweetly glows.
While thus she wanton'd, now beneath the wave
But ill conceal'd, and now with streaming locks,
That half embraced her in a humid veil,
Rising again, the latent Damon drew
Such maddening draughts of beauty to the soul,
As for awhile o'erwhelm'd his raptured thought
With luxury too daring. Check'd, at last,
By love's respectful modesty, he deem'd
The theft profane, if aught profane to love
Can e'er be deem'd ; and, struggling from the shade,
With headlong hurry fled : but first these lines,
Traced by his ready pencil, on the bank
With trembling hand he threw. "Bathe on, my fair,
Yet unbeheld, save by the sacred eye
Of faithful love : I go to guard thy haunt,
To keep from thy recess each vagrant foot,
And each licentious eye." With wild surprise,
As if to marble struck, devoid of sense,
A stupid moment motionless she stood :
So stands the statue* that enchants the world,
So bending tries to veil the matchless boast,
The mingled beauties of exulting Greece.
Recovering, swift she flew to find those robes
Which blissful Eden knew not ; and, array'd
In careless haste, the alarming paper snatch'd.
But, when her Damon's well-known hand she saw,
Her terrors vanish'd, and a softer train
Of mix'd emotions, hard to be described,
Her sudden bosom seized : shame void of guilt,
The charming blush of innocence, esteem,
And admiration of her lover's flame,
By modesty exalted : even a sense
Of self-approving beauty stole across
Her busy thought. At length a tender calm
Hush'd by degrees the tumult of her soul ;

* The Venus de' Medici.

And on the spreading beech, that o'er the stream
Incumbent hung, she with the silvan pen
Of rural lovers this confession carved,
Which soon her Damon kiss'd with weeping joy:
"Dear youth, sole judge of what these verses mean,
By fortune too much favour'd, but by love,
Alas! not favour'd less, be still as now
Discreet: the time may come you need not fly."
The sun has lost his rage: his downward orb
Shoots nothing now but animating warmth,
And vital lustre; that, with various ray,
Lights up the clouds, those beauteous robes of heaven,
Incessant roll'd into romantic shapes,
The dream of waking Fancy. Broad below,
Cover'd with ripening fruits, and swelling fast
Into the perfect year, the pregnant earth
And all her tribes rejoice. Now the soft hour
Of walking comes: for him who lonely loves
To seek the distant hills, and there converse
With Nature; there to harmonise his heart,
And in pathetic song to breathe around
The harmony to others. Social friends,
Attuned to happy unison of soul;
To whose exalting eye a fairer world,
Of which the vulgar never had a glimpse,
Displays its charms; whose minds are richly fraught
With philosophic stores, superior light;
And in whose breast, enthusiastic, burns
Virtue, the sons of interest deem romance;
Now call'd abroad enjoy the falling day:
Now to the verdant Portico of woods,
To Nature's vast Lyceum forth they walk;
By that kind school where no proud master reigns,
The full free converse of the friendly heart,
Improving and improved. Now from the world,
Sacred to sweet retirement, lovers steal,
And pour their souls in transport, which the sire
Of love approving hears, and calls it good.
Which way, Amanda, shall we bend our course?
The choice perplexes. Wherefore should we chuse?
All is the same with thee. Say, shall we wind
Along the streams? or walk the smiling mead?
Or court the forest-glades? or wander wild
Among the waving harvests? or ascend,
While radiant Summer opens all its pride,
Thy hill, delightful Shene*? Here let us sweep
The boundless landscape: now the raptured eye,
Exulting, swift to huge Augusta send,
Now to the Sister-Hills† that skirt her plain;
To lofty Harrow now, and now to where
Majestic Windsor lifts his princely brow.
In lovely contrast to this glorious view,
Calmly magnificent, then will we turn
To where the silver Thames first rural grows.
There let the feasted eye unwearied stray:
Luxurious, there, rove through the pendent woods
That nodding hang o'er Harrington's retreat:
And, stooping thence to Ham's embowering walks,
Beneath whose shades, in spotless peace retired,
With Her the pleasing partner of his heart,
The worthy Queensberry yet laments his Gay,
And polish'd Cornbury woos the willing Muse,
Slow let us trace the matchless vale of Thames;
Fair winding up to where the muses haunt
In Twick'nam's bowers, and for their Pope implore
The healing God‡; to royal Hampton's pile,
To Clermont's terraced height, and Esher's groves,
Where in the sweetest solitude, embraced
By the soft windings of the silent Mole,
From courts and senates Pelham finds repose.
Enchanting vale! beyond whate'er the Muse
Has of Achaia or Hesperia sung!
O vale of bliss! O softly-swelling hills!
On which the Power of Cultivation lies,
And joys to see the wonders of his toil.
Heavens! what a goodly prospect spreads around,
Of hills, and dales, and woods, and lawns, and spires,
And glittering towns, and gilded streams, till all
The stretching landscape into smoke decays!
Happy Britannia! where the Queen of Arts,
Inspiring vigour, Liberty abroad
Walks unconfined, even to thy farthest cots,
And scatters plenty with unsparing hand.
Rich is thy soil, and merciful thy clime;
Thy streams unfailing in the Summer's drought;
Unmatched thy guardian-oaks; thy valleys float
With golden waves; and on thy mountains flocks
Bleat numberless; while, roving round their sides,
Bellow the blackening herds in lusty droves.
Beneath, thy meadows glow, and rise unquelled
Against the mower's scythe. On every hand
Thy villas shine. Thy country teems with wealth;
And property assures it to the swain,
Pleased, and unwearied, in his guarded toil.
Full are thy cities with the sons of Art
And trade and joy, in every busy street,
Mingling are heard: e'en Drudgery himself,
As at the car he sweats, or dusty hews
The palace-stone, looks gay. Thy crowded ports,
Where rising masts an endless prospect yield,
With labour burn, and echo to the shouts
Of hurried sailor, as he hearty waves
His last adieu, and loosening every sheet,
Resigns the spreading vessel to the wind.
Bold, firm, and graceful, are thy generous youth,
By hardship sinewed, and by danger fired,
Scattering the nations where they go; and first
Or on the listed plain, or stormy seas.
Mild are thy glories too, as o'er the plains
Of thriving peace thy thoughtful sires preside
In genius, and substantial learning, high;
For every virtue, every worth, renown'd;
Sincere, plain-hearted, hospitable, kind;
Yet like the mustering thunder when provoked,
The dread of tyrants, and the sole resource
Of those that under grim oppression groan.
Thy sons of Glory many! Alfred thine,
In whom the splendour of heroic war,
And more heroic peace, when govern'd well,
Combine; whose hallow'd name the Virtues saint
And his own Muses love; the best of kings!
With him thy Edwards and thy Henries shine,
Names dear to fame; the first who deep impress'd
On haughty Gaul the terror of thy arms,
That awes her genius still. In statesmen thou,
And patriots, fertile. Thine a steady More,
Who, with a generous though mistaken zeal,
Withstood a brutal tyrant's useful rage,
Like Cato firm, like Aristides just,
Like rigid Cincinnatus nobly poor,
A dauntless soul erect, who smiled on death.
Frugal and wise, a Walsingham is thine;
A Drake, who made thee mistress of the deep,

* The old name of Richmond; signifying, in Saxon, *shining* or *splendour*.

† Highgate and Hampstead.

‡ In his last sickness.

And bore thy name in thunder round the world.
Then flamed thy spirit high ; but who can speak
The numerous worthies of the Maiden Reign?
In Raleigh mark their every glory mix'd ; [all
Raleigh, the scourge of Spain ! whose breast with
The sage, the patriot, and the hero burn'd ;
Nor sunk his vigour, when a coward reign
The warrior fetter'd, and at last resign'd,
To glut the vengeance of a vanquish'd foe.
Then, active still and unrestrain'd, his mind
Explored the vast extent of ages past,
And with his prison-hours enrich'd the world ;
Yet found no times, in all the long research,
So glorious, or so base, as those he proved,
In which he conquer'd, and in which he bled.
Nor can the Muse the gallant Sidney pass,
The plume of war ! with early laurels crown'd,
The lover's myrtle, and the poet's bay.
A Hampden too is thine, illustrious land !
Wise, strenuous, firm, of unsubmitting soul,
Who stemm'd the torrent of a downward age
To slavery prone, and bade thee rise again
In all thy native pomp of freedom bold.
Bright, at his call, thy Age of Men effulged,
Of men on whom late time a kindling eye
Shall turn, and tyrants tremble while they read.
Bring every sweetest flower, and let me strew
The grave where Russel lies; whose temper'd blood,
With calmest cheerfulness for thee resign'd,
Stain'd the sad annals of a giddy reign ;
Aiming at lawless power, though meanly sunk
In loose inglorious luxury. With him
His friend, the British Cassius *, fearless bled;
Of high determined spirit, roughly brave,
By ancient learning to the enlighten'd love
Of ancient freedom warm'd. Fair thy renown
In awful sages and in noble bards ;
Soon as the light of dawning Science spread
Her orient ray, and waked the Muses' song.
Thine is a Bacon ; hapless in his choice,
Unfit to stand the civil storm of state,
And through the smooth barbarity of courts,
With firm but pliant virtue, forward still
To urge his course : him for the studious shade
Kind Nature form'd, deep, comprehensive, clear,
Exact, and elegant : in one rich soul
Plato, the Stagyrite, and Tully, join'd.
The great deliverer he ! who from the gloom
Of cloister'd monks, and jargon-teaching schools,
Led forth the true Philosophy, there long
Held in the magic chain of words and forms,
And definitions void : he led her forth,
Daughter of Heaven ! that slow ascending still,
Investigating sure the chain of things,
With radiant finger points to Heaven again.
The generous Ashley † thine, the friend of man ;
Who scann'd his nature with a brother's eye,
His weakness prompt to shade, to raise his aim,
To touch the finer movements of the mind,
And with the moral beauty charm the heart.
Why need I name thy Boyle, whose pious search
Amid the dark recesses of his works
The great Creator sought? And why thy Locke,
Who made the whole internal world his own?
Let Newton, pure intelligence, whom God
To mortals lent, to trace his boundless works

* Algernon Sidney.

† Anthony Ashley Cooper, earl of Shaftesbury.

From laws sublimely simple, speak thy fame
In all philosophy For lofty sense,
Creative fancy, and inspection keen
Through the deep windings of the human heart,
Is not wild Shakspeare thine and Nature's boast
Is not each great, each amiable Muse
Of classic ages in thy Milton met?
A genius universal as his theme,
Astonishing as Chaos, as the bloom
Of blowing Eden fair, as Heaven sublime?
Nor shall my verse that elder bard forget,
The gentle Spenser, Fancy's pleasing son ;
Who, like a copious river, pour'd his song
O'er all the mazes of enchanted ground :
Nor thee, his ancient master, laughing sage,
Chaucer, whose native manners-painting verse,
Well moralised, shines through the Gothic cloud
Of time and language o'er thy genius thrown.
May my song soften, as thy daughters I,
Britannia, hail ! for beauty is their own,
The feeling heart, simplicity of life,
And elegance, and taste : the faultless form,
Shaped by the hand of Harmony ; the cheek,
Where the live crimson, through the native white
Soft-shooting, o'er the face diffuses bloom,
And every nameless grace ; the parted lip,
Like the red rose-bud moist with morning-dew,
Breathing delight ; and, under flowing jet,
Or sunny ringlets, or of circling brown,
The neck slight-shaded, and the swelling breast
The look resistless, piercing to the soul,
And by the soul inform'd, when dress'd in love
She sits high-smiling in the conscious eye.
Island of bliss ! amid the subject seas,
That thunder round thy rocky coasts, set up,
At once, the wonder, terror, and delight,
Of distant nations, whose remotest shores
Can soon be shaken by thy naval arm ;
Not to be shook thyself, but all assaults
Baffling, as thy hoar cliffs the loud sea-wave.
O Thou ! by whose Almighty nod the scale
Of empire rises, or alternate falls,
Send forth the saving Virtues round the land,
In bright patrol : white Peace, and social Love ;
The tender-looking Charity, intent
On gentle deeds, and shedding tears through smiles;
Undaunted Truth, and Dignity of mind ;
Courage composed, and keen ; sound Temperance
Healthful in heart and look ; clear Chastity,
With blushes reddening as she moves along,
Disorder'd at the deep regard she draws ;
Rough Industry ; Activity untired,
With copious life inform'd, and all awake ;
While in the radiant front superior shines
That first paternal virtue, Public Zeal ;
Who throws o'er all an equal wide survey,
And, ever musing on the common weal,
Still labours glorious with some great design.
Low walks the sun, and broadens by degrees,
Just o'er the verge of day. The shifting clouds
Assembled gay, a richly gorgeous train,
In all their pomp attend his setting throne.
Air, earth, and ocean smile immense. And now
As if his weary chariot sought the bowers
Of Amphitrite, and her tending nymphs,
(So Grecian fable sung) he dips his orb ;
Now half-immersed, and now a golden curve,
Gives one bright glance, then total disappears.
For ever running an enchanted round,
Passes the day, deceitful, vain, and void

As fleets the vision o'er the formful brain,
This moment hurrying wild the impassion'd soul,
The next in nothing lost. 'Tis so to him,
The dreamer of this earth, an idle blank:
A sight of horror to the cruel wretch,
Who all day long in sordid pleasure roll'd,
Himself a useless load, has squander'd vile,
Upon his scoundrel train, what might have cheer'd
A drooping family of modest worth.
But to the generous still-improving mind,
That gives the hopeless heart to sing for joy,
Diffusing kind beneficence around,
Boastless, as now descends the silent dew;
To him the long review of order'd life
Is inward rapture, only to be felt.
Confess'd from yonder slow-extinguish'd cloud,
All ether softening, sober Evening takes
Her wonted station in the middle air;
A thousand shadows at her beck. First this
She sends on earth; then that of deeper dye
Steals soft behind; and then a deeper still,
In circle following circle, gathers round,
To close the face of things. A fresher gale
Begins to wave the wood, and stir the stream,
Sweeping with shadowy gust the fields of corn;
While the quail clamours for his running mate.
Wide o'er the thistly lawn, as swells the breeze,
A whitening shower of vegetable down
Amusive floats. The kind impartial care
Of Nature nought disdains: thoughtful to feed
Her lowest sons, and clothe the coming year,
From field to field the feather'd seed she wings.
His folded flock secure, the shepherd home
Hies, merry-hearted; and by turns relieves
The ruddy milkmaid of her brimming pail;
The beauty whom perhaps his witless heart,
Unknowing what the joy-mix'd anguish means,
Sincerely loves, by that best language shown
Of cordial glances, and obliging deeds.
Onward they pass, o'er many a panting height,
And valley sunk, and unfrequented; where
At fall of eve the fairy people throng,
In various game, and revelry, to pass
The summer night, as village-stories tell.
But far about they wander from the grave
Of him, whom his ungentle fortune urged
Against his own sad breast to lift the hand
Of impious violence. The lonely tower
Is also shunn'd; whose mournful chambers hold,
So night-struck Fancy dreams, the yelling ghost.
Among the crooked lanes, on every hedge,
The glow-worm lights his gems; and, through the dark,
A moving radiance twinkles. Evening yields
The world to Night; not in her winter robe
Of massy Stygian woof, but loose array'd
In mantle dun. A faint erroneous ray,
Glanced from the imperfect surfaces of things,
Flings half an image on the straining eye;
While wavering woods, and villages and streams,
And rocks, and mountain-tops, that long retain'd
The ascending gleam, are all one swimming scene,
Uncertain if beheld. Sudden to heaven
Thence weary vision turns, where, leading soft
The silent hours of love, with purest ray
Sweet Venus shines; and from her genial rise,
When day-light sickens till it springs afresh,
Unrival'd reigns, the fairest lamp of Night.
As thus th' effulgence tremulous I drink,
With cherish'd gaze, the lambent lightnings shoot
Across the sky, or horizontal dart
In wondrous shapes: by fearful murmuring crowds
Portentous deem'd. Amid the radiant orbs
That more than deck, that animate the sky,
The life-infusing suns of other worlds;
Lo! from the dread immensity of space
Returning, with accelerated course,
The rushing comet to the sun descends;
And as he sinks below the shading earth,
With awful train projected o'er the heavens,
The guilty nations tremble. But, above
Those superstitious horrors that enslave
The fond sequacious herd, to mystic faith
And blind amazement prone, the enlightened few,
Whose godlike minds Philosophy exalts,
The glorious stranger hail. They feel a joy
Divinely great; they in their powers exult,
That wondrous force of thought which mounting spurns
This dusky spot, and measures all the sky;
While, from his far excursion through the wilds
Of barren ether, faithful to his time,
They see the blazing wonder rise anew,
In seeming terror clad, but kindly bent
To work the will of all-sustaining Love:
From his huge vapoury train perhaps to shake
Reviving moisture on the numerous orbs,
Through which his long ellipsis winds; perhaps
To lend new fuel to declining suns,
To light up worlds, and feed the eternal fire.
With thee, serene Philosophy, with thee,
And thy bright garland, let me crown my song!
Effusive source of evidence, and truth!
A lustre shedding o'er the ennobled mind,
Stronger than summer-noon; and pure as that
Whose mild vibrations soothe the parted soul,
New to the dawning of celestial day.
Hence through her nourish'd powers, enlarged by thee,
She springs aloft with elevated pride,
Above the tangling mass of low desires,
That bind the fluttering crowd, and, angel-wing'd,
The heights of science and of virtue gains,
Where all is calm and clear; with Nature round,
Or in the starry regions, or the abyss,
To Reason's and to Fancy's eye display'd:
The first up-tracing, from the dreary void,
The chain of causes and effects to Him,
The world-producing Essence, who alone
Possesses being; while the last receives
The whole magnificence of heaven and earth,
And every beauty, delicate or bold,
Obvious or more remote, with livelier sense,
Diffusive painted on the rapid mind.
Tutor'd by thee, hence Poetry exalts
Her voice to ages, and informs the page
With music, image, sentiment, and thought,
Never to die! the treasure of mankind!
Their highest honour, and their truest joy!
Without thee what were unenlighten'd man?
A savage roaming through the woods and wilds
In quest of prey; and with the unfashion'd fur
Rough clad; devoid of every finer art,
And elegance of life. Nor happiness
Domestic, mix'd of tenderness and care,
Nor moral excellence, nor social bliss,
Nor guardian law were his; nor various skill
To turn the furrow, or to guide the tool
Mechanic, nor the heaven-conducted prow
Of navigation bold, that fearless braves
The burning line or dares the wintry pole:

Mother severe of infinite delights!
Nothing, save rapine, indolence, and guile,
And woes on woes, a still-revolving train!
Whose horrid circle had made human life
Than non-existence worse: but, taught by thee,
Ours are the plans of policy and peace,
To live like brothers, and conjunctive all
Embellish life. While thus laborious crowds
Ply the tough oar, Philosophy directs
The ruling helm; or, like the liberal breath
Of potent Heaven, invisible, the sail
Swells out, and bears th' inferior world along.
Nor to this evanescent speck of earth
Poorly confined, the radiant tracts on high
Are her exalted range; intent to gaze
Creation through; and, from that full complex
Of never-ending wonders, to conceive
Of the Sole Being right, who spoke the Word,
And Nature moved complete. With inward view
Thence on th' ideal kingdom swift she turns
Her eye; and, instant, at her powerful glance,
Th' obedient phantoms vanish or appear;
Compound, divide, and into order shift,
Each to his rank, from plain perception up
To the fair forms of Fancy's fleeting train:
To reason then, deducing truth from truth;
And notion quite abstract; where first begins
The world of spirits, action all, and life
Unfettered and unmixed. But here the cloud,
(So wills eternal Providence) sits deep.
Enough for us to know that this dark state,
In wayward passions lost, and vain pursuits,
This Infancy of Being, cannot prove
The final issue of the works of God,
By boundless Love and perfect Wisdom formed,
And ever rising with the rising mind.

AUTUMN.

INSCRIBED

TO THE RIGHT HONOURABLE ARTHUR ONSLOW, ESQ.,

SPEAKER OF THE HOUSE OF COMMONS.

ARGUMENT.

The subject proposed. Addressed to Mr. Onslow. A prospect of the fields ready for harvest. Reflections in praise of industry, raised by that view. Reaping. A tale relative to it. A harvest-storm. Shooting and hunting; their barbarity. A ludicrous account of fox-hunting. A view of an orchard. Wall-fruit. A vineyard. A description of fogs frequent in the latter part of Autumn; whence a digression, inquiring into the rise of fountains and rivers. Birds of season considered, that now shift their habitation. The prodigious number of them that cover the northern and western isles of Scotland. Hence a view of the country. A prospect of the discoloured, fading woods. After a gentle dusky day, moonlight. Autumnal meteors. Morning: to which succeeds a calm, pure, sunshiny day, such as usually shuts up the season. The harvest being gathered in, the country dissolved in joy. The whole concludes with a panegyric on a philosophical country life.

CROWN'D with the sickle and the wheaten sheaf,
While Autumn, nodding o'er the yellow plain,
Comes jovial on; the Doric reed once more,
Well pleased, I tune. Whate'er the wintry frost
Nitrous prepared; the various-blossom'd Spring
Put in white promise forth; and Summer-suns
Concocted strong, rush boundless now to view,
Full, perfect all, and swell my glorious theme.
  Onslow! the Muse, ambitious of thy name,
To grace, inspire, and dignify her song,
Would from the public voice thy gentle ear
Awhile engage. Thy noble cares she knows,
The patriot virtues that distend thy thought,
Spread on thy front, and in thy bosom glow;
While listening senates hang upon thy tongue,
Devolving through the maze of eloquence
A roll of periods, sweeter than her song.
But she too pants for public virtue, she,
Though weak of power, yet strong in ardent will,
Whene'er her country rushes on her heart,
Assumes a bolder note, and fondly tries
To mix the patriot's with the poet's flame.
  When the bright Virgin gives the beauteous days,
And Libra weighs in equal scales the year;
From heaven's high cope the fierce effulgence [shook
Of parting Summer, a serener blue,
With golden light enliven'd, wide invests
The happy world. Attemper'd suns arise,
Sweet-beam'd, and shedding oft through lucid clouds
A pleasing calm; while broad, and brown, below
Extensive harvests hang the heavy head.
Rich, silent, deep, they stand; for not a gale
Rolls its light billows o'er the bending plain:
A calm of plenty! till the ruffled air
Falls from its poise, and gives the breeze to blow.
Rent is the fleecy mantle of the sky;
The clouds fly different; and the sudden sun
By fits effulgent gilds the illumined field,
And black by fits the shadows sweep along:
A gaily-checker'd heart-expanding view,
Far as the circling eye can shoot around,
Unbounded tossing in a flood of corn.
  These are thy blessings, Industry! rough power!
Whom labour still attends, and sweat and pain
Yet the kind source of every gentle art,
And all the soft civility of life:
Raiser of human kind! by Nature cast,
Naked, and helpless, out amid the woods
And wilds, to rude inclement elements;
With various seeds of art deep in the mind
Implanted, and profusely pour'd around,
Materials infinite, but idle all.
Still unexerted, in the unconscious breast,
Slept the lethargic powers; Corruption still,
Voracious, swallow'd what the liberal hand
Of bounty scatter'd o'er the savage year:
And still the sad barbarian, roving, mix'd
With beasts of prey; or for his acorn-meal
Fought the fierce tusky boar; a shivering wretch!
Aghast, and comfortless, when the bleak north,
With Winter charged, let the mix'd tempest fly,
Hail, rain, and snow, and bitter-breathing frost:
Then to the shelter of the hut he fled;
And the wild season, sordid, pined away.
For home he had not; home is the resort
Of love, of joy, of peace and plenty, where,
Supporting and supported, polish'd friends,
And dear relations, mingle into bliss.
But this the rugged savage never felt,
Even desolate in crowds; and thus his days
Roll'd heavy, dark, and unenjoy'd along,
A waste of time! till Industry approach'd,
And roused him from his miserable sloth:
His faculties unfolded; pointed out,
Where lavish Nature the directing hand
Of Art demanded; show'd him how to raise
His feeble force by the mechanic powers,
To dig the mineral from the vaulted earth,
On what to turn the piercing rage of fire,
On what the torrent, and the gather'd blast;
Gave the tall ancient forest to his axe;
Taught him to chip the wood, and hew the stone,
Till by degrees the finish'd fabric rose;
Tore from his limbs the blood-polluted fur,
And wrapt them in the woolly vestment warm,
Or bright in glossy silk, and flowing lawn,
With wholesome viands fill'd his table, pour'd
The generous glass around, inspired to wake

WINTER.

The life-refining soul of decent wit,
Nor stopp'd at barren bare necessity;
But still advancing bolder, led him on
To pomp, to pleasure, elegance, and grace;
And, breathing high ambition through his soul,
Set science, wisdom, glory, in his view,
And bade him be the lord of all below.
Then gathering men their natural powers combined,
And form'd a Public; to the general good
Submitting, aiming, and conducting all.
For this the Patriot-Council met, the full,
The free, and fairly represented Whole;
For this they plann'd the holy guardian laws,
Distinguish'd orders, animated arts,
And, with joint force Oppression chaining, set
Imperial Justice at the helm, yet still
To them accountable: nor slavish dream'd
That toiling millions must resign their weal,
And all the honey of their search, to such
As for themselves alone themselves have raised.
Hence every form of cultivated life
In order set, protected, and inspired,
Into perfection wrought. Uniting all,
Society grew numerous, high, polite,
And happy. Nurse of art! the city rear'd
In beauteous pride her tower-encircled head;
And, stretching street on street, by thousands drew,
From twining woody haunts, or the tough yew
To bows strong-straining, her aspiring sons.
Then Commerce brought into the public walk
The busy merchant; the big warehouse built;
Raised the strong crane; choked up the loaded street
With foreign plenty; and thy stream, O Thames,
Large, gentle, deep, majestic, king of floods!
Chose for his grand resort. On either hand,
Like a long wintry forest, groves of masts
Shot up their spires; the bellying sheet between
Possess'd the breezy void; the sooty hulk
Steer'd sluggish on; the splendid barge along
Row'd, regular, to harmony; around,
The boat, light-skimming, stretch'd its oary wings;
While deep the various voice of fervent toil
From bank to bank increased; whence ribb'd with oak,
To bear the British thunder, black and bold,
The roaring vessel rush'd into the main.
Then too the pillar'd dome, magnific, heaved
Its ample roof; and Luxury within
Pour'd out her glittering stores: the canvas smooth,
With glowing life protuberant, to the view
Embodied rose; the statue seem'd to breathe,
And soften into flesh, beneath the touch
Of forming art, imagination-flush'd.
All is the gift of industry! whate'er
Exalts, embellishes, and renders life
Delightful. Pensive Winter, cheer'd by him,
Sits at the social fire, and happy hears
The excluded tempest idly rave along;
His harden'd fingers deck the gaudy Spring;
Without him Summer were an arid waste;
Nor to the autumnal months could thus transmit
Those full, mature, immeasurable stores,
That, waving round, recal my wandering song.
Soon as the morning trembles o'er the sky,
And, unperceived, unfolds the spreading day;
Before the ripen'd field the reapers stand,
In fair array, each by the lass he loves,
To bear the rougher part, and mitigate
By nameless gentle offices her toil.
At once they stoop, and swell the lusty sheaves;
While through their cheerful band the rural talk,
The rural scandal, and the rural jest,
Fly harmless to deceive the tedious time,
And steal unfelt the sultry hours away.
Behind the master walks, builds up the shocks;
And, conscious, glancing oft on every side
His sated eye, feels his heart heave with joy.
The gleaners spread around, and here and there,
Spike after spike, their scanty harvest pick.
Be not too narrow, husbandmen! but fling
From the full sheaf, with charitable stealth,
The liberal handful. Think, oh grateful think!
How good the God of Harvest is to you;
Who pours abundance o'er your flowing fields;
While these unhappy partners of your kind
Wide-hover round you, like the fowls of heaven,
And ask their humble dole. The various turns
Of fortune ponder; that your sons may want
What now, with hard reluctance, faint, ye give.
The lovely young Lavinia once had friends;
And fortune smiled, deceitful, on her birth.
For, in her helpless years deprived of all,
Of every stay, save Innocence and Heaven,
She, with her widow'd mother, feeble, old,
And poor, lived in a cottage, far retired
Among the windings of a woody vale;
By solitude and deep surrounding shades,
But more by bashful modesty, conceal'd.
Together thus they shunn'd the cruel scorn
Which virtue, sunk to poverty, would meet
From giddy passion and low-minded pride;
Almost on Nature's common bounty fed;
Like the gay birds that sung them to repose,
Content, and careless of to-morrow's fare.
Her form was fresher than the morning rose.
When the dew wets its leaves; unstain'd and pure
As is the lily, or the mountain snow.
The modest Virtues mingled in her eyes,
Still on the ground dejected, darting all
Their humid beams into the blooming flowers:
Or when the mournful tale her mother told,
Of what her faithless fortune promised once
Thrill'd in her thought, they, like the dewy star
Of evening, shone in tears. A native grace
Sat fair-proportion'd on her polish'd limbs,
Veil'd in a simple robe, their best attire,
Beyond the pomp of dress; for loveliness
Needs not the foreign aid of ornament,
But is, when unadorn'd, adorn'd the most.
Thoughtless of beauty, she was Beauty's self,
Recluse amid the close-embowering woods.
As in the hollow breast of Apennine,
Beneath the shelter of encircling hills,
A myrtle rises, far from human eye,
And breathes its balmy fragrance o'er the wild;
So flourish'd blooming, and unseen by all,
The sweet Lavinia; till, at length, compell'd
By strong necessity's supreme command,
With smiling patience in her looks, she went
To glean Palemon's fields. The pride of swains
Palemon was, the generous, and the rich;
Who led the rural life in all its joy
And elegance, such as Arcadian song
Transmits from ancient uncorrupted times,
When tyrant custom had not shackled man,
But free to follow Nature was the mode.
He then, his fancy with autumnal scenes
Amusing, chanced beside his reaper-train
To walk, when poor Lavinia drew his eye;
Unconscious of her power, and turning quick
With unaffected blushes from his gaze:

He saw her charming, but he saw not half
The charms her downcast modesty conceal'd.
That very moment love and chaste desire
Sprung in his bosom, to himself unknown:
For still the world prevail'd and its dread laugh,
Which scarce the firm philosopher can scorn,
Should his heart own a gleaner in the field;
And thus in secret to his soul he sigh'd:—
"What pity! that so delicate a form,
By beauty kindled, where enlivening sense
And more than vulgar goodness seem to dwell,
Should be devoted to the rude embrace
Of some indecent clown! she looks, methinks,
Of old Acasto's line; and to my mind
Recals that patron of my happy life,
From whom my liberal fortune took its rise;
Now to the dust gone down; his houses, lands,
And once fair-spreading family, dissolved
'Tis said that in some lone obscure retreat,
Urged by remembrance sad, and decent pride,
Far from those scenes which knew their better days,
His aged widow and his daughter live,
Whom yet my fruitless search could never find.
Romantic wish! would this the daughter were!"
When, strict inquiring, from herself he found
She was the same, the daughter of his friend,
Of bountiful Acasto; who can speak
The mingled passions that surprised his heart,
And through his nerves in shivering transport ran?
Then blazed his smother'd flame, avow'd, and bold;
And as he view'd her, ardent, o'er and o'er,
Love, gratitude, and pity wept at once.
Confused, and frighten'd at his sudden tears,
Her rising beauties flush'd a higher bloom,
As thus Palemon, passionate and just,
Pour'd out the pious rapture of his soul.
"And art thou then Acasto's dear remains?
She whom my restless gratitude has sought
So long in vain? O heavens! the very same,
The soften'd image of my noble friend;
Alive his every look, his every feature,
More elegantly touch'd. Sweeter than Spring!
Thou sole surviving blossom from the root
That nourish'd up my fortune! Say, ah where,
In what sequester'd desert hast thou drawn
The kindest aspect of delighted Heaven?
Into such beauty spread, and blown so fair;
Though Poverty's cold wind, and crushing rain,
Beat keen and heavy on thy tender years?
O let me now into a richer soil
Transplant thee safe! where vernal suns and showers
Diffuse their warmest, largest influence;
And of my garden be the pride and joy!
Ill it befits thee, oh it ill befits
Acasto's daughter, his whose open stores,
Though vast, were little to his ampler heart,
The father of a country, thus to pick
The very refuse of those harvest-fields
Which from his bounteous friendship I enjoy.
Then throw that shameful pittance from thy hand,
But ill applied to such a rugged task;
The fields, the master, all, my fair, are thine;
If to the various blessings which thy house
Has on me lavish'd thou wilt add that bliss,
That dearest bliss, the power of blessing thee!"
Here ceased the youth: yet still his speaking eye
Express'd the sacred triumph of his soul,
With conscious virtue, gratitude, and love,
Above the vulgar joy divinely raised.
Nor waited he reply. Won by the charm
Of goodness irresistible, and all
In sweet disorder lost, she blush'd consent.
The news immediate to her mother brought,
While, pierced with anxious thought, she pined away
The lonely moments for Lavinia's fate;
Amazed, and scarce believing what she heard,
Joy seized her wither'd veins, and one bright gleam
Of setting life shone on her evening-hours:
Not less enraptured than the happy pair,
Who flourish'd long in tender bliss, and rear'd
A numerous offspring, lovely like themselves,
And good, the grace of all the country round.
Defeating oft the labours of the year,
The sultry south collects a potent blast.
At first the groves are scarcely seen to stir
Their trembling tops, and a still murmur runs
Along the soft-inclining fields of corn.
But as the aërial tempest fuller swells,
And in one mighty stream, invisible,
Immense, the whole excited atmosphere
Impetuous rushes o'er the sounding world:
Strain'd to the root, the stooping forest pours
A rustling shower of yet untimely leaves.
High-beat, the circling mountains eddy in,
From the bare wild, the dissipated storm,
And send it in a torrent down the vale.
Exposed, and naked, to its utmost rage,
Through all the sea of harvest rolling round
The billowy plain floats wide, nor can evade,
Though pliant to the blast, its seizing force;
Or whirl'd in air, or into vacant chaff
Shook waste. And sometimes too a burst of rain,
Swept from the black horizon, broad, descends
In one continuous flood. Still over head
The mingling tempest waves its gloom, and still
The deluge deepens, till the fields around
Lie sunk, and flatted, in the sordid wave.
Sudden the ditches swell, the meadows swim.
Red, from the hills, innumerable streams
Tumultuous roar, and high above its banks
The river lift, before whose rushing tide
Herds, flocks, and harvests, cottages, and swains,
Roll mingled down; all that the winds had spared
In one wild moment ruin'd; the big hopes
And well-earn'd treasures of the painful year.
Fled to some eminence, the husbandman
Helpless beholds the miserable wreck
Driving along; his drowning ox at once
Descending, with his labours scatter'd round,
He sees; and instant o'er his shivering thought
Comes Winter unprovided, and a train
Of clamant children dear. Ye masters, then,
Be mindful of the rough laborious hand
That sinks you soft in elegance and ease;
Be mindful of those limbs, in russet clad,
Whose toil to yours is warmth and graceful pride;
And, oh! be mindful of that sparing board
Which covers yours with luxury profuse,
Makes your glass sparkle, and your sense rejoice!
Nor cruelly demand what the deep rains
And all-involving winds have swept away.
Here the rude clamour of the sportsman's joy,
The gun fast-thundering, and the winded horn,
Would tempt the Muse to sing the rural game:
How, in his mid-career, the spaniel struck,
Stiff, by the tainted gale, with open nose,
Outstretch'd and finely sensible, draws full,
Fearful and cautious, on the latent prey;
As in the sun the circling covey bask
Their varied plumes, and watchful every way,

Through the rough stubble turn the secret eye.
Caught in the meshy snare, in vain they beat
Their idle wings, entangled more and more:
Nor on the surges of the boundless air,
Though borne triumphant, are they safe ; the gun,
Glanced just and sudden, from the fowler's eye,
O'ertakes their sounding pinions ; and again,
Immediate, brings them from the towering wing,
Dead to the ground ; or drives them wide-dispersed,
Wounded, and wheeling various, down the wind.
These are not subjects for the peaceful Muse,
Nor will she stain with such her spotless song ;
Then most delighted, when she social sees
The whole mix'd animal creation round
Alive and happy. 'Tis not joy to her,
The falsely-cheerful barbarous game of death,
This rage of pleasure, which the restless youth
Awakes, impatient, with the gleaming morn ;
When beasts of prey retire, that all night long,
Urged by necessity, had ranged the dark,
As if their conscious ravage shunn'd the light,
Ashamed. Not so the steady tyrant man,
Who with the thoughtless insolence of power
Inflamed, beyond the most infuriate wrath
Of the worst monster that e'er roam'd the waste,
For sport alone pursues the cruel chase,
Amid the beamings of the gentle days.
Upbraid, ye ravening tribes, our wanton rage,
For hunger kindles you, and lawless want ;
But lavish fed, in Nature's bounty roll'd,
To joy at anguish, and delight in blood,
Is what your horrid bosoms never knew.
Poor is the triumph o'er the timid hare !
Scared from the corn, and now to some lone seat
Retired: the rushy fen ; the ragged furze,
Stretch'd o'er the stony heath ; the stubble chapt ;
The thistly lawn ; the thick-entangled broom ;
Of the same friendly hue, the wither'd fern ;
The fallow ground laid open to the sun,
Concoctive ; and the nodding sandy bank,
Hung o'er the mazes of the mountain brook.
Vain is her best precaution ; though she sits
Conceal'd, with folded ears ; unsleeping eyes,
By Nature raised to take the horizon in ;
And head couch'd close between her hairy feet,
In act to spring away. The scented dew
Betrays her early labyrinth ; and deep,
In scatter'd sullen openings, far behind,
With every breeze she hears the coming storm.
But nearer, and more frequent, as it loads
The sighing gale, she springs amazed, and all
The savage soul of game is up at once:
The pack full-opening, various ; the shrill horn
Resounded from the hills ; the neighing steed,
Wild for the chase ; and the loud hunter's shout ;
O'er a weak, harmless, flying creature, all
Mix'd in mad tumult, and discordant joy.
The stag too, singled from the herd where long
He ranged the branching monarch of the shades,
Before the tempest drives. At first, in speed
He, sprightly, puts his faith ; and, roused by fear,
Gives all his swift aërial soul to flight ;
Against the breeze he darts, that way the more
To leave the lessening murderous cry behind:
Deception short ! though fleeter than the winds
Blown o'er the keen-air'd mountain by the north,
He bursts the thickets, glances through the glades,
And plunges deep into the wildest wood;
If slow, yet sure, adhesive to the track
Hot-steaming, up behind him come again
The inhuman rout, and from the shady depth
Expel him, circling through his every shift.
He sweeps the forest oft ; and sobbing sees
The glades, mild opening to the golden day ;
Where, in kind contest, with his butting friends
He wont to struggle, or his loves enjoy.
Oft in the full-descending flood he tries
To lose the scent, and lave his burning sides:
Oft seeks the herd ; the watchful herd, alarm'd,
With selfish care avoid a brother's woe.
What shall he do ? His once so vivid nerves,
So full of buoyant spirit, now no more
Inspire the course ; but fainting breathless toil,
Sick, seizes on his heart: he stands at bay,
And puts his last weak refuge in despair.
The big round tears run down his dappled face ;
He groans in anguish ; while the growling pack,
Blood-happy, hang at his fair jutting chest,
And mark his beauteous checker'd sides with [gore.
Of this enough. But if the sylvan youth,
Whose fervent blood boils into violence,
Must have the chase ; behold, despising flight,
The roused-up lion, resolute, and slow,
Advancing full on the protended spear,
And coward band, that circling wheel aloof.
Slunk from the cavern, and the troubled wood,
See the grim wolf ; on him his shaggy foe
Vindictive fix, and let the ruffian die:
Or, growling horrid, as the brindled boar
Grins fell destruction, to the monster's heart
Let the dart lighten from the nervous arm.
These Britain knows not ; give, ye Britons, then
Your sportive fury, pitiless, to pour
Loose on the nightly robber of the fold ;
Him, from his craggy winding haunts unearth'd,
Let all the thunder of the chase pursue.
Throw the broad ditch behind you ; o'er the hedge
High bound, resistless ; nor the deep morass
Refuse, but through the shaking wilderness
Pick your nice way ; into the perilous flood
Bear fearless, of the raging instinct full ;
And, as you ride the torrent, to the banks
Your triumph sound sonorous, running round,
From rock to rock, in circling echoes toss'd ;
Then scale the mountains to their woody tops ;
Rush down the dangerous steep ; and o'er the lawn,
In fancy swallowing up the space between,
Pour all your speed into the rapid game.
For happy he ! who tops the wheeling chase ;
Has every maze evolved, and every guile
Disclosed ; who knows the merits of the pack ;
Who saw the villain seized, and dying hard,
Without complaint, though by a hundred mouths
Relentless torn. O glorious he, beyond
His daring peers ! when the retreating horn
Calls them to ghostly halls of grey renown,
With woodland honours graced ; the fox's fur
Depending decent from the roof ; and spread
Round the drear walls, with antic figures fierce,
The stag's large front: he then is loudest heard,
When the night staggers with severer toils,
With feasts Thessalian centaurs never knew,
And their repeated wonders shake the dome.
But first the fuel'd chimney blazes wide ;
The tankards foam ; and the strong table groans
Beneath the smoking sirloin, stretch'd immense
From side to side ; in which, with desperate knife,
They deep incision make, and talk the while
Of England's glory, ne'er to be defaced,
While hence they borrow vigour : or amain

Into the pasty plunged, at intervals,
If stomach keen can intervals allow,
Relating all the glories of the chase.
Then sated Hunger bids his brother Thirst
Produce the mighty bowl; the mighty bowl,
Swell'd high with fiery juice, steams liberal round
A potent gale, delicious, as the breath
Of Maia to the love-sick shepherdess,
On violets diffused, while soft she hears
Her panting shepherd stealing to her arms.
Nor wanting is the brown October, drawn,
Mature and perfect, from his dark retreat
Of thirty years; and now his honest front
Flames in the light refulgent, not afraid
Even with the vineyard's best produce to vie.
To cheat the thirsty moments, Whist a while
Walks his dull round beneath a cloud of smoke,
Wreathed, fragrant, from the pipe; or the quick dice,
In thunder leaping from the box, awake
The sounding gammon; while romp-loving miss
Is haul'd about, in gallantry robust.
At last, these puling idlenesses laid
Aside, frequent and full, the dry divan
Close in firm circle; and set, ardent, in
For serious drinking. Nor evasion sly,
Nor sober shift, is to the puking wretch
Indulged apart; but earnest, brimming bowls
Lave every soul, the table floating round,
And pavement, faithless to the fuddled foot.
Thus as they swim in mutual swill, the talk,
Vociferous at once from twenty tongues,
Reels fast from theme to theme; from horses, hounds,
To church or mistress, politics or ghost,
In endless mazes, intricate, perplex'd.
Meantime, with sudden interruption, loud,
The impatient catch bursts from the joyous heart:
That moment touch'd is every kindred soul;
And, opening in a full-mouth'd cry of joy,
The laugh, the slap, the jocund curse go round;
While, from their slumbers shook, the kennel'd hounds
Mix in the music of the day again.
As when the tempest, that has vex'd the deep
The dark night long, with fainter murmurs falls,
So gradual sinks their mirth. Their feeble tongues,
Unable to take up the cumbrous word,
Lie quite dissolved. Before their maudlin eyes,
Seen dim and blue, the double tapers dance,
Like the sun wading through the misty sky.
Then, sliding soft, they drop. Confused above,
Glasses and bottles, pipes and gazetteers,
As if the table even itself was drunk,
Lie a wet broken scene; and wide, below,
Is heap'd the social slaughter: where astride
The lubber Power in filthy triumph sits,
Slumbrous, inclining still from side to side,
And steeps them drench'd in potent sleep till morn.
Perhaps some doctor, of tremendous paunch,
Awful and deep, a black abyss of drink,
Outlives them all; and from his buried flock
Retiring, full of rumination sad,
Laments the weakness of these latter times.
But if the rougher sex by this fierce sport
Is hurried wild, let not such horrid joy
E'er stain the bosom of the British fair.
Far be the spirit of the chase from them!
Uncomely courage, unbeseeming skill;
To spring the fence, to rein the prancing steed;
The cap, the whip, the masculine attire,
In which they roughen to the sense, and all
The winning softness of their sex is lost.
In them 'tis graceful to dissolve at woe;
With every motion, every word, to wave
Quick o'er the kindling cheek the ready blush;
And from the smallest violence to shrink
Unequal, then the loveliest in their fears;
And by this silent adulation, soft,
To their protection more engaging man.
O may their eyes no miserable sight,
Save weeping lovers, see; a nobler game,
Through love's enchanting wiles pursued, yet fled,
In chase ambiguous. May their tender limbs
Float in the loose simplicity of dress!
And, fashion'd all to harmony, alone
Know they to seize the captivated soul,
In rapture warbled from love-breathing lips;
To teach the lute to languish; with smooth step,
Disclosing motion in its every charm,
To swim along, and swell the mazy dance;
To train the foliage o'er the snowy lawn;
To guide the pencil, turn the tuneful page;
To lend new flavour to the fruitful year,
And heighten Nature's dainties; in their race
To rear their graces into second life;
To give society its highest taste;
Well-order'd home man's best delight to make;
And by submissive wisdom, modest skill,
With every gentle care-eluding art,
To raise the virtues, animate the bliss,
And sweeten all the toils of human life:
This be the female dignity and praise.
Ye swains, now hasten to the hazel bank,
Where, down yon dale, the wildly-winding brook
Falls hoarse from steep to steep. In close array
Fit for the thickets and the tangling shrub,
Ye virgins, come. For you their latest song
The woodlands raise; the clustering nuts for you
The lover finds amid the secret shade;
And, where they burnish on the topmost bough,
With active vigour crushes down the tree;
Or shakes them ripe from the resigning husk,
A glossy shower, and of an ardent brown,
As are the ringlets of Melinda's hair:
Melinda! form'd with every grace complete;
Yet these neglecting, above beauty wise,
And far transcending such a vulgar praise.
Hence from the busy joy-resounding fields,
In cheerful error, let us tread the maze
Of Autumn, unconfined; and taste, revived,
The breath of orchard big with bending fruit;
Obedient to the breeze and beating ray,
From the deep-loaded bough a mellow shower
Incessant melts away. The juicy pear
Lies, in a soft profusion scatter'd round.
A various sweetness swells the gentle race,
By Nature's all-refining hand prepared;
Of temper'd sun, and water, earth, and air,
In ever-changing composition mix'd.
Such, falling frequent through the chiller night,
The fragrant stores, the wide-projected heaps
Of apples, which the lusty-handed Year,
Innumerous, o'er the blushing orchard shakes.
A various spirit, fresh, delicious, keen,
Dwells in their gelid pores; and, active, points
The piercing cider for the thirsty tongue:
Thy native theme, and boon inspirer too,
Philips, Pomona's bard, the second thou
Who nobly durst, in rhyme-unfetter'd verse,
With British freedom sing the British song:
How, from Silurian vats, high-sparkling wines
Foam in transparent floods; some strong to cheer

The wintry revels of the labouring hind;
And tasteful some, to cool the summer hours.
In this glad season, while his sweetest beams
The sun sheds equal o'er the meeken'd day,
Oh lose me in the green delightful walks
Of, Dodington, thy seat, serene and plain;
Where simple Nature reigns; and every view,
Diffusive, spreads the pure Dorsetian downs,
In boundless prospect; yonder shagg'd with wood,
Here rich with harvest, and there white with flocks;
Meantime the grandeur of thy lofty dome,
Far-splendid, seizes on the ravish'd eye.
New beauties rise with each revolving day;
New columns swell; and still the fresh Spring finds
New plants to quicken, and new groves to green.
Full of thy genius all! the Muses' seat:
Where in the secret bower, and winding walk,
For virtuous Young and thee they twine the bay.
Here wandering oft, fired with the restless thirst
Of thy applause, I solitary court
The inspiring breeze, and meditate the book
Of Nature, ever open; aiming thence,
Warm from the heart, to learn the moral song.
Here, as I steal along the sunny wall
Where Autumn basks, with fruit empurpled deep,
My pleasing theme continual prompts my thought:
Presents the downy peach, the shining plum,
The ruddy fragrant nectarine, and, dark
Beneath his ample leaf, the luscious fig.
The vine too here her curling tendrils shoots,
Hangs out her clusters, glowing to the south,
And scarcely wishes for a warmer sky.
Turn we a moment Fancy's rapid flight
To vigorous soils, and climes of fair extent;
Where, by the potent sun elated high,
The vineyard swells refulgent on the day,
Spreads o'er the vale, or up the mountain climbs,
Profuse, and drinks amid the sunny rocks,
From cliff to cliff increased, the heighten'd blaze.
Low bend the weighty boughs. The clusters clear,
Half through the foliage seen, or ardent flame,
Or shine transparent; while perfection breathes
White o'er the turgent film the living dew.
As thus they brighten with exalted juice,
Touch'd into flavour by the mingling ray;
The rural youth and virgins o'er the field,
Each fond for each to cull the autumnal prime,
Exulting rove, and speak the vintage nigh.
Then comes the crushing swain; the country floats,
And foams unbounded with the mashy flood;
That by degrees fermented, and refined,
Round the raised nations pours the cup of joy;
The claret smooth, red as the lip we press
In sparkling fancy, while we drain the bowl;
The mellow-tasted Burgundy; and, quick
As is the wit it gives, the gay Champagne.
Now, by the cool declining year condensed,
Descend the copious exhalations, check'd
As up the middle sky unseen they stole,
And roll the doubling fogs around the hill.
No more the mountain, horrid, vast, sublime,
Which pours a sweep of rivers from its sides,
And high between contending kingdoms rears
The rocky long division, fills the view
With great variety; but, in a night
Of gathering vapour, from the baffled sense
Sinks dark and dreary. Thence expanding far,
The huge dusk, gradual, swallows up the plain:
Vanish the woods; the dim-seen river seems
Sullen, and slow, to roll the misty wave.
Even in the height of noon oppress'd, the sun
Sheds weak, and blunt, his wide-refracted ray:
Whence glaring oft, with many a broaden'd orb,
He frights the nations. Indistinct on earth,
Seen through the turbid air, beyond the life
Objects appear; and, wilder'd, o'er the waste
The shepherd stalks gigantic. Till at last
Wreathed dun around, in deeper circles still
Successive closing, sits the general fog
Unbounded o'er the world; and, mingling thick
A formless grey confusion covers all.
As when of old (so sung the Hebrew Bard)
Light, uncollected, through the chaos urged
Its infant way; nor Order yet had drawn
His lovely train from out the dubious gloom.
These roving mists, that constant now begin
To smoke along the hilly country, these,
With weightier rains, and melted Alpine snows,
The mountain-cisterns fill, those ample stores
Of water, scoop'd among the hollow rocks;
Whence gush the streams, the ceaseless fountains play,
And their unfailing wealth the rivers draw.
Some sages say, that, where the numerous wave
For ever lashes the resounding shore,
Drill'd through the sandy stratum, every way,
The waters with the sandy stratum rise;
Amid whose angles, infinitely strain'd,
They joyful leave their jaggy salts behind,
And clear and sweeten as they soak along.
Nor stops the restless fluid, mounting still,
Though oft amidst the irriguous vale it springs;
But to the mountain courted by the sand,
That leads it darkling on in faithful maze,
Far from the parent-main, it boils again
Fresh into day, and all the glittering hill
Is bright with spouting rills. But hence this vain
Amusive dream! why should the waters love
To take so far a journey to the hills,
When the sweet valleys offer to their toil
Inviting quiet, and a nearer bed?
Or if, by blind ambition led astray,
They must aspire, why should they sudden stop
Among the broken mountain's rushy dells,
And, ere they gain its highest peak, desert
The attractive sand that charm'd their course so long?
Besides, the hard agglomerating salts,
The spoil of ages, would impervious choke
Their secret channels; or, by slow degrees,
High as the hills protrude the swelling vales:
Old Ocean too, suck'd through the porous globe,
Had long ere now forsook his horrid bed,
And brought Deucalion's watery times again.
Say, then, where lurk the vast eternal springs,
That, like creating Nature, lie conceal'd
From mortal eye, yet with their lavish stores
Refresh the globe, and all its joyous tribes!
O thou pervading Genius, given to man,
To trace the secrets of the dark abyss,
O lay the mountains bare! and wide display
Their hidden structure to the astonish'd view!
Strip from the branching Alps their piny load;
The huge incumbrance of horrific woods
From Asian Taurus, from Imaus stretch'd
Athwart the roving Tartar's sullen bounds!
Give opening Hemus to my searching eye,
And high Olympus pouring many a stream;
O from the sounding summits of the north,
The Dofrine Hills, through Scandinavia roll'd
To farthest Lapland and the frozen main;

From lofty Caucasus, far seen by those
Who in the Caspian and black Euxine toil;
From cold Riphæan rocks, which the wild Russ
Believes the stony girdle of the world*;
And all the dreadful mountains, wrapt in storm,
Whence wide Siberia draws her lonely floods;
O sweep the eternal snows! Hung o'er the deep,
That ever works beneath his sounding base,
Bid Atlas, propping heaven, as poets feign,
His subterranean wonders spread! Unveil
The miny caverns, blazing on the day,
Of Abyssinia's cloud-compelling cliffs,
And of the bending Mountains of the Moon†!
O'ertopping all these giant-sons of earth,
Let the dire Andes, from the radiant line
Stretch'd to the stormy seas that thunder round
The southern pole, their hideous deeps unfold!
Amazing scene! Behold! the glooms disclose,
I see the rivers in their infant beds!
Deep, deep, I hear them, labouring to get free;
I see the leaning strata, artful ranged;
The gaping fissures to receive the rains,
The melting snows, and ever-dripping fogs.
Strow'd bibulous above I see the sands,
The pebbly gravel next, the layers then
Of mingled moulds, of more retentive earths,
The gutter'd rocks and mazy-running clefts;
That, while the stealing moisture they transmit,
Retard its motion, and forbid its waste.
Beneath the incessant weeping of these drains,
I see the rocky siphons stretch'd immense,
The mighty reservoirs, of harden'd chalk,
Or stiff-compacted clay, capacious form'd.
O'erflowing thence, the congregated stores,
The crystal treasures of the liquid world,
Through the stirr'd sands a bubbling passage burst;
And welling out, around the middle steep,
Or from the bottoms of the bosom'd hills,
In pure effusion flow. United, thus,
The exhaling sun, the vapour-burden'd air,
The gelid mountains, that to rain condensed
These vapours in continual current draw,
And send them, o'er the fair-divided earth,
In bounteous rivers to the deep again,
A social commerce hold, and firm support
The full-adjusted harmony of things.
When Autumn scatters his departing gleams,
Warn'd of approaching Winter, gather'd, play
The swallow-people; and toss'd wide around,
O'er the calm sky, in convolution swift,
The feather'd eddy floats; rejoicing once,
Ere to their wintry slumbers they retire;
In clusters clung, beneath the mouldering bank,
And where, unpierced by frost, the cavern sweats.
Or rather into warmer climes convey'd
With other kindred birds of season, there
They twitter cheerful, till the vernal months
Invite them welcome back: for, thronging, now
Innumerous wings are in commotion all.
Where the Rhine loses his majestic force
In Belgian plains, won from the raging deep,
By diligence amazing, and the strong
Unconquerable hand of Liberty,
The stork-assembly meets; for many a day,
Consulting deep, and various, ere they take
Their arduous voyage through the liquid sky:
And now their route design'd, their leaders chose,
Their tribes adjusted, clean'd their vigorous wings;
And many a circle, many a short essay,
Wheel'd round and round, in congregation full,
The figured flight ascends; and, riding high
The aërial billows, mixes with the clouds.
Or where the Northern Ocean, in vast whirls,
Boils round the naked melancholy isles
Of farthest Thule, and the Atlantic surge
Pours in among the stormy Hebrides;
Who can recount what transmigrations there
Are annual made? what nations come and go?
And how the living clouds on clouds arise?
Infinite wings! till all the plume-dark air
And rude-resounding shore are one wild cry.
Here the plain harmless native his small flock
And herd diminutive of many hues,
Tends on the little island's verdant swell,
The shepherd's sea-girt reign; or to the rocks
Dire-clinging, gathers his ovarious food;
Or sweeps the fishy shore; or treasures up
The plumage, rising full, to form the bed
Of luxury. And here awhile the Muse,
High hovering o'er the broad cerulean scene,
Sees Caledonia, in romantic view:
Her airy mountains, from the waving main,
Invested with a keen diffusive sky,
Breathing the soul acute; her forests large,
Incult, robust, and tall, by Nature's hand
Planted of old; her azure lakes between,
Pour'd out extensive, and of watery wealth
Full; winding deep, and green, her fertile vales
With many a cool translucent brimming flood
Wash'd lovely, from the Tweed (pure parent stream,
Whose pastoral banks first heard my Doric reed
With, sylvan Jed, thy tributary brook)
To where the north-inflated tempest foams
O'er Orca's or Betubium's highest peak:
Nurse of a people, in Misfortune's school
Train'd up to hardy deeds; soon visited
By Learning, when before the Gothic rage
She took her western flight. A manly race,
Of unsubmitting spirit, wise, and brave;
Who still through bleeding ages struggled hard
(As well unhappy Wallace can attest,
Great patriot hero! ill-requited chief!)
To hold a generous undiminish'd state;
Too much in vain! Hence of unequal bounds
Impatient, and by tempting glory borne
O'er every land, for every land their life
Has flow'd profuse, their piercing genius plann'd
And swell'd the pomp of peace their faithful toil.
As from their own clear north, in radiant streams
Bright over Europe bursts the Boreal morn.
Oh! is there not some patriot, in whose power
That best, that god-like luxury is placed,
Of blessing thousands, thousands yet unborn,
Through late posterity? some large of soul,
To cheer dejected industry? to give
A double harvest to the pining swain,
And teach the labouring hind the sweets of toil?
How, by the finest art, the native robe
To weave; how, white as hyperborean snow,
To form the lucid lawn; with venturous oar
How to dash wide the billow; nor look on,
Shamefully passive, while Batavian fleets
Defraud us of the glittering finny swarms,
That heave our friths, and crowd upon our shores
How all-enlivening trade to rouse, and wing

* The Muscovites call the Riphean Mountains *Weliki Camenypois*, that is, the *Great Stony Girdle*; because they suppose them to encompass the whole earth.

† A range of mountains in Africa, that surround almost all Monomotapa.

The prosperous sail, from every growing port,
Uninjured, round the sea-encircled globe;
And thus, in soul united as in name,
Bid Britain reign the mistress of the deep?
Yes, there are such. And, full on thee, Argyle,
Her hope, her stay, her darling, and her boast,
From her first patriots and her heroes sprung,
Thy fond imploring country turns her eye;
In thee, with all a mother's triumph, sees
Her every virtue, every grace combined,
Her genius, wisdom, her engaging turn,
Her pride of honour, and her courage tried,
Calm, and intrepid in the very throat
Of sulphurous war, on Tenier's dreadful field.
Nor less the palm of peace inwreathes thy brow:
For, powerful as thy sword, from thy rich tongue
Persuasion flows, and wins the high debate;
While mix'd in thee combine the charm of youth,
The force of manhood, and the depth of age.
Thee, Forbes, too, whom every worth attends,
As truth sincere, as weeping friendship kind,
Thee, truly generous, and in silence great,
Thy country feels through her reviving arts
Plann'd by thy wisdom, by thy soul inform'd;
And seldom has she known a friend like thee.
But see the fading many-colour'd woods,
Shade deepening over shade, the country round
Imbrown, a crowded umbrage, dusk, and dun,
Of every hue, from wan declining green
To sooty dark. These now the lonesome Muse,
Low-whispering, lead into their leaf-strown walks,
And give the Season in its latest view.
Meantime, light shadowing all, a sober calm
Fleeces unbounded ether; whose least wave
Stands tremulous, uncertain where to turn
The gentle current; while, illumined wide,
The dewy-skirted clouds imbibe the sun,
And through their lucid veil his soften'd force
Shed o'er the peaceful world. Then is the time,
For those whom Wisdom and whom Nature charm,
To steal themselves from the degenerate crowd,
And soar above this little scene of things;
To tread low-thoughted Vice beneath their feet;
To soothe the throbbing passions into peace;
And woo lone Quiet in her silent walks.
Thus solitary, and in pensive guise,
Oft let me wander o'er the russet mead,
And through the sadden'd grove, where scarce is heard
One dying strain, to cheer the woodman's toil.
Haply some widow'd songster pours his plaint,
Far, in faint warblings, through the tawny copse;
While congregated thrushes, linnets, larks,
And each wild throat, whose artless strains so late
Swell'd all the music of the swarming shades,
Robb'd of their tuneful souls, now shivering sit
On the dead tree, a dull despondent flock;
With not a brightness waving o'er their plumes,
And nought save chattering discord in their note.
O! let not, aim'd from some inhuman eye,
The gun the music of the coming year
Destroy; and harmless, unsuspecting harm,
Lay the weak tribes a miserable prey,
In mingled murder, fluttering on the ground!
The pale descending year, yet pleasing still,
A gentler mood inspires; for now the leaf
Incessant rustles from the mournful grove;
Oft startling such as, studious, walk below;
And slowly circles through the waving air.
But should a quicker breeze amid the boughs
Sob, o'er the sky the leafy deluge streams;
Till choked and matted with the dreary shower,
The forest walks, at every rising gale,
Roll wide the wither'd waste, and whistle bleak.
Fled is the blasted verdure of the fields;
And, shrunk into their beds, the flowery race
Their sunny robes resign. E'en what remain'd
Of stronger fruits falls from the naked tree;
And woods, fields, gardens, orchards, all around
The desolated prospect thrills the soul.
He comes! he comes! in every breeze the Power
Of Philosophic Melancholy comes!
His near approach the sudden starting tear,
The glowing cheek, the mild dejected air,
The soften'd feature, and the beating heart,
Pierced deep with many a virtuous pang, declare
O'er all the soul his sacred influence breathes!
Inflames imagination; through the breast
Infuses every tenderness; and far
Beyond dim earth exalts the swelling thought.
Ten thousand thousand fleet ideas, such
As never mingled with the vulgar dream,
Crowd fast into the mind's creative eye.
As fast the correspondent passions rise,
As varied, and as high: Devotion raised
To rapture, and divine astonishment;
The love of Nature unconfined, and, chief,
Of human race; the large ambitious wish
To make them blest; the sigh for suffering worth
Lost in obscurity; the noble scorn
Of tyrant-pride; the fearless great resolve;
The wonder which the dying patriot draws,
Inspiring glory through remotest time;
The awakened throb for virtue, and for fame;
The sympathies of love, and friendship dear;
With all the social offspring of the heart.
Oh! bear me then to vast embowering shades.
To twilight groves, and visionary vales;
To weeping grottoes, and prophetic glooms;
Where angel forms athwart the solemn dusk
Tremendous sweep, or seem to sweep along;
And voices more than human, through the void
Deep-sounding, seize the enthusiastic ear
Or is this gloom too much? Then lead, ye powers,
That o'er the garden and the rural seat
Preside, which shining through the cheerful land
In countless numbers blest Britannia sees;
O, lead me to the wide-extended walks,
The fair majestic paradise of Stowe*!
Not Persian Cyrus on Ionia's shore
E'er saw such sylvan scenes; such various art
By genius fired, such ardent genius tamed
By cool judicious art; that, in the strife,
All beauteous Nature fears to be outdone.
And there, O Pitt, thy country's early boast,
There let me sit beneath the shelter'd slopes,
Or in that Temple† where, in future times,
Thou well shalt merit a distinguish'd name;
And, with thy converse blest, catch the last smiles
Of Autumn beaming o'er the yellow woods.
While there with thee the enchanted round I walk,
The regulated wild, gay Fancy then
Will tread in thought the groves of Attic land;
Will from thy standard taste refine her own,
Correct thy pencil to the purest truth
Of Nature, or, the unimpassion'd shades
Forsaking, raise it to the human mind.
Or if hereafter she, with juster hand,

* The seat of Lord Cobham.

† The Temple of Virtue in Stowe Gardens

Shall draw the tragic scene, instruct her, thou,
To mark the varied movements of the heart,
What every decent character requires,
And every passion speaks: O! through her strain
Breathe thy pathetic eloquence, that moulds
The attentive senate, charms, persuades, exalts,
Of honest Zeal the indignant lightning throws,
And shakes Corruption on her venal throne!
While thus we talk, and through Elysian vales
Delighted rove, perhaps a sigh escapes:
What pity, Cobham, thou thy verdant files
Of order'd trees shouldst here inglorious range,
Instead of squadrons flaming o'er the field,
And long embattled hosts! when the proud foe,
The faithless vain disturber of mankind,
Insulting Gaul has roused the world to war;
When keen, once more, within their bounds to press
Those polish'd robbers, those ambitious slaves,
The British youth would hail thy wise command,
Thy temper'd ardour and thy veteran skill.
 The western sun withdraws the shorten'd day;
And humid Evening, gliding o'er the sky,
In her chill progress, to the ground condensed
The vapours throws. Where creeping waters ooze,
Where marshes stagnate, and where rivers wind,
Cluster the rolling fogs, and swim along
The dusky-mantled lawn. Meanwhile the Moon,
Full-orb'd, and breaking through the scatter'd clouds,
Shows her broad visage in the crimson'd east.
Turn'd to the sun direct, her spotted disk,
Where mountains rise, umbrageous dales descend,
And caverns deep, as optic tube descries,
A smaller earth, gives us his blaze again,
Void of its flame, and sheds a softer day.
Now through the passing cloud she seems to stoop,
Now up the pure cerulean rides sublime.
Wide the pale deluge floats, and streaming mild
O'er the skyed mountain to the shadowy vale,
While rocks and floods reflect the quivering gleam,
The whole air whitens with a boundless tide
Of silver radiance, trembling round the world.
 But when half blotted from the sky her light,
Fainting, permits the starry fires to burn
With keener lustre through the depth of heaven;
Or near extinct her deaden'd orb appears,
And scarce appears, of sickly beamless white;
Oft in this season, silent from the north
A blaze of meteors shoots: ensweeping first
The lower skies, they all at once converge
High to the crown of heaven, and all at once
Relapsing quick, as quickly reascend,
And mix, and thwart, extinguish and renew,
All ether coursing in a maze of light.
From look to look, contagious through the crowd,
The panic runs, and into wondrous shapes
The appearance throws: armies in meet array,
Throng'd with aërial spears, and steeds of fire;
Till, the long lines of full-extended war
In bleeding fight commix'd, the sanguine flood
Rolls a broad slaughter o'er the plains of heaven.
As thus they scan the visionary scene,
On all sides swells the superstitious din,
Incontinent; and busy Frenzy talks
Of blood and battle; cities overturn'd,
And late at night in swallowing earthquake sunk,
Or hideous wrapt in fierce ascending flame;
Of sallow famine, inundation, storm;
Of pestilence, and every great distress;
Empires subversed, when ruling fate has struck
The unalterable hour: even Nature's self
Is deem'd to totter on the brink of time.
Not so the man of philosophic eye,
And inspect sage; the waving brightness he
Curious surveys, inquisitive to know
The causes, and materials, yet unfix'd,
Of this appearance beautiful and new.
 Now black, and deep, the night begins to fall,
A shade immense! sunk in the quenching gloom,
Magnificent and vast, are heaven and earth.
Order confounded lies; all beauty void;
Distinction lost; and gay variety
One universal blot: such the fair power
Of light, to kindle and create the whole.
Drear is the state of the benighted wretch,
Who then, bewilder'd, wanders through the dark,
Full of pale fancies, and chimeras huge;
Nor visited by one directive ray,
From cottage streaming, or from airy hall.
Perhaps impatient as he stumbles on,
Struck from the root of slimy rushes, blue,
The wildfire scatters round, or gather'd trails
A length of flame deceitful o'er the moss:
Whither decoy'd by the fantastic blaze,
Now lost and now renew'd, he sinks absorb'd,
Rider and horse, amid the miry gulf:
While still, from day to day, his pining wife
And plaintive children his return await,
In wild conjecture lost. At other times,
Sent by the better Genius of the night,
Innoxious, gleaming on the horse's mane,
The meteor sits; and shows the narrow path,
That winding leads through pits of death, or else
Instructs him how to take the dangerous ford.
 The lengthen'd night elapsed, the morning shines
Serene, in all her dewy beauty bright,
Unfolding fair the last autumnal day.
And now the mounting sun dispels the fog;
The rigid hoar-frost melts before his beam;
And hung on every spray, on every blade
Of grass, the myriad dew-drops twinkle round.
 Ah, see where, robb'd and murder'd in that pit
Lies the still-heaving hive! at evening snatch'd
Beneath the cloud of guilt-concealing night,
And fix'd o'er sulphur; while, not dreaming ill,
The happy people, in their waxen cells,
Sat tending public cares, and planning schemes
Of temperance, for winter poor; rejoiced
To mark, full flowing round, their copious stores.
Sudden the dark oppressive steam ascends;
And, used to milder scents, the tender race,
By thousands, tumble from their honey'd domes,
Convolved, and agonizing in the dust.
And was it then for this you roam'd the Spring,
Intent from flower to flower? for this you toil'd
Ceaseless the burning Summer-heats away?
For this in Autumn search'd the blooming waste,
Nor lost one sunny gleam? for this sad fate?
O man! tyrannic lord! how long, how long
Shall prostrate Nature groan beneath your rage,
Awaiting renovation?—When obliged,
Must you destroy? of their ambrosial food
Can you not borrow; and, in just return,
Afford them shelter from the wintry winds?
Or, as the sharp year pinches, with their own
Again regale them on some smiling day?
See where the stony bottom of their town
Looks desolate, and wild; with here and there
A helpless number, who the ruin'd state
Survive, lamenting weak, cast out to death.

Thus a proud city, populous and rich,
Full of the works of peace, and high in joy,
At theatre or feast, or sunk in sleep,
(As late, Palermo, was thy fate) is seized
By some dread earthquake, and convulsive hurl'd
Sheer from the black foundation, stench-involved,
Into a gulf of blue sulphureous flame.
Hence every harsher sight! for now the day,
O'er heaven and earth diffused, grows warm, and high;
Infinite splendour! wide investing all.
How still the breeze! save what the filmy thread
Of dew evaporate brushes from the plain.
How clear the cloudless sky! how deeply tinged
With a peculiar blue! the ethereal arch
How swell'd immense! amid whose azure throned,
The radiant sun how gay! how calm below
The gilded earth! the harvest-treasures all
Now gather'd in, beyond the rage of storms,
Sure to the swain; the circling fence shut up;
And instant Winter's utmost rage defied;
While, loose to festive joy, the country round
Laughs with the loud sincerity of mirth,
Shook to the wind their cares. The toil-strung youth,
By the quick sense of music taught alone,
Leaps wildly graceful in the lively dance.
Her every charm abroad, the village-toast,
Young, buxom, warm, in native beauty rich,
Darts not unmeaning looks; and, where her eye
Points an approving smile, with double force
The cudgel rattles, and the wrestler twines.
Age too shines out; and, garrulous, recounts
The feats of youth. Thus they rejoice; nor think
That, with to-morrow's sun, their annual toil
Begins again the never-ceasing round.
Oh, knew he but his happiness, of men
The happiest he! who far from public rage
Deep in the vale, with a choice few retired,
Drinks the pure pleasures of the rural life.
What though the dome be wanting, whose proud gate,
Each morning, vomits out the sneaking crowd
Of flatterers false, and in their turn abused?
Vile intercourse! What though the glittering robe,
Of every hue reflected light can give,
Or floating loose, or stiff with mazy gold,
The pride and gaze of fools, oppress him not?
What though, from utmost land and sea purvey'd,
For him each rarer tributary life
Bleeds not, and his insatiate table heaps
With luxury and death? What though his bowl
Flames not with costly juice; nor sunk in beds,
Oft of gay care, he tosses out the night,
Or melts the thoughtless hours in idle state?
What though he knows not those fantastic joys
That still amuse the wanton, still deceive;
A face of pleasure, but a heart of pain;
Their hollow moments undelighted all?
Sure peace is his; a solid life, estranged
To disappointment and fallacious hope:
Rich in content, in Nature's bounty rich,
In herbs and fruits; whatever greens the Spring,
When heaven descends in showers; or bends the bough,
When Summer reddens, and when Autumn beams;
Or in the wintry glebe whatever lies
Conceal'd, and fattens with the richest sap:
These are not wanting; nor the milky drove,
Luxuriant, spread o'er all the lowing vale;
Nor bleating mountains; nor the chide of streams,
And hum of bees, inviting sleep sincere
Into the guiltless breast, beneath the shade,
Or thrown at large amid the fragrant hay;
Nor aught besides of prospect, grove, or song,
Dim grottoes, gleaming lakes, and fountain clear.
Here too dwells simple Truth; plain Innocence;
Unsullied Beauty; sound unbroken Youth,
Patient of labour, with a little pleased;
Health ever blooming; unambitious Toil;
Calm Contemplation, and poetic Ease.
Let others brave the flood in quest of gain,
And beat, for joyless months, the gloomy wave.
Let such as deem it glory to destroy,
Rush into blood, the sack of cities seek;
Unpierced, exulting in the widow's wail,
The virgin's shriek, and infant's trembling cry.
Let some, far distant from their native soil,
Urged or by want or harden'd avarice,
Find other lands beneath another sun.
Let this through cities work his eager way,
By legal outrage and establish'd guile,
The social sense extinct; and that ferment
Mad into tumult the seditious herd,
Or melt them down to slavery. Let these
Ensnare the wretched in the toils of law,
Fomenting discord, and perplexing right,
An iron race! and those of fairer front,
But equal inhumanity, in courts,
Delusive pomp and dark cabals, delight;
Wreathe the deep bow, diffuse the lying smile,
And tread the weary labyrinth of state.
While he, from all the stormy passions free
That restless men involve, hears, and but hears,
At distance safe, the human tempest roar,
Wrapp'd close in conscious peace. The fall of kings,
The rage of nations, and the crush of states,
Move not the man, who, from the world escaped,
In still retreats and flowery solitudes,
To Nature's voice attends, from month to month,
And day to day, through the revolving year;
Admiring, sees her in her every shape;
Feels all her sweet emotions at his heart;
Takes what she liberal gives, nor thinks of more.
He, when young Spring protrudes the bursting germs,
Marks the first bud, and sucks the healthful gale
Into his freshen'd soul; her genial hours
He full enjoys; and not a beauty blows,
And not an opening blossom breathes in vain.
In Summer he, beneath the living shade,
Such as o'er frigid Tempe wont to wave,
Or Hemus cool, reads what the Muse, of these,
Perhaps, has in immortal numbers sung;
Or, what she dictates writes; and, oft an eye
Shot round, rejoices in the vigorous year.
When Autumn's yellow lustre gilds the world,
And tempts the sickled swain into the field,
Seized by the general joy, his heart distends
With gentle throes; and, through the tepid gleams
Deep musing, then he best exerts his song.
Even Winter wild to him is full of bliss.
The mighty tempest, and the hoary waste,
Abrupt and deep, stretch'd o'er the buried earth,
Awake to solemn thought. At night the skies,
Disclosed, and kindled, by refining frost,
Pour every lustre on the exalted eye.
A friend, a book, the stealing hours secure,
And mark them down for wisdom. With swift wing
O'er land and sea imagination roams;

Or truth, divinely breaking on his mind,
Elates his being, and unfolds his powers;
Or in his breast heroic virtue burns.
The touch of kindred too and love he feels;
The modest eye, whose beams on his alone
Ecstatic shine; the little strong embrace
Of prattling children, twined around his neck,
And emulous to please him, calling forth
The fond parental soul. Nor purpose gay,
Amusement, dance, or song, he sternly scorns;
For happiness and true philosophy
Are of the social, still, and smiling kind.
This is the life which those who fret in guilt
And guilty cities, never knew; the life
Led by primeval ages, uncorrupt,
When angels dwelt, and God himself, with man!
Oh Nature! all-sufficient! over all!
Enrich me with the knowledge of thy works:
Snatch me to heaven; thy rolling wonders there,
World beyond world, in infinite extent,
Profusely scatter'd o'er the blue immense,
Show me; their motions, periods, and their laws,
Give me to scan; through the disclosing deep
Light my blind way: the mineral strata there;
Thrust blooming thence, the vegetable world;
O'er that the rising system, more complex,
Of animals; and, higher still, the mind,
The varied scene of quick-compounded thought,
And where the mixing passions endless shift;
These ever open to my ravish'd eye;
A search, the flight of time can ne'er exhaust!
But if to that unequal,—if the blood,
In sluggish streams about my heart, forbid
That best ambition,—under closing shades,
Inglorious, lay me by the lowly brook,
And whisper to my dreams. From Thee begin,
Dwell all on Thee, with Thee conclude my song;
And let me never, never stray from Thee!

WINTER.

. . . . . Horrida cano
Bruma gelu. . . . . . .—Virg.

TO

THE RIGHT HONOURABLE SIR SPENCER COMPTON.

Sir,

The author of the following Poem begs leave to inscribe this, his first performance, to your name and patronage. Unknown himself, and only introduced by the Muse, he yet ventures to approach you with a modest cheerfulness; for whoever attempts to excel in any generous art, though he comes alone, and unregarded by the world, may hope for your notice and esteem. Happy if I can, in any degree, merit this good fortune: as every ornament and grace of polite learning is yours, your single approbation will be my fame.

I dare not indulge my heart by dwelling on your public character; on that exalted honour and integrity which distinguish you in that august assembly where you preside; that unshaken loyalty to your sovereign; that disinterested concern for his people, which shine out united in all your behaviour, and finish the patriot. I am conscious of my want of strength and skill for so delicate an undertaking; and yet, as the shepherd in his cottage may feel and acknowledge the influence of the sun with as lively a gratitude as the great man in his palace, even I may be allowed to publish my sense of those blessings which, from so many powerful virtues, are derived to the nation they adorn.

I conclude with saying, that your fine discernment and humanity, in your private capacity, are so conspicuous, that if this address is not received with some indulgence, it will be a severe conviction that what I have written has not the least share of merit. I am, with the profoundest respect, Sir,

Your most devoted and most faithful humble servant,

James Thomson.

ARGUMENT.

The subject proposed. Address to the Earl of Wilmingtou. First approach of Winter. According to the natural course of the season, various storms described. Rain. Wind. Snow. The driving of the snows; a man perishing among them; whence reflections on the wants and miseries of human life. The wolves descending from the Alps and Apennines. A winter-evening described; as spent by philosophers; by the country people; in the city. Frost. A view of winter within the polar circle. A thaw. The whole concluding with moral reflections on a future state.

See, Winter comes, to rule the varied year,
Sullen and sad, with all his rising train,
Vapours, and clouds, and storms. Be these my theme,
These! that exalt the soul to solemn thought,
And heavenly musing. Welcome, kindred glooms!
Congenial horrors, hail! with frequent foot,
Pleased have I, in my cheerful morn of life,
When nursed by careless Solitude I lived,
And sung of Nature with unceasing joy,
Pleased have I wander'd through your rough domain;
Trod the pure virgin-snows, myself as pure;
Heard the winds roar, and the big torrent burst;
Or seen the deep-fermenting tempest brew'd
In the grim evening sky. Thus pass'd the time,
Till through the lucid chambers of the south
Look'd out the joyous Spring, look'd out, and smiled.
To thee, the patron of her first essay,
The Muse, O Wilmington! renews her song.
Since has she rounded the revolving year:
Skimm'd the gay Spring; on eagle-pinions borne,
Attempted through the Summer-blaze to rise;
Then swept o'er Autumn with the shadowy gale;
And now among the wintry clouds again,
Roll'd in the doubling storm, she tries to soar;
To swell her note with all the rushing winds;
To suit her sounding cadence to the floods;
As is her theme, her numbers wildly great:
Thrice happy could she fill thy judging ear
With bold description, and with manly thought.
Nor art thou skill'd in awful schemes alone,
And how to make a mighty people thrive;
But equal goodness, sound integrity,
A firm, unshaken, uncorrupted soul
Amid a sliding age, and burning strong,
Not vainly blazing, for thy country's weal.
A steady spirit regularly free;

These, each exalting each, the statesman light
Into the patriot ; these, the public hope
And eye to thee converting, bid the Muse
Record what Envy dares not flattery call.
Now when the cheerless empire of the sky
To Capricorn the Centaur Archer yields,
And fierce Aquarius stains the inverted year ;
Hung o'er the farthest verge of heaven, the sun
Scarce spreads through ether the dejected day.
Faint are his gleams, and ineffectual shoot
His struggling rays, in horizontal lines,
Through the thick air ; as clothed in cloudy storm,
Weak, wan, and broad, he skirts the southern sky ;
And, soon descending, to the long dark night,
Wide-shading all, the prostrate world resigns.
Nor is the night unwish'd ; while vital heat,
Light, life, and joy, the dubious day forsake.
Meantime, in sable cincture, shadows vast,
Deep-tinged and damp, and congregated clouds,
And all the vapoury turbulence of heaven,
Involve the face of things. Thus Winter falls,
A heavy gloom oppressive o'er the world,
Through Nature shedding influence malign,
And rouses up the seeds of dark disease ;
The soul of man dies in him, loathing life,
And black with more than melancholy views.
The cattle droop ; and o'er the furrow'd land,
Fresh from the plough, the dun discolour'd flocks,
Untended spreading, crop the wholesome root.
Along the woods, along the moorish fens,
Sighs the sad Genius of the coming storm ;
And up among the loose disjointed cliffs,
And fractured mountains wild, the brawling brook
And cave, presageful, send a hollow moan,
Resounding long in listening Fancy's ear.
Then comes the father of the tempest forth,
Wrapt in black glooms. First joyless rains obscure
Drive through the mingling skies with vapour foul ;
Dash on the mountain's brow, and shake the woods,
That grumbling wave below. The unsightly plain
Lies a brown deluge ; as the low-bent clouds
Pour flood on flood, yet, unexhausted, still
Combine, and deepening into night shut up
The day's fair face. The wanderers of heaven,
Each to his home, retire ; save those that love
To take their pastime in the troubled air,
Or skimming flutter round the dimply pool.
The cattle from the untasted fields return,
And ask, with meaning low, their wonted stalls,
Or ruminate in the contiguous shade.
Thither the household feathery people crowd,
The crested cock, with all his female train,
Pensive, and dripping ; while the cottage hind
Hangs o'er the enlivening blaze, and taleful there
Recounts his simple frolic : much he talks,
And much he laughs, nor recks the storm that
Without, and rattles on his humble roof. [blows
Wide o'er the brim, with many a torrent swell'd,
And the mix'd ruin of its banks o'erspread,
At last the roused-up river pours along :
Resistless, roaring, dreadful, down it comes
From the rude mountain, and the mossy wild,
Tumbling through rocks abrupt, and sounding far ;
Then o'er the sanded valley floating spreads,
Calm, sluggish, silent ; till again, constrain'd
Between two meeting hills, it bursts away,
Where rocks and woods o'erhang the turbid stream ;
There gathering triple force, rapid, and deep,
It boils, and wheels, and foams, and thunders
through.

Nature ! great parent ! whose unceasing hand
Rolls round the seasons of the changeful year,
How mighty, how majestic, are thy works !
With what a pleasing dread they swell the soul,
That sees astonish'd, and astonish'd sings !
Ye too, ye winds ! that now begin to blow
With boisterous sweep, I raise my voice to you.
Where are your stores, ye powerful beings ! say,
Where your aërial magazines reserved,
To swell the brooding terrors of the storm ?
In what far distant region of the sky,
Hush'd in deep silence, sleep ye when 'tis calm ?
When from the pallid sky the sun descends,
With many a spot, that o'er his glaring orb
Uncertain wanders, stain'd ; red fiery streaks
Begin to flush around. The reeling clouds
Stagger with dizzy poise, as doubting yet
Which master to obey ; while rising slow,
Blank, in the leaden-colour'd east, the moon
Wears a wan circle round her blunted horns.
Seen through the turbid fluctuating air,
The stars obtuse emit a shiver'd ray ;
Or frequent seem to shoot athwart the gloom,
And long behind them trail the whitening blaze.
Snatch'd in short eddies, plays the wither'd leaf ;
And on the flood the dancing feather floats.
With broaden'd nostrils to the sky up-turn'd,
The conscious heifer snuffs the stormy gale.
Even as the matron, at her nightly task,
With pensive labour draws the flaxen thread,
The wasted taper and the crackling flame
Foretel the blast. But chief the plumy race,
The tenants of the sky, its changes speak.
Retiring from the downs, where all day long
They pick'd their scanty fare, a blackening train
Of clamorous rooks thick-urge their weary flight,
And seek the closing shelter of the grove.
Assiduous, in his bower, the wailing owl
Plies his sad song. The cormorant on high
Wheels from the deep, and screams along the land.
Loud shrieks the soaring hern ; and with wild wing
The circling sea-fowl cleave the flaky clouds.
Ocean, unequal press'd, with broken tide
And blind commotion heaves ; while from the shore,
Eat into caverns by the restless wave,
And forest-rustling mountains, comes a voice,
That solemn sounding bids the world prepare.
Then issues forth the storm with sudden burst,
And hurls the whole precipitated air
Down in a torrent. On the passive main
Descends the ethereal force, and with strong gust
Turns from its bottom the discolour'd deep.
Through the black night that sits immense around,
Lash'd into foam, the fierce conflicting brine
Seems o'er a thousand raging waves to burn :
Meantime the mountain-billows, to the clouds
In dreadful tumult swell'd, surge above surge,
Burst into chaos with tremendous roar
And anchor'd navies from their stations drive,
Wild as the winds, across the howling waste
Of mighty waters : now the inflated wave
Straining they scale, and now impetuous shoot
Into the secret chambers of the deep,
The wintry Baltic thundering o'er their head.
Emerging thence again, before the breath
Of full-exerted heaven they wing their course,
And dart on distant coasts ; if some sharp rock,
Or shoal insidious, break not their career,
And in loose fragments fling them floating round.
Nor less on land the loosen'd tempest reigns.

The mountain thunders; and its sturdy sons
Stoop to the bottom of the rocks they shade.
Lone on the midnight steep, and all aghast,
The dark way-faring stranger breathless toils,
And, often falling, climbs against the blast.
Low waves the rooted forest, vex'd, and sheds
What of its tarnish'd honours yet remain;
Dash'd down, and scatter'd, by the tearing wind's
Assiduous fury, its gigantic limbs
Thus struggling through the dissipated grove,
The whirling tempest raves along the plain;
And on the cottage thatch'd, or lordly roof,
Keen-fastening, shakes them to the solid base.
Sleep frighted flies; and round the rocking dome,
For entrance eager, howls the savage blast.
Then too, they say, through all the burden'd air,
Long groans are heard, shrill sounds, and distant
That, utter'd by the Demon of the night, [sighs,
Warn the devoted wretch of woe and death.
Huge Uproar lords it wide. The clouds commix'd
With stars swift gliding sweep along the sky.
All Nature reels. Till Nature's King, who oft
Amid tempestuous darkness dwells alone,
And on the wings of the careering wind
Walks dreadfully serene, commands a calm;
Then straight air, sea, and earth, are hush'd at once.
As yet 'tis midnight deep. The weary clouds,
Slow-meeting, mingle into solid gloom.
Now, while the drowsy world lies lost in sleep,
Let me associate with the serious Night,
And Contemplation, her sedate compeer;
Let me shake off the intrusive cares of day
And lay the meddling senses all aside.
Where now, ye lying vanities of life!
Ye ever-tempting, ever-cheating train!
Where are you now? and what is your amount?
Vexation, disappointment, and remorse.
Sad, sickening thought! and yet deluded man,
A scene of crude disjointed visions pass'd,
And broken slumbers, rises still resolved,
With new-flush'd hopes, to run the giddy round.
Father of light and life! thou Good Supreme!
O teach me what is good! teach me Thyself!
Save me from folly, vanity, and vice,
From every low pursuit! and feed my soul
With knowledge, conscious peace, and virtue pure;
Sacred, substantial, never-fading bliss!
The keener tempests rise: and fuming dun
From all the livid east, or piercing north,
Thick clouds ascend; in whose capacious womb
A vapoury deluge lies, to snow congeal'd;
Heavy they roll their fleecy world along,
And the sky saddens with the gather'd storm.
Through the hush'd air the whitening shower
descends,
At first thin wavering; till at last the flakes
Fall broad, and wide, and fast, dimming the day
With a continual flow. The cherish'd fields
Put on their winter-robe of purest white.
'Tis brightness all, save where the new snow melts
Along the mazy current. Low the woods
Bow their hoar head; and ere the languid sun
Faint from the west emits his evening ray,
Earth's universal face, deep hid, and chill,
Is one wild dazzling waste, that buries wide
The works of man. Drooping, the labourer ox
Stands cover'd o'er with snow, and then demands
The fruit of all his toil. The fowls of heaven,
Tamed by the cruel season, crowd around
The winnowing store, and claim the little boon
Which Providence assigns them. One alone,
The red-breast, sacred to the household gods,
Wisely regardful of the embroiling sky,
In joyless fields and thorny thickets leaves
His shivering mates, and pays to trusted man
His annual visit. Half afraid, he first
Against the window beats; then, brisk, alights
On the warm hearth; then, hopping o'er the floor,
Eyes all the smiling family askance,
And pecks, and starts, and wonders where he is:
Till, more familiar grown, the table-crumbs
Attract his slender feet.—The foodless wilds
Pour forth their brown inhabitants. The hare,
Though timorous of heart, and hard beset
By death in various forms, dark snares, and dogs,
And more unpitying men, the garden seeks,
Urged on by fearless want. The bleating kind
Eye the bleak heaven, and next the glistening earth,
With looks of dumb despair; then, sad-dispersed,
Dig for the wither'd herb through heaps of snow.
Now, shepherds, to your helpless charge be kind,
Baffle the raging year, and fill their pens
With food at will; lodge them below the storm,
And watch them strict; for from the bellowing east,
In this dire season, oft the whirlwind's wing
Sweeps up the burden of whole wintry plains
At one wide waft, and o'er the hapless flocks,
Hid in the hollow of two neighbouring hills,
The billowy tempest whelms; till, upward urged,
The valley to a shining mountain swells,
Tipp'd with a wreath high-curling in the sky.
As thus the snows arise; and foul, and fierce,
All Winter drives along the darken'd air;
In his own loose-revolving fields the swain
Disaster'd stands; sees other hills ascend,
Of unknown joyless brow; and other scenes,
Of horrid prospect, shag the trackless plain:
Nor finds the river, nor the forest, hid
Beneath the formless wild; but wanders on
From hill to dale, still more and more astray;
Impatient flouncing through the drifted heaps,
Stung with the thoughts of home; the thoughts of
home
Rush on his nerves, and call their vigour forth
In many a vain attempt. How sinks his soul!
What black despair, what horror fills his heart!
When for the dusky spot, which fancy feign'd
His tufted cottage rising through the snow,
He meets the roughness of the middle waste,
Far from the track and blest abode of man;
While round him night resistless closes fast,
And every tempest, howling o'er his head,
Renders the savage wilderness more wild.
Then throng the busy shapes into his mind
Of cover'd pits, unfathomably deep,
A dire descent! beyond the power of frost;
Of faithless bogs; of precipices huge,
Smooth'd up with snow; and what is land unknown,
What water of the still unfrozen spring,
In the loose marsh or solitary lake,
Where the fresh fountain from the bottom boils.
These check his fearful steps; and down he sinks,
Beneath the shelter of the shapeless drift,
Thinking o'er all the bitterness of death;
Mix'd with the tender anguish Nature shoots
Through the wrung bosom of the dying man,
His wife, his children, and his friends unseen.
In vain for him the officious wife prepares
The fire fair-blazing, and the vestment warm;
In vain his little children, peeping out

Into the mingling storm, demand their sire,
With tears of artless innocence. Alas!
Nor wife, nor children, more shall he behold;
Nor friends, nor sacred home. On every nerve
The deadly Winter seizes; shuts up sense;
And, o'er his inmost vitals creeping cold,
Lays him along the snows a stiffen'd corse,
Stretch'd out, and bleaching in the northern blast.
Ah! little think the gay licentious proud,
Whom pleasure, power, and affluence surround;
They who their thoughtless hours in giddy mirth,
And wanton, often cruel, riot waste;
Ah! little think they, while they dance along,
How many feel, this very moment, death,
And all the sad variety of pain.
How many sink in the devouring flood,
Or more devouring flame. How many bleed,
By shameful variance betwixt man and man.
How many pine in want, and dungeon glooms;
Shut from the common air and common use
Of their own limbs. How many drink the cup
Of baleful grief, or eat the bitter bread
Of misery. Sore pierced by wintry winds,
How many shrink into the sordid hut
Of cheerless poverty. How many shake
With all the fiercer tortures of the mind,
Unbounded passion, madness, guilt, remorse;
Whence tumbled headlong from the height of life,
They furnish matter for the tragic Muse;
Even in the vale where Wisdom loves to dwell,
With Friendship, Peace, and Contemplation join'd,
How many, rack'd with honest passions, droop
In deep retired distress. How many stand
Around the death-bed of their dearest friends,
And point the parting anguish. Thought, fond man!
Of these, and all the thousand nameless ills,
That one incessant struggle render life,
One scene of toil, of suffering, and of fate,
Vice in his high career would stand appall'd,
And heedless rambling Impulse learn to think;
The conscious heart of Charity would warm,
And her wide wish Benevolence dilate;
The social tear would rise, the social sigh;
And into clear perfection, gradual bliss,
Refining still, the social passions work.
And here can I forget the generous band *,
Who, touch'd with human woe, redressive search'd
Into the horrors of the gloomy gaol,
Unpitied, and unheard, where Misery moans,
Where Sickness pines, where Thirst and Hunger
burn,
And poor Misfortune feels the lash of Vice?
While in the land of Liberty, the land
Whose every street and public meeting glow
With open freedom, little tyrants raged;
Snatch'd the lean morsel from the starving mouth;
Tore from cold wintry limbs the tatter'd weed;
Even robb'd them of the last of comforts, sleep;
The free-born Briton to the dungeon chain'd,
Or, as the lust of cruelty prevail'd,
At pleasure mark'd him with inglorious stripes;
And crush'd out lives, by secret barbarous ways,
That for their country would have toil'd or bled.
O great design! if executed well,
With patient care, and wisdom-temper'd zeal.
Ye sons of Mercy! yet resume the search,
Drag forth the legal monsters into light,
Wrench from their hands oppression's iron rod,

* The Gaol Committee, in the year 1729.

And bid the cruel feel the pains they give.
Much still untouch'd remains; in this rank age,
Much is the patriot's weeding hand required.
The toils of law, (what dark insidious men
Have cumbrous added to perplex the truth,
And lengthen simple justice into trade)
How glorious were the day that saw these broke,
And every man within the reach of right!
By wintry famine roused, from all the tract
Of horrid mountains which the shining Alps,
And wavy Apennine, and Pyrenees,
Branch out stupendous into distant lands;
Cruel as death, and hungry as the grave!
Burning for blood, bony, and gaunt, and grim!
Assembling wolves in raging troops descend;
And, pouring o'er the country, bear along,
Keen as the north-wind sweeps the glossy snow.
All is their prize. They fasten on the steed,
Press him to earth, and pierce his mighty heart.
Nor can the bull his awful front defend,
Or shake the murdering savages away.
Rapacious, at the mother's throat they fly,
And tear the screaming infant from her breast.
The godlike face of man avails him nought.
Even beauty, force divine! at whose bright glance
The generous lion stands in soften'd gaze,
Here bleeds, a hapless undistinguish'd prey.
But if, apprised of the severe attack,
The country be shut up, lured by the scent,
On churchyards drear (inhuman to relate!)
The disappointed prowlers fall, and dig
The shrouded body from the grave; o'er which,
Mix'd with foul shades and frighted ghosts, they
howl.
Among those hilly regions, where embraced
In peaceful vales the happy Grisons dwell;
Oft, rushing sudden from the loaded cliffs,
Mountains of snow their gathering terrors roll.
From steep to steep, loud-thundering down they
A wintry waste in dire commotion all; [come,
And herds, and flocks, and travellers, and swains,
And sometimes whole brigades of marching troops,
Or hamlets sleeping in the dead of night,
Are deep beneath the smothering ruin whelm'd.
Now, all amid the rigours of the year,
In the wild depth of Winter, while without
The ceaseless winds blow ice, be my retreat,
Between the groaning forest and the shore
Beat by the boundless multitude of waves,
A rural, shelter'd, solitary scene;
Where ruddy fire and beaming tapers join
To cheer the gloom. There studious let me sit,
And hold high converse with the mighty Dead;
Sages of ancient time, as gods revered,
As gods beneficent, who bless'd mankind
With arts, with arms, and humanised a world.
Roused at the inspiring thought, I throw aside
The long-lived volume; and, deep-musing, hail
The sacred shades, that slowly-rising pass
Before my wondering eyes. First Socrates,
Who, firmly good in a corrupted state,
Against the rage of tyrants single stood,
Invincible! calm Reason's holy law,
That Voice of God within the attentive mind,
Obeying, fearless, or in life, or death:
Great moral teacher! wisest of mankind!
Solon the next, who built his common weal
On equity's wide base; by tender laws
A lively people curbing, yet undamp'd;
Preserving still that quick peculiar fire,

Whence in the laurel'd field of finer arts
And of bold freedom, they unequal'd shone,
The pride of smiling Greece, and humankind.
Lycurgus then, who bow'd beneath the force
Of strictest discipline, severely wise,
All human passions. Following him, I see,
As at Thermopylæ he glorious fell,
The firm devoted chief *, who proved by deeds
The hardest lesson which the other taught.
Then Aristides lifts his honest front;
Spotless of heart, to whom the unflattering voice
Of Freedom gave the noblest name of Just;
In pure majestic poverty revered;
Who, even his glory to his country's weal
Submitting, swell'd a haughty rival's † fame.
Rear'd by his care, of softer ray appears
Cimon, sweet-soul'd; whose genius, rising strong,
Shook off the load of young debauch; abroad
The scourge of Persian pride, at home the friend
Of every worth and every splendid art;
Modest, and simple, in the pomp of wealth.
Then the last worthies of declining Greece,
Late call'd to glory, in unequal times,
Pensive, appear. The fair Corinthian boast,
Timoleon, happy temper! mild, and firm,
Who wept the brother while the tyrant bled.
And, equal to the best, the Theban pair ‡,
Whose virtues, in heroic concord join'd,
Their country raised to freedom, empire, fame.
He too, with whom Athenian honour sunk,
And left a mass of sordid lees behind,
Phocion the Good; in public life severe,
To virtue still inexorably firm;
But when, beneath his low illustrious roof,
Sweet Peace and happy Wisdom smooth'd his brow,
Not Friendship softer was, nor Love more kind.
And he, the last of old Lycurgus' sons,
The generous victim to that vain attempt,
To save a rotten state, Agis, who saw
Even Sparta's self to servile avarice sunk.
The two Achaian heroes close the train:
Aratus, who awhile relumed the soul
Of fondly lingering Liberty in Greece;
And he her darling, as her latest hope,
The gallant Philopœmen; who to arms
Turn'd the luxurious pomp he could not cure;
Or toiling in his farm, a simple swain,
Or, bold and skilful, thundering in the field.
Of rougher front, a mighty people come!
A race of heroes! in those virtuous times
Which knew no stain, save that with partial flame
Their dearest country they too fondly loved:
Her better Founder first, the light of Rome,
Numa, who soften'd her rapacious sons;
Servius the king, who laid the solid base
On which o'er earth the vast republic spread.
Then the great consuls venerable rise:
The public Father § who the private quell'd,
As on the dread tribunal sternly sad;
He, whom his thankless country could not lose,
Camillus, only vengeful to her foes;
Fabricius, scorner of all-conquering gold;
And Cincinnatus, awful from the plough:
Thy willing victim ||, Carthage, bursting loose
From all that pleading Nature could oppose,
From a whole city's tears, by rigid faith
Imperious call'd, and Honour's dire command;
Scipio, the gentle chief, humanely brave,
Who soon the race of spotless glory ran,
And, warm in youth, to the poetic shade
With friendship and philosophy retired;
Tully, whose powerful eloquence awhile
Restrain'd the rapid fate of rushing Rome;
Unconquer'd Cato, virtuous in extreme;
And thou, unhappy Brutus, kind of heart,
Whose steady arm, by awful virtue urged,
Lifted the Roman steel against thy friend:
Thousands besides the tribute of a verse
Demand; but who can count the stars of heaven
Who sing their influence on this lower world?
Behold, who yonder comes! in sober state,
Fair, mild, and strong, as is a vernal sun:
'Tis Phœbus' self, or else the Mantuan Swain!
Great Homer too appears, of daring wing,
Parent of song! and, equal by his side,
The British Muse; join'd hand in hand they walk
Darkling, full up the middle steep to fame.
Nor absent are those shades, whose skilful touch
Pathetic drew the impassion'd heart, and charm'd
Transported Athens with the moral scene;
Nor those who, tuneful, waked the enchanting lyre
First of your kind! society divine!
Still visit thus my nights, for you reserved,
And mount my soaring soul to thoughts like yours,
Silence, thou lonely power! the door be thine;
See on the hallow'd hour that none intrude,
Save a few chosen friends, who sometimes deign
To bless my humble roof, with sense refined,
Learning digested well, exalted faith,
Unstudied wit, and humour ever gay.
Or from the Muses' hill will Pope descend,
To raise the sacred hour, to bid it smile,
And with the social spirit warm the heart?
For though not sweeter his own Homer sings,
Yet is his life the more endearing song. [pride,
Where art thou, Hammond? thou, the darling
The friend and lover of the tuneful throng!
Ah why, dear youth, in all the blooming prime
Of vernal genius, where disclosing fast
Each active worth, each manly virtue lay,
Why wert thou ravish'd from our hope so soon?
What now avails that noble thirst of fame,
Which stung thy fervent breast? that treasured store
Of knowledge early gain'd? that eager zeal
To serve thy country, glowing in the band
Of youthful patriots, who sustain her name?
What now, alas! that life-diffusing charm
Of sprightly wit? that rapture for the Muse,
That heart of friendship, and that soul of joy,
Which bade with softest light thy virtues smile?
Ah! only show'd, to check our fond pursuits,
And teach our humbled hopes that life is vain!
Thus in some deep retirement would I pass
The winter-glooms, with friends of pliant soul,
Or blithe, or solemn, as the theme inspired,
With them would search, if Nature's boundless frame
Was call'd, late-rising from the void of night,
Or sprung eternal from the Eternal Mind;
Its life, its laws, its progress, and its end.
Hence larger prospects of the beauteous whole
Would, gradual, open on our opening minds;
And each diffusive harmony unite
In full perfection to the astonish'd eye.
Then would we try to scan the moral world,
Which, though to us it seems embroil'd, moves on

* Leonidas. † Themistocles.
‡ Pelopidas and Epaminondas.
§ Marcus Junius Brutus. || Regulus.

In higher order; fitted and impell'd
By Wisdom's finest hand, and issuing all
In general good. The sage historic Muse
Should next conduct us through the deeps of time:
Show us how empire grew, declined, and fell,
In scatter'd states; what makes the nations smile,
Improves their soil, and gives them double suns;
And why they pine beneath the brightest skies,
In Nature's richest lap. As thus we talk'd,
Our hearts would burn within us, would inhale
That portion of divinity, that ray
Of purest heaven, which lights the public soul
Of patriots and of heroes. But if doom'd,
In powerless humble fortune, to repress
These ardent risings of the kindling soul;
Then, even superior to ambition, we
Would learn the private virtues: how to glide
Through shades and plains, along the smoothest stream
Of rural life; or snatch'd away by hope,
Through the dim spaces of futurity,
With earnest eye anticipate those scenes
Of happiness and wonder; where the mind,
In endless growth and infinite ascent,
Rises from state to state, and world to world.
But, when with these the serious thought is foil'd,
We, shifting for relief, would play the shapes
Of frolic Fancy; and incessant form
Those rapid pictures, that assembled train
Of fleet ideas, never join'd before,
Whence lively Wit excites to gay surprise;
Or folly-painting Humour, grave himself,
Calls Laughter forth, deep-shaking every nerve.
Meantime the village rouses up the fire;
While well-attested, and as well believed,
Heard solemn, goes the goblin story round;
Till superstitious horror creeps o'er all.
Or, frequent in the sounding hall, they wake
The rural gambol. Rustic mirth goes round;
The simple joke that takes the shepherd's heart,
Easily pleased; the long loud laugh, sincere;
The kiss, snatch'd hasty from the side-long maid,
On purpose guardless, or pretending sleep:
The leap, the slap, the haul; and, shook to notes
Of native music, the respondent dance.
Thus jocund fleets with them the winter-night.
The city swarms intense. The public haunt,
Full of each theme, and warm with mix'd discourse,
Hums indistinct. The sons of riot flow
Down the loose stream of false enchanted joy,
To swift destruction. On the rankled soul
The gaming fury fails; and in one gulf
Of total ruin, honour, virtue, peace,
Friends, families, and fortune, headlong sink.
Up-springs the dance along the lighted dome,
Mix'd and evolved, a thousand sprightly ways.
The glittering court effuses every pomp;
The circle deepens: beam'd from gaudy robes,
Tapers, and sparkling gems, and radiant eyes,
A soft effulgence o'er the palace waves:
While, a gay insect in his summer-shine,
The fop, light-fluttering, spreads his mealy wings.
Dread o'er the scene, the ghost of Hamlet stalks;
Othello rages; poor Monimia mourns;
And Belvidera pours her soul in love.
Terror alarms the breast; the comely tear
Steals o'er the cheek: or else the Comic Muse
Holds to the world a picture of itself,
And raises sly the fair impartial laugh.
Sometimes she lifts her strain, and paints the scenes
Of beauteous life; whate'er can deck mankind,
Or charm the heart, in generous Bevil* show'd
O Thou, whose wisdom, solid yet refined,
Whose patriot virtues, and consummate skill
To touch the finer springs that move the world,
Join'd to whate'er the Graces can bestow,
And all Apollo's animating fire,
Give thee, with pleasing dignity, to shine
At once the guardian, ornament, and joy
Of polish'd life; permit the rural Muse,
O Chesterfield! to grace with thee her song,
Ere to the shades again she humbly flies,
Indulge her fond ambition, in thy train,
(For every Muse has in thy train a place)
To mark thy various full-accomplish'd mind:
To mark that spirit, which, with British scorn,
Rejects the allurements of corrupted power;
That elegant politeness, which excels,
Even in the judgment of presumptuous France,
The boasted manners of her shining court;
That wit, the vivid energy of sense,
The truth of Nature, which, with Attic point,
And kind well-temper'd satire, smoothly keen,
Steals through the soul, and without pain corrects.
Or, rising thence with yet a brighter flame,
O let me hail thee on some glorious day,
When to the listening senate, ardent, crowd
Britannia's sons to hear her pleaded cause.
Then, dress'd by thee, more amiably fair,
Truth the soft robe of mild Persuasion wears;
Thou to assenting Reason givest again
Her own enlighten'd thoughts; call'd from the heart,
The obedient passions on thy voice attend;
And even reluctant Party feels awhile
Thy gracious power, as through the varied maze
Of eloquence, now smooth, now quick, now strong,
Profound and clear, you roll the copious flood.
To thy loved haunt return, my happy Muse;
For now, behold, the joyous winter-days,
Frosty, succeed; and through the blue serene,
For sight too fine, the ethereal nitre flies,
Killing infectious damps, and the spent air
Storing afresh with elemental life.
Close crowds the shining atmosphere, and binds
Our strengthen'd bodies in its cold embrace,
Constringent; feeds and animates our blood;
Refines our spirits, through the new-strung nerves
In swifter sallies darting to the brain;
Where sits the soul, intense, collected, cool,
Bright as the skies, and as the season keen.
All Nature feels the renovating force
Of Winter, only to the thoughtless eye
In ruin seen. The frost-concocted glebe
Draws in abundant vegetable soul,
And gathers vigour for the coming year.
A stronger glow sits on the lively cheek
Of ruddy Fire, and luculent along
The purer rivers flow; their sullen deeps,
Transparent, open to the shepherd's gaze,
And murmur hoarser at the fixing frost.
What art thou, frost? and whence are thy keen [stores
Derived, thou secret all-invading power,
Whom even the illusive fluid cannot fly?
Is not thy potent energy, unseen,
Myriads of little salts or hook'd, or shaped
Like double wedges, and diffused immense
Through water, earth, and ether? Hence at eve,

* A character in "The Conscious Lovers," by Sir R. Steele.

Steam'd eager from the red horizon round,
With the fierce rage of Winter deep suffused,
An icy gale, oft shifting, o'er the pool
Breathes a blue film, and in its mid career
Arrests the bickering stream. The loosen'd ice,
Let down the flood, and half dissolved by day,
Rustles no more ; but to the sedgy bank
Fast grows, or gathers round the pointed stone,
A crystal pavement, by the breath of heaven
Cemented firm ; till, seized from shore to shore,
The whole imprison'd river growls below.
Loud rings the frozen earth, and hard reflects
A double noise ; while, at his evening watch,
The village dog deters the nightly thief ;
The heifer lows ; the distant water-fall
Swells in the breeze ; and, with the hasty tread
Of traveller, the hollow-sounding plain
Shakes from afar. The full ethereal round,
Infinite worlds disclosing to the view,
Shines out intensely keen ; and, all one cope
Of starry glitter, glows from pole to pole.
From pole to pole the rigid influence falls,
Through the still night, incessant, heavy, strong,
And seizes Nature fast. It freezes on :
Till Morn, late rising o'er the drooping world,
Lifts her pale eye unjoyous. Then appears
The various labour of the silent night :
Prone from the dripping cave, and dumb cascade,
Whose idle torrents only seem to roar,
The pendent icicle ; the frost-work fair,
Where transient hues, and fancied figures rise ;
Wide spouted o'er the hill, the frozen brook,
A livid tract, cold-gleaming on the morn ;
The forest bent beneath the plumy wave ;
And by the frost refined the whiter snow,
Encrusted hard, and sounding to the tread
Of early shepherd, as he pensive seeks
His pining flock, or from the mountain top,
Pleased with the slippery surface, swift descends.
On blithesome frolics bent, the youthful swains,
While every work of man is laid at rest,
Fond o'er the river crowd, in various sport
And revelry dissolved ; where mixing glad,
Happiest of all the train ! the raptured boy
Lashes the whirling top. Or, where the Rhine
Branch'd out in many a long canal extends,
From every province swarming, void of care,
Batavia rushes forth ; and as they sweep,
On sounding skates, a thousand different ways,
In circling poise, swift as the winds, along,
The then gay land is madden'd all to joy.
Nor less the northern courts, wide o'er the snow,
Pour a new pomp. Eager on rapid sleds,
Their vigorous youth in bold contention wheel
The long-resounding course. Meantime to raise
The manly strife, with highly blooming charms,
Flush'd by the season, Scandinavia's dames,
Or Russia's buxom daughters, glow around.
Pure, quick, and sportful is the wholesome day :
But soon elapsed. The horizontal sun,
Broad o'er the south, hangs at its utmost noon,
And, ineffectual, strikes the gelid cliff ;
His azure gloss the mountain still maintains,
Nor feels the feeble touch. Perhaps the vale
Relents awhile to the reflected ray ;
Or from the forest falls the cluster'd snow,
Myriads of gems, that in the waving gleam
Gay-twinkle as they scatter. Thick around
Thunders the sport of those, who with the gun,
And dog impatient bounding at the shot,
Worse than the season desolate the fields ;
And, adding to the ruins of the year,
Distress the footed or the feather'd game.
But what is this ? our infant Winter sinks,
Divested of his grandeur, should our eye
Astonish'd shoot into the frigid zone,
Where, for relentless months, continual Night
Holds o'er the glittering waste her starry reign.
There, through the prison of unbounded wilds
Barr'd by the hand of Nature from escape,
Wide roams the Russian exile. Nought around
Strikes his sad eye but deserts lost in snow ;
And heavy-loaded groves ; and solid floods
That stretch athwart the solitary waste
Their icy horrors to the frozen main ;
And cheerless towns far distant, never bless'd
Save when its annual course the caravan
Bends to the golden coast of rich Cathay *,
With news of human kind. Yet there life glows,
Yet cherish'd there, beneath the shining waste,
The furry nations harbour : tipp'd with jet,
Fair ermines, spotless as the snows they press ;
Sables, of glossy black ; and dark embrown'd,
Or beauteous freak'd with many a mingled hue,
Thousands besides, the costly pride of courts.
There, warm together press'd, the trooping deer
Sleep on the new-fallen snows ; and, scarce his head
Raised o'er the heapy wreath, the branching elk
Lies slumbering sullen in the white abyss.
The ruthless hunter wants nor dogs nor toils,
Nor with the dread of sounding bows he drives
The fearful flying race ; with ponderous clubs,
As weak against the mountain heaps they push
Their beating breast in vain, and piteous bray,
He lays them quivering on the ensanguined snows,
And with loud shouts rejoicing bears them home.
There through the piny forest half absorb'd,
Rough tenant of these shades, the shapeless bear,
With dangling ice all horrid, stalks forlorn ;
Slow-paced, and sourer as the storms increase,
He makes his bed beneath the inclement drift,
And with stern patience, scorning weak complaint,
Hardens his heart against assailing want.
Wide o'er the spacious regions of the north,
That see Boötes urge his tardy wain,
A boisterous race, by frosty Caurus † pierced,
Who little pleasure know and fear no pain,
Prolific swarm. They once relumed the flame
Of lost mankind, in polish'd slavery sunk ;
Drove martial horde on horde ‡, with dreadful sweep
Resistless rushing o'er the enfeebled south,
And gave the vanquish'd world another form.
Not such the sons of Lapland : wisely they
Despise the insensate barbarous trade of war ;
They ask no more than simple Nature gives ;
They love their mountains and enjoy their storms
No false desires, no pride-created wants,
Disturb the peaceful current of their time ;
And through the restless ever-tortured maze
Of pleasure, or ambition, bid it rage. [tents,
Their rein-deer form their riches. These their
Their robes, their beds, and all their homely wealth
Supply, their wholesome fare and cheerful cups.
Obsequious at their call, the docile tribe
Yield to the sled their necks, and whirl them swift
O'er hill and dale, heap'd into one expanse
Of marbled snow, as far as eye can sweep,
With a blue crust of ice unbounded glazed.

* The old name for China. † The north-west wind.
‡ The wandering Scythian clans.

By dancing meteors then, that ceaseless shake
A waving blaze refracted o'er the heavens,
And vivid moons, and stars that keener play
With doubled lustre from the glossy waste,
Even in the depth of polar night they find
A wondrous day ; enough to light the chase,
Or guide their daring steps to Finland fairs.
Wish'd Spring returns ; and from the hazy south,
While dim Aurora slowly moves before,
The welcome sun, just verging up at first,
By small degrees extends the swelling curve,
Till seen at last for gay rejoicing months,
Still round and round his spiral course he winds,
And, as he nearly dips his flaming orb,
Wheels up again, and re-ascends the sky.
In that glad season, from the lakes and floods,
Where pure Niemi's* fairy mountains rise,
And fringed with roses Tenglio † rolls his stream,
They draw the copious fry. With these, at eve,
They cheerful loaded to their tents repair;
Where, all day long in useful cares employ'd,
Their kind unblemish'd wives the fire prepare.
Thrice happy race ! by poverty secured
From legal plunder and rapacious power
In whom fell interest never yet has sown
The seeds of vice: whose spotless swains ne'er knew
Injurious deed, nor, blasted by the breath
Of faithless love, their blooming daughters woe.
  Still pressing on, beyond Tornea's lake,
And Hecla flaming through a waste of snow,
And farthest Greenland, to the pole itself,
Where, failing gradual, life at length goes out,
The Muse expands her solitary flight ;
And, hovering o'er the wild stupendous scene,
Beholds new seas beneath another sky ‡.
Throned in his palace of cerulean ice,
Here Winter holds his unrejoicing court ;
And through his airy hall the loud misrule
Of driving tempest is for ever heard ;
Here the grim tyrant meditates his wrath ;
Here arms his winds with all-subduing frost,
Moulds his fierce hail, and treasures up his snows,
With which he now oppresses half the globe.
  Thence winding eastward to the Tartar's coast,
She sweeps the bowling margin of the main ;
Where undissolving, from the first of time,
Snows swell on snows amazing to the sky ;
And icy mountains high on mountains piled
Seem to the shivering sailor from afar,
Shapeless and white, an atmosphere of clouds.
Projected huge, and horrid o'er the surge,
Alps frown on Alps ; or rushing hideous down,
As if old Chaos were again return'd,
Wide-rend the deep, and shake the solid pole.
Ocean itself no longer can resist
The binding fury ; but, in all its rage
Of tempest taken by the boundless frost,

* M. de Maupertuis, in his book on the "Figure of the Earth," after having described the beautiful lake and mountain of Niemi in Lapland, says, "From this height we had opportunity several times to see those vapours rise from the lake which the people of the country call Haltios, and which they deem to be the guardian spirits of the mountains. We had been frighted with stories of bears that haunted this place, but saw none. It seemed rather a place of resort for fairies and genii than bears."

† The same author observes, "I was surprised to see upon the banks of this river (the Tenglio) roses of as lively a red as any that are in our gardens."

‡ The other hemisphere.

Is many a fathom to the bottom chain'd,
And bid to roar no more : a bleak expanse,
Shagg'd o'er with wavy rocks, cheerless, and void
Of every life, that from the dreary months
Flies conscious southward. Miserable they !
Who, here entangled in the gathering ice,
Take their last look of the descending sun ;
While, full of death, and fierce with tenfold frost,
The long long night, incumbent o'er their heads,
Falls horrible. Such was the Briton's * fate,
As with first prow (what have not Britons dared!)
He for the passage sought, attempted since
So much in vain, and seeming to be shut
By jealous Nature with eternal bars.
In these fell regions, in Arzina caught,
And to the stony deep his idle ship
Immediate seal'd, he with his hapless crew,
Each full exerted at his several task,
Froze into statues ; to the cordage glued
The sailor, and the pilot to the helm.
  Hard by these shores, where scarce his freezing stream
Rolls the wild Oby, live the last of men ;
And half enliven'd by the distant sun,
That rears and ripens man, as well as plants,
Here human nature wears its rudest form.
Deep from the piercing season sunk in caves,
Here by dull fires, and with unjoyous cheer,
They waste the tedious gloom. Immersed in furs,
Doze the gross race. Nor sprightly jest, nor song,
Nor tenderness they know ; nor aught of life
Beyond the kindred bears that stalk without.
Till Morn at length, her roses drooping all,
Sheds a long twilight brightening o'er their fields,
And calls the quiver'd savage to the chase.
  What cannot active government perform,
New-moulding man ? Wide-stretching from these shores,
A people savage from remotest time,
A huge neglected empire, one vast mind,
By heaven inspired, from Gothic darkness call'd.
Immortal Peter ! first of monarchs ! He
His stubborn country tamed, her rocks, her fens,
Her floods, her seas, her ill-submitting sons ;
And while the fierce barbarian he subdued,
To more exalted soul he raised the man.
Ye shades of ancient heroes, ye who toil'd
Through long successive ages to build up
A labouring plan of state, behold at once
The wonder done ! behold the matchless prince !
Who left his native throne, where reign'd till then
A mighty shadow of unreal power ;
Who greatly spurn'd the slothful pomp of courts ;
And roaming every land, in every port
His sceptre laid aside, with glorious hand
Unwearied plying the mechanic tool,
Gather'd the seeds of trade, of useful arts,
Of civil wisdom, and of martial skill.
Charged with the stores of Europe home he goes !
Then cities rise amid the illumined waste ;
O'er joyless deserts smiles the rural reign ;
Far-distant flood to flood is social join'd ;
The astonish'd Euxine hears the Baltic roar ;
Proud navies ride on seas that never foam'd
With daring keel before ; and armies stretch
Each way their dazzling files, repressing here
The frantic Alexander of the North,
And awing there stern Othman's shrinking sons.
Sloth flies the land, and Ignorance, and Vice,

* Sir Hugh Willoughby, sent by Queen Elizabeth to discover the north-east passage.

Of old dishonour proud ; it glows around,
Taught by the royal hand that roused the whole,
One scene of arts, of arms, of rising trade ;
For what his wisdom plann'd, and power enforced,
More potent still, his great example show'd.
 Muttering the winds at eve, with blunted point,
Blow hollow-blustering from the south. Subdued,
The frost resolves into a trickling thaw.
Spotted the mountains shine ; loose sleet descends,
And floods the country round. The rivers swell,
Of bonds impatient. Sudden from the hills,
O'er rocks and woods, in broad brown cataracts,
A thousand snow-fed torrents shoot at once ;
And, where they rush, the wide resounding plain
Is left one slimy waste. Those sullen seas,
That wash'd the ungenial pole, will rest no more
Beneath the shackles of the mighty north ;
But, rousing all their waves, resistless heave.
And hark ! the lengthening roar continuous runs
Athwart the rifted deep : at once it bursts,
And piles a thousand mountains to the clouds.
Ill fares the bark, with trembling wretches charged,
That, toss'd amid the floating fragments, moors
Beneath the shelter of an icy isle,
While night o'erwhelms the sea, and horror looks
More horrible. Can human force endure
The assembled mischiefs that besiege them round?
Heart-gnawing hunger, fainting weariness,
The roar of winds and waves, the crush of ice,
Now ceasing, now renew'd with louder rage,
And in dire echoes bellowing round the main.
More to embroil the deep, Leviathan
And his unwieldy train, in dreadful sport,
Tempest the loosen'd brine, while through the gloom,
Far from the bleak inhospitable shore,
Loading the winds, is heard the hungry how
Of famish'd monsters, there awaiting wrecks.
But Providence, that ever-waking eye,
Looks down with pity on the feeble toil
Of mortals lost to hope, and lights them safe
Through all this dreary labyrinth of fate.
 'Tis done! dread Winter spreads his latest glooms,
And reigns tremendous o'er the conquer'd Year.
How dead the vegetable kingdom lies !
How dumb the tuneful ! Horror wide extends
His desolate domain. Behold, fond man!
See here thy pictured life ; pass some few years,
Thy flowering Spring, thy Summer's ardent strength,
Thy sober Autumn fading into age,
And pale concluding Winter comes at last,
And shuts the scene. Ah ! whither now are fled
Those dreams of greatness ? those unsolid hopes
Of happiness ? those longings after fame ?
Those restless cares ? those busy bustling days ?
Those gay-spent, festive nights ? those veering thoughts,
Lost between good and ill, that shared thy life ?
All now are vanish'd ! Virtue sole survives,
Immortal never-failing friend of man,
His guide to happiness on high. And see !
'Tis come, the glorious morn ! the second birth
Of heaven and earth. Awakening Nature hears
The new-creating word, and starts to life,
In every heighten'd form, from pain and death
For ever free. The great eternal scheme,
Involving all, and in a perfect whole
Uniting, as the prospect wider spreads,
To Reason's eye refined clears up apace.
Ye vainly wise ! ye blind presumptuous ! now,
Confounded in the dust, adore that Power
And wisdom oft arraign'd : see now the cause
Why unassuming Worth in secret lived,
And died neglected ; why the good man's share
In life was gall and bitterness of soul ;
Why the lone widow and her orphans pined
In starving solitude, while Luxury
In palaces lay straining her low thought
To form unreal wants ; why heaven-born Truth,
And Moderation fair, wore the red marks
Of Superstition's scourge ; why licensed Pain,
That cruel spoiler, that embosom'd foe,
Embitter'd all our bliss. Ye good distress'd !
Ye noble few ! who here unbending stand
Beneath life's pressure, yet bear up awhile,
And what your bounded view, which only saw
A little part, deem'd evil, is no more :
The storms of Wintry Time will quickly pass,
And one unbounded Spring encircle all.

A HYMN.

THESE, as they change, Almighty Father, these
Are but the varied God. The rolling year
Is full of Thee. Forth in the pleasing Spring
Thy beauty walks, thy tenderness and love.
Wide flush the fields ; the softening air is balm ;
Echo the mountains round ; the forest smiles ;
And every sense and every heart is joy.
Then comes thy glory in the Summer-months,
With light and heat refulgent. Then thy sun
Shoots full perfection through the swelling year ;
And oft thy voice in dreadful thunder speaks ;
And oft at dawn, deep noon, or falling eve,
By brooks and groves, in hollow-whispering gales,
Thy bounty shines in Autumn unconfined,
And spreads a common feast for all that lives.
In Winter awful Thou ! with clouds and storms
Around Thee thrown, tempest o'er tempest roll'd.
Majestic darkness ! on the whirlwind's wing
Riding sublime, Thou bidd'st the world adore,
And humblest Nature with thy northern blast.
 Mysterious round ! what skill, what force divine,
Deep felt, in these appear ! a simple train,
Yet so delightful mix'd, with such kind art,
Such beauty and beneficence combined,
Shade, unperceived, so softening into shade,
And all so forming an harmonious whole,
That, as they still succeed, they ravish still.
But wandering oft, with brute unconscious gaze,
Man marks not Thee, marks not the mighty hand
That, ever-busy, wheels the silent spheres ;

Works in the secret deep ; shoots, steaming, thence
The fair profusion that o'erspreads the Spring ;
Flings from the sun direct the flaming day ;
Feeds every creature ; hurls the tempest forth ;
And, as on earth this grateful change revolves,
With transport touches all the springs of life.
  Nature, attend ! join every living soul
Beneath the spacious temple of the sky,
In adoration join ; and, ardent, raise
One general song ! To Him, ye vocal gales,
Breathe soft, whose spirit in your freshness breathes:
Oh, talk of Him in solitary glooms!
Where, o'er the rock, the scarcely waving pine
Fills the brown shade with a religious awe.
And ye, whose bolder note is heard afar,
Who shake the astonish'd world, lift high to heaven
The impetuous song, and say from whom you rage.
His praise, ye brooks, attune, ye trembling rills ·
And let me catch it as I muse along.
Ye headlong torrents, rapid and profound ,
Ye softer floods, that lead the humid maze
Along the vale ; and thou, majestic main,
A secret world of wonders in thyself,
Sound His stupendous praise ; whose greater voice
Or bids you roar, or bids your roarings fall.
Soft roll your incense, herbs, and fruits and flowers,
In mingled clouds to him ; whose sun exalts,
Whose breath perfumes you, and whose pencil paints.
Ye forests, bend, ye harvests, wave to Him ;
Breathe your still song into the reaper's heart,
As home he goes beneath the joyous moon.
Ye that keep watch in heaven, as earth asleep
Unconscious lies, effuse your mildest beams,
Ye constellations, while your angels strike,
Amid the spangled sky, the silver lyre.
Great source of day ! best image here below
Of thy Creator, ever pouring wide,
From world to world, the vital ocean round,
On Nature write with every beam His praise.
The thunder rolls : be hush'd the prostrate world ;
While cloud to cloud returns the solemn hymn.
Bleat out afresh, ye hills : ye mossy rocks,
Retain the sound : the broad responsive low,
Ye valleys, raise ; for the Great Shepherd reigns,
And his unsuffering kingdom yet will come.
Ye woodlands all, awake : a boundless song
Burst from the groves ! and when the restless day,
Expiring, lays the warbling world asleep,
Sweetest of birds, sweet Philomela, charm
The listening shades, and teach the night His praise.
Ye chief, for whom the whole creation smiles,
At once the head, the heart, and tongue of all,
Crown the great Hymn ! In swarming cities vast,
Assembled men, to the deep organ join
The long-resounding voice, oft breaking clear,
At solemn pauses, through the swelling base ;
And, as each mingling flame increases each,
In one united ardour rise to heaven.
Or if you rather chuse the rural shade,
And find a fane in every sacred grove ;
There let the shepherd's flute, the virgin's lay,
The prompting seraph, and the poet's lyre,
Still sing the God of Seasons as they roll !
For me, when I forget the darling theme,
Whether the blossom blows, the Summer ray
Russets the plain, inspiring Autumn gleams,
Or Winter rises in the blackening east ;
Be my tongue mute, may Fancy paint no more,
And, dead to joy, forget my heart to beat !
  Should fate command me to the farthest verge
Of the green earth, to distant barbarous climes,
Rivers unknown to song ; where first the sun
Gilds Indian mountains, or his setting beam
Flames on the Atlantic isles ; 'tis nought to me :
Since God is ever present, ever felt,
In the void waste as in the city full ;
And where He vital breathes there must be joy.
When even at last the solemn hour shall come,
And wing my mystic flight to future worlds,
I cheerful will obey ; there, with new powers,
Will rising wonders sing : I cannot go
Where Universal Love not smiles around,
Sustaining all yon orbs, and all their suns;
From seeming Evil still educing Good,
And better thence again, and better still,
In infinite progression. But I lose
Myself in Him, in Light Ineffable !
Come then, expressive Silence, muse His praise.

THE

CASTLE OF INDOLENCE.

An Allegorical Poem.

ADVERTISEMENT.

This Poem being writ in the manner of Spenser, the obsolete words, and a simplicity of diction in some of the lines, which border on the ludicrous, were necessary to make the imitation more perfect. And the style of that admirable poet, as well as the measure in which he wrote, are, as it were, appropriated by custom to all allegorical poems written in our language; just as in French the style of Marot, who lived under Francis I., has been used in tales and familiar epistles by the politest writers in the age of Lewis XIV.

EXPLANATION OF THE OBSOLETE WORDS USED IN THIS POEM.

Archimage, the chief or greatest of magicians or enchanters.
Apaid, paid.
Appal, affright.
Atween, between.
Aye, always.
Bale, sorrow, trouble, misfortune.
Benempt, named.
Blazon, painting, displaying.
Breme, cold, raw.
Carol, to sing songs of joy.
Caurus, the north-east wind.
Certes, certainly.
Dan, a word prefixed to names.
Deftly, skilfully.
Depainted, painted.
Drowsihead, drowsiness.
Eath, easy.
Eftsoons, immediately, often, afterwards.
Eke, also.
Fays, fairies.
Fone, foes.
Gear or *Geer*, furniture, equipage, dress
Glaive, sword. (Fr.)
Glee, joy, pleasure.
Han, have.
Hight, named, called: and sometimes it is used for *is called*. See c. i. s. vii.
Idless, idleness.
Imp, child or offspring; from the Saxon impan, to graft or plant.
Kest, for cast.
Lad, for led.
Lea, a piece of land or meadow.
Libbard, leopard.
Lig, to lie.
Lithe, loose, lax.
Losel, a loose idle fellow.
Louting, bowing, bending.
Mell, mingle.
Moe, more.
Moil, to labour.
Mote, might.
Muchel or *Mochel*, much, great.
Nathless, nevertheless.
Ne, nor.
Needments, necessaries.
Noursling, a child that is nursed.
Noyance, harm.
Perdie (Fr. par Dieu), an old oath.
Prankt, coloured, adorned gaily.
Prick'd thro' the forest, rode through the forest.
Sear, dry, burnt up.
Sheen, bright, shining.
Sicker, sure, surely.
Smackt, savoured.
Soot, sweet, or sweetly.
Sooth, true, or truth.
Stound, misfortune, pang.
Sweltry, sultry, consuming with heat.
Swink, to labour.
Thrall, slave.
Transmew'd, transformed.
Unkempt (Lat. incomptus), unadorned.
Vild, vile.
Ween, to think, be of opinion.
Weet, to know; to weet, to wit.
Whilom, ere-while, formerly.
Wight, man.
Wis, for *Wist*, to know, think, understand.
Wonne (a noun), dwelling.
Wroke, wreakt.

N.B.—The letter Y is frequently placed in the beginning of a word by Spenser, to lengthen it a syllable; and *en* at the end of a word for the same reason, as *withouten*, *casten*, &c.

Yblent, or *blent*, blended, mingled.
Yborn, born.
Yclad, clad.
Ycleped, called, named.
Yfere, together.
Ymolten, melted.
Yode (preter tense of *yede*), went.

CANTO I.

The castle hight of Indolence,
And its false luxury:
Where for a little time, alas!
We lived right jollily.

I.

O MORTAL man, who livest here by toil,
Do not complain of this thy hard estate;
That like an emmet thou must ever moil,
Is a sad sentence of an ancient date;
And, certes, there is for it reason great;
For though sometimes it makes thee weep and wail,
And curse thy star, and early drudge and late,
Withouten that would come a heavier bale,
Loose life, unruly passions, and diseases pale.

II.

In lowly dale, fast by a river's side,
With woody hill o'er hill encompass'd round,
A most enchanting Wizard did abide,
Than whom a fiend more fell is nowhere found.
It was, I ween, a lovely spot of ground:
And there a season atween June and May,
Half prankt with spring, with summer half imbrown'd,
A listless climate made, where, sooth to say,
No living wight could work, ne cared e'en for play.

III.

Was nought around but images of rest:
Sleep-soothing groves, and quiet lawns between;
And flowery beds that slumbrous influence kest,
From poppies breathed; and beds of pleasant green,
Where never yet was creeping creature seen.
Meantime unnumber'd glittering streamlets play'd,
And hurled everywhere their waters sheen;
That, as they bicker'd through the sunny glade,
Though restless still themselves, a lulling murmur made.

IV.

Join'd to the prattle of the purling rills
Were heard the lowing herds along the vale,
And flocks loud bleating from the distant hills,
And vacant shepherds piping in the dale:
And, now and then, sweet Philomel would wail,
Or stock-doves plain amid the forest deep,
That drowsy rustled to the sighing gale;
And still a coil the grasshopper did keep;
Yet all these sounds yblent inclined all to sleep.

V.

Full in the passage of the vale, above,
A sable, silent, solemn forest stood,
Where nought but shadowy forms was seen to move,
As Idless fancied in her dreaming mood.
And up the hills, on either side, a wood
Of blackening pines, aye waving to and fro,
Sent forth a sleepy horror through the blood;
And where this valley winded out below,
The murmuring main was heard, and scarcely heard, to flow.

VI.

A pleasing land of drowsihead it was,
Of dreams that wave before the half-shut eye;
And of gay castles in the clouds that pass,
For ever flushing round a summer-sky:
There eke the soft Delights, that witchingly
Instil a wanton sweetness through the breast,
And the calm Pleasures always hover'd nigh;
But whate'er smack'd of noyance, or unrest,
Was far, far off expell'd from this delicious nest.

VII.

The landscape such, inspiring perfect ease,
Where INDOLENCE (for so the wizard hight)
Close hid his castle 'mid embowering trees,
That half shut out the beams of Phœbus bright,
And made a kind of checker'd day and night;
Meanwhile, unceasing at the massy gate,
Beneath a spacious palm, the wicked wight
Was placed; and to his lute, of cruel fate
And labour harsh, complain'd, lamenting man's estate.

VIII.

Thither continual pilgrims crowded still,
From all the roads of earth that pass thereby:
For, as they chaunced to breathe on neighbouring hill,
The freshness of this valley smote their eye,
And drew them ever and anon more nigh;
Till clustering round the enchanter false they hung,
Ymolten with his syren melody;
While o'er the enfeebling lute his hand he flung,
And to the trembling chords these tempting verses sung:—

IX.

"Behold! ye pilgrims of this earth, behold!
See all, but man, with unearn'd pleasure gay:
See her bright robes the butterfly unfold,
Broke from her wintry tomb in prime of May!
What youthful bride can equal her array?
Who can with her for easy pleasure vie?
From mead to mead with gentle wing to stray,
From flower to flower on balmy gales to fly,
Is all she has to do beneath the radiant sky.

X.

"Behold the merry minstrels of the morn,
The swarming songsters of the careless grove,
Ten thousand throats! that, from the flowering thorn,
Hymn their good God, and carol sweet of love,
Such grateful kindly raptures them emove:
They neither plough, nor sow; ne, fit for flail,
E'er to the barn the nodden sheaves they drove;
Yet theirs each harvest dancing in the gale,
Whatever crowns the hill, or smiles along the vale.

XI.

"Outcast of nature, man! the wretched thrall
Of bitter dropping sweat, of sweltry pain,
Of cares that eat away the heart with gall,
And of the vices, an inhuman train,
That all proceed from savage thirst of gain:
For when hard-hearted Interest first began
To poison earth, Astræa left the plain:
Guile, Violence, and Murder seized on man,
And, for soft milky streams, with blood the rivers ran.

XII.

"Come, ye, who still the cumbrous load of life
Push hard up hill ; but as the farthest steep
You trust to gain, and put an end to strife,
Down thunders back the stone with mighty sweep,
And hurls your labours to the valley deep,
For ever vain : come, and withouten fee,
I in oblivion will your sorrows steep,
Your cares, your toils ; will steep you in a sea
Of full delight : O come, ye weary wights, to me !

XIII.

"With me, you need not rise at early dawn,
To pass the joyless day in various stounds ;
Or, louting low, on upstart Fortune fawn,
And sell fair honour for some paltry pounds ;
Or through the city take your dirty rounds,
To cheat, and dun, and lie, and visit pay,
Now flattering base, now giving secret wounds ;
Or prowl in courts of law for human prey,
In venal senate thieve, or rob on broad highway.

XIV.

No cocks, with me, to rustic labour call,
From village on to village sounding clear ;
To tardy swain no shrill-voiced matrons squall ;
No dogs, no babes, no wives, to stun your ear ;
No hammers thump ; no horrid blacksmith sear,
Ne noisy tradesman your sweet slumbers start,
With sounds that are a misery to hear :
But all is calm, as would delight the heart
Of Sybarite of old, all nature, and all art.

XV.

"Here nought but candour reigns, indulgent ease,
Good-nature lounging, sauntering up and down :
They who are pleased themselves must always please;
On others' ways they never squint a frown,
Nor heed what haps in hamlet or in town :
Thus, from the source of tender Indolence,
With milky blood the heart is overflown,
Is soothed and sweeten'd by the social sense ;
For Interest, Envy, Pride, and Strife are banish'd hence.

XVI.

"What, what is virtue, but repose of mind,
A pure ethereal calm, that knows no storm,
Above the reach of wild Ambition's wind,
Above those passions that this world deform,
And torture man, a proud malignant worm ?
But here, instead, soft gales of passion play,
And gently stir the heart, thereby to form
A quicker sense of joy ; as breezes stray
Across the enliven'd skies, and make them still more gay.

XVII.

"The best of men have ever loved repose :
They hate to mingle in the filthy fray ;
Where the soul sours, and gradual rancour grows,
Embitter'd more from peevish day to day.
Even those whom Fame has lent her fairest ray,
The most renown'd of worthy wights of yore,
From a base world at last have stolen away :
So Scipio, to the soft Cumæan shore
Retiring, tasted joy he never knew before.

XVIII.

"But if a little exercise you chuse,
Some zest for ease, 'tis not forbidden here :
Amid the groves you may indulge the Muse,
Or tend the blooms, and deck the vernal year ;
Or softly stealing, with your watery gear,
Along the brooks, the crimson-spotted fry
You may delude : the whilst, amused, you hear
Now the hoarse stream, and now the zephyr's sigh,
Attuned to the birds, and woodland melody.

XIX.

"O grievous folly ! to heap up estate,
Losing the days you see beneath the sun ;
When, sudden, comes blind unrelenting Fate,
And gives the untasted portion you have won
With ruthless toil, and many a wretch undone,
To those who mock you, gone to Pluto's reign,
There with sad ghosts to pine, and shadows dun
But sure it is of vanities most vain,
To toil for what you here untoiling may obtain."

XX.

He ceased. But still their trembling ears retain'd
The deep vibrations of his witching song ;
That, by a kind of magic power, constrain'd
To enter in, pell-mell, the listening throng.
Heaps pour'd on heaps, and yet they slipt along,
In silent ease ; as when beneath the beam
Of summer-moons, the distant woods among,
Or by some flood all silver'd with the gleam,
The soft-embodied fays through airy portal stream:

XXI.

By the smooth demon so it order'd was,
And here his baneful bounty first began :
Though some there were who would not further pass,
And his alluring baits suspected han :
The wise distrust the too fair-spoken man.
Yet through the gate they cast a wishful eye :
Not to move on, perdie, is all they can :
For do their very best they cannot fly,
But often each way look, and often sorely sigh.

XXII.

When this the watchful wicked wizard saw,
With sudden spring he leap'd upon them straight :
And soon as touch'd by his unhallow'd paw,
They found themselves within the cursed gate ;
Full hard to be repass'd, like that of fate.
Not stronger were of old the giant crew,
Who sought to pull high Jove from regal state ;
Though feeble wretch he seem'd, of sallow hue :
Certes, who bides his grasp, will that encounter rue.

XXIII.

For whomsoe'er the villain takes in hand,
Their joints unknit, their sinews melt apace ;
As lithe they grow as any willow-wand,
And of their vanish'd force remains no trace :
So when a maiden fair, of modest grace,
In all her buxom blooming May of charms,
Is seized in some losel's hot embrace,
She waxeth very weakly, as she warms,
Then sighing yields her up to love's delicious harms.

XXIV.

Waked by the crowd, slow from his bench arose
A comely, full-spread porter, swoln with sleep :
His calm, broad, thoughtless aspect breathed
And in sweet torpor he was plunged deep, [repose;
Ne could himself from ceaseless yawning keep ;
While o'er his eyes the drowsy liquor ran, [peep :
Through which his half-waked soul would faintly
Then, taking his black staff, he call'd his man,
And roused himself as much as rouse himself he can.

XXV.

The lad leap'd lightly at his master's call :
He was, to weet, a little roguish page,
Save sleep and play who minded nought at all,
Like most the untaught striplings of his age.
This boy he kept each band to disengage,
Garters and buckles, task for him unfit,
But ill becoming his grave personage,
And which his portly paunch would not permit :
So this same limber page to all performed it.

XXVI.

Meantime, the master-porter wide display'd
Great store of caps, of slippers, and of gowns ;
Wherewith he those who enter'd in array'd,
Loose as the breeze that plays along the downs,
And waves the summer woods when evening frowns:
O fair undress, best dress ! it checks no vein,
But every flowing limb in pleasure drowns, [fain,
And heightens ease with grace. This done, right
Sir Porter sat him down, and turn'd to sleep again.

XXVII.

Thus easy robed, they to the fountain sped
That in the middle of the court up-threw
A stream, high spouting from its liquid bed,
And falling back again in drizzly dew ;
There each deep draughts, as deep he thirsted.
It was a fountain of nepenthe rare, [drew :
Whence, as Dan Homer sings, huge pleasaunce
And sweet oblivion of vile earthly care ; [grew,
Fair gladsome waking thoughts, and joyous dreams
more fair.

XXVIII.

This rite perform'd, all inly pleased and still,
Withouten tromp, was proclamation made :
"Ye sons of Indolence, do what you will ;
And wander where you list, through hall or glade ;
Be no man's pleasure for another staid ;
Let each as likes him best his hours employ,
And cursed be he who minds his neighbour's trade !
Here dwells kind Ease and unreproving Joy :
He little merits bliss who others can annoy."

XXIX.

Straight of these endless numbers, swarming round,
As thick as idle motes in sunny ray,
Not one eftsoons in view was to be found,
But every man stroll'd off his own glad way,
Wide o'er this ample court's blank area,
With all the lodges that thereto pertain'd,
No living creature could be seen to stray ;
While solitude, and perfect silence reign'd ;
So that to think you dreamt you almost were con-
strain'd.

XXX.

As when a shepherd of the Hebrid-Isles*,
Placed far amid the melancholy main,
(Whether it be lone Fancy him beguiles ;
Or that aërial beings sometimes deign
To stand, embodied, to our senses plain)
Sees on the naked hill, or valley low,
The whilst in ocean Phœbus dips his wain,
A vast assembly moving to and fro :
Then all at once in air dissolves the wondrous show.

XXXI.

Ye gods of quiet, and of sleep profound !
Whose soft dominion o'er this castle sways,
And all the widely silent places round,
Forgive me, if my trembling pen displays
What never yet was sung in mortal lays.
But how shall I attempt such arduous string ?
I who have spent my nights, and nightly days,
In this soul-deadening place loose loitering :
Ah ! how shall I for this uprear my moulted wing ?

XXXII.

Come on, my Muse, nor stoop to low despair,
Thou imp of Jove, touch'd by celestial fire !
Thou yet shalt sing of war, and actions fair,
Which the bold sons of Britain will inspire ;
Of ancient bards thou yet shalt sweep the lyre ;
Thou yet shalt tread in tragic pall the stage,
Paint love's enchanting woes, the hero's ire,
The sage's calm, the patriot's noble rage,
Dashing Corruption down through every worthless
age.

XXXIII.

The doors, that knew no shrill alarming bell,
Ne cursed knocker plied by villain's hand,
Self-open'd into halls, where, who can tell
What elegance and grandeur wide expand ;
The pride of Turkey and of Persia land ?
Soft quilts on quilts, on carpets carpets spread,
And couches stretch'd around in seemly band ;
And endless pillows rise to prop the head ;
So that each spacious room was one full-swelling
bed ;

XXXIV.

And everywhere huge cover'd tables stood,
With wines high flavour'd and rich viands crown'd,
Whatever sprightly juice or tasteful food
On the green bosom of this earth are found,
And all old Ocean 'genders in his round :
Some hand unseen these silently display'd,
Even undemanded by a sign or sound ;
You need but wish, and, instantly obey'd,
Fair ranged the dishes rose, and thick the glasses
play'd.

XXXV.

Here freedom reign'd, without the least alloy ;
Nor gossip's tale, nor ancient maiden's gall,
Nor saintly spleen durst murmur at our joy,
And with envenom'd tongue our pleasures pall.
For why ? there was but one great rule for all ;
To wit, that each should work his own desire,
And eat, drink, study, sleep, as it may fall,
Or melt the time in love, or wake the lyre,
And carol what, unbid, the Muses might inspire.

* Those islands on the western coast of Scotland called the Hebrides.

XXXVI.

The rooms with costly tapestry were hung,
Where was inwoven many a gentle tale;
Such as of old the rural poets sung,
Or of Arcadian or Sicilian vale:
Reclining lovers, in the lonely dale,
Pour'd forth at large the sweetly tortured heart;
Or, sighing tender passion, swell'd the gale,
And taught charm'd Echo to resound their smart;
While flocks, woods, streams around, repose and peace impart.

XXXVII.

Those pleased the most, where, by a cunning hand,
Depainted was the patriarchal age;
What time Dan Abra'am left the Chaldee land,
And pastured on from verdant stage to stage,
Where fields and fountains fresh could best engage.
Toil was not then: of nothing took they heed,
But with wild beasts the sylvan war to wage,
And o'er vast plains their herds and flocks to feed:
Bless'd sons of Nature they! true golden age indeed.

XXXVIII.

Sometimes the pencil, in cool airy halls,
Bade the gay bloom of vernal landscapes rise,
Or Autumn's varied shades imbrown the walls:
Now the black tempest strikes the astonish'd eyes;
Now down the steep the flashing torrent flies;
The trembling sun now plays o'er ocean blue,
And now rude mountains frown amid the skies;
Whate'er Lorraine light-touch'd with softening hue,
Or savage Rosa dash'd, or learned Poussin drew.

XXXIX.

Each sound too here to languishment inclined,
Lull'd the weak bosom, and induced ease:
Aërial music in the warbling wind,
At distance rising oft, by small degrees,
Nearer and nearer came, till o'er the trees
It hung, and breathed such soul-dissolving airs,
As did, alas! with soft perdition please:
Entangled deep in its enchanting snares,
The listening heart forgot all duties and all cares.

XL.

A certain music, never known before,
Here lull'd the pensive, melancholy mind;
Full easily obtain'd. Behoves no more,
But sidelong, to the gently waving wind,
To lay the well-tuned instrument reclined;
From which, with airy-flying fingers light,
Beyond each mortal touch the most refined,
The god of winds drew sounds of deep delight:
Whence, with just cause, the harp of Æolus* it hight.

XLI.

Ah me! what hand can touch the string so fine?
Who up the lofty diapason roll
Such sweet, such sad, such solemn airs divine,
Then let them down again into the soul?
Now rising love they fann'd; now pleasing dole
They breathed, in tender musings, through the heart;
And now a graver sacred strain they stole,
As when seraphic hands a hymn impart:
Wild warbling nature all, above the reach of art!

* This is not an imagination of the author; there being in fact such an instrument, called Æolus's harp, which, when placed against a little rushing or current of air, produces the effect here described.

XLII.

Such the gay splendour, the luxurious state,
Of caliphs old, who on the Tigris' shore,
In mighty Bagdat, populous and great,
Held their bright court, where was of ladies store;
And verse, love, music, still the garland wore:
When Sleep was coy, the bard,* in waiting there,
Cheer'd the lone midnight with the Muse's lore;
Composing music bade his dreams be fair,
And music lent new gladness to the morning air.

XLIII.

Near the pavilions where we slept, still ran
Soft tinkling streams, and dashing waters fell,
And sobbing breezes sigh'd, and oft began
(So work'd the wizard) wintry storms to swell,
As heaven and earth they would together mell:
At doors and windows threatening, seem'd to call
The demons of the tempest, growling fell,
Yet the least entrance found they none at all,
When sweeter grew our sleep, secure in massy hall.

XLIV.

And hither Morpheus sent his kindest dreams,
Raising a world of gayer tinct and grace,
O'er which were shadowy cast Elysian gleams,
That play'd in waving lights, from place to place,
And shed a roseate smile on Nature's face.
Not Titian's pencil e'er could so array,
So fleece with clouds the pure ethereal space;
Ne could it e'er such melting forms display,
As loose on flowery beds all languishingly lay.

XLV.

No, fair illusions! artful phantoms, no!
My Muse will not attempt your fairy land:
She has no colours that like you can glow:
To catch your vivid scenes too gross her hand.
But, sure it is, was ne'er a subtler band
Than these same guileful angel-seeming sprites,
Who thus in dreams voluptuous, soft, and bland,
Pour'd all the Arabian heaven upon our nights,
And bless'd them oft besides with more refined delights.

XLVI.

They were, in sooth, a most enchanting train,
E'en feigning virtue; skilful to unite
With evil good, and strew with pleasure pain.
But for those fiends, whom blood and broils delight,
Who hurl the wretch, as if to hell outright,
Down down black gulfs, where sullen waters sleep,
Or hold him clambering all the fearful night
On beetling cliffs, or pent in ruins deep;
They, till due time should serve, were bid far hence to keep.

XLVII.

Ye guardian spirits, to whom man is dear,
From these foul demons shield the midnight gloom:
Angels of fancy and of love, be near,
And o'er the blank of sleep diffuse a bloom:
Evoke the sacred shades of Greece and Rome,
And let them virtue with a look impart:
But chief, awhile, O! lend us from the tomb
Those long-lost friends for whom in love we smart,
And fill with pious awe and joy-mix'd woe the heart.

* The Arabian caliphs had poets among the officers of their court, whose office it was to do what is here mentioned.

XLVIII.

Or are you sportive?——Bid the morn of youth
Rise to new light, and beam afresh the days
Of innocence, simplicity, and truth;
To cares estranged, and manhood's thorny ways.
What transport, to retrace our boyish plays,
Our easy bliss, when each thing joy supplied;
The woods, the mountains, and the warbling maze
Of the wild brooks!—but, fondly wandering wide,
My Muse, resume the task that yet doth thee abide.

XLIX.

One great amusement of our household was,
In a huge crystal magic globe to spy,
Still as you turn'd it, all things that do pass
Upon this ant-hill earth, where constantly
Of idly busy men the restless fry
Run bustling to and fro with foolish haste,
In search of pleasures vain that from them fly;
Or which, obtain'd, the caitiffs dare not taste:
When nothing is enjoy'd, can there be greater waste?

L.

"Of vanity the mirrour," this was call'd:
Here you a muckworm of the town might see
At his dull desk, amid his ledgers stall'd,
Eat up with carking care and penury;
Most like to carcase parch'd on gallow-tree,
"A penny saved is a penny got:"
Firm to this scoundrel maxim keepeth he,
Ne of its rigour will he bate a jot,
Till it has quench'd his fire, and banished his pot.

LI.

Straight from the filth of this low grub, behold!
Comes fluttering forth a gaudy spendthrift heir,
All glossy gay, enamel'd all with gold,
The silly tenant of the summer air,
In folly lost, of nothing takes he care;
Pimps, lawyers, stewards, harlots, flatterers vile,
And thieving tradesmen him among them share:
His father's ghost from limbo lake, the while,
Sees this, which more damnation doth upon him pile.

LII.

This globe pourtray'd the race of learned men,
Still at their books, and turning o'er the page,
Backwards and forwards: oft they snatch the pen,
As if inspired, and in a Thespian rage;
Then write, and blot, as would your ruth engage;
Why, authors, all this scrawl and scribbling sore?
To lose the present, gain the future age,
Praised to be when you can hear no more,
And much enrich'd with fame, when useless worldly store.

LIII.

Then would a splendid city rise to view,
With carts, and cars, and coaches roaring all:
Wide-pour'd abroad behold the giddy crew:
See how they dash along from wall to wall!
At every door, hark how they thundering call!
Good lord! what can this giddy rout excite?
Why, on each other with fell tooth to fall,
A neighbour's fortune, fame or peace, to blight,
And make new tiresome parties for the coming night

LIV.

The puzzling sons of party next appear'd,
In dark cabals and nightly juntos met;
And now they whisper'd close, now shrugging rear'd
The important shoulder; then, as if to get
New light, their twinkling eyes were inward set.
No sooner Lucifer* recals affairs,
Than forth they various rush in mighty fret;
When lo! push'd up to power, and crown'd their cares,
In comes another set, and kicketh them down stairs.

LV.

But what most show'd the vanity of life
Was to behold the nations all on fire,
In cruel broils engaged, and deadly strife:
Most Christian kings, inflamed by black desire,
With honourable ruffians in their hire,
Cause war to rage, and blood around to pour;
Of this sad work when each begins to tire,
They sit them down just where they were before,
Till for new scenes of woe peace shall their force restore.

LVI.

To number up the thousands dwelling here,
A useless were, and eke an endless task;
From kings, and those who at the helm appear,
To gipsies brown in summer-glades who bask.
Yea many a man, perdie, I could unmask,
Whose desk and table make a solemn show,
With tape-tied trash, and suits of fools that ask
For place or pension, laid in decent row;
But these I passen by, with nameless numbers moe.

LVII.

Of all the gentle tenants of the place,
There was a man of special grave remark;
A certain tender gloom o'erspread his face,
Pensive, not sad; in thought involved, not dark,
As soot this man could sing as morning lark,
And teach the noblest morals of the heart:
But these his talents were yburied stark;
Of the fine stores he nothing would impart,
Which or boon Nature gave, or nature-painting Art.

LVIII.

To noon-tide shades incontinent he ran,
Where purls the brook with sleep-inviting sound;
Or when Dan Sol to slope his wheels began,
Amid the broom he bask'd him on the ground,
Where the wild thyme and camomile are found:
There would he linger, till the latest ray
Of light sat trembling on the welkin's bound;
Then homeward through the twilight shadows stray,
Sauntering and slow. So had he passed many a day!

LIX.

Yet not in thoughtless slumber were they pass'd;
For oft the heavenly fire, that lay conceal'd
Beneath the sleeping embers, mounted fast,
And all its native light anew reveal'd:
Oft as he traversed the cerulean field,
And mark'd the clouds that drove before the wind,
Ten thousand glorious systems would he build,
Ten thousand great ideas fill'd his mind;
But with the clouds they fled, and left no trace behind.

* The morning star.

LX.

With him was sometimes join'd, in silent walk,
(Profoundly silent, for they never spoke)
One* shyer still, who quite detested talk :
Oft, stung by spleen, at once away he broke,
To groves of pine, and broad o'ershadowing oak;
There, inly thrill'd, he wander'd all alone,
And on himself his pensive fury wroke,
Ne ever utter'd word, save when first shone
The glittering star of eve—"Thank heaven! the day is done."

LXI.

Here lurk'd a wretch, who had not crept abroad
For forty years, ne face of mortal seen ;
In chamber brooding like a loathly toad :
And sure his linen was not very clean.
Through secret loop-holes,that had practised been
Near to his bed, his dinner vile he took ;
Unkempt, and rough, of squalid face and mien,
Our Castle's shame! whence, from his filthy nook,
We drove the villain out, for fitter lair to look.

LXII.

One day there chaunced into these halls to rove
A joyous youth, who took you at first sight ;
Him the wild wave of pleasure hither drove,
Before the sprightly tempest tossing light :
Certes, he was a most engaging wight,
Of social glee, and wit humane though keen,
Turning the night to day and day to night :
For him the merry bells had rung, I ween,
If, in this nook of quiet, bells had ever been.

LXIII.

But not e'en pleasure to excess is good .
What most elates, then sinks the soul as low:
When springtide joy pours in with copious flood,
The higher still the exulting billows flow,
The farther back again they flagging go,
And leave us groveling on the dreary shore :
Taught by this son of joy, we found it so,
Who, whilst he stay'd, kept in a gay uproar
Our madden'd Castle all, the abode of sleep no more.

LXIV.

As when in prime of June a burnish'd fly,
Sprung from the meads, o'er which he sweeps along,
Cheer'd by the breathing bloom and vital sky,
Tunes up amid these airy halls his song,
Soothing at first the gay reposing throng :
And oft he sips their bowl ; or, nearly drown'd,
He, thence recovering, drives their beds among,
And scares their tender sleep, with trump profound;
Then out again he flies, to wing his mazy round.

LXV.

Another guest† there was, of sense refined,
Who felt each worth, for every worth he had ;
Serene yet warm, humane yet firm his mind,
As little touch'd as any man's with bad ;
Him through their inmost walks the Muses lad,
To him the sacred love of nature lent,
And sometimes would he make our valley glad ;
When as we found he would not here be pent,
To him the better sort this friendly message sent :

* Conjecture has applied this to Dr. Armstrong the poet.
† George Lord Lyttleton.

LXVI.

"Come, dwell with us ! true son of Virtue, come !
But if, alas ! we cannot thee persuade
To lie content beneath our peaceful dome,
Ne ever more to quit our quiet glade ;
Yet when at last thy toils but ill apaid
Shall dead thy fire, and damp its heavenly spark,
Thou wilt be glad to seek the rural shade,
There to indulge the Muse, and nature mark :
We then a lodge for thee will rear in Hagley Park."

LXVII.

Here whilom ligg'd the Esopus* of the age ;
But call'd by fame, in soul ypricked deep,
A noble pride restored him to the stage,
And roused him like a giant from his sleep.
Even from his slumbers we advantage reap :
With double force the enliven'd scene he wakes,
Yet quits not nature's bounds. He knows to keep
Each due decorum : now the heart he shakes,
And now with well-urged sense the enlighten'd judgment takes.

LXVIII.

A bard here dwelt, more fat than bard beseems,
Who void of envy, guile, and lust of gain†,
On virtue still, and nature's pleasing themes,
Pour'd forth his unpremeditated strain :
The world forsaking with a calm disdain,
Here laugh'd he careless in his easy seat;
Here quaff'd encircled with the joyous train,
Oft moralizing sage: his ditty sweet
He loathed much to write, ne cared to repeat.

LXIX.

Full oft by holy feet our ground was trod,
Of clerks good plenty here you mote espy.
A little, round, fat, oily man‡ of God,
Was one I chiefly mark'd among the fry:
He had a roguish twinkle in his eye,
And shone all glittering with ungodly dew,
If a tight damsel chaunced to trippen by ;
Which when observed, he shrunk into his mew,
And straight would recollect his piety anew.

LXX.

Nor be forgot a tribe, who minded nought
(Old inmates of the place) but state affairs:
They look'd, perdie, as if they deeply thought,
And on their brow sat every nation's cares;
The world by them is parcel'd out in shares,
When in the Hall of Smoke they congress hold,
And the sage berry sun-burnt Mocha bears
Has clear'd their inward eye: then, smoke-enroll'd,
Their oracles break forth, mysterious as of old.

* Mr. Quin.

† The following lines of this stanza were written by a friend of the author (since understood to have been Lord Lyttleton), and were designed to portray the character of Thomson.

‡ The Rev. Mr. Murdoch, Thomson's friend and biographer.

LXXI.

Here languid Beauty kept her pale-faced court:
Bevies of dainty dames, of high degree,
From every quarter thither made resort;
Where, from gross mortal care and business free,
They lay pour'd out in ease and luxury.
Or should they a vain show of work assume,
Alas! and well-a-day! what can it be?
To knot, to twist, to range the vernal bloom;
But far is cast the distaff, spinning-wheel, and loom.

LXXII.

Their only labour was to kill the time
(And labour dire it is, and weary woe;)
They sit, they loll, turn o'er some idle rhyme;
Then, rising sudden, to the glass they go,
Or saunter forth, with tottering step and slow:
This soon too rude an exercise they find;
Straight on the couch their limbs again they throw,
Where hours on hours they sighing lie reclined,
And court the vapoury god, soft breathing in the wind.

LXXIII.

One nymph there was, methought, in bloom of May,
On whom the idle Fiend glanced many a look,
In hopes to lead her down the slippery way
To taste of Pleasure's deep deceitful brook:
No virtues yet her gentle mind forsook:
No idle whims, no vapours fill'd her brain;
But Prudence for her youthful guide she took,
And Goodness, which no earthly vice could stain,
Dwelt in her mind; she was ne proud, I ween, or vain.

LXXIV.

Now must I mark the villany we found,
But ah! too late, as shall eftsoons be shown.
A place here was, deep, dreary, under ground;
Where still our inmates when unpleasing grown,
Diseased, and loathsome, privily were thrown:
Far from the light of heaven, they languish'd there,
Unpitied uttering many a bitter groan;
For of these wretches taken was no care:
Fierce fiends, and hags of hell, their only nurses were.

LXXV.

Alas! the change! from scenes of joy and rest,
To this dark den, where sickness toss'd alway.
Here Lethargy, with deadly sleep oppress'd,
Stretch'd on his back, a mighty lubbard, lay,
Heaving his sides, and snored night and day;
To stir him from his traunce it was not eath,
And his half-open'd eyne he shut straightway;
He led, I wot, the softest way to death,
And taught withouten pain and strife to yield the breath.

LXXVI.

Of limbs enormous, but withal unsound,
Soft-swoln and pale, here lay the Hydropsy:
Unwieldy man, with belly monstrous round,
For ever fed with watery supply;
For still he drank, and yet he still was dry.
And moping here did Hypochondria sit,
Mother of Spleen, in robes of various dye,
Who vexed was full oft with ugly fit;
And some her frantic deem'd, and some her deem'd a wit.

LXXVII.

A lady proud she was of ancient blood,
Yet oft her fear her pride made crouchen low:
She felt, or fancied in her fluttering mood,
All the diseases which the spittles know,
And sought all physic which the shops bestow,
And still new leeches and new drugs would try,
Her humour ever wavering to and fro:
For sometimes she would laugh and sometimes cry,
Then sudden waxed wroth, and all she knew not why.

LXXVIII.

Fast by her side a listless maiden pined,
With aching head and squeamish heart-burnings;
Pale, bloated, cold, she seem'd to hate mankind,
Yet loved in secret all forbidden things.
And here the Tertian shakes his chilling wings;
The sleepless Gout here counts the crowing cocks,
A wolf now gnaws him, now a serpent stings;
Whilst Apoplexy cramm'd Intemperance knocks
Down to the ground at once as butcher felleth ox *.

CANTO II.

The Knight of Arts and Industry,
And his achievements fair,
That by this Castle's overthrow,
Secured, and crowned were.

I.

ESCAPED the castle of the sire of sin,
Ah! where shall I so sweet a dwelling find?
For all around, without, and all within,
Nothing save what delightful was and kind,
Of goodness savouring and a tender mind,
E'er rose to view. But now another strain,
Of doleful note, alas! remains behind:
I now must sing of pleasure turn'd to pain,
And of the false enchanter INDOLENCE complain.

II.

Is there no patron to protect the Muse,
And fence for her Parnassus' barren soil?
To every labour its reward accrues,
And they are sure of bread who swink and moil;
But a fell tribe the Aonian hive despoil,
As ruthless wasps oft rob the painful bee:
Thus while the laws not guard that noblest toil,
Ne for the Muses other meed decree,
They praised are alone, and starve right merrily.

III.

I care not, Fortune, what you me deny:
You cannot rob me of free Nature's grace:
You cannot shut the windows of the sky,
Through which Aurora shows her brightening face;
You cannot bar my constant feet to trace
The woods and lawns, by living stream, at eve:
Let health my nerves and finer fibres brace,
And I their toys to the great children leave:
Of fancy, reason, virtue, nought can me bereave.

* These four concluding stanzas were claimed by Dr Armstrong, and inserted in his "Miscellanies."

IV.

Come then, my Muse, and raise a bolder song ;
Come lig no more upon the bed of sloth,
Dragging the lazy languid line along,
Fond to begin, but still to finish loth,
Thy half-writ scrolls all eaten by the moth :
Arise, and sing that generous imp of fame,
Who, with the sons of Softness nobly wroth,
To sweep away this human lumber came,
Or in a chosen few to rouse the slumbering flame.

V.

In Fairy Land there lived a knight of old,
Of feature stern, Selvaggio well yclep'd,
A rough unpolish'd man, robust and bold,
But wondrous poor : he neither sow'd nor reap'd,
Ne stores in summer for cold winter heap'd ;
In hunting all his days away he wore ;
Now scorch'd by June, now in November steep'd,
Now pinch'd by biting January sore,
He still in woods pursued the libbard and the boar.

VI.

As he one morning, long before the dawn,
Prick'd through the forest to dislodge his prey,
Deep in the winding bosom of a lawn,
With wood wild-fringed, he mark'd a taper's ray,
That from the beating rain and wintry fray,
Did to a lonely cot his steps decoy ;
There, up to earn the needments of the day,
He found dame Poverty, nor fair nor coy :
Her he compress'd, and fill'd her with a lusty boy.

VII.

Amid the greenwood shade this boy was bred,
And grew at last a knight of muchel fame,
Of active mind and vigorous lustyhed,
The Knight of Arts and Industry by name.
Earth was his bed, the boughs his roof did frame ;
He knew no beverage but the flowing stream ;
His tasteful well-earn'd food the sylvan game,
Or the brown fruit with which the woodlands teem:
The same to him glad summer, or the winter breme.

VIII.

So pass'd his youthly morning, void of care,
Wild as the colts that through the commons run :
For him no tender parents troubled were ;
He of the forest seem'd to be the son,
And, certes, had been utterly undone,
But that Minerva pity of him took,
With all the gods that love the rural wonne,
That teach to tame the soil and rule the crook ;
Ne did the sacred Nine disdain a gentle look.

IX.

Of fertile genius, him they nurtured well,
In every science, and in every art,
By which mankind the thoughtless brutes excel,
That can or use, or joy, or grace impart,
Disclosing all the powers of head and heart :
Ne were the goodly exercises spared,
That brace the nerves, or make the limbs alert,
And mix elastic force with firmness hard :
Was never knight on ground mote be with him compared.

X.

Sometimes, with early dawn, he mounted gay,
The hunter steed, exulting o'er the dale,
And drew the roseate breath of orient day ;
Sometimes retiring to the secret vale,
Yclad in steel, and bright with burnish'd mail,
He strain'd the bow, or toss'd the sounding spear,
Or, darting on the goal, outstripp'd the gale,
Or wheel'd the chariot in its mid career,
Or strenuous wrestled hard with many a tough compeer.

XI.

At other times he pried through Nature s store,
Whate'er she in the ethereal round contains,
Whate'er she hides beneath her verdant floor,
The vegetable and the mineral reigns ;
Or else he scann'd the globe, those small domains,
Where restless mortals such a turmoil keep,
Its seas, its floods, its mountains, and its plains :
But more he search'd the mind, and roused from sleep
Those moral seeds whence we heroic actions reap.

XII.

Nor would he scorn to stoop from high pursuits
Of heavenly Truth, and practise what she taught:
Vain is the tree of knowledge without fruits !
Sometimes in hand the spade or plough he caught,
Forth calling all with which boon earth is fraught;
Sometimes he plied the strong mechanic tool,
Or rear'd the fabric from the finest draught ;
And oft he put himself to Neptune's school,
Fighting with winds and waves on the vex'd ocean pool.

XIII.

To solace then these rougher toils, he tried
To touch the kindling canvass into life ;
With nature his creating pencil vied,
With nature joyous at the mimic strife :
Or, to such shapes as graced Pygmalion's wife,
He hew'd the marble ; or, with varied fire,
He roused the trumpet, and the martial fife,
Or bade the lute sweet tenderness inspire,
Or verses framed that well might wake Apollo's lyre.

XIV.

Accomplish'd thus, he from the woods issued,
Full of great aims, and bent on bold emprize ;
The work, which long he in his breast had brew'd,
Now to perform he ardent did devise ;
To wit, a barbarous world to civilize.
Earth was till then a boundless forest wild ;
Nought to be seen but savage wood and skies ;
No cities nourish'd arts, no culture smiled,
No government, no laws, no gentle manners mild.

XV.

A rugged wight, the worst of brutes, was man :
On his own wretched kind he, ruthless, prey'd :
The strongest still the weakest overran ;
In every country mighty robbers sway'd,
And guile and ruffian force were all their trade.
Life was a scene of rapine, want, and woe ;
Which this brave knight, in noble anger, made
To swear he would the rascal rout o'erthrow,
For, by the powers divine, it should no more be so !

XVI.

It would exceed the purport of my song,
To say how this best sun, from orient climes,
Came beaming life and beauty all along,
Before him chasing indolence and crimes.
Still as he pass'd the nations he sublimes,
And calls forth arts and virtues with his ray :
Then Egypt, Greece, and Rome, their golden times
Successive had ; but now in ruins grey
They lie, to slavish sloth and tyranny a prey.

XVII.

To crown his toils, Sir Industry then spread
The swelling sail, and made for Britain's coast.
A sylvan life till then the natives led,
In the brown shades and green-wood forest lost,
All careless rambling where it liked them most :
Their wealth the wild deer bouncing through the glade ;
They lodged at large, and lived at Nature's cost ;
Save spear and bow, withouten other aid ;
Yet not the Roman steel their naked breast dismay'd.

XVIII.

He liked the soil, he liked the clement skies,
He liked the verdant hills and flowery plains :
" Be this my great, my chosen isle," he cries,
" This, whilst my labours Liberty sustains,
This queen of ocean all assault disdains."
Nor liked he less the genius of the land,
To freedom apt and persevering pains,
Mild to obey, and generous to command,
Temper'd by forming Heaven with kindest, firmest hand.

XIX.

Here, by degrees, his master-work arose,
Whatever arts and industry can frame :
Whatever finish'd Agriculture knows,
Fair queen of arts ! from heaven itself who came,
When Eden flourish'd in unspotted fame :
And still with her sweet Innocence we find,
And tender Peace, and joys without a name,
That while they ravish, tranquillise the mind :
Nature and art at once, delight and use combined.

XX.

Then towns he quicken'd by mechanic arts,
And bade the fervent city glow with toil ;
Bade social commerce raise renowned marts,
Join land to land, and marry soil to soil ;
Unite the poles, and without bloody spoil
Bring home of either Ind the gorgeous stores ;
Or, should despotic rage the world embroil,
Bade tyrants tremble on remotest shores,
While o'er the encircling deep Britannia's thunder roars.

XXI.

The drooping Muses then he westward call'd
From the famed city* by Propontic Sea,
What time the Turk the enfeebled Grecian thrall'd;
Thence from their cloister'd walks he set them [free,
And brought them to another Castalie,
Where Isis many a famous nursling breeds ;
Or where old Cam soft-paces o'er the lea
In pensive mood, and tunes his Doric reeds,
The whilst his flocks at large the lonely shepherd feeds.

* Constantinople.

XXII.

Yet the fine arts were what he finish'd least.
For why ? They are the quintessence of all,
The growth of labouring time, and slow increased;
Unless, as seldom chances, it should fall
That mighty patrons the coy sisters call
Up to the sunshine of uncumber'd ease,
Where no rude care the mounting thought may thrall,
And where they nothing have to do but please :
Ah ! gracious God ! thou know'st they ask no other fees.

XXIII.

But now, alas ! we live too late in time :
Our patrons now even grudge that little claim,
Except to such as sleek the soothing rhyme ;
And yet, forsooth, they wear Mæcenas' name,
Poor sons of puft-up vanity, not fame.
Unbroken spirits, cheer ! still, still remains
The eternal patron, Liberty ; whose flame,
While she protects, inspires the noblest strains :
The best and sweetest far, are toil-created gains.

XXIV.

When as the knight had framed, in Britain-land,
A matchless form of glorious government,
In which the sovereign laws alone command,
Laws 'stablish'd by the public free consent,
Whose majesty is to the sceptre lent ;
When this great plan, with each dependent art,
Was settled firm, and to his heart's content,
Then sought he from the toilsome scene to part,
And let life's vacant eve breathe quiet through the heart.

XXV.

For this he chose a farm in Deva's vale,
Where his long alleys peep'd upon the main :
In this calm seat he drew the healthful gale ;
Here mix'd the chief, the patriot, and the swain.
The happy monarch of his sylvan train,
Here, sided by the guardians of the fold,
He walk'd his rounds, and cheer'd his blest domain.
His days, the days of unstain'd nature, roll'd
Replete with peace and joy, like patriarchs' of old.

XXVI.

Witness, ye lowing herds, who gave him milk,
Witness, ye flocks, whose woolly vestments far
Exceed soft India's cotton, or her silk ;
Witness, with Autumn charged the nodding car,
That homeward came beneath sweet evening's star,
Or of September-moons the radiance mild.
O hide thy head, abominable War !
Of crimes and ruffian idleness the child !
From Heaven this life ysprung, from hell thy glories vild !

XXVII.

Nor from this deep retirement banish'd was
The amusing care of rural industry.
Still, as with grateful change the seasons pass,
New scenes arise, new landscapes strike the eye,
And all the enliven'd country beautify :
Gay plains extend where marshes slept before ;
O'er recent meads the exulting streamlets fly ;
Dark frowning heaths grow bright with Ceres' store,
And woods imbrown the steep, or wave along the shore.

XXVIII.

As nearer to his farm you made approach,
He polish'd Nature with a finer hand:
Yet on her beauties durst not Art encroach;
'Tis Art's alone these beauties to expand.
In graceful dance immingled, o'er the land,
Pan, Pales, Flora, and Pomona play'd:
Here, too, brisk gales the rude wild common fann'd,
A happy place, where free, and unafraid,
Amid the flowering brakes each coyer creature stray'd.

XXIX.

But in prime vigour what can last for aye?
That soul-enfeebling wizard, Indolence,
I whilom sung, wrought in his works decay:
Spread far and wide was his cursed influence;
Of public virtue much he dull'd the sense,
Even much of private; ate our spirit out,
And fed our rank luxurious vices: whence
The land was overlaid with many a lout;
Not, as old Fame reports, wise, generous, bold, and stout.

XXX.

A rage of pleasure madden'd every breast;
Down to the lowest lees the ferment ran;
To his licentious wish each must be bless'd,
With joy be fever'd, snatch it as he can.
Thus Vice the standard rear'd; her arrier-ban
Corruption call'd, and loud she gave the word,
"Mind, mind yourselves! why should the vulgar man,
The lacquey be more virtuous than his lord?
Enjoy this span of life! 'tis all the gods afford."

XXXI.

The tidings reach'd to where, in quiet hall,
The good old knight enjoy'd well-earn'd repose:
"Come, come, Sir Knight! thy children on thee call;
Come, save us yet, ere ruin round us close!
The demon Indolence thy toils o'erthrows."
On this the noble colour stain'd his cheeks,
Indignant, glowing through the whitening snows
Of venerable eld; his eye full speaks
His ardent soul, and from his couch at once he breaks.

XXXII.

"I will," he cried, "so help me, God! destroy
That villain Archimage."—His page then straight
He to him call'd, a fiery-footed boy,
Benempt Despatch:—"My steed be at the gate;
My bard attend; quick bring the net of fate."
This net was twisted by the Sisters three,
Which, when once cast o'er harden'd wretch, too late
Repentance comes; replevy cannot be
From the strong iron grasp of vengeful Destiny.

XXXIII.

He came, the bard, a little Druid wight,
Of wither'd aspect; but his eye was keen,
With sweetness mix'd. In russet brown bedight,
As is his sister* of the copses green,
He crept along, unpromising of mien.
Gross he who judges so. His soul was fair,
Bright as the children of yon azure sheen!
True comeliness, which nothing can impair,
Dwells in the mind: all else is vanity and glare.

* The nightingale.

XXXIV.

"Come," quoth the knight, "a voice has reach'd mine ear:
The demon Indolence threats overthrow
To all that to mankind is good and dear:
Come, Philomelus, let us instant go,
O'erturn his bowers, and lay his castle low
Those men, those wretched men, who will be slaves,
Must drink a bitter wrathful cup of woe:
But some there be, thy song, as from their graves,
Shall raise. Thrice happy he who without rigour saves!"

XXXV.

Issuing forth, the knight bestrode his steed,
Of ardent bay, and on whose front a star
Shone blazing bright: sprung from the generous breed
That whirl of active day the rapid car,
He pranced along, disdaining gate or bar.
Meantime, the bard on milk-white palfrey rode,
An honest sober beast, that did not mar
His meditations, but full softly trode;
And much they moralised as thus yfere they yode.

XXXVI.

They talk'd of virtue and of human bliss.
What else so fit for man to settle well?
And still their long researches met in this,
This truth of truths, which nothing can refel:
"From virtue's fount the purest joys outwell,
Sweet rills of thought that cheer the conscious soul;
While vice pours forth the troubled streams of hell,
The which, howe'er disguised, at last with dole
Will, through the tortured breast, their fiery torrent roll."

XXXVII.

At length it dawn'd, that fatal valley gay,
O'er which high wood-crown'd hills their summits rear:
On the cool height awhile our palmers stay,
And spite e'en of themselves their senses cheer;
Then to the wizard's wonne their steps they steer
Like a green isle, it broad beneath them spread,
With gardens round, and wandering currents clear,
And tufted groves to shade the meadow bed,
Sweet airs and song; and without hurry all seem'd glad.

XXXVIII.

"As God shall judge me, knight, we must forgive
(The half-enraptured Philomelus cried)
The frail good man deluded here to live,
And in these groves his musing fancy hide.
Ah! nought is pure. It cannot be denied,
That virtue still some tincture has of vice,
And vice of virtue. What should then betide,
But that our charity be not too nice?
Come, let us those we can to real bliss entice."

XXXIX.

"Ay, sicker," quoth the knight, "all flesh is frail,
To pleasant sin and joyous dalliance bent;
But let not brutish Vice of this avail,
And think to 'scape deserved punishment.
Justice were cruel weakly to relent;
From Mercy's self she got her sacred glaive:
Grace be to those who can, and will, repent;
But penance long, and dreary, to the slave,
Who must in floods of fire his gross foul spirit lave."

XL.

Thus, holding high discourse, they came to where
The cursed carle was at his wonted trade ;
Still tempting heedless men into his snare,
In witching wise, as I before have said.
But when he saw, in goodly gear array'd,
The grave majestic knight approaching nigh,
And by his side the bard so sage and staid,
His countenance fell ; yet oft his anxious eye
Mark'd them, like wily fox who roosted cock doth spy.

XLI.

Nathless, with feign'd respect, he bade give back
The rabble rout, and welcomed them full kind ;
Struck with the noble train, they were not slack
His orders to obey, and fall behind.
Then he resumed his song ; and unconfined
Pour'd all his music, ran through all his strings :
With magic dust their eyne he tries to blind,
And virtue's tender airs o'er weakness flings.
What pity base his song who so divinely sings !

XLII.

Elate in thought, he counted them his own,
They listen'd so intent with fix'd delight :
But they instead, as if transmew'd to stone,
Marvel'd he could with such sweet art unite
The lights and shades of manners, wrong and right.
Meantime, the silly crowd the charm devour,
Wide pressing to the gate. Swift on the knight
He darted fierce, to drag him to his bower,
Who backening shunn'd his touch, for well he knew its power.

XLIII.

As in throng'd amphitheatre of old
The wary Retiarius * trapp'd his foe,
Even so the knight, returning on him bold,
At once involved him in the Net of Woe
Whereof I mention made not along ago.
Enraged at first, he scorn'd so weak a jail,
And leap'd, and flew, and flounced, to and fro :
But, when he found that nothing could avail,
He sat him felly down, and gnaw'd his bitter nail.

XLIV.

Alarm'd, the inferior demons of the place
Raised rueful shrieks and hideous yells around ;
Black stormy clouds deform'd the welkin's face,
And from beneath was heard a wailing sound,
As of infernal sprites in cavern bound ;
A solemn sadness every creature strook,
And lightnings flash'd, and horror rock'd the ground :
Huge crowds on crowds outpour'd with blemish'd [look,
As if on time's last verge this frame of things had shook.

XLV.

Soon as the short-lived tempest was yspent,
Steam'd from the jaws of vex'd Avernus' hole,
And hush'd the hubbub of the rabblement,
Sir Industry the first calm moment stole :
"There must," he cried, "amid so vast a shoal,
Be some who are not tainted at the heart,
Not poison'd quite by this same villain's bowl :
Come then, my bard, thy heavenly fire impart ;
Touch soul with soul, till forth the latent spirit start."

* A gladiator, who made use of a net, which he threw over his adversary.

XLVI.

The bard obey'd ; and taking from his side,
Where it in seemly sort depending hung,
His British harp, its speaking strings he tried,
The which with skilful touch he deftly strung,
Till tinkling in clear symphony they rung.
Then, as he felt the Muses come along,
Light o'er the chords his raptured hand he flung,
And play'd a prelude to his rising song :
The whilst, like midnight mute, ten thousands round him throng.

XLVII.

Thus, ardent, burst his strain : "Ye hapless race,
Dire labouring here to smother Reason's ray,
That lights our Maker's image in our face,
And gives us wide o'er earth unquestion'd sway,
What is the adored Supreme Perfection, say ?
What, but eternal never-resting soul,
Almighty power, and all-directing day ;
By whom each atom stirs, the planets roll ;
Who fills, surrounds, informs, and agitates the whole ?

XLVIII.

"Come, to the beaming God your hearts unfold !
Draw from its fountain life ! 'Tis thence, alone,
We can excel. Up from unfeeling mould,
To seraphs burning round the Almighty's throne,
Life rising still on life, in higher tone,
Perfection forms, and with perfection bliss.
In universal nature this clear shown,
Not needeth proof ; to prove it were, I wis,
To prove the beauteous world excels the brute abyss.

XLIX.

"Is not the field, with lively culture green,
A sight more joyous than the dead morass ?
Do not the skies, with active ether clean,
And fann'd by sprightly zephyrs, far surpass
The foul November fogs and slumbrous mass
With which sad Nature veils her drooping face ?
Does not the mountain stream, as clear as glass,
Gay-dancing on, the putrid pool disgrace ?
The same in all holds true, but chief in human race.

L.

"It was not by vile loitering in ease,
That Greece obtain'd the brighter palm of art ;
That soft yet ardent Athens learn'd to please,
To keen the wit, and to sublime the heart,
In all supreme ! complete in every part !
It was not thence majestic Rome arose,
And o'er the nations shook her conquering dart :
For sluggard's brow the laurel never grows ;
Renown is not the child of indolent Repose.

LI.

"Had unambitious mortals minded nought,
But in loose joy their time to wear away ;
Had they alone the lap of Dalliance sought,
Pleased on her pillow their dull heads to lay,
Rude nature's state had been our state to-day ;
No cities e'er their towery fronts had raised,
No arts had made us opulent and gay ;
With brother-brutes the human race had grazed ;
None e'er had soar'd to fame, none honour'd been, none praised.

LII.

"Great Homer's song had never fired the breast
To thirst of glory and heroic deeds;
Sweet Maro's muse, sunk in inglorious rest,
Had silent slept amid the Mincian reeds;
The wits of modern time had told their beads,
And monkish legends been their only strains;
Our Milton's Eden had lain wrapt in weeds,
Our Shakspeare stroll'd and laugh'd with Warwick swains,
Ne had my master Spenser charm'd his Mulla's plains.

LIII.

"Dumb too had been the sage historic muse,
And perish'd all the sons of ancient Fame;
Those starry lights of virtue, that diffuse
Through the dark depth of time their vivid flame,
Had all been lost with such as have no name.
Who then had scorn'd his ease for others' good?
Who then had toil'd rapacious men to tame?
Who in the public breach devoted stood,
And for his country's cause been prodigal of blood?

LIV.

"But, should to fame your hearts unfeeling be,
If right I read, you pleasure all require:
Then hear how best may be obtain'd this fee,
How best enjoy'd this nature's wide desire.
Toil and be glad! let Industry inspire
Into your quicken'd limbs her buoyant breath!
Who does not act is dead; absorpt entire
In miry sloth, no pride, no joy he hath:
O leaden-hearted men, to be in love with death!

LV.

"Ah! what avail the largest gifts of Heaven,
When drooping health and spirits go amiss?
How tasteless then whatever can be given!
Health is the vital principle of bliss,
And exercise of health. In proof of this,
Behold the wretch, who slugs his life away,
Soon swallow'd in disease's sad abyss;
While he whom toil has braced, or manly play,
Has light as air each limb, each thought as clear as day.

LVI.

"O who can speak the vigorous joys of health!
Unclogg'd the body, unobscured the mind:
The morning rises gay, with pleasing stealth;
The temperate evening falls serene and kind.
In health the wiser brutes true gladness find:
See! how the younglings frisk along the meads,
As May comes on, and wakes the balmy wind;
Rampant with life, their joy all joy exceeds:
Yet what but high-strung health this dancing pleasaunce breeds?

LVII.

"But here, instead, is foster'd every ill
Which or distemper'd minds or bodies know.
Come then, my kindred spirits, do not spill
Your talents here: this place is but a show,
Whose charms delude you to the den of woe.
Come, follow me, I will direct you right,
Where pleasure's roses, void of serpents, grow,
Sincere as sweet; come, follow this good Knight,
And you will bless the day that brought him to your sight.

LVIII.

"Some he will lead to courts, and some to camps,
To senates some, and public sage debates,
Where, by the solemn gleam of midnight lamps,
The world is poised, and managed mighty states;
To high discovery some, that new creates
The face of earth; some to the thriving mart;
Some to the rural reign, and softer fates;
To the sweet Muses some, who raise the heart:
All glory shall be yours, all nature, and all art!

LIX.

"There are, I see, who listen to my lay,
Who wretched sigh for virtue, but despair:
'All may be done,' methinks I hear them say,
'Even death despised by generous actions fair;
All, but for those who to these bowers repair,
Their every power dissolved in luxury,
To quit of torpid sluggishness the lair,
And from the powerful arms of Sloth get free:
'Tis rising from the dead—Alas! it cannot be!'

LX.

"Would you then learn to dissipate the band
Of these huge threatening difficulties dire,
That in the weak man's way like lions stand,
His soul appal, and damp his rising fire?
Resolve, resolve, and to be men aspire.
Exert that noblest privilege, alone
Here to mankind indulged; control desire:
Let godlike Reason, from her sovereign throne,
Speak the commanding word, 'I will!' and it is done.

LXI.

"Heavens! can you then thus waste, in shameful wise,
Your few important days of trial here?
Heirs of eternity! yborn to rise
Through endless states of being, still more near
To bliss approaching, and perfection clear;
Can you renounce a fortune so sublime,
Such glorious hopes, your backward steps to steer,
And roll, with vilest brutes, through mud and slime?
No! no!—Your heaven-touch'd hearts disdain the sordid crime!"

LXII.

"Enough! enough!" they cried—straight, from the crowd,
The better sort on wings of transport fly:
As when amid the lifeless summits proud
Of Alpine cliffs, where to the gelid sky
Snows piled on snows in wintry torpor lie,
The rays divine of vernal Phœbus play;
The awaken'd heaps, in streamlets from on high,
Roused into action, lively leap away,
Glad warbling through the vales, in their new being gay.

LXIII.

Not less the life, the vivid joy serene,
That lighted up these new-created men,
Than that which wings the exulting spirit clean,
When, just deliver'd from this fleshly den,
It soaring seeks its native skies agen:
How light its essence! how unclogg'd its powers
Beyond the blazon of my mortal pen!
Even so we glad forsook these sinful bowers,
Even such enraptured life, such energy was ours

LXIV.

But far the greater part, with rage inflamed,
Dire mutter'd curses, and blasphemed high Jove :
" Ye sons of hate !" they bitterly exclaim'd,
" What brought you to this seat of peace and love ?
While with kind Nature, here amid the grove,
We pass'd the harmless sabbath of our time,
What to disturb it could, fell men, emove
Your barbarous hearts ? Is happiness a crime ?
Then do the fiends of hell rule in yon Heaven sublime."

LXV.

" Ye impious wretches," quoth the Knight in wrath,
" Your happiness behold !"—Then straight a wand
He waved, an anti-magic power that hath
Truth from illusive falsehood to command.
Sudden the landscape sinks on every hand ;
The pure quick streams are marshy puddles found ;
On baleful heaths the groves all blacken'd stand,
And o'er the weedy, foul, abhorred ground,
Snakes, adders, toads, each loathsome creature crawls around.

LXVI.

And here and there, on trees by lightning scath'd,
Unhappy wights who loathed life yhung ;
Or, in fresh gore and recent murder bathed,
They weltering lay ; or else, infuriate flung
Into the gloomy flood, while ravens sung
The funeral dirge, they down the torrent roll'd :
These, by distemper'd blood to madness stung,
Had doom'd themselves ; whence oft, when night controll'd
The world, returning hither their sad spirits howl'd.

LXVII.

Meantime a moving scene was open laid ;
That lazar-house, I whilom in my lay
Depainted have, its horrors deep display'd,
And gave unnumber'd wretches to the day,
Who tossing there in squalid misery lay,
Soon as of sacred light the unwonted smile
Pour'd on these living catacombs its ray,
Through the drear caverns stretching many a mile,
The sick upraised their heads, and dropp'd their woes awhile.

LXVIII.

" O Heaven !" they cried, " and do we once more see
Yon blessed sun, and this green earth so fair ?
Are we from noisome damps of pesthouse free ?
And drink our souls the sweet ethereal air ?
O thou ! or Knight, or God ! who holdest there
That fiend, oh keep him in eternal chains !
But what for us, the children of Despair,
Brought to the brink of hell, what hope remains ?
Repentance does itself but aggravate our pains."

LXIX.

The gentle Knight, who saw their rueful case,
Let fall adown his silver beard some tears.
" Certes," quoth he, " it is not even in grace
T' undo the past, and eke your broken years :
Nathless, to nobler worlds Repentance rears,
With humble hope, her eye ; to her is given
A power the truly contrite hearts that cheers ;
She quells the brand by which the rocks are riven ;
She more than merely softens, she rejoices Heaven.

LXX.

" Then patient bear the sufferings you have earn'd,
And by these sufferings purify the mind ;
Let wisdom be by past misconduct learn'd ;
Or pious die, with penitence resign'd ;
And to a life more happy and refined,
Doubt not, you shall, new creatures, yet arise.
Till then, you may expect in me to find
One who will wipe your sorrow from your eyes,
One who will soothe your pangs, and wing you to the skies."

LXXI.

They silent heard, and pour'd their thanks in tears ;
" For you," resumed the Knight with sterner tone,
" Whose hard dry hearts the obdurate demon sears,
That villain's gifts will cause you many a groan ;
In dolorous mansion long you must bemoan
His fatal charms, and weep your stains away :
Till, soft and pure as infant goodness grown,
You feel a perfect change : then, who can say
What grace may yet shine forth in Heaven's eternal day ?"

LXXII.

This said, his powerful wand he waved anew :
Instant, a glorious angel-train descends,
The Charities, to wit, of rosy hue ;
Sweet love their looks a gentle radiance lends,
And with seraphic flame compassion blends.
At once, delighted, to their charge they fly :
When lo ! a goodly hospital ascends,
In which they bade each lenient aid be nigh,
That could the sick-bed smooth of that sad company

LXXIII.

It was a worthy edifying sight,
And gives to human kind peculiar grace,
To see kind hands attending day and night,
With tender ministry, from place to place.
Some prop the head ; some from the pallid face
Wipe off the faint cold dews weak Nature sheds ;
Some reach the healing draught: the whilst, to chase
The fear supreme, around their soften'd beds,
Some holy man by prayer all opening Heaven dispreds.

LXXIV.

Attended by a glad acclaiming train,
Of those he rescued had from gaping hell,
Then turn'd the Knight ; and, to his hall again
Soft-pacing, sought of peace the mossy cell :
Yet down his cheeks the gems of pity fell,
To see the helpless wretches that remain'd,
There left through delves and deserts dire to yell ;
Amazed, their looks with pale dismay were stain'd,
And spreading wide their hands, they meek repentance feign'd.

LXXV.

But ah ! their scorned day of grace was past :
For (horrible to tell !) a desert wild
Before them stretch'd, bare, comfortless, and vast !
With gibbets, bones, and carcases defiled,
There nor trim field, nor lively culture smiled ,
Nor waving shade was seen, nor fountain fair ;
But sands abrupt on sands lay loosely piled, [care,
Through which they floundering toil'd with painful
Whilst Phœbus smote them sore, and fired the cloudless air.

LXXVI.

Then, varying to a joyless land of bogs,
The sadden'd country a grey waste appear'd,
Where nought but putrid steams and noisome fogs
For ever hung on drizzly Auster's beard;
Or else the ground, by piercing Caurus sear'd,
Was jagg'd with frost, or heap'd with glazed snow;
Through these extremes a ceaseless round they [steer'd,
By cruel fiends still hurried to and fro,
Gaunt Beggary and Scorn, with many hell-hounds moe.

LXXVII.

The first was with base dunghill rags yclad,
Tainting the gale, in which they flutter'd light;
Of morbid hue his features, sunk and sad!
His hollow eyne shook forth a sickly light;
And o'er his lank jawbone, in piteous plight,
His black rough beard was matted rank and vile;
Direful to see! a heart-appalling sight!
Meantime foul scurf and blotches him defile;
And dogs, where'er he went, still barked all the while.

LXXVIII.

The other was a fell despightful fiend:
Hell holds none worse in baleful bower below;
By pride, and wit, and rage, and rancour, keen'd!
Of man alike. if good or bad, the foe!
With nose upturn'd he always made a show
As if he smelt some nauseous scent; his eye
Was cold and keen, like blast from boreal snow;
And taunts he casten forth most bitterly.
Such were the twain that off drove this ungodly fry

LXXIX.

Even so through Brentford town, a town of mud,
A herd of bristly swine is prick'd along;
The filthy beasts, that never chew the cud, [song,
Still grunt, and squeak, and sing their troublous
And oft they plunge themselves the mire among;
But aye the ruthless driver goads them on,
And aye of barking dogs the bitter throng
Makes them renew their unmelodious moan;
Ne ever find they rest from their unresting fone.

A POEM,

SACRED

TO THE MEMORY OF SIR ISAAC NEWTON.

INSCRIBED TO

THE RIGHT HONOURABLE SIR ROBERT WALPOLE.

SHALL the great soul of Newton quit this earth,
To mingle with his stars ; and every Muse,
Astonish'd into silence, shun the weight
Of honours due to his illustrious name?
But what can man?—Even now the sons of light
In strains high-warbled to seraphic lyre,
Hail his arrival on the coast of bliss.
Yet am not I deterr'd, though high the theme,
And sung to harps of angels ; for with you,
Ethereal flames! ambitious, I aspire
In Nature's general symphony to join.
And what new wonders can ye show your guest!
Who, while on this dim spot, where mortals toil
Clouded in dust, from motion's simple laws,
Could trace the secret hand of Providence,
Wide-working through this universal frame.
Have ye not listen'd while he bound the suns
And planets to their spheres! the unequal task
Of human-kind till then. Oft had they roll'd
O'er erring man the year, and oft disgraced
The pride of schools, before their course was known
Full in its causes and effects to him,
All-piercing sage! who sat not down and dream'd
Romantic schemes, defended by the din
Of specious words, and tyranny of names ;
But, bidding his amazing mind attend,
And with heroic patience years on years
Deep-searching, saw at last the System dawn,
And shine, of all his race, on him alone.
What were his raptures then! how pure! how strong!
And what the triumphs of old Greece and Rome,
By his diminish'd, but the pride of boys
In some small fray victorious! when instead
Of shatter'd parcels of this earth usurp'd
By violence unmanly, and sore deeds
Of cruelty and blood, Nature herself
Stood all-subdued by him, and open laid
Her ever-latent glory to his view.
All intellectual eye, our solar round
First gazing through, he by the blended power
Of gravitation and projection saw
The whole in silent harmony revolve.
From unassisted vision hid, the moons
To cheer remoter planets numerous form'd,
By him in all their mingled tracts were seen.
He also fix'd our wandering queen of night,
Whether she wanes into a scanty orb,
Or, waxing broad, with her pale shadowy light,
In a soft deluge overflows the sky.
Her every motion clear-discerning, he
Adjusted to the mutual main, and taught
Why now the mighty mass of water swells
Resistless, heaving on the broken rocks,
And the full river turning : till again
The tide revertive, unattracted, leaves
A yellow waste of idle sands behind.
Then breaking hence, he took his ardent flight
Through the blue infinite ; and every star,
Which the clear concave of a winter's night
Pours on the eye, or astronomic tube,
Far-stretching, snatches from the dark abyss ;
Or such as farther in successive skies
To fancy shine alone, at his approach
Blazed into suns, the living centre each
Of an harmonious system : all combined,
And ruled unerring by that single power,
Which draws the stone projected to the ground.
O unprofuse magnificence divine!
O wisdom truly perfect! thus to call
From a few causes such a scheme of things,
Effects so various, beautiful, and great,
An universe complete! And, O beloved
Of Heaven! whose well-purged penetrative eye,
The mystic veil transpiercing, inly scann'd
The rising, moving, wide-establish'd frame.
He, first of men, with awful wing pursued
The comet through the long elliptic curve,
As round innumerous worlds he wound his way ;
Till, to the forehead of our evening sky
Return'd, the blazing wonder glares anew,
And o'er the trembling nations shakes dismay.
The heavens are all his own ; from the wild rule
Of whirling vortices, and circling spheres,
To their first great simplicity restored.
The schools astonish'd stood ; but found it vain

To combat still with demonstration strong,
And, unawaken'd, dream beneath the blaze
Of truth At once their pleasing visions fled
With the gay shadows of the morning mix'd,
When Newton rose, our philosophic sun.
The aërial flow of sound was known to him,
From whence it first in wavy circles breaks,
Till the touch'd organ takes the message in.
Nor could the darting beam of speed, immense,
Escape his swift pursuit, and measuring eye.
Even light itself, which everything displays,
Shone undiscover'd, till his brighter mind
Untwisted all the shining robe of day;
And, from the whitening undistinguish'd blaze,
Collecting every ray into his kind,
To the charm'd eye educed the gorgeous train
Of parent colour. First the flaming red
Sprung vivid forth; the tawny orange next;
And next delicious yellow; by whose side
Fell the kind beams of all-refreshing green:
Then the pure blue, that swells autumnal skies,
Ethereal play'd; and then, of sadder hue,
Emerged the deepen'd indico, as when
The heavy-skirted evening droops with frost;
While the last gleamings of refracted light
Died in the fainting violet away.
These, when the clouds distil the rosy shower,
Shine out distinct adown the watery bow;
While o'er our heads the dewy vision bends
Delightful, melting on the fields beneath.
Myriads of mingling dyes from these result,
And myriads still remain:—infinite source
Of beauty, ever flushing, ever new!
Did ever poet image aught so fair,
Dreaming in whispering groves, by the hoarse brook?
Or prophet, to whose rapture heaven descends?
Even now the setting sun and shifting clouds,
Seen, Greenwich, from thy lovely heights, declare
How just, how beauteous the refractive law.
The noiseless tide of time, all bearing down
To vast eternity's unbounded sea,
Where the green islands of the happy shine,
He stemm'd alone: and to the source (involved
Deep in primeval gloom) ascending, raised
His lights at equal distances, to guide
Historian, wilder'd on his darksome way.
But who can number up his labours? who
His high discoveries sing? when but a few
Of the deep-studying race can stretch their minds
To what he knew. In fancy's lighter thought,
How shall the Muse then grasp the mighty theme?
What wonder thence that his devotion swell'd
Responsive to his knowledge! for could he,
Whose piercing mental eye diffusive saw
The finish'd university of things,
In all its order, magnitude and parts,
Forbear incessant to adore that Power
Who fills, sustains, and actuates the whole?
Say, ye who best can tell, ye happy few,
Who saw him in the softest lights of life,
All unwithheld, indulging to his friends
The vast unborrow'd treasures of his mind,
Oh speak the wondrous man! how mild, how calm,
How greatly humble, how divinely good;
How firm establish'd on eternal truth;
Fervent in doing well, with every nerve
Still pressing on, forgetful of the past,
And panting for perfection: far above
Those little cares, and visionary joys,
That so perplex the fond impassion'd heart
Of ever cheated, ever trusting man.
And you, ye hopeless gloomy-minded tribe,
You who, unconscious of those nobler flights
That reach impatient at immortal life,
Against the prime endearing privilege
Of being dare contend, say, can a soul
Of such extensive, deep, tremendous powers,
Enlarging still, be but a finer breath
Of spirits dancing through their tubes awhile,
And then for ever lost in vacant air?
But hark! methinks I hear a warning voice,
Solemn as when some awful change is come,
Sound through the world—'Tis done! The measure 's full;
And I resign my charge.—Ye mouldering stones,
That build the towering pyramid, the proud
Triumphal arch, the monument effaced
By ruthless ruin, and whate'er supports
The worship'd name of hoar antiquity,
Down to the dust! what grandeur can ye boast
While Newton lifts his column to the skies,
Beyond the waste of time. Let no weak drop
Be shed for him. The virgin in her bloom
Cut off, the joyous youth, and darling child,
These are the tombs that claim the tender tear,
And elegiac song. But Newton calls
For other notes of gratulation high,
That now he wanders through those endless worlds
He here so well described, and wondering talks
And hymns their Author with his glad compeers.
Oh, Britain's boast! whether with angels thou
Sittest in dread discourse, or fellow-blest,
Who joy to see the honour of their kind;
Or whether, mounted on cherubic wing,
Thy swift career is with the whirling orbs,
Comparing things with things, in rapture lost,
And grateful adoration, for that light
So plenteous ray'd into thy mind below,
From Light himself; oh, look with pity down
On human-kind, a frail erroneous race!
Exalt the spirit of a downward world!
O'er thy dejected country chief preside,
And be her genius call'd! her studies raise,
Correct her manners, and inspire her youth.
For, though depraved and sunk, she brought thee forth,
And glories in thy name; she points thee out
To all her sons, and bids them eye thy star:
While in expectance of the second life,
When time shall be no more, thy sacred dust
Sleeps with her kings, and dignifies the scene.

A POEM,

TO

THE MEMORY OF THE RIGHT HON. THE LORD TALBOT,

LATE CHANCELLOR OF GREAT BRITAIN.

ADDRESSED TO HIS SON.

WHILE, with the public, you, my Lord, lament
A friend and father lost; permit the Muse,—
The Muse assign'd of old a double theme,—
To praise dead worth and humble living pride,
Whose generous task begins where interest ends:
Permit her on a Talbot's tomb to lay
This cordial verse sincere, by truth inspired,
Which means not to bestow but borrow fame.
Yes, she may sing his matchless virtues now—
Unhappy that she may. But where begin?
How from the diamond single out each ray,
Where all, though trembling with ten thousand hues,
Effuse one dazzling undivided light?
Let the low-minded of these narrow days
No more presume to deem the lofty tale
Of ancient times, in pity to their own,
Romance. In Talbot, we united saw
The piercing eye, the quick enlighten'd soul,
The graceful ease, the flowing tongue of Greece,
Join'd to the virtues and the force of Rome.
Eternal Wisdom, that all-quickening sun,
Whence every life, in just proportion, draws
Directing light and actuating flame,
Ne'er with a larger portion of its beams
Awaken'd mortal clay. Hence steady, calm,
Diffusive, deep, and clear, his reason saw,
With instantaneous view, the truth of things;
Chief what to human life and human bliss
Pertains, that noblest science, fit for man:
And hence, responsive to his knowledge, glow'd
His ardent virtue. Ignorance and vice,
In consort foul, agree; each heightening each;
While virtue draws from knowledge brighter fire.
What grand, what comely, or what tender sense,
What talent, or what virtue, was not his?
What that can render man or great or good,
Give useful worth, or amiable grace?
Nor could he brook in studious shade to lie,
In soft retirement, indolently pleased
With selfish peace. The siren of the wise,
(Who steals the Aönian song, and, in the shape
Of virtue, wooes them from a worthless world)
Though deep he felt her charms, could never melt
His strenuous spirit, recollected, calm,
As silent night, yet active as the day.
The more the bold, the bustling, and the bad,
Press to usurp the reins of power, the more
Behoves it virtue, with indignant zeal,
To check their combination. Shall low views
Of sneaking interest or luxurious vice,
The villain's passions, quicken more to toil,
And dart a livelier vigour through the soul,
Than these that, mingled with our truest good,
With present honour and immortal fame,
Involve the good of all? An empty form
Is the weak virtue, that amid the shade
Lamenting lies, with future schemes amused,
While wickedness and folly, kindred powers,
Confound the world. A Talbot's, different far,
Sprung ardent into action, that disdain'd
To lose in deathlike sloth one pulse of life,
That might be saved; disdain'd for coward ease,
And her insipid pleasures, to resign
The prize of glory, the keen sweets of toil,
And those high joys that teach the truly great
To live for others, and for others die.
Early, behold! he breaks benign on life.
Not breathing more beneficence, the Spring
Leads in her swelling train the gentle airs:
While gay, behind her, smiles the kindling waste
Of ruffian storms and winter's lawless rage.
In him Astræa, to this dim abode
Of ever wandering men, return'd again:
To bless them his delight, to bring them back,
From thorny error, from unjoyous wrong,
Into the paths of kind primeval faith,
Of happiness and justice. All his parts,
His virtues all, collected, sought the good
Of human kind. For *that* he, fervent, felt
The throb of patriots, when they model states:
Anxious for that, nor needful sleep could hold
His still-awaken'd soul; nor friends had charms
To steal, with pleasing guile, one useful hour,
Toil knew no languor, no attraction joy.
Thus with unwearied steps, by virtue led,
He gain'd the summit of that sacred hill,
Where, raised above black Envy's darkening clouds,
Her spotless temple lifts its radiant front.
Be named, victorious ravagers, no more!
Vanish, ye human comets! shrink your blaze!

Ye that your glory to your terrors owe,
As, o'er the gazing desolated earth,
You scatter famine, pestilence, and war;
Vanish! before this vernal sun of fame;
Effulgent sweetness! beaming life and joy.
How the heart listen'd, while he, pleading, spoke!
While on the enlighten'd mind, with winning art,
His gentle reason so persuasive stole,
That the charm'd hearer thought it was his own.
Ah! when, ye studious of the laws, again
Shall such enchanting lessons bless your ear?
When shall again the darkest truths, perplex'd,
Be set in ample day? when shall the harsh
And arduous open into smiling ease?
The solid mix with elegant delight?
His was the talent with the purest light
At once to pour conviction on the soul,
And warm with lawful flame the impassion'd heart.
That dangerous gift with him was safely lodged
By Heaven. He, sacred to his country's cause,
To trample want and worth, to suffering right,
To the lone widow's and her orphan's woes,
Reserved the mighty charm. With equal brow,
Despising then the smiles or frowns of power,
He all that noblest eloquence effused,
Which generous passion, taught by reason, breathes:
Then spoke the man; and, over barren art,
Prevail'd abundant nature. Freedom then
His client was, humanity and truth.
Placed on the seat of justice, there he reign'd,
In a superior sphere of cloudless day,
A pure intelligence. No tumult there,
No dark emotion, no intemperate heat,
No passion e'er disturb'd the clear serene
That round him spread. A zeal for right alone,
The love of justice, like the steady sun,
Its equal ardour lent; and sometimes raised
Against the sons of violence, of pride,
And bold deceit, his indignation gleam'd,
Yet still by sober dignity restrain'd.
As intuition quick, he snatch'd the truth,
Yet with progressive patience, step by step,
Self-diffident, or to the slower kind,
He through the maze of falsehood traced it on,
Till, at the last, evolved, it full appear'd,
And even the loser own'd the just decree.
But when, in senates, he, to freedom firm,
Enlighten'd freedom, plann'd salubrious laws,
His various learning, his wide knowledge, then,
His insight deep into Britannia's weal,
Spontaneous seem'd from simple sense to flow,
And the plain patriot smooth'd the brow of
No specious swell, no frothy pomp of words
Fell on the cheated ear; no studied maze
Of declamation, to perplex the right,
He, darkening, threw around: safe in itself,
In its own force, all-powerful reason spoke;
While on the great, the ruling point, at once,
He stream'd decisive day, and show'd it vain
To lengthen farther out the clear debate.
Conviction breathes conviction; to the heart,
Pour'd ardent forth in eloquence unbid,
The heart attends. for let the venal try
Their every hardening stupifying art,
Truth must prevail, zeal will enkindle zeal,
And Nature, skilful touch'd, is honest still.
Behold him in the councils of his prince,
What faithful light he lends! How rare, in courts,
Such wisdom! such abilities! and join'd
To virtue so determined, public zeal,
And honour of such adamantine proof,
As even corruption, hopeless, and o'er-awed,
Durst not have tempted! Yet of manners mild,
And winning every heart, he knew to please,
Nobly to please; while equally he scorn'd
Or adulation to receive, or give.
Happy the state, where wakes a ruling eye
Of such inspection keen, and general care!
Beneath a guard so vigilant, so pure,
Toil may resign his careless head to rest,
And ever-jealous freedom sleep in peace.
Ah! lost untimely! lost in downward days!
And many a patriot counsel with him lost!
Counsels that might have humbled Britain's foe,
Her native foe, from eldest time by fate
Appointed, as did once a Talbot's arms.
Let learning, arts, let universal worth,
Lament a patron lost, a friend and judge:
Unlike the sons of vanity, that, veil'd
Beneath the patron's prostituted name,
Dare sacrifice a worthy man to pride,
And flush confusion o'er an honest cheek.
When he conferr'd a grace, it seem'd a debt
Which he to merit, to the public, paid,
And to the great all-bounteous Source of Good.
His sympathising heart itself received
The generous obligation he bestow'd.
This, this indeed, is patronizing worth.
Their kind protector him the Muses own,
But scorn with noble pride the boasted aid
Of tasteless vanity's insulting hand.
The gracious stream, that cheers the letter'd world,
Is not the noisy gift of summer's noon,
Whose sudden current, from the naked root,
Washes the little soil which yet remain'd,
And only more dejects the blushing flowers:
No, 'tis the soft descending dews at eve,
The silent treasures of the vernal year,
Indulging deep their stores, the still night long:
Till, with returning morn, the freshen'd world
Is fragrance all, all beauty, joy, and song.
Still let me view him in the pleasing light
Of private life, where pomp forgets to glare,
And where the plain unguarded soul is seen.
There, with that truest greatness he appear'd
Which thinks not of appearing; kindly veil'd
In the soft graces of the friendly scene,
Inspiring social confidence and ease.
As free the converse of the wise and good,
As joyous, disentangling every power,
And breathing mix'd improvement with delight,
As when amid the various-blossom'd spring,
Or gentle-beaming autumn's pensive shade,
The philosophic mind with nature talks.
Say ye, his sons, his dear remains, with whom
The father laid superfluous state aside,
Yet raised your filial duty thence the more,
With friendship raised it, with esteem, with love
Beyond the ties of blood, oh! speak the joy,
The pure serene, the cheerful wisdom mild,
The virtuous spirit, which his vacant hours,
In semblance of amusement, through the breast
Infused. And thou, O Rundle*! lend thy strain,
Thou darling friend! thou brother of his soul!
In whom the head and heart their stores unite:
Whatever fancy paints, invention pours,
Judgment digests, the well-tuned bosom feels,
Truth natural, moral, or divine, has taught,

* Dr. Rundle, late bishop of Derry in Ireland.

The virtues dictate or the Muses sing.
Lend me the plaint, which, to the lonely main,
With memory conversing, you will pour,
As on the pebbled shore you, pensive, stray,
Where Derry's mountains a bleak crescent form,
And mid their ample round receive the waves,
That from the frozen pole, resounding, rush,
Impetuous. Though from native sun-shine driven,
Driven from your friends, the sun-shine of the soul,
By slanderous zeal, and politics infirm,
Jealous of worth ; yet will you bless your lot,
Yet will you triumph in your glorious fate,
Whence Talbot's friendship glows to future times,
Intrepid, warm ! of kindred tempers born ;
Nursed, by experience, into slow esteem,
Calm confidence unbounded, love not blind,
And the sweet light from mingled minds disclosed,
From mingled chymic oils as bursts the fire.
  I too remember well that cheerful bowl,
Which round his table flow'd. The serious there
Mix'd with the sportive, with the learn'd the plain ;
Mirth soften'd wisdom, candour temper'd mirth ;
And wit its honey lent, without the sting.
Not simple nature's unaffected sons,
The blameless Indians, round the forest-cheer,
In sunny lawn or shady covert set,
Hold more unspotted converse : nor, of old,
Rome's awful consuls, her dictator-swains,
As on the product of their Sabine farms
They fared, with stricter virtue fed the soul :
Nor yet in Athens, at an Attic meal,
Where Socrates presided, fairer truth,
More elegant humanity, more grace,
Wit more refined, or deeper science reign'd.
  But far beyond the little vulgar bounds
Of family, or friends, or native land,
By just degrees, and with proportion'd flame,
Extended his benevolence : a friend
To human kind, to parent nature's works.
Of free access, and of engaging grace,
Such as a brother to a brother owes,
He kept an open judging ear for all,
And spread an open countenance, where smiled
The fair effulgence of an open heart :
While on the rich, the poor, the high, the low,
With equal ray, his ready goodness shone :
For nothing human foreign was to him.
  Thus to a dread inheritance, my Lord,
And hard to be supported, you succeed :
But kept by virtue, as by virtue gain'd,
It will, through latest time, enrich your race,
When grosser wealth shall moulder into dust,
And with their authors in oblivion sunk
Vain titles lie, the servile badges oft
Of mean submission, not the meed of worth.
True genuine honour its large patent holds
Of all mankind, through every land and age,
Of universal reason's various sons,
And even of God himself, sole perfect Judge !
Yet know these noblest honours of the mind
On rigid terms descend : the high-placed heir,
Scann'd by the public eye, that, with keen gaze,
Malignant seeks out faults, cannot through life,
Amid the nameless insects of a court,
Unheeded steal : but, with his sire compared,
He must be glorious, or he must be scorn'd.
This truth to you, who merit well to bear
A name to Britons dear, the officious Muse
May safely sing, and sing without reserve.
  Vain were the plaint, and ignorant the tear,
That should a Talbot mourn. Ourselves, indeed,
Our country robb'd of her delight and strength,
We may lament Yet let us, grateful, joy,
That we such virtues knew, such virtues felt,
And feel them still, teaching our views to rise
Through ever-brightening scenes of future worlds.
Be dumb, ye worst of zealots ! ye that, prone
To thoughtless dust, renounce that generous hope
Whence every joy below its spirit draws,
And every pain its balm : a Talbot's light,
A Talbot's virtues claim another source,
Than the blind maze of undesigning blood ;
Nor when that vital fountain plays no more,
Can they be quench'd amid the gelid stream.
  Methinks I see his mounting spirit, freed
From tangling earth, regain the realms of day,
Its native country, whence, to bless mankind,
Eternal Goodness, on this darksome spot,
Had ray'd it down a while. Behold ! approved
By the tremendous Judge of heaven and earth,
And to the Almighty Father's presence join'd,
He takes his rank, in glory, and in bliss,
Amid the human worthies. Glad around
Crowd his compatriot shades, and point him out
With joyful pride, Britannia's blameless boast.
Ah ! who is he, that with a fonder eye
Meets thine enraptured ?—'Tis the best of sons!
The best of friends ! —Too soon is realized
That hope, which once forbad thy tears to flow !
Meanwhile the kindred souls of every land,
(Howe'er divided in the fretful days
Of prejudice and error) mingled now,
In one selected never-jarring state,
Where God himself their only monarch reigns,
Partake the joy : yet, such the sense that still
Remains of earthly woes, for us below,
And for our loss they drop a pitying tear.
But cease, presumptuous Muse, nor vainly strive
To quit this cloudy sphere that binds thee down :
'Tis not for mortal hand to trace these scenes,
Scenes, that our gross ideas groveling cast
Behind, and strike our boldest language dumb.
  Forgive, immortal shade ! if aught from earth,
From dust low-warbled, to those groves can rise,
Where flows celestial harmony, forgive
This fond superfluous verse. With deep-felt voice,
On every heart impress'd, thy deeds themselves
Attest thy praise. Thy praise the widow's sighs,
And orphan's tears embalm. The good, the bad,
The sons of justice and the sons of strife,
All who or freedom or who interest prize,
A deep-divided nation's parties all,
Conspire to swell thy spotless praise to heaven.
Glad heaven receives it, and seraphic lyres
With songs of triumph thy arrival hail.
How vain this tribute then ! this lowly lay !
Yet nought is vain which gratitude inspires.
The Muse, besides, her duty thus approves
To virtue, to her country, to mankind,
To ruling nature, that, in glorious charge,
As to her priestess, gives it her, to hymn
Whatever good and excellent she forms.

POEMS

ON SEVERAL OCCASIONS.

EPITAPH ON MISS STANLEY.

HERE, STANLEY! rest, escaped this mortal strife,
Above the joys, beyond the woes of life.
Fierce pangs no more thy lively beauties stain,
And sternly try thee with a year of pain:
No more sweet patience, feigning oft relief,
Lights thy sick eye, to cheat a parent's grief:
With tender art, to save her anxious groan,
No more thy bosom presses down its own:
Now well-earn'd peace is thine, and bliss sincere:
Ours be the lenient, not unpleasing tear!
 O born to bloom, then sink beneath the storm;
To show us Virtue in her fairest form;
To show us artless Reason's moral reign,
What boastful Science arrogates in vain;
The obedient passions, knowing each their part;
Calm light the head, and harmony the heart!
 Yes, we must follow soon, will glad obey,
When a few suns have roll'd their cares away,
Tired with vain life, will close the willing eye:
'Tis the great birth-right of mankind to die.
Blest be the bark, that wafts us to the shore,
Where death-divided friends shall part no more!
To join thee there, here with thy dust repose,
Is all the hope thy hapless mother knows.

TO THE REV. MR. MURDOCH,

RECTOR OF STRADDISHALL IN SUFFOLK. 1738.

THUS safely low, my friend, thou canst not fall:
Here reigns a deep tranquillity o'er all;
No noise, no care, no vanity, no strife;
Men, woods, and fields, all breathe untroubled life.
Then keep each passion down, however dear;
Trust me, the tender are the most severe.
Guard, while 'tis thine, thy philosophic ease,
And ask no joy but that of virtuous peace;
That bids defiance to the storms of fate:
High bliss is only for a higher state.

A PARAPHRASE ON THE LATTER PART OF THE SIXTH CHAPTER OF ST. MATTHEW.

WHEN my breast labours with oppressive care,
And o'er my cheek descends the falling tear;
While all my warring passions are at strife,
Oh, let me listen to the words of life!
Raptures deep-felt his doctrine did impart,
And thus he raised from earth the drooping heart:
 Think not, when all your scanty stores afford
Is spread at once upon the sparing board;
Think not, when worn the homely robe appears,
While, on the roof, the howling tempest bears;
What farther shall this feeble life sustain,
And what shall clothe these shivering limbs again.
Say, does not life its nourishment exceed?
And the fair body its investing weed?
 Behold! and look away your low despair——
See the light tenants of the barren air:
To them, nor stores, nor granaries, belong,
Nought but the woodland, and the pleasing song;
Yet, your kind heavenly Father bends his eye
On the least wing, that flits along the sky.
To him they sing when Spring renews the plain,
To him they cry in Winter's pinching reign;
Nor is their music nor their plaint in vain:
He hears the gay, and the distressful call,
And with unsparing bounty fills them all.
 Observe the rising lily's snowy grace,
Observe the various vegetable race;
They neither toil, nor spin, but careless grow,
Yet see how warm they blush! how bright they glow!
What regal vestments can with them compare!
What king so shining! or what queen so fair!
 If, ceaseless, thus the fowls of heaven he feeds;
If o'er the fields such lucid robes he spreads;
Will he not care for you, ye faithless, say?
Is he unwise? or, are ye less than they?

SONG.

O THOU, whose tender serious eyes
Expressive speak the mind I love;
The gentle azure of the skies,
The pensive shadows of the grove:

O mix their beauteous beams with mine,
And let us interchange our hearts;
Let all their sweetness on me shine,
Pour'd through my soul be all their darts.

Ah! 'tis too much! I cannot bear
At once so soft, so keen, a ray:
In pity, then, my lovely fair,
O turn these killing eyes away!

But what avails it to conceal
One charm, where nought but charms we see!
Their lustre then again reveal,
And let me, Myra, die of thee.

SONG.

One day the god of fond desire,
  On mischief bent, to Damon said,
Why not disclose your tender fire,
  Not own it to the lovely maid?

The shepherd mark'd his treacherous art,
  And, softly sighing, thus replied:
'Tis true you have subdued my heart,
  But shall not triumph o'er my pride.

The slave in private only bears
  Your bondage, who his love conceals:
But when his passion he declares,
  You drag him at your chariot-wheels.

SONG.

Hard is the fate of him who loves,
  Yet dares not tell his trembling pain,
But to the sympathetic groves,
  But to the lonely listening plain.

Oh! when she blesses next your shade,
  Oh! when her footsteps next are seen
In flowery tracks along the mead,
  In fresher mazes o'er the green,

Ye gentle spirits of the vale,
  To whom the tears of love are dear,
From dying lilies waft a gale,
  And sigh my sorrows in her ear.

Oh tell her what she cannot blame,
  Though fear my tongue must ever bind;
Oh tell her that my virtuous flame
  Is as her spotless soul refined.

Not her own guardian angel eyes
  With chaster tenderness his care,
Not purer her own wishes rise,
  Not holier her own sighs in prayer.

But if, at first, her virgin fear
  Should start at love's suspected name,
With that of friendship soothe her ear—
  True love and friendship are the same.

SONG.

Unless with my Amanda blest,
  In vain I twine the woodbine bower;
Unless to deck her sweeter breast,
  In vain I rear the breathing flower.

Awaken'd by the genial year,
  In vain the birds around me sing;
In vain the freshening fields appear:
  Without my love there is no spring.

SONG.

For ever, Fortune, wilt thou prove
An unrelenting foe to love,
And when we meet a mutual heart,
Come in between, and bid us part:

Bid us sigh on from day to day,
And wish, and wish the soul away;
Till youth and genial years are flown,
And all the life of life is gone?

But busy, busy still art thou,
To bind the loveless joyless vow,
The heart from pleasure to delude,
To join the gentle to the rude.

For once, O Fortune! hear my prayer.
And I absolve thy future care;
All other blessings I resign,
Make but the dear Amanda mine.

SONG.

Come, gentle god of soft desire,
  Come and possess my happy breast,
Not fury-like in flames and fire,
  Or frantic folly's wildness drest;

But come in friendship's angel-guise:
  Yet dearer thou than friendship art,
More tender spirit in thy eyes,
  More sweet emotions at the heart.

O come with goodness in thy train,
  With peace and pleasure void of storm,
And wouldst thou me for ever gain,
  Put on Amanda's winning form.

ODE.

Tell me, thou soul of her I love,
  Ah! tell me, whither art thou fled?
To what delightful world above,
  Appointed for the happy dead?

Or dost thou, free, at pleasure, roam,
  And sometimes share thy lover's woe;
Where, void of thee, his cheerless home
  Can now, alas! no comfort know?

Oh! if thou hover'st round my walk,
  While, under every well-known tree,
I to thy fancied shadow talk,
  And every tear is full of thee;

Should then the weary eye of grief,
  Beside some sympathetic stream,
In slumber find a short relief,
  Oh visit thou my soothing dream!

ODE.

O NIGHTINGALE, best poet of the grove,
That plaintive strain can ne'er belong to thee,
Blest in the full possession of thy love:
O lend that strain, sweet Nightingale, to me!

'Tis mine, alas! to mourn my wretched fate:
I love a maid who all my bosom charms,
Yet lose my days without this lovely mate;
Inhuman Fortune keeps her from my arms.

You, happy birds! by nature's simple laws
Lead your soft lives, sustain'd by nature's fare;
You dwell wherever roving fancy draws,
And love and song is all your pleasing care:

But we, vain slaves of interest and of pride,
Dare not be blest, lest envious tongues should [blame:
And hence in vain I languish for my bride;
O mourn with me, sweet bird, my hapless flame.

ODE TO SERAPHINA.

THE wanton's charms, however bright,
Are like the false illusive light,
Whose flattering unauspicious blaze
To precipices oft betrays:
But that sweet ray your beauties dart,
Which clears the mind, and cleans the heart,
Is like the sacred queen of night,
Who pours a lovely gentle light
Wide o'er the dark, by wanderers blest,
Conducting them to peace and rest.
A vicious love depraves the mind,
'Tis anguish, guilt, and folly join'd;
But Seraphina's eyes dispense
A mild and gracious influence;
Such as in visions angels shed
Around the heaven-illumined head.
To love thee, Seraphina, sure
Is to be tender, happy, pure;
'Tis from low passions to escape,
And woo bright Virtue's fairest shape;
'Tis ecstasy with wisdom join'd,
And heaven infused into the mind.

ODE ON ÆOLUS'S HARP *.

ETHEREAL race, inhabitants of air,
Who hymn your God amid the secret grove;
Ye unseen beings to my harp repair,
And raise majestic strains, or melt in love.

Those tender notes, how kindly they upbraid,
With what soft woe they thrill the lover's heart!
Sure from the hand of some unhappy maid,
Who died of love, these sweet complainings part.

But hark! that strain was of a graver tone,
On the deep strings his hand some hermit throws;
Or he the sacred bard † who sat alone,
In the drear waste, and wept his people's woes.

Such was the song which Zion's children sung,
When by Euphrates' stream they made their [plaint;
And to such sadly solemn notes are strung
Angelic harps, to soothe a dying saint.

Methinks I hear the full celestial choir,
Through heaven's high dome their awful anthem raise;
Now chanting clear, and now they all conspire
To swell the lofty hymn, from praise to praise.

Let me, ye wandering spirits of the wind,
Who, as wild fancy prompts you, touch the string,
Smit with your theme, be in your chorus join'd;
For till you cease, my Muse forgets to sing.

* Æolus's harp is a musical instrument which plays with the wind, invented by Mr. Oswald. † Jeremiah.

HYMN ON SOLITUDE

HAIL, mildly pleasing Solitude,
Companion of the wise and good!
But from whose holy piercing eye
The herd of fools and villains fly.
Oh! how I love with thee to walk,
And listen to thy whisper'd talk,
Which innocence and truth imparts,
And melts the most obdurate hearts.
A thousand shapes you wear with ease,
And still in every shape you please.
Now wrapt in some mysterious dream,
A lone philosopher you seem;
Now quick from hill to vale you fly,
And now you sweep the vaulted sky.
A shepherd next, you haunt the plain,
And warble forth your oaten strain:—
A lover now, with all the grace
Of that sweet passion in your face:
Then, calm'd to friendship, you assume
The gentle-looking Hartford's bloom,
As, with her Musidora, she,
(Her Musidora fond of thee)
Amid the long withdrawing vale,
Awakes the rival'd nightingale.
Thine is the balmy breath of morn,
Just as the dew-bent rose is born;
And while meridian fervours beat,
Thine is the woodland dumb retreat;
But chief, when evening scenes decay,
And the faint landscape swims away,
Thine is the doubtful soft decline,
And that best hour of musing thine.
Descending angels bless thy train,
The virtues of the sage, and swain;
Plain Innocence, in white array'd,
Before thee lifts her fearless head:
Religion's beams around thee shine,
And cheer thy glooms with light divine:
About thee sports sweet Liberty;
And rapt Urania sings to thee.
Oh, let me pierce thy secret cell,
And in thy deep recesses dwell!
Perhaps from Norwood's oak-clad hill,
When Meditation has her fill,
I just may cast my careless eyes
Where London's spiry turrets rise,
Think of its crimes, its cares, its pain,
Then shield me in the woods again.

ON THE DEATH OF HIS MOTHER.

Ye fabled Muses, I your aid disclaim,
Your airy raptures, and your fancied flame:
True genuine woe my throbbing breast inspires,
Love prompts my lays, and filial duty fires;
The soul springs instant at the warm design,
And the heart dictates every flowing line.
See! where the kindest, best of mothers lies,
And death has shut her ever-weeping eyes;
Has lodged at last peace in her weary breast,
And lull'd her many piercing cares to rest.
No more the orphan train around her stands,
While her full heart upbraids her needy hands!
No more the widow's lonely fate she feels,
The shock severe that modest want conceals,
The oppressor's scourge, the scorn of wealthy pride,
And poverty's unnumber'd ills beside.
For see! attended by the angelic throng,
Through yonder worlds of light she glides along,
And claims the well-earn'd raptures of the sky.—
Yet fond concern recals the mother's eye;
She seeks the helpless orphans left behind;
So hardly left! so bitterly resign'd!
Still, still! is she my soul's divinest theme,
The waking vision, and the wailing dream:
Amid the ruddy sun's enlivening blaze
O'er my dark eyes her dewy image plays,
And in the dread dominion of the night
Shines out again the sadly pleasing sight.
Triumphant virtue all around her darts,
And more than volumes every look imparts—
Looks soft yet awful, melting yet serene,
Where both the mother and the saint are seen.
But ah! that night—that torturing night remains;
May darkness dye it with its deepest stains,
May joy on it forsake her rosy bowers,
And screaming sorrow blast its baleful hours,
When on the margin of the briny flood
Chill'd with a sad presaging damp I stood,
Took the last look, ne'er to behold her more,
And mix'd our murmurs with the wavy roar,
Heard the last words fall from her pious tongue,
Then, wild into the bulging vessel flung,
Which soon, too soon convey'd me from her sight
Dearer than life, and liberty and light!
Why was I then, ye powers, reserved for this?
Nor sunk that moment in the vast abyss?
Devour'd at once by the relentless wave,
And whelm'd for ever in a watery grave?—
Down, ye wild wishes of unruly woe!—
I see her with immortal beauty glow,
The early wrinkle care-contracted gone,
Her tears all wiped, and all her sorrows flown;
The exalting voice of Heaven I hear her breathe,
To soothe her soul in agonies of death;
I see her through the mansions blest above,
And now she meets her dear expecting love.
Heart-cheering sight! but yet, alas! o'erspread
By the damp gloom of Grief's uncheerful shade.
Come then of reason the reflecting hour,
And let me trust the kind o'er-ruling Power
Who from the night commands the shining day,
The poor man's portion, and the orphan's stay!

ELEGY ON THE DEATH OF AIKMAN,

THE PAINTER.

Oh could I draw, my friend, thy genuine mind,
Just, as the living forms by thee design'd,
Of Raphael's figures none should fairer shine,
Nor Titian's colours longer last than mine.
A mind in wisdom old, in lenience young,
From fervent truth where every virtue sprung;
Where all was real, modest, plain, sincere:
Worth above show, and goodness unsevere:
View'd round and round, as lucid diamonds throw
Still as you turn them a revolving glow;
So did his mind reflect with secret ray,
In various virtues, heaven's internal day,
Whether in high discourse it soar'd sublime,
And sprung impatient o'er the bounds of Time,
Or wandering nature through with raptured eye,
Adored the hand that turn'd yon azure sky:
Whether to social life he bent his thought,
And the right poise of mingling passions sought,
Gay converse bless'd; or in the thoughtful grove
Bid the heart open every source of love.
New varying light still set before your eyes
The just, the good, the social, or the wise.
For such a death who can, who would, refuse
The friend a tear, a verse the mournful Muse!
Yet pay we just acknowledgment to Heaven,
Though snatch'd so soon, that Aikman e'er was given.
A friend, when dead, is but removed from sight,
Hid in the lustre of eternal light:
Oft with the mind he wonted converse keeps
In the lone walk, or when the body sleeps
Lets in a wandering ray, and all elate
Wings and attracts her to another state!
And when the parting storms of life are o'er,
May yet rejoin him on a happier shore.
As those we love decay, we die in part,
String after string is sever'd from the heart;
Till loosen'd life at last—but breathing clay,
Without one pang, is glad to fall away.
Unhappy he who latest feels the blow,
Whose eyes have wept o'er every friend laid low,
Dragg'd lingering on from partial death to death,
And dying, all he can resign is breath.

TO DR. DE LA COUR, IN IRELAND.

ON HIS PROSPECT OF POETRY.

Hail gently-warbling De la Cour, whose fame,
Spurning Hibernia's solitary coast,
Where small rewards attend the tuneful throng,
Pervades Britannia's well-discerning isle:
In spite of all the gloomy-minded tribe
That would eclipse thy fame, still shall the Muse,
High soaring o'er the tall Parnassian mount
With spreading pinions—sing thy wondrous praise,
In strains attuned to the seraphic lyre.
Sing unappall'd, though mighty be the theme!
Oh! could she in thy own harmonious strain,
Where softest numbers smoothly flowing glide
In trickling cadence; where the milky maze
Devolves in silence; by the harsher sound
Of hoarser periods still unruffled, could

Her lines but like thine own Euphrates flow—
Then might she sing in numbers worthy thee.
But what can language do, when Fancy finds
Herself unequal to the lovely task ?
Can feeble words thy vivid colours paint,
Or show the sweets which inexhaustive flow ?
Hearken, ye woods, and long-resounding groves ;
Listen, ye streams, soft purling through the meads,
And hymning horrid, all ye tempests roar.
Awake, ye woodlands ! sing, ye warbling larks,
In wildly luscious notes ! But most of all,
Attend, ye grateful fair, attend the youth
Who sweetly sings of nature and of you :
From you alone his conscious breast expects
Its soft rewards, by sordid love of gain
Unbiass'd, undebased ; to meaner minds
Belong such narrow views ; his nobler soul,
Transported wlth a generous thirst of fame,
Sublimely rises with expanded wings,
And through the lucid empyrean soars.
So the young eagle wings its rapid way
Through heaven's broad azure ; sometimes springs aloft,
Now drops, now cleaves with even-waving wings
The yielding air, nor seas nor mountains stop
Its flight impetuous, gazing at the sun
With irretorted eye, whilst he pervades
A trackless void, and unexplored before.
Long had the curious traveller strove to find
The ruins of aspiring Babylon—
In vain—for nought the nicest eye could trace
Save one wide, watery, undistinguish'd waste :
But you with more than magic art have raised
Semiramis's city from its grave ;
You have reversed the scripture curse, which said,
Dragons shall here inhabit ; in your page
We view the rising spires ; the hurried eye
Distracted wanders through the verdant maze ;
In middle air the pendent gardens hang,
Tremendous ceiling !—whilst no solar beam
Falls on the lengthen'd gloom beneath ; the woods
Project above a steep-alluring shade ;
The finish'd garden opens to the view
Wide-stretching vistas, while the whispering wind
Dimples along the breezy-ruffled lake.
Now every tree irregular and bush
Are prodigal of harmony : the birds
Frequent the aërial wood, and nature blushes,
Ashamed to find herself outdone by art :
These and a thousand beauties could I sing,
Collecting like the ever-toiling bee
From yonder mingled wilderness of flowers
The aromatic sweets ; while you, great youth !
O'er thy decaying country chief preside ;
Be thou her genius call'd, inspire her youth
With noble emulation to arrive
At Helicon's fair font, which few, alas !
Save you, have tasted, of Hibernian youth.
Thy country, though corrupted, brought thee forth,
And deem'd her greatest ornament ; and now
Regards thee as her brightest northern star.
Long may you reign as such ; and should grim Time,
With iron teeth, deprive us of our Pope,
Then we'll transplant thy blooming laurels fresh
From your bleak shore to Albion's happier coast.

VERSES ADDRESSED TO MISS YOUNG.

Ah urge too late ! from beauty's bondage free,
Why did I trust my liberty with thee ?
And thou, why didst thou, with inhuman art,
If not resolved to take, seduce my heart ?
Yes, yes, you said (for lovers' eyes speak true) ,
You must have seen how fast my passion grew :
And when your glances chanced on me to shine,
How my fond soul ecstatic sprung to thine !
But mark me, fair one, what I now declare
Thy deep attention claims, and serious care :
It is no common passion fires my breast,
I must be wretched, or I must be blest !
My woes all other remedy deny ;
Or, pitying, give me hope, or bid me die !

TO MISS YOUNG,

WITH A PRESENT OF HIS SEASONS.

Accept, loved nymph ! this tribute due
To tender friendship, love, and you ;
But with it take what breathed the whole,
Oh ! take to thine the poet's soul.
If fancy here her power displays,
And if a heart exalts these lays—
You fairest in that fancy shine,
And all that heart is fondly thine.

ON HIS ROYAL HIGHNESS THE PRINCE OF WALES.

While secret-leaguing nations frown around,
Ready to pour the long-expected storm ;
While she, who wont the restless Gaul to bound,
Britannia, drooping, grows an empty form ;
While on our vitals selfish parties prey,
And deep corruption eats our soul away :

Yet in the goddess of the main appears
A gleam of joy, gay-flushing every grace,
As she the cordial voice of millions hears,
Rejoicing, zealous, o'er thy rising race :
Straight her rekindling eyes resume their fire,
The virtues smile, the Muses tune the lyre.

But more enchanting than the Muses' song,
United Britons thy dear offspring hail :
The city triumphs through her glowing throng ;
The shepherd tells his transport to the dale ;
The sons of roughest toil forget their pain,
And the glad sailor cheers the midnight main.

Can aught from fair Augusta's gentle blood,
And thine, thou friend of liberty ! be born :
Can aught save what is lovely, generous, good ;
What will, at once, defend us, and adorn ?
From thence prophetic joy new Edwards eyes,
New Henrys, Annas, and Elizas rise.

May fate my fond devoted days extend,
To sing the promised glories of thy reign ! [bend !
What though, by years depress'd, my muse might
My heart will teach her still a nobler strain :
How with recover'd Britain, will she soar,
When France insults, and Spain shall rob no more !

THE INCOMPARABLE SOPORIFIC DOCTOR.

Sweet, sleepy doctor ! dear pacific soul !
Lay at the beef, and suck the vital bowl !
Still let the involving smoke around thee fly,
And broad-look'd dulness settle in thine eye.
Ah ! soft in down these dainty limbs repose,
And in the very lap of slumber doze ;
But chiefly, on the lazy day of grace,
Call forth the lambent glories of thy face ;
If aught the thoughts of dinner can prevail,
And sure the Sunday's dinner cannot fail.
To the thin church in sleepy pomp proceed,
And lean on the lethargic book thy head.
These eyes wipe often with the hallow'd lawn,
Profoundly nod, immeasurably yawn.
Slow let the prayers by the meek lips be sung,
Nor let thy thoughts be distanced by thy tongue ;
If e'er the lingerers are within a call,
Or if on prayers thou deign'st to think at all.
Yet—only yet—the swimming head we bend ;
But when serene, the pulpit you ascend,
Through every joint a gentle horror creeps,
And round you the consenting audience sleeps.
So when an ass with sluggish front appears,
The horses start, and prick their quivering ears ;
But soon as e'er the sage is heard to bray,
The fields all thunder, and they bound away.

THE HAPPY MAN.

He's not the happy man, to whom is given
A plenteous fortune by indulgent Heaven ;
Whose gilded roofs on shining columns rise,
And painted walls enchant the gazer's eyes :
Whose table flows with hospitable cheer,
And all the various bounty of the year ; [spring,
Whose valleys smile, whose gardens breathe the
Whose carved mountains bleat, and forests sing ;
For whom the cooling shade in summer twines,
While his full cellars give their generous wines ;
From whose wide fields unbounded autumn pours
A golden tide into his swelling stores :
Whose winter laughs ; for whom the liberal gales
Stretch the big sheet, and toiling commerce sails ;
When yielding crowds attend, and pleasure serves ;
While youth, and health, and vigour, string his nerves.
Even not all these, in one rich lot combined,
Can make the happy man, without the mind ;
Where judgment sits clear-sighted, and surveys
The chain of reason with unerring gaze ;
Where fancy lives, and to the brightening eyes,
His fairer scenes, and bolder figures rise ;
Where social love exerts her soft command,
And plays the passions with a tender hand ;
Whence every virtue flows, in rival strife,
And all the moral harmony of life.
Nor canst thou, Dodington, this truth decline,
Thine is the fortune, and the mind is thine.

ON THE REPORT OF A WOODEN BRIDGE TO BE BUILT AT WESTMINSTER.

By Rufus' hall, where Thames polluted flows,
Provoked, the Genius of the river rose,
And thus exclaim'd : "Have I, ye British swains,
Have I for ages laved your fertile plains ?
Given herds, and flocks, and villages increase,
And fed a richer than a golden fleece ?
Have I, ye merchants, with each swelling tide,
Pour'd Afric's treasure in, and India's pride ?
Lent you the fruit of every nation's toil ?
Made every climate yours, and every soil ?
Yet pilfer'd from the poor, by gaming base,
Yet must a wooden bridge my waves disgrace ?
Tell not to foreign streams the shameful tale,
And be it publish'd in no Gallic vale."
He said ; and plunging to his crystal dome,
While o'er his head the circling waters foam.

PROLOGUE TO MR. MALLET'S "MUSTAPHA."

Since Athens first began to draw mankind,
To picture life, and show the impassion'd mind,
The truly wise have ever deem'd the stage
The moral school of each enlighten'd age.
There, in full pomp, the tragic Muse appears,
Queen of soft sorrows, and of useful fears.
Faint is the lesson reason'd rules impart :
She pours it strong and instant through the heart.
If virtue is the theme, we sudden glow
With generous flame ; and what we feel, we grow
If vice she paints, indignant passions rise ;
The villain sees himself with loathing eyes.
His soul starts, conscious, at another's groan ;
And the pale tyrant trembles on his throne.
To-night our meaning scene attempts to show
What fell events from dark suspicion flow ;
Chief when it taints a lawless monarch's mind,
To the false herd of flattering slaves confined.
The soul sinks gradual to so dire a state ;
Even excellence but serves to feed its hate :
To hate remorseless, cruelty succeeds,
And every worth, and every virtue bleeds.
Behold, our author at your bar appears,
His modest hopes depress'd by conscious fears.
Faults he has many—But to balance those,
His verse with heartfelt love of virtue glows :
All slighter errors let indulgence spare,
And be his equal trial full and fair.
For this best British privilege we call ;
Then—as he merits, let him stand, or fall.

BRITANNIA,

A Poem.

—— Et tantas audetis tollere moles?
Quos ego—sed motos præstat componere fluctus.
Post mihi non simili pœna commissa luetis.
Maturate fugam, regique hæc dicite vestro:
Non illi imperium pelagi, sævumque tridentem,
Sed mihi sorte datum.———VIRG.

As on the sea-beat shore Britannia sat,
Of her degenerate sons the faded fame
Deep in her anxious heart revolving sad:
Bare was her throbbing bosom to the gale,
That hoarse, and hollow, from the bleak surge blew;
Loose flow'd her tresses, rent her azure robe.
Hung o'er the deep, from her majestic brow
She tore the laurel, and she tore the bay.
Nor ceased the copious grief to bathe her cheek;
Nor ceased her sobs to murmur to the main.
Peace discontented nigh, departing, stretch'd
Her dove-like wings; and War, though greatly roused,
Yet mourns his fetter'd hands; while thus the queen
Of nations spoke; and what she said the Muse
Recorded, faithful, in unbidden verse.
Even not yon sail, that, from the sky-mixt wave,
Dawns on the sight, and wafts the Royal Youth*,
A freight of future glory to my shore;
Even not the flattering view of golden days,
And rising periods yet of bright renown,
Beneath the Parents, and their endless line
Through late revolving time, can soothe my rage;
While, unchastised, the insulting Spaniard dares
Infest the trading flood, full of vain war
Despise my navies, and my merchants seize;
As, trusting to false peace they fearless roam
The world of waters wild, made, by the toil,
And liberal blood of glorious ages, mine:
Nor bursts my sleeping thunder on their head.
Whence this unwonted patience? this weak doubt?
This tame beseeching of rejected peace?
This meek forbearance? this unnative fear,
To generous Britons never known before?
And sail'd my fleets for this; on Indian tides
To float, unactive, with the veering winds?
The mockery of war! while hot disease,
And sloth distemper'd, swept off burning crowds,
For action ardent! and amid the deep,
Inglorious, sunk them in a watery grave.
There now they lie beneath the rolling flood,
Far from their friends and country, unavenged;
And back the drooping war-ship comes again,
Dispirited, and thin; her sons ashamed,
Thus idly to review their native shore;
With not one glory sparkling in their eye,
One triumph in their tongue. A passenger,
The violated merchant comes along;
That far-sought wealth, for which the noxious gale
He drew, and sweat beneath equator suns,
By lawless force detain'd; a force that soon
Would melt away, and every spoil resign,
Were once the British lion heard to roar.
Whence is it that the proud Iberian thus,
In their own well-asserted element,
Dares rouse to wrath the masters of the main?
Who told him, that the big incumbent war
Would not, ere this, have roll'd his trembling ports
In smoky ruin? and his guilty stores,
Won by the ravage of a butcher'd world,
Yet unatoned, sunk in the swallowing deep,
Or led the glittering prize into the Thames?
There was a time (O let my languid sons
Resume their spirit at the rousing thought!)
When all the pride of Spain, in one dread fleet,
Swell'd o'er the labouring surge; like a whole heaven
Of clouds, wide-roll'd before the boundless breeze.
Gaily the splendid armament along
Exultant plough'd, reflecting a red gleam,
As sunk the sun, o'er all the flaming vast;
Tall, gorgeous, and elate; drunk with the dream
Of easy conquest; while their bloated war,
Stretch'd out from sky to sky, the gather'd force
Of ages held in its capacious womb.
But soon, regardless of the cumbrous pomp,
My dauntless Britons came, a gloomy few,
With tempest black, the goodly scene deform'd,
And laid their glory waste. The bolts of fate
Resistless thunder'd through their yielding sides;
Fierce o'er their beauty blazed the lurid flame;
And seized in horrid grasp, or shatter'd wide,
Amid the mighty waters deep they sunk.
Then too from every promontory chill,
Rank fen, and cavern where the wild wave works,
I swept confederate winds, and swell'd a storm.
Round the glad isle, snatch'd by the vengeful blast,

* Frederic Prince of Wales, then lately arrived.

The scatter'd remnants drove; on the blind shelve
And pointed rock, that marks the indented shore,
Relentless dash'd, where loud the northern main
Howls through the fractured Caledonian isles.
Such were the dawnings of my watery reign;
But since how vast it grew, how absolute,
Even in those troubled times, when dreadful Blake
Awed angry nations with the British name,
Let every humbled state, let Europe say,
Sustain'd and balanced, by my naval arm.
Ah what must those immortal spirits think
Of your poor shifts? Those, for their country's good,
Who faced the blackest danger, knew no fear,
No mean submission, but commanded peace.
Ah how with indignation must they burn,
(If aught, but joy, can touch ethereal breasts)
With shame! with grief! to see their feeble sons
Shrink from that empire o'er the conquer'd seas,
For which their wisdom plann'd, their councils glow'd,
And their veins bled through many a toiling age.
Oh first of human blessings! and supreme!
Fair Peace! how lovely, how delightful thou!
By whose wide tie, the kindred sons of men,
Like brothers live, in amity combined,
And unsuspicious faith; while honest toil
Gives every joy, and to those joys a right,
Which idle, barbarous rapine but usurps.
Pure is thy reign; when, unaccursed by blood,
Nought, save the sweetness of indulgent showers,
Trickling distils into the verdant glebe;
Instead of mangled carcases, sad-seen,
When the blithe sheaves lie scatter'd o'er the field;
When only shining shares, the crooked knife,
And hooks imprint the vegetable wound;
When the land blushes with the rose alone,
The falling fruitage and the bleeding vine.
Oh, Peace! thou source, and soul of social life!
Beneath whose calm inspiring influence,
Science his views enlarges, Art refines,
And swelling Commerce opens all her ports;
Blest be the man divine, who gives us thee!
Who bids the trumpet hush his horrid clang,
Nor blow the giddy nations into rage;
Who sheaths the murderous blade; the deadly gun
Into the well-piled armoury returns;
And, every vigour from the work of death
To grateful industry converting, makes
The country flourish, and the city smile.
Unviolated, him the virgin sings;
And him the smiling mother to her train.
Of him the shepherd, in the peaceful dale
Chaunts; and the treasures of his labours sure,
The husbandman of him, as at the plough,
Or team, he toils. With him the sailor soothes,
Beneath the trembling moon, the midnight wave;
And the full city, warm, from street to street,
And shop to shop, responsive, rings of him.
Nor joys one land alone; his praise extends
Far as the sun rolls the diffusive day;
Far as the breeze can bear the gifts of peace,
Till all the happy nations catch the song.
What would not, Peace! the patriot bear for thee?
What painful patience? What incessant care?
What mix'd anxiety? What sleepless toil?
Even from the rash protected, what reproach?
For he thy value knows; thy friendship he
To human nature: but the better thou,
The richer of delight, sometimes the more
Inevitable, war; when ruffian force
Awakes the fury of an injured state.
Even the good patient man, whom reason rules,
Roused by bold insult, and injurious rage,
With sharp and sudden check, the astonish'd sons
Of violence confounds; firm as his cause,
His bolder heart; in awful justice clad;
His eyes effulging a peculiar fire:
And, as he charges through the prostrate war,
His keen arm teaches faithless men, no more
To dare the sacred vengeance of the just.
And what, my thoughtless sons, should fire you more
Than when your well-earn'd empire of the deep
The least beginning injury receives?
What better cause can call your lightning forth?
Your thunder wake? your dearest life demand?
What better cause, than when your country sees
The sly destruction at her vitals aim'd?
For oh it much imports you, 'tis your all,
To keep your trade entire, entire the force
And honour of your fleets; o'er that to watch,
Even with a hand severe, and jealous eye.
In intercourse be gentle, generous, just,
By wisdom polish'd, and of manners fair;
But on the sea be terrible, untamed,
Unconquerable still; let none escape,
Who shall but aim to touch your glory there.
Is there the man, into the lion's den
Who dares intrude, to snatch his young away?
And is a Briton seized? and seized beneath
The slumbering terrors of a British fleet?
Then ardent rise! Oh great in vengeance rise!
O'erturn the proud, teach rapine to restore:
And as you ride sublimely round the world,
Make every vessel stoop, make every state
At once their welfare and their duty know.
This is your glory; this your wisdom; this
The native power for which you were design'd
By fate, when fate design'd the firmest state,
That e'er was seated on the subject sea;
A state alone where Liberty should live,
In these late times, this evening of mankind,
When Athens, Rome, and Carthage are no more,
The world almost in slavish sloth dissolved.
For this, these rocks around your coast were thrown;
For this, your oaks, peculiar harden'd, shoot
Strong into sturdy growth; for this, your hearts
Swell with a sullen courage, growing still
As danger grows; and strength and toil for this
Are liberal pour'd o'er all the fervent land.
Then cherish this, this unexpensive power,
Undangerous to the public, ever prompt,
By lavish nature thrust into your hand:
And, unencumber'd with the bulk immense
Of conquest, whence huge empires rose, and fell
Self-crush'd, extend your reign from shore to shore,
Where'er the winds your high behests can blow;
And fix it deep on this eternal base.
For should the sliding fabric once give way,
Soon slacken'd quite, and past recovery broke,
It gathers ruin as it rolls along,
Steep-rushing down to that devouring gulf,
Where many a mighty empire buried lies.
And should the big redundant flood of trade,
In which ten thousand thousand labours join
Their several currents, till the boundless tide
Rolls in a radiant deluge o'er the land;
Should this bright stream, the least inflected, point
Its course another way, o'er other lands
The various treasure would resistless pour,
Ne'er to be won again; its ancient tract

Left a vile channel, desolate, and dead,
With all around a miserable waste.
Not Egypt, were, her better heaven, the Nile
Turn'd in the pride of flow ; when o'er his rocks,
And roaring cataracts, beyond the reach
Of dizzy vision piled, in one wide flash
An Ethiopian deluge foams amain ;
(Whence wondering fable traced him from the sky)
Even not that prime of earth, where harvests crowd
On untill'd harvests, all the teeming year,
If of the fat o'erflowing culture robb'd,
Were then a more uncomfortable wild,
Steril, and void ; than of her trade deprived,
Britons, your boasted isle : her princes sunk ;
Her high-built honour moulder'd to the dust;
Unnerved her force ; her spirit vanish'd quite ;
With rapid wing her riches fled away ;
Her unfrequented ports alone the sign
Of what she was ; her merchants scatter'd wide ;
Her hollow shops shut up ; and in her streets,
Her fields, woods, markets, villages, and roads,
The cheerful voice of labour heard no more.
Oh let not then waste Luxury impair
That manly soul of toil, which strings your nerves,
And your own proper happiness creates.
Oh let not the soft penetrating plague
Creep on the free-born mind : and working there,
With the sharp tooth of many a new-form'd want,
Endless, and idle all, eat out the heart
Of Liberty ; the high conception blast ;
The noble sentiment, the impatient scorn
Of base subjection, and the swelling wish
For general good, erasing from the mind :
While nought save narrow selfishness succeeds,
And low design, the sneaking passions all
Let loose, and reigning in the rankled breast.
Induced at last, by scarce-perceived degrees,
Sapping the very frame of government,
And life, a total dissolution comes ;
Sloth, ignorance, dejection, flattery, fear,
Oppression raging o'er the waste he makes ;
The human being almost quite extinct ;
And the whole state in broad corruption sinks.
Oh shun that gulf ; that gaping ruin shun !
And countless ages roll it far away
From you, ye heaven-beloved ! may Liberty,
The light of life ! the sun of human-kind !
Whence heroes, bards, and patriots borrow flame,
Even where the keen depressive North descends,
Still spread, exalt, and actuate your powers !
While slavish southern climates beam in vain.
And may a public spirit from the throne,
Where every virtue sits, go copious forth,
Live o'er the land ; the finer arts inspire ;
Make thoughtful science raise his pensive head,
Blow the fresh bay, bid industry rejoice,
And the rough sons of lowest labour smile.
As when, profuse of spring, the loosen'd west
Lifts up the pining year, and balmy breathes
Youth, life, and love, and beauty o'er the world.
But haste we from these melancholy shores,
Nor to deaf winds, and waves, our fruitless plaint
Pour weak ; the country claims our active aid ;
That let us roam ; and where we find a spark
Of public virtue, blow it into flame.
Lo ! now my sons, the sons of freedom ! meet
In awful senate ; thither let us fly ;
Burn in the patriot's thought, flow from his tongue
In fearless truth ; myself, transform'd, preside,
And shed the spirit of Britannia round.
This said ; her fleeting form, and airy train,
Sunk in the gale ; and nought but ragged rocks
Rush'd on the broken eye ; and nought was heard
But the rough cadence of the dashing wave.

LIBERTY;

A Poem.

TO

HIS ROYAL HIGHNESS FREDERIC PRINCE OF WALES.

Sir,

When I reflect upon that ready condescension, that preventing generosity, with which your Royal Highness received the following Poem under your protection, I can alone ascribe it to the recommendation and influence of the subject. In you the cause and concerns of Liberty have so zealous a patron, as entitles whatever may have the least tendency to promote them, to the distinction of your favour. And who can entertain this delightful reflection without feeling a pleasure far superior to that of the fondest author, and of which all true lovers of their country must participate? To behold the noblest dispositions of the prince and of the patriot united; an overflowing benevolence, generosity, and candour of heart, joined to an enlightened zeal for liberty—an intimate persuasion that on it depend the happiness and glory both of kings and people: to see these shining out in public virtues, as they have hitherto smiled in all the social lights and private accomplishments of life, is a prospect that cannot but inspire a general sentiment of satisfaction and gladness more easy to be felt than expressed.

If the following attempt to trace Liberty from the first ages down to her excellent establishment in Great Britain can at all merit your approbation, and prove an entertainment to your Royal Highness; if it can in any degree answer the dignity of the subject, and of the name under which I presume to shelter it; I have my best reward,—particularly as it affords me an opportunity of declaring that I am, with the greatest zeal and respect,

Sir,

Your Royal Highness's most obedient and most devoted servant,

James Thomson.

ANCIENT AND MODERN HISTORY COMPARED;

BEING

THE FIRST PART OF LIBERTY, A POEM.

CONTENTS.

The following poem is thrown into the form of a poetical vision. Its scene, the ruins of ancient Rome. The goddess of Liberty. who is supposed to speak through the whole, appears, characterised as British Liberty. Gives a view of ancient Italy, and particularly of republican Rome, in all her magnificence and glory. This contrasted by modern Italy; its valleys, mountains, culture, cities, people: the difference appearing strongest in the capital city Rome. The ruins of the great works of Liberty more magnificent than the borrowed pomp of Oppression; and from them revived sculpture, painting, and architecture. The old Romans apostrophised, with regard to the several melancholy changes in Italy: Horace, Tully, and Virgil, with regard to their Tibur, Tusculum, and Naples. That once finest and most ornamented part of Italy, all along the coast of Baiæ, how changed. This desolation of Italy applied to Britain. Address to the goddess of Liberty, that she would deduce from the first ages, her chief establishments, the description of which constitute the subject of the following parts of this poem. She assents, and commands what she says to be sung in Britain; whose happiness, arising from freedom, and a limited monarchy, she marks. An immediate vision attends, and paints her words. Invocation.

O my lamented Talbot! while with thee
The Muse gay roved the glad Hesperian round,
And drew the inspiring breath of ancient arts;
Ah! little thought she her returning verse
Should sing her darling subject to thy shade.
And does the mystic veil, from mortal beam,
Involve those eyes where every virtue smiles,
And all thy father's candid spirit shone?
The light of reason, pure, without a cloud;

Full of the generous heart, the mild regard;
Honour disdaining blemish, cordial faith,
And limpid truth, that looks the very soul.
But to the death of mighty nations turn,
My strain; be there absorpt the private tear.
Musing, I lay; warm from the sacred walks,
Where at each step imagination burns:
While scatter'd wide around, awful, and hoar,
Lies, a vast monument, once-glorious Rome,
The tomb of empire! ruins! that efface
Whate'er, of finish'd, modern-pomp can boast.
Snatch'd by these wonders to that world where thought
Unfetter'd ranges, Fancy's magic hand
Led me anew o'er all the solemn scene,
Still in the mind's pure eye more solemn drest;
When straight, methought, the fair majestic power
Of Liberty appear'd. Not, as of old,
Extended in her hand the cap, and rod,
Whose slave-enlarging touch gave double life:
But her bright temples bound with British oak,
And naval honours nodded on her brow.
Sublime of port: loose o'er her shoulder flow'd
Her sea-green robe, with constellations gay.
An island-goddess now; and her high care
The Queen of Isles, the mistress of the main.
My heart beat filial transport at the sight;
And, as she moved to speak, the awaken'd Muse
Listen'd intense. A while she look'd around,
With mournful eye the well-known ruins mark'd,
And then, her sighs repressing, thus began.
Mine are these wonders, all thou see'st is mine;
But ah how changed! the falling poor remains
Of what exalted once the Ausonian shore.
Look back through time; and, rising from the gloom,
Mark the dread scene, that paints whate'er I say.
The great republic see! that glow'd, sublime,
With the mix'd freedom of a thousand states!
Raised on the thrones of kings her curule chair,
And by her fasces awed the subject world.
See busy millions quickening all the land,
With cities throng'd, and teeming culture high:
For nature then smiled on her free-born sons,
And pour'd the plenty that belongs to men.
Behold, the country cheering, villas rise,
In lively prospect; by the secret lapse
Of brooks now lost and streams renown'd in song:
In Umbria's closing vales, or on the brow
Of her brown hills that breathe the scented gale:
On Baiæ's viny coast; where peaceful seas,
Fann'd by kind zephyrs, ever kiss the shore;
And suns unclouded shine, through purest air:
Or in the spacious neighbourhood of Rome;
Far-shining upward to the Sabine hills,
To Anio's shore, and Tibur's olive shade;
To where Preneste lifts her airy brow;
Or downward spreading to the sunny shore,
Where Alba breathes the freshness of the main.
See distant mountains leave their valleys dry,
And o'er the proud arcade the tribute pour,
To lave imperial Rome. For ages laid,
Deep, massy, firm, diverging every way,
With tombs of heroes sacred, see her roads,
By various nations trod, and suppliant kings;
With legions flaming, or with triumph gay.
Full in the centre of these wondrous works,
The pride of earth! Rome in her glory see!
Behold her demigods, in senate met;
All head to counsel, and all heart to act:
The commonweal inspiring every tongue
With fervent eloquence, unbribed, and bold;
Ere tame corruption taught the servile herd
To rank obedient to a master's voice.
Her forum see, warm, popular, and loud,
In trembling wonder hush'd, when the two sires*,
As they the private father greatly quell'd,
Stood up the public fathers of the state.
See justice judging there in human shape.
Hark! how with freedom's voice it thunders high,
Or in soft murmurs sinks to Tully's tongue.
Her tribes, her census, see; her generous troops,
Whose pay was glory, and their best reward
Free for their country, and for me to die;
Ere mercenary murder grew a trade.
Mark, as the purple triumph waves along,
The highest pomp and lowest fall of life.
Her festive games, the school of heroes, see;
Her circus, ardent with contending youth;
Her streets, her temples, palaces, and baths,
Full of fair forms, of beauty's eldest born,
And of a people cast in virtue's mould:
While sculpture lives around, and Asian hills
Lend their best stores to heave the pillar'd dome;
All that to Roman strength the softer touch
Of Grecian art can join. But language fails
To paint this sun, this centre of mankind;
Where every virtue, glory, treasure, art,
Attracted strong, in heighten'd lustre met.
Need I the contrast mark? unjoyous view!
A land in all, in government, and arts,
In virtue, genius, earth and heaven, reversed.
Who but these far-famed ruins to behold,
Proofs of a people, whose heroic aims
Soar'd far above the little selfish sphere
Of doubting modern life; who but inflamed
With classic zeal, these consecrated scenes
Of men and deeds to trace: unhappy land,
Would trust thy wilds, and cities loose of sway?
Are these the vales, that, once, exulting states
In their warm bosom fed? The mountains these,
On whose high-blooming sides my sons, of old,
I bred to glory? These dejected towns,
Where, mean, and sordid, life can scarce subsist,
The scenes of ancient opulence, and pomp?
Come! by whatever sacred name disguised,
Oppression, come! and in thy works rejoice!
See nature's richest plains to putrid fens
Turn'd by thy fury. From their cheerful bounds,
See razed the enlivening village, farm, and seat.
First, rural toil, by thy rapacious hand
Robb'd of his poor reward, resign'd the plough;
And now he dares not turn the noxious glebe.
'Tis thine entire. The lonely swain himself,
Who loves at large along the grassy downs
His flocks to pasture, thy drear champain flies.
Far as the sickening eye can sweep around,
'Tis all one desert, desolate, and grey,
Grazed by the sullen buffalo alone;
And where the rank uncultivated growth
Of rotting ages taints the passing gale.
Beneath the baleful blast the city pines,
Or sinks enfeebled, or infected burns.
Beneath it mourns the solitary road,
Roll'd in rude mazes o'er the abandon'd waste;
While ancient ways, ingulf'd, are seen no more.
Such thy dire plains, thou self-destroyer! Foe
To human-kind! Thy mountains too, profuse,
Where savage nature blooms, seem their sad plaint
To raise against thy desolating rod.

* L. J. Brutus, and Virginius.

There on the breezy brow, where thriving states,
And famous cities, once, to the pleased sun,
Far other scenes of rising culture spread,
Pale shine thy ragged towns. Neglected round,
Each harvest pines; the livid, lean produce
Of heartless labour: while thy hated joys,
Not proper pleasure, lift the lazy hand.
Better to sink in sloth the woes of life,
Than wake their rage with unavailing toil.
Hence drooping art almost to nature leaves
The rude unguided year. Thin wave the gifts
Of yellow Ceres, thin the radiant blush
Of orchard reddens in the warmest ray.
To weedy wildness run, no rural wealth
(Such as dictators fed) the garden pours.
Crude the wild olive flows, and foul the vine;
Nor juice Cœcubian, nor Falernian, more,
Streams life and joy, save in the Muse's bowl.
Unseconded by art, the spinning race
Draw the bright thread in vain, and idly toil.
In vain, forlorn in wilds, the citron blows;
And flowering plants perfume the desert gale.
Through the vile thorn the tender myrtle twines.
Inglorious droops the laurel, dead to song,
And long a stranger to the hero's brow.
Nor half thy triumph this: cast from brute fields,
Into the haunts of men thy ruthless eye.
There buxom plenty never turns her horn;
The grace and virtue of exterior life,
No clean convenience reigns; even sleep itself,
Least delicate of powers, reluctant, there,
Lays on the bed impure his heavy head.
Thy horrid walk! dead, empty, unadorn'd,
See streets whose echoes never know the voice
Of cheerful hurry, commerce many-tongued,
And art mechanic at his various task,
Fervent employ'd. Mark the desponding race,
Of occupation void, as void of hope;
Hope, the glad ray, glanced from Eternal Good,
That life enlivens, and exalts its powers,
With views of fortune—madness all to them!
By thee relentless seized their better joys,
To the soft aid of cordial airs they fly,
Breathing a kind oblivion o'er their woes,
And love and music melt their souls away.
From feeble justice see how rash revenge,
Trembling, the balance snatches; and the sword,
Fearful himself, to venal ruffians gives.
See where God's altar, nursing murder, stands,
With the red touch of dark assassins stain'd.
But chief let Rome, the mighty city! speak
The full-exerted genius of thy reign.
Behold her rise amid the lifeless waste,
Expiring nature all corrupted round!
While the lone Tiber, through the desert plain,
Winds his waste stores, and sullen sweeps along.
Patch'd from my fragments, in unsolid pomp,
Mark how the temple glares; and, artful dress'd,
Amusive, draws the superstitious train.
Mark how the palace lifts a lying front,
Concealing often, in magnific jail,
Proud want; a deep unanimated gloom!
And oft adjoining to the drear abode
Of misery, whose melancholy walls
Seem its voracious grandeur to reproach.
Within the city bounds, the desert see.
See the rank vine o'er subterranean roofs,
Indecent, spread; beneath whose fretted gold
It once, exulting, flow'd. The people mark,
Matchless, while fired by me; to public good
Inexorably firm, just, generous, brave,
Afraid of nothing but unworthy life,
Elate with glory, an heroic soul
Known to the vulgar breast: behold then now
A thin despairing number, all-subdued,
The slaves of slaves, by superstition fool'd,
By vice unmann'd, and a licentious rule,
In guile ingenious, and in murder brave.
Such in one land, beneath the same fair clime,
Thy sons, Oppression, are; and such were mine.
Even with thy labour'd pomp, for whose vain show
Deluded thousands starve; all age-begrimed,
Torn, robb'd, and scatter'd in unnumber'd sacks,
And by the tempest of two thousand years
Continual shaken, let my ruins vie:
These roads that yet the Roman hand assert,
Beyond the weak repair of modern toil;
These fractured arches, that the chiding stream
No more delighted hear; these rich remains
Of marbles now unknown, where shines imbibed
Each parent ray; these massy columns, hew'd
From Afric's farthest shore; one granite all,
These obelisks high-towering to the sky,
Mysterious mark'd with dark Egyptian lore;
These endless wonders that this sacred way*
Illumine still, and consecrate to fame;
These fountains, vases, urns, and statues, charged
With the fine stores of art-completing Greece.
Mine is, besides, thy every later boast;
Thy Buonarotis†, thy Palladios† mine;
And mine the fair designs, which Raphael's† soul
O'er the live canvass, emanating, breathed.
What would you say, ye conquerors of earth!
Ye Romans! could you raise the laurel'd head;
Could you the country see, by seas of blood,
And the dread toil of ages, won so dear;
Your pride, your tiumph, your supreme delight.
For whose defence oft, in the doubtful hour,
You rush'd with rapture down the gulf of fate,
Of death ambitious! till by awful deeds,
Virtues, and courage, that amaze mankind,
The queen of nations rose; possess'd of all
Which nature, art, and glory could bestow:
What would you say, deep in the last abyss
Of slavery, vice, and unambitious want,
Thus to behold her sunk? Your crowded plains,
Void of their cities; unadorn'd your hills;
Ungraced your lakes; your ports to ships unknown;
Your lawless floods, and your abandon'd streams:
These could you know? these could you love again?
Thy Tibur, Horace, could it now inspire
Content, poetic ease, and rural joy,
Soon bursting into song: while through the groves
Of headlong Anio, dashing to the vale,
In many a tortured stream, you mused along?
Yon wild retreat‡, where superstition dreams,
Could, Tully, you your Tusculum believe?
And could you deem yon naked hills, that form,
Famed in old song, the ship-forsaken bay§,
Your Formian shore? once the delight of earth,
Where art and nature, ever-smiling, join'd

* Via Sacra.

† M. Angelo Buonaroti, Palladio, and Raphael d'Urbino; the three great modern masters in sculpture, architecture, and painting.

‡ Tusculum is reckoned to have stood at a place now called Grotta Ferrata, a convent of monks.

§ The bay of Mola (anciently Formiæ) into which Homer brings Ulysses and his companions. Near Formiæ Cicero had a villa.

land to lavish all their stores.
How changed, how vacant, Virgil, wide around,
Would now your Naples seem ? Disaster'd less
By black Vesuvius thundering o'er the coast,
His midnight earthquakes, and his mining fires,
Than by despotic rage* : that inward gnaws,
A native foe ; a foreign, tears without.
First from your flatter'd Cæsars this began :
Till, doom'd to tyrants an eternal prey,
Thin-peopled spreads, at last, the syren plain†,
That the dire soul of Hannibal disarm'd ;
And wrapt in weeds the shore of Venus‡ lies.
There Baiæ sees no more the joyous throng ;
Her bank ail beaming with the pride of Rome :
No generous vines now bask along the hills,
Where sport the breezes of the Tyrrhene main :
With baths and temples mixt, no villas rise ;
Nor, art-sustain'd amid reluctant waves,
Draw the cool murmurs of the breathing deep :
No spreading ports their sacred arms extend :
No mighty moles the big intrusive storm,
From the calm station, roll resounding back.
An almost total desolation sits,
A dreary stillness, saddening o'er the coast ;
Where, when soft suns and tepid winters rose,
Rejoicing crowds inhaled the balm of peace ;
Where city'd hill to hill reflected blaze ;
And where, with Ceres, Bacchus wont to hold
A genial strife§. Her youthful form, robust,
Even Nature yields ; by fire, and earthquake rent :
Whole stately cities in the dark abrupt
Swallow'd at once, or vile in rubbish laid,
A nest for serpents ; from the red abyss
New hills, explosive, thrown ; the Lucrine lake
A reedy pool ; and all to Cuma's point,
The sea recovering his usurp'd domain,
And pour'd triumphant o'er the buried dome.
Hence, Britain, learn ; my best-establish'd, last,
And more than Greece, or Rome, my steady reign ;
The land where, king and people equal bound
By guardian laws, my fullest blessings flow ;
And where my jealous unsubmitting soul,
The dread of tyrants ! burns in every breast ;
Learn hence, if such the miserable fate
Of an heroic race, the masters once
Of human-kind ; what, when deprived of me,
How grievous must be thine ? In spite of climes,
Whose sun-enliven'd ether wakes the soul
To higher powers ; in spite of happy soils,
That, but by labour's slightest aid impell'd,
With treasures teem to thy cold clime unknown ;
If there desponding fail the common arts,
And sustenance of life : could life itself,
Far less a thoughtless tyrant's hollow pomp,
Subsist with thee ? Against depressing skies,
Join'd to full-spread oppression's cloudy brow,
How could thy spirits hold ? where vigour find,
Forced fruits to tear from their unnative soil ?
Or, storing every harvest in thy ports,
To plough the dreadful all-producing wave ?
Here paused the goddess. By the pause assured,
In trembling accents thus I moved my prayer.
"Oh, first, and most benevolent of powers !
Come from eternal splendours, here on earth,
Against despotic pride, and rage, and lust,
To shield mankind ! to raise them to assert
The native rights and honour of their race :
Teach me thy lowest subject, but in zeal
Yielding to none, the progress of thy reign,
And with a strain from thee enrich the Muse.
As thee alone she serves, her patron, thou,
And great inspirer be ! then will she joy
Through narrow life her lot, and private shade :
And when her venal voice she barters vile,
Or to thy open or thy secret foes,
May ne'er those sacred raptures touch her more,
By slavish hearts unfelt ! and may her song
Sink in oblivion with the nameless crew !
Vermin of state ! to thy o'erflowing light
That owe their being, yet betray thy cause."
Then, condescending kind, the heavenly Power
Return'd.——" What here, suggested by the scene,
I slight unfold, record and sing at home,
In that blest isle, where (so we spirits move)
With one quick effort of my will I am.
There Truth, unlicensed, walks ; and dares accost
Even kings themselves, the monarchs of the free !
Fix'd on my rock, there, an indulgent race
O'er Britons wield the sceptre of their choice .
And there, to finish what his sires began,
A prince behold ! for me who burns sincere,
Even with a subject's zeal. He my great work
Will parent-like sustain ; and added give
The touch, the Graces and the Muses owe.
For Britain's glory swells his panting breast ;
And ancient arts he emulous revolves :
His pride to let the smiling heart abroad,
Through clouds of pomp, that but conceal the man ;
To please, his pleasure ; bounty his delight ;
And all the soul of Titus dwells in him."
Hail, glorious theme ! But how, alas ! shall verse,
From the crude stores of mortal language drawn,
How faint and tedious, sing, what piercing deep,
The goddess flash'd at once upon my soul ?
For, clear precision all, the tongue of gods
Is harmony itself ; to every ear
Familiar known, like light to every eye.
Meantime disclosing ages, as she spoke,
In long succession pour'd their empires forth ;
Scene after scene, the human drama spread ;
And still the embodied picture rose to sight.
Oh thou ! to whom the Muses owe their flame ;
Who bidd'st, beneath the pole, Parnassus rise,
And Hippocrene flow ; with thy bold ease,
The striking force, the lightning of thy thought,
And thy strong phrase, that rolls profound and clear ;
Oh, gracious goddess ! re-inspire my song ;
While I, to nobler than poetic fame
Aspiring, thy commands to Britons bear.

* Naples, then under the Austrian government.

† Campagna Felice, adjoining to Capua.

‡ The coast of Baiæ, which was formerly adorned with the works mentioned in the following lines ; and where, amidst many magnificent ruins, those of a temple erected to Venus are still to be seen.

§ All along this coast, the ancient Romans had their winter retreats ; and several populous cities stood.

GREECE;

BEING

THE SECOND PART OF LIBERTY, A POEM.

CONTENTS.

LIBERTY traced from the pastoral ages, and the first uniting of neighbouring families into civil government. The several establishments of Liberty, in Egypt, Persia, Phœnicia, Palestine, slightly touched upon, down to her great establishment in Greece. Geographical description of Greece. Sparta, and Athens, the two principal states of Greece, described. Influence of Liberty over all the Grecian states; with regard to their government, their politeness, their virtues, their arts and sciences. The vast superiority it gave them, in point of force and bravery, over the Persians, exemplified by the action of Thermopylæ, the battle of Marathon, and the retreat of the Ten Thousand. Its full exertion and most beautiful effects in Athens. Liberty the source of free philosophy. The various schools, which took their rise from Socrates. Enumeration of fine arts: eloquence, poetry, music, sculpture, painting, and architecture; the effects of Liberty in Greece, and brought to their utmost perfection there. Transition to the modern state of Greece. Why Liberty declined, and was at last entirely lost among the Greeks. Concluding reflection.

THUS spoke the goddess of the fearless eye;
And at her voice, renew'd, the Vision rose.
First, in the dawn of time, with Eastern swains,
In woods, and tents, and cottages, I lived;
While on from plain to plain they led their flocks,
In search of clearer spring, and fresher field.
These, as increasing families disclosed
The tender state, I taught an equal sway.
Few were offences, properties, and laws.
Beneath the rural portal, palm-o'erspread,
The father-senate met. There Justice dealt,
With reason then and equity the same,
Free as the common air, her prompt decree;
Nor yet had stain'd her sword with subjects' blood.
The simpler arts were all their simple wants
Had urged to light. But instant, these supplied,
Another set of fonder wants arose,
And other arts with them of finer aim;
Till, from refining want to want impell'd,
The mind by thinking push'd her latent powers,
And life began to glow, and arts to shine.
At first, on brutes alone the rustic war
Launch'd the rude spear; swift, as he glared along,
On the grim lion, or the robber-wolf.
For then young sportive life was void of toil,
Demanding little, and with little pleased:
But when to manhood grown, and endless joys,
Led on by equal toils, the bosom fired;
Lewd lazy rapine broke primeval peace,
And, hid in caves and idle forests drear,
From the lone pilgrim and the wandering swain
Seized what he durst not earn. Then brother's blood
First, horrid, smoked on the polluted skies.
Awful in justice, then the burning youth,
Led by their temper'd sires, on lawless men,
The last worst monsters of the shaggy wood,
Turn'd the keen arrow, and the sharpen'd spear.
Then war grew glorious. Heroes then arose;
Who, scorning coward self, for others lived,
Toil'd for their ease, and for their safety bled.
West with the living day to Greece I came:
Earth smiled beneath my beam: the Muse before
Sonorous flew, that low till then in woods
Had tuned the reed, and sigh'd the shepherd's pain;
But now, to sing heroic deeds, she swell'd
A nobler note, and bade the banquet burn.
For Greece my sons of Egypt I forsook;
A boastful race, that in the vain abyss
Of fabling ages loved to lose their source,
And with their river traced it from the skies.
While there my laws alone despotic reign'd,
And king, as well as people, proud obey'd;
I taught them science, virtue, wisdom, arts;
By poets, sages, legislators sought;
The school of polish'd life, and human-kind.
But when mysterious Superstition came,
And, with her civil sister* leagued, involved
In studied darkness the desponding mind;
Then tyrant power the righteous scourge unloosed:
For yielding reason speaks the soul a slave.
Instead of useful works, like nature's, great,
Enormous, cruel wonders crush'd the land;
And round a tyrant's tomb†, who none deserved,
For one vile carcass perish'd countless lives.
Then the great dragon‡, couch'd amid his floods,
Swell'd his fierce heart, and cried—"This flood is mine,
"'Tis I that bid it flow."—But, undeceived,
His frenzy soon the proud blasphemer felt;
Felt that, without my fertilising power,
Suns lost their force, and Niles o'erflow'd in vain.
Nought could retard me: nor the frugal state
Of rising Persia, sober in extreme,
Beyond the pitch of man, and thence reversed
Into luxurious waste: nor yet the ports
Of old Phoenicia; first for letters famed,
That paint the voice, and silent speak to sight,
Of arts prime source, and guardian! by fair stars,
First tempted out into the lonely deep;
To whom I first disclosed mechanic arts,
The winds to conquer, to subdue the waves,
With all the peaceful power of ruling trade;

---

* Civil tyranny. † The Pyramids.
‡ The tyrants of Egypt.

Earnest of Britain. Nor by these retain'd ;
Nor by the neighbouring land, whose palmy shore
The silver Jordan laves : before me lay
The promised Land of Arts, and urged my flight.
Hail Nature's utmost boast! unrival'd Greece !
My fairest reign ! where every power benign
Conspired to blow the flower of human-kind,
And lavish'd all that genius can inspire.
Clear sunny climates, by the breezy main,
Iönian or Ægean, temper'd kind :
Light, airy soils : a country rich, and gay ;
Broke into hills with balmy odours crown'd,
And, bright with purple harvest, joyous vales :
Mountains and streams, where verse spontaneous flow'd ;
Whence deem'd by wondering men the seat of gods,
And still the mountains and the streams of song.
All that boon nature could luxuriant pour
Of high materials, and my restless Arts
Frame into finish'd life. How many states,
And clustering towns, and monuments of fame,
And scenes of glorious deeds, in little bounds !
From the rough tract of bending mountains, beat
By Adria's here, there by Ægean waves ;
To where the deep-adorning Cyclade Isles
In shining prospect rise, and on the shore
Of farthest Crete resounds the Lybian main.
O'er all two rival cities rear'd the brow,
And balanced all. Spread on Eurotas' bank,
Amid a circle of soft-rising hills,
The patient Sparta one : the sober, hard,
And man-subduing city ; which no shape
Of pain could conquer, nor of pleasure charm.
Lycurgus there built, on the solid base
Of equal life, so well a temper'd state ;
Where mix'd each government, in such just poise ;
Each power so checking, and supporting, each ;
That firm for ages, and unmoved, it stood,
The fort of Greece ! without one giddy hour,
One shock of faction, or of party rage.
For, drain'd the springs of wealth, corruption there
Lay wither'd at the root. Thrice happy land !
Had not neglected art, with weedy vice
Confounded, sunk. But if Athenian arts
Loved not the soil ; yet there the calm abode
Of wisdom, virtue, philosophic ease,
Of manly sense and wit, in frugal phrase
Confined, and press'd into Laconic force.
There too, by rooting thence still treacherous self,
The public and the private grew the same.
The children of the nursing public all,
And at its table fed, for that they toil'd,
For that they lived entire, and even for that
The tender mother urged her son to die.
Of softer genius, but not less intent
To seize the palm of empire, Athens rose.
Where, with bright marbles big and future pomp,
Hymettus* spread, amid the scented sky,
His thymy treasures to the labouring bee,
And to botanic hand the stores of health ;
Wrapt in a soul-attenuating clime,
Between Ilissus and Cephissus† glow'd
This hive of science, shedding sweets divine,
Of active arts, and animated arms.
There, passionate for me, an easy-moved,
A quick, refined, a delicate, humane,
Enlighten'd people reign'd. Oft on the brink
Of ruin, hurried by the charm of speech,

* A mountain near Athens.

† Two rivers, betwixt which Athens was situated.

Inforcing hasty counsel immature,
Totter'd the rash democracy ; unpoised.
And by the rage devour'd, that ever tears
A populace unequal ; part too rich,
And part or fierce with want or abject grown.
Solon, at last, their mild restorer, rose :
Allay'd the tempest ; to the calm of laws
Reduced the settling whole ; and, with the weight
Which the two senates* to the public lent,
As with an anchor fix'd the driving state.
Nor was my forming care to these confined.
For emulation through the whole I pour'd,
Noble contention ! who should most excel
In government well-poised, adjusted best
To public weal : in countries cultured high :
In ornamented towns, where order reigns,
Free social life, and polish'd manners fair :
In exercise, and arms ; arms only drawn
For common Greece, to quell the Persian pride :
In moral science, and in graceful arts.
Hence, as for glory peacefully they strove,
The prize grew greater, and the prize of all.
By contest brighten'd, hence the radiant youth
Pour'd every beam ; by generous pride inflamed,
Felt every ardour burn : their great reward
The verdant wreath, which sounding Pisa† gave.
Hence flourish'd Greece ; and hence a race of men,
As gods by conscious future times adored :
In whom each virtue wore a smiling air,
Each science shed o'er life a friendly light,
Each art was nature. Spartan valour hence,
At the famed pass‡ firm as an isthmus stood ;
And the whole eastern ocean, waving far
As eye could dart its vision, nobly check'd.
While in extended battle, at the field
Of Marathon, my keen Athenians drove
Before their ardent band an host of slaves.
Hence through the continent ten thousand Greeks
Urged a retreat, whose glory not the prime
Of victories can reach. Deserts, in vain,
Opposed their course ; and hostile lands, unknown,
And deep rapacious floods, dire-bank'd with death ;
And mountains, in whose jaws destruction grinn'd,
Hunger, and toil ; Armenian snows, and storms ;
And circling myriads still of barbarous foes.
Greece in their view, and glory yet untouch'd,
Their steady column pierced the scattering herds,
Which a whole empire pour'd ; and held its way
Triumphant, by the Sage-exalted Chief §
Fired and sustain'd. Oh light and force of mind,
Almost almighty in severe extremes !
The sea at last from Colchian mountains seen,
Kind-hearted transport round their captains threw
The soldier's fond embrace ; o'erflow'd their eyes
With tender floods, and loosed the general voice
To cries resounding loud—The sea ! The sea !
In Attic bounds hence heroes, sages, wits,
Shone thick as stars, the milky-way of Greece !
And though gay wit, and pleasing grace was theirs,
All the soft modes of elegance and ease ;
Yet was not courage less, the patient touch
Of toiling art, and disquisition deep.

* The Areopagus, or supreme court of judicature, which Solon reformed, and improved : and the council of four hundred, by him instituted. In this council all affairs of state were deliberated, before they came to be voted in the assembly of the people.

† Or Olympia, the city where the Olympic games were celebrated.

‡ The straits of Thermopylæ. § Xenophon.

My Spirit pours a vigour through the soul,
The unfetter'd thought with energy inspires,
Invincible in arts, in the bright field
Of nobler science, as in that of arms.
Athenians thus not less intrepid burst
The bonds of tyrant darkness, than they spurn'd
The Persian chains: while through the city, full
Of mirthful quarrel and of witty war,
Incessant struggled taste refining taste,
And friendly free discussion, calling forth
From the fair jewel Truth its latent ray.
O'er all shone out the great Athenian Sage*,
And father of philosophy: the sun,
From whose white blaze emerged each various sect
Took various teints, but with diminish'd beam.
Tutor of Athens! he, in every street,
Dealt priceless treasure: goodness his delight,
Wisdom his wealth, and glory his reward.
Deep through the human heart, with playful art,
His simple question stole; as into truth,
And serious deeds, he smiled the laughing race;
Taught moral happy life, whate'er can bless,
Or grace mankind; and what he taught he was.
Compounded high, though plain, his doctrine broke
In different Schools. The bold poetic phrase
Of figured Plato; Xenophon's pure strain,
Like the clear brook that steals along the vale;
Dissecting truth, the Stagyrite's keen eye;
The exalted Stoic pride; the Cynic sneer;
The slow-consenting Academic doubt;
And, joining bliss to virtue, the glad ease
Of Epicurus, seldom understood.
They, ever-candid, reason still opposed
To reason; and, since virtue was their aim,
Each by sure practice tried to prove his way
The best. Then stood untouch'd the solid base
Of Liberty, the Liberty of Mind:
For systems yet, and soul-enslaving creeds,
Slept with the monsters of succeeding times.
From priestly darkness sprung the enlightening arts
Of fire, and sword, and rage, and horrid names.
O Greece! thou sapient nurse of Finer Arts!
Which to bright science blooming fancy bore,
Be this thy praise, that thou, and thou alone,
In these hast led the way, in these excell'd,
Crown'd with the laurel of assenting time.
In thy full language, speaking mighty things;
Like a clear torrent close, or else diffused
A broad majestic stream, and rolling on
Through all the winding harmony of sound:
In it the power of Eloquence, at large,
Breathed the persuasive or pathetic soul;
Still'd by degrees the democratic storm,
Or bade it threatening rise, and tyrants shook,
Flush'd at the head of their victorious troops.
In it the Muse, her fury never quench'd
By mean unyielding phrase, or jarring sound,
Her unconfined divinity display'd;
And, still harmonious, form'd it to her will:
Or soft depress'd it to the shepherd's moan,
Or raised it swelling to the tongue of gods.
Heroic song was thine; the Fountain-Bard†,
Whence each poetic stream derives its course.
Thine the dread moral scene, thy chief delight!
Where idle fancy durst not mix her voice,
When reason spoke august; the fervent heart
Or plain'd, or storm'd; and in the impassion'd man,
Concealing art with art, the poet sunk.
This potent school of manners, but when left
To loose neglect, a land-corrupting plague,
Was not unworthy deem'd of public care
And boundless cost, by thee; whose every son,
Even last mechanic, the true taste possess'd
Of what had flavour to the nourish'd soul.
The sweet enforcer of the poet's strain,
Thine was the meaning Music of the heart;
Not the vain trill, that, void of passion, runs
In giddy mazes, tickling idle ears;
But that deep-searching voice, and artful hand,
To which respondent shakes the varied soul.
Thy fair ideas, thy delightful forms,
By love imagined, by the graces touch'd,
The boast of well-pleased nature! Sculpture seized
And bade them ever smile in Parian stone.
Selecting Beauty's choice, and that again
Exalting, blending in a perfect whole,
Thy workmen left even nature's self behind.
From those far different, whose prolific hand
Peoples a nation; they for years on years,
By the cool touches of judicious toil,
Their rapid genius curbing, pour'd it all
Through the live features of one breathing stone.
There, beaming full, it shone; expressing gods:
Jove's awful brow, Apollo's air divine,
The fierce atrocious frown of sinew'd Mars,
Or the sly graces of the Cyprian Queen.
Minutely perfect all! Each dimple sunk,
And every muscle swell'd, as nature taught.
In tresses, braided gay, the marble waved;
Flow'd in loose robes, or thin transparent veils;
Sprung into motion; soften'd into flesh;
Was fired to passion, or refined to soul.
Nor less thy Pencil, with creative touch,
Shed mimic life, when all thy brightest dames,
Assembled, Zeuxis in his Helen mix'd;
And when Apelles, who peculiar knew
To give a grace that more than mortal smiled,
The soul of beauty! call'd the queen of love,
Fresh from the billows, blushing orient charms.
Even such enchantment then thy pencil pour'd,
That cruel-thoughted War, the impatient torch
Dash'd to the ground; and, rather than destroy
The patriot picture*, let the city 'scape.
First elder Sculpture taught her sister art
Correct design; where great ideas shone,
And in the secret trace expression spoke:
Taught her the graceful attitude; the turn,
And beauteous airs of head; the native act,
Or bold, or easy; and, cast free behind,
The swelling mantle's well-adjusted flow.
Then the bright Muse, their eldest sister, came;
And bade her follow where she led the way:
Bade earth, and sea, and air, in colours rise;
And copious action on the canvass glow;
Gave her gay fable; spread invention's store;
Enlarged her view; taught composition high,
And just arrangement, circling round one point,
That starts to sight, binds and commands the whole.
Caught from the heavenly Muse a nobler aim,
And scorning the soft trade of mere delight,
O'er all thy temples, porticoes, and schools,
Heroic deeds she traced, and warm display'd
Each moral beauty to the ravish'd eye.

* Socrates. † Homer.

* When Demetrius besieged Rhodes, and could have reduced the city, by setting fire to that quarter of it where stood the house of the celebrated Protogenes; he chose rather to raise the siege, than hazard the burning of a famous picture called Jalysus, the masterpiece of that painter.

There, as the imagined presence of the god
Aroused the mind, or vacant hours induced
Calm contemplation, or assembled youth
Burn'd in ambitious circle round the sage,
The living lesson stole into the heart,
With more prevailing force than dwells in words.
These rouse to glory ; while, to rural life,
The softer canvass oft reposed the soul.
There gaily broke the sun-illumined cloud ;
The lessening prospect, and the mountain blue,
Vanish'd in air ; the precipice frown'd, dire ;
White, down the rock, the rushing torrent dash'd;
The sun shone, trembling, o'er the distant main ;
The tempest foam'd, immense ; the driving storm
Sadden'd the skies, and, from the doubling gloom,
On the scathed oak the ragged lightning fell ;
In closing shades, and where the current strays,
With peace, and love, and innocence around,
Piped the lone shepherd to his feeding flock :
Round happy parents smiled their younger selves;
And friends conversed, by death divided long.
To public virtue thus the smiling arts,
Unblemish'd handmaids, served ; the graces they
To dress this fairest Venus. Thus revered,
And placed beyond the reach of sordid care,
The high awarders of immortal fame,
Alone for glory thy great masters strove ;
Courted by kings, and by contending states
Assumed the boasted honour of their birth.
In Architecture too thy rank supreme !
That art where most magnificent appears
The little builder man ; by thee refined,
And, smiling high, to full perfection brought.
Such thy sure rules, that Goths of every age,
Who scorn'd their aid, have only loaded earth
With labour'd heavy monuments of shame :
Not those gay domes that o'er thy splendid shore
Shot, all proportion, up. First unadorn'd,
And nobly plain, the manly Doric rose ;
The Ionic then, with decent matron grace,
Her airy pillar heaved ; luxuriant last,
The rich Corinthian spread her wanton wreath :
The whole so measured true, so lessen'd off
By fine proportion, that the marble pile,
Form'd to repel the still or stormy waste
Of rolling ages, light as fabrics look'd
That from the magic wand aërial rise.
These were the wonders that illumined Greece,
From end to end———Here interrupting warm,
Where are they now ? (I cried,) say, goddess, where?
And what the land thy darling thus of old ?
Sunk ! she resumed ; deep in the kindred gloom
Of superstition, and of slavery, sunk !
No glory now can touch their hearts, benumb'd
By loose dejected sloth and servile fear ;
No science pierce the darkness of their minds ;
No nobler art the quick ambitious soul
Of imitation in their breast awake.
Even, to supply the needful arts of life,
Mechanic toil denies the hopeless hand.
Scarce any trace remaining, vestige grey,
Or nodding column on the desert shore,
To point where Corinth, or where Athens stood.
A faithless land of violence, and death !
Where commerce parleys, dubious, on the shore ;
And his wild impulse curious search restrains,
Afraid to trust the inhospitable clime.
Neglected nature fails ; in sordid want
Sunk, and debased, their beauty beams no more.
The sun himself seems, angry to regard,
Of light unworthy, the degenerate race ;
And fires them oft with pestilential rays :
While earth, blue poison steaming on the skies,
Indignant, shakes them from her troubled sides.
But as from man to man, fate's first decree,
Impartial death the tide of riches rolls,
So states must die and Liberty go round.
Fierce was the stand, ere virtue, valour, arts,
And the soul fired by me (that often, stung
With thoughts of better times and old renown,
From hydra-tyrants tried to clear the land)
Lay quite extinct in Greece, their works effaced,
And gross o'er all, unfeeling bondage spread.
Sooner I moved my much-reluctant flight,
Poised on the doubtful wing : when Greece with Greece
Embroil'd in foul contention fought no more
For common glory, and for common weal :
But false to freedom, sought to quell the free ;
Broke the firm band of peace, and sacred love,
That lent the whole irrefragable force ;
And, as around the partial trophy blush'd,
Prepared the way for total overthrow.
Then to the Persian power, whose pride they scorn'd,
When Xerxes pour'd his millions o'er the land,
Sparta, by turns, and Athens, vilely sued ;
Sued to be venal parricides, to spill
Their country's bravest blood, and on themselves
To turn their matchless mercenary arms.
Peaceful in Susa, then, sat the Great King* ;
And by the trick of treaties, the still waste
Of sly corruption, and barbaric gold,
Effected what his steel could ne'er perform.
Profuse he gave them the luxurious draught,
Inflaming all the land : unbalanced wide
Their tottering states ; their wild assemblies ruled,
As the winds turn at every blast the seas :
And by their listed orators, whose breath
Still with a factious storm infested Greece,
Roused them to civil war, or dash'd them down
To sordid peace—† Peace ! that, when Sparta shook
Astonish'd Artaxerxes on his throne,
Gave up, fair-spread o'er Asia's sunny shore,
Their kindred cities to perpetual chains.
What could so base, so infamous a thought
In Spartan hearts inspire? Jealous, they saw
Respiring Athens‡ rear again her walls ;
And the pale fury fired them, once again
To crush this rival city to the dust.
For now no more the noble social soul
Of Liberty my families combined ;
But by short views, and selfish passions, broke,
Dire as when friends are rankled into foes,
They mix'd severe, and waged eternal war :
Nor felt they, furious, their exhausted force ;
Nor, with false glory, discord, madness blind,
Saw how the blackening storm from Thracia came.
Long years roll'd on, by many a battle stain'd§,
The blush and boast of fame ! where courage, art,
And military glory shone supreme :
But let detesting ages, from the scene

* So the kings of Persia were called by the Greeks.

† The peace made by Antalcidas, the Lacedemonian admiral, with the Persians ; by which the Lacedemonians abandoned all the Greeks established in the Lesser Asia to the dominion of the king of Persia.

‡ Athens had been dismantled by the Lacedemonians, at the end of the first Peloponnesian war, and was at this time restored by Conon to its former splendour.

§ The Peloponnesian war.

Of Greece self-mangled, turn the sickening eye.
At last, when, bleeding from a thousand wounds,
She felt her spirits fail; and in the dust
Her latest heroes, Nicias, Conon, lay,
Agesilaus, and the Theban Friends *:
The Macedonian vulture mark'd his time,
By the dire scent of Cheronæa † lured,
And, fierce-descending, seized his hapless prey.
Thus tame submitted to the victor's yoke
Greece, once the gay, the turbulent, the bold;
For every grace, and muse, and science born;
With arts of war, of government, elate;
To tyrants dreadful, dreadful to the best;
Whom I myself could scarcely rule: and thus
The Persian fetters, that inthrall'd the mind,
Were turn'd to formal and apparent chains.
Unless corruption first deject the pride,
And guardian vigour of the free-born soul,
All crude attempts of violence are vain;
For firm within, and while at heart untouch'd,
Ne'er yet by force was freedom overcome.
But soon as independence stoops the head,
To vice enslaved, and vice-created wants;
Then to some foul corrupting hand, whose waste
These heighten'd wants with fatal bounty feeds:
From man to man the slackening ruin runs,
Till the whole state unnerved in slavery sinks.

ROME;

BEING

THE THIRD PART OF LIBERTY, A POEM.

CONTENTS.

As this Part contains a description of the establishment of Liberty in Rome, it begins with a view of the Grecian colonies settled in the southern parts of Italy, which with Sicily constituted the Great Greece of the ancients. With these Colonies the spirit of Liberty, and of republics, spreads over Italy. Transition to Pythagoras and his philosophy, which he taught through those free states and cities. Amidst the many small republics in Italy, Rome the destined seat of Liberty. Her establishment there dated from the expulsion of the Tarquins. How differing from that in Greece. Reference to a view of the Roman republic given in the first part of this poem; to mark its rise and fall the peculiar purport of this. During its first ages, the greatest force of Liberty, and virtue, exerted. The source whence derived the heroic virtues of the Romans. Enumeration of these virtues. Thence their security at home; their glory, success, and empire, abroad. Bounds of the Roman empire geographically described. The states of Greece restored to Liberty, by Titus Quintus Flaminius, the highest instance of public generosity and beneficence. The loss of Liberty in Rome. Its causes, progress, and completion in the death of Brutus. Rome under the Emperors. From Rome the Goddess of Liberty goes among the northern nations; where, by infusing into them her spirit and general principles, she lays the groundwork of her future establishments; sends them in vengeance on the Roman empire, now totally enslaved; and then, with arts and sciences in her train, quits earth during the dark ages. The celestial regions, to which Liberty retired, not proper to be opened to the view of mortals.

Here melting mix'd with air the ideal forms,
That painted still whate'er the goddess sung.
Then I, impatient—"From extinguish'd Greece,
To what new region stream'd the Human Day?"
She softly sighing, as when Zephyr leaves,
Resign'd to Boreas, the declining year,
Resumed.——Indignant, these last scenes‡ I fled;
And long ere then, Leucadia's cloudy cliff,
And the Ceraunian hills behind me thrown,
All Latium stood aroused. Ages before,
Great mother of republics! Greece had pour'd,
Swarm after swarm, her ardent youth around.
On Asia, Afric, Sicily, they stoop'd,
But chief on fair Hesperia's winding shore;
Where, from Lacinium* to Etrurian vales,
They roll'd increasing colonies along,
And lent materials for my Roman reign.
With them my spirit spread; and numerous states,
And cities rose, on Grecian models form'd;
As its parental policy, and arts,
Each had imbibed. Besides, to each assign'd
A guardian genius, o'er the public weal,
Kept an unclosing eye; tried to sustain,
Or more, sublime the soul infused by me:
And strong the battle rose, with various wave,
Against the tyrant demons of the land.
Thus they their little wars and triumphs knew;
Their flows of fortune, and receding times,
But almost all below the proud regard
Of story vow'd to Rome, on deeds intent,
That truth beyond the flight of fable bore.
Not so the Samian sage†; to him belongs
The brightest witness of recording fame.
For these free states his native isle‡ forsook,
And a vain tyrant's transitory smile,
He sought Crotona's pure salubrious air,
And through Great Greece§ his gentle wisdom taught;
Wisdom that calm'd for listening years¶ the mind,
Nor ever heard amid the storm of zeal.
His mental eye first launch'd into the deeps
Of boundless ether; where unnumber'd orbs,
Myriads on myriads, through the pathless sky
Unerring roll, and wind their steady way.
There he the full consenting choir beheld;
There first discern'd the secret band of love,

* Pelopidas, and Epaminondas.
† The battle of Cheronæa, in which Philip of Macedon utterly defeated the Greeks.
‡ The last struggles of Liberty in Greece.

* A promontory in Calabria.
† Pythagoras.
‡ Samos, over which then reigned the tyrant Polycrates.
§ The southern parts of Italy and Sicily, so called because of the Grecian colonies there settled.
¶ His scholars were enjoined silence for five years.

The kind attraction, that to central suns
Binds circling earths, and world with world unites.
Instructed thence he great ideas form'd
Of the whole-moving, all-informing God,
The Sun of beings! beaming unconfined
Light, life, and love, and ever-active power:
Whom nought can image, and who best approves
The silent worship of the moral heart,
That joys in bounteous Heaven, and spreads the joy.
Nor scorn'd the soaring sage to stoop to life,
And bound his reason to the sphere of man.
He gave the four yet reigning virtues*. name;
Inspired the study of the finer arts,
That civilised mankind, and laws devised
Where with enlighten'd justice mercy mix'd.
He even, into his tender system, took
Whatever shares the brotherhood of life:
He taught that life's indissoluble flame,
From brute to man, and man to brute again,
For ever shifting, runs the eternal round;
Thence tried against the blood-polluted meal,
And limbs yet quivering with some kindred soul,
To turn the human heart. Delightful truth!
Had he beheld the living chain ascend,
And not a circling form, but rising whole.
  Amid these small republics one arose,
On yellow Tiber's bank, almighty Rome,
Fated for me. A nobler spirit warm'd
Her sons; and, roused by tyrants, nobler still
It burn'd in Brutus; the proud Tarquins chased
With all their crimes; bade radiant eras rise,
And the long honours of the consul-line.
  Here from the fairer, not the greater, plan
Of Greece I varied; whose unmixing states,
By the keen soul of emulation pierced,
Long waged alone the bloodless war of arts,
And their best empire gain'd. But to diffuse
O'er men an empire was my purpose now:
To let my martial majesty abroad;
Into the vortex of one state to draw
The whole mix'd force, and liberty, on earth;
To conquer tyrants, and set nations free.
  Already have I given, with flying touch,
A broken view of this my amplest reign.
Now, while its first, last, periods you survey,
Mark how it labouring rose, and rapid fell.
  When Rome in noon-tide empire grasp'd the
And, soon as her resistless legions shone, [world,
The nations stoop'd around; though then appear'd
Her grandeur most, yet in her dawn of power,
By many a jealous equal people press'd,
Then was the toil, the mighty struggle then;
Then for each Roman I an hero told;
And every passing sun, and Latian scene,
Saw patriot virtues then, and awful deeds,
That or surpass the faith of modern times,
Or, if believed, with sacred horror strike.
  For then, to prove my most exalted power,
I to the point of full perfection push'd,
To fondness and enthusiastic zeal,
The great, the reigning passion of the free;
That godlike passion! which, the bounds of self
Divinely bursting, the whole public takes
Into the heart, enlarged, and burning high
With the mix'd ardour of unnumber'd selves;
Of all who safe beneath the voted laws
Of the same parent state, fraternal, live.
From this kind sun of moral nature flow'd
Virtues, that shine the light of human-kind,

* The four cardinal virtues.

And, ray'd through story, warm remotest time.
These virtues too, reflected to their source,
Increased its flame. The social charm went round,
The fair idea, more attractive still,
As more by virtue mark'd; till Romans, all
One band of friends, unconquerable grew. [voice,
  Hence, when their country raised her plaintive
The voice of pleading nature was not heard;
And in their hearts the fathers throbb'd no more:
Stern to themselves, but gentle to the whole.
Hence sweeten'd pain, the luxury of toil;
Patience, that baffled fortune's utmost rage;
High-minded hope, which at the lowest ebb,
When Brennus conquer'd and when Cannæ bled,
The bravest impulse felt, and scorn'd despair.
Hence moderation a new conquest gain'd;
As on the vanquish'd, like descending Heaven,
Their dewy mercy dropp'd, their bounty beam'd,
And by the labouring hand were crowns bestow'd.
Fruitful of men, hence hard laborious life,
Which no fatigue can quell, no season pierce.
Hence, independence, with his little pleased
Serene, and self-sufficient, like a god;
In whom corruption could not lodge one charm,
While he his honest roots to gold preferr'd;
While truly rich, and by his Sabine field
The man maintain'd, the Roman's splendour all
Was in the public wealth and glory placed:
Or ready, a rough swain, to guide the plough;
Or else, the purple o'er his shoulder thrown,
In long majestic flow, to rule the state,
With wisdom's purest eye; or, clad in steel,
To drive the steady battle on the foe.
Hence every passion, even the proudest, stoop'd,
To common good: Camillus, thy revenge;
Thy glory, Fabius. All submissive hence,
Consuls, Dictators, still resign'd their rule,
The very moment that the laws ordain'd.
Though conquest o'er them clapp'd her eagle-wings,
Her laurels wreathed, and yoked her snowy steeds
To the triumphal car; soon as expired
The latest hour of sway, taught to submit,
(A harder lesson that than to command)
Into the private Roman sunk the chief.
If Rome was served, and glorious, careless they
By whom. Their country's fame they deem'd their
And above envy, in a rival's train, [own;
Sung the loud Iös by themselves deserved.
Hence matchless courage. On Cremera's bank,
Hence fell the Fabii; hence the Decii died;
And Curtius plunged into the flaming gulf.
Hence Regulus the wavering fathers firm'd,
By dreadful counsel never given before;
For Roman honour sued, and his own doom.
Hence he sustain'd to dare a death prepared
By Punic rage. On earth his manly look
Relentless fix'd, he from a last embrace,
By chains polluted, put his wife aside,
His little children climbing for a kiss;
Then dumb through rows of weeping wondering
A new illustrious exile! press'd along. [friends,
Nor less impatient did he pierce the crowds
Opposing his return, than if, escaped
From long litigious suits, he glad forsook
The noisy town a while and city cloud,
To breathe Venafrian or Tarentine air.
Need I these high particulars recount?
The meanest bosom felt a thirst for fame;
Flight their worst death, and shame their only fear.
Life had no charms, nor any terrors fate,

When Rome and glory call'd. But, in one view,
Mark the rare boast of these unequal'd times.
Ages revolved unsullied by a crime:
Astræa reign'd, and scarcely needed laws
To bind a race elated with the pride
Of virtue, and disdaining to descend
To meanness, mutual violence, and wrongs.
While war around them raged, in happy Rome
All peaceful smiled, all save the passing clouds
That often hang on Freedom's jealous brow;
And fair unblemish'd centuries elapsed,
When not a Roman bled but in the field.
Their virtue such, that an unbalanced state,
Still between noble and plebeian tost,
As flow'd the wave of fluctuating power,
Was thence kept firm, and with triumphant prow
Rode out the storms. Oft though the native feuds,
That from the first their constitution shook,
(A latent ruin, growing as it grew)
Stood on the threatening point of civil war
Ready to rush: yet could the lenient voice
Of wisdom, soothing the tumultuous soul,
Those sons of virtue calm. Their generous hearts,
Unpetrified by self, so naked lay
And sensible to truth, that o'er the rage
Of giddy faction, by oppression swell'd,
Prevail'd a simple fable, and at once
To peace recover'd the divided state.
But if their often-cheated hopes refused
The soothing touch; still, in the love of Rome,
The dread Dictator found a sure resource.
Was she assaulted? was her glory stain'd?
One common quarrel wide inflamed the whole.
Foes in the forum in the field were friends,
By social danger bound; each fond for each,
And for their dearest country all, to die.
Thus up the hill of empire slow they toil'd:
Till, the bold summit gain'd, the thousand states
Of proud Italia blended into one:
Then o'er the nations they resistless rush'd,
And touch'd the limits of the failing world.
Let fancy's eye the distant lines unite.
See that which borders wild the western main,
Where storms at large resound, and tides immense:
From Caledonia's dim cerulean coast,
And moist Hibernia, to where Atlas, lodged
Amid the restless clouds and leaning heaven,
Hangs o'er the deep that borrows thence its name.
Mark that opposed, where first the springing morn
Her roses sheds, and shakes around her dews:
From the dire deserts by the Caspian laved,
To where the Tigris and Euphrates, join'd,
Impetuous tear the Babylonian plain;
And blest Arabia aromatic breathes.
See that dividing far the watery north,
Parent of floods! from the majestic Rhine,
Drunk by Batavian meads, to where, seven-mouth'd,
In Euxine waves the flashing Danube roars;
To where the frozen Tanais scarcely stirs
The dead Mæotic pool, or the long Rha*,
In the black Scythian sea† his torrent throws.
Last, that beneath the burning zone behold.
See where it runs, from the deep-loaded plains
Of Mauritania to the Lybian sands,
Where Ammon lifts amid the torrid waste
A verdant isle with shade and fountain fresh;
And farther to the full Egyptian shore,

* The ancient name of the Volga.
† The Caspian Sea.

To where the Nile from Ethiopian clouds,
His never-drain'd ethereal urn, descends.
In this vast space what various tongues, and states
What bounding rocks, and mountains, floods, and seas!
What purple tyrants quell'd, and nations freed!
O'er Greece descended chief, with stealth divine,
The Roman bounty in a flood of day:
As at her Isthmian games, a fading pomp!
Her full-assembled youth innumerous swarm'd.
On a tribunal raised Flaminius sat;
A victor he, from the deep phalanx pierced
Of iron-coated Macedon, and back
The Grecian tyrant* to his bounds repell'd.
In the high thoughtless gaiety of game,
While sport alone their unambitious hearts
Possess'd; the sudden trumpet, sounding hoarse,
Bade silence o'er the bright assembly reign.
Then thus a herald—"To the states of Greece
The Roman people, unconfined, restore
Their countries, cities, liberties, and laws:
Taxes remit, and garrisons withdraw."
The crowd astonish'd half, and half inform'd,
Stared dubious round; some question'd, some exclaim'd,
(Like one who dreaming, between hope and fear,
Is lost in anxious joy) "Be that again,
Be that again proclaim'd, distinct, and loud."
Loud, and distinct, it was again proclaim'd;
And still as midnight in the rural shade,
When the gale slumbers, they the words devour'd.
A while severe amazement held them mute,
Then, bursting broad, the boundless shout to heaven
From many a thousand hearts ecstatic sprung.
On every hand rebellow'd to their joy
The swelling sea, the rocks, and vocal hills:
Through all her turrets stately Corinth† shook;
And, from the void above of shatter'd air,
The flitting bird fell breathless to the ground.
What piercing bliss! how keen a sense of fame,
Did then, Flaminius, reach thy inmost soul?
And with what deep-felt glory didst thou then
Escape the fondness of transported Greece?
Mix'd in a tempest of superior joy,
They left the sports; like Bacchanals they flew,
Each other straining in a strict embrace,
Nor strain'd a slave; and loud acclaims till night
Round the proconsul's tent repeated rung.
Then, crown'd with garlands, came the festive hours;
And music, sparkling wine, and converse warm,
Their raptures waked anew.—"Ye gods!" they cried,
"Ye guardian gods of Greece! And are we free?
Was it not madness deem'd the very thought?
And is it true? How did we purchase chains?
At what a dire expense of kindred blood?
And are they now dissolved? And scarce one drop
For the fair first of blessings have we paid?
Courage, and conduct, in the doubtful field,
When rages wide the storm of mingling war,
Are rare indeed; but how to generous ends
To turn success, and conquest, rarer still:
That the great gods and Romans only know.
Lives there on earth, almost to Greece unknown,
A people so magnanimous, to quit
Their native soil, traverse the stormy deep,
And by their blood and treasure, spent for us,

* The king of Macedonia.
† The Isthmian games were celebrated at Corinth.

Redeem our states, our liberties, and laws;
There does! there does! O saviour Titus! Rome!"
Thus through the happy night they pour'd their
And in my last reflected beams rejoiced. [souls,
As when the shepherd, on the mountain brow,
Sits piping to his flocks, and gamesome kids;
Meantime the sun, beneath the green earth sunk,
Slants upward o'er the scene a parting gleam:
Short is the glory that the mountain gilds,
Plays on the glittering flocks, and glads the swain;
To western worlds irrevocable roll'd,
Rapid, the source of light recals his ray.
Here interposing I—"Oh queen of men!
Beneath whose sceptre in essential rights
Equal they live; though placed, for common good,
Various, or in subjection or command;
And that by common choice: alas! the scene,
With virtue, freedom, and with glory bright,
Streams into blood, and darkens into woe."
Thus she pursued—Near this great era, Rome
Began to feel the swift approach of fate,
That now her vitals gain'd: still more and more
Her deep divisions kindling into rage,
And war with chains and desolation charged.
From an unequal balance of her sons
These fierce contentions sprung; and as increased
This hated inequality, more fierce
They flamed to tumult. Independence fail'd;
Here by luxurious wants, by real there;
And with this virtue every virtue sunk,
As, with the sliding rock, the pile sustain'd
A last attempt, too late, the Gracchi made,
To fix the flying scale, and poise the state.
On one side swell'd aristocratic pride;
With usury, the villain! whose fell gripe
Bends by degrees to baseness the free soul;
And luxury rapacious, cruel, mean,
Mother of vice! While on the other crept
A populace in want, with pleasure fired;
Fit for proscriptions, for the darkest deeds,
As the proud feeder bade: inconstant, blind,
Deserting friends at need, and duped by foes;
Loud and seditious, when a chief inspired
Their headlong fury, but, of him deprived,
Already slaves that lick'd the scourging hand.
This firm republic, that against the blast
Of opposition rose; that (like an oak,
Nursed on feracious Algidum, whose boughs
Still stronger shoot beneath the rigid axe)
By loss, by slaughter, from the steel itself,
Even force and spirit drew; smit with the calm,
The dead serene of prosperous fortune, pined.
Nought now her weighty legions could oppose;
Her terror* once, on Afric's tawny shore,
Now smoked in dust, a stabling now for wolves;
And every dreaded power received the yoke.
Besides, destructive, from the conquer'd east,
In the soft plunder came that worst of plague,
That pestilence of mind, a fever'd thirst
For the false joys which luxury prepares;
Unworthy joys! that wasteful leave behind
No mark of honour, in reflecting hour,
No secret ray to glad the conscious soul;
At once involving in one ruin wealth,
And wealth-acquiring powers: while stupid self,
Of narrow gust, and hebetating sense,
Devour the nobler faculties of bliss.
Hence Roman virtue slacken'd into sloth;
Security relax'd the softening state;

* Carthage.

And the broad eye of government lay closed.
No more the laws inviolable reign'd,
And public weal no more: but party raged;
And partial power, and licence unrestrain'd,
Let discord through the deathful city loose.
First, mild Tiberius*, on thy sacred head
The fury's vengeance fell; the first, whose blood
Had since the consuls stain'd contending Rome.
Of precedent pernicious! With thee bled
Three hundred Romans; with thy brother, next,
Three thousand more: till, into battles turn'd
Debates of peace, and forced the trembling laws,
The forum and comitia horrid grew,
A scene of barter'd power, or reeking gore.
When, half-ashamed, corruption's thievish arts,
And ruffian force begin to sap the mounds
And majesty of laws; if not in time
Repress'd severe, for human aid too strong
The torrent turns, and overbears the whole.
Thus luxury, dissension, a mix'd rage
Of boundless pleasure and of boundless wealth,
Want wishing change, and waste repairing war,
Rapine for ever lost to peaceful toil,
Guilt unatoned, profuse of blood revenge,
Corruption all avow'd, and lawless force,
Each heightening each, alternate shook the state.
Meantime ambition, at the dazzling head
Of hardy legions, with the laurels heap'd
And spoil of nations, in one circling blast
Combined in various storm, and from its base
The broad republic tore. By virtue built
It touch'd the skies, and spread o'er shelter'd earth
An ample roof: by virtue too sustain'd,
And balanced steady, every tempest sung
Innoxious by, or bade it firmer stand.
But when, with sudden and enormous change,
The first of mankind sunk into the last,
As once in virtue, so in vice extreme,
This universal fabric yielded loose,
Before ambition still; and thundering down,
At last, beneath its ruins crush'd a world.
A conquering people, to themselves a prey,
Must ever fall; when their victorious troops,
In blood and rapine savage grown, can find
No land to sack and pillage but their own.
By brutal Marius, and keen Sylla, first
Effused the deluge dire of civil blood,
Unceasing woes began, and this, or that,
(Deep-drenching their revenge) nor virtue spared,
Nor sex, nor age, nor quality, nor name;
Till Rome, into a human shambles turn'd,
Made desarts lovely.—Oh, to well-earn'd chains
Devoted race?—If no true Roman then,
No Scævola there was, to raise for me
A vengeful hand: was there no father, robb'd
Of blooming youth to prop his wither'd age?
No son, a witness to his hoary sire
In dust and gore defiled? No friend forlorn?
No wretch that doubtful trembled for himself?
None brave, or wild, to pierce a monster's heart,
Who, heaping horror round, no more deserved
The sacred shelter of the laws he spurn'd?
No. Sad o'er all profound dejection sat;
And nerveless fear. The slave's asylum theirs:
Or flight, ill-judging, that the timid back
Turns weak to slaughter; or partaken guilt.
In vain from Sylla's vanity I drew
An unexampled deed. The power resign'd,
And all unhoped the common-wealth restored,

* Tib. Gracchus.

Amazed the public, and effaced his crimes.
Through streets yet streaming from his murderous hand
Unarm'd he stray'd, unguarded, unassail'd,
And on the bed of peace his ashes laid ;
A grace, which I to his demission gave.
But with him died not the despotic soul.
Ambition saw that stooping Rome could bear
A master, nor had virtue to be free.
Hence, for succeeding years, my troubled reign
No certain peace, no spreading prospect knew.
Destruction gather'd round. Still the black soul,
Or of a Catiline, or Rullus *, swell'd
With fell designs ; and all the watchful art
Of Cicero demanded, all the force,
All the state-wielding magic of his tongue ;
And all the thunder of my Cato's zeal.
With these I linger'd ; till the flame anew
Burst out in blaze immense, and wrapt the world.
The shameful contest sprung ; to whom mankind
Should yield the neck : to Pompey, who conceal'd
A rage impatient of an equal name ;
Or to the nobler Cæsar, on whose brow
O'er daring vice deluding virtue smiled,
And who no less a vain superior scorn'd.
Both bled, but bled in vain. New traitors rose.
The venal will be bought, the base have lords.
To these vile wars I left ambitious slaves ;
And from Philippi's field, from where in dust
The last of Romans, matchless Brutus ! lay,
Spread to the north untamed a rapid wing.
What though the first smooth Cæsar's arts caress'd
Merit, and virtue, simulating me ?
Severly tender ! cruelly humane !
The chain to clinch, and make it softer sit
On the new-broken still ferocious state ;
From the dark third †, succeeding, I beheld
The imperial monsters all.—A race on earth
Vindictive, sent the scourge of human-kind !
Whose blind profusion drain'd a bankrupt world ;
Whose lust to forming nature seems disgrace ;
And whose infernal rage bade every drop
Of ancient blood, that yet retain'd my flame,
To that of Pætus ‡, in the peaceful bath,
Or Rome's affrighted streets, inglorious flow.
But almost just the meanly-patient death,
That waits a tyrant's unprevented stroke.
Titus indeed gave one short evening gleam ;
More cordial felt, as in the midst it spread
Of storm, and horror. The delight of men
He who the day, when his o'erflowing hand
Had made no happy heart, concluded lost ;
Trajan and he, with the mild sire and son,§
His son of virtue ! eased awhile mankind ;
And arts revived beneath their gentle beam.
Then was their last effort : what sculpture raised
To Trajan's glory, following triumphs stole ;
And mix'd with Gothic forms (the chisel's shame)
On that triumphal arch *, the forms of Greece.
Meantime o'er rocky Thrace, and the deep vales
Of gelid Hæmus, I pursued my flight ;
And, piercing farthest Scythia, westward swept
Sarmatia †, traversed by a thousand streams :
A sullen land of lakes, and fens immense,
Of rocks, resounding torrents, gloomy heaths,
And cruel desarts black with sounding pine ;
Where nature frowns : though sometimes into smiles
She softens ; and immediate, at the touch
Of southern gales, throws from the sudden glebe
Luxuriant pasture, and a waste of flowers.
But, cold-comprest, when the whole loaded heaven
Descends in snow, lost in one white abrupt,
Lies undistinguish'd earth ; and, seized by frost,
Lakes, headlong streams, and floods, and oceans sleep.
Yet there life glows , the furry millions there
Deep-dig their dens beneath the sheltering snows :
And there a race of men prolific swarms,
To various pain, to little pleasure used ;
On whom, keen-parching, beat Riphæan winds ;
Hard like their soil, and like their climate fierce,
The nursery of nations !—These I roused,
Drove land on land, on people people pour'd ;
Till from almost perpetual night they broke,
As if in search of day ; and o'er the banks
Of yielding empire, only slave-sustain'd,
Resistless raged, in vengeance urged by me.
Long in the barbarous heart the buried seeds
Of freedom lay, for many a wintry age ;
And though my spirit work'd, by slow degrees,
Nought but its pride and fierceness yet appear'd.
Then was the night of time, that parted worlds.
I quitted earth the while. As when the tribes
Aërial, warn'd of rising winter, ride
Autumnal winds, to warmer climates borne ;
So, arts and each good genius in my train,
I cut the closing gloom, and soar'd to heaven.
In the bright regions there of purest day,
Far other scenes, and palaces, arise,
Adorn'd profuse with other arts divine.
All beauty here below, to them compared,
Would, like a rose before the mid-day sun,
Shrink up its blossom ; like a bubble break
The passing poor magnificence of kings.
For there the King of Nature, in full blaze,
Calls every splendour forth ; and there his court
Amid etherial powers, and virtues, holds :
Angel, archangel, tutelary gods
Of cities, nations, empires, and of worlds.
But sacred be the veil, that kindly clouds
A light too keen for mortals ; wraps a view
Too softening fair, for those that here in dust
Must cheerful toil out their appointed years.
A sense of higher life would only damp
The schoolboy's task, and spoil his playful hours.
Nor could the child of reason, feeble man,
With vigour through this infant being drudge ;
Did brighter worlds, their unimagined bliss
Disclosing, dazzle and dissolve his mind.

* Pub. Servilius Rullus, tribune of the people, proposed an Agrarian law, in appearance very advantageous for the people, but destructive of their liberty ; and which was defeated by the eloquence of Cicero, in his speech against Rullus.

† Tiberius.

‡ Thrasea Pætus, put to death by Nero. Tacitus introduces the account he gives of his death thus :—" After having inhumanly slaughtered so many illustrious men, he (Nero) burned at last with a desire of cutting off virtue itself in the person of Thrasea," &c.

§ Antoninus Pius, and his adopted son Marcus Aurelius, afterwards called Antoninus Philosophus.

* Constantine's arch, to build which, that of Trajan was destroyed, sculpture having been then almost entirely lost.

† The ancient Sarmatia contained a vast tract of country running all along the north of Europe and Asia

BRITAIN;

BEING

THE FOURTH PART OF LIBERTY, A POEM.

CONTENTS.

DIFFERENCE betwixt the ancients and moderns slightly touched upon. Description of the dark ages. The Goddess of Liberty, who during these is supposed to have left earth, returns, attended with Arts and Science. She first descends on Italy. Sculpture, painting, and architecture fix at Rome, to revive their several arts by the great models of antiquity there, which many barbarous invasions had not been able to destroy. The revival of these arts marked out. That sometimes arts may flourish for a while under despotic governments, though never the natural and genuine production of them. Learning begins to dawn. The Muse and Science attend Liberty, who in her progress towards Great Britain raises several free states and cities. These enumerated. Author's exclamation of joy, upon seeing the British seas and coasts rise in the vision, which painted whatever the Goddess of Liberty said. She resumes her narration. The Genius of the Deep appears, and, addressing Liberty, associates Great Britain into his dominion. Liberty received and congratulated by Britannia, and the native genii or virtues of the island. These described. Animated by the presence of Liberty, they begin their operations. Their beneficent influence contrasted with the works and delusions of opposing demons. Concludes with an abstract of the English history, marking the several advances of Liberty, down to her complete establishment at the Revolution.

STRUCK with the rising scene, thus I, amazed—
"Ah, goddess, what a change! Is earth the same?
Of the same kind the ruthless race she feeds?
And does the same fair sun and ether spread
Round this vile spot their all-enlivening soul?
Lo! beauty fails; lost in unlovely forms
Of little pomp, magnificence no more
Exalts the mind, and bids the public smile.
While to rapacious interest glory leaves
Mankind, and every grace of life is gone."
  To this the Power, whose vital radiance calls
From the brute mass of man an order'd world:
  Wait till the morning shines, and from the depth
Of Gothic darkness springs another day.
True, genius droops; the tender ancient taste
Of beauty, then fresh-blooming in her prime,
But faintly trembles through the callous soul;
And grandeur, or of morals, or of life,
Sinks into safe pursuits, and creeping cares.
Even cautious virtue seems to stoop her flight,
And aged life to deem the generous deeds
Of youth romantic. Yet in cooler thought
Well reason'd, in researches piercing deep
Through nature's works, in profitable arts,
And all that calm experience can disclose,
(Slow guide, but sure) behold the world anew
Exalted rise, with other honours crown'd;
And where my spirit wakes the finer powers
Athenian laurels still afresh shall bloom.
  Oblivious ages pass'd; while earth forsook
By her best genii, lay to demons foul,
And unchain'd furies, an abandon'd prey.
Contention led the van; first small of size,
But soon dilating to the skies she towers:
Then, wide as air, the livid fury spread,
And high her head above the stormy clouds,
She blazed in omens, swell'd the groaning winds
With wild surmises, battlings, sounds of war:
From land to land the maddening trumpet blew,
And pour'd her venom through the heart of man,
Shook to the pole, the north obey'd her call.
Forth rush'd the bloody power of Gothic war,
War against human-kind: rapine that led
Millions of raging robbers in his train:
Unlistening, barbarous force, to whom the sword
Is reason, honour, law: the foe of arts
By monsters follow'd, hideous to behold,
That claim'd their place. Outrageous mix'd with these
Another species of tyrannic rule*,
Unknown before, whose cankerous shackles seized
The envenom'd soul; a wilder fury, she
Even o'er her elder sister† tyrannized;
Or, if perchance agreed, inflamed her rage.
Dire was her train, and loud: the sable band,
Thundering,—"Submit, ye laity! Ye prophane!
Earth is the Lord's, and therefore ours; let kings
Allow the common claim, and half be theirs;
If not, behold! the sacred lightning flies:"
Scholastic discord, with an hundred tongues,
For science uttering jangling words obscure,
Where frighted reason never yet could dwell:
Of peremptory feature, cleric pride,
Whose reddening cheek no contradiction bears;
And holy slander, his associate firm,
On whom the lying spirit still descends:
Mother of tortures! persecuting zeal,
High-flashing in her hand the ready torch,
Or poniard bathed in unbelieving blood;
Hell's fiercest fiend! of saintly brow demure,
Assuming a celestial seraph's name,
While she, beneath the blasphemous pretence
Of pleasing Parent Heaven, the source of love!
Has wrought more horrors more detested deeds,
Than all the rest combined. Led on by her,

---

* Church power or ecclesiastical tyranny.
† Civil tyranny.

And wild of head to work her fell designs,
Came idiot superstition ; round with ears
Innumerous strow'd, ten thousand monkish forms
With legends plied them, and with tenets, meant
To charm or scare the simple into slaves,
And poison reason ; gross, she swallows all,
The most absurd believing ever most.
Broad o'er the whole her universal night,
The gloom still doubling, ignorance diffused.
  Nought to be seen, but visionary monks
To councils strolling, and embroiling creeds ;
Banditti saints*, disturbing distant lands ;
And unknown nations, wandering for a home.
All lay reversed : the sacred arts of rule
Turn'd to flagitious leagues against mankind,
And arts of plunder more and more avow'd ;
Pure plain devotion to a solemn farce† ;
To holy dotage virtue, even to guile,
To murder, and a mockery of oaths ;
Brave ancient freedom to the rage of slaves‡,
Proud of their state, and fighting for their chains ;
Dishonour'd courage to the bravo's§ trade,
To civil broil ; and glory to romance.
Thus human life unhinged to ruin reel'd,
And giddy reason totter'd on her throne.
  At last Heaven's best inexplicable scheme,
Disclosing, bade new brightening eras smile.
The high command gone forth, arts in my train,
And azure-mantled science, swift we spread
A sounding pinion. Eager pity, mixt
With indignation, urged her downward flight.
On Latium first we stoop'd, for doubtful life
That panted, sunk beneath unnumber'd woes.
Ah poor Italia ! what a bitter cup
Of vengeance hast thou drain'd ? Goths, Vandals,
    Huns,
Lombards, barbarians broke from every land,
How many a ruffian form hast thou beheld ?
What horrid jargons heard, where rage alone
Was all thy frighted ear could comprehend ?
How frequent by the red inhuman hand,
Yet warm with brother's, husband's, father's blood,
Hast thou thy matrons and thy virgins seen
To violation dragg'd, and mingled death ?
What conflagrations, earthquakes, ravage, floods,
Have turn'd thy cities into stony wilds ;
And succourless, and bare, the poor remains
Of wretches forth to nature's common cast ?
Added to these, the still-continued waste
Of inbred foes¶, that on thy vitals prey,
And, double tyrants, seize the very soul.
Where hadst thou treasures for this rapine all ?
These hungry myriads, that thy bowels tore,
Heap'd sack on sack, and buried in their rage
Wonders of art ; whence this grey scene a mine
Of more than gold becomes and orient gems,
Where Egypt, Greece, and Rome united glow.
  Here sculpture, painting, architecture, bent
From ancient models to restore their arts,
Remain'd. A little trace we how they rose.
  Amid the hoary ruins sculpture first,
Deep-digging, from the cavern dark and damp,
Their grave for ages, bid her marble race
Spring to new light. Joy sparkled in her eyes,
And old remembrance thrill'd in every thought,
As she the pleasing resurrection saw.

* Crusades.

† The corruptions of the church of Rome.

‡ Vassalage, whence the attachment of clans to their chief.

§ Duelling.

¶ The Hierarchy.

In leaning site, respiring from his toils,
The well-known hero*, who deliver'd Greece,
His ample chest, all tempested with force,
Unconquerable rear'd. She saw the head,
Breathing the hero, small, of Grecian size,
Scarce more extensive than the sinewy neck,
The spreading shoulders, muscular, and broad ;
The whole a mass of swelling sinews, touch'd
Into harmonious shape ; she saw, and joy'd.
The yellow hunter, Meleager, raised
His beauteous front, and through the finish'd whole
Shows what ideas smiled of old in Greece.
Of raging aspect, rush'd impetuous forth
The gladiator†. Pitiless his look,
And each keen sinew braced, the storm of war,
Ruffling, o'er all his nervous body frowns.
The dying other‡ from the gloom she drew.
Supported on his shorten'd arm he leans,
Prone agonising ; with incumbent fate,
Heavy declines his head ; yet dark beneath
The suffering feature sullen vengeance lowrs,
Shame, indignation, unaccomplish'd rage ;
And still the cheated eye expects his fall.
All conquest-flush'd, from prostrate Python, came
The quiver'd god§. In graceful act he stands,
His arm extended with the slacken'd bow.
Light flows his easy robe, and fair displays
A manly-soften'd form. The bloom of gods
Seems youthful o'er the beardless cheek to wave.
His features yet heroic ardour warms ;
And sweet subsiding to a native smile,
Mix'd with the joy elating conquest gives,
A scatter'd frown exalts his matchless air.
On Flora moved ; her full-proportion'd limbs
Rise through the mantle fluttering in the breeze
The queen of love¶ arose, as from the deep
She sprung in all the melting pomp of charms ;
Bashful she bends, her well-taught look aside
Turns in enchanting guise, where dubious mix
Vain conscious beauty, a dissembled sense
Of modest shame, and slippery looks of love.
The gazer grows enamour'd, and the stone,
As if exulting in its conquest, smiles.
So turn'd each limb, so swell'd with softening art,
That the deluded eye the marble doubts.
At last her utmost masterpiece‖ she found,
That Maro** fired ; the miserable sire,
Wrapt with his sons in fate's severest grasp.
The serpents, twisting round, their stringent folds
Inextricable tie. Such passion here,
Such agonies, such bitterness of pain,
Seem so to tremble through the tortured stone,
That the touch'd heart engrosses all the view.
Almost unmark'd the best proportions pass,
That ever Greece beheld ; and, seen alone,
On the rapt eye the imperious passions seize :
The father's double pangs, both for himself
And sons convulsed ; to heaven his rueful look,
Imploring aid, and half-accusing, cast ;
His fell despair with indignation mix'd,
As the strong-curling monsters from his side
His full-extended fury cannot tear.
More tender touch'd, with varied art, his sons
All the soft rage of younger passions show :
In a boy's helpless fate one sinks oppress'd ;

* The Hercules of Farnese.

† The fighting gladiator.

‡ The dying gladiator.

§ The Apollo of Belvidere.

¶ The Venus of Medici.

‖ The group of Laocoon and his two sons, destroyed by two serpents.

** See Æneid, ii. ver. 199—227.

While, yet unpierced, the frighted other tries
His foot to steal out of the horrid twine.
She bore no more, but straight from Gothic rust
Her chisel clear'd, and dust* and fragments drove
Impetuous round. Successive as it went
From son to son, with more enlivening touch,
From the brute rock, it call'd the breathing form;
Till, in a legislator's awful grace
Dress'd, Buonaroti bid a Moses† rise.
And, looking love immense, a Saviour-God†.
Of these observant, Painting felt the fire
Burn inward Then ecstatic she diffused
The canvass, seized the pallet, with quick hand
The colours brew'd; and on the void expanse
Her gay creation pour'd, her mimic world.
Poor was the manner of her eldest race,
Barren, and dry; just struggling from the taste,
That had for ages scared in cloisters dim
The superstitious herd: yet glorious then
Were deem'd their works; where undevelop'd lay
The future wonders that enrich'd mankind,
And a new light and grace o'er Europe cast.
Arts gradual gather streams. Enlarging this
To each his portion of her various gifts
The goddess dealt, to none indulging all;
No, not to Raphael. At kind distance still
Perfection stands, like happiness, to tempt
The eternal chase. In elegant design
Improving nature; in ideas fair,
Or great, extracted from the fine antique;
In attitude, expression, airs divine;
Her sons of Rome and Florence bore the prize.
To those of Venice she the magic art
Of colours melting into colours gave.
Theirs too it was by one embracing mass
Of light and shade, that settles round the whole,
Or varies tremulous from part to part,
O'er all a binding harmony to throw,
To raise the picture, and repose the sight.
The Lombard school‡ succeeding, mingled both.
Meantime dread fanes and palaces, around,
Rear'd the magnific front. Music again
Her universal language of the heart
Renew'd; and, rising from the plaintive vale,
To the full concert spread, and solemn quire.
Even bigots smiled; to their protection took
Arts not their own, and from them borrow'd pomp:
For in a tyrant's garden these a while
May bloom, though freedom be their parent soil.
And now confest, with gently-growing gleam,
The morning shone, and westward stream'd its
light.
The Muse awoke. Not sooner on the wing
Is the gay bird of dawn. Artless her voice,
Untaught and wild, yet warbling through the woods
Romantic lays. But as her northern course
She, with her tutor science, in my train,
Ardent pursued, her strains more noble grew:
While reason drew the plan, the heart inform'd
The moral page, and fancy lent it grace.
Rome and her circling deserts cast behind,
I pass'd not idle to my great sojourn.
On Arno's§ fertile plain, where the rich vine
Luxuriant o'er Etrurian mountains roves,
Safe in the lap reposed of private bliss,
I small republics* raised. Thrice happy they!
Had social freedom bound their peace, and arts,
Instead of ruling power, ne'er meant for them,
Employ'd their little cares, and saved their fate.
Beyond the rugged Apennines, that roll
Far through Italian bounds their wavy tops,
My path too I with public blessings strow'd;
Free states and cities, where the Lombard plain,
In spite of culture negligent and gross,
From her deep bosom pours unbidden joys,
And green o'er all the land a garden spreads.
The barren rocks themselves beneath my foot,
Relenting bloom'd on the Ligurian shore.
Thick-swarming people† there like emmets, seized,
Amid surrounding cliffs, the scatter'd spots
Which nature left in her destroying rage‡,
Made their own fields, nor sigh'd for other lands.
There, in white prospect, from the rocky hill
Gradual descending to the shelter'd shore,
By me proud Genoa's marble turrets rose.
And while my genuine spirit warm'd her sons,
Beneath her Dorias, not unworthy, she
Vied for the trident of the narrow seas,
Ere Britain yet had open'd all the main.
Nor be the then triumphant state§ forgot;
Where¶, push'd from plunder'd earth, a remnant
still,
Inspired by me, through the dark ages kept
Of my old Roman flame some sparks alive:
The seeming god-built city! which my hand
Deep in the bosom fix'd of wondering seas.
Astonish'd mortals sail'd, with pleasing awe,
Around the sea-girt walls, by Neptune fenced,
And down the briny street; where on each hand,
Amazing seen amid unstable waves,
The splendid palace shines; and rising tides,
The green steps marking, murmur at the door.
To this fair queen of Adria's stormy gulf,
The mart of nations! long, obedient seas
Roll'd all the treasure of the radiant east.
But now no more. Than one great tyrant worse
(Whose shared oppression lightens, as diffused)
Each subject tearing, many tyrants rose;
The least the proudest. Join'd in dark cabal,
They jealous, watchful, silent, and severe,
Cast o'er the whole indissoluble chains:
The softer shackles of luxurious ease
They likewise added, to secure their sway.
Thus Venice fainter shines; and commerce thus,
Of toil impatient, flags the drooping sail.
Bursting, besides, his ancient bounds, he took
A larger circle‖; found another seat**,

* It is reported of Michael Angelo Buonaroti, the most celebrated master of modern sculpture, that he wrought with a kind of inspiration, or enthusiastical fury, which produced the effect here mentioned.

† Esteemed the two finest pieces of modern sculpture.

‡ The school of the Caracci.

§ The river Arno runs through Florence.

* The republics of Florence, Pisa, Lucca, and Sienna. They formerly have had very cruel wars together, but are now all peaceably subject to the great duke of Tuscany, except it be Lucca, which still maintains the form of a republic.

† The Genoese territory is reckoned very populous, but the towns and villages for the most part lie hid among the Apennine rocks and mountains.

‡ According to Dr Burnet's system of the deluge.

§ Venice was the most flourishing city in Europe, with regard to trade, before the passage to the East Indies by the Cape of Good Hope, and America, were discovered.

¶ Those who fled to some marshes in the Adriatic gulf, from the desolation spread over Italy by an irruption of the Huns, first founded there this famous city, about the beginning of the fifth century.

‖ The main ocean. ** Great Britain.

Opening a thousand ports, and, charm'd with toil,
Whom nothing can dismay, far other sons.
The mountains then, clad with eternal snow,
Confess'd my power. Deep as the rampant rocks,
By nature thrown insuperable round,
I planted there a league of friendly states*,
And bade plain freedom their ambition be.
There in the vale, where rural plenty fills,
From lakes, and meads, and furrow'd fields, her horn,
Chief, where the Leman† pure emits the Rhone,
Rare to be seen! unguilty cities rise,
Cities of brothers form'd; while equal life,
Accorded gracious with revolving power,
Maintains them free; and, in their happy streets,
Nor cruel deed, nor misery, is known.
For valour, faith, and innocence of life,
Renown'd, a rough laborious people, there,
Not only give the dreadful Alps to smile,
And press their culture on retiring snows;
But, to firm order train'd and patient war,
They likewise know, beyond the nerve remiss
Of mercenary force, how to defend
The tasteful little their hard toil has earn'd,
And the proud arm of Bourbon to defy.
Even, cheer'd by me, their shaggy mountains charm,
More than or Gallic or Italian plains:
And sickening fancy oft, when absent long,
Pines to behold their Alpine views again‡:
The hollow-winding stream: the vale, fair-spread
Amid an amphitheatre of hills;
Whence, vapour-wing'd, the sudden tempest springs:
From steep to steep ascending, the gay train
Of fogs, thick-roll'd into romantic shapes:
The flitting cloud, against the summit dash'd;
And, by the sun illumined, pouring bright
A gemmy shower: hung o'er amazing rocks,
The mountain ash, and solemn-sounding pine:
The snow-fed torrent, in white mazes tost,
Down to the clear etherial lake below:
And, high o'er-topping all the broken scene,
The mountain fading into sky; where shines
On winter winter shivering, and whose top
Licks from their cloudy magazine the snows.
From these descending, as I waved my course
O'er vast Germania, the ferocious nurse
Of hardy men and hearts affronting death,
I gave some favour'd cities§ there to lift
A nobler brow, and through their swarming streets,
More busy, wealthy, cheerful, and alive,
In each contented face to look my soul.
Thence the loud Baltic passing, black with storm,
To wintry Scandinavia's utmost bound;
There, I the manly race¶, the parent-hive
Of the mix'd kingdoms, form'd into a state
More regularly free.* By keener air
Their genius purged, and temper'd hard by frost,
Tempest and toil their nerves, the sons of those
Whose only terror was a bloodless death‖,
They wise and dauntless, still sustain my cause.
Yet there I fix'd not. Turning to the south,
The whispering zephyrs sigh'd at my delay.
Here, with the shifted vision, burst my joy.
"O the dear prospect! O majestic view!
See Britain's empire! Lo! the watery vast
Wide-waves, diffusing the cerulean plain.
And now, methinks, like clouds at distance seen,
Emerging white from deeps of ether, dawn
My kindred cliffs; whence, wafted in the gale,
Ineffable, a secret sweetness breathes.
Goddess, forgive!—My heart, surprised, o'erflows
With filial fondness for the land you bless."
As parents to a child complacent deign
Approvance, the celestial brightness smiled;
Then thus—As o'er the wave-resounding deep,
To my near reign, the happy isle, I steer'd
With easy wing; behold! from surge to surge,
Stalk'd the tremendous Genius of the Deep.
Around him clouds, in mingled tempest, hung;
Thick-flashing meteors crown'd his starry head;
And ready thunder redden'd in his hand,
Or from it stream'd compress the gloomy cloud.
Where'er he look'd, the trembling waves recoil'd.
He needs but strike the conscious flood, and shook
From shore to shore, in agitation dire,
It works his dreadful will. To me his voice
(Like that hoarse blast that round the cavern howls,
Mix'd with the murmurs of the falling main)
Address'd, began—"By fate commission'd, go,
My sister-goddess now, to yon blest Isle,
Henceforth the partner of my rough domain.
All my dread walks to Britons open lie.
Those that refulgent, or with rosy morn,
Or yellow evening, flame; those that, profuse
Drunk by equator-suns, severely shine;
Or those that, to the poles approaching, rise
In billows rolling into Alps of ice.
Even, yet untouch'd by daring keel, be theirs
The vast Pacific; that on other worlds,
Their future conquest, rolls resounding tides.
Long I maintain'd inviolate my reign;
Nor Alexanders me, nor Cæsars braved.
Still, in the crook of shore, the coward sail
Till now low-crept; and peddling commerce plied
Between near-joining lands. For Britons, chief,
It was reserved, with star-directed prow,
To dare the middle deep, and drive assured
To distant nations through the pathless main.
Chief, for their fearless hearts the glory waits,
Long months from land while the black stormy night
Around them rages, on the groaning mast
With unshook knee to know their giddy way;
To sing, unquell'd, amid the lashing wave;
To laugh at danger. Theirs the triumph be,
By deep invention's keen pervading eye,
The heart of courage, and the hand of toil,
Each conquer'd ocean staining with their blood,
Instead of treasure robb'd by ruffian war,
Round social earth to circle fair exchange,
And bind the nations in a golden chain.
To these I honour'd stoop. Rushing to light
A race of men behold! whose daring deeds
Will in renown exalt my nameless plains
O'er those of fabling earth, as hers to mine
In terror yield. Nay, could my savage heart
Such glories check, their unsubmitting soul
Would all my fury brave, my tempest climb,
And might in spite of me my kingdom force."
Here, waiting no reply, the shadowy power

* The Swiss cantons.

† Geneva, situated on the Lacus Lemanus, a small state, but noble example of the blessings of civil and religious liberty.

‡ The Swiss, after having been long absent from their native country, are seized with such a violent desire of seeing it again, as affects them with a kind of languishing indisposition, called the Swiss sickness.

§ The Hans Towns. ¶ The Swedes.

‖ See page 386, col. 2, note**.

Eased the dark sky, and to the deeps return'd :
While the loud thunder rattling from his hand,
Auspicious, shook opponent Gallia's shore.
  Of this encounter glad, my way to land
I quick pursued, that from the smiling sea
Received me joyous Loud acclaims were heard,
And music, more than mortal, warbling, fill'd
With pleased astonishment the labouring hind,
Who for a while the unfinish'd furrow left,
And let the listening steer forget his toil.
Unseen by grosser eye, Britannia breathed,
And her aërial train, these sounds of joy;
For of old time, since first the rushing flood,
Urged by Almighty Power, this favour'd isle
Turu'd flashing from the continent aside,
Indented shore to shore responsive still,
Its guardian she—the goddess, whose staid eye
Beams the dark azure of the doubtful dawn.
Her tresses, like a flood of soften'd light
Through clouds imbrown'd, in waving circles play.
Warm on her cheek sits beauty's brightest rose.
Of high demeanour, stately, shedding grace
With every motion. Full her rising chest;
And new ideas, from her finish'd shape,
Charm'd sculpture taking might improve her art.
Such the fair guardian of an isle that boasts,
Profuse as vernal blooms, the fairest dames.
High-shining on the promontory's brow,
Awaiting me, she stood ; with hope inflamed,
By my mix'd spirit burning in her sons,
To firm, to polish, and exalt the state.
  The native genii, round her, radiant smiled.
Courage, of soft deportment, aspect calm,
Unboastful, suffering long, and, till provoked,
As mild and harmless as the sporting child ;
But, on just reason, once his fury roused,
No lion springs more eager to his prey :
Blood is a pastime; and his heart, elate,
Knows no depressing fear. That virtue known
By the relenting look, whose equal heart
For others feels, as for another self :
Of various name, as various objects wake,
Warm into action, the kind sense within :
Whether the blameless poor, the nobly maim'd,
The lost to reason, the declined in life,
The helpless young that kiss no mother's hand,
And the grey second infancy of age,
She gives in public families to live,
A sight to gladden Heaven ! whether she stands
Fair beckoning at the hospitable gate,
And bids the stranger take repose and joy :
Whether, to solace honest labour, she
Rejoices those that make the land rejoice :
Or whether to philosophy, and arts,
(At once the basis and the finish'd pride
Of government and life) she spreads her hand ;
Nor knows her gift profuse, nor seems to know,
Doubling her bounty, that she gives at all.
Justice to these her awful presence join'd,
The mother of the state! No low revenge,
No turbid passions in her breast ferment :
Tender, serene, compassionate of vice,
As the last woe that can afflict mankind,
She punishment awards ; yet of the good
More piteous still, and of the suffering whole,
Awards it firm. So fair her just decree,
That, in his judging peers, each on himself
Pronounces his own doom. O happy land !
Which reigns alone this justice of the free !
And one bright group sincerity his front,
Diffusive, rear'd ; his pure untroubled eye
The fount of truth. The thoughtful power apart,
Now, pensive, cast on earth his fix'd regard,
Now, touch'd celestial, launch'd it on the sky.
The genius he whence Britain shines supreme,
The land of light, and rectitude of mind.
He too the fire of fancy feeds intense,
With all the train of passions thence derived :
Not kindling quick, a noisy transient blaze,
But gradual, silent, lasting, and profound.
Near him retirement, pointing to the shade,
And independence stood : the generous pair,
That simple life, the quiet-whispering grove,
And the still raptures of the free-born soul,
To cates prefer by virtue bought, not earn'd,
Proudly prefer them to the servile pomp,
And to the heart-embitter'd joys of slaves.
Or should the latter, to the public scene
Demanded, quit his sylvan friend awhile ;
Nought can his firmness shake, nothing seduce
His zeal, still active for the common-weal ;
Nor stormy tyrants, nor corruption's tools,
Foul ministers, dark-working by the force
Of secret-sapping gold. All their vile arts,
Their shameful honours, their perfidious gifts,
He greatly scorns ; and, if he must betray
His plunder'd country, or his power resign,
A moment's parley were eternal shame :
Illustrious into private life again,
From dirty levees he unstain'd ascends,
And firm in senates stands the patriot's ground,
Or draws new vigour in the peaceful shade.
Aloof the bashful virtue hover'd coy,
Proving by sweet distrust distrusted worth.
Rough labour closed the train : and in his hand
Rude, callous, sinew-swell'd, and black with toil,
Came manly indignation. Sour he seems,
And more than seems, by lawless pride assail'd ;
Yet kind at heart, and just, and generous, there
No vengeance lurks, no pale insidious gall :
Even in the very luxury of rage,
He softening can forgive a gallant foe ;
The nerve, support, and glory of the land !
Nor be religion, rational, and free,
Here pass'd in silence ; whose enraptured eye
Sees heaven with earth connected, human things
Link'd to divine : who not from servile fear,
By rites for some weak tyrant incense fit,
The God of Love adores, but from a heart
Effusing gladness, into pleasing awe
That now astonish'd swells, now in a calm
Of fearless confidence that smiles serene ;
That lives devotion, one continual hymn,
And then most grateful, when Heaven's bounty most
Is right enjoy'd. This ever-cheerful power
O'er the raised circle ray'd superior day.
  I joy'd to join the virtues whence my reign
O'er Albion was to rise. Each cheering each,
And, like the circling planets from the sun,
All borrowing beams from me, a heighten'd zeal
Impatient fired us to commence our toils,
Or pleasures rather. Long the pungent time
Pass'd not in mutual hails ; but, through the land
Darting our light, we shone the fogs away.
  The virtues conquer with a single look.
Such grace, such beauty, such victorious light,
Live in their presence, stream in every glance,
That the soul won, enamour'd, and refined,
Grows their own image, pure ethereal flame.
Hence the foul demons, that oppose our reign,

Would still from us deluded mortals wrap;
Or in gross shades they drown the visual ray,
Or by the fogs of prejudice, where mix'd
Falsehood and truth confounded, foil the sense
With vain refracted images of bliss.
But chief around the court of flatter'd kings
They roll the dusky rampart, wall o'er wall
Of darkness pile, and with their thickest shade
Secure the throne. No savage Alp, the den
Of wolves, and bears, the monstrous things obscene,
That vex the swain, and waste the country round,
Protected lies beneath a deeper cloud.
Yet there we sometimes send a searching ray.
As, at the sacred opening of the morn,
The prowling race retire; so, pierced severe,
Before our potent blaze these demons fly,
And all their works dissolve—The whisper'd tale,
That, like the fabling Nile, no fountain knows;
Fair-faced deceit, whose wily conscious eye
Ne'er looks direct; the tongue that licks the dust,
But, when it safely dares, as prompt to sting;
Smooth crocodile destruction, whose fell tears
Ensnare; the Janus face of courtly pride;
One to superiors heaves submissive eyes,
On hapless worth the other scowls disdain;
Cheeks that for some weak tenderness alone,
Some virtuous slip, can wear a blush; the laugh
Profane, when midnight bowls disclose the heart,
At starving virtue, and at virtue's fools;
Determined to be broke, the plighted faith;
Nay more, the godless oath, that knows no ties;
Soft buzzing slander; silky moths, that eat
An honest name; the harpy hand, and maw,
Of avaricious luxury; who makes
The throne his shelter, venal laws his fort,
And, by his service, who betrays his king.
Now turn your view, and mark from Celtic * night
To present grandeur how my Britain rose.
Bold were those Britons, who, the careless sons
Of nature, roam'd the forest-bounds, at once
Their verdant city, high-embowering fane,
And the gay circle of their woodland wars:
For by the Druid † taught, that death but shifts
The vital scene, they that prime fear despised;
And, prone to rush on steel, disdain'd to spare
An ill-saved life that must again return.
Erect from nature's hand, by tyrant force,
And still more tyrant custom, unsubdued,
Man knows no master save creating Heaven,
Or such as choice and common good ordain.
This general sense, with which the nations I
Promiscuous fire, in Britons burn'd intense,
Of future times prophetic. Witness, Rome
Who saw'st thy Cæsar, from the naked land,
Whose only fort was British hearts, repell'd,
To seek Pharsalian wreaths. Witness, the toil,
The blood of ages, bootless to secure,
Beneath an empire's ‡ yoke, a stubborn isle,
Disputed hard, and never quite subdued. [scorn'd
The north || remain'd untouch'd, where those who
To stoop retired; and, to their keen effort
Yielding at last, recoil'd the Roman power.
In vain, unable to sustain the shock,

* Great Britain was peopled by the Celtæ or Gauls.

† The Druids, among the ancient Gauls and Britons, had the care and direction of all religious matters.

‡ The Roman empire.

|| Caledonia, inhabited by the Scots and Picts; whither a great many Britons, who would not submit to the Romans, retired.

From sea to sea desponding legions raised
The wall * immense, and yet, on summer's eve,
While sport his lambkins round, the shepherd's gaze
Continual o'er it burst the northern storm†,
As often, check'd, receded; threatening hoarse
A swift return. But the devouring flood
No more endured control, when, to support
The last remains of empire ‡, was recall'd
The weary Roman, and the Briton lay
Unnerved, exhausted, spiritless, and sunk.
Great proof! how men enfeeble into slaves.
The sword behind him flash'd; before him roar'd,
Deaf to his woes, the deep ||. Forlorn, around
He roll'd his eye, not sparkling ardent flame,
As when Caractacus§ to battle led
Silurian swains, and Boadicea¶ taught
Her raging troops the miseries of slaves.
Then (sad relief!) from the bleak coast, that hears
The German Ocean roar, deep-blooming, strong,
And yellow-hair'd, the blue-eyed Saxon came.
He came implored, but came with other aim
Than to protect. For conquest and defence
Suffices the same arm. With the fierce race
Pour'd in a fresh invigorating stream,
Blood, where unquell'd a mighty spirit glow'd.
Rash war, and perilous battle, their delight;
And immature, and red with glorious wounds,
Unpeaceful death their choice**: deriving thence
A right to feast, and drain immortal bowls,
In Odin's hall; whose blazing roof resounds
The genial uproar of those shades, who fall
In desperate fight, or by some brave attempt;
And though more polish'd times the martial creed
Disown, yet still the fearless habit lives.

* The wall of Severus, built upon Adrian's rampart, which ran for eighty miles quite across the country, from the mouth of the Tyne to Solway Frith.

† Irruptions of the Scots and Picts.

‡ The Roman empire being miserably torn by the northern nations, Britain was for ever abandoned by the Romans in the year 426 or 427.

|| The Britons applying to Ætius the Roman general for assistance, thus expressed their miserable condition:—"We know not which way to turn us. The barbarians drive us to sea, and the sea forces us back to the barbarians; between which we have only the choice of two deaths, either to be swallowed up by the waves, or butchered by the sword."

§ King of the Silures, famous for his great exploits, and accounted the best general Great Britain had ever produced. The Silures were esteemed the bravest and most powerful of all the Britons: they inhabited Herefordshire, Radnorshire, Brecknockshire, Monmouthshire, and Glamorganshire.

¶ Queen of the Iceni: her story is well known.

** It is certain, that an opinion was fixed and general among them (the Goths), that death was but the entrance into another life; that all men who lived lazy and unactive lives, and died natural deaths, by sickness or by age, went into vast caves under ground, all dark and miry, full of noisome creatures usual to such places, and there for ever groveled in endless stench and misery. On the contrary, all who gave themselves to warlike actions and enterprises, to the conquest of their neighbours and the slaughter of their enemies, and died in battle, or of violent deaths upon bold adventures or resolutions, went immediately to the vast hall or palace of Odin, their god of war, who eternally kept open house for all such guests, where they were entertained at infinite tables, in perpetual feasts and mirth, carousing in bowls made of the skulls of their enemies they had slain: according to the number of whom, every one in these mansions of pleasure was the most honoured and best entertained.

SIR WILLIAM TEMPLE's *Essay on Heroic Virtue.*

Nor were the surly gifts of war their all.
Wisdom was likewise theirs, indulgent laws,
The calm gradations of art-nursing peace,
And matchless orders, the deep basis still
On which ascends my British reign. Untamed
To the refining subtleties of slaves,
They brought an happy government along!
Form'd by that freedom, which, with secret voice,
Impartial nature teaches all her sons,
And which of old through the whole Scythian mass
I strong inspired. Monarchical their state,
But prudently confined, and mingled wise
Of each harmonious power: only, too much,
Imperious war into their rule infused,
Prevail'd their general-king, and chieftain-thanes.
In many a field, by civil fury stain'd,
Bled the discordant Heptarchy *; and long
(Educing good from ill) the battle groan'd:
Ere, blood-cemented, Anglo-Saxons saw
Egbert † and peace on one united throne.
No sooner dawn'd the fair-disclosing calm
Of brighter days, when lo! the north anew,
With stormy nations black, on England pour'd
Woes the severest e'er a people felt.
The Danish Raven ‡, lured by annual prey,
Hung o'er the land incessant. Fleet on fleet
Of barbarous pirates unremitting tore
The miserable coast. Before them stalk'd,
Far seen, the demon of devouring flame;
Rapine, and murder, all with blood besmear'd,
Without or ear, or eye, or feeling heart;
While close behind them march'd the sallow power
Of desolating famine, who delights
In grass-grown cities, and in desert fields;
And purple-spotted pestilence, by whom
Even friendship scared, in sickening horror sinks
Each social sense and tenderness of life.
Fixing at last, the sanguinary race
Spread, from the Humber's loud-resounding shore,
To where the Thames devolves his gentle maze,
And with superior arm the Saxon awed.
But superstition first, and monkish dreams,
And monk-directed cloister-seeking kings,
Had ate away his vigour, ate away
His edge of courage, and depress'd the soul
Of conquering freedom, which he once respired.
Thus cruel ages pass'd; and rare appear'd
White-mantled peace, exulting o'er the vale,
As when, with Alfred §, from the wilds she came
To policed cities and protected plains.
Thus by degrees the Saxon empire sunk,
Then set entire in Hastings' ‖ bloody field.
Compendious war! (on Britain's glory bent
So fate ordain'd) in that decisive day,
The haughty Norman seized at once an isle,
For which, through many a century, in vain,
The Roman, Saxon, Dane, had toil'd and bled.
Of Gothic nations this the final burst;
And, mix'd the genius of these people all,
Their virtues mix'd in one exalted stream,
Here the rich tide of English blood grew full.
Awhile my spirit slept; the land a while,
Affrighted, droop'd beneath despotic rage.
Instead of Edward's equal gentle laws*,
The furious victor's partial will prevail'd.
All prostrate lay; and, in the secret shade,
Deep-stung but fearful indignation gnash'd
His teeth. Of freedom, property, despoil'd,
And of their bulwark, arms; with castles crush'd,
With ruffians quarter'd o'er the bridled land;
The shivering wretches at the curfew † sound,
Dejected shrunk into their sordid beds,
And, through the mournful gloom, of ancient times
Mused sad, or dreamt of better. Even to feed
A tyrant's idle sport the peasant starved:
To the wild herd, the pasture of the tame,
The cheerful hamlet, spiry town, was given,
And the brown forest ‡ roughen'd wide around.
But this so dead, so vile submission, long
Endured not. Gathering force, my gradual flame
Shook off the mountain of tyrannic sway.
Unused to bend, impatient of control,
Tyrants themselves the common tyrant check'd.
The church, by kings intractable and fierce,
Denied her portion of the plunder'd state,
Or tempted, by the timorous and weak,
To gain new ground, first taught their rapine law.
The Barons next a nobler league began,
Both those of English and of Norman race
In one fraternal nation blended now,
The nation of the free! press'd by a band
Of patriots §, ardent as the summer's noon
That looks delighted on, the tyrant see!
Mark! how with feign'd alacrity he bears
His strong reluctance down, his dark revenge,
And gives the Charter, by which life indeed
Becomes of price, a glory to be man. [affirm'd,
Through this and through succeeding reigns
These long-contested rights, the wholesome winds
Of opposition ‖ hence began to blow,
And often since have lent the country life.
Before their breath corruption's insect-blights,
The darkening clouds of evil counsel, fly;
Or should they sounding swell, a putrid court,
A pestilential ministry, they purge,
And ventilated states renew their bloom.
Though with the temper'd monarchy here mix'd
Aristocratic sway, the people still,

* The seven kingdoms of the Anglo-Saxons, considered as being united into one common government, under a general in chief or monarch, and by the means of an assembly-general, or Wittenagemot.

† Egbert king of Wessex, who, after having reduced all the other kingdoms of the Heptarchy under his dominion, was the first king of England.

‡ A famous Danish standard was called Reafan, or Raven. The Danes imagined that, before a battle, the Raven wrought upon this standard clapt its wings or hung down its head, in token of victory or defeat.

§ Alfred the Great, renowned in war, and no less famous in peace for his many excellent institutions, particularly that of juries.

‖ The battle of Hastings, in which Harold II. the last of the Saxon kings, was slain, and William the Conqueror made himself master of England.

* Edward III. the Confessor, who reduced the West-Saxon, Mercian, and Danish laws into one body; which from that time became common to all England, under the name of the Laws of Edward.

† The curfew bell (from the French *couvre-feu*), which was rung every night at eight of the clock, to warn the English to put out their fires and candles, under the penalty of a severe fine.

‡ The New Forest in Hampshire; to make which, the country for above thirty miles in compass was laid waste.

§ On the 5th of June 1215, king John, met by the barons on Runnemede, signed the great charter of liberties, or Magna Charta.

‖ The league formed by the barons, during the reign of John, in the year 1213, was the first confederacy made in England, in defence of the nation's interest, against the king.

Flatter'd by this or that, as interest lean'd,
No full protection knew. For me reserved,
And for my commons, was that glorious turn.
They crown'd my first attempt, in senates * rose
The fort of freedom ! Slow till then, alone,
Had work'd that general liberty, that soul
Which generous nature breathes, and which, when left
By me to bondage was corrupted Rome,
I through the northern nations wide diffused.
Hence many a people, fierce with freedom, rush'd
From the rude iron regions of the north,
To Libyan deserts swarm protruding swarm ;
And pour'd new spirit through a slavish world.
Yet, o'er these Gothic states, the king and chiefs
Retain'd the high prerogative of war,
And with enormous property engross'd
The mingled power. But on Britannia's shore
Now present, I to raise my reign began
By raising the democracy, the third
And broadest bulwark of the guarded state.
Then was the full, the perfect plan disclosed
Of Britain's matchless constitution, mix'd
Of mutual checking and supporting powers,
King, Lords, and Commons ; nor the name of free
Deserving, while the vassal-many droop'd :
For since the moment of the whole they form,
So, as depress'd or raised, the balance they
Of public welfare and of glory cast.
Mark, from this period, the continual proof.
When kings of narrow genius, minion-rid,
Neglecting faithful worth for fawning slaves ;
Proudly regardless of their people's plaints,
And poorly passive of insulting foes ;
Double, not prudent ; obstinate, not firm ;
Their mercy, fear ; necessity their faith ;
Instead of generous fire, presumptuous, hot ;
Rash to resolve, and slothful to perform ;
Tyrants at once, and slaves ; imperious, mean ;
To want rapacious joining shameful waste ;
By counsels weak and wicked, easy roused
To paltry schemes of absolute command ;
To seek their splendour in their sure disgrace ;
And in a broken ruin'd people, wealth :
When such o'ercast the state, no bond of love,
No heart, no soul, no unity, no nerve,
Combined the loose disjointed public, lost
To fame abroad, to happiness at home.
But when an Edward † and an Henry ‡ breathed
Through the charm'd whole one all-exerting soul :
Drawn sympathetic from his dark retreat,
When wide-attracted merit round them glow'd :
When counsels just, extensive, generous, firm,
Amid the maze of state, determined kept
Some ruling point in view : when, on the stock
Of public good and glory grafted, spread
Their palms, their laurels; or, if thence they stray'd,
Swift to return, and patient of restraint :
When regal state, pre-eminence of place,
They scorn'd to deem pre-eminence of ease,
To be luxurious drones, that only rob
The busy hive : as in distinction, power,
Indulgence, honour, and advantage, first ;
When they too claim'd in virtue, danger, toil,
Superior rank ; with equal hand, prepared
To guard the subject, and to quell the foe :
When such with me their vital influence shed,
No mutter'd grievance, hopeless sigh, was heard ;
No foul distrust through wary senates ran,
Confined their bounty, and their ardour quench'd :
On aid, unquestion'd, liberal aid was given .
Safe in their conduct, by their valour fired,
Fond where they led, victorious armies rush'd ;
And Cressy, Poitiers, Agincourt * proclaim
What kings supported by almighty love,
And people fired with liberty, can do.
Be veil'd the savage reigns †, when kindred rage
The numerous-once Plantagenets devour'd,
A race to vengeance vow'd ! and when, oppress'd
By private feuds, almost extinguish'd lay
My quivering flame. But, in the next, behold !
A cautious tyrant ‡ lend it oil anew.
Proud, dark, suspicious, brooding o'er his gold,
As how to fix his throne he jealous cast
His crafty views around ; pierced with a ray,
Which on his timid mind I darted full,
He mark'd the barons of excessive sway,
At pleasure making and unmaking kings § ;
And hence, to crush these petty tyrants, plann'd
A law ¶, that let them, by the silent waste
Of luxury, their landed wealth diffuse,
And with that wealth their implicated power.
By soft degrees a mighty change ensued,
Even working to this day. With streams, deduced
From these diminish'd floods, the country smiled :
As when impetuous from the snow-heap'd Alps,
To vernal suns relenting, pours the Rhine ;
While undivided, oft, with wasteful sweep,
He foams along ; but, through Batavian meads,
Branch'd into fair canals, indulgent flows ;
Waters a thousand fields ; and culture, trade,
Towns, meadows, gliding ships, and villas mix'd,
A rich, a wondrous landskip, rises round.
His furious son || the soul-enslaving chain **
Which many a doating venerable age
Had link by link strong-twisted round the land,
Shook off. No longer could be borne a power,
From Heaven pretended, to deceive, to void
Each solemn tie, to plunder without bounds,
To curb the generous soul, to fool mankind ;
And, wild at last, to plunge into a sea
Of blood and horror. The returning light,
That first through Wickliff †† streak'd the priestly gloom,
Now burst in open day. Bared to the blaze,
Forth from the haunts of superstition ‡‡ crawl'd
Her motley sons, fantastic figures all ;

* The commons are generally thought to have been first represented in parliament towards the end of Henry the Third's reign. To a parliament called in the year 1264, each county was ordered to send four knights, as representatives of their respective shires: and to a parliament called in the year following, each county was ordered to send, as their representatives, two knights ; and each city and borough, as many citizens and burgesses. Till then, history makes no mention of them ; whence a very strong argument may be drawn, to fix the original of the house of commons to that era.

† Edward III. ‡ Henry V.

* Three famous battles, gained by the English over the French.

† During the civil wars betwixt the families of York and Lancaster.

‡ Henry VII.

§ The famous earl of Warwick, during the reigns of Henry VI. and Edward IV., was called the king-maker.

¶ Permitting the barons to alienate their lands.

|| Henry VIII. ** Of papal dominion.

†† John Wickliff, doctor of divinity, who towards the close of the fourteenth century published doctrines very contrary to those of the Church of Rome, and particularly denying the papal authority. His followers grew very numerous, and were called Lollards.

‡‡ Suppression of monasteries.

And, wide-dispersed, their useless fetid wealth
In graceful labour bloom'd, and fruits of peace.
Trade, join'd to these, on every sea display'd
A daring canvass, pour'd with every tide
A golden flood. From other worlds * were roll'd
The guilty glittering stores, whose fatal charms,
By the plain Indian happily despised,
Yet work'd his woe; and to the blissful groves,
Where nature lived herself among her sons,
And innocence and joy for ever dwelt,
Drew rage unknown to Pagan climes before,
The worst, the zeal-inflamed barbarian drew.
Be no such horrid commerce, Britain, thine!
But want for want, with mutual aid, supply.
The commons thus enrich'd, and powerful grown,
Against the barons weigh'd. Eliza then,
Amid these doubtful motions steady, gave
The beam to fix. She! like the Secret Eye
That never closes on a guarded world,
So sought, so mark'd, so seized the public good,
That self-supported, without one ally,
She awed her inward, quell'd her circling, foes.
Inspired by me, beneath her sheltering arm,
In spite of raging universal sway †,
And raging seas repress'd, the Belgic states,
My bulwark on the continent, arose.
Matchless in all the spirit of her days!
With confidence unbounded, fearless love
Elate, her fervent people waited gay,
Cheerful demanded the long-threaten'd fleet‡,
And dash'd the pride of Spain around their isle.
Nor ceased the British thunder here to rage:
The deep, reclaim'd, obey'd its awful call;
In fire and smoke Iberian ports involved,
The trembling foe, even to the centre shook
Of their new-conquer'd world, and skulking stole,
By veering winds, their Indian treasure home.
Meantime, peace, plenty, justice, science, arts,
With softer laurels crown'd her happy reign.
As yet uncircumscribed the regal power,
And wild and vague prerogative remain'd
A wide voracious gulf, where swallow'd oft
The helpless subject lay. This to reduce
To the just limit was my great effort.
By means, that evil seem to narrow man,
Superior beings work their mystic will:
From storm and trouble thus a settled calm,
At last, effulgent o'er Britannia smiled.
The gathering tempest, heaven-commission'd, came,
Came in the Prince§, who, drunk with flattery, [dreamt
His vain pacific counsels ruled the world;
Though scorn'd abroad, bewilder'd in a maze
Of fruitless treaties; while at home enslaved,
And by a worthless crew insatiate drain'd,
He lost his people's confidence and love:
Irreparable loss! whence crowns become
An anxious burden. Years inglorious pass'd:
Triumphant Spain the vengeful draught enjoy'd:
Abandon'd Frederick‖ pined, and Raleigh bled.
But nothing that to these internal broils,
That rancour, he began; while lawless sway,
He, with his slavish doctors, tried to rear
On metaphysic, on enchanted ground*,
And all the mazy quibbles of the schools:
As if for one, and sometimes for the worst,
Heaven had mankind in vengeance only made.
Vain the pretence! not so the dire effect,
The fierce, the foolish discord† thence derived,
That tears the country still, by party-rage
And ministerial clamour kept alive.
In action weak, and for the wordy war
Best fitted, faint this prince pursued his claim:
Content to teach the subject-herd, how great,
How sacred he! how despicable they!
But his unyielding son‡ those doctrines drank,
With all a bigot's rage (who never damps
By reasoning his fire;) and what they taught,
Warm and tenacious, into practice push'd.
Senates, in vain, their kind restraint applied:
The more they struggled to support the laws,
His justice-dreading ministers the more
Drove him beyond their bounds. Tired with the check
Of faithful love, and with the flattery pleased
Of false designing guilt, the fountain§ he
Of public wisdom and of justice shut.
Wide mourn'd the land. Straight to the voted aid,
Free, cordial, large, of never failing source,
The illegal imposition follow'd harsh,
With execration given, or ruthless squeezed
From an insulted people, by a band
Of the worst ruffians, those of tyrant power.
Oppression walk'd at large, and pour'd abroad
Her unrelenting train: informers, spies,
Blood-hounds, that sturdy freedom to the grove
Pursue; projectors of aggrieving schemes,
Commerce‖ to load for unprotected seas,
To sell the starving many to the few,¶
And drain a thousand ways the exhausted land.
Even from that place, whence healing peace should [flow,
And gospel truth, inhuman bigots shed
Their poison** round; and on the venal bench,
Instead of justice, party held the scale,
And violence the sword. Afflicted years,
Too patient, felt at last their vengeance full.
'Mid the low murmurs of submissive fear
And mingled rage, my Hambden raised his voice
And to the laws appeal'd; the laws no more
In judgment sat, behoved some other ear:
When instant from the keen resentive north,
By long oppression, by religion roused,
The guardian army came. Beneath its wing
Was call'd, though meant to furnish hostile aid,
The more than Roman senate. There a flame
Broke out, that clear'd, consumed, renew'd the land,
In deep emotion hurl'd, nor Greece, nor Rome,
Indignant bursting from a tyrant's chain,
While, full of me, each agitated soul
Strung every nerve and flamed in every eye,
Had e'er beheld such light and heat combined!
Such heads and hearts! such dreadful zeal, led on

* The Spanish West Indies.

† The dominion of the house of Austria.

‡ The Spanish Armada. Rapin says, that after proper measures had been taken, the enemy was expected with uncommon alacrity.

§ James I.

‖ Elector Palatine, and who had been chosen king of Bohemia, but was stript of all his dominions and dignities by the Emperor Ferdinand, while James the First, his father-in-law, being amused from time to time, endeavoured to mediate a peace.

* The monstrous, and till then unheard-of, doctrines of divine indefeasible hereditary right, passive obedience, &c

† The parties of Whig and Tory.

‡ Charles I.

§ Parliaments.

‖ Ship-money.

¶ Monopolies.

** The raging high-church sermons of these times, inspiring at once a spirit of slavish submission to the court, and of bitter persecution against those whom they call church and state puritans.

By calm majestic wisdom ! taught its course
What nuisance to devour; such wisdom fired
With unabating zeal, and aim'd sincere
To clear the weedy state, restore the laws,
And for the future to secure their sway.
This then the purpose of my mildest sons.
But man is blind. A nation once inflamed
(Chief, should the breath of factious fury blow,
With the wild rage of mad enthusiast swell'd)
Not easy cools again. From breast to breast,
From eye to eye, the kindling passions mix
In heighten'd blaze; and, ever wise and just,
High Heaven to gracious ends directs the storm.
Thus in one conflagration Britain wrapt,
And by confusion's lawless sons despoil'd,
King, Lords, and Commons, thundering to the ground,
Successive rush'd.—Lo ! from their ashes rose,
Gay-beaming radiant youth, the Phœnix state*.
The grievous yoke of vassalage, the yoke
Of private life, lay by those flames dissolved:
And, from the wasteful, the luxurious king†,
Was purchased‡ that which taught the young to bend.
Stronger restored, the commons tax'd the whole,
And built on that eternal rock their power.
The crown, of its hereditary wealth
Despoil'd, on senates more dependant grew,
And they more frequent, more assured. Yet lived,
And in full vigour spread that bitter root,
The passive doctrines, by their patrons first
Opposed ferocious, when they touch themselves.
This wild delusive cant; the rash cabal
Of hungry courtiers, ravenous for prey;
The bigot, restless in a double chain
To bind anew the land; the constant need
Of finding faithless means, of shifting forms,
And flattering senates, to supply his waste;
These tore some moments from the careless prince,
And in his breast awaked the kindred plan.
By dangerous softness long he mined his way;
By subtle arts, dissimulation deep;
By sharing what corruption shower'd, profuse;
By breathing wide the gay licentious plague,
And pleasing manners, fitted to deceive.
At last subsided the delirious joy,
On whose high billow, from the saintly reign,
The nation drove too far. A pension'd king,
Against his country bribed by Gallic gold,
The port§ pernicious sold, the Scylla since
And fell Charybdis of the British seas;
Freedom attack'd abroad||, with surer blow
To cut it off at home; the saviour-league¶
Of Europe broke; the progress even advanced
Of universal sway**, which to reduce
Such seas of blood and treasure Britain cost;
The millions, by a generous people given,
Or squander'd vile, or to corrupt disgrace,
And awe the land with forces†† not their own,
Employ'd; the darling Church herself betray'd;
All these, broad glaring, oped the general eye,
And waked my spirit, the resisting soul.
Mild was, at first, and half ashamed, the check
Of senates, shook from the fantastic dream
Of absolute submission, tenets vile!
Which slaves would blush to own, and which, reduced
To practice, always honest nature shock.
Not even the mask removed, and the fierce front
Of tyranny disclosed; nor trampled laws;
Nor seized each badge of freedom* through the land;
Nor Sidney bleeding for the unpublish'd page;
Nor on the bench avow'd corruption placed,
And murderous rage itself, in Jefferies' form:
Nor endless acts of arbitrary power,
Cruel, and false, could raise the public arm.
Distrustful, scatter'd, of combining chiefs
Devoid, and dreading blind rapacious war,
The patient public turns not, till impell'd
To the near verge of ruin. Hence I roused
The bigot king†, and hurried fated on
His measures immature. But chief his zeal,
Out-flaming Rome herself, portentous scared
The troubled nation: Mary's horrid days
To fancy bleeding rose, and the dire glare
Of Smithfield lighten'd in its eyes anew.
Yet silence reign'd. Each on another scowl'd
Rueful amazement, pressing down his rage:
As, mustering vengeance, the deep thunder frowns,
Awfully still, waiting the high command
To spring. Straight from his country Europe saved,
To save Britannia, lo! my darling son,
Than hero more! the patriot of mankind!
Immortal Nassau came. I hush'd the deep
By demons roused, and bade the listed winds‡,
Still shifting as behoved, with various breath,
Waft the deliverer to the longing shore.
See! wide alive, the foaming channel§ bright
With swelling sails, and all the pride of war;
Delightful view! when justice draws the sword:
And mark! diffusing ardent soul around
And sweet contempt of death, my streaming flag||,
Even adverse navies¶ bless'd the binding gale,
Kept down the glad acclaim, and silent joy'd.
Arrived, the pomp, and not the waste of arms,
His progress mark'd. The faint opposing host**
For once, in yielding, their best victory found,
And by desertion proved exalted faith;
While his the bloodless conquest of the heart,
Shouts without groan, and triumph without war.
Then dawn'd the period destined to confine
The surge of wild prerogative, to raise
A mound restraining its imperious rage,
And bid the raving deep no farther flow.
Nor were, without that fence, the swallow'd state

---

* At the Restoration. † Charles II.
‡ Court of Wards. § Dunkirk.
|| The war, in conjunction with France, against the Dutch.
¶ The triple alliance. ** Under Lewis XIV.
†† A standing army, raised without the consent of parliament.

* The charters of corporations. † James II.
‡ The Prince of Orange, in his passage to England, though his fleet had been at first dispersed by a storm, was afterwards extremely favoured by several changes of wind.
§ Rapin in his History of England:—The third of November the fleet entered the Channel, and lay by between Calais and Dover, to stay for the ships that were behind. Here the Prince called a council of war. It is easy to imagine what a glorious show the fleet made. Five or six hundred ships in so narrow a channel, and both the English and French shores covered with numberless spectators, are no common sight. For my part, who was then on board the fleet, I own it struck me extremely.
|| The Prince placed himself in the main body, carrying a flag with English colours, and their Highnesses' arms surrounded with this motto,—"The Protestant Religion and the Liberties of England;" and underneath the motto of the house of Nassau, "Je maintiendrai, I will maintain." Rapin.
¶ The English fleet. ** The King's army.

Better than Belgian plains without their dykes,
Sustaining weighty seas. This, often saved
By more than human hand, the public saw,
And seized the white-wing'd moment. Pleased to
Destructive power*, a wise heroic prince† [yield
Even lent his aid—Thrice happy did they know
Their happiness, Britannia's bounded kings!
What though not theirs the boast, in dungeon glooms
To plunge bold freedom; or, to cheerless wilds,
To drive him from the cordial face of friend;
Or fierce to strike him at the midnight hour,
By mandate blind, not justice, that delights
To dare the keenest eye of open day.
What though no glory to control the laws,
And make injurious will their only rule,
They deem it! What though, tools of wanton power,
Pestiferous armies swarm not at their call!
What though they give not a relentless crew
Of civil furies, proud oppression's fangs,
To tear at pleasure the dejected land,
With starving labour pampering idle waste!
To clothe the naked, feed the hungry, wipe
The guiltless tear from lone affliction's eye;
To raise hid merit, set the alluring light
Of virtue high to view; to nourish arts,
Direct the thunder of an injured state,
Make a whole glorious people sing for joy,
Bless human kind, and through the downward depth
Of future times, to spread that better sun
Which lights up British soul: for deeds like these
The dazzling fair career unbounded lies;
While (still superior bliss!) the dark abrupt
Is kindly barr'd, the precipice of ill.
O luxury divine! O poor to this,
Ye giddy glories of despotic thrones!
By this, by this indeed, is imaged Heaven,
By boundless good, without the power of ill.
And now behold! exalted as the cope
That swells immense o'er many-peopled earth,
And like it, free, my fabric stands complete,
The palace of the laws. To the four heavens
Four gates impartial thrown, unceasing crowds,
With kings themselves the hearty peasant mix'd,
Pour urgent in. And though to different ranks
Responsive place belongs, yet equal spreads
The sheltering roof o'er all; while plenty flows,
And glad contentment echoes round the whole.
Ye floods descend! Ye winds, confirming, blow!
Nor outward tempest, nor corrosive time,
Nought but the felon undermining hand
Of dark corruption, can its frame dissolve,
And lay the toil of ages in the dust.

THE PROSPECT;

BEING

THE FIFTH PART OF LIBERTY, A POEM.

CONTENTS.

Author addresses the Goddess of Liberty, marking the happiness and grandeur of Great Britain, as arising from her influence. She resumes her discourse, and points out the chief virtues which are necessary to maintain her establishment there. Recommends, as its last ornament and finishing, sciences, fine arts, and public works. The encouragement of these urged from the example of France, though under a despotic government. The whole concludes with a prospect of future times, given by the Goddess of Liberty: this described by the author, as it passes in vision before him.

HERE interposion, as the goddess paused;——
"Oh, blest Britannia! in thy presence blest,
Thou guardian of mankind! whence spring, alone,
All human grandeur, happiness, and fame:
For toil, by thee protected, feels no pain;
The poor's man's lot with milk and honey flows;
And, gilded with thy rays, even death looks gay.
Let other lands the potent blessings boast
Of more exalting suns. Let Asia's woods,
Untended, yield the vegetable fleece:
And let the little insect-artist form,
On higher life intent, its silken tomb.
Let wondering rocks, in radiant birth, disclose
The various-tinctured children of the sun.
From the prone beam let more delicious fruits
A flavour drink, that in one piercing taste
Bids each combine. Let Gallic vineyards burst
With floods of joy; with mild balsamic juice
The Tuscan olive. Let Arabia breathe
Her spicy gales, her vital gums distil.
Turbid with gold, let southern rivers flow;
And orient floods draw soft, o'er pearls, their maze.
Let Afric vaunt her treasures; let Peru
Deep in her bowels her own ruin breed,
The yellow traitor that her bliss betray'd—
Unequal'd bliss!—and to unequal'd rage!
Yet nor the gorgeous east, nor golden south,
Nor, in full prime, that new-discover'd world,
Where flames the falling day, in wealth and praise
Shall with Britannia vie, while, goddess, she
Derives her praise from thee, her matchless charms.
Her hearty fruits the hand of freedom own;
And, warm with culture, her thick-clustering fields
Prolific teem. Eternal verdure crowns
Her meads; her gardens smile eternal spring.
She gives the hunter-horse, unquell'd by toil,
Ardent to rush into the rapid chase:
She, whitening o'er her downs, diffusive pours
Unnumber'd flocks; she weaves the fleecy robe
That wraps the nations: she, to lusty droves,
The richest pasture spreads; and, hers, deep-wave
Autumnal seas of pleasing plenty round.
These her delights; and by no baneful herb,
No darting tiger, no grim lion's glare,
No fierce-descending wolf, no serpent roll'd
In spires immense progressive o'er the land,

* By the Bill of Rights, and the Act of Succession.
† William III.

Disturb'd. Enlivening these, add cities, full
Of wealth, of trade, of cheerful-toiling crowds:
Add thriving towns; add villages and farms,
Innumerous sow'd along the lively vale,
Where bold unrival'd peasants happy dwell;
Add ancient seats, with venerable oaks
Embosom'd high, while kindred floods below
Wind through the mead; and those of modern hand,
More pompous, add, that splendid shine afar.
Need I her limpid lakes, her rivers name,
Where swarm the finny race? Thee, chief, O Thames!
On whose each tide, glad with returning sails,
Flows in the mingled harvest of mankind?
And thee, thou Severn, whose prodigious swell,
And waves resounding, imitate the main?
Why need I name her deep capacious ports,
That point around the world? And why her seas?
All ocean is her own, and every land
To whom her ruling thunder ocean bears.
She too the mineral feeds: the obedient lead,
The warlike iron, nor the peaceful less,
Forming of life, art-civilised, the bond;
And that the Tyrian merchant sought of old*,
Not dreaming then of Britain's brighter fame.
She rears to freedom an undaunted race:
Compatriot, zealous, hospitable, kind,
Hers the warm Cambrian: hers the lofty Scot,
To hardship tamed, active in arts and arms,
Fired with a restless, an impatient flame,
That leads him raptured where ambition calls:
And English merit hers; where meet, combined,
Whate'er high fancy, sound judicious thought,
An ample generous heart, undrooping soul,
And firm tenacious valour, can bestow.
Great nurse of fruits, of flocks, of commerce, she!
Great nurse of men! By thee, O goddess, taught,
Her old renown I trace; disclose her source
Of wealth, of grandeur, and to Britons sing
A strain the Muses never touch'd before.
 But how shall this thy mighty kingdom stand?
On what unyielding base? how finish'd shine?"
 At this her eye, collecting all its fire,
Beam'd more than human; and her awful voice,
Majestic, thus she raised:—"To Britons bear
This closing strain, and with intenser note
Loud let it sound in their awaken'd ear."
 On virtue can alone my kingdom stand,
On public virtue, every virtue join'd:
For, lost this social cement of mankind,
The greatest empires, by scarce-felt degrees,
Will moulder soft away; till, tottering loose,
They prone at last to total ruin rush.
Unblest by virtue, government a league
Becomes, a circling junto of the great,
To rob by law; religion mild, a yoke
To tame the stooping soul, a trick of state
To mask their rapine, and to share the prey.
What are without it senates, save a face
Of consultation deep, and reason free;
While the determined voice and heart are sold?
What boasted freedom, save a sounding name?
And what election, but a market vile
Of slaves self-barter'd? Virtue! without thee,
There is no ruling eye, no nerve, in states;
War has no vigour, and no safety peace:
Even justice warps to party; laws oppress;
Wide through the land their weak protection fails,
First broke the balance, and then scorn'd the sword.

* Tin.

Thus nations sink, society dissolves;
Rapine, and guile, and violence, break loose,
Everting life, and turning love to gall;
Man hates the face of man, and Indian woods,
And Libya's hissing sands, to him are tame.
 By those three virtues be the frame sustain'd
Of British freedom:—independent life;
Integrity in office; and, o'er all
Supreme, a passion for the common-weal.
 Hail! independence, hail! Heaven's next best gift
To that of life and an immortal soul!
The life of life! that to the banquet high
And sober meal gives taste; to the bow'd roof
Fair-dream'd repose, and to the cottage charms.
Of public freedom, hail, thou secret source!
Whose streams, from every quarter confluent, form
My better Nile, that nurses human life.
By rills from thee deduced, irriguous, fed,
The private field looks gay, with nature's wealth
Abundant flows, and blooms with each delight
That nature craves. Its happy master there,
The only freeman, walks his pleasing round;
Sweet-featured peace attending; fearless truth;
Firm resolution; goodness, blessing all
That can rejoice; contentment, surest friend;
And still fresh stores from nature's book derived,
Philosophy, companion ever new.
These cheer his rural, and sustain or fire,
When into action call'd, his busy hours.
Meantime, true-judging moderate desires,
Economy and taste combined, direct
His clear affairs, and from debauching fiends
Secure his little kingdom. Nor can those
Whom fortune heaps, without these virtues, reach
That truce with pain, that animated ease,
That self-enjoyment springing from within;
That independence, active, or retired,
Which make the soundest bliss of man below;
But, lost beneath the rubbish of their means,
And drain'd by wants to nature all unknown,
A wandering, tasteless, gaily-wretched train,
Though rich, are beggars; and though noble, slaves.
 Lo! damn'd to wealth, at what a gross expense,
They purchase disappointment, pain, and shame.
Instead of hearty hospitable cheer,
See! how the hall with brutal riot flows;
While in the foaming flood, fermenting, steep'd,
The country maddens into party rage.
Mark! those disgraceful piles of wood and stone;
Those parks and gardens, where, his haunts betrimm'd,
And nature by presumptuous art oppress'd,
The woodland genius mourns. See! the full board
That steams disgust, and bowls that give no joy:
No truth invited there to feed the mind,
Nor wit, the wine-rejoicing reason quaffs.
Hark! how the dome with insolence resounds,
With those retain'd by vanity to scare
Repose and friends. To tyrant fashion, mark!
The costly worship paid, to the broad gaze
Of fools. From still delusive day to day,
Led an eternal round of lying hope,
See! self-abandon'd, how they roam adrift,
Dash'd o'er the town, a miserable wreck!
Then to adore some warbling eunuch turn'd,
With Midas' ears they crowd; or to the buzz
Of masquerade unblushing; or, to show
Their scorn of nature, at the tragic scene
They mirthful sit, or prove the comic true.
But, chief, behold! around the rattling board

The civil robbers ranged ; and even the fair,
The tender fair, each sweetness laid aside,
As fierce for plunder as all-licensed troops
In some sack'd city. Thus dissolved their wealth,
Without one generous luxury dissolved,
Or quarter'd on it many a needless want,
At the throng'd levee bends the venal tribe :
With fair, but faithless smiles, each varnish'd o'er,
Each smooth as those that mutually deceive,
And for their falsehood each despising each :
Till shook their patron by the wintry winds,
Wide flies the wither'd shower, and leaves him bare.
O far superior Afric's sable sons,
By merchant pilfer'd, to these willing slaves !
And, rich, as unsqueezed favourite, to them,
Is he who can his virtue boast alone !
Britons ! be firm !—nor let corruption sly
Twine round your heart indissoluble chains !
The steel of Brutus burst the grosser bonds
By Cæsar cast o'er Rome ; but still remain'd
The soft enchanting fetters of the mind,
And other Cæsars rose. Determined, hold
Your independence ; for, that once destroy'd,
Unfounded, freedom is a morning dream,
That flits aërial from the spreading eye.
Forbid it, Heaven ! that ever I need urge
Integrity in office on my sons !
Inculcate common honour——not to rob——
And whom ?—the gracious, the confiding hand,
That lavishly rewards ; the toiling poor,
Whose cup with many a bitter drop is mixt ;
The guardian public ; every face they see,
And every friend ; nay, in effect, themselves.
As in familiar life, the villain's fate
Admits no cure ; so, when a desperate age
At this arrives, I the devoted race
Indignant spurn, and, hopeless, soar away.
But, ah too little known to modern times !
Be not the noblest passion past unsung ;
That ray peculiar, from unbounded love
Effused, which kindles the heroic soul ;
Devotion to the public. Glorious flame !
Celestial ardour ! in what unknown worlds,
Profusely scatter'd through the blue immense,
Hast thou been blessing myriads, since in Rome,
Old virtuous Rome, so many deathless names
From thee their lustre drew ? since, taught by thee,
Their poverty put splendour to the blush,
Pain grew luxurious, and even death delight ?
O wilt thou ne'er, in thy long period, look,
With blaze direct, on this my last retreat ?
'Tis not enough, from self right understood
Reflected, that thy rays inflame the heart :
Though virtue not disdains appeals to self,
Dreads not the trial ; all her joys are true,
Nor is there any real joy save hers.
Far less the tepid, the declaiming race,
Foes to corruption, to its wages friends,
Or those whom private passions, for a while,
Beneath my standard list, can they suffice
To raise and fix the glory of my reign ?
An active flood of universal love
Must swell the breast. First, in effusion wide,
The restless spirit roves creation round,
And seizes every being : stronger then
It tends to life, whate'er the kindred search
Of bliss allies : then, more collected still,
It urges human-kind : a passion grown,
At last, the central parent-public calls
Its utmost effort forth, awakes each sense;
The comely, grand, and tender. Without this,
This awful pant, shook from sublimer powers
Than those of self, this heaven-infused delight,
This moral gravitation, rushing prone
To press the public good, my system soon,
Traverse, to several selfish centres drawn,
Will reel to ruin : while for ever shut
Stand the bright portals of desponding fame.
From sordid self shoot up no shining deeds,
None of those ancient lights that gladden earth,
Give grace to being, and arouse the brave
To just ambition, virtue's quickening fire !
Life tedious grows, an idly-bustling round,
Fill'd up with actions animal and mean ;
A dull gazette ! The impatient reader scorns
The poor historic page ; till kindly comes
Oblivion, and redeems a people's shame.
Not so the times when, emulation-stung,
Greece shone in genius, science, and in arts ;
And Rome in virtues dreadful to be told !
To live was glory then ! and charm'd mankind :
Through the deep periods of devolving time,
Those, raptured, copy ; these, astonish'd, read.
True, a corrupted state, with every vice
And every meanness foul, this passion damps.
Who can, unshock'd, behold the cruel eye ?
The pale inveigling smile ? The ruffian front ?
The wretch abandon'd to relentless self,
Equally vile if miser or profuse ?
Powers not of God, assiduous to corrupt ?
The fell deputed tyrant, who devours
The poor and weak, at distance from redress ?*
Delirious faction bellowing loud my name ?
The false fair-seeming patriot's hollow boast?
A race resolved on bondage, fierce for chains,
My sacred rights a merchandise alone
Esteeming, and to work their feeder's will
By deeds, a horror to mankind, prepared,
As were the dregs of Romulus of old ?
Who these indeed can undetesting see ?—
But who unpitying ? To the generous eye
Distress is virtue ; and, though self-betray'd,
A people struggling with their fate must rouse
The hero's throb. Nor can a land, at once,
Be lost to virtue quite. How glorious then !
Fit luxury for gods ! to save the good,
Protect the feeble, dash bold vice aside,
Depress the wicked, and restore the frail.
Posterity, besides, the young are pure,
And sons may tinge their fathers' cheek with shame.
Should then the times arrive (which Heaven avert !)
That Britons bend unnerved, not by the force
Of arms, more generous and more manly, quell'd,
But by corruption's soul-dejecting arts,
Arts impudent ! and gross ! by their own gold,
In part bestow'd, to bribe them to give all ;
With party raging, or immersed in sloth,
Should they Britannia's well-fought laurels yield
To slily-conquering Gaul ; even from her brow
Let her own naval oak be basely torn
By such as tremble at the stiffening gale,
And nerveless sink, while others sing rejoiced.
Or (darker prospect ! scarce one gleam behind
Disclosing) should the broad corruptive plague

* Lord Molesworth, in his account of Denmark, says,—It is observed, that in limited monarchies and commonwealths a neighbourhood to the seat of the government is advantageous to the subjects ; whilst the distant provinces are less thriving, and more liable to oppression.

Breathe from the city to the farthest hut
That sits serene within the forest-shade,
The fever'd people fire, inflame their wants,
And their luxurious thirst, so gathering rage,
That, were a buyer found, they stand prepared
To sell their birthright for a cooling draught:
Should shameless pens for plain corruption plead;
The hired assassins of the common-weal!
Deem'd the declaiming rant of Greece and Rome,
Should public virtue grow the public scoff,
Till private, failing, staggers through the land;
Till round the city loose mechanic want,
Dire-prowling nightly, makes the cheerful haunts
Of men more hideous than Numidian wilds;
Nor from its fury sleeps the vale in peace;
And murders, horrors, perjuries abound:
Nay, till to lowest deeds the highest stoop;
The rich, like starving wretches, thirst for gold;
And those, on whom the vernal showers of Heaven
All-bounteous fall, and that prime lot bestow,
A power to live to nature and themselves,
In sick attendance wear their anxious days,
With fortune, joyless, and with honours, mean:
Meantime, perhaps, profusion flows around,
The waste of war, without the works of peace;
No mark of millions in the gulf absorpt
Of uncreating vice, none but the rage
Of roused corruption still demanding more:
That very portion, which (by faithful skill
Employ'd) might make the smiling public rear
Her ornamented head, drill'd through the hands
Of mercenary tools, serves but to nurse
A locust-band within, and in the bud
Leaves starved each work of dignity and use.
I paint the worst. But should these times arrive,
If any nobler passion yet remain,
Let all my sons all parties fling aside,
Despise their nonsense, and together join;
Let worth and virtue, scorning low despair,
Exerted full, from every quarter shine
Commix'd in heighten'd blaze. Light flash'd to [light,
Moral or intellectual, more intense
By giving glows. As on pure winter's eve,
Gradual, the stars effulge; fainter, at first,
They, straggling, rise; but when the radiant host,
In thick profusion pour'd, shine out immense,
Each casting vivid influence on each,
From pole to pole a glittering deluge plays,
And worlds above rejoice, and men below.
But why to Britons this superfluous strain?—
Good-nature, honest truth even somewhat blunt,
Of crooked baseness an indignant scorn,
A zeal unyielding in their country's cause,
And ready bounty, wont to dwell with them—
Nor only wont—Wide o'er the land diffused,
In many a blest retirement still they dwell.
To softer prospect turn we now the view,
To laurel'd science, arts, and public works,
That lend my finish'd fabric comely pride,
Grandeur and grace. Of sullen genius he!
Cursed by the Muses; by the Graces loathed!
Who deems beneath the public's high regard
These last enlivening touches of my reign.
However puff'd with power, and gorged with wealth,
A nation be; let trade enormous rise,
Let east and south their mingled treasures pour,
Till, swell'd, impetuous the corrupting flood
Burst o'er the city and devour the land:
Yet these neglected, these recording arts,
Wealth rots a nuisance; and, oblivious sunk,
That nation must another Carthage lie;
If not by them, on monumental brass,
On sculptured marble, on the deathless page,
Impress, renown had left no trace behind:
In vain, to future times, the sage had thought,
The legislator plann'd, the hero found
A beauteous death, the patriot toil'd in vain.
The awarders they of fame's immortal wreath,
They rouse ambition, they the mind exalt,
Give great ideas, lovely forms infuse,
Delight the general eye, and, drest by them,
The moral Venus glows with double charms.
Science, my close associate, still attends
Where'er I go. Sometimes, in simple guise,
She walks the furrow with the consul swain,
Whispering unletter'd wisdom to the heart
Direct; or, sometimes, in the pompous robe
Of Fancy drest, she charms Athenian wits,
And a whole sapient city round her burns.
Then o'er her brow Minerva's terrors nod:
With Xenophon, sometimes, in dire extremes,
She breathes deliberate soul, and makes retreat*
Unequal'd glory: with the Theban sage,
Epaminondas, first and best of men!
Sometimes she bids the deep-embattled host,
Above the vulgar reach resistless form'd,
March to sure conquest—never gain'd before†!
Nor on the treacherous seas of giddy state
Unskilful she: when the triumphant tide
Of high-swoln empire wears one boundless smile,
And the gale tempts to new pursuits of fame,
Sometimes, with Scipio, she collects her sail,
And seeks the blissful shore of rural ease,
Where, but the Aonian maids, no sirens sing;
Or should the deep-brew'd tempest muttering rise,
While rocks and shoals perfidious lurk around,
With Tully she her wide-reviving light
To senates holds, a Catiline confounds,
And saves a while from Cæsar sinking Rome.
Such the kind power, whose piercing eye dissolves
Each mental fetter, and sets reason free;
For me inspiring an enlighten'd zeal,
The more tenacious as the more convinced,
How happy freemen, and how wretched slaves.
To Britons not unknown, to Britons full
The Goddess spreads her stores, the secret soul
That quickens trade, the breath unseen that wafts
To them the treasures of a balanced world.
But finer arts (save what the Muse has sung
In daring flight, above all modern wing)
Neglected droop the head; and public works,
Broke by corruption into private gain,
Not ornament, disgrace; not serve, destroy.
Shall Britons, by their own joint wisdom ruled
Beneath one royal head, whose vital power
Connects, enlivens, and exerts the whole;
In finer arts, and public works, shall they
To Gallia yield? yield to a land that bends,
Deprest, and broke, beneath the will of one?
Of one who, should the unkingly thirst of gold,
Or tyrant passions, or ambition, prompt,
Calls locust-armies o'er the blasted land:

* The famous retreat of the Ten Thousand was chiefly conducted by Xenophon.

† Epaminondas, after having beat the Lacedæmonians and their allies in the battle of Leuctra, made an incursion, at the head of a powerful army, into Laconia. It was now six hundred years since the Dorians had possessed this country, and in all that time the face of an enemy had not been seen within their territories. PLUTARCH in AGESILAUS.

Drains from its thirsty bounds the springs of wealth,
His own insatiate reservoir to fill;
To the lone desert patriot-merit frowns,
Or into dungeons, arts; when they, their chains
Indignant bursting, for their nobler works
All other licence scorn but truth's and mine.
Oh shame to think! shall Britons, in the field
Unconquer'd still, the better laurel lose?
Even in that monarch's * reign, who vainly dreamt,
By giddy power betray'd, and flatter'd pride,
To grasp unbounded sway; while, swarming round,
His armies dared all Europe to the field;
To hostile hands while treasure flow'd profuse,
And, that great source of treasure, subjects' blood,
Inhuman squander'd, sicken'd every land;
From Britain, chief, while my superior sons,
In vengeance rushing, dash'd his idle hopes,
And bade his agonizing heart be low:
Even then, as in the golden calm of peace,
What public works at home, what arts arose!
What various science shone! what genius glow'd!
'Tis not for me to paint, diffusive shot
O'er fair extents of land, the shining road;
The flood-compelling arch; the long canal†,
Through mountains piercing, and uniting seas;
The dome ‡ resounding sweet with infant joy,
From famine saved, or cruel-handed shame;
And that where valour counts his noble scars ‡;
The land where social pleasure loves to dwell,
Of the fierce demon, gothic duel, freed;
The robber from his farthest forest chased;
The turbid city clear'd, and, by degrees,
Into sure peace the best police refined,
Magnificence, and grace, and decent joy.
Let Gallic bards record, how honour'd arts
And science, by despotic bounty bless'd,
At distance flourish'd from my parent-eye,
Restoring ancient taste; how Boileau rose;
How the big Roman soul shook, in Corneille,
The trembling stage: in elegant Racine,
How the more powerful though more humble voice
Of nature-painting Greece, resistless breathed
The whole-awaken'd heart: how Moliere's scene,
Chastised and regular, with well-judged wit,
Not scatter'd wild, and native humour, graced,
Was life itself. To public honours raised,
How learning in warm seminaries § spread;
And, more for glory than the small reward,
How emulation strove. How their pure tongue
Almost obtain'd what was denied their arms.
From Rome, awhile, how painting, courted long,
With Poussin came; ancient design, that lifts
A fairer front, and looks another soul.
How the kind art, || that of unvalued price
The famed and only picture easy gives,
Refined her touch, and, through the shadow'd piece,
All the live spirit of the painter pour'd.
Coyest of arts, how sculpture northward deign'd
A look, and bade her Girardon arise.
How lavish grandeur blazed; the barren waste,
Astonish'd, saw the sudden palace swell,
And fountains spout amid its arid shades.
For leagues bright vistas opening to the view,
How forests in majestic gardens smiled.
How menial Arts, by their gay sisters taught,
Wove the deep flower, the blooming foliage train'd
In joyous figures o'er the silky lawn,
The palace cheer'd, illumed the storied wall,
And with the pencil vied the glowing loom. *
These laurels, Louis, by the droppings raised
Of thy profusion, its dishonour shade.
And, green through future times, shall bind thy brow;
While the vain honours of perfidious war
Wither abhorr'd, or in oblivion lost:
With what prevailing vigour had they shot,
And stole a deeper root, by the full tide
Of war-sunk millions fed? Superior still,
How had they branch'd luxuriant to the skies,
In Britain planted, by the potent juice
Of freedom swell'd? Forced is the bloom of arts,
A false uncertain spring, when bounty gives,
Weak without me, a transitory gleam.
Fair shine the slippery days, enticing skies
Of favour smile, and courtly breezes blow;
Till arts, betray'd, trust to the flattering air
Their tender blossom: then malignant rise
The blights of envy, of those insect-clouds,
That, blasting merit, often cover courts:
Nay, should, perchance, some kind Mecænas ai
The doubtful beamings of his prince's soul,
His wavering ardour fix, and unconfined
Diffuse his warm beneficence around;
Yet death, at last, and wintry tyrants come,
Each sprig of genius killing at the root.
But when with me imperial bounty joins,
Wide o'er the public blows eternal spring;
While mingled autumn every harvest pours
Of every land; whate'er invention, art,
Creating toil, and nature, can produce.
Here ceased the goddess; and her ardent wings,
Dipt in the colours of the heavenly bow,
Stood waving radiance round, for sudden flight
Prepared; when thus, impatient, burst my prayer:
"O forming light of life! O better sun!
Sun of mankind! by whom the cloudy north
Sublimed, not envies Languedocian skies,
That, unstain'd ether all, diffusive smile:
When shall we call these ancient laurels ours?
And when thy work complete?"—Straight with her hand,
Celestial red, she touch'd my darken'd eyes.
As at the touch of day the shades dissolve,
So quick, methought, the misty circle clear'd,
That dims the dawn of being here below:
The future shone disclosed, and, in long view,
Bright-rising eras instant rush'd to light.
"They come! great goddess! I the times behold!
The times our fathers, in the bloody field,
Have earn'd so dear; and, not with less renown,
In the warm struggles of the senate fight.
The times I see! whose glory to supply,
For toiling ages, commerce round the world
Has wing'd unnumber'd sails, and from each land
Materials heap'd, that, well-employ'd, with Rome
Might vie our grandeur, and with Greece our art.
Lo! princes I behold! contriving still,
And still conducting firm some brave design;
Kings! that the narrow joyless circle scorn,
Burst the blockade of false designing men,
Of treacherous smiles, of adulation fell,
And of the blinding clouds around them thrown
Their court rejoicing millions; worth alone,
And virtue, dear to them; their best delight,
In just proportion, to give general joy;
Their jealous care thy kingdom to maintain;
The public glory theirs; unsparing love

* Lewis XIV. † The canal of Languedoc.
‡ The hospitals for foundlings and invalids
§ The Academies of Sciences, of the Belles Lettres, and of Painting. || Engraving.

* The tapestry of the Gobelins.

Their endless treasure; and their deeds their praise.
With thee they work. Nought can resist your force:
Life feels it quickening in her dark retreats:
Strong spread the blooms of genius, science, art;
His bashful bounds disclosing merit breaks;
And, big with fruits of glory, virtue blows
Expansive o'er the land. Another race
Of generous youth, of patriot-sires, I see!
Not those vain insects fluttering in the blaze
Of court, and ball, and play; those venal souls,
Corruption's veteran unrelenting bands,
That, to their vices slaves, can ne'er be free.
I see the fountains purged, whence life derives
A clear or turbid flow; see the young mind
Not fed impure by chance, by flattery fool'd,
Or by scholastic jargon bloated proud,
But fill'd and nourish'd by the light of truth;
Then, beam'd through fancy the refining ray,
And pouring on the heart, the passions feel
At once informing light and moving flame;
Till moral, public, graceful action crowns
The whole. Behold! the fair contention glows,
In all that mind or body can adorn,
And form to life. Instead of barren heads,
Barbarian pedants, wrangling sons of pride,
And truth-perplexing metaphysic wits;
Men, patriots, chiefs, and citizens, are form'd.
Lo! justice, like the liberal light of heaven,
Unpurchased, shines on all; and from her beam,
Appalling guilt, retire the savage crew
That prowl amid the darkness they themselves
Have thrown around the laws. Oppression grieves;
See! how her legal furies bite the lip,
While Yorkes and Talbots their deep snares detect,
And seize swift justice through the clouds they raise.
See! social labour lifts his guarded head,
And men not yield to government in vain.
From the sure land is rooted ruffian force,
And the lewd nurse of villains, idle waste; [bowl,
Lo! razed their haunts, down dash'd their maddening
A nation's poison! Beauteous order reigns:
Manly submission, unimposing toil,
Trade without guile, civility that marks
From the foul herd of brutal slaves thy sons,
And fearless peace. Or should affronting war
To slow but dreadful vengeance rouse the just,
Unfailing fields of freemen I behold!
That know, with their own proper arm to guard
Their own blest isle against a leaguing world.
Despairing Gaul her boiling youth restrains,
Dissolved her dream of universal sway:
The winds and seas are Britain's wide domain;
And not a sail, but by permission, spreads.
Lo! swarming southward on rejoicing suns,
Gay colonies extend; the calm retreat
Of undeserved distress; the better home
Of those whom bigots chase from foreign lands.
Not built on rapine, servitude, and woe,
And in their turn some petty tyrant's prey;
But, bound by social freedom, firm they rise;
Such as, of late, an Oglethorpe has form'd,
And, crowding round, the charm'd Savannah sees.
Horrid with want and misery, no more
Our streets the tender passenger afflict:
Nor shivering age, nor sickness without friend,
Or home, or bed to bear his burning load;
Nor agonizing infant, that ne'er earn'd
Its guiltless pangs, I see! The stores, profuse,
Which British bounty has to these assign'd,
No more the sacrilegious riot swell
Of cannibal devourers! Right applied,
No starving wretch the land of Freedom stains:
If poor, employment finds; if old, demands,
If sick, if maim'd, his miserable due;
And will, if young, repay the fondest care.
Sweet sets the sun of stormy life, and sweet
The morning shines, in mercy's dews array'd.
Lo! how they rise! these families of Heaven!
That, chief, (but why—ye bigots!—why so late?)
Where blooms and warbles glad a rising age*:
What smiles of praise! And, while their song ascends,
The listening seraph lays his lute aside.
Hark! the gay Muses raise a nobler strain
With active nature, warm impassion'd truth,
Engaging fable, lucid order, notes
Of various string, and heart-felt image fill'd.
Behold! I see the dread delightful school
Of temper'd passions, and of polish'd life,
Restored: behold! the well-dissembled scene
Calls from embellish'd eyes the lovely tear,
Or lights up mirth in modest cheeks again.
Lo! vanish'd monster-land.—Lo! driven away
Those that Apollo's sacred walks profane:
Their wild creation scatter'd, where a world
Unknown to nature, Chaos more confused,
O'er the brute scene its ouran-outangs† pours;
Detested forms! that, on the mind imprest,
Corrupt, confound, and barbarise an age.
Behold! all thine again the sister-arts,
Thy graces they, knit in harmonious dance.
Nursed by the treasure from a nation drain'd
Their works to purchase, they to nobler rouse
Their untamed genius, their unfetter'd thought;
Of pompous tyrants, and of dreaming monks,
The gaudy tools, and prisoners, no more.
Lo! numerous domes a Burlington confess:
For kings and senates fit, the palace see!
The temple breathing a religious awe;
Even framed with elegance the plain retreat,
The private dwelling. Certain in his aim,
Taste, never idly working, saves expense.
See! sylvan scenes, where art, alone, pretends
To dress her mistress, and disclose her charms:
Such as a Pope in miniature has shown;
A Bathurst o'er the widening forest‡ spreads;
And such as form a Richmond, Chiswick, Stowe.
August, around, what public works I see!
Lo! stately streets, lo! squares that court the breeze,
In spite of those to whom pertains the care,
Ingulfing more than founded Roman ways,
Lo! ray'd from cities o'er the brighten'd land,
Connecting sea to sea, the solid road.
Lo! the proud arch (no vile exactor's stand)
With easy sweep bestrides the chasing flood.
See! long canals, and deepen'd rivers join
Each part with each, and with the circling main
The whole enliven'd isle. Lo! ports expand,
Free as the winds and waves, their sheltering arms.
Lo! streaming comfort o'er the troubled deep,
On every pointed coast the light-house towers:
And, by the broad imperious mole repell'd,
Hark! how the baffled storm indignant roars."
As thick to view these varied wonders rose,
Shook all my soul with transport, unassured,
The vision broke; and, on my waking eye,
Rush'd the still ruins of dejected Rome.

* An hospital for foundlings.

† A creature which, of all brutes, most resembles man.—See Dr. Tyson's treatise on this animal.

‡ Okely woods, near Cirencester.

SOPHONISBA;

A Tragedy.

TO THE QUEEN.

Madam,

The notice your Majesty has condescended to take of the following Tragedy, emboldens me to lay it, in the humblest manner, at your Majesty's feet. And to whom can this illustrious Carthaginian so properly fly for protection, as to a Queen who commands the hearts of a people more powerful at sea than Carthage; more flourishing in commerce than those first merchants; more secure against conquest; and, under a monarchy, more free than a commonwealth itself?

I dare not, nor indeed need I, here attempt a character where both the great and the amiable qualities shine forth in full perfection. All words are faint to speak what is universally felt and acknowledged by a happy people. Permit me, therefore, only to subscribe myself, with the truest zeal and veneration, Madam,

Your Majesty's most humble, most dutiful, and most devoted servant,

James Thomson.

PREFACE.

It is not my intention, in this preface, to defend any faults that may be found in the following piece. I am afraid there are too many; but those who are best able to discover, will be most ready to pardon them. They alone know how difficult an undertaking the writing of a tragedy is: and this is a first attempt.

I beg leave only to mention the reason that determined me to make choice of this subject. What pleased me particularly, though perhaps it will not be least liable to objection with ordinary readers, was the great simplicity of the story. It is one, regular, and uniform, not charged with a multiplicity of incidents, and yet affording several revolutions of fortune, by which the passions may be excited, varied, and driven to their full tumult of emotion.

This unity of design was always sought after and admired by the ancients; and the most eminent among the moderns, who understood their writings, have chosen to imitate them in this, from an entire conviction that the reason of it must hold good in all ages. And here allow me to translate a passage from the celebrated Monsieur Racine, which contains all that I have to say on this head.

"We must not fancy that this rule has no other foundation but the caprice of those who made it. Nothing can touch us in tragedy but what is probable; and what probability is there that, in one day, should happen a multitude of things, which could scarce happen in several weeks? There are some who think that this simplicity is a mark of barrenness of invention; but they do not consider that, on the contrary, invention consists of making something out of nothing; and that this huddle of incidents has always been the refuge of poets who did not find in their genius either richness or force enough to engage their spectators for five acts together by a simple action, supported by the violence of passions, the beauty of sentiments, and the nobleness of expression."— I would not be understood to mean that all these things are to be found in my performance: I only show the reader what I aimed at, and how I would have pleased him, had it been in my power.

As to the character of *Sophonisba*, in drawing it I have confined myself to the truth of history. It were an affront to the age to suppose such a character out of nature, especially in a country which has produced so many great examples of public spirit and heroic virtues, even in the softer sex: and I had destroyed her character entirely, had I not marked it with that strong love to her country, disdain of servitude, and inborn aversion to the Romans, by which all historians have distinguished her. Nor ought her marrying *Masinissa*, while her former husband was still alive, to be reckoned a blemish in her character; for, by the laws of Rome and Carthage, the captivity of the husband dissolved the marriage of course: as, among us, impotence or adultery; not to mention the reasons of a moral and public nature, which I have put into her own mouth in the scene betwixt her and *Syphax*

This is all I have to say of the play itself; but I cannot conclude without owning my obligations to those concerned in the representation. They have indeed done me more than justice. Whatever was designed as amiable and engaging in *Masinissa*, shines out in Mr. Wilks's action. Mrs. Oldfield, in the character of *Sophonisba*, has excelled what, even in the fondness of an author, I could either wish or imagine. The grace, dignity, and happy variety of her action, have been universally applauded, and are truly admirable.

PERSONS REPRESENTED.

Masinissa, *King of Massylia.*
Syphax, *King of Masæsylia.*
Narva, *friend to Masinissa.*
Scipio, *the Roman General.*
Lælius, *his Lieutenant.*
Sophonisba.
Phœnissa, *her friend.*

Messenger, Slave, Guards, *and* Attendants.

Scene.—*The Palace of Cirtha.*

ACT I.

SCENE I.

Sophonisba Phœnissa.

Soph. This hour, Phœnissa, this important hour,
Or fixes me a queen, or from a throne
Throws Sophonisba into Roman chains.
Detested thought! For now his utmost force
Collected, desperate, distress'd, and sore
From battles lost; with all the rage of war,
Ill-fated Syphax his last effort makes.
But say, thou partner of my hopes and fears,
Phœnissa, say; while from the lofty tower
Our straining eyes the field of battle sought,
Ah! thought you not that our Numidian troops
Gave up the bloody field, and scattering fled,
Wild o'er the hills, from the rapacious sons
Of still triumphant Rome?
Phœn. Perhaps they wheel'd,
As is their custom, to return more fierce.
Distrust not fortune, while you yet may hope;
And think not, madam, Syphax can resign,
But with his ebbing life, in this last field,
At once a kingdom, and a queen he loves
Beyond ambition's brightest wish: for whom,
Nor moved by threats, nor bound by plighted faith,
He scorn'd the Roman friendship (that fair name
For slavery) and from the engagements broke
Of Scipio, famed for every winning art,
The towering genius of recover'd Rome. [blood
Soph. Oh, name him not! These Romans stir my
To too much rage. I cannot bear the fortune
Of that proud people.—Said you not, Phœnissa,
That Syphax loved me; which would fire his soul,
And urge him on to death or conquest?—True,
He loves me with the madness of desire;
His every passion is a slave to love;
Nor heeds he danger where I bid him go,
Nor leagues, nor interest. Hence these endless wars,
These ravaged countries, these successless fights,
Sustain'd by Carthage; whose defence alone,
Not love, engaged my marriage-vows with his.
But know you not, that in the Roman camp
I have a lover too; a gallant, brave,
And disappointed lover, full of wrath,
Returning to a kingdom, whence the sword
Of Syphax drove him?
Phœn. Masinissa?
Soph. He:
Young Masinissa, the Massylian king,
The first addresser of my youth; for whom
My bosom felt a fond beginning wish,
Extinguish'd soon, when once by Scipio's arts
Won over he became the slave of Rome.
E'er since, my heart has held him in contempt
And thrown out each idea of his worth,
That there began to grow: nay, had it been
As much enthrall'd and soft as hers who sits
In secret shades, or by the falling stream,
And wastes her being in unutter'd pangs,
I would have broke, or cured it of its fondness.
Phœn. Heroic Sophonisba!
Soph. No, Phœnissa;
It is not for the daughter of great Asdrubal,
Descended from a long illustrious line
Of Carthaginian heroes, who have oft
Fill'd Italy with terror and dismay,
And shook the walls of Rome, to pine in love,
Like a deluded maid; to give her life,
And heart high-beating in her country's cause,
To mean domestic cares, and idle joys;
Much less to one who stoops his neck to Rome,
An enemy to Carthage—Masinissa. [flame,
Phœn. Think not I mean to check that glorious
That just ambition which exalts your soul,

Glows on your cheek, and lightens in your eye.
Yet would he had been yours, this rising prince !
For, trust me, fame is fond of Masinissa.
His courage, conduct, deep-experienced youth,
And vast unbroken spirit in distress,
Still rising stronger from the last defeat,
Are all the talk, and terror too, of Afric.
Who has not heard the story of his woes ?
How hard he came to his paternal realm :
Whence soon by Syphax' unrelenting hate,
And jealous Carthage driven, he with a few
Fled to the mountains. Then, I think, it was,
Hemm'd in a circle of impending rocks,
That all his followers fell, save fifty horse,
Who, thence escaped through secret paths abrupt,
Gain'd the Clupean plain. There overtook,
And urged by fierce surrounding foes, he burst
With four alone, sore wounded, through their ranks,
And all amidst a deep-swoln torrent plunged.
Seized with the whirling gulf two sunk ; and two,
With him obliquely hurried down the stream,
Swam to the farther shore. The astonish'd foes
Stood check'd and shivering on the gloomy brink,
And deem'd him lost in the devouring flood.
Meantime, the dauntless undespairing youth
Lay in a cave conceal'd ; curing his wounds
With mountain herbs, and on his horses fed.
Nor here, even at the lowest ebb of life,
Stoop'd his aspiring mind. What need I say,
How once again restored, and once again
Expell'd, among the Garamantian hills
He since has wander'd till the Roman arm
Revived his cause ? and who shall reign alone,
Syphax or he, this day decides.
Soph. Enough.
Thou need'st not blazon thus his fame, Phœnissa :
Were he as glorious as the pride of woman
Could wish, in all her wantonness of thought ;
The joy of human-kind ; wise, valiant, good ;
With every praise, with every laurel crown'd ;
The warrior's wonder, and the virgin's sigh :
Yet this would cloud him o'er, this blemish all,
His means submission to the Roman yoke ;
That, false to Carthage, Afric, and himself,
With proffer'd hand and knee, he hither led
These ravagers of earth.—But while we talk,
The work of fate goes on ; even now perhaps
My dying country bleeds in every vein,
And the proud victor thunders at our gate.

SCENE II.

SOPHONISBA, PHŒNISSA, *and to them a* Messenger *from the battle.*

Soph. Ha ! whence art thou ? Speak ; though thy bleeding wounds
Might well excuse thy tongue.
Mess. Madam, escaped
From yon dire field, alas ! I come——
Soph. No more.
At once thy meaning flashes o'er my soul.
O all my vanish'd hopes ! O fatal chance
Of undiscerning war ! And is all lost ?—
An universal ruin ?
Mess. Madam, all.
Of all our numerous host, scarce one is saved.
The king——
Soph. Ah ! what of him ?
Mess. His fiery steed,
By Masinissa, the Massylian prince,
Pierced, threw him headlong to his clustering foes:
And now he comes in chains.
Soph. O worst of ills !
Absolute gods ! All Afric is in chains !
The weeping world in chains !—Oh, is there not
A time, a righteous time, reserved in fate,
When these oppressors of mankind shall feel
The miseries they give ; and blindly fight
For their own fetters too ?—The conquering troops,
How points their motion ?
Mess. At my heels they came,
Loud-shouting, dreadful in a cloud of dust,
By Masinissa headed.
Soph. Hark ! arrived :
The murmuring cloud rolls frighted to the palace.—
Thou bleed'st to death, poor faithful wretch ; away,
And dress thy wounds, if life be worth thy care ;
Though Rome, methinks, will lose a slave in thee.
Would Sophonisba were as near the verge
Of boundless and immortal liberty !

SCENE III.

SOPHONISBA, PHŒNISSA.

(After a pause.

Soph. And wherefore not ? When liberty is lost,
Let abject cowards live ; but in the brave
It were a treachery to themselves, enough
To merit chains. And is it fit for me,
Who in my veins, from Asdrubal derived,
Hold Carthaginian enmity to Rome ;
Who sold my joyless youth to Syphax' arms,
For her destruction ; is it fit for me
To sit in feeble grief, and trembling wait
The approaching victor's rage ? reserved in chains
To grace his triumph, and become the scorn
Of every Roman dame ?—Gods ! how my soul
Disdains the thought ! This, this shall set it free.

(Offers to stab herself.

Phœn. Hold, Sophonisba, hold ! my friend ! my queen !
For whom alone I live ! hold your rash hand,
Nor through your guardian bosom stab your country.
This is our last resort, and always sure.
The gracious gods are liberal of death ;
To that last blessing lend a thousand ways.
Think not I'd have you live to drag a chain,
And walk the triumph of insulting Rome.
No, by these tears of loyalty and love !
Ere I beheld so vile a sight, this hand
Should urge the faithful poniard to your heart,
And glory in the deed. But, while hope lives,
Let not the generous die. 'Tis late before
The brave despair.
Soph. Thou copy of my soul !
And now my friend indeed ! Show me but hope,
One glimpse of hope, and I'll renew my toils ;
Call patience, labour, fortitude again,
The vext unjoyous day, and sleepless night ;
Nor shrink at danger, any shape of death :
Show me the smallest hope ! Alas, Phœnissa,
Too fondly confident ! Hope lives not here,
Fled with her sister liberty beyond
The Garamantian hills, to some steep wild,
Some undiscover'd country, where the foot
Of Roman cannot come.
Phœn. Yes, there she lived

With Masinissa wounded and forlorn,
Amidst the serpent's hiss, and tiger's yell.——
Soph. Why namest thou him ?
Phœn. Madam, in this forgive
My forward zeal ; from him proceeds our hope.
He loved you once ; nor is your form impair'd,
Time has matured it into stronger charms :
Ask his protection from the Roman power :
You must prevail ; for Sophonisba sure
From Masinissa cannot ask in vain. [country !
Soph. Now, by the prompting Genius of my
I thank thee for the thought. True, there is pain
Even in descending thus to beg protection
From that degenerate youth. But, oh ! for thee,
My sinking country, and again to gall
This hated Rome, what would I not endure ?
It shall be done, Phœnissa ; though disgust
Hold back my struggling heart, it shall be done.—
But hark ; they come ; in this disorder'd tumult
It fits not Sophonisba to be seen.
I'll wait a calmer hour.—Let us retire.

SCENE IV.

MASINISSA, SYPHAX *in chains*, NARVA, Guards, &c.

Syph. Is there no dungeon in this city, dark
As is my troubled soul ? That thus I am brought
To my own palace ; to those rooms of state,
Wont in another manner to receive me,
With other signs of royalty than these.
(*Looking on his chains.*
Mas. I will not wound thee, nor insult thee,
With a recital of thy tyrant crimes. [Syphax,
A captive here I see thee, fallen below
My most revengeful wish ; and all the rage,
The nobly fury that this morn inflamed me,
Is sunk to soft compassion. In the field,
The perilous front of war, there is the scene
Of brave revenge : and I have sought thee there.
Keen as the wounded lion seeks his foe.
But when a broken enemy disarm'd
And helpless lies ; a falling sword, an eye
With pity flowing, and an arm as weak
As infant softness, then become the brave.
Believe it, Syphax, my relenting soul
Melts at thy fate.
Syph. This, this, is all I dread,
All I detest ; this insolence refined,
This affectation of superior goodness.
Pitied by thee !—Is there a form of death,
Of torture, and of infamy like that ?
Ye partial gods, to what have you debased me ?
I felt your worst ; why should I fear you more ?
Hear me, vain youth ? take notice—I abhor
Thy mercy, loath it.—Use me like a slave ;
As I would thee, (delicious thought !) wert thou
Here crouching in my power.
Mas. Outrageous man !
Thou canst not drive me, by thy bitterest rage,
To an unmanly deed ; not all thy wrongs
Can force my patient soul to stain its virtue.
Syph. I cannot wrong thee. When we drive the spear
Into the monster's heart, or crush the serpent,
Can that be call'd a wrong ? 'Tis self-defence.
Mas. I'm loth to hurt thee more.—The tyrant works
Too fierce already in thy rankled breast.
But since thou seem'st to rank me with thyself,
With great destroyers, with perfidious kings ;
I must reply to thy licentious tongue ;
Bid thee remember, whose accursed sword
Began this work of death ; who broke the ties,
The holy ties, attested by the gods,
Which bind the nations in the bond of peace ;
Who meanly took advantage of my youth,
Unskill'd in arms, unsettled on my throne,
And drove me to the desert, there to dwell
With kinder monsters ; who my cities sack'd,
My country pillaged, and my subjects murder'd ;
Who still pursued me with inveterate hate ;
When open force proved vain, with ruffian arts,
The villain's dagger, base assassination.
And for no reason all. Brute violence
Alone thy plea.—What the least provocation,
Say, canst thou but pretend ?
Syph. I needed none.
Nature has in my being sown the seeds
Of enmity to thine.—Nay, mark me this :
Couldst thou restore me to my former state,
Strike off these chains, give me my crown again ;
Yet must I still, implacable to thee,
Seek eagerly thy death, or die myself.
Life cannot hold us both !—Unequal gods !
Who love to disappoint mankind, and take
All vengeance to yourselves ; why to the point
Of my long-flatter'd wishes did ye lift me ;
Then sink me down so low ? Just as I aim'd
The glorious stroke that was to make me happy,
Why did you blast my strong-extended arm ?
But that to mock us is your cruel sport ?
What else is human life ?
Mas. Thus always join'd
With an inhuman heart, and brutal manners,
Is irreligion to the ruling gods ;
Whose schemes our peevish ignorance arraigns,
Our thoughtless pride.—Thy lost condition, Syphax,
Is nothing to the tumult of thy breast.
There lies the sting of evil, there the drop
That poisons nature. Ye mysterious powers !
Whose ways are ever-gracious, ever-just,
As ye think wisest, best, dispose of me ;
But, whether through your gloomy depths I wander,
Or on your mountains walk ; give me the calm,
The steady, smiling soul ; where wisdom sheds
Eternal sunshine and eternal peace.
Then, if misfortune comes, she brings along
The bravest virtues. And so many great
Illustrious spirits have conversed with woe,
Have in her school been taught, as are enough
To consecrate distress, and make ambition
Even wish the frown beyond the smile of fortune.
Syph. Torture and racks ! This is the common trick
Of insolent success, unsuffering pride ;
This prate of patience, and I know not what :
'Tis all a lie, impracticable rant ;
And only tends to make me scorn thee more.
But why this talk ? In mercy send me hence ;
Yet—ere I go—Oh save me from distraction !
I know, hot youth, thou burnest for my queen ;
But by the majesty of ruin'd kings,
And that commanding glory which surrounds her,
I charge thee touch her not !
Mas. No, Syphax, no.
Thou need'st not charge me. That were mean indeed,
A triumph that to thee. But could I stoop
Again to love her ; thou, what right hast thou,
A captive, to her bed ? Thy bonds divorce
And free her from thy power. All laws in this,
Roman and Carthaginian, all agree.

Syph. Here, here, begins the bitterness of ruin;
Here my chains grind me first!
Mas. Poor Sophonisba!
She too becomes the prize of conquering Rome;
What most her heart abhors. Alas, how hard
Will slavery sit on her exalted soul!
She never will endure it, she will die.
For not a Roman burns with nobler ardour,
A higher sense of liberty than she;
And though she married thee, her only stain,
False to my youth, and faithless to her vows,
Yet, I must own it, from a worthy cause,
From public spirit, did her fault proceed.
Syph. Must I then hear her praise from thee?
Confusion!
Oh! for a lonely dungeon! where I rather
Would talk with my own groans, and breathe revenge,
Than in the mansions of the bless'd with thee.
Hell! Whither must I go?
Mas. Unhappy man!
And is thy breast determined against peace,
On comfort shut?
Syph. On all, but death, from thee.
Mas. Narva, be Syphax thy peculiar care;
And use him well, with tenderness and honour:
This evening Lælius, and to-morrow Scipio,
To Cirtha comes. Then let the Romans take
Their prisoner.
Syph. There shines a gleam of hope
Across the gloom.—From thee deliver'd!—Ease
Breathes in that thought—Lead on—My heart grows lighter!

SCENE V

Mas. What dreadful havock in the human breast
The passions make, when unconfined, and mad,
They burst unguided by the mental eye,
The light of reason, which in various ways
Points them to good, or turns them back from ill!
O save me from the tumult of the soul!
From the wild beast within!—For circling sands,
When the swift whirlwind whelms them o'er the lands;
The roaring deeps that to the clouds arise,
While through the storm the darting lightning flies,
The monster-brood to which the land gives birth,
The blazing city, and the gaping earth;
All deaths, all tortures, in one pang combined,
Are gentle, to the tempest of the mind.

ACT II.

SCENE I.

MASINISSA, NARVA.

Mas. THOU good old man, by whom my youth was form'd,
The firm companion of my various life,
I own, 'tis true, that Sophonisba's image
Lives in my bosom still; and at each glance
I take in secret of the bright idea,
A strange disorder seizes on my soul,
Which burns with stronger glory. Need I say,
How once she had my vows? Till Scipio came,
(Resistless man!) like a descending god,
And snatch'd me from the Carthaginian side,
To nobler Rome; beneath whose laurel'd brow,
And favouring eye, the nations grow polite,
Humane, and happy. Then thou mayst remember,
Such is this woman's high impetuous spirit,
That all-controlling love she bears her country,
Her Carthage; that for this she sacrificed
To Syphax, unbeloved, her blooming years,
And won him off from Rome.
Nar. My generous prince!
Applauding Afric of thy choice approves:
Fame claps her wings, and virtue smiles on thee;
Of peace thou softener, and thou soul of war!
But, oh! beware of that fair foe to glory,
Woman! and most, of Carthaginian woman!
Who has not heard of fatal Punic guile?
Of their stolen conquests? their insidious leagues?
Their Asdrubals? their Hannibals? with all
Their wily heroes? And, if such their men,
What must their women be?
Mas. You make me smile.
I thank thy honest zeal. But never dread
The firmness of my heart; the strong attachment
I hold to Rome, to Scipio, and to glory.
Indeed, I cannot, would not quite forget
The grace of Sophonisba: how she look'd,
And talk'd, and moved, a Pallas or a Juno!
Accomplish'd even in trifles, when she stoop'd
From higher thoughts, and with a soften'd eye,
Gave her quick spirit into gayer life:
Then every word was liveliness and wit;
We heard the Muses' song; and the dance swam
Through all the maze of harmony. Believe me
I do not flatter; yet my panting soul
To Scipio's friendship, to the fair pursuit
Of fame, and for my people's happiness,
Resign'd this Sophonisba; and though now
Constrain'd by sweet necessity to see her
A captive in my power, yet will I still
Resign her.
Nar. I'll not doubt thy fortitude,
My Masinissa, thy exalted purpose
Not to be lost in love; but ah! we know not
Oft, till experience sighs it to the soul,
The boundless witchcraft of ensnaring woman,
And our own slippery hearts. From Scipio learn
The temperance of heroes. I'll recount
The instructive story, what these eyes beheld:
Perhaps you've heard it; but 'tis pleasing still,
Though told a thousand times.
Mas. I burn to hear it.
Lost by my late misfortunes in the desert,
I lived a stranger to the voice of fame,
To Scipio's last exploits. Indulge me now.
Great actions, even recounted, raise the mind;
But when a friend has done them, then, my Narva,
They doubly charm us; then with more than wonder,
Even with a sort of vanity, we listen.
Nar. When to his glorious first essay in war,
New Carthage fell; there all the flower of Spain
Were kept in hostage; a full field presenting
For Scipio's generosity to shine.
And then it was, that when the hero heard

How I to thee belong'd, he with large gifts,
And friendly words, dismiss'd me.
Mas. I remember;
And in his favour that engaged me first.
But to thy story.
Nar. What with admiration
Struck every heart, was this:—A noble virgin,
Conspicuous far o'er all the captive dames,
Was mark'd the general's prize. She wept, and blush'd,
Young, fresh, and blooming like the morn. An eye,
As when the blue sky trembles through a cloud
Of purest white. A secret charm combined
Her features, and infused enchantment through them.
Her shape was harmony.—But eloquence
Beneath her beauty fails: which seem'd on purpose,
By nature lavish'd on her, that mankind
Might see the virtue of a hero tried
Almost beyond the stretch of human force.
Soft as she past along, with downcast eyes,
Where gentle sorrow swell'd, and now and then
Dropt o'er her modest cheek a trickling tear,
The Roman legions languish'd; and hard war
Felt more than pity. Even their chief himself,
As on his high tribunal raised he sat,
Turn'd from the dangerous sight, and chiding ask'd
His officers, if by this gift they meant
To cloud his glory in its very dawn.
Mas. Oh gods! my fluttering heart! On; stop not, Narva.
Nar. She, question'd of her birth, in trembling accents,
With tears and blushes broken, told her tale.
But when he found her royally descended,
Of her old captive parents the sole joy;
And that a hapless Celtiberian prince,
Her lover, and beloved, forgot his chains,
His lost dominions, and for her alone
Wept out his tender soul; sudden the heart
Of this young, conquering, loving, godlike Roman,
Felt all the great divinity of virtue.
His wishing youth stood check'd, his tempting power
Restrain'd by kind humanity.—At once
He for her parents and her lover call'd.—
The various scene imagine: how his troops
Look'd dubious on, and wonder'd what he meant:
While, stretch'd below, the trembling suppliants lay,
Rack'd by a thousand mingling passions; fear,
Hope, jealousy, disdain, submission, grief,
Anxiety, and love in every shape:
To these as different sentiments succeeded,
As mix'd emotions, when the man divine
Thus the dread silence to the lover broke:
"We both are young, both charm'd. The right of war
Has put thy beauteous mistress in my power;
With whom I could, in the most sacred ties,
Live out a happy life; but know that Romans
Their hearts as well as enemies can conquer.
Then take her to thy soul; and with her take
Thy liberty and kingdom. In return
I ask but this. When you behold these eyes,
These charms, with transport; be a friend to Rome."
Mas. There spoke the soul of Scipio.—But the lovers?
Nar. Joy and ecstatic wonder held them mute;
While the loud camp, and all the clustering crowd
That hung around, rang with repeated shouts.
Fame took the alarm, and through resounding Spain
Blew fast the fair report; which, more than arms,
Admiring nations to the Romans gain'd.
Mas. My friend in glory! thy awaken'd prince
Springs at thy noble tale. It fires my soul,
And nerves each thought anew; apt oft, perhaps
Too much, too much, to slacken into love.
But now the soft oppression flies; and all
My mounting powers expand to deeds like these.
Who, who would live, my Narva, just to breathe
This idle air, and indolently run,
Day after day, the still-returning round
Of life's mean offices, and sickly joys?
But, in the service of mankind, to be
A guardian god below:—still to employ
The mind's brave ardour in heroic aims,
Such as may raise us o'er the groveling herd,
And make us shine for ever?—That is life.
Bleed every vein about me; every nerve
With anguish tremble; every sinew ache;
The third time may I lose my crown; again
Wander the false inhospitable Syrts;
If, to reward my toils, the gods will grant me
To share the wreath of fame on Scipio's brow.
But see, she comes, the beauteous Sophonisba!
Behold, my friend, mark her majestic port!

SCENE II.

MASINISSA, SOPHONISBA, NARVA, PHŒNISSA.

Soph. Behold, victorious prince! the scene reversed;
And Sophonisba kneeling here; a captive,
O'er whom the gods, thy fortune, and thy virtue,
Give thee unquestion'd power of life and death.
If such a one may raise her suppliant voice,
Once music to thy ear; if she may touch
Thy knee, thy purple, and thy victor-hand;
O listen, Masinissa! Let thy soul
Intensely listen; while I fervent pray,
And strong adjure thee, by that regal state,
In which with equal pomp we lately shone;
By the Numidian name, our common boast;
And by those household gods (who may, I wish,
With better omens take thee to this palace,
Than Syphax hence they sent;) as is thy pleasure
In all beside determine of my fate;
This, this alone I beg: never, O never!
Into the cruel, proud, and hated power
Of Romans let me fall. Since angry Heaven
Will have it so, that I must be a slave,
And that a galling chain must bind these hands,
It were some little softening in my doom,
To call a kindred son of the same clime,
A native of Numidia, my lord.
But if thou canst not save me from the Romans,
If this sad favour be beyond thy power;
At least to give me death is what thou canst:—
Here strike—my naked bosom courts thy sword;
And my last breath shall bless thee, Masinissa!
Mas. Rise, Sophonisba, rise. To see thee thus
Is a revenge I scorn; and all the man
Within me, though much injured by thy pride,
And spirit too tempestuous for thy sex,
Yet blushes to behold thus at my feet,
Thus prostrate low, her for whom kings have kneel'd;
The fairest, but the falsest of her sex.
Soph. Spare thy reproach.—'Tis cruel thus to lose,
In rankling discord, and ungenerous strife,
The few remaining moments that divide me

From the most loathed of evils, Roman bondage!—
Yes, shut thy heart against me; shut thy heart
Against compassion, every human thought,
Even recollected love: yet know, rash youth!
That when thou seest me swell their lofty triumph,
Thou seest thyself in me. This is my day;
To-morrow will be thine But here, be sure,
Here will I lie on this vile earth forlorn,
Of hope abandon'd, since despised by thee;
These locks all loose and sordid in the dust;
This sullied bosom growing to the ground;
Till the remorseless soldier comes, more fierce
From recent blood; and, in thy very eye,
Lays raging his rude sanguinary grasp
On these weak limbs, and tortures them with chains.
Then if no friendly steel, no nectar'd draught
Of deadly poison, can enlarge my soul,
It will indignant burst from a slave's body,
And, join'd to mighty Dido, scorn ye all.

Mas. Oh, Sophonisba! 'tis not safe to hear thee;
And I mistook my heart, to trust it thus.
Hence let me fly.

Soph. You shall not, Masinissa!
Here will I hold you, tremble here for ever;
Here unremitting grow, till you consent.
And canst thou think, oh! canst thou think to leave
Exposed, defenceless, wretched, here alone, [me,
A prey to Romans flush'd with blood and conquest,
The subject of their scorn, or baser love?
Sure Masinissa cannot: and though changed,
Though cold as that averted look he wears,
Sure love can ne'er in generous breasts be lost
To that degree, as not from shame and outrage
To save what once they loved.

Mas. Enchantment! madness!—
What wouldst thou, Sophonisba?—O my heart!
My treacherous heart!

Soph. What would I, Masinissa?—
My mean request sits blushing on my cheek.
To be thy slave, young prince, is what I beg;
Here Sophonisba kneels to be thy slave;
Yet kneels in vain.—But thou'rt a slave thyself,
And canst not from the Romans save one woman;
Her who was once the triumph of thy soul,
Ere they seduced it by their lying glory.
Immortal gods! and am I fallen so low?
Scorn'd by a lover? by the man whom once
My heart, alas! too much inclined to love,
Before he sunk into the slave of Rome?—
Nought can be worth this baseness, life nor empire.
I loathe me for it.—On this kinder earth
Then leave me, leave me to despair and death!

Mas. I cannot bear her tears.—Rise, quickly
In all the conquering majesty of charms, [rise;
O Sophonisba! rise; while here I swear,
By the tremendous powers that rule mankind!
By heaven, and earth, and hell! by love and glory!
The Romans shall not hurt you—Romans cannot;
For Rome is generous as the gods themselves;
And honours, not insults, a generous foe.
Yet, since you dread them, take this royal hand,
The pledge of surety, by which kings are bound;
By which I hold you mine, and vow to treat you,
With all the softness of remember'd love,
All that can soothe thy fate, and make thee happy.

Soph. I thank thee, Masinissa: now the same,
The same bright youth, exalted, full of soul,
With whom, in happier days, I used to pass
The tender hour; while, dawning fair in love,
All song and sweetness, life set joyous out;
Ere the black tempest of ambition rose,
And drove us different ways.—Thus dress'd in war,
In nodding plumes, o'ercast with sullen thought,
With purposed vengeance dark, I knew thee not;
But now breaks out the beauteous sun anew,
The gay Numidian shines, who warm'd me once,
Whose love was glory.—Vain ideas, hence!
Long since, my heart, to nobler passions known,
Has your acquaintance scorn'd.

Mas. Oh! while you talk,
Enchanting fair one! my deluded thought
Runs back to days of love; when fancy still
Found worlds of beauty, ever rising new
To the transported eye: when flattering hope
Form'd endless prospects of increasing bliss;
And still the credulous heart believed them all,
Even more than love could promise.—But the scene
Is full of danger for a youthful eye;
I must not, dare not, will not look that way:
O hide it, wisdom, glory, from my view!
Or in sweet ruin I shall sink again.
Distemper clouds thy cheek; thy colour goes.—
Retire, and from the troubles of the day
Repose thy weary soul, worn out with care,
And rough unhappy thought.

Soph. May Masinissa
Ne'er want the goodness he has shown to me.

SCENE III.

MASINISSA, NARVA.

Mas. The danger's o'er: I've heard the siren's
Yet still to virtue hold my steady course. [sung;
I mark'd thy kind concern, thy friendly fears,
And own them just; for she has beauty, Narva,
So full, so perfect, with so great a soul
Inform'd, so raised with animating spirit,
As strikes like lightning from the hand of Jove,
And raises love to glory.

Nar. Ah, my prince!
Too true, it is too true; her fatal charms
Are powerful, and to Masinissa's heart
Know but too well the way. And art thou sure,
That the soft poison, which within thy veins
Lay unextinguish'd, is not roused anew,
Is not this moment working through thy soul?
Dost thou not love?—Confess.

Mas. What said my friend
Of poison?—love?—of loving Sophonisba?—
Yes, I admire her, wonder at her beauty,
And he who does not is as dull as earth,
The cold unanimated form of man,
Ere lighted up with the celestial fire.
Where'er she goes, still admiration gazes,
And listens while she talks. Even thou thyself,
Who saw'st her with the malice of a friend,
Even thou thyself admirest her.—Dost thou not?—
Say, speak sincerely.

Nar. She has charms indeed;
But has she charms like virtue? Though majestic,
Does she command us with a force like glory?

Mas. All glory's in her eye! Perfection thence
Looks from its throne; and on her ample brow
Sits majesty. Her features glow with life,
Warm with heroic soul. Her mien! she walks
As when a towering goddess treads the earth.
But when her language flows; when such a mind
Descends to soothe, to sigh, to weep, to grasp

The tottering knee! oh! Narva, Narva, oh!
Expression here is dumb.
Nar. Alas! my lord,
Is this the talk of sober admiration?
Are these the sallies of a heart at ease?
Of Scipio's friend? Is this thy steady virtue?
Mas. I tell thee once again, too cautious man,
That when a woman begs, a matchless woman,
A woman once beloved, a fallen queen,
A Sophonisba! when she twines her charms
Around our soul, and all her power of looks,
Of tears, of sighs, of softness, plays upon us;
He's more or less than man who can resist her.
For me, my steadfast soul approves, nay more,
Exults in the protection it has promised:
And nought, though plighted honour did not bind me,
Should shake the virtuous purpose of my heart;
Nought, by the avenging gods! who heard my vow,
And hear me now again.
Nar. And was it then
For this you conquer'd?
Mas. Yes, and triumph in it.
This was my fondest wish; the very point,
The plume of glory, the delicious prize
Of bleeding years. I must have been a brute,
A greater monster than Numidia breeds,
A horror to myself; if, on the ground,
Cast vilely from me, I the illustrious fair
Had left to bondage, bitterness, and death.
Nor is there aught in war worth what I feel;
In pomp and hollow state, like the sweet sense
Of infelt bliss, which the reflection gives me,
Of saving thus such excellence and beauty
From what her generous soul abhors the most.
Nar. My friend! my royal lord! alas! you slide,
You sink from virtue.—On the giddy brink
Of fate you stand.—One step, and all is lost!
Mas. No more, no more! if this is being lost,
And rushing down the precipice of fate,
Then down I go, far, far beyond the reach
Of scrupulous dull precaution.—Leave me, Narva;
I want to be alone, to find some shade,
Some solitary gloom; there to shake off
These harsh tumultuous cares that vex my life,
This sick ambition on itself recoiling;
And there to listen to the gentle voice,
The sigh of peace, something, I know not what,
That whispers transport to my heart.—Farewell.

SCENE IV.

Nar. (*alone.*) Struck, and he knows it not.—So when the field,
Elate in heart, the warrior scorns to yield;
The streaming blood can scarce convince his eyes,
Nor will he feel the wound by which he dies.

ACT III.

SCENE I.

Mas. (*alone.*) In vain I wander through the shade for peace;
'Tis with the calm alone, the pure of heart,
That there the goddess talks:—but in my breast,
Some busy thought, some secret eating pang,
Still restless throbs; on Sophonisba still
Earnest, intent, devoted all to her.—
What may this mean?—'tis love, almighty love!
Returning on me with a stronger tide.
Come to my breast, thou rosy, smiling god!
Come unconfined! bring all thy joys along,
All thy soft cares, and mix them copious here.—
Quick, let me fly to her; and there forget
This tedious absence, war, ambition, noise,
Friendship itself, the vanity of fame,
And all but love—for love is more than all.

SCENE II.

Masinissa, Narva.

Mas. Welcome again, my friend.—Come nearer, Narva;
Lend me thine arm, and I will tell thee all;
Unfold my secret heart, whose every pulse
With Sophonisba beats—Nay, hear me out.—
Swift, as I mused, the conflagration spread;
At once too strong, too general, to be quench'd.
I love, and I approve it; doat upon her;
Even think these minutes lost I talk with thee.
Heavens! what emotions have possess'd my soul!
Snatch'd by a moment into years of passion.
Nar. Ah, Masinissa!——
Mas. Argue not against me.
Talk down the circling winds that lift the desert;
And when, by lightning fired, the forests blaze,
Talk down the flame, but not my stronger love.
I have for love a thousand thousand reasons,
Dear to the heart and potent o'er the soul.
My every thought, reflection, memory, all
Are a perpetual spring of tenderness;
Oh, Sophonisba! I am wholly thine.
Nar. Is this deceitful day then come to nought,
This day that set thee on a double throne?
That gave thee Syphax chain'd, thy deadly foe?
With perfect conquest crown'd thee, perfect glory?
Is it so soon eclipsed? And does yon sun,
Yon setting sun, who this fair morning saw thee
Ride through the ranks of long-extended war,
As radiant as himself; and when the storm
Began, beheld thee tread the rising surge
Of battle high, and drive it on the foe;
Does he now, blushing, see thee sunk so weak?
Caught in a smile? the captive of a look?—
I cannot name it without tears.
Mas. Away!
I'm sick of war, of the destroying trade,
Smoothed o'er and gilded with the name of glory.
In vain you spread the martial field to me,
My happier eyes are turn'd another way,
Behold it not; or, if they do, behold it
Shrunk up, far off, a visionary scene;
As to the waking man appears the dream.
Nar. Or rather as realities appear,
The virtue, pomp, and dignities of life,
In sick disorder'd dreams.
Mas. Think not I scorn

The task of heroes, when oppression rages,
And lawless violence confounds the world.
Who would not bleed with transport for his country,
Tear every tender passion from his heart,
And greatly die to make a people happy,
Ought not to taste of happiness himself,
And is low-soul'd indeed.—But sure, my friend,
There is a time for love; or life were vile,
A tedious circle of unjoyous days,
With senseless hurry fill'd, distasteful, wretched;
Till love comes smiling in, and brings his sweets,
His healing sweets, soft cares, transporting joys,
That make the poor account of life complete,
And justify the gods.

Nar. Mistaken prince,
I blame not love. But——

Mas. Slander not my passion.
I've suffer'd thee too far.—Take heed, old man;—
Love will not bear an accusation, Narva.

Nar. I'll speak the truth, when truth and friendship call,
Nor fear thy frown unkind. Thou hast no right
To Sophonisba; she belongs to Rome.

Mas. Ha! she belongs to Rome.—'Tis true.—My thoughts,
Where have you wander'd, not to think of this?
Think ere I promised? ere I loved?—Confusion!
I know not what to say.—I should have loved,
Though Jove in muttering thunder had forbid it.
But Rome will not refuse so small a boon,
Whose gifts are kingdoms: Rome must grant it sure,
One captive to my wish, one poor request;
So small to them, but oh! so dear to me.
In this my heart confides.

Nar. Delusive love!
Through what wild projects is the frantic mind
Beguiled by thee.—And think'st thou that the Romans,
The senators of Rome, these gods on earth,
Wise, steady to the right, severely just,
All uncorrupt, and, like eternal fate,
Not to be moved, will listen to the sigh
Of idle love? They who, when virtue calls,
Will not the voice itself of nature hear,
But bid their children bleed before their eyes;
Will they regard the light fantastic pangs
Of a fond heart; and with thy kingdom give thee
Their most inveterate foe, from their firm side,
Like Syphax, to delude thee, and the point
Of their own bounty on themselves to turn?—
Thou canst not hope it sure.—Impossible!

Mas. What shall I do?—Be now the friend exerted.
For love and honour press me; love and honour,
All that is dear and excellent in life,
All that or soothes the man or lifts the hero,
Engage my soul.

Nar. Rash was your vow, my lord.
I know not what to counsel. When you vow'd,
You vow'd what was not in your power to grant;
And therefore 'tis not binding.

Mas. Never! Never!
Oh never will I falsify that vow!
Ere then destruction seize me!—Yes, ye Romans,
If it be so, there, take your kingdoms back,
Your friendship, your esteem, all, all but her.——
Hold—Let me think a while—It shall be so!
By all the inspiring gods that prompt my thought,
This very night shall solemnise our vows;
And the next joyous sun that visits Afric,
See Sophonisba seated on my throne.——
Then must they spare my queen.—They will not, surely,
They will not dare to force my consort from me.

Nar. And is it possible?—Ye gods that rule us!
Can Masinissa, in his pride of youth,
In his meridian glory shining wide,
The light of Afric, can the friend of Scipio
Take a false woman to his nuptial bed,
Who scorn'd him for a tyrant old and cruel,
His rancorous foe, and gave her untouch'd bloom,
Her spring of charms, to Syphax?

Mas. Cursed remembrance!
This, this, has thrown a serpent to my heart,
While it o'erflow'd with tenderness, with joy,
With all the sweetness of exulting love:
Now nought but gall is there, and burning poison.—
Yes, it was so.—Curse on her vain ambition!
What had her meddling sex to do with states?
Forsook for him, just gods! for hateful Syphax,
My tender faithful love for his gross passion!
The thought is hell!—Oh, I had treasured up
A world of indignation, years of scorn;
But her sad suppliant witchcraft soothed it down.—
Where is she now, that it may burst upon her?
Haste, bring her to me; though my plighted faith
Shall save her from the Romans, yet I'll tell her,
That I will never, never see her more!—
Ha! there she comes.—Pernicious fair one!—
Leave me.

SCENE III.

SOPHONISBA, MASINISSA.

Soph. Forgive this quick return.—The rage, confusion,
And mingled passions of this luckless day,
Made me forget another warm request
I had to beg of generous Masinissa:
For oh! to whom, save to the generous, can
The miserable fly?—But much disturb'd
You look, and scowl upon me a denial.
Repentance frowns on your contracted brow;
Already, weary of my sinking fate,
You seem to droop; and for unhappy Syphax
I shall implore in vain.

Mas. For Syphax? vengeance!
And canst thou mention him? Oh! grant me breath.

Soph. I know, young prince, how deep he has provoked thee;
How keen he sought thy youth; through what a fire
Of great distress, from which you come the brighter.
On mere indifferent objects, common bounty
Will shower relief; but when our bitterest foe
Lies sunk, disarm'd, and desolate, then! then!
To feel the mercies of a pitying god,
To raise him from the dust, and that best way
To triumph o'er him, is heroic goodness.
Oh, let unhappy Syphax touch thy heart,
Victorious Masinissa!

Mas. Monstrous this!
Still dost thou blast me with that cursed name!
The very name thy conscious guilt should shun.
Had he but driven me from my native throne,
From regal pomp and luxury, to dwell
Among the forest beasts; to bear the beam
Of red Numidian suns, and the dank dew
Of cold unshelter'd nights: to mix with wolves,

To hunt with hungry tigers for my prey,
And thirst with dipsads on the burning sand;
I could have thank'd him for his angry lesson;
The fair occasion that his rage afforded
Of learning patience, fortitude, and hope,
Still rising stronger on incumbent fate.
But there is one unpardonable outrage,
That scorches up the tear in pity's eye,
And even sweet mercy's self converts to gall.
I cannot—will not name it.—Down my heart,
My swelling heart!

Soph. Ah! whence this sudden storm,
That hurries all thy soul?

Mas. And dost thou ask?
Ask thy own faithless heart; snatch'd from my vows,
From the warm wishes of my springing youth,
And given to that old hated monster Syphax—
Perfidious Sophonisba!

Soph. Nay, no more;
With too much truth I can return thy charge.
Why didst thou drive me to that cruel choice?
Why leave me, with my country, to destruction?
Why break thy love, thy faith, and join the Romans?

Mas. By heavens! the Romans were my better genius,
Saved me from shame, and form'd my youth to glory.
But for the Romans, I had been a savage,
A wretch like Syphax, a forgotten thing,
The tool of Carthage.

Soph. Meddle not with Carthage,
Impatient youth! for that I will not bear;
Though I am here thy slave, I will not bear it.
Not one base word of Carthage—on thy soul!

Mas. How vain thy frenzy!—Go, command thy slaves,
Thy fools, thy Syphaxes: but I will speak,
Speak loud of Carthage, call it false, ungenerous.
The Romans are the light, the glory——

Soph. Romans!
Perdition on the Romans!—on their friends!
On all—but thee. The Romans are the scourge
Of the vext world, destroyers of mankind,
And all beneath the smooth dissembling mask
Of justice and compassion! as if slave
Was but another name for civilised.
Against her tyrant power, each generous sword
Of every nation should be drawn.—While Carthage
Unblemish'd rises on the base of commerce,
Founds her fair empire on that common good,
And asks of Heaven nought but the winds and tides
To carry plenty, letters, science, wealth,
Civility, and grandeur, round the world.

Mas. No more compare them; for the gods [themselves
Declare for Rome.

Soph. It was not always so.
The gods declared for Hannibal, when Italy
Blazed all around him, all her streams ran blood;
And when at Trebia, Thrasymene, and Cannæ,
The Carthaginian sword with Roman blood
Was drunk.—Oh! that he then, on that dread day,
While lifeless consternation blacken'd Rome,
Had razed the accursed city to the ground,
And saved the world!—When will it come again,
A day so glorious, and so big with vengeance
On those my soul abhors?

Mas. Avert it, Heaven!
The Romans not enslave, but save the world
From Carthaginian rage——

Soph. I'll bear no more!
Nor tenderness, nor life, nor liberty,
Nothing shall make me bear it.—Rather, rather,
Detested as ye are, ye Romans, take me;
Oh! pitying take me to your nobler chains,
And save me from this abject youth, your slave!—
How canst thou kill me thus?——

Mas. I meant it not.
I only meant to tell thee, haughty fair one!
How this alone might bind me to the Romans;
That, in a frail and sliding hour, they snatch'd me
From the perdition of thy love, which fell,
Like baleful lightning, where I most could wish,
And proved destruction to my mortal foe.—
Oh, pleasing! fortunate!

Soph. I thank them too.
By heavens! for once, I love them; since they turn'd
My better thoughts from thee; thou—but I will not
Give thee the name thy mean servility
From my just scorn deserves.

Mas. Oh! freely call me
By every name thy fury can inspire;
Delight me with thy hate.—I love no more—
It will not hurt me, Sophonisba.——Love!
Long since I gave it to the passing winds,
And would not be a lover for the world.
A lover is the very fool of nature,
Made sick by his own wantonness of thought,
His fever'd fancy: while, to your own charms
Imputing all, you swell with boundless pride.
Shame on the wretch! he should be driven from [men,
To live with Asian slaves, in one soft herd;
All worthless, all ridiculous together.
For me this moment here I mean to bid
Farewell, a glad farewell, to love and thee.

Soph. With all my soul, farewell!—Yet ere you go,
Know that my spirit burns as high as thine,
As high to glory, and as low to love.
Thy promises are void; and I absolve thee,
Here in the presence of the listening gods.—
Take thy repented vows.—To proud Cornelia
I'd rather be a slave, to Scipio's mother,
Than queen of all Numidia, by the favour
Of him who dares insult the helpless thus.
[*Pausing.*

Still dost thou stay? behold me then again,
Hopeless and wild, a lost abandon'd slave.
And now thy brutal purpose must be gain'd,
Away, thou cruel and ungenerous, go!

Mas. No, not for worlds would I resume my [vow!
Dishonour blast me then! all kind of ills
Fill up my cup of bitterness and shame,
When I resign thee to triumphant Rome.
Oh, lean not thus dejected to the ground!
The sight is misery.—What roots me here?
[*Aside.*

Alas! I have urged my foolish heart too far;
And love depress'd, recoils with greater force.—
Oh, Sophonisba!

Soph. By thy pride she dies
Inhuman prince!

Mas. Thine is the triumph, love!
By heaven and earth! I cannot hold it more.
Wretch that I was, to crush the unhappy thus;
The fairest too, the dearest of her sex;
For whom my soul could die.—Turn, quickly turn,
O Sophonisba! my beloved! my glory!
Turn and forgive the violence of love,
Of love that knows no bounds!

Soph. And can it be?
Can that soft passion prove so fierce of heart,
As on the tears of misery, the sighs
Of death, to feast; to torture what it loves?
Mas. Yes, it can be, thou goddess of my soul,
Whose each emotion is but varied love;
All over love, its powers, its passions, all;
Its anger, indignation, fury, love;
Its pride, disdain, even detestation, love:
And when it, wild, resolves to love no more,
Then is the triumph of excessive love.
Didst thou not mark me, mark the dubious rage
That tore my heart with anguish while I talk'd?
Thou didst; and must forgive so kind a fault.—
What would thy trembling lips?
Soph. Oh! let me die.—
For such another storm, so much contempt
Thrown out on Carthage, so much praise on Rome,
Were worse than death. Why should I longer tire
My weary fate? The most relentless Roman
What could he more?
Mas. O Sophonisba, hear!
See me thy suppliant now. Talk not of death,
I have no life but thee.—Alas! alas!
Hadst thou a little tenderness for me,
The smallest part of what I feel, thou wouldst—
(What wouldst thou not) forgive? But how indeed,
How can I hope it? Yet I from this moment
Will so devote my being to thy pleasure,
So live alone to gain thee, that thou must,
If there is human nature in thy breast,
Feel some relenting warmth.
Soph. Well, well, 'tis past:
To be inexorable suits not slaves.
Mas. Spare, spare that word; it stabs me to the soul;
My crown, my life, and liberty are thine.
Oh! give my passion way: my heart is full,
Oppress'd by love; and I could number tears,
With all the dews that sprinkle o'er the morn.
Oh! thou hast melted down my stubborn soul
To female tenderness.—Enough, enough,
Have we been cheated by the trick of state,
For Rome and Carthage suffer'd much too long;
And, led by gaudy phantoms, wander'd far,
Far from our bliss. But now since met again,
Since here I hold thee, circle all perfection
In these bless'd arms; since fate too presses hard,
Since Rome and slavery drive thee to the brink,
Let this immediate night exchange our vows,
Secure my bliss, our future fortunes blend;
Set thee, the queen of beauty, on my throne,
And on these lovely brows, for empire form'd,
Place Afric's noblest crown.—A wretched gift,
To what my love would give.
Soph. What? marry thee?
This night?
Mas. Thou dear one! yes, this very night
Let injured Hymen have his rights restored,
And bind our broken vows.—Think, serious think
On what I plead.—A thousand reasons urge.—
Captivity dissolves thy former marriage;
And if the meanest vulgar thus are freed,
Can Sophonisba, to a slave, to Syphax!
The most exalted of her sex, be bound?
Besides it is the best, perhaps sole way,
To save thee from the Romans; and must sure
Bar their pretensions: or if ruin comes,
To perish with thee is to perish happy.
Soph. Yet must I still insist——
Mas. It shall be so.
I know thy purpose; it would plead for Syphax.
He shall have all, thou dearest! shall have all,
Crowns, trifles, kingdoms, all again, but thee,
But thee, thou more than all! [*Aside.*
Soph. Bear witness, Heaven!
This is alone for Carthage. [*To him.*
Gain'd by goodness,
I may be thine. Expect no love, no sighing.
Perhaps, hereafter, I may learn again
To hold thee dear. If on these terms thou canst,
Here take me, take me to thy wishes.
Mas. Yes,
Yes, Sophonisba! as a wretch takes life
From off the rack.—All wild with frantic joy,
Thus hold thee, press thee to my bounding heart;
And bless the bounteous gods.—Can Heaven give more?
Oh happy! happy! happy!—Come, my fair,
This ready minute sees thy will perform'd;
From Syphax knocks his chains; and I myself,
Even in his favour, will request the Romans.
Oh, thou hast smiled my passions into peace!—
So, while conflicting winds embroil'd the seas,
In perfect bloom, warm with immortal blood,
Young Venus rear'd her o'er the raging flood:
She smiled around, like thine her beauties glow'd;
When smooth, in gentle swells, the surges flow'd;
Sunk, by degress, into a liquid plain,
And one bright calm sat trembling on the main.

ACT IV.

SCENE I.

SOPHONISBA, PHŒNISSA.

Phœn. Hail! queen ot Masæsylia once again,
And fair Massylia join'd. This rising day
Saw Sophonisba, from the height of life,
Thrown to the very brink of slavery;
State, honours, armies vanish'd, nothing left
But her own great unconquerable mind.
And yet, ere evening comes, to larger power
Restored, I see my royal friend, and kneel
In grateful homage to the gods, and her.
Ye powers, what awful changes often mark
The fortunes of the great!
Soph. Phœnissa, true;
'Tis awful all, the wondrous work of fate.
But, ah! this sudden marriage damps my soul:
I like it not, that wild precipitance
Of youth, that ardour, that impetuous stream
In which his love return'd. At first, my friend,
He vainly raged with disappointed love;
And, as the hasty storm subsided, then
To softness varied, to returning fondness,
To sighs, to tears, to supplicating vows.
But all his vows were idle, till at last
He shook my heart by Rome.—To be his queen
Could only save me from their horrid power.
And there is madness in that thought, enough

In that strong thought alone to make me run
From nature.
Phœn. Was it not auspicious, madam;
Just as we hoped, just as our wishes plann'd?—
Nor let your spirits sink: your serious hours,
When you behold the Roman ravage check'd,
From their enchantment Masinissa freed,
And Carthage mistress of the world again,
This marriage will approve: then will it rise
In all its glory, virtuous, wise, and great,
While happy nations, then deliver'd, join
Their loud acclaim. And, had the bless'd occasion
Neglected flown, where now had been your hopes,
Your liberty, your country, where your all?
Think well of this; you cannot but exult
In what is done.
Soph. So may my hopes succeed,
As love alone to Carthage, to the public,
Led me a marriage-victim to the temple,
And justifies my vows!—Ha! Syphax here!—
What would his rage with me?—Phœnissa, stay.—
But this one trial more.—Heroic truth,
Support me now!

SCENE II.

SYPHAX, SOPHONISBA, PHŒNISSA.

Syph. You seem to fly me, madam,
To shun my gratulations.—Here I come,
To join the general joy; and I, sure I,
Who have to dotage, have to ruin loved you,
Must take a tender part in your success,
In your recover'd state.
Soph. 'Tis very well;
I thank you, sir.
Syph. And gentle Masinissa,
Say, will he prove a very coming fool;
All pliant, all devoted to your will;
A duteous wretch like Syphax?—Ha! not moved!
Speak, thou perfidious! canst thou bear it thus,
With such a steady countenance? canst thou
Here see the man thou hast so grossly wrong'd,
And yet not sink in shame? and yet not shake
In every guilty nerve?
Soph. What have I done,
That I should tremble? that I should not dare
To bear thy presence?—Was my heart to blame,
I'd tremble at myself, and not at thee,
Proud man.—Nor would I live to be ashamed;
For of all evils, to the generous, shame
Is the most deadly pang.—But you behold
My late engagement with a jealous, false,
And selfish eye.
Syph. Avenging Juno, hear!
And canst thou think to justify thyself?—
I blush to hear thee, traitress!
Soph. O my soul!
Canst thou hear this, this base opprobrious language,
And yet be tamely calm?—Well, for this once
It shall be so, in pity to thy madness.—
Impatient spirit, down!—Yes, Syphax, yes,
Yes, I will greatly justify myself:
Even by the consort of the thundering Jove,
Who binds the holy marriage-vow, be judged:
And every generous heart, not meanly lost
In little low pursuits, will sure absolve me.
But in the tempest of the soul, when rage,
Loud indignation, unattentive pride,
And jealousy confound it, how can then
The nobler public sentiments be heard?—
Yet let me tell thee——
Syph. Thou canst tell me nought.
Away! away! nought but illusion, falsehood——
Soph. My heart will burst, in justice to myself,
If here I speak not: though thy rage, I know,
Can never be convinced, yet shall it be
Confounded.—What! must I renounce my freedom?
Forego the power of doing general good?
Yield myself up the slave, the barbarous triumph,
Of insolent, enraged, inveterate Rome?
And all for nothing but to grace thy fall?
Nay, singly perish, to retain the name,
The empty title of a captive's wife?—
For thee, the Romans may be mild to thee;
But I, a Carthaginian, I, whose blood
Holds unrelenting enmity to theirs;
Who have myself much hurt them, and who live
Only to work them woe; what, what can I
Hope from their vengeance, but the very dregs
Of the worst fate, the bitterness of bondage?
Yet thou, kind man, thou in thy generous love,
Wouldst have me suffer that; be bound to thee,
For that dire end alone, beyond the stretch
Of nature and of law.
Syph. Confusion! law!—
I know the laws permit thee; the gross laws
That rule the vulgar.—I'm a captive; true;
And therefore mayst thou plead a shameful right
To leave me to my chains.—But say, thou base one!
Ungrateful, say, for whom am I a captive?
For whom has battle after battle bled!
For whom my crown, my kingdom, and my all,
Been vilely cast away?—For one, ye gods!
Who leaves me for the victor, for the foe
I hold in utter endless detestation.
Fire! fury! hell!—Oh, I am richly paid!
But this it is to love a woman—woman!
The source of all disaster, all perdition!—
Man in himself is social, would be happy,
Too happy, but the gods, to keep him wretched,
Cursed him with woman! fond, enchanting, smooth,
And harmless-seeming woman; but at heart
All poison, serpents, tigers, furies, all
That is destructive, in one breast combined,
And gilded o'er with beauty!
Soph. Hapless man!
I pity thee: this madness only stirs
My bosom to compassion, not to rage.—
Think as you list of our unhappy sex,
Too much subjected to your tyrant force:
Yet know that all, we were not all at least
Form'd for your trifles, for your wanton hours;
Our passions too can sometimes soar above
The household task assign'd us, can extend
Beyond the narrow sphere of families,
And take great states into the expanded heart,
As well as yours, ye partial to yourselves!
And this is my support, my joy, my glory;
On these great principles, and these alone,
I still direct my conduct.
Syph. False as hell!
I loath your sex when it pretends to virtue.
You talk of honour, conscience, patriotism!
A female patriot!—Vanity!—absurd!—
Even doating dull credulity would laugh
To hear you prate. Did ever woman yet
Form any better purpose in her thought,
Than how to please her pride or wanton will?

Those are the principles on which you act;
Yes, those alone.
Soph. Must I then, must I, Syphax,
Give thee a bitter proof of what I say?
I would not seem to heighten thy distress,
Not in the least insult thee. Thou art fallen,
So fate severe has will'd it, fallen by me;
I therefore have been patient: from another,
Such language, such indignity, had fired
My soul to madness. But since driven so far,
I must remind thy blind, injurious rage,
Of our unhappy marriage——
Syph. Darest thou name it,
After such perfidy?
Soph. Allow me, Syphax—
Hear me but once! If what I here declare
Shines not with reason, and the clearest truth,
May I be base, despised, and dumb for ever!
I pray thee think, when unpropitious Hymen
Our hands united, how I stood engaged.—
Was I not blooming in the pride of youth,
And youthful hopes? sunk in a passion too
Which few resign?—Yet then I married thee,
Because to Carthage deem'd a stronger friend:—
For that alone. On these conditions, say,
Didst thou not take me, court me to thy throne?
Have I deceived thee since? Have I dissembled?
To gain one purpose, e'er pretended what
I never felt?—Thou canst not say I have.
And if that principle, which then inspired
My marrying thee, was right, it cannot now
Be wrong: nay, since my native city wants
Assistance more, and sinking calls for aid,
'Tis still more right.
Syph. This reasoning is insult!
Soph. I'm sorry that thou dost oblige me to it:
Then, in a word, take my full-open'd soul:—
All love, but that of Carthage, I despise.
I formerly to Masinissa thee
Preferr'd not, nor to thee now Masinissa;
But Carthage to you both. And if preferring
Thousands to one, a whole collected people,
All nature's tenderness, whate'er is sacred,
The liberty, the welfare of a state,
To one man's frantic happiness, be shame;
Here, Syphax, I invoke it on my head!
This set aside; I, careless of myself,
And scorning prosperous state, had still been thine;
In all the depth of misery proudly thine.
But since the public good, the law supreme,
Forbids it; I will leave thee with a kingdom,
The same I found thee, or not reign myself.
Alas! I see thee hurt.—Why camest thou here,
Thus to inflame thee more?
Syph. Why, sorceress! why?—
Thou complication of all deadly mischief!
Thou lying, soothing, specious, charming fury!
I'll tell thee why:—To breathe my great revenge,
To throw this load of burning madness from me—
To stab thee!——
Soph. Ha!—
Syph. —And, springing from thy heart,
To quench me with thy blood.
[Phœnissa *interposes.*
Soph. Off, give me way,
Phœnissa; tempt not thou his brutal rage.
Me, me, he dares not murder: if he dares,
Here let his fury strike; for I dare die.—
What holds thy trembling hand?
Phœn. Guards!
Soph. Seize the king.
But look you treat him well, with all the state
His dignity demands.
Syph. That care from thee
Is worse than death.—The Roman trumpets!—Ha!
Now I bethink me, Rome will do me justice.
Yes, I shall see thee walk the slave of Rome;
Forget my wrongs, and glut me with the sight.
Be that my best revenge.
Soph. Inhuman!—that,
If there is death in Afric, shall not be.

SCENE III.

Lælius, Syphax.

Læl. Syphax!—alas! how fallen! how changed! from what
I here beheld thee once in pomp and splendour,
At that illustrious interview, when Rome
And Carthage met beneath this very roof;
Their two great generals, Asdrubal and Scipio,
To court thy friendship. Of the same repast
Both gracefully partook, and both reclined
On the same couch: for personal distaste
And hatred seldom burn between the brave.
Then the superior virtues of the Roman
Gain'd all thy heart. Even Asdrubal himself,
With admiration struck and just despair,
Own'd him as powerful at the social feast
As in the battle. This thou mayst remember;
And how thy faith was given before the gods,
And sworn and seal'd to Scipio: yet how false
Thou since hast proved, I need not now recount:
But let thy sufferings for thy guilt atone,
The captive for the king. A Roman tongue
Scorns to pursue the triumph of the sword
With mean upbraidings.
Syph. Lælius, 'tis too true.
Curse on the cause!
Læl. But where is Masinissa?
The brave young victor, the Numidian Roman,
Where is he? that my joy, my glad applause,
From envy pure, may hail his happy state.—
Why that contemptuous smile?
Syph. Too credulous Roman,
I smile to think how this brave Masinissa,
This Rome-devoted hero, must still more
Attract thy praises, by a late exploit;
In every thing successful.
Læl. What is this—
These public shouts? A strange unusual joy
O'er all the captive city blazes wide.
What wanton riot reigns to-night in Cirtha,
Within these conquer'd walls?
Syph. This, Lælius, is
A night of triumph o'er my conqueror,
O'er Masinissa.
Læl. Masinissa!—How?
Syph. Why, he to-night is married to my queen.
Læl. Impossible!——
Syph. Yes, she, the fury! she,
Who put the nuptial torch into my hand,
That set my throne, my palace, and my kingdom,
All in a blaze; she now has seized on him;
Will turn him soon from Rome.—I know her power,
Her lips distil unconquerable poison.—
O glorious thought! her arts, her fatal love

Will crush him deep, beneath the mighty ruins
Of falling Carthage.

Læl. Can it be?—Amazement!

Syph. Nay learn it from himself.—He comes.—Away,
Ye furies, snatch me from his sight!—For hell,
Its tortures all are gentle to the presence
Of a triumphant rival!

Læl. What is man!

SCENE IV.

MASINISSA, LÆLIUS.

Mas. Thou more than partner of this glorious day,
Which has from Carthage torn her chief support,
And tottering left her, I rejoice to see thee.—
To Cirtha welcome, Lælius. Thy brave legions
Now taste the sweet repose by valour purchased:
This city pours refreshment on their toils.—
I order'd Narva—

Læl. Thanks to Masinissa,
All that is well.—But I observed the king
More loosely guarded than befits the state
Of such a captive. True, indeed, from him
There is not much to fear. The dangerous spirit
Is his imperious queen, his Sophonisba:
The pride, the rage of Carthage, live in her.—
How? where is she?

Mas. She, Lælius!—in my care.
Think not of her. I'll answer for her conduct.

Læl. Yes, if in chains. Till then, believe me, prince,
It were as safe to answer for the winds,
That their loosed fury will not rouse the waves;
Or that the darted lightning will be harmless;
As promise peace from her.—But why so dark?—
You shift your place, your countenance grows warm:
It is not usual this in Masinissa.—
Pray, what offence can asking for the queen,
The Roman captive, give?

Mas. Lælius, no more.—
You know my marriage.—Syphax has been busy.—
It is unkind to dally with my passion.

Læl. Ah, Masinissa! was it then for this,
Thy hurry hither from the recent battle?
Is the first instance of the Roman bounty
Thus, thus abused?—They give thee back thy kingdom;
And, in return are of their captive robb'd;
Of all they valued—Sophonisba.—

Mas. Robb'd!—
How, Lælius, robb'd!

Læl. Yes, Masinissa, robb'd:
What is it else?—But I, this very night,
Will here assert the majesty of Rome,
And (mark me!) tear her from the nuptial bed.

Mas. O gods! O patience!—As soon, fiery Roman,
As soon thy rage might from her azure sphere
Tear yonder moon.—The man who seizes her,
Shall set his foot first on my bleeding heart—
Of that be sure.—And is it thus you treat [you?
Your firm allies?—Thus, kings in friendship with
Of human passions strip them?—Slaves indeed!
If thus denied the common privilege
Of nature, what the weakest creatures claim—
A right to what they love.

Læl. Out! out!—For shame!
This passion makes thee blind. Here is a war,
Which desolates the nations, has almost
Laid waste the world. How many widows, orphans,
And tender virgins weep its rage in Rome!
Even her great senate droops; her nobles fail.
Nature herself, by frequent prodigies,
Seems at this havoc of her works to sicken:
And our Ausonian plains are now become
A horror to the sight: at each sad step,
Remembrance weeps.—Yet her, the greatest prize
It hitherto has yielded; her, whose charms
Are only turn'd to whet its cruel point;
Thou to thy wedded breast hast wildly taken,
Hast purchased thee her beauties by the blood
Of thy protecting friends; and on a throne
Set her, this day recover'd by their arms.—
Canst thou do this, and call thyself a king
Allied to Rome?—Rash youth, the Roman people,
To kings who dare offend them thus, vouchsafe not
The honour of their friendship.—Thou hast thrown
That glory from thee, and must now be taught
To dread their wrath.

Mas. Be not so haughty, Lælius.
It scarce becomes the gentle Scipio's friend;
Suits not thy character, the tender manners
I still have mark'd in thee. I honour Rome:
But honour too myself, my vows, my queen:
Nor will, nor can I tamely hear thee threaten
To seize her like a slave.

Læl. I will be calm.
This thy rash deed, this unexpected shock,
Such a peculiar injury to me,
Thy friend and fellow-soldier, has perhaps
Snatch'd me too far. For hast thou not dishonour'd,
By this last action, a successful war,
Our common charge, trusted to us by Scipio?

Mas. Our charge from Scipio was to conquer Syphax;
Not by a barbarous triumph to insult
His beauteous queen. Was Sophonisba made
To follow weeping a proud victor's chariot?
She, the first mistress of my heart, who still
Reigns in my soul, and there will reign for ever.
At such a sight, the warrior's eye might wet
His burning cheek; and all the Roman matrons,
Who lined the laurel'd way, ashamed and sad,
Turn from a captive brighter than themselves.—
But Scipio will be milder.

Læl. I disdain
This thy surmise, and give it up to Scipio.—
These passions are not comely.—Here to-morrow
Comes the proconsul. Meantime, Masinissa,
Ah! harden not thyself in flattering hope.
Scipio is mild, but steady.—Ha! the queen.—
I think she hates a Roman—and will leave thee.

SCENE V.

SOPHONISBA, MASINISSA.

Soph. Was not that Roman Lælius, as I enter'd,
Who parted gloomy hence?

Mas. Madam, the same.

Soph. Unhappy Afric! since these haughty Romans
Have in this lordly manner trod thy courts.
I read his fresh reproaches in thy face;
The lesson'd pupil in thy fallen look,
In that forced smile which sickens on thy cheek.

Mas. Oh, say not so, thou rapture of my soul!
For while I fondly gaze upon thy charms,
I smile as joyous as the sun in May;
Nor can my heart, by thee possess'd, retain
One painful thought.
Soph. Nay, tell me, Masinissa,
How feels their tyranny when 'tis brought home;
When, lawless grown, it touches what is dear?—
Pomp for a while may dazzle thoughtless man,
False glory blind him; but there is a time,
When even the slave in heart will spurn his chains,
Nor know submission more.—What said thy tyrant?
Mas. His disappointment for a moment only
Burst in vain passion, and—
Soph. You stood abash'd;
You bore his threats, and, tamely silent, heard him,
Heard the fierce Roman mark me for his triumph.
Oh! meanness!
Mas. Banish that unkind suspicion.
The thought inflamed my soul. I vow'd my life,
My last Massylian to the sword, ere he
Should touch thy freedom with the least dishonour.
But that from Scipio—
Soph. Scipio!
Mas. That from him—
Soph. I tell thee, Masinissa, if from him
You gain my freedom, from myself conceal it.
I shall disdain such freedom.
Mas. Sophonisba,
Thou all my heart holds precious, doubt no more.
Nor Rome, nor Scipio, nor a world combined,
Shall tear thee from me; till outstretch'd I lie,
A nameless corpse.
Soph. If thy protection fails,
Of this at least be sure, be very sure,
To give me timely death.
Mas. Cease thus to talk,
Of death, of Romans, of unkind ambition:
My softer thoughts those rugged themes refuse,
And turn alone to love. All, all, but thee,
All nature is a passing dream to me.
Fix'd in my view, thou dost for ever shine,
Thy form forth-beaming from the soul divine.
A spirit thine, which mortals might adore;
Despising love, and thence creating more.
Thou the high passions, I the tender prove,
Thy heart was form'd for glory, mine for love.

ACT V.

SCENE I.

MASINISSA, NARVA.

Mas. Hail to the joyous day! With purple clouds
The whole horizon glows. The breezy spring
Stands loosely floating on the mountain top,
And deals her sweets around. The sun too seems,
As conscious of my joy, with brighter beams
To gild the happy world; and all things smile
Like Sophonisba. Love and friendship sure
Have mark'd this day with all their choicest blessing:
Oh! Sophonisba's mine! and Scipio comes!
Nar. My lord, the trumpets speak his near approach.
Mas. I want his secret audience.—Leave us, Narva.

SCENE II.

SCIPIO, MASINISSA.

Mas. Scipio! more welcome than my tongue can speak!
Oh, greatly, dearly welcome!
Scip. Masinissa!
My heart beats back thy joy.—A happy friend,
Raised by his prudence, fortitude, and valour,
O'er all his foes; and on his native throne,
Amidst his rescued shouting subjects, set.
Say, can the gods in lavish bounty give
A sight more pleasing?
Mas. My great friend and patron!
It was thy timely, thy restoring aid,
That brought me from the fearful desert-life,
To live again in state and purple splendour.
Thy friendship arm'd me with the strength of Rome,
And now I wield the sceptre of my fathers.
See my dear people from the tyrant's scourge,
From Syphax freed; I hear their glad applauses:
And, to complete my happiness, have gain'd
A friend worth all. O gratitude, esteem,
And love like mine, with what divine delight
Ye fill the heart!
Scip. Heroic youth! thy virtue
Has earn'd whate'er thy fortune can bestow.
It was thy patience, Masinissa, patience,
A champion clad in steel, that in the waste
Attended still thy step, and saved my friend
For better days. What cannot patience do!—
A great design is seldom snatch'd at once;
'Tis patience heaves it on. From savage nature,
'Tis patience that has built up human life,
The nurse of arts; and Rome exalts her head,
An everlasting monument of patience.
Mas. If I have that, or any virtue, Scipio,
'Tis copied all from thee.
Scip. No, Masinissa,
'Tis all unborrow'd, the spontaneous growth
Of nature in thy breast.—Friendship for once
Must, though thou blushest, wear a liberal tongue;
Must tell thee, noble youth, that long experience
In councils, battles, many a hard event,
Has found thee still so constant, so sincere,
So wise, so brave, so generous, so humane,
So well attemper'd, and so fitly turn'd
For what is either great or good in life,
As casts distinguish'd honour on thy country,
And cannot but endear thee to the Romans.
For me, I think my labours all repaid,
My wars in Afric.—Masinissa's friendship
Rewards them all.—Be that my dearest triumph,
To have assisted thy forlorn estate,
And lent a happy hand in raising thee
To thy paternal throne, usurp'd by Syphax.
The greatest service could be done my country,

Distracted Afric, and mankind in general,
Was thus to aid thy worth. To put the power
Of sovereign rule into the good man's hand,
Is giving peace and happiness to millions.
But has my friend, since late we parted armies,
Since he with Lælius acted such a brave,
Auspicious part, against the common foe;
Has he been blameless quite? has he consider'd,
How pleasure often on the youthful heart,
Beneath the rosy soft disguise of love
(All sweetness, smiles, and seeming innocence)
Steals unperceived, and lays the victor low?—
I would not, cannot put thee to the pain—
It pains me deeper—of the least reproach.—
Let thy too faithful memory supply
The rest. [*Pausing.*
Thy silence, that dejected look,
That honest colour flushing o'er thy cheek,
Impart thy better soul.

Mas. Oh, my good lord!
Oh, Scipio! Love has seized me; tyrant Love
Inthrals my soul.—I am undone by love.

Scip. And art thou then to ruin reconciled?
Tamed to destruction?—Wilt thou be undone?
Resign the towering thought? the vast design,
With future glories big? the warrior's wreath?
The praise of senates, an applauding world?
All for a sigh? all for a soft embrace?
For a gay transient fancy, Masinissa?—
For shame, my friend!—For honour's sake, for virtue's,
Sit not with folded arms, despairing, weak,
Like a sick virgin sighing to the gale,
Till sure destruction comes.—Alas! how changed
From him, the man I loved!

Mas. How changed indeed!—
The time has been, when, fired from Scipio's tongue,
My soul had mounted in a flame with his.—
Where is ambition flown?—Hopeless attempt!—
Can love like mine be quell'd? Can I forget
What still possesses, charms my thoughts for ever?
Throw scornful from me what I hold most dear?
Not feel the force of excellence? to joy
Be dead? and undelighted with delight?—
Hold, let me think a moment.—No! no! no!
I am unequal to thy virtue, Scipio.

Scip. Fie, Masinissa, fie!—By heavens! I blush
At thy dejection, this degenerate language.
What! perish for a woman! ruin all,
All the fair deeds which an admiring world
Hopes from thy riper years; only to soothe
A stubborn fancy, a luxurious will?
How must it, think you, sound in future story?—
Young Masinissa was a virtuous prince,
And Afric smiled beneath his early ray;
But that a Carthaginian captive came,
By whom untimely in the common fate
Of love he fell.—The wise will scorn the page;
And all thy praise be some fond maid exclaiming,
Where are those lovers now?—O rather, rather
Had I ne'er seen the vital light of heaven,
Than like the vulgar live, and like them die!—
Ambition sickens at the very thought.——
To puff and bustle here from day to day,
Lost in the passions of inglorious life,
Joys which the careless brutes possess above us;
And when some years, each duller than another,
Are thus elapsed, in nauseous pangs to die;
And pass away, like those forgotten things
That soon become as they had never been.

Mas. And am I dead to this!

Scip. The gods, my friend,
Who train up heroes in misfortune's school,
Have shook thee with adversity; with each
Illustrious evil that can raise, expand,
And fortify the mind. Thy rooted worth
Has stood these wintry blasts, grown stronger by them.
Shall then, in prosperous times, while all is mild,
All vernal fair, and glory blows around thee;
Shall then the dead serene of pleasure come,
And lay thy faded honours in the dust?

Mas. O, gentle Scipio! spare me, spare my weakness.

Scip. Remember Hannibal.—A signal proof,
A fresh example of destructive pleasure.
He was the dread of nations, once of Rome:
When from Bellona's bosom, nursed in camps,
And hard with toil, he down the rugged Alps
Rush'd like a torrent over Italy;
Unconquer'd, till the loose delights of Capua
Sunk his victorious arm, his genius broke,
Perfumed, and made a lover of the hero.
Lo! now he droops in Bruttium, fear'd no more.—
Remember him; and yet resume thy spirit,
Ere it be quite dissolved.

Mas. Shall Scipio stoop
Thus to regard, to teach me wisdom thus,
And yet a stupid anguish at my heart
Repel whate'er he says?—But why, my friend,
Why should we kill the best of passions, love?
It aids the hero, bids ambition rise
To nobler heights, inspires immortal deeds,
Even softens brutes, and adds a grace to virtue.

Scip. There is a holy tenderness indeed,
A virtuous, social, sympathetic love,
That binds, supports, and sweetens human life.
But is thy passion such?—List, Masinissa,
While I the hardest office of a friend
Discharge; and, with a necessary hand,
A hand, though harsh at present, truly tender,
I paint this passion: and if then thou still
Art bent to soothe it, I must sighing leave thee,
To what the gods think fit.

Mas. O never, Scipio,
O never leave me to myself!—Speak on:
I dread, and yet desire thy friendly hand.

Scip. I hope that Masinissa needs not now
Be told, how much his happiness is mine;
With what a warm benevolence I'd spring
To raise, confirm it, to prevent his wishes
In every right pursuit.—But while he rages,
Burns in a fever, shall I let him quaff
Delicious poison for a cooling draught,
In foolish pity to his thirst? shall I
Let a swift flame consume him as he sleeps,
Because his dreams are gay? shall I indulge
A frenzy flash'd from an infectious eye,
A sudden impulse unapproved by reason?
Nay, by thy cool deliberate thought condemn'd,
Resolved against?—A passion for a woman,
Who has abused thee basely? left thy youth,
Thy love as sweet, as tender as the spring,
The blooming hero for the hoary tyrant?
And now, who makes thy sheltering arms alone
Her last retreat, to save her from the vengeance
Which even her very perfidy to thee
Has brought upon her head?—Nor is this all:—
A woman who will ply her deepest arts
(Ah! too prevailing, as appears already)

Will never rest till Syphax' fate is thine;
Till friendship weeping flies, we join no more
In glorious deeds, and thou fall off from Rome?
I could add too, that there is something cruel,
Inhuman in thy passion. Does not Syphax,
While thou rejoicest, die? The generous heart
Should scorn a pleasure which gives others pain.—
If this, my friend, all this consider'd deep,
Alarm thee not, nor rouse thy resolution,
And call the hero from his wanton slumber,
Then Masinissa's lost.

Mas. Oh, I am pierced!
In every thought am pierced!—'Tis all too true.—
I would, but can't deny it.—Whither, whither,
Through what enchanted wilds have I been wandering?
They seem'd Elysium, the delightful plains,
The happy groves of heroes and of lovers;
But the divinity that breathes in thee
Has broke the charm, and I am in a desert,
Far from the land of peace. It was but lately
That a pure joyous calm o'erspread my soul,
And reason tuned my passions into bliss;
When love came hurrying in, and with rash hand
Mix'd them delirious, till they now ferment
To misery.—There is no reasoning down
This deep, deep anguish! this continual pang!—
A thousand things, whene'er my raptured thought
Runs back a little—But I will not think.—
And yet I must.—Oh gods! that I could lose
What a few hours have on my memory graved
In adamant!

Scip. But one strong effort more,
And the fair field is thine—A conquest far
Excelling that o'er Syphax. What remains,
Since now thy madness to thyself appears,
But an immediate manly resolution,
To shake off this effeminate disease;
These soft ideas which seduce thy soul,
Make it all idle, weak, inglorious, wild,
A scene of dreams; to give them to the winds,
And be my former friend, thyself again?——
I joy to find thee touch'd by generous motives,
And that I need not bid thee recollect
Whose awful property thou hast usurp'd;
Need not assure thee, that the Roman people,
The senators of Rome, will never suffer
A dangerous woman, their devoted foe,
A woman, whose irrefragable spirit
Has in great part sustain'd this bloody war,
Whose charms corrupted Syphax from their side,
To ruin thee too, taint thy faithful breast,
And kindle future war. No, fate itself
Is not more steady to the right than they.
And where the public good but seems concern'd,
No motive their impenetrable hearts,
Nor fear nor tenderness, can touch: such is
The spirit that has raised imperial Rome.

Mas. Ah, killing truth!—But I have promised, Scipio,
Have sworn to save her from the Roman power:
My plighted faith is pass'd, my hand is given;
And, by the conscious gods! who mark'd my vows,
The whole united world shall never have her.
For I will die a thousand thousand deaths,
With all Massylia in one field expire;
Ere to the lowest wretch, much less to her
I love, to Sophonisba, to my queen,
I violate my word.

Scip. My heart approves
Thy resolution, thy determined honour.
For ever sacred be thy word, and oath.
But, thus divided, how to keep thy faith
At once to Rome and Sophonisba; how
To save her from our chains, and yet thyself
From greater bondage; this thy secret thought
Can best inform thee.

Mas. Agony! distraction!—
These wilful tears!—O look not on me, Scipio,
For I'm a child again.

Scip. Thy tears are no reproach
Tears oft look graceful on the manly cheek.
The cruel cannot weep. Lo! friendship's eye
Gives thee the drop it would refuse itself.
I know 'tis hard, wounds every bleeding nerve
About thy heart, thus to tear off thy passion;
But for that very reason, Masinissa,
'Tis hoped from thee. The harder, thence results
The greater glory.—Why should we pretend
To conquer nations, and to rule mankind,
Pre-eminent in glory, place, and power,
While slaves at heart? while by fantastic turns
Our frantic passions reign?—This very thought
Should turn our pomp to shame, disgrace our triumphs;
And, when the shouts of millions rend our ears,
Whisper reproach.—O ye celestial powers!
What is it, in a torrent of success,
To overflow the world; if by the stream
Our own enfeebled minds are borne away
From reason and from virtue? Real glory
Springs from the silent conquest of ourselves;
And without that the conqueror is nought
But the first slave.—Then rouse thee, Masinissa!
Nor in one weakness all thy virtues lose;
And, oh! beware of long, of vain repentance.

Mas. Well! well! no more.—It is but dying too.

SCENE III.

Scip. (*alone.*) I wish I have not urged the truth to rigour!
There is a time when virtue grows severe,
Too much for nature, and almost even cruel.

SCENE IV.

SCIPIO, LÆLIUS.

Scip. Poor Masinissa, Lælius, is undone;
Betwixt his passion and his reason tost
In miserable conflict.

Læl. Entering, Scipio,
He shot athwart me, nor vouchsafed one look.
Hung on his clouded brow, I mark'd despair,
And his eye glaring with some dire resolve.
Fast o'er his cheek too ran the hasty tear.—
It were great pity that he should be lost.

Scip. By heavens! to lose him were a shock as if
I lost thee, Lælius, lost my dearest brother.
Bound up in friendship from our infant years,
A thousand lovely qualities endear him;
Only too warm of heart.

Læl. What shall be done?

Scip. Here let it rest, till time abates his passion.

Nature is nature, Lælius, let the wise
Say what they please. But now perhaps he dies.—
Haste! haste! and give him hope—I have not time
To tell thee what.—Thy prudence will direct.—
Whatever is consistent with my honour,
My duty to the public, and my friendship
To him himself, say, promise shall be done.
I hope returning reason will prevent
Our farther care.

Læl. I fly with joy.

Scip. His life
Not only save, but Sophonisba's too;
For both I fear are in this passion mixt.

Læl. It shall be done.

SCENE V.

Scip. (alone.) If friendship suffers thus;
When love pours in his added violence,
What are the pangs which Masinissa feels!

SCENE VI.

SOPHONISBA, PHŒNISSA.

Soph. Yes, Masinissa loves me—Heavens! how fond!
But yet I know not what hangs on my spirit,
A dismal boding: for this fatal Scipio,
I dread his virtues: this prevailing Roman
Even now perhaps deludes the generous king,
Fires his ambition with mistaken glory;
Demands me from him: for full well he knows,
That while I live I must intend their ruin.

Phœn. Madam, these fears——

Soph. And yet it cannot be.
Can Scipio, whom even hostile fame proclaims
Of perfect honour, and of polish'd manners,
Smooth, artful, winning, moderate, and wise,
Make such a wild demand?—Or, if he could,
Can Masinissa grant it? give his queen,
Whom love and honour bind him to protect,
Yield her a captive to triumphant Rome?—
'Tis baseness to suspect it; 'tis inhuman.—
What then remains?—Suppose they should resolve
By right of war to seize me for their prize——
Ay, there it kills!—What can his single arm
Against the Roman power? that very power
By which he stands restored?—Distracting thought!
Still o'er my head the rod of bondage hangs.
Shame on my weakness!—This poor catching hope,
This transient taste of joy, will only more
Imbitter death.

Phœn. A moment will decide.
Madam, till then——

Soph. Would I had died before!—
And am I dreaming here? Here! from the Romans
Beseeching I may live to swell their triumph?
When my free spirit should ere now have join'd
That great assembly, those devoted shades,
Who scorn'd to live till liberty was lost,
But, ere their country fell, abhorr'd the light.—
Whence this pale slave?—he trembles with his message.

SCENE VII.

SOPHONISBA, PHŒNISSA; *and to them a* Slave, *with a letter and poison from* MASINISSA.

Slave (kneeling). This, madam, from the king, and this.

Soph. Ha!—Stay.— [*Reads the letter.*
Rejoice, Phœnissa! Give me joy, my friend!
For here is liberty! my fears are vain:
The hand of Rome can never touch me more.
Hail! perfect freedom, hail!

Phœn. How? what? my queen!—
Ah! what is this? [*Pointing to the poison.*

Soph. The first of blessings—death.

Phœn. Alas! alas! can I rejoice in that?

Soph. Shift not thy colour at the sound of death;
For death appears not in a dreary light,
Seems not a blank to me, a loss of all
Those fond sensations, those enchanting dreams,
Which cheat a toiling world from day to day,
And form the whole of happiness they know.
It is to me perfection, glory, triumph.
Nay, fondly would I chuse it, though persuaded
It were a long dark night without a morning:
To bondage far prefer it, since it is
Deliverance from a world where Romans rule,
Where violence prevails.—And timely too,
Before my country falls; before I feel
As many stripes, as many chains, and deaths,
As there are lives in Carthage.—Glorious charter!
By which I hold immortal life and freedom,
Come, let me read thee once again; and then,
Obey the mandate. [*Reads the letter aloud.*

"MASINISSA *to his* QUEEN.

"The gods know with what pleasure I would have kept my faith to Sophonisba in another manner.—But since this fatal bowl alone can deliver thee from the Romans; call to mind thy father, thy country, that thou hast been the wife of two kings; and act up to the dictates of thy own heart. I will not long survive thee."

Oh, 'tis wondrous well!
Ye gods of death who rule the Stygian gloom!
Ye who have greatly died! I come! I come!
I die contented, since I die a queen,
By Rome untouch'd, unsullied by their power;
So much their terror that I must not live.——
And thou, go tell the king, if this is all
The nuptial present he can send his bride,
I thank him for it; but that death had worn
An easier face, before I trusted him.—
Add, hither had he come, I could have taught
Him how to die.—I linger not, remember;
I stand not shivering on the brink of life;
And, but these votive drops, which grateful thus [*Taking from him the poison.*
To Jove the high deliverer I shed,
Assure him that I drank it, drank it all,
With an unalter'd smile.——Away. [*Drinks.*

SCENE VIII.

SOPHONISBA, PHŒNISSA.

Soph. My friend!
In tears, my friend!—Dishonour not my death
With womanish complaints. Weep not for me;
Weep for thyself, Phœnissa, for thy country,

But not for me. There is a certain hour,
Which one would wish all undisturb'd and bright,
No care, no sorrow, no dejected passions;
And that is when we die, when hence we go,
Ne'er to be seen again; then let us spread
A bold exalted wing, and the last voice
We hear, be that of wonder and applause.

Phœn. Who with such virtue wishes not to die?

Soph. And is the sacred moment then so near?
The moment, when yon sun, those heavens, this earth,
Hateful to me, polluted by the Romans,
And all the busy slavish race of men,
Shall sink at once; and straight another state,
New scenes, new joys, new faculties, new wonders,
Rise on a sudden round: but this the gods
In clouds and horror wrap, or none would live.—
Oh! to be there.—My breast begins to burn;
My tainted heart grows sick.—Ah me! Phœnissa!
How many virgins, infants, tender wretches!
Must feel these pangs, ere Carthage is no more.—
Soft, lead me to my couch.—My shivering limbs,
Do this last office, and then rest for ever.—
I pray thee weep not, pierce me not with groans.—
The king too here!—Nay then my death is full.

SCENE IX.

SOPHONISBA, PHŒNISSA, MASINISSA, LÆLIUS, NARVA.

Mas. Has Sophonisba drank this cursed bowl?—
Oh, horror! horror! what a sight is here!

Soph. Had I not drank it, Masinissa, then
I had deserved it.

Mas. Exquisite distress!
Oh, bitter, bitter fate! and this last hope
Completes my woe.

Soph. When will these ears be deaf
To misery's complaint? These eyes be blind
To mischief wrought by Rome?

Mas. Too soon! too soon!
Ah! why so hasty? But a little while
Hadst thou delay'd this horrid draught, I then
Had been as happy as I now am wretched.

Soph. What means this talk of hope? of coward waiting?

Mas. What have I done? O heavens! I cannot think
On my rash deed!—But while I talk, she dies!—
And how? what? where am I then?—Say, canst thou
Forgive me, Sophonisba?

Soph. Yes, and more,
More than forgive thee, thank thee, Masinissa.—
Hadst thou been weak, and dallied with my freedom
Till by proud Rome enslaved, that injury
I never had forgiven.

Mas. I came with life.
Lælius and I from Scipio hasted hither;
But death was here before us—this vile poison!

Soph. With life!—There was some merit in the poison;
But this destroys it all.—And couldst thou think
Me mean enough to take it?—Oh! Phœnissa!
This mortal toil is almost at an end.—
Receive my parting soul.

Phœn. Alas, my queen!

Mas. Dies! dies! and scorns me! Mercy, Sophonisba!
Grant one forgiving look, while yet thou canst;
Or death itself, the grave cannot relieve me:
But with the furies join'd, my frantic ghost
Will howl for ever.--Quivering! and pale!—
Have I done this!

Soph. But for Rome,
We might have been most happy.—I conjure thee,
Be mild to Syphax; for my sake regard him,
And let thy rage against him die with me.—
Farewell!—'Tis done!—O never, never, Carthage,
Shall I behold thee more. [*Dies.*

Mas. Dead! dead!—oh! dead.—
Is there no death for me?
[*Snatches Lælius' sword to stab himself.*

Læl. Hold, Masinissa!

Mas. And wouldst thou make a coward of me, Lælius?
Have me survive that murder'd excellence?—
Did she not stir?—Ha! who has shock'd my brain!
It whirls, it blazes!—Was it thou, old man?

Nar. Alas! alas!—good Masinissa, softly!—
Let me conduct thee to thy couch.

Mas. The grave
Shall be my couch.—Ye cannot make me live;
Ye strive in vain.—Off!— crowd not thus around me:
For I will hear, see, think no more!—Thou sun,
Withhold thy hated beams! And all I want
Of thee, kind earth, is an immediate grave!—
Ay, there she lies!—Why to that pallid sweetness
Cannot I, Nature, lay my lips, and die!
[*Throws himself beside her.*

Læl. See there the ruins of the noble mind,
When, from calm reason, passion tears the sway.—
What pity she should perish!—Cruel war,
'Tis not the least misfortune in thy train,
That oft by thee the brave destroy the brave.—
She had a Roman soul; for every one
Who loves, like her, his country, is a Roman:
Whether on Afric's sandy plains he glows,
Or lives untamed among Riphæan snows,
If generous liberty the breast inflame,
The gloomy Libyan then deserves that name;
And, warm with freedom, under frozen skies,
In farthest Britain, Romans yet may rise.

A NUPTIAL SONG,

INTENDED TO HAVE BEEN INSERTED IN THE FOURTH ACT

Come, gentle Venus! and assuage
A warring world, a bleeding age:
For nature lives beneath thy ray,
The wintry tempests haste away,
A lucid calm invests the sea,
Thy native deep is full of thee:
The flowering earth, where'er you fly,
Is all o'er spring, all sun the sky;
A genial spirit warms the breeze;
Unseen among the blooming trees,
The feather'd lovers tune their throat;
The desert growls a soften'd note;
Glad o'er the meads the cattle bound,
And love and harmony go round.

But chief into the human heart
You strike the dear delicious dart;
You teach us pleasing pangs to know,
To languish in luxurious woe,
To feel the generous passions rise,
Grow good by gazing, mild by sighs;
Each happy moment to improve,
And fill the perfect year with love.

Come, thou delight of heaven and earth!
To whom all creatures owe their birth;
Oh! come, sweet-smiling, tender, come,
And yet prevent our final doom.
For long the furious god of war
Has crush'd us with his iron car;
Has raged along our ruin'd plains,
Has soil'd them with his cruel stains;
Has sunk our youth in endless sleep,
And made the widow'd virgin weep:
Now let him feel thy wonted charms;
Oh! take him to thy twining arms:
And, while thy bosom heaves on his,
While deep he prints the humid kiss,
Ah! then his stormy heart control,
And sigh thyself into his soul.

EDWARD AND ELEONORA.

A Tragedy.

TO

HER ROYAL HIGHNESS THE PRINCESS OF WALES.

MADAM,

If I take the liberty once more to crave the protection of your Royal Highness for another Tragedy of my writing, it is because I am led almost unavoidably to it by my subject. In the character of *Eleonora* I have endeavoured to represent, however faintly, a princess distinguished for all the virtues that render greatness amiable. I have aimed particularly to do justice to her inviolable affection and generous tenderness for a prince who was the darling of a great and free people.

Their descendants, even now, will own with pleasure how properly this address is made to your Royal Highness. I am, with the profoundest respect, Madam,

Your Royal Highness's most humble and most devoted servant,

JAMES THOMSON.

PERSONS REPRESENTED.

EDWARD, *Prince of England.*
EARL OF GLOSTER.
THEALD, *Archdeacon of Liege.*
SELIM, *Sultan of Jaffa.*

ELEONORA, *Princess of England.*
DARAXA, *an Arabian Princess.*

Assassin, Officers, &c.

SCENE.—EDWARD'S *Tent in the Camp before Jaffa, a City on the Coast of Palestine.*

ACT I.

SCENE I.

Prince EDWARD, THEALD, *Earl of* GLOSTER.

Edw. I will no longer doubt. 'Tis plain, my friends,
That with our little band of English troops,
By all allies, all western powers deserted,
All but the noble knights that guard this land,
The flower of Europe and of Christian valour,
Nought can be done, nought worthy of our cause,
Worthy of England's heir, and of the name
Of Lion-hearted Richard ; whose renown,
After almost a century elapsed,
Shakes through its wide extent this eastern world.
What else could bend the Saracen to peace,
Who might, with better policy, refuse
To grant it us ?—Yes, to the prince of Jaffa
I will accord the peace he has demanded :
And though my troops, impatient, wait the signal
To storm yon walls, yet will I not expose,
In vain attempts, valour that should be saved
For better days, and for the public welfare.
Rash fruitless war, from wanton glory waged,
Is only splendid murder.—What says Theald ?
Approves my reverend father of my purpose ?
The. Edward, illustrious heir of England's crown,
I must indeed be blinded with the zeal
Of this our holy cause, to think your arms,
Thus all-forsaken, thus betray'd, sufficient
To reach the grandeur of your first design,
And, from the yoke of infidels, to free
The sacred city, object of our vows ;
Yet this, methinks, this Jaffa might be seized :
That still were something, an auspicious omen
Of future conquest.—But, unskill'd in war,
To you, my lord, and Gloster's wise experience,
I this submit.

Edw. Speak, Gloster, your advice,
Before I fix my latest resolution.
Glo. You know, my lord, I never was a friend
To this crusado. My unchanged advice
Is strenuous still for peace. Nor this I urge,
From our deserted arms, and cause betray'd,
But from the state of our unhappy country.
Behold her, Edward, with a filial eye,
And say, is this a time for these adventures?
Behold her then with deep commotion shook,
Beneath a false delusive face of quiet:
Behold her bleeding yet from civil war,
Exhausted, sunk; drain'd by ten thousand arts
Of lawless imposition, priestly fraud,
Italian leeches, and insatiate Rome;
That never raged before with such gross insult,
With such abandon'd avarice. Besides,
Who knows what evil counsellors, again,
Are gather'd round the throne?—In times like these,
Disturb'd, and lowering with unsettled freedom,
One step to lawless power, one bold attempt
Renew'd, the least infringement of our charters,
Would in the giddy nation raise a tempest.—
Return, my prince. You have already saved
Your father from his foes, from haughty Leister:
Now save him from his ministers, from those
Who hold him captive in the worst of chains.
Edw. You, Gloster, saved us both.
Glo. I did my duty;
Even while I join'd with Leister, did my duty—
I hope I did—He, who contends for freedom,
Can ne'er be justly deem'd his sovereign's foe:
No, 'tis the wretch that tempts him to subvert it,
The soothing slave, the traitor in the bosom,
Who best deserves that name; he is a worm
That eats out all the happiness of kingdoms.—
Edward, return; lose not a day, an hour,
Before this city. Though your cause be holy,
Believe me, 'tis a much more pious office,
To save your father's old and broken years,
His mild and easy temper, from the snares
Of low, corrupt, insinuating traitors:
A nobler office far! on the firm base
Of well-proportion'd liberty, to build
The common quiet, happiness, and glory
Of king and people, England's rising grandeur.
To you, my prince, this task, of right, belongs.
Has not the royal heir a juster claim
To share his father's inmost heart and counsels,
Than aliens to his interest, those who make
A property, a market of his honour?—
One reason more allow me to suggest
For peace, immediate peace:—should blind misfortune,
In this far-distant hostile land, oppress us;
A chance to which our weakness stands exposed;
What, Edward, of thy princess would become,
Thy Eleonora; she, whose tender love,
Through stormy seas and in fierce camps, attends thee?
What of thy blooming offspring?—Charged with these,
To give our courage scope were cruel rashness.
Edw. Enough, my lord, I stand resolved on peace:
And will to England straight.—But where, alas!
Where shall we cover our inglorious heads;
When gay with hope the people round us press,
To hear by what exploits we have sustain'd
The fame of Richard, and of English valour?—
Shall I, my generous country, I be rank'd
With those weak princes, who consume thy wealth,
And sink thy name in idle expeditions?—
Perfidious France!—Be this the ruling point
Of my whole life and passion of my soul,
To humble thee, proud nation!—Meantime, Gloster,
See that the captive princess be restored,
Daraxa, to the sultan of this city,
Whose bride she is: we wage not war with women.

SCENE II.

EDWARD, THEALD, GLOSTER, *an* Officer *belonging to the Prince.*

Officer. One from the prince of Jaffa, sir, demands
Your secret ear on some important message.
Edw. Conduct him to my tent.——
[Officer *goes out.*
He brings, I judge,
The sultan's last instructions for this peace.
Here wait: I may your faithful counsel want.

SCENE III.

THEALD, GLOSTER.

The. Whatever woes, of late, have clouded England;
Yet must I, Gloster, call that nation happy,
On whose horizon smiles a dawning prince
Of Edward's worth and virtues.
Glo. True, my friend;
Edward has great, has amiable virtues;
That virtue chiefly which befits a prince—
He loves the people he must one day rule;
With fondness loves them, with a noble pride;
Esteems their good, esteems their glory his.
One instance it becomes me to recount,
That shows the genuine greatness of his soul.
Though I have met him in the bloody field,
He fighting for his father, I for freedom;
Yet bears his bosom no remaining grudge
Of those distracted times: to me his heart
Is greatly reconciled.—Virtue! beyond
The little unforgiving soul of tyrants!
Now will I tell thee, Theald, whence I stoop
To wear the gaudy chains of court-attendance,
At these grey years, that should in calm retirement
Pass the soft evening of a bustling life,
And plume my parting soul for better worlds.
Amidst his many virtues, youthful Edward
Is lofty, warm, and absolute of temper:
I therefore seek to moderate his heat,
To guide his fiery virtues, that, misled
By dazzling power and flattering sycophants,
Might finish what his father's weaker measures
Have tried in vain. And hence I here attend him,
In expeditions which I ne'er approved,
In holy wars—your pardon, reverend father—
I must declare I think such wars the fruit
Of idle courage, or mistaken zeal,
Sometimes of rapine and religious rage,
To every mischief prompt.
The. You wrong, my lord,
You wrong them much. To set this matter only

Upon a civil footing: say, what right
Had robbers rushing from Arabian deserts,
Fierce as the suns that kindled up their rage,
Thus, in a barbarous torrent, to bear down
All Asia, Afric, and profane their altars?—
And to repel brute force by force is just.
Nay, does not even our duty, interest, glory,
The common honour of the Christian name,
Require us to repress their wild ambition,
That labours westward still, and threatens Europe?

Glo. Yes, when they burst their limits, let us check them:
And with a firmer hand than those loose Christians,
The most corrupt and abject of mankind,
Slaves, doubly slaves, who suffer'd these Arabians,
In virtue their superiors as in valour,
Without resistance to o'er-run the world.
By rage and zeal, 'tis true, their empire rose:
But now some settled ages of possession
Create a right, than which, I fear, few nations
Can show a better. Sure I am 'tis madness,
Inhuman madness, thus, from half the world,
To drain its blood and treasure; to neglect
Each art of peace, each care of government!
And all for what?—By spreading desolation,
Rapine and slaughter o'er the other half,
To gain a conquest we can never hold.—
I venerate this land. Those sacred hills,
Those vales, those cities, trod by saints and prophets,
By God himself! the scenes of heavenly wonders,
Inspire me with a certain awful joy.
But the same God, my friend, pervades, sustains,
Surrounds and fills this universal frame;
And every land where spreads his vital presence,
His all-enlivening breath, to me is holy.—
Excuse me, Theald, if I go too far:
I meant alone to say, I think these wars
A kind of persecution. And when that,
That most absurd and cruel of all vices,
Is once begun, where shall it find an end?
Each in his turn, or has or claims a right
To wield its dagger, to return its furies;
And, first or last, they fall upon ourselves.

Edw. (*behind the scenes*). Inhuman villain! is thy message murder?

The. Ha! heard you not the prince exclaiming murder?

Glo. Should this barbarian messenger—
[*Moving towards the noise.*
'Tis so!

SCENE IV.

THEALD, GLOSTER; *to them Prince* EDWARD, *wounded in the arm, and dragging in the assassin.*

Edw. Detested wretch! and does the prince of Jaffa
Send base assassins to transact his treaties?
There—take thy answer, ruffian!—
[*Stabs him with the dagger he had wrested from him.*
Blow too hasty!
I should have saved thee for a fitter death.

Ass. I would have triumph'd, Christian, in thy rage.
For know, thou vile destroyer of the faithful!
That though my erring dagger miss'd thy heart,
Yet has it fired thy veins with mortal poison,
Whose very touch is death.—Allah be praised!
O glorious fate! Prophet, receive my soul! [*Dies.*

Edw. (*after a short pause*). Why gaze you with amazement on each other?
Are we not men, to whom the various chances
Of life are known?

Glo. Ha! poison did he say?
Then is at once my prince and country lost!—
O fatal wound to England!

The. Quick, my lord,
Retire and have it drest without delay,
Ere the fell poison can diffuse its rage,
And deeply taint your blood.

Edw. The princess comes!
O save me from her tenderness!

SCENE V.

EDWARD, THEALD, GLOSTER; *to them the Princess* ELEONORA.

Ele. My Edward!
Support me!—Oh!

Edw. She faints—My Eleonora!
Look up, and bless me with thy gentle eyes!—
The colour comes, her cheeks resume their beauty,
And all her charms revive.—Hence spurn that carcase;
A sight too shocking for my Eleonora.

Ele. And lives my Edward, lives my dearest lord,
From this assassin saved?—Alas! you bleed!

Edw. 'Tis nought, my lovely princess—A slight wound.

Ele. But, ah! methought, I entering heard of poison
Tainting the blood.—What! was the dagger poison'd?—
Ha! silent all? will none relieve my fears?—

Glo. Madam, restrain your tenderness a moment—
The prince delays too long—Let him retire.
Meanwhile, the troubled camp shall be my care;
Lest the base foe should make a sudden sally,
While yet our troops are stunn'd with this disaster.

Edw. I thank thee, noble Gloster.—Nor alone
Support my troops; go, rouse them to revenge;
Tell them their injured prince will try their love,
Their valour soon.—And you, my friend, good Theald,
Attend the princess.—Cheer thee, Eleonora!
I cannot, will not, leave thee long, to vex
Thy tender soul with aggravated fears.

The. Behold Daraxa, the false sultan's bride.

SCENE VI.

ELEONORA, THEALD, DARAXA.

Dar. Princess of England, let me share thy grief.
Whence flow these tears? and what this wild alarm,
This noise of murder and assassination?

Ele. Alas! the prince is wounded by a ruffian;
And with a poison'd dagger, as I fear,
Yet none will ease me of this racking thought.—
Nay, tell me, Theald, since to know the worst
Is oft a kind of miserable comfort,
What has befallen the prince? For this slight wound
Could never thus o'ercast the brave with terror.

The. I dare not, princess, dally with your fate.
An impious villain, from the sultan Selim,
Pretended to the prince a secret message
About the peace in treaty. Dreading nought,
He left us here, and to his tent retired,
There to receive this execrable envoy.
Straight with the prince alone, the fierce assassin
Attempted on his life; but in his arm
He took, it seems, the blow, and from the villain
Wresting the dagger, plunged it to his heart.
This last we saw; and heard the inhuman bigot,
Who deem'd himself a martyr in their cause,
Boast, as he died, the prince's wound was poison'd.
Ele. Then all I fear'd is true! then am I wretched
Beyond even hope!
Dar. A villain from the sultan!—
Ele. Ah the distracting thought! And is my life!
My love! my Edward! on the brink of fate!
Of fate that may this moment snatch him from me!
Dar. What! Selim send assassins? and beneath
A name so sacred? Selim, whose renown
Is incense breathing o'er the sweeten'd east;
For each humane, each generous virtue famed;
Selim! the rock of faith! and sun of honour!
Ele. O complicated woe! The Christian cause
Has now no more a patron and restorer;
England no more a prince, in whom she placed
Her glory, her delight, her only hope;
These desolated troops no more a chief;
No more a husband, a protector, I,
A friend, a lover! and my helpless children
No more a father!
Dar. Pardon, gentle princess,
If in this whirlwind of revolving passions,
That snatch my soul by turns, I have forgot
To pay the tribute which I owe thy sorrows—
But I myself, alas! am more unhappy!
Ele. What woes can equal mine? who lose, thus vilely,
The best! the bravest! loveliest of mankind!—
Dar. You only lose the man you love, but I
(O insupportable!) must learn to hate,
To scorn what once was all my pride and transport!
Should Edward die by this accursed crime,
(Which Heaven forbid!) he dies admired, beloved,
In the full bloom of fame and spotless honour.
To you, the daughter of illustrious grief,
Your tears remain, and sadly-sweet reflection;
You with his image, with his virtues, still,
Amidst the pensive gloom, may converse hold:—
While I—ah! nothing meets my blasted sight
But a black view of infamy and horror!
What is the loss of life to loss of virtue?
And yet how can this heavenly spark be lost?—
No! virtue burns with an immortal flame.
He is belied—some villain has abused him.
The. I honour, madam, this your virtuous grief:
But that the sultan did employ the assassin,
Is past all doubt—behold the false instructions,
By which he gain'd admittance.
[*Giving her the letter the prince had dropped.*
Dar. Ha!—'Tis so!—
His hand! his seal!—From my detesting heart,
I tear him thus for ever!—Perish, Selim!
Perish the feeble wretch who more bewails him!
That were to share his guilt!—Unhappy princess!
Now let me turn my soul to thy assistance—
There is a cure, 'tis true——
Ele. A cure, Daraxa!
O say, what cure?
Dar. No; it avails not, madam;
None can be found to risk it.
Ele. None to risk it?
Quick tell me what it is, my dear Daraxa.
Dar. To find some person, that, with friendly lip,
May draw the poison forth; at least, its rage
And mortal spirit. This will bring the wound
Within the power of art: but certain death
Attends the generous deed.
Ele. (kneeling). Then hear me, Heaven!
Prime source of love! Ye saints and angels, hear me!
I here devote me for the best of men,
Of princes, and of husbands. On this cross
I seal the cordial vow: confirm it, Heaven!
And grant me courage in the hour of trial!
The. O tenderness unequal'd!
Dar. Glorious princess.
Ele. Go, Theald, quickly find the earl of Gloster,
And with him break this matter to the prince.
As for the person, leave that task to me.
I with Daraxa will your call attend:—
O all ye powers of love! your influence lend.

ACT II.

SCENE I.

GLOSTER, THEALD.

Glo. No, Theald, no; he never will consent—
I know him well; he ne'er will purchase life,
At such a rate: besides, in aid of love,
His generous pride would come, and deem it baseness.
The. Then is yon sun his last. The blackening wound
Begins already to confess the poison:
Meantime, my lord, both friendship and our duty
Demand, at least, the trial. Well I know
That, poise his life with hers, he would as nothing
Esteem his own: but sure the life of thousands,
The mingled cause at once of heaven and earth,
Should o'er the best, the dearest life prevail.
Glo. Alas! my friend, you reason: Edward loves.
How weak the head contending with the heart!
Yet be the trial made.—Behold, he comes.

SCENE II.

EDWARD, GLOSTER, THEALD.

Edw. (entering.) O thou bright sun! now hastening to those climes,
That parent-isle, which I no more shall see;
And for whose welfare oft my youthful heart
Has vainly form'd so many a fond design;
O thither bear, resplendent orb of day,
To that dear spot of earth, my last farewell!—
And oh! eternal Providence, whose course,
Amidst the various maze of life, is fix'd
By boundless wisdom, and by boundless love,
I follow thee, with resignation, hope,
With confidence and joy; for thou art good,
And of thy rising goodness is no end!——
Well met, my dearest friends.—It was too true,
The villain's threatening, and I nearly touch
That awful hour which every man must prove,

Yet every man still shifts at distance from him.
Come then, and let us fill the space between
These last important moments, whence we take
Our latest tincture for eternity,
With solemn converse and exalting friendship.—
Nay—Theald—Gloster—wound me not with tears,
With tears that fall o'er venerable cheeks!
What could the princess more?—Ah! there, indeed,
At every thought of her, I feel a weight,
A dreadful weight of tenderness, that shakes
My firmest resolution.—Where is she?

The. She burns with fond impatience to attend you.

Edw. And how, brave Gloster, did you leave the camp?

Glo. The camp, Sir, is secure: each soldier there
From indignation draws new force and spirit.
O 'tis a glorious, an affecting sight!
Those furrow'd cheeks that never knew before
The dew of tears, now in a copious shower
Are bathed. Around your tent they, anxious, crowd,
Rank over rank: some pressing for a look;
Some sadly musing, with dejected eye;
Some, on their knees, preferring vows to heaven;
And, with extended arm, some breathing vengeance.
"Base Saracens," they cry, "perfidious cowards!—
But blood shall wash out blood. — Ah! poor atonement,
Did the whole bleeding city fall a victim!"

Edw. Alas, that to repay their faithful love
I cannot live!—Yet moderate their zeal;
And let the sword of justice only strike
The faithless Selim and his guilty council.
My new-departed spirit, just escaped
From the low feverish passions of this life,
Would grieve to see the blood of innocence,
With that of guilt confounded, stain my tomb.

The. Permit me, Sir, the hope, that you yourself—
I speak it on just cause—may live to punish
This breach of all the sacred rights of men.

Edw. Why will you turn my thoughts, from earth enlarged,
To soft enfeebling views of life again?

The. Not to a vain desire of life, my lord,
I would recal them; but inspire each hope,
Advise each possibility to save it.
And there is yet a remedy.

Edw. Delusion!

The. The fair Arabian princess mention'd one.

Edw. She one?—Daraxa?—Something to complete
Her lover's crime.

The. You could not wrong her thus,
Had you beheld the tempest of her soul,
Her grief, her rage, confusion, when she heard
Of Selim's baseness; had you seen that honour,
That glorious fire which darted from her eyes;
Till in a flood of virtuous sorrow sunk,
She almost equal'd Eleonora's tears.

Edw. What was it she proposed?

The. It was, my lord,
To find some person, who, with friendly lip,
Might draw the deadly spirit.—

Edw. I have heard
Of such a cure: but is it not, good Theald,
An action fatal to the kind performer?

The. Yes, surely fatal.

Edw. Name it then no more.
I should despise the paltry life it purchased.
Besides, what mortal can dispose so rashly
Of his own life? Talk not of low condition,
And of my public rank: when life or death
Becomes the question, all distinctions vanish:
Then the first monarch, and the lowest slave,
On the same level stand; in this the sons
Of equal nature all.

The. Allow me, Sir,
If 'tis a certain, an establish'd duty
(Than duty more, the height of human virtue)
To sacrifice a transitory life,
For that kind source from whence it is derived,
And all its guarded joys, our dearest country;
It may be justly sacrificed for those
On whom depends the welfare of the public.
And there is one, my lord, who stands devoted,
By solemn and irrevocable vows,
To die for you.

Edw. To die for me!—Kind nature!
Thanks to thy forming hand, I can myself
Cheerful sustain to pay this debt I owe thee,
Without the borrow'd sufferings of another.—
No, Theald, urge this argument no more.
I love not life to that degree, to purchase,
By the sure death of some brave guiltless friend,
A few uncertain days, that often rise
Like this, serene and gay, when, with swift wing,
A moment wraps them in disastrous fate.

Glo. Did we consult to save your single life,
Was that the present question, thy refusal
Were just, were generous. But, my lord, this person,
Who stands for you devoted, should, in that,
Be deem'd devoted for the Christian cause,
The common cause of Europe and thy country;
Dies for the brave companions of thy fortune,
Who weeping now around thy tent, conjure thee
To live for them, and England's promised glory.
O save our country, Edward! save a nation,
The chosen land, the last retreat of freedom,
Amidst a world enslaved!—Cast back thy view,
And trace from farthest times her old renown:
Think of the blood that, to maintain her rights,
And guard her sheltering laws, has flow'd in battle,
Or on the patriot's scaffold: think what cares,
What vigilance, what toils, what bright contention,
In councils, camps, and well-disputed senates,
It cost our generous ancestors, to raise
A matchless plan of freedom: whence we shine,
Even in the jealous eye of hostile nations,
The happiest of mankind.—Then see all this,
This virtue, wisdom, toil, and blood of ages,
Behold it ready to be lost for ever.
In this important, this decisive hour,
On thee, and thee alone, our weeping country
Turns her distressful eye; to thee she calls,
And with a helpless parent's piercing voice.—
Wilt thou not live for her? for her subdue
A graceful pride I own, but still a pride,
That more becomes thy courage and thy youth,
Than birth and public station? Nay, for her,
Say, wouldst thou not resign the dearest passions.

Edw. O, there is nothing, which for thee, my country
I, in my proper person, could not suffer!
But thus to skulk behind another's life,
'Tis what I have not courage to support;
It makes a kind of coward of me, Gloster.—
But let me see this friend, whose generous virtue
Exceeds what even my favourable thoughts
Had imaged in the selfish race of man.
The purpose claims the merit of the deed;
And ere I die, I must requite his friendship.—
Conduct him hither, Theald.

SCENE III.

EDWARD, GLOSTER.

Edw. Ah, my Gloster,
You have not touch'd on something that here pleads
For longer life, beyond the force of reason,
Perhaps too powerful pleads—my Eleonora!
To thee, my friend, I will not be ashamed
Even to avow my love in all its fondness.
For oh there shines in this my dearer self!
This partner of my soul! such a mild light
Of careless charms, of unaffected beauty,
Such more than beauty, such endearing goodness,
That when I meet her eye, where cordial faith,
And every gentle virtue mix their lustre,
I feel a transport that partakes of anguish!
How shall I then behold her, on the point
To leave her, Gloster, in a distant land?
For ever in a stormy world to leave her?—
There is no misery to be fear'd like that
Which from our greatest happiness proceeds.

SCENE IV.

EDWARD, GLOSTER, THEALD *presenting the princess* ELEONORA *as the person he went to bring*, DARAXA.

Edw. O Heaven!—what do I see?—I am betray'd!— [*Turning away.*
Ele. Edward!
Edw. O 'tis too much! O spare me, nature!
Ele. Not look upon me, Edward?
Edw. Eleonora!
How on this dreadful errand canst thou come?
Ele. Behold me kneel—
Edw. Why kneel you, best of women?
You ne'er offended, ne'er in thought offended:
Thou art all truth, and love, and angel-goodness!
Why do you kneel? O rise, my Eleonora!
Ele. Let me fulfil my vow.
Edw. O never! never!
Ele. Let me preserve a life, in which is wrapt
The life of thousands, dearer than my own!
Live thou, and let me die for thee, my Edward!
Edw. For me!—thy words are daggers to my soul.
And wouldst thou have me then thus meanly save
A despicable life? a life exposed
To that worst torment, to my own contempt!
A life still haunted by the cruel image
Of thy last pangs, thy agonizing throes,
The dire convulsions of these tender limbs:
And all for one—O infamy!—for one,
By love, by duty bound, each manly tie,
Even by a peasant's honour, to protect thee?—
Yet this, though strong, invincible, is nought
To what my wounded tenderness could urge
Against thy dire request.—Should fate demand
The life we love, then, then, we must exert
The greatest act of human resignation,
We must submit.—But wouldst thou have me, say,
Doom thee myself? with voluntary choice,
Nay, by a barbarous crime, untimely snatch
This worst of ills? would Eleonora make me
Of all mankind the most completely wretched?
Ele. Plead not the voice of honour. Well I know,
There is no danger, pain, no form of death,
Thou wouldst not meet with transport to protect me.
But I, alas! an unimportant woman,
Whose only boast and merit is to love thee;
Ah, what am I, with nameless numbers weigh'd?
With myriads yet unborn?—All ranks, all ages,
All arts, all virtues, all a state comprises?
These have a higher claim to thy protection.
Live then for them.—O make a generous effort!
What none but heroes can, bid the soft passions,
The private, stoop to those that grasp the public.
Live to possess the pleasure of a god,
To bless a people trusted to thy care.
Live to fulfil thy long career of glory,
But just begun. To die for thee be mine.
I ne'er can find a brighter, happier fate:
And fate will come at last, inglorious fate!
O grudge me not a portion of thy fame!
As join'd in love, O raise me to thy glory!
Edw. In vain is all thy eloquence. The more
Thou wouldst persuade, I with increasing horror
Fly from thy purpose.
Ele. Dost thou love me, Edward?
Edw. Oh!—If I love thee?—Witness heaven and earth!
Angels of death that hover round me, witness;
Witness these blinded eyes, these trembling arms,
This heart that beats unutterable fondness,
To what an agony I love thee.—
Ele. Then
Thou sure wilt save me from the worst of pains.
Edw. O that I could from all engross thy sufferings!
Pain felt for thee were pleasure!
Ele. Hear me, Edward.
I speak the strictest truth, no flight of passion,
I speak my naked heart.—To die, I own,
Is a dread passage, terrible to nature,
Chiefly to those who have, like me, been happy.—
But to survive thee—O, 'tis greatly worse!
'Tis a continual death!—I cannot bear
The very thought.—O leave me not behind thee!
Edw. Since nought can alter my determined breast,
Why dost thou pierce me with this killing image?
Ele. Ah! selfish that thou art! with thee the toil,
The tedious toil of life will soon be o'er;
Thou soon wilt hide thee in the quiet grave
While I, a lonely widow, with my orphans,
Am left defenceless to a troubled world,
A false, ungrateful, and injurious world!—
Oh! if thou lovest me, Edward, I conjure thee,
By that celestial flame which blends our souls!
By all a father, all a mother feels!
By every holy tenderness, I charge thee!
Live to protect the pledges of our love,
Our children.
Edw. Oh!——
Ele. Our young, our helpless—
Edw. Oh!—
Distraction!—Let me go!
Ele. Nay, drag me with thee
To the kind tomb.—Thou canst not leave our children,
Exposed, by being thine, beyond the lowest!
Surrounded with the perils of a throne!—
Edw. Cruel! no more embitter thus our last,
Our parting moments! Set no more the terrors
Of these best passions in array against me;
For by that Power, I swear, Father of life!
Whose universal love embraces all
That breathes this ample air; whose perfect wisdom
Brings light from darkness, and from evil good;

To whom I recommend thee, and my children:—
By him I swear! I never will submit
To what thy horrid tenderness proposes!
Glos. My lord—
Edw. Oh!—these emotions are too much—
I feel a heavy languor steal upon me:
The working poison clogs the springs of life.—
Conduct me to my couch,—Ah! Eleonora.
If we ne'er meet again—this one embrace—
Yet sink not to despair—Heaven may preserve me
By means superior to all human hope.
Ele. I will not, cannot quit thee!—

SCENE V.

ELEONORA, DARAXA.

Dar. Princess, stay.
Think not the hand of death is yet upon him;
Resistless sleep will first oppress his senses,
Before the last convulsive pangs come on;
For so the numbing poison oft begins
To spread its dark malignity.
Ele. Ha!—sleep?—
Then is the time—thanks to inspiring Heaven!
But come, and ere the venom sink too deep,
Swift let me seize the favouring hour of sleep.

ACT III.

SCENE I.

Glos. O miracle of love! O wonderous princess!
'Tis such as thou, who keep the gentle flame
That animates society alive;
Who make the dwellings of mankind delightful.
What is vain life? an idle flight of days,
A still-delusive round of sickly joys,
A scene of little cares and trifling passions,
If not ennobled by such deeds of virtue!—
And yet this matchless virtue, what avails it?
The afflicting angel has forsook the prince,
And now pours out his terrors on the princess.—
Forsook him, said I?—no; he must awake
To keener evils than the body knows,
Which minds alone, and generous minds, can feel.
O virtue! virtue! as thy joys excel,
So are thy woes transcendent; the gross world
Knows not the bliss or misery of either.——
The prince forsakes his couch—he seems renew'd
In health—ah, short deceitful gleam of ease!

SCENE II.

EDWARD, GLOSTER.

Edw. (*advancing from his couch.*) Hail to the fresher earth and brighter day!
I feel me lighten'd of the mortal load
That lay upon my spirits. This kind sleep
Has shed a balmy quiet through my veins.
Whence this amazing change?———
But be my first chief care, Author of good!
To bend my soul in gratitude to thee!
Thou, when blind mortals wander through the deeps
Of comfortless despair, with timely hand,
Invisible, and by unthought-of ways,
Thus lead'st them forth into thy light again.
Glos. How fares my lord the prince?
Edw. To health restored.
Only a kind of lassitude remains,
A not unpleasing weakness hangs upon me:
Like the soft trembling of the settled deep
After a storm.
Glos. Father of health be praised!
Edw. The moment that I sunk upon my couch,
A sick and troubled slumber fell upon me:
Chaos of gloomy unconnected thought!
That in black eddy whirl'd, made sleep more dreadful
Than the worst waking pang. While thus I toss'd,
Ready to bid farewell to suffering clay,
Methought an angel came and touch'd my wound.
At this the parting gloom clear'd up apace;
My slumbers soften'd; and, with health, return'd
Serenity of mind, and order'd thought,
And fair ideas gladdening all the soul.
Aërial music too, by fancy heard,
Sooth'd my late pangs and harmonized my breast.
Through shades of bliss I walk'd, where heavenly forms
Sung to their lutes my Eleonora's love.—
But where is she! the glory of her sex?
O dearer, justly dearer far than ever!
Quick, let me find her, pour into her bosom
My full, full soul, with tenderness o'ercharged,
With glad surprise, with gratitude and wonder.——
Ha! why this silence? this dejected look?—
You cast a drooping eye upon the ground.—
Where is the princess?
Glos. She, my lord, reposes.
Edw. Reposes!—no!—It is not likely, Gloster,
That she would yield her weeping eyes to sleep,
While I lay there in agonies.—Away!
I am too feeble then to know the truth.—
Say, is she well?
Glos. Now show thy courage, Edward.—
Edw. O all my fears! I shall start out to madness!—
What!—while I slept?
Glos. Yes.
Edw. Misery! distraction!
My peace, my honour is betray'd for ever!
O love! O shame! O murder'd Eleonora!

SCENE III.

Glos. Unhappy prince! go find thy Eleonora,
And in heart-easing grief exhale thy passion:
All other comfort, now, were to talk down
The winds and raging seas.—But yonder comes
The Arabian princess: from her tears I learn
The moving scene within.

SCENE IV

GLOSTER, DARAXA, *a* Messenger *from* SELIM *attending at some distance.*

Dar. O! 'tis too much!
I can no more support it.
Glos. Generous mourner,
How is it with the princess Eleonora?

Dar. Struck by the poison, on her couch she lies,
A rose soft-drooping in Sabæan vales
Beneath the fiery dog-star's noxious rage.
O christian chief! I never shall forget
The scene these melting eyes have just beheld,
With mingled tears of tenderness and wonder.

Glos. How was it, Madam?

Dar. When this pride of women,
This best of wives which in his radiant course
The sun beholds, when first she, sickening, felt
The imperious summons of approaching fate,
All robed in spotless white she sought the altar;
And, prostrate there, for her departing soul,
The prince her husband, and her orphan children,
Implored the Eternal Mind.—As yet she held
Her swelling tears, and in her bosom kept
Her sighs repress'd: nor did the near approach
Of the pale king of terrors dim her beauty;
No, rather adding to her charms, it breathed
A certain mournful sweetness through her features.
But as the increasing bane more desperate grew,
Wild to her bed she rush'd, and then, indeed,
The lovely fountains of her eyes were open'd;
Then flow'd her tears.—"Connubial bed," she cried,
"Chaste witness of my tenderness for him
To save whose life I unrepining die
In bloom of youth, farewell!—Thou shalt, perhaps,
Receive a fairer, a more happy bride;
But never a more faithful, never one
Who loves her husband with a fonder passion."—
Here flow'd her tears afresh; with burning lip
She press'd the humid couch, and wept again.
At last, while weary sorrow paused, she rose,
And, fearing lest immediate death might seize her,
Demanded to be led to see the prince
But fear of chasing from his eyes too soon
The salutary sleep that heal'd his pangs,
Restrain'd her trembling footsteps. On her couch,
Abandon'd to despair, she sunk anew,
And for her children call'd.—Her children came,
Awhile, supported on her arm, she eyed them,
With tears pursuing tears adown her cheek,
With all the speechless misery of woe.—
I see her still—O God!—the powerful image
Dissolves me into tears!—

Glos. Madam, proceed:
Such tears are virtue, and excel the joys
Of wanton pride.

Dar. Then, starting up, she went
To snatch them to a mother's last embrace;
When straight reflecting that the piercing poison
Might taint their tender years, she sudden shrunk
With horror back:—"O wretched Eleonora!
(She weeping cried) and must I then not taste
The poor remaining comfort of the dying,
To see a husband, clasp my dearest children,
And mix my parting soul with theirs I love?"—
Her sad attendants, that till then had mourn'd
In silent sorrow, all at this gave way
To loud laments.—She raised her languid eye,
And casting on them round a gracious smile,
To each by name she call'd, even to the lowest,
To each extended mild her friendly hand,
Gave, and by turns received, a last farewell.—
Such is the dreadful scene from which I come.

Glos. How heighten'd now with Edward's mingled woes?
Why are my lingering years reserved for this?

Dar. Come nearer, you, the messenger of Selim,
And bear him back this answer:—His chief aim,
He says, in stooping to solicit peace,
Was from the chains of infidels to save me.
What! was it then to rescue me he sent,
Beneath an all-revered and sacred name,
Beneath the shelter of his hand and seal,
A murdering wretch, a sacrilegious bigot,
To stab at once the gallant prince of England,
And public faith? nay, with a poison'd dagger
(Such his inhuman cowardice) to stab him?—
So well, 'tis true, he judged; the christian prince
Had now been mingled with the harmless dead,
If his bright princess, glorious Eleonora,
Had not redeem'd his dearer life with her's.
You heard in what extremity she lies.
Go, tell the tyrant then—O heaven and earth!
O vanity of virtue! that Daraxa
Should e'er to Selim send so fell a message——
I will suppress its bitterness—Yet tell him,
This crime has placed eternal bars between us.
See my last tear to love——Arabian wilds
Shall bury 'midst their rocks the lost Daraxa.—
Away!

Glo. Behold, they bear this way the princess,
Once more to taste the sweetness of the sun,
Ere yet to mortal light she bid farewell.

SCENE V.

GLOSTER, DARAXA, THEALD, EDWARD; ELEONORA, *borne in by her attendants, on a couch.*

Ele. (*entering.*) A little on, a little further on,
Bear me, my friends, into the cooling air.—
O cheerful sun! O vital light of day!

Edw. That sun is witness of our matchless woes,
Is witness of our innocence——Alas!
What have we done to merit this disaster?

Ele. O earth! O genial roofs! Oh the dear coast
Of Albion's isle! which I no more shall see!—

Edw. Nay, yield not to thy weakness, Eleonora!
Sustain thyself a little, nor desert me!
The all-ruling Goodness may relieve us still.

Ele. Edward! I tremble! terror seizes on me!
Through the rent veil of yon surrounding sky,
I had a glimpse, I saw the eternal world;
They call, they urge me hence—Yes, I obey.
But O forgive me, Heaven! if 'tis with pain,
With agonies, I tear my soul from his!

Edw. Heavens! what I suffer!—How thy plaintive voice
Shoots anguish through my soul!

Ele. Some power unseen—
Thy hand, my Edward—some dark power unseen
Is dragging me away.—O yet a little,
A little spare me!—Ah! how shall I leave
My weeping friends, my husband and my children?

Edw. Unhappy friends! O greatly wretched husband!
And O poor careless orphans, who not feel
The depth of your misfortune!

Ele. Lay me down;
Soft, lay me down—my powers are all dissolved—
A little forward bend me—Oh!

Edw. Oh Heaven!
How that soft frame is torn with cruel pangs!
Pangs robb'd from me!

Ele. 'Tis thence they borrow ease—
My children! O my children! you no more
Have now a mother: now, alas! no more
Have you a mother, O my hapless children!

Edw. What do I hear! What desolating words
Are these? more bitter than a thousand deaths!
Death to my soul! Call up thy failing spirit,
And leave me not to misery and ruin!

Ele. Edward, I feel an interval of ease:
And, ere I die, have something to impart
That will relieve my sufferings.

Edw. Speak, my soul!
Speak thy desire: I live but to fulfil it.

Ele. Thou seest in what a hopeless state I lie;
I who this morning rose in pride of youth,
High-blooming, promised many happy years:
I die for thee, I self-devoted die.
Think not, from this, that I repent my vow:
Or that, with little vanity, I boast it:
No; what I did from unrepenting love,
I cheerful did, from love that knows no fear,
No pain, no weak remission of its ardour.
And what, alas! what was it but the dictate
Of honour and of duty? nay, 'twas selfish,
To save me from unsufferable pain,
From dragging here a wretched life without thee.
Two fears yet stand betwixt my soul and peace.
One is for thee, lest thou disturb my grave
With tears of wild despair. Grieve not like those
Who have no hope. We yet shall meet again;
We still are in a kind Creator's hand;
Eternal Goodness reigns. Besides, this parting,
This parting, Edward, must have come at last,
When years of friendship had, perhaps, exalted
Our love, if that can be, to keener anguish.
Think what thy station, what thy fame demanded;
Nor yield thy virtue even to worthy passions.
My other care—my other care is idle—
From that thy equal tenderness with mine,
Thy love and generosity secure me—
Our children—

Edw. Yes, I penetrate thy fear.
But hear me, dying sweetness! On this hand,
This cold pale hand I vow, our children never,
Shall never call another by the name
Sacred to thee; my Eleonora's children
Shall never feel the hateful power thou fear'st.
As one in life, so death cannot divide us.
Nor high descent, nor beauty, nought that woman,
In her unbounded vanity of heart,
Can wish, shall ever tempt my faith from thee.
Shall ever, said I? Piteous boast indeed!
O nothing can!—I should be gross of heart,
Tasteless and dull as earth, to think with patience,
Without abhorrence, of a second hymen.
Where can I find such beauty? Where such grace,
The soul of beauty? where such winning charms?
Where such a soft divinity of goodness?
Such faith? such love? such tenderness unequal'd?
Such all that Heaven could give—to make me wretched!—
Talk not of comfort—Into what a gulf,
A lone abyss of misery I fall,
The moment that I lose thee—Oh! I know not—
I dare not think!—But these unhappy orphans—
Ah! the dire cause that makes it double duty—
Shall now be doubly mine; to shelter them,
These pledges of our love, I will attempt
To brave the horrors of loath'd life without thee.

Ele. Enough! it is enough!—On this condition
Receive them from my hands.

Edw. Dear hands! dear gift!
Dear, precious, dying, miserable gift!
With transport once received, but now with anguish!

Ele. All-softening time will heal thy woes. The dead
Soon leave the passions of the living free.

Edw. Detested life!—O take me, take me with thee!

Ele. No, Edward, live; or else I die in vain.

Edw. Raise, raise, my Eleonora, thy sweet eyes;
Once more behold thy children—

Ele. Oh!—'tis darkness—
A deadly weight.

Edw. Thou leavest me then for ever——

Ele. Where am I?—Ah!—a tenant still to pain;
The quivering flame of life leaps up a little.
Meantime, my Edward, 'tis my last request,
That thou wouldst leave me, while I yet enjoy
A parting gleam of thought.—Leave me to Heaven!—
Gloster, farewell; be careful of the prince;
Attend him hence, and double now thy friendship.

Edw. Barbarian! off!—Ah! whither wouldst thou drag me?

Glos. My lord, in pity to the princess—

Edw. Oh!

Ele. Farewell! farewell!—Receive my last adieu;
Edward, my dearest lord, farewell for ever!

Edw. O word of horror!—Can I?—No! I cannot!—
There, take me, lead me, hurl me to perdition!

SCENE VI.

ELEONORA, DARAXA, THEALD, *Attendants.*

Ele. 'Tis past, the bitterness of death is past.—
Alas! Daraxa, I can ne'er requite
Thy generous cares for me. Thou art the cause
My Edward lives, my children have a father,
Thy heaven-inspired proposal.—Tell him, Theald,
That, in the troubled moments of our parting,
I had forgot to beg he would restore
The Arabian princess to her friends and country.—
Thy hand—this sure, howe'er in faith we differ,
Humanity, the soul of all religion,
May well permit.

Dar. By virtue's sacred fire!
Our paradise, the garden of the blest,
Ne'er smiled upon a purer soul than thine.
For me, think not of me; such are my woes,
That I disdain all care, detest relief:
My name is trod in dust; thine beams for ever,
The richest gem that crowns the worth of woman.

Ele. The guilt of Selim cannot stain thy virtues:
It rather lends them lustre.—Bear me back,
My dear attendants: and good Theald, come,
Come, aid my mounting soul to spring away,
From the loved fetters of this kindred clay.

ACT IV.

SCENE I.

THEALD, *and a* Gentleman *belonging to him.*

The. To me a dervise!—Through the furious camp,
Yet raging at the perfidy of Selim,
How did he safely pass?
Gent. Sir, he had fallen
A victim to their vengeance: but he told them,
His life was of importance to the prince,
That he who struck him stabb'd the heart of Edward.
This stay'd their rage; then, after a strict search,
They let him pass through ranks of glaring eyes.
I have besides to say, an English ship,
And one from Italy, are just arrived:
The first brings great dispatches to prince Edward;
The other, holy father, these to you. [*Kneeling.*
The. Go, bid this dervise enter.

SCENE II.

THEALD: *he opens and looks on the dispatches.*

Awful Heaven!
Great ruler of the various heart of man!
Since thou hast raised me to conduct thy church,
Without the base cabal too often practised,
Beyond my wish, my thought; give me the lights,
The virtues which that sacred trust requires:
A loving, loved, unterrifying power,
Such as becomes a father: humble wisdom;
Plain, primitive sincerity; kind zeal
For truth and virtue, rather than opinions;
And, above all, the charitable soul
Of healing peace and christian moderation.
The dervise comes.

SCENE III.

THEALD, SELIM *disguised as a Dervise.*

The. With me what wouldst thou, dervise?
Selim. The princess Eleonora, lives she still?
The. She lives, and that is all.
Selim. Allah be praised!
Then lives the honour of the brightening name
Of Saracen and Mussulman.
The. How, dervise!
What can wipe out the horror of this deed?
Selim. The deed was execrable; but my hand
This instant shall prevent its dire effect.
I bring a certain remedy for poison;
Nor can it come too late, while wandering life
Yet, with faint impulse, stirs along the veins.
The. Ha! dervise, art thou sure of what thou say'st?
Selim. Christian, I am; and therefore am I here.
Haste, lead me to the princess; though she lay
Even in the last extremity, though call'd
By the fierce angel who compels the dead,
Yet bold experience gives me room to hope.
Oft have I seen its vital touch diffuse
New vigour through the poison'd streams of life,
When almost settled into dead stagnation;
Swift as a southern gale unbinds the flood.
Say, wilt thou trust me with the trial, christian?
The. Thou know'st we have great reason for distrust;
But fear in those who can no longer hope,
Were idle and absurd.
Selim. Bright Heaven! what fear?
Is there a slave of such inhuman baseness
To add fresh outrage to a dying princess?
For virtue dying? look into my eye:
Does one weak ray there shun the keenest gaze?
Say, dost thou there behold so foul a bottom?
The. No; seeming truth and generous candour shine
In what thou say'st. Come, follow me, good dervise.

SCENE IV.

THEALD, SELIM *disguised,* DARAXA.

Dar. At last through various pangs, the dying princess
Sees the delivering moment, and demands
Thy presence, reverend christian.
The. Dervise, come
Forbid it Heaven this aid should be too late!

SCENE V.

Dar. Heaven! can it be?—The very face of Selim!—
'Tis he himself—I know him, 'tis the sultan;
And, as he shot athwart me, from his eye
Flash'd the proud lightning of affronted virtue.
He must be innocent; his being here
Is radiant proof he must.—O weak Daraxa!
What man of virtue more would deign to lodge
His image in thy breast?—Ah! what avails
The light unfounded love, the treacherous friendship,
That, with inhuman cowardice, gives up
A worthy man, to infamy and slander?—
They talk'd of aid—what aid? [*A cry heard within.*
Alas! 'tis past!
Death must be in that cry.—O let me fly
To snatch one parting look.—But see the prince,
Roused by the sounds of sorrow, this way comes.
Unhappy prince! I venerate his tears.—
O gracious Allah! pity and support him. [*Exit.*

SCENE VI.

Edw. That cry was death.—Alas! she is no more!
The matchless Eleonora is no more!—
Where am I?—Heavens!—Ah! what a hideous desert
Is now this world, this blasted world around me!

O sun! I hate thee, I abhor thy light,
That shows not Eleonora! Earth, thy joy,
Thy sweetness all is fled; all, all that made
Thy ways to me delightful, Eleonora!
O Eleonora! perish'd Eleonora!
For ever lost!—That tent! ah me! that tent!—
[*Going into the tent, starts back.*
I dare not enter there. There death displays
His utmost terrors.—Pale and lifeless, there
She lies, whose looks were love, whose beauty smiled
The sweet effulgence of endearing virtue.—
And here I last beheld her—Ay, and how,
And how beheld her? The remorseless image
Will haunt me to the grave. I see her suffering,
With female softness, yet to pain superior;
Fearful and bold at once, with the strong hand
Of mighty love constraining feeble nature,
To steal me from affliction.—Let me fly
This fatal ground.—But whither shall I fly?—
To England—O I cannot bear the thought
Of e'er returning to that country more!
That country, witness of our happy days;
Where, at each step, remember'd bliss will sting
My soul to anguish. I already hear
Malice exclaim; nay, blushing valour sigh;
Where is thy princess: where the wish of thousands?
The charm, the transport of the public eye?
Base prince! and art thou not ashamed to bring
No trophy home but Eleonora's corse?——
The grave too is shut up, that last retreat
Of wretched mortals—Yes, my word is pass'd,
To Eleonora pass'd. Our orphan children
Bind me to life.—O dear, O dangerous passions!—
The valiant, in himself, what can he suffer?
Or what does he regard his single woes?
But when, alas! he multiplies himself
To dearer selves, to the loved tender fair;
To those whose bliss, whose beings hang upon him,
To helpless children; then, O! then, he feels
The point of misery festering in his heart,
And weakly weeps his fortune like a coward.
Such, such am I! undone—

SCENE VII.

EDWARD, GLOSTER.

Edw. My lord of Gloster,
I thought my orders were to be alone.
Glos. Forgive my fond intrusion—But I cannot
Be so regardless of thy welfare, Edward,
As to obey these orders.
Edw. But they shall,
Shall be obey'd.—I will enjoy my sorrows,
All that is left me now.
Glos. The more thy grief,
Just in its cause but frantic in degree,
Seeks aggravating solitude, the more
It suits my love and duty to attend thee,
To try to soothe—
Edw. Away! thou never shalt.
Not all that idle wisdom can suggest,
All the vain talk of proud unfeeling reason,
Shall rob me of one tear.
Glos. Of nature's tears
I would not rob thee: they invigorate virtue;
Soften, at once, and fortify the heart;
But when they rise to speak this desperate language,
They then grow tears of weakness; yes—
Edw. I care not.
Weakness, whate'er they be, I will indulge them;
Will, in despite of thee and all mankind,
Devote my joyless days for ever to them.
Glos. Reason and virtue then are empty names?
Edw. Hence! leave me to my fate.—You have undone me;
You have made shipwreck of my peace, among you;
My happiness and honour; and I now
Roam the detested world, a careless wretch.
Glos. Thy honour yet is safe; how long I know
For full it drives upon the rocks of passion. [not,
O all ye pitying powers that rule mankind!
Who so unworthy but may proudly deck him
With this fair-weather virtue, that exults,
Glad, o'er the summer main?—The tempest comes,
The rough winds rage aloud; when from the helm
This virtue shrinks, and in a corner lies
Lamenting.—Heavens! if privileged from trial,
How cheap a thing were virtue!
Edw. Do—insult me—
Rail, spare me not—rail, Gloster, all the world—
But know, meantime, thou canst not make me feel thee—
I have no more connexion with mankind. [thee—
Glos. Insult thee, Edward? Do these tears insult
These old man's tears?—Friendship, my prince, can weep,
As well as love.—But while I weep thy fortune,
Let me not weep thy virtue sunk beneath it.—
Thou hast no more connexion with mankind!—
Put off thy craving senses, the deep wants
And infinite dependencies of nature;
Put off that strongest passion of the soul,
Soul of the soul, love to society;
Put off all gratitude for what is past,
All generous hope of what is yet to come;
Put off each sense of honour and of duty;
Then use this language.—Let me tell thee, Edward,
Thou hast connexions with mankind, and great ones,
Thou know'st not of; connexions that might rouse
The smallest spark of honour in thy breast,
To wide-awaken'd life and fair ambition.
Edw. What dost thou mean?
Glos. What mean?—this day, in England,
How many ask of Palestine their king,
Edward their king.—Read these.
Edw. (*opening the dispatches.*) O Gloster!—
Alas! my royal father is no more: [Gloster!—
The gentlest of mankind, the most abused!
Of gracious nature, a fit soil for virtues,
Till there his creatures sow'd their flattering lies,
And made him—No, not all their cursed arts
Could ever make him insolent or cruel.
O my deluded father! Little joy
Hadst thou in life; led from thy real good,
And genuine glory, from thy people's love,
That noblest aim of kings, by smiling traitors.—
Thus weak of heart, thus desolate of soul,
Ah, how unfit am I, with steady hand,
To rule a troubled state!—She, she is gone,
Softener of care, the dear reward of toil,
The source of virtue! She, who to a crown
Had lent new splendour, who had graced a throne,
Like the sweet seraph mercy tempering justice.
O Eleonora! any life with thee,
The plainest could have charm'd; but pomp and
All that a loving people can bestow, [pleasure,
By thee unshared, will only serve to fret
The wounds of woe, and make me more unhappy.

Glos. Now is the time, now lift thy soul to virtue.
Behold a crisis, sent by Heaven, to save thee.
Whate'er, my prince, can touch or can command,
Can quicken or exalt the heart of man, [father,
Now speaks to thine.—Thy children claim their
Nay, more than father, claim their double parent;
For such thy promise was to Eleonora:
Thy subjects claim their king, thy troops their chief:
The manes of thy ancestors consign
Their long-descended glory to thy hands:
And thy dejected country calls upon thee
To save her, raise her, to restore her honour,
To spread her sure dominion o'er the deep,
And bid her yet arise the scourge of France.
Angels themselves might envy thee the joy
That waits thy will, of doing general good:
Of spreading virtue, cheering lonely worth;
Of dashing down the proud; of guarding arts,
The sacred rights of industry and freedom;
Of making a whole generous people happy.
O Edward! Edward! the most piercing transports
Of the best love can never equal these!——
And, need I add—thy Eleonora's death
Calls out for vengeance?——
Edw. Ha!
Glos. If thou, indeed,
Dost honour thus her memory, then show it,
Not by soft tears and womanish complaints,
But show it like a man.——
Edw. I will.
Glos. Yon towers—
Edw. 'Tis true—
Glos. Yon guilty towers—
Edw. Insult us still!
Glos. The murderer of thy princess riots there.
Edw. But shall not long!—Thou art my better genius:—
Thou brave old man! thou hast recall'd my virtue—
I was benumb'd with sorrow—what—or where—
I know not—never to have thought of this.
Bright virtue, welcome!—vigour of the mind,
The flame from Heaven that lights up higher being,
Thrice welcome! with thy noble servant anger,
And just revenge!—Hence, let us to the camp,
And there transfuse our soul into the troops.
This sultan's blood will ease my fever'd breast.—
Yes, I will take such vengeance on this city,
That all mankind shall turn their eyes to Jaffa,
And as they see her turrets sunk in dust,
Shall learn to dread the terrors of the just.

ACT V.

SCENE I.

Selim. O MY Daraxa! thou hast charm'd my soul!
This reconciling interview has soothed
My troubled bosom into tender joy:
As when the spring first, on the soften'd top
Of Lebanon unbinds her lovely tresses,
And shakes her blooming sweets from Carmel's
It only now remains to see the prince. [brow.—

The. He cannot long delay; for, as I enter'd,
I saw him parting from the hurried camp,
That lighten'd wide around him: burnish'd helms,
And glittering spears, and ardent thronging soldiers,
Demanding all the signal, when to storm
These walls devoted to their vengeance.—
Selim. Ha!
Then let us quickly find him.—But he comes.

SCENE II.

SELIM, THEALD.

The. I sought thee, worthy dervise.
Selim. Reverend Christian,
My toiling thoughts can find no fix'd repose,
Till the wrong'd sultan's vindicated honour
Shine out as bright as yon unsullied sky.
Conduct me to the prince—I claim that justice.—
It stings my conscious soul with sick impatience,
To think what Selim suffers. For a man,
Who loves the ways of truth and open virtue,
To lie beneath the burning imputation
Of baseness and of crimes—such horrid crimes!—
O 'tis a keen unsufferable torment!—
Come, let me then discharge this other part
Of my commission.
The. That thou soon shalt do.
He straight will come this way, the king of England,
Such now he is. Meantime, 'tis fit to tell thee,
He must be managed gently; for his passions
Are all abroad, in wild confusion hurl'd:
The winds, the floods, and lightning mix together.—
I need not say how little, in this uproar,
Avails the broken thwarted light of reason.
Selim. Fear not.—I trust in innocence and truth.

SCENE III.

SELIM, THEALD, EDWARD, GLOSTER.

Edw. Whence is it those barbarians here again,
Those base, those murdering cowards, dare be seen?
What new accursed attempt is now on foot?
What new assassination?—Start not, dervise,
Tinge not thy caitiff cheek with reddening honour.
What, thou!—Dost thou pretend to feel reproach?—
Art thou not of a shameless race of people,
Harden'd in arts of cruelty and blood,
Perfidious all?—Yes, have you not profaned
The faith of nations, broke the holy tie
That binds the families of earth together,
That gives even foes to meet with generous trust,
And teaches war security?—Your prince,
Your prince has done it.—And you should hereafter
Be hunted from your dens like savage beasts:
Be crush'd like serpents!
The. Sir, this dervise comes
To clear the sultan Selim from that crime, [him.
Which you, with strong appearance, charge upon
Edw. Appearance, Theald! with unquestion'd proof.
Doubtless the villain would be glad to change
The course by nature fix'd; enjoy his crimes,
Without their evil.—But he shall not 'scape me.
Selim. If, king of England, in this weighty matter,

On which depends the weal and life of thousands,
You love and seek the truth, let reason judge,
Cool, steady, quiet, and dispassion'd reason.
For never yet, since the proud selfish race
Of men began to jar, did passion give,
Nor ever can it give, a right decision.

Edw. Reason has judged, and passion shall chastise,
Shall make you howl, ye cowards of the east!—
What can be clearer?—This vile prince of Jaffa!
This infamy of princes! sends a ruffian [him)
(By his own hand and seal commission'd, sends
To treat of peace: and, as I read his letters,
The villain stabs me.—This, if this wants light,
There is no certainty in human reason;
If this not shines with all-convincing truth,
Yon sun is dark.—And yet these cowards come,
With lying shifts, and low elusive arts—
O! it inflames my anger into madness!
This added insult on our understanding,
This treacherous attempt to steal away
The only joy and treasure of my life—
Sweet sacred vengeance for my murder'd princess.

Selim. The cursed wretch who did assail thy life,
O king of England, was indeed an envoy
Sent by the prince of Jaffa: this we own;
But then he was an execrable bigot,
Who, for such horrid purposes, had crept
Into the cheated sultan's court and service,
As by the traitor's papers we have learn'd.
For know, there lives, upon the craggy cliffs
Of wild Phœnician mountains, a dire race,
A nation of assassins. Dreadful zeal,
Fierce and intolerant of all religion
That differs from their own, is the black soul
Of that infernal state. Soon as their chief,
The Old Man (so they style him) of the Mountains,
Gives out his baleful will, however fell,
However wicked and abhorr'd it be,
Though clothed in danger, the most cruel death,
They, swift and silent, glide through every land,
As fly the gloomy ministers of vengeance,
Famine and plague: they lie for years conceal'd,
Make light of oaths, nay sometimes change religion,
And never fail to execute his orders.
Of these the villain was, these ruffian saints,
The curse of earth, the terror of mankind:
And thy engagement, prince, in this crusade,
That was the reason whence they sought thy life.

Edw. False, false as hell! the lie of guilty fear!
You all are bigots, robbers, ruffians all!
It is the very genius of your nation.
Vindictive rage, the thirst of blood consumes you;
You live by rapine, thence your empire rose;
And your religion is a mere pretence
To rob and murder in the name of heaven.

Selim. Be patient, prince, be more humane and [just.
You have your virtues, have your vices too;
And we have ours. The liberal hand of nature
Has not created us, nor any nation
Beneath the blessed canopy of heaven,
Of such malignant clay, but each may boast
Their native virtues, and their Maker's bounty.
You call us bigots.—O! canst thou with that
Reproach us, christian prince? What brought thee hither?
What else but bigotry? What dost thou here?
What else but persecute?—The truth is great,
Greater than thou, and I will give it way:
Even thou thyself, in all thy rage, wilt hear it.—
From their remotest source, these holy wars,
What have they breathed but bigotry and rapine?
Did not the first Crusaders, when their zeal
Should have shone out the purest, did they not,
Led by the frantic hermit who began [spread
The murderous trade, through their own countries
The woes their vice could not reserve for ours?—
Though this exceeds the purport of my message,
Yet must I thus, insulted in my country,
Insulted in religion, bid thee think,
O king of England, on the different conduct
Of Saracens and Christians; when beneath
Your pious Godfrey, in the first crusade,
Jerusalem was sack'd; and when beneath
Our generous Saladin, it was retaken.——
O hideous scene! my soul within me shrinks,
Abhorrent, from the view!—Twelve thousand wretches,
Received to mercy, void of all defence,
Trusting to plighted faith, to purchased safety—
Behold these naked wretches, in cold blood,
Men, women, children, murder'd! basely murder'd!—
The holy temple, which you came to rescue,
Regorges with the barbarous profanation:—
The streets run dismal torrents: Drown'd in blood,
The very soldier sickens at his carnage.
Couldst thou, O sun! behold the blasting sight,
And lift again thy sacred eye on mortals?—
A ruthless race! who can do this, can do it,
To please the general Father of mankind!—
While nobler Saladin——

Edw. Away! be gone!
With thee, vile dervise, what have I to do?
I lose my hour of vengeance, I debase me,
To hold this talk with thee.

Selim. While truth and reason
Speak from my tongue, vile dervise as I am,
Yet am I greater than the highest monarch,
Who, from blind fury, grows the slave of passion.
Besides, I come to justify a prince,
Howe'er in other qualities below thee,
In love of goodness, truth, humanity,
And honour, Sir, thy equal—yes, thy equal.—

Edw. What! how! compare me with a damn'd assassin!
A matchless villain!—Ha! presumptuous dervise!
Thou gnaw'st thy quivering lip—A smother'd passion
Shakes through thy frame.—What villany is that
Thou darest not utter?—Wert thou not a wretch,
Protected by thy habit, this right hand
Should crush thee into atoms.—Hence! away!—
Go tell thy master that I hold him base,
Beyond the power of words to speak his baseness!
A coward! an assassinating coward!
And when I once have dragg'd him from his city—
Which I will straightway do—I then will make him,
In all the gall and bitterness of guilt,
Grinding the vengeful steel betwixt his teeth,
Will make the traitor own it.

Selim. (*discovering himself.*) Never!

Edw. Ha!

Selim. Thou canst not, haughty monarch:—I am [he!
I am this Selim! this insulted Selim!
Yet clear as day, and will confound thy passion.

Edw. Thou Selim?

Selim. I.

Edw. Was ever guilt so bold?

Selim. Did ever innocence descend to fear?

Edw. This bears some show of honour. Wilt
Decide it by the sword ? [thou then
Selim. I will do more—
Edw. How more ?
Selim. Decide it by superior reason.
Edw. No weak evasions.
Selim. If I not convince thee,
If by thyself I am not of this crime
Acquitted, then I grant thee thy demand.
Nay more, yon yielded city shall be thine :
For know, hot prince, I should disdain a throne
I could not fill with honour. Were I guilty,
I should not tremble at thy threatening voice ;
No, 'tis myself I fear.
Edw. What shall I think ?
Selim. Hear but one witness, and I ask no more,
To clear my name. The witness is a woman.
Her looks are truth ; fair uncorrupted faith
Beams from her eyes. Thou ne'er canst doubt such
For 'tis the expression of a spotless soul. [beauty;
Edw. Curse on thy mean luxurious eastern arts
Of cowardice! Thou wouldst seduce my vengeance;
But I detest all beauty—Barbarous sultan !
Ah ! thou hast murder'd beauty ! thy fell crime—
Haste, Gloster, haste—in sight of camp and city,
Prepare the lists—Now show thyself a prince,
Or die in shameful tortures like a slave.
Selim. I came not hither or to dread thy wrath,
Or court thy mercy.
Glos. Sir, you cannot justly
Refuse him his demand. The fervent soul
Of undissembled innocence, methinks,
Is felt in what he says. First hear this person ;
And if she gives not full conviction, then,
Have then recourse to what should always be
The last appeal of reasonable beings,
Brute force.
Edw. Well then, conduct her hither, sultan.—
[Selim *goes out.*
Ah ! my disorder'd mind ! from thought to thought,
Uncertain, toss'd, the wreck of stormy passion !
This rage a while supports me ; but I feel
It will desert me soon, and I again
Shall soon relapse to misery and weakness.—
O Eleonora ! little didst thou think,
How deeply wretched thy dire gift of life
Would make me !

SCENE IV.

Edward, Gloster, Theald ; *to them* Selim, *conducting* Eleonora ; Daraxa.

Selim. Raise thy eyes, O king of England,
To the bright witness of my blameless honour.
Edw. No ; beauty shall no more engage my eyes,
It shall no more profane the shrine devoted
To the sweet image of my Eleonora.—
Let her declare her knowledge in this matter.
Ele. Will not my Edward bless me with a look ?
Edw. What angel borrows Eleonora's voice !—
O thou pale shade of her I weep for ever !
Permit me thus to worship thee.—Thou art !—
Amazing !—Heaven !—thou art my Eleonora !
My Eleonora's self ! my dear, my true,
My living Eleonora !——What—to whom
Owe I this miracle ? this better life ?—
Oppressive joy !—owe I my Eleonora ?
Ele. To him, that generous prince, who put his life,
His honour on the desperate risk to save me,
When in the arms of death.—Deprived of voice,
Of motion, and of sense, benumb'd I lay ;
My frighted train around me thought me dead,
And fill'd the tent with cries ; my heart alone
Still feebly beat ; but soon the poison's force
Had driven out life from that its last retreat ;
If, in the moment of approaching fate,
He, like my guardian angel, had not brought
An antidote of wonderous power, by which
I am to light restored—to thee, my Edward !
Edw. Did he, did he preserve thee? He, whom thus
I have with such inhuman pride insulted ?
O blind, O brutish, O injurious rage !— [madness,
They, they are wise, who, when they feel thy
Seal up their lips.—And canst thou then forgive me,
Thou who hast o'er me gain'd that noblest triumph,
The triumph of humanity —Thou canst ;
'Tis easier for the generous to forgive,
Than for offence to ask it.
Selim. Use not, prince,
So harsh a word. More than forgive, I love
Thy noble heat, thy beautiful disorder.
O ! I am too much man ; I feel, myself,
Too much the charming force of human passions,
E'er to pretend, with supercilious brow,
With proud affected virtue, to disdain them. [thee!
Edw. How, generous sultan, how shall I requite
Here—take thy loved Daraxa, whom I meant
To have restored, when this misfortune happen'd
But secret-working Heaven ordain'd her stay,
To save us all.
Selim. Wert thou the lord of earth,
Thou couldst not give me more !—my dear Daraxa
Edw. Hence to the camp, my Gloster.—Bid the
Forsake the trenches—Let unbounded joy [soldiers
Reign, fearless, o'er the mingled camp and city.—
Go, tell my faithful soldiers, that their queen
My Eleonora lives !—A prize beyond
The chance of war to give !—She lives to soften
My too imperious temper, and to make them,
To make my people happy !—O my soul !
What love e'er equal'd thine ?—O dearest ! best !
Pride of thy sex ! inimitable goodness !
Whenever woman henceforth shall be praised
For conjugal affection, men will say,
There shine the virtues of an Eleonora !—
Transporting bliss !—How bountiful is Heaven !
Depressing often, but to raise us more.
Let never those despair who follow virtue.
Love—gratitude—divide me.—Once more, sultan,
Forgive me, pardon my mistaken zeal,
That left my country, cross'd the stormy seas,
To war with thee, brave prince—to war with honour.
Now that my passions give me leave to think :
The hand of Heaven appears in what I suffer'd ;
My erring zeal has suffer'd by a zealot.
Selim. It does, O king. And venerable Christian,
I know thy moderation will excuse me ;
But since by ruling wisdom (who unweigh'd,
Unmeant, does nought) men are so various made,
So various turn'd, that in opinions they
Must blindly think, or take a different way,
In spite of force, since judgment will be free ;
Then let us in this righteous mean agree :
Let holy rage, let persecution cease ;
Let the head argue, but the heart be peace ;
Let all mankind in love of what is right,
In virtue and humanity, unite.

AGAMEMNON.

A Tragedy.

TO

HER ROYAL HIGHNESS THE PRINCESS OF WALES.

MADAM,

I humbly beg leave to put this Tragedy under the protection of your Royal Highness; and hope you will condescend to accept of it, as a testimony of the most unfeigned and zealous respect, due no less to your amiable virtues than to your high rank, from, Madam,

Your Royal Highness's most dutiful and most obedient humble servant,

JAMES THOMSON.

PERSONS REPRESENTED.

AGAMEMNON.	CLYTEMNESTRA
EGISTHUS.	CASSANDRA.
MELISANDER.	ELECTRA.
ARCAS.	Attendant *of* CLYTEMNESTRA.
ORESTES.	
TALTHYBIUS, *Herald.*	Officers, Trojan Captives, *&c.*

SCENE.—*The Palace of Agamemnon, in Mycenæ.*

ACT I.

SCENE I.

CLYTEMNESTRA *sitting in a disconsolate posture, and her* Attendant.

Atten. O CLYTEMNESTRA! O my royal mistress!
Can then no comfort soothe your woes a while?
E'er since that flaming signal of sack'd Troy,
That signal fix'd and promised by the king,
Was seen some nights ago, nor food has pass'd
Your loathing lips, nor sleep has bless'd your eyes.
Or if perhaps a transient slumber hush'd
Your sighs a moment, and restrain'd your tears;
Sudden, you, starting wildly, would exclaim
Of guilt, Egisthus, Troy, and Agamemnon.
Sure 'tis too much, my queen.
Clyt. Away! Away!
Since my lost state admits of no relief,
To that sad comfort of the wretched leave me,
To yield me to my sorrows.
Atten. Hear me, Madam,
Once the dear burden of these aged arms!
My tender care from life's first opening bud!
My joy! my glory! hear your faithful servant,
And, let me add, your friend.—In reason's eye,
That never judges on a partial view,
Far less than your misfortune is your guilt.——
Your guilt.—Forgive me, 'tis too harsh a word,
For what deserves compassion more than blame.
I know the treacherous ways by which you sunk,
From pleasing peace, to these unhappy fears
This anxious tumult.——
Clyt. Hide me from the view
All comfort is in vain.—Away!
Atten. Allow me
To plead your injured cause against yourself.
When Agamemnon led the Greeks to Troy,
And left you, Madam, for the pomp of war;
Left you the pride of Greece in full-blown beauty,
The kindest mother and the fondest wife;
If fame says true, for Trojan captives left you—
But that apart.—How did he leave you, say?
Afflicted, out-raged, as a queen and mother;

Betray'd to Aulis with your first-born hope,
The blooming Iphigenia, under feint
Of her immediate marriage to Achilles;
And there no sooner at the wind-bound fleet
Arrived, but you beheld her spotless blood
Stream on the sullied altar of Diana,
The price of winds, of a dear-purchased gale,
To bear them on to Troy. Thus pierced with grief,
Then fired by turns to rage, almost to vengeance,
At an ambitious, cruel, haughty husband;
While all your passions were together mix'd,
And ready for a change; was you not left
In a submissive soothing lover's power,
Ordain'd your partner in the sovereign rule,
O'er Argos and Mycenæ, but to you
As pliant still as Agamemnon stately?

Clyt. (*rising.*) Alas! too true! you touch the source of woe.
Why did you leave me, barbarous Agamemnon?
Why leave me weeping o'er a murder'd daughter?
Why helpless leave me to a troubled mind?
Ah! why yourself betray me to a lover?
What arts Egisthus used too well I know;
All that can softly steal or gaily charm
The heart of woman——Hence dear sad ideas!
Destroyers hence! And dare you tempt me still,
Perfidious Sirens! in that very moment
When your false charms have wreck'd my peace for ever?
Oh, nature! wherefore, nature, are we form'd
One contradiction? the continual sport
Of fighting powers? Oh! wherefore hast thou sown
Such war within us, such unequal conflict,
Between slow reason and impetuous passion?
Passion resistless hurries us away,
Ere lingering reason to our aid can come,
And to upbraid us then it only serves.
Tormentor, cease!

Atten. You wrong yourself too much.
Think, Madam, how for years you baffled love:
Nor could Egisthus, though he touch'd your heart,
Though many a midnight tear, and secret sigh,
To me, and me alone, disclosed the pangs
That dimm'd your fading cheek; yet could he not,
With all his arts, his love, submission, charms,
O'ercome the struggling purpose of your soul;
Till Melisander, to a desart isle,
He banish'd from your ear.

Clyt. Ah, Melisander!
Given to the beasts a prey, or wilder famine;
Ah, perish'd friend! serene directing light,
By Agamemnon left to guide my counsels;
Whom every science, every muse adorn'd,
While the good honest heart enrich'd them all;
Oh hadst thou still remain'd, then I, this day,
Had been as glorious as I now am wretched!
There breathes a felt divinity in virtue,
In candid unassuming generous virtue,
Whose very silence speaks; and which inspires,
Without proud formal lessons, a disdain
Of mean injurious vice But lost with him,
With Melisander, reason, honour, pride,
Truth, sound advice, my better genius fled;
I friendless, flatter'd, importuned and charm'd,
Was left alone with all-seducing love;
Love to the future blind, each sober thought,
Each consequence despising, scorning all,
But what its own enchanting dreams suggest.
What could I do?—Away! self-flattering guilt!
I should have thought when honour once is sullied,
Not weeping mercy's tears can wash it clean;
And that one blot on mine diffused a stain
O'er the proud honour of a wedded king,
And o'er my children's, my poor blameless children's!
Whose cheeks will kindle at their mother's name:
I should have thought—Would I could think no more!
To think is torture!

Atten. What avails it, Madam—

Clyt. O Melisander! if the dead could hear,
I would invoke thy friendly influence now,
Would wish thee present in this hour of trouble.
Perhaps there is in wisdom, gentle wisdom,
That knows our frailties, therefore can forgive,
Some healing comfort for a guilty mind,
Some power to charm it into peace again,
And bid it smile anew with right affections.
No! fruitless wish!—It cannot, cannot be!
Egisthus who may henceforth give me laws,
Dread of discovery, that worst tyrant, shame,
And my own conscious blotted heart forbid it,
Forbid retreat ——

Atten. Madam, behold the man,
Who, then upon the watch, observed the signal
Of conquer'd Troy, and now attends your orders
To give a full account of what he saw.

SCENE II.

CLYTEMNESTRA, *her* Attendants, *and the* Man *who observed the signal.*

Clyt. Are you then sure that you beheld this signal?
Or was it not some vision of the brain,
That painted, while you slept, your waking wish?
Or else perhaps some meteor of the night?

Man. Madam, Troy doubtless lies one heap of ruins;
I saw the signal of its fate distinctly.
The night was dark and still. A heavier gloom
Ne'er cover'd earth. In lowering clouds, the stars
Were muffled deep; and not one ray, below,
O'er all Mycenæ glimmer'd, or around it.
When straight at farthest east, a ruddy light
Sprung up, and wide, increasing roll'd along;
By turns diminish'd, and by turns renew'd,
A wave of fire: at last, it flamed, confess'd,
From isle to isle, and beachy point to point;
Till the last blaze at Nauplia ended, plain.
A glorious sight, and as a Greek rejoiced me.

Clyt. How sits the wind?

Man. It blows from Troy, direct;
A bold and steady gale.

Clyt. 'Tis well. Retire.
Your care and faithful pains shall be rewarded.

SCENE III.

CLYTEMNESTRA, *her* Attendant.

Clyt. He comes! he comes! the hapless victor comes!
Even now his trophied vessel streaks the main,
And ploughs the billows with triumphant prow;
Or by glad crowds received, perhaps, he hails
His native shore, and presses on to shame.
Even now with glory charged, with conquest gay

Crown'd with the laurels of ten famous years,
He dreams to join them to the peaceful olive;
And after rugged toils and perilous war,
Soft to repose him on the myrtle bed
Of calm domestic bliss. How vain the hopes!
How short the prospect of believing man!
I dare not look before me, dare not paint
The rising storm.

Atten. Behold Egisthus, Madam.

Clyt. Leave me.

SCENE IV.

CLYTEMNESTRA, EGISTHUS.

Egis. (*after some silence.*) And is it thus, O Clytemnestra,
Thus that, in hours of danger, lovers meet? [*Pausing.*
Still coldly silent, still the look averted,
Where not one softness glows? While anger, fear,
Disgust, and sick repentance, shifting, cloud
Your varied cheek. 'Tis plain you never loved.

Clyt. Oh that I never had!

Egis. You never did.
The very power to wish it proves you did not.

Clyt. He ne'er deserved my love who dares suspect it.

Egis. Not to suspect it, weakness were and folly.

Clyt. Nor only doubt; believe your doubts.

Egis. I do.

Clyt. You do!

Egis. Nay more, am of their truth assured.

Clyt. 'Tis base, ungrateful, an ungenerous insult,
To tell me this. Urge not too far, Egisthus,
Urge not too far my guilt-dejected spirit.
Though you have trampled on my haughty virtue,
That noble pride of soul, which knows no fear,
And bears no insult; yet to you, at least,
To you of all mankind, I will be bold,
As I had never err'd, will be a queen,
The blood of Jove, be Clytemnestra still.

Egis. Be temperate, Madam: I have told you nothing,
But that I am not worthy of your love.

Clyt. Curse on that pride! which, with affected brow,
Humility conceals. And am I then so vile,
So lost to reason, honour, common honour;
As without love, that all-compelling fury,
Without debasing, thoughtless, blind blind love;
To bow me from the height of happy life,
To this low fearful state of coward shame?
Mistake me not—I would not waste one word,
One passing word, affronted thus to save you
From jealousy's worst rage; did not, alas!
A kind of mournful justice to myself
Tear from my swelling heart the mean confession.
How art thou fallen! to what dishonour fallen!
Unhappy Clytemnestra!

Egis. Harsh construction!
And yet these frowns delight, that anger charms me.
O more than lovely! O majestic fair one!
Since you then know the jealous force of love,
Forgive its tender fears, its fond offence;
Offence I could not mean.

Clyt. Ill-fated she!
Who must forgive.

Egis. Nay, rather cast me from you
Than thus upbraid me with so forced a pardon
O Clytemnestra, where are now those looks,
Those looks of smiling heaven, of radiant sweetness,
That waked our morn of love? Within whose sphere,
No evil durst approach, no sadness dwell;
While the charm'd gazer knew nor fear nor danger!
And set they then at last in gloomy quarrels?
Let us not quarrel, why should lovers quarrel?
Life is for that too short, too precious time;
These moments chiefly, these impetuous moments,
That to the brink of ruin seem to roll
Our mingled fate. Even now—

Clyt. 'Tis true! 'Tis true!
Alas! methinks in every hollow blast,
That shakes this palace, Agamemnon comes.
Yes, yes, Egisthus, still a proof remains,
A matchless proof of love, I mean to give you.
Glad will I throw this regal pomp aside,
And, instant, with you seek some distant country,
Some gloomy Thracian dale, where piny Hemus
May wrap us in impenetrable shade!
There, there, the coarsest life, fed by hard toil,
Will be luxurious ease to what I feel,
To this big pang that labours at my heart,
And fires my mingling passions into anguish.
Quick! let us fly, Egisthus, fly this moment!
The next may seize us, bind us down to shame,
Detested shame!

Egis. What! Clytemnestra! fly!
That is indeed the road direct to shame,
To infamy for ever. He who flies,
In war or peace, who his great purpose yields,
He is the only villain of this world:
But he who labours firm and gains his point,
Be what it will, which crowns him with success,
He is the son of fortune and of fame,
By those admired, those specious villains most,
That else had bellow'd out reproach against him.
Besides your husband, your vain-glorious husband,
Proud Agamemnon, who ten years has warr'd
At Troy, to scourge your sister Helen's rape,
Dream you that he would not pursue our flight,
Though we took shelter in Cimmerian shades,
And drag us back, the scorn of hissing Greece,
To then deserved, to true, unpitied shame?

Clyt. Excuse my weaker heart. But how, Egisthus,
How shall I bear an injured husband's eye?
The fiercest foe wears not a look so dreadful,
As does the man we wrong.

Egis. Madam, your fears
Cast a false glare upon your troubled reason,
That blinds it quite.—An injured husband he!
He wrong'd! No, Clytemnestra never, never,
Can never wrong her tyrant Agamemnon,
Tyrant of common Greece; can never wrong
The man who leaves her ten regardless years,
For the vain honours of a foolish war;
Nay, who consumed those years, if fame speaks true,
In nothing less than war; instead of war,
In shameful squabbles with his nobler friends,
About their captive females, training out
An amorous revel rather than a war,
Far from his country, family, and queen.
And can you wrong this false one? Think of Aulis,
How basely to that port you was betray'd,
And what dire nuptials waited there your daughter.
Think with what price he bought his cruel trophies.
Behold the first-born blossom of your youth,

Your Iphigenia, her mild eyes dejected,
Her cheek o'ercast with fear, her bosom bare,
An helpless, harmless, uncomplaining victim,
Stabb'd by the murderous Calchas; whilst her father,
Her unrelenting father, to protect
The sacrifice, stands by. Behold, she bleeds,
Pours the rich stream she drew from that fair bosom,
Falls like a drooping flower untimely cut;
And all to purchase for her sire's impatience,
From some fell demon that belied Diana,
A rising gale. The gale begins to blow,
The pendants flutter; when away he goes,
Gaily he goes; and leaves a wretched mother
To weep her murder'd child. If yet one spark
Of wonted spirit burns in Clytemnestra,
If she still lives to justice and to nature; [geance;
These, these are wrongs that call aloud for ven-
And there are hands that boldly—start not,
That will with pride avenge you. [madam—

Clyt. Ha! what hands?
What vengeance, say? Touch not so wild a string;
It wakes new discord in my jarring soul.
To the just gods, not us, pertaineth vengeance.
I cannot, will not, e'er consent to—Gods!
Where roves my tongue?—You did not mention that,
You did not mean it sure—O spare, Egisthus,
In pity spare my last remains of virtue!
Oh make me not beyond recovery vile!
A horror to myself!—how wretched they,
Who feel, yet cannot save, their dying virtue!
[*A shout heard.*
What means this transport of the maddening people?
Oh my presaging heart!—Save me!—Again!
Ah! little think they how their joy distracts me!

Egis. Some move this way—Resume your temper, Madam.

SCENE V.

To Clytemnestra *an* Officer *belonging to the court.*

Offi. Madam, the king is near, from Nauplia comes;
But such rejoicing crowds around him throng,
As makes his journey slow. Just now arrived
Talthybius brings the news, and craves admittance.

Clyt. Conduct him hither.

SCENE VI.

Clyt. (*alone.*) Oh too faithful signal!
Now must I take another step in vice.
Down, stubborn heart! and learn dissimulation:
Yes, learn to smile, though sorrow wrap thee round;
Learn to be friends with baseness.—See! how gay
This herald strides along! Mistaken man!

SCENE VII.

Clytemnestra, Talthybius, *with some* Grecian *soldiers that attend him.*

Clyt. Welcome, Talthybius; welcome, ye brave Greeks:
How fares the king?

Talth. Madam, the king is well;
Health, happiness, and glory, join to crown him.
His heart impatient to confer with yours,
Sends me before him with its warmest wishes,
Its warmest gratulations. "Tell," he said,
"Go tell my Clytemnestra, that the thoughts
Of meeting her awake a dearer joy
Than conquest ever gave: even tedious seems
My people's love, that loses me a moment."
This crown, which circled once the royal brows
Of Hecuba, of Priam's lofty queen,
He prays you to accept.

Clyt. There set it down.
I own, Talthybius, the soft moisture fills
My womanish eyes, while on the sudden turns
Of fate I think, on fortune's sad reverses.
Oft when blind mortals think themselves secure,
In height of bliss, they touch the brink of ruin.
But sure your voyage has been wondrous quick,
Not three full days.—Is all the fleet return'd?

Talth. No, madam; none, except this single ship,
Which bore the king: the rest are scatter'd wide.
When to the joyous breeze we spread our sails,
And left that bay, where Simois and Scamander
Mix with the rapid Hellespont; while Troy,
Or what was Troy, yet wreathing smoke to heaven,
And Ida's woody top, receding, sunk
Beneath the trembling main, the sky was fair;
And, wing'd our course with slender airs, we sail'd,
Till straight, as evening fell, the fluttering gale,
Increasing gradual from the red north-east,
Blew stiff and fierce. At last the tempest howl'd.
Next morning, nought but angry seas and skies
Appear'd, conflicting, round. Meantime, right on,
Our strong-ribb'd vessel drove before the blast,
That, falling somewhat of its fury, gave us
A quick auspicious voyage. Safe, we pass'd
The Cyclad isles, that, o'er the troubled deep,
Seem'd then to float amidst the mingling storm.
Only at one, with much ado, we touch'd,
Nor without risk.

Clyt. And why?

Talth. Madam, compell'd
By sacred pity. On the foaming beach,
A miserable figure beckoning stood,
Horrid and wild, with famine worn away.
His plaintive voice, half by the murmuring surge
Absorb'd, just reach'd our ears. In Greek he call'd,
And strong adjured us by the gentle gods,
That make the wretched their peculiar care,
To bear him thence, from savage solitude,
Into the cheerful haunts of men again.

Clyt. What?—Of condition look'd he?

Talth. So he seem'd;
Though dimm'd by helpless solitary life.
The king regards him much—Forgive me, Madam;
I see the rueful image but disturbs
Your generous soul.

Clyt. I thank you, good Talthybius,
And from the king himself will learn the rest.
This ring, on which a victory is carved
With curious art, befits the news you bring.
I am your debtor still; and, soldiers, yours.

ACT II.

SCENE I.

CLYTEMNESTRA, Attendant.

Clyt. ARRIVED so soon! I am not half prepared:
My features all are sunk with conscious shame;
My eyes are yet too tender to dissemble.
Atten. Madam, be firm. Wipe off these gloomy tears,
In which too plain is read your troubled soul.
Just now the trumpet spoke the king's approach.
Clyt. 'Tis come, at last, the trying hour is come!
Oh that my heart were hard, and features false!—
Again these trumpets swell——
Atten. A moment, Madam,
A moment will betray you.
Clyt. Open, earth,
And swallow up my shame!—What can I do?
Where look? what say? confusion! torture!
Atten. Madam——
Clyt. Ah, coward that I am! Was there no dagger
To save this tenfold death?
Atten. Hark! loud and near,
The triumph comes.
Clyt. Well—give me breath——
[*Endeavouring to compose her agitation.*
Agam. (*behind the scenes.*) A moment
Leave me, my friends.
Clyt. Ha! heard you not his voice?
Yes, yes, 'tis he! Go bring my children hither:
They may relieve me.
Atten. O remember!
Clyt. Heavens!

SCENE II.

AGAMEMNON, CLYTEMNESTRA.

Agam. Where is my life! my love! my Clytemnestra!
O let me press thee to my fluttering soul,
That is on wing to mix itself with thine!
O thou, for whom I live, for whom I conquer,
Than glory brighter! O my Clytemnestra!
Now, in this dear embrace, I lose the toils
Of ten years' war! absence, with all its pains,
Is by this charming moment wiped away.
All-bounteous gods! Sure, never was a heart
So full, so blest as mine.— [*Discovering her disorder.*
But whence, my fairest!
What mean these tears?—Not tears of happy love,
Such as I shed.—What means that clouded look,
Whose downcast sweetness will not shine upon me?
Why this cold meeting? Why unkindly damp'd
My ardour thus? Oh speak, my Clytemnestra!
Clyt. Forgive me, Agamemnon; but I cannot,
Alas! I cannot see your face again,
Without reflecting where I saw you last.
Aulis is present to my eyes anew,
The ships, the chiefs, the guards, the bloody Calchas,
All the dire pomp of sacrifice around:
Anew my daughter bleeds, basely deceived!
And when I see that awful brow, that doom'd her
Can Agamemnon wonder at my tears?
Agam. Why will my Clytemnestra add new stings
To what here rankles but too deep already?
Ah! why impute to me the work of fate?
'Tis not indulging private inclination,
The selfish passions, that sustains the world,
And lends its rulers grace; no, 'tis not thence
That glory springs, and high immortal deeds:
The public good, the good of others, still
Must bear fond nature down, in him who dares
Aspire to worthy rule; imperious honour
Still o'er the most distinguish'd lords it most.
Was it for me?—Let even your passions judge—
For Agamemnon was it, when ordain'd,
By common voice, the general of the Greeks;
While twenty kings beneath my banner march'd;
And while around me full-assembled Greece,
Indignant, kindled at your sister's rape,
On her old native foe demanding vengeance,
On faithless Asia: Was it then for me,
To quench this glorious flame? And to refuse
One life to thousands, to those generous thousands,
That for my honour, for the dearer honour
Of Clytemnestra's family, stood all
Prepared to die? If to the mingled voice,
Of honour, duty, glory, public good,
Of the commanding gods, I had been deaf;
And, in the feeble father, poorly sunk
The Greek, the chief, the patriot, and the king,
Greater than king, the general of the Greeks;
Then you yourself, my Clytemnestra's self,
Must (let her heart avow the truth) have scorn'd me.
Nor think it was an easy resignation.
Oh Clytemnestra! Had you seen within,
What here within my tortured bosom pass'd;
To that my battles since were only sport.
No, not the kindest mother, bathed in tears,
As o'er her agonising babe she hangs,
Feels what I suffer'd then—You may remember—
Again the father melts me at the thought—
You may remember how I hid my face;
Ashamed to let the Greeks around behold
The tears, that misbecame their general's cheek.
Then cease to blame what rather merits pity,
I might add, praise.—He, who the father's heart
More tender has than mine, too tender has it.
I love my children, as a father should;
Besides, I love them from a softer cause,
I love my Clytemnestra.
Clyt. Had, alas!
Had Agamemnon loved me, would he, nay,
Could he have left me in the rage of grief,
My daughter yet fresh bleeding in my sight?
Left me so long? love surely must have found,
In the wide round of ten revolving years,
Some way to see me, to prevent these sorrows—
Why was I thus abandon'd, Agamemnon?
Agam. Let me kiss off these tears. O beauteous tears!
If shed by doubting love, if shed for absence.

Instead of these reproaches, ask me rather,
How I that absence bore: and here all words,
All eloquence is dumb, to speak the pangs,
That lurk'd beneath the rugged brow of war.
When glaring day was closed, and hush'd the camp,
Oh! then, amid ten thousand other cares,
Those stung the keenest that remember'd thee,
That on my long-left Clytemnestra thought,
On what wild seas and mountains lay between us.

Clyt. Unhappy man!

Agam. What says my Clytemnestra?

Clyt. Unhappy mortals! by vain words deceived,
To their own pride, to joyless honour slaves.

Agam. He, he, alone, can claim a right to bliss,
Who has fulfill'd the painful task of honour.

Clyt. But what avails a right to vanish'd bliss?

Agam. Let me once more adjure thee, Clytemnestra,
By every tender name of love adjure thee,
To lose in kind oblivion these our past—
I would not call them quarrels—Ah! there was,
There was a time—I will indulge the thought—
When everlasting transport tuned our souls:
When join'd to vernal life, the spring of love
Around us gaily blow'd! and heaven and earth,
All smiling nature look'd delighted on.
Yet, would my Clytemnestra lend her aid,
I know a passion still more deeply charming
Than fever'd youth e'er felt; and that is love,
By long experience mellow'd into friendship.
How far beyond that froward child of fancy!
With beauty pleased awhile, anon disgusted,
Seeking some other toy; how far more noble
Is this bright offspring of unchanging reason,
That fonder grows with age, and charms for ever!
It is not often, Clytemnestra, thus,
That I submit to double my entreaties;
But, oh destroy not the collected hopes
Of life and love! Oh make not conquest hateful!
I shall abhor it, if it cost me thee,
Cost me thy love. A daughter was too much,
And ten years' absence from my Clytemnestra
Add not to these a loss I cannot bear,
The loss of thee, thou loveliest of thy sex!
And once the kindest!

Clyt. Oh!

Agam. Turn not away;
There is relenting goodness in thy look.

Clyt. Alas! untimely fondness—Agamemnon!
Too generous Agamemnon! you distress me.
Would you were not so kind, so tender, now!
Or ne'er had been so cruel!

Agam. 'Tis unjust
To call me cruel. Fate, the gods, our fortune,
Were cruel to us both—What could I more
To soothe our parting woes, and ease my absence?
I left you Melisander to advise you,
Left you the wisest, faithfullest and best—
Oh whispering nature! Are not these my children?

SCENE III.

AGAMEMNON, CLYTEMNESTRA, ELECTRA, ORESTES.

Agam. My daughter! my Electra!

Elec. O my father!

Agam. Come to my arms, my boy! my dear Orestes!
In whom I live anew, my younger self!
And thou, Electra! in thy opening cheek
I mark thy mother's bloom: even so she look'd,
Such the mild light with which her beauty dawn'd.
Oh thou soft image of my Clytemnestra!
My other Iphigenia!

Elec. Oh my father!
My joy! my pride! my glory! whom, in dreams,
I oft have seen, as if return'd from Troy;
But still unwelcome morning, with a tear,
Wiped out the dear illusion of the night.
And is it then no more a faithless vision?
Oh, 'tis my father! whose departure hence,
And Iphigenia's death, I just remember.
How glorious, Iphigenia, was thy death!
A death I envy rather than lament.
Who would not die to gain immortal fame,
Deliver Greece, and crown a father's glory?

Agam. Come to my arms again, my generous daughter!
And thou my son! O that thy tender years
Had suffer'd thee to share our toils at Troy!
'Tis war that forms the prince: 'tis hardship, toil;
'Tis sleepless nights, and never-resting days;
'Tis pain, 'tis danger, 'tis affronted death;
'Tis equal fate for all, and changing fortune;
That rear the mind to glory, that inspire
The noblest virtues and the gentlest manners.
Where shall I find, to teach thee these, Orestes,
Another Troy?

Orest. How happy had I been
To have beheld what I must only hear!
But I will hear it often, every day;
Will learn your story, study your example;
Will try to mix your virtues with your blood,
And not disgrace the laurels I inherit.
My bosom flutters with I know not what—
—Forgive me, Sir, I am too young to say it—
But something here I feel, which bids me hope
That I shall not betray my father's honour.

Agam. Son of my soul!—Look here, my Clytemnestra!
Look here and weep with tenderness and transport!
What is all tasteless luxury to this?
To these best joys, which holy love bestows?
O nature! parent nature! thou alone
Art the true judge of what can make us happy!

Enter an Officer *belonging to the court.*

Off. Egisthus, Sir, attends.

Agam. Go, bid him enter.
Retire, my Clytemnestra, my dear children:
We soon shall meet again, till then farewell.

SCENE IV.

Agam. Obey me, features, for one supple moment:
You shall not long be tortured. Here, in courts,
We must not wear the soldier's honest face.
He little thinks I have him in the snare
Of Melisander, whom, in my return,
I from that desart island chanced to save,
To which the ruffian——

SCENE V.

AGAMEMNON, EGISTHUS.

Egis. Health to Agamemnon!
And happiness responsive to his glory!
Agam. Cousin, I greet you well.
Egis. Forgive me, sir.
You have surprised us with this quick return:
For by that signal, whose illustrious flame
Rejoiced all Greece, we did not hope your presence
These three days hence. Forgive, that, unprepared,
We only with that joy, that loyal transport,
Which swell each Grecian bosom, thus receive you.
And truly such a burst I have not seen
Of that best triumph. City, country, all,
Is in a gay triumphant tempest tost.
I scarce could press along. The trumpet's voice
Is lost in loud repeated shouts that raise
Your name to heaven. Ten thousand eyes, below,
Ache to behold the conqueror of Troy.
Agam. The noblest praise that can salute my ear,
The sweetest music, is my people's joy.
But sure your tongue has done it ample justice;
Trust me, you blazon a description well.
I have not heard so much obliging speech
These many years.
Egis. Misconstrue not my zeal:
On the full heart obedient language waits.
I feel so deep your glory, Agamemnon,
As mingles with my joy a sort of passion,
That almost touches envy. O ye gods!
Has, while I lived, a war the most renown'd
Which any age e'er saw, or shall again
Be seen; a war, whose never-dying fame
Will cover earth, and reach remotest time,
Has such a war adorn'd my days, and I
Not shared its glory? Pining here, unknown,
In nameless peace—how have I lost my life?
Agam. This ardour is the mode. But know, Egisthus,
That ruling a free people well in peace,
Without or yielding or usurping power;
Maintaining firm the honour of the laws,
Yet sometimes softening their too rigid doom,
As mercy may require; steering the state,
Through factious storms, or the more dangerous calms
Of peace, by long continuance grown corrupt;
Besides the fair career which fortune opens
To the mild glories of protected arts,
To bounty, to beneficence, to deeds
That give the gods themselves their brightest beams:
Yes, know that these are, in true glory, equal,
If not superior, to deluding conquest:
Nor less demand thy conduct, courage, care,
And persevering toil.
Egis. Say, thankless toil,
Harsh and unpleasing; that instead of praise
And due reward, meets oftener scorn, reproach,
Fierce opposition to the clearest measures:
Injustice, banishment, or death itself:
Such is the nature of malignant man.
Not so the victor's meed: him all approve,
Him all admire.
Agam. Yet though a toilsome task,
Though an ungrateful labour oft to rule;
not so hardly of mankind, Egisthus,
Presume to judge. Truth, wisdom, courage, justice,
Munificence, and for the public good
A constant tenor of well-laid designs,
Must still be awful in the worst of times,
Be amiable, dear; while worth, at last,
Will light up worth, and virtue kindle virtue.
You was however eased of half the toil,
By him I left to counsel Clytemnestra,
By Melisander.
Egis. Would to heaven I had!
Agam. You much amaze me.—Is not Melisander
Wise, just, and faithful?
Egis. Sir, I must confess
He wore a specious mask———
Agam. Beware, Egisthus;
I know his steadfast worth, and will not bear
The farthest hint that stains the man I love.
Egis. Then urged by truth, and in my own defence
I boldly will assert him, Agamemnon,
To be more apt to trouble and embroil,
Than serve a state. A certain stubborn virtue,
I would say affectation of blunt virtue,
Beneath whose outside froth, fermenting lay
Pride, envy, faction, turbulence of soul,
And democrative views, in some sort made him
A secret traitor, equally unfit
Or to obey or rule. But that I check'd
His early treasons, here at your return,
You might have found your kingdom a republic.
Agam. Oh, I shall lose all patience!— [*Aside.*
You do well,
To give your accusation open speech.
Meantime, remember you must fully prove it,
You must!—And he who Melisander proves
The wretch you have described, proves man is vain,
And saps the broad foundations of all trust.
I know he would not patiently look on,
And suffer ill designs to gather strength,
Awaiting gentle seasons; yes, I know,
He had a troublesome old-fashion'd way
Of shocking courtly ears with horrid truth.
He was no civil ruffian; none of those,
Who lie with twisted looks, betray with shrugs——
I wax too warm—But he was none of those,
Is none of those dust-licking, reptile, close,
Insinuating, speckled, smooth court-serpents,
That make it so unsafe, chiefly for kings,
To walk this weedy world—Pardon my heat—
I wander from the purpose—You, Egisthus,
Must prove your charge, to Melisander's face
Must prove it.
Egis. Surely—Since the princely faith
Of your own blood you doubt——
Agam. Friendship and truth
Are more a-kin to me than blood.
Egis. You shall,
You shall have proof; but to his face you cannot.
Agam. But to his face I will!—I cannot! why?
Egis. He wanders far from hence, I know not where:
For when I found him an undoubted traitor,
Though he the heaviest punishment deserved;
Yet in regard to that esteem, which, once,
You deign'd to bear him, banishment alone
Was all I did inflict.
Agam. I thank you, sir—
O you are wondrous good!—But tell me, how,
How durst you meddle in the sphere assign'd
To Clytemnestra? He was left to her;
To be her counsellor I left my friend,
Left Melisander; left a man, whom long,
Whom well I knew! perhaps to check you, left him!

And you pretend, you !—But I will be calm—
These passions in a king to his inferiors,
Who cannot answer equal, are not comely.
Forgive my transport—A more quiet hour
Shall sift this matter to the bottom, shall
Do Melisander or Egisthus justice.

SCENE VI.

Egis. Now go thy way, weak, open-hearted man,
Thus to declare the ruin thou intendest.
Go, rate thy Trojan slaves; and elsewhere practise
This insolence of camps. Tame, as I seem,
Submissive, mild, and patient of thy threats;
Yet, ere to-morrow's sun beholds Mycenæ,
My sure-aim'd blow shall pierce thy swelling heart,
And cool this tyrant fever in thy veins.
Were not our blood, our kindred blood at variance,
And therefore burning with immortal hate;
Had not thy father Atreus, at a banquet,
A dreadful banquet! from whose sight the sun
Turn'd back eclipsed, served—Monstrous!—up to mine,
To his own brother, to the pale Thyestes,
His murder'd sons: didst thou not wear a crown
Then by thy father ravish'd from our line,
Mycenæ's crown, which he unjustly seized,
And added to his own, to that of Argos:
Had I not stain'd thy bed with Clytemnestra:
Though safety did not urge, and self-defence:
Yet this vile treatment, treatment fit for slaves;
Thanks to thy fury! this has fix'd thy doom.
Some foolish scruples, that still hung about me,
Are by this friendly tempest blown away.——
But Clytemnestra comes. How shall I calm
Her troubled mind? How bring her to my purpose?

SCENE VII.

CLYTEMNESTRA, EGISTHUS.

Clytem. Here let me kneel, Egisthus, grasp thy knees'
Here let me grow till my request be granted.
Now is the very crisis of my fate.

Egis. What sight is this I see? Rise, Clytemnestra!
Thou fairest, most majestic of thy sex!
It misbecomes thee much, this suppliant posture.
Oh, there is nothing, nothing, sure, which you
Need stoop to ask! Speak, and command it, madam.

Clytem. Then let us henceforth be, as if this love
Had never been betwixt us.

Egis. Cease to love thee!
What wild demand! Impossible!—Even now
Endear'd by danger, by distress endear'd,
I for thee feel a fonder pang, than e'er
I felt before.

Clytem. No! these deluding words
Can charm no longer; their enchantment flies;
And in my breast the guilty passions jar,
Unkind, unjoyous, unharmonious all.
Ah me! from real happiness we stray,
By vice bewilder'd; vice which always leads,
However fair at first, to wilds of woe.

Egis. Ah! Clytemnestra! didst thou love——

Clytem. No more!
Seduce my soul no more! Here will I stop——
Beyond this line 'tis misery, 'tis madness.
The furies flash their torches, vultures tear,
The mingled tortures of the damn'd await me.
Oh! if your passion be not merely selfish,
If the least tenderness for me you feel,
Drive me no farther down the gulf of woe!
To happiness I bid a last farewell;
I ask not happiness: no, that I leave
To innocence and virtue; peace, alone,
Some poor remains of peace is all I ask,
Not to be greatly wretched, plunged in horrors!
And yet who knows, the heavenly spark that sleeps
Beneath these embers, yet may spread anew
Its cheerful lustre—All may yet be well——
For Agamemnon was so kind, so gentle,
With such a holy tender flame he burn'd,
As might have kindled in a barbarous breast
Humanity and virtue.

Egis. All pretence.
I guess his aim! I penetrate his purpose.
On you he lavish'd fondness, while on me
He lower'd destruction. Doubtless, with his ear
Some villain has been busy; and he means
First to divide us, then with greater ease,
To ruin both—And can you then be caught,
Caught with the common prostituted speeches,
That oft have sicken'd on the glowing lip
Of many a Trojan slave? Chryseïs had them;
Briseïs too; and now Cassandra, she,
Who, more like a triumphant queen than captive,
Is every hour expected——

Clytem. What Cassandra?

Egis. Oh, it imports you little what Cassandra!
Thus poorly tame you ne'er will want Cassandras.
What is become of Clytemnestra's spirit,
That she can thus forget her high descent,
Forget her rank, her honour, nay forget
Her injuries?

Clytem. But what Cassandra, say?

Egis. Why, Priam's daughter! the prophetic princess,
The proud, the young, the beautiful Cassandra:
So vain of heart, she dreamt Apollo loved her,
And, on her plighted faith to crown his love,
Bestow'd the gift of prophecy; the gift
In her possession, she deceived the god;
Whence he, provoked, with this condition dash'd it,
Of never gaining credit. So the tale,
The fable runs—Yet on my soul, I think,
Did she give out, she would be queen of Argos,
She were indeed a prophetess.

Clytem. 'Tis well.
You mean it for an insult this, you do.
What else could tempt you to deride me, sir,
With such extravagance?

Egis. Mistake me not,
I mean it, madam, for a serious truth
I mean it for a certainty, if thus
You droop, unnerved with these dejecting fears.

Clytem. Cassandra queen of Argos!

Egis. Yes, of Argos;
While Clytemnestra in a prison pines;
Where she may weep and moralise at leisure.

Clytem. By heavens! she visits first her father's shade.

Egis. There shone your native self. Let bright revenge,
I should say justice, dissipate these clouds,

These melancholy whims of ill-judged virtue,
And show you burning with your former lustre.
Madam, our fates are blended : know, we stand
Or fall together. Shame, contempt, and ruin,
Or safety, love, and glory, is our choice.
And can we doubt a moment ?

Clytem. But Egisthus—

Egis. I know the purpose of thy pleading eye.
Of that hereafter—We shall meet again——
My presence now is wanted in the city.
Fear nothing—Thou shalt know before we act,
Thou for whose sake alone I act and live !

ACT III.

SCENE I.

ARCAS, MELISANDER.

Arcas. AND have I found my long lost-friend again?
My Melisander ! But so changed your look,
So sickly with a kind of thoughtful sadness,
So sunk each feature, by seven drooping years
Spent in that desert isle, as baffled quite
My wandering recollection.

Melis. True, dear Arcas :
For what a helpless creature, by himself,
Is the proud lord of this inferior world,
Vain feeble man ! The commoners of nature,
Each wing that flits along the spacious sky,
Is less dependant than their boasting master.
Hail social life ! into thy pleasing bounds
Again I come, to pay the common stock
My share of service ; and, in glad return,
To taste thy comforts, thy protected joys.

Arcas. O greatly welcome ! you deserve them well,
You well deserve the social life you polish.
Still on my thought your strange delivery dwells.
By Agamemnon left to aid the queen
With faithful counsel, while he warr'd at Troy ;
And thus by Agamemnon to be saved,
Returning from that conquest! wondrous chance !
Or rather wondrous conduct of the gods !
By mortals, from their blindness, chance misnamed.
Meantime, instruct me, while the king reposes,
How was you snatch'd away? and how, so long,
Could you this dreadful solitude support ?
I burn to know the whole.

Melis. 'Tis thus, my friend.
While sunk in unsuspecting sleep I lay,
Some midnight ruffians rush'd into my chamber,
Sent by Egisthus, who my presence deem'd
Obstructive (so I solve it) to his views ;
Black views I fear, as you perhaps may know.
Sudden they seized, and muffled up in darkness,
Straight bore me to the sea, whose instant prey
I did conclude myself, when first, around
The ship unmoor'd, I heard the chiding wave.
But these fell tools of cruel power, it seems,
Had orders in a desart isle to leave me ;
There hopeless, helpless, comfortless, to prove
The utmost gall and bitterness of death.
Thus malice often overshoots itself,
And some unguarded accident betrays
The man of blood.—Next night—a dreary night !
Cast on the wildest of the Cyclad Isles,
Where never human foot had mark'd the shore,
These ruffians left me—Yet believe me, Arcas,
Such is the rooted love we bear mankind,
All ruffians as they were, I never heard
A sound so dismal as their parting oars.——
Then horrid silence follow'd, broke alone
By the low murmurs of the restless deep,
Mix'd with the doubtful breeze, that now and then
Sigh'd through the mournful woods. Beneath a shade
I sat me down, more heavily oppress'd,
More desolate at heart, than e'er I felt
Before ; when Philomela, o'er my head,
Began to tune her melancholy strain,
As piteous of my woes ; till by degrees,
Composing sleep on wounded nature shed
A kind but short relief. At early morn,
Waked by the chaunt of birds, I look'd around
For usual objects : objects found I none,
Except before me stretch'd the toiling main,
And rocks and woods, in savage view, behind.
Wrapt for a moment in amazed confusion,
My thought turn'd giddy round ; when all at once,
To memory full my dire condition rush'd.

Arcas. But of each comfort, each convenience void,
How could you life sustain ? how fence against
Inclement skies ?

Melis. A mossy cave, that faced
The southern sea, and in whose deep recess
Boil'd up a crystal fountain, was my home.
Herbs were my food, those blessed stores of health!
Only when winter from my daily search
Withdrew my verdant meal, I was obliged
In faithless snares to seize, which truly grieved me,
My sylvan friends ; that ne'er till then had known,
And therefore dreaded less the tyrant man.
But these low hardships scarce deserve regard :
The pangs, that sharpest stung, were in my mind ;
There desolation reign'd ; and there, cut off
From social life, I felt a constant death.
And yet these pangs at last forgot to throb ·
What cannot lenient gentle time perform ?
I ate my lonely meal without a tear;
Nor sigh'd to see the dreadful night descend.
In my own breast, a world within myself,
In streams, in groves, in sunny hill and shade ;
In all that blooms with vegetable life,
Or joys with kindred animal sensation ;
In the full-peopled round of azure heaven ;
Whene'er I, studious, look'd, I found companions.
But, chief, the Muses lent their softening aid.
At their enchanting voice my sorrows fled,
Or learn'd to please ; while, through my troubled heart,
They breathed the soul of harmony anew.
Thus of the great community of nature
A denizen I lived ; and oft, in hymns,
And rapturous thought, even with the gods conversed,
That not disdain sometimes the walks of man.
So pass'd the time, when, lo ! within my call,
Arrived the ship, which hope had often promised—
The ship!—Oh, it surpass'd my fondest dream,
E'er to imagine the gay ship that came !
As on the deck I Agamemnon saw,
All glorious with the spoils of conquer'd Troy ;
Ye gods ! what transport, what amazement seized me !
What adoration of your wondrous ways!
Expression sinks beneath them.

Arcas. Sweet reward
Of manly patience! that, to fortune still
Superior, scorns despair.

Melis. This theme, my friend,
Will better suit a leisure hour; but now
The high concerns of life demand our care.
I have already to the king imparted
Suspicions of Egisthus, and remain
In this disguise, not to alarm his guilt,
Till it more full appear, and proper steps
To punish his misgovernment be taken.
If he has ill designs, you, Arcas, you [them.
Must, while you seem'd regardless, have discern'd
Your calm but keen inspection, not disturb'd
By the vain flutter of ill-timed discourse,
Must reach the very bottom of his purpose.
In you the king confides, of you demands,
As of his best-loved subject in Mycenæ,
The truth.

Arcas. Oh, I have precious truths in store!
And that best treasure will unlock before him.
Long has my silent observation traced
Egisthus, through the doubling maze of treason;
But now his ill designs are too, too plain,
To all Mycenæ plain; and who, indeed,
Who can have good ones that corrupts a people?
It was however, hard, a bitter task!
To wink at public villany; to wipe
Each honest passion from my livid face,
To bind my hands, and seal my quivering lips,
While my heart burn'd with rage, and treasured
A storm of indignation—— [up

Melis. Give it way!
Oh, 'tis a glorious luxury! Oppress'd,
For years beneath a load of wicked power
To heave it off indignant, and assert
The dear, dear freedom of a virtuous mind.
Curse on the coward or perfidious tongue,
That dares not, even to kings, avow the truth!
Let traitors wrap them in delusive incense,
On flattery flattery heap, on falsehood falsehood:
Truth is the living liberal breath of heaven;
That sweeps these fogs away, with all their vermin.
And on my soul, I think that Agamemnon
Deserves some touch of blame. To put the power,
The power of blessing or oppressing millions,
Of doing or great good or equal mischief,
Even into doubtful hands, is worse than careless.
Ye gods, avert the miseries that hence
On him and on his family may fall!
But, see, the king.

SCENE II.

AGAMEMNON, MELISANDER, ARCAS.

Agam. Nay, Arcas, to my bosom,
[*Arcas kneeling.*
Come, let me proudly take a faithful heart!

Arcas. Thrice welcome, sir, to Argos and
To virtue welcome! [Mycenæ!

Agam. In my own dominions
I am a stranger, Arcas. Ten full years,
Or even one day, is absence for a king,
Without some mighty reason, much too long.
For me a just and memorable war,
Whose actions future times perhaps may sing,
My own, my brother's, and my people's honour,
With that of common Greece, must plead my pardon.
Now shall my cares attend the works of peace:
Calm deeds that glare not on the vulgar eye;
And yet it equal courage oft demands,
To quell injustice, riot, factious rage,
Dark-working blind cabal and bold disorder,
As to confront the rigid face of war.
Then tell me, Arcas, for, till self-inform'd,
I mean to see with your discerning eyes,
And sure I am they never will mislead me,
Have I much subject for this peaceful courage
This fortitude of state?

Arcas. Too much, my lord.
Would to the gods, our virtues, here at home,
Could answer your heroic deeds abroad!
You, doubtless, from the rugged school of war,
Have brought sound manly hearts, and generous spirits:
While we, alas! we rot in weedy peace,
In slothful riot, luxury, profusion,
And every meanness to repair that waste—
I see the noble blood, indignant, mount,
At this relation, to my sovereign's cheek:
But as affairs now press, I were a traitor,
If with a sparing tongue I spoke the truth.

Agam. Immortal gods! have I, these ten long
Sustain'd a war at Troy; fill'd every day [years,
With cares incessant, councils, dangers, toils,
To cherish villains in licentious ease?
Have I thus squander'd vile, on Phrygian plains,
The bravest blood of Greece to shelter such;
And to assert their honour who have none?
But what can this perfidious, this Egisthus,
What can he, say, by such loose rule propose?
Is it his native bent? or does he push
Some dark design, by these detested means?

Arcas. There is no vice a stranger to his heart,
Conceal'd beneath refined dissimulation;
Dissimulation, that on you yourself
Imposed. Meantime, sir, his ourageous views
Invade the throne of Argos and Mycenæ.

Agam. Said you the throne of Argos and Mycenæ?
Already have I lost my noblest throne,
If he has robb'd me of my people's virtue;
'Tis but vain pomp, a tyrant's toy, the other.
And dares he bear a giddy look so high,
As to my throne? The villain! sure he dares not!

Arcas. Nay, more, my lord—he scales the dazzling height,
And almost grasps with impious hands your sceptre.

Agam. To touch it is perdition!—What! Egis-
Egisthus seize my throne! [thus!

Arcas. So means the traitor.

Agam. That creature of my power! that insect! raised
By the warm beams of my mistaken bounty!
Whom, when my father's vengeance razed his race,
I saved, train'd up, with favours, honours heap'd;
And trusted in his hands at last a jewel,
Too precious for the faithless heart of man—
O gross, gross blindness!—Half my kingly power!
Ay, there breaks out his father's treacherous blood!
There, there, too late, I find the base Thyestes!
Forgive me, Atreus! O my royal father!
Forgive my trusting thus the seed of him,
Of an abhorr'd, an execrable brother,
Who even profaned thy bed—But, ere yon orb
Shall from the purple ocean rise again,
O injured Atreus! by thy sacred shade
I swear, to make for this a full atonement.

Is then this people, Arcas, grown so vile,
So very vile, that he dares entertain
The smallest hope to rival me in empire?
I like not vaunting.—But, ungrateful people!
Can you prefer a nameless thing to me?
Am I not rough with scars on your account?
And for the careful love I always bore you,
Your father named? And yet prefer to me,
One who ne'er saw the glorious front of war,
For nothing famous but corrupting peace,
And whose sole merit was my ill-judged favour?
Can you?—Away!—Dishonour stains the thought!
How should this be?

Arcas. Not many, sir, stand fix'd
On the deep principles of reason'd virtue,
Whom time nor steals, nor passion bears away.
Mankind, in general, float along the stream
Of custom, good or bad; and oft the mind
To that familiar grows, by gradual use
And still-encroaching vice, whose first regard
Gave horror. Hence ten loosely-govern'd years
Have wrought such strange events, that you no more
Behold your ancient Argos and Mycenæ.
These cities now with slaves and villains swarm.
At first, Egisthus, popular and fair,
All smiles and softness, as if each man's friend,
By hidden ways proceeded, mining virtue:
He pride, he pomp, he luxury diffused;
He taught them wants, beyond their private means:
And straight, in bounty's pleasing chains involved,
They grew his slaves. Who cannot live on little,
Or as his various fortunes shall permit,
Stands in the market, ready to be sold.

Agam. Oh, damn'd detested traffic!—But proceed.

Arcas. While the luxurious fever thus increased,
Still, in proportion as it gather'd rage,
He lent it fuel: and, more bold, disclosed
His noon-day treason. Murmurs went about,
And spread at last into the common talk,
That you was proud, severe, beneath the notion
Of holding firm the helm of state, a tyrant;
That in vain wars, which nought imported them,
You spent their treasure, shed their noblest blood;
And that, Troy conquer'd once, to her rich plains
You meant from Argos to transplant your empire.
Meantime, in private, all, whom wild debauch
Has set adrift from every human tie;
Whom riot, want, and conscious guilt inflame,
Holding the gods and virtue in contempt,
Amidst their bowls; such are his bosom-friends:
And join'd to them, a meaner ruffian band,
Of villains bold in crimes, whose trade is murder,
Hang in black clouds around him; whence, I fear,
A sudden tempest is prepared to burst.
This, sir, from duty and a faithful zeal,
I plain unfold: nor on my word alone,
Believe these accusations; clear as day,
I for them will produce the strongest proof.

Agam. I thank thee, Arcas. Truth, though sometimes clad
In painful lustre, yet is always welcome,
Dear as the light that shows the lurking rock:
'Tis the fair star that, ne'er into the main
Descending, leads us safe through stormy life——
Gods! how it tears me from each calmer thought!
To think this traitor, that this double traitor,
This traitor to myself and to my people,
Should by such sneaking, such unmanly ways,
Thus filch away my crown!——
Why stand I chafing here? One timely deed
Is worth ten thousand words—Come then, my friends,
Come and behold me seize amidst his guards,
His coward guards—guilt ever was a coward—
This rival king, and with him crown my triumph.
Till then Troy smokes in vain, and Agamemnon
Cannot be said to conquer.

Melis. Sir, beware——

Agam. Of what beware? Where am I, Melisander?
Am I not in Mycenæ? in my palace?
Are not these crowds, that stream along the streets,
My subjects all? Of what should I beware?
Not seize a traitor in my own dominions!
Yes, I will seize him, Melisander,—will! [gives!

Melis. What grace to kings such generous ardour
But though brave deeds be warm at first conceived,
Let the best purpose cool, nor miss your blow.
More firm and sure the hand of courage strikes,
When it obeys the watchful eye of caution.
You hear from Arcas, sir, what ruffian bands,
What secret deaths, what daggers lurk around him:
Be cautious then; for virtue's, glory's sake!
And, when you strike, strike home.

Agam. O for those Greeks!
That this rude day are tossing on the seas;
Those hardy Greeks, whom ten years' war has steel'd;
With toils, with dangers, and with death familiar:
Then should you see what chaff before the wind
Are these weak sons of soft enfeebling peace,
These wretches, only bold where unresisted.

Melis. But since, my lord, you cannot now exert
This nobler force, let prudence take its place.
Have patience only, till you safely can,
And surely, seize him.

Agam. Well, till then I will.
And, though not made of patient mould, in this
I will have patience, will, some tedious hours,
Repress my vengeance—— [*Pausing.*
Yes, I like the thought—
He may be seized this evening at the banquet,
Be there surprised with ease—and shall!—
For, by the eternal gods that rule mankind!
The sleep of death alone shall seal these eyes,
While such a wretch holds power in my dominions.
Oh Clytemnestra! to the public, now,
Succeeds the private pang.—At thought of thee,
New rage, new vengeance shake my inmost soul!
Was my beloved, my queen, my Clytemnestra,
So long abandon'd in a villain's power,
Who knows, it seems, no limits, owns no laws,
Save those one vice imposes on another?
And now the secret cause, I fear, is plain,
Of that unusual damp, that strange dejection,
Which clouded her at meeting. Still the more
I pour'd my fondness, still the more distress'd
She seem'd; and, turning from my tender gaze,
The copious shower stole down her troubled cheek;
As if she pitied those my blind endearments,
And in her breast some horrid secret swell'd—
Should it be so—Confusion!—Can I stoop
Even to suppose it!—How from slight mistakes
Great evils spring! But the most fruitful source
Of every evil—O that I, in thunder,
Could sound it o'er the listening earth to kings—
Is delegated power to wicked hands.

Melis. My lord, let no suspicions of the queen
E'er taint your bosom: if I judge aright——

Agam. No, Melisander, no; I am not jealous;
In me that passion and contempt were one;

No, 'tis her situation gives me horror,
Her dreadful situation!—But of this
Enough.—Then tell me, Arcas, tell me truly;
Are there a few, say, do there yet remain
A faithful few! to save the sinking state?
Can you, ere night, collect an honest band,
A band of such as worthy are to rescue
Their king and country from impending fate?
Ah! little thought I, that amidst my subjects,
Embosom'd sweet in peace, I, like a tyrant,
Should e'er have needed guards.

Arcas. Yes, sir, I know
A band of generous youths, whom native virtue,
Unbroken yet by avarice or profusion,
Fits for our purpose: These I can collect——

Agam. About it quickly, Arcas; lose no time:
Go, bring me to the banquet those brave youths:
I long for their acquaintance. Till that hour,
Domestic cares and joys demand my presence:
The father's heart now bears me to my children.
Farewell! My all depends upon your conduct.

ACT IV.

SCENE I.

AGAMEMNON, MELISANDER.

Agam. DOMESTIC pleasures spread their charms in vain—
O for the hour of vengeance! I, till then,
But stalk about, the shadow of a king.
Heard you from Arcas aught?

Melis. Be patient, sir.
As yet the time permits not his return.
Arcas is zealous, ardent in your service,
And will not fail his duty.

Enter an Officer *belonging to the Court.*

Off. Sir, Cassandra
Is just arrived.

Agam. Conduct the princess hither.
This Priam's fairest daughter, Melisander,
Is a young princess of engaging beauty,
Raised by distress, of noble sense and spirit;
But, by poetic visions led astray,
She dreamt Apollo loved her, and the gift
Of prophecy bestow'd, to gain her promise:
The gift once hers, the chastely-faithless maid
Deceived the god; who therefore, in revenge,
Since he could not recal it, made it useless,
For ever doom'd to meet with disregard.
E'er since the lovely visionary raves
With dignity; foretels the fate of nations;
And, judging of the future from the past,
Has oft been wondrous happy in her guesses.
Some strange, some recent instances of this,
Confirm her in her venerable madness.

Melis. Be not too rash in judging, Agamemnon;
For we, blind mortals, but a little know
Of boundless nature—Hark! the princess comes;
I hear her voice, I hear the voice of sorrow.

SCENE II.

AGAMEMNON, MELISANDER, CASSANDRA, *attended by* Trojan Captives.

Cass. (*entering*). O hostile roofs! O Ilium! O my country!

Agam. I cannot blame your grief, unhappy princess,
But, if it can relieve you, here be sure
Of an asylum, safe as Priam's palace.

Cass. O sweet abode! O palace of my fathers!
My bleeding heart melts while I think of thee;
Think of the days of innocence and joy,
That shone upon me there. How changed art thou!
Ah! what a scene, when I beheld thee last!
Rage, blood, and flames, and shrieks of murder round me!
The sword of Pyrrhus, and a feeble father!
Where was your Hector then? Where all his sons?
O Priam's numerous race! what are you now
Become? Ah me, the desolating gods
Have laid their hands, their iron hands, upon us.

Agam. From past misfortunes, princess, turn your eye—

Cass. 'Tis true, the future may full well suffice.
The avenging sisters trace my footsteps still,
The hunters still pursue the trembling doe.
Where am I?—Gods!—Black heavy drops of blood
Run down the guilty walls—With the dun shades
Of night ascending, lo! successive troops
Of Trojan ghosts are flocking to the banquet:
Permitted by the infernal gods, they come,
To feast them with the horrors of this night,
To snuff the blood of victims—Ha! the car,
The gay triumphal car, is turn'd, at once,
Into a mournful bier, that nods along,
Solemn and slow—Yes, Troy shall be avenged:
I shall the vengeance see; and yet not see
Thy light, returning Phœbus.

Agam. Fair Cassandra,
Indulge no more these melancholy views,
These visions form'd by gloomy-minded grief.
We will each art, each tender art employ,
To soothe your sorrows, to restore your peace.
You come not to the proud unfeeling race
Of yesterday: we know the turns of fortune;
Have drunk the cup, the wholesome cup of sufferings,
That not inflames but moderates the mind.
Then fear not, princess; let me call you daughter!
Your treatment shall be such as well becomes
The dignity of woe, becomes the great,
The fair unhappy. Nought shall touch your honour.
I know, I feel your beauty: but here dwell
The gods of hospitality and faith;
The hymeneal powers are honour'd here.
Yes, I will shield thee, equal with Electra,
With my loved daughter in thy friendship blest.

Cass. In spite of swelling tears that choke the way,
Of bitter tears by big remembrance shed,
I own thy goodness, thank thee, Agamemnon.
Meantime, in vain are all thy generous cares,
On my account. The gods of death will, soon,
Extend o'er me their all-protecting wing.
I shall not long, I shall not want protection;
But who, devoted prince, will give it thee?
Even while we talk the secret wheels are turning,

That lift the vile, and lay the mighty low.
I pity thee, the house of Pelops pity:
Forgive me, Troy: I pity thy destroyers.

Enter an Officer.

Off. A messenger from Arcas, sir——
Agam. 'Tis well.
To my apartment lead him—you meanwhile
[*To* MELISANDER.
Attend the princess; grace her with such honours,
As suits her to receive, and me to give.

SCENE III.

CASSANDRA, CHORUS *of* Trojan Captives, MELISANDER.

Melis. Fair princess, stop these tears. Exert that best,
That noblest virtue, which can master fortune—
An equal mind.
Cass. Not for myself I weep?——
But, oh, my dear companions! How for you
My bosom yearns!
Cho. We have together lived!
Together let us die!
Cass. Together lived!
At this ten thousand images awake;
Ten thousand little tendernesses throb.
Cho. O days of youth! O careless days! Untaught
To weep, if love shed not the pleasing tear.
Cass. O woods! O fountains! O delightful meads!
That lent us flowers, the prime of blooming May,
To deck our tresses.
Cho. O the yellow banks
Of fair Scamander! in whose silver stream
We used to bathe, beneath the secret shade.
Cass. O cheerful Ida's airy summits! where
The gods delight to dwell.
Cho. O silent Troy!
Whose streets have often echo'd with our song.
Cass. O the lost labours of a ruin'd people!
O country! freedom! friends! relations! All,
That gives or taste or dignity to life,
All, all is gone, beyond recovery gone!
Cho. Then let us die!
Cass. For me, the hunted hart
More fervent pants not for the cooling stream,
Than I to wrap me in the quiet shades
Of death. But ah! my helpless friends, for you
I feel its keenest anguish.
Cho. Not for us,
Feel not for us. What comfort have we left?
What hope, what wish in life?—One healing pang,
And then we weep no more.
Cass Refreshing thought!
And then from bondage, pain, from every ill,
For ever free, we meet our friends again;
Our parents, brothers, sisters, lovers meet.
Cho. Then let us die! and sudden be the blow!
Cass. The gods assent.—Behold the happy shore!
But, ah! there lies a stormy sea betwixt!
Melis. So sings the plaining nightingale her woes.
Cass. Ah, far unlike the nightingale!—She sings,
Unceasing, through the balmy nights of May;
She sings from love and joy, while we, alas!—
Melis. Behold the queen.—Deep-wrapt in thought she seems—
Cass. Oh, direful musings!—Lead us from her presence.

SCENE IV.

Clyt. Sweet peace of mind! whence pleasure borrows taste,
Daughter of virtue! whither art thou fled!
To what calm cottage, to what blameless shade,
Far from these guilty walls! O walls! O race!
To horrors doom'd!—Before me gathers fast
A deepening gloom, with unknown terrors big.—
Not quite unknown.—Gods! what a dreadful hint
Flash'd from Egisthus, when I saw him last!
And to what desperate actions cannot safety,
Ambition, love, and vengeance drive the soul!—
Distraction lies that way—yet, how escape?
Shame urges on behind, unpitying shame,
That worst of furies, whose fell aspect frights
Each tender feeling from the human breast.
Goodness itself even turns in me to gall,
And only serves to heighten my despair.
How kind was Agamemnon! generous! fond!
How more than usual mild! As if, on purpose,
To give these tortures their severest sting.
Happy! compared to this tormented state,
Where honour only lives with inward lash,
To punish guilt, happy the harden'd wretch,
Who feels no conscience, and who fears no crime!—
Oh, horrid! horrid! Oh, flagitious thought!
How is it with the mind that can endure
A thought so dire!—My sole remaining hope
Is death, kind death, that amiable sleep
Which wakes no more,—at least to mortal care—
But then the dark hereafter that may come.—
There is no anchor that against this storm,
This mighty sea of doubts and fears, can hold.
Hopeless, I drive.—One thought destroys another.—
This stranger too!—Should it be Melisander—
Is there a fear, however idle, wild,
And even almost impossible, which guilt,
The feeble-hearted guilt not entertains?
I order'd his attendance.—See, he comes.

SCENE V.

CLYTEMNESTRA, MELISANDER.

Clyt. Stranger, are you not he, whom Agamemnon
By an amazing chance, in his return,
Saved from a desert isle?
Melis. Madam, the same.
Clyt. I much admire your fortunate deliverance
And wish to hear your story: why there left,
And how sustain'd. Indulge me with it, stranger.
Melis. Madam, I come this moment from the king,
Charged with a matter which requires dispatch:
But, that transacted once, without delay,
I will attend your orders.
Clyt. Then it seems,
You are not quite a stranger in Mycenæ.
What is your country?
Melis. Greece.
Clyt. What part of Greece?
Melis. At Athens I was born.
Clyt. But in Mycenæ,
Have you not in Mycenæ been before?
Melis. There are not, madam, many parts of Greece
To me unknown.

Clyt. Why thus avoid my question ?—
Have you been here before ?
Melis. Madam, I have.
Clyt. Here in this palace ?—Ha ! why stand you silent ?
You keep your eyes unmoved upon the ground.
What should this mean ? Beneath that rough disguise
There lurks, methinks, a form which somewhere I
Have seen.
Melis. The dream of fancy, that, the more
It is indulged, perplexes still the more.
I tarry here too long ; the king's commands
Admit of no delay.
Clyt. 'Tis so ! 'tis so !
Air, features, manners, voice, this studied haste,
The shifts of one unpractised in deceit,
All, all conspire—One image wakes another,
And thick they flash upon me !
Melis. You grow pale,
You tremble, madam ; that mistake, I find,
Concerning me turns wilder and disturbs you.
Let me retire——
Clyt. A moment—stay——
Melis. In vain,
I find it is in vain to wrap me longer
In these evasions.
Clyt. Melisander !
Melis. Madam——
Clyt. And can it be ? Behold I then the man,
Whom I so long have number'd with the dead ?
Almighty gods ! Behold I Melisander ?
But, ha ! how changed ! how darken'd with sus-
Yes, I am deem'd the author of his woes. [picion !
Melis. Madam, forgive——
Clyt. Why else from me conceal
Your wish'd return ?—I plainly am distrusted—
By Agamemnon too—It was unkind,
Unjust, unfriendly ; shocks me, Melisander.
Melis. Indeed you wrong me, madam, wrong me much,
To judge me apt or to conceive or spread
Distrust. I would have perish'd by myself,
Unknown, unwept, in helpless solitude,
Rather than here return to this full world,
To set my mistress and her lord at variance.
Oh, think me not a busy peace-destroyer !
Accursed is the wretch, to social life
The most inhuman foe, who in the nice,
The tender scenes of life, dares rashly meddle,
And sow division between friends and lovers.
Clyt. The generous heart is ever slow to blame;
But Melisander, not to me were owing,
Not in the least to me, those cruel woes,
This worse than death, which you so long have suffer'd.
Instead of that, your fate, how, whither gone,
If carried off, or secretly destroy'd,
Was all a mournful mystery to me,
Dark as the night on which you disappear'd.
Did you but know, here in my secret soul,
What undissembled pangs your absence roused;
What I have felt for you, and for myself,
In losing such a wise and faithful friend ;—
Knew you but these—oh, knew you, Melisander,
How your disaster has been truly mine,
You never could suspect me.
Melis. Witness, Heaven !
I never did—Your heart I know disdains
A thought that looks like cruelty or fraud.
From the first moment that his ruffians seized me,
I had no doubt, I knew it was Egisthus.
Some time before, I mark'd the rising storm,
And meant to warn you; but it sudden burst,
And bore me far away, far from all means,
Even from all hope of lending you assistance.
Ay ! there I suffer'd most. My fears for you,
At once by guile and violence beset,
Took off the point of my own proper woes.
But when your awful virtues struck my thought,
Your wisdom, spirit, resolution, truth ;
That dread effulgence of the spotless soul,
Which smites the hardest villain into shame ;
My fears appear'd impertinent and vain.
Yet doubtless, madam, you have had occasion
For a firm-ruling hand and watchful eye,
For every virtue ; and I truly joy,
That Agamemnon finds at his return
Egisthus by your conduct thus restrain'd.
Clyt. By heavens ! he tries me.—Oh, suspicious guilt ! [*Aside.*
Your words are friendly, but your deeds are doubtful.
No Melisander, friendship with distrust
Can never dwell. And that I am distrusted
To me is certain—In a matter too,
That much concern'd my peace, concern'd my honour.
For did you even ascribe your woes to me,
You could not manage with more distant caution.
Melis. Whence is it that the noble Clytemnestra,
Who used to shine in a superior sphere
Of fair serenity and candid peace,
Should to these doubts descend, these dark suspicions ?
For me, I here attest the gods, my soul
Ne'er knew a thought, that swell'd not with esteem,
With love and veneration of your virtues.
And for the king, no young enraptured lover,
In all the first effusions of his soul,
New to the mighty charm ; no friend, who meets
After long years of dark and silent absence,
His happy friend again, feels livelier joy,
Than Agamemnon feels, while his glad tongue
Runs out in endless praise of Clytemnestra—
But I must wait his orders.
Clyt. Do your duty.
I too must go, must to Egisthus straight [*Aside*
Impart this dreadful news.

SCENE VI.

Melis. (alone.) She went abruptly—
And as we talk'd, methought, strange passions shook
Her inward frame, and darken'd every feature.
Behold the black, the guilt-concealing night
Fast closes round. Wide, through this ample palace
The lamps begin to shine. The tempest falls ;
The weary winds sink, breathless. But, who knows
What fiercer tempest yet may shake this night !
Soul-cheering Phœbus, with thy sacred beams
O quickly come, and chase these sullen shadows !

ACT V.

SCENE I.

CLYTEMNESTRA, EGISTHUS.

Egis. Ah Clytemnestra! what a change is here!
And must I then thus steal an interview?
Are we alone?
Clyt. You fright me with that question:
You look astonish'd.
Egis. On the brink of ruin
We, tottering, stand.
Clyt. That is no news to me.
Egis. But——
Clyt. What?
Egis. We are discover'd.
Clyt. Ha! discover'd!
Egis. Yes, certainly discover'd. Arcas now,
By Agamemnon's orders, in the city
Collects a band to seize me at the banquet,
A short hour hence. And my accusers, madam,
You may be well assured, are not your friends.
Clyt. 'Tis plain! 'tis plain!—The parting fogs disperse:
And now the doubtful scene stands all reveal'd—
Who could have thought they should dissemble thus?
But I can tell you more.
Egis. What, madam? speak;
For danger presses on us.
Clyt. Saw you him,
This seeming stranger, saved by Agamemnon?
Egis. Arcas and he to-day, my friends inform me,
Were busy with the king; and, doubtless, then,
It was concerted that I should be seized.
Clyt. Ah! did you know, Egisthus, who he is!——
Egis. Who?
Clyt. Melisander.
Egis. Gods! and does he live?
For my confusion, saved! Oh, gross, gross folly!
To do an action of that kind by halves.
Had he been silent dust—To please you, madam,
From a false tenderness for you, he lives——
Clyt. A mighty merit! glorious boast indeed!
Hear him, ye gracious gentle powers of love!
From tenderness for me, he did not murder
A worthy blameless man, who never hurt him;
He murder'd not my friend, my faithful friend.
Ah! 'tis such tenderness, that makes me wretched;
Such tenderness, that still in blacker guilt,
In the last depth of misery will plunge me.
Egis. It is not, madam, now a time for this.
Think of our situation: close beset
By all those ills which mortals most abhor,
Whom have we to confide in but each other?
And this sad meeting is perhaps our last.
Concord alone, and vigorous measures, can
Prevent our ruin—But from Melisander
What did you learn? Are you yourself suspected?
Clyt. I cannot find I am:—And yet I must.
Egis. But as for me, my ruin is no secret.
Clyt. 'Tis true, some dark attempt goes on against you.
Egis. Then have I rightly done.
Clyt. What have you done?
Egis. What prudence, justice, love, and vengeance, all
Demand——
Clyt. Immortal Powers! you have not?—
Egis. No:
But must, and will—What else can you propose?
Clyt. Oh, anything besides! immediate flight,
Eternal absence, death!——
Egis. Let others die!
Let the proud, faithless, false, injurious tyrant;
The hero glorious in his daughter's murder;
The scourge of Greece, who has, from wild ambition,
Shed so much blood—let Agamemnon die!
Clyt. Oh, heavens and earth! you shock me to distraction!
I have, Egisthus, hitherto avoided
This dreadful point, still hoping you might drop
Your horrid resolution: now I tell you,
Before the listening gods, I plainly tell you,
That Agamemnon shall not fall unwarn'd:
You shall not rise by me into his throne:
I will not be the tool of your ambition;
Will not be wretched, infamous for ever,
The blush of women, the disgrace of nature!
That you may gain your execrable views,
Mask'd under smooth pretences.—I am guilty;
Alas, I am—But think not, therefore, tyrant!
To give me law. There are degrees in guilt;
And I have still my reason left, have left
Some resolution, some remains of virtue:
Yes, I dare die; and who dares die, Egisthus,
Needs not be driven to villanous extremes!
Mark me, insulting man!—My certain cure
Of every woe, my cordial draught is ready;
And if you do not promise me, here swear
To drop your fell designs on Agamemnon,
To quit this palace—You may still escape—
And never see me more; I go, I go
This moment, to discover all and die!
Egis. What! Clytemnestra!
Clyt. Nothing shall dissuade me.
I will not argue more—Say, only say,
Must I betake me to this cruel refuge?
This dire necessity?
Egis. Permit me, madam;
Hear me but once, and then pursue your purpose.
Suppose us guilty, what you will;—yet, madam,
Shall we acknowledge and proclaim that guilt?
Shall we, by patient waiting for our doom,
By pitiful neglect of self-defence,
Unheard-of meanness! stamp it into shame!
No; let us wipe it out with bold success.
It is success that colours all in life:
Success makes fools admired, makes villains honest;
All the proud virtue of this vaunting world
Fawns on success and power, howe'er acquired.
If then, supposing guilt, it were a meanness
To stoop to shame, can words express the madness
Of stopping short, with infamy and ruin,
When justice, love and vengeance, urge to glory!

Instead of being deem'd a generous queen,
The brave avenger of her sex's honour,
Famed for her spirit, for her just resentment;
Who greatly punish'd a perfidious husband,
A cruel tyrant; one, who from his bed,
His throne, proposed, with open shame to turn her,
And to her place to take his country's foe,
To take a Trojan captive, proud Cassandra:
Instead of such renown, can Clytemnestra—
Forgive the doubt—can she submit to pass,
Through future times, for an abandon'd woman?
A feeble, spiritless, abandon'd woman!—
Nay, madam, hear the truth, what now I tell you
Must, in a little scanty hour, take place:
In a few moments, you must be the first
Or last of women; be the public scorn,
Or admiration of approving Greece—
You know you must—be Agamemnon's slave,
Cassandra's slave, or nobly punish both,
And reign with me in happiness and glory.
Consult your heart; can you resolve on shame?
On voluntary shame? That only ill
The generous fear, which kills the soul itself.
Were those fair features, full of lovely grandeur,
Form'd for confusion? That majestic front,
To be bow'd down with infamy and vileness?
Ah! can you bear contempt? The venom'd tongue
Of those whom ruin pleases? The keen sneer,
The lewd reproaches of the rascal herd;
Who, for the self-same actions, if successful,
Would be as grossly lavish in your praise?—
To sum up all in one—Can you support
The scornful glances, the malignant joy,
Or more detested pity of a rival?
Of a triumphant rival?—No; you cannot.
That conscious worth, which kindles in your eye,
Tells me you cannot.—
But in vain disputes
No more to squander these important moments:
Know, that I have not, to the frail decision
Of wavering fear and female weakness, left
Our freedom, safety, happiness and honour.
Even in your own despite you shall be saved.
And could you be so lost to reason, wild,
To do what woman never did before,
What shocks humanity, accuse yourself;
You only court dishonour to no purpose:
For Agamemnon now cannot escape;
I am already master of this palace:
All is prepared, my people all are fix'd,
All properly disposed; and here I swear,
By sacred justice, glory, love, and vengeance!
He dies!—dies in the bath, before the banquet!—
And with him dies Cassandra, she, who dares,
In her presumptuous thought, usurp thy honours.
She weeps!—O my adored! my Clytemnestra!
Forgive this barbarous necessary truth!
Did I not love thee, love thee more than empire,
Than life and glory, would I thus disclose
These dangerous secrets? Could I not have veil'd,
And with more certain caution, gain'd my purpose?

Clyt. O that you had, Egisthus! then, alas!
I should have fondly thought myself less guilty.

Egis. I lose myself in softness, while the time,
With danger big, demands intrepid deeds.
Wipe off these tears—When next we meet again,
All will be well.

SCENE II.

Clyt. (*alone.*) Ah! when we meet again!—
I stand at last convinced, and must dissemble—
Yet how dissemble? Painted in my face,
Are the full horrors of this bloody deed.——
But who are these approaching?—Ha!—Cassandra!
How fair she seems! how lovely! hateful charms!
That well may rival mine, decay'd and sunk
By guilt and sorrow—She possess my bed!
Possess my sceptre!—This restores my spirit;——
I am abused! too patient!—Perish all!
Perish myself, Egisthus, Agamemnon!
So this proud rival, this Cassandra perish!

SCENE III.

CASSANDRA, Trojan Captives, MELISANDER.

Melis. Daughters of Ilium! By the king's command,
I come to ask your presence at the banquet.
Till then allow me to partake your woes:
I have a reverence for them. I myself, [fortune;
Thanks to the gracious gods! have known mis-
I am with grief acquainted; therefore can
For others feel. Sweet source of every virtue,
O sacred sorrow! he who knows not thee,
Knows not the best emotions of the heart,
Those tender tears that humanise the soul,
The sigh that charms, the pang that gives delight;
He dwells too near to cruelty and pride,
And is a novice in the school of virtue. [pity.

Cass. We thank thee, stranger, for thy generous
Heaven has, it seems, throughout diffused the good.
May the kind gods, the hospitable powers,
For this befriend thee! Thou must wander still,
Wilt their protection want.—But Agamemnon!
Where is the king?

Melis. He bathes him for the banquet,
The banquet earn'd by ten years' war and toil.

Cass. Short-sighted man! to dream of festal joy,
When his next banquet is perhaps with Pluto.
He comes! the god comes rushing on my soul!
O gently soothe me with the voice of music!
Assuage my pangs with harmony!—Methinks,
I hear Apollo's lyre.

Melis. Mysterious Powers!

Cass. 'Tis gone—And now harsh discord takes its place:
Dire yellings now affright my trembling ear!
What means this uproar of the howling forest?
The lioness and wolf, together leagued,
Pursue the lion's life.—Behold! the snare,
The infernal snare is set, spread by the stream,
Where, unsuspecting harm, he bathes at noon.
Soon will these guiltless waters blush with blood.

Melis. There is a sort of gloomy light in this,
That flashes horror on me.

Cass. A black swarm
Of fell ideas seize my fancy.—Hence!
O snatch me from this palace! shambles rather!
It smells of carnage; breathes a hideous steam,
As if from gaping sepulchres exhaled.
And lo! the spotless loves, the sports, the joys,
The weeping Lares fly: while in their place,
The vices all, the raging furies come;

And with them Comus, the flush'd god of banquets,
Besmear'd with gore. They sing the funeral hymn—
What do I see? what mean these mangled forms?
These pale, these nightly phantoms; such as rise,
To working fancy's eye, in troubled dreams?—
See! where they sit for ever at the gates,
Demanding vengeance—Vengeance is at hand—
Ha! 'tis the murder'd boys, whose limbs were here,
Served up to their own sire, to be devour'd!——

Melis. She wakes my dread--the story of Thyestes!

Cass. With this devoted race involved I fall:
Nor falls the slave alone—The master falls.
But man shall die for man, for woman woman:
Remember this.

Melis. The slave, the master fall!

Cass. Ah, bosom-traitress! Ill-persuaded queen!
And canst thou then the barbarous secret keep?—

Melis. What queen? what secret? Speak more plain, Cassandra!

Cass. From guilt, in vain, to greater guilt you fly,
From crime to crime precipitated—No!
The wicked find no peace—Distraction waits thee!—
One effort more—Yes, save thy lord, and die—
That throe belonged to virtue—Cannot then
The gentle powers prevail?—A moment yet,
The doubtful balance yet allows a moment—
Down, down it goes, for vengeance and for Troy!
But, ah! such vengeance, as even foes themselves
Abhor to see!

Melis. She staggers all my reason.
Unveil these dreadful oracles—Perhaps—

Cass. Yes, in a moment, they will be too plain.
The moment comes! The furies lash it on!
Ha! Now!

Melis. Unusual horror creeps——

Cass. Alas!
Keep from the murderous sacrificer's hand,
O keep the victim bull! Lo! seized, he spurns,
He foams in vain—Behold the lifted blow!
Behold the thirsty steel!—They strike him!—Hark!
What dismal echoes run from room to room!

Melis. I heard a distant noise!——

[*The noise of* AGAMEMNON'S *assassination heard indistinctly, and at a distance, behind the scenes.*

Cass. Again!—They strive,
The assassins labour who shall wound him most.
'Tis done!—He falls!—

[*The noise heard distinctly, and near.*

Agam. (*behind the Scenes.*) Off! villains! cowards!
By villains murder'd!—Oh! [off!—

Melis. Great gods! the king!

—•—

SCENE IV.

MELISANDER, CASSANDRA, Trojan Captives, ELECTRA, ORESTES.

Elec. Stop, generous stranger! Agamemnon's friend!

Melis. What would Electra? what with Melisander?

Elec. Heavens! Melisander!

Melis. To the king's assistance
I fly; detain me not.

Elec. He is no more!——

Melis. Ha! dead!

Elec. Yes, murder'd by Egisthus! dead!
Pierced with a thousand wounds! O horror! horror!
We have not time for grief—Orestes—Quick!
Fly! save my brother!

Orest. Leave my father!—No!
It is but once that I have ever seen him,
Shall I no more?

Elec. But to revenge his death,
O fly, Orestes, for that glorious purpose!
Tremendous gods! Methinks, I see his ghost,
That beckons you away!

Orest. I come! I come!
Oh, Melisander——

Elec. Brother!

Orest. Oh, my sister!
What will become of thee?

Elec. Good Melisander,
O guard my brother! save our only hope!—
I heard a noise——Farewell!

Orest. (*going.*) Ah! poor Electra!

—•—

SCENE V.

ELECTRA, CASSANDRA, Trojan Captives.

Elec. The murderers come! stain'd with my father's blood!
Hide me, Cassandra, hide me from a sight
I cannot bear, a scene to nature shocking!

—•—

SCENE VI.

The back-scene opening discovers, at a distance, AGAMEMNON'S *body.* ELECTRA *throws herself by it.*

CASSANDRA, Trojan Captives, EGISTHUS *with some of his party.*

Egis. Enough, my friends! How low, how silent, now,
The mighty boaster lies!—Another blow
Crowns my revenge.——

Cass. It shall not, base assassin!
The gods are just; amidst the crimes of men,
Are firmly just, supremely wise and good:
The gods are here, in all their terrors present!
See where in dreadful majesty they sit!
And write thy doom in Agamemnon's blood!

Egis. Think not to shake me with these gloomy fables:
This arm that has acquired, shall guard my power;
And since I now enjoy my long-wish'd vengeance,
All here is calm and cheerful.

Cass. The false boast
Of agonizing guilt! Thy soul, I see,
Beneath this harden'd pride, this brutal courage,
Boils with black torments, and with inward tempest.
I know whence breaks that gleam of joy athwart thee,
As lightning flashes o'er a troubled sky:
Thou dream'st the prince now falls beneath thy fury:
But hear and tremble—young Orestes lives!

Egis. Hence with thy vain predictions, doating woman!—

—•—

SCENE VII.

EGISTHUS, CASSANDRA, &c., *and to them* Assassins *sent to murder* ORESTES.

Egis. Well, is Orestes dead?

Ass. Ah, sir! escaped—
When all was in confusion, here, and tumult.

Egis. O nothing then is done: Fly! tardy villains!
Pursue him to the farthest verge of earth.——
No dark retreat, no country—But here comes
Another storm. Distraction wings her pace!

SCENE VIII.

CLYTEMNESTRA, EGISTHUS, CASSANDRA, &c.

Clyt. Off! give me way! to desarts let me fly!
The wildest savage there!——
Why pierce me thus with looks?—In every eye
There is a dagger; chief in thine [*to* EGISTHUS]—
Ha! villain!
I know thee; know these eyes, where smiling love
To the red glarings of a fury's torch
Is now transform'd.——Yes, traitor! turn away:
But, ere you go, give me my peace again;
Give me my happy family around;
Give me my virtue, honour—nay, my glory;
Or give me death, though death cannot relieve me.—
Are these the deeds of love!—I cannot step,
Unless I dip my shivering feet in blood.
Compared with this polluted, this dire palace,
The sepulchre is gay.—But whither fly?——
Ah! what avails it where the guilty fly,
Since from themselves they cannot!—Ha! behold!
The black abyss discloses to my view;
And down I go, a dark, a deep descent!——
Hell from beneath is moved at my approach:
Its princes flock around. Behold, they say,
The greatly wretched, greatly wicked woman!
She who preferr'd the villain to the hero!
The Trojan shades, with sharp derision, thank me:
The Grecian droop—Lo! where he comes himself!
See! how in sullen majesty he stalks!—
Oh, look not on me with that silent scorn!
I am too cursed already!——
[*Faints into the arms of her attendants.*
Egis. Bear her hence:
And look she be attended well.——But hark!
What new alarm?

SCENE IX.

EGISTHUS, CASSANDRA, &c., *and to them a* Messenger.

Mes. As Melisander, sir,
Bore off Orestes, to the assembled senate
He show'd the prince, and roused them to revenge.
'Tis nought but rage. The people, in a torrent,
By Arcas headed, pour upon the palace.
Besides, each moment, Agamemnon's troops—
Egis. Quick! summon here my friends—In Io's [grove
They ready wait. We this important day
Will or with conquest crown, or bravely die.
Cass. No, tyrant, no! the gods refuse thee that:
Not like the brave, but like the trembling coward,
The assassinating coward, thou shalt die;
There! in that spot, where Agamemnon lies!
Egis. Lead these ill-boding women to their fate;
And guard Electra.
Cass. The most grateful gift
A tyrant can bestow is instant death.
We shall be happy soon. But all the gods,
Combining all their mercy, from remorse,
From scorn and misery, cannot save the villain.

EPILOGUE.

OUR bard, to modern epilogue a foe,
Thinks such mean mirth but deadens generous woe;
Dispels in idle air the moral sigh,
And wipes the tender tear from pity's eye:
No more with social warmth the bosom burns;
But all the unfeeling selfish man returns.*

Thus he began:—And you approved the strain;
Till the next couplet sunk to light and vain.
You check'd him there.—To you, to reason just,
He owns he triumph'd in your kind disgust.
Charm'd by your frown, by your displeasure graced,
He hails the rising virtue of your taste.
Wide will its influence spread as soon as known:
Truth, to be loved, needs only to be shown.
Confirm it, once, the fashion to be good:
(Since fashion leads the fool, and awes the rude)
No petulance shall wound the public ear;
No hand applaud what honour shuns to hear:
No painful blush the modest cheek shall stain;
The worthy breast shall heave with no disdain.
Chastised to decency, the British stage
Shall oft invite the fair, invite the sage:
Both shall attend well-pleased, well-pleased depart;
Or if they doom the verse, absolve the heart.

* Another epilogue was spoken after the first representation of the play, which began with the first six lines of this: but the rest of that epilogue having been very justly disliked by the audience, this was substituted in its place.

ALFRED,

A Masque.

REPRESENTED BEFORE

THEIR ROYAL HIGHNESSES THE PRINCE AND PRINCESS OF WALES,

AT CLIFFDEN, ON THE 1ST OF AUGUST, 1740.

BY THOMSON AND MALLET.

Si velimus cum priorum temporum necessitate certare, vincemur. Ingeniosior est enim ad excogitandum simulatio, veritate; servitus, libertate; metus, amore.—PLIN. *Pan. Trajan.*

THE ARGUMENT.

After the Danes had made themselves masters of Chippenham, the strongest city in the kingdom of Wessex, Alfred was at once abandoned by all his subjects. In this universal defection, that monarch found himself obliged to retire into the little island of Athelney, in Somersetshire; a place then rough with woods and of difficult access. There, in the habit of a peasant, he lived unknown for some time, in a shepherd's cottage. He is supposed to be found in this retreat by the Earl of Devon, whose castle, upon the river Tau, was then besieged by the Danes.

PERSONS REPRESENTED.

ALFRED.
ELTRUDA.
HERMIT.
EARL OF DEVON.
CORIN, *a shepherd.*
EMMA, *his wife.*

A Bard, Soldiers, Spirits.

The SCENE *represents a plain, surrounded with woods. On one side, a cottage; on the other, flocks and herds in distant prospect. A hermit's cave in full view, overhung with trees, wild and grotesque.*

ACT I.

SCENE I.

CORIN, EMMA.

Emma. SHEPHERD, 'tis he. Beneath yon aged oak,
All on the flowery turf he lays him down.
Corin. Soft: let us not disturb him. Gentle Emma,
Poor though he be, unfriended and unknown,
My pity waits with reverence on his fortune.
Modest of carriage, and of speech most gracious,
As if some saint or angel, in disguise,
Had graced our lowly cottage with his presence,
He steals, I know not how, into the heart,
And makes it pant to serve him. Trust me, Emma,
He is no common man.
Emma. Some lord, perhaps,
Or valiant chief, that from our deadly foe,
The haughty, cruel, unbelieving Dane,
Seeks shelter here.
Corin. And shelter he shall find.
Who loves his country, is my friend and brother.

Behold him well. Fair virtue in his aspect,
Even through the homely russet that conceals him,
Shines forth and proves him noble. Seest thou, Emma,
Yon western clouds? the sun they strive to hide,
Yet darts his beam around.

Emma. Your thought is mine;
He is not what his present fortunes speak him.
But, ah! the raging foe is all around us:
We dare not keep him here.

Corin. Content thee, wife:
This island is of strength. Nature's own hand
Hath planted round a deep defence of woods,
The sounding ash, the mighty oak; each tree
A sheltering grove: and choked up all between
With wild encumbrance of perplexing thorns,
And horrid brakes. Beyond this woody verge,
Two rivers broad and rapid hem us in.
Along their channel spreads the gulfy pool,
And trembling quagmire, whose deceitful green
Betrays the foot it tempts. One path alone
Winds to this plain, so roughly difficult,
This single arm, poor shepherd as I am,
Could well dispute it with twice twenty Danes.

Emma. Yet think, my Corin, on the stern decree
Of that proud foe, "Who harbours or relieves
An English captain, dies the death of traitors:
But who their haunts discovers, shall be safe,
And high rewarded."

Corin. Now, just Heaven forbid,
A British man should ever count for gain
What villany must earn. No: are we poor?
Be honesty our riches. Are we mean,
And humbly born? The true heart makes us noble.
These hands can toil, can sow the ground, and reap
For thee and thy sweet babes. Our daily labour
Is daily wealth: it finds us bread and raiment.
Could Danish gold give more? And for the death
These tyrants threaten, let me rather meet it,
Than e'er betray my guest.——

Emma. Alas the while,
That loyal faith is fled from hall and bower,
To dwell with village-swains!

Corin. Ah, look! behold!
Where, like some goodly tree by wintry winds
Torn from the roots and withering, our sad guest
Lies on the ground diffused.

Emma. I weep to see it.

Corin. Thou hast a heart sweet pity loves to dwell in.
Dry up thy tears; and lean on this just hope:
If yet to do away his country's shame,
To serve her bravely on some blest occasion,
If for these ends this stranger sought our cottage,
The heavenly hosts are hovering here unseen,
To watch and to protect him.—But, oh! when—
My heart burns for it—shall I see the hour
Of vengeance on these Danish infidels,
That war with Heaven and us?

Emma. Alas, my love!
These passions are not for the poor man's state.
To Heaven and to the rulers of the land
Leave such ambitious thoughts. Be warn'd, my Corin:
And think our little all depends on thee.

SONG.

O Peace! the fairest child of Heaven,
To whom the sylvan reign was given,
The Vale, the fountain, and the grove,
With every softer scene of love:
Return, sweet Peace! and cheer the weeping swain!
Return, with Ease and Pleasure in thy train.

Corin. Hush: cease thy song—For see, our mournful guest
Has raised his head—and lo! who comes to greet him;
His friend, the woodman of the neighbouring dale,
Whom late, as yester evening-star arose,
At his request I found and hither brought.

SCENE II.

ALFRED. Earl of DEVON.

Alf. How long, O ever-gracious Heaven! how long
Shall war thus desolate this prostrate land?
All, all is lost—And Alfred lives to tell it!
His cities laid in dust! his subjects slaughter'd!
Or into slaves debased! the murderous foe
Proud and exulting in the general shame!——
Are these things so? and he without the means
Of great revenge? cast down below the hope
Of succouring those he weeps for? Oh, despair!
Oh, grief of griefs!

Dev. Old as I am, my liege,
In rough war harden'd, and with death familiar,
These eyes have long forgot to melt with softness.
But oh, my gracious master, they have seen——
All-pitying Heaven!—such sights of ruthless rage,
Of total desolation—

Alf. Oh, my people!
Oh, ruin'd England!—Devon, those were blest,
Who died before this time. Ha! and those robbers,
That violate the sanctity of leagues,
The reverend seal of oaths; that basely broke,
Like nightly ruffians, on the hour of peace,
And stole a victory from men unarm'd,
Those Danes enjoy their crimes! dread Vengeance! son
Of power and justice! come array'd in terrors,
Thy garment red with blood, thy keen sword drawn:
O come, and on the heads of faithless men
Pour ample retribution; men whose triumph
Upbraids eternal justice.—But no more:
Submission is Heaven's due.—I will not launch
Into that dark abyss where thought must drown.
Proceed, my lord: on with the mournful tale
My griefs broke off.

Dev. From yonder heath-crown'd hill,
This island's eastern point, where in one stream
The Thone and Parret roll their blending waves,
I look'd, and saw the progress of the foe,
As of some tempest, some devouring fire,
That ruins without mercy where it spreads.
The riches of the year, the golden grain
That liberal crown'd our plains, lies trampled wide
By hostile feet, or rooted up; and waste
Deforms the broad highway. From space to space,
Far as my straining eye could shoot its beam,
Trees, cottages, and castles smoke to heaven
In one ascending cloud. But oh for pity!
That way, my lord, where yonder verdant height
Declining slides into a fruitful vale,
Unsightly now and bare; a few poor hinds,
Grey-hair'd, and thinly clad, stood and beheld
The common ravage: motionless and mute
With hands to heaven up-raised, they stood, and wept—
My tears attended theirs——

Alf. If this sad sight
Could pain thee to such anguish, what must I
Their king and parent feel?—It is a torment
Beyond the strength of patience to endure.
Why end I not at once this wretched being?

The means are in my hand.—But shall a prince
Thus poorly shroud him in the grave from pain,
And sense of shame? The madman, nay the coward,
Has often dared the same. A monarch holds
His life in trust for others. I will live then:
Let Heaven dispose the rest.

Dev. Thrice noble Alfred,
And England's only hope, whose virtues raise
Our frail mortality, our human dust,
Up to angelic splendour and perfection;
With you to bear the worst of ills, the spoil
Of wasteful war, the loss of life or freedom,
Is happiness, is glory.

Alf. Ah! look round thee:
That mud-built cottage is thy sovereign's palace.
Yon hind, whose daily toil is all his wealth,
Lodges and feeds him. Are these times for flattery?
Or call it praise; such gaudy attributes
Would misbecome our best and proudest fortunes.
But what are mine? what is this high-praised Alfred?
Among ten thousand wretches, most undone.
That prince who sees his country laid in ruins,
His subjects perishing beneath the sword
Of foreign rage, who sees and cannot save them
Is but supreme in misery!

Dev. My liege!
Who has not known ill fortune, never knew
Himself, or his own virtue. Be of comfort:
We can but die at last. Till that hour comes,
Let noble anger keep our hopes alive.
A sudden thought, as if from heaven inspired,
Darts on my soul. One castle still is ours,
Though close begirt and shaken by the Danes.
In this disguise, my chance of passing on,
Of entering there unknown, is promising,
And wears a lucky face. 'Tis our last stake,
And I will play it like a man whose life,
Whose honour hangs upon a single cast.
Meanwhile, my lord——

Alf. Ha! Devon, thou hast roused
My slumbering virtue. I applaud thy thought.
The praise of this brave daring shall be thine:
The danger shall be common. We will both
Straight tempt the Danish camp, and gain this fort;
To animate our brothers of the war,
Those Englishmen who yet deserve that name.
And hear, eternal justice! if my life
Can make atonement for them, King of kings!
Accept thy willing victim. On my head
Be all their woes: to them be grace and mercy.
Come on, my noble friend.

Dev. Ah, good my liege,
What fits a private valour and might grace
The simple soldier's courage, would proclaim
His general's rashness. You are England's king:
Your infant children, and your much-loved queen;
Nay more, the public weal, ten thousand souls,
Whose hope you are, whose all depends on you,
Forbid this enterprise. 'Tis nobler virtue
To check this ardour, to reserve your sword
For some great day of known and high import;
That to your country, to the judging world
Shall justify all hazards you may run.
This trial suits but me.

Alf. Well, go, my friend;
If thou shalt prosper, thou wilt call me hence
To head my people from their fears recover'd.
May that good angel, who inspired thy thought,
Throw round thy steps a veil of cloudy air,
That thou mayst walk invisible and safe.
He's gone—and now without a friend to aid me,
I stand alone, abandon'd to the gloom
Of my sad thoughts—Said I without a friend!
Oh, blasphemous distrust! Have I not Thee,
All-powerful friend, and guardian of the righteous,
Have I not Thee to aid me? Let that thought
Support my drooping soul.—But, list. Ha! whence
These air-born notes that sound in measured sweetness
Through this vast silence?

SCENE III.

Solemn music is heard at a distance. It comes nearer in a full symphony: after which a single trumpet sounds a high and awakening air. Then the following stanzas are sung by two aërial Spirits, unseen.

First Spirit.

Hear, Alfred, father of the state,
Thy genius Heaven's high will declare!
What proves the hero truly great,
Is never, never to despair,
Is never to despair.

Second Spirit.

Thy hope awake, thy heart expand
With all its vigour, all its fires.
Arise! and save a sinking land!
Thy country calls, and Heaven inspires.

Both Spirits.

Earth calls, and Heaven inspires.

SCENE IV.

Alf. (*alone*) All hail, ye gentle ministers of heaven!
Your song inspires new patience through my breast,
And generous hope: it wings my mounting soul
Above the entangling mass of earthly passions,
That keep frail man, though struggling to be free,
Still fluttering in the dust.

SCENE V.

ALFRED, *the* HERMIT *advancing from his cave.*

Alf. Thrice-happy hermit!
Whom thus the heavenly habitants attend,
Blessing thy calm retreat; while ruthless war
Fills the polluted land with blood and crimes.
In this extremity of England's fate,
Led by thy sacred character, I come
For comfort and advice. Thy aged wisdom,
Purged from the stormy cloud of human passions,
And by a ray from heaven exalted, sees
Deep through futurity. Say what remains,
What yet remains to save our prostrate country!
Nor scorn this anxious question even from me,
A nameless stranger.

Hermit. Alfred, England's king,
All hail! and welcome to this humble cell.

Alf. Whence dost thou know me, venerable father?

Hermit. Last night, when with a draught from that cool fountain
I had my wholesome sober supper crown'd;
As is my stated custom, forth I walk'd,
Beneath the solemn gloom, and glittering sky,
To feed my soul with prayer and meditation.

And thus to inward harmony composed,
That sweetest music of the grateful heart,
Whose each emotion is a silent hymn,
I to my couch retired. Straight on mine eyes
A pleasing slumber fell, whose mystic power
Seal'd up my senses, but enlarged my soul.
At once, disclosed amid the dark waste night,
Appear'd a vision—not the dream of fancy,
But sent from heaven, prophetic and divine.
For know, this ample element contains
Unnumber'd spiritual beings, or malign,
Or good to man. These, when the grosser eye
Of nature sleeps, oft play their several parts,
As on a scene, before the attentive mind,
And to the favour'd man disclose the future.
Led by these spirits friendly to this isle,
I lived through future ages; felt the virtue,
The great, the glorious passions that will fire
Distant posterity: when guardian laws
Are by the patriot in the glowing senate
Won from corruption; when the impatient arm
Of liberty, invincible, shall scourge
The tyrants of mankind—and when the deep,
Through all her swelling waves, shall proudly joy
Beneath the boundless empire of thy sons.
I saw thee, Alfred, too—But o'er thy fortunes
Lay clouds impenetrable.

Alf. Ah, good hermit,
That scene is dark indeed! Ye awful powers!
To what am I reserved? Still must I roam
A wanderer here, inglorious and unknown?
Or am I destined your great instrument,
From fierce oppression to redeem this land?

Hermit. Perhaps, the last. But, prince, remember, then,
The vows, the noble uses, of affliction.
Preserve the quick humanity it gives,
The pitying, social sense of human weakness:
Yet keep thy stubborn fortitude entire,
The manly heart that to another's woe
Is tender, but superior to its own.
Learn to submit; yet learn to conquer fortune.
Attach thee firmly to the virtuous deeds
And offices of life; to life itself,
With all its vain and transient joys, sit loose.
Chief, let devotion to the Sovereign Mind,
A steady, cheerful, absolute dependance
On his best, wisest government, possess thee.
In thoughtless gay prosperity, when all
Attends our wish, when nought is seen around us
But kneeling flattery, and obedient fortune;
Then are blind mortals apt, within themselves
To fix their stay, forgetful of the giver.
But when thus humbled, Alfred, as thou art,
When to their feeble natural powers reduced,
'Tis then they feel this universal truth——
That Heaven is all in all—and man is nothing.

Alf. I thank thee, father, for thy pious counsel.
And witness, thou dread Power! who seest my [heart;
That if not to perform my regal task,
To be the common father of my people,
Patron of honour, virtue, and religion;
If not to shelter industry, to guard
Her honest portion from oppressive pride,
From wasteful riot, and the sons of rapine,
Who basely ravish what they dare not earn;
If not to deal out justice, like the sun,
With equal light; if not to spread thy bounty,
The treasures trusted to me, not my own,
On all the smiling ranks of nourish'd life;
If not to raise our drooping English name,
To clothe it yet with terror; make this land
Renown'd for peaceful arts to bless mankind,
And generous war to humble proud oppressors:
If not to build on an eternal base,
On liberty and laws, the public weal:
If not for these great ends I am ordain'd,
May I ne'er idly fill the throne of England!

Her. Still may thy breast these sentiments retain,
In prosperous life.

Alf. Prosperity were ruin,
Could it destroy or change such thoughts as these.
When those whom Heaven distinguishes o'er millions,
Profusely gives them honours, riches, power,
Whate'er the expanded heart can wish; when they,
Accepting the reward, neglect the duty;
Or worse, pervert those gifts to deeds of ruin:
Is there a wretch they rule so mean as they?
Guilty, at once, of sacrilege to Heaven,
And of perfidious robbery to men——
But hark! methinks I hear a plaintive voice
Sigh through the vale, and wake the mournful echo.

SONG.

Sweet valley, say, where, pensive lying,
For me, our children, England, sighing,
The best of mortals leans his head.
Ye fountains, dimpled by my sorrow,
Ye brooks that my complainings borrow,
O lead me to his lonely bed:
Or if my lover,
Deep woods, you cover,
Ah whisper where your shadows o'er him spread!

'Tis not the loss of pomp and pleasure,
Of empire or of tinsel treasure,
That drops this tear, that swells this groan;
No; from a nobler cause proceeding,
A heart with love and fondness bleeding
I breathe my sadly-pleasing moan.
With other anguish
I scorn to languish:
For love will feel no sorrows but his own.

SCENE VI.

ALFRED, HERMIT, ELTRUDA, *advancing.*

Alf. Sure by the voice, and purport of the song,
This generous mourner is my queen Eltruda.
And yet how can that be?—Oh, all good powers!
'Tis she! 'tis she!

Elt. My lord, my life, my Alfred!
Oh, take me to thy arms; with toil o'ercome,
And sudden transport, thus at once to find thee,
In this wild forest, pathless and perplex'd!

Alf. Come to my soul, thou dearest, best of women!
Come, and repose thy sorrows in my bosom.
Oh, all my passions mix in doubtful strife!
If pain or joy prevail, I scarce can say,
While thus I clasp thee, and recal the perils
To which thy trembling steps have been exposed.
Why hast thou left the convent where I placed thee?
Why, unprotected, trust thee to a land,
A barbarous land, where rages Danish war!
Our hospitable England is no more! [country,

Elt. Dire was the cause, my Alfred. The roused
All wild in breathless terror and confusion,
Inform'd us, a near party of the Danes,

Whose brutal fury spares no sex, no age,
No place however privileged or holy,
Were on full march that way. Instant I fled,
In this disguise with only these attendants:
But in our way oft cheer'd by airy voices,
To bear to this retreat our helpless children.
Alf. Ah, wanderers too young! ah, hapless children!
But more unhappy sire! who cannot give,
To those he loves, protection.
Elt. Thou too, Alfred,
Art thou not unattended? None to serve thee,
To soothe thy woes, to watch thy broken slumbers!
And when the silent tear o'erflows thy eye,
None, with the warm and cordial lip of love,
To kiss it off! There is in love a power,
There is a soft divinity, that draws
Transport even from distress; that gives the heart
A certain pang, excelling far the joys
Of gross unfeeling life. Besides, my Alfred,
Even had the fury of this barbarous foe
Not forced me from the convent, life is short;
And now it trembles on the wing of danger;
Why should we lose it then? One well-saved hour,
In such a tender circumstance to lovers,
Is better than an age of common time.
Alf. Oh, 'tis too much! thy tenderness o'ercomes me!
Nay, look not on me with that sweet dejection,
Through tears that pierce my soul!—Cheer thee, my love;
Hope still the best; that better days await us,
And fairer from remembrance.—Thou, Eltruda,
Thou art a pledge of happiness! On thee
Good angels wait; they led thy journey hither:
And I have heard them, in this wild retreat,
Warbling immortal airs, and strains of comfort.—
But, ah, the foe is round us: and this isle
Now holds my soul's best wealth, the treasured store
Of all my joys. I go to skirt it round,
To visit every creek and sedgy bank,
Where rustles through the reeds the shadowy gale;
Or where the bending umbrage drinks the stream;
Lest danger unawares should steal upon us.
And now, by slow degrees, solemn and sad,
Wide-falling o'er the world, the nightly shades
Hush the brown woods and deepen all their horrors:
While humbled into rest, and awed by darkness,
Each creature seeks the covert. To that cell
Retire, my life I will not long be absent.

ACT II.

SCENE I.

Alf. (*alone.*) 'Tis now the depth of darkness and repose.
All nature seems to rest: while Alfred wakes
To think, and to be wretched.—Where yon oak
With wide and dusky shade o'erhangs the stream,
That glides in silence by, I took my stand:
What time the glow-worm through the dewy path
First shot his twinkling flame. I stood attentive,
Listening each noise from wood-clad hill and dale;
But all was hush'd around. Nor trumpet's clang,
Nor shout of roving foe, nor hasty tread
Of evening passenger, disturb'd the wide
And awful stillness. Homeward as I sped,
O'er many a delve, through many a path perplex'd,
Maze running into maze; ill-boding thoughts
Haunted my steps.—Perhaps my gallant friend,
Discover'd to the Danes, this moment bleeds
Beneath their swords! or lies a breathless corse,
The prey of midnight wolves.—Some mournful sound
Strikes sudden on my sense.

SCENE II.

ALFRED, ELTRUDA.

Elt. Here will I lean
On this green bank, to wait the wish'd return
Of morning and my lord.
Alf. My gentle love,
Eltruda, why to this untimely sky
Expose thy health? The dews of night fall fast:
The chill breeze sighs aloud.
Elt. I could not rest.
Can love repose when apprehension wakes,
And whispers to the heart all dreadful things,
That walk with night and solitude? Methought,
In each low murmur of the woods, I heard
The invading foe—or heard my Alfred groan!
Our tender infants too—their fancied cries
Still sound within my ears!
Alf. Eltruda, there
I am a woman too: I who should cheer,
And shelter thee from every care. My children!
The thought of what may chance to them, completes
Their father's sum of woes. Oh, what safe shade
Can skreen their opening blossom from the storm
That beats severe on us! Not sweeter buds
The primrose in the vale, nor sooner shrinks
At winter's churlish blast——
Elt. Behold, my lord—
Good angels shield us—What a flood of brightness
Waves round our heads!
Alf. The hermit moves this way.
That wondrous man holds converse with the host
Of higher natures. These far-beaming fires
Were doubtless kindled up at his command.
Be silent and attentive.

SCENE III.

ALFRED, ELTRUDA, HERMIT.

Her. I have heard
Thy fond complainings, Alfred.
Alf. You have then,
Good father, heard the cause that wrings them from me.
Her. The human race are sons of sorrow born,
And each must have his portion. Vulgar minds
Refuse, or crouch beneath their load: the brave
Bear theirs without repining.
Alf. Who can bear
The shaft that wounds him through an infant's side?

When whom we love, to whom we owe protection,
Implore the hand we cannot reach to save them?
Her. Weep not, Eltruda.——Yet thou art a king,
All private passions fall before that name.
Thy subjects claim thee whole.
Alf. Can public trust,
O reverend sage! destroy the softer ties
That twine around the parent's yearning heart,
That holy passion Heaven itself infused,
And blended with the stream that feeds our life?
Her. You love your children, prince—
Alf. Lives there on earth,
In air, or ocean, creature tame or wild,
That has not known this universal love?
All nature feels it intimate and deep,
And all her sons of instinct or of reason.
Her. Then show that passion in its noblest form.
Season their tender years with every virtue,
Social or self-retired; of public greatness,
Or lovely in the hour of private life;
With all that can exalt, or can adorn
Their princely rank.
Alf. Alas! their hope must stoop,
Such my unhappy fate, to humbler aims:
Affliction and base want must be their teachers.
Her. Affliction is the wholesome soil of virtue:
Where patience, honour, sweet humanity,
Calm fortitude take root, and strongly flourish.
But prosperous fortune, that allures with pleasure,
Dazzles with pomp, and undermines with flattery,
Poisons the soil, and its best product kills.
Shouldst thou regain thy throne—
Alf. My throne? What glimpse,
What smallest ray of hope——
Her. That day may come—
What do I feel? My labouring breast expands
To give the glorious inspiration room.
And now the cloud that o'er thy future fate,
Like total night, lay heavy and obscure,
Fades into air: and all the brightening scene
Dawns gay before me! A long line of kings,
From thee descending, glorious and renown'd,
In shadowy pomp I see!

Genius of England! hovering near,
In all thy radiant charms appear.

O come and summon, from the world unknown,
Those mighty chiefs, those sons of future fame,
Who, ages hence, this island shall adorn,
And spread to distant realms her glorious name.
Slow let the visionary forms arise,
And solemn pass before our wondering eyes.

[*Music grand and awful. The Genius descending sings the following.*

SONG.

From those eternal regions bright,
Where suns, that never set in night,
Diffuse the golden day:
Where Spring, unfading, pours around,
O'er all the dew-impearled ground,
Her thousand colours gay:
O whether on the fountain's flowery side,
Whence living waters glide,
Or in the fragrant grove,
Whose shade embosoms peace and love,
New pleasures all our hours employ,
And ravish every sense with every joy!

Great heirs of empire! yet unborn,
Who shall this island late adorn;
A monarch's drooping thought to check,
Appear! appear! appear!

Spirits of EDWARD III., PHILIPPA *his queen, and the* BLACK PRINCE *his son, arise.*

Her. Alfred, look; and say,
What seest thou yonder?
Alf. Three majestic shapes:
Two habited like mighty warriors old;
A third in whose bright aspect beauty smiles
More soft and feminine. A lucid veil,
From her fair neck dependant floats around,
Light-hovering in the gale.
Her. O Alfred, man
Beloved of Heaven, behold a king *indeed*;
Matchless in arms; in arts of peaceful rule,
A sovereign's truest glory, yet more famed,
England's third Edward!—At his fear'd approach
Proud France, even now, through all her dukedoms quakes.
Her Genius sighs: and from the eternal shore,
The soul of her great Charles, a recent guest,
Looks back to earth, and mourns the distant woes
His realms are doom'd to feel from Edward's wrath.
Beneath his standard, Britain shall go forth,
Array'd for conquest, terrible in glory:
And nations shrink before her. Oh, what deaths,
What desolation shall her vengeance spread,
From engines yet unfound; whose lightnings flash,
Whose thunders roar, amazing, o'er the plain:
As if this king had summon'd from on high
Heaven's dread artillery to fight his battle!
Nor is renown in war his sole ambition:
A nobler passion labours in his breast——
Alfred, attend—to make his people blest!
The sacred rights that reason loudly claims
For free-born men—these, Alfred, are his care:
Oft to confirm, and fix them on the base
Of equal laws.—O father of mankind!
Successive praises from a grateful land
Shall saint thy name for ever!
Alf. Holy sage,
Whom angels thus enlighten and inspire,
My bosom kindles at thy heaven-born flame.
Great Edward! Be thy conquests and their praise
Unrival'd to thyself. But O thy fame
For care paternal of the public weal!
For England blest at home—my rapt heart pants
To equal that renown!
Her. Know farther, Alfred;
A sovereign's great example forms a people.
The public breast is noble, or is vile,
As he inspires it. In this Edward's time,
Warm'd by his courage, by his honour raised,
High flames the British spirit like the sun,
To shine o'er half the globe: and where it shines,
The cherish'd world to brighten and enrich.
Last see this monarch in his hour of leisure;
Even social on a throne, and tasting joys
To solitary greatness seldom known,
As friend, as husband, and as father blest.
That god-like youth remark, his eldest hope,
Who gives new lustre to the name he bears;
A hero ere a man.—I see him now
On Cressy's glorious plain! The father's heart,
With anxious love and wonder at his daring,
Beats high in mingled transport. Great himself,
Great above jealousy, the guilty mark
That brands all meaner minds, see, he applauds

The filial excellence, and gives him scope
To blaze in his full brightness!—Lo, again
He sends him dreadful to a nobler field:
The danger and the glory all his own!
A captive king, the rival of his arms,
I see adorn his triumph! Heaven! what grace,
What splendour from his gracious temper mild
That triumph draws! As gentle mercy kind,
He cheers the hostile prince whose fall he weeps!

Alf. A son so rich in virtues, and so graced
With all that gives those virtues fair to shine,
When I would ask of Heaven some mighty boon,
Should claim the foremost place.

Her. Remember then,
What to thy infant sons from thee is due,
As parent and as prince.

Elt. Forgive me, Hermit,
Forgive a queen and wife her anxious fondness.
Yon beauteous shade, that as I gaze her o'er,
My wonder draws, escapes your graver thought.

Her. O bright Eltruda! thou whose blooming youth,
Whose amiable sweetness promise blessings
To Alfred and to England! see, and mark,
In yonder pleasing form, the best of wives,
The happiest too, repaid with all the faith,
With all the friendship, love and duty claim.
She, powerful o'er the heart her charms enslave—
O virtue rarely practised!—uses nobly
That happy influence; to prompt each purpose
Fair honour kindles in her Edward's breast.
Amid the pomps, the pleasures of a court,
Humble of heart, severely good; the friend
Of modest worth, the parent of the poor.
Eltruda! oh, transmit these noblest charms
To that fair daughter, that unfolding rose, [loves.
With which, as on this day*, Heaven crown'd your

Spirit of Elizabeth *arises.*

Alf. Say, who is she, in whom the noble graces,
The engaging manner, dignity, and ease,
Are join'd with manly sense and resolution?

Her. The great Eliza. She, amid a world
That threatening swells in high commotion round
Each dangerous state her unrelenting foe, [her;
And chief a proud enormous empire stretch'd
O'er half mankind; with not one friendly power,
But what her kind creating hand shall raise
From out the marshes of the branching Rhine;
And mined, at home, her ever-tottering throne
By restless bigots, who, beneath the mask
Of mild religion, are to every crime
Set loose, the faithless sons of barbarous zeal:
Yet she shall crown this happy isle with peace,
With arts, with riches, grandeur, and renown;
And quell, by turns, the madness of her foes.
As when the winds, from different quarters, urge
The tempest on our shore; secure the cliffs
Repel its idle rage, and pour it back,
In broken billows, foaming to the main.

Alf. How shall she, Hermit, gain these glorious ends?

Her. By silent wisdom, whose informing power
Works unperceived: that seems in council slow;
But, when resolved, and ripe for execution,
That darts like lightning from the secret gloom:
By ever seizing the right point of view,
Her truest interest; which she firm pursues,
With steady patience, through the maze of state,
The storm of opposition, the mix'd views,
And thwarting managed passions of mankind:
By healing the divisions of her people,
And sowing the fell pest among her foes:
By saving, from the vermin of a court,
Her treasure; which, when fair occasion calls,
She knows to lavish, in protecting arts,
In guarding nations, and in nursing states:
By calling up to power, and public life,
Each virtue, each ability: yet she,
Amid the various worthies glowing round her
Still shines the first; the central sun that wakes
That rules their every motion: not the slave,
And passive property of her own creatures.
But the great soul that animates her reign,
That lights it to perfection, is the love,
The confidence unbounded, which her wisdom,
Her probity and justice, shall inspire
Into the public breast. Hence cordial faith,
Which nought can shake; hence unexhausted
And hence, above all mercenary force, [treasure:
The hand that by the free-born heart is raised.
And guards the blended weal of prince and people.
She too shall raise Britannia's naval power;
Shall greatly ravish, from insulting Spain,
The world-commanding sceptre of the deep.

Elt. O matchless queen! O glory of her sex!
The great idea, father, fills my soul,
And bids it glow beyond a woman's passions.

Spirit of William III. *arises.*

Her. Once more, O Alfred, raise thine eyes, and mark
Who next adorns the scene, yon laurel'd shade.
Ere yet the age that closed this female reign
Hath led around its train of circling years,
Shall Britain on the verge of ruin stand.
A monarch, lost to greatness, to renown,
The slave of dreaming monks, shall fill her throne,
Weak and aspiring; fond of lawless rule,
The lawless rule his mean ambition covets
Unequal to acquire. Yon prince thou saw'st
To glory tutor'd by the hand severe
Of sharp adversity, shall Heaven upraise,
And injured nations with joint call invoke,
Their last, their only refuge. Lo! he comes
Wide o'er the billows of the boundless deep
His navy rides triumphant: and the shores
Of shouting Albion echo with his name.
Immortal William! from before his face,
Flies Superstition, flies oppressive power,
With vile Servility that crouch'd and kiss'd
The whip he trembled at. From this great hour
Shall Britain date her rights and laws restored:
And one high purpose rule her sovereign's heart
To scourge the pride of France, that foe profess'
To England and to freedom. Yet I see,
From distant climes in peaceful triumph borne,
Another king arise! His early youth
With verdant laurel crown'd, for deeds of arms
That reason's voice approves; for courage, raised
Beyond all aid from passion, greatly calm!
Intrepidly serene!—In days of peace,
Around his throne the human virtues wait,
And fair adorn him with their mildest beams;
Good without show, above ambition great;
Wise, equal, merciful, the friend of man!

O Alfred! should thy fate, long ages hence,
In moving scenes recall'd, exalt the joy

* This masque was written to be acted at Clifden, on the birthday of her royal highness the princess Augusta.

Of some glad festal day, before a prince
Sprung from that king beloved—Hear, gracious [Heaven!
Thy soft humanity, thy patriot heart,
Thy manly virtue, steady, great, resolved,
Be his supreme ambition! and with these,
The happiness, the glory, that await
Thy better days, be shower'd upon his head!
Alf. O Hermit! thou hast raised me to new life!
New hopes, new triumphs swell my bounding heart—
Her. It comes! it comes!—The promised scene discloses!
Already the great work of fate begins!
The mighty wheels are turning, whence will spread,
Beyond the limits of our narrow world,
The fair dominions, Alfred, of thy sons.
Behold the warrior bright with Danish spoils!—
The raven droops his wings—and hark! the trumpet,
Exulting, speaks the rest.

SCENE IV.

Symphony of martial music.

ALFRED, ELTRUDA, HERMIT, *Earl of* DEVON, *followed by* Soldiers.

Alf. My friend return'd!
O welcome, welcome! but what happy tidings
Smile in thy cheerful countenance?
Dev. My liege,
Your troops have been successful. But to Heaven
Ascend the praise! For sure the event exceeds
The hand of man.
Alf. How was it, noble Devon?
Dev. You know my castle is not hence far distant.
Thither I sped: and in a Danish habit
The trenches passing, by a secret way,
Known to myself alone, emerged at once
Amid my joyful soldiers. There I found
A generous few, the veteran hardy gleanings
Of many a hapless fight. They with a fierce
Heroic fire inspirited each other;
Resolved on death, disdaining to survive
Their dearest country.—"If we fall," I cried,
"Let us not tamely fall like passive cowards!
No: let us live—or let us die, like men!
Come on, my friends: to Alfred we will cut
Our glorious way; or, as we nobly perish,
Will offer to the genius of our country
Whole hecatombs of Danes."—As if one soul
Had moved them all, around their heads they flash'd
Their flaming faulchions—"Lead us to those Danes!—
Our country?—vengeance!" was the general cry.
Straight on the careless drowsy camp we rush'd:
And rapid, as the flame devours the stubble,
Bore down the heartless Danes. With this success
Our enterprise increased. Not now contented
To hew a passage through the flying herd;
We, unremitting, urged a total rout.
The valiant Hubba bites the bloody field,
With twice six hundred Danes around him strow'd.
Alf. My glorious friend!—this action has restored
Our sinking country.—What reward can equal
A deed so great?—Is not yon pictured Raven
Their famous magic standard—Emblem fit
To speak the savage genius of the people—
That oft has scatter'd on our troops dismay,
And feeble consternation?
Dev. 'Tis the same,
Wrought by the sisters of the Danish king,
Of furious Ivar, in a midnight hour:
While the sick moon at their enchanted song,
Wrapt in pale tempest, labour'd through the clouds,
The demons of destruction then, they say,
Were all abroad, and mixing with the woof
Their baleful power: the sisters ever sung;
"Shake, standard, shake, this ruin on our foes!"
Her. So these infernal powers, with rays of truth,
Still deck their fables, to delude who trust them.
Alf. But where, my noble cousin, are the rest
Of your brave troops?
Dev. On t'other side the stream,
That half incloses this retreat, I left them.
Roused from the fear, with which it was congeal'd
As in a frost, the country pours amain.
The spirit of our ancestors is up,
The spirit of the free! and with a voice
That breathes success, they all demand their king.
Alf. Quick, let us join them, and improve their [ardour.
We cannot be too hasty to secure
The glances of occasion.

SCENE the Last.

To them CORIN, EMMA, *kneeling to* ALFRED.

Corin. Good my liege,
Pardon the poor unequal entertainment,
Which we, unknowing—
Alf. Rise, my honest shepherd,
I came to thee a peasant, not a prince:
Thy rural entertainment was sincere,
Plain, hospitable, kind: such as, I hope,
Will ever mark the manners of this nation.
You friendly lodged me, when by all deserted:
And shall have ample recompense.
Corin. One boon
Is all I crave.
Alf. Good shepherd, speak thy wish.
Corin. Permission, in your wars, to serve your grace:
For, though here lost in solitary shades,
A simple swain, I bear an English heart:
A heart that burns with rage to see those Danes,
Those foreign ruffians, those inhuman pirates,
Oft our inferiors proved, thus lord it o'er us.
Alf. Brave countryman, come on. 'Tis such as thou,
Who from affection serve, and free-born zeal,
To guard whate'er is dear and sacred to them,
That are a king's best honour and defence.

EMMA *sings the following* SONG.

If those who live in shepherd's bower
Press not the rich and stately bed,
The new-mown hay and breathing flower
A softer couch beneath them spread.

If those who sit at shepherd's board
Soothe not their taste by wanton art;
They take what nature's gifts afford,
And take it with a cheerful heart.

If those who drain the shepherd's bowl
No high and sparkling wines can boast,
With wholesome cups they cheer the soul,
And crown them with the village toast.

If those who join in shepherd's sport,
Gay-dancing on the daisied ground,
Have not the splendour of a court,
Yet love adorns the merry round

Alf. My loved Eltruda! thou shalt here remain,
With gentle Emma, and this reverend hermit.
Ye silver streams, that murmuring wind around
This dusky spot, to you I trust my all!
Oh, close around her, woods! for her, ye vales,
Throw forth your flowers, your softest lap diffuse!
And Thou! whose secret and expansive hand
Moves all the springs of this vast universe:
Whose government astonishes; who here,
In a few hours, beyond our utmost hope,
Beyond our thought, yet doubting, hast clear'd up
The storm of fate: preserve what thy kind will,
Thy bountiful appointment, makes so dear
To human hearts! preserve my queen and children!
Preserve the hopes of England! while I go
To finish thy great work, and save my country.
Elt. Go, pay the debt of honour to the public.
If ever woman, Alfred, loved her husband
More fondly than herself, I claim that virtue,
That heart-felt happiness. Yet by our loves
I swear that in a glorious death with thee
I rather would be wrapt, than live long years
To charm thee from the rugged paths of honour:
So much I think thee born for beauteous deeds,
And the bright course of glory.
Alf. Matchless woman!
Love, at thy voice, is kindled to ambition.
Be this my dearest triumph, to approve me
A husband worthy of the best Eltruda.
Her. Behold, my lord, our venerable bard,
Aged and blind, him whom the muses favour.
Yet ere you go, in our loved country's praise,
That noblest theme, hear what his rapture breathes.

AN ODE.

When Britain first, at Heaven's command,
Arose from out the azure main,
This was the charter of the land,
And guardian angels sung this strain:

"*Rule Britannia, rule the waves;*
"*Britons never will be slaves.*"

The nations, not so blest as thee,
Must in their turns to tyrants fall;
While thou shalt flourish, great and free,
The dread and envy of them all.

"*Rule, &c.*"

Still more majestic shalt thou rise,
More dreadful from each foreign stroke;
As the loud blast, that tears the skies,
Serves but to root thy native oak

"*Rule, &c.*"

Thee haughty tyrants ne'er shall tame:
All their attempts to bend thee down
Will but arouse thy generous flame;
But work their woe, and thy renown.

"*Rule, &c.*"

To thee belongs the rural reign;
Thy cities shall with commerce shine:
All thine shall be the subject main;
And every shore it circles, thine.

"*Rule, &c.*"

The muses, still with freedom found,
Shall to thy happy coast repair:
Blest isle! with matchless beauty crown'd,
And manly hearts to guard the fair.

"*Rule, Britannia, rule the waves;*
"*Britons never will be slaves.*"

Her. Alfred, go forth! lead on the radiant years,
To thee reveal'd in vision.—Lo! they rise!
Lo! patriots, heroes, sages, crowd to birth:
And bards to sing them in immortal verse!
I see thy commerce, Britain, grasp the world:
All nations serve thee; every foreign flood,
Subjected, pays its tribute to the Thames.
Thither the golden south obedient pours
His sunny treasures; thither the soft east
Her spices, delicacies, gentle gifts;
And thither his rough trade the stormy north.
See, where beyond the vast Atlantic surge,
By boldest keels untouch'd, a dreadful space!
Shores, yet unfound, arise! in youthful prime,
With towering forests, mighty rivers crown'd:
These stoop to Britain's thunder. This new world,
Shook to its centre, trembles at her name:
And there her sons, with aim exalted, sow
The seeds of rising empire, arts, and arms.

Britons, proceed, the subject deep command,
Awe with your navies every hostile land.
Vain are their threats, their armies all are vain:
They rule the balanced world, who rule the main.

TANCRED AND SIGISMUNDA.

A Tragedy.

ADVERTISEMENT.

This play is considerably shortened in the performance; but I hope it will not be disagreeable to the reader to see it as it was at first written, there being a great difference betwixt a play in the closet and upon the stage.

TO

HIS ROYAL HIGHNESS FREDERICK PRINCE OF WALES.

Sir,

The honour your Royal Highness has done me in the protection you was pleased to give to this tragedy, emboldens me to lay it now at your feet, and beg your permission to publish it under your royal patronage. The favouring and protecting of letters has been, in all ages and countries, one distinguishing mark of a great prince; and that with good reason, not only as it shows a justness of taste and elevation of mind, but as the influence of such a protection, by exciting good writers to labour with more emulation in the improvement of their several talents, not a little contributes to the embellishment and instruction of society. But of all the different species of writing, none has such an effect upon the lives and manners of men as the dramatic; and, therefore, that of all others most deserves the attention of princes; who, by a judicious approbation of such pieces as tend to promote all public and private virtue, may, more than by any coercive methods, secure the purity of the stage, and, in consequence thereof, greatly advance the morals and politeness of their people. How eminently your Royal Highness has always extended your favour and patronage to every art and science, and in a particular manner to dramatic performances, is too well known to the world for me to mention it here. Allow me only to wish, that what I have now the honour to offer to your Royal Highness may be judged not unworthy of your protection, at least in the sentiments which it inculcates. A warm and grateful sense of your goodness to me makes me desirous to seize every occasion of declaring in public with what profound respect and dutiful attachment I am, Sir,

Your Royal Highness's most obliged, most obedient, and most devoted servant,

James Thomson.

PROLOGUE.

Bold is the man! who, in this nicer age,
Presumes to tread the chaste corrected stage.
Now, with gay tinsel arts, we can no more
Conceal the want of nature's sterling ore.
Our spells are vanish'd, broke our magic wand,
That used to waft you over sea and land.
Before your light the fairy people fade,
The demons fly—the ghost itself is laid.
In vain of martial scenes the loud alarms,
The mighty prompter thundering out to arms,
The playhouse posse clattering from afar,
The close-wedged battle, and the din of war.
Now, even the senate seldom we convene;
The yawning fathers nod behind the scene.
Your taste rejects the glittering false sublime,
To sigh in metaphor, and die in rhyme.

High rant is tumbled from his gallery throne:
Description dreams—nay, similes are gone.

What shall we then? to please you how devise,
Whose judgment sits not in your ears and eyes?
Thrice happy! could we catch great Shakspeare's art,
To trace the deep recesses of the heart;
His simple plain sublime, to which is given
To strike the soul with darted flame from heaven:
Could we awake soft Otway's tender woe,
The pomp of verse and golden lines of Rowe.
We to your hearts apply: let them attend;
Before their silent candid bar we bend.
If warm'd, they listen, 'tis our noblest praise;
If cold, they wither all the muse's bays.

PERSONS REPRESENTED.

TANCRED, *Count of Lecce.*
MATTEO SIFFREDI, *Lord High Chancellor of Sicily.*
EARL OSMOND, *Lord High Constable of Sicily.*
RODOLPHO, *friend to Tancred, and Captain of the Guards.*
SIGISMUNDA, *daughter of Siffredi.*
LAURA. *sister of Rodolpho, and friend to Sigismunda.*

Barons, Officers, Guards, &c.

SCENE.—*The City of Palermo, in Sicily.*

ACT I.

SCENE I.

SIGISMUNDA, LAURA.

Sigis. AH fatal day to Sicily! The king
Approaches his last moments!
Lau. So 'tis fear'd.
Sigis. The death of those distinguish'd by their station,
But by their virtue more, awakes the mind
To solemn dread, and strikes a saddening awe:
Not that we grieve for them, but for ourselves,
Left to the toil of life—And yet the best
Are, by the playful children of this world,
At once forgot, as they had never been.
Laura, 'tis said—the heart is sometimes charged
With a prophetic sadness: such, methinks,
Now hangs on mine. The king's approaching death
Suggests a thousand fears. What troubles thence
May throw the state once more into confusion,
What sudden changes in my father's house
May rise, and part me from my dearest Tancred,
Alarms my thought.
Lau. The fears of love-sick fancy!
Perversely busy to torment itself.
But be assured, your father's steady friendship,
Join'd to a certain genius, that commands,
Not kneels to fortune, will support and cherish,
Here in the public eye of Sicily,
This—I may call him—his adopted son,
The noble Tancred, form'd to all his virtues.
Sigis. Ah, form'd to charm his daughter!—This fair morn
Has tempted far the chase. Is he not yet
Return'd?
Lau. No.—When your father to the king,
Who now expiring lies, was call'd in haste,
He sent each way his messengers to find him;
With such a look of ardour and impatience,
As if this near event was to count Tancred
Of more importance than I comprehend.
Sigis. There lies, my Laura, o'er my Tancred' birth
A cloud I cannot pierce. With princely cost,
Nay, with respect, which oft I have observed,
Stealing at times submissive o'er his features,
In Belmont's woods my father rear'd this youth—
Ah woods! where first my artless bosom learnt
The sighs of love.—He gives him out the son
Of an old friend, a baron of Apulia,
Who in the late crusado bravely fell.
But then 'tis strange; is all his family
As well as father dead? and all their friends,
Except my sire, the generous good Siffredi?
Had he a mother, sister, brother, left,
The last remain of kindred; with what pride,
What rapture, might they fly o'er earth and sea,
To claim this rising honour of their blood!
This bright unknown! this all-accomplish'd youth
Who charms—too much—the heart of Sigismunda!
Laura, perhaps your brother knows him better,
The friend and partner of his freest hours.
What says Rodolpho? Does he truly credit
This story of his birth?
Lau. He has sometimes,
Like you, his doubts; yet when maturely weigh'd,
Believes it true. As for lord Tancred's self,
He never entertain'd the slightest thought
That verged to doubt; but oft laments his state,
By cruel fortune so ill-pair'd to yours.
Sigis. Merit like his, the fortune of the mind,
Beggars all wealth—Then, to your brother, Laura,
He talks of me?
Lau. Of nothing else. Howe'er
The talk begin, it ends with Sigismunda.
Their morning, noontide, and their evening walks
Are full of you; and all the woods of Belmont
Enamour'd with your name——
Sigis. Away! my friend;
You flatter——Yet the dear delusion charms.
Lau. No, Sigismunda, 'tis the strictest truth,
Nor half the truth, I tell you. Even with fondness

My brother talks for ever of the passion
That fires young Tancred's breast. So much it
He praises love as if he were a lover. [strikes him,
He blames the false pursuits of vagrant youth,
Calls them gay folly, a mistaken struggle
Against best-judging nature. Heaven, he says,
In lavish bounty form'd the heart for love;
In love included all the finer seeds
Of honour, virtue, friendship, purest bliss——

Sigis. Virtuous Rodolpho!

Lau. Then his pleasing theme
He varies to the praises of your lover——

Sigis. And what, my Laura, says he on the subject?

Lau. He says, that, though he were not nobly born,
Nature has form'd him noble, generous, brave,
Truly magnanimous, and warmly scorning
Whatever bears the smallest taint of baseness:
That every easy virtue is his own;
Not learnt by painful labour, but inspired,
Implanted in his soul—Chiefly one charm
He in his graceful character observes;
That though his passions burn with high impatience,
And sometimes, from a noble heat of nature,
Are ready to fly off; yet the least check
Of ruling reason brings them back to temper,
And gentle softness.

Sigis. True! oh true, Rodolpho!
Blest be thy kindred worth for loving his!
He is all warmth, all amiable fire,
All quick heroic ardour! temper'd soft
With gentleness of heart, and manly reason!
If virtue were to wear a human form,
To light it with her dignity and flame,
Then softening mix her smiles and tender graces;
Oh, she would choose the person of my Tancred!
Go on, my friend, go on, and ever praise him;
The subject knows no bounds, nor can I tire,
While my breast trembles to that sweetest music!
The heart of woman tastes no truer joy,
Is never flatter'd with such dear enchantment—
'Tis more than selfish vanity—as when
She hears the praises of the man she loves——

Lau. Madam, your father comes.

SCENE II.

SIFFREDI, SIGISMUNDA, LAURA.

Sif. [*To an* Attendant *as he enters.*
Lord Tancred then
Is found?

Atten. My lord, he quickly will be here.
I scarce could keep before him, though he bid me
Speed on, to say he would attend your orders.

Sif. 'Tis well—retire—You, too, my daughter, leave me.

Sigis. I go, my father. But how fares the king?

Sif. He is no more. Gone to that awful state,
Where kings the crown wear only of their virtues.

Sigis. How bright must then be his!—This stroke is sudden.
He was this morning well, when to the chase
Lord Tancred went.

Sif. 'Tis true. But at his years
Death gives short notice—Drooping nature then,
Without a gust of pain to shake it, falls.
His death, my daughter, was that happy period
Which few attain. The duties of his day
Were all discharged, and gratefully enjoy'd
Its noblest blessings; calm as evening skies,
Was his pure mind, and lighted up with hopes
That open heaven; when, for his last long sleep
Timely prepared, a lassitude of life,
A pleasing weariness of mortal joy,
Fell on his soul, and down he sunk to rest.
Oh, may my death be such!——He but one wish
Left unfulfill'd, which was to see count Tancred——

Sigis. To see count Tancred!—Pardon me, my lord——

Sif. For what, my daughter?—But, with such emotion,
Why did you start at mention of count Tancred?

Sigis. Nothing—I only hoped the dying king
Might mean to make some generous just provision
For this your worthy charge, this noble orphan.

Sif. And he has done it largely—Leave me now—
I want some private conference with lord Tancred.

SCENE III.

Sif. (*alone.*) My doubts are but too true—If these old eyes
Can trace the marks of love, a mutual passion
Has seized, I fear, my daughter and this prince,
My sovereign now—Should it be so? Ah, there,
There lurks a brooding tempest, that may shake
My long-concerted scheme, to settle firm
The public peace and welfare, which the king
Has made the prudent basis of his will——
Away! unworthy views! you shall not tempt me!
Nor interest nor ambition shall seduce
My fix'd resolve——Perish the selfish thought,
Which our own good prefers to that of millions!—
He comes—my king—unconscious of his fortune.

SCENE IV.

TANCRED, SIFFREDI.

Tan. My lord Siffredi, in your looks I read,
Confirm'd, the mournful news that fly abroad
From tongue to tongue—We then, at last, have lost
The good old king?

Sif. Yes, we have lost a father!
The greatest blessing Heaven bestows on mortals,
And seldom found amidst these wilds of time;
A good, a worthy king!—Hear me, my Tancred,
And I will tell thee, in a few plain words,
How he deserved that best, that glorious title:
'Tis nought complex, 'tis clear as truth and virtue
He loved his people, deem'd them all his children;
The good exalted, and depress'd the bad.
He spurn'd the flattering crew, with scorn rejected
Their smooth advice that only means themselves,
Their schemes to aggrandise him into baseness:
Nor did he less disdain the secret breath,
The whisper'd tale, that blights a virtuous name.
He sought alone the good of those for whom
He was entrusted with the sovereign power:
Well knowing that a people in their rights
And industry protected; living safe
Beneath the sacred shelter of the laws,
Encouraged in their genius, arts, and labours,
And happy each as he himself deserves,

Are ne'er ungrateful. With unsparing hand
They will for him provide: their filial love
And confidence are his unfailing treasure,
And every honest man his faithful guard.

Tan. A general face of grief o'erspreads the
I mark'd the people, as I hither came, [city.
In crowds assembled, struck with silent sorrow,
And pouring forth the noblest praise of tears.
Those whom remembrance of their former woes,
And long experience of the vain illusions
Of youthful hope, had into wise consent
And fear of change corrected, wrung their hands,
And often casting up their eyes to heaven,
Gave sign of sad conjecture. Others show'd,
Athwart their grief, or real or affected,
A gleam of expectation, from what chance
And change might bring. A mingled murmur ran
Along the streets; and, from the lonely court
Of him who can no more assist their fortunes,
I saw the courtier-fry, with eager haste,
All hurrying to Constantia.

Sif. Noble youth!
I joy to hear from thee these just reflections,
Worthy of riper years—But if they seek
Constantia, trust me, they mistake their course.

Tan. How! is she not, my lord, the late king's sister,
Heir to the crown of Sicily? the last
Of our famed Norman line, and now our queen?

Sif. Tancred, 'tis true; she is the late king's sister,
The sole surviving offspring of that tyrant
William the Bad—so for his vices styled;
Who spilt much noble blood, and sore oppress'd
The exhausted land: whence grievous wars arose,
And many a dire convulsion shook the state,
When he, whose death Sicilia mourns to-day,
William, who has and well deserved the name
Of Good, succeeding to his father's throne,
Relieved his country's woes—But to return—
She is the late king's sister, born some months
After the tyrant's death, but not next heir.

Tan. You much surprise me—May I then pre-
To ask who is? [sume

Sif. Come nearer, noble Tancred,
Son of my care! I must, on this occasion,
Consult thy generous heart; which, when conducted
By rectitude of mind and honest virtues,
Gives better counsel than the hoary head—
Then know, there lives a prince, here in Palermo,
The lineal offspring of our famous hero,
Roger the First.

Tan. Great Heaven!—How far removed
From that our mighty founder?

Sif. His great-grandson:
Sprung from his eldest son, who died untimely,
Before his father.

Tan. Ha! the prince you mean,
Is he not Manfred's son? The generous, brave,
Unhappy Manfred! whom the tyrant William
You just now mention'd, not content to spoil
Of his paternal crown, threw into fetters,
And infamously murder'd?

Sif. Yes—the same.

Tan. By Heavens! I joy to find our Norman reign,
The world's sole light amidst these barbarous ages!
Yet rears its head; and shall not, from the lance,
Pass to the feeble distaff—But this prince,
Where has he lain conceal'd?

Sif. The late good king,
By noble pity moved, contrived to save him
From his dire father's unrelenting rage,
And had him rear'd in private, as became
His birth and hopes, with high and princely nurture.
Till now, too young to rule a troubled state,
By civil broils most miserably torn,
He in his safe retreat has lain conceal'd,
His birth and fortune to himself unknown;
But when the dying king to me entrusted,
As to the chancellor of the realm, his will,
His successor he named him.

Tan. Happy youth!
He then will triumph o'er his father's foes,
O'er haughty Osmond, and the tyrant's daughter.

Sif. Ay, that is what I dread—that heat of youth;
There lurks, I fear, perdition to the state.
I dread the horrors of rekindled war:
Though dead, the tyrant still is to be fear'd;
His daughter's party still is strong, and numerous:
Her friend, earl Osmond, constable of Sicily,
Experienced, brave, high-born, of mighty interest.
Better the prince and princess should by marriage
Unite their friends, their interest and their claims;
Then will the peace and welfare of the land
On a firm basis rise.

Tan. My lord Siffredi,
If by myself I of this prince may judge,
That scheme will scarce succeed—Your prudent
In vain will counsel, if the heart forbid it— [age
But wherefore fear? The right is clearly his;
And, under your direction, with each man
Of worth, and steadfast loyalty, to back
At once the king's appointment and his birthright,
There is no ground for fear. They have great odds,
Against the astonish'd sons of violence,
Who fight with awful justice on their side.
All Sicily will rouse, all faithful hearts
Will range themselves around prince Manfred's
For me, I here devote me to the service [son.
Of this young prince; I every drop of blood
Will lose with joy, with transport in his cause—
Pardon my warmth—but that, my lord, will never
To this decision come—Then find the prince;
Lose not a moment to awaken in him
The royal soul. Perhaps he now desponding
Pines in a corner, and laments his fortune;
That in the narrower bounds of private life
He must confine his aims, those swelling virtues
Which from his noble father he inherits.

Sif. Perhaps, regardless, in the common bane
Of youth he melts, in vanity and love.
But if the seeds of virtue glow within him,
I will awake a higher sense, a love
That grasps the loves and happiness of millions.

Tan. Why that surmise? Or should he love, Siffredi,
I doubt not, it is nobly, which will raise
And animate his virtues—Oh, permit me
To plead the cause of youth—Their virtue oft
In pleasure's soft enchantment lull'd a while
Forgets itself; it sleeps and gaily dreams,
Till great occasion rouse it: then all flame,
It walks abroad, with heighten'd soul and vigour,
And by the change astonishes the world.
Even with a kind of sympathy, I feel
The joy that waits this prince; when all the powers,
The expanding heart can wish, of doing good:
Whatever swells ambition, or exalts

The human soul into divine emotions,
All crowd at once upon him.
Sif. Ah, my Tancred,
Nothing so easy as in speculation,
And at a distance seen, the course of honour,
A fair delightful champain strew'd with flowers.
But when the practice comes; when our fond passions,
Pleasure, and pride, and self-indulgence, throw
Their magic dust around, the prospect roughens:
Then dreadful passes, craggy mountains rise,
Cliffs to be scaled, and torrents to be stemm'd:
Then toil ensues, and perseverance stern;
And endless combats with our grosser sense,
Oft lost, and oft renew'd; and generous pain
For others felt; and, harder lesson still!
Our honest bliss for others sacrificed;
And all the rugged task of virtue quails
The stoutest heart of common resolution.
Few get above this turbid scene of strife.
Few gain the summit, breathe that purest air,
That heavenly ether, which untroubled sees
The storm of vice and passion rage below.
Tan. Most true, my lord. But why thus augur ill?
You seem to doubt this prince. I know him not.
Yet oh, methinks, my heart could answer for him!
The juncture is so high, so strong the gale
That blows from heaven, as through the deadest soul
Might breathe the godlike energy of virtue.
Sif. Hear him, immortal shades of his great fathers!—
Forgive me, sir, this trial of your heart:
Thou! thou art he!
Tan. Siffredi!
Sif. Tancred, thou!
Thou art the man, of all the many thousands
That toil upon the bosom of this isle,
By Heaven elected to command the rest,
To rule, protect them, and to make them happy!
Tan. Manfred my father! I the last support
Of the famed Norman line, that awes the world!
I! who this morning wander'd forth an orphan,
Outcast of all but thee, my second father!
Thus call'd to glory! to the first great lot
Of human kind! O wonder-working Hand
That, in majestic silence, sways at will
The mighty movements of unbounded nature;
Oh, grant me, Heaven! the virtues to sustain
This awful burden of so many heroes!
Let me not be exalted into shame,
Set up the worthless pageant of vain grandeur.
Meantime I thank the justice of the king,
Who has my right bequeath'd me. Thee, Siffredi,
I thank thee—Oh, I ne'er enough can thank thee!
Yes, thou hast been—thou art—shalt be my father!
Thou shalt direct my unexperienced years,
Shalt be the ruling head, and I the hand.
Sif. It is enough for me—to see my sovereign
Assert his virtues, and maintain his honour.
Tan. I think, my lord, you said the king committed
To you his will. I hope it is not clogg'd
With any base conditions, any clause,
To tyrannise my heart, and to Constantia
Enslave my hand devoted to another.
The hint you just now gave of that alliance,
You must imagine, wakes my fear. But know,
In this alone I will not bear dispute,
Not even from thee, Siffredi!—Let the council
Be straight assembled, and the will there open'd:
Thence issue speedy orders to convene,
This day ere noon, the senate: where those barons,
Who now are in Palermo, will attend,
To pay their ready homage to the king,
Their rightful king, who claims his native crown,
And will not be a king by deeds and parchments.
Sif. I go, my liege. But once again permit me
To tell you——Now, now, is the trying crisis,
That must determine of your future reign.
Oh, with heroic rigour watch your heart!
And to the sovereign duties of the king,
The unequal'd pleasures of a god on earth,
Submit the common joys, the common passions—
Nay, even the virtues of the private man.
Tan. Of that no more. They not oppose, but aid,
Invigorate, cherish, and reward each other.
The kind all-ruling Wisdom is no tyrant.

SCENE V.

Tan. (*alone.*) Now, generous Sigsmunda, comes my turn
To show my love was not of thine unworthy,
When fortune bade me blush to look to thee.
But what is fortune to the wish of love?
A miserable bankrupt! Oh, 'tis poor,
'Tis scanty all, whate'er we can bestow!
The wealth of kings is wretchedness and want!—
Quick, let me find her! taste that highest joy,
The exalted heart can know, the mix'd effusion
Of gratitude and love!—Behold, she comes!

SCENE VI.

TANCRED, SIGISMUNDA.

Tan. My fluttering soul was all on wing to find
My love! my Sigismunda! [thee,
Sigis. Oh, my Tancred!
Tell me, what means this mystery and gloom
That lowers around? Just now, involved in thought,
My father shot athwart me—You, my lord,
Seem strangely moved—I fear some dark event
From the king's death to trouble our repose,
That tender calm we in the woods of Belmont
So happily enjoy'd——Explain this hurry,
What means it? Say.
Tan. It means that we are happy!
Beyond our most romantic wishes happy!
Sigis. You but perplex me more.
Tan. It means, my fairest!
That thou art queen of Sicily, and I
The happiest of mankind! than monarch more!
Because with thee I can adorn my throne.
Manfred, who fell by tyrant William's rage,
Famed Roger's lineal issue, was my father. [*Pausing.*
You droop, my love; dejected on a sudden;
You seem to mourn my fortune—The soft tear
Springs in thy eye—Oh, let me kiss it off——
Why this, my Sigismunda?
Sigis. Royal Tancred,
None at your glorious fortune can like me
Rejoice;—yet me alone, of all Sicilians,
It makes unhappy.
Tan. I should hate it then!
Should throw, with scorn, the splendid ruin from me!—
No, Sigismunda, 'tis my hope with thee
To share it, whence it draws its richest value.

Sigis. You are my sovereign—I at humble distance——

Tan. Thou art my queen! the sovereign of my soul!
You never reign'd with such triumphant lustre,
Such winning charms as now; yet, thou art still
The dear, the tender, generous Sigismunda!
Who, with a heart exalted far above
Those selfish views that charm the common breast,
Stoop'd from the height of life and courted beauty,
Then, then, to love me, when I seem'd of fortune
The hopeless outcast, when I had no friend,
None to protect and own me but thy father.
And wouldst thou claim all goodness to thyself?
Canst thou thy Tancred deem so dully form'd,
Of such gross clay, just as I reach the point—
A point my wildest hopes could never image—
In that great moment, full of every virtue,
That I should then so mean a traitor prove
To the best bliss and honour of mankind,
So much disgrace the human heart, as then,
For the dead form of flattery and pomp,
The faithless joys of courts, to quit kind truth,
The cordial sweets of friendship and of love,
The life of life! my all, my Sigismunda!
I could upbraid thy fears, call them unkind,
Cruel, unjust, an outrage to my heart,
Did they not spring from love.

Sigis. Think not, my lord,
That to such vulgar doubts I can descend.
Your heart, I know, disdains the little thought
Of changing with the vain external change
Of circumstance and fortune. Rather thence
It would, with rising ardour, greatly feel
A noble pride to show itself the same.
But, ah! the hearts of kings are not their own:
There is a haughty duty that subjects them
To chains of state, to wed the public welfare,
And not indulge the tender private virtues.
Some high-descended princess, who will bring
New power and interest to your throne, demands
Your royal hand—perhaps Constantia——

Tan. She!
Oh, name her not! Were I this moment free,
And disengaged as he who never felt
The powerful eye of beauty, never sigh'd
For matchless worth like thine, I should abhor
All thoughts of that alliance. Her fell father
Most basely murder'd mine; and she, his daughter,
Supported by his barbarous party still,
His pride inherits, his imperious spirit,
And insolent pretensions to my throne.
And canst thou deem me then so poorly tame,
So cool a traitor to my father's blood,
As from the prudent cowardice of state
E'er to submit to such a base proposal?
Detested thought! Oh, doubly, doubly hateful!
From the two strongest passions; from aversion
To this Constantia—and from love to thee.
Custom, 'tis true, a venerable tyrant,
O'er servile man extends her blind dominion:
The pride of kings enslaves them; their ambition,
Or interest, lords it o'er the better passions.
But vain their talk, mask'd under specious words
Of station, duty, and of public good:
They whom just Heaven has to a throne exalted,
To guard the rights and liberties of others,
What duty binds them to betray their own?
For me, my free-born heart shall bear no dictates,
But those of truth and honour; wear no chains,
But the dear chains of love and Sigismunda!
Or if indeed my choice must be directed
By views of public good, whom shall I chuse
So fit to grace, to dignify a crown,
And beam sweet mercy on a happy people,
As thee, my love? whom place upon my throne
But thee, descended from the good Siffredi?
'Tis fit that heart be thine, which drew from him
Whate'er can make it worthy thy acceptance.

Sigis. Cease, cease, to raise my hopes above my duty.
Charm me no more, my Tancred!—O that we
In those blest woods, where first you won my soul,
Had pass'd our gentle days; far from the toil
And pomp of courts! Such is the wish of love;
Of love, that, with delightful weakness, knows
No bliss and no ambition but itself.
But, in the world's full light, those charming dreams,
Those fond illusions vanish. Awful duties,
The tyranny of men, even your own heart,
Where lurks a sense your passion stifles now,
And proud imperious honour, call you from me.
'Tis all in vain—You cannot hush a voice
That murmurs here—I must not be persuaded!

Tan. (*kneeling.*) Hear me, thou soul of all my hopes and wishes!
And witness, Heaven! prime source of love and joy!
Not a whole warring world combined against me:
Its pride, its splendour, its imposing forms,
Nor interest, nor ambition, nor the face
Of solemn state, not even thy father's wisdom,
Shall ever shake my faith to Sigismunda!

[*Trumpets and acclamations heard.*

But, hark! the public voice to duties calls me,
Which with unwearied zeal I will discharge;
And thou, yes thou, shalt be my bright reward—
Yet—ere I go—to hush thy lovely fears,
Thy delicate objections—— [*Writes his name.*
Take this blank,
Sign'd with my name, and give it to thy father:
Tell him, 'tis my command it be fill'd up
With a most strict and solemn marriage-contract.
How dear each tie! how charming to my soul!
That more unites me to my Sigismunda.

For thee and for my people's good to live,
Is all the bliss which sovereign power can give.

ACT II.

SCENE I.

Sif. (*alone.*) So far 'tis well—The late king's will proceeds
Upon the plan I counsel'd ; that prince Tancred
Shall make Constantia partner of his throne.
O great, O wish'd event ! whence the dire seeds
Of dark intestine broils, of civil war,
And all its dreadful miseries and crimes,
Shall be for ever rooted from the land.
May these dim eyes, long blasted by the rage
Of cruel faction and my country's woes,
Tired with the toils and vanities of life,
Behold this period, then be closed in peace !
But how this mighty obstacle surmount,
Which love has thrown betwixt? Love, that disturbs
The schemes of wisdom still ; that, wing'd with [passion,
Blind and impetuous in its fond pursuits,
Leaves the grey-headed reason far behind.
Alas ! how frail the state of human bliss !
When even our honest passions oft destroy it.
I was to blame, in solitude and shades,
Infectious scenes ! to trust their youthful hearts.
Would I had mark'd the rising flame ! that now
Burns out with dangerous force—My daughter owns
Her passion for the king ; she trembling own'd it,
With prayers and tears and tender supplications,
That almost shook my firmness—And this blank,
Which his rash fondness gave her, shows how much,
To what a wild extravagance he loves—
I see no means—it foils my deepest thought—
How to control this madness of the king,
That wears the face of virtue, and will thence
Disdain restraint, will from his generous heart
Borrow new rage, even speciously oppose
To reason reason—But it must be done.
My own advice, of which I more and more
Approve, the strict conditions of the will,
Highly demand his marriage with Constantia ;
Or else her party has a fair pretence——
And all, at once, is horror and confusion——
How issue from this maze ?—The crowding barons,
Here summon'd to the palace, meet already,
To pay their homage, and confirm the will.
On a few moments hangs the public fate,
On a few hasty moments—Ha ! there shone
A gleam of hope—Yes—with this very paper
I yet will save him—Necessary means
For good and noble ends can ne'er be wrong.
In that resistless, that peculiar case,
Deceit is truth and virtue—But how hold
This lion in the toil ?—Oh, I will form it
Of such a fatal thread, twist it so strong
With all the ties of honour and of duty,
That his most desperate fury shall not break
The honest snare—Here is the royal hand—
I will beneath it write a perfect, full,
And absolute agreement to the will ;
Which read before the nobles of the realm
Assembled, in the sacred face of Sicily,
Constantia present, every heart and eye
Fix'd on their monarch, every tongue applauding,
He must submit, his dream of love must vanish—
It shall be done ?——To me, I know, 'tis ruin ;
But safety to the public, to the king.
I will not reason more, I will not listen
Even to the voice of honour—No—'tis fix'd !
I here devote me for my prince and country ;
Let them be safe, and let me nobly perish !
Behold earl Osmond comes ; without his aid
My schemes are all in vain.

SCENE II.

OSMOND, SIFFREDI.

Osm. My lord Siffredi,
I from the council hasten'd to Constantia,
And have accomplish'd what we there proposed.
The princess to the will submits her claims.
She with her presence means to grace the senate,
And of your royal charge young Tancred's hand
Accept. At first, indeed it shock'd her hopes
Of reigning sole, this new surprising scene
Of Manfred's son, appointed by the king,
With her, joint heir——But I so fully show'd
The justice of the case, the public good
And sure establish'd peace which thence would rise,
Join'd to the strong necessity that urged her,
If on Sicilia's throne she meant to sit,
As to the wise disposal of the will
Her high ambition tamed. Methought, besides,
I could discern that not from prudence merely
She to this choice submitted.

Sif. Noble Osmond,
You have in this done to the public great
And signal service. Yes, I must avow it ;
This frank and ready instance of your zeal,
In such a trying crisis of the state,
When interest and ambition might have warp'd
Your views ; I own, this truly generous virtue
Upbraids the rashness of my former judgment.

Osm. Siffredi, no.—To you belongs the praise ;
The glorious work is yours. Had I not seized,
Improved the wish'd occasion to root out
Division from the land, and save my country,
I had been base, been infamous for ever.
'Tis you, my lord, to whom the many thousands,
That by the barbarous sword of civil war
Had fallen inglorious, owe their lives ; to you
The sons of this fair isle, from her first peers
Down to the swain who tills her golden plains,
Owe their safe homes, their soft domestic hours ;
And through late time posterity shall bless you,
You who advised this will—I blush to think
I have so long opposed the best good man
In Sicily——With what impartial care
Ought we to watch o'er prejudice and passion,
Nor trust too much the jaundiced eye of party
Henceforth its vain delusions I renounce,
Its hot determinations, that confine
All merit and all virtue to itself.
To yours I join my hand ; with you will own
No interest and no party but my country.
Nor is your friendship only my ambition :

There is a dearer name, the name of father,
By which I should rejoice to call Siffredi.
Your daughter's hand would to the public weal
Unite my private happiness.

Sif. My lord,
You have my glad consent. To be allied
To your distinguish'd family, and merit,
I shall esteem an honour. From my soul,
I here embrace earl Osmond as my friend,
And son.

Osm. You make him happy. This assent,
So frank and warm, to what I long have wish'd,
Engages all my gratitude ; at once,
In the first blossom, it matures our friendship.
I from this moment vow myself the friend
And zealous servant of Siffredi's house.

Enter an Officer belonging to the Court.

Off. to Sif. The king, my lord, demands your speedy presence. [lord :

Sif. I will attend him straight—Farewell, my
The senate meets : there, a few moments hence,
I will rejoin you.

Osm. There, my noble lord,
We will complete this salutary work.
Will there begin a new auspicious era.

—•—

SCENE III.

Osm. (*alone.*) Siffredi gives his daughter to my wishes—
But does she give herself ? Gay, young, and flatter'd,
Perhaps engaged, will she her youthful heart
Yield to my harsher uncomplying years ?
I am not form'd by flattery and praise,
By sighs and tears, and all the whining trade
Of love, to feed a fair one's vanity ;
To charm at once and spoil her. These soft arts
Nor suit my years nor temper ; these be left
To boys and doating age. A prudent father,
By nature charged to guide and rule her choice,
Resigns his daughter to a husband's power,
Who with superior dignity, with reason,
And manly tenderness will ever love her ;
Not first a kneeling slave, and then a tyrant.

—•—

SCENE IV.

OSMOND, Barons.

Osm. My lords, I greet you well. This wondrous
Unites us all in amity and friendship. [day
We meet to-day with open hearts, and looks
Not gloom'd by party scowling on each other,
But all the children of one happy isle,
The social sons of liberty. No pride,
No passion now, no thwarting views divide us :
Prince Manfred's line, at last, to William's join'd,
Combines us in one family of brothers.
This to the late good king's well-order'd will,
And wise Siffredi's generous care, we owe.
I truly give you joy. First of you all,
I here renounce those errors and divisions
That have so long disturb'd our peace, and seem'd,
Fermenting still, to threaten new commotions—
By time instructed let us not disdain
To quit mistakes. We all, my lords, have err'd.
Men may, I find, be honest, though they differ.

1st Baron. Who follows not, my lord, the fair
You set us all, whate'er be his pretence, [example
Loves not with single and unbias'd heart
His country as he ought.

2nd Baron. O beauteous Peace !
Sweet union of a state ! What else, but thou,
Gives safety, strength, and glory to a people
I bow, lord constable, beneath the snow
Of many years ; yet in my breast revives
A youthful flame. Methinks, I see again
Those gentle days renew'd, that bless'd our isle,
Ere by this wasteful fury of division,
Worse than our Ætna's most destructive fires,
It desolated sunk. I see our plains
Unbounded waving with the gifts of harvest ;
Our seas with commerce throng'd, our busy ports
With cheerful toil. Our Enna blooms afresh ;
Afresh the sweets of thymy Hybla flow.
Our nymphs and shepherds, sporting in each vale,
Inspire new song, and wake the pastoral reed—
The tongue of age is fond—Come, come, my sons;
I long to see this prince, of whom the world
Speaks largely well—His father was my friend,
The brave unhappy Manfred—Come, my lords ;
We tarry here too long.

—•—

SCENE V.

Two Officers keeping off the Crowd.

One of the Crowd. Show us our king,
The valiant Manfred's son, who loved the people—
We must, we will behold him—Give us way.

1st Off. Pray, gentlemen, give back—it must not
Give back, I pray—on such a glad occasion [be—
I would not ill entreat the lowest of you.

2nd Man of the Crowd. Nay, give us but a glimpse of our young king.
We more than any baron of them all
Will pay him true allegiance.

2nd Off. Friends—indeed—
You cannot pass this way—We have strict orders,
To keep for him himself, and for the barons,
All these apartments clear—Go to the gate
That fronts the sea—You there will find admission.

All. Long live king Tancred ! Manfred's son—
Huzza ! [*Crowd goes off.*

1st Off. I do not marvel at their rage of joy :
He is a brave and amiable prince.
When in my lord Siffredi's house I lived,
Ere by his favour I obtain'd this office,
I there remember well the young count Tancred.
To see him and to love him were the same.
He was so noble in his ways, yet still
So affable and mild—Well, well, old Sicily,
Yet happy days await thee !

2nd Off. Grant it, Heaven !
We have seen sad and troublous times enough.
He is, they say, to wed the late king's sister,
Constantia.

1st Off. Friend, of that I greatly doubt.
Or I mistake, or lord Siffredi's daughter,
The gentle Sigismunda, has his heart.
If one may judge by kindly cordial looks,
And fond assiduous care to please each other,
Most certainly they love——Oh, be they blest,
As they deserve ! It were great pity aught
Should part a matchless pair : the glory he,
And she the blooming grace of Sicily !

2nd Off. My lord Rodolpho comes.

SCENE VI.

RODOLPHO, *from the Senate.*

Rod. My honest friends,
You may retire. [Officers *go out.*
A storm is in the wind.
This will perplexes all. No, Tancred never
Can stoop to these conditions, which at once
Attack his rights, his honour, and his love. [dants,
Those wise old men, those plodding grave state pe-
Forget the course of youth; their crooked prudence,
To baseness verging still, forgets to take
Into their fine-spun schemes the generous heart,
That through the cobweb system bursting lays
Their labours waste—So will this business prove,
Or I mistake the king—back from the pomp
He seem'd at first to shrink; and round his brow
I mark'd a gathering cloud, when by his side,
As if design'd to share the public homage,
He saw the tyrant's daughter. But confess'd,
At least to me, the doubling tempest frown'd,
And shook his swelling bosom, when he heard
The unjust, the base conditions of the will.
Uncertain, tost in cruel agitation,
He oft, methought, address'd himself to speak
And interrupt Siffredi; who appear'd,
With conscious haste, to dread that interruption,
And hurried on—But hark! I hear a noise,
As if the assembly rose—Ha! Sigismunda,
Oppress'd with grief and wrapt in pensive sorrow,
Passes along——

[SIGISMUNDA *and* Attendants *pass through the back scene.* LAURA *advances.*

SCENE VII.

RODOLPHO, LAURA.

Lau. Your high-praised friend, the king,
Is false, most vilely false! The meanest slave
Had shown a nobler heart; nor grossly thus,
By the first bait ambition spread, been gull'd.
He Manfred's son! away! it cannot be!
The son of that brave prince could ne'er betray
Those rights so long usurp'd from his great fathers,
Which he, this day, by such amazing fortune,
Had just regain'd; he ne'er could sacrifice
All faith, all honour, gratitude, and love,
Even just resentment of his father's fate,
And pride itself, whate'er exalts a man
Above the groveling sons of peasant-mud,
All in a moment—And for what? why truly,
For kind permission, gracious leave, to sit
On his own throne with tyrant William's daughter!

Rod. I stand amazed—You surely wrong him,
There must be some mistake. [Laura.

Lau. There can be none!
Siffredi read his full and free consent
Before the applauding senate. True indeed,
A small remain of shame, a timorous weakness,
Even dastardly in falsehood, made him blush
To act this scene in Sigismunda's eye,
Who sunk beneath his perfidy and baseness.
Hence, till to-morrow he adjourn'd the senate—
To-morrow fix'd with infamy to crown him!
Then, leading off his gay triumphant princess,
He left the poor unhappy Sigismunda,
To bend her trembling steps to that sad home
His faithless vows will render hateful to her—
He comes—Farewell—I cannot bear his presence!

SCENE VIII.

TANCRED, SIFFREDI, RODOLPHO.

Tan. (*entering to Sif.*) Avoid me, hoary traitor
—Go, Rodolpho,
Give orders that all passages this way
Be shut—Defend me from a hateful world,
The bane of peace and honour—then return—
What! dost thou haunt me still? Oh, monstrous
Unparallel'd indignity! Just Heaven! [insult!
Was ever king, was ever man so treated!
So trampled into baseness!

Sif. Here, my liege,
Here strike! I nor deserve nor ask for mercy.

Tan. Distraction!—Oh, my soul—Hold, reason,
Thy giddy seat—Oh, this inhuman outrage [hold
Unhinges thought!

Sif. Exterminate thy servant!

Tan. All, all but this I could have borne—but this!
This daring insolence beyond example!
This murderous stroke that stabs my peace for ever!
That wounds me there—there! where the human
Most exquisitely feels—— [heart

Sif. Oh, bear it not,
My royal lord! appease on me your vengeance

Tan. Did ever tyrant image aught so cruel!
The lowest slave that crawls upon the earth,
Robb'd of each comfort Heaven bestows on mortals,
On the bare ground, has still his virtue left,
The sacred treasures of an honest heart,
Which thou hast dared, with rash audacious hand,
And impious fraud, in me to violate——

Sif. Behold, my liege, that rash audacious hand,
Which not repents its crime——Oh, glorious!
If by my ruin I can save your honour. [happy!

Tan. Such honour I renounce! with sovereign
Greatly detest it, and its mean adviser! [scorn
Hast thou not dared beneath my name to shelter—
My name for other purposes design'd,
Given from the fondness of a faithful heart,
With the best love o'erflowing—hast thou not
Beneath thy sovereign's name basely presumed
To shield a lie? a lie! in public utter'd,
To all deluded Sicily? But know,
This poor contrivance is as weak as base.
In such a wretched toil none can be held
But fools and cowards—Soon thy flimsy arts,
Touch'd by my just, my burning indignation,
Shall burst like threads in flame!—Thy doating
prudence
But more secures the purpose it would shake.
Had my resolves been wavering and doubtful,
This would confirm them, make them fix'd as fate;
This adds the only motive that was wanting
To urge them on through war and desolation—
What! marry her! Constantia! Her! the daughter
Of the fell tyrant who destroy'd my father!
The very thought is madness! Ere thou seest
The torch of Hymen light these hated nuptials,
Thou shalt behold Sicilia wrapt in flames,
Her cities razed, her valleys drench'd with
slaughter—
Love set aside—my pride assumes the quarrel.
My honour now is up; in spite of thee,
A world combined against me, I will give
This scatter'd will in fragments to the winds,
Assert my rights, the freedom of my heart,
Crush all who dare oppose me to the dust,
And heap perdition on thee!

Sif. Sir, 'tis just.
Exhaust on me your rage; I claim it all.
But for these public threats thy passion utters,
'Tis what thou canst not do!
Tan. I cannot! ha!
Driven to the dreadful brink of such dishonour,
Enough to make the tamest coward brave,
And into fierceness rouse the mildest nature,
What shall arrest my vengeance? who?
Sif. Thyself!
Tan. Away! dare not to justify thy crime
That, that alone can aggravate its horror,
Add insolence to insolence—perhaps
May make my rage forget!——
Sif. Oh, let it burst,
On this grey head devoted to thy service!
But when the storm has vented all its fury,
Thou then must hear—nay more, I know, thou wilt—
Wilt hear the calm, yet stronger voice of reason.
Thou must reflect that a whole people's safety,
The weal of trusted millions should bear down,
Thyself the judge, thy fondest partial pleasure.
Thou must reflect that there are other duties,
A nobler pride, a more exalted honour,
Superior pleasures far, that will oblige,
Compel thee, to abide by this my deed,
Unwarranted perhaps in common justice,
But which necessity, even virtue's tyrant,
With awful voice commanded—Yes, thou must,
In calmer hours, divest thee of thy love,
These common passions of the vulgar breast,
This boiling heat of youth, and be a king!
The lover of thy people!
Tan. Truths ill employ'd!
Abused to colour guilt!—a king! a king!
Yes, I will be a king, but not a slave!
In this will be a king! in this my people
Shall learn to judge how I will guard their rights,
When they behold me vindicate my own.
But have I, say, been treated like a king?——
Heavens! could I stoop to such outrageous usage,
I were a mean, a shameless wretch, unworthy
To wield a sceptre in a land of slaves,
A soil abhorr'd of virtue should belie
My father's blood, belie those very maxims,
At other times, you taught my youth—Siffredi!
[*In a softened tone of voice.*
Sif. Behold, my prince, behold thy poor old servant,
Whose darling care, these twenty years, has been
To nurse thee up to virtue; who for thee,
Thy glory and thy weal, renounces all,
All interest or ambition can pour forth;
What many a selfish father would pursue
Through treachery and crimes: behold him here.
Bent on his feeble knees, to beg, conjure thee,
With tears to beg thee, to control thy passion,
And save thyself, thy honour, and thy people!
Kneeling with me behold the many thousands
To thy protection trusted: fathers, mothers,
The sacred front of venerable age,
The tender virgin and the helpless infant;
The ministers of Heaven, those, who maintain,
Around thy throne, the majesty of rule;
And those, whose labour, scorch'd by winds and sun,
Feeds the rejoicing public: see them all,
Here at thy feet, conjuring thee to save them,
From misery and war, from crimes and rapine!
Can there be aught, kind Heaven! in self-indulgence
To weigh down these? This aggregate of love
With which compared, the dearest private passion
Is but the wafted dust upon the balance?
Turn not away—Oh, is there not some part
In thy great heart, so sensible to kindness
And generous warmth, some nobler part, to feel
The prayers and tears of these, the mingled voice
Of Heaven and earth!
Tan. There is! and thou hast touch'd it.
Rise, rise, Siffredi—Oh! thou hast undone me,
Unkind old man! O ill-entreated Tancred!
Which way soe'er I turn, dishonour rears
Her hideous front—and misery and ruin!
Was it for this you took such care to form me?
For this imbued me with the quickest sense
Of shame; those finer feelings, that ne'er vex
The common mass of mortals, dully happy
In blest insensibility? Oh, rather
You should have sear'd my heart; taught me that power
And splendid interest lord it still o'er virtue;
That, gilded by prosperity and pride,
There is no shame, no meanness; temper'd thus,
It had been fit to rule a venal world.
Alas! what meant thy wantonness of prudence?
Why have you raised this miserable conflict
Betwixt the duties of the king and man?
Set virtue against virtue?—Ah, Siffredi!
'Tis thy superfluous, thy unfeeling wisdom,
That has involved me in a maze of error,
Almost beyond retreat—But hold, my soul,
Thy steady purpose—Toss'd by various passions,
To this eternal anchor keep—There is,
Can be, no public without private virtue——
Then mark me well, observe what I command;
It is the sole expedient now remaining—
To-morrow, when the senate meets again,
Unfold the whole, unravel the deceit;
Nor that alone, try to repair its mischief;
There all thy power, thy eloquence and interest
Exert, to reinstate me in my rights,
And from thy own dark snares to disembroil me—
Start not, my lord—This must and shall be done!
Or here, our friendship ends—Howe'er disguised,
Whatever thy pretence, thou art a traitor.
Sif. I should indeed deserve the name of traitor,
And even a traitor's fate, had I so slightly,
From principles so weak, done what I did,
As e'er to disavow it——
Tan. Ha!
Sif. My liege,
Expect not this—Though practised long in courts,
I have not so far learn'd their subtle trade,
To veer obedient with each gust of passion.
I honour thee, I venerate thy orders,
But honour more my duty. Nought on earth
Shall ever shake me from that solid rock,
Nor smiles nor frowns.——
Tan. You will not then?
Sif. I cannot?
Tan. Away! begone!—O my Rodolpho, come,
And save me from this traitor!—Hence, I say.—
Avoid my presence straight! and know, old man,
Thou my worst foe beneath the mask of friendship,
Who, not content to trample in the dust
My dearest rights, dost with cool insolence
Persist, and call it duty; hadst thou not
A daughter that protects thee, thou shouldst feel
The vengeance thou deservest—No reply!
Away!

SCENE IX.

TANCRED, RODOLPHO.

Rod. What can incense my prince so highly
Against his friend Siffredi?

Tan. Friend! Rodolpho!
When I have told thee what this friend has done,
How play'd me like a boy, a base-born wretch,
Who had nor heart nor spirit! thou wilt stand
Amazed, and wonder at my stupid patience.

Rod. I heard, with mix'd astonishment and grief,
The king's unjust dishonourable will,
Void in itself—I saw you stung with rage,
And writhing in the snare; just as I went,
At your command, to wait you here—but that
Was the king's deed, not his.

Tan. Oh, he advised it!
These many years he has in secret hatch'd
This black contrivance, glories in the scheme,
And proudly plumes him with his traitorous virtue.
But that was nought, Rodolpho, nothing, nothing!
O that was gentle, blameless to what follow'd!
I had, my friend, to Sigismunda given,
To hush her fears, in the full gush of fondness,
A blank sign'd by my hand—and he, O Heavens!
Was ever such a wild attempt!—he wrote
Beneath my name an absolute compliance
To this detested will; nay, dared to read it
Before myself, on my insulted throne
His idle pageant placed—Oh, words are weak
To paint the pangs, the rage, the indignation,
That whirl'd from thought to thought my soul in tempest;
Now on the point to burst, and now by shame
Repress'd—But in the face of Sicily,
All mad with acclamation, what, Rodolpho,
What could I do? The sole relief that rose
To my distracted mind, was to adjourn
The assembly till to-morrow—But to-morrow
What can be done?—Oh, it avails not what!
I care not what is done—My only care
Is how to clear my faith to Sigismunda.
She thinks me false! She cast a look that kill'd me!
Oh, I am base in Sigismunda's eye!
The lowest of mankind, the most perfidious!

Rod. This was a strain of insolence indeed,
A daring outrage of so strange a nature,
As stuns me quite——

Tan. Cursed be my timid prudence!
That dash'd not back, that moment, in his face
The bold presumptuous lie—and cursed this hand!
That from a start of poor dissimulation,
Led off my Sigismunda's hated rival.
Ah then! what, poison'd by the false appearance,
What, Sigismunda, were thy thoughts of me!
How, in the silent bitterness of soul,
How didst thou scorn me! hate mankind, thyself,
For trusting to the vows of faithless Tancred!
For such I seem'd—I was!—The thought distracts me!
I should have cast a flattering world aside,
Rush'd from my throne, before them all avow'd her,
The choice, the glory of my free-born heart,
And spurn'd the shameful fetters thrown upon it—
Instead of that—confusion!——what I did
Has clinch'd the chain, confirm'd Siffredi's crime,
And fix'd me down to infamy!

Rod. My lord,
Blame not the conduct, which your situation
Tore from your tortured heart—What could you do!—
Had you, so circumstanced, in open senate,
Before the astonish'd public, with no friends
Prepared, no party form'd, affronted thus
The haughty princess and her powerful faction,
Supported by this will, the sudden stroke,
Abrupt and premature, might have recoil'd
Upon yourself, even your own friends revolted,
And turn'd at once the public scale against you.
Besides, consider, had you then detected
In its fresh guilt this action of Siffredi,
You must with signal vengeance have chastised
The treasonable deed—Nothing so mean
As weak insulted power that dares not punish.
And how would that have suited with your love?
His daughter present too? Trust me, your conduct,
Howe'er abhorrent to a heart like yours,
Was fortunate and wise—Not that I mean
E'er to advise submission——

Tan. Heavens! Submission!
Could I descend to bear it, even in thought,
Despise me, you, the world, and Sigismunda!
Submission!—No!—To-morrow's glorious light
Shall flash discovery on the scene of baseness.
Whatever be the risk, by heavens! to-morrow
I will o'erturn the dirty lie-built schemes
Of these old men, and show my faithful senate,
That Manfred's son knows to assert and wear,
With undiminish'd dignity, that crown
This unexpected day has placed upon him.
But this, my friend, these stormy gusts of pride,
Are foreign to my love—Till Sigismunda
Be disabused, my breast is tumult all,
And can obey no settled course of reason.
I see her still, I feel her powerful image,
That look, where with reproach complaint was mix'd,
Big with soft woe and gentle indignation,
Which seem'd at once to pity and to scorn me—
Oh, let me find her! I too long have left
My Sigismunda to converse with tears,
A prey to thoughts that picture me a villain.
But, ah! how, clogg'd with this accursed state,
A tedious world, shall I now find access?
Her father too—Ten thousand horrors crowd
Into the wild fantastic eye of love——
Who knows what he may do? Come then, my friend,
And, by thy sister's hand, oh let me steal
A letter to her bosom!—I no longer
Can bear her absence, by the just contempt
She now must brand me with, inflamed to madness.
Fly, my Rodolpho, fly! engage thy sister
To aid my letter, and this very evening
Secure an interview—I would not bear
This rack another day, not for my kingdom!
Till then, deep-plunged in solitude and shades,
I will not see the hated face of man.
Thought drives on thought, on passions passions roll;
Her smiles alone can calm my raging soul.

ACT III.

SCENE I.

SIGISMUNDA *alone, sitting in a disconsolate posture.*

Ah, tyrant prince! ah, more than faithless Tancred!
Ungenerous and inhuman in thy falsehood!
Hadst thou, this morning, when my hopeless heart,
Submissive to my fortune and my duty,
Had so much spirit left, as to be willing
To give thee back thy vows, ah! hadst thou then
Confess'd the sad necessity thy state
Imposed upon thee, and with gentle friendship,
Since we must part at last, our parting soften'd;
I should indeed—I should have been unhappy,
But not to this extreme—Amidst my grief,
I had, with pensive pleasure, cherish'd still
The sweet remembrance of thy former love,
Thy image still had dwelt upon my soul,
And made our guiltless woes not undelightful.
But coolly thus—How couldst thou be so cruel?
Thus to revive my hopes, to soothe my love
And call forth all its tenderness, then sink me
In black despair—What unrelenting pride
Possess'd thy breast, that thou couldst bear unmoved
To see me bent beneath a weight of shame?
Pangs thou canst never feel! how couldst thou drag me
In barbarous triumph at a rival's car?
How make me witness to a sight of horror
That hand, which, but a few short hours ago,
So wantonly abused my simple faith,
Before the attesting world given to another,
Irrevocably given!—There was a time,
When the least cloud that hung upon my brow,
Perhaps imagined only, touch'd thy pity.
Then, brighten'd often by the ready tear,
Thy looks were softness all; then the quick heart,
In every nerve alive forgot itself,
And for each other then we felt alone.
But now, alas! those tender days are fled;
Now thou canst see me wretched, pierced with anguish,
With studied anguish of thy own creating,
Nor wet thy harden'd eye—Hold, let me think—
I wrong thee sure; thou canst not be so base,
As meanly in my misery to triumph——
What is it then?—Why should I search for pain?—
O, 'tis as bad!—'Tis fickleness of nature,
'Tis sickly love extinguish'd by ambition——
Is there, kind Heaven! no constancy in man?
No steadfast truth, no generous fix'd affection,
That can bear up against a selfish world?
No, there is none—Even Tancred is inconstant! [*Rising.*

Hence! let me fly this scene!—Whate'er I see,
These roofs, these walls, each object that surrounds [me,
Are tainted with his vows—But whither fly?
The groves are worse, the soft retreat of Belmont,
Its deepening glooms, gay lawns, and airy summits,
Will wound my busy memory to torture,
And all its shades will whisper—faithless Tancred!—
My father comes—How, sunk in this disorder,
Shall I sustain his presence?

SCENE II.

SIFFREDI, SIGISMUNDA.

Sif. Sigismunda,
My dearest child! I grieve to find thee thus
A prey to tears. I know the powerful cause
From which they flow, and therefore can excuse
But not their wilful obstinate continuance. [them,
Come, rouse thee, then, call up thy drooping spirit—
Come, wake to reason from this dream of love,
And show the world thou art Siffredi's daughter.

Sigis. Alas! I am unworthy of that name.

Sif. Thou art indeed to blame; thou hast too rashly
Engaged thy heart, without a father's sanction.
But this I can forgive. The king has virtues,
That plead thy full excuse; nor was I void
Of blame, to trust thee to those dangerous virtues.
Then dread not my reproaches. Though he blames,
Thy tender father pities more than blames thee.
Thou art my daughter still; and if thy heart
Will now resume its pride, assert itself,
And greatly rise superior to this trial,
I to my warmest confidence again
Will take thee, and esteem thee more my daughter.

Sigis. Oh, you are gentler far than I deserve!
It is, it ever was my darling pride,
To bend my soul to your supreme commands,
Your wisest will; and though by love betray'd—
Alas! and punish'd too—I have transgress'd
The nicest bounds of duty, yet I feel
A sentiment of tenderness, a source
Of filial nature springing in my breast,
That, should it kill me, shall control this passion,
And make me all submission and obedience
To you my honour'd lord, the best of fathers.

Sif. Come to my arms, thou comfort of my age!
Thou only joy and hope of these grey hairs!
Come! let me take thee to a parent's heart;
There with the kindly aid of my advice,
Even with the dew of these paternal tears,
Revive and nourish this becoming spirit——
Then thou dost promise me, my Sigismunda—
Thy father stoops to make it his request—
Thou wilt resign thy fond presumptuous hopes,
And henceforth never more indulge one thought
That in the light of love regards the king?

Sigis. Hopes I have none!—Those by this fatal [day
Are blasted all—But from my soul to banish,
While weeping memory there retains her seat,
Thoughts which the purest bosom might have cherish'd,
Once my delight, now even in anguish charming,
Is more, alas! my lord, than I can promise.

Sif. Absence and time, the softener of our passions,
Will conquer this. Meantime, I hope from thee
A generous great effort; that thou wilt now
Exert thy utmost force, nor languish thus
Beneath the vain extravagance of love.
Let not thy father blush to hear it said,
His daughter was so weak, e'er to admit

A thought so void of reason, that a king
Should to his rank, his honour, and his glory,
The high important duties of a throne,
Even to his throne itself, madly prefer
A wild romantic passion, the fond child
Of youthful dreaming thought and vacant hours;
That he should quit his heaven-appointed station,
Desert his awful charge, the care of all
The toiling millions which this isle contains;
Nay more, should plunge them into war and ruin:
And all to soothe a sick imagination,
A miserable weakness—Must for thee,
To make thee blest, Sicilia be unhappy?
The king himself, lost to the nobler sense
Of manly praise, become the piteous hero
Of some soft tale, and rush on sure destruction?
Canst thou, my daughter, let the monstrous thought
Possess one moment thy perverted fancy?
Rouse thee, for shame! and if a spark of virtue
Lies slumbering in thy soul, bid it blaze forth;
Nor sink unequal to the glorious lesson,
This day thy lover gave thee from his throne.

Sigis. Ah! that was not from virtue!—Had, my father,
That been his aim, I yield to what you say;
'Tis powerful truth, unanswerable reason.
Then, then, with sad but duteous resignation,
I had submitted as became your daughter;
But in that moment, when my humbled hopes
Were to my duty reconciled, to raise them
To yet a fonder height than e'er they knew,
Then rudely dash them down—There is the sting!
The blasting view is ever present to me——
Why did you drag me to a sight so cruel?

Sif. It was a scene to fire thy emulation

Sigis. It was a scene of perfidy!—But know
I will do more than imitate the king—
For he is false!—I, though sincerely pierced
With the best, truest passion, ever touch'd
A virgin's breast, here vow to Heaven and you,
Though from my heart I cannot, from my hopes
To cast this prince—What would you more, my father?

Sif. Yes, one thing more—thy father then is happy—
Though by the voice of innocence and virtue
Absolved, we live not to ourselves alone:
A rigorous world, with peremptory sway,
Subjects us all, and even the noblest most.
This world from thee, my honour and thy own,
Demands one step; a step, by which convinced
The king may see thy heart disdains to wear
A chain which his has greatly thrown aside.
'Tis fitting too, thy sex's pride commands thee,
To show the approving world thou canst resign,
As well as he, nor with inferior spirit,
A passion fatal to the public weal.
But above all, thou must root out for ever
From the king's breast the least remain of hope,
And henceforth make his mention'd love dishonour.
These things, my daughter, that must needs be done,
Can but this way be done—by the safe refuge,
The sacred shelter of a husband's arms.
And there is one—

Sigis. Good Heavens! what means my lord?

Sif. One of illustrious family, high rank,
Yet still of higher dignity and merit,
Who can and will protect thee; one to awe
The king himself—Nay, hear me, Sigismunda—
The noble Osmond courts thee for his bride,
And has my plighted word—This day—

Sigis. (kneeling.) My father!
Let me with trembling arms embrace thy knees!
Oh, if you ever wish to see me happy;
If e'er in infant years I gave you joy,
When, as I prattling twined around your neck,
You snatch'd me to your bosom, kiss'd my eyes,
And melting said you saw my mother there;
Oh, save me from that worst severity
Of fate! Oh, outrage not my breaking heart
To that degree!—I cannot! 'tis impossible!—
So soon withdraw it, give it to another—
Hear me, my dearest father! hear the voice
Of nature and humanity, that plead
As well as justice for me!—Not to chuse
Without your wise direction may be duty;
But still my choice is free—That is a right,
Which even the lowest slave can never lose.
And would you thus degrade me? make me base!
For such it were to give my worthless person
Without my heart, an injury to Osmond,
The highest can be done—Let me, my lord—
Or I shall die, shall by the sudden change
Be to distraction shock'd—Let me wear out
My hapless days in solitude and silence,
Far from the malice of a prying world!
At least—you cannot sure refuse me this——
Give me a little time—I will do all,
All I can do, to please you!—Oh, your eye
Sheds a kind beam——

Sif. My daughter! you abuse
The softness of my nature—

Sigis. Here, my father,
Till you relent, here will I grow for ever!

Sif. Rise, Sigismunda.—Though you touch my
Nothing can shake the inexorable dictates [heart,
Of honour, duty, and determined reason.
Then by the holy ties of filial love,
Resolve, I charge thee, to receive earl Osmond,
As suits the man who is thy father's choice,
And worthy of thy hand—I go to bring him—

Sigis. Spare me, my dearest father!

Sif. (aside.) I must rush
From her soft grasp, or nature will betray me!
Oh, grant us, Heaven! that fortitude of mind,
Which listens to our duty, not our passions—
Quit me, my child!

Sigis. You cannot, O my father!
You cannot leave me thus!

Sif. Come hither, Laura,
Come to thy friend. Now show thyself a friend.
Combat her weakness; dissipate her tears;
Cherish and reconcile her to her duty.

SCENE III.

SIGISMUNDA, LAURA.

Sigis. Oh, woe on woe! distress'd by love and
Oh, every way unhappy Sigismunda! [duty!

Lau. Forgive me, madam, if I blame your grief.
How can you waste your tears on one so false?
Unworthy of your tenderness? to whom
Nought but contempt is due and indignation?

Sigis. You know not half the horrors of my fate!
I might perhaps have learn'd to scorn his falsehood;
Nay, when the first sad burst of tears was past,

I might have roused my pride and scorn'd himself—
But 'tis too much, this greatest last misfortune—
Oh, whither shall I fly? Where hide me, Laura,
From the dire scene my father now prepares?
Lau. What thus alarms you, madam?
Sigis. Can it be?
Can I——ah no!——at once give to another
My violated heart? in one wild moment?
He brings earl Osmond to receive my vows!
Oh, dreadful change! for Tancred haughty Osmond!
Lau. Now, on my soul, 'tis what an outraged heart
Like yours, should wish!—I should, by Heavens, [esteem it
Most exquisite revenge!
Sigis. Revenge on whom?
On my own heart, already but too wretched!
Lau. On him! this Tancred! who has basely sold,
For the dull form of despicable grandeur,
His faith, his love!—At once a slave and tyrant!
Sigis. Oh, rail at me, at my believing folly,
My vain ill-founded hopes, but spare him, Laura!
Lau. Who raised those hopes? who triumphs o'er that weakness?
Pardon the word—You greatly merit him;
Better than him, with all his giddy pomp;
You raised him by your smiles when he was nothing!
Where is your woman's pride? that guardian spirit
Given us to dash the perfidy of man? [patience—
Ye Powers! I cannot bear the thought with
Yet recent from the most unsparing vows
The tongue of love e'er lavish'd; from your hopes
So vainly, idly, cruelly deluded;
Before the public thus, before your father,
By an irrevocable solemn deed,
With such inhuman scorn, to throw you from him!
To give his faithless hand yet warm from thine,
With complicated meanness, to Constantia!
And to complete his crime, when thy weak limbs
Could scarce support thee, then, of thee regardless,
To lead her off!
Sigis. That was indeed a sight
To poison love! to turn it into rage [weakness
And keen contempt!—What means this stupid
That hangs upon me? Hence unworthy tears!
Disgrace my cheek no more! No more, my heart,
For one so coolly false or meanly fickle—
Oh, it imports not which—dare to suggest
The least excuse!—Yes, traitor, I will wring
Thy pride, will turn thy triumph to confusion!
I will not pine away my days for thee,
Sighing to brooks and groves; while, with vain pity,
You in a rival's arms lament my fate——
No! let me perish! ere I tamely be
That soft, that patient, gentle Sigismunda,
Who can console her with the wretched boast,
She was for thee unhappy!—If I am,
I will be nobly so!——Sicilia's daughters
Shall wondering see in me a great example
Of one who punish'd an ill-judging heart,
Who made it bow to what it most abhorr'd!
Crush'd it to misery! for having thus
So lightly listen'd to a worthless lover!
Lau. At last it mounts! the kindling pride of virtue!
Trust me, thy marriage will embitter his——
Sigis. O may the furies light his nuptial torch!
Be it accursed as mine! for the fair peace,
The tender joys, of hymeneal love,
May jealousy awaked, and fell remorse,
Pour all their fiercest venom through his breast!——
Where the fates lead, and blind revenge, I follow!—
Let me not think.—By injured love! I vow,
Thou shalt, base prince! perfidious and inhuman!
Thou shalt behold me in another's arms!
In his thou hatest! Osmond's!
Lau. That will grind
His heart with secret rage! Ay, that will sting
His soul to madness! set him up a terror,
A spectacle of woe to faithless lovers!——
Your cooler thought, besides, will of the change
Approve, and think it happy. Noble Osmond
From the same stock with him derives his birth,
First of Sicilian barons, prudent, brave,
Of strictest honour, and by all revered——
Sigis. Talk not of Osmond, but perfidious Tancred!
Rail at him, rail! invent new names of scorn!
Assist me, Laura; lend my rage fresh fuel;
Support my staggering purpose, which already
Begins to fail me—Ah, my vaunts how vain!
How have I lied to my own heart!—Alas!
My tears return, the mighty flood o'erwhelms me!
Ten thousand crowding images distract
My tortured thought——And is it come to this?
Our hopes? our vows? our oft-repeated wishes,
Breathed from the fervent soul, and full of heaven,
To make each other happy?—come to this!
Lau. If thy own peace and honour cannot keep
Thy resolution fix'd, yet, Sigismunda,
O think, how deeply, how beyond retreat,
Thy father is engaged.
Sigis. Ah wretched weakness!
That thus enthrals my soul, that chases thence
Each nobler thought, the sense of every duty!—
And have I then no tears for thee, my father?
Can I forget thy cares, from helpless years,
Thy tenderness for me? an eye still beam'd
With love? a brow that never knew a frown?
Nor a harsh word thy tongue? Shall I for these
Repay thy stooping venerable age,
With shame, disquiet, anguish, and dishonour?
It must not be!—Thou first of angels! come,
Sweet filial piety! and firm my breast;
Yes, let one daughter to her fate submit,
Be nobly wretched—but her father happy!——
Laura!—they come!—O Heavens! I cannot stand
The horrid trial!—Open, open, earth!
And hide me from their view!
Lau. Madam!

SCENE IV.

SIFFREDI, OSMOND, SIGISMUNDA, LAURA.

Sif. My daughter,
Behold my noble friend who courts thy hand,
And whom to call my son I shall be proud;
Nor shall I less be pleased in his alliance,
To see thee happy.
Osm. Think not, I presume,
Madam, on this your father's kind consent,
To make me blest. I love you from a heart,
That seeks your good superior to my own;
And will, by every art of tender friendship,
Consult your dearest welfare. May I hope,
Yours does not disavow your father's choice?
Sigis. I am a daughter, Sir—and have no power
O'er my own heart—I die—Support me, Laura.
[*Faints.*

Sif. Help—Bear her off—She breathes—my daughter !—

Sigis. Oh !—
Forgive my weakness—soft—my Laura, lead me—
To my apartment.

Sif. Pardon me, my lord,
If by this sudden accident alarm'd,
I leave you for a moment.

SCENE V.

Osm. (*alone.*) Let me think——
What can this mean ?——Is it to me aversion ?
Or is it, as I fear'd, she loves another ?
Ha !—yes—perhaps the king, the young count Tancred !
They were bred up together——Surely that,
That cannot be—Has he not given his hand,
In the most solemn manner, to Constantia ?
Does not his crown depend upon the deed ?
No—if they loved, and this old statesman knew it,
He could not to a king prefer a subject.
His virtues I esteem—nay more, I trust them——
So far as virtue goes—but could he place
His daughter on the throne of Sicily——
Oh, 'tis a glorious bribe, too much for man !——
What is it then ?—I care not what it be.
My honour now, my dignity demands,
That my proposed alliance, by her father,
And even herself accepted, be not scorn'd.
I love her too—I never knew till now
To what a pitch I loved her. Oh, she shot
Ten thousand charms into my inmost soul !
She look'd so mild, so amiably gentle,
She bow'd her head, she glow'd with such confusion,
Such loveliness of modesty! She is,
In gracious mind, in manners, and in person,
The perfect model of all female beauty!—
She must be mine—She is !—If yet her heart
Consents not to my happiness, her duty,
Join'd to my tender cares, will gain so much
Upon her generous nature—That will follow.

The man of sense, who acts a prudent part,
Not flattering steals, but forms himself the heart.

ACT IV.

SCENE I.

The garden belonging to SIFFREDI'S *house.*

SIGISMUNDA, LAURA.

Sigis. (*with a letter in her hand.*) 'Tis done!—I am a slave !—The fatal vow
Has pass'd my lips !—Methought in those sad moments,
The tombs around, the saints, the darken'd altar,
And all the trembling shrines, with horror shook.
But here is still new matter of distress.
O Tancred, cease to persecute me more !
Oh, grudge me not some calmer state of woe!
Some quiet gloom to shade my hopeless days,
Where I may never hear of love and thee !——
Has Laura too conspired against my peace ?
Why did you take this letter ?—bear it back—
[*Giving her the letter.*
I will not court new pain.

Lau. Madam, Rodolpho
Urged me so much, nay, even with tears conjured me,
But this once more to serve the unhappy king—
For such he said he was—that though enraged,
Equal with thee, at his inhuman falsehood,
I could not to my brother's fervent prayers
Refuse this office—Read it—His excuses
Will only more expose his falsehood.

Sigis. No.
It suits not Osmond's wife to read one line
From that contagious hand—she knows too well!

Lau. He paints him out distress'd beyond expression,
Even on the point of madness. Wild as winds,
And fighting seas, he raves. His passions mix,
With ceaseless rage, all in each giddy moment.
He dies to see you and to clear his faith.

Sigis. Save me from that!—That would be worse than all !

Lau. I but report my brother's words; who then
Began to talk of some dark imposition,
That had deceived us all ; when, interrupted,
We heard your father and earl Osmond near,
As summon'd to Constantia's court they went.

Sigis. Ha! imposition!—Well! If I am doom'd
To be, o'er all my sex, the wretch of love,
In vain I would resist—Give me the letter—
To know the worst is some relief——Alas!
It was not thus, with such dire palpitations,
That, Tancred, once I used to read thy letters.
[*Attempting to read the letter, but gives it to* LAURA.
Ah, fond remembrance blinds me!—Read it, Laura.

LAURA *reads.*

"Deliver me, Sigismunda, from that most exquisite misery which a faithful heart can suffer—To be thought base by her, from whose esteem even virtue borrows new charms. When I submitted to my cruel situation, it was not falsehood you beheld, but an excess of love. Rather than endanger that, I for a while gave up my honour. Every moment till I see you stabs me with severer pangs than real guilt itself can feel. Let me then conjure you to meet me in the garden, towards the close of the day, when I will explain this mystery. We have been most inhumanly abused; and that by the means of the very paper which I gave you, from the warmest sincerity of love, to assure to you the heart and hand of "TANCRED."

Sigis. There, Laura, there, the dreadful secret sprung!
That paper! ah that paper! it suggests
A thousand horrid thoughts—I to my father
Gave it ; and he perhaps—I dare not cast
A look that way—If yet indeed you love me,
Oh, blast me not, kind Tancred, with the truth!
Oh, pitying keep me ignorant for ever!
What strange peculiar misery is mine ?
Reduced to wish the man I love were false ?
Why was I hurried to a step so rash ?
Repairless woe !—I might have waited, sure,

A few short hours—No duty that forbade—
I owed thy love that justice ; till this day
Thy love an image of all-perfect goodness !
A beam from Heaven that glow'd with every virtue!
And have I thrown this prize of life away ?
The piteous wreck of one distracted moment ?
Ah the cold prudence of remorseless age !
Ah parents, traitors to your children's bliss !
Ah cursed, ah blind revenge !—On every hand
I was betray'd—You, Laura, too, betray'd me !

Lau. Who, who, but he, whate'er he writes, betray'd you ?
Or false or pusillanimous. For once,
I will with you suppose, that his agreement
To the king's will was forged—Though forged by whom ?
Your father scorns the crime—Yet what avails it?
This, if it clears his truth, condemns his spirit.
A youthful king, by love and honour fired,
Patient to sit on his insulted throne,
And let an outrage, of so high a nature,
Unpunish'd pass, uncheck'd, uncontradicted—
Oh, 'tis a meanness equal even to falsehood.

Sigis. Laura, no more—We have already judged
Too largely without knowledge. Oft, what seems
A trifle, a mere nothing, by itself,
In some nice situations turns the scale
Of fate, and rules the most important actions.
Yes, I begin to feel a sad presage :
I am undone, from that eternal source
Of human woes—the judgment of the passions.
But what have I to do with these excuses ?
O cease my treacherous heart to give them room!
It suits not thee to plead a lover's cause ;
Even to lament my fate is now dishonour.
Nought now remains, but with relentless purpose,
To shun all interviews, all clearing up
Of this dark scene ; to wrap myself in gloom,
In solitude and shades ; there to devour
The silent sorrows ever swelling here ;
And since I must be wretched—for I must——
To claim the mighty misery myself,
Engross it all, and spare a hapless father.
Hence, let me fly !—the hour approaches——

Lau. Madam,
Behold he comes—the king—

Sigis. Heavens ! how escape ?
No—I will stay—This one last meeting—Leave me.

SCENE II.

TANCRED, SIGISMUNDA.

Tan. And are these long, long hours of torture
My life ! my Sigismunda ! [past ?
[*Throwing himself at her feet.*

Sigis. Rise, my lord.
To see my sovereign thus no more becomes me.

Tan. Oh, let me kiss the ground on which you tread!
Let me exhale my soul in softest transport !
Since I again embrace my Sigismunda ! [*Rising.*
Unkind ! how couldst thou ever deem me false?
How thus dishonour love?—Oh, I could much
Embitter my complaint !—How low were then
Thy thoughts of me ? How didst thou then affront
The human heart itself ? After the vows,
The fervent truth, the tender protestations,
Which mine has often pour'd, to let thy breast,
Whate'er the appearance was, admit suspicion?

Sigis. How ! when I heard myself your full con-
To the late king's so just and prudent will ? [sent
Heard it before you read, in solemn senate ?
When I beheld you give your royal hand
To her, whose birth and dignity of right
Demands that high alliance ? Yes, my lord,
You have done well. The man whom Heaven appoints
To govern others, should himself first learn
To bend his passions to the sway of reason.
In all you have done well ; but when you bid
My humbled hopes look up to you again,
And soothed with wanton cruelty my weakness—
That too was well—My vanity deserved
The sharp rebuke, whose fond extravagance
Could ever dream to balance your repose,
Your glory and the welfare of a people. [now,

Tan. Chide on, chide on. Thy soft reproaches
Instead of wounding, only soothe my fondness.
No, no, thou charming consort of my soul !
I never loved thee with such faithful ardour,
As in that cruel miserable moment [stoop'd
You thought me false ; when even my honour
To wear for thee a baffled face of baseness.
It was thy barbarous father, Sigismunda,
Who caught me in the toil. He turn'd that paper,
Meant for the assuring bond of nuptial love,
To ruin it for ever ; he, he wrote
That forged consent, you heard, beneath my name—
Nay, dared before my outraged throne to read it !
Had he not been thy father—Ha ! my love !
You tremble, you grow pale.

Sigis. Oh, leave me, Tancred!

Tan. No !—Leave thee ?—Never ! never ! till you set
My heart at peace, till these dear lips again
Pronounce thee mine ! Without thee I renounce
Myself, my friends, the world—Here on this hand—

Sigis. My lord, forget that hand, which never
Can be to thine united—— [now

Tan. Sigismunda!
What dost thou mean ?—Thy words, thy look, thy manner,
Seem to conceal some horrid secret—Heavens !—
No — That was wild — Distraction fires the thought !—

Sigis. Inquire no more——I never can be thine.

Tan. What, who shall interpose ? who dares
To brave the fury of an injured king ? [attempt
Who, ere he sees thee ravish'd from his hopes,
Will wrap all blazing Sicily in flames—

Sigis. In vain your power, my lord—This fatal
Join'd to my father's unrelenting will, [error,
Has placed an everlasting bar betwixt us—
I am—earl Osmond's—wife.

Tan. Earl Osmond's wife!——

[*After a long pause, during which they look at one another with the highest agitation and most tender distress.*

Heavens ! did I hear thee right ! what ! married ! married !
Lost to thy faithful Tancred ! lost for ever !
Couldst thou then doom me to such matchless woe,
Without so much as hearing me ?—Distraction !—
Alas ! what hast thou done ? Ah Sigismunda !
Thy rash credulity has done a deed,
Which of two happiest lovers—that e'er felt
The blissful power, has made two finish'd wretches !
But—Madness !——Sure, thou know'st it cannot be!
This hand is mine ! a thousand thousand vows—

SCENE III.

TANCRED, OSMOND, SIGISMUNDA.

Osm. [*Snatching her hand from the king.*
Madam, this hand, by the most solemn [rites,
A little hour ago, was given to me,
And did not sovereign honour now command me,
Never but with my life to quit my claim,
I would renounce it——thus!
Tan. Ha! who art thou?
Presumptuous man!
Sigis. (*aside.*) Where is my father? Heavens!
[*Goes out.*
Osm. One thou shouldst better know—Yes—view me—one!
Who can and will maintain his rights and honour,
Against a faithless prince, an upstart king,
Whose first base deed is what a harden'd tyrant
Would blush to act.
Tan. Insolent Osmond! know,
This upstart king will hurl confusion on thee,
And all who shall invade his sacred rights,
Prior to thine—thine founded on compulsion,
On infamous deceit, while his proceed
From mutual love and free long-plighted faith.
She is, and shall be mine!—I will annul,
By the high power with which the laws invest me,
Those guilty forms in which you have entrapp'd,
Basely entrapp'd, to thy detested nuptials,
My queen betroth'd! who has my heart, my hand,
And shall partake my throne—If, haughty lord,
If this thou didst not know, then know it now!
And know besides, as I have told thee this,
Shouldst thou but think to urge thy treason further—
Than treason more! Treason against my love!—
Thy life shall answer for it!
Osm. Ha! my life!——
It moves my scorn to hear thy empty threats.
When was it that a Norman baron's life
Became so vile, as on the frown of kings
To hang?—Of that, my lord, the law must judge:
Or if the law be weak, my guardian sword—
Tan. Dare not to touch it, traitor! lest my rage
Break loose, and do a deed that misbecomes me.

SCENE IV.

TANCRED, SIFFREDI, OSMOND.

Sif. (*entering.*) My gracious lord! what is it I behold!
My sovereign in contention with his subjects?
Surely this house deserves from royal Tancred
A little more regard, than to be made
A scene of trouble and unseemly jars.
It grieves my soul, it baffles every hope,
It makes me sick of life, to see thy glory
Thus blasted in the bud.—Heavens! can your [highness
From your exalted character descend,
The dignity of virtue; and, instead
Of being the protector of our rights,
The holy guardian of domestic bliss,
Unkindly thus disturb the sweet repose,
The secret peace of families, for which
Alone the freeborn race of man to laws
And government submitted?
Tan. My lord Siffredi,
Spare thy rebuke. The duties of my station
Are not to me unknown.—But thou, old man,
Dost thou not blush to talk of rights invaded!
And of our best, our dearest bliss disturb'd?
Thou! who with more than barbarous perfidy
Hast trampled all allegiance, justice, truth,
Humanity itself, beneath thy feet?
Thou know'st thou hast—I could, to thy confusion,
Return thy hard reproaches; but I spare thee
Before this lord, for whose ill-sorted friendship
Thou hast most basely sacrificed thy daughter.
Farewell, my lord!—For thee, lord constable,
Who dost presume to lift thy surly eye
To my soft love, my gentle Sigismunda,
I once again command thee, on thy life,——
Yes—chew thy rage—but mark me—on thy life,
No further urge thy arrogant pretensions!

SCENE V.

SIFFREDI, OSMOND.

Osm. Ha! arrogant pretensions! heaven and [earth!
What! arrogant pretensions to my wife!
My wedded wife! Where are we? In a land
Of civil rule, of liberty and laws?——
Not on my life pursue them?—Giddy prince!
My life disdains thy nod. It is the gift
Of parent heaven, who gave me too an arm,
A spirit to defend it against tyrants.
The Norman race, the sons of mighty Rollo,
Who rushing in a tempest from the north,
Great nurse of generous freemen! bravely won
With their own swords their seats, and still possess
By the same noble tenure, are not used [them
To hear such language—If I now desist,
Then brand me for a coward! deem me villain!
A traitor to the public! By this conduct
Deceived, betray'd, insulted, tyrannised.
Mine is a common cause. My arm shall guard,
Mix'd with my own, the rights of each Sicilian,
Of social life, and of mankind in general.
Ere to thy tyrant rage they fall a prey,
I shall find means to shake thy tottering throne,
Which this illegal, this perfidious usage
Forfeits at once, and crush thee in the ruins!
Constantia is my queen!
Sif. Lord constable,
Let us be stedfast in the right; but let us
Act with cool prudence, and with manly temper,
As well as manly firmness. True, I own,
The indignities you suffer are so high,
As might even justify what now you threaten.
But if, my lord, we can prevent the woes,
The cruel horrors of intestine war,
Yet hold untouch'd our liberties and laws;
Oh, let us, raised above the turbid sphere
Of little selfish passions, nobly do it!
Nor to our hot intemperate pride pour out
A dire libation of Sicilian blood.
'Tis god-like magnanimity, to keep,
When most provoked, our reason calm and clear,
And execute her will, from a strong sense
Of what is right, without the vulgar aid
Of heat and passion, which, though honest, bear us
Often too far. Remember that my house
Protects my daughter still; and ere I saw her
Thus ravish'd from us, by the arm of power,
This hand should act the Roman father's part.
Fear not: be temperate; all will yet be well.

I know the king. At first his passions burst
Quick as the lightning's flash ; but in his breast
Honour and justice dwell—Trust me, to reason
He will return.
Osm. He will!—By Heavens, he shall!—
You know the king—I wish, my lord Siffredi,
That you had deign'd to tell me all you knew—
And would you have me wait with duteous patience,
Till he return to reason ? Ye just Powers!
When he has planted on our necks his foot,
And trod us into slaves ; when his vain pride
Is cloy'd with our submission; if, at last,
He finds his arm too weak to shake the frame
Of wide-establish'd order out of joint,
And overturn all justice ; then, perchance,
He, in a fit of sickly kind repentance,
May make a merit to return to reason.
No, no, my lord !—There is a nobler way,
To teach the blind oppressive *fury* reason :
Oft has the lustre of avenging steel
Unseal'd her stupid eyes—The sword is reason !

SCENE VI.

SIFFREDI, OSMOND, RODOLPHO, *with Guards.*

Rod. My lord high constable of Sicily,
In the king's name, and by his special order,
I here arrest you prisoner of state.
Osm. What king ? I know no king of Sicily,
Unless he be the husband of Constantia.
Rod. Then know him now——Behold his royal
To bear you to the castle of Palermo. [orders
Sif. Let the big torrent foam its madness off.
Submit, my lord—No castle long can hold
Our wrongs—This, more than friendship or alliance,
Confirms me thine ; this binds me to thy fortunes,
By the strong tie of common injury,
Which nothing can dissolve——I grieve, Rodolpho,
To see the reign in such unhappy sort
Begin.
Osm. The reign! the usurpation call it!
This meteor king may blaze awhile, but soon
Must spend his idle terrors—Sir, lead on——
Farewell, my lord——More than my life and fortune,
Remember well, is in your hands——my honour !
Sif. Our honour is the same. My son, farewell—
We shall not long be parted. On these eyes
Sleep shall not shed his balm, till I behold thee
Restored to freedom, or partake thy bonds.

Even noble courage is not void of blame,
Till nobler patience sanctifies its flame.

ACT V.

SCENE I.

Sif. (*alone.*) THE prospect lowers around. found the king,
Though calm'd a little, with subsiding tempest,
As suits his generous nature, yet in love
Abated nought, most ardent in his purpose ;
Inexorably fix'd, whate'er the risk,
To claim my daughter, and dissolve this marriage—
I have embark'd, upon a perilous sea,
A mighty treasure. Here the rapid youth,
The impetuous passions of a lover-king
Check my bold course; and there, the jealous pride,
The impatient honour of a haughty lord
Of the first rank, in interest and dependants
Near equal to the king, forbid retreat.
My honour too, the same unchanged conviction,
That these my measures were, and still remain
Of absolute necessity, to save
The land from civil fury, urge me on.
But how proceed ? I only faster rush
Upon the desperate evils I would shun.
Whate'er the motive be, deceit, I fear,
And harsh unnatural force are not the means
Of public welfare or of private bliss——
Bear witness, Heaven ! Thou mind-inspecting eye!
My breast is pure. I have preferr'd my duty,
The good and safety of my fellow-subjects,
To all those views that fire the selfish race
Of men, and mix them in eternal broils.

Enter an Officer belonging to SIFFREDI.

Off. My lord, a man of noble port, his face
Wrapp'd in disguise, is earnest for admission.
Sif. Go bid him enter— [Officer *goes out.*
Ha ! wrapp'd in disguise!
And at this late unseasonable hour !
When o'er the world tremendous midnight reigns,
By the dire gloom of raging tempest doubled—

SCENE II.

SIFFREDI, OSMOND, *discovering himself.*

Sif. What! ha ! earl Osmond, you ?—Welcome, once more,
To this glad roof !—But why in this disguise ?
Would I could hope the king exceeds his promise
I have his faith, soon as to-morrow's sun
Shall gild Sicilia's cliffs, you shall be free.
Has some good angel turn'd his heart to justice ?
Osm. It is not by the favour of count Tancred
That I am here. As much I scorn his favour,
As I defy his tyranny and threats——
Our friend Goffredo, who commands the castle,
On my parole, ere dawn, to render back
My person, has permitted me this freedom.
Know then ; the faithless outrage of to-day,
By him committed whom you call the king,
Has roused Constantia's court. Our friends, the
Of virtue, justice, and of public faith, [friends
Ripe for revolt, are in high ferment all.
This, this, they say, exceeds whate'er deform'd
The miserable days we saw beneath
William the Bad. This saps the solid base,
At once of government and private life ;
This shameless imposition on the faith,
The majesty of senates, this lewd insult,

This violation of the rights of men.
Added to these, his ignominious treatment
Of her, the illustrious offspring of our kings,
Sicilia's hope, and now our royal mistress.
You know, my lord, how grossly these infringe
The late king's will: which orders, if count Tancred
Make not Constantia partner of his throne,
That he be quite excluded the succession,
And she to Henry given, king of the Romans,
The potent emperor Barbarossa's son,
Who seeks with earnest instance her alliance.
I thence of you, as guardian of the laws,
As guardian of this will to you entrusted,
Desire—nay, more, demand your instant aid,
To see it put in vigorous execution.

Sif. You cannot doubt, my lord, of my concurrence.
Who more than I have labour'd this great point?
'Tis my own plan. And if I drop it now,
I should be justly branded with the shame
Of rash advice, or despicable weakness.
But let us not precipitate the matter:
Constantia's friends are numerous and strong;
Yet Tancred's, trust me, are of equal force.
E'er since the secret of his birth was known,
The people all are in a tumult hurl'd
Of boundless joy, to hear there lives a prince
Of mighty Guiscard's line. Numbers, besides,
Of powerful barons, who at heart had pined,
To see the reign of their renown'd forefathers,
Won by immortal deeds of matchless valour,
Pass from the gallant Normans to the Suevi,
Will with a kind of rage espouse his cause—
'Tis so, my lord—be not by passion blinded——
'Tis surely so—Oh, if our prating virtue
Dwells not in words alone—Oh, let us join,
My generous Osmond, to avert these woes,
And yet sustain our tottering Norman kingdom!

Osm. But how, Siffredi? how?—If by soft means
We can maintain our rights, and save our country,
May his unnatural blood first stain the sword,
Who with unpitying fury first shall draw it!

Sif. I have a thought—The glorious work be thine.
But it requires an awful flight of virtue,
Above the passions of the vulgar breast;
And thence from thee I hope it, noble Osmond—
Suppose my daughter, to her God devoted,
Were placed within some convent's sacred verge,
Beneath the dread protection of the altar—

Osm. Ere then, by Heavens! I would devoutly shave
My holy scalp, turn whining monk myself,
And pray incessant for the tyrant's safety!
What! How! because an insolent invader,
A sacrilegious tyrant, in contempt
Of all those noblest rights, which to maintain
Is man's peculiar pride, demands my wife;
That I shall thus betray the common cause
Of human kind, and tamely yield her up,
Even in the manner you propose—Oh, then
I were supremely vile! degraded! shamed!
The scorn of manhood! and abhorr'd of honour!

Sif. There is, my lord, an honour, the calm child
Of reason, of humanity and mercy,
Superior far to this punctilious demon,
That singly minds itself, and oft embroils
With proud barbarian niceties the world!

Osm. My lord, my lord!—I cannot brook your prudence—
It holds a pulse unequal to my blood——
Unblemish'd honour is the flower of virtue!
The vivifying soul! and he who slights it
Will leave the other dull and lifeless dross.

Sif. No more——You are too warm.

Osm. You are too cool.

Sif. Too cool, my lord! I were indeed too cool,
Not to resent this language, and to tell thee
I wish earl Osmond were as cool as I
To his own selfish bliss—ay, and as warm
To that of others—But of this no more—
My daughter is thy wife—I gave her to thee,
And will against all force maintain her thine.
But think not I will catch thy headlong passions,
Whirl'd in a blaze of madness o'er the land;
Or till the last extremity compel me,
Risk the dire means of war. The king to-morrow
Will set you free; and if by gentle means
He does not yield my daughter to your arms,
And wed Constantia, as the will requires,
Why then expect me on the side of justice——
Let that suffice.

Osm. It does—forgive my heat.
My rankled mind, by injuries inflamed,
May be too prompt to take and give offence.

Sif. 'Tis past—Your wrongs, I own, may well transport.
The wisest mind—But henceforth, noble Osmond,
Do me more justice, honour more my truth,
Nor mark me with an eye of squint suspicion—
These jars apart—You may repose your soul
On my firm faith and unremitting friendship.
Of that I sure have given exalted proof,
And the next sun we see, shall prove it further—
Return, my son, and from your friend Goffredo
Release your word. There try, by soft repose,
To calm your breast.

Osm. Bid the vex'd ocean sleep,
Swept by the pinions of the raging north——
But your frail age, by care and toil exhausted,
Demands the balm of all-repairing rest.

Sif. Soon as to-morrow's dawn shall streak the skies,
I, with my friends in solemn state assembled,
Will to the palace, and demand your freedom.
Then by calm reason, or by higher means,
The king shall quit his claim, and in the face
Of Sicily, my daughter shall be yours.
Farewell.

Osm. My lord, good night.

SCENE III.

Osm. (*alone; after a long pause.*) I like him not——
Yes—I have mighty matter of suspicion.
'Tis plain—I see it lurking in his breast,
He has a foolish fondness for this king—
My honour is not safe, while here my wife
Remains—Who knows but he this very night
May bear her to some convent as he mention'd—
The king too—though I smother'd up my rage,
I mark'd it well—will set me free to-morrow.
Why not to-night? He has some dark design—
By heavens! he has—I am abused most grossly;
Made the vile tool of this old statesman's schemes;
Married to one—Ay, and he knew it,—one
Who loves young Tancred! Hence her swooning, tears,

And all her soft distress, when she disgraced me
By basely giving her perfidious hand
Without her heart—Hell and perdition! this,
This is the perfidy! This is the fell,
The keen, envenom'd, exquisite disgrace!
Which to a man of honour even exceeds
The falsehood of the person—But I now
Will rouse me from the poor tame lethargy,
By my believing fondness cast upon me
I will not wait his crawling timid motions,
Perhaps to blind me meant, which he to-morrow
Has promised to pursue. No! ere his eyes
Shall open on to-morrow's orient beam,
I will convince him that earl Osmond never
Was form'd to be his dupe—I know full well
The important weight and danger of the deed:
But to a man, whom greater dangers press,
Driven to the brink of infamy and horror,
Rashness itself, and utter desperation,
Are the best prudence—I will bear her off
This night, and lodge her in a place of safety.
I have a trusty band that waits not far.
Hence! let me lose no time—One rapid moment
Should ardent form, at once, and execute
A bold design—'Tis fix'd—'Tis done!—Yes, then,
When I have seized the prize of love and honour,
And with a friend secured her; to the castle
I will repair, and claim Goffredo's promise
To rise with all his garrison—my friends
With brave impatience wait. The mine is laid,
And only wants my kindling touch to spring.

SCENE IV.

SIGISMUNDA'S *Apartment.*

SIGISMUNDA, LAURA.

Lau. Heavens! 'tis a fearful night!
Sigis. Ah! the black rage
Of midnight tempest, or the assuring smiles
Of radiant morn are equal all to me.
Nought now has charms or terrors to my breast,
The seat of stupid woe!—Leave me, my Laura.
Kind rest, perhaps, may hush my woes a little—
O for that quiet sleep that knows no morning!
Lau. Madam, indeed I know not how to go.
Indulge my fondness—Let me watch a while
By your sad bed, till these dread hours shall pass.
Sigis. Alas! what is the toil of elements,
This idle perturbation of the sky,
To what I feel within!—O that the fires
Of pitying Heaven would point their fury here!
Good night, my dearest Laura!
Lau. Oh, I know not
What this oppression means—But 'tis with pain,
With tears, I can persuade myself to leave you—
Well then—Good night, my dearest Sigismunda!

SCENE V.

Sigis. And am I then alone?—The most undone,
Most wretched being now beneath the cope
Of this affrighting gloom that wraps the world!—
I said I did not fear—Ah me! I feel
A shivering horror run through all my powers!
Oh, I am nought but tumult, fears, and weakness!
And yet how idle fear when hope is gone,
Gone, gone for ever!—O thou gentle scene
[*Looking towards her bed.*
Of sweet repose, where by the oblivious draught
Of each sad toilsome day, to peace restored
Unhappy mortals lose their woes awhile,
Thou hast no peace for me!—What shall I do?
How pass this dreadful night, so big with terror?—
Here with the midnight shades, here will I sit,
[*Sitting down.*
A prey to dire despair, and ceaseless weep
The hours away—Bless me—I heard a noise—
[*Starting up.*
No—I mistook—Nothing but silence reigns
And awful midnight round—Again! O heavens!
My lord the king!

SCENE VI.

TANCRED, SIGISMUNDA.

Tan. Be not alarm'd, my love!
Sigis. My royal lord! why at this midnight hour?
How came you hither?
Tan. By that secret way
My love contrived, when we, in happier days,
Used to devote these hours, so much in vain,
To vows of love and everlasting friendship.
Sigis. Why will you thus persist to add new stings
To her distress, who never can be thine?
Oh, fly me! fly! You know——
Tan. I know too much.
Oh, how I could reproach thee, Sigismunda!
Pour out my injured soul in just complaints!
But now the time permits not, these swift moments—
I told thee how thy father's artifice
Forced me to seem perfidious in thy eyes.
Ah, fatal blindness! not to have observed
The mingled pangs of rage and love that shook me,
When, by my cruel public situation
Compell'd, I only feign'd consent, to gain
A little time, and more secure thee mine.
E'er since—a dreadful interval of care!
My thoughts have been employ'd, not without hope,
How to defeat Siffredi's barbarous purpose.
But thy credulity has ruin'd all,—
Thy rash, thy wild—I know not what to name it——
Oh, it has proved the giddy hopes of man
To be delusion all, and sickening folly!
Sigis. Ah, generous Tancred! ah, thy truth destroys me;
Yes, yes, 'tis I, 'tis I alone am false!
My hasty rage, join'd to my tame submission,
More than the most exalted filial duty
Could e'er demand, has dash'd our cup of fate
With bitterness unequal'd—But, alas!
What are thy woes to mine?—to mine!—just Heaven!—
Now is thy turn of vengeance—hate, renounce me!
Oh, leave me to the fate I well deserve,
To sink in hopeless misery!—at least,
Try to forget the worthless Sigismunda!
Tan. Forget thee! No! Thou art my soul itself!
I have no thought, no hope, no wish but thee!
Even this repented injury, the fears,
That rouse me all to madness, at the thought
Of losing thee, the whole collected pains
Of my full heart, serve but to make thee dearer!
Ah, how forget thee!—Much must be forgot,
Ere Tancred can forget his Sigismunda!
Sigis. But you, my lord, must make that great effort.

Tan. Can Sigismunda make it?
Sigis. Ah! I know not
With what success—But all that feeble woman
And love-entangled reason can perform,
I, to the utmost, will exert to do it.
Tan. Fear not—'tis done!—If thou canst form the thought,
Success is sure—I am forgot already! [more.
Sigis. Ah, Tancred?—But, my lord, respect me
Think who I am—What can you now propose?
Tan. To claim the plighted vows which Heaven has heard,
To vindicate the rights of holy love
By faith and honour bound, to which compared
These empty forms, which have ensnared thy hand,
Are impious guile, abuse, and profanation——
Nay, as a king, whose high prerogative
By this unlicensed marriage is affronted,
To bid the laws themselves pronounce it void.
Sigis. Honour, my lord, is much too proud to catch
At every slender twig of nice distinctions.
These for the unfeeling vulgar may do well:
But those, whose souls are by the nicer rule
Of virtuous delicacy nobly sway'd,
Stand at another bar than that of laws.
Then cease to urge me—Since I am not born
To that exalted fate to be your queen—
Or, yet a dearer name—to be your wife!
I am the wife of an illustrious lord
Of your own princely blood; and what I am,
I will with proper dignity remain.
Retire, my royal lord—There is no means
To cure the wounds this fatal day has given.
We meet no more!
Tan. O barbarous Sigismunda!
And canst thou talk thus steadily? thus treat me
With such unpitying, unrelenting rigour?
Poor is the love, that rather than give up
A little pride, a little formal pride,
The breath of vanity! can bear to see
The man, whose heart was once so dear to thine,
By many a tender vow so mix'd together,
A prey to anguish, fury and distraction!—
Thou canst not surely make me such a wretch,
Thou canst not, Sigismunda!—Yet relent,
O save us yet!—Rodolpho, with my guards,
Waits in the garden—Let us seize the moments
We ne'er may have again—With more than power
I will assert thee mine, with fairest honour.
The world shall even approve; each honest bosom
Swell with a kindred joy to see us happy.
Sigis. The world approve! What is the world to me?
The conscious mind is its own awful world.——
And yet, perhaps, if thou wert not a king,
I know not, Tancred, what I might have done.
Then, then, my conduct, sanctified by love,
Could not be deem'd, by the severest judge,
The mean effect of interest or ambition.
But now not all my partial heart can plead,
Shall ever shake the unalterable dictates
That tyrannise my breast.
Tan. 'Tis well—no more—
I yield me to my fate—Yes, yes, inhuman!
Since thy barbarian heart is steel'd by pride,
Shut up to love and pity, here behold me
Cast on the ground, a vile and abject wretch!
Lost to all cares, all dignities, all duties!
Here will I grow, breathe out my faithful soul,
Here at thy feet—Death, death alone shall part us!
Sigis. Have you then vow'd to drive me to perdition?
What can I more?—Yes, Tancred! once again
I will forget the dignity my station
Commands me to sustain—for the last time
Will tell thee, that I fear, no ties, no duty,
Can ever root thee from my hapless bosom.
O leave me! fly me! were it but in pity!
To see what once we tenderly have loved,
Cut off from every hope—cut off for ever!
Is pain thy generosity should spare me.
Then rise, my lord; and if you truly love me;
If you respect my honour,—nay, my peace;
Retire! for though the emotions of my heart
Can ne'er alarm my virtue; yet, alas!
They tear it so, they pierce it with such anguish—
Oh, 'tis too much!—I cannot bear the conflict!

SCENE VII.

TANCRED, OSMOND, SIGISMUNDA.

Osm. (*entering.*) Turn, tyrant! turn! and answer to my honour,
For this thy base insufferable outrage!
Tan. Isolent traitor! think not to escape
Thyself my vengeance! [*They fight.* OSMOND *falls.*
Sigis. Help here! help!—O Heavens!
[*Throwing herself down by him.*
Alas! my lord, what meant your headlong rage?
That faith, which I this day upon the altar,
To you devoted, is unblemish'd, pure,
As vestal truth; was resolutely yours,
Beyond the power of aught on earth to shake it.
Osm. Perfidious woman! die!——
[*Shortening his sword, he plunges it into her breast.*
And to the grave
Attend a husband, yet but half avenged?
Tan. O horror! horror! execrable villain!
Osm. And, tyrant! thou!—Thou shalt not o'er my tomb
Exult—'Tis well—'Tis great;—I die content!—
[*Dies.*

SCENE VIII.

TANCRED, SIFFREDI, RODOLPHO, SIGISMUNDA, LAURA.

TANCRED, (*Throwing himself down by* SIGISMUNDA.)
Quick! here! bring aid!—All in Palermo bring
Whose skill can save her!—Ah! that gentle bosom
Pours fast the streams of life.
Sigis. All aid is vain,
I feel the powerful hand of death upon me—
But, oh! it sheds a sweetness through my fate,
That I am thine again; and without blame,
May in my Tancred's arms resign my soul!
Tan. Oh, death is in that voice! so gently mild,
So sadly sweet, as mixes even with mine
The tears of hovering angels!—Mine again!—
And is it thus the cruel fates have join'd us;
Are these the horrid nuptials they prepare
For love like ours? Is virtue thus rewarded?
Let not my impious rage accuse just Heaven!
Thou, Tancred! Thou! hast murder'd Sigismunda!
That furious man was but the tool of fate,
I, I the cause!—But I will do thee justice
On this deaf heart! that to thy tender wisdom
Refused an ear—Yes, death shall soon unite us!

Sigis. Live, live, my Tancred!—Let my death suffice
To expiate all that may have been amiss.
May it appease the fates, avert their fury
From thy propitious reign! Meantime, of me
And of thy glory mindful, live, I charge thee,
To guard our friends, and make thy people happy—
[*Observing* SIFFREDI *fixed in astonishment and grief.*
My father!——Oh! how shall I lift my eyes
To thee, my sinking father!
Sif. Awful Heaven!
I am chastised——My dearest child!——
Sigis. Where am I?
A fearful darkness closes all around—
My friends! We needs must part—I must obey
The imperious call—Farewell, my Laura! cherish
My poor afflicted father's age—Rodolpho,
Now is the time to watch the unhappy king,
With all the care and tenderness of friendship—
O my dear father! bow'd beneath the weight
Of age and grief—the victim even of virtue,
Receive my last adieu!—Where art thou, Tancred?
Give me thy hand—But, ah!—it cannot save me
From the dire king of terrors, whose cold power
Creeps o'er my heart——Oh!
Tan. How these pangs distract me!
Oh, lift thy gracious eyes!——Thou leavest me then;
Thou leavest me, Sigismunda!
Sigis. Yet a moment—
I had, my Tancred, something more to say—
Yes——but thy love and tenderness for me
Sure makes it needless—Harbour no resentment
Against my father; venerate his zeal,
That acted from a principle of goodness,
From faithful love to thee—Live and maintain
My innocence imbalm'd, with holiest care
Preserve my spotless memory!——I die—
Eternal Mercy take my trembling soul!
Oh! 'tis the only sting of death to part
From those we love—from thee—farewell, my Tancred! [*Dies.*
Tan. Thus then!
[*Flying to his sword, is held by* RODOLPHO.
Rod. Hold! hold! my lord!—Have you forgot
Your Sigismunda's last request already?
Tan. Off! set me free! Think not to bind me down,
With barbarous friendship, to the rack of life!
What hand can shut the thousand thousand gates,
Which death still opens to the woes of mortals?—
I shall find means—No power in earth or heaven
Can force me to endure the hateful light,
Thus robb'd of all that lent it joy and sweetness!
Off! traitors! off! or my distracted soul
Will burst indignant from this jail of nature,
To where she beckons yonder—No, mild seraph!
Point not to life——I cannot linger here,
Cut off from thee, the miserable pity,
The scorn of human kind!——A trampled king!
Who let his mean poor-hearted love, one moment,
To coward prudence stoop; who made it not
The first undoubting action of his reign,
To snatch thee to his throne, and there to shield thee,
Thy helpless bosom from a ruffian's fury!——
O shame! O agony! O the fell stings
Of late, of vain repentance!——Ha! my brain
Is all on fire! a wild abyss of thought!
The infernal world discloses! See! behold him!
Lo! with fierce smiles he shakes the bloody steel,
And mocks my feeble tears!—Hence! quickly, hence!
Spurn his vile carcass! give it to the dogs!
Expose it to the winds and screaming ravens!
Or hurl it down that fiery steep to hell,
There with his soul to toss in flames for ever!——
Ah, impotence of rage!—What am I? where?
Sad, silent, all? The forms of dumb despair,
Around some mournful tomb! What do I see?
This soft abode of innocence and love
Turn'd to the house of death! a place of horror!——
Ah! that poor corse! pale! pale! deform'd with murder!
Is that my Sigismunda?
[*Throwing himself down by her.*

Sif. (*after a pathetic pause, looking on the scene before him.*) Have I lived
To these enfeebled years, by Heaven reserved
To be a dreadful monument of justice!——
Rodolpho, raise the king, and bear him hence
From this distracting scene of blood and death.
Alas! I dare not give him my assistance;
My care would only more inflame his rage.

Behold the fatal work of my dark hand,
That by rude force the passions would command,
That ruthless sought to root them from the breast;
They may be ruled, but will not be opprest.
Taught hence, ye parents, who from nature stray
And the great ties of social life betray;
Ne'er with your children act a tyrant's part:
'Tis yours to guide, not violate the heart:
Ye vainly wise who o'er mankind preside,
Behold my righteous woes, and drop your pride!
Keep virtue's simple path before your eyes,
Nor think from evil good can ever rise.

EPILOGUE.

CRAMM'D to the throat with wholesome moral stuff,
Alas! poor audience! you have had enough.
Was ever hapless heroine of a play
In such a piteous plight as ours to-day!
Was ever woman so by love betray'd?
Match'd with two husbands, and yet—die a maid.
But bless me!—hold—What sounds are these I hear!
I see the Tragic Muse herself appear.

The back-scene opens, and discovers a romantic sylvan landscape; from which Mrs. Cibber, in the character of the Tragic Muse, advances slowly to music, and speaks the following lines:

Hence with your flippant epilogue, that tries
To wipe the virtuous tear from British eyes;
That dares my mortal tragic scene profane,
With strains—at best, unsuiting, light and vain.
Hence from the pure unsullied beams that play
In yon fair eyes where virtue shines—Away!

Britons, to you from chaste Castalian groves,
Where dwell the tender, oft unhappy loves;
Where shades of heroes roam, each mighty name,
And court my aid to rise again to fame;
To you I come, to freedom's noblest seat,
And in Britannia fix my last retreat.

In Greece and Rome, I watch'd the public weal;
The purple tyrant trembled at my steel:
Nor did I less o'er private sorrows reign,
And mend the melting heart with softer pain.
On France and You then rose my brightening star,
With social ray The arts are ne'er at war.
Oh, as your fire and genius stronger blaze,
As yours are generous freedom's bolder lays,
Let not the Gallic taste leave yours behind,
In decent manners and in life refined;
Banish the motley mode, to tag low verse,
The laughing ballad to the mournful hearse.
When through five acts your hearts have learnt to glow,
Touch'd with the sacred force of honest woe;
O keep the dear impression on your breast,
Nor idly lose it for a wretched jest.

CORIOLANUS.

A Tragedy.

PERSONS REPRESENTED.

CAIUS MARCIUS CORIOLANUS.
ATTIUS TULLUS, *General of the Volscian army.*
GALESUS, *one of the Deputies of the Volscian States attending the camp.*
The other Deputies of the Volscian States.
VOLUSIUS, *one of the principal Volscian officers.*
TITUS, *freed-man of Galesus.*
MARCUS MINUCIUS, *Consul and principal of the Deputation from Rome to Coriolanus.*
POSTHUMUS COMINIUS, *a Consular Senator, one of the Deputation, and who had been the Roman General at the taking of Corioli.*
VETURIA, *mother of Coriolanus.*
VOLUMNIA, *wife of Coriolanus.*

Roman Senators, Priests, Augurs, *&c., of the first Deputation.* Roman Ladies *in the train of* VETURIA *and* VOLUMNIA, *of the second Deputation.*

Volscian Officers, Lictors, Soldiers, *&c.*

SCENE.—*The Volscian Camp.*

ACT I.

SCENE I.

The Volscian Camp.

ATTIUS TULLUS, VOLUSIUS.

Vol. WHENCE is it, Tullus, that our arms are stopp'd
Here on the borders of the Roman state?
Why sleeps that spirit whose heroic ardour
Urged you to break the truce, and pour'd our host,
From all the united cantons of the Volsci,
On their unguarded frontier? Such designs
Brook not an hour's delay; their whole success
Depends on instant vigorous execution.
Tul. Volusius, I approve thy brave impatience:
And will to thee, in confidence of friendship,
Disclose my secret soul. Thou know'st Galesus,
Whose freedom Caius Marcius, once his guest,
Of all the spoil of sack'd Corioli,
Alone demanded; and who thence to Rome,
From gratitude and friendship, follow'd Marcius;
Whence lately to our Antium he return'd,
With overtures of peace proposed by Rome.
Vol. I know him well; an antiquated sage
Of that romantic school Pythagoras
Establish'd here on our Hesperian shore;
Whose gentle dictates only serve to tame
Enfeebled mortals into slaves.
Tul. Galesus
Doubtless possesses many civil virtues;
Is gentle, good; for rectitude of heart
And innocence of life by all revered.
Vol. Pardon me, Tullus, if my faithful bluntness
Deems you too liberal in his praise. In peace
Such may perhaps do well, when prating rules
An idle world; but in tempestuous times
They are stark naught, these visionary statesmen,
Fit rulers only for their golden age.
The rugged genius of rapacious Rome
For other men, and other counsels, calls.
Tul. Your thoughts are mine—I only meant to tell thee
The part he bears in this ill-timed delay.
Soon as our gather'd army march'd from Antium,
The Roman senate, whose attentive caution
Watch'd all our motions, took at once the alarm!
And sent a herald, ere we pass'd their borders,
With formal ceremony, to demand
The cause of our approach.—Had I been master,
I would have answer'd at the gates of Rome.
But this Galesus, who attends our camp
Among the Volscian deputies, so pleaded
The laws of nations, made such loud complaints
Against the infraction of the public faith,

So teazed us with the pedantry of states,
That I was forced, unwilling, to permit
His freedman, Titus, to be sent to Rome
With our demands. If these the senate grants,
We then are in the toils of peace entangled,
In spite of all my efforts to avoid them.

Vol. Oh, 'tis a wild chimera! Peace with Rome!
Dream not of that, unless the Volscian courage
Is quite subdued, and only seeks to gild
A vile submission with that specious name.
Learn wisdom from your neighbours. Peace with Rome
Has quell'd the Latines, tamed their free-born spirit,
And by her friendship honour'd them with chains.

Tul. She ne'er will grant it on the just conditions
I now have brought the Volsci to demand:
The restitution of our conquer'd cities,
And fair alliance upon equal terms.
I know the Roman insolence will scorn
To yield to this: and Titus must return,
Within three days, the longest term allow'd him;
Of which the third is near elapsed already.
Then even Galesus will not dare to stop us
With superstitious forms, and solemn trifles,
From letting loose the unbridled rage of war
Against those hated tyrants of Hesperia.

Vol. Thanks to the gods! my sword will then be [free.
Then, poor Corioli! thy bleeding wounds,
Thy treasures sack'd, thy captivated matrons,
Shall amply be revenged by thy Volusius;
Then, Tullus, from the lofty brows of Marcius
Thou mayst regain the wreaths his conquering hand,
By partial fortune aided, tore from thine.

Tul. O my Volusius! thou, who art a soldier,
A tried and brave one too, say, in thy heart
Dost thou not scorn me? thou who saw'st me bend
Beneath the half-spent thunder of a foe,
Warm from the conquest of Corioli,
Which, rushing furious in with those whose sally
He had repell'd, he seized almost alone,
And gave to fire and sword. Yet thence he flew
Scorning the plunder of our richest city,
His wounds undress'd, without a moment's respite,
To where our armies on the fearful edge
Of battle stood; and, asking of the consul
To be opposed to me, with mighty rage,
Resistless, bore us down.

Vol. True valour, Tullus,
Lies in the mind, the never-yielding purpose,
Nor owns the blind award of giddy fortune.

Tul. My soul, my friend, my soul is all on fire!
Thirst of revenge consumes me! the revenge
Of generous emulation, not of hatred.
This happy Roman, this proud Marcius haunts me.
Each troubled night when slaves and captives sleep,
Forgetful of their chains, I, in my dreams,
Anew am vanquish'd; and, beneath the sword
With horror sinking, feel a tenfold death,
The death of honour. But I will redeem—
Yes, Marcius, I will yet redeem my fame.
To face thee once again is the great purpose
For which alone I live—Till then how slow, [me,
How tedious lags the time! while shame corrodes
With many a bitter thought; and injured honour
Sick and desponding preys upon itself.

Vol. It fast approaches now, the hour of vengeance,
To this famed land. to ancient Latium due.
Unbalanced Rome, at variance with herself,
To order lost, in deep and hot commotion,
Stands on the dangerous point of civil war;
Her haughty nobles, and seditious commons
Reviling, fearing, hating one another;
While, on our part, all wears a prosperous face;
Our troops united, numerous, high in spirit,
As if their general's soul inform'd them all.
O long-expected day!

Tul. Go, brave Volusius,
Go breathe thy ardour into every breast,
That when the Volscian envoy shall return,
Whom ere the close of evening I expect,
One spirit may unite us in the cause
Of generous freedom, and our native rights,
So long oppress'd by Rome's encroaching power.

SCENE II.

Tul. (*alone.*) Galesus said that Marcius stands for consul.
Oh favour thou his suit, propitious Jove!
That I may brave him at his army's head,
In all the majesty of sovereign power!
That the whole conduct of the war may rest
On us alone, and prove by its decision,
Which of the two is worthiest to command——

SCENE III.

TULLUS, Officer.

Tul. Ha! why this haste? you look alarm'd.

Off. My lord,
One of exalted port, his visage hid,
Has placed himself upon your sacred hearth,
Beneath the dread protection of your Lares;
And sits majestic there in solemn silence.

Tul. Did you not ask him who, and what he was?

Off. My lord, I could not speak; I felt appall'd,
As if the presence of some god had struck me.

Tul. Come, dastard! let me find this man of terrors.

SCENE IV.

The back-scene opens and discovers CORIOLANUS *as described above.*

CORIOLANUS, TULLUS.

Tul. (*after some silence.*) Illustrious stranger—for thy high demeanour
Bespeaks thee such—who art thou?

Cor. (*rising and unmuffling his face.*) View me, Tullus— (*After some pause.*
Dost thou not know me?

Tul. No. That noble front
I never saw before. What is thy name?

Cor. Does not the secret voice of hostile instinct,
Does not thy swelling heart declare me to thee?

Tul. Gods! can it be?—

Cor. Yes. I am Caius Marcius;
Known to thy smarting country by the name
Of Coriolanus. That alone is left me,
That empty name, for all my toils, my service,
The blood which I have shed for thankless Rome.
Behold me banish'd thence, a victim yielded
By her weak nobles to the maddening rabble.
I seek revenge. Thou mayst employ my sword,

With keener edge, with heavier force against her,
Than e'er it fell upon the Volscian nation.
But if thou, Tullus, dost refuse me this,
The only wish of my collected heart,
Where every passion in one burning point
Concentres, give me death: death from thy hand
I sure have well deserved—Nor shall I blush
To take or life or death from Attius Tullus.

Tul. O Caius Marcius! in this one short moment,
That we have friendly talk'd, my ravish'd heart
Has undergone a great, a wondrous change.
I ever held thee in my best esteem;
But this heroic confidence has won me,
Stamp'd me at once thy friend. I were indeed
A wretch as mean as this thy trust is noble,
Could I refuse thee thy demand—Yes, Marcius!
Thou hast thy wish! take half of my command:
If that be not enough, then take the whole.
We have, my friend, a gallant force on foot,
An army, Marcius, fit to follow thee.
Go lead them on, and take thy full revenge.
All should unite to punish the ungrateful;
Ingratitude is treason to mankind.

Cor. (*embracing him.*) Thus, generous Tullus, take a soldier's thanks,
Who is not practised in the gloss of words——
Thou friend in deed! friend to my cause, my quarrel!
Friend to the darling passion of my soul!
All else I set at nought!—Immortal gods!
I am new-made, and wonder at myself!
A little while ago, and I was nothing;
A powerless reptile, crawling on the earth,
Cursed with a soul that restless wish'd to wield
The bolts of Jove! I dwelt in Erebus,
I wander'd through the hopeless gloom of hell,
Stung with revenge, tormented by the furies!
Now, Tullus, like a god, you draw me thence,
Throne me amidst the skies, with tempest charged,
And put the ready thunder in my hand!

Tul. What I have promised, Marcius, I will do.
Within an hour at farthest we expect
The freedman of Galesus back from Rome,
Who carried to the senate our demands.
Their answer will, I doubt not, end the truce,
And instant draw our angry swords against them.
Till then retire within my inmost tent,
Unknown to all but me, that when our chiefs
Meet in full council to declare for war,
I may produce thee to their wondering eyes,
As if descended from avenging Heaven
To humble lofty Rome, and teach her justice.

Cor. To thy direction, Tullus, I resign
My future life: my fate is in thy hands;
And, if I judge aright, the fate of Rome.

ACT II.

SCENE I.

GALESUS, TITUS.

Gal. INDEED! my Titus, I had hopes that Rome,
Vext as she is with her domestic broils,
Her frontier weak, her armies unprepared,
Might have complied with our demands, and given us
The same alliance granted to the Latines.

Tit. The senate scarce would hear the terms I offer'd;
But order'd me to bear this answer back:
"If first the Volsci take up arms, the Romans
Will be the last to lay them down."

Gal. Alas!
This answer seals the doom of many a wretch.
Unchain'd Bellona from her temple rushes,
With all the crimes and vices in her train.
Earth fades at her approach. To rural peace,
Fair plenty, and the social joy of cities,
Soon will succeed rage, rapine, devastation,
Each cruel horror sanctified by names.
O mortals! mortals! when will you, content
With nature's bounty, that in fuller flow,
Still as your labours open more its sources,
Abundant gushes o'er the happy world;
When will you banish violence and outrage,
To dwell with beasts of prey in woods and deserts?

Tit. Never till Rome shall change her conquering maxims.

Gal. Her haughty spirit now will soar beyond
Its usual pitch, upborne by Caius Marcius.
Stands he not for the consulate?

Tit. He did;
But is no more a citizen of Rome.

Gal. What mean'st thou, Titus?

Tit. Marcius is from Rome
Banish'd for ever.

Gal. O immortal powers!
On what pretence could they to exile doom
Their wisest captain, and their bravest soldier?
Nor less renown'd for piety, for justice,
An uncorrupted heart, and purest manners.

Tit. The charge against him was entirely groundless,
What not his enemies themselves believed,
Affecting of tyrannic power in Rome.
His real crime was only some hot words,
Struck from his fiery temper, in the senate,
Against those factious ministers of discord,
The tribunes of the people. They to rage,
And frantic fury, roused the mad plebeians;
By whom supported in their bold attempt,
They durst presume to summon to the bar
Of an enraged and partial populace,
The most illustrious senator of Rome.
To this the nobles yielded—and, with his,
Gave up their own and children's rights for ever.

Gal. Oh, shameful weakness in a Roman senate,
So much renown'd for firmness! yet my Titus,
Spite of my love to Marcius, I must own it,
The vigorous soil whence his heroic virtues
Luxuriant rise, if not with careful hand
Severely weeded, teems with imperfections.
His lofty spirit brooks no opposition.
His rage, if once offended, knows no bounds.
He deems plebeian, with patrician blood
Compared, the creatures of a lower species,
Mere menial hands by nature meant to serve him.

Tit. It was this high patrician pride undid him.
The furious people triumph'd in his ruin,
As if they had expell'd another Tarquin:

While, like a captive train, the vanquish'd nobles
Hung their dejected heads in silent shame.
Marcius alone seem'd unconcern'd; though deep
The latent tempest boil'd within his breast,
Choked up and smother'd with excessive rage.

Gal. You were his guest at Rome, and therefore, Titus,
Might on this sad occasion be permitted
To join your tears with his domestic friends.
Saw you that moving scene?

Tit. I did, Galesus.
I follow'd Marcius home—His mother, there,
Veturia, the most venerable matron
These eyes have e'er beheld, and soft Volumnia,
His lovely virtuous wife, amidst his children,
Spread on the ground, lay lost in dumb despair.
He swelling stood a while, and could not speak,
The affronted hero struggling with the man;
Then thus at last he broke the gloomy silence:
"'Tis done. The guilty sentence is pronounced,
Ungrateful Rome has cast me from her bosom.
Support this blow with fortitude and courage,
As it becomes two generous Roman matrons:
I recommend my children to your care.
Farewell. I go, I quit, without regret,
A city grown an enemy to virtue."

Gal. Oh, godlike Marcius! oh, unconquer'd strength
And dignity of mind! How much superior
Is such a soul to all the power of fortune!

Tit. This said, he sternly tried to break away:
When, holding in his hand his eldest son,
Veturia follow'd; while the poor Volumnia,
All drown'd in tears, and bearing in one arm
Their youngest, yet an infant, with the other
Hung clinging at his knees—he turning to them,
Half soften'd, half severe, breathed from his soul
These broken accents— "Cease your vain complaints,
Mother, you have no more a son; and thou,
Thou best of women! thou, my dear Volumnia!
No more a husband."—Pierced with these dire words
Volumnia lifeless sunk: and off he flung,
With wild precipitation.

Gal. Thy sad tale
Blinds my old eyes with tears—But whither, tell me,
O whither, Titus, bent he then his course?

Tit. Where the blind genius of regardless rage
And desperation led. On to the gate
Capena call'd, attended by the nobles,
He stalk'd in sullen majesty along;
Nor deign'd a word. A godlike virtuous anger
Beam'd through his features, and sublimed his air.
With downcast eyes he walk'd; or, if aside
He chanced to look, each look was great reproach.
Thus in emphatic silence, that made words
Void and insipid all, he parted from them,
The day preceding my return from Rome;
Nor has been heard of since, lost in the abyss
Of his own woes.

Gal. O Marcius, noble Marcius!
How shall my friendship succour thy distress?
Where shall I find thee to partake thy sorrows,
And make myself companion of thy exile?
But, Titus, we indulge discourse too long—
Go, and assemble thou the Volscian chiefs,
Whilst I repair to Tullus, to inform,
And bring him to the council, there to hear
The fatal answer thou hast brought from Rome.

SCENE II.

Changes to TULLUS's *Tent.*

CORIOLANUS, TULLUS.

Cor. Forgive me, Tullus, if I count the moments
That stop the purpose of thy noble kindness,
And keep me here confined in tame inaction.
Why lingers Titus?

Tul. Calm thy restless heart,
Brave Marcius; every minute I expect him.
Soon from the cloud that hides thee, shalt thou break
With double brightness; soon thy fiery rage
Shall wither all the strength and pride of Rome.

Cor. O righteous Jove, protector of the injured!
If from my earliest youth, with pious awe,
I still have reverenced thy all-powerful justice,
Still by her sacred dictates ruled my actions;
O let that justice now support my cause,
And arm my strong right-hand with all her terrors!
When that is done, be life or death my lot,
As thy almighty pleasure shall determine.

[*Enter an* Officer *to* TULLUS.

Off. My lord, Galesus asks admittance to you.

Tul. Marcius, retire an instant, till I hear
The business brings him hither—Bid him enter.

[*Exeunt* Officer *and* CORIOLANUS.

[*Enter* GALESUS.

SCENE III.

TULLUS, GALESUS.

Gal. Tullus, the Roman senate has return'd
No other answer, to our late demands,
But absolute denial and defiance.

Tul. It is what I expected—We shall teach them
An humbler language soon—Hast thou assembled,
As I desired, the Volscian chiefs in council?

Gal. Titus is gone to summon their attendance.

Tul. It is enough; come forth, my noble guest!
And show Galesus how the gods assist us.

SCENE IV

CORIOLANUS, TULLUS, GALESUS.

Gal. Oh, my astonish'd soul! what do I see?
What! Caius Marcius! Caius Marcius here,
Beneath one tent with Tullus!

Tul. Ay, and more,
With Tullus, now his friend and fellow-soldier.
Yes, thou shalt see him thundering at the head
Of Volscian armies—he, who oft has carried
Destruction through their ranks—Your leave a moment,
While to our chiefs and fathers I announce
Their unexpected guest.

SCENE V.

CORIOLANUS, GALESUS.

Cor. Thou good old man!
Close let me strain thee to my faithful heart,
Which now is doubly thine, united more
By the protection which thy country gives me,
Than by our former friendship.

Gal. Strange event!
This is thy work, almighty Providence!
Whose power, beyond the stretch of human thought,
Revolves the orbs of empire; bids them sink
Deep in the deadening night of thy displeasure,
Or rise majestic o'er a wondering world.
The gods by thee—I see it, Coriolanus—
Mean to exalt us, and depress the Romans.

Cor. Galesus, yes, the gods have sent me hither;
Those righteous gods, who, when vindictive justice
Excites them to destroy a worthless people,
Make their own crimes and follies strike the blow.

Gal. Cherish these thoughts that teach us what we are,
And tame the pride of man. There is a power
Unseen that rules the illimitable world,
That guides its motions, from the brightest star,
To the least dust of this sin-tainted mold;
While man, who madly deems himself the lord
Of all, is nought but weakness and dependance.
This sacred truth, by sure experience taught,
Thou must have learnt, when, wandering all alone,
Each bird, each insect, flitting through the sky,
Was more sufficient for itself than thou——
Ah the full image of thy woes dissolves me!
The pangs that must have torn, at parting from thee,
Thy mother and thy wife. I cannot think
Of that sad scene, without some drops of pity!

Cor. Who was it forced me to that bitter parting?
Who, in one cruel, hasty moment, chased me
From wife, from children, friends, and household gods,
Me! who so often had protected theirs?
Who, from the sacred city of my fathers,
Drove me with nature's commoners to dwell,
To lodge beneath their wide unshelter'd roof,
And at their table feed? O blast me, gods!
With every woe! debility of mind,
Dishonour, just contempt, and palsied weakness,
If I forgive the villains! yes, Galesus,
Yes, I will offer to the powers of vengeance
A great, a glorious victim—a whole city!——
Why, Tullus, this delay?

Gal. May Coriolanus
Be to the Volscian nation, and himself,
The dread, the godlike instrument of justice!
But let not rage and vengeance mix their rancour;
Let them not trouble with their fretful storm,
Their angry gleams, that azure, where enthroned
The calm divinity of justice sits,
And pities, while she punishes, mankind.

Cor. What saidst thou? What, against the powers of vengeance?
The gods gave honest anger, just revenge,
To be the awful guardians of the rights
And native dignity of human kind.
O were it not for them, the saucy world
Would grow a noisome nest of little tyrants!
Each carrion crow, on eagle merit perch'd,
Would peck his eyes out, and the mongrel cur
At pleasure bait the lion—No, Galesus,
I would not rashly, nor on light occasion,
Receive the deep impression in my breast;
But when the base, the brutal and unjust,
Or worse than all, the ungrateful, stamp it there;
O I will then, with luxury supreme,
Enjoy the pleasure of offended gods,
A righteous, just revenge!—Behold my soul.

Enter an Officer.

Off. My lords, the assembled chiefs desire your presence.

Gal. Come, noble Marcius; let my joyful hand
Conduct thee thither—Doubt not thy reception
Will be proportion'd to thy fame and merit.

SCENE VI.

The back-scene opens, and discovers the Deputies of the Volscian States assembled in council. They rise and salute CORIOLANUS; *then resume their places.*

GALESUS, TULLUS, CORIOLANUS, Senators.

Gal. Assembled states, and captains of the Volsci,
Behold the chief so much renown'd in war;
Our once so formidable foe, but now
Our proffer'd friend and soldier—Caius Marcius.

1st Sen. We give him hearty welcome from our souls.

Cor. Most noble chiefs, and fathers of the Volsci,
I need not say, how by the people's rage,
And the poor weakness of the timid nobles,
I am expell'd from Rome. Had I confined
My wishes merely to a safe retreat,
Some Latine city might have given me that;
Or any nameless corner. What imports it,
Where a tame patient exile rots in silence!
But, Volscian lords, permit me to declare,
I would at once cut short my useless days,
Rather than be that despicable wretch,
Who neither can take vengeance on his foes,
Nor serve his friends. That is my temper, chiefs.
I shall be glad to merit, by my sword,
The asylum which I seek among the Volsci.
Rome is our common foe. Then let us join
Our common sufferings, passions, and resentments.
Yes, though but one, I bring so many wrongs,
So large a share of powerful enmity,
Into the war, as gives me the presumption,
To offer to the Volscian states the alliance
Even of my single arm.——

Tul. That single arm
Is in itself a numerous army, Marcius;
The Volscians so esteem it—But proceed.

Cor. I will not mention, Volscian chiefs, what talent
The world allows me to possess in war:
But be that what it will, you may employ it.
Soldier, or captain, in whatever station
You place me, I will lose each drop of blood,
Or with this hand I'll fix the Volscian standard
On the proud towers of Capitolian Jove.

Tul. Chiefs of the Volscian league, I give you joy
Of our new citizen, the noble Marcius.
The genius of the Volscian state has sent him,
Whetted by wrongs into a keener hatred
Than that we bear to Rome. It were contemning,
With impious self-sufficient arrogance,
This bounty of the gods, not to accept,
With every mark of honour, of his service.
I, Volscians, I, even Attius Tullus, give,
First of you all, my voice, that Caius Marcius
Be now received to high command among us;
That instantly we do appoint him general
Of half our troops, which here, with your consent,
I to him yield.—Speak, chiefs, is this your pleasure?

1st Sen. It is—We give unanimous consent.
Tul. (embracing him.) Marcius, I joy to call thee [my companion,
And colleague in this war.
Cor. By all the gods!
Thou art the generous victor of my soul!
Yes, Tullus, I am conquer'd by thy virtue.
Gal. Though I have oft, on great occasions, [Tullus,
Beheld thee in the senate, and the field,
Cover'd with glory; yet, I must avow,
I never saw thee show such genuine greatness,
Such true sublimity of soul, as now.
To scorn the all powerful charm of selfish passions,
Chiefly the dazzling pride of emulation,
That noble weakness of heroic minds,
To sink thyself that thou mayst raise thy country;
To put the sword into thy rival's hand,
And twine thy promised laurels round his brow—
O 'tis a flight beyond the highest point
Of martial glory! and what few can reach.
Go forth, ye chosen ministers of justice;
And may that awful Power, whose secret hand
Sways all our passions, turns our partial views
All to its own dread purposes, attend you!
Cor. I burn to enter on the glorious task
You now have mark'd me out. How slow the time
To the warm soul, that, in the very instant
It forms, would execute, a great design.
'Tis my advice we march direct to Rome;
We cannot be too quick. Let the first dawn
See us in bright array before her walls.
Perhaps when they behold their exile there,
Back'd by your force, some conscious hearts among [them
May feel the alarm of guilt.
Tul. I much approve
Of this advice. 'Tis what I thought before,
Ere strengthen'd, Marcius, by thy mighty arm:
But now 'tis doubly right. Here, Volscian chiefs,
Here let our council terminate—The troops
Have had repose sufficient. Straight to Rome—
Come, let us urge our march—As yet the stars
Ride in their middle watch; we shall with ease
Reach it by dawn——
Cor. Yes, we have time—too much!
Six tedious hours till morn—But hence! away!
My soul on fire anticipates the dawn.

ACT III.

SCENE I.

CORIOLANUS, TULLUS, VOLUSIUS, TITUS, *with a crowd of Volscian Officers. Acclamations behind the scenes.*

Cor. No more—I merit not this lavish praise.
True, we have driven the Roman legions back,
Defeated and disgraced—But what is this?
Nothing, ye Volsci, nothing yet is done.
We but begin the wondrous leaf of story,
That marks the Roman doom. At length it dawns,
The destined hour, that eases of their fears
The nations round, and sets Hesperia free.
Come on, my brave companions of the war!
Come, let us finish at one mighty stroke
This toil of labouring fate.—We will, or perish!
While, noble Tullus, you protect the camp,
I, with my troops, all men of chosen valour,
And well approved to-day, will storm the city.
Tit. Beneath thy animating conduct, Marcius,
What can the Volscian valour not perform?
Thy very sight and voice subdues the Romans.
When, lifting up your helm, you show'd your face,
That like a comet glared destruction on them,
I saw their bravest veterans fly before thee.
Their ancient spirit has with thee forsook them,
And ruin hangs o'er yon devoted walls.

Enter an Officer, *who addresses himself to* CORIOLANUS.

Off. My lord, a herald is arrived from Rome,
To say, a deputation from the senate,
Attended by the ministers of Heaven,
A venerable train of priests and flamens,
Is on the way, address'd to you.
Cor. To me!
What can this message mean! Stand to your arms,
Ye Volscian troops; and let these Romans pass
Betwixt the lowering frown of double files.
What! do they think me such a milky boy,
To pay my vengeance with a few soft words?
Come, fellow soldiers, Tullus, come, and see,
If I betray the honours you have done me.
[*Goes out with a train of Volscian Officers.*

SCENE II.

TULLUS, VOLUSIUS, *who remain.*

Vol. (after some silence.) Are we not, Tullus, failing in our duty
Not to attend our general?
Tul. How! what saidst thou?
Vol. Methought, my lord, his parting orders were,
We should attend the triumph now preparing
O'er all his foes at once—Romans and Volsci!
Come, we shall give offence.
Tul. Of this no more.
I pray thee spare thy bitter irony.
Vol. Shall I then speak without disguise?
Tul. Speak out
With all the honest bluntness of a friend.
Think'st thou I fear the truth?
Vol. Then, Tullus, know,
Thou art no more the general of the Volsci.
Thou hast, by this thy generous weakness, sunk
Thyself into a private man of Antium.
Yes, thou hast taken from thy laurel'd brow
The well-earn'd trophies of thy toils and perils,
Thy springing hopes, the fairest ever budded,
And heap'd them on a man too proud before.
Tul. He bears it high.
Vol. Death and perdition! high!
With uncontrol'd command!—You see, already,
He will not be incumber'd with the fetters
Of our advice. He speaks his sovereign will;
On every hand he issues out his orders,
As to his natural slaves.—For you, my lord,
He has, I think, confined you to your camp,
There in inglorious indolence to languish;
While he, beneath your blasted eyes, shall reap
The harvest of your honour.
Tul. No, Volusius,
Whatever honour shall by him be gain'd
Reverts to me, from whose superior bounty
He drew the means of all his glorious deeds.

This mighty chief, this conqueror of Rome,
Is but my creature.——

Vol. Wretched self-delusion!
He and the Volscians know he is thy master.
He acts as such in all things.—Now, by Mars,
Could my abhorrent soul endure the thought
Of stooping to a Roman chief, I here
Would leave thee in thy solitary camp,
And go where glory calls.

Tul. Indeed, Volusius,
I did expect more equal treatment from him.
But what of that?—The generous pride of virtue
Disdains to weigh too nicely the returns
Her bounty meets with—Like the liberal gods,
From her own gracious nature she bestows,
Nor stoops to ask reward—Yet must I own,
I thought he would not have so soon forgot
What he so lately was, and what I am.

Vol. Gods! knew ye not his character before?
Did you not know his genius was to yours
Averse, as are antipathies in nature?
High, over-weening, tyrannously proud,
And only fit to hold command o'er slaves?
Hence, as repugnant to that equal life,
Which is the quickening soul of all republics,
The Roman people cast him forth; and we,
Shall we receive the bane of their repose,
Into our breast? Are we less free than they?
Or shall we be more patient of a tyrant?

Tul. All this I knew. But while his imperfections
Are thy glad theme, thou hast forgot his virtues.

Vol. I leave that subject to the smooth Galesus,
And these his Volscian flatterers—His virtues!
Trust me there is no insolence that treads
So high as that which rears itself on virtue.

Tul. Well, be it so—I meant, that even his vices
Should, on this great occasion, serve the Volsci.

Vol. Confusion! there it is! there lurks the sting
Of our dishonour! While this Marcius leads
The Roman armies, ours are driven before him.
Behold, he changes sides; when with him changes
The fortune of the war. Straight they grow Volsci,
And we victorious Romans—Such no doubt,
Such is his secret boast—Ay, this vile brand
Success itself will fix for ever on us;
And, Tullus, thou, 'tis thou must answer for it.

Tul. (*aside.*) His words are daggers to my heart; I feel
Their truth, but am ashamed to own my folly.

Vol. O shame! O infamy! the thought consumes me,
It scalds my eyes with tears, to see a Roman
Borne on our shoulders to immortal fame:
Just in the happy moment that decided
The long dispute of ages, that for which
Our generous ancestors had toil'd and bled,
To see him then step in and steal our glory!
O that we first had perish'd all! A people,
Who cannot find in their own proper force
Their own protection, are not worth the saving!

Tul. It must have way! I will no more suppress it—
Know then, my rough old friend, no less than thee
His conduct hurts me and upbraids my folly.
I wake as from a dream. What demon moved me?
What doting generosity? his woes,
Was it his woes? To see the brave reduced
To trust his mortal foe? perhaps, a little
That work'd within my bosom—But, Volusius,
That was not all—I will to thee confess
The weakness of my heart—Yes, it was pride,
The dazzling pride to see my rival-warrior,
The great Coriolanus, bend his soul,
His haughty soul, to sue for my protection.
Protection, said I? were it that alone,
I had been base to have refused him that,
To have refused him aught a gallant foe
Owes to a gallant foe.—But to exalt him
To the same level, nay, above myself;
To yield him the command of half my troops,
The choicest acting half—That, that was madness!
Was weak, was mean, unworthy of a man!——

Vol. I scorn to flatter thee—It was indeed.

Tul. Curse on the slave Galesus! soothing, he
Seized the fond moment of infatuation,
And clinch'd the chains my generous folly forged.
How shall I from this labyrinth escape?
Must it then be! what cruel genius dooms me,
In war or peace, to creep beneath his fortune?

Vol. That genius is thyself. If thou canst bear
The very thought of stooping to this Roman,
Thou from that moment art his vassal, Tullus;
By that thou dost acknowledge parent nature
Has form'd him thy superior. But if fix'd
Upon the base of manly resolution,
Thou say'st—I will be free! I will command!
I and my country! then—O never doubt it—
We shall find means to crush this vain intruder!
Even I myself—this hand——
Nay, hear me, Tullus,
'Tis not yet come to that, that last resource.
I do not say we should employ the dagger,
While other, better means are in our power.

Tul. No, my Volusius, fortune will not drive us,
Or I am much deceived, to that extreme:
We shall not want the strongest fairest plea,
To give a solemn sanction to his fate.
He will betray himself. Whate'er his rage
Of passion talks, a weakness for his country
Sticks in his soul, and he is still a Roman.
Soon shall we see him tempted to the brink
Of this sure precipice—Then down, at once,
Without remorse, we hurl him to perdition!
But hark! the trumpet calls us to a scene
I should detest, if not from hope we thence
May gather matter to mature our purpose.

SCENE III.

The back-scene opens, and discovers CORIOLANUS *sitting on his tribunal, attended by his* Lictors, *and a crowd of* Volscian Officers. *Files of troops drawn up on either hand. In the depth of the scene appear the Deputies from the Roman Senate,* M. MINUCIUS, POSTHUMUS COMINIUS, SP. LARTIUS, P. PINNARIUS, *and* Q. SULPITIUS, *all* Consular Senators, *who had been his most zealous friends. And behind them march the* Priests, *the* Sacrificers, *the* Augurs, *and the* Guardians *of the sacred things, dressed in their ceremonial habits. These advance slowly betwixt the files of* Soldiers, *under arms. As* TULLUS *enters,* CORIOLANUS, *rising, salutes him.*

Cor. Here, noble Tullus, sit and judge my conduct;
Nor spare to check me, if I act amiss.

Tul. Marcius, the Volscian fate is in thy hands.

[CORIOLANUS *is seated again, and* TULLUS *places himself upon a tribunal on his left hand. Meantime the Roman Deputies advance up to* CORIOLANUS *and salute him, which he returns.*

Cor. What, Romans, from the generals of the [Volsci
Is your demand?

Min. O Coriolanus, Rome,
Nurse of thy tender years, thy parent-city,
Her senators, her people, priests, and augurs,
Her every order and degree, by us,
Thy ever-zealous, still unshaken friends,
Sue in the most pathetic terms for peace.
And if in this constrain'd, we from our maxim,
Never to ask but give it, must depart;
It is some consolation, in the state
To which thou hast by thy superior valour
Reduced us, that we ask it from a Roman.

Cor. I was a Roman once, and thought the name
Was not dishonour'd by me; but it pleased
Your lords, the mob of Rome, to take it from me;
Nor will I now receive it back again.

Min. The name thou mayst reject, but canst not throw
The duties from thee which that name imports;
Indissoluble duties, bound upon thee
By the strong hand of nature, and confirm'd
By the dread sanction of all-ruling Jove.
Then hear thy country's supplicating voice;
By all those duties I conjure thee hear us.

Cor. Well—I will hear thee; speak, declare thy message.

Min. Give peace, give healing peace, to two brave nations,
Fatigued with war, and sick of cruel deeds!
To carry on destruction's easy trade,
Afflict mankind, and scourge the world with war,
Is what each wicked, each ambitious man,
Who lets his furious passions loose, may do:
But in the flattering torrent of success,
To check his rage, and drop the avenging sword,
When a repenting people ask it of him,
That is the genuine bounty of a god.
Then urge no farther this your just resentment;
Which, injured as you are, you needs must feel,
But never ought to carry into action,
Against your sacred country; whence you drew
Your life, your virtues, every mortal good,
That very valour you employ against her.
Stop, Coriolanus, ere, beyond retreat,
You plunge yourself in crimes. To the fierce joy
Of vengeance push'd to barbarous excess,
Repentance will succeed, and sickening horror.
Consider too the slippery state of fortune.
The gods take pleasure oft, when haughty mortals
On their own pride erect a mighty fabric,
By slightest means, to lay their towering schemes
Low in the dust, and teach them they are nothing.
Return, thou virtuous Roman! to the bosom
Of thy imploring country. Lo! her arms
She fondly spreads to take thee back again,
And by redoubled love efface her harshness.
Return, and crown thee with the noblest wreath
Which glory can bestow—the palm of mercy!

Cor. Marcus Minucius, and ye other Romans,
Respected senators, and holy flamens,
Attend, and take to your demand this answer:
Why court you me, the servant of the Volsci?
It is to them that you must bend for peace,
Which on these only terms they will accord you.
"Restore the conquer'd lands, your former wars
Have ravish'd from them: from their towns and cities,
Won by your arms, withdraw your colonies;
And to the full immunities of Rome
Frankly admit them, as you have the Latines."
Then Romans, ye have peace, and not till then!
If these are terms which suit not your ambition,
They suit the state to which the Volscian arms
Have now reduced you—We have learn'd from Rome
To use our fortune, and command the vanquish'd.

Tul. (*aside.*) Death to my hopes! I'm now his slave for ever.

Cor. (*addressing himself to the Volsci.*) This, my illustrious patrons and protectors,
Volsci, to you I owed. Permit me now
To do myself and injured honour justice.
[*Turning again to the Romans.*
As to the liberty you idly vaunt
To give me of returning to your city,
'Tis what I hold unworthy of acceptance.
Can I return into the ungrateful bosom
Of a distracted state, where to the rage
Of a vile senseless populace, the laws
Are by your shameful weakness given a prey?
Who are the men that hold the sway among you?
And whom have you expell'd as even unworthy
To live within the cincture of your walls!—
O the wild thought breaks in and troubles reason!—
With what, ye Romans, can the sourest censor,
The most envenom'd malice, justly charge me?
Did I e'er break your laws? Nay, did I e'er
Do aught that could disturb the sacred order,
The peace and social harmony of life;
Or taint your ancient sanctity of manners?
What was my crime? I could not bear to see
Your dignity debased, to see the rabble
Tread on the reverend grey authority
Of senatorial wisdom: Yes, for you,
In your defence I did enrage this monster;
And yet you basely left me to its fury.
Then talk no more of services and friendship:
A friend, who can, and does not shield, betrays me.
Or if the power was wanting, then your senate
Is sunk into servility and bondage,
Nor should a freeman deign to sit among you.

Min. The wisest are sometimes compell'd to yield
To popular storms: yet I defend not, Marcius,
Our timid conduct; we have felt our error,
And now invite thee back to aid the senate,
With thy heroic spirit to restrain
The giddy rage of faction, and to hold
The reins of government more firm hereafter.
As to the appeal which thou hast nobly made
In vindication of thy spotless fame,
With pleasure we confirm it, and bear witness
To all thy public and thy private virtues:
But let us also beg thee not to stain
The brightness of that glory by a crime,
Which, unrepented, would disgrace them all;
A dire rebellious war against thy country.

Cor. Absurd! what can you mean? To call a people,
Who with the last indignity have used me,
To call my foes my country! No, Minucius,
It is the generous nation of the Volsci;
These brave, these virtuous men, you see around me,
Who, when I wander'd a poor helpless exile,
Took pity of my injuries and woes;
Forgot the former mischiefs of my sword;
Heap'd on me kindness, honours, dignities;
Fear'd not to trust me with this high command,
And placed me here the guardian of their cause:—

Be witness, Jove !—It is alone their nation
I henceforth will acknowledge for my country !
Let this suffice—You have my answer, Romans.

Com. This answer, Coriolanus, is the dictate
More of thy pride than magnanimity:
'Tis thy revenge that gives it, not thy virtue.
Art thou above the gods ? who joy to shower
Their double goodness on repenting mortals ?
But think not I intend by this to urge
Our proffer'd peace, so harshly treated, further;
That were a weakness ill becoming Romans.
Yet I must tell thee, it would better suit
A fierce despotic chief of barbarous slaves,
Than the calm dignity of one who sits
In the grave senate of a free republic,
To talk so high, and as it were to thrust
Plebeians from the native rights of man.——

Cor. Ha ! dost thou come the people's advocate
To me, Cominius ! comest thou to insult me !

Com. Nay, hear me, Marcius : — These grey hairs empower me
To set thee right before this great assembly :
And there was once a time, thou wouldst have heard
Thy general with more deference and patience—
I tell thee then, whoe'er amidst the sons
Of reason, valour, liberty, and virtue,
Displays distinguish'd merit, is a noble
Of nature's own creating. Such have risen,
Sprung from the dust ; or where had been our honours ?
And such in radiant bands will rise again,
In yon immortal city, that, when most
Depress'd by fate, and near apparent ruin,
Returns, as with an energy divine,
On her astonish'd foes, and shakes them from her—
Your pardon, Volsci—But this, Coriolanus,
Is what I had to say.

Cor. And I have heard it—

[*Rising from his tribunal ; and the* Priests *advancing to address him, he prevents them.*

For you, ye awful ministers of Heaven,
Let me not hear your holy lips profaned
By urging what my duty must refuse.
I bow in adoration to the gods ;
I venerate their servants. But there is,
There is a power, their chief, their darling care,
The guardian of mankind, which to betray
Were violating all—And that is justice.
So far my public character demands ;
So far my honour.—Now, what should forbid
The man, and friend, to be indulged a little ?
Permit me to embrace thee, good Minucius,
Thee, Lartius ; you, Pinnarius and Sulpitius :
But chiefly thee, Cominius, who first raised me
To deeds of arms : who from thy consular brow
Took thy own crown, and with it circled mine.
Though nought can shake my purpose, yet I wish
That Rome had sent me others on this errand.
I thank you for your friendship. The protection,
Which you have given to those, whom once I call'd
By tender names, I would not now remember.
How shall I—say—return your generous goodness?
Oh, there is nothing you, as friends, can ask,
My grateful heart will not with pleasure grant you.

Com. We thank thee, Coriolanus—But a Roman
Disdains that favour you refuse his country.

Cor. [*To the* Volscian Officers.
See that they be, with due regard and safety,
Conducted back. [*To the* Roman Senators
I will suspend the assault,
Till to these terms, of which we will not bate
The smallest part, your senate may have time
To send their latest answer. Then we cut
All further treaty off. Romans, farewell.

ACT IV.

SCENE I.

Tul. (*alone.*) WHAT is the mind of man ? A restless scene
Of vanity and weakness ; shifting still,
As shift the lights of our uncertain knowledge ;
Or as the various gale of passion breathes.
None ever thought himself more deeply founded
On what is right, nor felt a nobler ardour,
Than I, when I invested Caius Marcius
With this ill-judged command. Now it appears
Distraction, folly, monstrous folly ! meanness !
And down I plunge, betray'd even by my virtue,
From gulf to gulf, from shame to deeper shame.

SCENE II.

TULLUS, GALESUS.

Gal. I listen'd, Tullus, to the important scene
That lately pass'd before us, with most strict
Unprejudiced attention ; and have since
Revolved it in my mind, both as a man,
Allied to all mankind, and as a Volscian.
Indeed our terms are high, and by the manner
In which they were prescribed by Coriolanus,
Are what we cannot hope will e'er be granted.
They should be soften'd. Let us yield a little,
Conscious ourselves to a great nation's pride,
The pride of human nature. Could the Romans
Stoop to such peace, commanded by the sword,
They then were slaves, unworthy our alliance.

Tul. Gods ! do I hear in thee, one of the chiefs
Intrusted with the honour of the Volsci,
An advocate for Rome ?

Gal. I glory, Tullus,
To own myself an advocate for peace.
Peace is the happy natural state of man ;
War his corruption, his disgrace—

Tul. His safeguard !
His pride ! his glory !—What but war, just war,
Gave Greece her heroes? Those who drew the sword
(As we do now) against the sons of rapine ;
To quell proud tyrants, and to free mankind.

Gal. Yes, Tullus, when to just defence the warrior
Confines his force, he is a worship'd name,
Dear to mankind, the first and best of mortals !
Yet still if this can by soft means be done,
And fair accommodation, that is better.
Why should we purchase with the blood of thousands
What may be gain'd by mutual just concession ?
Why give up peace, the best of human blessings,
For the vain cruel pride of useless conquest ?

Tul. These soothing dreams of philosophic quiet
Are only fit for unfrequented shades.
The sage should quit the busy bustling world,
Ill suited to his gentle meditations,
And in some desart find that peace he loves.

Gal. Mistaken man! Philosophy consists not
In airy schemes, or idle speculations:
The rule and conduct of all social life
Is her great province. Not in lonely cells
Obscure she lurks, but holds her heavenly light
To senates and to kings to guide their councils,
And teach them to reform and bless mankind.
All policy but hers is false and rotten;
All valour not conducted by her precepts
Is a destroying fury sent from hell
To plague unhappy man, and ruin nations.

Tul. To stop the waste of that destroying fury
Is the great cause and purpose of this war.
Art thou a friend to peace?—subdue the Romans.
Who, who, but they have turn'd this ancient land,
Where, from Saturnian times, harmonious concord
Still loved to dwell, into a scene of blood,
Of endless discord, and perpetual rapine?
The sword, the vengeful sword, must drain away
This boiling blood, that thus disturbs the nations!
Talk not of terms. It is a vain attempt
To bind the ambitious and unjust by treaties:
These they elude a thousand specious ways;
Or if they cannot find a fair pretext,
They blush not in the face of Heaven to break them.

Gal. Why then affronted Heaven will combat [for us.
Set justice on our side, and then my voice
Shall be as loud for war as thine; my sword
Shall strike as deep, at least my blood shall flow
As freely, Tullus, in my country's cause.
But as I then would die to serve the Volscians,
So now I dare to serve them by opposing,
Even with my single voice, the impetuous torrent
That hurries us away beyond the bounds
Of temperate wisdom; and presume to tell thee,
It is thy passion, not thy prudence, dictates
This haughty language.

Tul. Yes, it is my passion,
A passion for the glory of my country,
That scorns your narrow views of timid prudence.
Our injured honour drew our swords, and never
Shall they be sheath'd while I command the [Volscians,
Till Rome submits to Antium.

Gal. Rome will perish
Ere she submit; and she has still her walls,
The strength of her allies, her native valour,
Which oft hath saved her in the worst extremes,
And, stronger yet than all, despair, to aid her.

Tul. All these will nought avail her, if our fears
Come not to her assistance—But, Galesus,
Why urge you this to me? Go, talk to Marcius.
The war has given him all his pride could hope for,
To see Rome's senate humbled at his feet:
He now may wish to reign in peace at Antium,
And thou, perhaps, art come an envoy from him,
To learn if I shall prove a quiet subject.

Gal. Through this unguarded opening of thy soul,
I see what stings thee—Ah! beware of envy!
If that pale fury seize thee, thou art lost!
Tullus, 'tis easier far, from the clear breast,
To keep out treacherous vice, than to expel it.
Farewell. Remember I have done my duty. [*Goes out.*

Tul. (*alone.*) This man discerns my heart—
Well: What of that?
Am I afraid its movements should be seen?
I, whose clear thoughts have never shunn'd the light,
Must I now seek to hide them? O misfortune!
To have reduced myself to such a state,
So much beneath the greatness of my soul,
That, like a coward, I must learn to practise
The wretched arts of vile dissimulation!
By Heaven, I will not do it—I will not stoop
To veil my discontent a moment longer.
But see! my rival comes, the happy Marcius.
His haughty mien, his very looks, affront me.

SCENE III.

CORIOLANUS, TULLUS.

Cor. Tullus, I have received intelligence,
That a strong body of the Latine troops
Is in full march to raise the siege of Rome:
Another day will bring them to its aid.
But go thou forth, and lead the valiant bands,
By thee commanded, to repel these succours
Go, and cut off from Rome its last resource.

Tul. I lead my troops from the great scene of action,
From falling Rome, which ere to-morrow's sun
Shall set, may be our prey! sure you forget
My rank and station—I disdain the service:
Give it to some you may command. For me,
I own no master but the Volscian states.
Rome is my object. I from Antium brought
The noblest army ever shook her walls.
And shall I now, on that decisive day,
Doom'd by the gods to lay her pride in ashes,
Shall I be absent from the glorious work?
It is the highest outrage even to think it.—
Just gods! dost thou presume to give thy orders
To me? to me! thy equal in command?
Nay, thy superior? was it not my hand,
My lavish hand, bestow'd thy power upon thee?
And know, proud Roman, that the man who gave it
Can at his will resume it.

Cor. I proposed
This expedition to thee as thy friend,
Not as thy general, Tullus. We are both
Commanders here; and for my share of power,
Whene'er the council of the Volscian states,
Who clothed me with it, shall again demand it,
I at their feet will lay it down, persuaded,
The canker'd tongue of envy's self must own,
That by my service I have well deserved it.

Tul. Was it to them, or me, you hither came
To crave protection? Was not then your fortune,
Your liberty, your life, at my disposal?
I raised you from the dust, a wretched exile,
An outcast, helpless, friendless, driven to beg,
The lowest refuge which despair can seek,
Shelter amidst thy foes. My pitying goodness
Protected, trusted, and believed you grateful.
Oh, ill-placed confidence!

Cor. Immortal gods!
Hear I these words from Tullus!

Tul. What for all this
Is thy return? Pride; self-sufficiency;
Councils apart from mine; despotic orders;
The glory of the war all pilfer'd from me:
And, to complete the whole, a Latine army
Now conjured up to draw me from the siege;
Till by cajoling our tame chiefs, and dazzling

The senseless eyes of the low mob of soldiers,
Thou shalt be solely seated in the power
Which, thank my folly! now is shared betwixt us.
Cor. Oh indignation! — Down, thou swelling heart—
I will be calm—I will.—Thou dost accuse me
Of the worst vice that can debase mankind,
Of black ingratitude. On what foundations?
What have I done to merit such a charge?
Is it my fault, if in the Volscian army
My name is as revered and great as thine?
Can I forbid authority, and fame,
To follow merit and success?—You knew
The man whom you employ'd, and should have known
He would not be a cipher in employment.
Tul. Think'st thou my heart can better brook than thine
To be that cipher; that dishonour'd tool!
Subservient to the ambition of another?
Gods! I had rather live a drudging peasant
Unknown to glory, in some Alpine village,
Than at the head of these victorious legions
Bear the high name of chief, without the power.
No, Marcius, no. I will command indeed:
And thou shalt learn, with all the Volscian army,
To treat their general with respect.
Cor. Respect!
O Tullus! Tullus! by the powers divine!
I bore thee once respect, as high as man
Can show to man. From thee, my foe, my rival,
I nor disdain'd nor fear'd to ask protection.
You gave me all I ask'd, you gave me more,
With noble warmth of heart! which to esteem,
Added the ties of gratitude and friendship.
Whatever since, in council or in arms,
Has been by me achieved, was done for thee.
My glory all was thine. The palms I gain'd
Only composed a garland for his brow,
Who raised this banish'd man to tread on Rome.
Tul. To tread on him who raised him—That, I know,
Is thy ambitious purpose: but be certain,
However Rome may bend beneath thy fortune,
Thou shalt not find an easy conquest here.
Cor. May Jove with lightning strike me to the centre,
If from the day I saw thy face at Antium,
My heart has ever form'd one secret thought
To hurt thy honour, or depress thy greatness:
I was thy friend, thy soldier, and thy servant.
But now I will as openly avow,
Thy jealousy has, with envenom'd breath,
Made such a sudden ravage in our friendship,
I know not what to think——
Tul. Think me thy foe.
There is no lasting friendship with the proud.
Cor. Nor with the jealous——But of this enough.
Come let us turn our fire a nobler way:
We have a worthier quarrel to pursue.——
It were unjust, dishonourable, base,
Our pride should hurt the Volscian cause.
Tul. No, Marcius,
I mean to guard it better for the future:
The Volscian cause is safest with a Volscian.
I therefore claim, insist upon my right;
That you shall yield me my command in turn.
The first attack was yours: 'tis scanty justice,
The second should be mine.
Cor. Tullus, 'tis yours.
Oh it imports not which of us command!
Give me the lowest rank among your troops:
All Italy will know, the voice of fame
Will tell all future times, that I was present;
That Coriolanus in the Volscian army
Assisted, when imperial Rome was sack'd;
That city which, while he maintain'd her cause,
Invincible herself, made Antium tremble.
Tul. What arrogant presumption!

SCENE IV.

To them Volusius *entering hastily.*

Tul. Ha! Volusius,
Thy looks declare some message of importance.
Vol. Tullus, they do—I was to find thee, Marcius
To thee a second deputation comes,
Thy mother, and thy wife, with a long train
Of all the noblest ladies Rome can boast,
In mourning habits clad, approach our camp,
Preceded by a herald, to demand
Another audience of thee.
Cor. How, Volusius!
Said you, the Roman ladies? Low, indeed,
Must be the state of Rome, when thus her matrons
She sends amidst the tumults of a camp,
To beg protection for the men, who lie
Trembling behind their ramparts—come! once more!
And see me put an end to prayers and treaty!

SCENE V.

Tullus, Volusius.

Vol. Tullus, 'tis well. This answers to my wishes.
Tul. How? What is well? That humbled Rome once more
Shall deck him with the trophies of our arms?
Vol. And hopest thou nothing from this blest event?
They who have often blasted mighty heroes,
Who oft have stolen into the firmest hearts,
And melted them to folly; they, my friend,
Will do what wisdom never could effect.
Tul. Think'st thou the prayers and tears of wailing women
Can shake the man, who with such cold disdain
Stood firm against those venerable consuls,
And spurn'd the genius of his kneeling country?
Vol. It was his pride alone that made him ours.
That passion kept him firm; the flattering charm
Of humbling those, who in their persons bore
The whole collected majesty of Rome.
These women are no proper objects for it:
He cannot triumph o'er his wife and mother.
On this my hopes are founded, that these women
May by their gentler influence subdue him.
Tul. Whate'er the event, he shall no longer here,
As wave his passions, dictate peace or war.
Whether his stubborn soul maintains its firmness,
Or yields to female prayers, the Volscian honour
Will be alike betray'd. If Rome prevails,
He stops our conquering arms from her destruction;
If he rejects her suit, he reigns our tyrant.
But, by the immortal gods! his short-lived empire
Shall never see yon radiant sun descend.
Vol. Blest be those gods that have at last inspired thee

With resolution equal to thy cause,
The cause of liberty!
Tul. Be sure, Volusius,
If that should happen which thy hopes portend;
Should he, by nature tamed, disarm'd by love,
Respite the Roman doom—he seals his own:
By Heaven! he dies.
Vol. Let me embrace thee, Tullus!
Now breaking from the cloud, which, like the sun,
Thy own too bounteous beams had drawn around thee.
Tul. You was deceived, my friend, when I with tameness,
With tameness which astonish'd thy brave spirit,
Seem'd to submit to that unequal sway
He arrogated o'er me; know, my heart
Ne'er swell'd so high as in that cruel moment.
My indignation, like the imprison'd fire
Pent in the troubled breast of glowing Ætna,
Burnt deep and silent: but, collected now,
It shall beneath its fury bury Marcius!
'Tis fix'd. Our tyrant dies.
Vol. Tullus, my sword
Here claims to be employ'd. Nor mine alone—
There are some worthy Volsci still remaining,
Who think with us, and pine beneath the laurels
A Roman chief bestows.
Tul. Go find them straight,
And bring them to the space before his tent;
'Tis there he will receive this deputation.
Then if he sinks beneath these women's prayers—
Or if he does not—But, Volusius, wait,
I give thee strictest charge to wait my signal.
Perhaps I may find means to free the Volsci
Without his blood. If not—we will be free.

ACT V.

SCENE I.

Trumpets sounding.

The scene discovers the camp, a crowd of Volscian Officers *with files of* Soldiers *drawn up as before. Enter* CORIOLANUS, TULLUS, GALESUS, VOLUSIUS. *The* Roman Ladies *advance slowly from the depth of the stage, with* VETURIA *the mother of* CORIOLANUS, *and* VOLUMNIA *his wife, at their head, all clad in habits of mourning;* CORIOLANUS *stands at the head of the* Volsci, *surrounded by his* Lictors; *but when he perceives his mother and wife, after some struggle, he advances, and goes hastily to embrace them.*

Cor. (*advancing.*) LOWER your fasces, lictors—
Oh Veturia!
Thou best of parents!
Vet. Coriolanus, stop.
Whom am I to embrace? A son, or foe?
Say, in what light am I regarded here?
Thy mother, or thy captive?
Cor. Justly, madam,
You check my fondness, that by nature hurried,
Forgot I was the general of the Volsci,
And you a deputy from hostile Rome.
[*He goes back to his former station.*
I hear you with respect. Speak your commission.
Vet. Think not I come a deputy from Rome:
Rome once rejected, scorns a second suit.
You have already heard whate'er the tongue
Of eloquence can plead, whate'er the wisdom
Of sacred age, the dignity of senates,
And virtue can enforce. Behold me here,
Sent by the shades of your immortal fathers,
Sent by the genius of the Marcian line,
Commission'd by my own maternal heart,
To try the soft, yet stronger powers of nature.
Thus authorised, I ask, nay claim a peace,
On equal, fair, and honourable terms,
To thee, to Rome, and to the Volscian people.
Grant it, my son, Thy mother begs it of thee!
Thy wife, the best, the kindest of her sex,
And these illustrious matrons, who have soothed
The gloomy hours thou hast been absent from us.
We, by whate'er is great and good in nature,
By every duty, by the gods, conjure thee!
To grant us peace, and turn on other foes
Thy arms, where thou mayst purchase virtuous [glory.
Cor. I should, Veturia, break those holy bonds
That hold the wide republic of mankind,
Society, together; I should grow,
A wretch, unworthy to be call'd thy son;
I should, with my Volumnia's fair esteem,
Forfeit her love; these matrons would despise me—
Could I betray the Volscian cause, thus trusted,
Thus recommended to me. No, my mother,
You cannot sure, you cannot ask it of me!
Vet. And does my son so little know me? me,
Who took such care to form his tender years,
Left to my conduct by his dying father?
Have I so ill deserved that trust? alas!
Am I so low in thy esteem, that thou
Should e'er imagine I could urge a part
Which in the least might stain the Marcian honour
No, let me perish rather! perish all!
Life has no charms compared with spotless glory!
I only ask, thou wouldst forbid thy troops
To waste our lands, and to assault yon city,
Till time be given for mild and righteous measures.
Grant us but one year's truce: meanwhile thou mayst,
With honour and advantage to both nations,
Between us mediate a perpetual peace.
Cor. Alas! my mother! that were granting all.
Vet. Canst thou refuse me such a just petition,
The first request thy mother ever made thee
Canst thou to her intreaties, prayers, and tears,
Prefer a savage, obstinate revenge?
Have love and nature lost all power within thee?
Cor. No,—in my heart they reign as strong as ever.
Come, I conjure you, quit ungrateful Rome,
Come, and complete my happiness at Antium,
You, and my dear Volumnia—There, Veturia,
There shall you see with what respect the Volsci
Will treat the wife and mother of their general.
Vet. Treat me thyself with more respect, my son;
Nor dare to shock my ears with such proposals.
Shall I desert my country, I who come
To plead her cause? Ah no! A grave in Rome
Would better please me, than a throne at Antium.
How hast thou thus forsaken all my precepts!
How hast thou thus forgot thy love to Rome!
Oh, Coriolanus, when with hostile arms,

With fire and sword, you enter'd on our borders,
Did not the fostering air, that breathes around us,
Allay thy guilty fury, and instil
A certain native sweetness through thy soul?
Did not your heart thus murmur to itself:
"These walls contain whatever can command
Respect from virtue, or is dear to nature,
The monuments of piety and valour,
The sculptured forms, the trophies of my fathers,
My household gods, my mother, wife, and children!"
Cor. Ah! you seduce me with too tender views!
These walls contain the most corrupt of men,
A base seditious herd; who trample order,
Distinction, justice, laws beneath their feet,
Insolent foes to worth, the foes of virtue!
Vet. Thou hast not thence a right to lift thy hand
Against the whole community, which forms
Thy ever-sacred country—That consists
Not of coeval citizens alone:
It knows no bounds: it has a retrospect
To ages past; it looks on those to come,
And grasps of all the general worth and virtue.
Suppose, my son, that I to thee had been
A harsh obdurate parent, even unjust:
How would the monstrous thought with horror strike thee,
Of plunging, from revenge, thy raging steel
Into her breast who nurst thy infant years!
Cor. Rome is no more! that Rome which nursed my youth:
That Rome, conducted by Patrician virtue,
She is no more! My sword shall now chastise
These sons of pride and dirt! Her upstart tyrants!
Who have debased the noblest state on earth
Into a sordid democratic faction.
Why will my mother join her cause to theirs?
Vet. Forbid it, Jove! that I should e'er distinguish
My interest from the general cause of Rome;
Or live to see a foreign hostile arm
Reform the abuses of our land of freedom.
[*Pausing.*
But 'tis in vain, I find, to reason more.
Is there no way to reach thy filial heart,
Once famed as much for piety as courage?
Oft hast thou justly triumph'd, Coriolanus;
Now yield one triumph to thy widow'd mother;
And send me back amidst the loud acclaims,
The grateful transports of deliver'd Rome,
The happiest far, the most renown'd of women!
Cor. Why, why, Veturia, wilt thou plead in vain?
Tul. (*aside to* Vol.) See, see, Volusius, how the strong emotions
Of powerful nature shake his inmost soul!
See how they tear him.—If he long resists them,
He is a god, or something worse than man.
Vet. O Marcius, Marcius! canst thou treat me thus?
Canst thou complain of Rome's ingratitude,
Yet be to me so cruelly ungrateful?
To me! who anxious rear'd thy youth to glory?
Whose only joy, these many years, has been
To boast that Coriolanus was my son?
And dost thou then renounce me for thy mother?
Spurn me before these chiefs, before those soldiers,
That weep thy stubborn cruelty? Art thou
The hardest man to me in this assembly?
Look at me! Speak!
[*Pausing, during which he appears in great agitation.*
Still dost thou turn away?
Inexorable? silent?—Then, behold me,
Behold thy mother, at whose feet thou oft
Hast kneel'd with fondness, kneeling now at thine,
Wetting thy stern tribunal with her tears.
[*Raises her*
Cor. Veturia, rise. I cannot see thee thus.
It is a sight uncomely, to behold
My mother at my feet, and that to urge
A suit, relentless honour must refuse.
Vol. (*advancing.*) Since, Coriolanus, thou dost still retain,
In spite of all thy mother now has pleaded,
Thy dreadful purpose, ah! how much in vain
Were it for me to join my supplications!
The voice of thy Volumnia, once so pleasing,
How shall it hope to touch the husband's heart,
When proof against the tears of such a parent?
I dare not urge what to thy mother thou
So firmly hast denied——But I must weep
Must weep, if not thy harsh severity,
At least thy situation. O permit me
[*Taking his hand.*
To shed my gushing tears upon thy hand!
To press it with the cordial lips of love!
And take my last farewell!
Cor. Yet, yet, my soul!
Be firm, and persevere—
Vol. Ah Coriolanus!
Is then this hand, this hand to be devoted,
The pledge of nuptial love, that has so long
Protected, bless'd and shelter'd us with kindness,
Now lifted up against us? Yet I love it,
And, with submissive veneration, bow
Beneath the affliction which it heaps upon us.
But O! what nobler transports would it give thee!
What joy beyond expression! couldst thou once
Surmount the furious storm of fierce revenge,
And yield ye to the charms of love and mercy.
Oh make the glorious trial!
Cor. Mother! wife!
Are all the powers of nature leagued against me?
I cannot! will not—Leave me, my Volumnia!
Vol. Well, I obey—How bitter thus to part!
Upon such terms to part! perhaps for ever!
But tell me, ere I hence unroot my feet,
When to my lonely home I shall return,
What from their father, to our little slaves,
Unconscious of the shame to which you doom them,
What shall I say? [*Pausing: he highly agitated*
Nay, tell me, Coriolanus!
Cor. Tell thee! What shall I tell thee? these tears!
These tears will tell thee what exceeds the power
Of words to speak, whate'er the son, the husband
And father, in one complicated pang
Can feel—But leave me;—even in pity leave!
Cease, cease to torture me, my dear Volumnia!
You only tear my heart, but cannot shake it;
For by the immortal gods, the dread avengers
Of broken faith!——
Vol. (*kneeling.*) Oh swear not, Coriolanus!
O vow not our destruction!
Vet. Daughter, rise.
Let us no more before the Volscian people
Expose ourselves a spectacle of shame.
It is in vain we try to melt a breast,
That to the best affections nature gives us,
Prefers the worst—Hear me, proud man! I have
A heart as stout as thine. I came not hither,
To be sent back rejected, baffled, shamed,
Hateful to Rome, because I am thy mother:

A Roman matron knows, in such extremes,
What part to take—And thus I came provided.
[*Drawing from under her robe a dagger.*
Go! barbarous son! go! double parricide!
Rush o'er my corse to thy beloved revenge!
Tread on the bleeding breast of her, to whom
Thou owest thy life!—Lo, thy first victim!

Cor. Ha! [*Seizing her hand.*
What dost thou mean?

Vet. To die, while Rome is free,
To seize the moment ere thou art her tyrant.

Cor. O use thy power more justly! Set not thus
My treacherous heart in arms against my reason.
Here! here! thy dagger will be well employ'd;
Strike here! and reconcile my fighting duties.

Vet. Off! Set me free!—Think'st thou that grasp, which binds
My feeble hand, can fetter too my will?
No, my proud son! Thou canst not make me live,
If Rome must fall!—No power on earth can do it!

Cor. Pity me, generous Volsci!—You are men—
Must it then be?—Confusion!—Do I yield?
What is it? Is it weakness? Is it virtue?—
Well!—

Vet. What? Speak!

Cor. O, no!—my stifled words refuse
A passage to the throes that wring my heart.

Vet. Nay, if thou yieldest, yield like Coriolanus;
And what thou dost, do nobly!

Cor. (*quitting her hand.*) There!—'Tis done!—
Thine is the triumph, nature!
[*To* VETURIA, *in a low tone of voice.*
Ah Veturia!
Rome by thy aid is saved—but thy son lost.

Vet. He never can be lost, who saves his country.

Cor. [*Turning to the* Roman Ladies.
Ye matrons, guardians of the Roman safety,
You to the senate may report this answer.
We grant the truce you ask. But on these terms:
That Rome, meantime, shall to a peace agree,
Fair, equal, just, and such as may secure
The safety, rights, and honour of the Volsci.
[*To the troops.*
Volsci, we raise the siege. Go, and prepare,
By the first dawn, for your return to Antium.
[*As the troops retire, and* CORIOLANUS *turns to the* Roman Ladies.

Tul. [*To* VOLUSIUS *aside.*
'Tis as we wish'd, Volusius—To your station.
But mark me well—Till thou shalt hear my call,
I charge thee not to stir. One offer more
My honour bids me make to this proud man,
Before we strike the blow—If he rejects it,
His blood be on his head.

Vol. Well, I obey you.
[*He goes out.*

Cor. Be it thy care, Galesus, that a safeguard
Attend these noble matrons back to Rome.

—•—

SCENE II.

CORIOLANUS, TULLUS.

Cor. I plainly, Tullus, by your looks discern
You disapprove my conduct.

Tul. Caius Marcius,
I mean not to assail thee with the clamour
Of loud reproaches, and the war of words;
But, pride apart, and all that can pervert
The light of steady reason, here to make
A candid fair proposal.

Cor. Speak. I hear thee.

Tul. I need not tell thee, that I have perform'd
My utmost promise. Thou hast been protected;
Hast had thy amplest, most ambitious wish;
Thy wounded pride is heal'd, thy dear revenge
Completely sated; and to crown thy fortune,
At the same time, thy peace with Rome restored.
Thou art no more a Volscian, but a Roman.
Return, return; thy duty calls upon thee,
Still to protect the city thou hast saved:
It still may be in danger from our arms.

Cor. Insolent man! Is this thy fair proposal?

Tul. Be patient—Hear me speak—I have already
From Rome protected thee; now from the Volsci,
From their just vengeance, I will still protect thee.
Retire. I will take care thou mayst with safety.

Cor. With safety!—Heavens!—And think'st thou Coriolanus
Will stoop to thee for safety? No! my safeguard
Is in myself, a bosom void of blame,
And the great gods, protectors of the just.—
O 'tis an act of cowardice and baseness,
To seize the very time my hands were fetter'd
By the strong chain of former obligations,
The safe sure moment to insult me—Gods!
Were I now free, as on that day I was,
When at Corioli I tamed thy pride,
This had not been.

Tul. Thou speak'st the truth: It had not.
O for that time again! Propitious gods,
If you will bless me, grant it!—Know, for that,
For that dear purpose, I have now proposed
Thou shouldst return. I pray thee, Marcius, do it!
And we shall meet again on nobler terms.

Cor. When to the Volsci I have clear'd my faith,
Doubt not I shall find means to meet thee nobly.
We then our generous quarrel may decide
In the bright front of some embattled field,
And not in private brawls, like fierce barbarians.

Tul. Thou canst not hope acquittal from the Volsci.

Cor. I do: nay more, expect their approbation,
Their thanks! I will obtain them such a peace
As thou durst never ask; a perfect union
Of their whole nation with imperial Rome
In all her privileges, all her rights.
By the just gods, I will! What wouldst thou more?

Tul. What would I more! Proud Roman! this I would:
Fire the cursed forest where these Roman wolves
Haunt and infest their nobler neighbours round them;
Extirpate from the bosom of this land,
A false perfidious people, who, beneath
The mask of freedom, are a combination
Against the liberty of human-kind,
The genuine seed of outlaws and of robbers.

Cor. The seed of gods! 'Tis not for thee, vain boaster!
'Tis not for such as thou, so often spared
By her victorious sword, to talk of Rome,
But with respect and awful veneration.
Whate'er her blots, whate'er her giddy factions
There is more virtue in one single year

Of Roman story, than your Volscian annals
Can boast through all your creeping dark duration!

Tul. I thank thy rage. This full displays the traitor.

Cor. Ha! traitor!

Tul. First, to thy own country, traitor;
And traitor, now, to mine!

Cor. Ye heavenly powers!
I shall break loose—My rage—But let us part—
Lest my rash hand should do a hasty deed
My cooler thought forbids.

Tul. Begone—Return—
To head the Roman troops. I grant thee quittance
Full and complete of all those obligations
Thou hast so oft insultingly complain'd
Fetter'd thy hands. They now are free. I court
The worst thy sword can do; whilst thou from me
Hast nothing to expect but sure destruction.
Quit then this hostile camp. Once more I tell thee,
Thou art not here one single hour in safety.

Cor. Think'st thou to fright me hence?

Tul. Thou wilt not, then?
Thou wilt not take the safety which I offer?

Cor. Till I have clear'd my honour in your council,
And proved before them all, to thy confusion,
The falsehood of thy charge; as soon in battle
I would before thee fly, and howl for mercy,
As quit the station they have here assign'd me.

Tul. Volusius! Hoa!

SCENE III.

To them VOLUSIUS, *and* Conspirators, *with their swords drawn.*

Tul. Seize and secure the traitor!

Cor. [*Laying his hand upon his sword.*
Who dares approach me, dies!

Vol. Die thou!

[*As* CORIOLANUS *draws his sword,* VOLUSIUS *and the* Conspirators *rush upon and stab him.* TULLUS *standing by without having drawn his sword.*

Cor. [*Endeavouring to free himself.*
Off!—Villains!
[*Falling.*
O murdering slaves! Assassinating cowards!
[*Dies.*

SCENE IV.

[*Upon the noise of the tumult, enter hastily to them* GALESUS, *the other deputies of the* Volscian *States,* Officers, *friends of* CORIOLANUS, *and* TITUS *with a large band of Soldiers.*

Gal. [*As he enters.*
Are we a nation ruled by laws, or fury?
How? whence this tumult? [*Pausing.*
Gods! what do I see?
The noble Marcius slain!

Tul. You see a traitor
Punish'd as he deserved, the Roman yoke
That thrall'd us broken, and the Volsci free!

Gal. Hear me, great Jove! Hear, all you injured powers
Of friendship, hospitality, and faith!
By that heroic blood, which from the ground,
Reeking to you for vengeance cries, I swear!
This impious breach of your eternal laws,
This daring outrage on the Volscian honour,
Shall find in me a rigorous avenger!
On the same earth, polluted by their crime,
I will not live with these unpunish'd ruffians!

Tul. This deed is mine: I claim it all!—These men,
These valiant men, were but my instruments,
To punish him who to our face betray'd us.
We shall not fear to answer to the Volsci,
In a full council of the states at Antium,
The glorious charge of having stabb'd their traitor!

Gal. Titus, till then secure them.
[TULLUS *and* Conspirators *are led off.*

[GALESUS, *standing over the body of* CORIOLANUS, *after a short pause, proceeds.*
Volscian fathers,
And ye, brave soldiers, see an awful scene,
Demanding serious solemn meditation
This man was once the glory of his age,
Disinterested, just, with every virtue
Of civil life adorn'd, in arms unequal'd.
His only blot was this; that, much provoked,
He raised his vengeful arm against his country.
And, lo! the righteous gods have now chastised him,
Even by the hands of those for whom he fought.

Whatever private views and passions plead,
No cause can justify so black a deed:
These, when the angry tempest clouds the soul,
May darken reason, and her course control;
But when the prospect clears, her startled eye
Must from the treacherous gulf with horror fly,
On whose wild wave, by stormy passions tost,
So many hapless wretches have been lost.
Then be this truth the star by which we steer,
Above ourselves our Country should be dear.

THE

POETICAL WORKS

OF

HENRY KIRKE WHITE.

MEMOIR.

HENRY KIRKE WHITE, whose splendid talents and untimely fate have excited wonder and regret, was born at Nottingham, on the 21st of March, 1785. His father was a butcher, and his son was destined by him to follow the same trade. Henry's aptitude for learning was very early apparent; it was difficult even then to persuade him to lay by his book for his meals; and when he was about seven years old he used to steal into the kitchen, to teach the servant to read and write; but with the modesty inseparable from merit, he carefully concealed this good deed until, by accident, his occupation was discovered. At this time, one whole day in the week and his leisure hours on the others were devoted to the pursuit of his father's business, and the young poet, who was afterwards the pride and hope of the University of Cambridge, might be seen traversing the streets of Nottingham bearing a butcher's basket. All the school education he received amounted only to the acquirement of reading and writing his mother tongue, with some instruction in arithmetic and French; but he thirsted for more ample supplies; and, already an ardent admirer of the beauties of nature, he revolted both from the occupations of a butcher and of a hosier, to which latter business he was placed when fourteen years of age. His own poems, "On being confined to School one pleasant morning in Spring," and his "Address to Contemplation," written about this time, exemplify his state of mind.

To his mother he spoke his feelings openly. He said he could not bear to spend his days in stocking-spinning and folding; that he *wanted something to occupy his brain;* and he should be wretched if he continued any longer at this trade, or indeed any thing except one of the learned professions. At length he obtained his wish, and he was placed in the office of Messrs. Coldham and Enfield, attorneys and town-clerks of Nottingham; but, as no premium could be given, the terms fixed on were, that he should serve two years before he was articled. He entered on this new pursuit with pleasure, and became fond of his profession; but the ambition which, until it became modified by religious feelings, was the leading characteristic of his mind, led him, before many years had passed, to aim at higher things.

He was fifteen years old when he entered the office of Messrs. Coldham and Enfield; he died six years afterwards; yet the acquirements he gained and the works he achieved in that short space were such as have not frequently been equalled. On entering the profession of the law, he was advised to make himself master of the Latin language. With very trifling assistance he enabled himself to read Horace with facility, and had made some progress in Greek, in *ten months.* In his walks to and from the office, he used to exercise himself in declining the Greek nouns and verbs, and contracted a habit he ever afterwards practised, of studying in his walks. Every moment that could be snatched from the day, and but too many from the night, were now employed by the enthusiastic student in the pursuit of multifarious knowledge. Professional lore took the first place in his studies; Greek, Latin, Italian, Spanish, Portuguese, chemistry, drawing, music, and mechanics, each in turn occupied his unwearied mind.

He now began a correspondence with several magazines, and by the success he met with was encouraged to attempt the publication of a small collection of poems: this was about the close of the year 1802. His chief object was to obtain a fund which might enable him to go to college, and eventually enter the church; a step which had now become the first wish, the eager desire of his heart. He was not averse to his profession; on the contrary, he took pleasure in it, and had cherished a hope that some day he might win his way to the bar; but a distressing deafness, which increased upon him, greatly impeded the practice of the law, and the religious fervour which had succeeded the deistical opinions he had once entertained, caused him to look to the church as the great object towards which all his exertions should now be directed.

The reception his Poems met with was not very encouraging, and an unfavourable notice of them in the Monthly Review greatly distressed him. The unfairness of this article induced Southey, with all the generosity of true genius, to address a letter to Kirke White, encouraging him to persevere. A correspondence ensued, and when the Poet sunk into an untimely grave, it was Southey's friendly hand which gathered his scattered works together, and gave them to the world.

The change in Henry's sentiments from deism to Christianity was accelerated by the conduct of his friend Mr. Almond, who pointedly shunned his society, fearing his ridicule of the serious views of religion which he himself entertained. Henry sought an explanation, and expressed to him the doubts which he felt (doubts which were happily of no long continuance), and the dreadful effect they had upon his mind. Before this period, as he himself acknowledges, he had wished to enter the church from motives of ambition. "Now," he says, in a statement of his reasons for wishing to enter into the ministry, published in the supplementary volume of his Remains, "I trust I may now say that I would be a minister, that I may do good; and, although I am sensible of the awful importance of the pastoral charge, I would sacrifice every thing for it, in the hope that I should be strengthened to discharge the duties of that sacred office."

His desire of entering the church had now become so predominant, that his friends, although able to do little to assist his views, would no longer oppose them; and Mr. Pigott and Mr. Dashwood, both clergymen at Nottingham, and his friend Mr. Almond, who was now at Queen's College, Cambridge, undertook to do their best to procure an adequate support for him during his university studies. At this period he obtained a month's leave of absence from his employers, which he spent in seclusion in the village of Wilford, near Clifton Woods, the theme of his chief poem. At the expiration of this term he returned, with all his fond hopes withered; the efforts in his favour had not yet been attended with success, and he appears to have despaired of accomplishing the wish of his heart. He now applied himself with even redoubled diligence to the prosecution of all his former studies; night and day was he occupied, and despite all the tender care of his mother, who too truly foresaw the consequences of such desperate exertions, he persevered till his health sank under it, and he experienced an attack of illness, from the effects of which he, in the opinion of his friends, never completely recovered.

On his recovery he, in consequence of an introduction which had been procured by Mr. Dashwood, waited on Mr. Simeon, of King's College, who at once took up his cause with all the zeal of a friendship of old standing. He promised him a sizarship at St. John's College, and undertook, with the assistance of a friend, to supply him with 30*l.* a year. His brother Neville promised him 20*l.* more, and on this he determined to enter the University. He accordingly quitted the law in October, 1804; his employers, although unwilling to part with one who had uniformly conducted himself with strict propriety, and was now become of considerable value to them, meeting his present views with cordiality, and offering to give up the remainder of his time.

By the advice of Mr. Simeon he passed the next year in the family of a clergyman, Mr. Grainger, of Winteringham, who received pupils into his house, for preparation for the University. Here, pursuing his former habits of excessive study, he was again attacked by severe illness; and although he was, during his convalescence, obliged to slacken somewhat in his exertions, he even then frequently studied fourteen hours a day. The consequence was, that he went to college with so shattered a frame, as to cause his friends to fear already for his life. During his first term a university scholarship fell vacant; he was advised to study for it, and did so; but the effort was too great for his weakened frame, and he was compelled to decline. By the help of strong medicines only was he enabled to pass the general college examination: he was pronounced the first man of his year, but he was a dying man. He went to London afterwards for relaxation, perhaps the worst place in the world he could have gone to; but in no place was his mind suffered to unbend: his walks were not refreshing, for his studies were pursued even there; and while at Cambridge he in this manner committed a whole tragedy of Euripides to memory. The next year he was again highly distinguished, was again pronounced first at the great college examination, and also one of the three best theme writers, between whom the examiners could not decide. The college offered him, at their expense, a private tutor in mathematics during the long vacation; and exhibitions to the amount of 66*l.* per annum being procured for him, he was enabled to dispense with the assistance afforded by Mr. Simeon and his friend.

During the course of the summer, it being expected that the mastership of the Free School of Nottingham would shortly become vacant, the situation was offered to him, but he declined it, because, had he accepted it, it would have interfered with his intentions respecting the ministry. His studies were continued, and the long vacation, instead of affording him the relaxation he so much needed, was spent with his mathematical tutor; his strength, which had appeared increasing, failed as the year advanced; he again went to London, but experienced no benefit, and he returned to the college but to die. On the 19th October, 1806, this victim to impetuous ardour in the pursuit of knowledge, sank beneath a struggle which had worn out both mind and body, for his physicians expressed their opinion, that had he recovered this last attack his intellects would have been affected. He died universally regretted by all who knew him, and especially by his college acquaintances, who, though comparatively of recent date, yet universally esteemed him as he deserved, and deeply lamented the untimely loss of one who had appeared destined to do equal honour to his college, by his worldly acquirements, and to the church to which he had devoted himself, by his ardent zeal and fervent piety.

His works, which can only be regarded as the fair blossoms of a richly fruitful tree, may nevertheless claim an equal rank with many more mature productions. Almost all were composed before he was nineteen; for after he went to Mr. Grainger's he seldom permitted himself to dally with the muses: a self-denial which one so gifted as himself would scarcely be able to resolve on, were he not supported by the strong feelings of duty which actuated Kirke White. His example may be a useful one, but whilst we lament the effects of his excessive and unwisely severe labours, we cannot but admire the firmness of soul which induced him to undergo them.

We cannot better conclude this sketch of a highly interesting and instructive life, which shows to what lengths a spirit determined to obtain the golden fruits of knowledge may proceed in the right path, against all imaginable obstacles, than by quoting the epitaph written by Professor Smyth, and inscribed on a tablet, erected by an American gentleman, Mr. Francis Boott of Boston, who, visiting the poet's grave and finding only a plain stone with his initials, caused this memorial to be placed in All Saints Church, Cambridge:—

Warm with fond hope and learning's sacred flame,
To Granta's bowers the youthful poet came;
Unconquer'd powers the immortal mind display'd,
But, worn with anxious thought, the frame decay'd;
Pale o'er his lamp, and in his cell retired,
The martyr-student faded, and expired.
Oh! genius, taste, and piety sincere,
Too early lost, 'midst studies too severe!
Foremost to mourn was generous Southey seen,
He told the tale and show'd what White had been;
Nor told in vain.—Far o'er the Atlantic wave
A wanderer came, and sought the poet's grave:
On yon low stone he saw his lonely name,
And raised this fond memorial to his fame.

THE

Poetical Works

OF

HENRY KIRKE WHITE.

CLIFTON GROVE:

A SKETCH.

Lo! in the west fast fades the lingering light,
And day's last vestige takes its silent flight:
No more is heard the woodman's measured stroke,
Which, with the dawn, from yonder dingle broke;
No more, hoarse clamouring o'er the uplifted head,
The crows assembling, seek their wind-rocked bed;
Stilled is the village hum—the woodland sounds
Have ceased to echo o'er the dewy grounds;
And general silence reigns, save when, below,
The murmuring Trent is scarcely heard to flow;
And save when, swung by 'nighted rustic late,
Oft, on its hinge, rebounds the jarring gate;
Or when the sheep-bell, in the distant vale,
Breathes its wild music on the downy gale.

Now, when the rustic wears the social smile,
Released from day and its attendant toil,
And draws his household round their evening fire,
And tells the oft-told tales that never tire;
Or where the town's blue turrets dimly rise,
And manufacture taints the ambient skies,
The pale mechanic leaves the labouring loom,
The air-pent hold, the pestilential room,
And rushes out, impatient to begin
The stated course of customary sin;
Now, now my solitary way I bend
Where solemn groves in awful state impend:
And cliffs, that boldly rise above the plain,
Bespeak, blest Clifton! thy sublime domain.
Here lonely wandering o'er the sylvan bower,
I come to pass the meditative hour;
To bid awhile the strife of passion cease,
And woo the calms of solitude and peace.
And oh! thou sacred power, who rear'st on high
Thy leafy throne where waving poplars sigh!
Genius of woodland shades! whose mild control
Steals with resistless witchery to the soul,
Come with thy wonted ardour, and inspire
My glowing bosom with thy hallowed fire.
And thou too, Fancy, from thy starry sphere,
Where to the hymning orbs thou lend'st thine car,
Do thou descend, and bless my ravished sight,
Veiled in soft visions of serene delight.
At thy command the gale that passes by
Bears in its whispers mystic harmony:
Thou wav'st thy wand, and lo! what forms appear!
On the dark cloud what giant shapes career!
The ghosts of Ossian skim the misty vale,
And hosts of sylphids on the moonbeams sail.

This gloomy alcove darkling to the sight,
Where meeting trees create eternal night;
Save, when from yonder stream, the sunny ray,
Reflected, gives a dubious gleam of day;
Recalls, endearing to my altered mind,
Times, when beneath the boxen hedge reclined,
I watched the lapwing to her clamorous brood;
Or lured the robin to its scattered food;
Or woke with song the woodland echo wild,
And at each gay response delighted smiled.
How oft, when childhood threw its golden ray
Of gay romance o'er every happy day,
Here would I run, a visionary boy,
When the hoarse tempest shook the vaulted sky,
And, fancy-led, beheld the' Almighty's form
Sternly careering on the eddying storm;
And heard, while awe congealed my inmost soul,
His voice terrific in the thunders roll.
With secret joy, I viewed with vivid glare
The volleyed lightnings cleave the sullen air;
And, as the warring winds around reviled,
With awful pleasure big, I heard and smiled.
Beloved remembrance! Memory which endears
This silent spot to my advancing years:
Here dwells eternal peace, eternal rest;
In shades like these to live is to be bless'd.
While happiness evades the busy crowd,
In rural coverts loves the maid to shroud:
And thou too, Inspiration, whose wild flame
Shoots with electric swiftness through the frame,
Thou here dost love to sit with upturned eye,
And listen to the stream that murmurs by,
The woods that wave, the grey owl's silken flight,
The mellow music of the listening night.
Congenial calms more welcome to my breast
Than maddening joy in dazzling lustre dressed,
To Heaven my prayers, my daily prayers, I raise,
That ye may bless my unambitious days,
Withdrawn, remote, from all the haunts of strife,
May trace with me the lowly vale of life,
And when her banner Death shall o'er me wave,
May keep your peaceful vigils on my grave.
Now as I rove, where wide the prospect grows,
A livelier light upon my vision flows;
No more above the embracing branches meet,
No more the river gurgles at my feet,
But seen deep down the cliff's impending side,
Through hanging woods, now gleams its silver tide.

Dim is my upland path,—across the green
Fantastic shadows fling, yet oft between
The chequered glooms the moon her chaste ray sheds,
Where knots of bluebells droop their graceful heads,
And beds of violets blooming 'mid the trees,
Load with waste fragrance the nocturnal breeze.

Say, why does man, while to his opening sight
Each shrub presents a source of chaste delight,
And Nature bids for him her treasures flow,
And gives to him alone his bliss to know,
Why does he pant for Vice's deadly charms?
Why clasp the siren Pleasure to his arms,
And suck deep draughts of her voluptuous breath,
Though fraught with ruin, infamy, and death?
Could he who thus to vile enjoyment clings,
Know what calm joy from purer sources springs;
Could he but feel how sweet, how free from strife,
The harmless pleasures of a harmless life,
No more his soul would pant for joys impure;
The deadly chalice would no more allure;
But the sweet potion he was wont to sip
Would turn to poison on his conscious lip.

Fair Nature! thee, in all thy varied charms,
Fain would I clasp for ever in my arms!
Thine are the sweets which never, never sate,
Thine still remain through all the storms of fate.
Though not for me 'twas Heaven's divine command
To roll in acres of paternal land;
Yet still my lot is blest, while I enjoy
Thine opening beauties with a lover's eye.

Happy is he, who, though the cup of bliss
Has ever shunned him when he thought to kiss,
Who, still in abject poverty or pain,
Can count with pleasure what small joys remain:
Though were his sight conveyed from zone to zone,
He would not find one spot of ground his own,
Yet, as he looks around, he cries with glee,
These bounding prospects all were made for me:
For me yon waving fields their burden bear,
For me yon labourer guides the shining share,
While happy I in idle ease recline,
And mark the glorious visions as they shine.
This is the charm, by sages often told,
Converting all it touches into gold!
Content can soothe, where'er by fortune placed,
Can rear a garden in the desert waste.

How lovely, from this hill's superior height,
Spreads the wide view before my straining sight!
O'er many a varied mile of lengthening ground,
E'en to the blue-ridged hill's remotest bound,
My ken is borne; while o'er my head serene
The silver moon illumes the misty scene;
Now shining clear, now darkening in the glade,
In all the soft varieties of shade.

Behind me, lo! the peaceful hamlet lies,
The drowsy god has sealed the cotter's eyes.
No more, where late the social faggot blazed,
The vacant peal resounds, by little raised;
But locked in silence, o'er Arion's* star,
The slumbering night rolls on her velvet car.
The church-bell tolls, deep sounding down the glade,
The solemn hour for walking spectres made;
The simple ploughboy, wakening with the sound,
Listens aghast, and turns him startled round,
Then stops his ears, and strives to close his eyes,
Lest at the sound some grisly ghost should rise!
Now ceased the long and monitory toll,
Returning silence stagnates in the soul;
Save when, disturbed by dreams, with wild affright,
The deep-mouthed mastiff bays the troubled night:
Or where the village alehouse crowns the vale,
The creaking signpost whistles to the gale.
A little onward let me bend my way,
Where the mossed seat invites the traveller's stay:
That spot, oh! yet it is the very same;
That hawthorn gives it shade, and gave it name:
There yet the primrose opes its earliest bloom,
There yet the violet sheds its first perfume,
And in the branch that rears above the rest
The robin unmolested builds its nest.
'Twas here, when Hope, presiding o'er my breast,
In vivid colours every prospect dressed:
'Twas here, reclining, I indulged her dreams,
And lost the hour in visionary schemes.
Here, as I press once more the ancient seat,
Why, bland deceiver! not renew the cheat?
Say, can a few short years this change achieve,
That thy illusions can no more deceive?
Time's sombrous tints have every view o'erspread,
And thou too, gay seducer! art *thou* fled?
Though vain thy promise, and the suit severe,
Yet thou couldst guile Misfortune of her tear,
And oft thy smiles across life's gloomy way
Could throw a gleam of transitory day.
How gay, in youth, the flattering future seems,
How sweet is manhood in the infant's dreams;
The dire mistake too soon is brought to light,
And all is buried in redoubled night!
Yet some can rise superior to their pain,
And in their breasts the charmer Hope retain;
While others, dead to feeling, can survey,
Unmoved, their fairest prospects fade away:
But yet a few there be—too soon o'ercast!—
Who shrink unhappy from the adverse blast,
And woo the first bright gleam which breaks the gloom,
To gild the silent slumbers of the tomb!
So in these shades the early primrose blows,
Too soon deceived by suns and melting snows,
So falls untimely on the desert waste;
Its blossoms withering in the northern blast.

Now passed whate'er the upland heights display,
Down the steep cliff I wind my devious way;
Oft rousing, as the rustling path I beat,
The timid hare from its accustomed seat.
And oh! how sweet this walk o'erhung with wood,
That winds the margin of the solemn flood!
What rural objects steal upon the sight!
What rising views prolong the calm delight;
The brooklet branching from the silver Trent,
The whispering birch by every zephyr bent,
The woody island, and the naked mead,
The lowly hut half hid in groves of reed,
The rural wicket, and the rural stile,
And, frequent interspersed, the woodman's pile:
Above, below, where'er I turn my eyes,
Rocks, waters, woods, in grand succession rise.
High up the cliff the varied groves ascend,
And mournful larches o'er the wave impend.
Around, what sounds, what magic sounds, arise,
What glimmering scenes salute my ravished eyes!
Soft sleep the waters on their pebbly bed,
The woods wave gently o'er my drooping head,

* The constellation Delphinus. For authority for this appellation, see Ovid's *Fasti*, b. xi. 113.

And, swelling slow, comes wafted on the wind,
Lorn Progne's note from distant copse behind.
Still, every rising sound of calm delight
Stamps but the fearful silence of the night,
Save when is heard, between each dreary rest,
Discordant from her solitary nest,
The owl, dull screaming to the wandering moon;
Now riding, cloud-wrapped, near her highest noon:
Or when the wild duck, southering, hither rides,
And plunges sullen in the sounding tides.
How oft, in this sequestered spot, when youth
Gave to each tale the holy force of truth,
Have I long lingered, while the milk-maid sung
The tragic legend, till the woodland rung;
That tale, so sad! which still to memory dear,
From its sweet source can call the sacred tear,
And (lulled to rest stern Reason's harsh control)
Steal its soft magic to the passive soul.
These hallowed shades, these trees that woo the wind
Recall its faintest features to my mind.

A hundred passing years, with march sublime,
Have swept beneath the silent wing of time,
Since, in yon hamlet's solitary shade,
Reclusely dwelt the far-famed Clifton Maid,
The beauteous Margaret; for her each swain
Confessed in private his peculiar pain,
In secret sighed, a victim to despair,
Nor dared to hope to win the peerless fair.
No more the shepherd on the blooming mead
Attuned to gaiety his artless reed,
No more intwined the pansied wreath, to deck
His favourite wether's unpolluted neck;
But listless, by yon bubbling stream reclined,
He mixed his sobbings with the passing wind,
Bemoaned his helpless love; or, boldly bent,
Far from these smiling fields, a rover went,
O'er distant lands, in search of ease, to roam,
A self-willed exile from his native home.

Yet not to all the maid expressed disdain;
Her Bateman loved, nor loved the youth in vain.
Full oft, low whispering o'er these arching boughs,
The echoing vault responded to their vows,
As here deep hidden from the glare of day,
Enamoured oft, they took their secret way.
Yon bosky dingle still the rustics name;
'Twas there the blushing maid confessed her flame.
Down yon green lane they oft were seen to hie,
When evening slumbered on the western sky.
That blasted yew—that mouldering walnut bare,
Each bears mementoes of the fated pair.

One eve, when Autumn loaded every breeze
With the fallen honours of the mourning trees,
The maiden waited at the' accustomed bower,
And waited long beyond the' appointed hour,
Yet Bateman came not,—o'er the woodland drear,
Howling portentous, did the winds career;
And bleak and dismal on the leafless woods,
The fitful rains rushed down in sullen floods;
The night was dark!—As, now and then, the gale
Paused for a moment, Margaret listened pale;
But through the covert to her anxious ear,
No rustling footstep spoke her lover near.
Strange fears now fill'd her breast—she knew not why,
She sighed, and Bateman's name was in each sigh.
She hears a noise,—'tis he,—he comes at last;
Alas! 'twas but the gale which hurried past:
But now she hears a quickening footstep sound,
Lightly it comes, and nearer does it bound—
'Tis Bateman's self; he springs into her arms;
'Tis he that clasps, and chides her vain alarms.
"Yet why this silence?—I have waited long,
And the cold storm has yelled the trees among:
And now thou'rt here my fears are fled—yet speak,
Why does the salt tear moisten on thy cheek?
Say, what is wrong?"—Now through a parting cloud
The pale moon peered from her tempestuous shroud,
And Bateman's face was seen—'twas deadly white,
And sorrow seemed to sicken in his sight.
"O, speak, my love!" again the maid conjured,
"Why is thy heart in sullen woe immured?"
He raised his head, and thrice essayed to tell,
Thrice from his lips the' unfinish'd accents fell;
When thus at last reluctantly he broke
His boding silence, and the maid bespoke:
"Grieve not, my love; but ere the morn advance
I on these fields must cast my parting glance;
For three long years, by cruel fate's command,
I go to languish in a foreign land.
O, Margaret! omens dire have met my view;
Say, when far distant, wilt thou bear me true?
Should honours tempt thee, and should riches fee,
Wouldst thou forget thine ardent vows to me,
And, on the silken couch of wealth reclined,
Banish thy faithful Bateman from thy mind?"

"O! why," replies the maid, "my faith thus prove?
Canst thou! ah! canst thou, then, suspect my love?
Hear me, just God! if from my traitorous heart
My Bateman's fond remembrance e'er shall part,
If, when he hail again his native shore,
He finds his Margaret true to him no more,
May fiends of hell, and every power of dread,
Conjoin'd, then drag me from my perjured bed,
And hurl me headlong down these awful steeps,
To find deservéd death in yonder deeps*!"
Thus spake the maid, and from her finger drew
A golden ring, and broke it quick in two;
One half she in her lovely bosom hides,
The other, trembling, to her love confides.
"This bind the vow," she said: "this mystic charm
No future recantation can disarm;
The right vindictive does the fates involve;
No tears can move it, no regrets dissolve."

She ceased: the death-bird gave a dismal cry,
The river moaned, the wild gale whistled by,
And once again the lady of the night
Behind a heavy cloud withdrew her light.
Trembling she viewed these portents with dismay;
But gently Bateman kissed her fears away:
Yet still he felt concealed a secret smart,
Still melancholy bodings filled his heart.

When to the distant land the youth was sped,
A lonely life the moody maiden led.
Still would she trace each dear, each well-known walk,
Still by the moonlight to her love would talk,
And fancy, as she paced among the trees,
She heard his whispers in the dying breeze.
Thus two years glided on in silent grief;
The third her bosom owned the kind relief:
Absence had cooled her love—the' impoverished flame
Was dwindling fast, when lo! the tempter came,
He offered wealth, and all the joys of life,
And the weak maid became another's wife!

* This part of the Trent is commonly called the Clifton Deeps.

Six guilty months had marked the false one's crime,
When Bateman hailed once more his native clime:
Sure of her constancy, elate he came,
The lovely partner of his soul to claim;
Light was his heart, as up the well-known way
He bent his steps—and all his thoughts were gay.
O! who can paint his agonizing throes,
When on his ear the fatal news arose!
Chilled with amazement, senseless at the blow,
He stood a marble monument of woe;
Till called to all the horrors of despair,
He smote his brow, and tore his horrent hair;
Then rushed impetuous from the dreadful spot,
And sought those scenes (by memory ne'er forgot),
Those scenes, the witness of their growing flame,
And now like witnesses of Margaret's shame.

'Twas night—he sought the river's lonely shore,
And traced again their former wanderings o'er.
Now on the bank in silent grief he stood,
And gazed intently on the stealing flood:
Death in his mien and madness in his eye,
He watched the waters as they murmur'd by;
Bade the base murderess triumph o'er his grave—
Prepared to plunge into the whelming wave!
Yet still he stood irresolutely bent;
Religion sternly stayed his rash intent:
He knelt; cool played upon his cheek the wind,
And fanned the fever of his maddening mind.
The willows waved, the stream it sweetly swept,
The paly moonbeam on its surface slept,
And all was peace; he felt the general calm
O'er his racked bosom shed a genial balm;
When casting far behind his streaming eye,
He saw the Grove—in fancy saw her lie,
His Margaret, lulled in Germain's* arms to rest,
And all the demon rose within his breast.
Convulsive now, he clenched his trembling hand,
Cast his dark eye once more upon the land,
Then at one spring he spurned the yielding bank,
And in the calm deceitful current sank.

Sad, on the solitude of night, the sound,
As in the stream he plunged, was heard around:
Then all was still—the wave was rough no more,
The river swept as sweetly as before;
The willows waved, the moonbeams shone serene,
And peace returning brooded o'er the scene.

Now, see upon the perjured fair one hang
Remorse's glooms and never-ceasing pang.
Full well she knew, repentant now too late,
She soon must bow beneath the stroke of fate:
But, for the babe she bore beneath her breast,
The' offended God prolonged her life unblest.
But fast the fleeting moments rolled away,
And near and nearer drew the dreaded day;
That day, foredoomed to give her child the light,
And hurl its mother to the shades of night!
The hour arrived, and from the wretched wife
The guiltless baby struggled into life:
As night drew on, around her bed, a band
Of friends and kindred kindly took their stand;
In holy prayer they passed the creeping time,
Intent to expiate her awful crime.
Their prayers were fruitless: as the midnight came,
A heavy sleep oppressed each weary frame;
In vain they strove against the' o'erwhelming load,
Some power unseen their drowsy lids bestrode.

* Germain is the traditionary name of her husband.

They slept, till in the blushing eastern sky
The blooming morning oped her dewy eye;
Then wakening wide, they sought the ravished bed,
But lo! the hapless Margaret was fled;
And never more the weeping train were doomed
To view the false one, in the deeps entombed.

The neighbouring rustics told that in the night
They heard such screams as froze them with affright;
And many an infant, at its mother's breast,
Started, dismayed, from its unthinking rest.
And even now, upon the heath forlorn,
They show the path down which the fair was borne,
By the fell demons, to the yawning wave,
Her own, and murdered lover's, mutual grave!

Such is the tale, so sad, to memory dear,
Which oft in youth has charmed my listening ear;
That tale, which bade me find redoubled sweets
In the drear silence of these dark retreats,
And even now, with melancholy power,
Adds a new pleasure to the lonely hour.
'Mid all the charms by magic Nature given
To this wild spot, this sublunary heaven,
With double joy enthusiast Fancy leans
On the attendant legend of the scenes.
This sheds a fairy lustre on the floods,
And breathes a mellower gloom upon the woods;
This, as the distant cataract swells around,
Gives a romantic cadence to the sound;
This, and the deepening glen, the alley green,
The silver stream with sedgy tufts between,
The massy rock, the wood-encompassed leas,'
The broom-clad islands, and the nodding trees,
The lengthening vista, and the present gloom,
The verdant pathway breathing waste perfume;
These are thy charms: the joys which these impart
Bind thee, blest Clifton! close around my heart.

Dear native Grove! where'er my devious track,
To thee will Memory lead the wanderer back.
Whether in Arno's polished vales I stray,
Or where "Oswego's swamps" obstruct the day;
Or wander lone, where, wildering and wide,
The tumbling torrent laves St. Gothard's side;
Or by old Tejo's classic margent muse,
Or stand entranced with Pyrenean views;
Still, still to thee, where'er my footsteps roam,
My heart shall point, and lead the wanderer home.
When Splendour offers, and when Fame incites,
I'll pause, and think of all thy dear delights,
Reject the boon, and, wearied with the change,
Renounce the wish which first induced to range;
Turn to these scenes, these well-known scenes,
once more,
Trace once again old Trent's romantic shore,
And, tired with worlds and all their busy ways,
Here waste the little remnant of my days.
But, if the Fates should this last wish deny,
And doom me on some foreign shore to die;
O! should it please the world's supernal King
That weltering waves my funeral dirge shall sing;
Or that my corse should, on some desert-strand,
Lie stretched beneath the simoom's blasting hand;
Still, though unwept I find a stranger-tomb,
My sprite shall wander through this favourite gloom,
Ride on the wind that sweeps the leafless grove,
Sigh on the wood-blast of the dark alcove,
Sit a lorn spectre on yon well-known grave,
And mix its moanings with the desert-wave.

GONDOLINE:

A BALLAD.

THE night it was still, and the moon it shone
  Serenely on the sea,
And the waves at the foot of the rifted rock
  They murmured pleasantly.

When Gondoline roamed along the shore,
  A maiden full fair to the sight,
Though love had made bleak the rose on her cheek,
  And turned it to deadly white.

Her thoughts they were drear, and the silent tear
  It filled her faint blue eye,
As oft she heard, in fancy's ear,
  Her Bertrand's dying sigh.

Her Bertrand was the bravest youth
  Of all our good king's men,
And he was gone to the Holy Land
  To fight the Saracen.

And many a month had passed away,
  And many a rolling year,
But nothing the maid from Palestine
  Could of her lover hear.

Full oft she vainly tried to pierce
  The ocean's misty face;
Full oft she thought her lover's bark
  She on the wave could trace.

And every night she placed a light
  In the high rock's lonely tower,
To guide her lover to the land,
  Should the murky tempest lower.

But now despair had seized her breast,
  And sunken in her eye;
"Oh, tell me but if Bertrand live,
  And I in peace will die."

She wandered o'er the lonely shore,
  The curlew screamed above—
She heard the scream with a sickening heart,
  Much boding of her love.

Yet still she kept her lonely way,
  And this was all her cry,
"Oh, tell me but if Bertrand live,
  And I in peace shall die."

And now she came to a horrible rift,
  All in the rock's hard side,
A bleak and blasted oak o'erspread
  The cavern yawning wide.

And pendent from its dismal top
  The deadly nightshade hung;
The hemlock and the aconite
  Across the mouth were flung.

And all within was dark and drear,
  And all without was calm;
Yet Gondoline entered, her soul upheld
  By some deep-working charm.

And as she entered the cavern wide,
  The moonbeam gleamed pale,
And she saw a snake on the craggy rock,
  It clung by its slimy tail.

Her foot it slipped, and she stood aghast,
  She trod on a bloated toad;
Yet, still upheld by the secret charm,
  She kept upon her road.

And now upon her frozen ear
  Mysterious sounds arose;
So, on the mountain's piny top,
  The blustering north wind blows.

Then furious peals of laughter loud
  Were heard with thundering sound,
Till they died away in soft decay,
  Low whispering o'er the ground.

Yet still the maiden onward went,
  The charm yet onward led,
Though each big glaring ball of sight
  Seemed bursting from her head.

But now a pale blue light she saw,
  It from a distance came;
She followed, till upon her sight
  Burst full a flood of flame.

She stood appalled; yet still the charm
  Upheld her sinking soul;
Yet each bent knee the other smote,
  And each wild eye did roll.

And such a sight as she saw there,
  No mortal saw before,
And such a sight as she saw there,
  No mortal shall see more.

A burning cauldron stood in the midst,
  The flame was fierce and high,
And all the cave, so wide and long,
  Was plainly seen thereby.

And round about the cauldron stout
  Twelve withered witches stood;
Their waists were bound with living snakes,
  And their hair was stiff with blood.

Their hands were gory too, and red
  And fiercely flamed their eyes;
And they were muttering indistinct
  Their hellish mysteries.

And suddenly they joined their hands,
  And uttered a joyous cry,
And round about the cauldron stout
  They danced right merrily.

And now they stopped; and each prepared
  To tell what she had done
Since last the lady of the night
  Her waning course had run.

Behind a rock stood Gondoline,
  Thick weeds her face did veil,
And she leaned fearful forwarder,
  To hear the dreadful tale.

The first arose: she said she had seen
  Rare sport since the blind cat mewed,
She had been to sea in a leaky sieve,
  And a jovial storm had brewed.

She called around the wingèd winds,
  And raised a devilish rout;
And she laughed so loud, the peals were heard
  Full fifteen leagues about.

She said there was a little bark
  Upon the roaring wave,
And there was a woman there, who had been
  To see her husband's grave.

And she had got a child in her arms,
  It was her only child,
And oft its little infant pranks
  Her heavy heart beguiled.

And there was too, in that same bark,
  A father and his son;
The lad was sickly, and the sire
  Was old and woe-begone.

And when the tempest waxëd strong,
  And the bark could no more it bide,
She said it was jovial fun to hear
  How the poor devils cried!

The mother clasped her orphan child
  Unto her breast and wept;
And, sweetly folded in her arms,
  The careless baby slept.

And she told how, in the shape of the wind,
  As manfully it roared,
She twisted her hand in the infant's hair,
  And threw it overboard.

And to have seen the mother's pangs,
  'Twas a glorious sight to see;
The crew could scarcely hold her down
  From jumping in the sea.

The hag held a lock of the hair in her hand,
  And it was soft and fair:
It must have been a lovely child,
  To have had such lovely hair.

And she said, the father in his arms
  He held his sickly son,
And his dying throes they fast arose,
  His pains were nearly done.

And she throttled the youth with her sinewy [hands,
  And his face grew deadly blue;
And the father he tore his thin grey hair,
  And kissed the livid hue.

And then she told, how she bored a hole
  In the bark, and it filled away;
And 'twas rare to hear, how some did swear,
  And some did vow and pray.

The man and woman they soon were dead,
  The sailors their strength did urge,
But the billows that beat were their winding-sheet,
  And the winds sung their funeral dirge.

She threw the infant's hair in the fire,
  The red flame flamëd high,
And round about the cauldron stout
  They danced right merrily.

The second begun: she said she had done
  The task that Queen Hecate had set her,
And that the devil, the father of evil,
  Had never accomplished a better.

She said, there was an aged woman,
  And she had a daughter fair,
Whose evil habits filled her heart
  With misery and care.

The daughter had a paramour,
  A wicked man was he,
And oft the woman him against
  Did murmur grievously.

And the hag had worked the daughter up
  To murder her old mother,
That then she might seize on all her goods,
  And wanton with her lover.

And one night as the old woman
  Was sick and ill in bed,
And pondering sorely on the life
  Her wicked daughter led,

She heard her footstep on the floor,
  And she raised her pallid head,
And she saw her daughter, with a knife,
  Approaching to her bed,

And said, My child, I am very ill,
  I have not long to live,
Now kiss my cheek, that ere I die,
  Thy sins I may forgive.

And the murderess bent to kiss her cheek,
  And she lifted the sharp bright knife,
And the mother saw her fell intent,
  And hard she begged for life.

But prayers would nothing her avail,
  And she screamed aloud with fear,
But the house was lone, and the piercing screams
  Could reach no human ear.

And though that she was sick, and old,
  She struggled hard, and fought;
The murderess cut three fingers through
  Ere she could reach her throat.

And the hag she held the fingers up,
  The skin was mangled sore,
And they all agreed a nobler deed
  Was never done before.

And she threw the fingers in the fire,
  The red flame flamëd high,
And round about the cauldron stout
  They danced right merrily.

The third arose: she said she had been
  To Holy Palestine,
And seen more blood in one short day
  Than they had all seen in nine.

Now Gondoline, with fearful steps,
  Drew nearer to the flame;
For much she dreaded now to hear
  Her hapless lover's name.

The hag related then the sports
  Of that eventful day,
When on the well-contested field
  Full fifteen thousand lay.

She said that she in human gore
  Above the knees did wade,
And that no tongue could truly tell
  The tricks she there had played.

There was a gallant-featured youth,
  Who like a hero fought;
He kissed a bracelet on his wrist,
  And every danger sought.

And in a vassal's garb disguised,
Unto the knight she sues,
And tells him she from Britain comes,
And brings unwelcome news.

That three days ere she had embarked
His love had given her hand
Unto a wealthy thane—and thought
Him dead in Holy Land.

And to have seen how he did writhe
When this her tale she told,
It would have made a wizard's bleed
Within his heart run cold.

Then fierce he spurred his warrior steed,
And sought the battle's bed;
And soon, all mangled o'er with wounds
He on the cold turf bled.

And from his smoking corse she tore
His head, half clove in two—
She ceased, and from beneath her garb
The bloody trophy drew.

The eyes were starting from their socks,
The mouth it ghastly grinned,
And there was a gash across the brow,
The scalp was nearly skinned.

'Twas Bertrand's head!—With a terrible scream
The maiden gave a spring,
And from her fearful hiding-place
She fell into the ring.

The lights they fled, the cauldron sunk,
Deep thunders shook the dome,
And hollow peals of laughter came
Resounding through the gloom.

Insensible the maiden lay
Upon the hellish ground,
And still mysterious sounds were heard
At intervals around.

She woke—she half arose—and wild,
She cast a horrid glare;
The sounds had ceased, the lights had fled,
And all was stillness there.

And through an awning in the rock,
The moon it sweetly shone,
And showed a river in the cave
Which dismally did moan.

The stream was black, it sounded deep,
As it rushed the rocks between;
It offered well, for madness fired
The breast of Gondoline.

She plungëd in, the torrent moaned
With its accustomed sound;
And hollow peals of laughter loud
Again rebellowed round.

The maid was seen no more!—But oft
Her ghost is known to glide,
At midnight's silent, solemn hour,
Along the ocean's side.

LINES

SUPPOSED TO BE SPOKEN BY A LOVER AT THE GRAVE OF HIS MISTRESS.

OCCASIONED BY A SITUATION IN A ROMANCE.

MARY, the moon is sleeping on thy grave,
And on the turf thy lover sad is kneeling,
The big tear in his eye. Mary, awake;
From thy dark house arise, and bless his sight
On the pale moonbeam gliding. Soft and low
Pour on the silver ear of night thy tale,
Thy whispered tale of comfort and of love,
To soothe thy Edward's lorn, distracted soul,
And cheer his breaking heart. Come, as thou didst,
When o'er the barren moors the night wind howled,
And the deep thunders shook the ebon throne
Of the startled night. O then, as lone reclining,
I listened sadly to the dismal storm,
Thou on the lambent lightnings wild careering
Didst strike my moody eye: dead pale thou wert,
Yet passing lovely. Thou didst smile upon me,
And O! thy voice it rose so musical,
Betwixt the hollow pauses of the storm,
That at the sound the winds forgot to rave,
And the stern demon of the tempest, charmed,
Sunk on his rocking throne to still repose,
Locked in the arms of silence.

Spirit of her!
My only love! O, now again arise,
And let once more thine airy accents fall
Soft on my listening ear. The night is calm,
The gloomy willows wave in sinking cadence
With the stream that sweeps below. Divinely [swelling
On the still air, the distant waterfall
Mingles its melody; and high above,
The pensive empress of the solemn night,
Fitful, emerging from the rapid clouds,
Shows her chaste face in the meridian sky.
No wicked elves upon the *Warlock-knoll*
Dare now assemble at their mystic revels;
It is a night, when from their primrose beds
The gentle ghosts of injured innocents
Are known to rise, and wander on the breeze,
Or take their stand by the oppressor's couch,
And strike grim terror to his guilty soul.
The spirit of my love might now awake,
And hold its customed converse.

Mary, lo!
Thy Edward kneels upon thy verdant grave,
And calls upon thy name. The breeze that blows
On his wan cheek will soon sweep over him,
In solemn music, a funereal dirge,
Wild and most sorrowful. His cheek is pale;
The worm that preyed upon thy youthful bloom,
It cankered green on his. Now lost he stands,
The ghost of what he was, and the cold dew
Which bathes his aching temples gives sure omen
Of speedy dissolution. Mary, soon
Thy love will lay his pallid cheek to thine,
And sweetly will he sleep with thee in death!

LINES

WRITTEN ON A SURVEY OF THE HEAVENS, IN THE MORNING, BEFORE DAYBREAK.

Ye many twinkling stars, who yet do hold
Your brilliant places in the sable vault
Of night's dominions!—Planets and central orbs
Of other systems; big as the burning sun
Which lights this nether globe, yet to our eye
Small as the glow-worm's lamp!—To you I raise
My lowly orisons, while, all bewildered,
My vision strays o'er your ethereal hosts;
Too vast, too boundless for our narrow mind,
Warped with low prejudices, to unfold
And sagely comprehend. Thence higher soaring,
Through ye I raise my solemn thoughts to him,
The mighty Founder of this wondrous maze,
The great Creator; him, who now sublime,
Wrapped in the solitary amplitude
Of boundless space, above the rolling spheres,
Sits on his silent throne, and meditates.

The angelic hosts, in their inferior heaven,
Hymn to the golden harps his praise sublime,
Repeating loud, "The Lord our God is great,"
In varied harmonies: the glorious sounds
Roll o'er the air serene. The' Æolian spheres,
Harping along their viewless boundaries,
Catch the full note, and cry, "The Lord is great,"
Responding to the seraphim. O'er all,
From orb to orb, to the remotest verge
Of the created world, the sound is borne,
Till the whole universe is full of him.

O! 'tis this heavenly harmony which now
In fancy strikes upon my listening ear,
And thrills my inmost soul. It bids me smile
On the vain world, and all its bustling cares,
And gives a shadowy glimpse of future bliss.
O! what is man, when at ambition's height,
What e'en are kings, when balanced in the scale
Of these stupendous worlds! Almighty God!
Thou the dread author of these wondrous works!
Say, canst thou cast on me, poor passing worm,
One look of kind benevolence?—Thou canst;
For thou art full of universal love,
And in thy boundless goodness wilt impart
Thy beams as well to me as to the proud,
The pageant insects of a glittering hour!

O! when reflecting on these truths sublime,
How insignificant do all the joys,
The gauds, and honours of the world appear!
How vain, ambition! Why has my wakeful lamp
Outwatched the slow-paced night?—Why on the page,
The schoolman's laboured page, have I employed
The hours devoted by the world to rest,
And needful to recruit exhausted nature?
Say, can the voice of narrow fame repay
The loss of health?—Or can the hope of glory
Lend a new throb unto my languid heart,
Cool, even now, my feverish aching brow,
Relume the fires of this deep-sunken eye,
Or paint new colours on this pallid cheek?

Say, foolish one, can that unbodied fame,
For which thou barterest health and happiness,
Say, can it soothe the slumbers of the grave?—
Give a new zest to bliss, or chase the pangs
Of everlasting punishment condign?
Alas! how vain are mortal man's desires!
How fruitless his pursuits! Eternal God,
Guide thou my footsteps in the way of truth,
And oh assist me so to live on earth,
That I may die in peace, and claim a place
In thy high dwelling. All but this is folly,
The vain illusions of deceitful life.

MY STUDY:

A LETTER IN HUDIBRASTIC VERSE.

You bid me, Ned, describe the place
Where I, one of the rhyming race,
Pursue my studies, *con amore*,
And wanton with the Muse in glory.

Well, figure to your senses straight,
Upon the house's topmost height,
A closet, just six feet by four,
With white-washed walls and plaster floor,
So nobly large, 'tis scarcely able
To' admit a single chair and table:
And (lest the Muse should die with cold)
A smoky grate my fire to hold;
So wondrous small, 'twould much it pose
To melt the icedrop on one's nose;
And yet so big, it covers o'er
Full half the spacious room and more.

A window, vainly stuffed about
To keep November's breezes out,
So crazy, that the panes proclaim,
That soon they mean to leave the frame.

My furniture I sure may crack—
A broken chair without a back;
A table wanting just two legs,
One end sustained by wooden pegs;
A desk—of that I am not fervent,
The work of, sir, your humble servant
(Who, though I say't, am no such fumbler);
A glass decanter and a tumbler,
From which my night-parched throat I lave,
Luxurious, with the limpid wave:
A chest of drawers, in antique sections,
And sawed by me in all directions;
So small, sir, that whoever views 'em
Swears nothing but a doll could use 'em.
To these, if you will add a store
Of oddities upon the floor,
A pair of globes, electric balls,
Scales, quadrants, prisms, and cobbler's awls,
And crowds of books, on rotten shelves,
Octavos, folios, quartos, twelves;
I think, dear Ned, you curious dog!
You'll have my earthly catalogue.

But stay, I nearly had left out
My bellows, destitute of snout;
And on the walls, good Heavens! why there
I've such a load of precious ware,
Of heads, and coins, and silver medals,
And organ works, and broken pedals
(For I was once a-building music,
Though soon of that employ I grew sick);
And skeletons of law, which shoot
All out of one primordial root;
That you, at such a sight would swear
Confusion's self had settled there.

There stands, just by a broken spire,
A Cicero without an ear,
A neck, on which, by logic good,
I know for sure a head *once* stood;
But who it was the able master
Had moulded in the mimic plaster,
Whether 'twas Pope, or Coke, or Burn,
I never yet could justly learn:
But knowing well, that any head
Is made to answer for the dead,
(And sculptors first their faces frame,
And after pitch upon a name,
Nor think it aught of a misnomer
To christen Chaucer's busto Homer,
Because they both have beards, which, you know,
Will mark them well from Joan and Juno,)
For some great man, I could not tell
But Neck might answer just as well,
So perched it up, all in a row
With Chatham and with Cicero.

Then all around in just degree,
A range of portraits you may see,
Of mighty men and eke of women,
Who are no whit inferior *to* men.

With these fair dames, and heroes round,
I call my garret classic ground;
For though confined, 'twill well contain
The ideal flights of Madam Brain:
No dungeon's walls, no cell confined,
Can cramp the energies of mind!
Thus, though my heart may seem so small,
I've friends, and 'twill contain them all;
And should it e'er become so cold
That these it will no longer hold,
No more may Heaven her blessings give—
I shall not then be fit to live.

DESCRIPTION OF A SUMMER'S EVE.

Down the sultry arc of day
The burning wheels have urged their way;
And eve along the western skies
Sheds her intermingling dyes.
Down the deep, the miry lane,
Creaking comes the empty wain;
And driver on the shaft-horse sits,
Whistling now and then by fits;
And oft with his accumstomed call,
Urging on the sluggish ball.
The barn is still, the master's gone,
And thrasher puts his jacket on,
While Dick, upon the ladder tall,
Nails the dead kite to the wall.
Here comes shepherd Jack at last,
He has penned the sheepcote fast,
For, 'twas but two nights before,
A lamb was eaten on the moor:
His empty wallet Rover carries,
Nor for Jack, when near home, tarries;
With lolling tongue he runs to try
If the horse-trough be not dry.
The milk is settled in the pans,
And supper messes in the cans:
In the hovel carts are wheeled,
And both the colts are drove a-field;
The horses are all bedded up,
And the ewe is with the tup:
The snare for Mister Fox is set,
The leaven laid, the thatching wet;
And Bess has slinked away to talk
With Roger in the holly-walk.

Now, on the settle all but Bess
Are set to eat their supper mess;
And little Tom and roguish Kate
Are swinging on the meadow-gate.
Now they chat on various things,
Of taxes, ministers, and kings,
Or else tell all the village news,
How madam did the squire refuse;
How parson on his tithes was bent,
And landlord oft distrained for rent.
Thus do they talk, till in the sky,
The pale-eyed moon is mounted high,
And from the ale-house drunken Ned
Has reeled—then hasten all to bed.
The mistress sees that lazy Kate
The happing-coal on kitchen grate
Has laid—while master goes throughout,
Sees shutters fast, the mastiff out,
The candles safe, the hearths all clear,
And naught from thieves or fire to fear;
Then both to bed together creep,
And join the general troop of sleep.

A BALLAD.

Be hushed, be hushed, ye bitter winds;
Ye pelting rains, a little rest;
Lie still, lie still, ye busy thoughts,
That wring with grief my aching breast!

Oh, cruel was my faithless love,
To triumph o'er an artless maid;
Oh, cruel was my faithless love,
To leave the breast by him betrayed!

When exiled from my native home,
He should have wiped the bitter tear;
Nor left me faint and lone to roam,
A heart-sick weary wanderer here.

My child moans sadly in my arms,
The winds they will not let it sleep:
Ah, little knows the hapless babe
What makes its wretched mother weep!

Now lie thee still, my infant dear;
I cannot bear thy sobs to see;
Harsh is thy father, little one,
And never will he shelter thee.

Oh, that I were but in my grave,
And winds were piping o'er me loud;
And thou, my poor, my orphan babe,
Wert nestling in thy mother's shroud!

ODE,

ADDRESSED TO H. FUSELI, ESQ., R. A., ON SEEING ENGRAVINGS FROM HIS DESIGNS.

Mighty magician! who on Torneo's brow,
When sullen tempests wrap the throne of night,
Art wont to sit and catch the gleam of light
That shoots athwart the gloom opaque below;

And listen to the distant death-shriek long
From lonely mariner foundering in the deep,
Which rises slowly up the rocky steep,
While the weird sisters weave the horrid song:
Or, when along the liquid sky
Serenely chant the orbs on high,
Dost love to sit in musing trance,
And mark the northern meteor's dance,
(While far below the fitful oar
Flings its faint pauses on the steepy shore,)
And list the music of the breeze,
That sweeps by fits the bending seas;
And often bears with sudden swell
The shipwreck'd sailor's funeral knell,
By the spirits sung, who keep
Their night-watch on the treacherous deep,
And guide the wakeful helms-man's eye
To Helicé in northern sky;
And there upon the rock inclined
With mighty visions fill'st the mind,
Such as bound in magic spell
Him* who grasped the gates of Hell,
And bursting Pluto's dark domain,
Held to the day the terrors of his reign.

Genius of horror and romantic awe,
Whose eye explores the secrets of the deep,
Whose power can bid the rebel fluids creep,
Can force the inmost soul to own its law;
Who shall now, sublimest spirit,
Who shall now thy wand inherit,
From him* thy darling child who best
Thy shuddering images expressed?
Sullen of soul, and stern, and proud,
His gloomy spirit spurned the crowd;
And now he lays his aching head
In the dark mansion of the silent dead.

Mighty magician! long thy wand has lain
Buried beneath the unfathomable deep;
And oh, for ever must its efforts sleep?
May none the mystic sceptre e'er regain?
Oh yes, 'tis his!—Thy other son!
He throws thy dark-wrought tunic on,
Fuesslin waves thy wand; again they rise, [eyes.
Again thy wildering forms salute our ravished
Him didst thou cradle on the dizzy steep, [flung,
Where round his head the volleyed lightnings
And the loud winds that round his pillow rung
Wooed the stern infant to the arms of sleep:

Or on the highest top of Teneriffe
Seated the fearless boy, and bade him look
Where far below the weather-beaten skiff
On the gulf bottom of the ocean strook.
Thou mark'dst him drink with ruthless ear
The death-sob; and, disdaining rest,
Thou saw'st how danger fired his breast,
And in his young hand couched the visionary spear.
Then, Superstition, at thy call,
She bore the boy to Odin's Hall,
And set before his awe-struck sight
The savage feast and spectred fight;
And summoned from his mountain-tomb
The ghastly warrior son of gloom,
His fabled Runic rhymes to sing,
While fierce Hresvelger flapped his wing;
Thou show'dst the trains the shepherd sees,
Laid on the stormy Hebrides,

* Dante.

Which on the mists of evening gleam,
Or crowd the foaming desert-stream:
Lastly, her storied hand she waves,
And lays him in Florentian caves:
There milder fables, lovelier themes,
Inwrap his soul in heavenly dreams;
There Pity's lute arrests his ear,
And draws the half-reluctant tear:
And now at noon of night he roves
Along the embowering moonlight groves;
And as from many a caverned dell
The hollow wind is heard to swell,
He thinks some troubled spirit sighs;
And as upon the turf he lies,
Where sleeps the silent beam of night,
He sees below the gliding sprite,
And hears in Fancy's organ sound
Aërial music warbling round.
Taste lastly comes and smooths the whole,
And breathes her polish o'er his soul:
Glowing with wild, yet chastened heat,
The wondrous work is now complete.

The Poet dreams!—The shadow flies,
And fainting fast, its image dies.
But lo! the Painter's magic force
Arrests the phantom's fleeting course:
It lives—it lives—the canvas glows,
And tenfold vigour o'er it flows.
The Bard beholds the work achieved,
And as he sees the shadow rise,
Sublime before his wondering eyes,
Starts at the image his own mind conceived!

LINES,

Written impromptu, on reading the following passage in Mr. Capel Lofft's beautiful and interesting Preface to Nathaniel Bloomfield's Poems, just published. "It has a mixture of the sportive, which deepens the impression of its melancholy close. I could have wished, as I have said in a short note, the conclusion had been otherwise: the sours of life less offend my taste than its sweets delight it."

Go to the raging sea, and say, "Be still!"
Bid the wild lawless winds obey thy will;
Preach to the storm, and reason with Despair,
But tell not Misery's son *that life is fair!*

Thou, who in Plenty's lavish lap hast rolled,
And every year with new delight hast told;
Thou, who, recumbent on the lackered barge,
Hast dropp'd down joy's gay stream of pleasant [marge,
Thou may'st extol life's calm, untroubled sea,
The storms of misery never burst on *thee*.
Go to the mat, where squalid Want reclines;
Go to the shade obscure, where Merit pines;
Abide with him whom Penury's charms control,
And bind the rising yearnings of his soul,
Survey his sleepless couch, and, standing there,
Tell the poor pallid wretch *that life is fair!*

Press thou the lonely pillow of his head,
And ask why sleep his languid eyes has fled;
Mark his dewed temples, and his half-shut eye,
His trembling nostrils, and his deep-drawn sigh,
His muttering mouth contorted with despair,
And ask if Genius could inhabit there?
Oh, yes! that sunken eye with fire once gleamed,
And rays of light from its full circlet streamed;

But now neglect has stung him to the core,
And Hope's wild raptures thrill his breast no more;
Domestic Anguish winds his vitals round,
And added Grief compels him to the ground.
Lo! o'er his manly form, decayed and wan,
The shades of death with gradual steps steal on;
And the pale mother, pining to decay,
Weeps for her boy her wretched life away.

Go, child of Fortune! to his early grave,
Where o'er his head obscure the rank weeds wave;
Behold the heart-wrung parent lay her head
On the cold turf, and ask to share his bed.
Go, child of Fortune! take thy lesson there,
And tell us then *that life is wondrous fair!*

Yet, Lofft, in thee, whose hand is still stretched forth
To' encourage genius and to foster worth,
On thee, the unhappy's firm, unfailing friend,
'Tis just that every blessing should descend;
'Tis just that life to thee should only show
Her fairer side but little mixed with woe.

TO CONTEMPLATION:

AN ODE.

Come, pensive sage, who lov'st to dwell
In some retired Lapponian cell,
Where, far from noise and riot rude,
Resides sequestered solitude.
Come, and o'er my longing soul
Throw thy dark and russet stole,
And open to my duteous eyes
The volume of thy mysteries.

I will meet thee on the hill,
Where, with printless footsteps still,
The morning in her buskin grey
Springs upon her eastern way;
While the frolic zephyrs stir,
Playing with the gossamer,
And, on ruder pinions borne,
Shake the dewdrops from the thorn.
There, as o'er the fields we pass,
Brushing with hasty feet the grass,
We will startle from her nest
The lively lark with speckled breast,
And hear the floating clouds among
Her gale-transported matin song;
Or on the upland stile embowered,
With fragrant hawthorn snowy flowered,
Will sauntering sit, and listen still
To the herdman's oaten quill,
Wafted from the plain below;
Or the heifer's frequent low;
Or the milkmaid in the grove,
Singing of one that died for love.
Or when the noontide heats oppress,
We will seek the dark recess,
Where, in the embowered translucent stream
The cattle shun the sultry beam,
And o'er us on the marge reclined
The drowsy fly her horn shall wind,
While Echo, from her ancient oak,
Shall answer to the woodman's stroke;
Or the little peasant's song,
Wandering lone the glens among,
His artless lip with berries dyed,
And feet through ragged shoes descried.

But oh, when evening's virgin queen
Sits on her fringëd throne serene,
And mingling whispers rising near,
Steal on the still, reposing ear;
While distant brooks decaying round
Augment the mixed dissolving sound,
And the zephyr flitting by
Whispers mystic harmony;
We will seek the woody lane,
By the hamlet on the plain,
Where the weary rustic nigh
Shall whistle his wild melody,
And the croaking wicket oft
Shall echo from the neighbouring croft:
And as we trace the green path lone,
With moss and rank weeds overgrown,
We will muse on pensive lore,
Till the full soul brimming o'er,
Shall in our upturned eyes appear,
Embodied in a quivering tear,
Or else, serenely silent, sit
By the brawling rivulet,
Which on its calm unruffled breast
Bears the old mossy arch impressed,
That clasps its secret stream of glass
Half hid in shrubs and waving grass,
The wood-nymph's lone secure retreat,
Unpressed by fawn or sylvan's feet,
We'll watch in eve's ethereal braid,
The rich vermilion slowly fade;
Or catch, faint twinkling from afar,
The first glimpse of the eastern star,
Fair Vesper, mildest lamp of light,
That heralds in imperial night:
Meanwhile, upon our wondering ear,
Shall rise, though low, yet sweetly clear,
The distant sounds of pastoral lute,
Invoking soft the sober suit
Of dimmest darkness—fitting well
With love or sorrow's pensive spell
(So erst did music's silver tone
Wake slumbering Chaos on his throne).
And haply then, with sudden swell,
Shall roar the distant curfew bell,
While in the castle's mouldering tower
The hooting owl is heard to pour
Her melancholy song, and scare
Dull Silence brooding in the air.
Meanwhile her dusk and slumbering car,
Black-suited Night drives on from far,
And Cynthia, 'merging from her rear,
Arrests the waxing darkness drear,
And summons to her silent call,
Sweeping, in their airy pall,
The unshrived ghosts, in fairy trance,
To join her moonshine morris-dance;
While around the mystic ring
The shadowy shapes elastic spring,
Then with a passing shriek they fly,
Wrapped in mists, along the sky,
And oft are by the shepherd seen,
In his lone night-watch on the green.
Then, hermit, let us turn our feet
To the low abbey's still retreat,
Embowered in the distant glen,
Far from the haunts of busy men,
Where, as we sit upon the tomb,
The glow-worm's light may gild the gloom,
And show to Fancy's saddest eye
Where some lost hero's ashes lie.

And oh, as through the mouldering arch,
With ivy filled, and weeping larch,
The night-gale whispers sadly clear,
Speaking drear things to Fancy's ear,
We'll hold communion with the shade
Of some deep-wailing, ruined maid—
Or call the ghost of Spenser down,
To tell of woe and fortune's frown;
And bid us cast the eye of hope
Beyond this bad world's narrow scope.
Or if these joys, to us denied,
To linger by the forest's side;
Or in the meadow, or the wood,
Or by the lone romantic flood;
Let us in the busy town
When sleep's dull streams the people drown,
Far from drowsy pillows flee,
And turn the church's massy key;
Then, as through the painted glass
The moon's faint beams obscurely pass,
And, darkly on the trophied wall
Her faint ambiguous shadows fall,
Let us, while the faint winds wail
Through the long reluctant aisle,
As we pace with reverence meet,
Count the echoings of our feet;
While from the tombs, with confest breath,
Distinct responds the voice of death.
If thou, mild sage, wilt condescend
Thus on my footsteps to attend,
To thee my lonely lamp shall burn
By fallen Genius' sainted urn,
As o'er the scroll of time I pore,
And sagely spell of ancient lore,
Till I can rightly guess of all
That Plato could to memory call,
And scan the formless view of things;
Or, with old Egypt's fettered kings,
Arrange the mystic trains that shine
In Night's high philosophic mine:
And to thy name shall e'er belong
The honours of undying song.

EPIGRAM ON ROBERT BLOOMFIELD.

Bloomfield, thy happy-omened name
Insures continuance to thy fame:
Both sense and truth this verdict give—
While *fields* shall *bloom*, thy name shall live!

WRITTEN IN THE PROSPECT OF DEATH.

Sad solitary Thought, who keep'st thy vigils,
Thy solemn vigils, in the sick man's mind;
Communing lonely with his sinking soul,
And musing on the dubious glooms that lie
In dim obscurity before him,—thee,
Wrapped in thy dark magnificence, I call
At this still midnight hour, this awful season,
When on my bed, in wakeful restlessness,
I turn me wearisome: while all around,
All, all save me, sink in forgetfulness;
I only wake to watch the sickly taper
Which lights me to my tomb!—Yea, 'tis the hand
Of Death I feel press heavy on my vitals,
Slow sapping the warm current of existence!
My moments now are few—the sand of life
Ebbs fastly to its finish! Yet a little,
And the last fleeting particle will fall,
Silent, unseen, unnoticed, unlamented.
Come then, sad Thought, and let us meditate
While meditate we may. We have now
But a small portion of what men call time
To hold communion; for e'en now the knife,
The separating knife, I feel divide
The tender bond that binds my soul to earth.
Yes, I must die—I feel that I must die;
And though to me has life been dark and dreary,
Though Hope for me has smiled but to deceive,
And Disappointment still pursued her blandishments,
Yet do I feel my soul recoil within me
As I contemplate the dim gulf of death,
The shuddering void, the awful blank—futurity.
Ay, I had planned full many a sanguine scheme
Of earthly happiness—romantic schemes,
And fraught with loveliness; and it is hard
To feel the hand of Death arrest one's steps,
Throw a chill blight o'er all one's budding hopes,
And hurl one's soul untimely to the shades,
Lost in the gaping gulf of blank oblivion.
Fifty years hence, and who will hear of Henry?—
Oh, none! Another busy brood of beings
Will shoot up in the interim, and none
Will hold him in remembrance. I shall sink,
As sinks a stranger in the crowded streets
Of busy London!—Some short bustle's caused,
A few inquiries, and the crowds close in,
And all's forgotten. On my grassy grave
The men of future times will careless tread,
And read my name upon the sculptured stone;
Nor will the sound, familiar to their ears,
Recall my vanished memory. I did hope
For better things!—I hoped I should not leave
The earth without a vestige!—Fate decrees
It shall be otherwise; and I submit.
Henceforth, oh world, no more of thy desires!—
No more of Hope—the wanton vagrant Hope!—
I abjure all. Now other cares engross me,
And my tired soul, with emulative haste,
Looks to its God, and prunes its wings for Heaven.

TO MY LYRE:

AN ODE.

Thou simple Lyre! thy music wild
Has served to charm the weary hour,
And many a lonely night has 'guiled,
When even pain has owned, and smiled,
Its fascinating power.

Yet, oh my Lyre! the busy crowd
Will little heed thy simple tones:
Them mightier minstrels harping loud
Engross; and thou and I must shroud
Where dark oblivion 'thrones.

No hand, thy diapason o'er,
Well skilled, I throw with sweep sublime;
For me, no academic lore
Has taught the solemn strain to pour,
Or build the polished rhyme.

Yet thou to sylvan themes canst soar;
Thou know'st to charm the woodland train;
The rustic swains believe thy power
Can hush the wild winds when they roar,
And still the billowy main!

These honours, Lyre, we yet may keep;
I, still unknown, may live with thee;
And gentle zephyr's wing will sweep
Thy solemn string, where low I sleep,
Beneath the alder tree.

This little dirge will please me more
Than the full requiem's swelling peal;
I'd rather than that crowds should sigh
For me, that from some kindred eye
The trickling tear should steal.

Yet dear to me the wreath of bay,
Perhaps from me debarred;
And dear to me the classic zone,
Which, snatched from learning's laboured throne,
Adorns the' accepted bard.

And oh, if yet 'twere mine to dwell
Where Cam or Isis winds along,
Perchance, inspired with ardour chaste,
I yet might call the ear of taste
To listen to my song.

Oh, then, my little friend, thy style
I'd change to happier lays;
Oh, then the cloistered glooms should smile,
And through the long, the fretted aisle
Should swell the note of praise.

MELODY.

Yes, once more that dying strain—
Anna, touch thy lute for me;
Sweet, when pity's tones complain,
Doubly sweet is melody.

While the virtues thus inweave
Mildly soft the thrilling song,
Winter's long and lonesome eve
Glides unfelt, unseen, along.

Thus, when life hath stolen away,
And the wintry night is near,
Thus shall virtue's friendly ray
Age's closing evening cheer.

TO AN EARLY PRIMROSE.

Mild offspring of a dark and sullen sire,
Whose modest form, so delicately fine,
Was nursed in whirling storms,
And cradled in the winds;

Thee, when young Spring first questioned Winter's sway,
And dared the sturdy blusterer to the fight,
Thee on this bank he threw
To mark his victory.

In this low vale, the promise of the year,
Serene, thou openest to the nipping gale,
Unnoticed and alone,
Thy tender elegance.

So virtue blooms, brought forth amid the storms
Of chill adversity: in some lone walk
Of life she rears her head,
Obscure and unobserved;

While every bleaching breeze that on her blows,
Chastens her spotless purity of breast,
And hardens her to bear
Serene the ills of life.

THE LULLABY OF A FEMALE CONVICT TO HER CHILD,

THE NIGHT PREVIOUS TO EXECUTION.

Sleep, baby mine;* enkerchieft on my bosom,
Thy cries they pierce again my bleeding breast:
Sleep, baby mine; not long thou'lt have a mother
To lull thee fondly in her arms to rest.

Baby, why dost thou keep this sad complaining?
Long from mine eyes have kindly slumbers fled;
Hush, hush, my babe, the night is quickly waning,
And I would fain compose my aching head.

Poor wayward wretch! and who will heed thy weeping,
When soon an outcast on the world thou'lt be:
Who then will soothe thee, when thy mother's sleeping
In her low grave of shame and infamy!

Sleep, baby mine!—To-morrow I must leave thee,
And I would snatch an interval of rest:
Sleep these last moments, ere the laws bereave thee,
For never more thou'lt press a mother's breast.

ODE TO MIDNIGHT.

Season of general rest, whose solemn still
Strikes to the trembling heart a fearful chill,
But speaks to philosophic souls delight,
Thee do I hail, as at my casement high,
My candle waning melancholy by,
I sit and taste the holy calm of night.

Yon pensive orb, that through the ether sails,
And gilds the misty shadows of the vales,
Hanging in thy dull rear her vestal flame,
To her, while all around in sleep recline,
Wakeful I raise my orisons divine,
And sing the gentle honours of her name;

While Fancy lone o'er me, her votary, bends,
To lift my soul her fairy visions sends,
And pours upon my ear her thrilling song;
And Superstition's gentle terrors come;
See, see yon dim ghost gliding through the gloom!
See round yon churchyard elm what spectres throng!

Meanwhile I tune, to some romantic lay,
My flagelet—and, as I pensive play,
The sweet notes echo o'er the mountain scene:
The traveller late journeying o'er the moors
Hears them aghast, (while still the dull owl pours
Her hollow screams each dreary pause between,)

Till in the lonely tower he spies the light
Now faintly flashing on the glooms of night,
Where I, poor muser, my lone vigils keep,
And, 'mid the dreary solitude serene,
Cast a much-meaning glance upon the scene,
And raise my mournful eye to Heaven, and weep.

* Sir Philip Sidney has a poem beginning "Sleep, baby mine."

CANZONET.

Maiden! wrap thy mantle round thee,
Cold the rain beats on thy breast:
Why should Horror's voice astound thee?
Death can bid the wretched rest!
All under the tree
Thy bed may be,
And thou mayst slumber peacefully.

Maiden! once gay pleasure knew thee,
Now thy cheeks are pale and deep;
Love has been a felon to thee,
Yet, poor maiden, do not weep!
There's rest for thee
All under the tree,
Where thou wilt sleep most peacefully.

ODE TO THOUGHT.

WRITTEN AT MIDNIGHT.

Hence, away, vindictive Thought!
Thy pictures are of pain;
The visions through thy dark eye caught,
They with no gentle charms are fraught,
So prythee back again.
I would not weep,
I wish to sleep,
Then why, thou busy foe, with me thy vigils keep?

Why dost o'er bed and couch recline?
Is this thy new delight?
Pale visitant, it is not thine
To keep thy sentry through the mine,
The dark vault of the night:
'Tis thine to die,
While o'er the eye
The dews of slumber press, and waking sorrows fly.

Go thou, and bide with him who guides
His bark through lonely seas;
And, as reclining on his helm,
Sadly he marks the starry realm,
To him thou mayst bring ease;
But thou to me
Art misery,
So prythee, prythee, plume thy wings, and from my pillow flee.

And, Memory, pray what art thou?
Art thou of Pleasure born?
Does bliss untainted from thee flow?
The rose that gems thy pensive brow,
Is it without a thorn?
With all thy smiles,
And witching wiles,
Yet not unfrequent bitterness thy mournful sway defiles.

The drowsy night-watch has forgot
To call the solemn hour;
Lulled by the winds he slumbers deep,
While I in vain, capricious Sleep,
Invoke thy tardy power;
And restless lie,
With unclosed eye,
To count the tedious hours as slow they minute by.

TO A FRIEND IN DISTRESS,

WHO, WHEN THE AUTHOR REASONED WITH HIM CALMLY, ASKED, "IF HE DID NOT FEEL FOR HIM."

"*Do I not feel?*" The doubt is keen as steel.
Yea, I do feel—most exquisitely feel;
My heart can weep, when from my downcast eye
I chase the tear, and stem the rising sigh:
Deep buried there I close the rankling dart,
And smile the most when heaviest is my heart.
On this I act—whatever pangs surround,
'Tis magnanimity to hide the wound!
When all was new, and life was in its spring,
I lived an unloved solitary thing;
E'en then I learn'd to bury deep from day
The piercing cares that wore my youth away;
E'en then I learn'd for others' cares to feel;
E'en then I wept I had not power to heal;
E'en then, deep sounding thro' the nightly gloom,
I heard the wretched's groan, and mourned the wretched's doom.
Who were my friends in youth?—The midnight fire,
The silent moonbeam, or the starry choir;
To these I 'plained; or turned from outer sight,
To bless my lonely taper's friendly light:
I never yet could ask, howe'er forlorn,
For vulgar pity mix'd with vulgar scorn;
The sacred source of woe I never ope,
My breast's my coffer, and my God's my hope.
But that I *do* feel, Time, my friend, will show,
Though the cold crowd the secret never know;
With them I laugh—yet, when no eye can see,
I weep for nature, and I weep for thee.
Yes, thou didst wrong me,——; I fondly thought
In thee I'd found the friend my heart had sought;
I fondly thought, that thou couldst pierce the guise,
And read the truth that in my bosom lies;
I fondly thought, ere Time's last days were gone,
Thy heart and mine had mingled into one!
Yes—and they yet will mingle. Days and years
Will fly, and leave us partners in our tears:
We then shall feel that friendship has a power
To soothe affliction in her darkest hour;
Time's trial o'er, shall clasp each other's hand,
And wait the passport to a better land.

Thine,
H. K. White.

Half past Eleven o'Clock at Night.

A PASTORAL SONG.

Come, Anna, come! the morning dawns,
Faint streaks of radiance tinge the skies;
Come, let us seek the dewy lawns,
And watch the early lark arise;
While Nature, clad in vesture gay,
Hails the loved return of day.

Our flocks, that nip the scanty blade
Upon the moor, shall seek the vale;
And then, secure beneath the shade,
We'll listen to the throstle's tale,
And watch the silver clouds above,
As o'er the azure vault they rove.

Come, Anna, come, and bring thy lute,
 That with its tones, so softly sweet
In cadence with my mellow flute,
 We may beguile the noontide heat;
 While near the mellow bee shall join,
 To raise a harmony divine.

And then at eve, when silence reigns,
 Except when heard the beetle's hum,
We'll leave the sober-tinted plains,
 To these sweet heights again we'll come;
 And thou to thy soft lute shalt play
 A solemn vesper to departing day.

ELEGY

OCCASIONED BY THE DEATH OF MR. GILL, WHO WAS DROWNED IN THE RIVER TRENT, WHILE BATHING 9TH AUGUST, 1802.

He sunk!—The' impetuous river rolled along,
 The sullen wave betrayed his dying breath;
And rising sad the rustling sedge among,
 The gale of evening touched the chords of death!

Nymph of the Trent! why didst not thou appear
 To snatch the victim from thy felon wave?
Alas! too late thou cam'st to' embalm his bier,
 And deck with water-flags his early grave.

Triumphant, riding o'er its tumid prey,
 Rolls the red stream in sanguinary pride;
While anxious crowds, in vain, expectant stay,
 And ask the swoln corse from the murdering tide.

The stealing tear-drop stagnates in the eye,
 The sudden sigh by friendship's bosom proved,
I mark them rise—I mark the general sigh;
 Unhappy youth! and wert thou so beloved?

On thee, as lone I trace the Trent's green brink,
 When the dim twilight slumbers on the glade;
On thee my thoughts shall dwell, nor Fancy shrink
 To hold mysterious converse with thy shade.

Of thee, as early I, with vagrant feet,
 Hail the grey-sandalled morn in Colwick's vale,
Of thee my sylvan reed shall warble sweet,
 And wild-wood echoes shall repeat the tale.

And oh, ye nymphs of Pæon! who preside
 O'er running rill and salutary stream,
Guard ye in future well the halcyon tide
 From the rude death-shriek and the dying scream.

ODE,

ADDRESSED TO THE EARL OF CARLISLE, K.G.

I. 1.

Retired, remote from human noise,
 A humble Poet dwelt serene;
His lot was lowly, yet his joys
 Were manifold, I ween.
He laid him by the brawling brook
 At eventide to ruminate,
 He watched the swallow skimming round,
 And mused, in reverie profound,
On wayward man's unhappy state,
And pondered much, and paused on deeds of ancient date.

II. 1.

"Oh, 'twas not always thus," he cried;
 "There was a time, when Genius claimed
Respect from even towering Pride,
 Nor hung her head ashamed:
But now to Wealth alone we bow;
 The titled and the rich alone
 Are honoured, while meek Merit pines,
 On Penury's wretched couch reclines,
Unheeded in his dying moan,
As overwhelmed with want and woe, he sinks unknown.

III. 1.

"Yet was the Muse not always seen
In Poverty's dejected mien,
 Not always did repining rue
 And misery her steps pursue.
Time was, when nobles thought their titles graced
. By the sweet honours of poetic bays,
 When Sidney sung his melting song,
 When Sheffield joined the' harmonious throng,
And Lyttleton attuned to love his lays.
 Those days are gone—alas, for ever gone!
 No more our nobles love to grace
 Their brows with anadems, by genius won,
 But arrogantly deem the Muse as base;
How different thought the sires of this degenerate race!"

I. 2.

Thus sang the minstrel: still at eve
 The upland's woody shades among,
In broken measures did he grieve,
 With solitary song.
And still his theme was aye the same,
 Neglect had stung him to the core;
And he with pensive joy did love
 To seek the still congenial grove,
 And muse on all his sorrows o'er,
And vow that he would join the abjured world no more.

II. 2.

But human vows, how frail they be!
 Fame brought Carlisle unto his view,
And all amazed, he thought to see
 The Augustan age anew.
Filled with wild rapture, up he rose,
 No more he ponders on the woes
 Which erst he felt that forward goes,
 Regrets he'd sunk in impotence,
And hails the ideal day of virtuous eminence.

III. 2.

Ah! silly man, yet smarting sore
With ills which in the world he bore,
Again on futile hopes to rest,
An unsubstantial prop at best,
And not to know one swallow makes no summer!
 Ah! soon he'll find the brilliant gleam
Which flashed across the hemisphere,
Illumining the darkness there,
 Was but a single solitary beam,
While all around remained in customed night.
 Still leaden Ignorance reigns serene
In the false court's delusive height,
 And only one Carlisle is seen
To illume the heavy gloom with pure and steady light.

I 'M PLEASED, AND YET I 'M SAD.

When twilight steals along the ground,
And all the bells are ringing round,
One, two, three, four, and five,
I at my study-window sit,
And, wrapped in many a musing fit,
To bliss am all alive.

But though impressions calm and sweet
Thrill round my heart a holy heat,
And I am inly glad;
The tear-drop stands in either eye,
And yet I cannot tell thee why—
I'm pleased, and yet I'm sad.

The silvery rack that flies away,
Like mortal life or pleasure's ray,
Does that disturb my breast?
Nay; what have I, a studious man,
To do with life's unstable plan,
Or pleasure's fading vest?

Is it that here I must not stop,
But o'er yon blue hill's woody top
Must bend my lonely way?
No, surely no! for, give but me
My own fireside, and I shall be
At home where'er I stray.

Then is it that yon steeple there,
With music sweet shall fill the air
When thou no more canst hear?
Oh, no! oh, no! for then, forgiven,
I shall be with my God in Heaven,
Released from every fear.

Then whence it is I cannot tell;
But there is some mysterious spell
That holds me when I'm glad;
And so the tear drop fills my eye,
When yet in truth I know not why,
Or wherefore I am sad.

TO A FRIEND.

WRITTEN AT A VERY EARLY AGE.

I've read, my friend, of Dioclesian,
And many another noble Grecian,
Who wealth and palaces resigned,
In cots the joys of peace to find;
Maximian's meal of turnip-tops,
(Disgusting food to dainty chops,)
I've also read of, without wonder;
But such a curst egregious blunder,
As that a man of wit and sense
Should leave his books to hoard up pence,
Forsake the loved Aonian maids
For all the petty tricks of trades,
I never, either now or long since,
Have heard of such a piece of nonsense;
That one who learning's joys hath felt,
And at the Muses' altar knelt,
Should leave a life of sacred leisure,
To taste the' accumulating pleasure;
And, metamorphosed to an alley duck,
Grovel in loads of kindred muck.
Oh, 'tis beyond my comprehension!
A courtier throwing up his pension,
A lawyer working without a fee,
A parson giving charity,
A truly pious Methodist preacher,
Are not, egad, so out of nature.
Had nature made thee half a fool,
But given thee wit to keep a school,
I had not stared at thy backsliding:
But when thy wit I can confide in;
When well I know thy just pretence
To solid and exalted sense;
When well I know that on thy head
Philosophy her lights hath shed;
I stand aghast! thy virtues sum too,
And wonder what this world will come to!

Yet, whence this strain?—Shall I repine
That thou alone dost singly shine?
Shall I lament that thou alone,
Of men of parts, hast prudence known?

SOLITUDE.

It is not that my lot is low,
That bids this silent tear to flow;
It is not grief that bids me moan;
It is that I am all alone.

In woods and glens I love to roam,
When the tired hedger hies him home;
Or by the woodland pool to rest,
When pale the star looks on its breast.

Yet when the silent evening sighs,
With hallowed airs and symphonies,
My spirit takes another tone,
And sighs that it is all alone.

The autumn leaf is sere and dead,
It floats upon the water's bed;
I would not be a leaf to die
Without recording sorrow's sigh!

The woods and winds, with sullen wail,
Tell all the same unvaried tale;
I've none to smile when I am free,
And when I sigh, to sigh with me.

Yet in my dreams a form I view,
That thinks on me, and loves me too:
I start, and then, the vision flown,
I weep that I am all alone.

If far from me the Fates remove
Domestic peace, connubial love,
The prattling ring, the social cheer,
Affection's voice, affection's tear,
Ye sterner powers that bind the heart,
To me your iron aid impart!
O teach me, when the nights are chill,
And my fireside is lone and still;
When to the blaze that crackles near,
I turn a tired and pensive ear,
And Nature conquering bids me sigh
For love's soft accents whispering nigh;
O teach me, on that heavenly road
That leads to Truth's occult abode,
To wrap my soul in dreams sublime,
Till earth and care no more be mine.
Let blest Philosophy impart
Her soothing measures to my heart;

And while with Plato's ravished ears
I list the music of the spheres,
Or on the mystic symbols pore,
That hide the Chald's sublimer lore,
I shall not brood on summers gone,
Nor think that I am all alone.

FANNY! upon thy breast I may not lie!—
Fanny! thou dost not hear me when I speak!—
Where art thou, love? Around I turn my eye;
And as I turn, the tear is on my cheek.
Was it a dream?—Or did my love behold
Indeed my lonely couch? Methought the breath
Fanned not her bloodless lip: her eye was cold
And hollow; and the livery of death
Invested her pale forehead. Sainted maid!
My thoughts oft rest with thee in thy cold grave
Through the long wintry night, when wind and wave
Rock the dark house where thy poor head is laid.
Yet, hush! my fond heart, hush! there is a shore
Of better promise; and I know at last,
When the long sabbath of the tomb is past,
We two shall meet in Christ—to part no more.

GENIUS:

AN ODE.

I. 1.

MANY there be, who, through the vale of life,
With velvet pace, unnoticed, softly go,
While jarring discord's inharmonious strife
Awakes them not to woe.
By them unheeded, carking care,
Green-eyed grief, and dull despair;
Smoothly they pursue their way,
With even tenor and with equal breath,
Alike through cloudy and through sunny day,
Then sink in peace to death.

II. 1.

But, ah! a few there be whom griefs devour,
And weeping woe, and disappointment keen,
Repining penury, and sorrow sour,
And self-consuming spleen.
And these are Genius' favourites: these
Know the thought-throned mind to please,
And from her fleshy seat to draw
To realms where Fancy's golden orbits roll,
Disdaining all but wildering rapture's law,
The captivated soul.

III. 1.

Genius, from thy starry throne,
High above the burning zone,
In radiant robe of light arrayed,
Oh, hear the moan by thy sad favourite made,
His melancholy moan.
He tells of scorn, he tells of broken vows,
Of sleepless nights, of anguish-ridden days,
Pangs that his sensibility uprouse
To curse his being and his thirst for praise.
Thou gav'st to him with treble force to feel
The sting of keen neglect, the rich man's scorn;
And what o'er all does in his soul preside
Predominant, and tempers him to steel
His high indignant pride.

I. 2.

Lament not ye, who humbly steal through life,
That Genius visits not your lowly shed;
For, ah! what woes and sorrows ever rife
Distract his hapless head!
For him awaits no balmy sleep,
He wakes all night, and wakes to weep;
Or by his lonely lamp he sits
At solemn midnight, when the peasant sleeps,
In feverish study, and in moody fits
His mournful vigils keeps.

II. 2.

And oh, for what consumes his watchful oil?
For what does thus he waste life's fleeting breath?
'Tis for neglect and penury he doth toil,
'Tis for untimely death.
Lo! where dejected pale he lies,
Despair depicted in his eyes,
He feels the vital flame decrease,
He sees the grave wide yawning for its prey,
Without a friend to soothe his soul to peace,
And cheer the expiring ray.

III. 2.

By Sulmo's bard of mournful fame,
By gentle Otway's magic name,
By him, the youth, who smiled at death,
And rashly dared to stop his vital breath,
Will I thy pangs proclaim;
For still to misery closely thou'rt allied,
Though gaudy pageants glitter by thy side,
And far-resounding fame.
What though to thee the dazzled millions bow,
And to thy posthumous merit bend them low;
Though unto thee the monarch looks with awe;
And thou at thy flashed car dost nations draw;
Yet, ah! unseen behind thee fly
Corroding anguish, soul-subduing pain,
And discontent that clouds the fairest sky,
A melancholy train.
Yes, Genius, thee a thousand cares await,
Mocking thy derided state;
Thee chill adversity will still attend,
Before whose face flies fast the summer's friend,
And leaves thee all forlorn;
While leaden ignorance rears her head and laughs,
And fat stupidity shakes his jolly sides,
And while the cup of affluence he quaffs
With bee-eyed wisdom, Genius he derides,
Who toils, and every hardship doth outbrave,
To gain the meed of praise, when he is mouldering in his grave.

THE SAVOYARD'S RETURN.

OH, yonder is the well-known spot,
My dear, my long-lost native home!
Oh, welcome is yon little cot,
Where I shall rest, no more to roam!
Oh, I have travell'd far and wide,
O'er many a distant foreign land;
Each place, each province I have tried,
And sung and danced my saraband.
But all their charms could not prevail
To steal my heart from yonder vale.

Of distant climes the false report
It lured me from my native land;
It bade me rove—my sole support
My cymbals and my saraband.

The woody dell, the hanging rock,
The chamois skipping o'er the heights;
The plain adorned with many a flock,
And oh, a thousand more delights,
That grace yon dear, beloved retreat,
Have backward won my weary feet.

Now safe returned, with wandering tired,
No more my little home I'll leave;
And many a tale of what I've seen
Shall while away the winter's eve.
Oh, I have wandered far and wide,
O'er many a distant foreign land;
Each place, each province I have tried,
And sung and danced my saraband.
But all their charms could not prevail
To steal my heart from yonder vale.

LINES

ON READING THE POEMS OF WARTON.

WRITTEN AT THE AGE OF FOURTEEN.

Oh, Warton! to thy soothing shell,
Stretched remote in hermit cell,
Where the brook runs babbling by,
For ever I could listening lie;
And catching all the Muses' fire,
Hold converse with the tuneful choir.

What pleasing themes thy page adorn—
The ruddy streaks of cheerful morn,
The pastoral pipe, the ode sublime,
And Melancholy's mournful chime!
Each with unwonted graces shines
In thy ever lovely lines.

Thy Muse deserves the lasting meed:
Attuning sweet the Dorian reed,
Now the love-lorn swain complains,
And sings his sorrows to the plains;
Now the sylvan scenes appear
Through all the changes of the year;
Or the elegiac strain
Softly sings of mental pain,
And mournful diapasons sail
On the faintly-dying gale.

But, ah! the soothing scene is o'er!
On middle flight we cease to soar,
For now the Muse assumes a bolder sweep,
Strikes on the lyric string her sorrows deep,
In strains unheard before.
Now, now the rising fire thrills high,
Now, now to heaven's high realms we fly,
And every throne explore:
The soul entranced, on mighty wings,
With all the poet's heat, upsprings,
And loses earthly woes;
Till all alarmed at the giddy height,
The Muse descends on gentler flight,
And lulls the wearied soul to soft repose.

TO THE MUSE.

WRITTEN AT THE AGE OF FOURTEEN.

Ill-fated maid! in whose unhappy train
Chill poverty and misery are seen,
Anguish and discontent, the unhappy bane
Of life, and blackener of each brighter scene,
Why to thy votaries dost thou give to feel
So keenly all the scorns, the jeers of life?—
Why not endow them to endure the strife
With apathy's invulnerable steel,
Of self-content and ease, each torturing wound to heal?

Ah, who would taste your self-deluding joys,
That lure the unwary to a wretched doom,
That bid fair views and flattering hopes arise,
Then hurl them headlong to a lasting tomb?
What is the charm which leads thy victims on
To persevere in paths that lead to woe?
What can induce them in that route to go,
In which innumerous before have gone,
And died in misery, poor and woe-begone?

Yet can I ask what charms in thee are found—
I, who have drank from thine ethereal rill,
And tasted all the pleasures that abound
Upon Parnassus' loved Aonian hill— [thrill!
I through whose soul the Muses' strains aye
Oh, I do feel the spell with which I'm tied;
And though our annals fearful stories tell,
How Savage languished, and how Otway died,
Yet must I persevere, let whate'er will betide.

TO LOVE.

Why should I blush to own I love?
'Tis Love that rules the realms above;
Why should I blush to say to all,
That Virtue holds my heart in thrall?

Why should I seek the thickest shade,
Lest Love's dear secret be betray'd?
Why the stern brow deceitful move,
When I am languishing with love?

Is it weakness thus to dwell
On passion that I dare not tell?
Such weakness I would ever prove—
'Tis painful though 'tis sweet to love!

THE EVE OF DEATH.

IRREGULAR.

Silence of death—portentous calm,
Those airy forms that yonder fly
Denote that your void foreruns a storm,
That the hour of fate is nigh.
I see, I see, on the dim mist borne,
The spirit of battles rear his crest:
I see, I see, that ere the morn
His spear will forsake its hated rest,
And the widowed wife of Larrendill will beat her naked breast.

O'er the smooth bosom of the sullen deep
No softly ruffling zephyrs fly;
But Nature sleeps a deathless sleep,
For the hour of battle is nigh.
Not a loose leaf waves on the dusky oak,
But a creeping stillness reigns around;
Except when the raven, with ominous croak,
On the ear does unwelcomely sound.
I know, I know what this silence means;
I know what the raven saith—
Strike, oh ye bards! the melancholy harp,
For this is the eve of death.

Behold, how along the twilight air
The shades of our fathers glide!
There Morven fled, with the blood-drenched hair,
And Colma with grey side.
No gale around its coolness flings,
Yet sadly sigh the gloomy trees;
And, hark! how the harp's unvisited strings
Sound sweet, as if swept by a whispering breeze!
'Tis done! the sun he has set in blood;
He will never set more to the brave;
Let us pour to the hero the dirge of death—
For to-morrow he hies to the grave.

THANATOS.

Oh! who would cherish life,
And cling unto this heavy clog of clay,
Love this rude world of strife,
Where glooms and tempests cloud the fairest day;
And where, 'neath outward smiles,
Concealed, the snake lies feeding on its prey,
Where pitfalls lie in every flowery way,
And sirens lure the wanderer to their wiles!
Hateful it is to me,
Its riotous railings and revengeful strife;
I'm tired with all its screams and brutal shouts
Dinning the ear!—Away—away with life!
And welcome, oh thou silent maid,
Who in some foggy vault art laid,
Where never daylight's dazzling ray
Comes to disturb thy dismal sway;
And there amid unwholesome damps dost sleep,
In such forgetful slumbers deep,
That all thy senses stupified
Are to marble petrified.
Sleepy death, I welcome thee!
Sweet are thy calms to misery.
Poppies I will ask no more,
Nor the fatal hellebore;
Death is the best, the only cure,
His are slumbers ever sure.
Lay me in the Gothic tomb,
In whose solemn fretted gloom
I may lie in mouldering state,
With all the grandeur of the great:
Over me, magnificent,
Carve a stately monument;
Then thereon my statue lay,
With hands in attitude to pray,
And angels serve to hold my head,
Weeping o'er the father dead.
Duly too, at close of day,
Let the pealing organ play;
And while the harmonious thunders roll,
Chant a vesper to my soul:
Thus how sweet my sleep will be,
Shut out from thoughtful misery!

ATHANATOS.

Away with Death—away
With all her sluggish sleeps and chilling damps,
Impervious to the day,
Where Nature sinks into inanity.
How can the soul desire
Such hateful nothingness to crave,
And yield with joy the vital fire,
To moulder in the grave!
Yet mortal life is sad,
Eternal storms molest its sullen sky;
And sorrows ever rife
Drain the sacred fountain dry—
Away with mortal life!
But, hail the calm reality,
The seraph Immortality!
Hail the heavenly bowers of peace,
Where all the storms of passion cease.
Wild Life's dismaying struggle o'er,
The wearied spirit weeps no more;
But wears the eternal smile of joy,
Tasting bliss without alloy.
Welcome, welcome, happy bowers,
Where no passing tempest lowers;
But the azure heavens display
The everlasting smile of day:
Where the choral seraph choir
Strike to praise the harmonious lyre;
And the spirit sinks to ease,
Lulled by distant symphonies.
Oh! to think of meeting there
The friends whose graves received our tear,
The daughter loved, the wife adored,
To our widowed arms restored;
And all the joys which death did sever,
Given to us again for ever!
Who would cling to wretched life,
And hug the poisoned thorn of strife;
Who would not long from earth to fly,
A sluggish senseless lump to lie,
When the glorious prospect lies
Full before his raptured eyes?

ON BEING CONFINED TO SCHOOL ONE PLEASANT MORNING IN SPRING.

WRITTEN AT THE AGE OF THIRTEEN.

The morning sun's enchanting rays
Now call forth every songster's praise;
Now the lark with upward flight,
Gaily ushers in the light;
While wildly warbling from each tree,
The birds sing songs to Liberty.

But for me no songster sings,
For me no joyous lark upsprings;
For I, confined in gloomy school,
Must own the pedant's iron rule,
And, far from sylvan shades and bowers,
In durance vile must pass the hours;
There con the scholiast's dreary lines,
Where no bright ray of genius shines,
And close to rugged learning cling,
While laughs around the jocund spring.

How gladly would my soul forego
All that arithmeticians know,
Or stiff grammarians quaintly teach,
Or all that industry can reach,
To taste each morn of all the joys
That with the laughing sun arise;
And unconstrained to rove along
The bushy brakes and glens among;
And woo the Muses' gentle power,
In unfrequented rural bower!
But, ah! such heaven-approaching joys
Will never greet my longing eyes;
Still will they cheat in vision fine,
Yet never but in fancy shine.

Oh, that I were the little wren
That shrilly chirps from yonder glen!
Oh, far away I then would rove,
To some secluded bushy grove;
There hop and sing with careless glee,
Hop and sing at liberty;
And till death should stop my lays,
Far from men would spend my days.

ON WHITMONDAY.

Hark, how the merry bells ring jocund round!
And now they die upon the veering breeze;
Anon they thunder loud
Full on the musing ear.

Wafted in varying cadence, by the shore
Of the still twinkling river, they bespeak
A day of jubilee
An ancient holiday.

And lo! the rural revels are begun;
And gaily echoing to the laughing sky;
On the smooth-shaven green,
Resounds the voice of Mirth.

Alas! regardless of the tongue of Fate,
That tells them 'tis but as an hour since they
Who now are in their graves,
Kept up the Whitsun dance:

And that another hour, and they must fall
Like those who went before, and sleep as still
Beneath the silent sod,
A cold and cheerless sleep.

Yet why should thoughts like these intrude to scare
The vagrant Happiness, when she will deign
To smile upon us here,
A transient visitor?

Mortals! be gladsome while ye have the power,
And laugh and seize the glittering lapse of joy;
In time the bell will toll
That warns ye to your graves.

I to the woodland solitude will bend [shout
My lonesome way; where Mirth's obstreperous
Shall not intrude to break
The meditative hour.

There will I ponder on the state of man,
Joyless and sad of heart, and consecrate
This day of Jubilee
To sad Reflection's shrine;

And I will cast my fond eye far beyond
This world of care, to where the steeple loud
Shall rock above the sod,
Where I shall sleep in peace.

MUSIC.

WRITTEN BETWEEN THE AGES OF FOURTEEN AND FIFTEEN, WITH A FEW SUBSEQUENT VERBAL ALTERATIONS.

Music, all-powerful o'er the human mind,
Can still each mental storm, each tumult calm,
Soothe anxious Care on sleepless couch reclined,
And e'en fierce Anger's furious rage disarm.

At her command the various passions lie—
She stirs to battle, or she lulls to peace;
Melts the charm'd soul to thrilling ecstasy,
And bids the jarring world's harsh clangour cease.

Her martial sounds can fainting troops inspire
With strength unwonted, and enthusiasm raise;
Infuse new ardour, and with youthful fire
Urge on the warrior, grey with length of days.

Far better she, when with her soothing lyre
She charms the falchion from the savage grasp,
And melting into pity, vengeful Ire
Looses the bloody breastplate's iron clasp.

With her in pensive mood I long to roam,
At midnight's hour, or evening's calm decline,
And thoughtful o'er the falling streamlet's foam,
In calm Seclusion's hermit walks recline.

Whilst mellow sounds from distant copse arise,
Of softest flute or reeds harmonic joined,
With rapture thrilled each worldly passion dies,
And pleased attention claims the passive mind.

Soft through the dell the dying strains retire,
Then burst majestic in the varied swell;
Now breathe melodious as the Grecian lyre,
Or on the ear in sinking cadence dwell.

Romantic sounds! such is the bliss ye give,
That heaven's bright scenes seem bursting on the
With joy I'd yield each sensual wish, to live [soul,
For ever 'neath your undefiled control.

Oh, surely melody from heaven was sent
To cheer the soul when tired with human strife,
To soothe the wayward heart by sorrow rent,
And soften down the rugged road of life.

TO THE MORNING.

WRITTEN DURING ILLNESS.

Beams of the daybreak faint! I hail
Your dubious hues, as on the robe
Of night, which wraps the slumbering globe,
I mark your traces pale.
Tired with the taper's sickly light,
And with the wearying, numbered night,
I hail the streaks of morn divine:
And lo! they break between the dewy wreaths
That round my rural casement twine:
The fresh gale o'er the green lawn breathes;
It fans my feverish brow, it calms the mental strife,
And cheerily re-illumes the lambent flame of life.

The lark has her gay song begun,
She leaves her grassy nest,
And soars till the *unrisen sun*
Gleams on her speckled breast.
Now let me leave my restless bed,
And o'er the spangled uplands tread:
Now through the customed wood-walk wend
By many a green lane lies my way,
Where high o'erhead the wild briars bend,
Till on the mountain's summit grey
I sit me down, and mark the glorious dawn of day.

Oh, Heaven! the soft refreshing gale
It breathes into my breast!
My sunk eye gleams; my cheek, so pale,
Is with new colours dressed.

Blithe Health! thou soul of life and ease!
Come thou too, on the balmy breeze,
Invigorate my frame:
I'll join with thee the buskined chase,
With thee the distant clime will trace,
Beyond those clouds of flame.

Above, below, what charms unfold
In all the varied view!
Before me all is burnished gold,
Behind the twilight's hue.
The mists which on old Night await,
Far to the west they hold their state,
They shun the clear blue face of morn:
Along the fine cerulean sky
The fleecy clouds successive fly,
While bright prismatic beams their shadowy folds adorn.

And hark! the thatcher has begun
His whistle on the eaves,
And oft the hedger's bill is heard
Among the rustling leaves.
The slow team creaks upon the road,
The noisy whip resounds,
The driver's voice—his carol blithe,
The mower's stroke—his whetting scythe,
Mix with the morning's sounds.

Who would not rather take his seat
Beneath these clumps of trees,
The early dawn of day to greet,
And catch the healthy breeze,
Than on the silken couch of Sloth
Luxurious to lie?
Who would not from life's dreary waste
Snatch, when he could, with eager haste,
An interval of joy?

To him who simply thus recounts
The morning's pleasures o'er,
Fate dooms, ere long, the scene must close,
To ope on him no more.
Yet, Morning! unrepining still
He'll greet thy beams awhile;
And surely thou, when o'er his grave
Solemn the whispering willows wave,
Wilt sweetly on him smile;
And the pale glow-worm's pensive light
Will guide his ghostly walks in the drear moonless night.

TO THE HERB ROSEMARY*.

Sweet-scented flower! who art wont to bloom
On January's front severe,
And o'er the wintry desert drear
To waft thy waste perfume!
Come, thou shalt form my nosegay now,
And I will bind thee round my brow;
And as I twine the mournful wreath
I'll weave a melancholy song;
And sweet the strain shall be, and long,
The melody of death.

Come, funeral flower! who lov'st to dwell
With the pale corse in lonely tomb,
And throw across the desert gloom
A sweet decaying smell.
Come, press my lips, and lie with me
Beneath the lowly alder tree:
And we will sleep a pleasant sleep,
And not a care shall dare intrude
To break the marble solitude,
So peaceful and so deep.

And hark! the wind-god, as he flies,
Moans hollow in the forest trees,
And sailing on the gusty breeze,
Mysterious music dies.
Sweet flower! that requiem wild is mine
It warns me to the lonely shrine,
The cold turf altar of the dead!
My grave shall be in yon lone spot,
Where as I lie, by all forgot,
A dying fragrance thou wilt o'er my ashes shed.

* The rosemary buds in January. It is the flower commonly put in the coffins of the dead.

TO THE HARVEST MOON.

Cum ruit imbriferum ver:
Spicea jam campis cum messis inhorruit, et cum
Frumenta in viridi stipula lactentia turgent.
Cuncta tibi Cererem pubes agrestis adoret.—VIRGIL.

Moon of Harvest, herald mild
Of plenty, rustic labour's child,
Hail, oh hail! I greet thy beam,
As soft it trembles o'er the stream,
And gilds the straw-thatched hamlet wide,
Where Innocence and Peace reside;
'Tis thou that gladd'st with joy the rustic throng,
Promptest the tripping dance, th' exhilarating song.

Moon of harvest, I do love
O'er the uplands now to rove,
While thy modest ray serene
Gilds the wide surrounding scene;
And to watch thee riding high
In the blue vault of the sky,
Where no thin vapour intercepts thy ray,
But in unclouded majesty thou walkest on thy way.

Pleasing 'tis, oh, modest Moon!
Now the night is at her noon,
'Neath thy sway to musing lie,
While around the zephyrs sigh,
Fanning soft the sun-tanned wheat,
Ripened by the summer's heat;
Picturing all the rustic's joy
When boundless plenty greets his eye,
And thinking soon,
Oh, modest Moon!
How many a female eye will roam
Along the road,
To see the load,
The last dear load of harvest-home.

Storms and tempests, floods and rains,
Stern despoilers of the plains,
Hence away, the season flee,
Foes to light-heart jollity:
May no winds careering high
Drive the clouds along the sky,
But may all nature smile with aspect boon,
When in the heavens thou show'st thy face, oh, Harvest Moon!

'Neath yon lowly roof he lies,
The husbandman, with sleep-sealed eyes;

He dreams of crowded barns, and round
The yard he hears the flail resound.
Oh, may no hurricane destroy
His visionary views of joy!
God of the winds! oh, hear his humble prayer,
And while the moon of harvest shines, thy blustering whirlwind spare.

Sons of luxury! to you
Leave I Sleep's dull power to woo:
Press ye still the downy bed,
While feverish dreams surround your head;
I will seek the woodland glade,
Penetrate the thickest shade,
Wrapped in Contemplation's dreams,
Musing high on holy themes,
While on the gale
Shall softly sail
The nightingale's enchanting tune,
And oft my eyes
Shall grateful rise
To thee, the modest Harvest Moon!

TO CONTEMPLATION.

Thee do I own the prompter of my joys,
The soother of my cares, inspiring peace,
And I will ne'er forsake thee. Men may rave,
And blame and censure me, that I don't tie
My every thought down to the desk, and spend
The morning of my life in adding figures
With accurate monotony; that so
The good things of the world may be my lot,
And I might taste the blessedness of wealth:
But, oh! I was not made for money-getting;
For me no much-respected plum awaits,
Nor civic honour, envied. For as still
I tried to cast with school dexterity
The interesting sums, my vagrant thoughts
Would quick revert to many a woodland haunt,
Which fond remembrance cherished, and the pen
Dropped from my senseless fingers as I pictured,
In my mind's eye, how on the shores of Trent
I erewhile wandered with my early friends
In social intercourse. And then I'd think
How contrary pursuits had thrown us wide,
One from the other, scattered o'er the globe.
They were set down with sober steadiness,
Each to his occupation: I alone,
A wayward youth, misled by Fancy's vagaries,
Remained unsettled, insecure, and veering
With every wind to every point of the' compass.
Yes, in the counting-house I could indulge
In fits of close abstraction; yea, amid
The busy bustling crowds could meditate,
And send my thoughts ten thousand leagues away
Beyond the Atlantic, resting on my friend.
Ay, Contemplation, e'en in earliest youth
I wooed thy heavenly influence! I would walk
A weary way when all my toils were done,
To lay myself at night in some lone wood,
And hear the sweet song of the nightingale.
Oh, those were times of happiness, and still
To memory doubly dear; for growing years
Had not then taught me man was made to mourn;
And a short hour of solitary pleasure,
Stolen from sleep, was ample recompense
For all the hateful bustles of the day.
My opening mind was ductile then, and plastic,
And soon the marks of care were worn away,
While I was swayed by every novel impulse,
Yielding to all the fancies of the hour.
But it has now assumed its character;
Marked by strong lineaments, its haughty tone,
Like the firm oak, would sooner break than bend.
Yet still, oh Contemplation! I do love
To indulge thy solemn musings; still the same
With thee alone I know to melt and weep,
In thee alone delighting. Why along
The dusky track of commerce should I toil,
When, with an easy competence content,
I can alone be happy; where with thee
I may enjoy the loveliness of Nature,
And loose the wings of Fancy?—Thus alone
Can I partake of happiness on earth;
And to be happy here is man's chief end,
For to be happy he must needs be good.

INSCRIPTION FOR A MONUMENT TO THE MEMORY OF COWPER.

Reader! if with no vulgar sympathy
Thou view'st the wreck of genius and of worth,
Stay thou thy footsteps near this hallowed spot.
Here Cowper rests. Although renown have made
His name familiar to thine ear, this stone
May tell thee that his virtues were above
The common portion; that the voice, now hushed
In death, was once serenely querulous
With pity's tones, and in the ear of woe
Spake music. Now forgetful, at thy feet,
His tired head presses on its last long rest,
Still tenant of the tomb; and on the cheek
Once warm with animation's lambent flush,
Sits the pale image of unmarked decay.
Yet mourn not: he had chosen the better part;
And these sad garments of Mortality
Put off, we trust that to a happier land
He went a light and gladsome passenger.
Sigh'st thou for honours, reader? Call to mind
That glory's voice is impotent to pierce
The silence of the tomb! But virtue blooms
E'en on the wreck of life, and mounts the skies.
So gird thy loins with lowliness, and walk
With Cowper on the pilgrimage of Christ.

THE SHIPWRECKED SOLITARY'S SONG TO THE NIGHT.

Thou spirit of the spangled night!
I woo thee from the watch-tower high,
Where thou dost sit to guide the bark
Of lonely mariner.

The winds are whistling o'er the welds,
The distant main is moaning low;
Come, let us sit and weave a song—
A melancholy song!

Sweet is the scented gale of morn,
And sweet the noontide's fervid beam,
But sweeter far the solemn calm,
That marks thy mournful reign.

I've passed here many a lonely year,
And never human voice have heard;
I've passed here many a lonely year
A solitary man.

And I have lingered in the shade,
From sultry noon's hot beams; and I
Have knelt before my wicker door,
To sing my evening song.

And I have hailed the grey morn high,
On the blue mountain's misty brow;
And tried to tune my little reed
To hymns of harmony.

But never could I tune my reed
At morn, or noon, or eve, so sweet,
As when upon the ocean shore
I hailed thy star-beam mild.

The dayspring brings not joy to me,
The moon it whispers not of peace;
But oh! when darkness robes the heavens,
My woes are mixed with joy.

And then I talk, and often think
Aërial voices answer me;
And oh! I am not then alone—
A solitary man.

And when the blustering winter winds
Howl in the woods that clothe my cave,
I lay me on my lonely mat,
And pleasant are my dreams.

And Fancy gives me back my wife;
And Fancy gives me back my child;
She gives me back my little home,
And all its placid joys.

Then hateful is the morning hour,
That calls me from the dream of bliss,
To find myself still lone, and hear
The same dull sounds again.

The deep-toned winds, the moaning sea,
The whispering of the boding trees,
The brook's eternal flow, and oft
The condor's hollow scream.

ON DISAPPOINTMENT.

Come, Disappointment, come!
Not in thy terrors clad;
Come in thy meekest, saddest guise;
Thy chastening rod but terrifies
The restless and the bad.
But I recline
Beneath thy shrine,
And round my brow resigned, thy peaceful cypress twine.

Though Fancy flies away
Before thy hollow tread,
Yet Meditation, in her cell,
Hears with faint ear the lingering knell,
That tells her hopes are dead;
And though the tear
By chance appear,
Yet she can smile, and say, "My all was not laid here."

Come, Disappointment, come!
Though from Hope's summit hurled,
Still, rigid nurse, thou art forgiven,
For thou severe was sent from heaven
To win me from the world;
To turn my eye
From vanity,
And point to scenes of bliss that never, never die.

What is this passing scene?
A peevish April day!
A little sun—a little rain,
And then night sweeps along the plain,
And all things fade away.
Man (soon discussed)
Yields up his trust,
And all his hopes and fears lie with him in the dust.

Oh, what is Beauty's power?
It flourishes and dies!
Will the cold earth its silence break,
To tell how soft, how smooth a cheek
Beneath its surface lies?
Mute, mute is all
O'er Beauty's fall;
Her praise resounds no more when mantled in her pall.

The most beloved on earth
Not long survives to-day;
So music past is obsolete,
And yet 'twas sweet, 'twas passing sweet,
But now 'tis gone away.
Thus does the shade
In memory fade,
When in forsaken tomb the form beloved is laid.

Then since this world is vain,
And volatile, and fleet,
Why should I lay up earthly joys,
Where rust corrupts, and moth destroys,
And cares and sorrows eat?
Why fly from ill
With anxious skill,
When soon this hand will freeze, this throbbing heart be still?

Come, Disappointment, come!
Thou art not stern to me:
Sad monitress! I own thy sway,
A votary sad in early day,
I bend my knee to thee.
From sun to sun
My race will run,
I only bow, and say, "My God, thy will be done!"

[On another paper were a few lines, written probably in the freshness of our author's disappointment.]

I dream no more—the vision flies away,
And Disappointment . . . .
There fell my hopes—I lost my all in this,
My cherished all of visionary bliss.
Now hope farewell, farewell all joys below;
Now welcome sorrow, and now welcome woe.
Plunge me in glooms . . . .

[His health soon sunk under these habits; he became pale and emaciated, and at length had a sharp fit of sickness. On his recovery he wrote the following lines in the church-yard of his favourite village.]

LINES

WRITTEN IN WILFORD CHURCH-YARD, ON RECOVERY FROM SICKNESS.

Here would I wish to sleep.—This is the spot
Which I have long marked out to lay my bones in;
Tired out and wearied with the riotous world,
Beneath this yew I would be sepulchred.
It is a lovely spot! The sultry sun,
From his meridian height, endeavours vainly

To pierce the shadowy foliage, while the zephyr
Comes wafting gently o'er the rippling Trent,
And plays about my wan cheek. It is a nook
Most pleasant: such a one, perchance, did Gray
Frequent, as with a vagrant Muse he wantoned.
Come, I will sit me down and meditate,
For I am wearied with my summer's walk,
And here I may repose in silent ease;
And thus, perchance, when life's sad journey's o'er,
My harassed soul, in this same spot, may find
The haven of its rest—beneath this sod
Perchance may sleep it sweetly, sound as death.

I would not have my corpse cemented down
With brick and stone, defrauding the poor earth-
Of its predestined dues; no, I would lie [worm
Beneath a little hillock, grass-o'ergrown,
Swathed down with osiers, just as sleep the cotters.
Yet may not undistinguished be my grave;
But there at eve may some congenial soul
Duly resort, and shed a pious tear,
The good man's benison—no more I ask.
And, oh! (if heavenly beings may look down
From where, with cherubim, inspired they sit,
Upon this little dim-discovered spot,
The earth,) then will I cast a glance below,
On him who thus my ashes shall embalm;
And I will weep too, and will bless the wanderer,
Wishing he may not long be doomed to pine
In this low-thoughted world of darkling woe,
But that, ere long, he reach his kindred skies.

Yet 'twas a silly thought, as if the body,
Mouldering beneath the surface of the earth,
Could taste the sweets of summer scenery,
And feel the freshness of the balmy breeze!
Yet nature speaks within the human bosom,
And, spite of reason, bids it look beyond
His narrow verge of being, and provide
A decent residence for its clayey shell,
Endeared to it by time. And who would lay
His body in the city burial-place,
To be thrown up again by some rude sexton,
And yield its narrow house another tenant,
Ere the moist flesh had mingled with the dust,
Ere the tenacious hair had left the scalp,
Exposed to insult lewd, and wantonness?
No, I will lay me in the *village* ground;
There are the dead respected. The poor hind,
Unlettered as he is, would scorn to invade
The silent resting-place of death. I've seen
The labourer, returning from his toil,
Here stay his steps, and call his children round,
And slowly spell the rudely sculptured rhymes,
And, in his rustic manner, moralize.
I've marked with what a silent awe he'd spoken,
With head uncovered, his respectful manner,
And all the honours which he paid the grave,
And thought on cities, where e'en cemeteries,
Bestrewed with all the emblems of mortality,
Are not protected from the drunken insolence
Of wassailers profane, and wanton havoc.
Grant, heaven, that here my pilgrimage may close!
Yet, if this be denied, where'er my bones
May lie—or in the city's crowded bounds,
Or scattered wide o'er the huge sweep of waters,
Or left a prey on some deserted shore
To the rapacious cormorant,—yet still,
(For why should sober reason cast away
A thought which soothes the soul?) yet still my spirit
Shall wing its way to these my native regions,
And hover o'er this spot. Oh, then I'll think
Of times when I was seated 'neath this yew
In solemn rumination; and will smile
With joy that I have got my longed release.

THE WANDERING BOY.

A SONG.

When the winter winds whistle along the wild moor,
And the cottager shuts on the beggar his door;
When the chilling tear stands in my comfortless eye,
Oh, how hard is the lot of the Wandering Boy.

The winter is cold, and I have no vest,
And my heart it is cold as it beats in my breast;
No father, no mother, no kindred have I—
Oh, I am a parentless Wandering Boy.

Yet I once had a home, and I once had a sire,
A mother who granted each infant desire;
Our cottage it stood in a wood-embowered vale,
Where the ringdove would warble its sorrowful tale.

But my father and mother were summoned away,
And they left me to hard-hearted strangers a prey;
I fled from their rigour with many a sigh,
And now I'm a poor little Wandering Boy.

The wind it is keen, and the snow loads the gale,
And no one will list to my innocent tale;
I'll go to the grave where my parents both lie,
And Death shall befriend the poor Wandering Boy.

LINES.

Yes, my stray steps have wandered, wandered far
From thee, and long, heart-soothing Poesy!
And many a flower, which in the passing time
My heart hath registered, nipped by the chill
Of undeserved neglect, hath shrunk and died.
Heart-soothing Poesy! though thou hast ceased
To hover o'er the many-voicèd strings
Of my long silent lyre, yet thou canst still
Call the warm tear from its thrice hallowed cell,
And with recallèd images of bliss
Warm my reluctant heart: yes, I would throw,
Once more would throw, a quick and hurried hand
O'er the responding chords. It hath not ceased—
It cannot, will not cease; the heavenly warmth
Plays round my heart, and mantles o'er my cheek;
Still, though unbidden, plays. Fair Poesy!
The summer and the spring, the wind and rain,
Sunshine and storm, with various interchange,
Have marked full many a day, and week, and month,
Since by dark wood, or hamlet far retired,
Spell-struck, with thee I loitered. Sorceress!
I cannot burst thy bonds! It is but lift
Thy blue eyes to that deep-bespangled vault,
Wreathe thy enchanted tresses round thine arm,
And mutter some obscure and charmèd rhyme,
And I could follow thee, on thy night's work,
Up to the regions of thrice chastened fire,
Or, in the caverns of the ocean flood,
Thrid the light mazes of thy volant foot.
Yet other duties call me, and mine ear
Must turn away from the high minstrelsy
Of thy soul-trancing harp, unwillingly
Must turn away; there are severer strains,

(And surely they are sweet as ever smote
The ear of spirit, from this mortal coil
Released and disembodied,) there are strains
Forbid to all, save those whom solemn thought,
Through the probation of revolving years,
And mighty converse with the Spirit of Truth,
Have purged and purified. To these my soul
Aspireth; and to this sublimer end
I gird myself, and climb the toilsome steep
With patient expectation: yea, sometimes
Foretaste of bliss rewards me; and sometimes
Spirits unseen upon my footsteps wait,
And minister strange music, which doth seem
Now near, now distant, now on high, now low,
Then swelling from all sides, with bliss complete,
And full fruition filling all the soul.
Surely such ministry, though rare, may soothe
The steep ascent, and cheat the lassitude
Of toil; and but that my fond heart
Reverts to day-dreams of the summer gone,
When by clear fountain, or embowered brake,
I lay a listless muser, prizing, far
Above all other lore, the poet's theme;
But for such recollections I could brace
My stubborn spirit for the arduous path
Of science unregretting; eye afar
Philosophy upon her steepest height,
And with bold step and resolute attempt
Pursue her to the innermost recess,
Where throned in light she sits, the Queen of Truth.

SONG.

BY WALLER.

[A lady of Cambridge lent Waller's Poems to Henry, and when he returned them to her, she discovered an additional stanza written by him at the bottom of the song here copied.]

"Go, lovely rose!
Tell her, that wastes her time on me,
That now she knows,
When I resemble her to thee,
How sweet and fair she seems to be.

"Tell her that's young,
And shuns to have her graces spied,
That hadst thou sprung
In deserts where no men abide,
Thou must have uncommended died.

"Small is the worth
Of beauty from the light retired;
Bid her come forth,
Suffer herself to be desired,
And not blush so to be admired.

"Then die, that she
The common fate of all things rare
May read in thee;
How small a part of time they share
That are so wondrous sweet and fair."

Yet, though thou fade,
From thy dead leaves let fragrance rise;
And teach the maid
That Goodness Time's rude hand defies;
That Virtue lives when Beauty dies.

H. K. White.

ON

THE DEATH OF DERMODY THE POET.

Child of Misfortune! Offspring of the Muse!
Mark like the meteor's gleam his mad career;
With hollow cheeks and haggard eye,
Behold he shrieking passes by;
I see, I see him near:
That hollow scream, that deepening groan,
It rings upon mine ear.

Oh come, ye thoughtless, ye deluded youth,
Who clasp the siren Pleasure to your breast,
Behold the wreck of genius here,
And drop, oh drop the silent tear
For Dermody at rest:
His fate is yours, then from your loins
Tear quick the silken vest.

Saw'st thou his dying bed: saw'st thou his eye,
Once flashing fire, despair's dim tear distil;
How ghastly did it seem!
And then his dying scream:
Oh God! I hear it still!
It sounds upon my fainting sense,
It strikes with deathly chill.

Say, didst thou mark the brilliant poet's death,
Saw'st thou an anxious father by his bed,
Or pitying friends around him stand?
Or didst thou see a mother's hand
Support his languid head?
Oh none of these—no friend o'er him
The balm of pity shed.

Now come around, ye flippant sons of wealth,
Sarcastic smile on genius fallen low;
Now come around who pant for fame,
And learn from hence a poet's name
Is purchased but by woe:
And when ambition prompts to rise,
Oh think of him below.

For me, poor moralizer, I will run,
Dejected, to some solitary state:
The Muse has set her seal on me,
She set her seal on Dermody,
It is the seal of fate:
In some lone spot my bones may lie,
Secure from human hate.

Yet ere I go I'll drop one silent tear,
While lies unwept the poet's fallen head:
May Peace her banners o'er him wave!
For me in my deserted grave
No friend a tear shall shed:
Yet may the lily and the rose
Bloom on my grassy bed.

THE PROSTITUTE.

DACTYLICS.

Woman of weeping eye, ah! for thy wretched lot,
Putting on smiles to lure the lewd passenger,
Smiling while anguish gnaws at thy heavy heart;

Sad is thy chance, thou daughter of misery,
Vice and disease are wearing thee fast away,
While the unfeeling ones sport with thy sufferings.

Destined to pamper the vicious one's appetite;
Spurned by the beings who lured thee from innocence;
Sinking unnoticed in sorrow and indigence;

Thou hast no friends, for they with thy virtue fled;
Thou art an outcast from house and from happiness;
Wandering alone on the wide world's unfeeling stage!

Daughter of misery, sad is thy prospect here;
Thou hast no friend to sooth down the bed of death;
None after thee inquires with solicitude;

Famine and fell disease shortly will wear thee down,
Yet thou hast still to brave often the winter's wind,
Loathsome to those thou wouldst court with thine hollow eyes.

Soon wilt thou sink into death's silent slumbering,
And not a tear shall fall on thy early grave,
Nor shall a single stone tell where thy bones are laid.

Once wert thou happy—thou wert once innocent;
But the seducer beguiled thee in artlessness,
Then he abandoned thee unto thine infamy.

Now he perhaps is reclined on a bed of down:
But if a wretch like him sleeps in security,
God of the red right arm! where is thy thunderbolt?

SONG.

WRITTEN AT THE AGE OF FOURTEEN.

Softly, softly blow, ye breezes,
Gently o'er my Edwy fly;
Lo! he slumbers, slumbers sweetly:
Softly, zephyrs, pass him by!
My love is asleep,
He lies by the deep,
All along where the salt waves sigh.

I have covered him with rushes,
Water-flags, and branches dry.
Edwy, long have been thy slumbers;
Edwy, Edwy, ope thine eye!
My love is asleep,
He lies by the deep,
All along where the salt waves sigh.

Still he sleeps, he will not waken,
Fastly closèd is his eye;
Paler is his cheek, and chiller
Than the icy moon on high.
Alas! he is dead,
He has chose his death-bed
All along where the salt waves sigh.

Is it, is it so, my Edwy?
Will thy slumbers never fly?
Couldst thou think I would survive thee?
No, my love, thou bidd'st me die.
Thou bidd'st me seek
Thy death-bed bleak
All along where the salt waves sigh.

I will gently kiss thy cold lips,
On thy breast I'll lay my head,
And the winds shall sing our death-dirge,
And our shroud the waters spread;
The moon will smile sweet,
And the wild wave will beat,
Oh! so softly o'er our lonely bed.

THE WONDERFUL JUGGLER:

A SONG.

Come, all ye true hearts, who, Old England to save,
Now shoulder the musket, or plough the rough wave,
I will sing you a song of a wonderful fellow,
Who has ruin'd Jack Pudding, and broke Punchinello.
Derry down, down, high derry down.

This juggler is little, and ugly, and black,
But, like Atlas, he stalks with the world at his back;
'Tis certain, all fear of the devil he seorns;
Some say they are cousins; we know he wears horns.
Derry down.

At hop, skip, and jump, who so famous as he?
He hopped o'er an army, he skipped o'er the sea;
And he jumped from the desk of a village attorney
To the throne of the Bourbons; a pretty long journey.
Derry down.

He tosses up kingdoms the same as a ball,
And his cup is so fashioned it catches them all;
The Pope and Grand Turk have been heard to declare
His skill at the long-bow has made them both stare.
Derry down.

He has shown off his tricks in France, Italy, Spain;
And Germany too knows his legerdemain;
So hearing John Bull has a taste for strange sights,
He's coming to London to put us to rights.
Derry down.

To encourage his puppets to venture this trip,
He has built them such boats as can conquer a ship;
With a gun of good metal, that shoots out so far,
It can silence the broadsides of three men of war.
Derry down.

This new Katerfelto, his show to complete,
Means his boats should all sink as they pass by our fleet;
Then, as under the ocean their course they steer right on,
They can pepper their foes from the bed of old Triton.
Derry down.

If this project should fail, he has others in store;
Wooden horses, for instance, may bring them safe o'er;
Or the genius of France (as the Moniteur tells)
May order balloons, or provide diving-bells.
Derry down.

When Philip of Spain fitted out his Armada,
Britain saw his designs, and could meet her invader;
But how to meet Bony she never will know,
If he comes in the style of a fish or a crow.
Derry down.

Now if our rude tars will so crowd up the seas,
That his boats have not room to go down when they please,
Can't he wait till the channel is quite frozen over,
And a pair of stout skates will transport him to Dover.
Derry down.

How welcome he'll be it were needless to say;
Neither he nor his puppets will e'er go away;
I am sure at his heels we shall constantly stick,
Till we know he has played off his very last trick.
Derry down, down, high derry down.

UNFINISHED PIECES,

INCLUDING SOME MINOR FRAGMENTS.

TIME: A POEM.

[This was commenced about the period when "Clifton Grove" was published: some of the detached parts were among our author's latest productions.]

GENIUS of musings, who the midnight hour
Wasting in woods or haunted forests wild,
Dost watch Orion in his arctic tower,
Thy dark eye fix'd as in some holy trance;
Or when the volleyed lightnings cleave the air,
And Ruin gaunt bestrides the winged storm,
Sitt'st in some lonely watch-tower, where thy lamp,
Faint blazing, strikes the fisher's eye from far,
And, mid the howl of elements, unmoved,
Dost ponder on the awful scene, and trace
The vast effect to its superior source;
Spirit, my lowly benison attend!
For now I strike to themes of import high
The solitary lyre; and, borne by thee
Above this narrow cell, I celebrate
The mysteries of Time!
Him who, august,
Was ere these worlds were fashioned, ere the sun
Sprang from the east, or Lucifer displayed
His glowing cresset in the arch of morn,
Or Vesper gilded the serener eve.
Yea, he had been for an eternity!
Had swept unvarying from eternity
The harp of desolation—ere his tones,
At God's command, assumed a milder strain,
And startled on his watch, in the vast deep,
Chaos's sluggish sentry, and evoked
From the dark void the smiling universe.

Chained to the grovelling frailties of the flesh,
Mere mortal man, unpurged from earthly dross,
Cannot survey, with fix'd and steady eye,
The dim uncertain gulf, which now the muse,
Adventurous, would explore; but dizzy grown,
He topples down the abyss. If he would scan
The fearful chasm, and catch a transient glimpse
Of its unfathomable depths, that so
His mind may turn with double joy to God,
His only certainty and resting-place;
He must put off awhile this mortal vest,
And learn to follow, without giddiness,
To heights where all is vision, and surprise,
And vague conjecture; he must waste by night
The studious taper, far from all resort
Of crowds and folly, in some still retreat—
High on the beetling promontory's crest,
Or in the caves of the vast wilderness,
Where, compassed round with Nature's wildest shapes,
He may be driven to centre all his thoughts
In the great architect, who lives confessed
In rocks, and seas, and solitary wastes.

So has divine philosophy, with voice
Mild as the murmurs of the moonlight wave,
Tutored the heart of him who now awakes,
Touching the chords of solemn minstrelsy,
His faint, neglected song—intent to snatch
Some vagrant blossom from the dangerous steep
Of poesy, a bloom of such a hue,
So sober, as may not unseemly suit
With Truth's severer brow; and one withal
So hardy, as shall brave the passing wind
Of many winters, rearing its meek head
In loveliness, when he who gathered it
Is numbered with the generations gone.
Yet not to me hath God's good providence
Given studious leisure*, or unbroken thought,
Such as he owns—a meditative man;
Who from the blush of morn to quiet eve
Ponders, or turns the page of wisdom o'er,
Far from the busy crowd's tumultuous din;
From noise and wrangling far, and undisturbed
With mirth's unholy shouts. For me the day
Hath duties which require the vigorous hand
Of steadfast application, but which leave
No deep improving trace upon the mind.
But be the day another's—let it pass!—
The night's my own!—They cannot steal my night!
When evening lights her folding star on high,
I live and breathe; and in the sacred hours
Of quiet and repose my spirit flies,
Free as the morning, o'er the realms of space,
And mounts the skies, and imps her wing for Heaven.

Hence do I love the sober-suited maid;
Hence Night's my friend, my mistress, and my theme,
And she shall aid me now to magnify
The night of ages—now when the pale ray
Of starlight penetrates the studious gloom,
And, at my window seated, while mankind
Are locked in sleep, I feel the freshening breeze
Of stillness blow, while, in her saddest stole,
Thought, like a wakeful vestal at her shrine,
Assumes her wonted sway.
Behold, the world
Rests, and her tired inhabitants have paused
From trouble and turmoil. The widow now
Has ceased to weep, and her twin orphans lie
Locked in each arm, partakers of her rest.
The man of sorrow has forget his woes;
The outcast that his head is shelterless,
His griefs unshared. The mother tends no more
Her daughter's dying slumbers, but surprised
With heaviness, and sunk upon her couch,
Dreams of her bridals. E'en the hectic, lulled
On Death's lean arm to rest, in visions wrapped,
Crowning with Hope's bland wreath his shuddering nurse,
Poor victim! smiles. Silence and deep repose
Reign o'er the nations; and the warning voice
Of Nature utters audibly within
The general moral; tells us, that repose,
Deathlike as this, but of far longer span,
Is coming on us; that the weary crowds,
Who now enjoy a temporary calm,
Shall soon taste lasting quiet, wrapped around
With gravclothes, and their aching restless heads
Mouldering in holes and corners unobserved,
Till the last trump shall break their sullen sleep.

* The author was then in an attorney's office.

Who needs a teacher to admonish him
That flesh is grass, that earthly things are mist?
What are our joys but dreams, and what our hopes
But goodly shadows in the summer cloud?
There's not a wind that blows but bears with it
Some rainbow promise!—Not a moment flies
But puts its sickle in the fields of life,
And mows its thousands, with their joys and cares!
'Tis but as yesterday since on yon stars,
Which now I view, the Chaldee shepherd* gazed,
In his midwatch observant, and disposed
The twinkling hosts as fancy gave them shape;
Yet, in the interim what mighty shocks
Have buffeted mankind!—Whole nations razed;
Cities made desolate; the polished sunk
To barbarism, and once barbaric states
Swaying the wand of science and of arts;
Illustrious deeds and memorable names
Blotted from record, and upon the tongue
Of grey Tradition voluble no more!

Where are the heroes of the ages past?—
Where the brave chieftains, where the mighty ones
Who flourished in the infancy of days?
All to the grave gone down! On their fallen fame,
Exultant, mocking at the pride of man,
Sits grim Forgetfulness. The warrior's arm
Lies nerveless on the pillow of its shame,
Hushed is his stormy voice and quenched the blaze
Of his red eye-ball. Yesterday, his name
Was mighty on the earth; to-day, 'tis—what?
The meteor of the night of distant years,
That flashed unnoticed, save by wrinkled eld,
Musing at midnight upon prophecies,
Who at her lonely lattice saw the gleam
Point to the mist-poised shroud, then quietly
Closed her pale lips, and locked the secret up
Safe in the charnel's treasures.

Oh, how weak
Is mortal man! how trifling, how confined
His scope of vision! Puffed with confidence,
His phrase grows big with immortality,
And he, poor insect of a summer's day,
Dreams of eternal honours to his name,
Of endless glory, and perennial bays!
He idly reasons of eternity
As of the train of ages, when, alas,
Ten thousand thousand of his centuries
Are, in comparison, a little point
Too trivial for account! Oh, it is strange,
'Tis passing strange, to mark his fallacies;
Behold him proudly view some pompous pile,
Whose high dome swells to emulate the skies,
And smile, and say, "My name shall live with this
Till Time shall be no more," while at his feet—
Yea, at his very feet—the crumbling dust
Of the fallen fabric of the other day
Preaches the solemn lesson! He should know
That Time must conquer; that the loudest blast
That ever filled Renown's obstreperous trump
Fades in the lapse of ages, and expires.
Who lies inhumed in the terrific gloom
Of the gigantic pyramid, or who
Reared its huge walls? Oblivion laughs, and says,
"The prey is mine!" They sleep, and never more
Their names shall strike upon the ear of man;
Their memory bursts its fetters.

Where is Rome?
She lives but in the tale of other times:
Her proud pavilions are the hermit's home;
And her long colonnades, her public walks,
Now faintly echo to the pilgrim's feet,
Who comes to muse in solitude, and trace,
Through the rank moss revealed, her honoured dust.
But not to Rome alone has fate confined
The doom of ruin: cities numberless,
Tyre, Sidon, Carthage, Babylon, and Troy,
And rich Phœnicia—they are blotted out,
Half razed from memory, and their very name
And being in dispute! Has Athens fallen?—
Is polished Greece become the savage seat
Of ignorance and sloth?—And shall we dare

. . . .
. . . .

And empire seeks another hemisphere.

Where now is Britain?—Where her laurelled names,
Her palaces and halls? Dashed in the dust.
Some second Vandal hath reduced her pride,
And with one big recoil hath thrown her back
To primitive barbarity! Again,
Through her depopulated vales, the scream
Of bloody Superstition hollow rings,
And the scared native to the tempest howls
The yell of deprecation. O'er her marts,
Her crowded ports, broods silence; and the cry
Of the low curlew, and the pensive dash
Of distant billows, break alone the void.
E'en as the savage, sits upon the stone
That marks where stood her capitols, and hears
The bittern booming in the weeds, he shrinks
From the dismaying solitude. Her bards
Sing in a language that hath perished;
And their wild harps, suspended o'er their graves,
Sigh to the desert winds a dying strain.

Meanwhile the Arts, in second infancy,
Rise in some distant clime, and then, perchance,
Some bold adventurer, filled with golden dreams,
Steering his bark through trackless solitudes,
Where, to his wandering thoughts, no daring prow
Hath ever ploughed before, espies the cliffs
Of fallen Albion. To the land unknown
He journeys joyful, and perhaps descries
Some vestige of her ancient stateliness:
Then he with vain conjecture fills his mind
Of the unheard-of race, which had arrived,
At science in that solitary nook,
Far from the civil world; and sagely sighs,
And moralises on the state of man.

Still on its march, unnoticed and unfelt,
Moves on our being. We do live and breathe,
And we are gone! The spoiler heeds us not:
We have our springtime and our rottenness;
And as we fall, another race succeeds,
To perish likewise. Meanwhile Nature smiles,
The seasons run their round, the sun fulfils
His annual course; and heaven and earth remain
Still changing, yet unchanged—still doomed to feel
Endless mutation in perpetual rest.
Where are concealed the days which have elapsed?
Hid in the mighty cavern of the past,
They rise upon us only to appal,
By indistinct and half-glimpsed images,
Misty, gigantic, huge, obscure, remote.

* Alluding to the first astronomical observations made by the Chaldean shepherds.

Oh, it is fearful, on the midnight couch,
When the rude rushing winds forget to rave,
And the pale moon, that through the casement high
Surveys the sleepless muser, stamps the hour
Of utter silence, it is fearful then
To steer the mind in deadly solitude,
Up the vague stream of probability;
To wind the mighty secrets of the past,
And turn the key of Time! Oh, who can strive
To comprehend the vast, the awful truth,
Of the eternity that hath gone by,
And not recoil from the dismaying sense
Of human impotence! The life of man
Is summed in birthdays and in sepulchres:
But the Eternal God hath no beginning,
He hath no end! Time had been with him
For everlasting, ere the dædal world
Rose from the gulf in loveliness. Like him
It knew no source, like him 'twas uncreate.
What is it then?—The past eternity!
We comprehend a *future without end;*
We feel it possible that e'en yon sun
May roll for ever; but we shrink amazed—
We stand aghast, when we reflect that Time
Knew no commencement; that heap age on age,
And million upon million, without end,
And we shall never span the void of days
That were, and are not but in retrospect!
The past is an unfathomable depth,
Beyond the span of thought; 'tis an elapse
Which hath no mensuration, but hath been
For ever and for ever!
Change of days
To us is sensible; and each revolve
Of the recording sun conducts us on
Further in life, and nearer to our goal.
Not so with Time, mysterious chronicler!
He knoweth not mutation: centuries
Are to his being as a day, a day
As centuries. Time past, and Time to come,
Are always equal; when the world began,
God had existed from eternity.

. . . .
. . . .

Now look on man
Myriads of ages hence. Hath Time elapsed?—
Is he not standing in the selfsame place
Where once we stood? The same eternity
Hath gone before him, and is yet to come;
His past is not of longer span than ours,
Though myriads of ages intervened;
For who can add to what has neither sum,
Nor bound, nor source, nor estimate, nor end?—
Oh, who can compass the Almighty mind?—
Who can unlock the secrets of the High?
In speculations of an altitude
Sublime as this, our reason stands confessed
Foolish, and insignificant, and mean.
Who can apply the futile argument
Of finite beings to infinity?
He might as well compress the universe
Into the hollow compass of a gourd,
Scooped out by human art; or bid the whale
Drink up the sea it swims in! Can the less
Contain the greater?—Or the dark obscure
Infold the glories of meridian day?
What does Philosophy impart to man
But undiscovered wonders? Let her soar
E'en to the proudest heights—to where she caught
The soul of Newton and of Socrates,
She but extends the scope of wild amaze
And admiration. All her lessons end
In wider views of God's unfathomed depths.

Lo! the unlettered hind, who never knew
To raise his mind excursive to the heights
Of abstract contemplation, as he sits
On the green hillock by the hedge-row side,
What time the insect swarms are murmuring,
And marks in silent thought the broken clouds
That fringe with loveliest hues the evening sky,
Feels in his soul the hand of Nature rouse
The thrill of gratitude to him who formed
The goodly prospect: he beholds the God
Throned in the west, and his reposing ear
Hears sounds angelic in the fitful breeze
That floats through neighbouring copse or fairy brake,
Or lingers playful on the haunted stream.
Go with the cotter to his winter fire,
Where o'er the moors the loud blast whistles shrill,
And the hoarse bandog bays the icy moon;
Mark with what awe he lists the wild uproar,
Silent, and big with thought; and hear him bless
The God that rides on the tempestuous clouds
For his snug hearth, and all his little joys;
Hear him compare his happier lot with his
Who bends his way across the wintry wolds,
A poor night-traveller, while the dismal snow
Beats in his face, and, dubious of his path,
He stops, and thinks, in every lengthening blast,
He hears some village-mastiff's distant howl,
And sees, far streaming, some lone cottage light;
Then, undeceived, upturns his streaming eyes,
And clasps his shivering hands; or, overpowered,
Sinks on the frozen ground, weighed down with sleep,
From which the hapless wretch shall never wake!
Thus the poor rustic warms his heart with praise
And glowing gratitude; he turns to bless,
With honest warmth, his Maker and his God!
And shall it e'er be said, that a poor hind,
Nursed in the lap of ignorance, and bred
In want and labour, glows with nobler zeal
To laud his Maker's attributes; while he
Whom starry Science in her cradle rocked,
And Castaly enchastened with its dews,
Closes his eyes upon the holy word,
And, blind to all but arrogance and pride,
Dares to declare his infidelity,
And openly contemn the Lord of Hosts?
What is philosophy, if it impart
Irreverence for the Deity, or teach
A mortal man to set his judgment up
Against his Maker's will? The Polygar,
Who kneels to sun or moon, compared with him
Who thus perverts the talents he enjoys,
Is the most blest of men! Oh, I would walk
A weary journey—to the furthest verge
Of the big world, to kiss that good man's hand,
Who, in the blaze of wisdom and of art,
Preserves a lowly mind; and to his God,
Feeling the sense of his own littleness,
Is as a child in meek simplicity!
What is the pomp of learning—the parade
Of letters and of tongues? E'en as the mists
Of the grey morn before the rising sun,
That pass away and perish!
Earthly things
Are but the transient pageants of an hour;
And earthly pride is like the passing flower,

That springs to fall, and blossoms but to die:
'Tis as the tower erected on a cloud,
Baseless and silly as the schoolboy's dream.
Ages and epochs that destroy our pride,
And then record its downfall, what are they
But the poor creatures of man's teeming brain?
Hath Heaven its ages—or doth Heaven preserve
Its stated eras? Doth the Omnipotent
Hear of to-morrows or of yesterdays?
There is to God nor future nor a past:
Throned in his might, all times to him are present;
He hath no lapse, no past, no time to come;
He sees before him one eternal *now*.
Time moveth not!—Our being 'tis that moves;
And we, swift gliding down life's rapid stream,
Dream of swift ages and revolving years,
Ordained to chronicle our passing days:
So the young sailor in the gallant bark,
Scudding before the wind, beholds the coast
Receding from his eyes, and thinks the while,
Struck with amaze, that he is motionless,
And that the land is sailing!

Such, alas,
Are the illusions of this Proteus life!
All, all is false: through every phasis still
'Tis shadowy and deceitful. It assumes
The semblances of things and specious shapes;
But the lost traveller might as soon rely
On the evasive spirit of the marsh,
Whose lantern beams, and vanishes, and flits,
O'er bog, and rock, and pit, and hollow way,
As we on its appearances.

On earth
There is nor certainty nor stable hope.
As well the weary mariner, whose bark
Is tossed beyond Cimmerian Bosphorus,
Where Storm and Darkness hold their drear domain,
And sunbeams never penetrate, might trust
To expectation of serener skies,
And linger in the very jaws of death,
Because some peevish cloud were opening,
Or the loud storm had bated in its rage;
As we look forward in this vale of tears
To permanent delight, from some slight glimpse
Of shadowy unsubstantial happiness.

The good man's hope is laid far, far beyond
The sway of tempests, or the furious sweep
Of mortal desolation. He beholds,
Unapprehensive, the gigantic stride
Of rampant ruin, or the unstable waves
Of dark vicissitude. Even in death,
In that dread hour, when, with a giant pang
Tearing the tender fibres of the heart,
The immortal spirit struggles to be free,
Then, even then, that hope forsakes him not,
For it exists beyond the narrow verge
Of the cold sepulchre: the petty joys
Of fleeting life indignantly it spurned,
And rested on the bosom of its God.
This is man's only reasonable hope;
And 'tis a hope which, cherished in the breast,
Shall not be disappointed. Even he,
The Holy One—Almighty, who elanced
The rolling world along its airy way,
Even he will deign to smile upon the good,
And welcome him to these celestial seats,
Where joy and gladness hold their changeless reign.

Thou proud man, look upon yon starry vault,
Survey the countless gems which richly stud
The Night's imperial chariot; telescopes
Will show thee myriads more innumerous
Than the sea sand: each of those little lamps
Is the great source of light, the central sun
Round which some other mighty sisterhood
Of planets travel, every planet stocked
With living beings impotent as thee.
Now, proud man, now, where is thy greatness fled?—
What art thou in the scale of universe?
Less, less than nothing! Yet of thee the God
Who built this wondrous frame of worlds is careful,
As well as of the mendicant who begs
The leavings of thy table. And shalt thou
Lift up thy thankless spirit and contemn
His heavenly providence! Deluded fool,
E'en now the thunderbolt is wing'd with death,
E'en now thou totterest on the brink of hell!

How insignificant is mortal man,
Bound to the hasty pinions of an hour!—
How poor, how trivial in the vast conceit
Of infinite duration, boundless space!
God of the universe, Almighty One,
Thou who dost walk upon the winged winds,
Or with the storm, thy rugged charioteer,
Swift and impetuous as the northern blast,
Ridest from pole to pole; thou who dost hold
The forked lightnings in thine awful grasp,
And reignest in the earthquake; when thy wrath
Goes down towards erring man, I would address
To thee my parting pæan; for of thee,
Great beyond comprehension, who thyself
Art Time and Space, sublime Infinitude,
Of thee has been my song. With awe I kneel
Trembling before the footstool of thy state,
My God, my Father!—I will sing to thee
A hymn of laud, a solemn canticle,
Ere on the cypress wreath, which overshades
The throne of Death, I hang my mournful lyre,
And give its wild strings to the desert gale.
Rise, Son of Salem! rise, and join the strain;
Sweep to accordant tones thy tuneful harp,
And leaving vain laments, arouse thy soul
To exultation. Sing hosanna, sing;
And hallelujah; for the Lord is great
And full of mercy!—He has thought of man;
Yea, compassed round with countless worlds, has thought
Of us poor worms, that batten in the dews
Of morn, and perish ere the noonday sun.
Sing to the Lord, for he is merciful:
He gave the Nubian lion but to live,
To rage its hour, and perish; but on man
He lavished immortality and heaven.
The eagle falls from her aërial tower,
And mingles with irrevocable dust;
But man from death springs joyful,
Springs up to life and to eternity.
Oh that, insensate of the favouring boon,
The great exclusive privilege bestowed
On us unworthy triflers, men should dare
To treat with slight regard the proffered Heaven,
And urge the lenient, but All-Just, to swear
In wrath, "They shall not enter in my rest."
Might I address the supplicative strain
To thy high footstool, I would pray that thou
Wouldst pity the deluded wanderers,
And fold them, ere they perish, in thy flock.

Yea, I would bid thee pity them, through him,
Thy Well-belovëd, who, upon the cross,
Bled a dead sacrifice for human sin,
And paid, with bitter agony, the debt
Of primitive transgression.
Oh, I shrink,
My very soul doth shrink, when I reflect
That the time hastens, when, in vengeance clothed,
Thou shalt come down to stamp the seal of fate
On erring mortal man! Thy chariot wheels
Then shall rebound to earth's remotest caves,
And stormy Ocean from his bed shall start
At the appalling summons. Oh, how dread,
On the dark eye of miserable man,
Chasing his sins in secrecy and gloom,
Will burst the effulgence of the opening Heaven;
When to the brazen trumpet's deafening roar
Thou and thy dazzling cohorts shall descend,
Proclaiming the fulfilment of the word!
The dead shall start astonished from their sleep;
The sepulchres shall groan and yield their prey;
The bellowing floods shall disembogue their charge
Of human victims! From the farthest nook
Of the wide world shall troop their risen souls,
From him whose bones are bleaching in the waste
Of polar solitudes, or him whose corpse,
Whelmed in the loud Atlantic's vexëd tides,
Is washed on some Caribbean prominence,
To the lone tenant of some secret cell
In the Pacific's vast . . . realm,
Where never plummet's sound was heard to part
The wilderness of water; they shall come
To greet the solemn advent of the Judge.

Thou first shalt summon the elected saints,
To their apportioned Heaven; and thy Son,
At thy right hand, shall smile with conscious joy
On all his past distresses, when for them
He bore humanity's severest pangs.
Then shalt thou seize the avenging scimitar,
And, with a roar as loud and horrible
As the stern earthquake's monitory voice,
The wicked shall be driven to their abode,
Down the immitigable gulf, to wail
And gnash their teeth in endless agony.

. . . .

Rear thou aloft thy standard.—Spirit, rear
Thy flag on high!—Invincible and throned
In unparticipated might. Behold
Earth's proudest boasts, beneath thy silent sway,
Sweep headlong to destruction, thou the while,
Unmoved and heedless, thou dost hear the rush
Of mighty generations, as they pass
To the broad gulf of ruin, and dost stamp
Thy signet on them, and they rise no morë.
Who shall contend with Time—unvanquished Time,
The conqueror of conquerors, the lord
Of desolations?—Lo! the shadows fly,
The hours and days, and years and centuries,
They fly, they fly, and nations rise and fall;
The young are old, the old are in their graves.
Heard'st thou that shout? It rent the vaulted skies;
It was the voice of people—mighty crowds—
Again! 'tis hushed—Time speaks, and all is hushed!
In the vast multitude now reigns alone
Unruffled solitude. They all are still;
All—yea, the whole—the incalculable mass,
Still as the ground that clasps their cold remains.
Rear thou aloft thy standard.—Spirit, rear
Thy flag on high, and glory in thy strength!

But do thou know the season yet shall come,
When from its base thine adamantine throne
Shall tumble; when thine arm shall cease to strike,
Thy voice forget its petrifying power;
When saints shall shout, and Time shall be no more.
Yea, he doth come—the Mighty Champion comes,
Whose potent spear shall give thee thy death-wound,
Shall crush the conqueror of conquerors,
And desolate stern Desolation's lord.
Lo! where he cometh!—The Messiah comes!
The King! the Comforter! the Christ!—He comes
To burst the bonds of Death, and overturn
The power of Time.—Hark! the loud trumpet's blast
Rings o'er the heavens! They rise, the myriads rise,
E'en from their graves they spring, and burst the
Of torpor!—He has ransomed them [chains

. . . .

Forgotten generations live again,
Assume the bodily shapes they owned of old,
Beyond the flood: the righteous of their times
Embrace and weep, they weep the tears of joy.
The sainted mother wakes, and in her lap
Clasps her dear babe, the partner of her grave,
And heritor with her of Heaven, a flower
Washed by the blood of Jesus from the stain
Of native guilt, e'en in its early bud.
And, hark! those strains, how solemnly serene
They fall, as from the skies—at distance fall—
Again more loud—the hallelujahs swell;
The newly-risen catch the joyful sound;
They glow, they burn; and now with one accord
Bursts forth sublime from every mouth the song
Of praise to God on high, and to the Lamb
Who bled for mortals.

. . . .

Yet there is peace for mam—Yea, there is peace
E'en in this noisy, this unsettled scene;
When from the crowd, and from the city far,
Haply he may be set (in his late walk
O'ertaken with deep thought) beneath the boughs
Of honeysuckle, when the sun is gone,
And with fix'd eye, and wistful, he surveys
The solemn shadows of the heavens sail,
And thinks the season yet shall come, when Time
Will waft him to repose, to deep repose,
Far from the unquietness of life—from noise
And tumult far—beyond the flying clouds,
Beyond the stars, and all this passing scene,
Where change shall cease, and Time shall be no more.

. . . .

CHILDHOOD: A Poem.

[This appears to be one of the author's earliest productions: written when about the age of fourteen.]

PART I.

Pictured in memory's mellowing glass, how sweet
Our infant days, our infant joys, to greet;
To roam in fancy in each cherished scene,
The village churchyard, and the village green,
The woodland walk remote, the greenwood glade,
The mossy seat beneath the hawthorn's shade,
The whitewashed cottage, where the woodbine grew,
And all the favourite haunts our childhood knew!
How sweet, while all the evil shuns the gaze,
To view the unclouded skies of former days!

Belovëd age of innocence and smiles,
When each wing'd hour some new delight beguiles;

When the gay heart, to life's sweet dayspring true,
Still finds some insect pleasure to pursue.
Blest childhood, hail!—Thee simply will I sing,
And from myself the artless picture bring:
These long-lost scenes to me the past restore,
Each humble friend, each pleasure now no more;
And every stump familiar to my sight
Recalls some fond idea of delight.

This shrubby knoll was once my favourite seat;
Here did I love at evening to retreat,
And muse alone, till in the vault of night,
Hesper, aspiring, showed his golden light.
Here once again, remote from human noise,
I sit me down to think of former joys;
Pause on each scene, each treasured scene, once
And once again each infant walk explore: [more,
While as each grove and lawn I recognise,
My melted soul suffuses in my eyes.

And oh, thou power, whose myriad trains resort
To distant scenes, and picture them to thought—
Whose mirror, held unto the mourner's eye,
Flings to his soul a borrowed gleam of joy—
Blest Memory! guide, with finger nicely true,
Back to my youth my retrospective view;
Recall with faithful vigour to my mind
Each face familiar, each relation kind;
And all the finer traits of them afford,
Whose general outline in my heart is stored.

In yonder cot, along whose mouldering walls
In many a fold the mantling woodbine falls,
The village matron kept her little school,
Gentle of heart, yet knowing well to rule;
Staid was the dame, and modest was her mien;
Her garb was coarse, yet whole, and nicely clean:
Her neatly bordered cap, as lily fair,
Beneath her chin was pinned with decent care:
And pendent ruffles, of the whitest lawn,
Of ancient make, her elbows did adorn.
Faint with old age and dim were grown her eyes,
A pair of spectacles their want supplies;
These does she guard secure, in leathern case,
From thoughtless wights, in some unweeted place.

Here first I entered, though with toil and pain,
The lowly vestibule of learning's fane;
Entered with pain, yet soon I found the way,
Though sometimes toilsome, many a sweet display.
Much did I grieve, on that ill-fated morn,
While I was first to school reluctant borne:
Severe I thought the dame, though oft she tried
To soothe my swelling spirits when I sighed;
And oft, when harshly she reproved, I wept,
To my lone corner broken-hearted crept, [kept.
And thought of tender home, where anger never

But soon inured to alphabetic toils,
Alert I met the dame with jocund smiles;
First at the form, my task for ever true,
A little favourite rapidly I grew:
And oft she stroked my head with fond delight,
Held me a pattern to the dunce's sight;
And as she gave my diligence her praise,
Talked of the honours of my future days.

Oh! had the venerable matron thought
Of all the ills by talent often brought;
Could she have seen me when revolving years
Had brought me deeper in the vale of tears,
Then had she wept, and wished my wayward fate
Had been a lowlier, an unlettered state;
Wished that, remote from worldly woes and strife,
Unknown, unheard, I might have passed through life.

Where in the busy scene, by peace unbless'd,
Shall the poor wanderer find a place of rest?
A lonely mariner on the stormy main,
Without a hope the calms of peace to gain;
Long tossed by tempest o'er the world's wide shore,
When shall his spirit rest to toil no more?
Not till the light foam of the sea shall lave
The sandy surface of his unwept grave.
Childhood, to thee I turn, from life's alarms,
Serenest season of perpetual calms,
Turn with delight, and bid the passions cease,
And joy to think with thee I tasted peace.
Sweet reign of innocence, when no crime defiles,
But each new object brings attendant smiles;
When future evils never haunt the sight,
But all is pregnant with unmixed delight;
To thee I turn, from riot and from noise,
Turn to partake of more congenial joys.

'Neath yonder elm, that stands upon the moor,
When the clock spoke the hour of labour o'er,
What clamorous throngs, what happy groups were
seen,
In various postures scattering o'er the green!
Some shoot the marble, others join the chase,
Of self-made stag, or run the emulous race;
While others, seated on the dappled grass,
With doleful tales the light-wing'd minutes pass.
Well I remember how, with gesture starched,
A band of soldiers, oft with pride we marched;
For banners, to a tall ash we did bind
Our handkerchiefs, flapping to the whistling wind;
And for our warlike arms we sought the mead,
And guns and spears we made of brittle reed;
Then, in uncouth array, our feats to crown,
We stormed some ruined pigsty for a town.

Pleased with our gay disports, the dame was wont
To set her wheel before the cottage front,
And o'er her spectacles would often peer,
To view our gambols and our boyish geer.
Still as she looked, her wheel kept turning round,
With its beloved monotony of sound.
When tired with play, we'd set us by her side,
(For out of school she never knew to chide,)
And wonder at her skill—well-known to fame,
For who could match in spinning with the dame?
Her sheets, her linen, which she showed with pride
To strangers, still her thriftness testified;
Though we poor wights did wonder much in troth,
How 'twas her spinning manufactured cloth.

Oft we would leave, though well-beloved, our play,
To chat at home the vacant hour away.
Many's the time I've scampered down the glade,
To ask the promised ditty from the maid,
Which well she loved, as well she knew to sing,
While we around her formed a little ring:
She told of innocence foredoomed to bleed,
Of wicked guardians bent on bloody deed,
Or little children murdered as they slept;
While at each pause we wrung our hands and wept.
Sad was such tale, and wonder much did we,
Such hearts of stone there in the world could be.
Poor simple wights, ah! little did we ween
The ills that wait on man in life's sad scene!
Ah, little thought that we ourselves should know,
This world's a world of weeping and of woe!

Belovèd moment! then 'twas first I caught
The first foundation of romantic thought;
Then first I shed bold Fancy's thrilling tear,
Then first that poesy charmed mine infant ear.
Soon stored with much of legendary lore,
The sports of Childhood charmed my soul no more.

Far from the scene of gaiety and noise,
Far, far from turbulent and empty joys,
I hied me to the thick o'er-arching shade,
And there, on mossy carpet, listless laid,
While at my feet the rippling runnel ran,
The days of wild romance antique I'd scan;
Soar on the wings of fancy through the air,
To realms of light, and pierce the radiance there.

. . . . . .

PART II.

There are who think that childhood does not share
With age the cup, the bitter cup of care:
Alas! they know not this unhappy truth,
That every age, and rank, is born to ruth.

From the first dawn of reason in the mind,
Man is foredoomed the thorns of grief to find!
At every step has farther cause to know,
The draught of pleasure still is dashed with woe.

Yet in the youthful breast, for ever caught
With some new object for romantic thought,
The' impression of the moment quickly flies,
And with the morrow every sorrow dies.

How different manhood! Then does Thought's control
Sink every pang still deeper in the soul;
Then keen Affliction's sad unceasing smart
Becomes a painful resident in the heart;
And Care, whom not the gayest can outbrave,
Pursues its feeble victim to the grave.
Then, as each long-known friend is summoned hence,
We feel a void no joy can recompense,
And as we weep o'er every new-made tomb,
Wish that ourselves the next may meet our doom.

Yes, Childhood, thee no rankling woes pursue,
No forms of future ills salute thy view,
No pangs repentant bid thee wake to weep,
But halcyon Peace protects thy downy sleep,
And sanguine Hope, through every storm of life,
Shoots her bright beams, and calms the internal strife.
Yet e'en round childhood's heart, a thoughtless shrine,
Affection's little thread will ever twine;
And though but frail may seem each tender tie,
The soul foregoes them but with many a sigh.
Thus, when the long-expected moment came,
When forced to leave the gentle-hearted dame,
Reluctant throbbings rose within my breast,
And a still tear my silent grief expressed.
When to the public school compelled to go,
What novel scenes did on my senses flow!
There in each breast each active power dilates,
Which broils whole nations, and convulses states;
There reigns by turns alternate, love and hate,
Ambition burns, and factious rebels prate;
And in a smaller range, a smaller sphere,
The dark deformities of man appear.
Yet there the gentler virtues kindred claim,
There Friendship lights her pure untainted flame,
There mild Benevolence delights to dwell,
And sweet Contentment rests without her cell;
And there, mid many a stormy soul, we find
The good of heart, the intelligent of mind.

'Twas there, oh George, with thee I learn'd to join
In Friendship's bands—in amity divine.
Oh, mournful thought!—Where is thy spirit now
As here I sit on favourite Logar's brow,
And trace below each well-remembered glade,
Where arm-in-arm erewhile with thee I strayed,
Where art thou laid—on what untrodden shore,
Where naught is heard save ocean's sullen roar,
Dost thou in lowly unlamented state,
At last repose from all the storms of fate?
Methinks I see thee struggling with the wave,
Without one aiding hand stretched out to save;
See thee convulsed, thy looks to heaven bend,
And send thy parting sigh unto thy friend;
Or where immeasurable wilds dismay,
Forlorn and sad thou bend'st thy weary way,
While sorrow and disease with anguish rife
Consume apace the ebbing springs of life.
Again I see his door against thee shut,
The unfeeling native turn thee from his hut;
I see thee spent with toil and worn with grief,
Sit on the grass, and wish the longed relief;
Then lie thee down, the stormy struggle o'er,
Think on thy native land—and rise no more!

Oh! that thou couldst, from thine august abode,
Survey thy friend in life's dismaying road,
That thou couldst see him at this moment here,
Embalm thy memory with a pious tear,
And hover o'er him as he gazes round,
Where all the scenes of infant joys surround.

Yes, yes, his spirit's near!—The whispering breeze
Conveys his voice sad sighing on the trees;
And lo! his form transparent I perceive,
Borne on the grey mist of the sullen eve:
He hovers near, clad in the night's dim robe,
While deathly silence reigns upon the globe.
Yet ah! whence comes this visionary scene?
'Tis Fancy's wild aërial dream, I ween;
By her inspired, when reason takes its flight,
What fond illusions beam upon the sight!
She waves her hand, and lo! what forms appear!
What magic sounds salute the wondering ear!
Once more o'er distant regions do we tread,
And the cold grave yields up its cherished dead;
While present sorrow's banished far away,
Unclouded azure gilds the placid day,
Or in the future's cloud-encircled face,
Fair scenes of bliss to come we fondly trace,
And draw minutely every little wile
Which shall the feathery hours of time beguile

So when forlorn and lonesome, at her gate,
The Royal Mary solitary sate,
And viewed the moonbeam trembling on the wave,
And heard the hollow surge her prison lave,
Towards France's distant coast she bent her sight,
For there her soul had winged its longing flight;
There did she form full many a scheme of joy,
Visions of bliss unclouded with alloy,
Which bright through Hope's deceitful optics beamed,
And all became the surety which it seemed;
She wept, yet felt, while all within was calm,
In every tear a melancholy charm.

To yonder hill, whose sides deformed and steep,
Just yield a scanty sustenance to the sheep,
With thee, my friend, I oftentimes have sped,
To see the sun rise from his healthy bed;
To watch the aspect of the summer morn,
Smiling upon the golden fields of corn,
And taste delighted of superior joys,
Beheld through Sympathy's enchanted eyes:
With silent admiration oft we viewed
The myriad hues o'er heaven's blue concave strewed;
The fleecy clouds, of every tint and shade,
Round which the silvery sunbeam glancing played,
And the round orb itself, in azure throne,
Just peeping o'er the blue hill's ridgy zone;
We marked delighted, how with aspect gay,
Reviving Nature hailed returning day; [heads,
Marked how the flowerets reared their drooping
And the wild lambkins bounded o'er the meads,
While from each tree, in tones of sweet delight,
The birds sung pæans to the source of light:
Oft have we watched the speckled lark arise,
Leave his grass bed, and soar to kindred skies,
And rise, and rise, till the pained sight no more
Could trace him in his high aërial tour;
Though on the ear, at intervals, his song
Came wafted slow the wavy breeze along;
And we have thought how happy were out lot,
Bless'd with some sweet, some solitary cot,
Where, from the peep of day, till russet eve
Began in every dell her forms to weave,
We might pursue our sports from day to day,
And in each other's arms wear life away.

At sultry noon too, when our toils were done,
We to the gloomy glen were wont to run:
There on the turf we lay, while at our feet
The cooling rivulet rippled softly sweet;
And mused on holy theme, and ancient lore,
Of deeds, and days, and heroes now no more;
Heard, as his solemn harp Isaiah swept,
Sung woe unto the wicked land—and wept;
Or, fancy-led, saw Jeremiah mourn
In solemn sorrow o'er Judea's urn.
Then to another shore perhaps would rove,
With Plato talk in his Ilyssian grove;
Or, wandering where the Thespian palace rose,
Weep once again o'er fair Jocasta's woes.
Sweet then to us was that romantic band,
The ancient legends of our native land—
Chivalric Britomart, and Una fair,
And courteous Constance, doomed to dark despair,
By turns our thoughts engaged; and oft we talked
Of times when monarch Superstition stalked,
And when the blood-fraught galliots of Rome
Brought the grand Druid fabric to its doom:
While, where the wood-hung Menai's waters flow,
The hoary harpers poured the strain of woe.

While thus employed, to us how sad the bell
Which summoned us to school! 'Twas Fancy's knell,
And, sadly sounding on the sullen ear,
It spoke of study pale and chilling fear.
Yet even then, (for oh! what chains can bind,
What powers control, the energies of mind?)
E'en then we soared to many a height sublime,
And many a day-dream charmed the lazy time.

At evening too, how pleasing was our walk,
Endeared by Friendship's unrestrained talk,
When to the upland heights we bent our way,
To view the last beam of departing day;
How calm was all around!—No playful breeze
Sighed 'mid the wavy foliage of the trees,
But all was still, save when, with drowsy song,
The grey-fly wound his sullen horn along;
And save when heard, in soft yet merry glee,
The distant church-bell's mellow harmony;
The silver mirror of the lucid brook,
That 'mid the tufted broom its still course took;
The rugged arch, that clasped its silent tides,
With moss and rank weeds hanging down its sides;
The craggy rock, that jutted on the sight;
The shrieking bat, that took its heavy flight;
All, all was pregnant with divine delight.
We loved to watch the swallow swimming high,
In the bright azure of the vaulted sky;
Or gaze upon the clouds, whose coloured pride
Was scattered thinly o'er the welkin wide,
And tinged with such variety of shade,
To the charmed soul sublimest thoughts conveyed.
In these what forms romantic did we trace,
While Fancy led us o'er the realms of space!
Now we espied the Thunderer in his car,
Leading the embattled seraphim to war,
Then stately towers descried, sublimely high,
In Gothic grandeur frowning on the sky—
Or saw, wide stretching o'er the azure height,
A ridge of glaciers in mural white,
Hugely terrific. But those times are o'er,
And the fond scene can charm mine eyes no more;
For thou art gone, and I am left below
Alone to struggle through this world of woe.

The scene is o'er:—Still seasons onward roll,
And each revolve conducts me towards the goal;
Yet all is blank, without one soft relief,
One endless continuity of grief;
And the tired soul, now led to thoughts sublime,
Looks but for rest beyond the bounds of time.

Toil on, toil on, ye busy crowds, that pant
For hoards of wealth which ye will never want:
And, lost to all but gain, with ease resign
The calms of peace and happiness divine!
Far other cares be mine—Men little crave
In this short journey to the silent grave;
And the poor peasant, bless'd with peace and health,
I envy more than Crœsus with his wealth.
Yet grieve not I, that Fate did not decree
Paternal acres to await on me;
She gave me more—she placed within my breast
A heart with little pleased, with little blest:
I look around me, where on every side
Extensive manors spread in wealthy pride;
And could my sight be borne to either zone,
I should not find one foot of land my own.

But whither do I wander?—Shall the Muse,
For golden baits, her simple theme refuse?
Oh, no; but while the weary spirit greets
The fading scenes of childhood's far-gone sweets,
It catches all the infant's wandering tongue,
And prattles on its desultory song.
That song must close—the gloomy mists of night
Obscure the pale stars' visionary light,
And ebon darkness, clad in vapoury wet,
Steals on the welkin in primeval jet.

The song must close.—Once more my adverse lot
Leads me reluctant from this cherished spot,
Again compels to plunge in busy life,
And brave the hurtful turbulence of strife.

Scenes of my youth, ere my unwilling feet
Are turned for ever from this loved retreat,
Ere on these fields, with plenty covered o'er,
My eyes are closed to ope on them no more,
Let me ejaculate, to feeling due,
One long, one last affectionate adieu.
Grant that, if ever Providence should please,
To give me an old age of peace and ease,
Grant that, in these sequestered shades, my days
May wear away in gradual decays ;
And oh! ye spirits, who unbodied play,
Unseen upon the pinions of the day,
Kind genii of my native fields benign,
Who were . . . . . .

THE CHRISTIAD: A Divine Poem.

BOOK I.

I.

I sing the Cross!—Ye white-robed angel choirs,
Who know the chords of harmony to sweep,
Ye who o'er holy David's varying wires
Were wont, of old, your hovering watch to keep,
Oh, now descend! and with your harpings deep,
Pouring sublime the full symphonious stream
Of music, such as soothes the saint's last sleep,
Awake my slumbering spirit from its dream,
And teach me how to exalt the high mysterious theme.

II.

Mourn! Salem, mourn! low lies thine humbled [state,
Thy glittering fanes are levelled with the ground!
Fallen is thy pride!—Thy halls are desolate!
Where erst was heard the timbrel's sprightly sound,
And frolic pleasures tripped the nightly round,
There breeds the wild fox lonely ; and aghast
Stands the mute pilgrim at the void profound,
Unbroke by noise, save when the hurrying blast
Sighs, like a spirit, deep along the cheerless waste.

III.

It is for this, proud Solyma! thy towers
Lie crumbling in the dust; for this forlorn
Thy genius wails along thy desert bowers,
While stern Destruction laughs, as if in scorn,
That thou didst dare insult God's eldest born ;
And with most bitter persecuting ire
Pursued his footsteps till the last day dawn
Rose on his fortunes; and thou saw'st the fire
That came to light the world, in one great flash expire.

IV.

Oh! for a pencil dipped in living light,
To paint the agonies that Jesus bore!
Oh! for the long-lost harp of Jesse's might,
To hymn the Saviour's praise from shore to shore;
While seraph hosts the lofty pæan pour,
And Heaven enraptured lists the loud acclaim!
May a frail mortal dare the theme explore?
May he to human ears his weak song frame?
Oh! may he dare to sing Messiah's glorious name?

V.

Spirits of pity! mild crusaders, come!
Buoyant on clouds around your minstrel float,
And give him eloquence who else were dumb,
And raise to feeling and to fire his note!
And thou, Urania! who dost still devote
Thy nights and days to God's eternal shrine,
Whose mild eyes 'lumined what Isaiah wrote,
Throw o'er thy bard that solemn stole of thine,
And clothe him for the fight with energy divine.

VI.

When from the temple's lofty summit prone,
Satan o'ercome, fell down ; and thronëd there,
The Son of God confessed, in splendour shone;
Swift as the glancing sunbeam cuts the air,
Mad with defeat, and yelling his despair,

. . . .

Fled the stern king of Hell—and with the glare
Of gliding meteors, ominous and red, [head.
Shot 'thwart the clouds that gathered round his

VII.

Right o'er the Euxine, and that gulf which late
The rude Massagetæ adored, he bent [state,
His northering course, while round, in dusky
The assembling fiends their summoned troops augment;
Clothed in dark mists, upon their way they went,
While, as they passed to regions more severe,
The Lapland sorcerer swelled with loud lament
The solitary gale, and, filled with fear,
The howling dogs bespoke unholy spirits near.

VIII.

Where the North Pole, in moody solitude,
Spreads her huge tracts and frozen wastes around,
There ice-rocks piled aloft, in order rude,
Form a gigantic hall, where never sound
Startled dull Silence' ear, save when profound
The smoke frost muttered: there drear Cold for aye
Thrones him ; and, fix'd on his primeval mound,
Ruin, the giant, sits ; while stern Dismay [way.
Stalks like some woe-struck man along the desert

IX.

In that drear spot, grim Desolation's lair,
No sweet remain of life encheers the sight;
The dancing heart's blood in an instant there
Would freeze to marble. Mingling day and night
(Sweet interchange, which makes our labours light,)
Are there unknown; while in the summer skies
The sun rolls ceaseless round his heavenly height,
Nor ever sets till from the scene he flies, [rise.
And leaves the long bleak night of half the year to

X.

'Twas there, yet shuddering from the burning [lake,
Satan had fix'd their next consistory,
When parting last he fondly hoped to shake
Messiah's constancy ; and thus to free
The powers of darkness from the dread decree
Of bondage brought by him, and circumvent
The unerring ways of him whose eye can see
The womb of Time, and, in its embryo pent,
Discern the colours clear of every dark event.

XI.

Here the stern monarch stayed his rapid flight,
And his thick hosts, as with a jetty pall,
Hovering, obscured the north star's peaceful light,
Waiting on wing their haughty chieftain's call.
He, meanwhile, downward, with a sullen fall,
Dropped on the echoing ice. Instant the sound
Of their broad vans was hushed, and o'er the hall,
Vast and obscure, the gloomy cohorts bound,
Till, wedged in ranks, the seat of Satan they surround.

XII.

High on a solium of the solid wave,
Pranked with rude shapes by the fantastic frost,

He stood in silence: now keen thoughts engrave
Dark figures on his front; and, tempest-toss'd,
He fears to say that every hope is lost.
Meanwhile the multitude as death are mute:
So, ere the tempest on Malacca's coast,
Sweet Quiet, gently touching her soft lute,
Sings to the whispering waves the prelude to dispute.

XIII.

At length collected, o'er the dark divan
The archfiend glanced, as by the Boreal blaze
Their downcast brows were seen, and thus began
His fierce harangue: "Spirits! our better days
Are now elapsed; Moloch and Belial's praise
Shall sound no more in groves by myriads trod.
Lo, the light breaks!—The astonished nations [gaze!
For us is lifted high the avenging rod!
For, spirits, this is he—this is the Son of God!

XIV.

"What, then! shall Satan's spirit crouch to fear?
Shall he who shook the pillars of God's reign
Drop from his unnerved arm the hostile spear?
Madness!—The very thought would make me fain
To tear the spanglets from yon gaudy plain,
And hurl them at their Maker! Fix'd as fate
I am his foe!—Yea, though his pride should deign
To soothe mine ire with half his regal state,
Still would I burn with fix'd, unalterable hate.

XV.

"Now hear the issue of my curst emprize,
When from our last sad synod I took flight,
Buoyed with false hopes, in some deep-laid disguise,
To tempt this vaunted Holy One to write
His own self-condemnation: in the plight
Of aged man in the lone wilderness,
Gathering a few stray sticks, I met his sight;
And, leaning on my staff, seemed much to guess
What cause could mortal bring to that forlorn recess.

XVI.

"Then thus in homely guise I featly framed
My lowly speech: 'Good sir, what leads this way
Your wandering steps?—Must hapless chance be blamed
That you so far from haunt of mortals stray?
Here have I dwelt for many a lingering day,
Nor trace of man have seen: but how! methought
Thou wert the youth on whom God's holy ray
I saw descend in Jordan, when John taught
That he to fallen man the saving promise brought?'

XVII.

"'I am that man,' said Jesus, 'I am He!
But truce to questions—canst thou point my feet
To some low hut, if haply such there be
In this wild labyrinth, where I may meet
With homely greeting, and may sit and eat?
For forty days I have tarried fasting here,
Hid in the dark glens of this lone retreat,
And now I hunger; and my fainting ear
Longs much to greet the sound of fountains gushing near.'

XVIII.

"Then thus I answered wily: 'If indeed,
Son of our God thou beest, what need to seek
For food from men?—Lo! on these flintstones feed,
Bid them be bread! Open thy lips and speak,
And living rills from yon parched rock will break.'
Instant as I had spoke, his piercing eye
Fix'd on my face; the blood forsook my cheek,
I could not bear his gaze; my mask slipped by;
I would have shunned his look, but had not power to fly.

XIX.

"Then he rebuked me with the holy word—
Accursëd sounds! but now my native pride
Returned, and by no foolish qualm deterred,
I bore him from the mountain's woody side,
Up to the summit, where extending wide
Kingdoms and cities, palaces and fanes,
Bright sparkling in the sunbeams were descried,
And in gay dance, amid luxuriant plains,
Tripped to the jocund reed the emasculated swains.

XX.

"'Behold,' I cried, 'these glories! scenes divine!
Thou whose sad prime in pining want decays;
And these, O rapture! these shall all be thine,
If thou wilt give to me, not God, the praise.
Hath he not given to indigence thy days?
Is not thy portion peril here and pain?
Oh! leave his temples, shun his wounding ways!
Seize the tiara! these mean weeds disdain,
Kneel, kneel, thou man of woe, and peace and splendour gain.'

XXI.

"'Is it not written,' sternly he replied, [spake,
'Tempt not the Lord thy God!' Frowning he
And instant sounds, as of the ocean tide,
Rose, and the whirlwind from its prison brake,
And caught me up aloft, till in one flake,
The sidelong volley met my swift career, [quake
And smote me earthward.—Jove himself might
At such a fall; my sinews cracked, and near
Obscure and dizzy sounds seemed ringing in mine ear.

XXII.

"Senseless and stunned I lay; till, casting round
My half unconscious gaze, I saw the foe
Borne on a car of roses to the ground,
By volant angels; and as sailing slow
He sunk, the hoary battlement below,
While on the tall spire slept the slant sunbeam,
Sweet on the enamoured zephyr was the flow
Of heavenly instruments. Such strains oft seem,
On starlit hill, to sooth the Syrian shepherd's dream.

XXIII.

"I saw, blaspheming: hate renewed my strength:
I smote the ether with my iron wing,
And left the accursëd scene.—Arrived at length
In these drear halls, to ye, my peers! I bring
The tidings of defeat. Hell's haughty king
Thrice vanquished, baffled, smitten and dismayed!
O shame! is this the hero who could fling
Defiance at his Maker, while arrayed, [played!
High o'er the walls of light rebellion's banners

XXIV.

"Yet shall not Heaven's bland minions triumph long;
Hell yet shall have revenge.—O glorious sight,
Prophetic visions on my fancy throng,
I see wild Agony's lean finger write
Sad figures on his forehead! Keenly bright
Revenge's flambeau burns! Now in his eyes
Stand the hot tears—immantled in the night,
Lo! he retires to mourn! I hear his cries!
He faints—he falls—and lo!—'tis true, ye powers, he dies."

XXV.

Thus spake the chieftain ; and as if he viewed
The scene he pictured, with his foot advanced
And chest inflated, motionless he stood,
While under his uplifted shield he glanced,
With straining eyeball fixed, like one entranced,
On viewless air : thither the dark platoon
Gazed wondering, nothing seen, save when there danced
The northern flash, or fiend late fled from noon,
Darkened the disk of the descending moon.

XXVI.

Silence crept stilly through the ranks ; the breeze
Spake most distinctly. As the sailor stands,
When all the midnight gasping from the seas
Break boding sobs, and to his sight expands
High on the shrouds the spirit that commands
The ocean-farer's life : so stiff, so sere
Stood each dark power ; while through their numerous bands
Beat not one heart ; and mingling hope and fear
Now told them all was lost, now bade revenge appear.

XXVII.

One there was there, whose loud defying tongue
Nor hope nor fear had silenced, but the swell
Of over-boiling malice. Utterance long
His passion mocked, and long he strove to tell
His labouring ire ; still syllable none fell
From his pale quivering lip, but died away
For very fury ; from each hollow cell
Half sprang his eyes, that cast a flamy ray
And . . . .

XXVIII.

"This comes," at length burst from the furious chief,
" This comes of distant counsels ! Here behold
The fruits of wily cunning, the relief
Which coward policy would fain unfold
To soothe the powers that warred with Heaven of old !
O wise, O potent, O sagacious snare !
And lo, our prince—the mighty and the bold,
There stands he spell-struck, gaping at the air,
While Heaven subverts his reign, and plants her standard there."

XXIX.

Here, as recovered, Satan fix'd his eye
Full on the speaker ; dark it was, and stern ;
He wrapped his black vest round him gloomily,
And stood like one whom weightiest thoughts concern.
Him Moloch marked, and strove again to turn
His soul to rage. " Behold, behold," he cried,
"The lord of Hell, who bade these legions spurn
Almighty rule—behold, he lays aside
The spear of just revenge, and shrinks by man defied."

XXX.

Thus ended Moloch, and his [burning] tongue
Hung quivering, as if [mad] to quench its heat
In slaughter. So, his native wilds among,
The famished tiger pants, when, near his seat,
Pressed on the sands he marks the traveller's feet.
Instant low murmurs rose, and many a sword
Had from its scabbard sprung ; but toward the seat
Of the archfiend all turned with one accord,
As loud he thus harangued the sanguinary horde.

. . . . . .

"Ye powers of Hell, I am no coward : I proved this of old. Who led your forces against the armies of Jehovah ?—Who coped with Ithuriel and the thunders of the Almighty ?—Who, when stunned and confused ye lay on the burning lake, who first awoke, and collected your scattered powers ?—Lastly, who led you across the unfathomable abyss to this delightful world, and established that reign here which now totters to its base ? How, therefore, dares yon treacherous fiend to cast a stain on Satan's bravery ?—He, who preys only on the defenceless, who sucks the blood of infants, and delights only in acts of ignoble cruelty and unequal contention ! Away with the boaster who never joins in action, but, like a cormorant, hovers over the field, to feed upon the wounded, and overwhelm the dying. True bravery is as remote from rashness as from hesitation : let us counsel coolly, but let us execute our counselled purposes determinately. In power we have learned, by that experiment which lost us Heaven, that we are inferior to the Thunder-bearer : in subtlety—in subtlety alone, we are his equals. Open war is impossible.

. . . .

" Thus we shall pierce our Conqueror through the race
Which as himself he loves ; thus, if we fall,
We fall not with the anguish, the disgrace
Of falling unrevenged. The stirring call
Of vengeance wrings within me ! Warriors all !
The word is vengeance, and the spur despair.
Away with coward wiles ! Death's coal-black pall
Be now our standard ! Be our torch the glare
Of cities fired ! Our fifes, the shrieks that fill the air."

Him answering rose Mecashpim, who of old,
Far in the silence of Chaldea's groves,
Was worshiped, god of fire, with charms untold,
And mystery. His wandering spirit roves,
Now vainly searching for the flame it loves
And sits and mourns like some white-robëd sire,
Where stood his temple, and where fragrant cloves
And cinnamon upheaped the sacred pyre,
And nightly magi watched the everlasting fire.

He waved his robe of flame, he crossed his breast,
And, sighing, his papyrus scarf surveyed,
Wove with dark characters ; then thus addressed
The troubled council. . . . .

. . . .

. . . .

I.

THUS far have I pursued my solemn theme
With self-rewarding toil ; thus far have sung
Of godlike deeds, far loftier than beseem
The lyre which I in early days have strung :
And now my spirits faint, and I have hung
The shell that solaced me in saddest hour
On the dark cypress ; and the strings which rung
With Jesu's praise, their harpings now are o'er,
Or, when the breeze comes by, moan, and are heard no more.

. . . .

And must the harp of Judah sleep again ?
Shall I no more reanimate the lay ?
Oh, thou who visitest the sons of men
Thou who dost listen when the humble pray,
One little space prolong my mournful day,

One little lapse suspend thy last decree!
I am a youthful traveller in the way,
And this slight boon would consecrate to thee
Ere I with death shake hands, and smile that I am free

. . . .
. . . .

TO THE WIND AT MIDNIGHT.

Not unfamiliar to mine ear,
Blasts of the night, ye howl as now
My shuddering casement loud
With fitful force ye beat.

Mine ear has dwelt in silent awe,
The howling sweep, the sudden rush;
And when the passing gale
Poured deep the hollow dirge.

VERSES.

When pride and envy, and the scorn
Of wealth, my heart with gall imbued,
I thought how pleasant were the morn
Of silence, in the solitude;
To hear the forest bee on wing,
Or by the stream or woodland spring
To lie and muse alone—alone,
While the tinkling waters moan,
Or such wild sounds arise, as say,
Man and noise are far away.

Now, surely, thought I, there's enow
To fill life's dusty way;
And who will miss a poet's feet,
Or wonder where he stray?
So to the woods and wastes I'll go,
And I will build an osier bower;
And sweetly there to me shall flow
The meditative hour.

And when the Autumn's withering hand
Shall strow with leaves the sylvan land,
I'll to the forest caverns hie:
And in the dark and stormy nights
I'll listen to the shrieking sprites,
Who in the wintry wolds and floods,
Keep jubilee, and shred the woods;
Or, as it drifted soft and slow,
Hurl in ten thousand shapes the snow.

. . . .

TO THE MOON.

Mild orb, who floatest through the realm of night,
A pathless wanderer o'er the lonely wild;
Welcome to me thy soft and pensive light,
Which oft in childhood my lone thoughts beguiled;
Now doubly dear as o'er my silent seat,
Nocturnal study's still retreat,
It casts a mournful melancholy gleam,
And through my lofty casement weaves,
Dim through the vine's encircling leaves,
An intermingled beam.

These feverish dews that on my temples hang,
This quivering lip, these eyes of dying flame;
These, the dread signs of many a secret pang,
These are the meed of him who pants for fame!
Pale Moon, from thoughts like these divert my soul;
Lowly I kneel before thy shrine on high;
My lamp expires; beneath thy mild control,
These restless dreams are ever wont to fly.

Come, kindred mourner, in my breast
Soothe these discordant tones to rest,
And breathe the soul of peace;
Mild visitor, I feel thee here,
It is not pain that brings this tear,
For thou hast bid it cease.

Oh, many a year has passed away
Since I, beneath thy fairy ray
Attuned my infant reed:
When wilt thou, Time, those days restore,
Those happy moments now no more

. . . .

When on the lake's damp marge I lay,
And marked the northern meteor's dance,
Bland Hope and Fancy, ye were there
To inspirate my trance.
Twin sisters, faintly now ye deign
Your magic sweets on me to shed,
In vain your powers are now essayed
To chase superior pain.

And art thou fled, thou welcome orb?
So swiftly pleasure flies;
So to mankind, in darkness lost,
The beam of ardour dies.
Wan Moon, thy nightly task is done,
And now, encurtained in the main,
Thou sinkest into rest;
But I, in vain, on thorny bed
Shall woo the god of soft repose

. . . .

Loud rage the winds without; the wintry cloud
O'er the cold north star casts her flitting shroud;
And silence, pausing in some snow-clad dale,
Starts as she hears, by fits, the shrieking gale:
Where now, shut out from every still retreat,
Her pine-clad summit, and her woodland seat,
Shall Meditation, in her saddest mood,
Retire o'er all her pensive stores to brood?
Shivering and blue the peasant eyes askance
The drifted fleeces that around him dance,
And hurries on his half-averted form,
Stemming the fury of the sidelong storm.
Him soon shall greet his snow-topped [cot of thatch,]
Soon shall his 'numbed hand tremble on the latch,
Soon from his chimney's nook the cheerful flame
Diffuse a genial warmth throughout his frame;
Round the light fire, while roars the north-wind loud,
What merry groups of vacant faces crowd;
These hail his coming—these his meal prepare,
And boast in all that cot no lurking care.
What though the social circle be denied,
E'en Sadness brightens at her own fireside,
Loves, with fixed eye, to watch the fluttering blaze,
While musing Memory dwells on former days;
Or Hope, blest spirit! smiles; and, still forgiven,
Forgets the passport while she points to Heaven.

Then heap the fire, shut out the biting air;
And from its station wheel the easy chair:
Thus fenced and warm, in silent fit, 'tis sweet
To hear without the bitter tempest beat,
All, all alone—to sit, and muse, and sigh,
The pensive tenant of obscurity.

. . . .

Oh, thou most fatal of Pandora's train,
Consumption! silent cheater of the eye;
Thou com'st not robed in agonizing pain,
Nor mark'st thy course with Death's delusive dye,
But silent and unnoticed thou dost lie;
O'er life's soft springs thy venom dost diffuse,
And, while thou giv'st new lustre to the eye,
While o'er the cheek are spread health's ruddy hues,
E'en then life's little rest thy cruel power subdues.
Oft I've beheld thee, in the glow of youth,
Hid'neath the blushing roses which there bloomed,
And dropped a tear, for then thy cankering tooth
I knew would never stay, till, all consumed,
In the cold vault of Death he there entombed.
But oh, what sorrow did I feel, as swift,
Insidious ravager! I saw thee fly
Through fair Lucina's breast of whitest snow,
Preparing swift her passage to the sky.
Though still intelligence beamed in the glance,
The liquid lustre of her fine blue eye;
Yet soon did languid listlessness advance,
And soon she calmly sunk in death's repugnant trance.
E'en when her end was swiftly drawing near,
And dissolution hovered o'er her head;
E'en then so beauteous did her form appear,
That none who saw her but admiring said,
"Sure so much beauty never could be dead."
Yet the dark lash of her expressive eye,
Bent lowly down upon the languid

. . . .

CHRISTMAS DAY.

1804.

Yet once more, and once more, awake, my harp,
From silence and neglect!—One lofty strain,
Lofty, yet wilder than the winds of heaven,
And speaking mysteries more than words can tell,
I ask of thee; for I, with hymnings high,
Would join the dirge of the departing year.
Yet with no wintry garland from the woods,
Wrought of the leafless branch, or ivy sere,
Wreathe I thy tresses, dark December, now!
Me higher quarrel calls, with loudest song,
And fearful joy, to celebrate the day
Of the Redeemer. Near two thousand suns
Have set their seals upon the rolling lapse
Of generations, since the dayspring first
Beamed from on high!—Now to the mighty mass
Of that increasing aggregate we add
One unit more. Space, in comparison,
How small, yet marked with how much misery—
Wars, famines, and the fury Pestilence
Over the nations hanging her dread scourge;
The oppressed, too, in silent bitterness
Weeping their sufferance; and the arm of Wrong
Forcing the scanty portion from the weak,
And steeping the lone widow's couch with tears.

So has the year been charactered with woe
In Christian land, and marked with wrongs and crimes:
Yet 'twas not thus *he* taught—not thus *he* lived,
Whose birth we this day celebrate with prayer
And much thanksgiving.—He, a man of woes,
Went on the way appointed—path, though rude,
Yet borne with patience still. He came to cheer
The broken-hearted, to raise up the sick,
And on the wandering and benighted mind
To pour the light of truth.—O, task divine!
O, more than angel teacher! He had words
To soothe the barking waves, and hush the winds;
And when the soul was tossed in troubled seas,
Wrapped in thick darkness and the howling storm,
He, pointing to the Star of Peace on high,
Armed it with fortitude, and bade it smile
At the surrounding wreck. . . .
When with deep agony his heart was racked,
Not for himself the teardrop dewed his cheek;
For them he wept, for them to Heaven he prayed
His persecutors—"Father, pardon them,
They know not what they do."

Angels of Heaven,
Ye who beheld him fainting on the cross,
And did him homage, say, may mortal join
The hallelujahs of the risen God?
Will the faint voice and grovelling song be heard
Amid the seraphim in light divine?
Yes, he will deign, the Prince of Peace will deign,
For mercy, to accept the hymn of faith,
Low though it be, and humble. Lord of life,
The Christ, the Comforter, thine advent now
Fills my uprising soul! I mount, I fly
Far o'er the skies, beyond the rolling orbs;
The bonds of flesh dissolve, and earth recedes;
And care, and pain, and sorrow are no more.

. . . .

NELSONI MORS.

Yet once again, my harp, yet once again—
One ditty more, and on the mountain ash
I will again suspend thee. I have felt
The warm tear frequent on my cheek, since last,
At eventide, when all the winds were hushed,
I woke to thee the melancholy song.
Since then with Thoughtfulness, a maid severe,
I've journeyed, and have learn'd to shape the freaks
Of frolic fancy to the line of truth;
Not unrepining—for my froward heart
Still turns to thee, mine harp, and to the flow
Of spring-gales past, the woods and storied haunts
Of my not songless boyhood. Yet once more,
Not fearless, I will wake thy tremulous tones,
My long neglected harp. He must not sink;
The good, the brave—he must not, shall not sink
Without the meed of some melodious tear.

Though from the Muse's chalice I may pour
No precious dews of Aganippe's well
Or Castaly; though from the morning cloud
I fetch no hues to scatter on his hearse;
Yet will I wreathe a garland for his brows,
Of simple flowers, such as the hedge-rows scent

Of Britain, my loved country ; and with tears,
Most eloquent, yet silent, I will bathe
Thy honoured corse, my Nelson—tears as warm
And honest as the ebbing blood that flowed
Fast from thy honest heart. Thou, Pity, too,
If ever I have loved, with faltering step,
To follow thee in the cold and starless night
To the top crag of some rain-beaten cliff,
And as I heard the deep gun bursting loud
Amid the pauses of the storm, have poured
Wild strains, and mournful, to the hurrying winds,
The dying soul's viaticum ; if oft
Amid the carnage of the field I 've sate
With thee upon the moonlight throne, and sung
To cheer the fainting soldier's dying soul
With mercy and forgiveness ; visitant
Of Heaven, sit thou upon my . . . harp,
And give it feeling, which were else too cold
For argument so great, for theme so high.

How dimly on that morn the sun arose,
Kerchiefed in mists, and tearful, when

. . . .
. . . .

TO THE GENIUS OF ROMANCE.

Oh, thou who, in my early youth,
When fancy wore the garb of truth,
Wert wont to win my infant feet
To some retired, deep-fabled seat,
Where, by the brooklet's secret tide,
The midnight ghost was known to glide ;
Or lay me in some lonely glade,
In native Sherwood's forest shade,
Where Robin Hood, the outlaw bold
Was wont his sylvan courts to hold ;
And there, as musing deep I lay,
Would steal my little soul away,
And all thy pictures represent,
Of siege and solemn tournament ;
Or bear me to the magic scene,
Where, clad in greaves and gaberdine,
The warrior knight of chivalry
Made many a fierce enchanter flee ;
And bore the high-born dame away,
Long held the fell magician's prey ;
Or oft would tell the shuddering tale
Of murders, and of goblins pale
Haunting the guilty baron's side,
(Whose floors with secret blood were dyed)
Which o'er the vaulted corridor
On stormy nights was heard to roar,
By old domestic, wakened wide
By the angry winds that chide ;
Or else the mystic tale would tell,
Of Greensleeve, or of Bluebeard fell.

. . . .

FRAGMENT OF AN ECCENTRIC DRAMA.

WRITTEN AT A VERY EARLY AGE.

THE DANCE OF THE CONSUMPTIVES.

Ding-dong ! ding-dong !
Merry, merry go the bells,
Ding-dong ! ding-dong !
Over the heath, over the moor, and over the dale,
"Swinging slow with sullen roar,"
Dance, dance away the jocund roundelay !
Ding-dong, ding-dong calls us away.

Round the oak, and round the elm
Merrily foot it o'er the ground !
The sentry ghost it stands aloof,
So merrily, merrily foot it round.
Ding-dong ! ding-dong !
Merry, merry go the bells,
Swelling in the nightly gale,
The sentry ghost,
It keeps its post,
And soon, and soon our sports must fail :
But let us trip the nightly ground,
While the merry, merry bells ring round.

Hark ! hark ! the death-watch ticks !
See, see, the winding sheet !
Our dance is done,
Our race is run,
And we must lie at the alder's feet !
Ding-dong ! ding-dong !
Merry, merry go the bells,
Swinging o'er the weltering wave !
And we must seek
Our death-beds bleak,
Where the green sod grows upon the grave.

[*They vanish: the* Goddess of Consumption *descends, habited in a sky-blue robe, attended by mournful music.*]

Come, Melancholy, sister mine,
Cold the dews, and chill the night !
Come from thy dreary shrine !
The wan moon climbs the heavenly height,
And underneath her sickly ray
Troops of squalid spectres play,
And the dying mortal's groan
Startles the night on her dusky throne.
Come, come, sister mine !
Gliding on the pale moon-shine :
We 'll ride at ease
On the tainted breeze,
And oh ! our sport will be divine.

[*The* Goddess of Melancholy *advances out of a deep glen in the rear, habited in black, and covered with a thick veil: she speaks.*]

Sister, from my dark abode,
Where nests the raven, sits the toad,
Hither I come, at thy command :
Sister, sister, join thy hand !
Sister, sister, join thy hand !
I will smooth the way for thee,
Thou shalt furnish food for me :
Come, let us speed our way
Where the troops of spectres play,
To charnel-houses, church-yards drear,
Where Death sits with a horrible leer,
A lasting grin, on a throne of bones,
And skim along the blue tomb-stones.

Come, let us speed away,
Lay our snares, and spread our tether !
I will smooth the way for thee,
Thou shalt furnish food for me ;
And the grass shall wave
O'er many a grave,
Where youth and beauty sleep together.

CONSUMPTION.

Come, let us speed our way!
Join our hands, and spread our tether!
I will furnish food for thee,
Thou shalt smooth the way for me;
And the grass shall wave
O'er many a grave,
Where youth and beauty sleep together.

MELANCHOLY.

Hist, sister, hist! who comes here?
Oh! I know her by that tear,
By that blue eye's languid glare,
By her skin, and by her hair:
She is mine,
And she is thine,
Now the deadliest draught prepare.

CONSUMPTION.

In the dismal night air dressed,
I will creep into her breast;
Flush her cheek, and bleach her skin,
And feed on the vital fire within.
Lover, do not trust her eyes—
When they sparkle most, she dies!
Mother, do not trust her breath—
Comfort she will breathe in death!
Father, do not strive to save her—
She is mine, and I must have her!
The coffin must be her bridal bed;
The winding-sheet must wrap her head;
The whispering winds must o'er her sigh,
For soon in the grave the maid must lie.
The worm it will riot
On heavenly diet,
When death has deflowered her eye.

[*They vanish. While* CONSUMPTION *speaks,* ANGELINA *enters.*]

ANGELINA.

With what a silent and dejected pace *
Dost thou, wan moon! upon thy way advance
In the blue welkin's vault!—Pale wanderer!
Hast thou too felt the pangs of hopeless love,
That thus, with such a melancholy grace,
Thou dost pursue thy solitary course?
Has thy Endymion, smooth-faced boy, forsook
Thy widowed breast—on which the spoiler oft
Has nestled fondly, while the silver clouds
Fantastic pillowed thee, and the dim night,
Obsequious to thy will, encurtained round
With its thick fringe thy couch? Wan traveller,
How like thy fate to mine!—Yet I have still
One heavenly hope remaining, which thou lack'st:
My woes will soon be buried in the grave
Of kind forgetfulness; my journey here,
Though it be darksome, joyless, and forlorn,
Is yet but short, and soon my weary feet
Will greet the peaceful inn of lasting rest.
But thou, unhappy queen! art doomed to trace
Thy lonely walk in the drear realms of night,
While many a lagging age shall sweep beneath
The leaden pinions of unshaken time;
Though not a hope shall spread its glittering hue
To cheat thy steps along the weary way.

O that the sum of human happiness
Should be so trifling, and so frail withal,
That when possessed, it is but lessened grief;
And even then there's scarce a sudden gust
That blows across the dismal waste of life,
But bears it from the view. Oh! who would shun
The hour that cuts from earth, and fear to press
The calm and peaceful pillows of the grave,
And yet endure the various ills of life,
And dark vicissitudes!—Soon, I hope, I feel,
And am assured, that I shall lay my head,
My weary aching head, on its last rest,
And on my lowly bed the grass-green sod
Will flourish sweetly. And then they will weep
That one so young, and what they're pleased to call
So beautiful, should die so soon: and tell
How painful disappointment's cankered fang
Withered the rose upon my maiden cheek.
Oh, foolish ones! why, I shall sleep so sweetly,
Laid in my darksome grave, that they themselves
Might envy me my rest!—And as for them,
Who, on the score of former intimacy,
May thus remembrance me, they must themselves
Successive fall.
Around the winter fire
(When out-o'-doors the biting frost congeals,
And shrill the skater's irons on the pool
Ring loud, as by the moonlight he performs
His graceful evolutions,) they not long
Shall sit and chat of older times, and feats
Of early youth, but silent, one by one,
Shall drop into their shrouds—some in their age
Ripe for the sickle; others young, like me,
And falling green beneath th' untimely stroke.
Thus, in short time, in the church-yard forlorn,
Where I shall lie, my friends will lay them down,
And dwell with me, a happy family.
And oh! thou cruel yet belovëd youth,
Who now hast left me hopeless here to mourn,
Do thou but shed one tear upon my corse,
And say that I was gentle, and deserved
A better lover, and I shall forgive
All, all thy wrongs; and then do thou forget
The hapless Margaret, and be as blest
As wish can make thee—laugh, and play, and sing
With thy dear choice, and never think of me.

Yet hist! I hear a step.—In this dark wood

. . . .

THE western gale,
Mild as the kisses of connubial love,
Plays round my languid limbs, as all dissolved,
Beneath the ancient elm's fantastic shade
I lie, exhausted with the noontide heat;
While rippling o'er his deep-worn pebble-bed,
The rapid rivulet rushes at my feet,
Dispensing coolness. On the fringëd marge
Full many a floweret rears its head—or pink,
Or gaudy daffodil. 'Tis here, at noon,
The buskined wood-nymphs from the heat retire,
And lave them in the fountain; here secure
From Pan, or savage satyr, they disport;
Or stretch supinely on the velvet turf,
Lulled by the laden bee, or sultry fly,
Invoke the god of slumber.

. . . .

And hark! how merrily, from distant tower,
Ring round the village bells! Now on the gale
They rise with gradual swell, distinct and loud;
Anon they die upon the pensive ear,

* With how sad steps, O moon! thou climb'st the skies,
How silently, and with how wan a face!
SIR P. SIDNEY.

Melting in faintest music: they bespeak
A day of jubilee, and oft they bear,
Commixed along the unfrequented shore,
The sound of village dance and tabor loud,
Startling the musing ear of solitude.

Such is the jocund wake of Whitsuntide,
When happy Superstition, gabbling eld!
Holds her unhurtful gambols. All the day
The rustic revellers ply the mazy dance
On the smooth-shaven green; and then at eve
Commence the harmless rites and auguries;
And many a tale of ancient days goes round.
They tell of wizard seer, whose potent spells
Could hold in dreadful thrall the labouring moon.
Or draw the fixed stars from their eminence,
And still the midnight tempest! Then anon
Tell of uncharneled spectres, seen to glide
Along the lone wood's unfrequented path,
Startling the 'nighted traveller; while the sound
Of undistinguished murmurs, heard to come
From the dark centre of the deepening glen,
Struck on his frozen ear.
Oh, ignorance,
Thou art fallen man's best friend!—With thee he speeds
In frigid apathy along his way.
And never does the tear of agony
Burn down his scorching cheek; or the keen steel
Of wounded feeling penetrate his breast.

E'en now, as leaning on this fragrant bank
I taste of all the keener happiness
Which sense refined affords—e'en now, my heart
Would fain induce me to forsake the world,
Throw off these garments, and in shepherd's weeds
With a small flock, and short suspended reed,
To sojourn in the woodland. Then my thought
Draws such gay pictures of ideal bliss,
That I could almost err in reason's spite,
And trespass on my judgment.
Such is life!—
The distant prospect always seems more fair,
And when attained, another still succeeds,
Far fairer than before, yet compassed round
With the same dangers and the same dismay:
And we poor pilgrims, in this dreary maze,
Still discontented, chase the fairy form
Of unsubstantial happiness, to find,
When life itself is sinking in the strife,
'Tis but an airy bubble and a cheat!

. . . . .

—•—

COMMENCEMENT OF A POEM ON DESPAIR.

Some to Aonian lyres of silver sound
With winning elegance attune their song,
Formed to sink lightly on the soothëd sense,
And charm the soul with softest harmony:
'Tis then that Hope with sanguine eye is seen
Roving through Fancy's gay futurity;
Her light heart dancing to the sounds of pleasure,
Pleasure of days to come. Memory, too, then
Comes with her sister Melancholy, sad,
Pensively musing on the scenes of youth,
Scenes never to return*.

. . . .

Such subjects merit poets used to raise
The Attic verse harmonious; but for me
A dreadlier theme demands my backward hand,
And bids me strike the strings of dissonance
With frantic energy.

. . . .

'Tis wan Despair I sing; if sing I can
Of him before whose blast the voice of Song,
And Mirth, and Hope, and Happiness all fly,
Nor ever dare return. His notes are heard
At noon of night, where, on the coast of blood,
The lacerated son of Angola
Howls forth his sufferings to the moaning wind;
And, when the awful silence of the night
Strikes the chill death-dew to the murderer's heart,
He speaks in every conscience-prompted word
Half uttered, half suppressed.
'Tis him I sing—Despair, terrific name!
Striking unsteadily the tremulous chord
Of timorous Terror—discord in the sound:
For to a theme revolting as is this,
Dare not I woo the maids of harmony,
Who love to sit and catch the soothing sound
Of lyre Æolian, or the martial bugle,
Calling the hero to the field of glory,
And firing him with deeds of high emprise
And warlike triumph: but from scenes like mine
Shrink they affrighted, and detest the bard
Who dares to sound the hollow tones of horror.

Hence, then, soft maids,
And woo the silken zephyr in the bowers
By Heliconia's sleep-inviting stream:
For aid like yours I seek not; 'tis for powers
Of darker hue to inspire a verse like mine!
'Tis work for wizards, sorcerers, and fiends!

Hither, ye furious imps of Acheron,
Nurslings of hell, and beings shunning light,
And all the myriads of the burning concave!
Souls of the damned!—Hither, oh, come and join
The infernal chorus. 'Tis Despair I sing;
He, whose sole tooth inflicts a deadlier pang
Than all your tortures joined. Sing, sing Despair!
Repeat the sound, and celebrate his power;
Unite shouts, screams, and agonizing shrieks,
Till the loud pæan ring through hell's high vault,
And the remotest spirits of the deep
Leap from the lake, and join the dreadful song!

. . . .
. . . .

* Alluding to the two pleasing poems, the Pleasures of Hope and of Memory.

MY OWN CHARACTER.

ADDRESSED, DURING ILLNESS, TO A LADY.

Dear Fanny, I mean, now I'm laid on the shelf,
To give you a sketch—ay, a sketch of myself.
'Tis a pitiful subject, I frankly confess,
And one it would puzzle a painter to dress;
But however, here goes! and as sure as a gun
I'll tell all my faults like a penitent nun;
For I know, for my Fanny, before I address her,
She wont be a cynical father confessor.

Come, come, 'twill not do! put that curling brow down;
You can't, for the soul of you, learn how to frown,
Well, first I premise, it's my honest conviction,
That my breast is a chaos of all contradiction;

Religious—deistic—now loyal and warm ;
Then a dagger-drawn democrat hot for reform :
This moment a fop ; *that*, sententious as Titus ;
Democritus now, and anon Heraclitus ;
Now laughing and pleased, like a child with a rattle ;
Then vexed to the soul with impertinent tattle ;
Now moody and sad, now unthinking and gay,
To all points of the compass I veer in a day.

I'm proud and disdainful to Fortune's gay child,
But to Poverty's offspring submissive and mild :
As rude as a boor, and as rough in dispute ;
Then as for politeness—oh dear, I'm a brute !
I show no respect where I never can feel it ;
And as for contempt, take no pains to conceal it ;
And so in the suit, by these laudable ends,
I've a great many foes, and a very few friends.

And yet, my dear Fanny, there are who can feel
That this proud heart of mine is not fashioned like
steel,
It can love (can it not?)—it can hate, I am sure ;
And it's friendly enough, though in friends it be poor.
For itself though it bleed not, for others it bleeds ;
If it have not *ripe* virtues, I'm sure it's the *seeds* :
And though far from faultless, or even so-so,
I think it may pass as our worldly things go.

Well, I've told you my frailties without any gloss ;
Then as to my virtues, I'm quite at a loss !
I think I'm devout, and yet I can't say,
But in process of time I may get the wrong way,
I'm a *general lover*, if that's commendation,
And yet can't withstand *you know whose* fascination.
But I find that amidst all my tricks and devices,
In fishing for virtues, I'm pulling up vices ;
So as for the *good*, why, if I possess it,
I am not yet learned enough to express it.

You yourself must examine the lovelier side,
And after your every art you have tried,
Whatever my faults, I may venture to say,
Hypocrisy never will come in your way.
I am upright, I hope ; I am downright, I'm clear !
And I think my worst foe must allow I'm sincere ;
And if ever sincerity glowed in my breast,
'Tis now when I swear . . . .

. . . .

VERSES.

THOU base repiner at another's joy,
Whose eye turns green at merit not thine own,
Oh, far away from generous Britons fly,
And find on meaner climes a fitter throne.
Away, away, it shall not be,
Thou shalt not dare defile our plains ;
The truly generous heart disdains
Thy meaner, lowlier fires, while he
Joys at another's joy, and smiles at others' jollity.

Triumphant monster ! though thy schemes succeed,
Schemes laid in Acheron, the brood of Night,
Yet but a little while, and nobly freed,
Thy happy victim will emerge to light ;
When o'er his head in silence that reposes,
Some kindred soul shall come to drop a tear ;
Then will his last cold pillow turn to roses,
Which thou hadst planted with a soul severe ;
Then will thy baseness stand confessed, and all
Will curse the ungenerous fate that bade a poet fall.

. . . .

YET, ah ! thy arrows are too keen, too sure :
Couldst thou not pitch upon another prey ?
Alas ! in robbing him thou robb'st the poor,
Who only boast what thou wouldst take away ;
See the lone bard at midnight study sitting,
O'er his pale features streams his dying lamp :
While o'er fond Fancy's pale perspective flitting,
Successive forms their fleet ideas stamp.
Yet say, is bliss upon his brow impressed ;
Does jocund Health in thought's still mansion live ?
Lo, the cold dews that on his temples rest,
That short quick sigh—their sad responses give.

And canst thou rob a poet of his song ;
Snatch from the bard his trivial meed of praise ?
Small are his gains, nor does he hold them long ;
Then leave, oh leave him to enjoy his lays
While yet he lives—for to his merits just,
Though future ages join his fame to raise,
Will the loud trump awake his cold unheeding dust ?

. . . .

[The Fragments which follow were written during the last year of our author's life, on the back of his mathematical papers.]

"SAW'ST thou that light?" exclaimed the youth, and paused :
"Through yon dark firs it glanced, and on the stream
That skirts the woods it for a moment played.
Again, more light it gleamed—or does some sprite
Delude mine eyes with shapes of woods and streams,
And lamp far-beaming through the thicket's gloom,
As from some bosomed cabin, where the voice
Of revelry, or thrifty watchfulness,
Keeps in the lights at this unwonted hour ?
No sprite deludes mine eyes—the beam now glows
With steady lustre. Can it be the moon,
Who, hidden long by the invidious veil
That blots the heavens, now *sets* behind the woods ?"
"No moon to-night has looked upon the sea
Of clouds beneath her," answered Rudiger :
"She has been sleeping with Endymion.

. . . .

THE pious man,
In this bad world, when mists and couchant storms
Hide Heaven's fine circlet, springs aloft in faith,
Above the clouds that threat him, to the fields
Of ether, where the day is never veiled
With intervening vapours ; and looks down
Serene upon the troublous sea, that hides
The earth's fair breast, that sea whose nether face
To grovelling mortals frowns and darkens all ;
But on whose billowy back, from man concealed,
The glaring sunbeam plays.

. . . .

Lo ! on the eastern summit, clad in grey,
Morn, like a horseman girt for travel, comes ;
And from his tower of mist
Night's watchman hurries down.

OH, give me music, for my soul doth faint ;
I'm sick of noise and care, and now mine ear
Longs for some air of peace, some dying plaint,
That may the spirit from its cell unsphere.

Hark, how it falls! and now it steals along,
Like distant bells upon the lake at eve,
When all is still; and now it grows more strong,
As when the choral train their dirges weave,
Mellow and many-voiced; where every close,
O'er the old minster roof, in echoing waves reflows.

Oh, I am wrapped aloft!—My spirit soars
Beyond the skies, and leaves the stars behind.
Lo! angels lead me to the happy shores,
And floating pæans fill the buoyant wind.
Farewell, base earth, farewell!—My soul is freed,
Far from its clayey cell it springs,

. . . .

There was a little bird upon that pile;
It perched upon a ruined pinnacle,
And made sweet melody.
The song was soft, yet cheerful, and most clear,
For other note none swelled the air but his.
It seemed as if the little chorister,
Sole tenant of the melancholy pile,
Were a lone hermit, outcast from his kind,
Yet withal cheerful. I have heard the note
Echoing so lonely o'er the aisle forlorn,
. . . much musing. . . . .

Oh, pale art thou, my lamp, and faint
Thy melancholy ray;
When the still night's unclouded saint
Is walking on her way.
Through my lattice leaf imbowered,
Fair she sheds her shadowy beam,
And o'er my silent sacred room
Casts a checkered twilight gloom;
I throw aside the learned sheet,
I cannot choose but gaze, she looks so mildly sweet.
Sad vestal, why art thou so fair,
Or why am I so frail?

Methinks thou lookest kindly on me, Moon,
And cheerest my lone hours with sweet regards!
Surely, like me, thou art sad, but dost not speak
Thy sadness to the cold unheeding crowd:
So mournfully composed, o'er yonder cloud
Thou shinest, like a cresset, beaming far
From the rude watch-tower, o'er the Atlantic wave.

. . . .

Ah, who can say, however fair his view,
Through what sad scenes his path may lie?
Ah, who can give to others' woes his sigh,
Secure his own will never need it too?

Let thoughtless youth its seeming joys pursue,
Soon will they learn to scan with thoughtful eye
The illusive past and dark futurity;
Soon will they know

When high romance o'er every wood and stream
Dark lustre shed, my infant mind to fire,
Spell-struck, and filled with many a wondering dream,
First in the groves I woke the pensive lyre.

All there was mystery then—the gust that woke
The midnight echo was a spirit's dirge,
And unseen fairies would the moon invoke,
To their light morrice by the restless surge.

Now to my sobered thought with life's false smiles
Too much . . . . . .
The vagrant Fancy spreads no more her wiles,
And dark forebodings now my bosom fill.

And must thou go, and must we part?
Yes!—Fate decrees, and I submit;
The pang that rends in twain my heart,
Oh, Fanny, dost thou share in it?

Thy sex is fickle!—When away,
Some happier youth may win thy
. . . .
. . . .

Once more, and yet once more,
I give unto my harp a dark-woven lay;
I heard the waters roar,
I heard the flood of ages pass away.

O thou stern spirit, who dost dwell
In thine eternal cell,
Noting, grey chronicler! the silent years;
I saw thee rise—I saw the scroll complete,
Thou spak'st, and at thy feet
The universe gave way.

. . . .

Hushed is the lyre!—The hand that swept
The low and pensive wires,
Robbed of its cunning, from the task retires.

Yes, it is still—the lyre is still;
The spirit which its slumbers broke
Hath passed away, and that weak hand that woke
Its forest melodies hath lost its skill.

Yet I would press you to my lips once more,
Ye wild yet withering flowers of poesy;
Yet would I drink the fragrance which ye pour
Mixed with decaying odours; for to me
Ye have beguiled the hours of infancy,
As in the wood-paths of my native

SONNETS.

TO THE RIVER TRENT.

WRITTEN ON RECOVERY FROM SICKNESS.

ONCE more, O Trent, along thy pebbly marge,
A pensive invalid, reduced and pale,
From the close sick room newly let at large,
Woos to his wan-worn cheek the pleasant gale.
O, to his ear how musical the tale
Which fills with joy the throstle's little throat;
And all the sounds which on the fresh breeze sail,
How wildly novel on his senses float!
It was on this that many a sleepless night,
As, lone, he watched the taper's sickly gleam,
And at his casement heard, with wild affright,
The owl's dull wing and melancholy scream,
On this he thought—this, this his sole desire,
Thus once again to hear the warbling woodland choir.

GIVE me a cottage on some Cambrian wild,
Where, far from cities, I may spend my days,
And, by the beauties of the scene beguiled,
May pity man's pursuits, and shun his ways.
While on the rock I mark the browsing goat,
List to the mountain-torrent's distant noise,
Or the hoarse bittern's solitary note,
I shall not want the world's delusive joys;
But with my little scrip, my book, my lyre,
Shall think my lot complete, nor covet more;
And when, with time shall wane the vital fire,
I'll raise my pillow on the desert shore,
And lay me down to rest where the wild wave
Shall make sweet music o'er my lonely grave.

SUPPOSED TO HAVE BEEN ADDRESSED BY A FEMALE LUNATIC TO A LADY*.

LADY, thou weepest for the maniac's woe;
And thou art fair, and thou, like me, art young;
Oh, may thy bosom never, never know
The pangs with which my wretched heart is wrung.
I had a mother once—a brother too—
Beneath yon yew my father rests his head—
I had a lover once, and kind and true!
But mother, brother, lover, all are fled!
Yet, whence the tear which dims thy lovely eye?
Oh, gentle lady! not for me thus weep;
The green sod soon upon my breast will lie,
And soft and sound will be my peaceful sleep.
Go thou and pluck the roses while they bloom—
My hopes lie buried in the silent tomb.

As thus oppressed with many a heavy care,
(Though young, yet sorrowful,) I turn my feet
To the dark woodland, longing much to greet
The form of peace, if chance she sojourn there,
Deep thoughts, and dismal, verging to despair,
Fill my sad breast; and, tired with this vain coil,
I shrink dismayed before life's upland toil.
And as amid the leaves, the evening air
Whispers still melody, I think, ere long,
When I no more can hear, these woods will speak;
And then a sad smile plays upon my cheek,
And mournful phantasies upon me throng,
And I do ponder with most strange delight
On the calm slumbers of the dead man's night.

* This quartorzain had its rise from an elegant sonnet, written by Mrs. Lofft, "Occasioned by seeing a young Female Lunatic."

SONNET

SUPPOSED TO HAVE BEEN WRITTEN BY THE UNHAPPY POET DERMODY, IN A STORM, WHILE ON BOARD A SHIP IN HIS MAJESTY'S SERVICE.

Lo! o'er the welkin the tempestuous clouds
Successive fly, and the loud piping wind
Rocks the poor sea-boy on the dripping shrouds,
While the pale pilot, o'er the helm reclined,
Lists to the changeful storm: and as he plies
His wakeful task, he oft bethinks him, sad,
Of wife, and little home, and chubby lad;
And the half-strangled tear bedews his eyes.
I, on the deck, musing on themes forlorn,
View the drear tempest and the yawning deep,
Nought dreading in the green sea's caves to sleep;
For not for me shall wife or children mourn,
And the wild winds will ring my funeral knell,
Sweetly as solemn peal of pious passing-bell.

WHAT art thou, Mighty One! and where thy seat?
Thou broodest on the calm that cheers the lands,
And thou dost bear within thine awful hands
The rolling thunders and the lightnings fleet.
Stern on thy dark-wrought car of cloud and wind,
Thou guid'st the northern storm at night's dead noon,
Or on the red wings of the fierce monsoon
Disturb'st the sleeping giant of the Ind.
In the drear silence of the polar span
Dost thou repose? or in the solitude
Of sultry tracts, where the lone caravan
Hears nightly howl the tiger's hungry brood?
Vain thought! the confines of his throne to trace,
Who glows through all the fields of boundless space.

THE WINTER TRAVELLER.

GOD help thee, traveller, on thy journey far;
The wind is bitter keen, the snow o'erlays
The hidden pits and dangerous hollow ways,
And darkness will involve thee. No kind star
To-night will guide thee, traveller; and the war
Of winds and elements on thy head will break,
And in thy agonizing ear the shriek
Of spirits howling on their stormy car
Will often ring appalling! I portend
A dismal night; and on my wakeful bed
Thoughts, traveller, of thee will fill my head,
And him who rides where winds and waves contend,
And strives, rude cradled on the seas, to guide
His lonely bark through the tempestuous tide.

SONNET.

BY CAPEL LOFFT, ESQ.

[This sonnet was addressed to the author of this volume, and was occasioned by several little quatorzains, misnomered sonnets, which he published in "The Monthly Mirror." He begs leave to return his thanks to the much-respected writer, for the permission so politely granted to insert it here, and for the good opinion he has been pleased to express of his productions.]

Ye, whose aspirings court the Muse of lays,
"Severest of those orders which belong,
Distinct and separate, to Delphic song,"
Why shun the Sonnet's undulating maze?
And why its name, boast of Petrarchian days,
Assume, its rules disowned? Whom from the throng
The Muse selects, their ear the charm obeys
Of its full harmony: they fear to wrong
The Sonnet, by adorning with a name
Of that distinguished import, lays, though sweet,
Yet not in magic texture taught to meet
Of that so varied and peculiar frame.
O think! to vindicate its genuine praise
Those it beseems, whose lyre a favouring impulse sways.

SONNET

RECANTATORY, IN REPLY TO THE FOREGOING ELEGANT ADMONITION.

Let the sublimer Muse, who, wrapped in night,
Rides on the raven pennons of the storm,
Or o'er the field, with purple havoc warm,
Lashes her steeds, and sings along the fight,
Let her, whom more ferocious strains delight,
Disdain the plaintive Sonnet's little form,
And scorn to its wild cadence to conform
The impetuous tenor of her hardy flight.
But me, far lowest of the sylvan train,
Who wake the wood-nymphs from the forest shade
With wildest song; me, much behoves thy aid
Of mingled melody, to grace my strain,
And give it power to please, as oft it flows
Through the smooth murmurs of thy frequent close.

TO CAPEL LOFFT, ESQ.

Lofft, unto thee one tributary song
The simple Muse, admiring, fain would bring;
She longs to lisp thee to the listening throng,
And with thy name to bid the woodlands ring.
Fain would she blazon all thy virtues forth,
Thy warm philanthropy, thy justice mild,
Would say how thou didst foster kindred worth,
And to thy bosom snatched Misfortune's child:
Firm she would paint thee, with becoming zeal,
Upright, and learned, as the Pylian sire,
Would say how sweetly thou couldst sweep the lyre,
And show thy labours for the public weal,
Ten thousand virtues tell with joys supreme,
But ah! she shrinks abashed before the arduous theme.

ON HEARING THE SOUNDS OF AN ÆOLIAN HARP.

So ravishingly soft upon the tide
Of the infuriate gust it did career,
It might have soothed its rugged charioteer,
And sunk him to a zephyr: then it died,
Melting in melody; and I descried,
Borne to some wizard stream, the form appear
Of druid sage, who on the far-off ear
Poured his lone song, to which the surge replied
Or thought I heard the hapless pilgrim's knell,
Lost in some wild enchanted forest's bounds,
By unseen beings sung; or are these sounds
Such, as 'tis said, at night are known to swell
By startled shepherd on the lonely heath,
Keeping his night-watch sad, portending death?

TO THE MOON.

WRITTEN IN NOVEMBER.

Sublime, emerging from the misty verge
Of the horizon dim, thee, Moon, I hail,
As sweeping o'er the leafless grove, the gale
Seems to repeat the year's funereal dirge.
Now autumn sickens on the languid sight,
And leaves bestrew the wanderer's lonely way;
Now unto thee, pale arbitress of night,
With double joy my homage do I pay.
When clouds disguise the glories of the day,
And stern November sheds her boisterous blight,
How doubly sweet to mark the moony ray
Shoot through the mist from the ethereal height,
And, still unchanged, back to the memory bring
The smiles Favonian of life's earliest spring.

WRITTEN AT THE GRAVE OF A FRIEND.

Fast from the west the fading day-streaks fly,
And ebon night assumes her solemn sway;
Yet here alone, unheeding time, I lie,
And o'er my friend still pour the plaintive lay.
Oh, 'tis not long since, George, with thee I wooed
The maid of musings by yon moaning wave;
And hailed the moon's mild beam, which now, renewed,
Seems sweetly sleeping on thy silent grave!
The busy world pursues its boisterous way,
The noise of revelry still echoes round,
Yet I am sad while all beside is gay,
Yet still I weep o'er thy deserted mound.
Oh that, like thee, I might bid sorrow cease,
And neath the greensward sleep the sleep of peace.

TO MISFORTUNE.

Misfortune, I am young, my chin is bare,
And I have wondered much when men have told,
How youth was free from sorrow and from care,
That thou shouldst dwell with me, and leave the old.
Sure dost not like me! Shrivelled hag of hate,
My phiz, and thanks to thee, is sadly long;
I am not either, beldame, over strong;
Nor do I wish at all to be thy mate,
For thou, sweet fury, art my bitter hate.
Nay, shake not thus thy miserable pate;

I am yet young, and do not like thy face;
And lest thou shouldst resume the wild-goose chase,
I'll tell thee something all thy heat to assuage—
Thou wilt not hit my fancy in my age.

TO APRIL.

Emblem of life, see changeful April sail
In varying vest along the shadowy skies,
Now bidding summer's softest zephyrs rise,
Anon recalling winter's stormy gale,
And pouring from the cloud her sudden hail;
Then, smiling through the tear that dims her eyes,
While Iris with her braid the welkin dyes,
Promise of sunshine, not so prone to fail.
So, to us sojourners in life's low vale,
The smiles of Fortune flatter to deceive,
While still the Fates the web of misery weave.
So Hope exultant spreads her airy sail,
And from the present gloom the soul conveys
To distant summers and far happier days.

Ye unseen spirits, whose wild melodies,
At evening rising slow, yet sweetly clear,
Steal on the musing poet's pensive ear,
As by the wood-spring stretched supine he lies;
When he, who now invokes you, low is laid,
His tired frame resting on the earth's cold bed,
Hold ye your nightly vigils o'er his head,
And chant a dirge to his reposing shade!
For he was wont to love your madrigals;
And often by the haunted stream that laves
The dark sequestered woodland's inmost caves,
Would sit and listen to the dying falls,
Till the full tear would quiver in his eye,
And his big heart would heave with mournful
    ecstacy.

TO A TAPER.

'Tis midnight. On the globe dead slumber sits,
And all is silence—in the hour of sleep,
Save when the hollow gust, that swells by fits,
In the dark wood roars fearfully and deep.
I wake alone to listen and to weep,
To watch my taper, thy pale beacon, burn;
And, as still Memory does her vigils keep,
To think of days that never can return.
By thy pale ray I raise my languid head,
My eye surveys the solitary gloom;
And the sad meaning tear, unmixed with dread,
Tells thou dost light me to the silent tomb.
Like thee I wane; like thine, my life's last ray
Will fade in loneliness, unwept, away.

Quick o'er the wintry waste dart fiery shafts,
Bleak blows the blast—now howls—then faintly
And oft upon its awful wings it wafts [dies,
The dying wanderer's distant, feeble cries.
Now, when athwart the gloom gaunt horror stalks,
And midnight hags their damnëd vigils hold,
The pensive poet 'mid the wild waste walks,
And ponders on the ills life's paths unfold.
Mindless of dangers hovering round, he goes,
Insensible to every outward ill;
Yet oft his bosom heaves with rending throes,
And oft big tears adown his worn cheeks trill.
Ah! 'tis the anguish of a mental sore,
Which gnaws his heart, and bids him hope no more.

TO MY MOTHER.

And canst thou, mother, for a moment think,
That we, thy children, when old age shall shed
Its blanching honours on thy weary head,
Could from our best of duties ever shrink?
Sooner the sun from his high sphere should sink
Than we, ungrateful, leave thee in that day
To pine in solitude thy life away,
Or shun thee, tottering on the grave's cold brink.
Banish the thought!—Where'er our steps may
    roam,
O'er smiling plains, or wastes without a tree,
Still will fond memory point our hearts to thee,
And paint the pleasures of thy peaceful home;
While duty bids us all thy griefs assuage,
And smooth the pillow of thy sinking age.

Yes, 'twill be over soon!—This sickly dream
Of life will vanish from my feverish brain;
And death my wearied spirit will redeem
From this wild region of unvaried pain.
Yon brook will glide as softly as before,
Yon landscape smile, yon golden harvest grow,
Yon sprightly lark on mounting wing will soar,
When Henry's name is heard no more below.
I sigh when all my youthful friends caress,
They laugh in health, and future evils brave;
Them shall a wife and smiling children bless,
While I am mouldering in the silent grave.
God of the just, thou gav'st the bitter cup;
I bow to thy behest, and drink it up.

TO CONSUMPTION.

Gently, most gently, on thy victim's head,
Consumption, lay thine hand!—Let me decay,
Like the expiring lamp, unseen, away,
And softly go to slumber with the dead.
And if 'tis true what holy men have said,
That strains angelic oft foretell the day
Of death, to those good men who fall thy prey,
O let the aërial music round my bed,
Dissolving sad in dying symphony,
Whisper the solemn warning in mine ear;
That I may bid my weeping friends good bye
Ere I depart upon my journey drear;
And, smiling faintly on the painful past,
Compose my decent head, and breathe my last.

Sweet to the gay of heart is Summer's smile,
Sweet the wild music of the laughing Spring;
But ah! my soul far other scenes beguile,
Where gloomy storms their sullen shadows fling.
Is it for me to strike the Idalian string—
Raise the soft music of the warbling wire,
While in my ears the howls of furies ring
And melancholy wastes the vital fire?
Away with thoughts like these!—To some lone cave
Where howls the shrill blast, and where sweeps
    the wave,
Direct my steps; there, in the lonely drear,
I'll sit remote from worldly noise, and muse
Till through my soul shall Peace her balm infuse,
And whisper sounds of comfort in mine ear.

TRANSLATION

FROM THE FRENCH OF M. DESBARREAUX.

THY judgments, Lord, are just; thou lov'st to wear
The face of pity, and of love divine;
But mine is guilt—thou must not, canst not spare,
While Heaven is true, and equity is thine.
Yes, oh my God, such crimes as mine, so dread,
Leave but the choice of punishment to thee;
Thy interest calls for judgment on my head,
And e'en thy mercy dares not plead for me!
Thy will be done—since 'tis thy glory's due,
Did from mine eyes the endless torrents flow;
Smite—it is time—though endless death ensue,
I bless the avenging hand that lays me low.
But on what spot shall fall thine anger's flood,
That has not first been drenched in Christ's atoning
blood?

WHEN I sit musing on the checkered past,
(A term much darkened with untimely woes,)
My thoughts revert to her, for whom still flows
The [illegible] a, though half disowned; and binding
fast [illegible]
Pride's stubborn cheat to my too yielding heart,
I say to her, she robbed me of my rest,
When that was all my wealth. 'Tis true, my
breast
Received from her this wearying, lingering smart;
Yet, ah! I cannot bid her form depart:
Though wronged, I love her—yet in anger love,
For she was most unworthy. Then I prove
Vindictive joy; and on my stern front gleams,
Throned in dark clouds, inflexible [illegible].
The native pride of my much-injured heart.

HYMNS.

FOR FAMILY WORSHIP.

O LORD, another day is flown,
And we, a lonely band,
Are met once more before thy throne,
To bless thy fostering hand.

And wilt thou bend a listening ear,
To praises low as ours?
Thou wilt! for thou dost love to hear
The song which meekness pours.

And, Jesus, thou thy smiles wilt deign,
As we before thee pray;
For thou didst bless the infant train,
And we are less than they.

O let thy grace perform its part,
And let contention cease;
And shed abroad in every heart
Thine everlasting peace!

Thus chastened, cleansed, entirely thine,
A flock by Jesus led;
The Sun of Holiness shall shine
In glory on our head.

And thou wilt turn our wandering feet,
And thou wilt bless our way;
Till worlds shall fade, and faith shall greet
The dawn of lasting day.

O LORD, my God, in mercy turn,
In mercy hear a sinner mourn!
To thee I call, to thee I cry,
O leave me, leave me not to die!

I strove against thee, Lord, I know,
I spurned thy grace, I mocked thy law;
The hour is past—the day's gone by,
And I am left alone to die.

O pleasures past, what are ye now
But thorns about my bleeding brow!
Spectres that hover round my brain,
And aggravate and mock my pain.

For pleasure I have given my soul;
Now, Justice, let thy thunders roll!
Now vengeance smile—and with a blow,
Lay the rebellious ingrate low.

Yet Jesus, Jesus! there I'll cling,
I'll crowd beneath his sheltering wing;
I'll clasp the cross, and holding there,
E'en me, oh bliss! his wrath may spare.

In Heaven we shall be purified, so as to be able to endure the splendours of the Deity.

AWAKE, sweet harp of Judah, wake,
Retune thy strings for Jesu's sake;
We sing the Saviour of our race,
The Lamb, our shield, and hiding-place.

When God's right arm is bared for war,
And thunders clothe his cloudy car,
Where, where, oh where shall man retire,
To escape the horrors of his ire?

'Tis he, the Lamb, to him we fly,
While the dread tempest passes by;
God sees his Well-belovèd's face,
And spares us in our hiding-place.

Thus while we dwell in this low scene,
The Lamb is our unfailing screen;
To him, though guilty, still we run,
And God still spares us for his Son.

While yet we sojourn here below,
Pollutions still our hearts o'erflow;
Fallen, abject, mean, a sentenced race,
We deeply need a hiding-place.

Yet courage—days and years will glide,
And we shall lay these clods aside;
Shall be baptized in Jordan's flood,
And washed in Jesu's cleansing blood.

Then pure, immortal, sinless, freed,
We through the Lamb shall be decreed;
Shall meet the Father face to face,
And need no more a hiding-place.*

* The last stanza of this hymn was added extemporaneously by our author, one summer evening, when he was with a few friends on the Trent, and singing it, as he was used to do on such occasions.

THE STAR OF BETHLEHEM.

When marshalled on the nightly plain,
  The glittering host bestud the sky;
One star alone, of all the train,
  Can fix the sinner's wandering eye.

Hark! hark! to God the chorus breaks,
  From every host, from every gem;
But one alone the Saviour speaks—
  It is the Star of Bethlehem.

Once on the raging seas I rode,
  The storm was loud, the night was dark,
The ocean yawned, and rudely blowed
  That wind that tossed my foundering bark.

Deep horror then my vitals froze,
  Death-struck, I ceased the tide to stem;
When suddenly a star arose—
  It was the Star of Bethlehem,

It was my guide, my light, my all,
  It bade my dark forebodings cease;
And through the storm and danger's thrall
  It led me to the port of peace.

Now safely moored—my perils o'er,
  I'll sing, first in night's diadem,
For ever, and for evermore,
  The Star—the Star of Bethlehem!

TRIBUTARY VERSES.

LINES BY LORD BYRON.

FROM THE "ENGLISH BARDS AND SCOTCH REVIEWERS."

Unhappy White* ! while life was in its spring,
And thy young Muse just waved her joyous wing,
The spoiler came; and all thy promise fair
Has sought the grave, to sleep for ever there.
Oh! what a noble heart was here undone,
When science' self destroyed her favourite son!
Yes! she too much indulged thy fond pursuit,
She sowed the seeds, but death has reaped the fruit.
'Twas thine own genius gave the final blow,
And helped to plant the wound that laid thee low.
So the struck eagle, stretched upon the plain,
No more through rolling clouds to soar again,
Viewed his own feather on the fatal dart,
And wing'd the shaft that quivered in his heart.
Keen were his pangs, but keener far to feel,
He nursed the pinion which impelled the steel;
While the same plumage that had warmed his nest
Drank the last life-drop of his bleeding breast.

SONNET ON HENRY KIRKE WHITE.

BY CAPEL LOFFT.

Master so early of the various lyre
Energic, pure, sublime!—Thus art thou gone!
In its bright dawn of fame that spirit flown,
Which breathed such sweetness, tenderness, and
Wert thou but shown to win us to admire, [fire!
And veil in death thy splendour?—But unknown
Their destination who least time have shone,
And brightest beamed.—When these the Eternal
  Sire:
Righteous, and wise, and good are all his ways—
Eclipses as their sun begins to rise,
Can mortal judge, for their diminished days,
What blest equivalent in changeless skies,
What sacred glory waits them?—His the praise;
Gracious, whate'er he gives, whate'er denies.

Oct. 24, 1806.

* Henry Kirke White died at Cambridge in October, 1806, in consequence of too much exertion in the pursuit of studies that would have matured a mind which disease and poverty could not impair, and which death itself destroyed rather than subdued. His poems abound in such beauties as must impress the reader with the liveliest regret that so short a period was allotted to talents, which would have dignified even the sacred functions he was destined to assume.

SONNET OCCASIONED BY THE SECOND OF HENRY KIRKE WHITE.

BY CAPEL LOFFT.

Yes, fled already is thy vital fire,
And the fair promise of thy early bloom
Lost, in youth's morn extinct; sunk in the tomb;
Mute in the grave sleeps thy enchanted lyre!
And is it vainly that our souls aspire?
Falsely does the presaging heart presume
That we shall live beyond life's cares and gloom;
Grasps it eternity with high desire,
But to imagine bliss, feel woe, and die;
Leaving survivors to worse pangs than death!
Not such the sanction of the Eternal Mind.
The harmonious order of the starry sky,
And awful revelation's angel breath,
Assure these hopes their full effect shall find.

Dec 25, 1806.

WRITTEN IN THE HOMER OF MR. H. K. WHITE,

PRESENTED TO ME BY HIS BROTHER, J. NEVILLE WHITE.

Bard of brief days, but ah, of deathless fame!
While on these awful leaves my fond eyes rest,
On which thine late have dwelt, thy hand late
  pressed,
I pause; and gaze regretful on thy name.
By neither chance nor envy, time nor flame,
Be it from this its mansion dispossessed,
But thee Eternity clasps to her breast,
And in celestial splendour thrones thy claim.
No more with mortal pencil shalt thou trace
An imitative radiance*: thy pure lyre
Springs from our changeful atmosphere's embrace,
And beams and breathes in empyreal fire:
The Homeric and Miltonian sacred tone
Responsive hail that lyre, congenial to their own.

Capel Lofft.

Bury, Jan. 11, 1807.

* Alluding to his pencilled sketch of a head surrounded with a glory.

SONNET TO HENRY KIRKE WHITE, ON HIS POEMS LATELY PUBLISHED.

BY ARTHUR OWEN, ESQ.

Hail, gifted youth, whose passion-breathing lay
Portrays a mind attuned to noblest themes—
A mind, which, wrapped in fancy's high-wrought dreams,
To nature's veriest bounds its daring way
Can wing: what charms through out thy pages shine,
To win with fairy thrill the melting soul!—
For though along impassioned grandeur roll,
Yet in full power simplicity is thine.
Proceed, sweet bard! and the heaven-granted fire
Of pity, glowing in thy feeling breast,
May naught destroy; may naught thy soul divest
Of joy, of rapture in the living lyre,
Thou tun'st so magically: but may fame
Each passing year add honours to thy name.

Richmond, September, 1803.

SONNET,

On seeing another written to H. K. White, in September, 1803, inserted in his "Remains, by Robert Southey."

BY ARTHUR OWEN, ESQ.

Ah! once again the long-left wires among,
Truants the Muse to weave her requiem song;
With sterner lore now busied, erst the lay
Cheered my dark morn of manhood, wont to stray
O'er fancy's fields in quest of musky flower;
To me nor fragrant less, though barred from view
And courtship of the world: hailed was the hour
That gave me, dripping fresh with nature's dew,
Poor Henry's budding beauties—to a clime
Hapless transplanted, whose exotic ray
Forced their young vigour into transient day,
And drained the stalk that reared them! and shall time [breathe
Trample these orphan blossoms?—No! they
Still lovelier charms—for Southey culls the wreath!

Oxford, Dec. 17, 1807.

SONNET TO H. K. WHITE, ON HIS POEMS LATELY PUBLISHED.

BY G. L. C.

Henry, I greet thine entrance into life,
Sure presage that the myrmidons of fate,
The fool's unmeaning laugh, the critic's hate,
Will dire assail thee; and the envious strife
Of bookish schoolmen, beings over-rife,
Whose pia-mater studious is filled
With unconnected matter, half distilled
From lettered page, shall bare for thee the knife,
Beneath whose edge the poet ofttimes sinks.
But, fear not; for thy modest work contains
The germ of worth: thy wild poetic strains,
How sweet to him, untutored bard, who thinks
Thy verse "has power to please, as soft it flows
Through the soft murmurs of the frequent close."

1803.

TO MR. HENRY KIRKE WHITE.

BY H. WELKER.

Hark! 'tis some sprite who sweeps a funeral knell
For Dermody, no more. That fitful tone
From Æolus' wild harp alone can swell,
Or Chatterton assumes the lyre unknown.

No; list again! 'tis Bateman's fatal sigh
Swells with the breeze, and dies upon the stream:
'Tis Margaret mourns, as swift she rushes by,
Roused by the demons from adulterous dream.

O say, sweet youth, what genius fires thy soul?
The same which tuned the frantic nervous strain
To the wild harp of Collins?—By the pole,
Or 'mid the seraphim and heavenly train,
Taught Milton everlasting secrets to unfold,
To sing Hell's flaming gulf, or Heaven high arched with gold?

VERSES OCCASIONED BY THE DEATH OF HENRY KIRKE WHITE.

BY JOSIAH CONDER.

What is this world at best,
Though decked in vernal bloom,
By hope and youthful fancy dressed,
What but a ceaseless toil for rest,
A passage to the tomb?
If flowerets strew
The avenue,
Though fair, alas! how fading, and how few!

And every hour comes arm'd
By sorrow or by woe:
Concealed beneath its little wings,
A scythe the soft-shod pilferer brings,
To lay some comfort low:
Some tie to' unbind,
By love entwined,
Some silken bond that holds the captive mind.

And every month displays
The ravages of time:
Faded the flowers—the Spring is past!
The scattered leaves, the wintry blast,
Warn to a milder clime:
The songsters flee
The leafless tree,
And bear to happier realms their melody.

Henry! the world no more
Can claim thee for her own!
In purer skies thy radiance beams!
Thy lyre employed in nobler themes;
Before the' eternal throne:
Yet, spirit dear,
Forgive the tear, [here
Which those must shed who are doomed to linger

Although a stranger, I
In friendship's train would weep:
Lost to the world, alas! so young,
And must thy lyre, in silence hung,
On the dark cypress sleep?
The poet, all
Their friend may call;
And Nature's self attends his funeral.

Although with feeble wing
Thy flight I would pursue,
With quickened zeal, with humbled pride,
Alike our object, hopes, and guide,
One heaven alike in view;
True, it was thine
To tower, to shine;
But I may make thy milder virtues mine.

If Jesus own my name,
(Though fame pronounced it never,)
Sweet spirit, not with thee alone,
But all whose absence here I moan,
Circling with harps the golden throne,
I shall unite for ever:
At death then why
Tremble or sigh?
Oh! who would wish to live but he who fears to die!

Dec. 5, 1807.

—•—

ON READING HENRY KIRKE WHITE'S POEM ON SOLITUDE.

BY JOSIAH CONDER.

But art thou thus indeed "alone,"
Quite unbefriended, and unknown?
And hast thou then his name forgot
Who formed thy frame, and fix'd thy lot?

Is not his voice in evening's gale?
Beams not with him the "star" so pale?
Is there a leaf can fade and die,
Unnoticed by his watchful eye?

Each fluttering hope, each anxious fear,
Each lonely sigh, each silent tear,
To thine Almighty Friend are known;
And say'st thou, thou art "all alone?"

—•—

LINES ON THE DEATH OF H. K. WHITE,

LATE OF ST. JOHN'S COLLEGE, CAMBRIDGE.

Sorrows are mine!—Then let me joys evade,
And seek for sympathies in this lone shade.
The glooms of death fall heavy on my heart,
And between life and me a truce impart:
Genius has vanished in its opening bloom,
And youth and beauty wither in the tomb!

Thought, ever prompt to lend the inquiring eye,
Pursues thy spirit through futurity.
Does thy aspiring mind new powers essay,
Or in suspended being wait the day,
When Earth shall fall before the awful train
Of Heaven and Virtue's everlasting reign?

May goodness, which thy heart did once enthrone,
Emit one ray to meliorate my own!
And for thy sake, when time my grief shall calm,
Science shall please, and poesy shall charm.

I turn my steps whence issued all my woes,
Where the dull courts monastic glooms impose;
Thence fled a spirit whose unbounded scope
Surpassed the fond creations e'en of hope.

Along this path thy living step has fled,
Along this path they bore thee to the dead.
All that this languid eye can now survey
Witnessed the vigour of thy fleeting day:
And witnessed all, as speaks this anguished tear,
The solemn progress of thy early bier.
Sacred the walls that took thy parting breath,
Owned thee in life, encompassed thee in death!

O, I can feel as felt the sorrowing friend
Who o'er thy corse in agony did bend;
Dead as thyself to all the world inspires,
Paid the last rites mortality requires;
Closed the dim eye that beamed with mind before;
Composed the icy limbs to move no more!
Some power the picture from my memory tear,
Or feeling will rush onward to despair!

Immortal hopes! come, lend your blest relief,
And raise the soul bowed down with mortal grief;
Teach it to look for comfort in the skies:
Earth cannot give what Heaven's high will denies.

Cambridge, November, 1806.

—•—

TO THE MEMORY OF H. K. WHITE.

BY THE REV. W. B. COLLYER, A.M.

Oh, lost too soon! accept the tear
A stranger to thy memory pays!
Dear to the Muse, to science dear,
In the young morning of thy days!

All the wild notes that pity loved,
Awoke, responsive still to thee,
While o'er the lyre thy fingers roved
In softest, sweetest harmony.

The chords that in the human heart
Compassion touches as her own,
Bore in thy symphonies a part—
With them in perfect unison.

Amidst accumulated woes,
That premature afflictions bring,
Submission's sacred hymn arose,
Warbled from every mournful string.

When o'er thy dawn the darkness spread,
And deeper every moment grew;
When rudely round thy youthful head,
The chilling blasts of sickness blew:

Religion heard no plainings loud;
The sigh in secret stole from thee;
And pity, from the "dropping cloud,"
Shed tears of holy sympathy.

Cold is that heart in which were met
More virtues than could ever die;
The morning-star of hope is set—
The sun adorns another sky.

O partial grief, to mourn the day
So suddenly o'erclouded here,
To rise with unextinguished ray,
To shine in a superior sphere!

Oft genius early quits this sod,
Impatient of a robe of clay,
Spreads the light pinion, spurns the clod,
And smiles, and soars, and steals away!

But more than genius urged thy flight,
And marked the way, dear youth, for thee
Henry sprang up to worlds of light,
On wings of immortality!

Blackheath Hill, June 24, 1808.

ODE ON THE LATE H. K. WHITE.

BY JUVENIS.

And is the minstrel's voyage o'er?
  And is the star of genius fled?
And will his magic harp no more,
  Mute in the mansions of the dead,
Its strains seraphic pour?

A pilgrim in this world of woe,
  Condemned, alas! awhile to stray,
Where bristly thorns, where briars grow,
  He bade, to cheer the gloomy way,
Its heavenly music flow.

And oft he bade, by fame inspired,
  Its wild notes seek the' ethereal plain,
Till angels by its music fired,
  Have, listening, caught the' ecstatic strain,
Have wondered, and admired.

But now secure on happier shores,
  With choirs of sainted souls he sings;
His harp the Omnipotent adores,
  And from its sweet, its silver strings,
Celestial music pours.

And though on earth no more he'll weave
  The lay that's fraught with magic fire,
Yet oft shall Fancy hear at eve
  His now exalted heavenly lyre
In sounds Æolian grieve.

Basingstoke.

SONNET IN MEMORY OF MR. H. K. WHITE.

BY J. G.

"'Tis now the dead of night," and I will go
To where the brook soft-murmuring glides along
In the still wood; yet does the plaintive song
Of Philomela through the welkin flow;
And while pale Cynthia carelessly doth throw
Her dewy beams the verdant boughs among,
Will sit beneath some spreading oak-tree strong,
And intermingle with the streams my woe:
Hushed in deep silence every gentle breeze;
No mortal breath disturbs the awful gloom;
Cold, chilling dewdrops trickle down the trees,
And every flower withholds its rich perfume:
'Tis sorrow leads me to that sacred ground
Where Henry moulders in a sleep profound!

ON THE DEATH OF MR. H. K. WHITE.

BY THE REV. J. PLUMPTRE.

Such talents and such piety combined,
With such unfeigned humility of mind,
Bespoke him fair to tread the way to fame,
And live an honour to the Christian name:
But Heaven was pleased to stop his fleeting hour,
And blight the fragrance of the opening flower.
We mourn—but not for him, removed from pain;
Our loss, we trust, is his eternal gain:
With him we'll strive to win the Saviour's love,
And hope to join him with the blest above.

October 24, 1806.

REFLECTIONS ON READING THE LIFE OF THE LATE H. K. WHITE.

BY WILLIAM HOLLOWAY, AUTHOR OF "THE PEASANT'S FATE."

Darling of science and the Muse,
How shall a son of song refuse
  To shed a tear for thee?
To us so soon for ever lost,
What hopes, what prospects have been crossed
  By Heaven's supreme decree?

How could a parent, love-beguiled,
In life's fair prime resign a child
  So duteous, good, and kind?
The warblers of the soothing strain
Must string the elegiac lyre in vain
  To soothe the wounded mind?

Yet Fancy, hovering round the tomb,
Half envies while she mourns thy doom,
  Dear poet, saint, and sage!
Who into one short span, at best,
The wisdom of an age compressed,
  A patriarch's lengthened age!

To him a genius sanctified,
And purged from literary pride,
  A sacred boon was given:
Chaste as the Psalmist's harp, his lyre
Celestial raptures could inspire,
  And lift the soul to Heaven.

'Twas not the laurel earth bestows,
'Twas not the praise from man that flows,
  With classic toil he sought:
He sought the crown that martyrs wear,
When rescued from a world of care;
  Their spirit too he caught.

Here come, ye thoughtless, vain, and gay,
Who idly range in folly's way,
  And learn the worth of time:
Learn ye, whose days have run to waste,
How to redeem this pearl at last,
  Atoning for your crime.

This flower, that drooped in one cold clime,
Transplanted from the soil of time
  To immortality,
In full perfection there shall bloom;
And those who now lament his doom
  Must bow to God's decree.

London, Feb. 27, 1808.

ON THE DEATH OF H. K. WHITE.

BY T. PARK.

Too, too prophetic did thy wild note swell,
Impassioned minstrel! when its pitying wail
Sighed o'er the vernal primrose as it fell
Untimely, withered by the northern gale.*
Thou wert that flower of promise and of prime,
Whose opening bloom, 'mid many an adverse blast,
Charmed the lone wanderer through this desert
  clime,
But charmed him with a rapture soon o'ercast,

* See "Clifton Grove."

To see thee languish into quick decay.
Yet was not thy departing immature;
For ripe in virtue thou wert reft away,
And pure in spirit, as the bless'd are pure—
Pure as the dewdrop freed from earthly leaven,
That sparkles, is exhaled, and blends with heaven!*

TO THE MEMORY OF H. K. WHITE.

BY A LADY.

If worth, if genius, to the world are dear,
To Henry's shade devote no common tear:
His worth on no precarious tenure hung,
From genuine piety his virtues sprung.
If pure benevolence, if steady sense,
Can to the feeling heart delight dispense;
If all the highest efforts of the mind,
Exalted, noble, elegant, refined,
Call for fond sympathy's heart-felt regret,
Ye sons of genius, pay the mournful debt:
His friends can truly speak how large his claim,
And "Life was only wanting to his fame."
Art thou, indeed, dear youth, for ever fled;
So quickly numbered with the silent dead?
Too sure I read it in the downcast eye,
Hear it in mourning friendship's stifled sigh.
Ah! could esteem, or admiration, save
So dear an object from the untimely grave,
This transcript faint had not essayed to tell
The loss of one beloved, revered so well.
Vainly I try, even eloquence were weak,
The silent sorrow that I feel, to speak.
No more my hours of pain thy voice will cheer,
And bind my spirit to this lower sphere;
Bend o'er this suffering frame with gentle sigh,
And bid new fire relume my languid eye:
No more the pencil's mimic art command,
And with kind pity guide my trembling hand;
Nor dwell upon the page in fond regard,
To trace the meaning of the Tuscan bard.
Vain all the pleasures thou canst not inspire,
And "in my breast the imperfect joys expire:"
I fondly hoped thy hand might grace my shrine,
And little dreamed I should have wept o'er thine:
In fancy's eye methought I saw thy lyre
With virtue's energies each bosom fire;
I saw admiring nations press around,
Eager to catch the animating sound:
And when, at length, sunk in the shades of night,
To brighter worlds thy spirit wing'd its flight,
Thy country hailed thy venerated shade,
And each graced honour to thy memory paid.
Such was the fate hope pictured to my view—
But who, alas! e'er found hope's visions true?
And ah! a dark presage, when last we met,
Saddened the social hour with deep regret;
When thou thy portrait from the Minstrel drew,
The living Edwin starting on my view—
Silent, I asked of Heaven a lengthened date;
His genius thine, but not like thine his fate;
Shuddering I gazed, and saw too sure revealed,
The fatal truth, by hope till then concealed.
Too strong the portion of celestial flame
For its weak tenement, the fragile frame;
Too soon for us it sought its native sky,
And soared impervious to the mortal eye;
Like some clear planet, shadowed from our sight,
Leaving behind long tracks of lucid light:
So shall thy bright example fire each youth
With love of virtue, piety, and truth.
Long o'er thy loss shall grateful Granta mourn,
And bid her sons revere thy favoured urn:
When thy loved flower "Spring's victory makes known,"
The primrose pale shall bloom for thee alone:
Around thy urn the rosemary we'll spread,
Whose "tender fragrance," emblem of the dead,
Shall "teach the maid, whose bloom no longer lives,"
That "virtue every perished grace survives."
Farewell, sweet moralist! heart-sickening grief
Tells me in duty's paths to seek relief,
With surer aim on faith's strong pinions rise,
And seek hope's vanished anchor in the skies.
Yet still on thee shall fond remembrance dwell,
And to the world thy worth delight to tell;
Though well I feel unworthy thee the lays
That to thy memory weeping friendship pays.

* Young, I think, says of Narcissa,
"She sparkled, was exhaled, and went to Heaven."

STANZAS

SUPPOSED TO HAVE BEEN WRITTEN AT THE GRAVE OF HENRY KIRKE WHITE.

BY A LADY.

Ye gentlest gales! oh, hither waft,
On airy undulating sweeps,
Your frequent sighs, so passing soft,
Where he, the youthful poet, sleeps;
He breathed the purest, tenderest sigh,
The sigh of sensibility.

And thou shalt lie, his favourite flower,
Pale primrose, on his grave reclined;
Sweet emblem of his fleeting hour,
And of his pure, his spotless mind!
Like thee, he sprung in lowly vale;
And felt, like thee, the trying gale.

Nor hence thy pensive eye seclude,
Oh thou, the fragrant rosemary,
Where he, "in marble solitude,
So peaceful, and so deep," doth lie!
His harp prophetic sung to thee
In notes of sweetest minstrelsy.

Ye falling dews! oh, ever leave
Your crystal drops these flowers to steep:
At earliest morn, at latest eve,
Oh let them for their poet weep!
For tears bedew his gentle eye,
The tears of heavenly sympathy.

Thou western sun, effuse thy beams;
For he was wont to pace the glade,
To watch in pale uncertain gleams
The crimson-zoned horizon fade—
Thy last, thy setting radiance pour,
Where he is set to rise no more.

THE END.

Five-Shilling Series.

ELEGANTLY BOUND IN CLOTH, AND ILLUSTRATED, SMALL POST 8VO, 5S, CLOTH.

1. Young Benjamin Franklin: Showing the Principles which raised a Printer's Boy to First Ambassador of the American Republic. By HENRY MAYHEW. 8 Illustrations by JOHN GILBERT.
2. Romance and Reality. By L. E. L, with a full Memoir and Portrait of the Author, and other Illustrations.

   "Thus have I begun;
   And 'tis my hope to end successfully."
3. The Royal Holiday and Young Student's Book: Being the "Holiday Book for the Young" and the "Young Student's Holiday Book" complete in One Volume. Numerous Illustrations.
4. Indoor and Outdoor Games for all Seasons: Being Parlour Pastimes and Games for all Seasons. Complete in One Volume. Numerous Illustrations.
5. Stories of the Conquests of Mexico and Peru, with a Sketch of the Adventures of Spaniards in the New World, retold for Youth. By WILLIAM DALTON. With 8 Illustrations by GILBERT.

Blackwood's Edition of the Poets.

LARGE FCAP. 8VO, ILLUSTRATED, 3S 6D, CLOTH EXTRA, GILT EDGES.

1. Choice Selections from the British Poets, from Spenser to Robert Montgomery. Eight Illustrations.
2. Poetical Works of . W. Longfellow. Eight Illustrations. From the last American edition.
3. Poetical Works of Alexander Pope, with a Memoir of the Author, Notes and Critical Notices of each Poem. By the Rev. Dr CROLY With Portrait and other Illustrations.
4. The Poetical Works of Robert Burns, with Memoir, complete Portrait and other Illustrations.
5. The Poetical Works of John Milton. Complete, with Channing's Essay. Portrait and other Illustrations on Steel.
6. The Poetical Works of Sir Walter Scott, with the Life of the Author. Portrait and other Illustrations on Steel.
7. Lamb's Tales from Shakespeare. By Charles and Mary Lamb. With Scenes illustrating each Tale. Edited by CHARLES KNIGHT. 16 Illustrations.

5\. The Life and Travels of Alexander Von Humboldt: with an Account of his Discoveries, and Notices of his Scientific Fellow-Labourers and Contemporaries. Eight Illustrations.

Contents.—Early Life—The Voyage and Visit to the Canary Islands—Excursions about Cumana—Towards the Orinoco—Up the Orinoco—To Cuba and Back—Colombia and Peru—Mexico—Results of Humboldt's Travels—Journey to Central Asia—Last Literary Labours.

6\. The Military Heroes of England, from the Invasion of Julius Cæsar to the Present Time. Eight Illustrations. Tenth Thousand.

Contents.—The Ancient Britons and their Roman Conquerors—Saxon and Danish Rule—William of Normandy—Richard the Lion Hearted—Reigns of John and Henry III.—Edward I., and his Wars with the Welsh and Scots—Edwards II. and III.—Wars with Scotland, Wales, and France—The Wars of the Roses—The Tudor Sovereigns—Cromwell—William of Orange—Marlborough—Jacobite Rebellions—Chatham, Wolfe, Clive—War with United States, India, &c.—Wellington, Moore—Wars with Affghans, Sikhs—Sir C. Napier—Crimea, Indian Mutiny, Havelock, Sir C. Campbell, &c., &c.

10\. A Popular Book on Flowers, Grasses, and Shrubs. With Anecdotes and Poetical Illustrations; a Glossary of Botanical Terms, and a Copious Index. By MARY PIRIE. Numerous Illustrations.

A most excellent Book for Young Ladies.

11\. Illustrious Men: Their Noble Deeds, Discoveries, and Attainments Tenth Thousand. Eight Illustrations.

Contents.—Alfred the Great—Geoffrey Chaucer—Cardinal Wolsey—Sir Thomas More—Thomas Cromwell, Earl of Essex—Hugh Latimer, Bishop of Worcester—John Jewell, Bishop of Salisbury—Sir Thomas Gresham—The Admirable Crichton—Sir Francis Drake—William Cecil, Lord Burleigh—William Shakespeare—Sir Walter Raleigh—Francis Bacon—Sir Edward Coke—Thomas Wentworth, Earl of Strafford—John Hamden—Dr William Harvey—Admiral Blake—Edward Hyde, Earl of Clarendon—John Milton—John Tillotson—John Locke—Gilbert Burnet, Bishop of Salisbury—William Penn—Joseph Addison—John Churchill, Duke of Marlborough—Sir Isaac Newton—Robert Walpole—John Dalrymple, Earl of Stair—Sir Hans Sloane—General Wolfe—George, Lord Anson—George, Lord Lyttelton—William Pitt, Earl of Chatham—Sir William Blackstone—Dr Samuel Johnson—Robert Lowth, Bishop of London—John Howard—William Murray, Earl of Mansfield.

12\. Illustrious Women who have Distinguished Themselves for Virtue, Piety, and Benevolence. Eight Illustrations.

Contents.—Queen Victoria—Princess Frederick William of Prussia, the Princess Royal—The Empress Eugenie—The Duchess of Kent—Queen Adelaide—Lady Jane Grey—Mary, Queen of Scots—Queen Caroline—Queen Marie Antoinette—Josephine, Queen and Empress—Lady Rachel Russell—Elizabeth Fry, the Prison Reformer—Harriet Martineau—Amelia Opie—Lady Huntingdon—Hannah More—Eliza Cook—Felicia Hemans—Mrs Bunyan—Charlotte Corday—Frederika Bremer—L. E. L.—Jenny Lind—Joan of Arc—Miss Coutts—Florence Nightingale—Elizabeth, Anna, and Emily Blackwell.

13. Mercantile Morals. A Book for Young Men entering upon the Duties of Active Life. With an Appendix, containing a popular Explanation of the principal Terms used in Law and Commerce, with the Moneys, Weights, and Measures of Foreign Countries, and their English Equivalents. Tenth Thousand.

Contents.—Wealth not the Chief End of Life—Mercantile Morality—Making Haste to be Rich—Dangers incident to Young Men in Large Cities—The Young Merchant needs a Guide—The Young Merchant in Society—Unsuccessful Merchandise, or, Sabbath Desecration—Forbidden Gains—The Young Merchant opposes the Bible—The Young Merchant a Novel Reader—The Young Man at the Theatre—Sketch of the History of English Trade and Commerce—Principal Terms used in Trade and Commerce, &c., &c.

14. The Remarkable Scenes of the Bible; or, The Places distinguished by Memorable Events recorded in Scripture. By the late Rev. DR HUGHES, Rector of St John's, London. Numerous Illustrations.

Contents.—Eden—Ararat—Babel—Ur, Haran, Moreh—Sodom and Gomorrah—Moriah—Bethel—Shechem—Dan and Beersheba—Egypt—The Red Sea—The Wilderness—Rephidim—Sinai—Hor and Pisgah—Jordan—Gilgal—Jericho—Gibbon—Shiloh—Ramoth-Gilead—Carmel—Bethlehem.

15. Lectures on the Parables of our Saviour. By Rev. Dr KIRK. With Preface by Professor McCRIE.

16. The Religion of Geology and its Connected Sciences. By EDWARD HITCHCOCK, D.D., LL.D. With Corrections and an Additional Lecture, giving a Summary of the Author's Present Views on the whole subject, and a copious Index. Extra Cloth. (Cheap Edition, 2s.)

Contents.—Revelation Illustrated by Science—The Epoch of the Earth's Creation Unrevealed—Death a Universal Law of Organic Beings on this Globe from the Beginning—The Noachian Deluge Compared with the Geological Deluges—The World's Supposed Eternity—Geological Proofs of the Divine Benevolence—Divine Benevolence as Exhibited in a Fallen World—Unity of the Divine Plan and Operation in all Ages of the World's History—The Hypothesis of Creation by Law—Special and Miraculous Providence—The Future Condition and Destiny of the Earth—The Telegraphic System of the Universe—The Vast Plans of Jehovah—Scientific Truth, Rightly Applied, is Religious Truth—Synoptical View of the Bearings of Geology upon Religion.

17. Dogs: Their Sagacity, Instinct, and Uses, with Descriptions of their several Varieties. By GEORGE FREDERICK PARDON. Illustrated by HARRISON WEIR.

18. The Holiday Book for the Young: Being Short Readings in History, Geography, Natural History, Theology, Physics, &c. By WILLIAM MARTIN. With numerous Illustrations. Seventh Edition.

"A work to amuse and instruct, to enlighten the mind and purify the affections."

Contents.—Ancient History—Bible Lessons—Boat-Building—Butterflies—Different Kinds of Ships—History, Geography, and Chronology—History of Ancient Egypt—Lessons on the Lord's Prayer—My Grandfather's Stories—

Natural History—Natural Theology—Physics—Picture Lessons—Poetry—Flowers—Teachings from Nature—Thanksgiving for Existence—The Birds—The Flowers—The Juvenile Lecturer—The Life, Travels, and Adventures of Reuben Ramble—The Moon—The Selfish Boy—The Stars—The Sun—The Wonders of Geology.

19. The Young Student's Holiday Book: Being Lessons on Architecture, Mechanics, Natural History, Manufacture of Pottery, &c. By WILLIAM MARTIN. Seventh Edition. With numerous Illustrations.

Contents.—A Chronological Epitome of the History of Architecture in England—Austrian Salt Mines—A Wild Boar Hunt—Bible Lessons—Cleanliness—Coal and Gas—Evening Prayer—History of Macedon—Persia—Lessons on Things—Lessons on the Lord's Prayer—Mechanics—Morning Prayer—My Grandfather's Stories—Natural History—Physics—Picture Lessons—Architecture—Poetry—Steam and the Steam-Engine—Teachings from Nature—The Electric Telegraph—The Juvenile Lecturer: Earthenware and Porcelain—Ancient Pottery—Porcelain Manufacture—Preparation of Clay and Flints—Manufacture of Pottery—Painting, Gilding, &c.—The Pump—The Stereoscope.

20. Story of the Peninsular War. By the late Marquis of LONDONDERRY, Colonel of the Second Regiment of Life-Guards. With continuation by G. R. GLEIG. With Portraits and Illustrations. This work contains a lucid description of the momentous period between 1789 and 1815. All the Battles are described and notices of the leading Generals inserted.

21. Life and Adventures of Dr Livingstone in the Interior of South Africa; comprising a Description of the Regions which he traversed, an Account of Missionary Pioneers, and Chapters on Cotton Cultivation, Slavery, Wild Animals, &c., &c. By H. G. ADAMS. With Portrait and Numerous Illustrations.

Contents.—The Boy, the Man, the Missionary—Missionary Pioneers—Mamaqualand and the Griguas—Among the Bechuanis—Lake Ngami—To St Paul de Loanda—Back to Linyanti—Visit to Moselekatse—Away to Quillimane—Wild Animals of South Africa—Cotton Cultivation and Slavery—Journey Home—Recent Information.

22. The Earth: Its Physical Condition, and most Remarkable Phenomena. By W. M. HIGGINS. Sixth Edition. Numerous Illustrations.

Contents.—The Earth in Relation to the Universe—Celestial Appearances—The Atmosphere and its Properties—Atmospherical Phenomena Dependent on the Distribution of Heat—Light—Electricity—Terrestrial Magnetism—Interior of the Earth—Land and Water—Superficial Temperature of the Earth.

23. Half-hours with our Sacred Poets. Edited, with Biographical Sketches, by ALEXANDER H. GRANT, M.A. Eight Illustrations. Nearly Two Hundred Select Pieces from the Writings of more than Eighty Authors of Sacred Poetry are embraced in this volume, from the Fourteenth Century to the Present Time.

24 Curiosities of Physical Geography, comprising Avalanches, Icebergs, Trade Winds, Earthquakes, Volcanoes, also Reflections on the connection between the Physical Condition of a Country and the Mental Development of its Inhabitants, &c. By W. WITTICH. Eight Illustrations.

Contents.—Snow Mountains—Glaciers—Avalanches—Mountain-slips—Icebergs and Ice-fields—The Gulf Stream—The Simoom—Trade-Winds—Monsoons—Plains and Deserts—The Sahara—The Selva, or Forest Desert of the Amasonas—The Pampas—The Llanos—Earthquakes—Volcanoes.

25. Popular Natural History and Characteristics of Animals, with Illustrative Anecdotes. By Captain T. BROWN.

Contents.—Anecdotes of Animals—The Horse Kind—The Cow Kind—The Sheep Kind—The Deer Kind—The Hog Kind—Of the Cat Kind—The Dog Kind—The Weasel Kind—The Hare Kind—The Rat Kind, &c.—The Bat Kind.

26. Habits and Characteristics of Animals and Birds, with numerous Anecdotes. By Captain T. BROWN.

Contents.—Amphibious Animals—Of the Monkey Kind—The Monkey Proper—Of Pouched Animals, the Great Kangaroo—Of the Elephant—Rhinoceros—Hippopotamus—Cameleopard or Giraffe—Camel and Dromedary—Bear—Badger—Racoon—Anecdotes of Birds, Ostrich, Emu, Cassowary, Dodo, Solitaire—Of Rapacious Birds, Eagle, Condor of America, Vulture, Falcon, Jer-Falcon, Common Falcon, Kestrel, Hobby, Merlin, Goshawk, Sparrow Hawk, Kite, Buzzard, Butcher Bird—The Owl Kind, Horned or Eagle Owl, Common Horned Owl, Long-eared Owl, Snowy Owl, Barn Owl, Tawny Owl—Of Birds of the Poultry Kind, The Cock, Peacock, Turkey, Pheasant, Guinea Hen, Bustard, The Grouse and Its Congeners—The Partridge and its Varieties—Birds of the Pie Kind—The Magpie and its Congeners—Jay—The Woodpecker and its Congeners, Wryneck, Nuthatch—The Cuckoo and its Varieties—The Parrot and its Congeners—The Pigeon and its Congeners, Rock Dove, Ring Dove—Birds of the Sparrow Kind, Song Thrush, Missel Thrush, Blackbird, Redwing, Fieldfare, Ring Ouzel, Water Ouzel, Starling, Sparrow, Greenfinch, Crossbill, Grossbeak, Chaffinch, Yellow Hammer, Bunting, Siskin, Wheat-ear—The Nightingale and other Soft-billed Birds, Nightingale, Redbreast, Sky-Lark, Wood-Lark, Grasshopper-Lark, Black-cap, Blue Titmouse, Wren, House Wren, Golden-crested Wren, Willow Wren, Wood Wren—White-ear—Pied Wagtail, Grey Wagtail, Yellow Wagtail, Rock or Shore Pipit—Meadow Pipit or Tit—The Canary and other Hard-billed Song Birds—Goldfinch—Bullfinch—Common or Brown Linnet—Mountain Finch or Brambling—The Swallow and its Congeners, House Swallow, Chimney Swallow, Swift, Cape Swallow, Sand Martin, Cliff Swallow, Esculent Swallow—European Goat-sucker—The Humming Bird and its Varieties.

27. Illustrative Anecdotes of Birds, Fishes, and Insects, &c. By Captain T. BROWN.

Birds of the Crane Kind—Small Birds of the Crane Kind—Water Fowl—The Penguin Kind—Birds of the Goose Kind—The Duck and its Varieties—Cetaceous Animals—Fishes in General—The Shark Tribe—The Ray Tribe in General—The Lamprey and its Congeners—Sturgeons in General—Spinous Fishes—The Mackerel Tribe—The Chætodon Tribe—The Perch

Tribe—Surmullets in General—Gurnards in General—The Doree Tribe—Sticklebacks—The Mullet Genus—Eels in General—The Cod Tribe—Flat Fish in General—The Sucking Fish Tribe—The Salmon and its Congeners—The Pike and its Congeners—The Herring and its Congeners—Flying Fish in General—The Carp and its Congeners—Crustaceous Animals in General—The Tortoise and its Congeners—Testaceous Shell Fish—The Frog Tribe—Lizards and their Congeners—Serpents in General—Anecdotes of Insects—Concluding Remarks on Insects—Worms—Zoophytes—Animalculæ.

28. The Pilgrim's Progress from this World to that which is to Come, delivered under the similitude of a dream, wherein is discovered the manner of his setting out, his dangerous journey, and his safe arrival at the desired country. In three parts. By JOHN BUNYAN. "I have used similitudes." Hosea xii. 10. With Eight Page Illustrations.

29. Lives of the British Admirals and Naval History of Great Britain, from the Days of Cæsar to the Present Time. By Dr JOHN CAMPBELL. Seventh Edition. Revised and Corrected. Illustrated by Portraits, Numerous Facsimiles and Engravings, and Plans of Battles.

Contents.—CHAPTER I.—The Britons—The Romans—The Saxons—The Danes—The Normans—Alfred—Cœur-de-Lion—Reign of Henry the Seventh—Origin of the Royal Navy as a distinct service—Henry the Eighth—Edward the Sixth—Mary—Sir John Cabot—Sebastian Cabot—Howard—Sir John Dudley.

CHAPTER II.—Reign of Elizabeth—Her precautions to restore her Fleet—The Spanish Armada—Howard of Effingham—Earl of Essex—Sir John Hawkins—Sir Francis Drake—Sir Martin Frobisher—Earl of Cumberland—Sir Robert Dudley—Sir Richard Grenville—James Lancaster.

CHAPTER III.—Reign of James the First—Sir William Monson—Quarrels with the Dutch—Sir Walter Raleigh—Reign of Charles the First—Sir Robert Mansel—Sir William Monson.

CHAPTER IV.—Naval History during the Commonwealth—The Protectorate—Wars with the Dutch—War with Spain—Admiral Blake—The Restoration—Charles II.—Struggle with the Dutch for the Sovereignty of the Seas—James II.—Duke of Albemarle—Earl of Sandwich—Prince Rupert—Lawson—Kempthorne—Ayscue—Spragge.

CHAPTER V.—Reign of William and Mary—War with France—Reign of Anne, 1689 to 1714—War with France and Spain—Admiral Benbow—Sir Cloudesley Shovel—Sir George Rooke, and others.

CHAPTER VI.—Reign of George I., 1714 to 1727—Byng, Lord Torrington—Action off Messina—Sir William Jumper—Reign of George II., 1727 to the Treaty of Aix la Chapelle in 1748—Capture of Portobello—Admiral Vernon—Sir Charles Wager—Sir John Norris—Sir Peter Warren—George II., from the Peace of Aix la Chapelle to his Death in 1760—The Seven Years' War—Admiral John Byng, his Trial and Execution—Taking of Quebec—Destruction of the French Fleet in Quiberon Bay—George III., from his Accession to the Peace of Paris in 1763—Successes in the West Indies—Actions with the Spanish—Admiral Boscawen—Hawke—Lord Anson, and others.

CHAPTER VII.—George III., 1763 to 1783—Progress of Discovery—Byron—Captain Cook—War of American Revolution—War with France—

CPSIA information can be obtained
at www.ICGtesting.com
Printed in the USA
BVHW04*1338180918
527831BV00012B/496/P

9 780484 423731